M/B	Market to book ratio
MCC	Marginal cost of capital
NPV	Net present value
P	Price of a share of stock
	P_0 = price of the stock today
P/E	Price/earnings ratio
PI	Profitability index
PV	Present value
PVIF	Present value interest factor for a lump sum
PVIFA	Present value interest factor for an annuity
r	(1) Rate of return
	(2) The IRR on a new project
	(3) Correlation coefficient
R_F	Rate of return on a risk-free security
ROA	Return on assets
ROE	Return on equity
ROI	Return on investment
S	(1) Sales
	(2) Stock, total market value
Σ	Summation sign (capital sigma)
σ	Standard deviation (lower case sigma)
t	(1) Tax rate
	(2) Time, when used as a subscript (for example, D_t = the dividend in Year t)
TIE	Times interest earned
V	Value
YTM	Yield to maturity

Financial Management

Financial Management

Third Edition

Theory and Practice

Eugene F. Brigham   University of Florida

 The Dryden Press

Chicago   New York   Philadelphia
San Francisco   Montreal   Toronto
London   Sydney   Tokyo   Mexico City
Rio de Janeiro   Madrid

Acquisitions Editor: Glenn Turner
Developmental Editor: Elizabeth Widdicombe
Managing Editor: Jane Perkins
Design Director: Alan Wendt

Text and cover design by James Buddenbaum/Design
Copy editing by Judith Lynn Bleicher

Address orders to:

383 Madison Avenue
New York, New York 10017

Address editorial correspondence to:

901 North Elm Street
Hinsdale, Illinois 60521

Library of Congress Catalog Card Number: 81-67228
ISBN: 0-03-059593-2
Printed in the United States of America
234-032-9876543

CBS College Publishing
The Dryden Press
Holt, Rinehart and Winston
Saunders College Publishing

Preface

Financial management has changed greatly in recent years. Strong inflationary pressures have pushed interest rates to unprecedented heights, and the resulting high cost of capital has led to profound changes in corporate financial policies and practices. Academic researchers have made significant advances, especially in the areas of capital budgeting and the cost of capital. At the same time, business practitioners are making increasing use of financial theory, and feedback from "the real world" has led to revisions in financial theory. To a large extent, these trends have dictated the revisions made in the third edition of *Financial Management*.

The book begins with basic valuation concepts, focusing on stocks and bonds, and then goes on to show how the principles of financial management can be used to help maximize the value of a firm. This organization has three important advantages:

1. Developing valuation models at the beginning of the book gives students an early familiarity with the time value of money and with risk analysis, permitting the use of these concepts throughout the book. This usage, in turn, not only makes the institutional aspects of finance more interesting and meaningful but also reinforces through use students' understanding of risk and time value concepts.
2. Structuring the book around valuation concepts provides a continuity that is missing in many texts. Most finance texts develop a series of topics in modular form, then attempt to integrate them in the later chapters. The present organization gives students a better and more continuous understanding of how the topics interact, and it also minimizes the danger of running out of class time before all the pieces have been fitted into place.
3. Students—even those who do not plan to major in finance—generally find the study of investments interesting. They enjoy working with stock and bond values, rates of return, and the like. Since people's ability to learn a subject is a function of their interest and motivations, and since *Financial Management* begins by showing the direct relationship between security values and corporate finance, this organization is good from a pedagogic standpoint.

Intended Market

The book is designed for use either as an introductory text for MBAs or better-than-average undergraduates, or in advanced courses. In introductory one-quarter or one-semester courses, the first sixteen chapters will typically be covered. Students who have the time and energy to study additional material on their own will gain added depth from the appendices and breadth from the last eight chapters. In advanced courses, the basic chapters can be reviewed, the appendices and special topic chapters can be covered in depth, and cases can be used to gain a better understanding of how financial theory and methodology are applied in practice. A third alternative, where the curriculum permits, is to cover the text in a two-term sequence. The book has been used in all three ways, and its structure provides the flexibility necessary for each of them.

Changes in the Third Edition

As in any revision, all sections were updated to incorporate the latest interest rates and other types of data, and a major effort was made to clarify and smooth out rough spots throughout the book. Specific changes worthy of note include the following:

1. The primary symbols and equations used in the book are set forth for easy reference on the inside front cover and in Appendix C.
2. A set of fairly difficult "self-test" problems, with detailed solutions, is given at the end of certain key chapters (3, 4, 5, 6, 7, 8, 11, 12, 15, 16). These problems serve both to test students' ability to set up problems for solution and also to explain the solution set-up for those needing help.
3. The end-of-chapter problems have been revised extensively. The number of problems has been increased, their range of difficulty has been expanded, and, in chapters where a discussion approach is especially useful (for example, Chapter 14, "Common Stock"), longer, case-like problems have been added. To make room for the expanded problem set, most of the regular cases were deleted in this edition. However, arrangements have been made through Dryden Press to allow instructors who want to use a few cases, but not enough to warrant having students purchase a casebook, to reproduce selected cases from our casebooks. A set of supplemental problems similar to the end-of-chapter problems is also available.
4. The list of end-of-chapter references has been shortened substantially. An emphasis has been placed on recent articles, which themselves contain extended bibliographies on selected topics.
5. Chapter 2 now includes a discussion of capital markets and institutions, plus a new appendix that discusses (1) the effect of inflation on interest rates and (2) the term structure of rates. A second appendix is also included to discuss the 1981 tax law changes and their effects on financial management.

6. Chapter 3 ("Time Value") now includes loan amortization and perpetuities.

7. Chapter 4 ("Stock and Bond Values") has a streamlined discussion of stock valuation models, plus an appendix which deals with after-tax returns on securities.

8. Chapter 5 ("Risk and Rates of Return") has been clarified significantly.

9. The credit policy section of Chapter 8 ("Accounts Receivable and Inventories") has been completely rewritten to reflect the incremental effects of changes in each credit policy variable on profits.

10. Chapter 9 ("Cash and Marketable Securities") now uses the basic inventory model as a framework for establishing the target cash balance and the mix of cash and marketable securities.

11. Major revisions have been made in the capital budgeting chapters. First, Chapter 11 ("The Basics of Capital Budgeting") has been streamlined. Second, and more important, Chapter 12, which deals largely with capital budgeting under uncertainty, has been greatly modified. Here the concept of beta risk in capital budgeting is clarified and extended, while the concepts of sensitivity analysis and computer simulation (which are what is really being done in industry today) are developed and explained in terms that beginning students can understand. The chapter concludes with a discussion of the process of setting risk-adjusted discount rates, along with a lead-in to a further discussion of this topic in the chapter appendices as well as in Chapter 15 ("Cost of Capital").

12. The chapters on cost of capital and capital structure have been changed in two ways. First, the weighted average and marginal cost of capital concepts are now developed before capital structure is discussed. Holding constant the capital structure simplifies the cost of capital chapter, and having already covered cost of capital concepts facilitates the capital structure discussion. Second, a completely new chapter, "The Theory of Capital Structure," has been added. This new chapter begins with the MM/NOI framework, and then in a systematic series of steps shows how corporate income taxes, bankruptcy-related costs, agency costs, and personal income taxes affect the optimal capital structure.

13. The new Bankruptcy Act, which became effective in October 1979, is incorporated into Chapter 21.

14. Chapter 22 ("Warrants and Convertibles") has been strengthened by incorporating the convertible bond model, which was formerly developed in an appendix, into the chapter.

Several additional items are available as aids to students and instructors:

Ancillary Materials

1. *Study Guide.* This supplement, coauthored with Robert T. LeClair,

outlines the key sections of the text, offers students self-testing questions for each chapter, and provides a set of solved problems similar to those in the text.

2. *Casebook.* A casebook, *Cases in Managerial Finance*, by E. F. Brigham, R. L. Crum, T. J. Nantell, R. T. Aubey, and R. H. Pettway, was designed specifically for use with this text. The cases show real-world applications of the methodologies and concepts developed in the text. A revised edition of the casebook is scheduled for 1982.

3. *Readings Books.* A number of readings books, including one designed specifically for use with this text (*Issues in Managerial Finance*, edited by E. F. Brigham and R. E. Johnson), can be used as supplements.

4. *Instructor's Manual.* A very complete, 400-page manual is available to instructors who adopt the book.

5. *Test Bank.* A completely new test bank with over 1,000 class-tested questions/problems in objective format is now available. The new test bank questions are, in general, more challenging than those in the old bank. In a sense, the new questions are more suitable for exams, whereas many of the old test bank questions were more suitable for quizzes than for midterm and final exams.

6. *Lecture notes and transparencies.* A set of lecture notes, together with 100 acetate transparencies, is available from Dryden Press to instructors who adopt the text. These notes were prepared on the basis of detailed student suggestions as to which parts of each chapter require the most explanation. Each instructor will want to modify the notes to suit his or her own situation, but the notes and transparencies can be used as the basis for lectures to both large and small classes.

7. *Supplemental problems.* Supplemental problems, which are similar to but generally somewhat more difficult than the end-of-chapter problems, are also available to instructors.

Acknowledgments

A great many people participated, directly or indirectly, in the preparation of this book, and I would like to acknowledge the help of the following:

Michael Adler	Moshe Ben-Horim	Mary Broske
Edward Altman	William Beranek	William Brueggeman
Robert Angell	Roger Bey	B. J. Campsey
Vincent Apilado	John Bildersee	Robert Carleson
Robert Aubey	Kenneth Boudreaux	Stephen Celec
Guilford Babcock	Donald Boyd	Donald Chance
Peter Bacon	Patricia Boyer	S. K. Choudhury
Thomas Bankston	Katherine Brigham	Lal Chugh
Charles Barngrover	Laura Brigham	Bruce Clements
William Beedles	Sue Brigham	Philip Cooley

David Crary
Roy Crum
Brent Dalrymple
Lois Day
Mark Dorfman
David Durst
Edward Dyl
A. Edwards
John Ezzell
Michael Ferri
John Finnerty
Louis Gapenski
James Garvin
Adam Gehr
Walt Goulet
Edwin Grossnickle
John Groth
Manak Gupta
Donald Hakala
Charles Haley
Robert Haugen
Stephen Hawk
Sally Heck
Robert Hehre
George Hettenhouse
Haws Heymann
Pearson Hunt
Kose John
Craig Johnson
Keith Johnson
Ramon Johnson
Ray Jones
Gus Kalogeras
Scott Karp
Michael Keenan
Donald Knight

Jaroslaw Komarynsky
Harold Krogh
Charles Kroncke
Larry Lang
P. Lange
Howard Lanser
Robert LeClair
Wayne Lee
John Lewis
Charles Linke
James Longstreet
Robert Magee
Philip Malone
Terrence Martell
Andrew McCollough
Kathleen McShane
Larry Merville
James Millar
Carol Moerdyk
Robert Moore
Frederic Morrissey
Stewart Myers
Timothy Nantell
Robert Nelson
William Nelson
Thomas O'Brien
Dennis O'Conner
James Pappas
James Pettijohn
Richardson Pettit
Richard Pettway
Hugo Phillips
John Pinkerton
Gerald Pogue
R. Potter

R. Powell
Howard Puckett
George Racette
Robert Radcliffe
William Rentz
Charles Rini
John Ritchie
Dexter Rowell
James Sachlis
M. J. Scheuer
Carl Schweser
Sol Shalit
Ronald Shrieves
Joseph Sinkey
Eric Smith
P. Smith
Stephen Smith
Donald Sorenson
Kenneth Stanley
Donald Stevens
Glen Strasburg
Albert Sweetser
Philip Swensen
Ernest Swift
Gary Tallman
Russell Taussig
George Trivoli
Milford Tysseland
Howard Van Auken
Pieter Vandenburg
Pretorius Van den Dool
Paul Vanderheiden
James Verbrugge
Steve Vinson
Donald Woods

In addition, all or major parts of the manuscript were reviewed by the following executives: James Dunn, Financial Vice-President, GT&E; Larry Hastie, Treasurer, Bendix Corporation; Victor Leavengood, Treasurer, General Telephone of Florida; Archie Long, Comptroller, General Motors; and James Taggart, Financial Vice-President, Tampa Electric Company.

Special thanks are due to Art Herrmann, who coauthored the bankruptcy chapter, to Hai Hong, who coauthored the chapter on multinational finance, and to Dilip Shome, who coauthored the capital structure chapter.

My colleagues at the University of Florida gave me many useful suggestions, and the Dryden Press staff—especially Glenn Turner, Liz Widdicombe, Jane Perkins, William Seabright, Alan Wendt, and Jo-Anne Naples—helped greatly in bringing out this third edition. I also wish to express my appreciation for the copy editing and proofreading done by Judith Lynn Bleicher, Mary Berry, and Shirley Moore.

Last, but certainly not least, I owe a special debt to Fred Weston, both for teaching me much of what I know about finance and for permitting me to draw from our coauthored texts.

Errors in the Text

At this point in the preface, authors generally say something like this: "I appreciate all the help I received from the people listed above, but any remaining errors are, of course, my own responsibility." And in many books there are plenty of remaining errors. Having experienced difficulties with errors myself, both as a student and as an instructor, I resolved to avoid this problem in *Financial Management*. As a result of the error detection procedures used, I am convinced that it is freer of mistakes than any other book with which I have been associated.

Some of my colleagues suggested that if I am so confident about the book's accuracy, I should offer a reward to people who find errors. With this in mind, and also because I want to detect any remaining errors and correct them in subsequent printings, I hereby offer a reward of $5 per error (misspelled word, arithmetic mistake, and the like) to the first person who reports it to me. (Any error that has follow-through effects is counted as two errors only.) Two accounting students have set up a foolproof audit system to make sure I pay off. Accounting students tend to be skeptics!

Conclusion

Finance is, in a real sense, the cornerstone of the enterprise system, so good financial management is vitally important to the economic health of business firms and hence to the nation and the world. Because of its importance, finance should be widely and thoroughly understood, but this is easier said than done. The field is relatively complex, and it is undergoing constant change in response to shifts in economic conditions. All of this makes finance stimulating and exciting but also challenging and sometimes perplexing. I sincerely hope that *Financial Management* will meet its own challenge by contributing to a better understanding of the financial system.

Eugene F. Brigham
College of Business
University of Florida
Gainesville, Florida 32611
September 1981

Contents

Financial Management

INTRODUCTION   I

Financial management can best be understood if we begin with a brief
survey of the history of the field, a summary of our goals, and a review
of the legal and economic framework within which financial management is practiced. These topics are covered in Part I.

An Overview of Financial Management

1

The study of *financial management* has undergone significant changes over the years. When finance first emerged as a separate field of study in the early 1900s, the emphasis was on legalistic matters such as mergers, consolidations, the formation of new firms, and the various types of securities issued by corporations. Industrialization was sweeping the country, and the critical problem firms faced was obtaining capital for expansion. The capital markets were relatively primitive, making transfers of funds from individual savers to businesses difficult. Reports of earnings and asset values in accounting statements were unreliable, while stock trading by insiders and manipulators caused prices to fluctuate wildly. Consequently, investors were reluctant to purchase stocks and bonds. As a result of these environmental conditions, finance in the early 1900s concentrated heavily on legal issues relating to the issuance of securities.

The emphasis remained on securities through the 1920s. However, radical changes occurred during the depression of the 1930s, when an unprecedented number of business failures caused finance to focus on bankruptcy and reorganization, on corporate liquidity, and on governmental regulation of securities markets. Finance was still a descriptive, legalistic subject, but the emphasis shifted from expansion to survival.

During the 1940s and early 1950s, finance continued to be taught as a descriptive, institutional subject, viewed from the outside rather than from the standpoint of management. However, methods of financial analysis designed to help firms maximize their profits and stock prices were beginning to receive attention. The evolutionary pace in this direction quickened during the late 1950s. Also, whereas the right-hand side of the balance sheet (liabilities and capital) had received more attention in the earlier era, the major emphasis began to shift to asset analysis. Mathematical models were developed and applied to inventories, cash, accounts receivable, and fixed assets. Increasingly, the focus of finance shifted from the outsider's to the insider's point of view, as financial decisions within the firm were recognized to be the critical issue in corporate finance. Descriptive, institutional materials on capital markets and financing instruments were still studied, but these topics were considered within the context of corporate financial decisions.

The 1960s witnessed a renewed interest in the liabilities-capital side of the balance sheet, with a focus on (1) the optimal mix of securities and

(2) the cost of capital. At the same time, the theory of security selection by individual investors, or "portfolio management," and its implications for corporate finance were being developed. Corporate financial management is designed to help general management take actions that will maximize the value of the firm and the wealth of its stockholders; therefore, sound corporate financial decisions are dependent upon how investors are likely to react to these decisions. Thus, there has been a merging of investments with corporate finance.

Thus far in the 1980s the major new issue has been inflation and how to deal with it. We have had to work inflation into the fabric of both financial theories and financial decision processes. Inflation has led to the creation of new financial institutions and industries—for example, money market funds and the interest rate futures markets. Older institutions have been forced into major structural changes; it is getting harder and harder to tell a bank from a savings and loan or an insurance company from a brokerage firm. The types of securities used to raise capital are also changing; a few years ago virtually all debt had fixed interest rates, but today floating rate bonds and variable mortgages are the rule.

Increasing Importance of Financial Management

These evolutionary changes have greatly increased the importance of financial management. In earlier times, the marketing manager would project sales, the engineering and production staffs would determine the assets necessary to meet these demands, and the financial manager's job was simply to raise the money needed to purchase the plant, equipment, and inventories. This mode of operation is no longer prevalent. Today, decisions are made in a much more coordinated manner, with the financial manager having direct responsibility for the control process.

Northeast Utilities can be used to illustrate this change. A few years ago, Northeast's economic forecasters would project power demand on the basis of historic trends and then give these forecasts to the engineers, who would then proceed to build the new plants necessary to meet the forecasted demand. The finance group simply had the task of raising the capital the engineers told them was needed. However, inflation, environmental regulations, and other factors combined to double or even triple plant construction costs, and this caused a corresponding increase in the need for new capital. At the same time, rising fuel costs caused dramatic increases in electricity prices, which lowered demand and made some of the new construction unnecessary. Thus, Northeast found itself building plants that it did not need and, at the same time, unable to raise the capital necessary to pay for them. The price of the company's stock declined from $20 to $5. As a result of this experience, Northeast Utilities (and other utilities and industrial companies) now places far more stress on the planning and control process, and this has greatly increased the importance of the finance staff.

The direction in which business is moving, as well as the increasing importance of finance, was described recently in *Fortune*. After pointing out that well over half of today's top executives had majored in business administration, versus about 25 percent a few years earlier, *Fortune* continued:

Career patterns have followed the educational trends. Like scientific and technical schooling, nuts-and-bolts business experience seems to have become less important. The proportion of executives with their primary experience in production, operations, engineering, design, and R. and D. has fallen from a third of the total to just over a quarter. And the number of top officers with legal and financial backgrounds has increased more than enough to make up the difference. Lawyers and financial men now head two out of five corporations.

It is fair to assume the changes in training, and in the paths that led these men to the top, reflect the shifting priorities and needs of their corporations. In fact, the expanding size and complexity of corporate organizations, coupled with their continued expansion overseas, have increased the importance of financial planning and controls. And the growth of government regulation and of obligations companies face under law has heightened the need for legal advice. The engineer and the production man have become, in consequence, less important in management than the finance man and the lawyer.

Today's chief executive officers have obviously perceived the shift in emphasis, and many of them wish they had personally been better prepared for it. Interestingly enough, a majority of them say they would have benefited from additional formal training, mainly in business administration, accounting, finance, and law.[1]

These same trends are evident at lower levels within firms of all sizes, as well as in nonprofit and governmental organizations. Thus, it is becoming increasingly important for people in marketing, accounting, production, personnel, and other areas to understand finance in order to do a good job in their own fields. Marketing people, for instance, must understand how marketing decisions affect and are affected by funds availability, by inventory levels, by excess plant capacity, and so on. Accountants, to cite another example, must understand how accounting data are used in corporate planning and viewed by investors. The function of accounting is to provide quantitative financial information for use in making economic decisions, while the main functions of financial management are to plan for, acquire, and utilize funds in order to maximize the efficiency and value of the enterprise.[2]

Thus, there are financial implications in virtually all business decisions, and

---

[1] C. G. Burck, "A Group Profile of the Fortune 500 Chief Executive," *Fortune* (May 1976), p. 173.

[2] American Institute of Certified Public Accountants, *Statement of the Accounting Principles Board No. 4* (New York, October 1970), p. 17.

nonfinancial executives simply must know enough finance to work these implications into their own specialized analyses.[3] This point is amplified in the following section.

Organization structures vary from firm to firm, but Figure 1-1 gives a fairly typical picture of the role of finance within a business. The chief financial officer, who has the title of vice-president: finance, reports to the president. Key subordinates are the treasurer and the controller. The treasurer has direct responsibility for managing the firm's cash and marketable securities, for planning the financial structure, and for selling stocks and bonds to raise capital. Under the treasurer (but in some firms under the controller) are the credit manager, the inventory manager, and

The Place of Finance in a Business Organization

Figure 1-1
Place of Finance in a Typical Business Organization

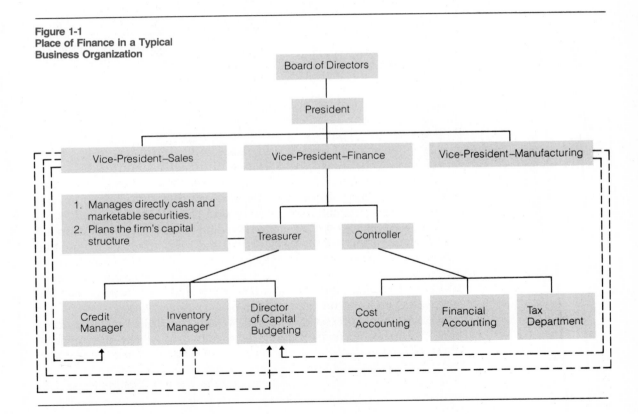

[3] It is an interesting fact that the course "Financial Analysis for Nonfinancial Executives" has the highest enrollment in most executive development programs.

the director of capital budgeting (who analyzes decisions relating to investments in fixed assets). The controller is responsible for the activities of the accounting and tax departments.

The Goals of the Firm

Decisions are not made in a vacuum—they are made with some objective in mind. *Throughout this book, we operate on the assumption that management's primary goal is to maximize the wealth of its stockholders.* As we shall see, this translates into *maximizing the price of the common stock.* Firms do, of course, have other objectives—managers, who make the actual decisions, are interested in their own personal satisfaction, in employees' welfare, and in the good of the community and society at large. Still, for the reasons set forth below, *stock price maximization is probably the most important goal of most firms (except public utilities),* and it is a reasonable operating objective upon which to build decision rules in a book such as this one.

Why Managers Try to Maximize Stockholders' Wealth

Stockholders own the firm and elect the management team. Management, in turn, is supposed to operate in the best interests of the stockholders. We know, however, that because the stock of most large firms is widely held, the managers of such firms have a great deal of autonomy. This being the case, might not managements pursue goals other than maximization of stockholder wealth? For example, some argue that the management of a large, well-entrenched corporation could work to keep stockholder returns at a fair or "reasonable" level and then devote part of its efforts and resources to public service activities, to employee benefits, to higher management salaries, or to golf.

Similarly, an entrenched management might avoid risky ventures, even when the possible gains to stockholders were high enough to warrant taking the gamble. The theory behind this argument is that stockholders are generally well diversified, holding portfolios of many different stocks, so if one company takes a chance and loses, the stockholders lose only a small part of their wealth. Managers, on the other hand, are not diversified, so setbacks affect them more seriously. Accordingly, some maintain that corporate managers tend to "play it safe" rather than aggressively seek to maximize the prices of their firms' stocks.

It is extremely difficult to determine whether a particular management team is trying to maximize shareholder wealth or is merely attempting to keep stockholders satisfied while pursuing other goals. For example, how can we tell whether or not voluntary employee or community benefit programs are in the long-run best interests of the stockholders? Are relatively high management salaries really necessary to attract and retain excellent managers who, in turn, will keep the firm ahead of its competition? When a risky venture is turned down, does this reflect management conservatism, or is it a correct judgment regarding the risks of the venture versus its potential rewards?

It is impossible to give definitive answers to these questions. Several studies have suggested that managers are not completely stockholder-oriented, but the evidence is cloudy. It is true that more and more firms are tying management's compensation to the company's performance, and research suggests that this motivates managers to operate in a manner consistent with stock price maximization.[4] Additionally, in recent years tender offers and proxy fights have removed a number of supposedly entrenched managements; the recognition that such actions can take place has probably stimulated many other firms to attempt to maximize share prices.[5] Finally, a firm operating in a competitive market, or almost any firm during an economic downturn, will be forced to undertake actions that are reasonably consistent with shareholder wealth maximization. Thus, while managers may have other goals in addition to stock price maximization, there are reasons to view this as the dominant goal for most firms.

Another point that deserves consideration is social responsibility: should businesses operate strictly in the stockholders' best interest, or are firms also partly responsible for the welfare of employees, customers, the communities in which they operate, and, indeed, society at large? In tackling this question, consider first those firms whose rates of return on investment are close to "normal," that is, close to the average for all firms. If such companies attempt to be social do-gooders, thereby increasing their costs over what they otherwise would have been, and if the other businesses in the industry do not follow suit, then the socially oriented firms will probably be forced to abandon their efforts. Thus, any socially responsible acts that raise costs will be difficult, if not impossible, in industries subject to keen competition.

Social Responsibility

What about firms with profits above normal levels—can they not devote resources to social projects? Undoubtedly they can; many large, successful firms do engage in community projects, employee benefit programs, and the like to a greater degree than would appear to be called for by pure profit or wealth maximization goals.[6] Still, publicly owned firms are constrained in such actions by capital market factors. Suppose a saver who has funds to invest is considering two alternative firms. One firm devotes a substantial part of its resources to social actions, while the other concentrates on profits and stock prices. Most investors are likely

---

[4] Wilbur G. Lewellen, "Management and Ownership in the Large Firm," *Journal of Finance* 24 (May 1969): 299-322. Lewellen concludes that managers seem to make decisions that are largely oriented toward stock price maximization.

[5] A *tender offer* is a bid by one company to buy the stock of another, while a *proxy fight* involves an attempt to gain control by getting stockholders to vote a new management group into office. Both actions are facilitated by low stock prices, so self-preservation can lead management to try to keep the stock value as high as possible.

[6] Even firms such as these often find it necessary to justify such programs at stockholder meetings by stating that they contribute to long-run profit maximization.

to shun the socially oriented firm, thus putting it at a disadvantage in the capital market. After all, why should the stockholders of one corporation subsidize society to a greater extent than stockholders of other businesses? For all these reasons, even highly profitable firms (unless they are closely held rather than publicly owned) are generally constrained against taking unilateral cost-increasing social actions.

Does all this mean that firms should not exercise social responsibility? Not at all—it simply means that most cost-increasing actions may have to be put on a *mandatory* rather than a voluntary basis, at least initially, to insure that the burden of such action falls uniformly across all businesses. Thus, fair hiring practices, minority training programs, product safety, pollution abatement, antitrust actions, and the like are more likely to be effective if realistic rules are established initially and then enforced by government agencies. It is critical that industry and government cooperate in establishing the rules of corporate behavior and that firms follow the spirit as well as the letter of the law in their actions. Thus, the rules of the game become constraints, and firms should strive to maximize stock prices subject to these constraints. Throughout the book, we shall assume that managements operate in this manner.

If firms attempt to maximize stock prices, is this good or bad for society? In general, it is good. Aside from such illegal actions as attempting to form monopolies, violating safety codes, and failing to meet pollution control requirements—all of which are constrained by the government— *the same actions that maximize stock prices also benefit society*. First, stock price maximization requires efficient, low-cost operations that get the most value out of a given set of resources. Second, price maximization also requires the development of products that consumers want and need, so the profit motive leads to new technology, new products, and new jobs. Finally, stock price maximization requires efficient and courteous service, adequate stocks of merchandise, and well-located business establishments, because these things are all necessary to make sales, and sales are certainly necessary for profits. Therefore, the types of actions that help a firm increase the price of its stock are also directly beneficial to society at large. This is why profit-motivated enterprise economies have been so much more successful than other types of economic systems. Since financial management plays a crucial role in the operation of successful firms, and since successful firms are absolutely necessary for a healthy, productive economy, it is easy to see why finance is important from a social standpoint.[7]

---

[7] People sometimes argue that firms, in their efforts to raise profits and stock prices, increase product prices and gouge the public. In a reasonably competitive economy, which we have, prices are constrained by competition and consumer resistance. If a firm raises its prices beyond reasonable levels, it will simply lose its market share. Even giant firms like Chrysler lose business to the Japanese and Germans, as well as to Ford and General Motors, if they do not set prices that merely cover production costs plus a "normal" profit. Of course, firms *want* to earn more, and they constantly try to cut costs, develop new products, and so on, and thereby earn excess profits. Yet these very excess profits attract competition, so the main beneficiary is the consumer.

Assuming that a firm's management team does indeed seek to maximize its stock price, what types of actions should it take? First, consider the question of stock prices versus profits: will profit maximization result in stock price maximization? In answering this question, we must analyze the matter of total corporate profits versus earnings per share (EPS).

Suppose Company X had one million shares outstanding and earned $2 million, or $2 per share, and you owned 100 shares of the stock. Now suppose the company sold another one million shares and invested the funds received in assets which produced $1 million of income. Total income would have risen to $3 million, but earnings per share would have declined from $2 to $3,000,000/2,000,000 shares = $1.50. Now your share of the firm's earnings would be only $150, down from $200. You (and the other original stockholders) would have suffered an earnings dilution, even though total corporate profits had risen. Therefore, other things held constant, *if management is interested in the well-being of its existing stockholders, it should concentrate on earnings per share rather than on total corporate profits.*

Will maximization of expected earnings per share always maximize stockholder welfare, or should other factors be considered? Think about the *timing of the earnings.* Suppose one project will cause earnings per share to rise by $0.20 per year for five years, or $1.00 in total, while another project has no effect on earnings for four years but increases earnings by $1.25 in the fifth year. Which project is better? The answer depends on which project adds the most to the value of the stock. This, in turn, depends on the time value of money to investors. In any event, timing is an important reason to concentrate on wealth as measured by the price of the stock rather than on earnings alone.

Still another issue relates to *risk.* Suppose one project is expected to increase earnings per share by $1.00, while another is expected to raise earnings by $1.20 per share. The first project is not very risky; if it is undertaken, earnings will almost certainly rise by about $1.00 per share. The other project is quite risky, so while our best guess is that earnings will rise by $1.20 per share, we must recognize the possibility that there may be no increase whatsoever. Depending on how averse stockholders are to risk, the first project may be preferable to the second.

The riskiness inherent in projected earnings per share (EPS) also depends on *how the firm is financed.* As we shall see, many firms go bankrupt every year, and the greater the use of debt, the greater the threat of bankruptcy. Consequently, *while the use of debt financing may increase projected EPS, debt also increases the riskiness of these projected earnings.*

Still another issue is the matter of paying dividends to stockholders versus retaining earnings and plowing them back into the business, thereby causing the earnings stream to grow over time. Stockholders like cash dividends, but they also like the growth in EPS that results from plowing earnings back into the business. The financial manager must decide exactly how much of current earnings should be paid out as divi-

What Can Managers Do to Maximize Stock Prices?

dends rather than retained and reinvested—this is called the *dividend policy decision*. The optimal dividend policy is the one that maximizes the firm's stock price.

We see, then, that the firm's stock price is dependent on the following factors:

1. projected earnings per share,
2. riskiness of these projected earnings,
3. timing of the earnings stream,
4. the manner of financing the firm, and
5. dividend policy.

Every significant corporate decision should be analyzed in terms of its effect on these factors, hence on the price of the firm's stock. For example, a coal company may be considering opening a new mine. If the mine is opened, can it be expected to increase EPS? Is there a chance that costs will exceed estimates, that prices and output will fall below projections, and that EPS will be reduced because the new mine was opened? How long will it take for the new mine to start showing a profit? How should the capital required to open the mine be raised? If debt is used, how much will this increase the firm's riskiness? Should the firm reduce its current dividends and use the cash thus saved to finance the project, or should it finance the mine with external capital? Financial management is designed to help answer such questions as these, plus many more.

The Economic Environment

Although managers can take actions which affect the values of their firms' stocks, there are also other factors which influence stock prices. Included among these are external constraints, the general level of economic activity, taxes, and conditions in the stock market. Figure 1-2 diagrams these general relationships. Working within the set of external constraints shown in the left box, management makes a set of long-run, strategic policy decisions which chart a future course for the firm. These policy decisions, along with the general level of economic activity and the level of corporate income taxes, influence the firm's expected profitability, the timing of its earnings, their eventual transfer to stockholders in the form of dividends, and the degree of uncertainty (or risk) inherent in projected earnings and dividends. Profitability, timing, and risk all affect the price of the firm's stock, but so does another factor, the state of the stock market as a whole, for all stock prices tend to move up and down together to some extent.

Organization of the Book

Finance cannot be studied in a vacuum—financial decisions are made within an economic and social environment which has a profound influence on these decisions. An introduction to the economic side of the en-

Figure 1-2
Summary of Major Factors Affecting Stock Prices

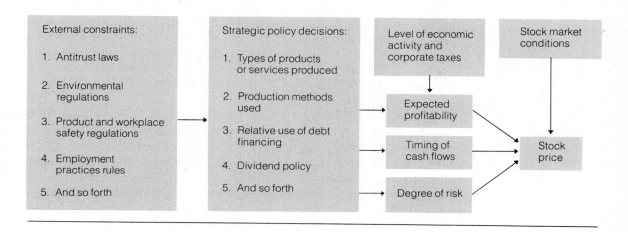

vironment is provided in Part I of the book, which consists of Chapters 1 and 2.

Part II develops some models which can be used to help evaluate financial decisions. The specific tasks of financial managers include (1) coordinating the planning process, (2) administering the control process, and (3) handling the specialized finance functions such as raising capital and paying bills. To perform these tasks properly, it is necessary to estimate stockholders' reactions to alternative actions or events. Accordingly, our first task is to develop a *stock valuation model* which can be used to gain insights into how different actions are likely to affect the price of the firm's stock. The concepts and models developed in Part II are used extensively throughout the remainder of the book.

Next, since both long- and short-run plans are analyzed in terms of future financial statements, Part III considers how these statements are developed and used by both managers and investors. Here we concentrate first on analyzing reports of past operations, then on projecting financial statements into the future under different strategic plans and operating conditions.

In Part IV we move into the execution phase of the financial management process. Here we examine current, ongoing operations, looking first at the role of finance in insuring that cash, inventories, and current assets are used most effectively, and then considering the question of how current operations should be financed.

Part V takes up the vital subject of fixed asset acquisitions, or capital budgeting. Since major capital expenditures take years to plan and execute, and since decisions in this area are generally not reversible and affect operations for many years, their impact on the value of the firm is obvious.

Part VI focuses on raising long-term capital. What are the principal sources and forms of long-term capital, how much does each type cost, and how does the method of financing affect the value of the firm? This section utilizes most of the valuation concepts developed throughout the book, so it not only addresses such key issues as the optimal debt/equity mix and dividend policy, but it also serves to integrate the book and to show how the parts fit together.

Finally, in Part VII we consider some subjects that, while important, are best studied within the basic framework of financial management as developed in Parts I through VI. Included here are multinational operations, mergers, bankruptcy, leasing, convertible securities, warrants, and small business finance.

Summary

This chapter has provided an overview of financial management. We began with a brief review of the evolution of finance as an academic discipline, tracing developments from 1900 to the present. We next examined the place of finance in the firm and saw that the financial manager has been playing an increasingly important role in the organization. We also considered the goals of financial management and concluded that *the key goal in most publicly owned firms is stock price maximization*. Managers do have other goals, both personal and social, but in a competitive economy, where managers serve at the pleasure of stockholders, stock price maximization must be the dominant goal (except for public utilities).

The book's organization reflects this primary goal. First, we shall develop valuation models that can be used to show how corporate actions affect stock prices. Then, in the remainder of the book, we shall examine actions that management can take to help maximize the price of the firm's stock.

Questions

1-1 Would the management of a firm in an oligopolistic or in a competitive industry be more likely to engage in what might be called "socially conscious" practices? Explain your reasoning.

1-2 What is the difference between stock price maximization and profit maximization? Would profit maximization not lead to stock price maximization?

1-3 If you were running a large, publicly owned corporation, would you make decisions to maximize stockholders' welfare or your own? What are some actions stockholders could take to insure that your interests and theirs coincided?

1-4 The president of Consolidated Mining Corporation made this statement in the company's annual report: "Consolidated's primary goal is to increase the value of the common stockholders' equity over time." Later on in the report, these announcements were made:

a. The company contributed $1 million to the symphony orchestra in the headquarters city.

b. The company is spending $300 million to open a new zinc mine in South America. No revenues will be produced by the mine for three years, so earnings will be depressed during this period versus what they would have been had the decision been made not to open the new mine.

c. The company is increasing its relative use of debt. Whereas assets were formerly financed with 40 percent debt, 60 percent equity, henceforth the financing mix will be 50-50.

d. The company uses a great deal of electricity in its smelting operations, and it generates most of this power itself. Plans are to utilize nuclear fuel, rather than coal, to produce electricity in the future.

Discuss how each of these factors might affect Consolidated's stock price.

Selected References

For a good summary of financial management, see

Pogue, Gerald A., and Kishore Lall, "Corporate Finance: An Overview," *Sloan Management Review*, Spring 1974, 19-38.

For alternative views on firms' goals and objectives, see the following articles:

Anthony, Robert N., "The Trouble with Profit Maximization," *Harvard Business Review*, vol. 38 (November-December 1960), 126-134.

Donaldson, Gordon, "Financial Goals: Management versus Stockholders," *Harvard Business Review*, vol. 41 (May-June 1963), 116-129.

Elliot, J. W., "Control, Size, Growth, and Financial Performance in the Firm," *Journal of Financial and Quantitative Analysis*, vol. 7 (January 1972), 1309-1320.

Findlay, M. C., and E. E. Williams, "A Positivist Evaluation of the New Finance," *Financial Management*, vol. 9 (Summer 1980), 7-17.

Lewellen, Wilbur G., "Management and Ownership in the Large Firm," *Journal of Finance*, vol. 24 (May 1969), 299-322.

For a general review of the state of the art in academic finance, together with an extensive bibliography of key research articles, see

Beranek, William, "Research Directions in Finance," *Quarterly Review of Business and Economics*, Spring 1981, 6-24.

Forms of Organization, Financial Markets, and Taxes

Financial management cannot be studied in a vacuum—if the value of a firm is to be maximized, the financial manager must understand the legal and economic environment in which financial decisions are made. Accordingly, this chapter presents some background information on forms of business organizations, financial markets, and the federal income tax system.

Alternative Forms of Business Organization

There are three major forms of business organization: the sole proprietorship, the partnership, and the corporation. In terms of numbers, about 80 percent of business firms are operated as sole proprietorships, while the remainder are divided equally between partnerships and corporations. By dollar value of sales, however, about 80 percent of business is conducted by corporations, about 13 percent by sole proprietorships, and about 7 percent by partnerships.

Sole Proprietorship

A proprietorship is a business owned by one individual. To go into business as a single proprietor is very simple—one merely begins business operations. However, most cities require even the smallest establishments to be licensed, and occasionally state licenses are required as well.

The proprietorship has key advantages for small operations. It is easily and inexpensively formed; no formal charter for operations is required; and a proprietorship is subject to few government regulations. Further, the business pays no corporate income taxes, although all earnings of the firm are subject to personal income taxes, whether they are reinvested in the business or withdrawn.

The proprietorship also has important limitations. Most significant is its inability to obtain large sums of capital. Further, the proprietor has unlimited personal liability for the business's debts. Finally, the life of a business organized as a proprietorship is limited to the life of the individual who created it. For all of these reasons, the individual proprietorship is restricted primarily to small business operations. However, businesses are frequently started as proprietorships and then converted to corporations if and when their growth causes the disadvantages of the proprietorship form to outweigh its advantages.

When two or more persons associate to conduct business, a partnership is said to exist. A partnership may operate under different degrees of formality, ranging from an informal oral understanding to a formal agreement filed with the secretary of the state. Like the proprietorship, the partnership has the advantages of ease and economy of formation, as well as freedom from special governmental regulations. Partnership profits are taxed as personal income in proportion to the partners' claims, whether they are distributed or retained in the business.

Partnership

If a new partner comes into the business, the old partnership ceases to exist and a new one must be created. The withdrawal or death of any one of the partners also dissolves the partnership. To prevent disputes under such circumstances, the articles of the partnership agreement should include terms and conditions under which assets are to be distributed upon dissolution. Of course, dissolution of the partnership does not necessarily mean the end of the business—the remaining partners may simply buy out the one who leaves the firm. To avoid financial pressures caused by the death of one of the partners, it is a common practice for each partner to carry life insurance naming the remaining partners as beneficiaries. The proceeds of such a policy may then be used to buy out the investment of the deceased partner.

Partnerships do have some drawbacks, including impermanence, difficulties of transferring ownership, and unlimited liability. Partners must risk their personal assets as well as their investments in the business, for under partnership law, the partners are liable for business debts. This means that if any partners are unable to meet their pro rata claims resulting from the bankruptcy of the partnership, the remaining partners must take over the unsatisfied claims, drawing on their personal assets if necessary.[1]

A corporation is a legal entity created by a state. It is separate and distinct from its owners and managers. This separateness gives the corporation three major advantages: (1) It has an *unlimited life*—it can continue after its original owners and managers are dead. (2) It permits *easy transferability of ownership interest* in the firm, as ownership interests can be divided into shares of stock, which can be transferred far more easily than can partnership interests. (3) It permits *limited liability*. To illustrate: if you invested $10,000 in a partnership and the partnership went bankrupt owing a considerable sum of money, you could be assessed for a share of these debts. Thus, an investor in a partnership is exposed to unlimited liability. On the other hand, if you invested $10,000 in the stock of a corporation, your potential loss on the investment would be $10,000—

Corporation

[1] However, it is possible to limit the liabilities of certain partners by establishing a *limited partnership*, wherein certain partners are designated *general partners* and others *limited partners*. Limited partnerships are quite common in the area of real estate investment, but they do not work well with most types of businesses.

your liability would be limited to the amount of your investment in the business.[2]

While a proprietorship or a partnership can commence operations without much paperwork, setting up a corporation is a bit more involved. The incorporators must prepare a charter and a set of bylaws. The *charter* includes the following information: (1) name of the proposed corporation, (2) type of activities it will pursue, (3) amount of capital stock, (4) number of directors, (5) names and addresses of directors, and (6) duration (if limited). The charter is filed with the secretary of the state in which the firm will be headquartered, and when it is approved, the corporation is officially in existence.

The *bylaws* are a set of rules drawn up by the founders of the corporation to aid in governing the internal management of the company. Included are such points as (1) how directors are to be elected (all elected each year or, say, one-third each year); (2) whether the existing stockholders shall have the first right to buy any new stock the firm issues; and (3) what provisions there are for management committees, such as an executive committee or a finance committee, and their duties. Also included is the procedure for changing the bylaws themselves, should conditions require it.

The value of any business other than a very small one will probably be maximized if it is organized as a corporation. The reasons are outlined below:

1. Limited liability reduces risk to investors, and the lower the risk, other things held constant, the higher the value of the firm.
2. Value is dependent on growth opportunities, which in turn are dependent on a firm's ability to attract capital. Since corporations can attract capital more easily than unincorporated businesses, they have superior growth opportunities.
3. The value of an asset also depends on its *liquidity*, which means the ease of selling the asset and converting it to cash. Since an investment in the stock of a corporation is much more liquid than a similar investment in a proprietorship or partnership, this too means that corporate organization can enhance the value of a business.
4. Corporations are taxed differently from proprietorships and partnerships. In some instances the tax laws favor corporations. This point is discussed in detail later in the chapter.

Since most firms are indeed managed with value maximization in mind, it is easy to see why most business is conducted by corporations.

---

[2] In the case of small corporations, the limited liability feature is often a fiction, as bankers and credit managers frequently require personal guarantees from the stockholders of small, weak businesses.

Business firms, as well as individuals and government units, often need to raise capital. For example, suppose Tampa Electric Company forecasts an increase in the demand for power in its service area and decides to build a new power plant. It almost certainly will not have the $500 million necessary to pay for the plant, so it will have to raise this capital in the market. Or suppose that Mr. Jones, the proprietor of a local hardware store, decides to expand into appliances. Where will he get the money to buy the initial inventory of TV sets, washers, and freezers? Similarly, if the Smith family wants to buy a home that costs $60,000, but they have only $10,000 in savings, how can the Smiths raise the additional $50,000? At the same time, if the City of Sacramento wants to borrow $20 million to finance a new sewer plant, while the federal government needs some $60 billion to cover its projected 1982 deficit, they each need sources for raising this capital.

On the other hand, some individuals and firms have incomes which are greater than their current expenditures, so they have funds available to invest. For example, Edgar Rice has an income of $36,000, but his expenses are only $30,000, and in 1981 Xerox Corporation had accumulated about $500 million of excess cash which it could make available for investment.

It is in the *financial markets* that entities wanting to borrow money are brought together with those having surplus funds. Note that "markets" is plural—there are a great many different financial markets in a developed economy. Each market deals with a somewhat different type of security, serves a different kind of customer, or operates in a different part of the country. Some of the major types of markets are listed below:

1. *Money markets* are defined as the markets for short-term (less than one year) debt securities. The New York money market is the world's largest, and it is dominated by the major U.S. banks, although branches of foreign banks also operate there.

2. *Capital markets* are defined as the markets for long-term debt and corporate stocks. The New York Stock Exchange, which handles the stocks of the largest corporations, is a prime example of a capital market. The stocks and bonds of smaller corporations are handled in other segments of the capital market.

3. *Mortgage markets* deal with loans on residential, commercial, and industrial real estate, and on farmland.

4. *Consumer credit markets* involve loans on autos and appliances, as well as loans for education, vacations, and so on.

5. *World, national, regional, and local markets* also exist. Thus, depending on an organization's size and scope of operations, it can borrow all around the world, or it may be confined to strictly local, even neighborhood, markets.

The Financial Markets

A healthy economy is vitally dependent on efficient transfers of funds from savers to firms and individuals who need capital, that is, on *efficient financial markets*. Without efficient transfers, the economy simply could not function: Tampa Electric could not raise capital, so Tampa's citizens would have no electricity; the Smith family would not have adequate housing; Edgar Rice would have no place to invest his savings; and so on. Obviously, our level of productivity, hence our standard of living, would be much lower, so it is absolutely essential that our financial markets function efficiently—not only quickly, but also at a low cost.[3]

Financial Intermediaries (Financial Institutions)

It is, of course, possible for individual savers to strike bargains with firms and others who need capital—some capital is transferred on a one-to-one basis between people who have money and those who need it. However, most transfers occur through specialized financial institutions which serve as *intermediaries* between savers and users of capital. The economic rationale for the development of a system of intermediaries is *market efficiency*: (1) the costs of transferring funds from those with excess funds to those who need funds are reduced, (2) the risks faced by savers are lessened, and (3) the liquidity of savers is increased.

To illustrate, if Tampa Electric Company tried to go out and borrow $500 million from individual savers, the costs would be prohibitive. The company does not have the marketing expertise required to locate people with money, to design securities whose features would appeal to these savers, or to convince them that the securities being offered are fairly priced and of good quality. Thus, the cost of direct transfers would be high, and these high costs not only would raise the cost of electricity to Tampa Electric's customers but also would lower the effective return to the savers who finally bought its stock and bonds.

The situation would be even worse for the Smiths, who want credit to buy a house. Edgar Rice might have $6,000 to lend, but the Smiths need $50,000. Also, Rice is not likely to know how to investigate the value of the Smiths' house, how to ascertain their credit standing, how to write the mortgage in proper legal form, and so on. Further, the Smiths would probably not be able to repay Rice on short notice if he wanted his $6,000 back, and Rice would probably not be willing to lend the money for 25 or 30 years with no possibility of getting it back if he needed it. At the same time, Rice would be taking quite a chance by putting all his money into one investment. A basic rule of investing is: Don't put all your eggs in one basket. Yet if Rice tried to spread his savings out among a number of borrowers, then his problems would multiply.

---

[3] When organizations such as the United Nations design plans to aid developing nations, just as much attention must be paid to the establishment of efficient financial markets as to electrical power, transportation, and communications systems. Economic efficiency is simply impossible without a good system for allocating capital within the economy.

The solution to Tampa Electric's, the Smiths', and Mr. Rice's problems is our system of specialized financial intermediaries, or *financial institutions*. A few of them are listed below:

1. *Commercial banks* are the "department stores" of finance, serving a wide variety of savers and those with needs for funds.

2. *Mutual savings banks* operate primarily in the Northeastern states, accept savings primarily from individuals, and lend mainly on a long-term basis to home buyers and large corporations.

3. *Savings and loan associations* generally serve individual savers and residential mortgage borrowers.

4. *Pension funds* are retirement plans funded by corporations or government agencies for their workers and administered primarily by the trust departments of commercial banks or by life insurance companies. Pension funds invest in bonds, stocks, mortgages, and real estate.

5. *Life insurance companies* take savings in the form of annual premiums, then invest the funds received in stocks, bonds, real estate, and mortgages, and, finally, upon the deaths of the insured parties, make payments to their beneficiaries.

6. *Investment banking houses* (or brokerage houses) are the organizations which help firms such as Tampa Electric sell stocks and bonds to investors. Investment bankers also facilitate the transfer of outstanding securities from one investor to another through markets such as the New York Stock Exchange. Making it possible to sell securities on short notice if one needs money is called "making the securities more *liquid*." The greater the degree of liquidity, the more willing investors are to commit their capital. Hence, the more liquid a security, the lower the rate of interest required to induce savers to buy it.

There are many other types of financial institutions, but these are the main ones. Without them, our economic system simply could not operate. Also, new financial institutions are periodically created as our economy evolves, and structural changes occur over time in the existing institutions. The major trend during the 1970s has been for the different institutions to become less specialized and more like one another. It remains to be seen just how far this trend will continue during the 1980s.

Regulatory Agencies

Our financial markets are regulated by government agencies. The banking system is regulated by several agencies, including the Federal Reserve System, which controls the volume of bank deposits (the money supply) in an effort to hold down inflation while still maintaining a growing economy. In addition, several other state and federal agencies try to insure the soundness of the banks and the safety of depositors' funds. The stock and bond markets are regulated by the Securities and Exchange Commission (SEC), which tries to insure (1) that investors are not given deceptive and misleading information and (2) that brokerage firms are financially sound. Savings and loans, life insurance companies, credit unions, and other institutions are all subject to similar regulation. The primary purpose of this regulation is to maintain investor confidence, which is vital to an efficient financial system.

Interest Rates and the Cost of Capital

Capital in a free economy is allocated through the price system. The interest rate is the price paid for borrowed capital, while in the case of equity capital, investors expect compensation in the form of dividends and capital gains. Firms with the most profitable investment projects can pay the most for capital, so they tend to attract it away from inefficient firms or from those whose products are not in demand. Of course, our economy is not completely free in the sense of being influenced only by market forces. Thus, the federal government has agencies which help individuals or groups as stipulated by Congress to obtain credit on favorable terms. Among those eligible for this kind of assistance are small businesses, certain minorities, firms willing to build plants in areas with high unemployment, and so on. Still, most capital in the U.S. economy is allocated through the price system.

Figure 2-1 shows how supply and demand interact to determine interest rates in two capital markets. Markets A and B represent two of the many capital markets in existence. The going interest rate (k) is 10 percent for the low-risk securities in Market A. Borrowers whose credit is strong enough to qualify for this market can obtain funds at a cost of 10 percent, and investors who want to put their money to work at low risk can obtain a 10 percent return. Riskier borrowers must obtain higher-cost funds in Market B. There, investors who are more willing to take risks invest with the expectation of receiving a 12 percent return but also with the realization that they might receive much less.

If the demand for funds in a market declines, as it typically does during a business recession, the demand curve will shift to the left (or down) as shown by Curve D_2 in Market A. The market clearing, or equilibrium, interest rate (k) in this example will decline to 8 percent. You can also visualize what will happen if the Federal Reserve tightens credit: The supply curve (S_1) will shift to the left, and this will raise interest rates and lower the demand for funds.

Capital markets are interdependent. For example, assuming that Markets A and B were in equilibrium before the demand shift to D_2 in Market A, then investors were willing to accept the higher risk in Market B in exchange for a *risk premium* of 12% − 10% = 2%. After the shift to D_2, the risk premium will immediately rise to 12% − 8% = 4%. In all likelihood, this much larger premium will induce some of the lenders in Market A to shift to Market B. This, in turn, will cause the supply curve in

Figure 2-1
Interest Rates as a Function of Supply and
Demand for Funds

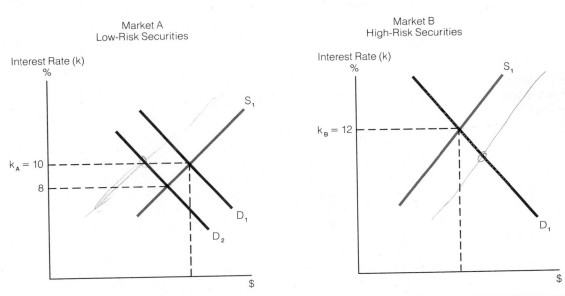

Market A
Low-Risk Securities

Market B
High-Risk Securities

Market A to shift to the left (or up) and that in Market B to shift to the right. This transfer of capital between markets will raise interest rates in Market A and lower them in Market B.

As we have seen, there are many, many capital markets in the United States. U.S. firms also raise capital throughout the world, while foreign borrowers obtain capital in the U.S. There are markets in the U.S. for real estate loans; farm loans; business loans; federal, state, and local government loans; and consumer loans. Within each category, there are also regional markets, as well as submarkets. For example, in real estate there are separate markets for first and second mortgages and for owner-occupied homes, apartments, office buildings, shopping centers, vacant land, and so on. Within the business sector, there are dozens of types of debt (see Chapters 10 and 13) and a sharply differentiated market for common stocks as opposed to debt.

There are as many prices as there are types of capital, and these prices change over time with changes in supply and demand conditions. Figure 2-2 shows how long- and short-term interest rates to business borrowers have varied over the last twenty-eight years. Notice that short-term interest rates are especially prone to rise during booms, then fall during recessions. (The shaded areas of the chart indicate recessions.) When the econ-

Figure 2-2
Long- and Short-Term Interest Rates, 1953-1981

Note: The shaded areas designate business recessions. Short-term rates are measured by four- to six-month A-rated commercial paper and long-term rates by A-rated corporate bonds.
Sources: Federal Reserve Bulletin, U.S. Department of Commerce, Moody's Investors Service.

omy is expanding, firms need capital, and this pressure to borrow pushes rates up. Also, inflationary pressures are strongest during business booms, so at such times the Federal Reserve tends to tighten the money supply, which also exerts an upward pressure on rates. Just the reverse holds true during recessions—the Fed increases the money supply, slack business reduces the demand for credit, and the result is a drop in interest rates.

These tendencies do not hold exactly—the early part of the 1974-1975 recession is a case in point. The price of oil increased dramatically in 1974, exerting inflationary pressures on other prices and raising fears of serious, long-term inflation. These fears pushed rates to high levels; investors "looked over the valley" of the 1974-1975 recession, forecasted a continued problem with inflation, and demanded an inflation premium that kept long-term rates high by historic standards.[4]

The relationship between inflation and long-term interest rates is highlighted in Figure 2-3, which plots rates of inflation along with long-term interest rates. From 1960 through 1964, when the average rate of inflation was 1.4 percent, interest rates on A-rated bonds ranged from 4 to 5 percent. As the war in Vietnam accelerated in the mid-1960s, the rate of inflation increased, and interest rates began to rise. The rate of inflation dropped after 1970, and so did long-term interest rates. However, the lifting of wage and price controls, in conjunction with the Arab oil embargo and a quadrupling of oil prices in 1974, caused a spurt in the price level, which drove interest rates to new record highs in 1974 and 1975. Inflationary pressures eased in late 1975 and 1976 but then rose again after 1976. In 1981, as this is written, inflation rates are at the highest levels on record, and fears of continued double digit inflation have pushed interest rates up to historic highs.

Figure 2-3
**Relationship between Annual Inflation Rates and
Long-Term Interest Rates, 1960-1981**

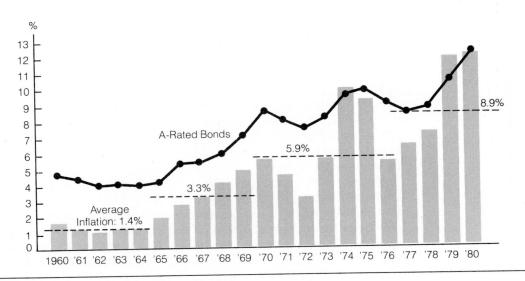

[4] Short-term rates are responsive to current economic conditions, while long-term rates primarily reflect long-run expectations for inflation. As a result, short-term rates are sometimes above and sometimes below long-term rates. The relationship between long-term and short-term rates is called the *term structure of interest rates*. This topic is discussed in Appendix 2A.

Interest rates also vary depending on the riskiness of the borrower—the greater the risk, the higher the interest rate that lenders charge. Thus, had AAA bonds (which are less risky than A bonds) been used in Figures 2-2 and 2-3, the interest rate lines would have been somewhat lower. Also, as we shall see in Chapters 4 and 5, common stock represents an investment security much like a bond. Whereas the interest rate represents the "price" paid for debt capital, there is a similar "price" associated with capital supplied in the form of common stock. This "price," which is called the *cost of common equity*, moves up when interest rates go up and down when rates fall. Further, since a firm's common stock is riskier than its bonds, the cost of equity capital exceeds the cost of bonds. Therefore, if the cost of equity were plotted in Figure 2-3, it would lie somewhat above the line for A-rated bonds and move up and down with bond rates. These points are analyzed in depth in later chapters.

The Federal Income Tax System

The value of any financial asset, including stocks, bonds, or even whole firms, depends on the stream of *usable* income produced by the asset. Usable income means income *after taxes*. Proprietorship and partnership income must be reported and taxed as personal income to the owners. Most corporations must first pay taxes on their own income, and stockholders must then pay taxes on corporate after-tax income distributed to them as dividends. Therefore, consideration must be given to both *personal* and *corporate* income taxes.

Federal income tax rates for individuals may be as high as 70 percent. When state income taxes are included, the marginal tax rate on an individual's income can approach 90 percent. Business income is also taxed heavily. The income from partnerships and proprietorships is reported by the individual owners and taxed at their own rates, while corporate profits are subject to federal income tax rates of up to 46 percent, in addition to state income taxes. Because of the magnitude of the tax bite, taxes play an important role in many financial decisions.

Taxes are so complicated that university law schools offer master's degrees in taxation to practicing lawyers, many of whom also have CPAs. In a field complicated enough to warrant such detailed study, we can only cover the highlights. This is all that is really necessary, because business people and investors should and do rely on tax specialists rather than trust their own limited knowledge. Still, it is important to know the basic elements of the tax system as a starting point for discussions with tax experts.[5]

---

[5] It should be noted that Congress changes the tax laws fairly often. The provisions given here are those for 1981 as they existed in the spring of 1981. At the time, a major rewrite of the tax laws was under active consideration. Tax rates will probably be lowered.

Individuals pay taxes on wages and salaries, on investment income (dividends, interest, and profits from the sale of securities), and on the profits of proprietorships and partnerships. Our tax rates are *progressive*; that is, the higher the income, the larger the percentage paid in taxes. Rates in 1981 ranged from 14 percent on the first $500 of taxable income to 70 percent on each dollar of income over $100,000, with a 50 percent limit on such earned income as salaries.[6]

The tax rate on the last unit of income is defined as the *marginal tax rate*. Thus, for a person with taxable income in excess of $100,000, the marginal tax rate is 70 percent. (The *average tax rate* on the $100,000 would be much lower than 70 percent.)

Taxes on Dividend and Interest Income. Dividend and interest income is fully taxed at rates going up to 70 percent.[7] Since corporations pay dividends out of earnings that have already been taxed, there is *double taxation* of corporate income. However, the first $200 of dividend or interest income ($400 for married couples filing joint returns) is *excluded* from personal income taxes.

no longer

Capital Gain versus Ordinary Income. Assets such as stocks, bonds, and real estate are defined as *capital assets*. If you buy a capital asset and later sell it for more than your purchase price, the profit is defined as a *capital gain*. If you suffer a loss, it is called a *capital loss*.

An asset sold within one year of the time it was purchased produces a *short-term gain or loss*, while an asset held for more than one year produces a *long-term gain or loss*. Thus, if you buy 100 shares of GM stock for $70 per share and sell it for $80, you make a capital gain of 100 × $10, or $1,000. If you sell the stock for $60, you have a $1,000 capital loss. If you hold the stock for more than one year, the gain or loss is long-term; otherwise, it is short-term.

Long-term capital gains are generally taxed at much lower rates than short-term gains (or other ordinary income). As a rule, 60 percent of any

---

[6] It is interesting to note what happens to taxes under inflation. Suppose you had a taxable income of $10,000. Your tax bill would be $2,090. Now suppose inflation causes prices to double, and your income, being tied to a cost of living index, rises to $20,000. Because our tax rates are progressive, your taxes would jump to $5,230. Your after-tax income has thus increased from $7,910 to $14,770, but, since prices have doubled, your real income has *declined* from $7,910 to $7,385 (calculated as $1/2$ of $14,770). You are in a higher tax bracket, so you are paying a higher percentage of your real income in taxes. If this happens to everyone, and if Congress fails to change tax rates sufficiently, then the federal government gets a larger share of the national product. This is exactly what happened during the 1970s. Indexing tax rates would eliminate this problem.

[7] However, interest on state and local government bonds is not subject to federal income taxes. Thus, for a taxpayer in the 70 percent bracket, a 3.6 percent state bond would provide as much after-tax income as a 12 percent corporate bond:

Tax exempt yield = Taxable yield (1 − Tax rate) = 12% (0.3) = 3.6%.

long-term gain is excluded from taxable income, so taxes are paid on only 40 percent of long-term gains income. Thus, if one individual has $1,000 of short-term capital gains (or dividends) and is in the 30 percent marginal tax bracket, the gains tax will be $300, while if another individual in the same bracket has $1,000 of long-term gains, the tax will be only 0.3 ($1,000 − $600) = $120. As a percentage, the long-term gains tax rate is 40 percent of the ordinary tax rate.[8]

The fact that capital gains income is taxed at a lower rate than dividend or interest income has an important bearing on financial management. As we shall see, most businesses have at least some flexibility in providing returns to investors in the form of dividends or capital gains. Since the tax treatment of income from an asset has a significant effect on the value of the asset, personal income taxes must be taken into account by a firm seeking to maximize the value of its stock.

Corporate Income Taxes

The corporate tax structure is relatively simple. In 1981, corporations were required to pay 17 percent on the first $25,000 of taxable income, and the rates progressed up to 46 percent on all income over $100,000:

1st $25,000:   17%
2nd $25,000:   20%
3rd $25,000:   30%
4th $25,000:   40%
Over $100,000: 46%

Therefore, if a firm had $200,000 of taxable income, its tax bill would be

$$
\begin{aligned}
\text{Taxes} &= 0.17\,(\$25,000) + 0.20\,(\$25,000) + 0.30\,(\$25,000) \\
&\quad + 0.40\,(\$25,000) + 0.46\,(\$100,000) \\
&= \$4,250 + \$5,000 + \$7,500 + \$10,000 + \$46,000 \\
&= \$72,750.
\end{aligned}
$$

Thus, the corporate tax is very progressive up to $100,000 of income, but it is constant thereafter.[9] Also, note that the marginal corporate tax rate is 46 percent if a firm earns over $100,000.

Interest and Dividend Income *Received* by a Corporation. Interest income received by a corporation is taxed as ordinary income at regular corporate tax rates. However, 85 percent of the dividends received by one corpo-

---

[8] Some complexities in long-term capital gains taxes are not discussed here: (1) Gains realized before October 31, 1978, are treated differently from those realized after that date. (2) Long-term gains are regarded as tax preference items; if tax preferences exceed $10,000, special tax rates apply. (3) Corporate capital gains are treated differently from the gains realized by individuals. (4) For individuals in very high tax brackets, the long-term capital gains tax is generally limited to 28 percent.

[9] Corporate capital gains and losses are also subject to special (more favorable) tax treatment, but the rules are too complicated to be described in this book. The interested reader is referred to *Federal Tax Course* (Englewood Cliffs, N.J.: Prentice-Hall, 1981).

ration from another is excluded from taxable income. The remaining 15 percent of dividends received is taxed at the ordinary tax rate. Thus, a corporation earning over $100,000 and paying a 46 percent tax rate would pay (0.15) (0.46) = 0.069 = 6.9 percent of its dividend income as taxes. If this corporation passes its own after-tax income on to its stockholders as dividends, the income is ultimately subjected to *triple taxation*. The original corporation is first taxed, then the second corporation is taxed, and finally the individual who receives the dividend is taxed. This is the reason for the 85 percent exclusion on intercorporate dividends.

Notice that for a corporation with surplus funds which can be invested in marketable securities, the tax factor favors investment in stocks, which pay dividends, rather than bonds, which pay interest. For example, suppose a firm had $100,000 to invest and it could buy bonds that paid interest of $10,000 per year or stock that paid dividends of $10,000. If the firm were in the 46 percent tax bracket, its tax on the interest would be 0.46 ($10,000) = $4,600, and its after-tax income would be $5,400. If it bought stock, its tax would be (0.15) ($10,000) (0.46) = $690, and its after-tax income would be $9,310. Other factors might lead the firm to invest in bonds, but the tax factor favors stock investments when the investor is a corporation.

Interest and Dividends *Paid* by a Corporation. A firm's operations can be financed with either debt or equity capital. If it uses debt, it must pay interest on this debt, while firms generally pay dividends to equity investors (stockholders). The interest paid by a corporation is deducted from its operating income to obtain its taxable income, but dividends paid are not deductible. Thus, interest is paid with before-tax dollars, while dividends are paid with after-tax dollars.

To illustrate, suppose a firm's assets produced $25,000 of income before taxes. If the firm were financed entirely by debt and had interest payments of $25,000, then, as we see in Table 2-1, taxable income to the firm would be zero, taxes would be zero, and investors would receive the entire $25,000. (The term *investors* includes both stockholders and bondholders.) If the firm had no debt and was therefore financed only by

	Use Bonds	Use Stock
Before-tax income	$25,000	$25,000
Interest	25,000	0
Taxable income	$ 0	$25,000
Taxes (17%)	0	4,250
After-tax income	$ 0	$20,750
Income to investors	$25,000	$20,750

Table 2-1
Cash Flows to Investors under Bond and Stock Financing

stock, the $25,000 would be taxable income to the corporation, the tax would be $25,000 (0.17) = $4,250, and investors would receive only $20,750 versus $25,000 under debt financing. Of course, it is generally not possible to finance exclusively with debt capital, and the risk of doing so would offset the benefits of the higher expected income. *Still, the fact that interest is a deductible expense has a profound effect on the way businesses are financed—our tax system favors debt financing over equity financing.* This point is discussed in more detail in Chapters 15, 16, and 17.

Corporate Loss Carry-Back and Carry-Forward. Ordinary corporate operating losses can be carried back to each of the three preceding years and forward for the following seven years and used to offset taxable income in those years. For example, an operating loss in 1981 can be used to reduce taxable income in 1978, 1979, or 1980, and then any remaining losses can be carried forward and used in 1982, 1983, 1984, 1985, 1986, 1987, and 1988. The loss must be first applied to the earliest year, then to the next earliest year, and so on.

To illustrate, suppose that the Detroit Dolphins, Inc., made $1 million every year except for 1981, when they had a bad season and lost $6 million. The Dolphins would use the carry-back feature to recompute taxes for 1978, using $1 million of the operating losses to reduce the 1978 profit to zero. This would permit them to recover the amount of taxes paid in 1978, so in 1982 the Dolphins would receive a refund of 1978 taxes because of the loss experienced in 1981. Since $5 million of unrecovered losses would still be available, the Dolphins would repeat this procedure for 1979 and 1980. Then in 1982, 1983, and 1984 they would apply the loss carry-forward to reduce profits to zero in each of these years. The purpose of permitting this loss averaging is, of course, to avoid penalizing corporations whose incomes fluctuate widely.

Improper Accumulation to Avoid Payment of Dividends. Corporations could refrain from paying dividends to permit their stockholders to avoid personal income taxes on dividends. To prevent this, the tax code states that earnings accumulated by a corporation are subject to penalty rates *if the purpose of the accumulation is to enable stockholders to avoid the personal income tax.* Of income not paid out in dividends, a cumulative total of $150,000 (the balance sheet item "retained earnings") is by law exempted from the improper accumulation tax. This is a benefit primarily to small corporations.

Although there is a penalty rate on all amounts over $150,000 *shown to be unnecessary to meet the reasonable needs of the business,* many companies do indeed have legitimate reasons for retaining earnings over $150,000 and are thus not subject to the penalty rate. Earnings during a given year may be retained and used to pay off debt, to finance growth, and to provide the corporation with a cushion against possible cash drains caused by losses. How much a firm should properly accumulate for uncertain contingencies is a matter of judgment. We shall consider this matter again in Chapter 18, which deals with corporate dividend policy.

Consolidated Corporate Tax Returns. If a corporation owns 80 percent or more of another corporation's stock, it can aggregate income and file one consolidated tax return. Thus, losses in one company can be used to offset profits in another company. (Similarly, one division's losses can offset another division's profits.) No business ever wants to incur losses (you can go broke losing $1 to save 46 cents in taxes), but tax offsets do make it more feasible for large, multidivisional corporations to undertake risky new ventures or ventures that will suffer losses during a developmental period.

Investment Tax Credit. The investment tax credit (ITC) is designed to stimulate business investment. The ITC is figured as a percentage of the cost of certain new assets used in any corporation, partnership, or proprietorship. Congress varies the ITC depending on economic conditions. In 1981 it was 10 percent for an asset with a life of seven years or more, $6^2/_3$ percent for an asset with a life of five or six years, $3^1/_3$ percent for an asset with a life of three or four years, and zero for an asset with a life of less than three years.

The ITC is a direct reduction of taxes. Suppose a firm estimates that its taxable income next year will be $100,000 and that its tax bill will be $26,750. Now it decides to buy equipment that costs $50,000 and has a ten year life. The company's tax bill will be reduced by (0.10) ($50,000) = $5,000. *Thus, the ITC reduces the effective cost of fixed assets, and this stimulates investment.*[10]

Subchapter S of the Internal Revenue Code provides that small businesses which meet certain restrictions as spelled out in the code may be set up as corporations and thus receive the benefits of the corporate form of organization—especially limited liability—yet still be taxed as proprietorships or as partnerships rather than as corporations. There are several reasons for a small firm's electing to be taxed under the Subchapter S procedures, including the following:

Taxation of Small Businesses: Subchapter S Corporations

1. If the firm is profitable, its income is reported on a pro rata basis by its owners. This avoids the double taxation that occurs when a corporation reports income, pays taxes, and then pays dividends that are taxable income to the stockholders.

---

[10] If a firm does not have sufficiently large income taxes, it cannot fully utilize the ITC immediately. The ITC can be carried forward and used in future years, but there are also financing arrangements that effectively transfer the ITC from low-profit to high-profit firms. The details are covered in the chapter on leasing.

2. If the firm has operating losses, these losses can be claimed on a pro rata basis by the stockholders as deductions against their ordinary income. This is an especially attractive feature for a new business that incurs heavy start-up costs and whose stockholders are in high marginal tax brackets because of income from other sources.

3. If the firm has investment tax credits, these credits can be passed along to the stockholders. Again, this is especially important for small, new firms that are making heavy capital investments yet whose income is insufficient to fully utilize the tax credits generated by these investments, but whose owners have outside income that can be offset by the firm's tax credits.

Many factors other than taxes bear on the question of whether or not a firm should be organized as a corporation. However, the existence of Subchapter S makes it possible for most small businesses to have the benefits of a corporation yet be taxed at the owners' personal tax rates.

Summary

This chapter presented some background information on forms of business organizations, interest rates, and income taxes. First, we saw that firms may be organized as *proprietorships,* as *partnerships,* or as *corporations.* The first two types are easy and inexpensive to form. However, corporations have a major advantage in terms of risk reduction, growth possibilities, and investment liquidity. These features make it possible to maximize the value of any business except very small ones by using the corporate form of organization. Accordingly, corporations are the dominant form of business.

Interest rates represent the price of borrowed money. Rates have been rising for the past twenty-five years, pushed up by rising inflation rates. Short-term rates are often lower than long-term rates, and short-term rates are also subject to wider swings. As a general rule, short-term rates fall during recessions, then rise when the economy is strong. An astute financial manager will recognize these tendencies and try to take advantage of them to finance growth with the lowest-cost capital. Such action, if successful, will help to maximize the value of the firm.

The value of any asset is dependent on the effective income it produces for its owner. *Effective income* means *after-tax income.* Since corporate income is taxed at rates going up to 46 percent, and since personal income is subjected to additional taxes of up to 70 percent, the tax consequences of various decisions have a most important impact on a firm's value. It is not necessary to memorize everything about taxes—indeed, this would be impossible. However, you should know the basic differences between corporate and personal taxes, that interest is a tax deduction to the payer of the interest, that capital gains and operating income are taxed differently, what the investment tax credit is, and so on. These matters will come up throughout the book as we examine various types of financial decisions.

2-1 What are the three principal forms of business organizations? What are the advantages and disadvantages of each?

2-2 Which fluctuate more, long-term or short-term interest rates?

2-3 You feel that the economy is just entering a recession. Your firm must raise capital immediately, and debt will be used. Would it be better to borrow on a long-term or a short-term basis? Explain.

2-4 What effect does inflation have on long-term interest rates?

2-5 Suppose you owned 100 shares of General Motors stock and the company just earned $6 per share. Suppose further that GM could either pay all its earnings out as dividends (in which case you would receive $600) or retain the earnings in the business, buy more assets, and cause the price of the stock to go up by $6 per share (in which case the value of your stock would rise by $600).

  a. How would the tax laws influence what you, as a typical stockholder, would want the company to do?

  b. Would your choice be influenced by how much other income you had?

  c. How might the corporation's decision with regard to dividend policy influence the price of its stock?

2-6 What does *double taxation of corporate income* mean?

2-7 If you were starting a business, what tax considerations might cause you to prefer to set it up as a proprietorship or a partnership rather than as a corporation?

2-8 Explain how the federal income tax structure affects the choice of financing (debt versus equity) used by U.S. business firms.

2-9 How can the federal government influence the level of business investment by adjusting the ITC?

2-10 Suppose interest rates on residential mortgages of equal risk were 14 percent in California and 16 percent in New York. Could this differential persist? What forces might tend to equalize rates? Would differences in borrowing costs for businesses of equal risk located in California and New York be more or less likely than mortgage rate differentials? Would differentials in the cost of money for New York and California firms be more likely to exist if the firms being compared were very large or if they were very small?

2-11 What would happen to the standard of living in the U.S. if people lost faith in the safety of our financial institutions? Explain.

2-12 How does a cost-efficient capital market hold down the prices of goods and services?

Questions

Problems

2-1 The Dyl Pickle Company had an income of $200,000 from operations after all operating costs but before (a) interest charges of $10,000, (b) dividends paid of $20,000, and (c) income taxes. What is Dyl Pickle's income tax liability?

2-2 a. The Thomas Corporation had $200,000 of taxable income from operations. What is the company's federal income tax bill for the year?

b. Assume Thomas receives an additional $20,000 interest income from some bonds it owns. What is the tax on this interest income?

c. Now assume that Thomas does not receive the interest income but that it does receive an additional $20,000 as dividends on some stock it owns. What is the tax on this dividend income?

2-3 The Columbus Construction Company has made $200,000 before taxes for each of the last fifteen years, and it expects to make $200,000 a year before taxes in the future. However, this year (1982) Columbus incurred a loss of $1,200,000. Columbus will claim a tax credit at the time it files its 1982 income tax returns and will receive a check from the U.S. Treasury. Show how it calculates this credit, and then indicate Columbus's tax liability for each of the next five years. Assume a 50 percent tax rate on *all* income to ease the calculations.

Selected References

There are many excellent textbooks on financial institutions, financial markets, and interest rates. One concise, excellent treatment, and a good starting point, is

Van Horne, James C., *Financial Market Rates and Flows* (Englewood Cliffs, N.J.: Prentice-Hall, 1978).

Another is

Rose, Peter, and Donald R. Fraser, *Financial Institutions* (Dallas, Tex.: Business Publications, 1980).

For current empirical data and a forecast of monetary conditions, see the most recent edition of this annual publication:

Salomon Brothers, *Supply and Demand for Credit* (New York Plaza, New York, N.Y.).

Perhaps the best reference on taxes is

Prentice-Hall, *Federal Tax Course* (Englewood Cliffs, N.J.: Updated annually).

Appendix 2A

The Term Structure of Interest Rates

A study of Figure 2-2 in Chapter 2 reveals that at certain times such as in 1975, short-term interest rates were lower than long-term rates, while at other times such as in 1980, short rates were above long rates. The relationship between long and short rates is important to corporate treasurers who must decide whether to borrow by issuing long- or short-term debt. It is also important to investors who must decide whether to buy long- or short-term bonds. The analysis that should precede such buy and sell decisions will be explored in depth later in the book, but it is essential to understand at this point (1) how long and short rates are related to one another and (2) what causes shifts in their relative positions.

	Interest Rate			Table 2A-1
Term to Maturity	December 1975	March 1980	September 1980	U.S. Treasury Bond Interest Rates on Different Dates
1 week	5.20%	17.19%	8.92%	
6 months	5.93	15.03	11.39	
1 year	6.16	14.03	11.61	
5 years	7.50	13.47	11.69	
10 years	7.58	12.75	11.70	

To begin, we can look up in a source such as the *Wall Street Journal* or the *Federal Reserve Bulletin* the interest rates on bonds of various maturities at a given point in time.[1] For example, Table 2A-1 presents interest rates for Treasury issues of different maturities on three dates.

The set of data for a given date, when plotted on a graph such as Figure 2A-1, is defined as *the term structure of interest rates,* or *the yield curve,* on that date. The yield curve changes over time as interest rates rise and fall. In December 1975, short-term rates were considerably lower than long-term rates, so the yield curve was *upward sloping*. In March 1980, short-term rates were much higher than long rates, so the yield curve on that date was *downward sloping*. However, from March to September, yields on short-term bonds fell sharply, and in September the yield curve was again *upward sloping*, but with all rates much higher than they had been in December 1975. Had we drawn the yield curve during June of 1980, it would have been essentially *horizontal*, for long and short bonds on that date had about the same rate of interest.

Why does the shape of the yield curve change over time? There are three major explanations, or theories, of yield curve patterns.

The expectations theory postulates that the term structure of interest rates is established through the following three-step process:

The Expectations Theory

1. Investors at any point in time have a set of expectations about the rate of inflation in each future year. A number of governmental and private organizations forecast future interest rates and give (or sell) these forecasts to investors. Most brokerage houses make inflation forecasts available to their customers.

[1] Since it is important to hold risk constant when analyzing the effects of maturity on bond yields, term structure studies must analyze the bonds of a given organization. We shall concentrate here on U.S. Treasury securities. The same general relationship would hold if we were to analyze the bonds of a corporation such as AT&T or IBM. Also, for simplicity we shall call all Treasury debt "bonds" even though the official terminology includes bonds, bills, notes, and certificates. These terminological differences are immaterial for our purposes.

Figure 2A-1
Yield Curves on U.S. Treasury Debt

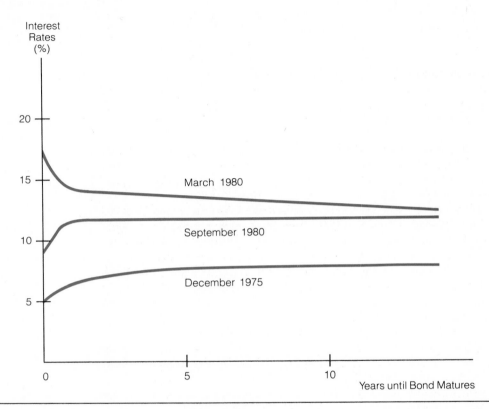

2. The short-term rate that is expected to exist at the beginning of a given future year is estimated by adding the rate of inflation expected during that year to a constant "real" or inflation-free rate. The level of the real risk-free rate is probably about 2 percent.[2] Therefore, if most investors expected a zero rate of inflation, then the market-clearing interest rate on short-term Treasury bonds would probably be about 2 percent. If inflation were expected to be 10 percent, then the interest rate on one year bonds would be about 12 percent.

3. Given the estimated set of future short-term interest rates, the long-

[2] Since we are dealing with *expectations*, or what is in the minds of investors on average, it is clearly impossible to measure exactly either expected inflation rates or the real rate of interest. A 1-to-3 percent range for the real short-term rate (and a 2-to-4 percent range for the real long-term rate) is frequently cited by such authorities as G. William Miller, former chairman of the Federal Reserve Board and later secretary of the Treasury.

term rate is then established as the geometric average of future short-term rates.

The following example illustrates the process. It is not complicated, but it can be confusing if it is not approached in a careful, step-by-step manner.

Step 1: Inflation Adjustment. Assume that on January 1, 1982, you have $1, which you plan to hold for one year. How much will it be worth, in beginning-of-year dollars, on December 31, 1982, if the rate of inflation (I) during 1982 is 12 percent, or 0.12? The answer is 89 cents:

$$\text{Value in } 1/1/82 \text{ dollars} = \frac{\$1}{1 + I} = \frac{\$1}{1.12} = \$0.8929.$$

Step 2: Offsetting Inflation. What rate of interest (k) would you have to earn on your $1 to end up on December 31, 1982, with as much purchasing power as you had on January 1, 1982; that is, to end up with $1 rather than 89 cents in 1/1/82 dollars? The answer is found by solving for k in this equation:

$$\$1 = \frac{\$1\ (1 + k)}{(1 + I)}$$

$$\$1 = \frac{\$1\ (1 + k)}{1.12}$$

$$1.12 = 1 + k$$

$$k = 1.12 - 1.00$$

$$= 0.12 \text{ or } 12\%.$$

Thus, if your money earned 12 percent, you would exactly "break even" in the battle against inflation.[3]

Step 3: The Real Rate of Return. What *nominal rate of interest* (k) would you have to earn on your money (disregarding taxes) in order to earn a given real rate of return (RR)? In general, this equation may be used:[4]

---

[3] Of course, most of us would have to pay taxes on the interest earned, so we would really have to earn 12% *after taxes* to break even in a world with 12% inflation.

[4] The proof of Equation 2A-1 is developed as follows: First, we want to end up with $1 + $RR, or 1 + RR after one year, with dollars expressed in beginning-of-year terms. We will actually end up with $1(1 + k) nominal, or end-of-year, dollars. Dividing $1(1 + k) by (1 + I) converts the end-of-year dollars to beginning-of-year values. Therefore, we can set (1 + RR) equal to $1(1 + k)/(1 + I) and solve for k to find the nominal k needed to produce a real return RR given an inflation rate of I percent:

$$1 + RR = \frac{\$1(1 + k)}{1 + I}$$

$$(1 + RR)(1 + I) = \$1(1 + k)$$

$$k = (1 + RR)(1 + I) - 1$$

$$= 1 + RR + I + RR(I) - 1$$

$$= RR + I + (RR)I. \tag{2A-1}$$

$$k = RR + I + RR(I). \qquad (2A\text{-}1)$$

In our example, with $I = 12\%$, the nominal rate required to produce RR $= 2\%$ must be 14.24%:

$$
\begin{aligned}
k &= 0.02 + 0.12 + (0.02)\,(0.12) \\
&= 0.02 + 0.12 + 0.0024 \\
&= 0.1424 \\
&= 14.24\%.
\end{aligned}
$$

Thus, if you started with \$1 (or \$1 million) and earned an interest rate of 14.24 percent during a period when inflation was 12 percent, then your real rate of return would be 2 percent:

$$\frac{\text{Ending nominal dollars}}{1 + \text{Inflation rate}} = \frac{\$1\,(1.1424)}{1.12} = \frac{\$1.02 \text{ in beginning-}}{\text{of-year dollars}}$$

Step 4: The Cross Product. As a practical matter, the cross-product term, or $RR(I) = 0.0024 = 0.24\%$ in the example, is generally dropped on the grounds that it is so small that we do not need to worry about it. Also, our ability to estimate expected inflation does not warrant four decimal place accuracy. Therefore, as a reasonable approximation, the nominal interest rate on one year Treasury bonds can be estimated as

$$k = RR + I \approx 2\% + I. \qquad (2A\text{-}2)$$

Here k is the nominal risk-free rate, or the rate of interest on Treasury bonds, the real rate (RR) is assumed to be 2 percent, and I stands for the expected inflation rate. Equation 2A-2 is known as the *Fisher Equation*; it is named after the great economist Irving Fisher, upon whose work this appendix is based.[5]

Step 5: The Fisher Equation. Thus far we have considered only one year bonds. Our goal, however, is to show how the interest rates on longer-term bonds such as those maturing in five, ten, or twenty years are related to the set of one year bond rates. As a general rule, the Fisher Equation holds reasonably well for interest rates on longer maturity bonds. *However, in the analysis of long-term bonds, the inflation rate which must be used is the geometric average expected inflation rate over the life of the bond in question.* To illustrate, we would find the interest rate on a three year bond, if RR $= 2\%$ and inflation is expected to be 12%, 10%, and 8% during the next three years, as follows:

1. *Find the geometric average interest rate:*

---

[5] Irving Fisher, *The Theory of Interest* (New York: Macmillan, 1930).

Average inflation rate $= [(1 + I_1)(1 + I_2) \cdots (1 + I_n)]^{1/n} - 1.0$
$$= [(1.12)(1.10)(1.08)]^{1/3} - 1.0$$
$$= (1.33056)^{0.3333} - 1.0$$
$$= 0.09988$$
$$= 9.988\%. \qquad\qquad (2A\text{-}3)$$

2. *Apply the Fisher Equation:*

$$R_F = RR + I = 2\% + 9.988\% = 11.988\%.$$

If you bought a three year bond which yielded 11.988%, it would provide a return equivalent to the return you would expect if you adopted the strategy of investing in a series of three one–year bonds:

Value of $1 at the end
of 3 years
if you buy a three year bond $= \$1(1.11988)^3 = \$1.40.$
which yields
11.988% per year

Value of $1 at the end
of 3 years
if you buy a series $= \$1(1.14)(1.12)(1.10) = \$1.40.$
of one year bonds which yield
14%, 12%, and 10%

Given the assumed one year inflation rates and, therefore, interest rates over the next three years, if the interest rate on a three year bond were anything other than 11.988 percent, a disequilibrium would exist. For example, if rates on three year bonds were below 11 percent, then you and others would refuse to buy these bonds, choosing instead to invest in the series of one year bonds with a higher expected total return. Conversely, if the rate were 12½ percent on the three year bonds, there would be an excess demand for these bonds. This would push their prices up and their yields down until an equilibrium was established at k = 11.988%.

This completes our discussion of the expectations theory of the term structure. As we have seen, the expectations theory postulates that interest rates are based almost entirely on expectations about future inflation. Therefore, changes in interest rates, according to the expectations theory, are dependent entirely on changes in expectations about future inflation. Empirical studies certainly support the expectations theory to a large extent, but the empirical evidence also suggests that factors in addition to inflationary expectations also affect interest rates. This point is explored in the following sections.

The liquidity preference theory states that investors generally prefer short-term bonds to long-term bonds, and, accordingly, that rates on long-term bonds will generally be above the level called for by the expec-

The Liquidity Preference Theory

tations theory. In Chapter 4 we will demonstrate (1) that the value of outstanding bonds will fall if interest rates rise, and (2) that such losses are much greater on long-term than on short-term bonds. For example, if the going rate of interest on both one year and thirty year bonds was 10 percent, and if you owned one of each type bond that paid an interest payment of $100 per year (so the bonds each had a 10 percent coupon), then your bonds would sell for $1,000 each, and the total value of your investment would be $2,000. Now if the expected rate of inflation increased, causing the going rate of interest to rise from 10 percent to 20 percent, the value of your one year bond would decline from $1,000 to $916.67, which would be bad, but the value of your thirty year bond would fall to $502.11, which would be terrible.

This decline in the values of outstanding bonds as a result of an increase in interest rates is known as *interest rate risk,* and it is greater the longer the maturity of the bond. Since investors prefer less risk to more, other things held constant, it follows that investors would, at the same expected rate of return, prefer to own short rather than long bonds. Therefore, long-term interest rates should have a tendency to exceed short rates, other things held constant.

The implications of liquidity preferences for the yield curve are shown in Figure 2A-2. The solid lines represent two yield curves that might exist on two different dates if the pattern of rates were determined by the expectations theory only, while the dashed lines show how liquidity premiums increase the interest rates on longer-term bonds. We have no way of knowing exactly how large the liquidity premium is, or how it increases as the term to maturity of a bond lengthens. However, the limited evidence which is available suggests that very long-term bonds (bonds that mature in twenty to thirty years) have liquidity premiums in the range of 1 to 2 percentage points over the rate called for by the pure expectations theory.[6]

Market Segmentation, or "Preferred Habitat", Theory

Some lenders are required by law or custom to lend primarily on a short-term basis—banks are an example. Other lenders, such as pension funds and life insurance companies, prefer to operate in the long-term market. Similarly, some borrowers need short-term money (for instance, retailers borrowing money to build inventories prior to the Christmas season),

---

[6] See J. Houston McCulloch, "An Estimate of the Liquidity Premium," *Journal of Political Economy*, vol. 83 (January 1975), 95-119. See also James C. Van Horne, *Financial Market Rates and Flows* (New York: Prentice-Hall, 1978), especially Chapter 4. Also, note that Treasury bonds are free of default risk but corporate bonds are exposed to possible default losses. Further, the longer the maturity of a corporate bond, the greater the danger of default. Thus, the liquidity premium for corporate bonds should be larger than that for U.S. Treasury bonds.

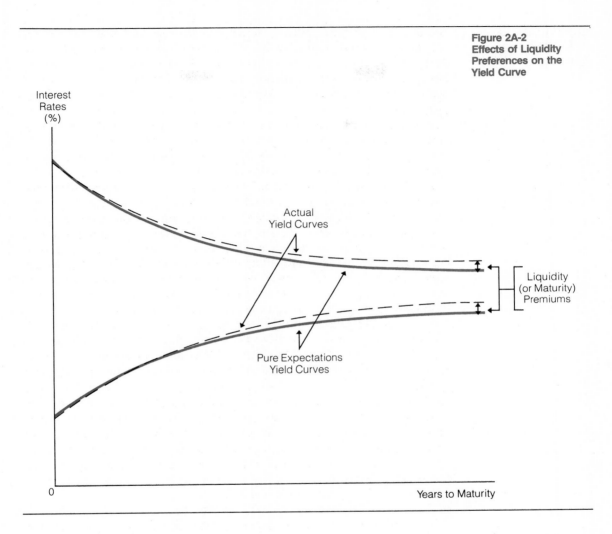

Figure 2A-2
Effects of Liquidity
Preferences on the
Yield Curve

while other borrowers need long-term capital (for example, people buying homes). Therefore, according to the market segmentation theory, if more funds are available in the short-term end of the market relative to demand than in the long-term market, then the yield curve will slope upward more steeply than would be called for by the expectations and liquidity preference theories. Since, at any given time, it is possible for either long-term or short-term money to be in relatively tight supply, market segmentation, or "preferred habitat," could cause the yield curve to slope either up or down.

Empirical Tests of Yield Curve Theories

A number of empirical tests of yield curve theories have been conducted. All three theories have some merit, although expectations about future inflation has definitely been the strongest factor in recent years. Further discussions of interest rate theories and empirical tests are, however, best deferred for advanced finance courses.[7]

Problems

2A-1 If the rate of interest on two year bonds is 9.4 percent and the rate on one year bills is 12 percent, what is the expected rate on one year bills one year from now? What does this suggest about the expected rate of inflation? Assume that RR = 2%.

2A-2 In late 1980, the U.S. Commerce Department released new figures which showed that inflation was running at an annual rate of close to 15 percent. However, many investors expected the new Reagan administration to be more effective in controlling inflation than the Carter administration had been. At the time, the prime rate of interest was 21 percent, a record high. However, many observers felt that the extremely high interest rates and generally tight credit, which were brought on by the Federal Reserve System's attempts to curb the inflation rate, would shortly bring about a recession, which would in turn lead to a decline in the inflation rate and also in the rate of interest. Assume that at the beginning of 1981 the expected rate of inflation for 1981 is 12 percent, for 1982 it is 10 percent, for 1983 it is 8 percent, and for 1984 and thereafter it is 6 percent.

a. What is the (geometric) average expected inflation rate over the five years?

b. What average *nominal* interest rate will, over the five year period, produce a 2 percent real rate of return? (Use the Fisher approximation.)

c. Assuming a real required rate of RR = 2%, estimate the interest rate on bonds that mature in 1, 2, 5, 10, and 20 years, and draw a yield curve based on these data. Use the Fisher Equation approximation.

d. Describe the general economic conditions that could be expected to produce an upward sloping yield curve.

e. If the consensus view of investors is that the expected rate of inflation for every future year is 10 percent, that is, $I_t = I_{t+1} = 10\%$ for $t = 1$ to ∞, what do you think the yield curve will look like? Consider all the factors that are likely to offset the curve. Does your answer here make you question the yield curve you drew in Part c?

2A-3 It is now January 1, 1982. The real rate of return is estimated to be 2 percent. A three year bond bought today would yield $k_d = 10.638\%$. A one year bond purchased today would yield $k_d = 14\%$. A one year bond purchased one year from today (on 1/1/83) is expected to carry an interest rate of 10 percent. What is the expected rate of inflation in the third year, according to the expectations theory?

---

[7] Van Horne, *Financial Market Rates and Flows*, provides a good summary of the empirical studies of term structure.

In August 1981, as this book was going into the final production stages, Congress voted to make a number of important changes in the federal income tax system as Part II of President Reagan's economic program. Part I of the program was a massive reduction in the federal budget, and the tax changes in Part II were, basically, a series of tax cuts which returned to the private sector the money saved by the budget reductions.

President Reagan's position, which not everyone agreed with, but which was supported by a good bit of tangible evidence, was based on these premises:

1. The federal government had gotten too big, and it was doing things that could be better done by state and local governments or by the private sector.
2. The steeply progressive nature of our personal income tax system, with rates going up to 70 percent on top of double taxation of corporate income, was not only destroying the incentive to work and to save but was also diverting savings into tax sheltered "gimmicks" rather than into truly productive, economically efficient investments.
3. "Entitlements" programs such as Medicare, Medicaid, Social Security, and general welfare programs, which had been taking an increasing share of the national income, were creating disincentives to work, hence hurting national productivity and at the same time limiting the funds available for capital expenditures, which would boost productivity.
4. The factors noted above were contributing to our accelerating rate of inflation.
5. Inflation, combined with our progressive tax rates, was leading to *de facto* tax rate increases which channeled an ever higher proportion of our national income to Washington and thus perpetuated and exacerbated all these problems (see footnote 6, page 25).

This philosophical position dictated the thrust of the tax law changes: Both personal and corporate taxes were generally reduced, and the reductions were made in a manner designed to encourage investment. Here are the key provisions of the 1981 law as they relate to the materials covered in this book:

1. The distinction between earned and unearned income is eliminated, and the top personal tax rate is set at 50 percent. This eliminates the penalty tax on dividend and interest income, and it simultaneously adds to the incentive to save and helps redirect savings from tax shelters into corporate stocks and bonds.
2. Since the effective capital gains tax rate is to be 40 percent of an individual's marginal personal tax rate, the top long-term capital gains rate is lowered from $0.4 (70\%) = 28\%$ to $0.4 (50\%) = 20\%$. This also increases the reward for saving and provides investment capital to industry.

Appendix 2B

1981 Changes in the Federal Tax Law

3. Tax rates on individuals' incomes will be reduced on an across-the-board basis by approximately 23 percent in three stages between 1981 and 1984. In effect, rates will decline from 1980 levels by 1.25 percent in 1981, by 10 percent in 1982, by 19 percent in 1983, and by 23 percent in 1984 and thereafter. Since the change relates to basic rates, it means, generally speaking, that everyone's taxes will fall by about 23 percent. Since wealthy people pay out far more of their incomes than poor people, the wealthy receive more benefits from the 1981 changes than they did from past changes. (The U.S. income tax system began in 1913. Since that time, whenever the federal government needed to increase revenues, the tendency was to raise rates for wealthy individuals and corporations by the largest amounts and, when excessive revenues permitted tax cuts, to cut the taxes most for those with lower incomes. This led to a very progressive tax system. The 1981 changes reduce somewhat the level of progressiveness in U.S. tax rates.)

4. The $200 or $400 interest/dividend exclusion from personal income taxes has been changed to an exclusion of $100 for a single taxpayer or ·$200 on a joint return, and it is applicable only to dividends received. However, several other provisions are made to reduce the tax on interest received from investments made in certain financial institutions, especially those associated with home financing.

5. Up to $750 ($1,500 for a joint return) of dividends received from a public utility and reinvested in the stock of the utility will be excluded from taxes for 1982, 1983, 1984, and 1985. (See Chapter 18 for a discussion of automatic dividend reinvestment plans.)

6. The investment tax credit on eligible equipment is set at 6 percent on property with a three-year life and at 10 percent on longer-lived property. Also, as discussed in Chapter 22, leasing is often used as a vehicle to permit businesses with low incomes and low taxes, which cannot use all available tax credits, to pass these credits on to a financial institution in exchange for lower rental payments. The new tax law facilitates this transfer by making it easier to qualify a transaction as a lease.

7. Corporate tax rates have been lowered on the first two brackets (from 17 percent down to 15 percent in 1983 and thereafter for up to $25,000 of income, and from 20 percent to 18 percent on the second $25,000), but corporate rates remain unchanged for the higher brackets. However, the changes in depreciation discussed below do lower effective corporate tax rates substantially for firms of all sizes.

8. Both operating losses and tax credits can now be carried forward for fifteen years rather than seven years. The three-year carry-back provision is unchanged.

9. The major benefit of the new tax law to larger businesses is a liberalization of depreciation procedures. Appendix 11D contains a de-

tailed discussion of depreciation and its effects on corporate cash flows. In essence, the shorter the period over which an asset must be written off, the greater the tax shelter to a business and the lower the business's taxes. The new law shortens assets' depreciable lives for tax purposes considerably, and this will (a) reduce corporations' tax payments, (b) increase their cash flows, (c) make investments more profitable, and (d) therefore increase the level of investment and the modernization of industry in the United States.

The new tax law is very complicated and detailed—Congress published a sixty-three page *summary of the highlights*— so this appendix hardly scratches the surface of either the law or the changes. However, it does update those aspects of the tax law that are used in the text.

Fundamental Concepts in Finance: Risk, Return, and Value II

Each financial decision must be analyzed in terms of its effect on the value of the firm's stock. This requires a knowledge of how alternative decisions will influence stock prices. A stock price model is essential to such knowledge. Accordingly, we develop in Part II a basic stock valuation model for use throughout the remainder of the book.

Part II begins with Chapter 3, which takes up the concept of the time value of money. Next, in Chapter 4, we use this concept to see how bond and stock values are determined. Finally, Chapter 5 discusses the concept of risk, including ways of measuring a security's risk and the impact risk has on stock prices and rates of return.

3   Time Value of Money

In Chapter 1 we saw that the primary goal of management is to maximize the value of a firm's stock. We also saw that stock values depend, in part, on the timing of the cash flows investors expect to receive—income expected soon is valued more highly than income expected far in the future. These concepts are extended and made more precise in this chapter, which shows how the timing of cash flows affects asset values and rates of return.

The principles of the time value of money as developed here also have many other applications, ranging from setting up schedules for paying off loans to making decisions about whether to acquire new equipment. *In fact, of all the techniques used in finance, none is more important than the time value of money.* This concept is used throughout the remainder of the book, so it is vital to understand the material in this chapter thoroughly before going on to other topics.

Future Value (or Compound Value)

A dollar in hand today is worth more than a dollar to be received in the future because, if you had it now, you could invest it and earn interest. To illustrate, suppose you had $100 and deposited it in a bank savings account that paid 5 percent interest compounded annually. How much would you have at the end of one year? Let us define terms as follows:

PV = present value of your account, or the beginning amount, $100.

k = interest rate the bank pays you = 5 percent per year, or, expressed as a decimal, 0.05.

I = dollars of interest you earn during the year = $k\,(PV)$.

FV_n = future value, or ending amount, of your account at the end of n years. Whereas PV is the value now, at the *present* time, FV_n is the value n years into the future, after compound interest has been earned. Note also that FV_0 is the future value *zero* years into the future, which is the *present*, so $FV_0 = PV$.

In our example, $n = 1$, so $FV_n = FV_1$, and it is calculated as follows:

$$
\begin{aligned}
FV_1 &= PV + I \\
&= PV + PV(k) \\
&= PV(1 + k).
\end{aligned}
\tag{3-1}
$$

We can now use Equation 3-1 to find how much your account is worth at the end of one year:

$$FV_1 = \$100(1 + 0.05) = \$100(1.05) = \$105.$$

Your account earned \$5 of interest (I = \$5), so you have \$105 at the end of the year.

Now suppose you leave your funds on deposit for five years; how much will you have at the end of the fifth year? The answer is \$127.63; this value is worked out in Table 3-1.

Year	Beginning Amount, PV	×	(1 + k)	=	Ending Amount, FV_n
1	\$100.00		1.05		\$105.00
2	105.00		1.05		110.25
3	110.25		1.05		115.76
4	115.76		1.05		121.55
5	121.55		1.05		127.63

**Table 3-1
Compound Interest
Calculations**

Notice that the Table 3-1 value for FV_2, the value of the account at the end of Year 2, is equal to

$$FV_2 = FV_1(1 + k) = PV(1 + k)(1 + k) = PV(1 + k)^2.$$

Continuing, we see that FV_3, the balance after three years, is

$$FV_3 = FV_2(1 + k) = PV(1 + k)^3.$$

In general, FV_n, the future value at the end of n years, is found as follows:

$$FV_n = PV(1 + k)^n. \qquad (3\text{-}2)$$

Applying Equation 3-2 to our five year, 5 percent case, we obtain

$$FV_5 = \$100(1.05)^5$$
$$= \$100(1.2763)$$
$$= \$127.63,$$

which is the same as the value worked out in Table 3-1.

If an electronic calculator is handy, it is easy enough to calculate $(1 + k)^n$ directly.[1] However, tables have been constructed for values of

---

[1] For example, to calculate $(1 + k)^n$ for k = 5% = 0.05 and n = 5 years, we multiply (1 + k) = (1.05) times (1.05); multiply this product by (1.05); and so on:

$$(1 + k)^n = (1.05)(1.05)(1.05)(1.05)(1.05) = (1.05)^5 = 1.2763.$$

This same result is obtained using the exponential function of a calculator.

$(1 + k)^n$ for wide ranges of k and n. Table 3-2 is illustrative. Notice that we have used the term *period* rather than *year* in Table 3-2. As we shall see later in the chapter, compounding can occur over periods of time different from one year. Thus, while compounding is often on an annual basis, it can be quarterly, semiannually, monthly, or for any other period.

Table 3-2
Future Value of $1 at the End of n Periods:
$$FVIF_{k,n} = (1 + k)^n$$

Period (n)	1%	2%	3%	4%	5%	6%	7%	8%	9%	10%
0	1.0000	1.0000	1.0000	1.0000	1.0000	1.0000	1.0000	1.0000	1.0000	1.0000
1	1.0100	1.0200	1.0300	1.0400	1.0500	1.0600	1.0700	1.0800	1.0900	1.1000
2	1.0201	1.0404	1.0609	1.0816	1.1025	1.1236	1.1449	1.1664	1.1881	1.2100
3	1.0303	1.0612	1.0927	1.1249	1.1576	1.1910	1.2250	1.2597	1.2950	1.3310
4	1.0406	1.0824	1.1255	1.1699	1.2155	1.2625	1.3108	1.3605	1.4116	1.4641
5	1.0510	1.1041	1.1593	1.2167	1.2763	1.3382	1.4026	1.4693	1.5386	1.6105
6	1.0615	1.1262	1.1941	1.2653	1.3401	1.4185	1.5007	1.5869	1.6771	1.7716
7	1.0721	1.1487	1.2299	1.3159	1.4071	1.5036	1.6058	1.7138	1.8280	1.9487
8	1.0829	1.1717	1.2668	1.3686	1.4775	1.5938	1.7182	1.8509	1.9926	2.1436
9	1.0937	1.1951	1.3048	1.4233	1.5513	1.6895	1.8385	1.9990	2.1719	2.3579
10	1.1046	1.2190	1.3439	1.4802	1.6289	1.7908	1.9672	2.1589	2.3674	2.5937
11	1.1157	1.2434	1.3842	1.5395	1.7103	1.8983	2.1049	2.3316	2.5804	2.8531
12	1.1268	1.2682	1.4258	1.6010	1.7959	2.0122	2.2522	2.5182	2.8127	3.1384
13	1.1381	1.2936	1.4685	1.6651	1.8856	2.1329	2.4098	2.7196	3.0658	3.4523
14	1.1495	1.3195	1.5126	1.7317	1.9799	2.2609	2.5785	2.9372	3.3417	3.7975
15	1.1610	1.3459	1.5580	1.8009	2.0789	2.3966	2.7590	3.1722	3.6425	4.1772

We define the term *future value interest factor for k,n* ($FVIF_{k,n}$) to equal $(1 + k)^n$. Therefore, Equation 3-2 may be written as $FV_n = PV(FVIF_{k,n})$. It is necessary only to go to an appropriate interest table to find the proper interest factor. For example, the correct interest factor for our five year, 5 percent illustration can be found in Table 3-2. We look down the period column to 5, then across this row to the 5 percent column to find the interest factor, 1.2763. Then, using this interest factor, we find the value of $100 after five years as $FV_5 = PV(FVIF_{5\%, 5}) = \$100(1.2763) = \$127.63$, which is identical to the value obtained by the long method in Table 3-1.

Graphic View of the Compounding Process: Growth

Figure 3-1 shows how $1 (or any other sum) grows over time at various rates of interest. The points plotted on the 5 percent and 10 percent curves are taken from the appropriate columns of Table 3-2. The higher the rate of interest, the faster the rate of growth. The interest rate is, in

Figure 3-1
Relationship between
Future Value Interest
Factors, Interest Rates,
and Time

fact, the growth rate; if a sum is deposited and earns 5 percent, then the funds on deposit grow at the rate of 5 percent per period.

Present Value

Suppose you are offered the alternative of receiving either $127.63 at the end of five years or X dollars today. There is no question that the $127.63 will be paid in full (perhaps the payer is the United States government). Having no current need for the money, you would deposit it in a bank account that pays 5 percent interest. (Five percent is defined to be your "opportunity cost," or the rate of interest you could earn on alternative investments of equal risk.) What value of X would make you indifferent between X dollars today and the promise of $127.63 five years hence?

Table 3-1 showed that the initial amount of $100 growing at 5 percent a year yields $127.63 at the end of five years. Thus, you should be indifferent in your choice between $100 today and $127.63 at the end of five years. The $100 is defined as the present value, or PV, of $127.63 due in five years when the applicable interest rate is 5 percent. Therefore, if X is anything less than $100, you would prefer the promise of $127.63 in five years to X dollars today.

In general, the present value of a sum due n years in the future is the amount which, if it were on hand today, would grow to equal the future sum. Since $100 would grow to $127.63 in five years at a 5 percent interest rate, $100 is defined to be the present value of $127.63 due five years in the future when the appropriate interest rate is 5 percent.

Finding present values (or *discounting,* as it is commonly called) is simply the reverse of compounding, and Equation 3-2 can readily be transformed into a present value formula:

$$FV_n = PV(1 + k)^n, \tag{3-2}$$

which, when solved for PV, gives

$$PV = \frac{FV_n}{(1 + k)^n} = FV_n(1 + k)^{-n} = FV_n \left[\frac{1}{(1 + k)} \right]^n \tag{3-3}$$

Tables have been constructed for the term in brackets for various values of k and n; Table 3-3 is an example. For a more complete table, see Table A-1 at the end of the book. For the illustrative case being considered, look down the 5 percent column in Table 3-3 to the fifth row. The figure shown there, 0.7835, is the *present value interest factor* ($PVIF_{k,n}$) used to determine the present value of $127.63 payable in five years, discounted at 5 percent:

$$PV = FV_5 \, (PVIF_{5\%,5})$$
$$= \$127.63(0.7835)$$
$$= \$100.$$

Graphic View of the Discounting Process

Figure 3-2 shows how interest factors for discounting decrease as the discounting period increases. The curves in the figure were plotted with data taken from Table 3-3; they show that the present value of a sum to be received at some future date decreases (1) as the payment date is ex-

Table 3-3
Present Values of $1 Due at the End of n Periods:

$$PVIF_{k,n} = \frac{1}{(1 + k)^n} = \left[\frac{1}{(1 + k)} \right]^n$$

Period (n)	1%	2%	3%	4%	5%	6%	7%	8%	9%	10%	12%	14%	15%
1	.9901	.9804	.9709	.9615	.9524	.9434	.9346	.9259	.9174	.9091	.8929	.8772	.8696
2	.9803	.9612	.9426	.9246	.9070	.8900	.8734	.8573	.8417	.8264	.7972	.7695	.7561
3	.9706	.9423	.9151	.8890	.8638	.8396	.8163	.7938	.7722	.7513	.7118	.6750	.6575
4	.9610	.9238	.8885	.8548	.8227	.7921	.7629	.7350	.7084	.6830	.6355	.5921	.5718
5	.9515	.9057	.8626	.8219	.7835	.7473	.7130	.6806	.6499	.6209	.5674	.5194	.4972
6	.9420	.8880	.8375	.7903	.7462	.7050	.6663	.6302	.5963	.5645	.5066	.4556	.4323
7	.9327	.8706	.8131	.7599	.7107	.6651	.6227	.5835	.5470	.5132	.4523	.3996	.3759
8	.9235	.8535	.7894	.7307	.6768	.6274	.5820	.5403	.5019	.4665	.4039	.3506	.3269
9	.9143	.8368	.7664	.7026	.6446	.5919	.5439	.5002	.4604	.4241	.3606	.3075	.2843
10	.9053	.8203	.7441	.6756	.6139	.5584	.5083	.4632	.4224	.3855	.3220	.2697	.2472

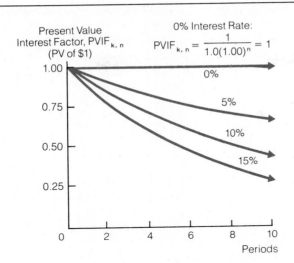

Present Value
Interest Factor, PVIF$_{k, n}$
(PV of $1)

0% Interest Rate:

$$PVIF_{k, n} = \frac{1}{1.0(1.00)^n} = 1$$

**Figure 3-2
Relationship between
Present Value Interest
Factors, Interest Rates,
and Time**

tended further into the future and (2) as the discount rate increases. If relatively high discount rates apply, funds due in the future are worth very little today. Even at relatively low discount rates, the present values of funds due in the distant future are quite small. For example, $1 due in ten years is worth about 61 cents today if the discount rate is 5 percent, but it is worth only 25 cents today at a 15 percent discount rate. Similarly, $1 due in five years at 10 percent is worth 62 cents today, but at the same discount rate $1 due in ten years is worth only 39 cents today.

Notice that Equation 3-2, the basic equation for compounding, was developed from the logical sequence set forth in Table 3-1; the equation merely presents in mathematical form the steps outlined in the table. The present value interest factor (PVIF$_{k,n}$) in Equation 3-3, the basic equation for discounting or finding present values, was found as the *reciprocal* of the future value interest factor (FVIF$_{k,n}$) for the same k,n combination. In other words,

**Future Value
versus
Present Value**

$$PVIF_{k,n} = \frac{1}{FVIF_{k,n}}.$$

For example, the *future value* interest factor for 5 percent over five years is seen in Table 3-2 to be 1.2763. The *present value* interest factor for 5 percent over five years must be the reciprocal of 1.2763:

$$PVIF_{5\%,\ 5\ years} = \frac{1}{1.2763} = 0.7835.$$

The $PVIF_{k,n}$ found in this manner does, of course, correspond with the $PVIF_{k,n}$ shown in Table 3-3.

The reciprocal nature of the relationship between present value and future value permits us to find present values in two ways—by multiplying or by dividing. Thus, the present value of $1,000 due in five years and discounted at 5 percent may be found as

$$PV = FV_n(PVIF_{k,n}) = FV_n\left[\frac{1}{1+k}\right]^n = \$1,000(0.7835) = \$783.50,$$

or as

$$PV = \frac{FV_n}{FVIF_{k,n}} = \frac{FV_5}{(1+k)^5} = \frac{\$1,000}{1.2763} = \$783.50.$$

To conclude this comparison of present and future values, compare Figures 3-1 and 3-2. Notice that the vertical intercept is at 1.0 in each case, but future value interest factors rise, while present value interest factors decline.[2]

Future Value of an Annuity

An annuity is defined as a series of payments of a fixed amount for a specified number of periods. If payments occur at the end of each period, as they typically do, then we have an *ordinary annuity*, or a *deferred payment annuity* as it is sometimes called. If payments are made at the beginning of each period, then we have an *annuity due.* Since ordinary (or deferred) annuities are far more common in finance, when the word *annuity* is used in this book, you may assume that payments are received at the end of each period unless otherwise indicated.

A promise to pay $1,000 a year for three years is a three year annuity. If you were to receive such an annuity and were to deposit each annual payment in a savings account paying 4 percent interest, how much would you have at the end of three years? The answer is shown graphically as a *time line* in Figure 3-3. The first payment is made at the end of Year 1, the second at the end of Year 2, and the third at the end of Year 3. Thus, the first payment is compounded over two years; the second payment is compounded for one year; and the last payment is not compounded at all. When the future values of each of the payments are added, their total is the sum of the annuity. In the example, this total is $3,121.60.[3]

---

[2] Notice that Figure 3-2 is not a mirror image of Figure 3-1. The curves in Figure 3-1 approach ∞ as n increases; in Figure 3-2 the curves approach zero, not −∞.

[3] Had the annuity been an annuity due, the first $1,000 payment would have occurred at time t = 0, the second at t = 1, and the third at t = 2. Thus, each payment would have been compounded for an extra year, so the future value would have been larger. (It would have been $3,246.46.)

Figure 3-3
Time Line for an
Annuity: Future Value
with k = 4%

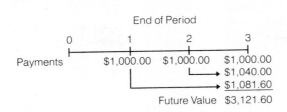

End of Period

	0	1	2	3
Payments		$1,000.00	$1,000.00	$1,000.00
				$1,040.00
				$1,081.60
			Future Value	$3,121.60

Expressed algebraically, with S_n defined as the future value of the annuity, R as the periodic receipt, n as the length of the annuity, and $FVIFA_{k,n}$ as the future value interest factor for an annuity, the formula is

$$S_n = R(1 + k)^{n-1} + R(1 + k)^{n-2} + \cdots + R(1 + k)^1 + R(1 + k)^0$$
$$= R[(1 + k)^{n-1} + (1 + k)^{n-2} + \cdots + (1 + k)^1 + (1 + k)^0]$$
$$= R \sum_{t=1}^{n} (1 + k)^{n-t}$$
$$= R[FVIFA_{k,n}].$$

The expression in brackets, $FVIFA_{k,n}$, has been calculated for various combinations of k and n.[4] An illustrative set of these annuity interest factors is given in Table 3-4.[5] To find the answer to the three year, $1,000 annuity problem, simply refer to Table 3-4, look down the 4 percent column to the row of the third period, and multiply the factor 3.1216 by $1,000. The answer is the same as the one derived by the long method illustrated in Figure 3-3:

$$S_n = R(FVIFA_{k,n}) \tag{3-4}$$
$$S_3 = \$1,000(3.1216) = \$3,121.60.$$

[4] The third equation is simply a shorthand expression in which sigma (Σ) signifies "sum up" or add the values of n factors. If $t = 1$, then $(1 + k)^{n-t} = (1 + k)^{n-1}$; if $t = 2$, then $(1 + k)^{n-t} = (1 + k)^{n-2}$; and so on until $t = n$, the last year the annuity provides any returns.

The symbol $\sum_{t=1}^{n}$ simply says, "Go through the following process: Let $t = 1$ and find the first factor. Then let $t = 2$ and find the second factor. Continue until each individual factor has been found, and then add these individual factors to find the value of the annuity."

[5] The equation given with Table 3-4 recognizes that an FVIFA factor is the sum of a geometric progression. The proof of this equation is given in all college algebra texts. Notice that it is easy to use the equation to develop annuity factors. This is especially useful if you need the FVIFA for some interest rate not given in the tables, for example, 6.5 percent. The equation is also useful for finding factors for fractional periods—for example, $2^{1/2}$ years—but one really needs a calculator with an exponential function for this. See Problem 3-23 for an example.

Table 3-4
Sum of an Annuity of $1 per Period for n Periods:

$$FVIFA_{k,n} = \sum_{t=1}^{n} (1 + k)^{n-t}$$
$$= \frac{(1 + k)^n - 1}{k}$$

Number of Periods	1%	2%	3%	4%	5%	6%	7%	8%
1	1.0000	1.0000	1.0000	1.0000	1.0000	1.0000	1.0000	1.0000
2	2.0100	2.0200	2.0300	2.0400	2.0500	2.0600	2.0700	2.0800
3	3.0301	3.0604	3.0909	3.1216	3.1525	3.1836	3.2149	3.2464
4	4.0604	4.1216	4.1836	4.2465	4.3101	4.3746	4.4399	4.5061
5	5.1010	5.2040	5.3091	5.4163	5.5256	5.6371	5.7507	5.8666
6	6.1520	6.3081	6.4684	6.6330	6.8019	6.9753	7.1533	7.3359
7	7.2135	7.4343	7.6625	7.8983	8.1420	8.3938	8.6540	8.9228
8	8.2857	8.5830	8.8923	9.2142	9.5491	9.8975	10.2598	10.6366
9	9.3685	9.7546	10.1591	10.5828	11.0266	11.4913	11.9780	12.4876
10	10.4622	10.9497	11.4639	12.0061	12.5779	13.1808	13.8164	14.4866

Notice that for all positive interest rates, the $FVIFA_{k,n}$ for the sum of an annuity is always equal to or greater than the number of periods the annuity runs.[6]

Present Value of an Annuity

Suppose you were offered the following alternatives: a three year annuity of $1,000 a year or a lump sum payment today. You have no need for the money during the next three years, so if you accept the annuity you would simply deposit the receipts in a savings account paying 4 percent interest. How large must the lump sum payment be to make it equivalent to the annuity? The time line shown in Figure 3-4 will help explain the problem.

The present value of the first receipt is $R[1/(1 + k)]$, the second is $R[1/(1 + k)]^2$, and so on. Defining the present value of an annuity of n

---

[6] It is worth noting that the entry for each period t in Table 3-4 is equal to the sum of the entries in Table 3-2 up to Period n − 1. For example, the entry for Period 3 under the 4 percent column in Table 3-4 is equal to 1.000 + 1.0400 + 1.0816 = 3.1216.

Also, had the annuity been an *annuity due,* then the three payments would have occurred at t = 0, t = 1, and t = 2. To find the future value of an annuity due, (1) look up the $FVIFA_{k,n}$ for n + 1 years, then subtract 1.0 from the amount to get the $FVIFA_{k,n}$ for the annuity due. In the example, the annuity due $FVIFA_{k,n}$ is 4.2465 − 1.0 = 3.2465 versus 3.1216 for an ordinary annuity. Because payments on an annuity due come earlier, it is a little more valuable than an ordinary (deferred) annuity.

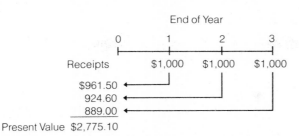

Figure 3-4
Time Line for an
Annuity: Present Value
with k = 4%

years as A_n, and with $PVIFA_{k,n}$ defined as the present value interest factor for an annuity, we may write the following equation in its several equivalent forms:

$$A_n = R\left(\frac{1}{1+k}\right)^1 + R\left(\frac{1}{1+k}\right)^2 + \cdots + R\left(\frac{1}{1+k}\right)^n$$

$$= R\left(\frac{1}{(1+k)} + \frac{1}{(1+k)^2} + \cdots + \frac{1}{(1+k)^n}\right)$$

$$= R\sum_{t=1}^{n}\left(\frac{1}{1+k}\right)^t$$

$$= R(PVIFA_{k,n}). \tag{3-5}$$

Again, tables have been worked out for $PVIFA_{k,n}$. Table 3-5 is illustrative; a more complete listing is found in Table A-2 in Appendix A.[7] From Table 3-5, the $PVIFA_{k,n}$ for a three year, 4 percent annuity is found to be 2.7751. Multiplying this factor by the $1,000 annual receipt gives $2,775.10, the present value of the annuity. This figure is identical to the long-method answer shown in Figure 3-4:

$$A_n = R(PVIFA_{k,n})$$
$$A_3 = \$1,000(2.7751)$$
$$= \$2,775.10.$$

Notice that the entry for each value of n in Table 3-5 is equal to the sum of the entries in Table 3-3 up to and including period n. For example,

---

[7] The second equation given at the top of Table 3-5 is derived in Appendix 4A, where we show that the PV of an annuity of n years is equal to the PV of a perpetuity minus the PV of the perpetuity discounted back for n years.

Table 3-5
Present Value of an Annuity of $1 per Period for
n Periods:

$$PVIFA_{k,n} = \sum_{t=1}^{n}\frac{1}{(1 + k)^t} = \frac{1 - \dfrac{1}{(1 + k)^n}}{k} = \frac{1}{k} - \frac{1}{k(1 + k)^n} \quad (3\text{-}6)$$

Number of Payments (n)	1%	2%	3%	4%	5%	6%	7%	8%	9%	10%
1	0.9901	0.9804	0.9709	0.9615	0.9524	0.9434	0.9346	0.9259	0.9174	0.9091
2	1.9704	1.9416	1.9135	1.8861	1.8594	1.8334	1.8080	1.7833	1.7591	1.7355
3	2.9410	2.8839	2.8286	2.7751	2.7232	2.6730	2.6243	2.5771	2.5313	2.4869
4	3.9020	3.8077	3.7171	3.6299	3.5460	3.4651	3.3872	3.3121	3.2397	3.1699
5	4.8534	4.7135	4.5797	4.4518	4.3295	4.2124	4.1002	3.9927	3.8897	3.7908
6	5.7955	5.6014	5.4172	5.2421	5.0757	4.9173	4.7665	4.6229	4.4859	4.3553
7	6.7282	6.4720	6.2303	6.0021	5.7864	5.5824	5.3893	5.2064	5.0330	4.8684
8	7.6517	7.3255	7.0197	6.7327	6.4632	6.2098	5.9713	5.7466	5.5348	5.3349
9	8.5660	8.1622	7.7861	7.4353	7.1078	6.8017	6.5152	6.2469	5.9952	5.7590
10	9.4713	8.9826	8.5302	8.1109	7.7217	7.3601	7.0236	6.7101	6.4177	6.1446

the PVIFA for 4 percent, three periods, as shown in Table 3-5, could have been calculated by summing values from Table 3-3:

$$0.9615 + 0.9246 + 0.8890 = 2.7751.$$

Notice also that for all positive interest rates, $PVIFA_{k,n}$ for the *present value* of an annuity is always less than the number of periods the annuity runs, whereas $FVIFA_{k,n}$ for the *sum* of an annuity is equal to or greater than the number of periods.[8]

Perpetuities

Most annuities call for payments to be made for some definite period of time: for example, $1,000 per year for three years. However, some annuities go on indefinitely; the payments represent an *infinite series*, and the

---

[8] Had the annuity been an *annuity due,* then in Figure 3-4 each $1,000 payment would have occurred one year earlier. Therefore, the PV of each individual payment would have been larger, and the PV of the annuity due, using the method in Figure 3-4, would have been $2,886.10 versus $2,775.10 for the ordinary annuity. Also, to find the $PVIFA_{k,n}$ for an *annuity due,* go through these steps: (1) look up the $PVIFA_{k,n}$ for n − 1 periods, then (2) add 1.0 to this amount to obtain the $PVIFA_{k,n}$ for the annuity due:

$$PVIFA_{k,n} = PVIFA_{k,n-1} + 1.0.$$
(Annuity due)

In the example, the $PVIFA_{k,n}$ for a 4 percent, three year annuity due is 1.8861 + 1.0 = 2.8861.

series is defined as a *perpetuity*. The value of a perpetuity is found by applying Equation 3-7:[9]

$$\text{Present value of a perpetuity} = \frac{\text{Receipt}}{\text{Discount rate}} = \frac{R}{k}. \quad (3\text{-}7)$$

To illustrate, after the Napoleonic Wars (1814), the British government sold a huge bond issue and used the proceeds to pay off many smaller issues that had been floated in prior years to pay for the war. Since the purpose of the new bonds was to consolidate past debts, the bonds were called "consols." Suppose each consol promised to pay $90 interest per year in perpetuity. (Actually, interest was stated in pounds.) What would each bond be worth if the going rate of interest, or the discount rate, were 8 percent? The answer is $1,125:

$$\text{Value} = \$90/0.08 = \$1,125.$$

Perpetuities are discussed further in Chapter 4, where procedures for finding the values of various types of securities (stocks and bonds) are analyzed.

Present Value of an Uneven Series of Receipts

The definition of an annuity includes the words *fixed amount*—in other words, annuities involve situations where cash flows are *identical* in every period. Although many financial decisions do involve constant cash flows, some important decisions are concerned with uneven flows of cash. In particular, common stock investments ordinarily involve uneven, hopefully increasing, dividend payments over time. Consequently, it is necessary to expand our analysis to deal with varying payment streams.

The PV of an uneven stream of future income is found as the sum of the PVs of the individual components of the stream. For example, suppose we are trying to find the PV of the stream of receipts shown in Table 3-6, discounted at 6 percent. As shown in the table, we multiply each receipt by the appropriate $PVIF_{k,n}$, then sum these products to obtain the PV of the stream, $1,413.24. Figure 3-5 gives a graphic view of the cash flow stream.[10]

The PV of the receipts shown in Table 3-6 and Figure 3-5 can also be

---

[9] The derivation of Equation 3-7 is given in Appendix 4A.

[10] This general equation may be used to find the PV of an uneven series of payments:

$$PV = \sum_{t=1}^{n} R_t \left(\frac{1}{1+k}\right)^t = \sum_{t=1}^{n} R_t (PVIF_{k,t}),$$

where R_t is the payment in any year t.

Table 3-6
Present Value of an
Uneven Stream of
Receipts

	Stream of Receipts	×	PVIF$_{k,n}$ (6%)	=	PV of Individual Receipts
Year 1	$ 100		0.9434		$ 94.34
Year 2	200		0.8900		178.00
Year 3	200		0.8396		167.92
Year 4	200		0.7921		158.42
Year 5	200		0.7473		149.46
Year 6	0		0.7050		0
Year 7	1,000		0.6651		665.10
				PV = sum =	$1,413.24

found by using the annuity equation; the steps in this alternative solution process are outlined below:

Step 1. Find PV of $100 due in Year 1:

$$\$100(0.9434) = \$94.34.$$

Step 2. Recognize that a $200 annuity will be received during Years 2 through 5. Thus, we could determine the value of a five year annuity, subtract from it the value of a one year annuity, and have remaining the value of a four year annuity whose first payment is due in two years. This result is achieved by subtracting the PVIFA for a one year, 6 percent

Figure 3-5
Time Line for an Uneven
Cash Flow Stream with
k = 6%

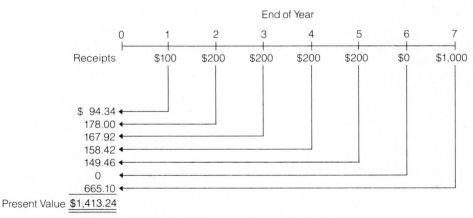

annuity from the PVIFA for a five year annuity and then multiplying the difference by $200:

$$\text{PV of the annuity} = \$200 \ (\text{PVIFA}_{6\%,5 \text{ yrs.}}) - \$200 \ (\text{PVIFA}_{6\%,1 \text{ yr.}})$$
$$= \$200 \ (\text{PVIFA}_{6\%,5 \text{ yrs.}} - \text{PVIFA}_{6\%,1 \text{ yr.}})$$
$$= \$200 \ (4.2124 - 0.9434)$$
$$= \$653.80.$$

Thus, the present value of the annuity component of the uneven stream is $653.80.

Step 3. Find the PV of the $1,000 due in Year 7:

$$\$1,000(0.6651) = \$665.10.$$

Step 4. Sum the components:

$$\$94.34 + \$653.80 + \$665.10 = \$1,413.24.$$

Either the Table 3-6 method or the method that utilizes the annuity formula can be used to solve problems of this type. However, the alternative annuity solution is easier if the annuity component runs for many years. For example, the alternative solution would be clearly superior for finding the PV of a stream consisting of $100 in Year 1, $200 in Years 2 through 29, and $1,000 in Year 30.[11]

We can use the basic equations developed above to determine the interest rates implicit in financial contracts.

Determining Interest Rates

Example 1. A bank offers to lend you $1,000 if you sign a note to repay $1,610.50 at the end of five years. What rate of interest are you paying?

1. Recognize that $1,000 is the PV of $1,610.50 due in five years:

$$\text{PV} = \$1,000 = \$1,610.50(\text{PVIF}_{k,5}).$$

2. Solve for $\text{PVIF}_{k,5}$:

$$\text{PVIF}_{k,5} = \$1,000/\$1,610.50 = 0.6209.$$

3. Now turn to Table 3-3 (or Table A-1). Look across the row for Period 5 until you find the value 0.6209. It is in the 10 percent column, so

---

[11] The future value of a series of uneven payments, often called the *terminal value*, is found by compounding each payment, then summing the individual future values:

$$\text{FV} = \sum_{t=1}^{n} R_t(1 + k)^{n-t}$$

you would be paying a 10 percent rate of interest if you were to take out the loan.

Example 2. A bank offers to lend you $25,000 to buy a home. You must sign a mortgage calling for payments of $2,545.16 at the end of each of the next twenty-five years. What interest rate is the bank charging you?

1. Recognize that $25,000 is the PV of a twenty-five year, $2,545.16 annuity:

$$PV = \$25,000 = \sum_{t=1}^{25} \$2,545.16 \left[\frac{1}{(1 + k)^t} \right] = \$2,545.16(PVIFA_{k,25}).$$

2. Solve for $PVIFA_{k,25}$.

$$PVIFA_{k,25} = \$25,000/\$2,545.16 = 9.8226.$$

3. Turn to Table A-2. Looking across the row for twenty-five periods, you find 9.8226 under the column for 9 percent. Therefore, the rate of interest on this mortgage loan is 9 percent.[12]

While the tables can be used to find the interest rate implicit in single payments and annuities, it is more difficult to find the interest rate implicit in an uneven series of payments. One can use a trial-and-error procedure, use more efficient but more complicated analytic procedures, or use a computer. We shall defer further discussion of this problem for now, but we will take it up later in our discussion of bond values and again in the capital budgeting chapters.

Semiannual and Other Compounding Periods

In all the examples used thus far, it has been assumed that returns were received once a year, or annually. Suppose, however, that you put your $1,000 in a bank that advertises that it pays 6 percent compounded *semiannually*. How much will you have at the end of one year? Semiannual

---

[12] Suppose the mortgage called for annual payments of $2,400. Then $PVIFA_{k,n}$ = $25,000/$2,400 = 10.4167. This value lies between the $PVIFA_{k,n}$ for 8 percent and 9 percent, but closer to 8 percent. The approximate rate for the mortgage could be found by using more extensive tables, by using one of the better hand-held calculators, or by "linear interpolation." To interpolate, we go through the following steps:

Step 1. Find the difference between 10.6748, the $PVIFA_{k,n}$ for 8 percent, and 9.8226, the $PVIFA_{k,n}$ for 9 percent. This difference is 0.8522.

Step 2. Find the difference between the calculated value, 10.4167, and 9.8226, the $PVIFA_{k,n}$ for 9 percent. This difference is 0.5941.

Step 3. Divide 0.5941 by 0.8522 to obtain 0.6971, the ratio expressing the distance of the calculated $PVIFA_{k,n}$ from the upper end of the range.

Step 4. The calculated $PVIFA_{k,n}$, 10.4167, represents 69.71 percent of the difference between 8 percent and 9 percent. Thus the interest rate represented by the $PVIFA_{k,n}$ of 10.4167 is 9% − 0.6971% = 8.3029%. (The exact rate, determined with a calculator, is 8.2887 percent.)

compounding means that interest is actually paid each six months; the procedures are illustrated in the tabular calculations in Table 3-7. Here the annual interest rate is divided by 2, but twice as many compounding periods are used, because interest is paid twice a year. Comparing the amount on hand at the end of the second six month period, $1,060.90, with what would have been on hand under annual compounding,$1,060, shows that semiannual compounding is better from the standpoint of the saver. This result occurs because you earn *interest on interest* more frequently.

Period	Beginning Amount, PV	×	(1 + k/2)	=	Ending Amount, FV$_n$
1	$1,000.00		(1.03)		$1,030.00
2	1,030.00		(1.03)		1,060.90

Table 3-7
Future Value Calculations with Semiannual Compounding

Throughout the economy, different types of investments use different compounding periods. For example, bank and savings and loan accounts generally pay interest quarterly; most bonds pay interest semiannually; and a few bonds pay annual interest. Thus, if we are to compare securities with different compounding periods, we need to put them on a common basis. This need has led to the development of the terms *nominal,* or *stated, interest rate* versus the *effective annual rate,* or *annual percentage rate* (APR). The stated, or nominal, rate is the quoted rate; thus, in our example the nominal rate is 6 percent. *The annual percentage rate is the rate that would have produced the final compound value, $1,060.90, under annual rather than semiannual compounding.* In this case, the effective annual rate is 6.09 percent:

$$\$1,000\ (1+k) = \$1,060.90$$

$$k = \frac{\$1,060.90}{\$1,000} - 1 = 0.0609 = 6.09\%.$$

Thus, if one bank offered 6 percent with semiannual compounding, while another offered 6.09 percent with annual compounding, they would both be paying the same effective rate of interest.

In general, we can determine the effective annual percentage rate, or APR, given the nominal rate, by solving Equation 3-8:

$$\text{Annual percentage rate (APR)} = \left(1 + \frac{k_{nom}}{m}\right)^m - 1.0. \qquad (3\text{-}8)$$

Here k_{nom} is the nominal rate, and m is the number of compounding periods per year. For example, to find the effective annual rate if the nominal rate is 6 percent, compounded semiannually, we make the calculations below:

$$\text{Effective annual rate (APR)} = \left(1 + \frac{0.06}{2}\right)^2 - 1.0$$
$$= (1.03)^2 - 1.0$$
$$= 1.0609 - 1.0$$
$$= 0.0609$$
$$= 6.09\%.$$

The points made about semiannual compounding can be generalized as follows. When compounding periods are more frequent than once a year, we use a modified version of Equation 3-2:

$$\text{Annual compounding: } FV_n = PV(1 + k)^n. \tag{3-2}$$

$$\text{More frequent compounding: } FV_n = PV\left(1 + \frac{k_{nom}}{m}\right)^{mn}. \tag{3-2a}$$

Here m is the number of times per year compounding occurs, and n is the number of years. When banks compute daily interest, the value of m is set at 365, and Equation 3-2a is applied.

The interest tables can be used when compounding occurs more than once a year. Simply divide the nominal, or stated, interest rate by the number of times compounding occurs, and multiply the years by the number of compounding periods per year. For example, to find the amount to which $1,000 will grow after five years if semiannual compounding is applied to a stated 4 percent interest rate, divide 4 percent by 2 and multiply the five years by 2. Then look in Table 3-2 under the 2 percent column and in the row for Period 10. You find an interest factor of 1.2190. Multiplying this by the initial $1,000 gives a value of $1,219, the amount to which $1,000 will grow in five years at 4 percent compounded semiannually. This compares with $1,216.70 for annual compounding.

The same procedure is applied in all the cases covered—compounding, discounting, single payments, and annuities. To illustrate semiannual discounting in finding the present value of an annuity, consider the case described in the section "Present Value of an Annuity": $1,000 a year for three years, discounted at 4 percent. With annual discounting, the interest factor is 2.7751 and the present value of the annuity is $2,775.10. For semiannual discounting, look under the 2 percent column and in the Period 6 row of Table 3-5 to find an interest factor of 5.6014. This is now multiplied by half of $1,000, or the $500 received each six months, to get the present value of the annuity, $2,800.70. The payments come a little more rapidly—the first $500 is paid after only six months (similarly with other payments), so the annuity is a little more valuable if payments are received semiannually rather than annually.

By letting m approach infinity, Equation 3-2a can be modified to the special case of *continuous compounding*. Continuous compounding is extremely useful in theoretical finance, and it also has practical applications. For example, banks and savings associations in New York and many other states pay interest on a continuous basis. Continuous compounding is discussed in Appendix 3A.[13]

Amortized Loans

One of the most important applications of compound interest concepts involves loans that are to be paid off in installments over time. Examples include automobile loans, home mortgage loans, and most business debt other than very short-term debt. If a loan is to be repaid in equal periodic amounts (monthly, quarterly, or annually), then it is said to be an *amortized loan*.[14]

To illustrate, suppose a firm borrows $1,000 to be repaid in three equal payments at the end of each of the next three years. The lender is to receive 6 percent interest on the funds that are outstanding at each point in time. The first task is to determine the amount the firm must repay each year, or the annual payment. To find this amount, recognize that the $1,000 represents the present value of an annuity of R dollars per year for 3 years, discounted at 6 percent:

$$\$1,000 = \text{PV of annuity} = R(\text{PVIFA}_{6\%,\ 3\ \text{yrs.}}). \qquad (3\text{-}5)$$

The PVIFA is 2.6730, so

$$\$1,000 = R(2.6730).$$

Solving for R, we obtain

$$R = \$1,000/2.6730 = \$374.11.$$

If the firm pays the lender $374.11 at the end of each of the next three years, the percentage cost to the borrower, and the return to the lender, will be 6 percent.

Each payment consists partly of interest and partly of a repayment of principal. This breakdown is given in the *amortization schedule* shown in Table 3-8. The interest component is largest in the first year, and it declines as the outstanding balance of the loan goes down. For tax pur-

---

[13] Before closing this section, it should be noted that many banks define the term APR simply as the nominal interest rate, that is, APR ≡ k_{nom}. Although this is a widespread practice, and although it apparently meets the minimum requirements of the "truth in lending" laws, it is somewhat deceptive because the true effective interest rate, which ought to be reported to borrowers, exceeds k_{nom} unless annual compounding is used.

[14] The word *amortized* comes from the Latin "mort," meaning dead, so an amortized loan is one that is "killed off" over time.

**Table 3-8
Loan Amortization
Schedule**

Year	Payment (1)	Interest[a] (2)	Repayment of Principal[b] (3)	Remaining Balance (4)
1	$ 374.11	$ 60.00	$ 314.11	$685.89
2	374.11	41.15	332.96	352.93
3	374.11	21.18	352.93	0
	$1,122.33	$122.33	$1,000.00	

[a]Interest is calculated by multiplying the loan balance at the beginning of the year by the interest rate. Therefore, interest in Year 1 is $1,000(0.06) = $60; in Year 2 interest is $685.89(0.06) = $41.15; and in Year 3 interest is $352.93(0.06) = $21.18.

[b]Repayment of principal is equal to the payment of $374.11 minus the interest charge.

poses, the borrower reports as a deductible cost each year the interest payments in Column 2, while the lender reports these same amounts as taxable income.

Summary

Financial decisions often involve determining the present value of a stream of future cash flows—this is true in stock, bond, and real estate valuation. Also, we often need to know the amount to which funds now on hand will grow during a specified time period. At other times we must calculate the interest rate built into a bond or loan contract. The basic concepts involved in these processes are called the "math of finance," which is the subject of this chapter.

The key procedures covered in the chapter are summarized below:

Future Value. $FV_n = PV(1 + k)^n$, where FV_n is the future value of an initial amount, PV, compounded at the rate k percent for n periods. The term $(1 + k)^n$ is defined as $FVIF_{k,n}$, the "future value interest factor." Values for FVIF are contained in tables.

Present Value. $PV = FV_n \left[\dfrac{1}{(1 + k)} \right]^n$. This equation is simply a transformation of the future value equation. The term $\left[\dfrac{1}{(1 + k)} \right]^n$ is defined as $PVIF_{k,n}$, the "present value interest factor." The term k, when used to find present values, is often called the *discount rate*.

Future Value of an Annuity. An annuity is defined as a series of constant or equal payments of R dollars per period. The sum, or future value of an annuity, is given the symbol S_n, and it is found as follows:

$$S_n = R \left[\sum_{t=1}^{n} (1 + k)^{n-t} \right].$$

The term $\left[\sum_{t=1}^{n}(1 + k)^{n-t}\right]$ is defined as $FVIFA_{k,n}$, the "future value interest factor for an annuity."

Present Value of an Annuity. The present value of an annuity is given the symbol A_n, and it is found as follows:

$$A_n = R\left[\sum_{t=1}^{n}\left(\frac{1}{1 + k}\right)^{t}\right].$$

The term $\left[\sum_{t=1}^{n}\left(\frac{1}{1 + k}\right)^{t}\right]$ is defined as $PVIFA_{k,n}$, the present value interest factor for an annuity.

These four basic equations can be used to find the present or the future value of any lump sum or series of cash flows, and also the interest rate built into any financial contract. These concepts will be used throughout the remainder of the book. In Chapter 4 we apply present value concepts to the process of valuing stocks and bonds. This discussion is extended in Chapter 5, where we examine the determinants of k, the interest rate, and in Chapter 6, where we analyze ways of estimating future cash flows. Then, in later chapters, the same basic concepts are applied to corporate decisions involving expenditures on capital assets as well as to decisions involving the types of capital that should be used to pay for assets.

Questions

3-1 Is it true that for all positive interest rates, the following conditions hold: $FVIF_{k,n} \geq 1.0$; $PVIF_{k,n} < 1.0$; $FVIFA_{k,n} \geq$ number of periods the annuity lasts; $PVIFA_{k,n} <$ number of periods the annuity lasts?

3-2 An annuity is defined as a series of payments of a fixed amount for a specific number of periods. Thus, $100 a year for ten years is an annuity, but $100 in Year 1, $200 in Year 2, and $400 a year in Years 3 through 10 is *not* an annuity. However, the second series *contains* an annuity. Is this statement true or false?

3-3 If a firm's earnings per share grew from $1 to $2 over a ten year period, the *total growth* was 100 percent, but the *annual growth rate* was *less than* 10 percent. Why is this so?

3-4 Would you rather have a deposit in a bank that uses annual, semiannual, or quarterly compounding? Explain.

3-5 To find the present value of an uneven series of payments, you must use the $PVIF_{k,n}$ tables; the $PVIFA_{k,n}$ tables can never be of use, even if some of the payments constitute an annuity (for example, $100 each for Years 3, 4, 5, and 6), because the entire series is not an annuity. Is this statement true or false?

3-6 The present value of a perpetual annuity is equal to the receipt on the annuity (R) divided by the discount rate (k): PV = R/k. What is the *sum* of a perpetuity of R dollars per year growing at a rate of k percent? (Hint: The answer is infinity, but explain why.)

Self-Test Problems

Work these self-test problems out, then check your solution and methodology against the solutions given at the end of the chapter.

ST3-1 Assume that it is now January 1, 1981. If you were to put $1,000 into a savings account on January 1, 1982, at an 8 percent interest rate, compounded annually, how much would you have in your account on January 1, 1985?

ST3-2 Suppose instead that you deposited the $1,000 in four payments of $250 each on January 1st of 1982, 1983, 1984, and 1985. How much would you have in your account on January 1, 1985, if you deposited the $1,000 in this fashion?

ST3-3 How large would each of your payments in Self-Test Problem 3-2 above have to be for you to obtain the same ending balance as you would have obtained by the single $1,000 deposit?

ST3-4 Going back to Self-Test Problem 3-1, what would your January 1, 1985, balance be if the bank used quarterly compounding rather than annual compounding?

ST3-5 If you needed $1,000 as an ending balance in your account on January 1, 1985, how much would you have to deposit on January 1, 1982? Only one deposit will be made, and the compounding rate is 8 percent annually.

ST3-6 If you want to make equal payments on each January 1st from 1982 through 1985 to accumulate the $1,000, then how large must each of the four payments be? The compounding rate is 8 percent annually.

ST3-7 If your father were to offer either to make the payments given in Self-Test Problem 3-6 above or to give you a lump sum of $750 on January 1, 1982, which would you choose?

ST3-8 If you have only $750 on January 1, 1982, what interest rate, compounded annually, would you have to earn to have the necessary $1,000 on January 1, 1985?

ST3-9 (Read Appendix 3A before trying to work Self-Test Problem 3-9.) By how much could you reduce the deposit in Self-Test Problem 3-5 above and still achieve the same $1,000 goal if your bank offered continuous compounding at an 8 percent rate?

ST3-10 Suppose you could only deposit $186.29 each January 1st from 1982 through 1985, but you still need $1,000 on January 1, 1985. What interest rate, with annual compounding, must you seek out to achieve your goal?

ST3-11 To help you reach your $1,000 goal, your father offers to give you $400 on January 1, 1982. You will get a part-time job and make six additional payments of equal amounts each six months thereafter. If all of this money is deposited in a bank which pays 8 percent compounded semiannually, how large must your payments be?

ST3-12 What is the effective annual percentage rate being paid by the bank in Self-Test Problem 3-11 above?

3-1 Find the following values *without using tables*, then work the problems *with tables* to check your answers. Disregard rounding errors.
   a. An initial $200 compounded for one year at 5 percent.
   b. An initial $200 compounded for two years at 5 percent.
   c. The present value of $200 due in one year at a discount rate of 5 percent.
   d. The present value of $200 due in two years at a discount rate of 5 percent.

3-2 Use the tables to find the following values:
   a. An initial $200 compounded for ten years at 5 percent.
   b. An initial $200 compounded for ten years at 10 percent.
   c. The present value of $200 due in ten years at a 5 percent discount rate.
   d. The present value of $518.80 due in ten years at a 10 percent discount rate.

3-3 To the closest year, how long will it take $200 to double if it is deposited and earns the following rates?
   a. 10 percent.
   b. 15 percent.
   c. 100 percent.

3-4 Find the *future value* of the following annuities. The first payment in these annuities is made at the *end* of Year 1:
   a. $200 per year for ten years at 10 percent.
   b. $100 per year for five years at 5 percent.
   c. $200 per year for five years at 0 percent.

3-5 Find the *present value* of the following annuities:
   a. $200 per year for ten years at 10 percent.
   b. $100 per year for five years at 5 percent.
   c. $200 per year for five years at 0 percent.

3-6 a. Find the present values of the following cash flow streams; the appropriate discount rate is 10 percent:

Year	Cash Stream A	Cash Stream B
1	$100	$300
2	$200	$200
3	$200	$200
4	$200	$200
5	$300	$100

b. What is the value of each cash flow stream at a zero percent discount rate?

3-7 Find the present value of the following cash flow stream, discounted at 5 percent: Year 1, $100; Years 2 to 20, $200.

3-8 Last year Carter Corporation's sales were $4 million. Sales were $2 million five years earlier. To the nearest percentage point, at what rate have sales been growing?

3-9 Suppose someone calculated the sales growth rate for Carter Corporation in Problem 3-8 as follows: "Sales doubled in five years. This represents a growth of 100 percent in five years, so, dividing 100 percent by 5, we find the growth rate to be 20 percent per year." Explain what is wrong with this calculation.

3-10 Find the interest rates, or rates of return, on each of the following:
a. You borrow $200 and promise to pay back $210 at the end of one year.
b. You lend $200, and you receive a promise of $210 at the end of one year.
c. You borrow $20,000 and promise to pay back $32,578 at the end of ten years.
d. You borrow $2,000 and promise to make payments of $514.18 per year for five years.

3-11 The Taussig Company buys a machine for $20,000 and expects a return of $4,770.42 per year for the next ten years. What is the expected rate of return on the machine?

3-12 Georgia-Atlantic invests $1 million to clear a tract of land and set out some young pine trees. The trees will mature in ten years, at which time Georgia-Atlantic plans to sell the forest at an expected price of $3 million. What is Georgia-Atlantic's expected rate of return?

3-13 Your broker offers to sell you a note for $2,395.62 that will pay $600 per year for five years. If you buy the note, what rate of interest will you be earning?

3-14 A mortgage company offers to lend you $50,000; the loan calls for payments of $5,477.36 per year for twenty years. What interest rate is the mortgage company charging you?

3-15 To enable you to complete your last year in the business school and then go through law school, you will need $7,000 per year for four years, starting next year (that is, you need the first payment of $7,000 one year from today). Your rich uncle offers to deposit a sum of money sufficient to put you through school in a bank time deposit that pays 8 percent interest; the deposit will be made today.
a. How large must the deposit be?
b. How much will be in the account immediately after you make the first withdrawal? After the last withdrawal?

3-16 Find the amount to which $200 will grow under each of the following conditions:

    a. 8 percent compounded annually for four years.

    b. 8 percent compounded semiannually for four years.

    c. 8 percent compounded quarterly for four years.

    d. 12 percent compounded monthly for one year.

3-17 Find the present values of $200 due in the future under each of the following conditions:

    a. 8 percent nominal rate, semiannual compounding, discounted back four years.

    b. 8 percent nominal rate, quarterly compounding, discounted back four years.

    c. 12 percent nominal rate, monthly compounding, discounted back one year.

3-18 Find the indicated value of the following annuities:

    a. FV of $200 each six months for four years at a nominal rate of 12 percent.

    b. PV of $200 each three months for four years at a nominal rate of 12 percent.

3-19 The First National Bank pays 13 percent interest compounded annually on time deposits. The Second National Bank pays 12 percent interest compounded quarterly.

    a. In which bank would you prefer to deposit your money?

    b. Could your choice of banks be influenced by the fact that you might want to withdraw your funds during the year as opposed to the end of a year? In answering this question, assume that funds must be left on deposit during the entire compounding period in order to receive any interest.

3-20 What is the present value of a perpetuity of $100 per year if the appropriate discount rate is 5 percent? If interest rates were to double and the appropriate discount rate were to rise to 10 percent, what would happen to the PV of the annuity?

3-21 Set up an amortization schedule for a $20,000 loan to be repaid in equal installments at the end of each of the next three years. The interest rate is 10 percent.

(These next three problems are quite difficult. Most introductory students cannot work them without guidance, so do not be surprised if you have trouble!)

3-22 As a financial consultant, you are helping a client who just won a fortune at Las Vegas plan his retirement. He will make a deposit today (January 1, 1982) in a time deposit that pays 8 percent interest, compounded annually. He will retire in twenty-five years (on January 1, 2007), and he expects to live for another thirty years beyond his retirement (until December 31, 2036). His wife is expected to live an additional five years (until December 31, 2041). He wants a retirement income of $30,000 per year during his retirement years, the first payment to be received on January 1, 2007, and the last on January 1, 2036. Further, he wants his wife to have an income of $20,000 after he is dead, or $20,000 on each January 1 from 2037 through 2041. Finally, he plans to take a trip to Saturn in 2012 and be gone for two years, so he wants to receive $60,000 on January 1, 2012, and nothing on January 1, 2013.

   a. How much must he deposit on January 1, 1982, in order to attain his retirement goal? (Hint: Use a time line.)

   b. In terms of current dollars, how much will his $30,000 of income in 2007 be worth in 1982 dollars if we experience a constant 10 percent rate of inflation?

   c. Are there any weaknesses in this financial plan? Assume this is your client's only source of retirement income and think about the assumptions used in the problem.

3-23 Assume that you deposited $100 in a bank time deposit account on January 1, 1980, and an additional $100 each six months thereafter until July 1, 1989. Thus, you made a total of twenty deposits of $100 each. The bank paid interest at the rate of 4 percent, compounded quarterly, from January 1, 1980, through December 31, 1982. The rate of interest goes to 6 percent, compounded semiannually, on January 1, 1983, and remains at that level until December 31, 1987. The interest rate then becomes 8 percent, compounded annually, on January 1, 1988, and stays at that level until December 31, 1989. How much will you have in your account on January 1, 1990?

(Hints: [1] This problem requires the use of a calculator with an exponential function. [2] Work the problem assuming that the deposits are $1 rather than $100, and then multiply by 100 to get the final answer.[3] Although it is possible to use annuity formulas to help solve this problem, it is probably easier for most people not to use them. However, the deferred annuity equation might be used for the period January 1, 1983, through December 31, 1987.)

3-24 Assume that your father is now fifty and plans an early retirement in eight years at age fifty-eight. He will be able to save $6,000 per year for the next four years, while he puts you through law school, and $20,000 per year for the following four years. In addition, he has $300,000 currently invested in undeveloped real estate.

   a. If his annual savings over the next eight years are deposited in a bank account that pays 6 percent compounded annually, while the value of his real estate appreciates at the rate of 10 percent per year, how much will your father have upon retirement at age fifty-eight? (Disregard taxes.)

   b. If your father expects to live to be eighty-eight, that is, he expects to live for thirty years after retirement, and at age fifty-eight he deposits all his wealth in a savings and loan account that pays 7 percent annual interest, how much can he withdraw at the end of each year to end up with a zero balance?

c. Assume all the conditions in Part b except that your father wants to leave an estate of $200,000 when he dies. How much can he draw out of the account each year after he reaches age fifty-eight?

d. How much will be in the account after one year of retirement but just before your father makes his first withdrawal?

e. Continuing Part d, how much will be in the account immediately after your father's first withdrawal? Assume he wishes to provide the estate as described in Part c.

f. Of your father's annual withdrawal at the end of Year 1, which was calculated in Part c and used in Part e, how much constituted withdrawal of principal, and how much was interest? Will this breakdown between principal and interest remain constant over the thirty years of your father's retirement?

ST3-1

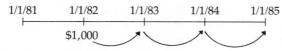

1/1/81   1/1/82   1/1/83   1/1/84   1/1/85

$1,000

$1,000 is being compounded for three years:

$$FV = PV(1 + k)^n$$
$$= \$1,000(1 + 0.08)^3$$
$$= \$1,259.71.$$

ST3-2

1/1/81   1/1/82   1/1/83   1/1/84   1/1/85

$250 $250 $250 $250

Future value of an annuity:

$$R(FVIFA_{k,n}) = \$250(4.5061) = \$1,126.53.$$

ST3-3 $FV = \$1,259.71$
$k = 8\%$
$n = 4$

$$R(FVIFA_{8\%,4}) = FV$$
$$R(4.5061) = \$1,259.71$$
$$R = \$1,259.71/4.5061 = \$279.56.$$

ST3-4 The effective annual rate, or APR, for 8 percent, quarterly compounding, is

$$APR = \left(1 + \frac{0.08}{4}\right)^4 - 1.0$$
$$= (1.02)^4 - 1.0 = 0.0824 = 8.24\%.$$

Therefore, $FV = \$1,000(1.0824)^3 = \$1,000(1.2681) = \$1,268.10$.

Alternatively, use FVIF for 2%, $3 \times 4 = 12$ periods:

$$FV = \$1,000 \ (FVIF_{2,12})$$
$$= \$1,000(1.2682)$$
$$= \$1,268.20. \ (\text{Rounding error})$$

ST3-5 $FV = \$1,000$
$n = 3$
$k = 8\%$

$$FV(PVIF_{8\%,3}) = PV$$
$$\$1,000(0.7938) = \$793.80 \ (= \text{initial deposit}$$
$$\text{necessary to accumulate } \$1,000).$$

ST3-6 $FV = \$1,000$
$n = 4$
$k = 8\%$

$$R(FVIFA_{8\%,4}) = FV$$
$$\frac{FV}{(FVIFA_{8\%,4})} = R$$
$$\frac{\$1,000}{4.5061} = \$221.92.$$

ST3-7 $R = \$221.92$
$k = 8\%$
$n = 4$

$$R(PVIFA_{8\%,4}) = PV$$
$$\$221.92(3.3121) = \$735.02.$$

This is less than the $750 lump sum offer, so your initial reaction might be to accept the lump sum of $750. However, this would be a mistake. Note that if you were to deposit the $750 on January 1, 1982, at an 8 percent interest rate, to be withdrawn on January 1, 1985, interest would only be compounded for three years, from January 1, 1982, to December 31, 1984, and the future value would be only

$$PV(FVIF_{8\%,3}) = \$750(1.2597)$$
$$= \$944.78.$$

The problem is that when you found the $735.02 PV of the annuity, you were finding the value of the annuity *today*, on January 1, 1981. You were comparing $735.02 today with the lump sum $750 one year from now. This is, of course, invalid. What you should have done was take the $735.02 found in Step 1, recognize that this is the PV of an annuity as of January 1, 1981, multiply $735.02 times 1.08 to get $793.82, and compare $793.82 with the lump sum of $750. You would then take your father's offer to pay off the loan rather than the lump sum on January 1, 1982.

ST3-8 PV = $750
FV = $1,000
n = 3
k = ?

$$PV(FVIF_{k,3}) = FV$$

$$\frac{FV}{PV} = (FVIF_{k,3})$$

$$\frac{\$1,000}{\$750} = FVIF_{k,3}$$

$$= 1.3333.$$

Use the Future Value of $1 Table (A-3) for three periods to find the interest rate corresponding to an FVIF of 1.3333. Look across the 3 period row of Table A-3 until you come to 1.3333. The closest value is 1.3310 in the 10 percent column. Therefore, you would require an interest rate of approximately 10 percent to achieve your $1,000 goal. The exact rate required, found with a financial calculator, is 10.0642 percent.

ST3-9 Continuous compounding:

FV = $1,000
k = 8%
t = 3

$$PV = \frac{FV_t}{e^{kt}}$$

$$PV = FV_t e^{-kt}$$

$$= \$1,000e^{-(0.08)(3)}$$

$$= \$1,000(0.78663)$$

$$= \$786.63.$$

ST3-10 FV = $1,000
R = $186.29
k = ?
n = 4

$$R(FVIFA_{k,4}) = FV$$

$$\$186.29(FVIFA_{k,4}) = \$1,000$$

$$\frac{\$1,000}{\$186.29} = (FVIFA_{k,4})$$

$$5.3680 = (FVIFA_{k,4}).$$

Using the Sum of an Annuity Table for 4 Periods (Table A-4 at the end of the book) we find that 5.3680 corresponds to a 20 percent interest rate. You might be able to find a borrower willing to offer you a 20 percent interest rate, but there would be some risk involved, and he might not actually pay you your $1,000!

ST3-11

Find the future value of the original $400 deposit:

$$FV = PV\ (FVIF_{4\%,6})$$
$$= \$400\ (1.2653)$$
$$= \$506.12.$$

This means that on January 1, 1985, you need an additional sum of

$$\begin{array}{r} \$1,000.00 \\ -\ \ 506.12 \\ \hline \$\ \ \ 493.88 \end{array}$$

This will be made in six equal payments:

FV = $493.88
n = 6
k = 4%

$$R(FVIFA_{4\%,6}) = FV$$
$$R = \frac{FV}{(FVIFA_{4\%,6})}$$

$$\frac{\$493.88}{6.6330} = \$74.46.$$

ST3-12

$$APR = \left(1 + \frac{k_{nom}}{m}\right)^{m} - 1.0$$
$$= \left(1 + \frac{0.08}{2}\right)^{2} - 1$$
$$= 1.0816 - 1$$
$$= 0.0816$$
$$= 8.16\%.$$

Appendix 3A

Continuous Compounding and Discounting

Continuous Compounding

In Chapter 3, we implicitly assumed that growth occurs at discrete intervals—annually, semiannually, and so forth. For some purposes it is better to assume instantaneous, or *continuous*, growth. The relationship between discrete and continuous compounding is illustrated in Figure 3A-1. The left panel shows the annual compounding case, where interest is added once a year; in the center panel compounding occurs twice a year; and in the right panel interest is earned continuously. As the graph shows, the more frequent the compounding period, the larger the final compound amount, because interest is earned on interest more often.

Figure 3A-1
Annual, Semiannual, and Continuous
Compounding (25% Rate)

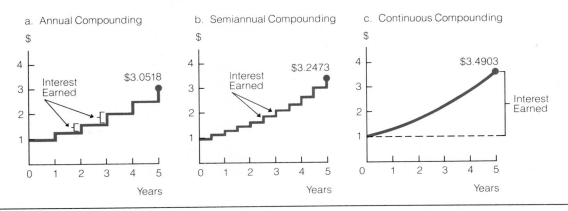

a. Annual Compounding   b. Semiannual Compounding   c. Continuous Compounding

In Chapter 3, Equation 3-2a was developed to allow for any number of compounding periods per year:

$$FV_n = PV\left(1 + \frac{k_{nom}}{m}\right)^{m \cdot n}. \qquad (3\text{-}2a)$$

Here k_{nom} = the stated interest rate, m = the number of compounding periods per year, and n = the number of years. To illustrate, let PV = $100, k = 10%, and n = 5. At various compounding periods per year, we obtain the following future values at the end of five years:

Annual: $FV_5 = \$100\left(1.0 + \frac{0.10}{1}\right)^{1 \cdot 5} = \$100(1.10)^5 = \$161.05.$

Semiannual: $FV_5 = \$100\left(1.0 + \frac{0.10}{2}\right)^{2 \cdot 5} = \$100(1.05)^{10} = \$162.89.$

Monthly: $FV_5 = \$100\left(1.0 + \frac{0.10}{12}\right)^{12 \cdot 5} = \$100(1.0083)^{60} = \$164.53.$

Daily: $FV_5 = \$100\left(1.0 + \frac{0.10}{365}\right)^{365 \cdot 5} = \$164.86.$

Hourly: $FV_5 = \$100\left(1.0 + \frac{0.10}{8,760}\right)^{365 \cdot 24 \cdot 5} = \$164.87.$

We could keep going, compounding every minute, every second, every 1/1000th of a second, and so on. At the limit, we could compound every instant, or *continuously*. The equation for continuous compounding is

$$FV_n = PV(e^{k \cdot n}), \tag{3A-1}$$

where e is the value 2.7183···.[1] In our example, FV_5 is computed as follows:[2]

$$\text{Continuous:} \quad FV_5 = \$100(e^{0.10 \cdot 5}) = \$100(2.7183···)^{0.5}$$
$$= \$164.872.$$

Continuous Discounting

Equation 3A-1 can be transformed into Equation 3A-2 and used to determine present values under continuous compounding:

$$PV = \frac{FV_n}{e^{kn}} = FV_n e^{-kn}. \tag{3A-2}$$

Thus, if \$1,649 is due in ten years and if the appropriate *continuous* discount rate, k, is 5 percent, the present value of this future payment is

$$PV = \$1,649 \left[\frac{1}{(2.7183···)^{0.5}} \right] = \frac{\$1,649}{1.649} \approx \$1,000.$$

---

[1] To derive Equation 3A-1, we proceed as follows:
1. We begin with Equation 3-2a, letting $k = k_{nom}$:

$$FV_n = PV \left(1 + \frac{k}{m} \right)^{m \cdot n} \tag{3-2a}$$

2. Multiply mn by k/k, obtaining mn = mn(k/k) = (m/k)(kn).
3. Substitute (m/k)(kn) for mn in Equation 3-2a:

$$FV_n = PV \left[\left(1 + \frac{k}{m} \right)^{m/k} \right]^{kn} \tag{3-2b}$$

4. Define x = m/k and note that k/m = 1/(m/k) = 1/x. Now rewrite Equation 3-2b as follows:

$$FV_n = PV \left[\left(1 + \frac{1}{x} \right)^{x} \right]^{kn} \tag{3-2c}$$

5. As the number of compounding periods, m, increases, x also increases; this causes the term in brackets in Equation 3-2c to increase. At the limit, when m and x approach infinity (and compounding is instantaneous, or continuous), the term in brackets approaches the value 2.7183···. The value e is defined as this limiting case:

$$e = \lim_{x \to \infty} \left(1 + \frac{1}{x} \right)^{x} = 2.7183···. \tag{3-2d}$$

6. We can substitute e for the bracketed term in Equation 3-2c to obtain the following expression:

$$FV_n = (PV)e^{kn}. \tag{3A-1}$$

[2] Scientific or financial calculators with exponential functions can be used to evaluate Equation 3A-1.

The treatment of continuous compounding for single values is more complex than that for discrete compounding, but it still involves nothing more than algebra. To continuously compound and discount *streams* of payments (annuities), however, elementary integral calculus must be employed. The procedures involved are outlined below.

Step 1. First look at Figure 3A-2a. An amount R is received at the end of each year. It is left on deposit and grows at the rate g; thus the accumulated sum at the end of any year n is

$$
\begin{aligned}
S_n &= R(1 + g)^{n-1} + R(1 + g)^{n-2} + R(1 + g)^{n-3} + \cdots + R(1 + g)^0 \\
&= R(1 + g)^{n-1} + R(1 + g)^{n-2} + \cdots + R \\
&= \sum_{t=1}^{n} R(1 + g)^{n-t}.
\end{aligned}
$$

The accumulated sum of the payments, S_n, is equal to the sum of the rectangles in Figure 3A-2(a); this is the area under the discontinuous curve formed by the tops of the rectangles. Note also that the term g has been substituted for k; here the growth rate, g, is equal to the interest rate, k.

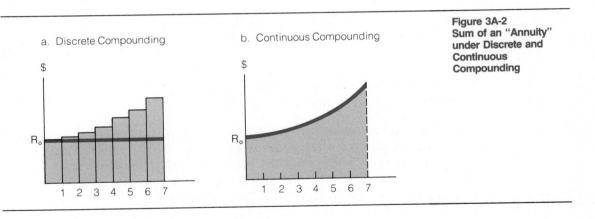

a. Discrete Compounding   b. Continuous Compounding

**Figure 3A-2
Sum of an "Annuity" under Discrete and Continuous Compounding**

Step 2. Exactly the same principle is involved in finding the accumulated sum of the continuous equivalent of an annuity, or a stream of receipts received continuously. The accumulated sum is again represented by the area under a curve, but now the curve is continuous as in Figure 3A-2b. In the discrete case, the area under the curve was obtained by adding the rectangles; in the continuous case, the area must be found by the process of integration.

Note that the stream of receipts, or the value of R_t, is found by using Equation 3A-1, taking the initial receipt, R_0 (*not* R_1), and letting it grow at the continuous rate g:

$$R_n = R_0 e^{gn}. \tag{3A-1}$$

Equation 3A-1 defines the curve; the area under the curve, S_n, is represented by the integral

$$S_n = \int_{n=0}^{N} R_0 e^{gn} \, dn = R_0 \int_{n=0}^{N} e^{gn} \, dn. \tag{3A-3}$$

Step 3. Given a discrete series of receipts, such as those shown in Figure 3A-2a, and a discount rate, k, we find their PV as

$$PV = \sum_{n=1}^{N} R_n (1 + k)^{-n}.$$

If the receipts accrue continuously, as do those in Figure 3A-2b, we must find the present value of the stream of payments by calculus. First, note that by Equation 3A-2 we find the PV of the instantaneous receipt for Period n as

$$PV = R_n e^{-kn}. \tag{3A-2}$$

The present value of the entire stream of receipts to Year n is given as the integral

$$PV = \int_{n=0}^{N} R_n e^{-kn} dn. \tag{3A-4}$$

Problem   **3A-1**   A firm has just borrowed $X at a rate of 10 percent, continuous compounding, for ten years. At the end of the tenth year, the firm must pay $1 million to satisfy the loan. To provide for the $1 million payment, the firm plans to invest a constant amount of money, $Y, each six months, *starting today*, in an account that pays 10 percent, compounded semiannually.

     a. How much money must be invested each six months in order to have the $1 million when it is needed; that is, what is the value of Y? (Hint: think about an annuity due.)

     b. How much money did the firm borrow in the first place; that is, what is the value of X?

     c. What is (1) the effective annual rate of 10 percent compounded semiannually versus (2) the effective annual rate of 10 percent compounded continuously?

     d. Would the firm be better off under the situation as described above or if it used the payment every six months to reduce the size of the loan; that is, to amortize the loan?

Stock and Bond Values   4

In the last chapter we examined the time value of money. The concepts developed there can be used to analyze the value of any financial asset, including real estate, factories, machinery, oil wells, coal mines, farmland, stocks, or bonds. In this chapter we use the time value concept to show how investors establish the values of stocks and bonds. The materials covered in the chapter are obviously important to investors and potential investors, and they are also important to corporate decision makers. *All important corporate decisions should be analyzed in terms of how a particular decision will affect the price of the firm's stock, so it is clearly important for management to know what determines a firm's stock price.*

Bond Values

Corporations raise capital in two primary forms—debt and common equity. Our first task in this chapter is to examine the valuation process for the primary type of long-term debt, bonds.

A *bond* is a promissory note issued by a business or governmental unit. For example, on October 1, 1981, the Carter Chemical Company borrowed $150 million by selling 150,000 individual bonds for $1,000 each. As a first step in explaining how bond values are determined, we need to define some of the terms associated with these securities.

1. *Par value.* This is the stated face value of the bond, and it is usually set at $1,000. The par value generally represents the amount of money that the firm borrows and promises to repay at some future date.
2. *Maturity date.* Bonds generally mature at a specified date; at maturity, the par value is repaid to each bondholder. Carter's bonds, which were issued in 1981, will mature in 1996. Thus, they had a fifteen year maturity at time of issue. Most bonds have maturities of from ten to forty years, but this is not a hard and fast rule.[1]

---

[1] Some bonds have a provision whereby the issuer may pay them off prior to maturity. This feature is termed a *call provision,* and it is discussed in detail in Chapter 13. If a bond is callable, and if interest rates on new bonds fall substantially below the coupon rate on the old bond, then the company will sell a new issue of low interest rate bonds and use the proceeds to retire the old high interest rate issue.

3. *Coupon interest rate.* The bond states that the issuer will pay a specified number of dollars of interest each year (or perhaps each six months). When this *coupon payment*, as it is called, is divided by the par value, the result is the *coupon interest rate.* For example, Carter Chemical's bonds have a $1,000 par value and pay $90 each year. The bond's coupon interest is $90, so its coupon interest rate is 9 percent. The $90 is the yearly "rent" on the $1,000 loan. This payment, which is fixed at the time the bond is issued, remains in force, by contract, during the life of the bond. Incidentally, each bond literally has fifteen small ($1/2$-by-2-inch), dated coupons attached to it, and on the interest payment date the owner clips one off and either cashes it at his or her bank or mails it to the company's paying agent, who then mails back a check for $90.

4. *New issues* versus *outstanding bonds.* As we shall see below, a bond's market price is determined in large part by its coupon interest payment—the higher the coupon, other things held constant, the higher the market price of the bond. At the time a bond is issued, the coupon is generally set at a level that will force the market price of the bond to equal its par value. If a lower coupon were set, investors simply would not be willing to pay $1,000 for the bond, while if a higher coupon were set, investors would clamor for the bond and bid its price up over $1,000. Issuers can judge quite precisely the coupon rate which will cause the bond to sell at its $1,000 par value.

A bond that has just been issued is defined as a *new issue.* (The *Wall Street Journal* classifies a new bond as a new issue for about two weeks after it has first been issued.) Once the bond has been on the market for a while, it is classified as an *outstanding* bond, also called a *seasoned issue.* As we shall see below, although newly issued bonds do generally sell at par, outstanding bonds do not always sell at par. Their coupon interest payments are constant, but economic conditions change, so although a bond with a $90 coupon may sell at par when it is issued, it can sell for more or less than $1,000 thereafter.

The Basic Bond Valuation Model[2]

As noted above, bonds call for the payment of a specified amount of interest for a stated number of years, and for the repayment of the par value on the bond's maturity date.[3] Thus, a bond represents an annuity plus a lump sum, and its value is found as the present value of this payment stream.

---

[2] In finance the term *model* refers to an equation or set of equations designed to show how one or more variables affect some other variable. Thus, a bond valuation model shows the mathematical relationship between a bond's price and the set of variables that determines this price.

[3] Actually, most bonds pay interest semiannually, not annually, which makes it necessary to modify our valuation equation slightly. We abstract from semiannual compounding at this point to avoid unnecessary detail. However, the subject is discussed later in the chapter.

The following equation is used to find a bond's value:

$$\text{Value} = V = \sum_{t=1}^{n} I\left(\frac{1}{1 + k_d}\right)^t + M\left(\frac{1}{1 + k_d}\right)^n$$
$$= I(\text{PVIFA}_{k_d,n}) + M(\text{PVIF}_{k_d,n}). \qquad (4-1)$$

Here:

I = dollars of interest paid each year = coupon interest rate × par value.

M = the par value, or maturity value, which is typically $1,000.

k_d = the appropriate rate of interest on the bond.[4]

n = the number of years until the bond matures; n declines each year after the bond is issued.

We can use the equation to find the value of Carter Chemical's bonds. Simply substitute in $90 for I, $1,000 for M, and the values of PVIFA and PVIF at 9 percent, 15 periods, as found in Tables A-1 and A-2 at the end of the book:

$$V = \$90(8.0607) + \$1,000(0.2745)$$
$$= \$725.46 + \$274.50$$
$$= \$999.96 \approx \$1,000 \text{ when } k_d = 9\%.$$

Figure 4-1 gives a graphic view of the bond valuation process.

If k_d remained constant at 9 percent, what would the value of the bond be one year after it was issued? We can find this value using the same valuation formula, but now the term to maturity is only fourteen years; that is, n = 14:

$$V = \$90(7.7862) + \$1,000(0.2992)$$
$$= \$999.96 \approx \$1,000.$$

This same result will hold for every year so long as the appropriate interest rate for the bond remains constant at 9 percent.[5]

---

[4] The matter of how the *appropriate interest rate* is determined will be taken up in the next chapter. The bond's riskiness and years to maturity, as well as supply and demand conditions in the capital markets, all have an influence. We shall go into detail on these points later, but for now just accept the statement that k_d is the appropriate interest rate for the bonds. k_d is also called the *required rate of return*, and on any risky investment it is equal to the rate of return on riskless investments (such as U.S. Treasury Securities), given the symbol R_F, plus a risk premium, ρ, pronounced "rho." All this is discussed in depth in Chapter 5.

[5] The bond prices quoted by brokers are calculated as described. However, if you bought a bond, you would have to pay this basic price plus accrued interest. Thus, if you purchased a Carter Chemical bond six months after it was issued, your broker would send you an invoice stating that you must pay $1,000 as the basic price of the bond plus $45 interest, representing one-half the annual interest of $90. The seller of the bond would receive $1,045. If you bought the bond the day before its interest payment date, you would pay $1,000 + 364/365 ($90) = $1,089.75. Of course, you would receive an interest payment of $90 at the end of the next day.

Figure 4-1
Time Line for Carter Chemical Bonds

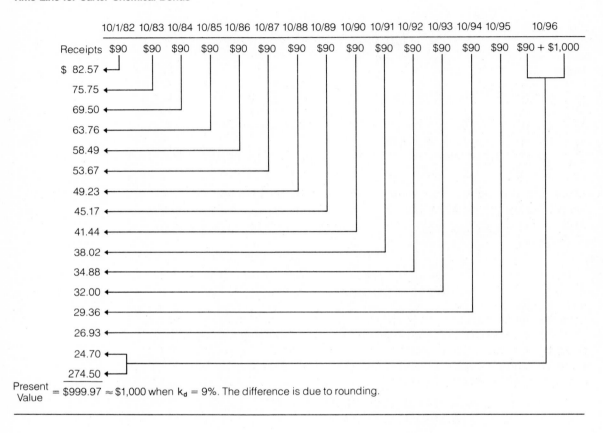

Present Value = $999.97 ≈ $1,000 when k_d = 9%. The difference is due to rounding.

Now suppose interest rates in the economy rose after the Carter Chemical bonds were issued, and as a result k_d increased from 9 percent to 10 percent. Both the coupon interest payments and the maturity value would remain constant, but now 10 percent values for PVIF and PVIFA would have to be used in Equation 4-1. The value of the bond at the end of the first year would be

$$V = \$90(\text{PVIFA}_{10\%,14 \text{ yrs.}}) + \$1,000(\text{PVIF}_{10\%,14 \text{ yrs.}})$$
$$= \$90(7.3667) + \$1,000(0.2633)$$
$$= \$663.00 + \$263.30$$
$$= \$926.30 \text{ when } k_d = 10\%.$$

Thus, the bond sells at a *discount* below its par value.

The arithmetic of the bond price decline should be clear, but what is the logic behind the decline? The reason for it is simple. The fact that k_d has risen to 10 percent means that, if you had $1,000 to invest, you could buy new bonds like Carter's (every day some ten to twelve companies sell new bonds) except that they would pay $100 of interest each year rather than $90. Naturally, you would prefer $100 to $90, so you would not be willing to pay $1,000 for Carter bonds when your $1,000 could buy you a higher-yielding bond. All investors would recognize these facts, and as a result the Carter bonds would be bid down in price to $926.30, at which price the Carter bonds would provide the same rate of return to a potential investor as the new bonds, 10 percent.

Assuming that interest rates remain constant at 10 percent for the next fourteen years, what will happen to the value of Carter's bonds? It will rise gradually from $926.30 at present to $1,000 at maturity, when Carter Chemical must redeem each bond for $1,000. This point is illustrated by calculating the value of the bond one year later, when it has thirteen years remaining to maturity:

$$V = \$90(PVIFA_{10\%,13\text{ yrs.}}) + \$1,000(PVIF_{10\%,13\text{ yrs.}})$$
$$= \$90(7.1034) + \$1,000(0.2897) = \$929.01.$$

Thus, the value of the bond has risen from $926.30 to $929.01, or by $2.71. If you were to calculate the value of the bond at other dates, the price would continue to rise as the maturity date approached.

Notice also that, if you purchased the bond at a price of $926.30 and then sold it one year later, you would receive $90 of interest income plus a capital gain of $2.71, or a total return of $92.71. Your percentage rate of return would consist of an *interest yield* (also called *current yield*) plus a *capital gains yield* calculated as follows:

$$\text{Interest or current yield} = \$90/\$926.30 = 0.0971 = 9.71\%$$
$$\text{Capital gains yield} = \$2.71/\$926.30 = 0.0029 = \underline{0.29\%}$$
$$\text{Total rate of return or yield} = \$92.71/\$926.30 = 0.1000 = \underline{10.00\%}$$

Had interest rates fallen to 8 percent during the first year rather than risen, the value of Carter's bonds would have increased to $1,082.48:

$$V = \$90(8.2442) + \$1,000(0.3405)$$
$$= \$741.98 + \$340.50$$
$$= \$1,082.48 \text{ when } k_d = 8\%.$$

In this case, the bond would sell at a *premium* above its par value. Its total expected future yield would again consist of a current interest yield and a capital gains yield, but the capital gains yield would be *negative* as the premium was amortized over time. The total yield would, of course, be 8 percent.

Figure 4-2 graphs the value of the bond over time, assuming that interest rates in the economy remain constant at 9 percent, rise to 10 per-

Figure 4-2
Time Path of the Value of a 9% Coupon, $1,000 Par Value Bond When Interest Rates Are 8%, 9%, and 10%

Note: The curves for 8% and 10% appear to be straight, but they actually have a slight bow.

cent, or fall to 8 percent. Of course, if interest rates do *not* remain constant, then the price of the bond will fluctuate. However, regardless of what interest rates do, the bond's price will approach $1,000 as the maturity date comes nearer (barring bankruptcy, in which case the bond's value might drop to zero).

Figure 4-2 illustrates the following key points:

1. Whenever the going rate of interest (k_d) is equal to the coupon rate, a bond will sell at its par value.
2. Whenever the going rate of interest is above the coupon rate, a bond will sell below its par value. Such a bond is called a *discount bond*.
3. Whenever the going rate of interest is below the coupon rate, a bond will sell above its par value. Such a bond is said to sell at a *premium*.
4. An increase in interest rates will cause the prices of outstanding bonds to fall, while a decrease in rates will cause bond prices to rise.
5. The market value of a bond will approach its par value as its maturity date approaches.

These points are very important to investors, for they show that bondholders may suffer capital losses or make capital gains, depending on whether interest rates rise or fall. And, as we saw in Chapter 2, interest rates do indeed change over time.

Finding the Interest Rate on a Bond: Yield to Maturity

Suppose you were offered a fourteen year, 9 percent coupon, $1,000 par value bond at a price of $1,082.48. What rate of interest would you earn if you bought the bond and held it to maturity? This rate is defined as the bond's *yield to maturity,* and it is the interest rate discussed by bond traders when they talk about rates of return. To find the yield to maturity, often called the YTM, you could solve the following equation for k_d:

$$V = \$1,082.48 = \frac{\$90}{(1 + k_d)^1} + \frac{\$90}{(1 + k_d)^2} + \cdots + \frac{\$90}{(1 + k_d)^{14}} + \frac{\$1,000}{(1 + k_d)^{14}}$$

$$= \$90(\text{PVIFA}_{k,n}) + \$1,000(\text{PVIF}_{k,n}).$$

We can substitute in values for PVIFA and PVIF until we find a pair that "works" and makes

$$\$1,082.48 = \$90(\text{PVIFA}_{k,n}) + \$1,000(\text{PVIF}_{k,n}).$$

What would be a good interest rate to use as a starting point? First, referring to Point 3 in the preceding subsection, we know that since the bond is selling at a premium over its par value ($1,082.48 vs. $1,000), the bond's yield is *below* the going 9 percent coupon rate. Therefore, we might try a rate of 7 percent. Substituting in factors for 7 percent, we obtain

$$\$90(8.7455) + \$1,000(0.3878) = \$1,174.90 \neq \$1,082.48.$$

Our calculated bond value, $1,174.90, is *above* the actual market price, so the yield to maturity is *not* 7 percent. To lower the calculated value, we must *raise* the interest rate used in the process. Inserting factors for 8 percent, we obtain

$$V = \$90(8.2442) + \$1,000(0.3405)$$
$$= \$741.98 + \$340.50$$
$$= \$1,082.48.$$

This calculated value is exactly equal to the market price of the bond; thus, 8 percent is the bond's yield to maturity: $k_d = \text{YTM} = 8.0\%$.[6]

The yield to maturity is identical to the total rate of return we calcu-

---

[6] We found the yield to maturity on this bond by trial and error. In Chapter 11 we will examine more efficient procedures for zeroing in on interest rates. It should also be noted that specialized hand-held calculators can be used to find the yield to maturity on a bond with very little effort. A few years ago traders all had specialized tables called *bond tables* that gave yields on bonds of different maturities selling at different premiums and discounts. Because the calculators are so much more efficient (and accurate), bond tables are rarely used any more.

There is also a formula that can be used to find the approximate yield to maturity on a bond:

$$k_d = \text{YTM} = \frac{I + (M - V)/n}{(M + V)/2}$$

In the situation where $I = \$90$, $M = \$1,000$, $V = \$1,082.48$, and $n = 14$,

$$k_d = \frac{\$90 + (\$1,000 - \$1,082.48)/14}{(\$1,000 + \$1,082.48)/2} = 0.0808 = 8.08\%.$$

This is close to the exact value, 8 percent. This formula can also be used to obtain a starting point for the trial-and-error method.

lated in the preceding section. The YTM for a bond that sells at par consists entirely of an interest yield, but if the bond sells at a price other than its par value, YTM consists of a positive or negative capital gains yield plus the interest yield. Note also that a bond's YTM changes whenever interest rates in the economy change, and this is almost daily. One who purchases a bond and holds it until it matures will receive the YTM that existed on the purchase date, but the bond's YTM will change frequently.[7]

Interest Rate Risk on a Bond

As we saw in Chapter 2, Figure 2-2, interest rates go up and down over time, and as interest rates change, the values of outstanding bonds also fluctuate. Suppose that you bought some 9 percent Carter bonds at a price of $1,000 and interest rates subsequently rose to 10 percent. The price of the bonds would fall to $926.30, so the value of the bonds would decline by $73.70 per bond. Interest rates can and do rise, and rising rates will cause a loss of value for bondholders. Thus, people or firms who invest in bonds are exposed to risk from changing interest rates, or *interest rate risk*.

One's exposure to interest rate risk is higher on bonds with long maturities than on those maturing in the near future. This point can be demonstrated by showing how the value of a one year, 9 percent coupon bond changes with changes in k_d, and then comparing these changes with those on a fourteen year bond as calculated above. The one year bond's values at different interest rates are shown below.

Value at $k_d = 8\%$:

$$V = \$90(\text{PVIFA}_{8\%,1 \text{ yr.}}) + \$1,000(\text{PVIF}_{8\%,1 \text{ yr.}})$$
$$= \$90(0.9259) + \$1,000(0.9259)$$
$$= \$83.33 + \$925.90 = \$1,009.23.$$

Value at $k_d = 9\%$:

$$V = \$90(0.9174) + \$1,000(0.9174)$$
$$= \$82.57 + \$917.40 = \$999.97 \approx \$1,000.$$

---

[7] If you had bought a bond that was callable (see Footnote 1), and the company called it, you would not have the option of holding the bond until it matured, so the YTM would not be applicable. For example, if a firm had callable 15 percent coupon bonds outstanding and interest rates fell from 15 percent to 10 percent, then the company could call in the 15 percent bonds, replace them with 10 percent bonds, and save $150 − $100 = $50 interest per bond per year. This is beneficial to the company, but not to bondholders.

If current interest rates are well below an outstanding bond's coupon rate, then the bond is likely to be called, and investors should estimate the expected rate of return on the bond as the *yield to call* (YTC) rather than as the yield to maturity (YTM). To calculate YTC, solve this equation for k_d:

$$\text{Price of bond} = \sum_{t=1}^{n} \frac{I}{(1 + k_d)^t} + \frac{\text{Call price}}{(1 + k_d)^n}.$$

Here n = years until the company can call the bond, call price is the price the company must pay in order to call the bond (it is often set equal to the par value plus one year's interest), and k_d is the YTC. Problem 4-11 at the end of the chapter deals with the YTC calculation.

Value at $k_d = 10\%$:
$$V = \$90(0.9091) + \$1,000(0.9091)$$
$$= \$81.82 + \$909.10 = \$990.92.$$

The values of the one year and fourteen year bonds, at different current market interest rates, are summarized in Table 4-1, and they are plotted in Figure 4-3. Notice how much more sensitive the price of the long-term bond is to changes in interest rates. At a 9 percent interest rate, both the long- and short-term bonds are valued at $1,000. When rates rise to 10 percent, the long-term bond falls to $926.30, while the short-term bond falls only to $990.92. A similar situation occurs when rates fall below 9 percent.

This differential sensitivity to changes in interest rates always holds true for bonds selling reasonably close to par—the longer the maturity of a security, the greater its price change in response to a given change in interest rates. Thus, even if the risk of default on two bonds is exactly the same, the one with the longer maturity is exposed to more risk from a rise in interest rates.[8]

The logical explanation for this difference in interest rate risk is simple. Suppose you bought a fifteen year bond that yielded 9 percent, or $90 a year. Now suppose interest rates on bonds of comparable risk rose to 10 percent. You would be stuck with only $90 interest for the next fifteen years. On the other hand, had you bought a one year bond, you

	Current Market Interest Rate (k_d)	Current Market Value	
		One Year Bond	Fourteen Year Bond
	8%	$1,009.23	$1,082.48
	9%	1,000.00	1,000.00
	10%	990.92	926.30

Table 4-1
Values of Long-Term and Short-Term, 9% Coupon Rate Bonds at Different Market Interest Rates

[8] The discount or premium on a bond may also be calculated as follows:

$$\frac{\text{Discount or}}{\text{premium}} = \left(\frac{\text{Interest payment}}{\text{on old bond}} - \frac{\text{Interest payment}}{\text{on new bond}}\right)\left(PVIFA_{k_d,n}\right),$$

where n = years to maturity on the old bond and k_d = current rate of interest, or yield to maturity, on the new bond. For example, when interest rates rose to 10 percent one year after they were issued, the discount on the Carter bonds could be calculated as follows:

$$\text{Discount} = (\$90 - \$100)(7.3667) = -\$73.67. \text{ (The minus sign indicates discount.)}$$

This value agrees (except for a rounding error) with the value calculated above:

$$\text{Discount} = \text{Par value} - \text{Price} = \$1,000 - \$926.30 = \$73.70.$$

In this form, we see that the discount is equal to the present value of the interest payment one sacrifices to buy a low-coupon old bond rather than a high-coupon new bond. The longer the bond has to run, the greater the sacrifice, hence the greater the discount.

**Figure 4-3
Values of Long-Term
and Short-Term, 9%
Coupon Rate Bonds at
Different Market Interest
Rates**

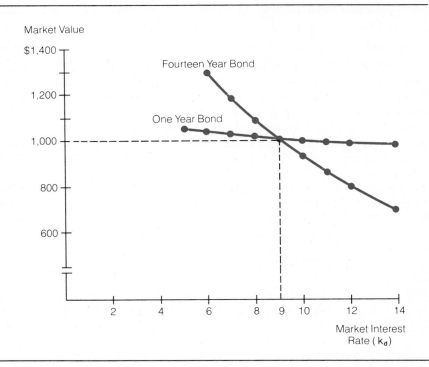

would only have a low return for one year. At the end of the year, you would get your $1,000 back, and you could then reinvest it and receive 10 percent, or $100 per year, for the next fourteen years. Thus, interest rate risk reflects the length of time one is committed to a given investment.[9]

Bond Values with Semiannual Compounding

Although many bonds do pay interest annually, most actually pay interest semiannually. To evaluate these bonds, we must modify the valuation formula (Equation 4-1) as follows:

1. Divide the annual coupon interest payment by 2 to determine the amount of interest paid each six months.
2. Determine the number of periods by multiplying the years to maturity, n, by 2.

[9] If a ten year bond were plotted in Figure 4-3, its curve would lie between those of the fourteen year bond and the one year bond. The curve of a one month bond would be almost horizontal, indicating that its price changes very little in response to interest rate changes.

3. Determine the semiannual interest rate by dividing the annual rate, k_d, by 2.

By making these changes, we arrive at the following equation for finding the value of a bond that pays interest semiannually:

$$V = \sum_{t=1}^{2n} \frac{I}{2}\left(\frac{1}{1 + \frac{k_d}{2}}\right)^t + M\left(\frac{1}{1 + \frac{k_d}{2}}\right)^{2n} \qquad (4\text{-}1a)$$

Assume, for example, that Carter Chemical's bonds pay $45 interest each six months rather than $90 at the end of each year. Thus, each interest payment is only half as large, but there are twice as many of them. When the going rate of interest is 8 percent, the value of this fifteen year bond is found as follows:

$$
\begin{aligned}
V &= \$45(PVIFA_{4\%,30}) + \$1,000(PVIF_{4\%,30}) \\
&= \$45(17.2920) + \$1,000(0.3083) \\
&= \$778.14 + \$308.30 \\
&= \$1,086.44.
\end{aligned}
$$

The $1,086.44 value with semiannual interest payments is slightly larger than $1,085.56, the value when interest is paid annually. This higher value occurs because interest payments are received somewhat faster under semiannual compounding.

Students sometimes discount the maturity value at 8 percent over 15 years, rather than at 4 percent over 30 six-month periods. This is incorrect—logically, all cash flows in a given contract must be discounted on the same basis, semiannually in this instance. For consistency, bond traders *must* apply semiannual compounding to the maturity value, and they do.

Common Stock Valuation

Common stock represents ownership of a corporation, but to the typical investor, a share of common stock is simply a piece of paper distinguished by two important features:

1. It entitles its owner to dividends.
2. It can be sold at some future date, hopefully for more than its purchase price.

If the stock is sold at a price above its purchase price, the investor will receive a *capital gain*. Generally, at the time people buy common stocks, they do expect to receive capital gains; otherwise they would not buy the stocks.

In Chapter 14 we shall discuss the rights and privileges of the common stockholder, the process by which new shares are issued, and the markets in which outstanding shares are traded. Our purpose in this chapter, however, is simply to analyze models that help explain how stock prices are determined.

Definitions of Terms Used in the Stock Valuation Models

Common stocks provide an expected future cash flow stream, and stock values are found in the same manner as the values of other financial assets, namely, as the present value of a future stream of income. The expected cash flows consist of two elements: (1) the dividend expected in each year and (2) the price investors expect to receive when they sell the stock. The final stock price includes the return of the original investment plus a capital gain (or minus a capital loss).

We shall develop some models to help determine the value of a share of stock under several different sets of conditions, but let us first define the following terms:

D_t = the dividend the stockholder expects to receive at the end of Year t.[10] D_0 is the most recent dividend, which has already been paid; D_1 is the next dividend, which will be paid at the end of this year; D_2 is the dividend expected at the end of two years, and so forth. D_1 represents the first cash flow a new purchaser of the stock will receive.

P_t = the price of the stock at the end of each year t. P_0 is the price of the stock today; P_1 is the price expected at the end of one year; and so on.

g = the expected rate of growth in the stock price. (In most of our models, g is also the expected rate of growth in earnings and dividends. In addition, we generally assume that g is expected to be constant over time.)

k_s = the minimum acceptable or *required rate of return* on the stock, considering both its riskiness and the returns available on other investments. The determinants of k_s will be discussed in detail in Chapter 5.

$\hat{k}_s$ = (pronounced "k hat") the *expected rate of return* which the individual who buys the stock actually expects to receive. The caret, or "hat," is used to indicate that $\hat{k}_s$ is a predicted value. $\hat{k}_s$ could be above or below k_s, but one would buy the stock only if $\hat{k}_s$ were equal to or greater than k_s.

D_1/P_0 = the expected *dividend yield* on the stock during the coming year. If the stock is expected to pay a dividend of $1 during

---

[10] We could speak here of periods rather than years, but in stock valuation it is typical to work on an annual rather than on a quarterly, semiannual, or other basis. The data used in stock valuation are simply not precise enough to warrant such refinements.

the next twelve months, and if its current price is $10, then the expected dividend yield is $1/\$10 = 0.10 = 10\%$.

$\dfrac{P_1 - P_0}{P_0} =$ the expected *capital gains yield* on the stock during the coming year. If the stock sells for $10 today, and if it is expected to rise to $10.50 at the end of one year, then the expected capital gain is $P_1 - P_0 = \$10.50 - \$10.00 = \$0.50$, and the expected capital gains yield is $\$0.50/\$10 = 0.05 = 5\%$. Notice that the growth rate that would cause the stock price to rise from $10 to $10.50 is 5%. This growth rate, g, is equal to the capital gains yield.

Expected total return $=$ the expected dividend yield plus the expected capital gains yield $= \hat{k}_s$ as defined above. In the example, $\hat{k}_s = 10\% + 5\% = 15\%$.

Expected Dividends as the Basis for Stock Values

In our discussion of bonds, we found the value of a bond as the present value of interest payments over the life of the bond, plus the present value of the bond's maturity (or par) value:

$$V = \frac{I}{(1 + k_d)} + \frac{I}{(1 + k_d)^2} + \cdots + \frac{I}{(1 + k_d)^n} + \frac{M}{(1 + k_d)^n}.$$

Stock prices are determined as the present value of a stream of cash flows, and the basic stock valuation equation turns out to be very similar to the bond value equation. What are the cash flows that corporations provide to their stockholders? First, think of yourself as an investor who buys a stock with the intention of holding it (in your family) forever. In this case, all you (and your heirs) will receive is a stream of dividends, and the value of the stock is calculated as the present value of an infinite stream of dividends:

$$\text{Value of stock} = P_0 = \text{PV of expected future dividends}$$
$$= \frac{D_1}{(1 + k_s)^1} + \frac{D_2}{(1 + k_s)^2} + \cdots + \frac{D_\infty}{(1 + k_s)^\infty}. \quad (4\text{-}2)$$

What about the more typical case, where you expect to hold the stock for a finite period, then to sell it? What will be the value of P_0 in this case? *The value of the stock is again determined by Equation 4-2.* To see this, recognize that for any individual investor, cash flows consist of dividends plus the sale price of the stock, but for all present and future investors in total, expected cash flows consist only of future dividends. Unless a firm is liquidated or is sold to another concern, the cash flows it provides to its stockholders consist only of a stream of dividends. Thus, the value of a share of common stock may be established as the present value of its stream of dividends.

The generalized nature of Equation 4-2 can also be seen by asking this question: Suppose I buy a stock expecting to hold it for one year. I will receive dividends during the year, and the value P_1 when I sell the stock at the end of the year. But what will determine the value of P_1? It will be determined as the present value of the dividends during Year 2 plus the stock price at the end of Year 2, which, in turn, will be determined as the present value of another set of future dividends and an even more distant stock price. This process can be continued ad infinitum, and the ultimate result is Equation 4-2.[11]

Equation 4-2 is a generalized stock valuation model in the sense that the time pattern of D_t can be anything: D_t can be rising, falling, constant, or it can even fluctuate randomly, and Equation 4-2 will still hold. For many purposes, however, it is useful to estimate a particular time pattern for D_t and then develop a simplified (that is, easier to evaluate) version of the stock valuation model expressed in Equation 4-2. In the following sections we consider the cases of zero growth, constant growth, and non-constant (or "supernormal") growth.

Stock Values with Zero Growth

Suppose dividends are not expected to grow. If they are expected to remain constant, we have a *zero growth stock*. In this case, the dividends expected in each future year are equal to some constant amount, $D_1 = D_2$

---

[11] Assume that you and all other investors buy a stock expecting to hold it for one year and then sell it at a price P_1. P_0 would be found as follows:

$$P_0 = \frac{D_1}{1 + k_s} + \frac{P_1}{1 + k_s}. \tag{1}$$

The value of P_1 would be found as the present value of D_2 and P_2:

$$P_1 = \frac{D_2}{1 + k_s} + \frac{P_2}{1 + k_s}. \tag{2}$$

We could substitute the Equation 2 value for P_1 into Equation 1, obtaining Equation 3:

$$P_0 = \frac{D_1}{1 + k_s} + \frac{\dfrac{D_2}{1 + k_s} + \dfrac{P_2}{1 + k_s}}{1 + k_s}$$

$$= \frac{D_1}{(1 + k_s)} + \frac{D_2}{(1 + k_s)^2} + \frac{P_2}{(1 + k_s)^2}. \tag{3}$$

We could continue in similar fashion, finding the values of P_2, P_3, and so forth, and at the limit we would have Equation 4-2:

$$P_0 = \frac{D_1}{(1 + k_s)} + \frac{D_2}{(1 + k_s)^2} + \dots + \frac{D_\infty}{(1 + k_s)^\infty}. \tag{4-2}$$

Here we developed Equation 4-2 on the assumption that investors have a one year investment horizon. If they had longer horizons, we would still get to Equation 4-2, but we would simply get there faster because, for example, we could start with Equation 3 if investors had two year horizons.

We should note that investors periodically lose sight of the long-run nature of stocks as investments and forget that in order to sell a stock at a profit, one must find a buyer who will pay the higher price. If you analyze a stock's value in accordance with Equation 4-2, conclude that the stock's market price exceeds a reasonable value, and then buy the stock anyway, then you are following the "bigger fool theory of investment." You think that you may be a fool to buy the stock at its excessive price, but you also think that when you get ready to sell it, you can find someone who is an even bigger fool. The bigger fool theory was widely followed in 1929.

= D_3 and so on. Therefore, we can drop the subscript and rewrite Equation 4-2 as follows:

$$P_0 = \frac{D}{(1 + k_s)^1} + \frac{D}{(1 + k_s)^2} + \cdots + \frac{D}{(1 + k_s)^n} + \cdots + \frac{D}{(1 + k_s)^\infty}. \quad (4\text{-}2a)$$

As we noted in Chapter 3 in connection with the British Consol bond, a security that is expected to pay a constant amount each period forever is defined as a *perpetuity*. Therefore, a zero growth stock may be thought of as a perpetuity.

The stock is expected to provide an infinite stream of future dividends, but each dividend has a smaller present value than the preceding one, and as n gets very large, the present value of the individual future dividends approaches zero. To illustrate, suppose D = $1.92 and k_s = 9% = 0.09. We can rewrite Equation 4-2a as follows:

$$P_0 = \frac{\$1.92}{(1.09)^1} + \frac{\$1.92}{(1.09)^2} + \frac{\$1.92}{(1.09)^3} + \cdots + \frac{\$1.92}{(1.09)^{50}} + \cdots + \frac{\$1.92}{(1.09)^{100}} + \cdots$$

$$= \$1.76 + \$1.62 + \$1.48 + \cdots + \$0.03 + \cdots + \$0.0003 + \cdots.$$

We can also show the perpetuity in graph form, as in Figure 4-4. The horizontal line shows the constant dividend stream, D_t = $1.92. The step function curve shows the present value of each future dividend. If we extended the analysis on out to infinity and then summed the PVs of all future dividends, the sum would be equal to the value of the stock.

It can be shown that Equation 4-2a, hence the value of a zero growth stock, reduces to this formula:[12]

$$P_0 = \frac{D_1}{k_s}. \qquad\qquad g = 0 \qquad (4\text{-}3)$$

Therefore, in our example, the value of the stock is $21.33:

$$P_0 = \frac{\$1.92}{0.09} = \$21.33.$$

Thus, if you were to extend Figure 4-4 on out forever and then add up the present values of each individual dividend, you would end up with the value of the stock, $21.33.[13]

We could transpose the P_0 and the k_s in Equation 4-3 to solve for k_s. We could then look up the value of the stock and the latest dividend, P_0

---

[12] The derivation of the formula in Equation 4-3 is shown in Appendix 4A.

[13] If you think that having a stock pay dividends forever is unrealistic, then think of it as lasting only for 50 or 100 years. Here we would have an annuity of $1.92 per year for 50 or 100 years. The PV of a 50 year annuity would be $1.92 (10.9617) = $21.04, while the PV of a 100 year annuity would be $21.329, versus $21.33 for the infinite annuity. Thus, the years from 50 to infinity do not contribute much to the value of the stock!

Figure 4-4
Present Values of Dividends of a Perpetuity (Zero Growth Stock)

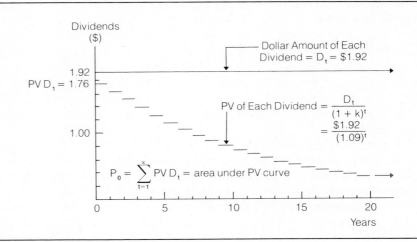

and D, in the newspaper, and the value k = D/P_0 would be the rate of return we would expect to earn if we bought the stock. Since we are dealing with an *expected rate of return,* we put a "hat" on the k value to produce Equation 4-4:

$$\hat{k}_s = \frac{D_1}{P_0}. \tag{4-4}$$

Thus, if we bought the stock at a price of $21.33 and expected to receive a constant dividend of $1.92, our expected rate of return would be

$$\hat{k}_s = \frac{\$1.92}{\$21.33} = 0.09 = 9\%.$$

Before leaving this section, we should note that Equations 4-3 and 4-4 are also applicable to *preferred stock,* a type of stock that pays a constant dividend. Preferred stock is discussed in detail in Chapter 13.

"Normal," or Constant, Growth

Although the zero growth model is applicable to some companies, the earnings and dividends of most companies increase each year. In general, this growth is expected to continue in the foreseeable future at about the same rate as that of the gross national product. On this basis, it is expected that an average, or "normal," company will grow at a rate of about 6 percent a year, and this rate will rise if the inflation rate increases.[14]

---

[14] Growth in dividends occurs primarily as a result of growth in earnings per share (EPS). Earnings growth, in turn, results from a number of factors, including the following: (1) EPS can grow simply because of inflation. If output is stable, and if both sales prices and input costs rise by the same

(continued)

Thus, if such a company's last dividend, which has already been paid, was D_0, its dividend in any future Year t may be forecast as $D_t = D_0(1 + g)^t$, where g is the expected rate of growth. For example, if Carter Chemical just paid a dividend of $1.92 (that is, $D_0 = \$1.92$) and investors expect a 4 percent growth rate, the estimated dividend one year hence will be $D_1 = (\$1.92)(1.04) = \$2$; D_2 will be $2.08; and the estimated dividend five years hence will be

$$D_t = D_0(1 + g)^t$$
$$= \$1.92(1.04)^5$$
$$= \$2.34.$$

Using this method of estimating future dividends, the current price, P_0, is determined by Equation 4-2, as described earlier. In other words, we find the expected future cash flow stream (the dividends), get the present value of each dividend payment, and sum them. The summation is the value of the stock. Thus, the stock price is equal to the present value of the expected future dividends.

If g is constant, Equation 4-2 may be simplified as follows:[15]

$$P_0 = \frac{D_1}{k_s - g}. \qquad (4\text{-}5)$$

Inserting values into the equation, we find the price of this stock to be $40:

$$P_0 = \frac{\$1.92(1.04)}{0.09 - 0.04} = \frac{\$2}{0.05} = \$40.$$

The constant growth model expressed in Equation 4-5 is often called the Gordon Model, after Myron J. Gordon, who did much to develop and popularize it.

Note that Equation 4-5 is sufficiently general to encompass the no growth case described above: if growth is zero, this is simply a special case, and Equation 4-5 is equal to Equation 4-3. Note also that a necessary condition for the derivation of Equation 4-5 is that k_s be greater than g. If the equation is used where k_s is not greater than g, the results are meaningless.

---

proportions, then EPS will grow. The purchasing power of EPS will not grow if the firm's costs and prices rise at the same rate as most other products—that is, there will be no "real" growth. Of course, there is no reason whatever to think that a firm's EPS will necessarily match the rate of general inflation, because some prices rise faster than others. (2) EPS will also grow as a result of the reinvestment, or plowback, of earnings. If the firm's earnings are not all paid out as dividends (some fraction of earnings is retained), then the investment behind each share will rise over time, and this rising investment per share should lead to rising earnings and dividends. The relationship between earnings retention and growth is discussed further in Chapter 18.

[15] The proof of Equation 4-5 is given in Appendix 4A.

The concept underlying the stock valuation process is graphed in Figure 4-5 for the case of a 4 percent growth rate. Dividends grow, but since $k_s > g$, the present value of each future dividend (the lower step-function curve) is declining. For example, the dividend in Year 1 is $D_1 = D_0 (1 + g)^1 = \$1.92(1.04) = \$2.00$. The present value of this dividend, discounted at 9 percent, is $PV\ D_1 = \$2.00/(1.09)^1 = \$2.00/1.09 = \$1.83$. The dividend expected in Year 2 is $D_2 = \$2.08$, and the PV of this dividend is \$1.75. Continuing, $D_3 = \$2.16$ and $PV\ D_3 = \$1.67$. Thus, the expected dividends are growing, but the PV of the successive dividends is declining because $k_s > g$.

Figure 4-5
Growing Dividend Stream and Present Value of the Stream: $D_0 = \$1.92$, g = 4%, $k_s = 9\%$

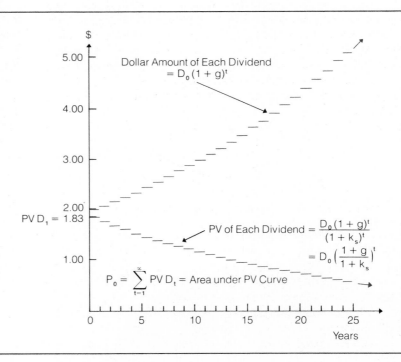

If we added up the PVs of each future dividend, this summation would be the value of the stock, P_0. And, as we saw above, when g is a constant, this summation is equal to $D_1/(k_s - g)$, the value of Equation 4-5. Therefore, if we extended the lower step-function curve in Figure 4-5 on out to infinity and added up the present values of each future dividend, the summation would be identical to the value given by the formula.

We could solve Equation 4-5 for k_s, again using the hat to denote that we are dealing with an expected rate of return:[16]

$$\hat{k}_s = \frac{D_1}{P_0} + g. \tag{4-6}$$

Thus, if you buy a stock for a price $P_0 = \$40$, and if the stock is expected to pay a dividend $D_1 = \$2$ next year and to grow at a constant rate $g = 4\%$ in the future, then your expected rate of return is 9 percent on your $40 investment:

$$\hat{k}_s = \frac{\$2}{\$40} + 4\% = 5\% + 4\% = 9\%.$$

In this form we see that $\hat{k}_s$ is the *expected total return* and that it consists of $D_1/P_0 = 5\%$, the *expected dividend yield*, and $g = 4\%$, the *expected growth rate or capital gains yield*.

Suppose the analysis above had been conducted on January 1, 1982, so $P_0 = \$40$ was the January 1, 1982, stock price and $D_1 = \$2$ was the dividend expected during 1982. What should the stock price be at the end of 1982 (or the beginning of 1983)? We would again apply Equation 4-5, but this time with the 1983 dividend, $D_2 = D_1 (1 + g) = \$2(1.04) = \$2.08$:

$$P_{1/1/83} = \frac{D_{1983}}{k_s - g} = \frac{\$2.08}{0.09 - 0.04} = \$41.60.$$

Now notice that $41.60 is exactly 4 percent greater than P_0, the $40 price on 1/1/82:

$$\$41.60 = \$40(1.04).$$

Thus, we expect to make a capital gain of $\$41.60 - \$40 = \$1.60$ during the year, for a capital gains yield of 4 percent:

$$\text{Capital gains yield} = \frac{\$1.60}{\$40} = 0.04 = 4\%.$$

---

[16] Equation 4-6 is derived from 4-5 as follows:

$$P_0 = \frac{D_1}{k_s - g} \tag{4-5}$$

$$k_s P_0 - g P_0 = D_1$$

$$k_s P_0 = D_1 + g P_0$$

$$\hat{k}_s = \frac{D_1}{P_0} + g. \tag{4-6}$$

The k value in Equation 4-5 is a *required* rate of return, but when we transform to form Equation 4-6 we are finding an *expected* rate of return. Obviously, the transformation requires that $k_s = \hat{k}_s$. This equality holds if the stock market is in equilibrium, a condition discussed at length in Chapter 5.

We could extend the analysis on out, and in each future year the expected capital gains yield would always equal g, the expected dividend growth rate.

The dividend yield in 1983 can be estimated as follows:

$$\text{Dividend yield}_{1983} = \frac{D_{1983}}{P_{1/1/83}} = \frac{\$2.08}{\$41.60} = 0.05 = 5\%.$$

The dividend yield for 1984 could also be calculated, and it would again be 5 percent. Thus, for a constant growth stock, (1) the dividend grows at a constant rate; (2) the stock price grows at this same rate; (3) the dividend yield is a constant; (4) the capital gains yield is also a constant, and it is equal to g, the expected dividend growth rate; and (5) the expected total rate of return, $\hat{k}_s$, is equal to the expected dividend yield plus the expected capital gains yield, as shown in Equation 4-6.

Nonconstant, or "Supernormal," Growth

Firms typically go through "life cycles" during part of which their growth is much faster than that of the economy as a whole. Automobile manufacturers in the 1920s and computer and office equipment manufacturers in the 1970s are examples. Figure 4-6 illustrates such nonconstant, or "su-

Figure 4-6
Illustrative Dividend
Growth Rates

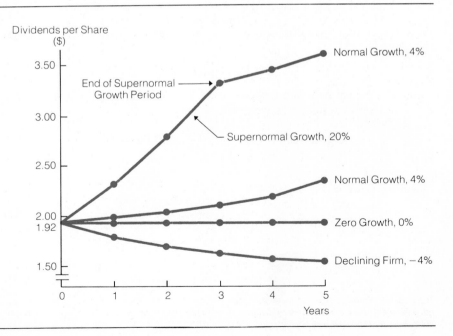

pernormal," growth and compares it with normal growth, zero growth, and negative growth.[17]

The dividends of the supernormal growth firm are expected to grow at a 20 percent rate for three years, after which the growth rate is expected to fall to 4 percent, the assumed norm for the economy. The value of this firm, like any other, is the present value of its expected future dividends as determined by Equation 4-2. In the case where D_t is growing at a constant rate, we simplified Equation 4-2 to $P_0 = D_1/(k_s - g)$. In the supernormal case, however, the expected growth rate is not a constant— it declines at the end of the period of supernormal growth. To find the value of such a stock, we proceed in three steps:

1. Find the PV of the dividends during the period of supernormal growth.
2. Find the price of the stock at the end of the supernormal growth period, and then discount this price back to the present.
3. Add these two components to find the present value of the stock, P_0.

To illustrate the process of growth stock valuation, suppose the following facts exist:

k_s = stockholders' required rate of return = 9 percent.
N = years of supernormal growth = 3.
g_s = rate of earnings and dividend growth during supernormal growth period = 20 percent.
g_n = rate of growth after supernormal period = 4 percent.
D_0 = last dividend that the company paid = \$1.92.

Step 1. Find the PV of dividends paid (PV D) at the end of Years 1 to 3 using this formula:

$$PV\ D_t = D_0(1 + g_s)^t \left(\frac{1}{1 + k_s}\right)^t = D_0(FVIF_{g_s, t})(PVIF_{k_s, t}):$$

	D_0	× $FVIF_{20\%, t}$	× $PVIF_{9\%, t}$	=	PV D_t
D_1:	\$1.92 ×	(1.200)	× 0.9174	=	\$2.1137
D_2:	1.92 ×	(1.440)	× 0.8417	=	2.3273
D_3:	1.92 ×	(1.728)	× 0.7722	=	2.5622
			Sum of PVs of supernormal period dividends	=	\$7.0032

---

[17] A negative growth rate indicates a declining company. A mining company whose profits are falling because of a declining ore body is an example.

Step 2. Find the PV of the stock's price at the end of Year 3:

a.
$$P_3 = \frac{D_4}{k_s - g_n} = \frac{D_0(1 + g_s)^3(1 + g_n)}{k_s - g_n} = \frac{D_3(1 + g_n)}{0.09 - 0.04}$$

$$= \frac{\$3.318(1.04)}{0.05} = \frac{\$3.45}{0.05} = \$69.$$

b. $PV\ P_3 = \$69\ (PVIF_{9\%,3\ yrs.}) = \$69(0.7722) = \$53.28.$

Step 3. Sum to find P_0, the value of the stock today:

$$P_0 = \$7.00 + \$53.28 = \$60.28.$$

A graphic view of this process, using a time line diagram, is given in Figure 4-7.

Figure 4-7
Time Line for Finding the Value of a Supernormal Growth Stock

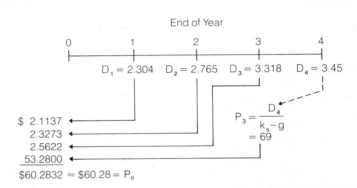

It is useful to summarize our discussion of stock valuation models by comparing companies with the four growth situations graphed in Figure 4-6. Here we had a zero growth company, one with a constant 4 percent expected growth rate, one whose earnings are expected to decline at the rate of 4 percent a year, and one whose growth rate is not a constant.

We can use the valuation equations developed above to determine the stock prices, dividend yields, capital gains yields, total expected returns, and price/earnings ratios (P/E ratios)[18] for the four companies. These data

Comparing Companies with Different Expected Growth Rates

---

[18] Price/earnings ratios relate a stock's price to its earnings per share (EPS). The higher the P/E ratio, the more investors are willing to pay for a dollar of the firm's current earnings. Other things held constant, investors will pay more for a dollar of current earnings of a rapidly growing firm than for one of a slow growth company; hence, rapid growth companies generally have high P/E ratios. These ratios are discussed in more detail in Chapter 6. The relationships among the P/E ratios, shown in the last column

(continued)

are shown in Table 4-2. We assume that each firm had earnings per share (EPS) of \$3.60 during the preceding reporting period (that is, $EPS_0 = $ \$3.60) and paid out 53.3 percent of its reported earnings as dividends. Therefore, dividends per share last year, D_0, were \$1.92 for each company, but the values of D_1 differ among the companies.

The expected and required return is 9 percent on each of the stocks; thus, $\hat{k}_s = k_s = 9\%$. For a declining firm this return consists of a relatively high current dividend yield combined with a capital loss amounting to 4 percent a year. For the no growth firm there is neither a capital gain nor a capital loss expectation, so the 9 percent return must be obtained entirely from the dividend yield. The normal growth firm provides a rela-

Table 4-2
Prices, Dividend Yields, and Price/Earnings Ratios for 9 Percent Returns under Different Growth Assumptions

		Price	Current Dividend Yield (D_1/P_0)	Capital Gains Yield in Year 1 $[(P_1 - P_0)/P_0]$	Total Expected Return	P/E Ratio[a]
Declining firm (-4%)	$P_0 = \dfrac{D_1}{k_s - g} = \dfrac{\$1.84}{0.09 - (-0.04)} =$	\$14.15	13%	-4.0%	9%	3.9
No growth firm (0%)	$P_0 = \dfrac{D_1}{k_s} = \dfrac{\$1.92}{0.09} =$	21.33	9	0.0	9	5.9
Normal growth firm (4%)	$P_0 = \dfrac{D_1}{k_s - g} = \dfrac{\$2.00}{0.09 - 0.04} =$	40.00	5	4.0	9	11.1
Supernormal growth firm	$P_0 = $ (see earlier section) $=$	60.28	3.8	5.2[b]	9	16.7

[a] It was assumed at the beginning of this example that each company is earning \$3.60 initially. This \$3.60, divided into the various prices, gives the indicated P/E ratios.

We might also note that as the supernormal growth rate declines toward the normal rate (or as the time when this decline will occur becomes more imminent), the high P/E ratio must approach the normal P/E ratio; that is, the P/E of 16.7 will decline year by year and equal 11.1, that of the normal growth company, in the third year.

Note also that D_1 differs for each firm, being calculated as follows:

$$D_1 = EPS_0(1 + g)(\text{Percentage of earnings paid out}) = \$3.60(1 + g)(0.533).$$

For the declining firm, $D_1 = \$3.60 (0.96) (0.533) = \$1.84$.

[b] With $k = 9\%$ and $D_1/P_0 = 3.8\%$, then the capital gains yield must be $9.0 - 3.8 = 5.2\%$. We could calculate the price of the stock at the end of the year (P_1) using the supernormal growth procedures to confirm that the capital gains yield in Year 1 is indeed 5.2%, but this is not necessary.

of Table 4-2, are similar to what one would intuitively expect—the higher the expected growth (all other things the same), the higher the P/E ratio.

We should note, too, that differences in P/E ratios among firms can also arise from differences in the required rates of return, k_s, which investors use in capitalizing the future dividend streams. If one company has a higher P/E than another, this could be caused by a higher g, a lower k_s, or a combination of these two factors.

tively low current dividend yield, but a 4 percent per year capital gains expectation. Finally, the supernormal growth firm has the lowest current dividend yield but the highest capital gains expectation.

What is expected to happen to the prices of the four illustrative firms' stocks over time? Three of the four cases are straightforward: The zero growth firm's price is expected to be constant (that is, $P_t = P_{t+1}$); the declining firm is expected to have a falling stock price; and the constant growth firm's stock is expected to grow at a constant rate, 4 percent. We do not prove it here, but we could show that the supernormal firm's stock price growth rate starts at 5.2 percent per year but declines to 4 percent as the supernormal growth period ends. So, the supernormal firm's stock price grows at a declining rate that levels off at 4 percent at the end of the supernormal growth period, when it becomes a "normal growth stock."

An Illustration: AT&T

AT&T can be used to illustrate the stock valuation equations. In January of 1981, AT&T's common stock sold at a price of $49 per share. Earnings for 1980 were $8.10 per share; the 1980 dividend was $5 per share; the 1981 dividend was projected to be in the range of $5.25 to $5.40; and AT&T's long-term growth rate was projected to be in the range of 5 to 6 percent.

The analysts for Murray Finch, Price, Emmer & Smithe, a major brokerage house, believed that investors would receive a return of about 17.5 percent on an average New York Stock Exchange (NYSE) stock bought in January, 1981. Further, they felt that AT&T's required rate of return was about 16.5 percent. (At the time, AT&T's bonds were yielding about 13.5 percent.) Under these conditions, does AT&T's stock represent a good buy?

The Murray Finch analysts calculated a range of values as shown below:

$$D_1 = \$5.25,\ g = 5\%: P_0 = \$5.25/(0.165 - 0.05) = \$45.65.$$
$$D_1 = \$5.25,\ g = 6\%: P_0 = \$5.25/(0.165 - 0.06) = \$50.00.$$
$$D_1 = \$5.40,\ g = 5\%: P_0 = \$5.40/(0.165 - 0.05) = \$46.96.$$
$$D_1 = \$5.40,\ g = 6\%: P_0 = \$5.40/(0.165 - 0.06) = \$51.43.$$

The stock does seem to be fairly priced, since its market price of $49 is near the middle of the calculated range of values.

The book value per share of AT&T's stock, which represented the amount of money per share that investors had supplied to allow the company to buy the assets needed to serve telephone subscribers, was about $65 in January 1981. The Federal Communications Commission (FCC) was holding hearings to decide how much to allow AT&T to earn. The procedure for making this decision should be to estimate the cost of equity for AT&T ($k_{AT\&T}$) and then allow the company to earn this return. Based on the information given above, and assuming a stock price of $49, what was the value of $k_{AT\&T}$, the expected and required rate of return on AT&T's stock? Again, a range of values may be calculated:

$$D_1 = \$5.25,\ g = 5\%:\ k_{AT\&T} = (\$5.25/\$49.00) + 5\%$$
$$= 10.7\% + 5\%$$
$$= 15.7\%.$$

$$D_1 = \$5.25,\ g = 6\%:\ k_{AT\&T} = (\$5.25/\$49.00) + 6\%$$
$$= 10.7\% + 6\%$$
$$= 16.7\%.$$

$$D_1 = \$5.40,\ g = 5\%:\ k_{AT\&T} = (\$5.40/\$49.00) + 5\%$$
$$= 11\% + 5\%$$
$$= 16.0\%.$$

$$D_1 = \$5.40,\ g = 6\%:\ k_{AT\&T} = (\$5.40/\$49.00) + 6\%$$
$$= 11\% + 6\%$$
$$= 17.0\%.$$

Thus, these data suggest that AT&T's expected (and required) rate of return on equity was in the range of 15.7 to 17.0 percent.

In 1980, AT&T had earned a return of about 12.5 percent on its book equity ($8.10/$65.00 = 12.5%). If during 1981 the FCC (and all the state commissions which also regulate Bell System operations) allowed the company to earn a return toward the lower end of the estimated range of required return figures found above, say 16 percent, earnings per share would be $65(0.16) = $10.40, up from $8.10. With these higher earnings, the dividend could be boosted considerably, and the rate of growth in earnings and dividends would also increase.[19] Suppose you anticipated that AT&T would be allowed to earn 16 percent on its common, that it would pay out 60 percent of earnings, so that the 1981 dividend would be $D_1 = 0.6(\$10.40) = \$6.24$, and that the long-term growth rate would be $g = 0.4(16\%) = 6.4\%$. Assuming that $k_s = 16\%$, what would have

---

[19] Think about putting $1,000 into a bank time deposit earning 12 percent interest. If you were to leave all of your interest income in the bank, then your principal would grow at a rate of 12 percent per year, that is, $g = 12\%$. If you were to pull all of your interest out, your principal would not grow at all, that is, $g = 0$. If you were to withdraw 60 percent of your interest, leaving 40 percent in the account, then your account would grow at a rate of $g = 0.4(12\%) = 3\%$. The same general situation holds for corporate earnings—the approximate average long-run growth rate in earnings per share (g) is equal to the rate of return on common equity capital (ROE) times the fraction of earnings retained (b): $g = b(ROE)$. Therefore, if AT&T or any other company had an increase in ROE and if its retention fraction (b) were left constant, then the growth rate in its earnings per share and dividends per share would increase.

been your January 1981 estimate of the value of AT&T's stock? The answer is $65:

$$P_0 = \$6.24/(0.16 - 0.064) = \$65.00.$$

We see, then, that if AT&T's regulators actually allowed it to earn its required rate of return, then (1) AT&T's stock price would be equal to its book value and (2) the investors who have supplied the capital that has been used to make the United States telephone system possible would have stock with a value equal to the capital that has been invested. This is exactly the result that regulation (for telephone and electric companies) is supposed to attain.

The AT&T example presents just one of the many ways the concepts and formulas developed in Chapter 4 can be used. Individual investors, the managers of financial institutions, corporate executives, regulators of electric and telephone companies, real estate analysts and investors, and many others use these concepts on a daily basis. We shall extend and clarify the basic valuation/rate of return concepts in Chapter 5 and elsewhere throughout the book.

Summary

Corporate decisions should be analyzed in terms of how alternative courses of action will affect the value of the firm's stock. Clearly, it is necessary to know how stock prices in general are established before attempting to measure how a given decision will affect a specific firm's stock price. Accordingly, this chapter shows how bond and stock values are established, as well as how investors go about estimating the rates of return they will receive on these securities if they purchase them at the existing market prices. In all cases, security values were found to be *the present value of the future cash flows expected from the security*. The cash flows from a bond consist of interest payments and the bond's maturity value, while stocks provide a stream of dividends plus a sale price which can include capital gains or losses.

The following equation is used to find the value of a bond:

$$V = I\ (PVIFA_{k_d,n}) + M\ (PVIF_{k_d,n}).$$

Here V is the value of the bond; I is the annual interest payment, or coupon; n is years to maturity; k_d is the appropriate interest rate; and M is the bond's maturity value, generally $1,000. This equation can also be solved for k_d, which is called the *yield to maturity* (YTM).

Several different stock valuation formulas were developed; the ones for zero and for constant growth are given below:

$$\text{Zero growth stock:}\quad P_0 = \frac{D_1}{k_s}.$$

Constant, or normal, growth stock: $P_0 = \dfrac{D_1}{k_s - g}$.

Here P_0 is the current price of the stock; D_1 is the dividend expected during the next year; k_s is the required rate of return on the stock; and g is the expected growth rate. In this equation, g is a constant; if g is not a constant, then the supernormal growth formula must be used to find the stock's value.

We can express the equation for the expected rate of return as follows:

$$\hat{k}_s = \dfrac{D_1}{P_0} + g.$$

In this form, we see that $\hat{k}_s$ is a total expected return, consisting of an *expected dividend yield* plus an *expected capital gains yield*. For a constant growth stock, the dividend and capital gains components of total yield are constant over time. For supernormal growth stocks, the dividend yield rises over time, while the capital gains component declines, with the total yield remaining constant.

Throughout the chapter we simply take as given both the "appropriate discount rate," k_s, and the expected growth rate of dividends and stock prices. In Chapter 5 we shall examine the factors that determine the discount rates, and in Chapter 6 we take up methods of estimating future growth. Then, in the remainder of the book, we consider the types of actions that a firm's financial manager can take to lower the discount rate and to increase the expected growth rate, thus increasing the value of the firm's stock.

Questions

4-1 Two investors are evaluating AT&T's stock for possible purchase. They agree on the expected value of D_1 and also on the expected future dividend growth rate. However, one investor normally holds stock for two years while the other holds stock for ten years. Based on the type of analysis done in Chapter 4, they should both be willing to pay the same price for AT&T's stock. True or false?

4-2 A bond that pays interest forever and has no maturity date is a perpetual bond. In what respect is a perpetual bond similar to a no growth stock and to a share of preferred stock?

4-3 Is it true that the following equation can be used to find the value of an n-year bond that pays interest once a year?

$$\text{Value} = \sum_{t=1}^{n} \dfrac{\text{Annual interest}}{(1 + k_d)^t} + \dfrac{\text{Par value}}{(1 + k_d)^n}.$$

4-4 "The values of outstanding bonds change whenever the going rate of interest changes. In general, short-term bond prices are more sensitive to interest rate changes than are long-term bond prices." Is this statement true or false? Explain.

4-5 The rate of return you would get if you bought a bond and held it to its maturity date is defined as the bond's yield to maturity (YTM). If interest rates in the economy rise after a bond has been issued, what will happen to the YTM? Does it matter how long the bond has before maturity?

4-6 If you buy a share of common stock, you will typically expect to receive dividends plus capital gains. Would you expect the distribution between dividends and capital gains to be influenced by a firm's decision to pay more dividends rather than retain and reinvest more earnings?

4-7 The next expected dividend, D_1, divided by the current price of a share of stock, P_0, is defined as the stock's expected dividend yield. What is the relationship between the dividend yield, the total yield, and the remaining years of supernormal growth for a supernormal growth firm?

4-8 Is it true that the following expression can be used to find the value of a constant growth stock?

$$P_0 = \frac{D_0}{k_s + g}.$$

4-9 You are considering buying the stock of two very similar companies. Both companies are expected to earn $3 per share this year. However, Company A is expected to pay all of its earnings out as dividends, while Company B is expected to pay out only one-third of its earnings, or $1. A's stock price is $20. Which of the following is most likely to be true?

  a. Company B will have a faster growth rate than Company A. Therefore, B's stock price should be greater than $20.

  b. Although B's growth rate should exceed A's, A's current dividend exceeds that of B, and this should cause A's price to exceed B's.

  c. An investor in Stock A will get his or her money back faster because A pays out more of its earnings as dividends. Thus, in a sense, A is like a short-term bond, and B is like a long-term bond. Therefore, if economic shifts cause k_d and k_s to increase, and if the expected streams of dividends from A and B remain constant, then Stocks A and B will both decline, but A's price should decline further.

  d. A's expected and required rate of return is $\hat{k}_s = k_s = 15$ percent. B's expected return will be higher because of its higher expected growth rate.

  e. Based on the available information, the best estimate of B's growth rate is 10 percent.

Self-Test Problems

ST4-1 A firm issued a new series of bonds on January 1, 1962. The bonds were sold at par ($1,000), have a 12 percent coupon, and mature in thirty years. Coupon payments are made semiannually (on June 30 and December 31).

  a. What was the yield to maturity of the bond on 1/1/62?

    b. What was the price of the bond on 1/1/67, five years later, assuming that the level of interest rates had fallen to 10 percent?

    c. Find the current yield and capital gains yield on the bond on 1/1/67, given the price as determined in Part b above.

    d. On July 1, 1982, the bonds sold for $896.64. What was the YTM at that date?

    e. What was the current yield and capital gains yield on 7/1/82?

    f. Now assume that you purchase an outstanding bond on March 1, 1982. The going rate of interest is 15.5 percent: How large a check must you write to complete the transaction?

ST4-2 You can buy a share of the Karp Company's stock today for $24. Karp's last dividend was $1.60. In view of Karp's low risk, its required rate of return is only 12 percent. If dividends are expected to grow at a constant rate, g, in the future, and if k is expected to remain at 12 percent, what is Karp Company's expected stock price five years from now?

ST4-3 Miniscule Computer Chips, Inc., is experiencing a period of rapid growth. Earnings and dividends are expected to grow at a rate of 18 percent during the next two years, 15 percent in the third year, and then at a constant rate of 6 percent thereafter. Miniscule's last dividend was $1.15, and the required rate of return on the stock is 12 percent.

    a. Calculate the price of the stock today.

    b. Calculate P_1 and P_2.

    c. Calculate the dividend yield and capital gains yield for Years 1, 2, and 3.

4-1   a. The Hayes Company's bonds pay $100 annual interest, mature in fifteen years, and pay $1,000 on maturity. What will be the value of these bonds when the going rate of interest is (1) 6 percent, (2) 9 percent, and (3) 12 percent?   **Problems**

    b. Now suppose Hayes has some other bonds that pay $100 interest per year, $1,000 at maturity, and mature in one year. What will be the value of these bonds at a going rate of interest of (1) 6 percent, (2) 9 percent, and (3) 12 percent? Assume there is only one more interest payment to be made.

    c. Why do the longer-term bonds fluctuate more when interest rates change than do the shorter-term bonds (the one year bonds)?

4-2   a. The Coronet Company's bonds have three years remaining to maturity. Interest is paid annually, the bonds have a $1,000 par value, and the coupon interest rate is 7 percent. What is the yield to maturity at a current market price (1) of $974 or (2) of $1,027?

    b. Would you pay $974 for the bond described in Part a if you thought that the appropriate rate of interest for these bonds is $7\frac{1}{2}$ percent; that is, $k_d = 7\frac{1}{2}\%$? Explain your answer.

4-3 Suppose Exxon sold an issue of bonds with a ten year maturity, a $1,000 par value, a 12 percent coupon rate, and semiannual interest payments.

a. Two years after the bonds were issued, the going rate of interest on bonds such as these fell to 8 percent. At what price would the bonds sell?

b. Suppose that, two years after issue, the going interest rate had risen to 14 percent. At what price would the bonds sell?

c. Suppose the conditions in Part a existed; that is, interest rates fell to 8 percent two years after the issue date. Suppose, further, that the interest rate remained at 8 percent for the next eight years. What would happen to the price of the Exxon bonds over time?

4-4 Your broker offers to sell you a share of common stock that paid a dividend of $1 *last year*. You expect the dividend to grow at the rate of 5 percent per year for the next three years, and you plan to hold the stock for three years, then to sell it, if you do indeed buy the stock.

a. What is the expected dividend for each of the next three years; that is, calculate D_1, D_2, and D_3. Note that $D_0 = \$1$.

b. If the appropriate discount rate is 10 percent, and the first of these dividend payments will occur one year from now, what is the present value of the dividend stream; that is, calculate the PV of D_1, D_2, and D_3, and sum these PVs.

c. You expect the price of the stock to be $24.31 three years from now; that is, you expect P_3 to equal $24.31. Discounted at a 10 percent rate, what is the present value of this expected future stock price; that is, calculate the PV of $24.31.

d. If you plan to buy the stock, hold it for three years, and then sell it for $24.31, what is the most you should pay for it?

e. Use Equation 4-5 to calculate the present value of this stock. Assume that $g = 5\%$ and is a constant.

f. Is the value of this stock dependent upon how long you plan to hold it? In other words, if your planned holding period were two years or five years rather than three years, would this affect the value of the stock today, P_0?

4-5 You buy a share of stock for $21.00. You expect the stock to pay dividends of $1.05, $1.1025, and $1.1576 in Years 1, 2, and 3, respectively, and you expect to sell the stock at a price of $24.31 at the end of three years.

a. Calculate the growth rate in dividends.

b. Calculate the current dividend yield.

c. Assuming the calculated growth rate is expected to continue, you can add the dividend yield to the expected growth rate to get the expected total rate of return. What is this expected total rate of return?

4-6 a. Investors require a 16 percent rate of return on Company X's stock ($k_s = 16\%$). At what price will the stock sell if the previous dividend was $D_0 = \$1$ and investors expect dividends to grow at a constant compound annual rate of (1) minus 5 percent, (2) 0 percent, (3) 5 percent, and (4) 15 percent? (Hint: Use $D_1 = D_0(1 + g)$, not D_0, in the formula.)

b. In Part a, what is the "formula price" for Company X's stock if the required rate of return is 16 percent and the expected growth rate is (1) 16 percent or (2) 20 percent? Are these reasonable results? Explain.

4-7 In February 1956 the Los Angeles Airport authority issued a series of 3.4 percent, thirty year bonds. Interest rates rose substantially in the years following the issue, and as rates rose, the price of the bonds declined. In February 1969, thirteen years later, the price of the bonds had dropped from $1,000 to $650. Assume annual interest payments.

 a. Each bond originally sold at its $1,000 par value. What was the yield to maturity of these bonds at their time of issue?

 b. Calculate the yield to maturity in February 1969. (Hint: Use the formula in Footnote 6 to get started. Also, note that the bonds have seventeen years remaining to maturity.)

 c. Assume that interest rates stabilize at the 1969 level and remain at this level for the remainder of the life of the bonds. What will be their price in February 1981, when they have five years remaining to maturity?

 d. What will the price of the bonds be the day before they mature in 1986?

 e. In 1969 the Los Angeles Airport bonds were called "discount bonds." What happens to the price of discount bonds as they approach maturity? Is there a "built-in capital gain" on discount bonds?

 f. The coupon interest divided by the market price of a bond is defined as the bond's *current yield*. What is the current yield of a Los Angeles Airport bond (1) in February 1969 and (2) in February 1981? What are its capital gains yields and total yields (total yield equals yield to maturity) on those same two dates?

4-8 Lehigh Mining Company's ore reserves are being depleted, and its costs of recovering a declining quantity of ore are rising each year. As a result, the company's earnings and dividends are declining at the rate of 10 percent per year. If $D_0 = \$6$ and $k_s = 15\%$, what is the value of Lehigh Mining's stock?

4-9 It is now January 1, 1982. Overthrust Oil's 1981 dividend, which was paid yesterday, was $2, that is, $D_0 = \$2$. Earnings and dividends are expected to grow at a rate of 15 percent per year for the next three years (that is, during 1982, 1983, and 1984) and thereafter to grow indefinitely at the same rate as the national economy, 6 percent. Thus $g_s = 15\%$ and $g_n = 6\%$, and the period of supernormal growth is three years. The required rate of return on the stock, k_s, is 12 percent.

 a. Calculate the expected dividends for 1982, 1983, and 1984.

 b. Calculate the price of the stock today. This is P_0. Proceed by finding the present value of the dividends expected during 1982, 1983, and 1984, plus the present value of the stock price at the end of 1984. The year-end 1984 stock price can be found by use of the constant growth equation. Notice that, to find the 12/31/1984 price, you use the dividend expected in 1985, which is 6 percent greater than the 1984 dividend.

c. Calculate the current dividend yield, D_1/P_0, the capital gains yield expected in 1982, $(P_1 - P_0)/P_0$, and the expected total return (dividend yield plus capital gains yield) for 1982. Also, calculate these same three yields for 1985.

d. How might an investor's tax situation affect his or her decision to purchase stocks of companies in the early stages of their lives, when they are growing rapidly, versus stocks of older, more mature firms? When does Overthrust Oil's stock become "mature" in this example?

4-10 a. Overseas Motors Corporation (OMC) has been growing at a rate of 25 percent per year in recent years. This same growth rate is expected to last for another two years. If $D_0 = \$2$, $k_s = 14\%$, and $g_n = 6\%$, what is OMC's stock worth today? What is its current dividend yield and capital gains yield?

b. Now assume that OMC's period of supernormal growth is five years rather than two years. How does this affect its price, dividend yield, and capital gains yield?

c. What will be OMC's dividend yield and capital gains yield the year after its period of supernormal growth ends? (Hint: These values will be the same regardless of whether you examine the case of two or five years of supernormal growth.)

d. Of what interest to investors is the changing relationship between dividend yield and capital gains yield over time?

4-11 It is now January 1, 1982, and you are considering the purchase of an outstanding bond that was issued on January 1, 1980. It has a 10.5 percent annual coupon, and a thirty year original maturity (the bond matures in 2010). There is a five year call protection (until December 31, 1984), after which time the bond is callable at 110 (that is, at 110 percent of par, or for $1,100). Interest rates have declined since the bond was issued, and the bond is now selling at 115.174 percent, or $1,151.74. You want to determine both the yield to maturity and the yield to call for this bond. (Note: The yield to call considers the impact of a call provision on the actual bond yield. In the calculation, we assume that the bond will be outstanding until the call date, at which time it will be called. Thus, the investor will have received interest payments for the call-protected period and then will receive the call price, in this case, $1,100.00.)

a. What is the yield to maturity for this bond? What is its yield to call?

b. Which return do you think investors would actually expect? Explain your reasoning.

c. Suppose that the bond had sold at a discount. Would YTM or YTC have been more relevant?

ST4-1   a. The bonds were sold at par. Therefore, the YTM equals the coupon rate. YTM = 12%.

**Solutions
to Self-Test
Problems**

b.
$$V = \sum_{t=1}^{50} \frac{\$120/2}{\left(1 + \dfrac{0.10}{2}\right)^t} + \frac{\$1,000}{\left(1 + \dfrac{0.10}{2}\right)^{50}}$$

$$= \$60(\text{PVIFA}_{5\%,50}) + \$1,000(\text{PVIF}_{5\%,50})$$
$$= \$60(18.2559) + \$1,000(0.0872)$$
$$= \$1,095.35 + \$87.20$$
$$= \$1,182.55.$$

c.
$$\text{Current yield} = \text{Coupon payment/Price}$$
$$= \$120/\$1,182.55$$
$$= 0.101476 = 10.15\%.$$

$$\text{Capital gains yield} = \text{Total yield} - \text{Current yield}$$
$$= 10\% - 10.15\% = -0.15\%.$$

d.
$$\$896.64 = \sum_{t=1}^{19} \frac{\$60}{\left(1 + \dfrac{k_d}{2}\right)^t} + \frac{\$1,000}{\left(1 + \dfrac{k_d}{2}\right)^{19}}.$$

Use the approximate YTM formula to get a starting point:

$$\text{Approximate YTM} = \frac{I + (M - V)/n}{(M + V)/2}$$

$$= \frac{\$60 + (\$1,000 - \$896.64)/19}{(\$1,000 + \$896.64)/2}$$

$$= 6.90\%, \therefore k_d \cong 13.8\%.$$

Try $k_d = 14\%$:

$$V = I(\text{PVIFA}_{7\%,19}) + M(\text{PVIF}_{7\%,19})$$
$$\$896.64 = \$60(10.3356) + \$1,000(0.2765)$$
$$= \$620.14 + \$276.50$$
$$= \$896.64.$$

Therefore, the YTM on 7/1/82 is 14 percent.

e. Current yield = $\$120/\$896.64 = 13.38\%$.
Capital gains yield = $14\% - 13.38\% = 0.62\%$.

f. The timeline below illustrates the years to maturity of the bond.

1/1/82	7/1/82	1/1/83	7/1/83	1/1/84	12/31/91

⊢——+——+——————+——————+——————+———— · · · ——⊣

March 31, 1982

$$V = \$60(PVIFA_{7.75\%,19\ 2/3}) + \$1,000(PVIF_{7.75\%,19\ 2/3}).$$

Substitute $k = 7.75\%$ and $n = 19^2/_3$ periods into the equations for PVIFA and PVIF:

$$PVIFA = \frac{1 - \dfrac{1}{(1 + k)^n}}{k} = \frac{1 - \dfrac{1}{(1 + 0.0775)^{19\ 2/3}}}{0.0775}$$
$$= 9.9305.$$

$$PVIF = \frac{1}{(1 + k)^n} = \frac{1}{\left(1 + \dfrac{0.155}{2}\right)^{19\ 2/3}} = 0.2304.$$

Therefore,

$$V = \$60(9.9305) + \$1,000(0.2304)$$
$$= \$595.83 + \$230.40$$
$$= \$826.23.$$

Since the bond was purchased between interest payment dates, the buyer must also pay the accrued interest, calculated as follows:

$$\text{Accrued interest} = \frac{2}{6}\,(\$60) = \$20.$$

Therefore, you must write a check for $846.23 on 3/1/82 to complete the transaction:

$$\text{Total check} = \text{Bond value} + \text{Accrued interest}$$
$$= \$826.23 + \$20$$
$$= \$846.23.$$

ST4-2   The first step is to solve for g, the unknown variable, in the constant growth equation. Since D_1 is unknown, substitute $D_0\,(1 + g)$ as follows:

$$P_0 = \frac{D_0\,(1 + g)}{k_s - g}$$

$$\$24 = \frac{\$1.60(1 + g)}{0.12 - g}.$$

Solving for g, we find the growth rate to be 5 percent. The next step is to use the growth rate to project the stock price five years hence:

$$P_5 = \frac{D_0\,(1 + g)^6}{k_s - g}$$
$$= \frac{\$1.60(1.05)^6}{0.12 - 0.05}$$
$$= \$30.63.$$

[Alternatively,] $P_5 = \$24(1.05)^5 = \$30.63$.

Therefore, Karp Company's expected stock price five years from now, P_5, is $30.63.

ST4-3 a. *Step 1:* Calculate the PV of the dividends paid during the supernormal growth period.

$$D_1 = \$1.15 \quad (1.18) = \$1.3570.$$
$$D_2 = \$1.3570 \ (1.18) = \$1.6013.$$
$$D_3 = \$1.6013 \ (1.15) = \$1.8415.$$

$$\text{PV D} = \$1.3570 \ (0.8929) + \$1.6013 \ (0.7972) + \$1.8415 \ (0.7118)$$
$$= \$1.2117 + \$1.2766 + \$1.3108$$
$$= \$3.7991 \cong \$3.80.$$

Step 2: Find the PV of the stock's price at the end of Year 3.

$$P_3 = \frac{D_4}{k_s - g} = \frac{D_3(1 + g)}{k_s - g}$$
$$= \frac{\$1.8415(1.06)}{0.12 - 0.06}$$
$$= \$32.53.$$

$$\text{PV } P_3 = \$32.53 \ (0.7118) = \$23.15.$$

Step 3: Sum the two components to find the price of the stock today:

$$P_0 = \$3.80 + \$23.15 = \$26.95.$$

b. $$P_1 = \$1.6013(0.8929) + \$1.8415(0.7972) + \$32.53(0.7972)$$
$$= \$1.4298 + \$1.4680 + \$25.9329$$
$$= \$28.8307 \cong \$28.83.$$

$$P_2 = \$1.8415(0.8929) + \$32.53(0.8929)$$
$$= \$1.6443 + \$29.0460$$
$$= \$30.6903 \cong \$30.69.$$

c.

Year	Dividend Yield		Capital Gains Yield		Total Return
1	$\dfrac{\$1.3570}{\$26.95}$	$= 5.04\%$	$\dfrac{\$28.83 - \$26.95}{\$26.95}$	$= 6.98\%$	$\cong 12\%$
2	$\dfrac{\$1.6013}{\$28.83}$	$= 5.55\%$	$\dfrac{\$30.69 - \$28.83}{\$28.83}$	$= 6.45\%$	12%
3	$\dfrac{\$1.8415}{\$30.69}$	$= 6.00\%$	$\dfrac{\$32.53 - \$30.69}{\$30.69}$	$= 6.00\%$	12%

**Selected
References**

Many investments textbooks cover stock and bond valuation models in depth and detail. These are some of the good recent ones:

Francis, Jack C., *Investments: Analysis and Management* (New York: McGraw-Hill, 1980).

Reilly, Frank K., *Investment Analysis: Portfolio Management* (Hinsdale, Ill.: The Dryden Press, 1979).

Sharpe, William F., *Investments* (Englewood Cliffs, N.J.: Prentice-Hall, 1981).

The classic works on stock valuation models are these:

Gordon, Myron J., and Eli Shapiro, "Capital Equipment Analysis: The Required Rate of Profit," *Management Science*, October 1956, 102-110.

Williams, John Burr, *The Theory of Investment Value* (Cambridge: Harvard University Press, 1938).

Appendix 4A

**Derivation of
Valuation
Equations**

**Zero Growth
Stock**

The derivation of the formula for the value of a perpetuity is explained here. First, we saw that the value of a zero growth stock, $P_0 = D/k_s$ (Equation 4-3), is as follows:

$$P_0 = \frac{D}{(1 + k_s)^1} + \frac{D}{(1 + k_s)^2} + \ldots + \frac{D}{(1 + k_s)^\infty}. \qquad (4A\text{-}1)$$

Equation 4A-1 may be rewritten as follows:

$$P_0 = D\left[\frac{1}{(1 + k_s)^1} + \frac{1}{(1 + k_s)^2} + \ldots + \frac{1}{(1 + k_s)^n}\right]. \qquad (4A\text{-}2)$$

Multiply both sides of Equation 4A-2 by $(1 + k_s)$:

$$P_0(1 + k_s) = D\left[1 + \frac{1}{(1 + k_s)^1} + \frac{1}{(1 + k_s)^2} + \ldots + \frac{1}{(1 + k_s)^{n-1}}\right]. \qquad (4A\text{-}3)$$

Subtract Equation 4A-2 from Equation 4A-3, obtaining

$$P_0(1 + k_s - 1) = D\left[1 - \frac{1}{(1 + k_s)^n}\right]. \qquad (4A\text{-}4)$$

As $n \to \infty$, $\dfrac{1}{(1 + k_s)^n} \to 0$, so Equation 4A-4 approaches

$$P_0(k_s) = D,$$

and

$$P_0 = \frac{D}{k_s}. \qquad (4\text{-}3)$$

**Constant
Growth Stock**

The proof for Equation 4-5, the formula for the value of a constant growth stock, $P_0 = D_1/(k_s - g)$, is developed as follows. Rewrite Equation 4-2 as

$$\text{Value} = P_0 = \frac{D_0(1 + g)^1}{(1 + k_s)^1} + \frac{D_0(1 + g)^2}{(1 + k_s)^2} + \frac{D_0(1 + g)^3}{(1 + k_s)^3} + \cdots$$

$$= D_0\left[\frac{(1 + g)}{(1 + k_s)} + \frac{(1 + g)^2}{(1 + k_s)^2} + \frac{(1 + g)^3}{(1 + k_s)^3} + \cdots + \frac{(1 + g)^n}{(1 + k_s)^n}\right]. \quad (4A\text{-}5)$$

Multiply both sides of Equation 4A-5 by $(1 + k_s)/(1 + g)$:

$$\left[\frac{(1 + k_s)}{(1 + g)}\right]P_0 = D_0\left[1 + \frac{(1 + g)}{(1 + k_s)} + \frac{(1 + g)^2}{(1 + k_s)^2} + \cdots + \frac{(1 + g)^{n-1}}{(1 + k_s)^{n-1}}\right]. \quad (4A\text{-}6)$$

Subtract Equation 4A-5 from Equation 4A-6 to obtain

$$\left[\frac{(1 + k_s)}{(1 + g)} - 1\right]P_0 = D_0\left[1 - \frac{(1 + g)^n}{(1 + k_s)^n}\right].$$

$$\left[\frac{(1 + k_s) - (1 + g)}{(1 + g)}\right]P_0 = D_0\left[1 - \frac{(1 + g)^n}{(1 + k_s)^n}\right].$$

Assuming $k_s > g$, as $n \rightarrow \infty$ the term in brackets on the right-hand side of the equation $\rightarrow 1.0$, leaving

$$\left[\frac{(1 + k_s) - (1 + g)}{(1 + g)}\right]P_0 = D_0,$$

which simplifies to

$$(k_s - g)P_0 = D_0(1 + g) = D_1$$

$$P_0 = \frac{D_1}{k_s - g}. \quad (4\text{-}5)$$

PV of an Annuity

In Chapter 3, at the top of Table 3-5, we gave this equation for the PV of an annuity:

$$\text{PVIFA}_{k,n} = \sum_{t=1}^{n} \frac{1}{(1 + k)^t} = \frac{1 - \dfrac{1}{(1 + k)^n}}{k}. \quad (4A\text{-}7)$$

The second term is not intuitively clear, but it is derived from the perpetuity equation developed earlier in this appendix, Equation 4-3, with V, R, and k substituted for P_0, D, and k_s, respectively:

$$P_0 = \frac{D}{k_s} = V = \frac{R}{k}. \quad (4A\text{-}8)$$

To better understand Equation 4A-7, consider (1) an *ordinary annuity* of $1 per year for ten years, (2) an *"immediate" perpetuity* of $1 per year forever whose first payment occurs one year from today, and (3) a *deferred perpetuity* of $1 per year whose first payment occurs 11 years from today and is thus deferred ten years into the future. The discount rate is 8 percent.

It is easy to find the present value of the two perpetuities:

$$\text{PV of immediate perpetuity} = V = \frac{R}{k} = \frac{\$1}{0.08} = \$12.50.$$

$$\text{PV of deferred perpetuity} = V = \frac{R}{k}\left(\frac{1}{(1 + k)^n}\right) = \frac{\$1}{0.08}\left(\frac{1}{(1.08)^{10}}\right) = \$12.50(0.4632) = \$5.7899.$$

The difference in present values between these two perpetuities, $12.50 − $5.7899 = $6.7101, must be the present value of the ten payments which the immediate perpetuity provides but the deferred perpetuity does not provide. This value, $6.7101, is the PV of a ten year annuity. You can confirm this by looking up $\text{PVIFA}_{8\%,10}$ in Table A-2; this PVIFA is 6.7101.

We can use the knowledge that the PV of an annuity is the difference between the values of an immediate perpetuity and a deferred perpetuity to derive Equation 4A-7:

$$\text{PV of annuity at k\% for n years} = \frac{R}{k} - \frac{R}{k}\left(\frac{1}{(1 + k)^n}\right).$$

Let R = 1, so

$$\text{PV} = \frac{1}{k} - \frac{1}{k}\left(\frac{1}{(1 + k)^n}\right),$$

which may be transformed to

$$\text{PV} = \text{PVIFA}_{k,n} = \frac{1 - \dfrac{1}{(1 + k)^n}}{k}. \tag{4A-7}$$

Equation 4A-7 is useful when one is calculating PVIFAs for k values not found in the tables, including fractional values, and when fractional years (say $5^{1}/_{3}$ years) are involved.

Appendix 4B

Effects of Personal Taxes

All of the calculations in Chapter 4 were based on cash flows to the investor *before personal taxes* (CF). However, for investors who must pay taxes, the cash flows which they actually get to keep are the after-tax cash flows, ATCF:

$$\text{ATCF} = \text{CF} - \text{Tax} = \text{CF} - \text{CF}(t) = \text{CF} (1 - t),$$

where t is the investor's tax rate. For example, if an investor in the 55 percent tax bracket bought for $1,000 a new 10 percent, twenty year, annual payment Exxon Corporation bond, then the before-tax rate of return would be 10 percent, but the after-tax rate of return would be

$$\text{Price of bond} = \sum_{t=1}^{n} \frac{\$I(1-t)}{(1+k_{d(AT)})^t} + \frac{\text{Maturity Value}}{(1+k_{d(AT)})^n}$$

$$\$1,000 = \sum_{t=1}^{20} \frac{\$100(0.45)}{(1+k_{d(AT)})^t} + \frac{\$1,000}{(1+k_{d(AT)})^{20}}$$

$$= \$45 \ (\text{PVIFA}_{k_{d(AT)},20}) + \$1,000 \ (\text{PVIF}_{k_{d(AT)},20}).$$

Using interest factors for 4.5 percent, we obtain

$$\$1,000 = \$45(13.0079) + \$1,000(0.4146) = \$1,000,$$

which demonstrates that 4.5 percent is the after-tax rate of return on a 10 percent taxable bond to a 55 percent bracket investor.

If a bond with a 10 percent yield to maturity is bought at a discount, then the after-tax return will be higher than that on a bond with a 10 percent YTM bought at par. This result occurs because capital gains are taxed at a lower rate than is interest income, and a discount bond provides some of its return in the form of capital gains. For example, suppose an investor is in the 55 percent tax bracket. Recall from Chapter 2 that 60 percent of all capital gains are excluded from income, leaving 40 percent of long-term gains to be taxed. Therefore, the effective tax rate on capital gains for this investor is (tax rate) $(1.0 - \text{percentage exclusion}) = 55\% \ (0.4) = 22\%$. Now assume that our investor buys an old 6 percent coupon Exxon bond that was issued years ago. This bond now has twenty years remaining to maturity, and its price is $659.42. The annual interest payment is $60, and the YTM on this bond is 10 percent, the same as that on a new 10 percent coupon Exxon bond bought at par. However, the investor's after-tax interest receipt would be $60 \ (1-t) = \$60 \ (0.45) = \$27$, and the rate of return on this discount bond would be

$$\text{Price of bond} = \sum_{t=1}^{20} \frac{\$27}{(1+k)^t} + \frac{\$1,000 - 0.22 \ (\$1,000 - \$659.42)}{(1+k)^{20}}$$

$$\$659.42 = \$27 \ (\text{PVIFA}_{k,20}) + \$925.07 \ (\text{PVIF}_{k,20}).$$

Using a financial calculator, we could solve for k; we find $k_{d(AT)} = 5.28\%$.

If you were in the 55 percent tax bracket and you found that you could buy these two Exxon bonds at the indicated prices, which would you choose? Obviously, the discount bond, because it would offer the higher after-tax return, 5.28 percent versus 4.5 percent. So you (and others) would tend to bid the price of the discount bond up relative to that of the par bond, and this action would continue until the *after-tax* returns on the two bonds were approximately equal.[1]

A similar situation holds with common stocks. Recall that a stock's total expected return, $\hat{k}_s$, consists of an expected dividend yield plus an expected capital gains yield. Suppose our 55 percent bracket investor is considering buying some stock of the High-Yield Corporation, with $P_0 = \$30$, $D_1 = \$3.60$, and $g = 3\%$, or, alternatively, the stock of High-Growth Company, with $P_0 = \$30$, $D_1 = \$0.90$, and $g = 12\%$. What would be the expected before-tax and after-tax rates of return on the two stocks?

Before-tax returns

$$\text{High-Yield:} \quad \hat{k} = D_1/P_0 + g = \$3.60/\$30 + 3\% = 15\%.$$

$$\text{High-Growth:} \quad \hat{k} = D_1/P_0 + g = \$0.90/\$30 + 12\% = 15\%.$$

After-tax returns

$$
\begin{aligned}
\text{High-Yield:} \quad \hat{k}_{AT} &= \text{Dividend yield} - t\,(\text{Dividend yield}) + \\
&\quad \text{Capital gains yield} - t[(0.4)\,(\text{Capital gains yield})] \\
&= \text{Dividend yield}\,(1 - t) + \text{Capital gains yield} \\
&\quad (1.0 - 0.4t) \\
&= 12\%\,(0.45) + 3\%\,(0.78) \\
&= 5.4\% + 2.3\% = 7.7\%.
\end{aligned}
$$

$$
\begin{aligned}
\text{High-Growth:} \quad \hat{k}_{AT} &= 3\%\,(0.45) + 12\%\,(0.78) \\
&= 1.3\% + 9.4\% = 10.7\%.
\end{aligned}
$$

The example above shows that, to a tax-paying investor, more capital gains income than dividend income flows through to spendable income. This suggests that stockholders might prefer to have corporations retain earnings, plow them back into the business, and provide capital gains instead of paying out dividends. Before accepting this as gospel, however, wait and consider in Chapter 18 some of the other points made in connection with dividend policy. In any event, it is obvious that, at least from the tax standpoint, an investor in a high tax bracket is better off if a high percentage of his or her total return comes as capital gains rather than as dividend income.

[1] The effect of a deep discount on the likelihood of a call would also have an effect on the bonds' relative prices. A deep discount bond has very good de facto protection against a call. See Chapter 13 for more on calls. Another factor which should also be noted is the fact that, if the two Exxon bonds were priced so as to provide the same after-tax returns to an investor in the 55 percent bracket, then a zero tax bracket investor such as a pension fund would obtain a higher return by buying the bond that is selling close to par. Therefore, the pension funds would tend to bid for these bonds and thus drive their yields up. The final set of equilibrium prices in the economy would reflect the amount of funds available to investors in different tax brackets. But, in any event, one would expect to find investors in high tax brackets buying primarily discount bonds, while zero tax rate investors would buy par (and premium) bonds.

Risk and Rates of Return 5

In Chapter 4, we referred frequently to the terms *appropriate interest rate on debt, k_d,* and *appropriate (or required) rate of return on a share of common stock, k_s.* These rates, which we used to help determine the values of bonds and stocks, depend primarily on the riskless rate of interest, R_F, and on the riskiness of the security in question. In this chapter, we define the term *risk* as it relates to securities, examine procedures for measuring it, and then discuss the relationships between risk, returns, and security prices.

Risk is defined in *Webster's* as "a hazard; a peril; exposure to loss or injury." Thus, risk refers to the chance that some unfavorable event will occur. If you engage in skydiving, you take a chance with your life—skydiving is risky. If you bet on the horses, you risk losing your money. If you invest in speculative stocks (or, really, *any* stock), you are taking a risk in the hope of making an appreciable capital gain.

To illustrate the riskiness of financial assets, suppose an investor buys $100,000 of short-term government bonds with an interest rate of 10 percent. In this case, the yield to maturity on the investment, 10 percent, can be estimated quite precisely, and the investment is defined as being risk-free. However, if the $100,000 were invested in the stock of a company just being organized to prospect for oil in the mid-Atlantic, then the investment's return could not be estimated precisely. The rate of return could range from some extremely large positive figure to minus 100 percent, and because there is a significant danger of loss, the stock is described as being relatively risky.

Investment risk, then, is related to the probability of low or negative returns—the greater the chance of low returns, the riskier the investment. However, we can define risk more precisely, and it is useful to do so.

An event's *probability* is defined as the chance that the event will occur. For example, a weather forecaster may state, "There is a 40 percent chance of rain today and a 60 percent chance that it will not rain." If all possible events, or outcomes, are listed, and if a probability is assigned to each event, then the listing is defined as a *probability distribution.* For our weather forecast, we could set up the following probability distribution:

Outcome (1)	Probability (2)
Rain	0.4 = 40%
No rain	0.6 = 60%
	1.0 = 100%

The possible outcomes are listed in Column 1, while the probabilities of these outcomes, expressed both as decimals and as percentages, are given in Column 2. Notice that the probabilities must sum to 1.0, or 100 percent.

In Chapter 4 we defined the expected rate of return on a stock, $\hat{k}_s$, as the sum of the expected dividend yield plus the expected capital gain: $\hat{k}_s = D_1/P_0 + g$. We now examine the probability distribution concept as related to rates of return. To begin, consider the possible rates of return (dividend yield plus capital gain or loss) that you might earn next year on a $10,000 stock investment in Kelly Services, Inc., or on a $10,000 investment in U.S. Water Company stock:

1. Kelly Services, Inc.

State of the Economy	Probability of This State Occurring	Rate of Return on Kelly Services' Stock under This State
Boom	0.3	100%
Normal	0.4	15
Recession	0.3	−70
	1.0	

2. U.S. Water Company

State of the Economy	Probability of This State Occurring	Rate of Return on U.S. Water's Stock under This State
Boom	0.3	20%
Normal	0.4	15
Recession	0.3	10
	1.0	

We can graph the rates of return to obtain a picture of the variability of possible outcomes; this is shown in the bar charts in Figure 5-1. The height of each bar signifies the probability that a given outcome will occur. The range of probable returns for Kelly Services is from 100 to −70 percent, with an average or expected return of 15 percent. The expected return for U.S. Water is also 15 percent, but its range is much narrower.

Thus far we have assumed that only three states of the economy can exist: recession, normal, and boom. Actually, of course, the state of the economy could range from a deep depression to a fantastic boom, and there are an unlimited number of possibilities in between. Suppose we had the time and patience to assign a probability to each possible state of the economy (with the sum of the probabilities still equaling 1.0), and to assign a rate of return to each stock for each state of the economy. We would have a table similar to Table 5-1 except that it would have many more entries in each column. This table could be used to calculate expected rates of return as shown above, and the probabilities and outcomes could be approximated by the continuous curves presented in Figure 5-2. Here we have changed the assumptions so that there is essen-

Continuous Probability Distributions

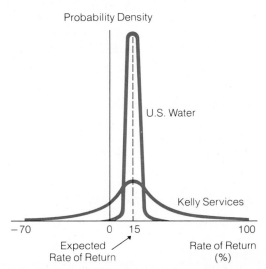

Probability Density

U.S. Water

Kelly Services

−70   0   15   100

Expected ╱   Rate of Return
Rate of Return   (%)

**Figure 5-2
Continuous Probability Distributions of Kelly Services' and U.S. Water's Rates of Return**

Note: The assumptions regarding the probabilities of various outcomes have been changed from those in Figure 5-1. The probability of obtaining exactly 15 percent was 40 percent in Figure 5-1; in Figure 5-2 it is *much smaller*, because here there are many possible outcomes instead of just three. With continuous distributions such as in Figure 5-2, it is more appropriate to ask what the probability is of obtaining *at least* some specified rate of return than to ask what the probability is of obtaining exactly that rate of return. This cumulative probability is equal to the area under the probability distribution curve to the right of the point of interest or 1 minus the area under the curve up to the point of interest. This topic is covered in detail in Appendix A to Chapter 12.

tially a zero probability that the return of Kelly Services will be less than −70 percent or more than 100 percent, or that U.S. Water will return less than 10 percent or more than 20 percent.

The tighter the probability distribution, the more likely it is that the actual outcome will be close to the expected value, and the less likely it is that the actual return will be far below the expected return. Thus, the tighter the probability distribution, the lower the risk assigned to a stock. Since U.S. Water has a relatively tight probability distribution, its *actual return* is likely to be closer to the 15 percent *expected return* than is that of Kelly Services.[3]

Measuring Risk: The Standard Deviation

Risk is a difficult concept to grasp, and a great deal of controversy has surrounded attempts to define and measure it. However, a common definition, and one that is satisfactory for many purposes, is stated in terms of probability distributions such as those presented in Figure 5-2: *The tighter the probability distribution of expected future returns, the smaller the risk of a given investment.* According to this definition, U.S. Water is less risky than Kelly Services *because the chances of returns below the expected level for U.S. Water are smaller than the chances of low returns for Kelly Services.*

To be most useful, any measure of risk should have a definite value— we need a measure of the tightness of the probability distribution. One such measure is the *standard deviation*, the symbol for which is σ, pronounced "sigma." The smaller the standard deviation, the tighter the probability distribution and, accordingly, the lower the riskiness of the stock. To calculate the standard deviation, we proceed as follows:

1. Calculate the expected rate of return:

$$\text{Expected rate of return} = \hat{k} = \sum_{i=1}^{n} P_i k_i. \qquad (5\text{-}1)$$

2. Subtract the expected rate of return from each possible outcome to obtain a set of deviations about the expected rate of return:

$$\text{Deviation}_i = k_i - \hat{k}.$$

3. Square each deviation, multiply the squared deviation by the probabil-

---

[3] Since we define risk in terms of the chance of low returns, it would seem logical to measure risk in terms of the probability of returns below the expected return, rather than by the entire distribution. Measures of below-expected returns, which are known as *semivariance measures,* have been developed, but they are difficult to analyze. In addition, such measures are unnecessary if the distribution of future returns is reasonably symmetric about the expected return. Returns on stocks tend to be skewed to the right rather than normal, but, if stock returns are converted to logarithms, then the returns distributions are approximately normal. Therefore, much empirical work on stock returns is done with logs.

ity of occurrence for its related outcome, and sum these products to obtain the *variance* of the probability distribution:

$$\text{Variance} = \sigma^2 = \sum_{i=1}^{n} (k_i - \hat{k})^2 P_i. \tag{5-2}$$

4. Now take the square root of the variance to obtain the standard deviation:

$$\text{Standard deviation} = \sigma = \sqrt{\sum_{i=1}^{n} (k_i - \hat{k})^2 P_i}. \tag{5-3}$$

We can illustrate these procedures by calculating the standard deviation for Kelly Services:

a. The expected rate of return, or the mean, was found in Table 5-1 to be 15 percent.

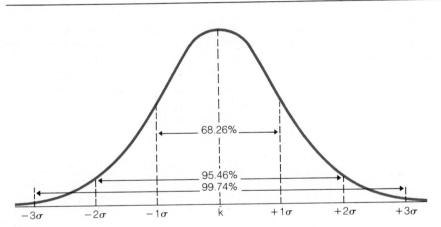

**Figure 5-3
Probability Ranges for a
Normal Distribution**

Notes:

a. The area under the normal curve equals 1.0, or 100 percent. *Thus, the areas under any pair of normal curves drawn on the same scale, whether they be peaked or flat, must be equal.*

b. Half of the area under a normal curve is to the left of the mean, indicating that there is a 50 percent probability that the actual outcome will be less than the mean and a 50 percent probability that it will be greater than the mean, or to the right of $\hat{k}$.

c. Of the area under the curve, 68.26 percent is within $\pm 1\sigma$ of the mean, indicating that the probability is 68.26 percent that the actual outcome will be within the range $\hat{k} - 1\sigma$ to $\hat{k} + 1\sigma$.

d. Procedures are available for finding the probability of other earnings ranges. These procedures are covered in Appendix 12A.

e. For a normal distribution, the larger the value of σ, the greater the probability that the actual outcome will vary widely from, hence perhaps be far below, the expected, or most likely, outcome. *Since the probability of having the actual results turn out to be bad is our definition of risk, and since σ measures this probability, we can use σ as a measure of risk.* This definition may not be a good one, however, if we are dealing with an asset held in a diversified portfolio. This point is covered later in the chapter.

b. Set up a table to work out the value for Equation 5-3:

$k_i - \hat{k}$	$(k_i - \hat{k})^2$	$(k_i - \hat{k})^2 P_i$
$100 - 15 = \quad 85$	7,225	$(7,225)(0.3) = 2,167.5$
$15 - 15 = \quad 0$	0	$(0)(0.4) = \quad\quad 0$
$-70 - 15 = -85$	7,225	$(7,225)(0.3) = 2,167.5$

$$\text{Variance} = \sigma_k^2 = \underline{4,335.0}$$

$$\text{Standard deviation} = \sigma_k = \sqrt{\sigma_k^2} = \sqrt{4,335} = 65.84\%.$$

Using these same procedures, we find U.S. Water's standard deviation to be 3.87 percent. Since Kelly's standard deviation is larger, it is the riskier stock according to this measure of risk.

If a probability distribution is normal, the *actual* return will be within ± 1 standard deviation of the *expected* return 68 percent of the time. Figure 5-3 illustrates this point and also shows the situation for $\pm 2\sigma$ and $\pm 3\sigma$. For Kelly Services, $\hat{k} = 15$ percent and $\sigma = 65.84$ percent. Thus, there is a 68.26 percent probability that the actual return will be in the range of 15 percent ± 65.84 percent, or from -50.84 to 80.84 percent. For U.S. Water, the 68 percent range is 15 percent ± 3.87 percent, or from 11.13 to 18.87 percent. With such a small σ, there is only a small probability that U.S. Water's return will be very low; hence, the stock is not very risky. For the average firm listed on the New York Stock Exchange, σ has been close to 30 percent in recent years.[4]

---

[4] In this section we have described the procedure for finding the mean and standard deviation where the data are in the form of a known probability distribution. If only sample returns data over some past period ($\bar{k}$, called "k bar") are available, then the standard deviation of returns can be estimated using this formula:

$$\text{Estimated } \sigma = S = \sqrt{\frac{\sum_{t=1}^{n} (\bar{k}_t - \bar{k}_{Avg.})^2}{n - 1}}. \tag{5-3a}$$

Example:

Year	$\bar{k}_t$
1978	15%
1979	-5
1980	20

$$\bar{k}_{Avg.} = \frac{(15 - 5 + 20)}{3} = 10.0\%.$$

$$\text{Estimated } \sigma \text{ (or S)} = \sqrt{\frac{(15 - 10)^2 + (-5 - 10)^2 + (20 - 10)^2}{3 - 1}}$$

(continued)

Suppose you have worked hard and saved $1 million, which you now plan to invest. You can buy a 10 percent Treasury note, and at the end of one year you will have a sure $1,100,000, which is your original investment plus $100,000 in interest. Alternatively, you can buy stock in R&D Enterprises. If R&D's research programs are successful, your stock will increase in value to $2.2 million; however, if the research is a failure, the value of your stock will go to zero and you will be penniless. You regard the chances of success or failure as being 50-50, so the expected value of the stock investment is 0.5($0) + 0.5($2.2 million) = $1,100,000. Subtracting out the $1 million cost of the stock, you will have an expected profit of $100,000, or an expected (but risky) 10 percent rate of return.

Thus, you have a choice between a sure $100,000 profit (a 10 percent rate of return) on the Treasury note, or a *risky* expected $100,000 profit (also a 10 percent expected rate of return) on the R&D Enterprises stock. Which one would you choose? *If you choose the less risky investment, you are risk averse. Most investors are indeed risk averse, and certainly the average investor is risk averse. Since this is a well-documented fact, we shall assume risk aversion throughout the remainder of the book.*

What are the implications of risk aversion for security prices and rates of return? The answer is that, other things held constant, the higher a security's risk, (1) the lower its price and (2) the higher its expected return. To see how this works, we can analyze the situation with U.S. Water and Kelly Services stocks. Suppose each stock sold for $100 per share and each had an expected dividend of $15 per share. No growth is anticipated, so the expected rate of return on each stock is $15/$100 = 0.15 = 15 percent. Investors are averse to risk, so there would be a general preference for U.S. Water. People with money to invest would bid for Water rather than Kelly stock, and Kelly stockholders would start selling it and buying Water stock. The buying pressure would tend to drive up the price of Water stock, and the selling pressure would cause Kelly's price to decline.

These price changes, in turn, would cause changes in the expected rates of return on the two securities. Suppose, for example, that the price of Water stock was bid up from $100 to $150, while the price of Kelly stock declined from $100 to $75. With the $15 expected dividend, this would cause Water's expected return to fall to $15/$150 = 0.10 = 10 percent, while Kelly's expected return would rise to $15/$75 = 0.20 = 20 percent. The difference in returns, 20% − 10% = 10%, is defined as a

$$= \sqrt{\frac{350}{2}} = 13.2\%.$$

Often, the historical σ is used as an estimate of the future σ. Much less often, $\overline{k}_{Average}$ is used as an estimate of $\hat{k}$.

risk premium, which represents the compensation investors require for assuming the additional risk of Kelly stock.

This example demonstrates a very important principle: *Riskier securities must have higher expected returns than less risky ones, for if this situation does not exist, then actions will occur in the stock market to force it to exist.* We will consider the question of *how much* higher the returns on risky securities must be later in the chapter, after we examine in more depth how risk should be measured.

Portfolio Risk and the Capital Asset Pricing Model

In the preceding section, we considered the riskiness of a stock held in isolation. Now we analyze the riskiness of stocks held in portfolios.[5] As we shall see, a stock held as part of a portfolio is less risky than the same stock held in isolation. This fact has been incorporated into a generalized framework for analyzing the relationship between risk and rates of return; this framework is called the *Capital Asset Pricing Model,* or CAPM. The CAPM framework is, as we shall see, an extremely important analytical tool in both financial management and investment analysis.

Portfolio Risk and Return

Most financial assets are not held in isolation; rather, they are held as parts of portfolios. Banks, pension funds, insurance companies, mutual funds, and other financial institutions are required by law to hold diversified portfolios. Even individual investors—at least those individuals whose security holdings constitute a significant part of their total wealth—generally hold stock portfolios, not just the stock of one firm. This being the case, from an investor's standpoint the fact that a particular stock goes up or down is not very important; *what is important is the return on the portfolio, and the portfolio's risk.* Logically, then, the risk and return of an individual security should be analyzed in terms of how the security affects the risk and return of the portfolio in which it is included.

Portfolio Returns. The expected return on a portfolio $(\hat{k}_p)$ is simply the weighted average return of the individual stocks in the portfolio, with the weights being the fraction of the total portfolio invested in each stock:

$$\hat{k}_p = w_1\hat{k}_1 + w_2\hat{k}_2 + \ldots + w_n\hat{k}_n$$
$$= \sum_{j=1}^{n} w_j\hat{k}_j. \tag{5-4}$$

Here the $\hat{k}$'s are the expected returns on individual stocks, the w's are the weights, and there are n stocks in the portfolio; the w's must sum to

---

[5] A *portfolio* is a collection of investment securities. If you owned some General Motors stock, some Exxon stock, and some IBM stock, you would be holding a three stock portfolio. For reasons set forth in this section, the vast majority of all stocks are held as parts of portfolios.

1.0. To illustrate, given the w's and $\hat{k}$'s shown below, the expected return on a hypothetical four stock portfolio is 11.8 percent:

$$\hat{k}_p = w_1\hat{k}_1 + w_2\hat{k}_2 + w_3\hat{k}_3 + w_4\hat{k}_4$$
$$= 0.20\ (10\%) + 0.25\ (12\%) + 0.30\ (11\%) + 0.25\ (14\%)$$
$$= 2.0\% + 3.0\% + 3.3\% + 3.5\%$$
$$= 11.8\%.$$

Portfolio Risk. Unlike returns, the riskiness of a portfolio, σ_p, is generally *not* a weighted average of the standard deviations of the individual securities in the portfolio, and each stock's contribution to the portfolio's risk is *not* $w_i\sigma_i$. It is theoretically possible to combine two stocks which are, individually, quite risky as measured by their standard deviations, and to form a portfolio which is completely riskless, with $\sigma_p = 0$. To illustrate, consider the situation in Figure 5-4. The top section gives data on rates of return for Stocks W and M, and for a portfolio invested 50 percent in each stock; the middle section plots the data in a time series format; and the bottom graph shows a probability distribution of returns, assuming the future is expected to be like the past. The two stocks would be quite risky if they were held in isolation, but, when they are combined to form Portfolio WM, they are not risky at all. (Note: These stocks are called W and M because their returns graphs in Figure 5-4 resemble a W and an M.)

The reason Stocks W and M can be combined to form a riskless portfolio is that their returns move countercyclically to one another—when W's returns fall, those of M rise, and vice versa. In statistical terms, we say that the returns on Stocks W and M are *perfectly negatively correlated*, with r = correlation coefficient = -1.0.[6]

The opposite of perfect negative correlation, with r = -1.0, is perfect positive correlation, with r = $+1.0$. Returns on two perfectly positively correlated stocks would move up and down together, and a portfolio consisting of two such stocks would be just as risky as the individual stocks. This point is illustrated in Figure 5-5. We see that the portfolio's standard deviation is equal to that of the individual stocks, indicating that diversification does nothing to reduce risk if the portfolio consists of perfectly positively correlated stocks.

Figures 5-4 and 5-5 demonstrate (1) that when stocks are perfectly negatively correlated (r = -1.0), all risk can be diversified away, but (2) that when stocks are perfectly positively correlated (r = $+1.0$), diver-

---

[6] *Correlation* is defined as the tendency of two variables to move together. The *correlation coefficient*, r, measures this tendency and can range from $+1.0$, denoting that the two variables move up and down in perfect synchronization, to -1.0, denoting that the variables always move in exactly opposite directions. A correlation coefficient of zero suggests that the two variables are not related to one another, that is, changes in one variable are *independent* of changes in the other.

Figure 5-4
Rate of Return Distributions for Two Perfectly
Negatively Correlated Stocks (r = −1.0), and for
Portfolio WM

a. Rate of Return Data

Year	Stock W k_W	Stock M k_M	Portfolio WM k_p
1976	40%	−10%	15%
1977	−10	40	15
1978	35	−5	15
1979	−5	35	15
1980	15	15	15
Average return	15%	15%	15%
Standard deviation	22.6%	22.6%	0.0%

b. Rate of Return Graphs

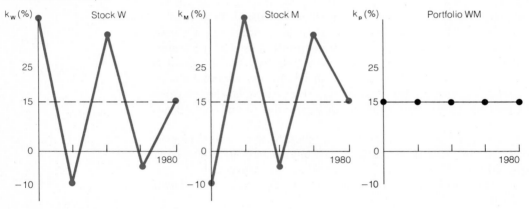

c. Probability Distribution of Returns

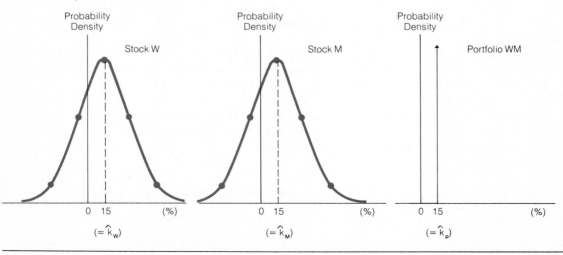

Figure 5-5
Rate of Return Distributions for Two Perfectly
Positively Correlated Stocks (r = +1.0), and for
Portfolio MM

a. Rate of Return Data

Year	Stock M k_M	Stock M k_M	Portfolio MM k_p
1976	−10%	−10%	−10%
1977	40	40	40
1978	−5	−5	−5
1979	35	35	35
1980	15	15	15
Average return	15%	15%	15%
Standard deviation	22.6%	22.6%	22.6%

b. Rate of Return Graph

c. Probability Distribution of Returns

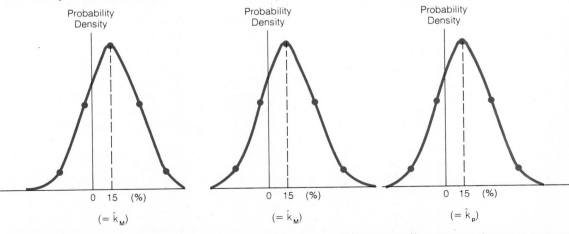

sification does no good whatever in terms of reducing risk. In reality, most stocks are positively correlated, but not perfectly so. On average, the correlation coefficient for the returns on two randomly selected stocks would be about +0.6, and for most pairs of stocks, r would lie in the range of +0.5 to +0.7. *Under such conditions, combining stocks into portfolios reduces risk but does not eliminate it completely.* Figure 5-6 illustrates this point with two stocks whose correlation coefficient is r = +0.65. The portfolio's average return is 15.0 percent, which is exactly the same as the average return for each of the two stocks, but the portfolio's standard deviation is 20.6 percent, which is less than the standard deviation of either stock. Thus, the portfolio's risk is *not* an average of the risks of its individual stocks—diversification has reduced, but has not eliminated, risk.

From these examples, we have seen that in one extreme case (r = −1.0), risk can be completely eliminated, while in the other extreme case (r = +1.0), diversification does no good whatever. In between these extremes, combining two stocks into a portfolio reduces but does not eliminate the riskiness inherent in the individual stocks.

What would happen if we added more stocks to the portfolio? *As a rule, the riskiness of a portfolio will be reduced as the number of stocks in the portfolio increases.* If we added enough partially correlated stocks, could we completely eliminate risk? In general, the answer is no, but the extent to which adding stocks to a portfolio reduces the portfolio's risk depends on the *degree of correlation* among the stocks. The smaller the correlation coefficient, the lower the remaining risk in a large portfolio. For a set of stocks whose correlation coefficients are zero or negative, all risk can be eliminated. *In the typical case, where the correlations among the individual stocks are positive but less than +1.0, some but not all risk can be eliminated.*[7]

As noted earlier, it is very difficult, if not impossible, to find stocks whose expected returns are not positively correlated—most stocks tend to do well when the economy is strong, and badly when the national economy is weak.[8] Thus, even very large portfolios end up with a material amount of risk. Consider, for example, Figure 5-7, which shows how portfolio risk is affected by forming larger and larger portfolios of average New York Stock Exchange (NYSE) stocks. Standard deviations are plotted for a one stock portfolio, a two stock portfolio, and so on, up to a portfolio consisting of all 1,576 common stocks that are listed on the NYSE.[9] The graph illustrates that, in general, the riskiness of a portfolio

---

[7] The relationship between correlations and portfolio risk is discussed in more detail in Appendix 5A.

[8] It is not too hard to find a stock that happened to decline because of a particular set of circumstances in the past while most other stocks were rising; it is much harder to find stocks that could logically be *expected* to decline in the future when other stocks are rising.

[9] In 1980, there were 1,576 common stocks listed on the NYSE. If we found the return and standard deviation of each of the 1,576 stocks, and then averaged these values, we would have the return and standard deviation of an *average* NYSE stock. For more precision, we would develop a weighted average based on each company's total market value.

Figure 5-6
Rate of Return Distributions for Two Partially
Correlated Stocks (r = +0.65),
and for Portfolio WY

a. Rates of Return

Year	Stock W k_W	Stock Y k_Y	Portfolio WY k_p
1976	40%	28%	34%
1977	−10	20	5
1978	35	41	38
1979	−5	−17	−11
1980	15	3	9
Average return	15%	15%	15%
Standard deviation	22.6%	22.6%	20.6%

b. Rate of Return Graphs

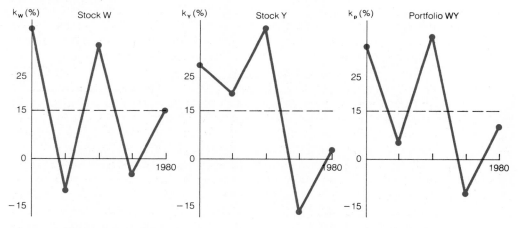

c. Probability Distribution of Returns

Figure 5-7
Effects of Portfolio Size on Portfolio Risk for
Average Stocks

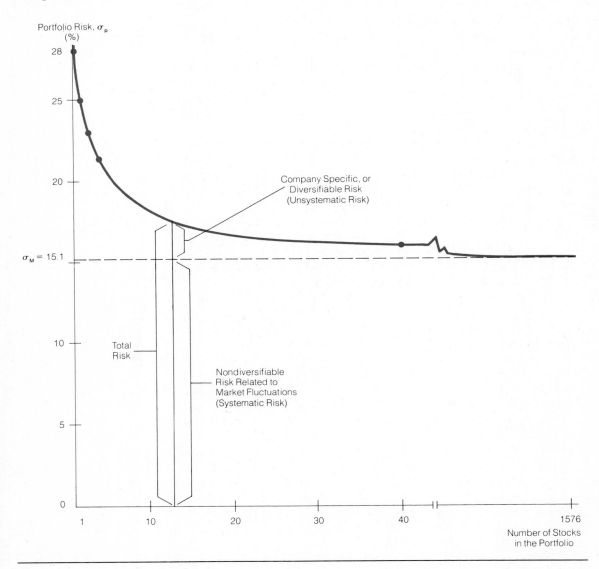

consisting of average NYSE stocks tends to decline and to asymptotically approach a limit as the size of the portfolio increases. According to data accumulated in recent years, σ_1, the standard deviation of a one stock portfolio (or an average stock), is approximately 28 percent. A portfolio consisting of all stocks, which is called "the market portfolio," would have a standard deviation of about 15.1 percent. The market portfolio's standard deviation is given the symbol σ_M, so $\sigma_M = 15.1\%$.

Thus, a great deal of the riskiness inherent in an average individual stock can be eliminated if the stock is held in a reasonably well-diversified portfolio, one containing about forty stocks. Some risk always remains, however, so it is virtually impossible to diversify away the effects of broad stock market declines that affect almost all stocks.

That part of the risk of an average stock which can be eliminated is called *diversifiable, or company-specific, risk*. That part which cannot be eliminated is called *nondiversifiable, or market, risk*. The name is not especially important, but the fact that part of the riskiness of any individual stock can be eliminated is vitally important.

Company-specific risk is caused by such things as lawsuits, strikes, successful and unsuccessful marketing programs, winning and losing major contracts, and other events that are unique to a particular firm. Since these events are essentially random, their effects on a portfolio can be eliminated by diversification—bad events in one firm will be offset by good events in another. *Market risk*, on the other hand, stems from such things as war, inflation, recessions, and high interest rates, factors which affect all firms simultaneously. Since all firms are affected simultaneously by these factors, this type of risk cannot be eliminated by diversification.

We know that investors demand a premium for bearing risk; that is, the higher the riskiness of a security, the higher its expected return must be to induce investors to buy (or to hold) it. But if investors are primarily concerned with *portfolio risk* rather than the risk of the individual securities in the portfolio, how should the riskiness of the individual stocks be measured? The answer is this: The *relevant riskiness of an individual stock is its contribution to the riskiness of a well-diversified portfolio*. In other words, the riskiness of Stock X to a doctor who has a portfolio of 40 stocks, or to a trust officer managing a 150 stock portfolio, is the contribution that Stock X makes to the portfolio's riskiness. The stock might be quite risky if held by itself, but if most of its risk can be eliminated by diversification, the stock's *relevant risk*, which is its *contribution to the portfolio's risk*, may be small.

A simple example will help make this point clear. Suppose you can flip a coin once. If a head comes up, you win $10,000, but you lose $8,000 if it comes up tails. Although this may be considered to be a good bet— the expected return is $1,000—it is a highly risky proposition. Alternatively, suppose you can flip 100 coins and win $100 for each head but lose $80 for each tail. It is possible that you would hit all heads and win

$10,000, and it is also possible that you would flip all tails and lose $8,000, but the chances are very high that you would actually flip about fifty heads and about fifty tails, winning a net $1,000. Although each individual flip is a risky bet, collectively you have a very low-risk proposition because you have diversified away most of the risk. This is the idea behind holding portfolios of stocks rather than just one stock, except that with stocks all of the risk cannot be eliminated by diversification—those risks related to broad changes in the stock market as reflected in the Dow Jones Index and other stock market averages will remain.

Are all stocks equally risky in the sense that adding them to a well-diversified portfolio would have the same effect on the portfolio's riskiness? The answer is no—different stocks will affect the portfolio differently; hence, different securities have different degrees of relevant risk. How can the relevant risk of an individual stock be measured? As we saw above, all risk except that related to broad market movements can, and presumably will, be diversified away. After all, why accept risk that can easily be eliminated? *The risk that remains after diversifying is market risk, or risk that is inherent in the market, and this risk can be measured by the degree to which a given stock tends to move up and down with the market.*

The Concept of Beta

The tendency of a stock to move with the market is reflected in its *beta coefficient*, which is a measure of the stock's *volatility* relative to an average stock. Betas are discussed at an intuitive level in this section, then in more detail later in the chapter.

An *average risk stock* is defined as one which tends to move up and down in step with the general market as measured by some index such as the Dow Jones or the New York Stock Exchange Index. Such a stock will, by definition, have a beta (b) of 1.0, which indicates that, in general, if the market moves up by 10 percent, the stock will also move up by 10 percent, while if the market falls by 10 percent, the stock will likewise fall by 10 percent. A portfolio of such b = 1.0 stocks will move up and down with the broad market averages and will be just as risky as the averages. If b = 0.5, the stock is only half as volatile as the market—it will rise and fall only half as much—and a portfolio of such stocks is half as risky as a portfolio of b = 1.0 stocks. On the other hand, if b = 2.0, the stock is twice as volatile as an average stock, so a portfolio of such stocks will be twice as risky as an average portfolio.

Betas are calculated and published by Merrill Lynch, Value Line, and numerous other organizations. The beta coefficients of some well-known companies, as calculated by Merrill Lynch, are shown in Table 5-2. Most stocks have betas in the range of 0.75 to 1.50. The average for all stocks is 1.0 by definition.[10]

---

[10] These betas are called "historic," or "ex post," betas because they are based strictly on historic, or past, data. Another type of beta, the "fundamental beta," which is based partly on past actions and

(continued)

Stock	Beta	
Campbell Soup Company	0.69	**Table 5-2**
Caterpillar Tractor	1.13	**Illustrative List of Beta**
Data 100 Corporation	2.02	**Coefficients**
Dean Foods Company	0.88	
Eastman Kodak	1.24	
General Electric	1.40	
General Motors	0.76	
Olympia Brewing Company	0.67	
Oceanic Drilling & Exploration	1.96	
Polaroid	2.17	
Safeway Stores	0.70	
St. Regis Paper	1.21	

Source: Merrill Lynch, Pierce, Fenner & Smith, November 1980.

If a high-beta stock (one whose beta is greater than 1.0) is added to an average risk (b = 1.0) portfolio, then the beta and consequently the riskiness of the portfolio will increase. Conversely, if a low-beta stock (one whose beta is less than 1.0) is added to an average risk portfolio, the portfolio's beta and risk will decline. *Thus, since a stock's beta measures its contribution to the riskiness of a portfolio, beta is the appropriate measure of the stock's riskiness.*

We can summarize our analysis to this point as follows:

1. A stock's risk consists of two components, market and company risk.
2. The company risk can be eliminated by diversification, and most investors do indeed diversify. We are left, then, with market risk, which is caused by general movements in the stock market. This market risk is the only relevant risk to a rational, diversified investor.
3. Investors must be compensated for bearing risk—the greater the riskiness of a stock, the higher its required return. However, compensation is required only for risk which cannot be eliminated by diversification. If risk premiums existed for diversifiable risk, well diversified investors would buy these securities and bid up their prices, and their final expected returns would reflect only nondiversifiable market risk.
4. The market risk of a stock is measured by its beta coefficient, which is an index of the stock's relative volatility. Some benchmark betas are given below:

   b = 0.5: Stock is only half as volatile, or risky, as the average stock.
   b = 1.0: Stock is of average risk.
   b = 2.0: Stock is twice as risky as the average stock.

partly on expected future conditions not yet reflected in historic data, is also in wide use today. For a discussion, see Barr Rosenberg and James Guy, "Beta and Investment Fundamentals," *Financial Analysts' Journal*, May-June 1976, 60-72.

5. *Since a stock's beta coefficient determines how it affects the riskiness of a diversified portfolio, beta is the most relevant measure of a stock's risk. Henceforth, we shall rely heavily on beta coefficients to measure security risk.*[11]

In the following section, we discuss the process of calculating beta coefficients for individual stocks.

Calculating Beta Coefficients

Professor William F. Sharpe developed the concept of beta coefficients and pioneered their use in separating the risk of an individual stock into market and company risk components.[12] Sharpe noted that the market risk of a given stock can be measured by its tendency to move with the general market. His procedure for determining market risk is illustrated in Figure 5-8, which is explained in the following paragraphs.

First, familiarize yourself with the definitions of the terms used in Figure 5-8:

$\bar{k}_J$ = historic realized rate of return on Stock J. ($\bar{k}$ is called "k bar.")

$\bar{k}_M$ = historic realized rate of return on the market.

α = Vertical axis intercept term, pronounced "alpha." α is often written as "a."

b = Slope coefficient, called the "beta coefficient."

e_J = Random error, reflecting the difference between the actual return on Stock J in a given year and the return predicted by the regression equation or line.

Each of these definitions is expanded in the paragraphs below.

To begin, if you have ever invested in stocks, you are well aware that there is often a big difference between expected returns ($\hat{k}$) and the actual returns that are realized on an investment. Accordingly, it is useful to define the term *historic realized rate of return,* $\bar{k}_J$, as the dividend yield plus capital gain or minus capital loss that actually occurred for Stock J in a given year. For example, people who bought General Public Utilities (GPU) stock at $18 per share in 1979, just prior to the accident at its Three Mile Island nuclear plant, expected to receive a dividend yield of about $1.87/$18 = 10.4% plus a capital gains yield of about 4%, for a total return $\hat{k}_{GPU}$ = 14.4%. However, after the accident, the company was forced to

---

[11] It should be noted that beta analysis in practice is much more difficult than this discussion makes it sound. Actually, a great deal of controversy has surrounded attempts to apply the theory.

[12] William F. Sharpe, "Capital Asset Prices: A Theory of Market Equilibrium under Conditions of Risk," *Journal of Finance* vol. 19 (September 1964), 425-442. It should also be noted that Sharpe, in his early work, defined market risk as "systematic risk" and company-specific risk as "unsystematic risk." These terms are still found in much of the finance literature, but Sharpe and others are now using the terminology employed here.

Figure 5-8
Calculating Beta Coefficients

Year	Stock J ($\bar{k}_J$)	The Market ($\bar{k}_M$)
1976	38.6%	23.8%
1977	−24.7	−7.2
1978	12.3	6.6
1979	8.2	20.5
1980	40.1	30.6
Average $\bar{k}$	14.9%	14.9%
σ_k	26.5%	15.1%

reduce the dividend to $1, and the stock price fell from $18 to $7, so the yield actually realized in 1979 on the $18 investment was

$$\bar{k}_{GPU} = D_1/P_0 + g$$

$$= \frac{\$1}{\$18} + \frac{\$7 - \$18}{\$18}$$

$$= 0.056 - 0.611 = -0.555 = -55.5\%.$$

This demonstrates that realized or historic returns are not necessarily equal to expected returns for risky assets like stocks.

The historic returns on Stock J are given in the upper section of Figure 5-8, along with historic returns on "the market," $\bar{k}_M$. In the lower section of the figure, we plot the data as a scatter diagram. For example, the data for 1979 are plotted as Point N, while those for 1976 are plotted as Point M. Notice that when returns on the market are high, returns on Stock J likewise tend to be high, and when the market is down, Stock J's returns are low. This general relationship is expressed more precisely in the regression line shown in Figure 5-8.

Recall what the term *regression line* or *regression equation* means: the equation Y = a + bX is the standard form of a simple linear regression. It states that the dependent variable, Y, is equal to a constant, a, plus b times X, where X is the "independent" variable. Thus, the rate of return on the stock during a given time period depends on what happens to the general stock market, which is measured by $\bar{k}_M$.

The regression equation is obtained by plotting the data points on graph paper and then drawing a line through the scatter of points "by eye."[13] There is a mathematical line of best fit, the *least squares regression line*, but unless the data points all line up neatly, the "by eye" regression line may differ from the least squares line, and different students will draw in somewhat different lines. The procedure for obtaining least squares estimates is explained in statistics courses.

Once the line has been drawn on the graph paper, we can estimate its intercept and slope, the a and b values in Y = a + bX. The intercept, a, is simply the point where the line cuts the vertical axis. The slope coefficient, b, can be estimated by the "rise over run" method. This involves calculating the amount by which $\bar{k}_J$ increases for a given increase in $\bar{k}_M$. For example, we observe (in Figure 5-8) that $\bar{k}_J$ increases from -8.9 percent to $+7.1$ percent (the rise) when $\bar{k}_M$ increases from 0 to 10.00 (the run). Thus, the b, or beta coefficient, can be measured as follows:

$$b = Beta = \frac{Rise}{Run} = \frac{\Delta Y}{\Delta X} = \frac{7.1 - (-8.9)}{10.00 - 0.00} = \frac{16.0}{10.00} = 1.6.$$

---

[13] In practical applications, the regression equation would always be fitted by the method of least squares, using one of the better hand-held calculators or a computer.

Note that rise over run is a ratio, and it would be the same if measured using any two arbitrarily selected points on the line.

The regression line or equation enables us to predict a rate of return for Stock J, given a value of $\bar{k}_M$. For example, if $\bar{k}_M = 15\%$, we would predict $\bar{k}_J = -8.9\% + 1.6(15\%) = 15.1\%$. The actual return will probably differ from the predicted return. This deviation is the error term, e, for the year, and it varies randomly from year to year depending on company-specific factors. The least squares method of fitting the line is designed to minimize the errors.[14]

Now that we have plotted the scatter diagram and estimated the regression equation and the beta coefficient, we can note the following points: First, the future returns on Stock J are presumed to bear a linear relationship of the following form to those of the market:

Some Observations about Betas

$$\bar{k}_J = \alpha_J + b_J \bar{k}_M + e_J$$
$$= -8.9 + 1.6\,\bar{k}_M + e_J.$$

In words, the return on the stock, $\bar{k}_J$, is equal to an intercept term, α (pronounced alpha), plus a regression coefficient, b_J, times the market portfolio return, $\bar{k}_M$, plus a random error term, e_J. The term b_J, called the *beta coefficient*, is generally positive, indicating that if the market return is high, the return on Stock J is also high, and conversely.

Second, in addition to general market movements, each firm also faces events that are peculiar to it and independent of the general economic climate. Such events tend to cause the returns on any Firm J's stock to move at least somewhat independently of those for the market as a whole. For example, GPU suffered a sharp price decline in 1979 despite a generally rising stock market. Such an event is accounted for by the random error term e_J. Before the fact, the expected value of the error term is zero; after the fact, it will generally be either positive or negative.

Third, the regression coefficient, b (the beta coefficient), is a *market sensitivity index; it measures the relative volatility of a given stock (J) versus the average stock, or the "market."* If a firm's beta is 1.0, then on average we would expect its rate of return to rise or fall in direct proportion to changes in market returns. Thus, if the market return falls one year by

---

[14] Statisticians have demonstrated that the beta coefficient may be calculated as follows:

$$b_J = \frac{\text{Covariance between Stock J and the Market}}{\text{Variance of market returns}} = \frac{\text{cov}(\bar{k}_J, \bar{k}_M)}{\sigma_M{}^2}$$
$$= \frac{r_{JM}\sigma_J\sigma_M}{\sigma_M{}^2} = r_{JM}\left(\frac{\sigma_J}{\sigma_M}\right). \tag{5-5}$$

In this form, we see that a stock's beta depends on (1) its correlation with the stock market as a whole, r_{JM}, (2) its own variability, σ_J, and (3) the variability of the market, σ_M. In the Figure 5-8 example, $r_{JM} = 0.91$, $\sigma_J = 26.5$ percent, and $\sigma_M = 15.1$ percent. Therefore, $b_J = 0.91(26.5\%/15.1\%) = 1.60$.

one percentage point, say from a 10 percent return to a 9 percent return, we would expect the firm's rate of return to experience a similar decline. This tendency of an individual stock to move with the market constitutes a risk, because the market does fluctuate, and these fluctuations cannot be diversified away. *This component of total risk is the stock's market, or non-diversifiable, risk.*

As noted earlier, a beta of 1.0 indicates a stock with "average" market risk—on the average, such a stock rises and falls by the same percentage as the market. What does b = 0.5 indicate? This means that if the market return rises or falls by X percentage points, the firm's rate of return rises or falls by only 0.5X, so this stock has less market risk than the average stock. Conversely, if beta = 2.0, then the stock's rate of return fluctuates twice as much as the market rate of return, so it has more than the average market risk. *From this it follows that the size of beta is an indicator of market risk: The larger the value of beta, the greater a stock's market, or nondiversifiable, risk.*

Finally, the relationship between a stock's total risk, market risk, and company risk can be expressed as follows:

$$\text{Total risk} = \text{Market risk} + \text{Company-specific risk}.$$

The company-specific risk should be eliminated by diversification, so we are left with the following:

$$\text{Relevant risk} = \text{Market risk}.$$

Several points about total and relevant risk are significant:

1. If, in a graph such as Figure 5-8, all the points plotted exactly on the regression line, then the error term would be zero and all of the stock's risk would be market related. On the other hand, if the points were widely scattered about the regression line, much of the stock's risk would be company specific. The shares of a large, well-diversified mutual fund would plot very close to the regression line, as would those of a highly diversified conglomerate corporation.
2. If the stock market never fluctuated, then stocks would have no market risk. Of course, the market does fluctuate, so market risk is present. In recent years the standard deviation of market returns, σ_M, has generally run about 15 percent annually, meaning that actual returns could easily be 15 percent below the expected return. Back in the "wild" days of the 1920s, before the SEC and other forces helped stabilize the market, fluctuations were even greater.
3. Although it is not demonstrated here, the market risk of any individual stock can be measured as follows:

$$\text{Market risk for Stock J} = b_J \sigma_M.$$

Therefore, for any given level of market volatility as measured by the standard deviation, σ_M, the higher a stock's beta, the higher its market risk. If beta were zero, the stock would have no market risk, while if beta were negative (that is, if the regression line in Figure 5-8 had a negative slope), the market risk would also be negative. As is shown in Problem 5-6, a negative beta has interesting implications.

4. If a given stock has b = 0.5, and if σ_M = 15 percent, then the stock's relevant risk equals $b_J\sigma_M$ = 0.5(15%) = 7.5%. A portfolio of such low-beta stocks would have a standard deviation of expected returns of σ_p = 7.5%, or one-half the standard deviation of expected returns on a portfolio of average (b = 1.0) stocks. Had Stock J been a high-beta stock (b = 2.0), then its relevant risk would have been $b_J\sigma_M$ = 2.0(15%) = 30%. A portfolio of b = 2.0 stocks would have σ_p = 30%, so such a portfolio would be twice as risky as a portfolio of average stocks.

Figure 5-9 demonstrates several of the points made above. First, note that the figure is divided into three sections. The top third deals with stocks whose betas are about equal to zero, the middle third with stocks whose betas are about 0.5, and the bottom third with stocks having betas of about 1.0. Within each section, the top row of the graph gives scatter diagrams between the market and 1 stock, 20 stock, and 200 stock portfolios. Here we see, for each of the three beta groups, that the scatter narrows and the points get closer to the regression line as the size of the portfolio increases. However, the regression lines for each beta group have exactly the same slope, regardless of the size of the portfolio.

Beneath each scatter diagram we show the portfolios' returns distributions. These distributions become tighter, indicating a lower σ_p, hence less risk, as the size of the portfolio increases. However, note that in the top section, where b ≈ 0, diversification completely eliminates risk; in the middle section, where b ≈ 0.5, the large portfolio has a relatively low level of risk; and in the bottom part, where b ≈ 1.0, the final portfolio still has quite a bit of risk. Indeed, a large portfolio of b = 0.5 stocks would be half as risky as the market, while a portfolio of b = 1.0 stocks would be exactly as risky as the market. Also, had we included an analysis for b = 2.0 stocks, the regression lines would have had a slope of 2.0, indicating twice the risk of a portfolio of average (b = 1.0) stocks.

Notice that the mean returns ($\bar{k}_p$) are constant for portfolios within each beta group, but increase from 10 percent to 13 percent as beta increases from zero to 1.0. This is reasonable, because investors must be compensated in the form of higher returns if a stock is exposed to more nondiversifiable risk.[15]

---

[15] Of course, in a bad year for stocks in general, the risky, high-beta stocks will have lower realized returns than the less risky, low-beta stocks: $\bar{k}$ (high beta) < $\bar{k}$ (low beta) after a market decline. However, on average, $\bar{k}$ is higher for high-beta stocks than for ones with lower betas. Also, in a forward-looking, or *ex ante* sense, the expected returns ($\hat{k}$) should *always* be higher for high- than for low-beta stocks: $\hat{k}$ (high beta) > $\hat{k}$ (low beta) at all times.

Figure 5-9
Effects of Beta and Size of Portfolio on
Portfolio Risk

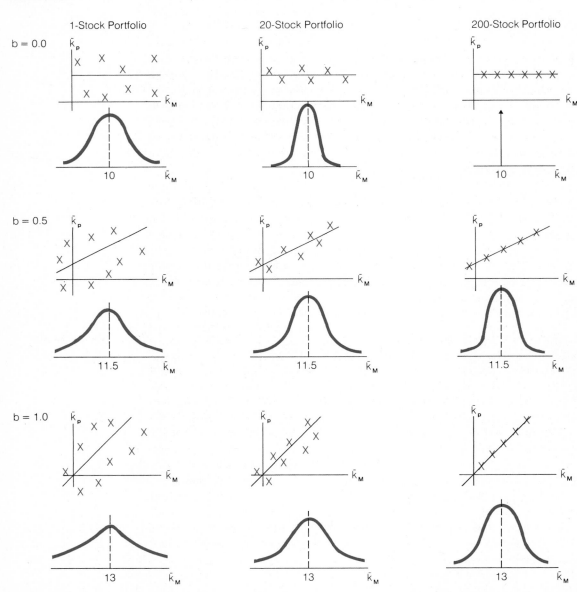

A portfolio consisting of low-beta securities will itself have a low beta, as the beta of any set of securities is a weighted average of the individual securities' betas:

$$b_p = \sum_{J=1}^{n} x_J b_J.$$

Here b_p is the beta of the portfolio, which reflects how volatile the portfolio is in relation to the market index; x_J is the fraction of the portfolio invested in the Jth stock; and b_J is the beta coefficient of the Jth stock.

If an investor holds a \$100,000 portfolio consisting of \$10,000 invested in each of ten stocks, and if each stock has a beta of 0.8, then the portfolio will have $b_p = 0.8$. Thus, the portfolio is less risky than the market, and it should experience relatively narrow price swings and have small rate of return fluctuations.

Now suppose one of the existing stocks is sold and replaced by a stock with $b = 2.0$. This action will increase the riskiness of the portfolio from $b_{p1} = 0.8$ to $b_{p2} = 0.92$:

$$b_{p2} = \sum_{J=1}^{n} x_J b_J = 0.9(0.8) + 0.1(2.0) = 0.92.$$

Had a stock with $b = 0.6$ been added, the portfolio beta would have declined from 0.8 to 0.78.

A word of caution about betas and the capital asset pricing model is in order. Although these concepts are very logical, the entire theory is based on *ex ante*, or expected, conditions, yet we have available only *ex post*, or past, data. Thus, the betas we calculate show how volatile a stock has been in the *past*, but conditions may change and alter its *future volatility*, which is the item of real concern to investors. This problem and others involved in actually using the CAPM are covered in depth in advanced finance courses.[16]

---

[16] The concept of beta was discovered and developed by academicians, and then seized upon and used by business practitioners. To some extent, betas seem to have been oversold—the beauty of the concept has been overemphasized, and the difficulties with actually implementing the theory in practice have not been pointed out sufficiently. In a recent article, Anise Wallace ("Is Beta Dead?" *Institutional Investor*, July 1980) reached this conclusion: "It took nearly a decade for money managers to learn to love beta. Now it looks as if they were sold a bill of goods—and the whole MPT [Modern Portfolio Theory] house of cards could come tumbling down." This judgment is, in the minds of most observers, far too harsh. The concept of beta obviously reflects the way sophisticated investors should and do look at the risk inherent in a security. Problems do arise when one attempts to measure *future* events on the basis of *past* data, but abandoning beta because of these difficulties would be like throwing out the baby with the bath water!

The Relationship between Risk and Rates of Return

Now that we have established beta as the conceptually best measure of a stock's risk, the next step in the capital asset pricing model (CAPM) framework is to specify the relationship between risk and return. This relationship is known as the *Security Market Line (SML)*, and it is expressed by this equation:

$$\text{SML: } k = R_F + b(k_M - R_F). \qquad (5\text{-}6)$$

Here:

k = the required rate of return on the stock in question. If the expected future return, $\hat{k}$, is less than k, then you would not purchase this stock, or you would sell it if you owned it.

R_F = the riskless rate of return, generally measured by the rate of return on U.S. Treasury securities.

b = the beta coefficient of the stock in question.

k_M = the required rate of return on an average (b = 1.0) stock. k_M is also the required rate of return on a portfolio consisting of all stocks, or the market portfolio.

$(k_M - R_F)$ = the market risk premium, or the price of risk for an average stock. It is the additional return over the riskless rate required to compensate investors for assuming an "average" amount of risk.

$b(k_M - R_F)$ = the risk premium on the stock in question. The stock's risk premium is less than, equal to, or greater than the premium on an average stock depending on whether its beta is less than, equal to, or greater than 1.0.

In words, the SML equation shows that the required rate of return on a given stock (k) is equal to the return required in the marketplace for securities that have no risk (R_F) plus a risk premium equal to the risk premium demanded on an average stock ($k_M - R_F$) scaled up or down by the relative riskiness of the firm as measured by its beta coefficient. Thus, if R_F = 8%, b = 0.5, and k_M = 12%, then

$$\begin{aligned} k &= 8\% + 0.5(12\% - 8\%) \\ &= 8\% + 0.5(4\%) \\ &= 10\%. \end{aligned}$$

An average firm, with b = 1.0, would have

$$k = 8\% + 1.0(4\%) = 12\%,$$

while a riskier firm, with b = 2.0, would have

$$k = 8\% + 2.0(4\%) = 16\%.$$

Figure 5-10 gives a graph of the SML and the required returns on the three illustrative stocks. Figure 5-10 is related to Figure 5-7, which showed that the relevant risk of a large portfolio of average stocks (i.e., stocks with b = 1.0) is the portfolio's standard deviation, σ_p = 15.1%. Since each of these average stocks has b = 1.0, each contributes equally to the portfolio's risk. In Figure 5-10 we see that the required return on an average stock is 12 percent, reflecting the 8 percent required return for riskless assets plus a 4 percent risk premium needed to induce investors to accept the level of risk in a portfolio of these average, or b = 1.0, stocks, with σ_p = 15.1%.[17]

Figure 5-10
The Security Market Line (SML)

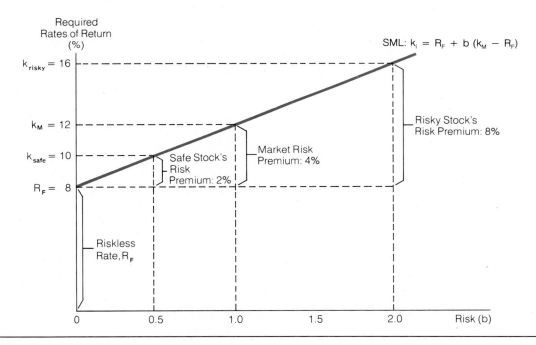

Interest amounts to "rent" on borrowed money, or the "price" of money. Thus, R_F is the price of money to a riskless borrower. The existing market risk-free rate is called the *nominal rate,* and it consists of two elements: (1) *a real or inflation-free rate of return,* RR_F, and (2) an *inflation premium,* IP,

The Impact of Inflation

[17] The risk premium of an average stock, $k_M - R_F$, cannot be measured with great precision because it is impossible to observe expected returns. However, empirical studies suggest that, where long-term U.S. Treasury bonds are used to measure R_F and where k_M is the return on the S&P 400 Industrial Stocks, the market risk premium varies somewhat from year to year, but it has averaged 5½ percent during the last twenty years. See Appendix 5B.

equal to the anticipated rate of inflation.[18] Thus, $R_F = RR_F + IP$. The real rate on risk-free government bonds has, historically, ranged from 2 to 4 percent, with a mean of about 3 percent. Thus, if no inflation were expected, government bonds would tend to yield about 3 percent.[19] However, as the expected rate of inflation increases, a premium must be added to the real rate of return to compensate investors for the loss of purchasing power that results from inflation.

To illustrate the effects of inflation, if you loaned the government $1,000 at 4 percent, you would have $1,040 at the end of the year. If inflation occurred at the rate of 5 percent during the year, you would end up with a purchasing power *loss* of 1 percent—your real rate of return would be *minus* 1 percent. If you (and other investors) anticipated a 5 percent inflation rate, you would add a 5 percent inflation premium to the 3 percent real required rate of return to produce a nominal R_F of about 8 percent. Thus, the 8 percent R_F shown in Figure 5-10 may be thought of as consisting of a 3 percent real rate of return plus a 5 percent inflation premium: $R_F = RR_F + IP = 3\% + 5\% = 8\%$.

If the expected rate of inflation rose to 7 percent, this would cause R_F to rise to 10 percent. Such a change is shown in Figure 5-11. Notice that the increase in R_F also causes an increase in the rate of return on all risky assets. For example, the rate of return on an average stock, k_M, increases from 12 to 14 percent. Other risky securities' returns also rise by two percentage points.

Changes in Risk Aversion

The slope of the Security Market Line (SML) reflects the extent to which investors are averse to risk—the steeper the slope of the line, the greater the average investor's risk aversion. If investors were not at all averse to risk, and if R_F were 8 percent, then risky assets would also sell to provide an expected return of 8 percent—with no risk aversion, there would be no risk premium, and the SML would be horizontal. As risk aversion increases, so does the risk premium and, thus, the slope of the SML.

Figure 5-12 illustrates an increase in risk aversion. The market risk premium rises from 4 percent to 6 percent, and k_M rises from 12 percent to 14 percent. The returns on other risky assets also rise, with the impact of this shift in risk aversion being more pronounced on riskier securities. For example, the required return on a stock with $b = 0.5$ increases by

---

[18] The terminology employed here is standard economics notation. We should note, however, that in accounting terminology *nominal rate of return* means what we call the *coupon interest rate*. As economists use the term, nominal rate of return is identical to yield to maturity.

[19] The real rate of return depends on the supply of and demand for money, which in turn depend on people's willingness to defer consumption (save), rates of return on investments in manufacturing plants, Federal Reserve policy, and so on. For example, during the depression of the 1930s, when investment opportunities were poor, the real rate of return was quite low. In a more booming period, the expected real rate tends to be high. RR_F cannot be measured with precision. See Appendix 2A for further discussion.

Figure 5-11
Shift in the SML Caused by an Increase in Inflation

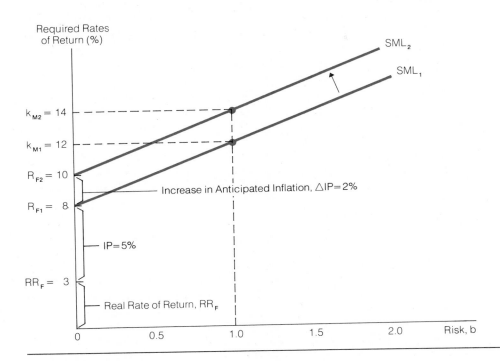

only one percentage point, from 10 to 11 percent, while the required return on a stock with b = 1.5 increases by three percentage points, from 14 to 17 percent.

As we shall see later in the book, a firm can affect its market, or beta, risk through changes in the nature and composition of its assets, and also through its use of debt financing. A company's beta can also change as a result of increased competition in its industry, the expiration of basic patents, a change in management, and the like. When such changes occur, the demanded or required rate of return also changes, and this will affect the price of the firm's stock. For example, suppose some action occurred that caused Carter Chemical's beta to increase from 1.0 to 1.5. If the conditions depicted in Figure 5-10 held, Carter's required rate of return would increase from

Changes in a Stock's Beta Coefficient

$$k_1 = R_F + b(k_M - R_F) = 8\% + 1.0(12\% - 8\%) = 12\%$$

to

$$k_2 = 8\% + 1.5(12\% - 8\%) = 14\%.$$

Figure 5-12
Shift in the SML Caused by Increased Risk
Aversion

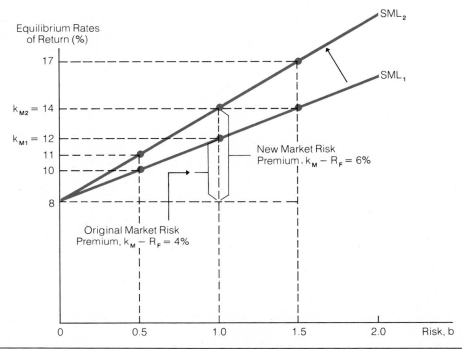

This change in k would cause a change in Carter's stock price, other things held constant:[20]

$$\text{Old price} = P = \frac{D_1}{k - g} = \frac{\$2.00}{0.12 - 0.05} = \$28.57.$$

$$\text{New price} = P = \frac{\$2.00}{0.14 - 0.05} = \$22.22.$$

Notice that at its new equilibrium price of $22.22, Carter's new expected rate of return is exactly equal to its new 14 percent required rate of return:

$$\hat{k} = \frac{D_1}{P_0} + g = \frac{\$2.00}{\$22.22} + 5\% = 14\% = 8\% + 1.5(12\% - 8\%) = k.$$

[20] Companies do sometimes deliberately increase their risk, but only if the action that raises risk also raises the expected earnings and the expected growth rate. Trying to determine the effects of a given action on risk and profitability, which affects growth, is one of the financial manager's central tasks.

Since the expected rate of return is equal to the required return, we know that $22.22 is Carter's new equilibrium stock price.

Suppose a "typical" investor's required rate of return on Stock X, with $b = 2$, is 16 percent, determined as follows:

Security Market Equilibrium

$$k_X = R_F + b_X(k_M - R_F)$$
$$= 8\% + 2.0(12\% - 8\%)$$
$$= 16\%.$$

This 16 percent required return is indicated in Figure 5–13.

Our typical investor will want to buy X if the expected rate of return is more than 16 percent, will want to sell it if the expected rate of return is less than 16 percent, and will be indifferent if the expected return is exactly 16 percent. Now suppose the investor, whose portfolio contains X, analyzes the stock's prospects and concludes that its earnings, dividends, and price can be expected to grow at the rate of 5 percent per year. The last dividend was $D_0 = \$2.8571$, so the next expected dividend is

$$D_1 = \$2.8571(1.05) = \$3.$$

The investor observes that the present price of the stock, P_0, is $30. Should more of Stock X be purchased, should the present holdings be sold, or should the present position be maintained? This investor can calculate Stock X's expected rate of return as follows:

$$\hat{k}_X = \frac{D_1}{P_0} + g = \frac{\$3}{\$30} + 5\% = 15\%.$$

The point is plotted on Figure 5-13 as Point X, which is below the SML.

Since the expected rate of return is less than the required return, this typical investor will want to sell the stock, as will other holders. However, few people will want to buy at the $30 price, so present owners will only be able to find buyers if they cut the price of the stock. Thus, the price will decline until it reaches $27.27, at which point the expected rate of return, 16 percent, is equal to the required rate of return:

$$\hat{k}_X = \frac{\$3}{\$27.27} + 5\% = 16\% = k_X.$$

Had the stock initially sold for less than $27.27, then events would have been reversed. Investors would have wanted to buy the stock, because its expected return would have exceeded its required rate of return. These buy orders would have driven the stock's price up to $27.27.

The price of $27.27 is defined as Stock X's *equilibrium price* because, given investors' feelings about the stock, this is the only stable price. If the price had exceeded $27.27, market forces would have driven it down,

Figure 5-13
Expected and Required Returns on Stock X

while if the current price had been less than $27.27, market forces would have driven it up.

**Changes in
Equilibrium
Stock Prices**

Stock market prices are *not* constant—they undergo violent changes at times. Let us assume that Stock X is in equilibrium, selling at a price of $27.27 per share. If all expectations were exactly met, over the next year the price would gradually rise to $28.63, or by 5 percent. However, many different events could occur to cause a change in the equilibrium price of the stock. To illustrate, consider again the set of inputs used to develop Stock X's price of $27.27, and a new set of assumed input variables:

| | Variable Value | |
	Original	New
Riskless rate, R_F	8%	7%
Market risk premium, $k_M - R_F$	4%	3%
Stock X's beta coefficient, b_x	2.0	1.0
Stock X's expected growth rate, g_x	5%	6%

The first three variables influence k_x, which declines as a result of the new set of variables from 16 to 10 percent:

$$\text{Original } k_x = 8\% + 2(4\%) = 16\%.$$
$$\text{New } k_x = 7\% + 1(3\%) = 10\%.$$

Using these values, together with the new D and g values, we find that P_0 rises from \$27.27 to \$75.71.[21]

$$\text{Original } P_0 = \frac{\$2.8571(1.05)}{0.16 - 0.05} = \frac{\$3}{0.11} = \$27.27.$$

$$\text{New } P_0 = \frac{\$2.8571(1.06)}{0.10 - 0.06} = \frac{\$3.0285}{0.04} = \$75.71.$$

At the new price, the expected and required rates of return will be equal:

$$\hat{k}_x = \frac{\$3.0285}{\$75.71} + 6\% = 10\% = k_x.$$

Evidence suggests that stocks, and especially those of large NYSE companies, adjust quite rapidly to disequilibrium situations. Consequently, equilibrium ordinarily exists for any given stock, and in general required and expected returns are equal. Stock prices certainly change, sometimes violently and rapidly, but this simply reflects changing conditions and expectations. There are, of course, times when a stock continues to react for several months to a favorable or unfavorable development, but this does not signify a long adjustment period; rather, it simply illustrates that as more new bits of information about the situation become available, the market adjusts to them.[22]

A body of theory called the *Efficient Markets Hypothesis* (EMH), which holds (1) that stocks are always in equilibrium and (2) that it is impossible for an investor to consistently "beat the market," has been developed. Essentially, the EMH states that there are some 100,000 or so full-time, well-trained, professional analysts and traders operating in the market and following some 2,000 major stocks. If each analyst followed only 20 stocks, there would still be 1,000 analysts following each stock. As new information about a stock became available, these 1,000 analysts all would receive and evaluate it at approximately the same time, and the price of the stock would adjust almost immediately to reflect the new information. Therefore, according to the EMH, at any given time all the infor-

---

[21] A price change of this magnitude is by no means rare. The prices of *many* New York Stock Exchange stocks double or halve during a year, and almost every day some stock goes up or down by 15 percent or more.

[22] It should be obvious that actual realized rates of return are not necessarily equal to expected and required returns. Thus, an investor might *expect* to receive a return of 15 percent if he or she bought General Motors stock in 1981, but after the fact, in 1982, the realized return will probably be above or below 15 percent.

mation about all the major stocks is reflected in the prices of these stocks.

If the EMH is correct, then it would be a waste of time to analyze stocks seeking to find some that are undervalued—if stock prices already reflect all available information, hence are fairly priced, one could "beat the market" only by luck, and it would be difficult if not impossible for anyone to consistently outperform the market averages. Empirical tests have shown that the EMH is, to a very large extent, valid. People such as corporate officers who have inside information can do better than the averages, and individuals and organizations that are especially good at digging out information on small, new companies also seem to do consistently well. However, the market for large firms such as those traded on the NYSE is highly efficient. Therefore, for NYSE companies, it is generally safe to assume that $\hat{k} = k$ and that stocks plot on the SML.

Summary

The primary goals of this chapter were (1) to show how risk is measured in financial analysis and (2) to explain how risk affects security prices and rates of return. We began by showing that risk is related to variability of expected future returns. However, we soon saw that most rational investors hold *portfolios of stocks,* and that such investors are more concerned with the risks of their portfolios than with the risks of individual stocks.

Next, we saw that the riskiness of a given stock can be split into two components—*market risk,* which is caused by changes in the broad stock market and which cannot be eliminated by diversification, and *company-specific risk,* which can be eliminated by holding a diversified portfolio. Since investors do diversify and eliminate company risk, the most *relevant risk* inherent in stocks is their market risk, which is measured by the *beta coefficient.*

Betas measure the tendency of stocks to move up and down with the market—a high-beta stock is more volatile than the market, while a low-beta stock is less volatile than average. An average stock has $b = 1.0$ by definition.

The required rate of return on a stock consists of the rate of return on riskless bonds, R_F, plus a risk premium that depends on the stock's beta coefficient:

$$k = R_F + b(k_M - R_F).$$

This formula is called the *Security Market Line (SML) equation,* or sometimes the *Capital Asset Pricing Model (CAPM) equation,* and it is of fundamental importance in finance.

We also saw that stocks are typically in equilibrium, with their expected and required rates of return equal to one another:

$$\hat{k} = \frac{D_1}{P_0} + g = R_F + b(k_M - R_F) = k.$$

Although stocks are generally in equilibrium, a number of things can happen to cause prices to change. The riskless rate can change because of changes in anticipated inflation; a stock's beta can change; or its rate of expected growth can increase or decrease. In the remainder of this book we will examine ways a firm's management can influence its stock's riskiness and expected growth rate, hence its price.

Questions

5-1 Define the following terms, using graphs or equations to illustrate your answers wherever feasible:
   a. Uncertainty
   b. Probability distribution
   c. *Expected* versus *required* versus *past realized* rate of return
   d. Standard deviation
   e. SML
   f. Market risk
   g. Company-specific risk
   h. Beta coefficient
   i. Relevant risk
   j. CAPM
   k. Risk premium
   l. Inflation premium
   m. Risk aversion
   n. Market equilibrium
   o. Correlation

5-2 The probability distribution of a less risky expected return is more peaked than that of a risky return. What shape would the probability distribution have (1) for completely certain returns and (2) for completely uncertain returns?

5-3 Security A has an expected return of 6 percent, a standard deviation of expected returns of 30 percent, a correlation coefficient with the market of minus 0.25, and a beta coefficient of minus 0.5. Security B has an expected return of 11 percent, a standard deviation of returns of 10 percent, a correlation with the market of 0.75, and a beta coefficient of 0.10. Which security is more risky? Why?

5-4 a. If you owned a portfolio consisting of $500,000 worth of long-term U.S. government bonds, would your portfolio be riskless?
   b. Suppose you held a portfolio consisting of $500,000 worth of thirty day Treasury bills. Every thirty days, your bills mature and you reinvest the proceeds ($500,000) in a new batch of bills. Would your portfolio be truly riskless? (Hint: Assume that you live on the investment income from your portfolio, and that you want to maintain a constant standard of living.)
   c. You should have concluded that both long-term and short-term portfolios of government securities have some element of risk. Can you think of any asset that would be completely riskless?

5-5 An insurance policy is a financial asset. The investment cost is the premium paid.

 a. How do you calculate the expected return on a life insurance policy?

 b. Suppose the owner of the life insurance policy has no other financial assets—the person's only other asset is "human capital" or lifetime earnings capacity. What is the correlation coefficient between returns on the insurance policy and returns on the policyholder's human capital?

 c. Life insurance companies have administrative costs and sales representatives' commissions; hence, the expected rate of return on insurance premiums is low or even negative. Use the portfolio concept to explain why people buy life insurance in spite of negative expected returns.

5-6 If investors' aversion to risk increases, would the risk premium on a high-beta stock increase more or less than that on a low-beta stock? Explain.

Self-Test Problems

ST5-1 Stocks A and B have the following historical dividend and price data:

Year	Stock A Dividend	Stock A Year-End Price	Stock B Dividend	Stock B Year-End Price
1976	—	$22.50	—	$43.75
1977	$2.00	16.00	$3.40	35.50
1978	2.20	17.00	3.65	38.75
1979	2.40	20.25	3.90	51.75
1980	2.60	17.25	4.05	44.50
1981	2.95	18.75	4.25	45.25

 a. Calculate the realized rate of return (or holding period return) for each stock in each year. Then assume that someone had held a portfolio consisting of 50 percent of A and 50 percent of B. What would the realized rate of return on the portfolio be in each year from 1977 through 1981? What are the average returns for each stock and for the portfolio?

 b. Now calculate the standard deviation of returns for each stock and for the portfolio.

 c. Based on the extent to which the portfolio has a lower risk than the stocks held individually, would you guess that the correlation coefficient between returns on the two stocks is closer to 0.9, 0.0, or −0.9?

 d. If you added more stocks at random to the portfolio, what is the most accurate statement of what would happen to σ_p?

 1. σ_p would remain constant.

 2. σ_p would decline to somewhere in the vicinity of 15 percent.

 3. σ_p would decline to zero if enough stocks were included.

ST5-2 You are given the following set of data:

	Historic Rates of Return, $(\bar{k})$	
Year	Stock X, $(\bar{k}_X)$	NYSE, $(\bar{k}_M)$
1974	−14.0%	−26.5%
1975	23.0	37.2
1976	17.5	23.8
1977	2.0	−7.2
1978	8.1	6.6
1979	19.4	20.5
1980	18.2	30.6
$\bar{k}_{Avg}$	10.6%	12.1%

a. Plot these data points on a scatter diagram, draw in the regression line, and then estimate the value of the beta coefficient.

b. Check the average returns $(\bar{k}_{Avg})$ given in the tabular data, and then calculate the standard deviation of returns for both Stock X and the NYSE from 1974 through 1980.

c. Assuming (1) that the 1974-1980 situation is expected to hold true in the future (that is, $\hat{k}_X = \bar{k}_X = 10.6\%$; $\hat{k}_M = \bar{k}_M = 12.1\%$; and both σ_X and b_X in the future will equal their past values) and (2) that Stock X is in equilibrium (that is, it plots on the Security Market Line), what is the risk-free rate?

d. Plot the Security Market Line.

e. Suppose you hold a large, well-diversified portfolio and are considering adding to the portfolio either Stock X or another stock, Stock Y, that has the same beta as Stock X but a higher standard deviation of returns. Stocks X and Y have the same expected returns, that is, $\hat{k}_X = \hat{k}_Y = 10.6\%$. Which stock would you choose?

f. If Stock X were expected to pay a dividend of $3.50 in 1981, and if its dividends were expected to grow at a rate of 5 percent in the future, what would be its equilibrium price at the beginning of 1981?

5-1 Stocks A and B have the following probability distributions of expected future returns:

Problems

Probability	A	B
0.1	−10%	−30%
0.2	5	0
0.4	15	17
0.2	25	34
0.1	40	64

a. Calculate the expected rate of return, $\hat{k}$, for Stock B. $\hat{k}_A = 15\%$.

b. Calculate the standard deviation of expected returns for Stock A. That for Stock B is 23.6 percent. Is it possible that most investors might regard Stock B as being *less* risky than Stock A? Explain.

5-2   a. Suppose $R_F = 10\%$, $k_M = 14\%$, and $b_A = 1.4$. What is k_A, the required rate of return on Stock A?

b. Now suppose R_F (1) increases to 11 percent, or (2) decreases to 9 percent. The slope of the SML remains constant. How will this affect k_M and k_A?

c. Now assume R_F remains at 10 percent, but k_M (1) increases to 15 percent, or (2) falls to 12 percent. The slope of the SML does *not* remain constant. How will this affect k_A?

d. Now assume that R_F remains at 10 percent and k_M at 14 percent, but beta (1) rises to 1.6, or (2) falls to 0.75. How will this affect k_A?

5-3   Suppose you are offered (a) \$1 million or (b) a gamble where you get \$2 million if a head is flipped but zero if a tail comes up.

a. What is the expected value of this gamble?

b. Would you take the sure \$1 million or the gamble?

c. If you take the sure \$1 million, are you a risk averter or a risk seeker?

d. Suppose you actually take the \$1 million. You can invest it in either a U.S. Treasury bond that will return \$1,075,000 at the end of a year or common stock that has a 50-50 chance of being either worthless or worth \$2,300,000 at the end of the year.

   1. What is the expected profit on the stock investment? The expected profit on the bond investment is \$75,000.

   2. What is the expected rate of return on the stock investment? The expected rate of return on the bond investment is 7.5 percent.

   3. Would you invest in the bond or the stock?

   4. Just how large would the expected profit and the expected rate of return have to be on the stock investment to make *you* invest in the stock?

   5. How might your decision be affected if, rather than buying one stock for \$1 million, you could construct a portfolio consisting of 100 stocks with \$10,000 in each? Each of these stocks has the same return characteristics as the one stock, that is, a 50-50 chance of being worth either zero or \$23,000 at year end. Would the correlation of returns on these stocks matter?

5-4   a. The risk-free rate of return is 10 percent, the required rate of return on the market, k_M, is 15 percent, and Stock X has a beta coefficient of 1.4. If the dividend expected during the coming year, D_1, is \$2.50 and $g = 5\%$, at what price should Stock X sell?

b. Now suppose the Federal Reserve Board increases the money supply, causing the riskless rate to drop to 9 percent. What will this do to the price of the stock?

c. In addition to the change in Part b, suppose investors' risk aversion

declines; this fact, combined with the decline in R_F, causes k_M to fall   *26.04*
to 13 percent. At what price will Stock X sell?

d. Now suppose Firm X has a change in management. The new group
institutes policies that increase the growth rate to 6 percent. Also, the   *34.05*
new management stabilizes sales and profits, and thus causes the
beta coefficient to decline from 1.4 to 1.1. After all these changes,
what is Stock X's new equilibrium price? (Note: D_1 goes to $2.52.)

5-5 a. Suppose Regal Chemical Company's management conducts a study
and concludes that, if Regal expands its consumer products division
(which is less risky than its primary business, industrial chemicals),
the firm's beta will decline from 1.2 to 0.9. However, consumer products have a somewhat lower profit margin, and this will cause Regal's
growth rate in earnings and dividends to fall from 7 percent to 5   *45*
percent. Should management make the change? Assume the follow-   *37.17*
ing: $k_M = 11\%$; $R_F = 7.5\%$; $D_0 = 2.

b. Assume all the facts as given in Part a except the change in the beta
coefficient. By how much would the beta have to decline to cause the   *β=.60353*
expansion to be a good one? (Hint: Set P_0 under the new policy equal
to P_0 under the old one, and find the new beta that produces this
equality.)

5-6 The beta coefficient for Stock C is $b_C = 0.4$, while that for Stock D is
$b_D = -0.5$. (Stock D's beta is negative, indicating that its rate of return
rises whenever returns on most other stocks fall. There are very few negative beta stocks, although gold mining stocks are often cited as an example.)

a. If the risk-free rate is 9 percent, and the expected rate of return on an
average stock is 13 percent, what are the required rates of return on
Stocks C and D?

b. For Stock C, suppose the current price, P_0, is $25, the next expected
dividend, D_1, is $1.50, and the stock's expected growth rate is 4 per-
cent. Is the stock in equilibrium? Explain, and describe what will happen if the stock is not in equilibrium.

5-7 The Sharpe Investment Fund has a total investment of $400 million in
five stocks:

Stock	Investment	Stock's Beta Coefficient
A	$120 million	0.5
B	$100 million	2.0
C	$60 million	4.0
D	$80 million	1.0
E	$40 million	3.0

The beta coefficient for a fund such as this can be found as a weighted average of the fund's investments. The current risk-free rate is 7 percent, while expected market returns, $\hat{k}_M$, have the following probability distribution for the next period:

Probability	Market Return
0.1	8%
0.2	10
0.4	12
0.2	14
0.1	16

a. What is the estimated equation for the security market line (SML)?

b. Compute the required rate of return on the Sharpe Fund for the next period.

c. Suppose management receives a proposal for a new stock. The investment needed to take a position in the stock is $50 million; it will have an expected return of 16 percent; and its estimated beta coefficient is 2.5. Should the new stock be purchased? At what expected rate of return would management be indifferent to purchasing the stock?

5-8 You are given the following set of data:

	Historic Rates of Return ($\bar{k}$)	
Year	NYSE ($\bar{k}_M$)	Stock Y ($\bar{k}_Y$)
1970	4.0%	3.0%
1971	14.3	18.2
1972	19.0	9.1
1973	−14.7	−6.0
1974	−26.5	−15.3
1975	37.2	33.1
1976	23.8	6.1
1977	−7.2	3.2
1978	6.6	14.8
1979	20.5	24.1
1980	30.6	18.0
Mean	9.8%	9.8%
σ	18.7%	13.1%

a. Construct a "standard" graph showing the relationship between returns on Stock Y and the market; then draw a freehand approximation of the regression line. What is the approximate value of the beta coefficient?

b. Give a verbal interpretation of what the regression line and the beta coefficient show about Stock Y's volatility and relative riskiness as compared to other stocks.

c. Suppose the scatter of points had been more spread out, but the regression line was exactly where your present graph shows it. How would this affect (1) the firm's risk if the stock is held in a one-asset portfolio and (2) the actual risk premium on the stock if the CAPM holds exactly?

d. Suppose the regression line had been downward-sloping, and the beta coefficient had been negative. What would this imply about (1) Stock Y's relative riskiness, (2) its correlation with k_M, and (3) its probable risk premium?

e. Construct an illustrative probability distribution graph of returns on portfolios consisting of (1) only Stock Y, (2) 1 percent each of 100 stocks with beta coefficients similar to that of Stock Y, and (3) all stocks (that is, the distribution of returns on the market). Use as the expected rate of return the arithmetic mean as given above for both Stock Y and the market, and assume that the distributions are normal. Are the expected returns "reasonable"; that is, is it reasonable for $\hat{k}_Y = \hat{k}_M = 9.8\%$?

5-9 You are given the following data on market returns, k_M, and the returns on Stocks A and B:

Year	$\bar{k}_M$	$\bar{k}_A$	$\bar{k}_B$
1975	37.2%	37.2%	26.1%
1976	23.8	23.8	19.4
1977	-7.2	-7.2	3.9
1978	6.6	6.6	10.8
1979	20.5	20.5	17.7
1980	30.6	30.6	22.8

R_F, the riskless rate, is 10 percent. Your probability distribution for $\hat{k}_M$ for next year is as follows:

Probability	$\hat{k}_M$
0.1	-15%
0.2	0
0.4	15
0.2	30
0.1	45

a. Determine graphically the beta coefficients for Stocks A and B.
b. Graph the market line, and give the equation for the SML.
c. Calculate the required rates of return on Stocks A and B.
d. Suppose Stock C has b = 2, D_1/P_0 = 8%, and an expected growth rate of 8 percent. Is the stock in equilibrium? Explain, and if the stock is not in equilibrium, explain how equilibrium will be restored.
e. What percentage of Stock A's total risk is market risk? Explain.

Solutions to Self-Test Problems

ST5-1   a. The realized return in Period t is estimated as follows:

$$\bar{k}_t = \frac{D_t + P_t - P_{t-1}}{P_{t-1}}.$$

For example, the realized return for Stock A in 1977 is −20.0%:

$$\bar{k}_{77} = \frac{D_{77} + P_{77} - P_{76}}{P_{76}}$$

$$= \frac{\$2.00 + \$16.00 - \$22.50}{\$22.50}$$

$$= -0.200 = -20.0\%.$$

The table that follows shows the realized returns for each stock in each year, the averages for the five years, and the same data for the portfolio:

Year	Stock A's Return, $\bar{k}_A$	Stock B's Return, $\bar{k}_B$	Portfolio AB's Return, $\bar{k}_{AB}$
1977	−20.0%	−11.1%	−15.6%
1978	20.0	19.4	19.7
1979	33.2	43.6	38.4
1980	−2.0	−6.2	−4.1
1981	25.8	11.2	18.5
$\bar{k}_{Avg.}$	11.4%	11.4%	11.4%

b. The standard deviation of returns is estimated, using Equation 5-3a, as follows:

$$\text{Estimated } \sigma = \sqrt{\frac{\sum_{t=1}^{n} (\bar{k}_t - \bar{k}_{Avg.})^2}{n-1}}. \tag{5-3a}$$

For Stock A, the estimated σ is 21.9%:

$$\sigma_A = \sqrt{\frac{(-20.0 - 11.4)^2 + (20.0 - 11.4)^2 + \ldots + (25.8 - 11.4)^2}{5 - 1}}$$

$$= \sqrt{\frac{1,922.08}{4}} = 21.9\%.$$

The standard deviations of returns for Stock B and for the portfolio are similarly determined, and they are shown below:

	Stock A	Stock B	Portfolio AB
Average return, $\bar{k}_{Avg.}$	11.4%	11.4%	11.4%
Standard deviation, σ	21.9%	21.9%	21.3%

c. Since the risk reduction from diversification is small (σ_{AB} falls only from 21.9% to 21.3%), the most likely value of the correlation coefficient is 0.9. If the correlation coefficient were 0.0 or -0.9, the risk reduction would have been much larger. In fact, the correlation coefficient between Stocks A and B is 0.9.

d. If more randomly selected stocks were added to the portfolio, σ_p would decline to somewhere in the vicinity of 15 percent. σ_p would have remained constant only if the correlation coefficient were $+1.0$, which is most unlikely. σ_p would have declined to zero only if the correlation coefficient r were less than or equal to zero, which is also unlikely.

ST5-2 a. A plot of the approximate regression line is shown in the figure on the next page. The equation of the regression line is

$$\bar{k}_i = a + b\bar{k}_M.$$

The stock's beta coefficient is given by the slope of the regression line:

$$b = \text{Slope} = \frac{\text{Rise}}{\text{Run}} = \frac{\Delta Y}{\Delta X} = \frac{22 - 10}{32 - 12} = \frac{12}{20} = 0.6.$$

The intercept a seems to be about 3.5. Note: Using a calculator with a least squares regression routine, we find the exact equation to be $\bar{k}_X = 3.7 + 0.56\bar{k}_M$, with r = 0.98.

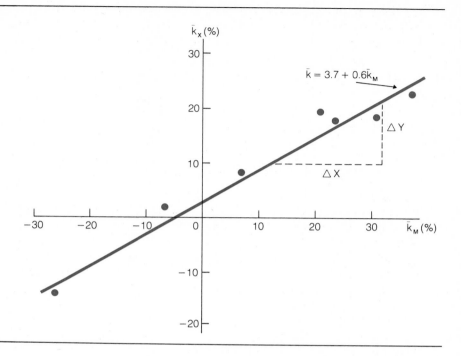

b. The average return for Stock X was calculated as follows:

$$\bar{k}_{Avg.} = \frac{(-14.0 + 23.0 + \cdots + 18.2)}{7} = 10.6\%.$$

The average return on the market portfolio was determined similarly.

The standard deviation of returns is estimated using Equation 5-3a:

$$\text{Estimated } \sigma = \sqrt{\frac{\sum_{t=1}^{n}(\bar{k}_t - \bar{k}_{Avg.})^2}{n - 1}}. \qquad (5\text{-}3a)$$

For Stock X, the estimated σ is 13.1%:

$$\sigma_X = \sqrt{\frac{(-14.0 - 10.6)^2 + (23.0 - 10.6)^2 + \cdots + (18.2 - 10.6)^2}{7 - 1}}$$

$$= 13.1\%.$$

The standard deviation of returns for the market portfolio is similarly determined to be 22.6 percent. The results are summarized below:

	Stock X	Market Portfolio
Average return, $\bar{k}_{Avg.}$	10.6%	12.1%
Standard deviation, σ	13.1%	22.6%

Several points should be noted: (1) σ_M over this particular period is higher than the historic average σ_M of about 15 percent, indicating that the stock market was relatively volatile during the late 1970s; (2) Stock X, with $\sigma_X = 13.1\%$, has much less total risk than an average stock, with $\sigma_{Avg.} \approx 28\%$; and (3) this example demonstrates that it is possible for a very low-risk single stock to have less risk than a portfolio of average stocks, since $\sigma_X < \sigma_M$.

c. Since Stock X is in equilibrium and plots on the security market line (SML), and given the further assumption that $\hat{k}_X = \bar{k}_X$ and $\hat{k}_M = \bar{k}_M$—and this assumption often does *not* hold—then this equation must hold:

$$\bar{k}_X = R_F + b\,(\bar{k}_M - R_F).$$

This equation can be solved for the risk-free rate, R_F, which is the only unknown:

$$10.6 = R_F + 0.6\,(12.1 - R_F)$$
$$= R_F + 7.3 - 0.6R_F$$
$$0.4R_F = 10.6 - 7.3 = 3.3$$
$$R_F = 3.3/0.4$$
$$= 8.3\%.$$

d. The SML is plotted on the following page. Data on the risk-free security ($b = 0$, $R_F = 8.3\%$)and Security X ($b = 0.6$, $\bar{k}_X = 10.6\%$) provide the two points through which the SML can be drawn. k_M provides a third point.

e. In theory, you would be indifferent between the two stocks. Since they have the same beta, their relevant risks are identical, and in equilibrium they should provide the same returns. The two stocks would be represented by a single point on the SML. Stock Y, with the higher standard deviation, has more diversifiable risk, but this risk will be eliminated in a well diversified portfolio, so the market will compensate the investor only for bearing market or relevant risk.

The Security Market Line

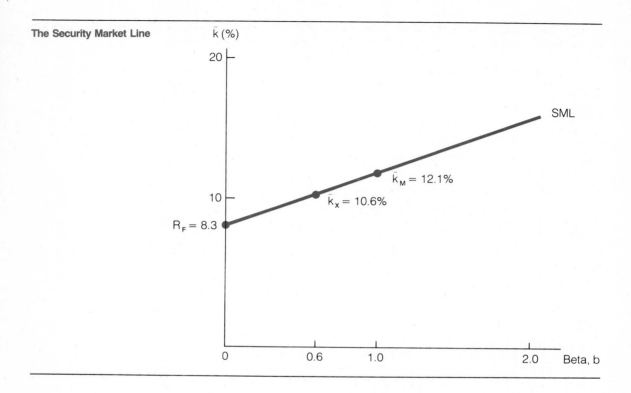

In practice, it is possible that Stock Y would have a slightly higher required return, but this premium for diversifiable risk would be small.

f. The equilibrium price is calculated using the Gordon equation:

$$P_0 = \frac{D_1}{k - g}.$$

Given the following facts,

$$D_1 = \$3.50,$$
$$g = 5.0\%, \text{ and}$$
$$k = \bar{k}_X = 10.6\%,$$

then,

$$P_0 = \frac{\$3.50}{0.106 - 0.050} = \$62.50.$$

Probably the best place to find an extension of the basic contents of Chapter 5 and the appendices is one of the investments textbooks listed in the Chapter 4 references. Those who want to start at the beginning in studying the CAPM in depth should see

Markowitz, Harry M., "Portfolio Selection," *Journal of Finance,* March 1952, 77-91.
Sharpe, William F., "Capital Asset Prices: A Theory of Market Equilibrium under Conditions of Risk," *Journal of Finance,* September 1964, 425-442.

Literally thousands of articles providing theoretical extensions and tests of the theory have appeared in the last twenty years. Some of the more important earlier papers appeared in a book compiled by Jensen:

Jensen, Michael C., ed., *Studies in the Theory of Capital Markets* (New York: Praeger, 1972).

However, the validity of the empirical tests has been questioned; see

Roll, Richard, "A Critique of the Asset Pricing Theory's Tests," *Journal of Financial Economics,* vol. 4 (March 1977), 129-176.
Wallace, Anise, "Is Beta Dead?" *Institutional Investor,* vol. 14 (July 1980), 23-30.

The following articles provide some valuable general insights into the use of the CAPM in financial management:

Beaver, W. H., Paul Kettler, and Myron Scholes, "The Association between Market Determined and Accounting Determined Risk Measures," *Accounting Review,* vol. 45 (October 1970), 654.
Blume, M. E., "Betas and Their Regression Tendencies," *Journal of Finance,* vol. 30 (June 1975), 785-795.
Bowman, R. G., "The Theoretical Relationship between Systematic Risk and Financial (Accounting) Variables," *Journal of Finance,* vol. 34 (June 1979), 617-630.
Rosenberg, Barr, and James Guy, "Beta and Investment Fundamentals," *Financial Analysts' Journal,* vol. 32 (May-June 1976), 60-72.

Additional references for the CAPM are given in Chapter 12.

Selected References

Chapter 5 dealt with the relationship between risk and rates of return in an intuitive, informal manner. This appendix examines the relationship more systematically. First, we examine the basic elements of portfolio theory. Second, we show how portfolio theory has been extended to relate assets' risks to their rates of return through the capital asset pricing model (CAPM). Finally, we discuss some of the empirical studies that have been undertaken (1) to test the validity of the CAPM and (2) to measure the specific relationship between risk and return.

Appendix 5A

Risk Aversion, Portfolio Theory, and the Capital Asset Pricing Model

A *portfolio* is defined as a combination of assets, and *portfolio theory* deals with the selection of *efficient* portfolios, or portfolios that provide either (1) the highest possible expected return for any specified degree of risk or (2) the lowest possible risk for any specified rate of return.

Portfolio Theory

The expected rate of return on a portfolio is always a linear function—it is simply a weighted average of the expected returns of the individual securities in the portfolio. For example, if 50 percent of the portfolio is

Expected Return on a Portfolio

invested in a security with a 6 percent expected return (Security A), and 50 percent in one with a 10 percent expected return (Security B), the expected rate of return on the portfolio is

$$\hat{k}_p = x(6\%) + (1 - x)(10\%) \qquad (5A\text{-}1)$$
$$= 0.5(6\%) + 0.5(10\%) = 8\%.$$

Here $\hat{k}_p$ is the expected return on the portfolio, x is the percentage of the portfolio invested in A, and $(1 - x)$ is the percentage invested in B. If all of the portfolio were invested in A, the expected return would be 6 percent. If all were invested in B, the expected return would be 10 percent. If the portfolio contained some of each, the expected portfolio return would be a linear combination of the two securities' expected returns—it is 8 percent in our present case. Therefore, given the expected returns on the individual securities, the expected return on the portfolio depends on the percentage of the total funds invested in each security.[1]

Figure 5A-1 illustrates the set of expected returns for our two-asset portfolio. The line AB represents all possible expected returns when Securities A and B are combined in different proportions.

**Figure 5A-1
Expected Rate of Return
on a Two-Asset Portfolio**

$$\hat{k}_p = \sum_{i=1}^{n} x_i \hat{k}_i. \qquad (5A\text{-}1a)$$

Here x_i is the percent of the portfolio invested in the ith asset, and $\hat{k}_i$ is the expected return on the ith asset.

The riskiness of a portfolio is measured by the standard deviation of expected returns. Equation 5A-2 is used to calculate the standard deviation of a portfolio:[2]

Riskiness of a Portfolio

$$\sigma_p = \sqrt{\sum_{j=1}^{n} (\hat{k}_{pj} - \hat{k}_p)^2 \, P_j}. \qquad (5A\text{-}2)$$

Here σ_p is the standard deviation of the portfolio's expected returns; $\hat{k}_{pj}$ is the expected return on the portfolio given the jth state of the economy; $\hat{k}_p$ is the expected value of the n possible returns; and P_j is the probability of occurrence of the jth state of the economy. Figure 5A-2 illustrates two

Probability Density

Portfolio Y

Portfolio X

$\hat{k}_p$

Return

**Figure 5A-2
Distributions of Portfolio Returns**

possible distributions of expected portfolio returns for two portfolios. Portfolio X has more variability than Portfolio Y; consequently, investors view Portfolio X as being riskier than Y. Incidentally, the graph shows the expected returns on the two portfolios as being equal. Typically, in equilibrium this equality would not hold—the expected return on the riskier portfolio, X, would be higher, so the entire distribution for Portfolio X in Figure 5A-2 would be shifted to the right.

A fundamental aspect of portfolio theory is the idea that the riskiness inherent in any single asset held in a portfolio is different from the riskiness of that asset held in isolation. As we shall see, it is possible for a given asset to be quite risky when held in isolation, but to be relatively safe if held in a portfolio.

---

[2] See Chapter 5 for an illustration of the procedure for calculating the standard deviation of the expected returns on an asset.

**Measuring the
Riskiness of a
Portfolio: The
Two-Asset Case**

Equation 5A-2 could be used to calculate the riskiness of a portfolio, but, under the assumption that the distributions of returns on the individual securities are normal, a complicated looking but operationally simple equation can be derived from Equation 5A-2 to determine the risk of a two-asset portfolio:[3]

$$\sigma_p = \sqrt{x^2\sigma_A^2 + (1 - x)^2\sigma_B^2 + 2x(1 - x)\, r_{AB}\sigma_A\sigma_B}. \qquad (5A\text{-}3)$$

Here σ_p is the standard deviation of the portfolio; x is the fraction of the portfolio invested in Security A; $(1 - x)$ is the fraction invested in Security B; σ_A and σ_B are the standard deviations of returns on Securities A and B; and r_{AB} is the correlation between the two securities. Look back at Figure 5-4 in Chapter 5 to get an "intuitive feel" for Equation 5A-3. Also, note that the term $r_{AB}\sigma_A\sigma_B$ is called the covariance (cov) between Securities A and B.

As was indicated at the beginning of the appendix, portfolio theory is used to select *efficient* portfolios—those portfolios which provide the highest expected return for any degree of risk, or the lowest degree of risk for any given expected return. To illustrate the concept, assume that two investment securities, A and B, are available, and that we have a specific amount of money to invest in these securities. We can allocate our funds between the securities in any proportion. Security A has an expected rate of return of $\hat{k}_A = 5\%$ and a standard deviation of returns $\sigma_A = 4\%$; for Security B the expected return is $\hat{k}_B = 8\%$ and the standard deviation is $\sigma_B = 10\%$. Our first task is to determine the set of *attainable* portfolios, and then we must select the subset of *efficient* portfolios.

We need data on the degree of correlation between the two securities' expected returns, r_{AB}, in order to construct the attainable and efficient sets of portfolios. Let us develop the portfolios' expected returns $\hat{k}_p$ and standard deviations of returns σ_p using three different degrees of correlation: $r_{AB} = +1.0$, $r_{AB} = 0$, and $r_{AB} = -1.0$. (Of course, only one correlation can exist; our example simply shows three alternative situations.)

To calculate $\hat{k}_p$ and σ_p, we use Equations 5A-1 and 5A-3:

$$\hat{k}_p = x\hat{k}_A + (1 - x)\hat{k}_B, \qquad (5A\text{-}1)$$

and

$$\sigma_p = \sqrt{x^2\sigma_A^2 + (1 - x)^2\sigma_B^2 + 2x(1 - x)r_{AB}\sigma_A\sigma_B}. \qquad (5A\text{-}3)$$

---

[3] Equation 5A-3 is derived from Equation 5A-2 in standard statistics books. Notice that if $x = 1$, all of the portfolio is invested in Security A, and Equation 5A-2 reduces to

$$\sigma_p = \sqrt{\sigma_A^2} = \sigma_A.$$

The portfolio contains but a single asset, so the risk of the portfolio and that of the asset are identical.

Equations 5A-2 and 5A-3 can be expanded to include any number of assets by adding additional terms, but we shall not do so here.

We now substitute in the given values for $\hat{k}_A$ and $\hat{k}_B$, then solve Equation 5A-1 for $\hat{k}_p$ at different values of x. For example, when x equals 0.75, then

$$\hat{k}_p = 0.75\,(5\%) + 0.25\,(8\%) = 5.75\%.$$

Similarly, we can substitute in the given values for σ_A, σ_B, and r_{AB}, then solve Equation 5A-3 for σ_p at different values of x. For example, when $r_{AB} = 0$ and x = 75%, then

$$\sigma_p = \sqrt{(0.5625)(16\%) + (0.0625)(100\%) + 2(0.75)(0.25)(0)(4\%)(10\%)}$$
$$= \sqrt{9\% + 6.25\%} = \sqrt{15.25\%} = 3.9\%.$$

The equations can be solved for other values of x and for the three cases, $r_{AB} = +1.0$, 0, and -1.0. Table 5A-1 gives the solution values for x = 100%, 75%, 50%, 25%, and 0%, and Figure 5A-3 gives plots of $\hat{k}_p$, σ_p, and the attainable set of portfolios for each case. In both the table and the graphs, note the following points:

Percent of Portfolio in Security A (value of x)	Percent of Portfolio in Security B (value of 1 − x)	$r_{AB} = +1.0$		$r_{AB} = 0$		$r_{AB} = -1.0$	
		$\hat{k}_p$	σ_p	$\hat{k}_p$	σ_p	$\hat{k}_p$	σ_p
100	0	5.00	4.0	5.00	4.0	5.00	4.0
75	25	5.75	5.5	5.75	3.9	5.75	0.5
50	50	6.50	7.0	6.50	5.4	6.50	3.0
25	75	7.25	8.5	7.25	7.6	7.25	6.5
0	100	8.00	10.0	8.00	10.0	8.00	10.0

Table 5A-1
$\hat{k}_p$ and σ_p under Various Assumptions

1. The three graphs across the top row of Figure 5A-3 designate Case I, where the two assets are perfectly positively correlated, that is, $r_{AB} = +1.0$. The middle row of graphs is for the zero correlation case, and the bottom row is for perfect negative correlation.
2. All three cases are theoretical. Case II (zero correlation) produces graphs which would most closely resemble those of a real world example, where the correlation would probably be in the range of 0.5 to 0.7.
3. The left column of graphs shows the expected returns with different combinations of A and B; the middle column shows risk in the three cases; and the right column shows the attainable set of risk-return combinations.
4. In the left column of graphs, since $\hat{k}_p$ is a linear function of x, the graphs are identical in each of the three cases. Thus, we see that $\hat{k}_p$ does not depend on correlation.
5. In the middle column of graphs we see that σ_p is linear in Case I,

Figure 5A-3
Illustrations of Portfolio Returns, Risk, and the
Attainable Set of Portfolios

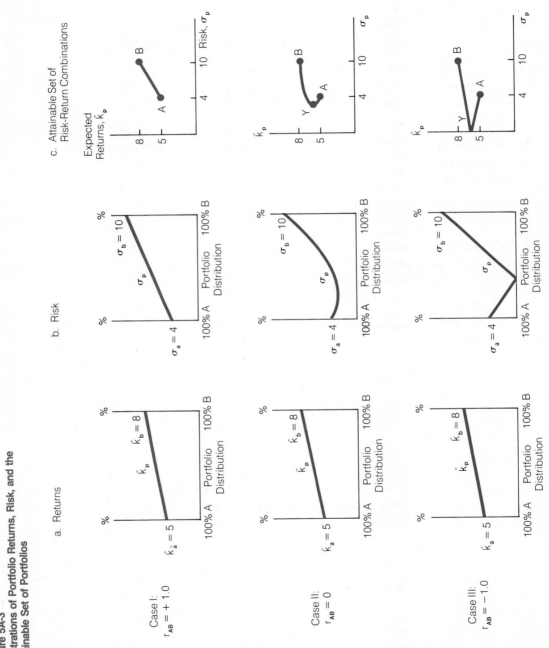

where $r_{AB} = +1.0$; it is nonlinear in Case II; and Case III of the figure shows that risk can be completely diversified away when $r_{AB} = -1.0$. Thus, σ_p does depend on correlation, although $\hat{k}_p$ does not.

6. The right column of graphs shows the attainable set of portfolios consisting of Securities A and B. With only two securities, the attainable set is a curve or line.[4]

7. That part of the attainable set from Y to B in Cases II and III is defined to be *efficient*; the part from A to Y is inefficient. That is, for any degree of risk on the line segment AY, a higher return can be found on segment YB.

With only two assets, the feasible set of portfolios is a line (or curve) as shown in the third column of graphs of Figure 5A-3. However, if we were to increase the number of assets, we would obtain a space, or area, such as the shaded area in Figure 5A-4. The points A, H, G, and F represent single securities (or portfolios containing only one security). All the other points in the shaded area, including its boundaries, represent portfolios of two or more securities. The space itself is called the *feasible* (or attainable) region. Each point in this area represents a particular portfolio with a risk of σ_p and an expected return of $\hat{k}_p$. For example, point X represents one such portfolio's risk and expected return, as do B, C, D, and E.

Expected Portfolio
Returns, $\hat{k}_p$

Efficient Set (BCDE)

E

D

F

C — X

G

B

Feasible, or
Attainable, Set

H

A

Portfolio Risk σ_p

**Figure 5A-4
The Efficient Set
of Investments**

[4] If we differentiate Equation 5A-3, set the derivative equal to zero, and then solve for x, we obtain the fraction of the portfolio which should be invested in Security A if we wish to have the least-risk portfolio. Here is the equation:

$$x = \frac{\sigma_B(\sigma_B - r_{AB}\sigma_A)}{\sigma_A^2 + \sigma_B^2 - 2r_{AB}\sigma_A\sigma_B}. \qquad (5A\text{-}4)$$

As a rule, we limit x to the range 0 to 1.0, that is, if the solution value is $x > 1.0$, set $x = 1.0$, while if x is negative, set $x = 0$.

The Efficient Frontier

Given the full set of potential portfolios that could be constructed from the available assets, which portfolio should *actually* be constructed? This choice involves two separate decisions: (1) determining the efficient set of portfolios, and (2) choosing from the efficient set the single portfolio that is best for the individual investor.

As we noted earlier, an *efficient portfolio* is defined as a portfolio that provides the highest possible expected return for any degree of risk, or the lowest possible degree of risk for any expected return. In Figure 5A-4, the boundary line BCDE defines the *efficient set of portfolios*.[5] Portfolios to the left of the efficient set are not possible because they lie outside of the attainable set. In other words, there is no set of x_i values that will yield a portfolio with an expected rate of return, $\hat{k}_p$, and risk, σ_p, represented by a point to the left of BCDE. Portfolios to the right of the boundary line are inefficient because some other portfolio would provide either a higher return with the same degree of risk or a lower risk for the same rate of return. To illustrate, consider Point X. Portfolio C provides the same rate of return as does Portfolio X, but C is less risky. At the same time, Portfolio D is as risky as Portfolio X, but D provides a higher expected rate of return. Points C and D (and other points on the boundary of the efficient set between C and D) are said to *dominate* Point X. Similarly, points on the curve from B to A and from E to F are dominated by points on the efficient set BCDE.

Risk-Return Indifference Curves

Given the efficient set of portfolio combinations, which specific portfolio should an investor choose? To determine the optimal portfolio for a particular investor, we must know the investor's attitude toward risk as reflected in his or her risk-return tradeoff function.

An investor's risk-return preference function is based on the standard economic concept of indifference curves as illustrated in Figure 5A-5. The curves labelled I_A and I_B represent the indifference curves of Individuals A and B. Ms. A is indifferent with regard to the riskless 5 percent portfolio, a portfolio with an expected return of 6 percent but with a risk of $\sigma_p = 1.5$ percent, and so on. Mr. B is equally well satisfied with a riskless 5 percent return, an expected 6 percent return with risk of $\sigma_p = 3.3$ percent, and so on.

Notice that Ms. A requires a higher expected rate of return to compensate her for a given amount of risk than does Mr. B; thus, Ms. A is said to be more *risk averse* than Mr. B. Her higher risk aversion causes

---

[5] A computational procedure for determining the efficient set of portfolios was developed by Harry Markowitz and first reported in his article, "Portfolio Selection," *Journal of Finance*, vol. 7 (March 1952), 77-91. In this article Markowitz developed the basic concepts of portfolio theory.

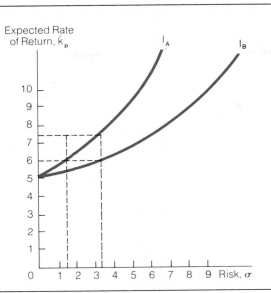

Ms. A to require a higher *risk premium*—defined as the difference between the 5 percent riskless return and the required return associated with any specific amount of risk—than does Mr. B. Thus, Ms. A requires a premium of 2.5 percent to compensate for a risk σ_p = 3.3 percent, while Mr. B's risk premium for this degree of risk is only 1 percent. *As a generalization, the steeper the slope of the indifference curve, the more risk averse the investor.* Thus, it is clear that Ms. A is more averse to risk than is Mr. B.

Each individual has a "map" of indifference curves; the indifference maps for Ms. A and Mr. B are shown in Figure 5A-6. (Aspects of this graph other than the indifference curves are discussed in the next section.) The higher curves denote a greater level of satisfaction (or utility). Thus, I_{B2} is better than I_{B1} because, for any level of risk such as σ_p = 3 percent, Mr. B has a higher expected return, hence greater utility. An infinite number of utility curves could be drawn for each individual, and different individuals are likely to have somewhat different sets of curves.

Figure 5A-6 also combines the feasible set of portfolios for the two-asset case with r_{AB} = 0 as it was developed in Figure 5A-3 with the indifference curves for Ms. A and Mr. B. The optimal portfolio for each investor is found at the tangency point between the efficient set of portfolios and one of the investor's indifference curves. This tangency point marks the highest level of satisfaction the investor can attain. Ms. A, who is more risk averse than Mr. B, chooses a portfolio with a lower expected return

The Optimal Portfolio
for an Investor

Figure 5A-6
Selecting the Optimal
Portfolio of Risky Assets

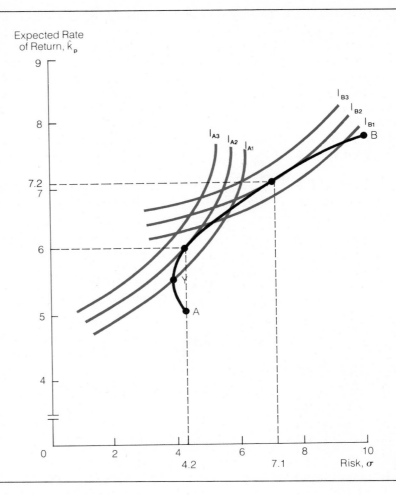

(about 6 percent) but a riskiness of only σ_p = 4.2 percent. Mr. B picks a combination of securities (a portfolio) that provides an expected return of about 7.2 percent and has a risk of about σ_p = 7.1 percent. Ms. A selects a portfolio more heavily weighted with the low-risk security, while Mr. B's portfolio contains a larger proportion of the more risky security.[6]

---

[6] Ms. A's portfolio would contain 67 percent Security A and 33 percent Security B, while Mr. B's portfolio would consist of 27 percent Security A and 73 percent Security B. These percentages can be determined from Figure 5A-3(a) or by Equation 5A-1 by simply seeing what percentage of the two securities is consistent with k_p = 6.0 percent and 7.2 percent. For example, x(5%) + (1 − x) (8%) = 7.2% when x = 0.27 and (1 − x) = 0.73.

As we have now seen, the riskiness of a portfolio of assets as measured by its standard deviation of returns is generally less than the average of the risks of the individual assets as measured by their standard deviations. This phenomenon, in turn, has direct implications for the required rate of return on a given security: Since investors generally hold portfolios of securities, not just one security, it is reasonable to consider the riskiness of a security in terms of its contribution to the riskiness of the portfolio rather than in terms of its riskiness if held in isolation. The *Capital Asset Pricing Model* (CAPM) was developed to analyze the riskiness and the required rates of return on assets when they are held in portfolios.

As in all financial theories, a number of assumptions were made in the development of the CAPM; they have been summarized by Michael C. Jensen as follows:[7]

1. All investors are single-period expected utility of terminal wealth maximizers who choose among alternative portfolios on the basis of means and standard deviations of portfolio returns.
2. All investors can borrow or lend an unlimited amount at a given risk-free rate of interest, R_F, and there are no restrictions on short sales of any asset.
3. All investors have identical subjective estimates of the means, variances, and covariances of return among all assets; that is, investors have homogeneous expectations.
4. All assets are perfectly divisible and perfectly liquid (that is, marketable at the going price), and there are no transactions costs.
5. There are no taxes.
6. All investors are price takers (that is, all investors assume that their own buying and selling activity will not affect stock prices).
7. The quantities of all assets are given and fixed.

Theoretical extensions in the literature, attempting to relax the basic CAPM assumptions, have yielded results that are generally consistent with the basic theory. However, the assumptions which underlie the model are both strong and unrealistic. Therefore, the validity of the model can only be established through empirical tests. More will be said later in this appendix about the empirical validity of the CAPM.

In Figure 5A-6 we graphed a set of portfolio opportunities for the two-asset case and illustrated a method of selecting the optimal portfolio. In Figure 5A-7 we have a similar diagram for the N-asset case, but here we also include a risk-free asset with a return R_F. The riskless asset has zero risk, so it is plotted on the vertical axis.

The Capital Asset Pricing Model (CAPM)

Basic Assumptions of the CAPM

The Capital Market Line (CML)

[7] M. C. Jensen, "Capital Markets: Theory and Evidence," *Bell Journal*, Autumn 1972, 357-398.

Figure 5A-7
Investor Equilibrium:
Combining the Risk-Free
Asset with the Market
Portfolio

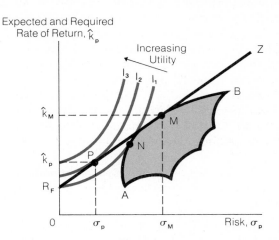

Figure 5A-7 shows the feasible set of portfolios of risky assets (the shaded area) and a set of indifference curves (I_1, I_2, I_3), which represent the tradeoff between risk and return for a particular investor. Point N, where the indifference curve is tangent to the efficient set ANMB, represents a possible equilibrium; it is the point on the efficient set where the investor obtains the highest return for a given amount of risk, σ_p, or the smallest risk for a given expected return, $\hat{k}_p$.

However, the investor can do better than Portfolio N; it is possible to reach a higher indifference curve. In addition to the risky securities represented in the feasible set of portfolios, we now have a risk-free asset that yields R_F. With the additional alternative of investing in the risk-free asset, the investor can create a new portfolio that combines the risk-free asset with a portfolio of risky assets. This enables us to achieve any combination of risk and return lying along a straight line connecting R_F and the point of tangency of that straight line at M on the portfolio opportunities curve.[8] All portfolios on the line R_FMZ are preferred to the other

---

[8] The risk-return combinations between a risk-free asset and a risky asset (a single stock or a portfolio of stocks) will always be linear. To see this, consider the equations for return, $\hat{k}_p$, and risk, σ_p, for any combination:

$$\hat{k}_p = xR_F + (1 - x)\hat{k}_M,\tag{5A-1}$$

and

$$\sigma_p = \sqrt{x^2\sigma_{R_F}^2 + (1 - x)^2\sigma_M^2 + 2x(1 - x)\, r_{R_FM}\sigma_{R_F}\sigma_M}.\tag{5A-3}$$

Equation 5A-1 is obviously linear. For Equation 5A-3, we know that R_F is the risk-free asset, so $\sigma_{R_F} =$
(continued)

risky portfolio opportunities on curve ANMB; the points on the line R_FMZ represent the best attainable combinations of risk and return.

Given the new opportunity set R_FMZ, our investor will move from Point N to Point P, which is on the highest attainable risk-return indifference curve. Note that line R_FMZ dominates the opportunities that could have been achieved from the portfolio opportunities curve ANMB alone. In general, since investors can include both the risk-free security and a fraction of the risky portfolio, M, in a portfolio, it will be possible to move to a point such as P. In addition, if the investor can borrow as well as lend (lending is equivalent to buying risk-free securities) at the riskless rate R_F, it is possible to move out the line segment MZ, and one would do so if the utility indifference curve were tangent to R_FMZ in that section.[9]

Under the conditions set forth in Figure 5A-7, all investors would hold portfolios lying on the line R_FMZ; this implies that they would hold only efficient portfolios that are linear combinations of the risk-free security and the risky portfolio M. For the capital market to be in equilibrium, M must be a portfolio that contains every asset in exact proportion to that asset's fraction of the total market value of all assets; that is, if Security i is x percent of the total market value of all securities, x percent of the market portfolio M will consist of Security i. In effect, M represents "the market." Thus, in equilibrium all investors will hold efficient portfolios with standard deviation, return combinations along the line R_FMZ. The particular location of a given individual on the line will be determined by the point at which the indifference curve is tangent to the line, and this in turn reflects the investor's attitude toward risk, or degree of risk aversion.

0; hence $\sigma_{R_F}^2$ is also zero. Using this information, we can simplify Equation 5A-3 as follows:

$$\sigma_p = \sqrt{(1 - x)^2 \sigma_M^2}$$
$$= (1 - x)\sigma_M.$$

Thus σ_p is also linear when a riskless asset is combined with a portfolio of risky assets.

We see, then, that a portfolio with x percent invested in the riskless asset and $(1 - x)$ invested in the market portfolio of risky assets will have a linear risk-return relationship. For example, if 100 percent of the portfolio is invested in $R_F = 8$ percent, the portfolio return will be 8 percent with $\sigma_p = 0$. If 100 percent is invested in M, with $\hat{k}_M = 12$ percent and $\sigma_M = 10$ percent, then $\sigma_p = 1.0(10$ percent$) = 10$ percent, and $k_p = 0(8$ percent$) + 1.0(12$ percent$) = 12$ percent. If 50 percent of the portfolio is invested in M and 50 percent in the risk-free asset, then $\sigma_p = 0.5(10$ percent$) = 5$ percent, and $\hat{k}_p = 0.5(8$ percent$) + 0.5(12$ percent$) = 10$ percent. Plotting these points will reveal the linear relationship given as R_FPMZ in Figure 5A-7.

[9] An investor who is relatively averse to risk will be at a point such as P, holding some of the risky market portfolio and some of the riskless asset. An investor less averse to risk will move out beyond M toward Z, borrowing to do so. Such an investor might be buying stocks on margin and using personal leverage. If the borrowing rate is higher than R_F, then the line R_FMZ will tilt down (i.e., be less steep) beyond M. This condition would invalidate the basic CAPM equation or at least require it to be modified. Therefore, the assumption of equal lending and borrowing rates is crucial to the pure CAPM theory.

The line R_FMZ in Figure 5A-7 is defined as the *capital market line* (CML). It has an intercept of R_F and a slope (using the "rise over run" concept) of $(\hat{k}_M - R_F)/\sigma_M$. Thus:

$$\hat{k}_p = R_F + \left(\frac{\hat{k}_M - R_F}{\sigma_M}\right)\sigma_p. \qquad (5A-5)$$

In words, the expected return on any portfolio is equal to the riskless rate plus a risk premium equal to $(\hat{k}_M - R_F)/\sigma_M$ times the portfolio's standard deviation. Therefore, the CML for efficient portfolios shows a linear relationship between expected return and risk, and it can be rewritten as follows:

$$\hat{k}_p = R_F + \lambda\sigma_p. \qquad (5A-6)$$

Here:

$\hat{k}_p$ = expected return on an efficient portfolio.
R_F = risk-free interest rate.
λ = market price of risk (pronounced "lambda"); $\lambda = (\hat{k}_M - R_F)/\sigma_M$ = slope of the CML.
σ_p = standard deviation of returns on an efficient portfolio.
$\hat{k}_M$ = expected return on the market portfolio.
σ_M = standard deviation of returns on the market portfolio.

All efficient portfolios, including the market portfolio, lie on the CML. Hence,

$$\hat{k}_M = R_F + \lambda\sigma_M. \qquad (5A-6a)$$

Both Equations 5A-6 and 5A-6a state that the expected return on an efficient portfolio in equilibrium is equal to a risk-free return plus the market price of risk multiplied by the standard deviation of the portfolio's returns. This relationship is graphed in Figure 5A-8. The CML is drawn as a straight line with an intercept at R_F, the risk-free return, and a slope equal to the market price of risk (λ), which is the market risk premium $(\hat{k}_M - R_F)$ divided by σ_M. The market price of risk, or the slope of the CML, reflects the attitudes of individuals in the aggregate (that is, all individuals) toward risk.

**The Security
Market Line**

The next step in the development of the CAPM calls for going from risk and returns on *portfolios* to risk and returns on *individual securities*. We stated in Chapter 5 that, under the CAPM theory, the riskiness of a security is measured by its beta coefficient (b), and that the required return (and, in equilibrium, the expected return also) is found by this equation:

$$\hat{k}_i = k_i = R_F + b_i(k_M - R_F). \qquad (5A-7)$$

Expected and Required
Rate of Return, $\hat{k}_p$

$CML = R_F + \lambda\sigma_p$

$\hat{k}_M$

R_F

0 $\quad$ σ_M $\quad$ Risk, σ_p

**Figure 5A-8
Expected Return on an
Efficient Portfolio**

Equation 5A-7 is actually derived from Equation 5A-6. However, the derivation involves some difficult mathematical statistics, so it is not presented here.[10]

The idea that risk should be associated with portfolios and that the relevant risk of an individual security depends upon the security's effect on portfolio risk is quite logical. Thus, the conclusions of the CAPM are intuitively appealing. As we noted earlier, however, the precise form of

**Empirical Tests
of the CAPM**[11]

---

[10] The interested reader is referred to E. F. Fama and M. H. Miller, *The Theory of Finance* (New York: Holt, Rinehart & Winston, 1972), for a derivation of Equation 5A-6. Essentially, the proof involves first showing how, given a security's covariance with the market ($\sigma_i\sigma_M r_{iM}$), the security affects the market portfolio's risk. This equation results:

$$\hat{k}_i = R_F + \left[\frac{\hat{k}_M - R_F}{\sigma_M^2}\right]\sigma_i\sigma_M r_{iM}. \tag{5A-8}$$

Then, it is demonstrated that the beta coefficient, which we found in Chapter 5 by regressing a stock's return on the market return, is equal to

$$b_i = \frac{\sigma_i r_{iM}}{\sigma_M}. \tag{5A-9}$$

Thus, a stock's CAPM risk index, which is its beta coefficient, is dependent on (1) its own standard deviation, (2) its correlation with other stocks (the market), and (3) the standard deviation of returns on the market. Individual firms cannot significantly affect the market's variability, σ_M, but they can take actions that will raise or lower their own variability, σ_i, and their correlation with the market, r_{iM}. Such actions will affect the firm's beta, its required rate of return, and consequently its stock price.

[11] This section draws heavily on F. Modigliani and G. A. Pogue, "An Introduction to Risk and Returns: Concepts and Evidence," *Financial Analysts' Journal,* Mar.-Apr. and May-June 1974, reprinted in E. F. Brigham and R. E. Johnson, *Issues in Managerial Finance* (Hinsdale, Ill.: Dryden Press, 1980).

the model was developed on the basis of a set of assumptions that are most unrealistic. Therefore, while the basic CAPM equation, $k_i = R_F + b_i (k_M - R_F)$, *might* represent an accurate description of how rates of return are established in the marketplace, the model could actually be invalid if investors do not actually behave as the model assumes they do. For example, if many investors are not fully diversified, hence have not eliminated all nonmarket (or nonsystematic) risk from their portfolios, then beta would not be an adequate measure of risk, and Equation 5A-7 would not explain how required returns are really set. Also, if the rate investors must pay for money is greater than the risk-free rate (in other words, if the borrowing rate is greater than the lending rate), then the CML will not be a straight line beyond Point M in Figure 5A-7, and this will produce a "bend" in the CML in Figure 5A-8 and also invalidate the basic CAPM equation, Equation 5A-7. Thus, like all theories, the CAPM must be tested empirically and validated before it can be used with any real confidence. The literature dealing with empirical tests of the CAPM is quite extensive. We give here a brief synopsis of some of the empirical tests.

Tests of the Stability of Beta Coefficients

According to the CAPM, the beta that should be used to estimate a stock's market risk reflects investors' estimates of the stock's *future* volatility in relation to that of the market; we define this "true" beta as β_i. Obviously, we do not know now how a stock will be related to the market in the future, nor do we know how the average investor views this expected future relative volatility. All we have are data on past volatility. We can use these data to calculate *historic betas;* we define a historic beta as b_i. If the historic betas are stable over time, then there would seem to be reason for investors to use past betas as estimators of future volatility. In other words, if b_i is stable over time, then b_i is probably a good proxy for β_i. By "stable" we mean that if b_i is calculated using data from the period of, say, 1970 to 1975, then this same beta (approximately) should be found from 1976 to 1980.

Robert A. Levy, Marshal E. Blume, and others have studied the question of the stability of betas in depth.[12] Levy calculated betas for individual securities, as well as for portfolios of securities, over a range of time intervals. He concluded (1) that the betas of individual stocks are unstable, hence that past betas for *individual securities* are *not* good estimators of future risk, but (2) that betas of portfolios of ten or more randomly selected stocks are quite stable, hence that past *portfolio* betas are good estimators of future volatility. In effect, in a portfolio the errors in estimating individual securities' betas tend to offset one another. This means

---

[12] R. A. Levy, "On the Short-Term Stationarity of Beta Coefficients," *Financial Analysts' Journal*, Nov.-Dec. 1971; M. E. Blume, "On the Assessment of Risk," *Journal of Finance*, Mar. 1971, and "Betas and Their Regression Tendencies," *Journal of Finance*, June 1975.

that the CAPM is better for selecting portfolios than it is for estimating the required rate of return on an individual stock. The work of Blume and others supports Levy's position.

Estimating the Slope of the SML

As we have seen, the CAPM states that a linear relationship should exist between a security's required rate of return and its beta. Further, when the SML is graphed, the vertical axis intercept should be R_F, and the required rate of return for a stock (or portfolio) with $b = 1.0$ should be k_M, the rate of return on the market. Various researchers have attempted to test the validity of the model by calculating betas and rates of return, plotting these values, and observing whether or not (1) the intercept is equal to R_F, (2) the regression line is linear, and (3) the line passes through the point $b = 1.0$, k_M. Monthly rates of return are often used for the stocks, and both thirty day Treasury bill rates and long-term Treasury bond rates are used to estimate the value of R_F. This point is illustrated by the line labeled "theoretical SML" in Figure 5A-9.

There have been many tests designed to see if the data conform to the theoretical SML. Most of these studies actually analyze portfolios rather than individual securities because security betas are so unstable. With several notable exceptions, most of the studies have reached the following conclusions:

1. The SML is indeed linear.
2. The intercept term is not consistently equal to R_F as measured either by thirty day Treasury bills or by long-term bonds.
3. The fitted slope of the SML is unstable when the regression is run for different time periods.
4. Both company-specific (σ_e) and market (b) risk seem to influence the required returns on individual securities.

However, in a recent article, Richard Roll[13] has questioned whether it is conceptually possible to even test the CAPM. Roll's work does not indicate that the CAPM is not a valid theory, but he does show that it is not possible to prove that investors behave in accordance with the theory. Other recent work suggests that the public utilities have a unique characteristic—their distributions of expected returns are skewed to the left rather than being symmetrical—which makes their nonmarket risk important. This in turn may invalidate the CAPM for this group of stocks.[14]

This brief discussion gives some of the background on the empirical

[13] "A Critique of the Asset Pricing Theory's Tests, Part 1. On Past and Potential Testability of the Theory," *Journal of Financial Economics*, vol. 4 (1977), 129-176.

[14] See the set of articles by E. F. Brigham and R. L. Crum, W. F. Sharpe, and others in the Fall 1978 issue of *Financial Management* for more on the use of the CAPM to estimate required returns on utility stocks.

Figure 5A-9
Tests of the CAPM

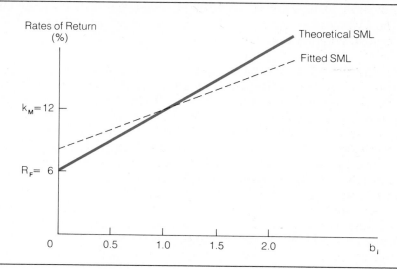

tests of the CAPM. Different observers may reach different conclusions, but most would probably agree with the following:

1. The evidence shows a significant positive relationship between realized returns and systematic risk. However, the slope of the relationship is usually less than predicted by the CAPM.
2. The relationship between risk and return appears to be linear. Empirical studies give no evidence of significant curvature in the risk-return relationship. However, Roll has suggested that this linearity may be a mathematical quirk rather than evidence that the CAPM is valid.
3. Tests that attempt to discriminate between the effects of market and company-specific risk do not yield definitive results. Both kinds of risk appear to be positively related to security returns, i.e., higher returns are required to compensate for both company-specific and market risk. However, it may be that the relationship between return and nonmarket risk is at least partly spurious—that is, it may reflect statistical problems rather than the true nature of capital markets.
4. The CAPM is an *ex ante*, or forward-looking model. The data used to test it are historical. There is no reason to believe that realized rates of return over past holding periods reflect *expected* rates of return such as the model deals with. Also, historical betas may not reflect either current or expected future risk. This lack of *ex ante* data makes it hard to really test the true CAPM.

We shall return to the empirical tests of the CAPM in Chapter 15, "The Cost of Capital," where we employ the CAPM framework to help estimate the cost of equity capital for a firm.

5A-1 An investor plans to invest in Stock A, Stock B, or some combination of the two stocks. The expected return for A is 9 percent and $\sigma_A = 4$ percent; the expected return for B is 10 percent and $\sigma_B = 5$ percent. $r_{AB} = 0.5$.

   a. Construct a table similar to Table 5A-1 giving $\hat{k}_p$ and σ_p for 100 percent, 75 percent, 50 percent, 25 percent, and 0 percent investment in Stock A. (Hint: For x = 75%, $\hat{k}_p = 9.25\%$ and $\sigma_p = 3.78\%$, while for x = 50%, $\hat{k}_p = 9.5\%$ and $\sigma_p = 3.9\%$.)

   b. Use your calculated $\hat{k}_p$ and σ_p values to graph the attainable set of portfolios, and indicate which part of the attainable set is efficient.

   c. Using hypothetical indifference curves, show how an investor might choose a portfolio consisting of Stocks A and B.

5A-2 You are planning to invest \$200,000. Two securities, A and B, are available, and you can invest in either of them or in a portfolio with some of each. Returns on A and B are correlated at the level $r_{AB} = -0.5$. You estimate that the following probability distributions of returns are applicable for A and B:

	Security A		Security B	
p_1	k_i		p_2	k_i
0.1	−10%		0.1	−30%
0.2	5		0.2	0
0.4	15		0.4	20
0.2	25		0.2	40
0.1	40		0.1	70
$\hat{k}_A =$			$\hat{k}_B =$	20.0%
$\sigma_A =$			$\sigma_B =$	25.7%

   a. The expected return for Security B is $\hat{k}_B = 20$ percent, and $\sigma_B = 25.7$ percent. Find $\hat{k}_A$ and σ_A.

   b. Use Equation 5A-4, discussed in Footnote 4, to find the value of x which produces the minimum risk portfolio. Assume $r_{AB} = -0.5$.

   c. Construct a table similar to Table 5A-1 giving $\hat{k}_p$ and σ_p for portfolios with x = 1.00, 0.75, 0.50, 0.25, 0.0, and the minimum risk value of x. (Hint: For x = 0.75, $\hat{k}_p = 16.25\%$ and $\sigma_p = 8.5\%$; for x = 0.5, $\hat{k}_p = 17.5\%$ and $\sigma_p = 11.1\%$; for x = 0.25, $\hat{k}_p = 18.75\%$ and $\sigma_p = 17.9\%$.)

   d. Graph the *feasible* set of portfolios, and identify the *efficient* section of the feasible set.

   e. Suppose your risk-return tradeoff function, or indifference curve, is tangent to the efficient set at the point where $\hat{k}_p = 18\%$. Use this information, plus the graph constructed in Part c above, to locate (approximately) your optimal portfolio. Draw in a reasonable indifference curve; indicate the percentage of your funds invested in each security; and determine the optimal portfolio's σ_p and $\hat{k}_p$. (Hint: Estimate σ_p and $\hat{k}_p$ graphically, then use the equation for $\hat{k}_p$ to determine x.)

f. Now suppose a riskless asset with a return $R_F = 10\%$ becomes available. How would this change the investment opportunity set? Explain *why* the investment opportunity set becomes linear.

g. Given the indifference curve in Part e above, would you change your portfolio? If so, how? (Hint: Assume the indifference curves are parallel.)

h. What are the beta coefficients of Stocks A and B? [Hints: (1) Recognize that $k_i = R_F + b_i(k_M - R_F)$ and solve for b_i, and (2) assume that your preferences match those of most other investors.]

5A-3 Stock A has an expected return $\hat{k}_A = 10\%$ and $\sigma_A = 10\%$. Stock B has $\hat{k}_B = 14\%$ and $\sigma_B = 15\%$. $r_{AB} = 0$. The rate of return on riskless assets is 6%.

a. Construct a graph that shows the feasible and efficient sets, giving consideration to the existence of the riskless asset.

b. Explain what would happen to the CML if the two stocks had (a) a positive correlation coefficient or (b) a negative correlation coefficient. Assume everything else is held constant.

c. Suppose these were the *only* three securities (A, B, and riskless) in the economy, and *everyone's* indifference curves were such that they were tangent to the CML *to the right* of the point where the CML was tangent to the efficient set of risky assets. Would this represent a stable equilibrium? If not, how would an equilibrium be produced? Do *not* assume that everything else is held constant.

Appendix 5B

Estimated Risk Premiums[1]

To use the CAPM equation for estimating the required rate of return on a stock, we need three elements: the risk-free rate (R_F), the beta coefficient (b_i), and the market risk premium ($k_M - R_F$). Selecting proper values for each of these three elements presents problems. First, unless the yield curve is perfectly horizontal, then the estimate of k_i depends on the choice of a long-term or a short-term Treasury bond rate for R_F. Second, betas based on *historic* data may not reflect investors' expectations for the company's *future* risk. And third, it is difficult to obtain a reliable estimate of k_M, the expected and required return on the market portfolio; this makes it difficult to obtain a reliable estimate of the market risk premium. This appendix addresses the third of these issues.

---

[1] Much of this appendix is based on the following papers: (1) E. F. Brigham and D. K. Shome, "The Risk Premium Approach to Estimating the Cost of Common Equity Capital," *Proceedings of the Iowa State Regulatory Conference,* May 1980; (2) E. F. Brigham and D. K. Shome, "The Effects of Inflation on Capital Structure and the Cost of Capital in the 1980s," *Journal of the Midwest Finance Association,* 1980; and (3) E. F. Brigham and D. K. Shome, "Estimating the Market Risk Premium," in F. Derkinderin and R. Crum, eds., *Risk, Capital Costs, and Project Financing Decisions* (Boston: Martinus Nijhoff, 1981).

One frequently used source of data on the market risk premium is the study by Ibbotson and Sinquefield (hereafter referred to as I&S).[2] I&S first determined the historic realized rate of return for each NYSE company for each year from 1926 through 1978, after which they developed a weighted average return for each year. Next, they determined the historic realized return on a yearly basis from 1926 through 1978 for thirty day Treasury bills and long-term Treasury bonds. These data can be used to calculate "historic risk premiums." For example, the realized return on common stocks in 1926 was 11.6 percent, while the return on Treasury bills was 3.3 percent. The difference, 8.3 percent, was the 1926 "risk premium" of stocks over bills. The average "historic risk premium" from 1926 through 1978 was 8.7 percent. Doing the same thing with long-term Treasury bonds produced an average 1926-1978 historic risk premium of 7.8 percent.[3]

To understand how these data could be used to estimate the required rate of return, consider the case of AT&T in January 1981. AT&T's beta (as reported by the Value Line Investment Survey) was 0.65, Treasury bills yielded 15 percent, and long-term Treasury bonds yielded 12.1 percent. These facts, combined with the I&S data, suggest that $k_{AT\&T}$ was in the range of 17.2 percent to 20.7 percent:

$$\text{CAPM, Bills: } k_{AT\&T} = 15.0\% + 0.65(8.7\%) = 20.7\%.$$
$$\text{CAPM, Bonds: } k_{AT\&T} = 12.1\% + 0.65(7.8\%) = 17.2\%.$$

Similar calculations at other points in time would show $k_{AT\&T}$ based on short-term bills to be extremely volatile, while $k_{AT\&T}$ based on long-term bonds would be more stable and probably more realistic. Hence, most real world users of the CAPM prefer to use long-term bond yields for R_F.

Using historic risk premiums requires two rather heroic assumptions: (1) Investors expect the same stock-bond differentials to exist in the future as existed in the past. (2) Expected risk premiums are stable over time. These two assumptions imply that both risk aversion and the relative riskiness of stocks and bonds (interest rate risk on Treasury bonds) are constant over time. Evidence exists which suggests that neither assumption is correct. Therefore, using historic risk premiums will probably lead to errors in estimating k for AT&T and other companies.

The CAPM is a forward-looking, or *ex ante*, model. Therefore, we need the values of R_F and k_M that investors expect in the future, not the values that happened to exist in the past. Yields-to-maturity currently being

[2] R. G. Ibbotson and R. A. Sinquefield, *Stocks, Bonds, Bills, and Inflation: Historical Returns (1926-1978)*, (Charlottesville, Va.: Financial Analysts Research Foundation, 1979).

[3] I&S also report "geometric mean risk premiums," but the averages shown above should be used in the CAPM equation.

Figure 5B-1
Expected Rates of Return on Dow Jones
Industrials and U.S. Treasury Bonds, 1966–1981

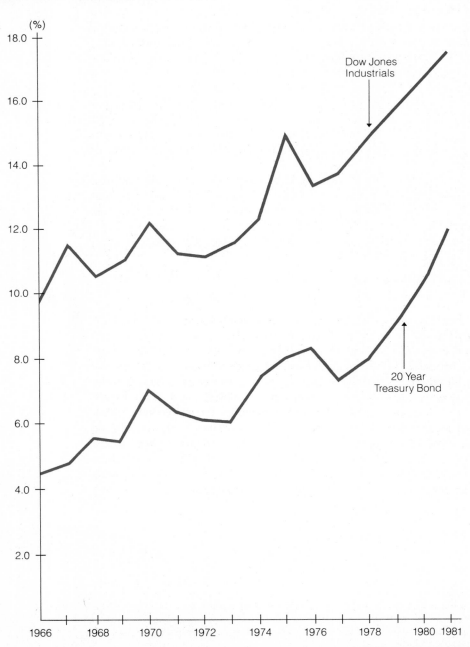

quoted on Treasury bills and bonds are forward-looking, expected returns. It is also possible to obtain data on the expected and required equilibrium returns on the market, $\hat{k}_M = k_M$. These data are developed in several ways:

1. Security analysts such as Charles Benore have surveyed samples of investors, asked for their expected returns (or risk premiums) on sets of stocks, and used the averages of the survey data to develop risk premium estimates.[4]

2. The major investment banking houses develop forecasts of future stock market returns which can be used to calculate expected risk premiums. Merrill Lynch recently reported a risk premium of 4.4 percent for stocks in general over AAA bonds; this corresponded to an expected risk premium over long-term governments of approximately 5.8 percent.[5]

3. One can obtain the dividend and growth rate forecasts of a number of analysts for a sample of stocks such as the Dow Jones Industrials or the S&P 500, determine the implied expected return on each stock, average these returns to form an expected return on a proxy for the market, and then subtract R_F to obtain an estimate of the market risk premium. Risk premiums estimated by this method are consistent with those of Benore and Merrill Lynch.

Figure 5B-1 shows a graph of expected rates of return on the market as represented by the Dow Jones Industrial stocks, along with yields-to-maturity on twenty year government bonds, from 1966 to 1981. Figure 5B-2 plots risk premiums (the difference between the two lines in Figure 5B-1) over the same time period; we can see that forward-looking risk premiums of stocks over long-term government bonds have varied from about 5 percent to about 7 percent over the last fifteen years.

Based on a Treasury bond rate of 12.1 percent, a beta of 0.65, and a market risk premium of 5.5 percent, a CAPM estimate of AT&T's cost of equity would be 15.7 percent:

$$k_{AT\&T} = 12.1\% + 0.65(5.5\%) = 15.7\%.$$

Given estimates of different companies' betas, estimates of their required rates of return could be found similarly.

---

[4] See Charles Benore, "A Survey of Investor Attitudes toward the Electric Power Industry," Paine Webber Mitchell Hutchins, various dates, generally twice a year. Benore's latest survey (June 1980) indicated a risk premium on electric utility stocks over Aa bonds of 4.23 percent, which is equivalent to a premium over Treasury bonds of about 6 percent.

[5] R. J. Hoffman and S. R. Resnick, *Investment Strategy*, Merrill Lynch, Pierce, Fenner & Smith, December 1980. Data are for September 1980.

Figure 5B-2
Risk Premiums for Dow Jones Industrials,
1966–1981

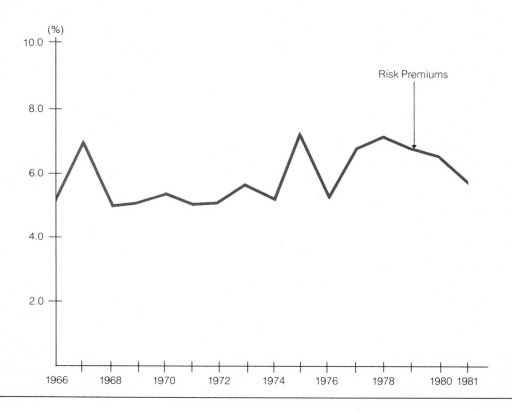

Effects of Inflation on Risk Premiums

The effects of inflation on the relative riskiness of stocks versus bonds has been hotly debated, but without definitive conclusions. Still, perhaps the most prevalent view in 1981 is expressed in Figure 5B-3. Here we see that Treasury bonds in 1978 were regarded as being somewhat risky (interest rate risk), and the observed forward-looking risk premium was about 6 percent. In 1980, interest rates fluctuated wildly, and "safe" bond portfolios lost as much as 35 percent of their values. This caused an upward revision in the perceived riskiness of bonds, so bonds moved to the right on the risk axis in Figure 5B-3. In 1981 the expected rate of future inflation was higher than it was in 1978, and this caused the SML to shift upward. Unlike the case of bonds, there is no reason to think that the perceived riskiness of equities increased from 1978 to 1981. Therefore, the risk differential between stocks and bonds narrowed between 1978 and

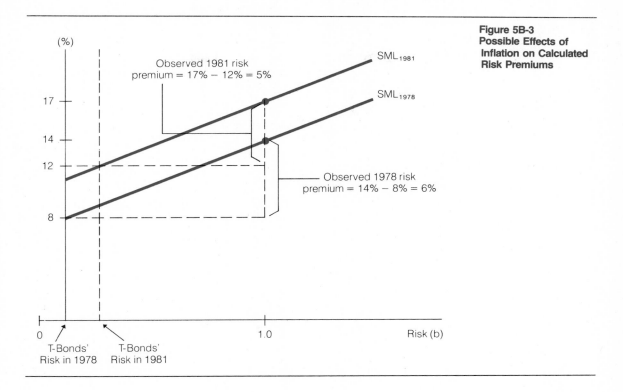

Figure 5B-3
Possible Effects of
Inflation on Calculated
Risk Premiums

1981, and this led to a decrease in the observed risk premium, from about 6 percent to about 5 percent. This scenario is somewhat speculative, but it is consistent with observed risk premium movements.

Financial Statements and Financial Forecasting

III

In order to use the valuation models developed in Part II, investors need information on companies' expected earnings, dividends, and growth rates, and on the riskiness of these items. The sources of this information are described in Chapter 6. Then, in Chapter 7, we see how financial managers make projections of future financial statements and use these projections to help plan future operations.

Analysis of Financial Statements

6

In Part II we examined compound interest and the time value of money, developed bond and stock valuation models, discussed the concept of risk, and saw that risk affects the value of financial assets. Up to this point, however, we have abstracted from the actual data used in financial analysis, as well as from the fundamental determinants of risk and profitability. In this chapter we first examine the basic financial data available to managers and investors, then look at some analytical techniques used by investors to appraise firms' relative riskiness, profit potential, and general management competence. Managers also use these same analytical techniques to measure and improve upon their own performance, judging it in terms of maximizing the firm's stock price.

The Basic Financial Statements

Of the various reports corporations issue to their stockholders, the *annual report* is by far the most important. Two types of information are given in this report. First, there is a verbal statement that describes the firm's operating results during the past year and discusses new developments that will affect future operations. Second, the report presents four basic financial statements—the *income statement*, the *balance sheet*, the *statement of retained earnings*, and the *statement of changes in financial position*. Taken together, these statements give an accounting picture of the firm's operations and financial position. Detailed data are provided for the two most recent years, along with historical summaries of key operating statistics for the past ten years.[1]

The quantitative information and the verbal information are equally important. The financial statements report *what has actually happened* to earnings and dividends over the past few years, while the verbal statements attempt to explain why things turned out the way they did. For example, suppose earnings dropped sharply last year. Management may report that the drop resulted from a strike at a key facility at the height of the busy season, but then go on to state that the strike has now been settled and that future profits are expected to bounce back. Of course, this return to profitability may not occur, and investors will want to com-

---

[1] Larger firms file even more detailed statements, giving the particulars of each major division or subsidiary, with the U.S. Securities and Exchange Commission (SEC). These reports, called *10-K reports*, are made available to stockholders upon request to a company's secretary.

pare management's past statements with subsequent results. *In any event, the information contained in the annual report is used by investors to form expectations about future earnings and dividends, and about the riskiness of these expected values.* Therefore, the annual report is obviously of great interest to investors.

Table 6-1 gives the 1980 and 1981 income statements for Carter Chemical Company, a major producer of industrial and consumer chemical products. Given at the top of the statements are net sales, from which various

The Income Statement

	1981	1980
Net sales	$3,000	$2,850
Costs and expenses		
Labor and materials	$2,544	$2,413
Depreciation	100	90
Selling	22	20
General and administrative	40	35
Lease payments on buildings	28	28
Total costs	$2,734	$2,586
Net operating income, or earnings before interest and taxes (EBIT)	$ 266	$ 264
Less interest expense		
Interest on notes payable	$ 8	$ 2
Interest on first mortgage bonds	40	42
Interest on debentures	18	3
Total interest	$ 66	$ 47
Earnings before tax	$ 200	$ 217
Federal income tax (at 40%)	80	87
Net income after taxes available to common stockholders	$ 120	$ 130
Disposition of net income		
Dividends to common stockholders	$ 100	$ 90
Addition to retained earnings	$ 20	$ 40
Per share of common stock		
Earnings per share (EPS)[a]	$ 2.40	$ 2.60
Dividends per share (DPS)[a]	$ 2.00	$ 1.80

Table 6-1
Carter Chemical Company: Income Statement for Year Ending December 31 ($ in Millions, except for per Share Data)

[a]There are 50 million shares outstanding: see Table 6-2. Calculations of EPS and DPS for 1981 are as follows:

$$EPS = \frac{\text{Net income after tax}}{\text{Shares outstanding}} = \frac{\$120,000,000}{50,000,000} = \$2.40.$$

$$DPS = \frac{\text{Dividends paid to common stockholders}}{\text{Shares outstanding}} = \frac{\$100,000,000}{50,000,000} = \$2.00.$$

costs, including income taxes, are subtracted to obtain the net income available to common stockholders.[2] A report on earnings and dividends per share is given at the bottom of the statement. In financial management, earnings per share (EPS) is called "the bottom line," denoting that of all the items on the income statement, EPS is the most important.[3] Carter earned $2.40 per share in 1981, down from $2.60 in 1980, but it raised the dividend from $1.80 to $2.00.

The Balance Sheet

The left-hand side of Carter's balance sheet, which is given in Table 6-2, shows the firm's assets, while the right-hand side of the statement shows

Table 6-2
Carter Chemical Company: Balance Sheet as of December 31 ($ in Millions)

Assets	1981	1980	Claims on Assets	1981	1980
Cash	$ 50	$ 55	Accounts payable	$ 60	$ 30
Marketable securities	0	25	Notes payable	100	60
Accounts receivable	350	315	Accrued wages	10	10
Inventories	300	215	Accrued federal income taxes	130	120
Total current assets	$ 700	$ 610	Total current liabilities	$ 300	$ 220
Gross plant and equipment	$1,800	$1,470	First mortgage bonds[a]	$ 500	$ 520
Less depreciation	500	400	Debentures	300	60
			Total long-term debt	$ 800	$ 580
Net plant and equipment	$1,300	$1,070	Stockholders' equity: Common stock		
			(50,000,000 shares, $1 par)	$ 50	$ 50
			Additional paid-in capital	100	100
			Retained earnings	750	730
			Total stockholders' equity (common net worth)	$ 900	$ 880
Total assets	$2,000	$1,680	Total claims on assets	$2,000	$1,680

[a]The sinking fund requirement for the first mortgage bonds is $20 million a year. Sinking funds are discussed in Chapter 13, but, in brief, a sinking fund simply involves the repayment of long-term debt. Thus Carter Chemical is required to pay off $20 million from 12/31/80 to 12/31/81. The current portion of the long-term debt is included in notes payable here, although in a more detailed balance sheet it would be shown as a separate item.

[2] We shall not devote much time to the question of the accounting methods used to calculate net income. It should, however, be noted that the methods for calculating depreciation, valuing inventory, determining pension fund liabilities, and so on have significant impacts on reported profits. Accounting methods are reported in detail in notes to the financial statements, especially in the 10-K report to the SEC, and security analysts are well aware of the degree of conservatism used to produce reported profits. In other words, analysts recognize differences in the "quality" of reported earnings, and these quality differences are reflected in k_s and consequently in stock prices.

[3] Dividends are important too, but the firm's ability to pay dividends is dependent on its earnings.

claims against these assets. The assets are listed in order of their "liquidity," or the length of time it typically takes to convert them to cash. The claims are listed in the order in which they must be paid: Trade accounts must generally be paid within thirty days; notes are payable within ninety days; and so on down to the stockholders' equity accounts, which represent ownership and need never be "paid off."

Some additional points about the balance sheet are significant:

1. *Cash versus Other Assets.* Although the assets are all stated in terms of dollars, *only cash* represents actual money. Receivables are bills others owe Carter; inventories consist of raw materials, work in process, and finished goods available for sale; and fixed assets consist of Carter's plant and equipment. Carter can write checks at present for a total of $50 million (versus current liabilities of $300 million due within a year). The noncash assets will presumably be converted to cash eventually, but they do not represent cash-in-hand.

2. *Liabilities versus Stockholders' Equity.* The claims against assets are of two types—liabilities, or money the company owes, and the stockholders' ownership position.[4] The equity, or net worth, is a residual; that is,

$$\text{Assets} - \text{Liabilities} = \text{Stockholders' equity.}$$
$$\$2{,}000{,}000{,}000 - \$1{,}100{,}000{,}000 = \$900{,}000{,}000.$$

Suppose assets decline in value—for example, suppose some of the accounts receivable are written off as bad debts. Liabilities remain constant, so the value of the net worth declines. Therefore, the risk of asset value fluctuations is borne entirely by the stockholders. Note, however, that if asset values rise, these benefits accrue exclusively to the stockholders.

3. *Breakdown of the Stockholders' Equity Account.* A detailed discussion of the equity accounts is given in Chapter 14, "Common Stock," but a brief preview of that discussion is useful here. First, note that the equity section is divided into three accounts—*common stock, paid-in capital,* and *retained earnings.* As explained below, the retained earnings account is built up over time by the firm's "saving" a part of its earnings rather than paying all earnings out as dividends. The other two accounts arise from the sale of stock by the firm to raise capital. Accountants generally assign a *par value* to common stock—Carter Chemical's stock has a par value of $1.[5] Now suppose Carter were to sell 1 million additional shares at a price of $30 per share.

---

[4] One could divide liabilities into (1) debts owed to someone and (2) other items such as deferred taxes, reserves, etc. We do not make this distinction, so the terms *debt* and *liabilities* are used synonymously.

[5] See Chapter 14 for a discussion of par value.

The company would raise $30 million, and the cash accounts would go up by this amount. Of the total, $1 million would be added to common stock, and $29 million would be added to paid-in capital. Thus, after the sale, common stock would show $51 million, paid-in capital would show $129 million, and there would be 51 million shares outstanding.

The breakdown of the equity accounts is important for some purposes but not for others. For example, a potential stockholder would want to know if the company had earned the funds in its equity accounts, or if funds had come mainly from selling stock. A potential creditor, on the other hand, would be more interested in the amount of money the owners had put up than in the form in which they put it up. In the remainder of this chapter, we generally aggregate the three equity accounts and call this sum *equity* or *net worth.*[6]

4. *The Time Dimension.* The balance sheet may be thought of as a snapshot of the firm's financial position *at a point in time*—for example, on December 31, 1981. The income statement, on the other hand, reports on operations *over a period of time*—for example, during the calendar year 1981.

The Cash Flow Cycle

Figure 6-1 shows the cash flow cycle within a firm. Rectangles represent balance sheet accounts—assets and claims against assets—while circles represent actions taken by the firm. Each rectangle may be thought of as a reservoir, and you can visualize a wavy line which designates the amount of the asset or liability in the reservoir (account) on a balance sheet date. Various transactions would cause changes in the accounts, just as adding or subtracting water would change the level in a reservoir. The diagram is by no means a complete representation of the cash flow cycle: To avoid undue complexity, it shows only the major flows.

The cash account is the focal point of the graph. Certain events, such as collecting accounts receivable or borrowing money from the bank, will cause the cash account to increase, while the payment of taxes, interest, and so on will cause the cash account to decline. Similar comments could be made about all the balance sheet accounts—their balances rise, fall, or remain constant depending on events that occur during the period under study, which for Carter Chemical is January 1, 1981, through December 31, 1981.

Projected sales increases may require the firm to raise cash by borrowing from its bank or selling new stock. For example, if Carter anticipates an increase in sales, it will (1) expend cash to buy or build fixed assets through the capital budgeting process, (2) step up purchases, thereby in-

---

[6] In Chapter 14 we will differentiate between *total equity*, which includes preferred stocks, and *common equity*, which does not.

Figure 6-1
Cash and Materials Flows within the Firm

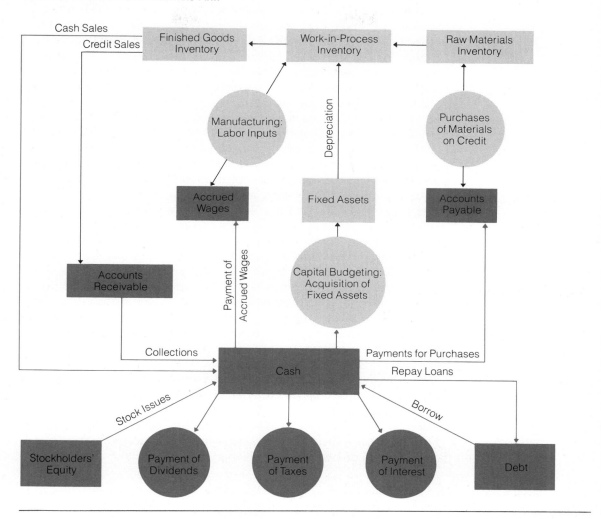

creasing both raw materials inventories and accounts payable, (3) increase production, which causes an increase in both accrued wages and work-in-process, and (4) eventually build up its finished goods inventory. Some cash will have been expended, hence removed from the cash account, and the firm will have obligated itself to expend still more cash to pay off its accounts payable and accrued wages within a few weeks. These events will have occurred *before* any new cash has been generated. Even when the expected sales do occur, there will still be a lag in the generation of cash until receivables are collected. For example, if Carter gives free credit for 30 days, then it will be about 30 days after a sale is made before cash comes in. Depending on how much cash the firm had at the beginning of the build-up, on the length of its production-sales-collection cycle, and on how long it can delay payment of its own payables and accrued wages, the firm may have to obtain significant amounts of additional cash by selling stock or bonds, or by borrowing from the bank.

If the firm is profitable, its sales revenues will exceed its costs, and its cash inflows will eventually exceed its cash outlays. However, even a profitable firm can experience a cash shortage if it is growing rapidly. It may have to pay for plant, materials, and labor before cash from the expanded sales starts flowing in. For this reason, rapidly growing firms often require large bank loans or capital from other sources.

An unprofitable firm, such as Chrysler in recent years, will have larger cash outlays than inflows. This, in turn, will typically cause a slow-down in the payment of accrued wages and accounts payable, and it may also lead to heavy borrowings. Thus, liabilities build up to excessive levels in unprofitable firms. Similarly, an overly ambitious expansion plan will be reflected in an excessive buildup of inventories and fixed assets, while a poor credit/collection policy will produce bad debts and reduced profits that first show up as high accounts receivable. Financial analysts are well aware of these relationships, and they use the analytical techniques discussed in the remainder of this chapter to help discover problems before they become too serious.

Statement of Retained Earnings

Changes in the equity accounts between balance sheet dates are reported in the statement of retained earnings; Carter's statement is shown in Table 6-3. The company earned $120 million during 1981, paid out $100 million in dividends, and plowed $20 million back into the business. Thus, the balance sheet item "retained earnings" increased from $730 million at the end of 1980 to $750 million at the end of 1981.

Table 6-3
Carter Chemical Company: Statement of Retained Earnings for Year Ending December 31, 1981 ($ in Millions)

Balance of retained earnings, December 31, 1980	$730
Add: Net income, 1981	120
Less: Dividends to stockholders	(100)
Balance of retained earnings, December 31, 1981	$750

Note that the balance sheet account "retained earnings" represents a *claim against assets,* not assets per se. Further, firms retain earnings primarily to expand the business. This means investing in plant and equipment, inventories, and so on, *not* in a bank account. *Thus, retained earnings as reported on the balance sheet do not represent cash and are not "available" for the payment of dividends or anything else.*[7]

The graphic analysis given earlier in Figure 6-1 is converted into numerical form and reported in annual reports as the *statement of changes in financial position*, often called the *sources and uses of funds statement*. This statement is designed to show how funds were obtained and how they were used. It helps answer questions such as these: Was the expansion program financed by sale of debt or equity? How much of its required capital has the firm been able to generate internally? Has the firm been building up its liquid assets, or is it becoming less liquid? Information such as this is useful both for investment analysis and for corporate planning, so the statement of changes in financial position is an important part of the annual report.

The Role of Depreciation. Before we discuss the statement of changes in financial position in detail, we should pause to consider one of its most important elements—depreciation. First, what is depreciation? In effect, it is an annual charge against income which reflects a rough estimate of the dollar cost of the capital equipment used in the production process. For example, suppose a machine with an expected useful life of ten years and a zero expected salvage value was purchased in 1978 for $100,000. This $100,000 cost must be charged against production over the machine's ten year life; otherwise, profits will be overstated. If the machine is depreciated by the straight-line method, the annual charge is $10,000. This amount is deducted from sales revenues, along with such other costs as labor and raw materials, to determine income. However, depreciation is not a cash outlay; funds were expended back in 1978, so the depreciation charged against the income in years 1979 through 1988 is not a cash outlay, as are labor or raw materials charges. *Depreciation is a noncash charge.*

This point is illustrated with data for Carter Chemical Company in Table 6-4. Here Column 1 shows an abbreviated version of Carter's income statement, while Column 2 shows the statement on a cash flow basis. Assume for the moment that (1) all sales are for cash, (2) all costs except depreciation were paid during 1981, and (3) no buildups occurred in inventories or other assets. How much cash would have been generated from operations? From Column 2 we see that the answer is $220

Statement of Changes in Financial Position

---

[7] Recall that the amount recorded in the retained earnings account is *not* an indication of the amount of cash the firm has. That amount (as of the balance sheet date) is found in the cash account—an asset account. A positive number in the retained earnings account indicates only that, in the past, according to generally accepted accounting principles, the firm has earned an income and its dividends have been less than that reported income. Also, recall the difference between accrual and cash accounting. Even though a company reports record earnings and shows an increase in the retained earnings account, it may still be short of cash.

**Table 6-4
Carter Chemical
Company: Cash Flows
for 1981 ($ in Millions)**

	Income Statement (1)	Cash Flows (2)
Sales	$3,000	$3,000
Costs and expenses:		
All costs except depreciation	2,634	2,634
Depreciation (D)	100	—
Earnings before interest and taxes (EBIT)	$ 266	$ 366
Interest expense	66	66
Earnings before taxes	$ 200	$ 300
Taxes	80	80
Net income (NI)	$ 120	
Cash flow: CF = NI + D = $120 + $100 =	$ 220	$ 220

million. The sales are all for cash, so the firm took in $3,000,000,000 in cash money. Its costs other than depreciation were $2,634,000,000, and these were paid in cash, leaving $366 million. Depreciation is *not* a cash charge—the firm does not pay out the $100 million of depreciation expenses—so $366 million of cash money is still left after depreciation. Taxes and interest, however, are paid in cash, so $66 million for interest and $80 million for taxes must be deducted from the $366 million EBIT cash flow, leaving a net cash flow from operations of $220 million. As shown in Column 1, this $220 million is, of course, exactly equal to profit after tax plus depreciation: $120 million plus $100 million equals $220 million. Thus, since depreciation is a noncash charge and is added back to net income to approximate cash flows from operations, it is included as a source of funds in the statement of changes in financial position.

Before leaving the subject of depreciation, we should sound a word of caution. Depreciation does not really *provide* funds; it is simply a noncash charge which is added back to net income to obtain an estimate of the cash flow from operations. However, if the firm made no sales, then depreciation would certainly not provide cash flows. To see this point more clearly, consider the situation of Communications Satellite Corporation (Comsat), which derives its income principally from two satellites, one positioned over the Atlantic and one over the Pacific. Comsat's cash flows are approximately equal to its net income plus its depreciation charges. Yet, if its satellites stopped working, sales would vanish, and while accountants might still calculate depreciation, this depreciation would provide no cash flows (except possibly some tax loss carrybacks).

Preparing the Statement of Changes in Financial Position. The statement of changes in financial position is designed to answer at a glance these three questions: (1) Where did the firm get its funds during the year?

(2) What did it do with its available funds? (3) Did operations during the year tend to increase or decrease the firm's liquidity as measured by the change in net working capital? (*Working capital* is defined as current assets, while *net working capital* is current assets minus current liabilities. In general, the firm's financial position is stronger if net working capital increases, weaker if it decreases.)

The starting point in preparing a statement of changes in financial position is to determine the change in each balance sheet item, and then to record it as either a source or a use of funds in accordance with the following rules:

Sources: 1. *Increase* in a claim, that is, in a liability or capital account. Borrowing is an example.
2. *Decrease* in an asset account. Selling some fixed assets is an example.

Uses: 1. *Decrease* in a claim against assets. Paying off a loan is an example.
2. *Increase* in an asset account. Buying fixed assets is an example.

Thus, sources of funds include bank loans and retained earnings, as well as money generated by selling assets, collecting receivables, and even drawing down the cash account. Uses include acquiring fixed assets, building up inventories, and paying off debts.

Table 6-5 shows the changes in Carter Chemical Company's balance sheet accounts during the calendar year 1981, with each change designated as a source or a use. Sources and uses each total $470 million.[8]

The data contained in Table 6-5 are next used to prepare the formal statement of changes in financial position, or sources and uses of funds statement. The one contained in Carter Chemical's annual report is shown in Table 6-6. Notice that the statement provides answers to the three questions asked above: (1) the top section answers the question regarding Carter's major sources of funds; (2) the middle section answers the question about how Carter used funds; and (3) the lower section, which deals with current assets and liabilities, shows how the company's liquidity position changed during the year. We see that Carter's major sources of funds were net income, depreciation, and the sale of debentures (a type of long-term debt which is described in Chapter 13). These funds were used to reduce the mortgage debt, to increase fixed assets, and to pay dividends on common stock. Also, $10 million was used to increase net working capital.

---

[8] Adjustments must be made if fixed assets were sold or retired during the year. Carter had no sales of assets or major retirements during 1981.

Table 6-5
Carter Chemical
Company: Changes in
Balance Sheet Accounts
during 1981
($ in Millions)

	12/31/81	12/31/80	Change Source	Use
Cash	$ 50	$ 55	$ 5	$
Marketable securities	0	25	25	
Accounts receivable	350	315		35
Inventories	300	215		85
Gross plant and equipment	1,800	1,470		330
Accumulated depreciation[a]	500	400	100	
Accounts payable	60	30	30	
Notes payable	100	60	40	
Accrued wages	10	10		
Accrued taxes	130	120	10	
Mortgage bonds	500	520		20
Debentures	300	60	240	
Common stock	50	50		
Paid-in capital	100	100		
Retained earnings	750	730	20	
Totals			$470	$470

[a]Depreciation is a "contra-asset," not an asset. Hence, an increase in depreciation is a source of funds.

As shown in the bottom section, Carter decreased its cash and marketable securities but increased accounts receivable and inventories, for a net increase in current assets of $90 million. Current liabilities increased by $80 million, so there was an increase of $10 million in net working capital (current assets minus current liabilities). This net increase in working capital is reported as a use in the middle section.

Notice also that every item in the "change" columns of Table 6-5 is carried over to Table 6-6 *except retained earnings*. The statement of changes in financial position reports net income as a source and dividends as a use, rather than netting these items out and just reporting the increase in retained earnings.

Carter Chemical is a strong, well-managed company, and its sources and uses statement shows nothing unusual or alarming. One does, however, occasionally see situations where huge increases in fixed assets are financed primarily by short-term debt, which must be repaid within a few months if the lender demands repayment. This would show up in the lower third of the table as a decrease in net working capital, and it is, as we shall see in detail later in the book, a dangerous situation.[9]

---

[9] It should be noted that statements of changes in financial position are especially useful for planning purposes. More will be said about this in Chapter 7, which deals with the analysis of projected financial statements.

**Table 6-6
Carter Chemical
Company: Statement of
Changes in Financial
Position ($ in Millions)**

Sources of funds:

Net income after taxes	$120
Depreciation	100
Funds from operations	$220
Proceeds from sale of debentures	240
Total sources	$460

Uses of funds:

Repayment of mortgage bonds	$ 20
Increase in fixed assets	330
Dividend payments to common stockholders	100
Net increase in working capital (see detail below)	10
Total uses	$460

Analysis of changes in working capital[a]

Increase (decrease) in current assets:	
Cash	$(5)[b]
Marketable securities	(25)
Accounts receivable	35
Inventories	85
Net increase in current assets	$90
Increase (decrease) in current liabilities:	
Accounts payable	$30
Notes payable	40
Accrued taxes	10
Net increase in current liabilities	$80
Net increase (decrease) in working capital	$10

[a]*Net working capital* is defined as current assets minus current liabilities.
[b]Parentheses denote negative numbers here and throughout the book.

In addition to the four statements described above, most annual reports today also give a summary of earnings, dividends, and stock prices over the last few years. For Carter Chemical, these data are given in Table 6-7 and plotted in Figure 6-2. Earnings were variable, but there was a definite upward trend over the period. In 1981 a strike caused earnings to drop somewhat, but management expects the growth trend to resume in 1982.

Eleven Year Earnings, Dividend, and Stock Price Record

Although dividends and dividend policy are discussed in detail in Chapter 18, we can make several comments about dividends at this point:

1. Dividends per share (DPS) represent the basic cash flows passed from the firm to its stockholders. As such, dividends are a key element in the stock valuation models developed in earlier chapters.

2. DPS in any given year can exceed EPS, but in the long run dividends are paid from earnings, so normally DPS is smaller than EPS. The

Table 6-7
Carter Chemical
Company: Eleven Year
Earnings, Dividend,
and Stock Price Record,
1971-1981

Year	Average Stock Price	Earnings per Share	Dividends per Share
1971	$20	$1.53	$1.25
1972	22	1.55	1.30
1973	22	1.80	1.35
1974	23	1.65	1.40
1975	24	2.00	1.50
1976	21	1.80	1.55
1977	30	1.25	1.65
1978	31	2.40	1.70
1979	30	2.43	1.75
1980	37	2.60	1.80
1981	33	2.40	2.00

Ten year growth rate[a]: EPS 5%
DPS 5%

[a]Growth rates were obtained by linear regression. The logs of EPS and DPS were regressed against years, and the slope coefficient represents the growth rate. The graphs in Figure 6-2 give plots of EPS and DPS over time and a trend line for EPS fitted by least squares regression. (The DPS growth is so smooth that a trend line is unnecessary.) By dividing the trend line figure for EPS in 1981 ($2.43) into the trend line figure for 1971 ($1.49), we obtain a PVIF for ten years (not eleven years; eleven years of data are needed to estimate ten years of *growth*). We can look up PVIF = $1.49/$2.43 = 0.6132 in Table A-1, across the row for 10 periods. The calculated interest factor is approximately equal to 0.6139, the factor for 5 percent. Thus, the growth rate in EPS is approximately 5 percent.

Calculated growth rates can be highly sensitive to the beginning and ending points. For example, Carter's growth rate in EPS was negative from 1971 to 1977, but positive from 1971 to 1981. A *great deal* of judgment, plus qualitative information about the company, is needed when interpreting past trends and forecasting future EPS growth rates. Indeed, the historic growth rate can almost never be used as more than a starting point for estimating the expected future growth rate.

percentage of earnings paid out in dividends, or the ratio of DPS to EPS, is defined as the *dividend payout ratio*. Carter Chemical's payout ratio has varied somewhat from year to year, but it has averaged about 80 percent.

3. In a graph such as Figure 6-2, the DPS line is typically below the EPS line, while the two lines generally have about the same slope, indicating that EPS and DPS are growing at about the same rate. As the data in Table 6-7 indicate, Carter's earnings and dividends have both been growing at an average rate of 5 percent per year. If the type of analysis undertaken in the next section suggests that this trend will continue, then 5 percent is the value of g that will be used in the valuation model to calculate Carter's stock price.

Analysis of
the Financial
Statements

Financial statements report both on a firm's position at a point in time and on its operations over some past period. However, their real value lies in the fact that they can be used to help predict the firm's future earnings and dividends, as well as the riskiness of these cash flows. From

Figure 6-2
Carter Chemical Company: Eleven Year Earnings
and Dividend Record, 1971-1981

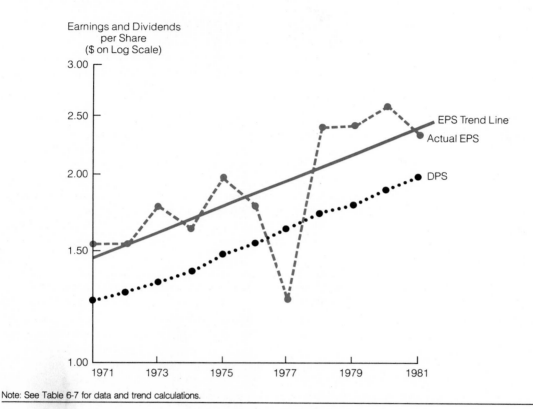

Note: See Table 6-7 for data and trend calculations.

an investor's standpoint, *predicting the future is what financial statement analysis is all about.* From management's standpoint, *financial statement analysis is useful both as a way to anticipate future conditions and, more important, as a starting point for planning actions that will influence the future course of events.* In the remainder of this chapter we discuss procedures used by both investors and managers to analyze and interpret financial statements.

Financial ratios are designed to show relationships among financial statement accounts. Ratios put numbers into perspective. For example, Firm

Ratio Analysis[10]

[10] In addition to the ratios discussed in this section, financial analysts also employ a tool known as *common size* balance sheets and income statements. To form a common size balance sheet, one
(continued)

A might have $5,248,760 of debt and annual interest charges of $419,900, while Firm B's debt totals $52,647,980 and its interest charges are $3,948,600. The true burden of these debts, and the companies' ability to repay them, can only be ascertained by comparing each firm's debt to its assets, and its interest charges to the income available for payment of interest. Such comparisons are made by *ratio analysis.*

Ratios may be categorized into five groups: (1) liquidity ratios, (2) asset management ratios, (3) debt management ratios, (4) profitability ratios, and (5) market value ratios. Some of the most useful ones in each category are discussed next.

Liquidity Ratios

One of the first concerns of the financial analyst is liquidity: Will the firm be able to meet its maturing obligations? Carter Chemical has debts totaling $300 million that must be paid off within the coming year. Can those obligations be satisfied? A full liquidity analysis requires the use of cash budgets (described in Chapter 9); however, by relating the amount of cash and other current assets to the current obligations, ratio analysis provides a quick and easy-to-use measure of liquidity. Two commonly used liquidity ratios are presented below.

Current Ratio. The current ratio is computed by dividing current assets by current liabilities. Current assets normally include cash, marketable securities, accounts receivable, and inventories; current liabilities consist of accounts payable, short-term notes payable, current maturities of long-term debt, accrued income taxes, and other accrued expenses (principally wages).

If a company is getting into financial difficulty, it begins paying its bills (accounts payable) slowly, building up bank loans, and so on. If these current liabilities are rising faster than current assets, the current ratio will fall, and this could spell trouble. Accordingly, the current ratio is the most commonly used measure of short-term solvency, since it provides the best single indicator of the extent to which the claims of short-term creditors are covered by assets that are expected to be converted to cash in a period roughly corresponding to the maturity of the claims.

The calculation of the current ratio for Carter Chemical at year-end 1981 is shown below. (All dollar amounts in this section are in millions.)

$$\text{Current ratio} = \frac{\text{Current assets}}{\text{Current liabilities}} = \frac{\$700}{\$300} = 2.3 \text{ times.}$$
$$\text{Industry average} = 2.5 \text{ times.}$$

Carter's current ratio is slightly below the average for the industry, 2.5,

simply divides each asset and liability item by total assets and expresses the result as a percentage. The resultant percentage statement can be compared with those of larger or smaller firms, or for the same firm over time. To form a common size income statement, one simply divides each item by sales.

but not low enough to cause concern. It appears that Carter is about in line with most other chemical firms. Since current assets are scheduled to be converted to cash in the near future, it is highly probable that they could be liquidated at close to their stated value. With a current ratio of 2.3, Carter could liquidate current assets at only 43 percent of book value and still pay off current creditors in full.[11]

Although industry average figures are discussed later in some detail, it should be stated at this point that an industry average is not a magic number that all firms should strive to maintain. In fact, some very well-managed firms will be above it, and other good firms will be below it. However, if a firm's ratios are very far removed from the average for its industry, the analyst must be concerned about why this variance occurs. Thus, a deviation from the industry average should signal the analyst to check further.

Note also that Carter's current ratio declined to 2.3 in 1981 from 2.8 in 1980. Thus, the *trend* is poor, and this could indicate potential future difficulties. More will be said about *trend analysis* later in the chapter.

Quick Ratio or Acid Test. The quick ratio is calculated by deducting inventories from current assets and dividing the remainder by current liabilities. Inventories are typically the least liquid of a firm's current assets, hence the assets on which losses are most likely to occur in the event of liquidation. Therefore, this measure of the firm's ability to pay off short-term obligations without relying on the sale of inventories is important.

$$\text{Quick, or acid test, ratio} = \frac{\text{Current assets} - \text{Inventory}}{\text{Current liabilities}} = \frac{\$400}{\$300}$$
$$= 1.3 \text{ times.}$$
$$\text{Industry average} = 1.0 \text{ times.}$$

The industry average quick ratio is 1.0, so Carter's 1.3 ratio compares favorably with other firms in the industry. If the accounts receivable can be collected, the company can pay off current liabilities even without selling any inventory. Again, however, it should be noted that the trend is downward: 1.3 in 1981 versus 1.8 in 1980.

The second group of ratios is designed to measure how effectively the firm is managing its assets. In particular, the asset management ratios answer this question: Does the total amount of each type of asset as reported on the balance sheet seem "reasonable," too high, or too low in view of current and projected operating levels? Carter Chemical and other companies must borrow or obtain capital from other sources in order to acquire assets. If they have too many assets, then their interest expenses

Asset Management Ratios

---

[11] (1/2.3) = 0.43, or 43 percent. Note that (0.43) ($700) ≈ $300, the amount of current liabilities.

are too high, hence profits are too low. On the other hand, if assets are too low, then operations will not be as efficient as possible.

Inventory Utilization. The inventory utilization ratio, sometimes called the *inventory turnover ratio*, is defined as sales divided by inventories.

$$\text{Inventory utilization (or turnover)} = \frac{\text{Sales}}{\text{Inventory}} = \frac{\$3,000}{\$300} = 10 \text{ times.}$$

$$\text{Industry average} = 9 \text{ times.}$$

Carter's ratio of 10 compares favorably with an industry average of 9 times. This suggests that the company does not hold excessive stocks of inventory; excess stocks are, of course, unproductive and represent an investment with a low or zero rate of return. This high inventory utilization ratio also reinforces our faith in the current ratio. If the turnover were low—say 3 or 4 times—we might wonder whether the firm was holding damaged or obsolete materials not actually worth their stated value.

Two problems arise in calculating and analyzing the inventory utilization ratio. First, sales are at market prices; if inventories are carried at cost, as they generally are, it would be more appropriate to use cost of goods sold in place of sales in the numerator of the formula. Established compilers of financial ratio statistics such as Dun & Bradstreet, however, use the ratio of sales to inventories carried at cost. To develop a figure that can be compared with those developed by Dun & Bradstreet, it is therefore necessary to measure inventory utilization with sales in the numerator, as we do here.

The second problem lies in the fact that sales occur over the entire year, whereas the inventory figure is for one point in time. This makes it better to use an average inventory.[12] If it is determined that the firm's business is highly seasonal, or if there has been a strong upward or downward sales trend during the year, it becomes essential to make some such adjustment. To maintain comparability with industry averages, we did not use the average inventory figure.

Average Collection Period. The average collection period, which is used to appraise the accounts receivable, is computed by dividing average daily sales into accounts receivable to find the number of days' sales tied up in receivables.[13] This is defined as the *average collection period* (ACP),

---

[12] Preferably, the average inventory would be calculated by summing the monthly figures during the year and dividing by 12. If monthly data are not available, one can add the beginning and ending figures and divide by 2. This will adjust for secular trends but not for seasonal fluctuations.

[13] Because information on credit sales is generally unavailable, total sales must be used. Since all firms do not have the same percentage of credit sales, there is a good chance that the average collection period will be somewhat in error. Also, note that for convenience, the financial community generally

(continued)

because it represents the average length of time that the firm must wait after making a sale before receiving cash. The calculations for Carter show an average collection period of forty-two days, slightly above the thirty-six day industry average.

$$\begin{matrix} \text{Average} \\ \text{collection} \\ \text{period} \end{matrix} = \frac{\text{Receivables}}{\text{Average sales per day}} = \frac{\text{Receivables}}{\text{Annual sales}/360}$$

$$= \frac{\$350}{\$3,000/360} = \frac{\$350}{\$8.333} = 42 \text{ days.}$$

$$\text{Industry average} = 36 \text{ days.}$$

The ACP can also be evaluated by comparison with the terms on which the firm sells its goods. For example, Carter's sales terms call for payment within thirty days, so the forty-two day collection period indicates that customers, on the average, are not paying their bills on time. If the trend in the collection period over the past few years had been rising while the credit policy had not changed, this would be even stronger evidence that steps should be taken to expedite the collection of accounts receivable.

Fixed Asset Utilization. The ratio of sales to fixed assets, often called the fixed asset turnover ratio, measures the utilization of plant and equipment:

$$\begin{matrix} \text{Fixed assets utilization} \\ \text{(or turnover)} \end{matrix} = \frac{\text{Sales}}{\text{Net fixed assets}} = \frac{\$3,000}{\$1,300} = 2.3 \text{ times.}$$

$$\text{Industry average} = 3.0 \text{ times.}$$

Carter's ratio of 2.3 times compares poorly with the industry average of 3 times, indicating that the firm is not using its fixed assets to as high a percentage of capacity as are the other firms in the industry. The financial manager should bear this fact in mind when production people request funds for new capital investments.

Total Assets Utilization. The final asset ratio measures the utilization or turnover of all the firm's assets—it is calculated by dividing sales by total assets.

$$\begin{matrix} \text{Total assets utilization} \\ \text{(or turnover)} \end{matrix} = \frac{\text{Sales}}{\text{Total assets}} = \frac{\$3,000}{\$2,000} = 1.5 \text{ times.}$$

$$\text{Industry average} = 1.8 \text{ times.}$$

uses 360 rather than 365 as the number of days in the year for purposes such as these. Finally, it would be better to use *average* receivables = (Beginning + Ending)/2 = (315 + 350)/2 = $332.5 in the formula. Had this been done, the ACP would have been $332.5/$8.333 = 40 days. The forty day figure is the more accurate one, but since the industry average was based on year-end receivables, we used forty-two days for the comparison.

Carter's ratio is somewhat below the industry average. The company is not generating a sufficient volume of business for the size of its asset investment. Sales should be increased, or some assets should be disposed of, or both steps should be taken.

Debt Management Ratios

The extent to which a firm uses debt financing, or financial leverage, has a number of implications. First, creditors look to the equity, or owner-supplied funds, to provide a margin of safety. Second, if owners have provided only a small proportion of total financing, the risks of the enterprise are borne mainly by the creditors. Third, by raising funds through debt, the owners gain the benefits of maintaining control of the firm with a limited investment. And fourth, if the firm earns more on the borrowed funds than it pays in interest, then the return on the owners' capital is magnified, or "leveraged."

To illustrate the last point, if the assets of a firm earned 10 percent while its debt cost only 8 percent, there would be a 2 percent differential accruing to the stockholders. If the firm had $200 in assets and was financed totally with common equity, then its operating income would be $(0.10)\ (\$200) = \$20$, and its return on equity would be $\$20/\$200 = 10\%$. However, if the firm used $150 of debt and only $50 of equity, its return on equity (ROE) would be[14]

$$
\begin{aligned}
\text{ROE} &= \frac{\text{Income available to common stockholders}}{\text{Common equity}} \\[6pt]
&= \frac{\text{Operating income} - \text{Interest} - \text{Taxes}}{\text{Common equity}} \\[6pt]
&= \frac{0.10\ (\$200) - 0.08\ (\$150)}{\$50} \\[6pt]
&= \frac{\$20 - \$12}{\$50} = \frac{\$8}{\$50} = 16\%.
\end{aligned}
$$

Thus, financial leverage can increase the rate of return on common stockholders' equity. However, financial leverage cuts both ways. In our example, if the return on assets fell to 5 percent, the differential between that return and the cost of debt would have to be made up from equity's share of total profits, resulting in

$$
\text{ROE} = \frac{0.05(\$200) - 0.08(\$150)}{\$50} = \frac{\$10 - \$12}{\$50} = -4\%.
$$

Thus, if operating income were low, financial leverage would reduce eq-

---

[14] In our example we disregarded income taxes in order to simplify the analysis. As we shall see later, taxes have an important effect on the firm's optimal capital structure. The problem of determining the optimum leverage for a firm is examined extensively in Chapters 16 and 17.

uity returns below the rate of return on assets. If the return on assets stayed at the 5 percent level, the firm would be unable to meet interest payments, which would eventually force it into bankruptcy and would result in total losses to the common stockholders.

We see, then, that firms with low amounts of debt have less risk of loss when the economy is in a recession, but they also have lower expected returns when the economy booms. Conversely, firms with high leverage ratios run the risk of large losses but also have a chance of gaining high profits. The prospects of high returns are desirable, but investors are averse to risk. Decisions about the use of leverage, then, must balance higher expected returns against increased risk.

In practice, leverage is approached in two ways: (1) by examining balance sheet ratios to determine the extent to which borrowed funds have been used to finance the firm, and (2) by examining income statement ratios to determine the number of times fixed charges are covered by operating profits. These two sets of ratios are complementary, and most analysts examine both types of leverage ratios.

Total Debt to Total Assets. The ratio of total debt to total assets, generally called the *debt ratio*, measures the percentage of total funds provided by creditors. Debt includes current liabilities and all bonds. Creditors prefer low debt ratios, since the lower the ratio, the greater the cushion against creditors' losses in the event of liquidation. The owners, on the other hand, may seek high leverage either (1) to magnify earnings or (2) because selling new stock means giving up some degree of control.

$$\text{Debt ratio} = \frac{\text{Total debt}}{\text{Total assets}} = \frac{\$1,100}{\$2,000} = 55\%.$$
$$\text{Industry average} = 40\%.$$

Carter's debt ratio is 55 percent; this means that creditors have supplied more than half the firm's total financing. Since the average debt ratio for this industry—and for manufacturing generally—is about 40 percent, Carter would find it difficult to borrow additional funds without first raising more equity capital. Creditors would be reluctant to lend the firm more money, and management would probably be subjecting the firm to the risk of bankruptcy if it sought to increase the debt ratio still more by borrowing.[15]

---

[15] The ratio of debt to equity is also used in financial analysis. The debt to assets (D/A) and debt to equity (D/E) ratios are simply transformations of one another.

$$D/E = \frac{D/A}{1 - D/A} \text{ and } D/A = \frac{D/E}{1 + D/E}.$$

Both ratios increase as a firm of a given size (total assets) uses a greater proportion of debt, but D/A

(continued)

Times Interest Earned. The times-interest-earned ratio (TIE) is determined by dividing earnings before interest and taxes (EBIT in Table 6-1) by the interest charges. The TIE ratio measures the extent to which earnings can decline without resultant financial embarrassment to the firm because of an inability to meet annual interest costs. Failure to meet this obligation can bring legal action by the creditors, possibly resulting in bankruptcy. Note that the before-tax profit figure is used in the numerator. Because income taxes are computed after interest expense is deducted, the ability to pay current interest is not affected by income taxes.

$$\text{TIE} = \frac{\text{EBIT}}{\text{Interest charges}} = \frac{\$266}{\$66} = 4 \text{ times.}$$
$$\text{Industry average} = 6 \text{ times.}$$

Carter's interest is covered 4 times. Since the industry average is 6 times, the company is covering its interest charges by a minimum margin of safety and deserves only a fair rating. This ratio reinforces the conclusion based on the debt ratio that the company might face some difficulties if it attempts to borrow additional funds.[16]

Profitability Ratios

Profitability is the net result of a large number of policies and decisions. The ratios examined thus far reveal some information about the way the firm is operating, but the profitability ratios show the combined effects of liquidity, asset management, and debt management on operating results.

Profit Margin on Sales. The profit margin on sales, computed by dividing net income after taxes by sales, gives the profit per dollar of sales.

$$\text{Profit margin} = \frac{\text{Net profit after taxes}}{\text{Sales}} = \frac{\$120}{\$3,000} = 4\%.$$
$$\text{Industry average} = 5\%.$$

Carter's profit margin is somewhat below the industry average of 5 percent, indicating that the firm's sales prices are relatively low or that its costs are relatively high, or both.

---

rises linearly and approaches a limit of 100 percent, while D/E rises exponentially and approaches infinity.

It should also be noted that, for certain purposes, the debt ratio is based on the market values of the firm's assets and its debt (outstanding bonds). Market values are especially important if the accounting values as shown on the balance sheet are significantly different from the market values, as is true of many oil companies and other firms that have large amounts of assets which have appreciated because of inflation. Market value ratios are discussed in detail in Chapters 16 and 17.

[16] More complete coverage ratios, which take account of mandatory lease payments, sinking fund payments, and other fixed financial charges, are also used in financial analysis. These refinements are covered in Chapter 13, which deals specifically with long-term debt.

Return on Total Assets (ROA). The ratio of net profit to total assets measures the return on total assets.

$$\text{Return on total assets (ROA)} = \frac{\text{Net profit after taxes}}{\text{Total assets}} = \frac{\$120}{\$2,000} = 6\%.$$
$$\text{Industry average} = 9\%.$$

Carter's 6 percent return is well below the 9 percent average for the industry. This low rate results from three primary factors: (1) the low profit margin on sales, (2) the low utilization of total assets, and (3) Carter's above average use of debt, which causes its interest payments to be high and its profits to be reduced.[17]

Return on Common Equity (ROE). The ratio of net profit after taxes to common equity measures the rate of return on the stockholders' investment, ROE.

$$\text{Return on common equity (ROE)} = \frac{\text{Net profit after taxes}}{\text{Common equity}} = \frac{\$120}{\$900} = 13.3\%.$$
$$\text{Industry average} = 15.0\%.$$

Carter's 13.3 percent return is below the 15.0 percent industry average, but not as far below as the return on total assets. This results from Carter's greater use of debt, a point analyzed in detail later in the chapter.

Market Value Ratios

A final group of ratios relates the firm's stock price to its earnings and book value per share. These ratios give management an indication of what investors think of the company's past performance and future prospects. If the firm's liquidity, asset management, debt management, and profitability ratios are all good, then its market value ratios will be high, and the stock price will probably be as high as can be expected.

Price/Earnings Ratios. The P/E ratio, which was discussed in Chapter 4, shows how much investors are willing to pay per dollar of reported prof-

---

[17] In calculating the return on total assets, it is sometimes desirable to add interest to net profits after taxes to form the numerator of the ratio. The logic here is that since assets are financed by both stockholders and creditors, the ratio should measure the productivity of assets in providing returns to both classes of investors. Alternatively, one can calculate a "basic earning power" ratio:

$$\text{Basic earning power} = \frac{\text{Earnings before interest and taxes}}{\text{Total assets}}$$

Also, if assets grew rapidly during the year, it would improve the analysis if average assets (beginning assets plus ending assets divided by 2) were used in the denominator. We have not made these adjustments because the published averages we use for comparative purposes do not include them.

its. Carter's stock sells for $28.50, so with an EPS of $2.40, its P/E ratio is 11.9.

$$\text{Price/earnings ratio} = \frac{\text{Price per share}}{\text{Earnings per share}} = \frac{\$28.50}{\$2.40} = 11.9 \text{ times.}$$
$$\text{Industry average} = 12.5 \text{ times.}$$

As we saw in Chapter 4, P/E ratios are higher for firms with high growth prospects, but lower for riskier firms. Carter's P/E ratio is slightly below those of other large chemical producers, which suggests that the company is regarded as being somewhat riskier than most, as having poorer growth prospects, or both.

Market/Book Ratios. The ratio of a stock's market price to its book value gives another indication of how investors regard the company. Companies with high rates of return on equity generally sell at higher multiples of book value than those with low returns. Carter's book value per share is $18.00:

$$\text{Book value per share} = \frac{\text{Stockholders' equity}}{\text{Shares outstanding}} = \frac{\$900}{50} = \$18.$$

Dividing this value into the price per share gives a market/book ratio of 1.6 times:

$$\text{Market/book ratio} = \frac{\$28.50}{\$18.00} = 1.6 \text{ times.}$$
$$\text{Industry average} = 1.8 \text{ times.}$$

Investors are willing to pay slightly less for Carter's book value than for that of an average chemical company.[18]

The typical railroad, which has a very low rate of return on assets, has a market/book value ratio of less than 0.5. Very successful firms such as IBM achieve high rates of return on their assets and have market values that are four or five times their book values.

Trend Analysis

It is important to analyze trends in ratios as well as their absolute levels, for the trends give clues as to whether the financial situation is improving or deteriorating. To do a trend analysis, one simply graphs a ratio against years, as shown in Figure 6-3. This graph shows that Carter's rate of return on common equity has been declining since 1978, even though the industry average has been relatively stable. Other ratios could be analyzed similarly.

---

[18] The degree of conservatism used by the company's accountants can also affect the market/book ratio. The more conservative the accountants, the higher the market/book ratio will be, other things held constant. The same holds true for the P/E ratio.

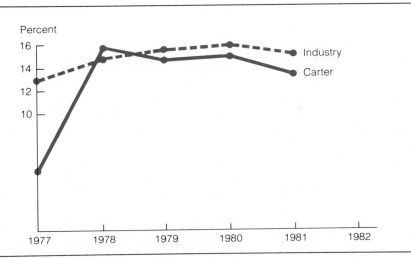

Figure 6-3
Rate of Return on
Common Equity,
1977-1981

Summary of Ratio Analysis: The du Pont System

Table 6-8 summarizes Carter Chemical's ratios, while Figure 6-4, which is called a *du Pont chart* because that company's managers developed the general approach, shows the relationships among debt, asset utilization, and profitability ratios. The left-hand side of the chart develops the *profit margin on sales*. The various expense items are listed, then summed to obtain Carter's total costs. Subtracting costs from sales yields the company's net income, which, when divided by sales, indicates that 4 percent of each sales dollar is left over for stockholders.

The right-hand side of the chart lists the various categories of assets, which are summed and then divided into sales to find the number of times Carter "turns its assets over" each year. Carter's total asset utilization, or "turnover," ratio is 1.5 times.

The profit margin times the total asset turnover ratio is defined as the *du Pont equation*, which gives the rate of return on assets, ROA:

$$\text{ROA} = \frac{\text{Rate of return}}{\text{on assets}} = \text{Profit margin} \times \text{Total asset turnover}$$

$$= \frac{\text{Net profit after taxes}}{\text{Sales}} \times \frac{\text{Sales}}{\text{Total assets}}$$

$$= 4\% \times 1.5 = 6\%.$$

Carter makes 4 percent, or four cents, on each dollar of sales. Assets were "turned over" 1.5 times during the year, so Carter earned a return of 6 percent on its assets.[19]

---

[19] The term *turnover* goes back to the days of the Yankee peddler. See Footnote 1, Chapter 8, for an explanation.

Table 6-8
Summary of Carter Chemical's Ratios

Ratio	Formula for Calculation	Calculation	Ratio	Industry Average	Evaluation
Liquidity					
Current	$\dfrac{\text{Current assets}}{\text{Current liabilities}}$	$\dfrac{\$\ 700}{\$\ 300}$ = 2.3 times		2.5 times	Good
Quick, or acid test	$\dfrac{\text{Current assets} - \text{Inventory}}{\text{Current liabilities}}$	$\dfrac{\$\ 400}{\$\ 300}$ = 1.3 times		1.0 times	Good
Asset management					
Inventory turnover	$\dfrac{\text{Sales}}{\text{Inventory}}$	$\dfrac{\$3,000}{\$\ 300}$ = 10 times		9 times	Good
Average collection period (ACP)	$\dfrac{\text{Receivables}}{\text{Sales}/360}$	$\dfrac{\$\ 350}{\$8.333}$ = 42 days		36 days	Bad
Fixed assets utilization	$\dfrac{\text{Sales}}{\text{Fixed assets}}$	$\dfrac{\$3,000}{\$1,300}$ = 2.3 times		3.0 times	Bad
Total assets utilization	$\dfrac{\text{Sales}}{\text{Total assets}}$	$\dfrac{\$3,000}{\$2,000}$ = 1.5 times		1.8 times	Bad
Debt management					
Debt to total assets	$\dfrac{\text{Total debt}}{\text{Total assets}}$	$\dfrac{\$1,100}{\$2,000}$ = 55 percent		40 percent	Bad
Times interest earned (TIE)	$\dfrac{\text{Earnings before interest and taxes}}{\text{Interest charges}}$	$\dfrac{\$\ 266}{\$\ 66}$ = 4.0 times		6 times	Bad
Profitability					
Profit margin on sales	$\dfrac{\text{Net profit after taxes}}{\text{Sales}}$	$\dfrac{\$\ 120}{\$3,000}$ = 4 percent		5.0 percent	Bad
Return on total assets (ROA)	$\dfrac{\text{Net profit after taxes}}{\text{Total assets}}$	$\dfrac{\$\ 120}{\$2,000}$ = 6 percent		9.0 percent	Bad
Return on common equity (ROE)	$\dfrac{\text{Net profit after taxes}}{\text{Common equity}}$	$\dfrac{\$\ 120}{\$\ 900}$ = 13.3 percent		15.0 percent	Bad
Market value					
Price/earnings (P/E)	$\dfrac{\text{Price per share}}{\text{Earnings per share}}$	$\dfrac{\$28.50}{\$\ 2.40}$ = 11.9 times		12.5 times	Bad
Market/book	$\dfrac{\text{Market price per share}}{\text{Book value per share}}$	$\dfrac{\$28.50}{\$18.00}$ = 1.6 times		1.8 times	Bad

If Carter used only equity, the 6 percent rate of return on assets would equal the rate of return on equity. However, 55 percent of the firm's capital is supplied by creditors. Since the 6 percent return on *total* assets all goes to stockholders, who put up only 45 percent of the capital, the return on equity is higher than 6 percent. Specifically, the rate of return

Figure 6-4
Modified du Pont Chart Applied to Carter
Chemical Company ($ in Millions)

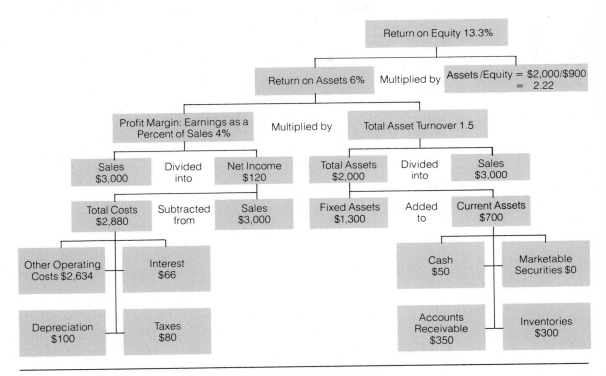

on assets (ROA) must be multiplied by the *equity multiplier*, which is the ratio of assets to common equity, to obtain the rate of return on equity, ROE:

$$\text{ROE} = \text{ROA} \times \text{Equity multiplier}$$
$$= \frac{\text{Net income}}{\text{Assets}} \times \frac{\text{Assets}}{\text{Common equity}}$$
$$= 6\% \times (\$2{,}000/\$900)$$
$$= 6\% \times 2.22 = 13.3\%.$$

This 13.3 percent rate of return could, of course, be calculated directly: net income after taxes/common equity = $120/$900 = 13.3 percent. However, the du Pont equation shows how the rate of return on assets and the use of debt interact to determine the return on equity.[20]

Management can use the du Pont system to analyze ways of improving the firm's performance. On the left, or "profit margin," side of the chart, marketing people can study the effects of raising sales prices (or lowering them to increase volume), of moving into new products or markets with higher margins, and so on. Cost accountants can study the expense items and, working with engineers, purchasing agents, and other operating personnel, seek ways of holding costs down. On the "turnover" side, financial analysts, working with both production and marketing people, can investigate ways of reducing investments in various types of assets. At the same time, the treasurer can analyze the effects of alternative financing strategies, seeking to hold down interest expenses and the risks of debt while still using debt to increase the rate of return on equity.

Comparative Ratios

The preceding analysis of Carter Chemical Company pointed out the usefulness of comparing a company's ratios with those of other firms in its industry. Comparative ratios are available from a number of sources. One useful set of comparative data is compiled by Dun & Bradstreet, Inc. D&B provides fourteen ratios calculated for a large number of industries. Useful ratios can also be found in the *Annual Statement Studies* published by Robert Morris Associates, the national association of bank loan officers. The Federal Trade Commission's *Quarterly Financial Report*, which is found in most libraries, gives a set of ratios for manufacturing firms by industry group and size of firm. Trade associations and individual firms' credit departments also compile industry average financial ratios. Finally, financial statement data are available on magnetic tapes for thousands of corporations, and since most of the larger brokerage houses, banks, and other financial institutions have access to these data, security analysts can and do generate comparative ratios tailored to their own individual needs.

Each of these organizations uses a somewhat different set of ratios, designed for its own purposes. For example, D&B deals mainly with small firms, many of which are proprietorships, and they are concerned

---

[20] Another ratio that is frequently used is the following:

$$\text{Rate of return on invested capital} = \frac{\text{Net income after taxes } + \text{ Interest}}{\text{Debt } + \text{ Equity}}.$$

This ratio is especially important in the public utility industries, where regulators are concerned about the companies' using their monopoly positions to earn excessive returns on invested capital. In fact, regulators try to set utility prices (service rates) at levels that will force the return on invested capital to equal a company's cost of capital as defined in Chapter 15.

largely with the creditors' viewpoint. Accordingly, their ratios emphasize current assets and liabilities, and D&B is completely unconcerned with market value ratios. Therefore, when you select your comparative data source, you should be sure that your emphasis is similar to that of the agency, or else recognize the limitations of their ratios for your purposes.

Although ratio analysis is useful in finance, it does have limitations, some of which are listed below.

Limitations of Ratio Analysis

1. Many large firms actually operate a number of different divisions in quite different industries, making it difficult to develop a meaningful set of industry averages for comparative purposes. This tends to make ratio analysis more useful for small than for large firms.

2. Most firms want to be better than average (although about half will be above and half below), so merely attaining average performance is not necessarily good. As a target for high-level performance, it is preferable to look at the industry leaders' ratios.

3. The ratios can be distorted. For example, the inventory turnover ratio for a food processor will be radically different if the balance sheet figure used for inventory is the one just before versus just after the close of the canning season. This problem can be minimized by using average inventory figures.

   Also, firms can employ "window dressing" techniques to make their financial statements look better to credit analysts. Recently, a firm sold its corporate aircraft for cash just prior to issuing a quarterly statement. This substantially improved its cash balance in time for the quarterly report.

4. Different operating and accounting practices distort comparisons. For example, if one firm leases a substantial amount of its productive equipment, then its assets may be low relative to sales because leased assets may not appear on the balance sheet. (Some airlines lease about half of their planes whereas others own virtually all of their equipment.) This improves turnover ratios. The accounting profession has recently taken steps which reduce but do not eliminate this problem. (See Chapter 22 for a discussion.)

5. It is difficult to generalize about whether a particular ratio is "good" or "bad." For example, a high current ratio may show a strong liquidity position, which is good, or excessive cash, which is bad because excess cash in the bank is a nonearning asset. Similarly, high asset utilization ratios may denote either a firm that uses assets efficiently

or an undercapitalized firm that simply cannot afford to buy enough assets.

6. A firm may have some ratios which look "good" and others which look "bad," making it difficult to tell whether the firm is, on balance, in a strong or a weak position. A procedure called *discriminant analysis* can be used to analyze the net effects of a set of ratios. See Appendix 6A for a discussion of this procedure.

Ratio analysis is useful, but analysts should be aware of these problems and make adjustments as necessary. Ratio analysis conducted in a mechanical, unthinking manner is dangerous. Used intelligently and with good judgment, however, ratios can provide useful insights into a firm's operations. Your judgment in interpreting a set of ratios is probably weak at this point, but it will be greatly enhanced as we go through the remainder of the book.

Summary

The primary purposes of this chapter were (1) to describe the basic financial statements and (2) to discuss techniques used by investors and managers to analyze these statements. Four basic statements were covered: *the income statement, the balance sheet, the statement of retained earnings, and the statement of changes in financial position.*

Financial analysis is designed to determine the relative strengths and weaknesses of a company—whether the firm is financially sound and profitable relative to other firms in its industry, and whether its position is improving or deteriorating over time. Investors need such information in order to estimate both future cash flows from the firm and the riskiness of these flows. Managers need to be aware of their firms' financial positions in order to detect and strengthen weaknesses in a continuous quest for improvement.

Our study of financial analysis concentrated on a set of ratios designed to highlight the key aspects of a firm's operations. These ratios were broken down into five categories: (1) liquidity ratios, (2) asset management ratios, (3) debt management ratios, (4) profitability ratios, and (5) market value ratios. The ratios for a given firm are calculated, then compared with those of other firms in the same industry to judge the relative strength of the firm in question. Trends in the ratios are also analyzed, and the du Pont system is used to pinpoint the cause of any weakness that is uncovered. Ratio analysis has limitations, but used with care and judgment, it can be most helpful.

Questions

6-1 What four statements are contained in most annual reports?

6-2 Is it true that if a "typical" firm reports $20 million of retained earnings on its balance sheet, that firm's directors could declare a $20 million cash dividend without any qualms whatsoever?

6-3 a. What would Carter Chemical's balance sheet item "retained earnings" for 1981 have been if, during 1980, the company had paid dividends of $150 million? (See Tables 6-1 and 6-2.)

b. What would Carter Chemical's 1981 EPS have been had net income for that year been $150 million rather than $120 million?

c. Suppose you knew that Carter's EPS was $2.40 and that net income was $120 million. Could you use this information to determine the number of shares outstanding?

d. If Carter sold inventories carried at $200 million for only $50 million, what effects would this have on the firm's balance sheet? (Disregard tax effects.)

e. Could the DPS line in Figure 6-2 rise more steeply (that is, have a steeper slope) than the EPS line (1) over a ten year period, (2) in the "long run" (that is, forever)?

f. 1. Examine Figure 6-4, and then explain how a reduction in other operating costs from $2,634 million to $2,534 million would affect the rate of return on equity.

2. Then, holding other operating costs at the original $2,634 million, show how a reduction of total assets from $2 billion to $1.8 billion, with an offsetting reduction in equity by payment of a $200 million extra dividend, would affect the rate of return on equity.

3. Finally, use the stock price model developed in Chapter 4 to explain how these actions could affect the growth rate of EPS and DPS, hence the value of the firm's stock.

g. Suppose Carter's profit margin had been 5 percent, its total assets turnover 2 times, and its assets/equity ratio 1.49 times. What would Carter's rate of return on equity have been?

h. Had Carter's accountants decided to *shorten* the average life used to calculate depreciation, this would have increased the company's depreciation expense. Would this action have affected the company's cash flows? If so, how?

6-4 What is the relationship between each rectangle in Figure 6-1 and each individual source and use in a sources and uses of funds statement?

6-5 How might (a) seasonal factors and (b) different growth rates over time or across companies distort a comparative ratio analysis? Give some examples.

ST6-1 H. Lanser & Co. had earnings per share of $2 last year, and it paid a $1 dividend. Book value per share at year end was $20, while total retained earnings increased by $6,000,000 during the year. Lanser has no preferred stock, and no new common stock was issued during the year. If Lanser's year-end debt (which equals its total liabilities) was $60,000,000, what was the company's year-end debt/assets ratio?

Self-Test Problems

ST6-2 The following data apply to Horrigan & Company:

	($ in Millions)
Cash and marketable securities	$100.00
Fixed assets	$283.50
Sales	$1,000.00
Net income	$50.00
Quick ratio	2.0×
Current ratio	3.0×
ACP	40 days
ROE	0.12 or 12%

Horrigan has no preferred stock, only common equity, current liabilities, and long-term debt. Find Horrigan's (a) accounts receivable, (b) current liabilities, (c) current assets, (d) total assets, (e) ROA, (f) common equity, and (g) long-term debt.

ST6-3 In the preceding problem, you should have found Horrigan's accounts receivable (A/R) = $111.1 million. If Horrigan could reduce its ACP from forty days to thirty days while holding other things constant, how much cash would it generate? If this cash were used to buy back common stock (at book value) and thus to reduce the amount of common equity, how would this affect (a) the ROE, (b) the ROA, and (c) the total debt/total assets ratio?

Problems

6-1 Data for the Core Computer Company, and its industry averages, are given below and on the next page.
  a. Calculate the indicated ratios for Core Computer.
  b. Outline Core Computer's strengths and weaknesses as revealed by your analysis.
  c. Suppose Core had doubled its sales and also its inventories, accounts receivable, and common equity during 1981. How would that information affect the validity of your ratio analysis?

Core Computer Company: Balance Sheet, December 31, 1981

Cash	$220,000	Accounts payable	$165,000
Receivables	275,000	Notes payable	220,000
Inventory	825,000	Other current liabilities	110,000
Total current assets	$1,320,000	Total current liabilities	$495,000
Net fixed assets	605,000	Long-term debt	220,000
		Common equity	1,210,000
Total assets	$1,925,000	Total claims on assets	$1,925,000

Sales		$2,750,000
Cost of goods sold		
Materials	$1,045,000	
Labor	660,000	
Heat, light, and power	99,000	
Indirect labor	165,000	
Depreciation	60,500	2,029,500
Gross profit		720,500
Selling expenses		275,000
General and administrative expenses		316,800
Earnings before interest and taxes		$128,700
Less interest expense		13,200
Net profit before taxes		$115,500
Less federal income taxes (50%)		57,750
Net profit		$ 57,750

Core Computer Company: Income Statement for Year Ended December 31, 1981

Ratio	Core	Ratios Industry Averages
Current assets/current liabilities	_____	2.4×
Average collection period	_____	43 days
Sales/inventories	_____	9.8×
Sales/total assets	_____	2×
Net profit/sales	_____	3.3%
Net profit/total assets	_____	6.6%
Net profit/net worth	_____	18.1%
Total debt/total assets	_____	63.5%

6-2 The Williamsburg Furniture Company, a manufacturer and wholesaler of high-quality home furnishings, has been experiencing low profitability in recent years. As a result, the Board of Directors has replaced the president of the firm with a new president, John Sharpe, who asks you to make an analysis of the firm's financial position using the du Pont system. The most recent financial statements are reproduced below and on the next page.

a. Calculate some ratios which you feel would be useful in this case.

b. Do the balance sheet accounts or the income statement figures seem to be primarily responsible for the low profits?

Industry Average Ratios

Current ratio	2×	Sales/fixed assets	6×
Debt/total assets	30%	Sales/total assets	3×
Times interest earned	7×	Net profit on sales	3%
Sales/inventory	10×	Return on total assets	9%
Average collection period	24 days	Return on common equity	12.8%

c. Which specific accounts seem to be most out of line in relation to other firms in the industry?

d. If Williamsburg had a pronounced seasonal sales pattern, or if it grew rapidly during the year, how might this affect the validity of your ratio analysis? How might you correct for such potential problems?

Williamsburg Furniture Company: Balance Sheet, December 31, 1981 ($ in Million)

Cash	$ 30	Accounts payable	$ 30	
Marketable securities	22	Notes payable	30	
Net receivables	44	Other current liabilities	14	
Inventories	106	Total current liabilities		$ 74
Total current assets	$202	Long-term debt		16
		Total liabilities		$ 90
Gross fixed assets	$150			
Less depreciation	52	Common stock	$ 76	
Net fixed assets	98	Retained earnings	134	
		Total stockholder equity		210
Total assets	$300	Total claims on assets		$300

Williamsburg Furniture Company: Income Statement for Year Ended December 31, 1981 ($ in Millions)

Net sales	$530	
Cost of goods sold	440	
Gross profit		$90
Operating expenses	49	
Depreciation expense	8	
Interest expense	3	
Total expenses		60
Net income before tax		$30
Taxes (50%)		15
Net income		$15

6-3   The consolidated balance sheets for the Oregon Lumber Company at the beginning and end of 1981 follow. The company bought $75 million worth of fixed assets. The charge for depreciation in 1981 was $15 million. Earnings after taxes were $38 million, and the company paid out $10 million in dividends.

a. Fill in the amount of source or use in the appropriate column.

Oregon Lumber Company: Balance Sheet, Beginning and End of 1981 ($ in Millions)

	Jan. 1	Dec. 31	Change Source	Use
Cash	$ 15	$ 7		
Marketable securities	11	0		
Net receivables	22	30		
Inventories	53	75		
Total current assets	$101	$112		
Gross fixed assets	75	150		
Less depreciation	(26)	(41)		
Net fixed assets	49	109		
Total assets	$150	$221		
Accounts payable	$ 15	$ 18		
Notes payable	15	3		
Other current liabilities	7	15		
Long-term debt	8	26		
Common stock	38	64		
Retained earnings	67	95		
Total claims on assets	$150	$221		

b. Prepare a statement of changes in financial position.

c. Briefly summarize your findings.

6-4 Indicate the effects of the transactions listed below on each of the following: total current assets, net working capital, current ratio, and net profit. Use (+) to indicate an increase, (−) to indicate a decrease, and (0) to indicate no effect or indeterminate effect. State necessary assumptions and assume an initial current ratio of more than 1 to 1.

	Total Current Assets	Net Working Capital[a]	Current Ratio	Effect on Net Profit
1. Cash is acquired through issuance of additional common stock.	+	↑	↑	0
2. Merchandise is sold for cash.	−	↑	↑	↑
3. Federal income tax due for the previous year is paid.	↓	0	↓	↓
4. A fixed asset is sold for less than book value.	↑	↑	↑	↑
5. A fixed asset is sold for more than book value.	↑	↑	↑	↑
6. Merchandise is sold on credit.	↑	↑	↑	↑

(continued)

	Total Current Assets	Net Working Capital[a]	Current Ratio	Effect on Net Profit
7. Payment is made to trade creditors for previous purchases.	↓	—	—	—
8. A cash dividend is declared and paid.	↓	↓	↓	↓
9. Cash is obtained through bank loans.	↑	—	—	—
10. Short-term notes receivable are sold at a discount.	↓	↓	↓	—
11. Previously issued stock rights are exercised by company stockholders.	↑			
12. A profitable firm increases its rate of depreciation on fixed assets.				
13. Marketable securities are sold below cost.				
14. Uncollectible accounts are written off against the bad debt reserve.				
15. Advances are made to employees.				
16. Current operating expenses are paid.				
17. Short-term promissory notes are issued to trade creditors for prior purchases.				
18. Ten year notes are issued to pay off accounts payable.				
19. A fully depreciated asset is retired.				
20. A cash sinking fund for the retirement of bonds is created; a reserve for a bond sinking fund is also created.				
21. Bonds are retired by use of the cash sinking fund.				
22. Accounts receivable are collected.				
23. A stock dividend is declared and paid.				
24. Equipment is purchased with short-term notes.				
25. The allowance for doubtful accounts is increased.				
26. Merchandise is purchased on credit.				
27. Controlling interest in another firm is acquired by the issuance of additional common stock.				
28. Earnings are added to the reserve for a bond sinking fund.				
29. An unconsolidated subsidiary pays the firm a cash dividend from current earnings.				
30. The estimated taxes payable are increased.				

[a]Net working capital is defined as current assets minus current liabilities.

6-5 The record of earnings and dividends per share for the American Container Company (ACC) is given below:

Year	EPS	DPS
1971	$2.00	$0.80
1972	2.15	0.80
1973	2.30	0.80
1974	2.45	1.30
1975	2.60	1.30
1976	2.75	1.30
1977	3.25	1.60
1978	2.95	1.60
1979	3.44	2.00
1980	4.00	2.00
1981	3.62	2.00

a. Calculate ACC's growth rates in EPS and DPS. (Round to nearest percent.)
b. Suppose you conclude that ACC's growth rate in EPS will probably be maintained into the indefinite future. Which growth rate, that of EPS or that of DPS, would you use in the stock valuation equation $P = D_1/(k_s - g)$?
c. Consider now how the financial decisions listed on page 230 would probably affect the indicated factors. Use $(+)$ to represent an increase, $(-)$ to represent a decrease, and (0) to represent either no effect or an unpredictable effect. (Note: This question is designed to encourage discussion, not to produce precise answers. While some of the answers are clear-cut, finance professors would argue among themselves about others!)

6-6 Kose Company has a quick ratio of 1.0, a current ratio of 3.0, an inventory turnover of 6 times, and current assets of $600,000. What are Kose's annual sales, and, if cash and marketable securities are negligible, its ACP?

ST6-1 Lanser paid $1 and retained $1 per share. Since total retained earnings rose by $6,000,000, there must be 6,000,000 shares outstanding. With a book value of $20 per share, total common equity must be $20(6,000,000) = $120,000,000. Thus, the debt ratio must be 33.3 percent:

Solutions to Self-Test Problems

$$\frac{\text{Debt}}{\text{Assets}} = \frac{\text{Debt}}{\text{Debt} + \text{Equity}} = \frac{\$60 \text{ million}}{\$60 \text{ million} + \$120 \text{ million}}$$

$$= 0.333 = 33.3\%.$$

	ACC's Expected EPS and Growth in EPS during the Coming Year	ACC's Required Rate of Return on Stock, k_s	ACC's Cost of Debt, k_d	Market Price of ACC's Stock
1. ACC increases its debt/assets ratio.	————	————	————	————
2. ACC decides to increase its cash position by selling long-term bonds.	————	————	————	————
3. Inventories are reduced by the introduction of a new control system.	————	————	————	————
4. ACC acquires through merger a firm whose beta is twice that of ACC.	————	————	————	————
5. The Federal Reserve System takes actions to lower interest rates in the economy.	————	————	————	————
6. ACC decides to pay out all of its earnings, each year, as dividends.	————	————	————	————
7. Optional question for accountants: ACC's "conservative" accountants are replaced by a group of more "liberal" accountants.	————	————	————	————

ST6-2 a.

$$ACP = \frac{\text{Accounts receivable}}{\text{Sales}/360}$$

$$40 = \frac{A/R}{\$1,000/360}$$

$$A/R = 40(\$2.778) = \$111.1 \text{ million.}$$

b.

$$\text{Quick ratio} = \frac{\text{Current assets } - \text{ Inventories}}{\text{Current liabilities}} = 2.0$$

$$= \frac{\text{Cash and marketable securities } + \text{ A/R}}{\text{Current liabilities}} = 2.0$$

$$\text{Current liabilities} = (\$100 + \$111.1)/2 = \$105.5 \text{ million.}$$

c.

$$\text{Current ratio} = \frac{\text{Current assets}}{\text{Current liabilities}} = 3.0$$

$$\text{Current assets} = 3.0(\$105.5) = \$316.50 \text{ million.}$$

d.

$$\text{Total assets} = \text{Current assets} + \text{Fixed assets}$$

$$= \$316.5 + \$283.5 = \$600.$$

e.
$$\text{ROA} = \text{Profit margin} \times \text{Total asset turnover}$$
$$= \frac{\text{Net income}}{\text{Sales}} \times \frac{\text{Sales}}{\text{Total assets}}$$
$$= \frac{\$50}{\$1,000} \times \frac{\$1,000}{\$600}$$
$$= 0.05 \times 1.667 = 0.0833 = 8.33\%.$$

f.
$$\text{ROE} = \text{ROA} \times \frac{\text{Assets}}{\text{Equity}}$$
$$12.0 = 8.33 \times \frac{\$600}{\text{Equity}}$$
$$\text{Equity} = \frac{(8.33)(\$600)}{12.0} = \$416.50 \text{ million.}$$

g.
$$\text{Total assets} = \text{Total claims} = \$600$$
$$\text{Current liabilities} + \text{Long-term debt} + \text{Equity} = \$600$$
$$\$105.5 + \text{Long-term debt} + \$416.5 = \$600$$
$$\text{Long-term debt} = \$600 - \$105.5 - \$416.5 = \$78 \text{ million.}$$

Note: We could have found equity as follows:

$$\text{ROE} = \frac{\text{Net income}}{\text{Equity}}$$
$$0.12 = \frac{\$50}{\text{Equity}}$$

Equity = $50/0.12 = $416.67 million (rounding error difference).

Then we could have gone on to find current liabilities and long-term debt.

ST6-3 Horrigan's average sales per day were $1,000/360 = $2.777777 million. Its ACP was 40, so A/R = 40($2,777,777) = $111,111,111. Its new ACP of 30 would cause A/R = 30($2,777,777) = $83,333,333. The reduction in A/R = $111,111,111 − $83,333,333 = $27,777,777, which would equal the amount of new cash generated.

a.
$$\text{New equity} = \text{Old equity} - \text{Stock bought back}$$
$$= \$416,500,000 - \$27,777,777$$
$$= \$388,722,223.$$

Thus,

$$\text{New ROE} = \frac{\text{Net income}}{\text{New equity}}$$

$$= \frac{\$50,000,000}{\$388,722,223}$$

$$= 12.86\% \text{ (versus old ROE of 12.00\%).}$$

b.

$$\text{New ROA} = \frac{\text{Net income}}{\text{Total assets} - \text{Reduction in A/R}}$$

$$= \frac{\$50,000,000}{\$600,000,000 - \$27,777,777}$$

$$= 8.74\% \text{ (versus old ROA of 8.33\%).}$$

c. The old debt is the same as the new debt:

$$\text{New debt} = \text{Total claims} - \text{Equity}$$
$$= \$600 - \$416.5 = \$183.5 \text{ million.}$$

The old total assets $= \$600,000,000.$

$$\text{New total assets} = \text{Old total assets} - \text{Reduction in A/R}$$
$$= \$600 - \$27.78$$
$$= \$572.22 \text{ million.}$$

Therefore,

$$\frac{\text{Old debt}}{\text{Total assets}} = \frac{\$183.5}{\$600} = 30.6\%,$$

while,

$$\frac{\text{New debt}}{\text{Total assets}} = \frac{\$183.5}{\$572.22} = 32.1\%.$$

Selected References

The effects of alternative accounting policies on both financial statements and ratios based on these statements are discussed in the many excellent texts on financial accounting. For example, see

Kieso, Donald E., and Jerry J. Weygandt, *Intermediate Accounting* (New York: Wiley, 1980).

Smith, Jay M., and Fred K. Skousen, *Intermediate Accounting* (Cincinnati: Southwestern Publishing, 1981).

For additional insights into the use of ratio analysis in financial management, see

Altman, Edward I., "Financial Ratios, Discriminant Analysis, and the Prediction of Corporate Bankruptcy," *Journal of Finance*, vol. 23 (September 1968), 589–609.

Altman, Edward I., R. G. Haldeman, and P. Narayanan, "Zeta Analysis: A New Model to Identify Bankruptcy Risk of Corporations," *Journal of Banking and Finance*, vol. 1 (June 1977), 29-54.

Beaver, William H., "Financial Ratios as Predictors of Failure," *Empirical Research in Accounting: Selected Studies* (Chicago: University of Chicago Press, 1966), 71-127.

Chen, Kung H., and Thomas A. Shimerda, "An Empirical Analysis of Useful Financial Ratios," *Financial Management,* vol. 10 (Spring 1980), 51-60.

Gonedes, N. J., "Evidence on the Information Content of Accounting Numbers: Accounting-Based and Market-Based Estimates of Systematic Risk," *Journal of Financial and Quantitative Analysis,* vol. 8 (June 1973), 407-443.

Horrigan, James C., "A Short History of Financial Ratio Analysis," *Accounting Review,* vol. 43 (April 1968), 284-294.

Regarding earnings and dividend growth rate prediction, see

Brown, Lawrence D., and Michael S. Rozeff, "The Superiority of Analyst Forecasts as a Measure of Expectations: Evidence from Earnings," *Journal of Finance,* vol. 33 (March 1978), 1-15.

For sources of ratios, see the following:

Dun & Bradstreet, *Key Business Ratios* (99 Church Street, New York, N.Y., 1981).

Financial Research Associates, *Financial Studies of the Small Business* (Arlington, Va.: Updated annually).

Robert Morris Associates, *Annual Statement Studies* (Philadelphia, Pa.: Updated annually).

Troy, Leo, *Almanac of Business and Industrial Financial Ratios* (Englewood Cliffs, N.J.: Prentice-Hall, 1980).

Although ratio analysis as described in Chapter 6 provides many insights into a firm's operations, it still leaves unanswered two very important classes of questions. First, how serious is below-average performance in a particular ratio? For example, suppose a firm's current ratio is 1.8 versus an industry average ratio of 2.1. Is this situation bad enough to cause concern? Second, to what extent can a strong ratio of one type offset a weak one of another type? For example, suppose a firm's debt ratio is above the industry average, but its current ratio is strong. To what extent would these two factors offset one another?

Perhaps the most successful approach to answering these questions is Multiple Discriminant Analysis (MDA), a statistical technique similar to regression analysis.[1] MDA can be used to classify companies into two groups, those with a high probability of going bankrupt and those not likely to fail. This classification is made on the basis of each company's characteristics as measured by its financial ratios.[2] The purpose of this appendix is to describe the basic elements of discriminant analysis and to show how it has been used to evaluate a corporation's financial strength.

Appendix 6A

Using Multiple Discriminant Analysis to Evaluate Financial Ratios

[1] This appendix is based largely on the work of Edward I. Altman, especially these two papers: (1) "Financial Ratios, Discriminant Analysis, and the Prediction of Corporate Bankruptcy," *Journal of Finance,* September 1968, and (2) with R. G. Haldeman, and P. Narayanan, "Zeta Analysis: A New Model to Identify Bankruptcy Risk of Corporations," *Journal of Banking and Finance,* June 1977.

[2] In general, MDA can use any quantifiable factor to help classify populations. For example, in the area of consumer credit, loan applicants may be classified into those likely to default and those not likely to default on the basis of such variables as years employed, annual income, whether the applicant has a telephone, and so on. This is called "credit scoring." Banks, small loan companies, credit card companies, and retailers use MDA extensively for this purpose.

Relationship between Ratios and the Probability of Bankruptcy

On the basis of both common sense and the discussion in Chapter 6, it is clear that the probability of bankruptcy is, other things held constant, higher for a firm with a low current ratio than a high one. Similarly, the probability of bankruptcy is higher the higher the debt/assets ratio, the lower the rate of return on assets, the lower the times interest earned ratio, and so on. Figure 6A-1 shows the general nature of the relationship between bankruptcy and a few illustrative ratios.

Figure 6A-1
General Relationship between Selected Financial Ratios and the Probability of Bankruptcy

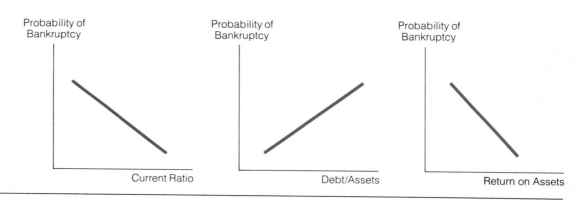

There are two difficulties with the type of analysis shown in Figure 6A-1: (1) It is difficult to measure the probability of bankruptcy, as firms either go bankrupt or remain solvent. (2) Some type of index which consolidates the effects of the current ratio, the debt ratio, the rate of return on assets, and all the other factors that affect the likelihood of bankruptcy is needed. Multiple discriminant analysis is designed to solve both of these problems.

Multiple Discriminant Analysis

Suppose a bank loan officer wants to segregate corporate loan applicants into those likely to default or not default. Assume that data for some past period is available on a group of firms that went bankrupt and another group that did not. For simplicity, we assume that only the current ratio and the debt/assets ratio are analyzed. These ratios for our sample of firms are given in Columns 2 and 3 of Table 6A-1.

The data given in Table 6A-1 are plotted in Figure 6A-2. The X's represent firms that went bankrupt, while the dots represent firms that remained solvent. For example, Point A in the upper left section is the

Firm Number (1)	Current Ratio (2)	Debt/Assets (Percent) (3)	Did Firm Go Bankrupt? (4)	Z Score (5)	Probability of Bankruptcy (6)
1	3.6	60%	No	−0.780	17.2%
2	3.0	20	No	−2.451	0.8
3	3.0	60	No	−0.135	42.0
4	3.0	76	Yes	0.791	81.2
5	2.8	44	No	−0.847	15.5
6	2.6	56	Yes	0.062	51.5
7	2.6	68	Yes	0.757	80.2
8	2.4	40	Yes[a]	−0.649	21.1
9	2.4	60	No[a]	0.509	71.5
10	2.2	28	No	−1.129	9.6
11	2.0	40	No	−0.220	38.1
12	2.0	48	No[a]	0.244	60.1
13	1.8	60	Yes	1.153	89.7
14	1.6	20	No	−0.948	13.1
15	1.6	44	Yes	0.441	68.8
16	1.2	44	Yes	0.871	83.5
17	1.0	24	No	−0.072	45.0
18	1.0	32	Yes	0.391	66.7
19	1.0	60	Yes	2.012	97.9

[a]Denotes a misclassification. Firm 8 had Z = −0.649, so MDA predicted no bankruptcy, but it did go bankrupt. Similarly, MDA predicted bankruptcy for Firms 9 and 12, but they did not go bankrupt. The following tabulation shows bankruptcy and solvency predictions and actual results.

	Z Positive: MDA Predicts Bankruptcy	Z Negative: MDA Predicts Solvency
Went bankrupt	8	1
Remained solvent	2	8

Had the MDA analysis been "perfect" as a bankruptcy predictor, all the firms would have fallen in the diagonal cells. The model did not perform perfectly, as two predicted bankrupts remained solvent, while one firm that was expected to remain solvent went bankrupt. Thus, the model misclassified three out of nineteen firms, or 16 percent of the sample.

point for Firm 2, which had a current ratio of 3.0 and a debt ratio of 20 percent. The dot at Point A indicates that the firm did not go bankrupt. Point B, in the lower right section, represents Firm 19, which had a current ratio of 1.0 and a debt ratio of 60 percent. It did go bankrupt.

The objective of discriminant analysis is to construct a boundary line through the graph such that, if the firm is to the left of the line, it is not likely to become insolvent. This boundary line is called the *discriminant function*, and in our example it takes this form:

$$Z = a + b_1 \text{ (Current ratio)} + b_2 \text{ (Debt ratio)}.$$

Here Z is defined as the "Z score," a is a constant term, and b_1 and b_2 indicate the effect that the current ratio and the debt ratio have on the probability of a firm's going bankrupt.

Although a full discussion of discriminant analysis would go well be-

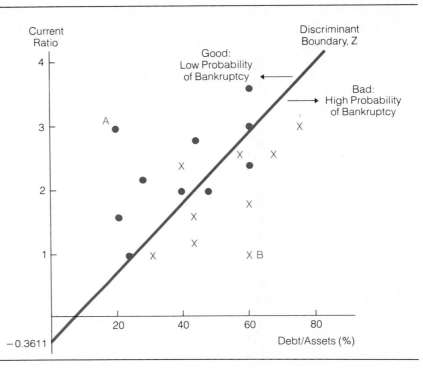

**Figure 6A-2
Discriminant Boundary
between Bankrupt and
Solvent Firms Based on
Current and Debt Ratios**

yond the scope of this book, some useful insights may be gained by observing these points:

1. The discriminant function is fitted (that is, the values of a, b_1, and b_2 are obtained) using historical data for a sample of firms that either went bankrupt or did not during some past period. Table 6A-1 gave the data for our illustrative sample. When the data were fed into a "canned" discriminant analysis program (the computing centers of most universities and large corporations have such programs), the following discriminant function was obtained:

$$Z = -0.3877 - 1.0736 \text{ (Current ratio)} + 0.0579 \text{ (Debt ratio)}.$$

2. This equation may be plotted on Figure 6A-2 as the locus of points for which $Z = 0$. All combinations of current ratio and debt ratio shown on the line result in $Z = 0$.[3] Companies that lie to the left of the line are not likely to go bankrupt, while those to the right are likely to fail. It may be seen from the graph that one X, indicating a

---

[3] To plot the boundary line, let D/A = 0% and 80%, then find the current ratio that forces Z = 0. For example, at D/A = 0,   *(continued)*

failed company, lies to the left of the line, while two dots, indicating nonbankrupt companies, lie to the right of the line. Thus, the discriminant analysis failed to classify properly three companies.

3. If we have determined the parameters of the discriminant function, then we can calculate the Z score for other companies, say loan applicants at a bank. The Z scores for our hypothetical companies are given in Column 5 of Table 6A-1, and they may be interpreted as follows:

   Z = 0: 50-50 probability of future bankruptcy (say within two years). The company lies on the boundary line.

   Z < 0: If Z is negative, there is less than a 50 percent probability of bankruptcy. The smaller the Z score, the lower the probability of bankruptcy. The computer output from MDA programs gives this probability. It is shown in Column 6 of Table 6A-1.

   Z > 0: If Z is positive, the probability of bankruptcy is greater than 50 percent. The larger Z is, the greater the probability of bankruptcy.

4. The mean Z score of our companies that did not go bankrupt is −0.583, while that for the bankrupt firms is +0.648. These means, along with approximations of the Z score probability distributions of the two groups, are shown in Figure 6A-3. We may interpret this graph as indicating that if Z is less than about −0.3, there is a very small probability that a firm will turn out to be in the bankrupt group, while if Z is greater than +0.3, there is only a small probability that it will remain solvent. If Z is in the range ±0.3, we are highly uncertain about how the firm should be classified. This range is called "the zone of ignorance."

5. The signs of the coefficients of the discriminant function are logical. Since its coefficient is negative, the larger the current ratio, the lower a company's Z score, and the lower the Z score, the smaller the probability of failure. Similarly, high debt ratios produce high Z scores, and this is directly translated into a higher probability of bankruptcy.

6. Our illustrative discriminant function has only two variables, but other characteristics could be introduced. For example, we could add such variables as the rate of return on assets, the times interest

$$Z = -0.3877 - 1.0736 \text{ (Current ratio)} + 0.0579 \text{ (0)} = 0$$
$$-1.0736 \text{ (Current ratio)} = 0.3877.$$
$$\text{Current ratio} = 0.3877/-1.0736 = -0.3611.$$

Thus, −0.3611 is the vertical axis intercept. Similarly, the current ratio at D/A = 80% is found to be 3.9533. Plotting these two points on Figure 6A-2 and then connecting them provides the discriminant boundary line. It is the line that best partitions the companies into bankrupt and nonbankrupt. It should be noted that *nonlinear* discriminant functions may also be used.

Figure 6A-3
Probability Distributions
of Z Scores

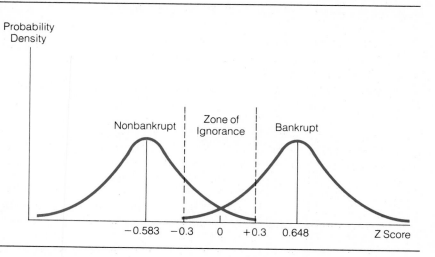

earned ratio, the quick ratio, and so forth.[4] Had the rate of return on assets been introduced, it might have turned out that Firm 8 (which failed) had a low ROA, while Firm 9 (which did not fail) had a high ROA. A new discriminant function would be calculated:

$$Z = a + b_1 \text{ (Current ratio)} + b_2 \text{ (D/A)} + b_3 \text{ (ROA)}.$$

Firm 8 might now have a positive Z, while Firm 9's Z might become negative. Thus, it is quite possible that by adding more characteristics we could improve the accuracy of our bankruptcy forecasts. In terms of Figure 6A-3, this would spread the probability distributions apart and narrow the zone of ignorance, while in terms of the matrix shown in the footnote to Table 6A-1, more firms would fall on the diagonal and fewer in the off-diagonal cells.

Altman's Studies

In his 1968 paper, Edward Altman applied MDA to a sample of corporations and developed a discriminant function that has seen wide use in actual practice.[5] Altman's function was fitted as follows:

$$Z = 0.012X_1 + 0.014X_2 + 0.033X_3 + 0.006X_4 + 0.999X_5.$$

[4] With more than two variables, it is difficult to graph the function, but this presents no problem in actual usage because graphs are only used to explain MDA.

[5] Altman, "Financial Ratios, Discriminant Analysis, and the Prediction of Corporate Bankruptcy."

Here,

X_1 = Net working capital/Total assets.
X_2 = Retained earnings (the balance sheet figure)/Total assets.
X_3 = EBIT/Total assets.
X_4 = Market value of common and preferred stock/Book value of debt.[6]
X_5 = Sales/Total assets.

The first four variables are expressed as percentages, not as decimals. Also, Altman's 50-50 point was 2.675, not 0.0 as in our hypothetical example; his zone of ignorance was from $Z = 1.81$ to $Z = 2.99$; and the *larger* the Z score, the less the probability of bankruptcy.[7]

Altman's function can be used to calculate a Z score for Carter Chemical based on the data in Chapter 6. (See Tables 6-1, 6-2, and 6-8.) This calculation is shown below:

$$
\begin{aligned}
X_1 &= 400/2{,}000 = 20.0\% & \times\ 0.012 &= 0.240 \\
X_2 &= 750/2{,}000 = 37.5\% & \times\ 0.014 &= 0.525 \\
X_3 &= 266/2{,}000 = 13.3\% & \times\ 0.033 &= 0.439 \\
X_4 &= (50 \times 28.50)/(300 + 800) = 129.5\% & \times\ 0.006 &= 0.777 \\
X_5 &= 3{,}000/2{,}000 = 1.5 & \times\ 0.999 &= \underline{1.499} \\
& & Z &= \underline{\underline{3.480}}
\end{aligned}
$$

Since Carter's Z score of 3.480 is well above the 2.99 upper limit of Altman's zone of ignorance, the data indicate that there is virtually no chance that Carter will go bankrupt within the next two years. (Altman's model could predict bankruptcy reasonably well for about two years into the future.)

Altman and his colleagues recently updated and improved the 1968 study.[8] In their more recent work, they explicitly considered such factors as capitalized lease obligations, and they used a larger sample with more current financial data. In addition, they applied smoothing techniques to level out random fluctuations in the data. The new model was able to predict bankruptcy with a high degree of accuracy for two years into the future, and with a slightly lower but still reasonable degree of accuracy (70 percent) for about five years.

---

[6] [(Shares of common outstanding × Price per share) + (Shares of preferred × Price per share of preferred)]/Balance sheet value of total debt.

[7] These differences reflect the software package used to generate the discriminant function. Altman's program operated from a base of 2.675 rather than 0.0, and his program simply reversed the sign of Z from ours.

[8] Altman, Haldeman, and Narayanan, "Zeta Analysis."

Summary

MDA has been used with success to quantify ratio analysis, to establish default probabilities for both consumer and corporate loan applicants, and in other financial applications. The technique is described in detail in many statistics texts, while articles cited at the end of Chapter 6 discuss financial applications of the model. The interested reader is urged to study this literature, for MDA does have many potential valuable applications in finance.

Appendix 6B

Effects of Inflation on Financial Statements[1]

Double-digit inflation has drawn increased attention to the need to assess both the impact of inflation on business and the success of management in coping with it. Numerous reporting methods have been proposed to provide such an assessment, but no consensus has been reached either on the preferability of any one method or on the practical usefulness of the resulting data. Nevertheless, in September 1979, the Financial Accounting Standards Board (FASB) issued Statement of Financial Accounting Standards No. 33, which requires businesses to disclose supplementary data to reflect the effects of general inflation.[2]

Traditionally, financial statements have been prepared on the basis of historical costs—the actual number of dollars exchanged at the time each transaction took place. Still, it is recognized that general inflation has caused the purchasing power of dollars to decline, resulting in the presentation of financial statement elements in dollars of varying purchasing power. To illustrate, a $100,000 machine purchased in 1981 will be quite different from a $100,000 machine purchased in 1965, so adding 1981 dollars and 1965 dollars is much like adding apples and oranges. To eliminate this disparity, such assets acquired in different years may be restated in "constant" dollars, each of which has equal purchasing power. To reflect the effects of inflation and thus express operating results in dollars of comparable purchasing power, Statement No. 33 requires a company to show what the FASB characterizes as "income from continuing operations" as if depreciation of plant assets had been based on asset amounts expressed in dollars of constant purchasing power. (This is shown for AT&T in Column b of Table 6B-1, stated in average 1979 dollars.) This adjustment is derived from the application of the Consumer Price Index for All Urban Consumers (CPI-U), a measure of inflation based on changes in the costs to consumers of a wide range of commodities and services.

Statement No. 33 also requires firms to present a supplementary five year comparison of selected financial data. The required information in

---

[1] This appendix draws heavily on the description of inflation accounting contained on pages 38-40 of AT&T'S 1979 *Annual Report*.

[2] In addition to reporting the effects of general inflation, certain companies are also required to report specific cost changes in their particular industries. This adjustment is not addressed in this appendix.

	As Reported in the Basic (Historical Cost) Financial Statements (a)	Adjusted for General Inflation (Constant Dollars) (b)	Table 6B-1 AT&T Financial Data Adjusted for Inflation December 31, 1979 ($ in Millions, except per Share Amounts)
Operating revenues	$45,408	$45,408	
Expenses:			
Depreciation	6,130	9,967	
Other operating expenses	24,075	24,075	
Operating federal income taxes	3,261	3,261	
Other operating taxes	3,960	3,960	
Other income	(775)	(775)	
Interest deductions	3,083	3,083	
Total expenses	39,734	43,571	
Net income from continuing operations	$ 5,674	$ 1,837	
Income per common share (after preferred dividend requirements)	$8.04	$2.45	

this report is to be stated in terms of the average purchasing power of the dollar during 1979. This type of comparison is shown in Table 6B-2, where selected financial data are given for AT&T for the years 1975 through 1979. The calculations for operating revenues, cash dividends per common share, and the price per share of common stock have been made by applying the average CPI-U for 1979 to the data for the years 1975 through 1978. The effect of these calculations is to increase the number of dollars shown for each year as compared to the actual number of dollars received or spent.

	1979	1978	1977	1976	1975	Table 6B-2 AT&T: Supplementary Five Year Comparison of Selected Financial Data Adjusted for the Effects of Changing Prices
Operating revenues in millions of average 1979 dollars	$45,408	$45,630	$43,657	$41,795	$39,001	
Cash dividends declared per common share:						
At historical cost	$5.00	$4.60	$4.20	$3.80	$3.40	
In average 1979 dollars	$5.00	$5.12	$5.03	$4.85	$4.59	
Market price per common share at year end:						
At historical cost	$52.13	$60.50	$60.50	$63.50	$50.88	
In average 1979 dollars	$49.10	$64.85	$70.71	$79.24	$66.54	
Average CPI-U	217.5	195.4	181.5	170.5	161.2	

It is clear from the data in Table 6B-1 that AT&T's reported income would have been much lower had depreciation been based on inflated assets rather than on the historical cost of depreciable assets, with other things held constant. However, it seems most unrealistic to report higher depreciation without recognizing that, if this higher depreciation were used in the basic income determination, then AT&T's regulators would have permitted it to charge higher rates. With higher rates, AT&T would have had higher revenues, and net income would have moved back toward, if not all the way up to, the level reported in Column a of Table 6B-1.

The data on dividends and market prices in Table 6B-2 make it clear that AT&T's stockholders have fared worse, considering inflation, than the raw data indicate. Using the raw data, it looks as if dividends have grown from $3.40 to $5.00, or by 10 percent per year. However, the purchasing power of the dividends received has only grown from $4.59 to $5.00, or by 2 percent per year. Further, the historical stock price data suggest that the value of AT&T's stock has been reasonably stable, but the price-adjusted data reveal that the real value of a share of AT&T stock has declined from $66.54 to $52.13, or by 22 percent.

Effects of Inflation on Ratio Analysis

If a ratio analysis is based on "regular" financial statements, unadjusted for inflation, then distortions can creep in. Obviously, there will be a tendency for the value of the fixed assets to be understated, and inventories will also be understated if the firm uses last-in, first-out (LIFO) accounting. At the same time, increasing rates of inflation will cause increases in interest rates, which will cause the value of the outstanding long-term debt to decline. Further, profits will vary from year to year as the inflation rate changes, and these variations will be especially severe if inventory is charged to cost of goods sold on the first-in, first-out (FIFO) basis.

These factors will make ratio comparisons over time for a given company, and across companies at a point in time, less reliable than would be the case in the absence of inflation. This is especially true if a company changes its accounting procedures (say, from straight line to accelerated depreciation or from FIFO to LIFO), or if various companies in a given industry use different accounting methods. Analysts can attempt to restate financial statements to put everything on a common basis, but at best this can only reduce the problem, not eliminate it. With the present state of the art, financial analysts cannot do much more than base their ratio analysis of a firm on the existing accounting data. They simply have to recognize that there are weaknesses in this approach and apply judgment in interpreting the data.·

Financial Forecasting

As noted in Chapter 6, both managers and investors are vitally concerned with *future* financial statements. Also, managers regularly construct *pro forma*, or projected, statements and consider alternative courses of action in terms of how these alternative actions affect the projected statements. In this chapter we discuss briefly how pro forma statements are constructed and how they are used to help estimate the need for different types of capital.

Demand Forecasts

The most important element in financial planning is a demand (or sales) forecast. Because such forecasts are critical for production scheduling, for plant design, for financial planning, and so on, the entire management team participates in their preparation. In fact, most of the larger firms have a *planning group* or *planning committee*, with its own staff of economists, which coordinates the corporation's sales forecast. Since demand forecasting is a rather specialized subject, we will not consider the mechanics of the forecasting process in this chapter. Rather, we will simply take the sales forecast as given and then use it to illustrate various types of financial decisions.[1]

Forecasting Financial Requirements: The Percentage of Sales Method

To use this simple but often practical method of forecasting financial requirements, we first express the various balance sheet items as percentages of sales, then use these percentages, together with expected future sales, to construct pro forma balance sheets. To illustrate, consider the Arinson Products Company, whose December 31, 1981, balance sheet is given in Table 7-1. Arinson is operating at full capacity. Its 1981 sales were $400,000; its profit margin on sales was 10 percent; and Arinson distributed 60 percent of its after-tax profits to stockholders as dividends. If Arinson Products expects sales to increase to $600,000 in 1982, what

---

[1] A sales forecast is actually the *expected value of a probability distribution* of possible levels of sales. Because any sales forecast is subject to a greater or lesser degree of uncertainty, for financial planning we are often just as interested in the degree of uncertainty inherent in the sales forecast (σ sales) as we are in the expected value of sales. See J. L. Pappas and E. F. Brigham, *Managerial Economics*, Chapter 5: "Demand Estimation" (Hinsdale, Ill.: Dryden Press, 1979), for a detailed discussion of procedures for making demand forecasts.

Table 7-1 Arinson Products Company: Balance Sheet, December 31, 1981 ($ in Thousands)	Cash	$ 10	Accounts payable	$ 40
	Receivables	90	Notes payable	10
	Inventories	200	Accrued wages and taxes	50
	Total current assets	$300	Total current liabilities	$100
	Net fixed assets	300	Mortgage bonds	150
			Common stock	50
			Retained earnings	300
	Total assets	$600	Total claims	$600

Current ratio = 300/100 = 3:1; Industry average = 2.6:1.
Total debt/total assets = 250/600 = 42%; Industry average = 45%.

will be its pro forma December 31, 1982, balance sheet, and how much additional financing will the company require?

Our first step is to isolate those balance sheet items that vary directly with sales. Since Arinson is operating at full capacity, each asset item must increase if the higher level of sales is to be attained. More cash will be needed for transactions; receivables will be higher; additional inventory must be stocked; and new plant must be added.[2]

If assets are to increase, liabilities and net worth must likewise rise—the balance sheet must balance, and increases in assets must be financed in some manner. Accounts payable and accruals will rise *spontaneously* with sales: as sales increase, so will purchases, and larger purchases will result in higher levels of accounts payable. Thus, if sales double, accounts payable will also double. Similarly, a higher level of operations will require more labor, so accrued wages will increase, and, assuming profit margins are maintained, an increase in profits will pull up accrued taxes. Retained earnings will also increase, but not in direct proportion to the increase in sales. Neither notes payable, mortgage bonds, nor common stock will rise spontaneously with sales—higher sales do not *automatically* trigger increases in these items.

We can construct a pro forma balance sheet for December 31, 1982, proceeding as outlined below.

Step 1. In Table 7-2, Column 1, we express those balance sheet items that vary directly with sales as a percentage of sales. An item such as notes payable that does not vary directly with sales is designated n.a., or "not applicable."

[2] Assets such as marketable securities, which are not tied directly to operations, do not vary directly with sales.

	Balance Sheet Items on 12/31/1981 (as a % of the $400 1981 Sales) (1)	Pro Forma Balance Sheet on 12/31/1982 (= Projected Sales of $600 Times Column 1) (2)	Table 7-2 Arinson Products Company: 12/31/1981 Balance Sheet Expressed as a Percentage of Sales and 12/31/1982 Pro Forma Balance Sheet ($ in Thousands)
Cash	2.5%	$ 15	
Receivables	22.5	135	
Inventories	50.0	300	
Total current assets	75.0%	$450	
Net fixed assets	75.0	450	
Total assets	150.0%	$900	
Accounts payable	10.0%	$ 60	
Notes payable	n.a.[a]	10[b]	
Accrued wages and taxes	12.5	75	
Total current liabilities	22.5%	$145	
Mortgage bonds	n.a.	150[b]	
Common stock	n.a.	50[b]	
Retained earnings	n.a.	324[c]	
	22.5%	Funds available $669	
		Additional funds needed[d] 231	
		$900	

[a]n.a. = not applicable.
[b]1982 projections picked up from 12/31/1981 balance sheet.
[c]12/31/1981 balance in retained earnings plus 1982 addition to retained earnings.
[d]"Additional funds needed" is a balancing figure: $900 − $669 = $231.

Step 2. Next, we multiply these percentages by the $600,000 projected 1982 sales to obtain the projected amounts as of December 31, 1982. These are shown in Column 2 of the table.

Step 3. We simply insert figures for notes payable, mortgage bonds, and common stock from the 12/31/1981 balance sheet. At least one of these accounts may have to be changed later in the analysis.

Step 4. We next add the addition to retained earnings estimated for 1982 to the figure shown on the December 31, 1981, balance sheet to obtain the 12/31/1982 projected retained earnings. Recall that Arinson expects to earn 10 percent on sales of $600,000, or $60,000, and to pay 60 percent of this out in dividends to stockholders. (The *dividend payout ratio* is 60 percent.) Thus, retained earnings for the year are projected to be $60,000 − 0.6($60,000) = $24,000. Adding the $24,000 addition to retained earnings to the $300,000 beginning balance gives the $324,000 projected retained earnings shown in Column 2.

Step 5. Next, we sum the asset accounts, obtaining a total projected assets figure of $900,000, and also add the projected liabilities and net worth items to obtain $669,000, the estimate of available funds. Since liabilities and net worth must total $900,000, but only $669,000 is projected, we have a shortfall of $231,000 "additional funds needed," which will presumably be raised by selling securities. For simplicity, we disregard depreciation by assuming that cash flows from depreciation are reinvested in fixed assets.

Step 6. Arinson could use short-term notes, mortgage bonds, common stock, or a combination of these securities to make up the shortfall. Ordinarily, it would make this choice on the basis of the relative costs of these different types of securities. However, in this case the company has a contractual agreement with its bondholders to keep total debt at or below 50 percent of total assets, and also to keep the current ratio at a level of 3.0 or greater. These provisions restrict the financing choices as follows:[3]

1. *Restriction on Additional Debt*

$$\text{Maximum debt permitted} = 0.5 \times \text{Total assets}$$
$$= 0.5 \times \$900,000 = \$450,000$$

Less debt already projected for 12/31/1982:		
Current liabilities	$145,000	
Mortgage bonds	150,000	= 295,000
Maximum additional debt		$155,000

2. *Restriction on Additional Current Liabilities*

$$\text{Maximum current liabilities} = \text{⅓ of current assets}$$
$$= \$450,000 \div 3 = \$150,000$$

Current liabilities already projected	145,000
Maximum additional current liabilities	$ 5,000

3. *Common Equity Requirements*

Total additional funds needed (from Table 7-2)	$231,000
Maximum additional debt permitted	155,000
Common equity funds required	$ 76,000

We see, then, that Arinson needs a total of $231,000 from external sources. Its existing debt contract limits new debt to $155,000, and of that amount only $5,000 can be short-term debt. Thus, Arinson must plan to sell common stock in the amount of $76,000, in addition to some debt financing, to cover its financial requirements.

[3] As we shall see in Chapter 13, restrictions such as these are contained in virtually all long-term debt agreements. They are designed to protect bondholders against imprudent managerial decisions that would increase the risk the bondholders face.

Arinson's financial manager can now construct a set of projected, or pro forma, financial statements and then analyze the ratios that are implied by these statements. Table 7-3 gives abbreviated versions of the final projected balance sheet, income statement, statement of changes in financial position, and a few key ratios. These statements, in turn, can be used by the financial manager to show the other executives the implications of the planned sales increase. For example, the projected rate of return on equity is 13.3 percent. Is this a reasonable target, or can it be improved? Also, the preliminary forecast calls for the sale of some common stock—but does top management really want to sell any new stock? Suppose Arinson Products is owned entirely by John Arinson, who does not want to sell any stock and thereby lose his exclusive control of the company. How then can the needed funds be raised, or what adjustments should be made? In the remainder of the chapter, we look at approaches to answering questions such as these.

Projected Financial Statements and Ratios

Table 7-3
Arinson Products Company: Projected Financial Statements for 1982 ($ in Thousands)

I. Projected Balance Sheet, 12/31/82

Cash	$ 15	Accounts payable	$ 60
Accounts receivable	135	Notes payable[a]	15
Inventories	300	Accruals	75
Total current assets	$450	Total current liabilities	$150
Net fixed assets	$450	Long-term debt[b]	$300
		Common stock[c]	126
		Retained earnings	324
		Total equity	$450
Total assets	$900	Total claims	$900

II. Projected Income Statement, 1982

Sales	$600
Total costs	500
Taxable income	$100
Taxes (40%)	40
Net income after taxes	$ 60
Dividends	36
Addition to retained earnings	$ 24

III. Projected Statement of Changes in Financial Position, 1982

Sources of funds:	
Net income	$ 60
Funds from operations[d]	60
Proceeds from sale of bonds	150
Proceeds from sale of common stock	76
Total sources	$286

Table 7-3 continued

Uses of funds:

Increase in net fixed assets	$150
Dividend payments	36
Increase in net working capital	100
Total uses	$286

Analysis of Changes in Working Capital

Increase (decrease) in current assets:

Cash	$ 5
Accounts receivable	45
Inventories	100
Net increase (decrease) in current assets	$150

Increase (decrease) in current liabilities:

Accounts payable	$ 20
Notes payable	5
Accruals	25
Net increase (decrease) in current liabilities	$ 50
Increase (decrease) in net working capital	$100

IV. Key Ratios Projected for 12/31/82

1. Current ratio	3.0 times
2. Total debt/total assets	50%
3. Rate of return on equity	13.3%

(Other ratios could be calculated and analyzed by the du Pont system.)

[a]Assumes $5,000 additional is borrowed from bank. This is the maximum permissible increase in short-term debt.

[b]Assumes $150,000 additional long-term debt is sold. This is the maximum permissible increase in long-term debt, given the $5,000 increase in notes payable.

[c]Assumes $76,000 additional common stock is sold to complete the financing.

[d]The figure for funds from operations normally includes depreciation. Here we have assumed that depreciation is reinvested in fixed assets; that is, depreciation is netted out against fixed asset additions.

The Relationship between Growth in Sales and Capital Requirements

Although the forecast of capital requirements can be made by constructing pro forma balance sheets as described above, it is often easier to use a simple forecasting formula. In addition, the formula can be used to make clear the relationship between sales growth and financial requirements:

$$\begin{matrix} \text{Additional} \\ \text{funds} \\ \text{needed} \end{matrix} = \begin{bmatrix} \text{Required} \\ \text{increase} \\ \text{in assets} \end{bmatrix} - \begin{bmatrix} \text{Spontaneous} \\ \text{increase in} \\ \text{liabilities} \end{bmatrix} - \begin{bmatrix} \text{Increase in} \\ \text{retained} \\ \text{earnings} \end{bmatrix}$$

$$\text{AFN} = \left(\frac{A}{S}\right)\Delta S - \left(\frac{L}{S}\right)\Delta S - MS_1(1 - d). \qquad (7\text{-}1)$$

Here,

AFN = additional funds needed.

A/S = assets that increase spontaneously with sales as a percent of sales, or required dollar increase in assets per $1 increase in sales. A/S = 150%, or 1.5, for Arinson.

L/S = liabilities that increase spontaneously with sales as a percent of sales, or spontaneously generated financing per $1 increase in sales. L/S = 22.5%, or 0.225, for Arinson.

S_1 = total sales projected for next year. Note that S_0 = last year's sales. S_1 = $600,000 for Arinson.

ΔS = change in sales = $S_1 - S_0$ = $600,000 − $400,000 = $200,000 for Arinson.

M = profit margin, or rate of profits per $1 of sales. M = 10%, or 0.10, for Arinson.

d = percentage of earnings paid out in dividends, or the dividend payout ratio; d = 60%. Notice that 1 − d = 1.0 − 0.6 = 0.4, or 40 percent. This is the percentage of earnings that Arinson retains, often called the *retention rate* or *retention ratio*.

Inserting values for Arinson Products into Equation 7-1, we find the additional funds needed as follows:

$$AFN = 1.5(\Delta S) - 0.225(\Delta S) - 0.1(S_1)(1 - 0.6)$$
$$= 1.5(\$200,000) - 0.225(\$200,000) - 0.1(\$600,000)(0.4)$$
$$= \$300,000 - \$45,000 - \$24,000$$
$$= \$231,000.$$

To increase sales by $200,000, Arinson must increase assets by $300,000. The $300,000 of new assets must be financed in some manner. Of the total, $45,000 will come from a spontaneous increase in liabilities, while another $24,000 will be raised from retained earnings. The remaining $231,000 must be obtained from external sources. This value must, of course, agree with the figure developed earlier in Table 7-2.

The faster Arinson's growth rate in sales, the greater its need for external financing; we can use Equation 7-1 to indicate this relationship. Consider Table 7-4, which shows Arinson Products' external financial requirements at various growth rates. These data also are plotted in Figure 7-1. Several points are apparent from the exhibits; they are discussed below.

Graph of the Relationship between Growth and Funds Requirements

Financial Planning. At low growth rates Arinson needs no external financing. However, if the company grows faster than 3.239 percent, it must raise capital from outside sources. If for any reason management foresees difficulties in raising this capital—perhaps because Arinson's owners do not want to sell additional stock—then the company might need to reconsider the feasibility of its expansion plans.

Table 7-4
Relationship between
Growth in Sales and
Financial Requirements,
Assuming S_0 = $400,000

Growth Rate in Sales (%) (1)	Dollar Increase (Decrease) in Sales (ΔS in Thousands) (2)	Forecasted Sales (S_1 in Thousands) (3)	External Funds Requirements (Surplus in Thousands) (4)
100%	$400	$800	$478.0
50	200	600	231.0
25	100	500	107.5
10	40	440	33.4
3.239	12.956	412.956	0.0
0	0	400	(16.0)
−10	(40)	360	(65.4)
−25	(100)	300	(139.5)

Note: *Explanation of Columns*
Col. 1 Growth rate in sales, g.
Col. 2 Increase (decrease) in sales, $\Delta S = g(S_0)$.
Col. 3 Forecasted sales, $S_1 = S_0 + g(S_0) = S_0(1 + g)$.
Col. 4 External funds required $= 1.5(\Delta S) - 0.225(\Delta S) - 0.04(S_1)$
$\qquad\qquad\qquad\qquad = 1.275(\Delta S) - 0.04(S_1)$
$\qquad\qquad\qquad\qquad = 1.275(g)(S_0) - 0.04(S_0)(1 + g)$
$\qquad\qquad\qquad\qquad = 510g - 16 - 16g$
$\qquad\qquad\qquad\qquad = -16 + 494g$
$\qquad\qquad\qquad\qquad =$ equation plotted in Figure 7-1.
Example: If g = 10%, or 0.10, then
External funds required $= -16 + 494g$
$\qquad\qquad\qquad\qquad = -16 + 494(0.10)$
$\qquad\qquad\qquad\qquad = 33.4$ or $33,400.
The maximum growth rate that can be financed without external funds is found by setting the equation equal to zero:
External funds required $= 0 = -16 + 494g$
$\qquad\qquad\qquad 494g = 16$
$\qquad\qquad g = 16/494 = 0.03239$ or 3.239%.

The Effect of Dividend Policy on Financing Needs. Dividend policy also affects external capital requirements, so if Arinson foresees difficulties in raising capital, it might want to consider a reduction in the dividend payout ratio. This would lower, or shift to the right, the line in Figure 7-1, indicating lower external capital requirements at all growth rates. However, before making this decision, management should consider the effects of changes in dividends on stock prices. These effects are described in Chapter 18.

Notice that the line in Figure 7-1 does *not* pass through the origin; thus, at low growth rates surplus funds (negative funds requirements) will be produced, because new retained earnings plus spontaneous funds will exceed the required asset increases. Only if the dividend payout ratio is 100 percent, meaning that the firm does not retain any of its earnings, will the "funds required" line pass through the origin.

Capital Intensity. The amount of assets required per dollar of sales, A/S

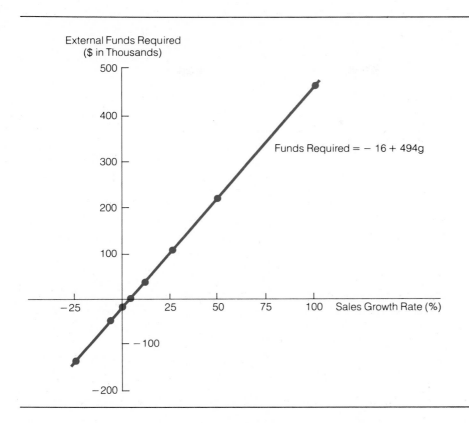

External Funds Required
($ in Thousands)

Funds Required = − 16 + 494g

Sales Growth Rate (%)

in Equation 7-1, is often called the *capital intensity ratio.* This factor has a major effect on capital requirements per unit of sales growth. If the capital intensity ratio is low, then sales can grow rapidly without much outside capital. However, if the firm is capital intensive, even a small growth in output will require a great deal of outside capital. This is precisely the problem facing the utility industry today. Utilities are very capital intensive, so they require large amounts of capital to expand output. Further, a conversion from an oil-based economy to one based more heavily on coal and nuclear energy will mean a substantial growth in demand for electricity. Since all this is coming at a time of tight money and high interest rates, financial executives in the utility industry have their work cut out for them.

The Profit Margin and the Need for External Funds. The profit margin, M, is also an important determinant of the funds required equation—the higher the margin, the lower the funds requirements, other things held constant. Arinson's profit margin was 10 percent. Now suppose M increased to 15 percent. This new value could be inserted into the funds required formula, and the following relationship between funds needs and growth would result: AFN $= -24 + 486g$. Thus, we see that an increase in the profit margin lowers both the intercept term and the slope coefficient, so for all positive growth rates there is a reduction in external funds needed. Because of the relationship between profit margins and external capital requirements, some very rapidly growing firms do not need much external capital. Thus, for example, Xerox grew very rapidly with very little borrowing or stock sales. However, as the company lost patent protection, and as competition intensified in the copier industry, Xerox's profit margin declined, its needs for external capital rose, and it began to borrow from banks and other sources.

Forecasting Financial Requirements When the Balance Sheet Ratios Are Subject to Change

To this point we have been assuming that the balance sheet ratios (A/S and L/S) are expected to remain constant over time. For the ratios to remain constant, each asset and liability item must increase at the same rate as sales. In graph form, this assumption suggests the existence of the type of relationship indicated in Panel a of Figure 7-2, a relationship that is linear and passes through the origin. Then, if the company grows and sales expand from $200 million to $400 million, inventories will increase proportionately, from $100 million to $200 million.

The assumption of constant ratios is appropriate at times, but there are times when it is incorrect. Three such conditions are described in the following sections.

Economies of Scale

There are economies of scale in the use of many kinds of assets, and where they occur, the ratios are likely to change over time as the size of the firm increases. Often, for example, firms need to maintain base stocks of different inventory items, even if sales levels are quite low. Then, as sales expand, inventories grow less rapidly than sales, so the ratio of inventory to sales (I/S) declines. This situation is depicted in Panel b of Figure 7-2. Here we see that the inventory/sales ratio is 1.5, or 150 percent, when sales are $200 million, but that the ratio declines to 1.0 when sales climb to $400 million.

The relationship shown for economies of scale is linear, but this is not necessarily the case. Indeed, as we shall see in Chapters 8 and 9, if a firm employs a basic model (the EOQ model) to establish inventory and cash levels, these items will rise with the square root of sales. This means that the line in Figure 7-2b would tend to be a curved line whose slope diminishes at higher sales levels.

"Lumpy" Assets

In many industries technological considerations dictate that if a firm is to be competitive, it must add fixed assets in large, discrete units. For example, in the paper industry there are strong economies of scale in basic

Figure 7-2
Three Possible Relationships between Assets and Sales ($ in Millions)

a. Constant Ratios

Inventory ($)

200/400 =
0.50 =
50%

100/200 =
0.50 =
50%

I/S

Sales ($)

b. Economies of Scale

Inventory ($)

300/200 =
1.50 =
150%

400/400 =
1.00 =
100%

I/S

Sales ($)

c. "Lumpy" Assets

Fixed Assets ($)

Capacity

FA/S

Excess Capacity
(Temporary)

A

B

Sales ($)

paper mill equipment, so when paper companies expand capacity, they must do so in large increments. This type of situation is depicted in Panel c of Figure 7-2. Here we assume that the minimum-sized feasible plant has a cost of $75 million, and that such a plant can produce enough output to attain a sales level of $100 million. If the firm is to be competitive, it simply must have at least $75 million of fixed assets.

This situation has a major effect on the fixed assets/sales (FA/S) ratio at different sales levels, and consequently effects on financial requirements. At Point A in Figure 7-2, which represents a sales level of $50 million, the fixed assets are $75 million, so the ratio FA/S = $75/$50 = 1.5. However, sales can expand by $50 million, out to $100 million, with no required increase in fixed assets. At that point, represented by Point B, the ratio FA/S = $75/$100 = 0.75. Here, though, even a small increase in sales would require the firm to double its plant capacity, so a small projected sales increase would bring with it very large financial requirements.[4]

Cyclical Changes

Panels a, b, and c of Figure 7-2 all focus on target, or projected, relationships between sales and assets. Actual sales, however, are often different from projected sales, and the actual asset/sales ratio for a given period may thus be quite different from the planned ratio. To illustrate, the firm depicted in Panel b might, when its sales are at $200 million and its inventories at $300 million, predict a sales expansion to $400 million and then increase its inventories to $400 million in anticipation of the sales expansion. Yet suppose an unforeseen economic downturn holds sales to only $300 million. In this case, inventories would be $400 million, but inventories of only about $350 million are needed to support sales of $300 million. Then if the firm were forecasting its financial requirements, it could expand sales by $100 million with no increase in inventories, but any sales expansion beyond $100 million would require additional financing to build inventories.

Modifying the Forecast of External Funds Needed

If any of the asset/sales ratios are subject to any of the types of changes noted above, then the simple percentage of sales method of forecasting financial requirements should not be used. Rather, it becomes necessary (1) to make separate forecasts of the requirements for each type of asset, given the projected sales level, (2) to forecast spontaneously generated funds, and then (3) to subtract to determine the external funds needed.

To illustrate, consider again the Arinson Products example set forth in Tables 7-1 and 7-2. Now suppose a ratio analysis along the lines described

---

[4] Several other points should be noted about Panel c of Figure 7-2. First, if the firm is operating at a sales level of $100 million or less, then any expansion that calls for a sales increase above $100 million will require a *doubling* of the firm's fixed assets. Much smaller percentage increases will be involved if the firm is large enough to be operating a number of plants. Second, firms generally go to multiple shifts and take other actions to minimize the need for new fixed asset capacity as they approach Point B. However, these efforts can go only so far, and eventually a fixed asset expansion is required. Third, firms often make arrangements to purchase excess capacity output from other firms in their industry, or to sell excess capacity to other firms. For example, consider the situation in the electric utility industry. It is very much like that depicted in Panel c. Electric companies often arrange to buy excess capacity from other companies in order to avoid building a new plant that will be underutilized. Sometimes they may sell excess power from a newly completed plant for a number of years, until their own customer demand catches up with their output capacity.

in Chapter 6 suggests that the cash, receivables, and inventories ratios indicated in Table 7-2 are appropriate, as are the liability ratios and the retained earnings calculations, but that excess capacity exists in fixed assets. Specifically, fixed assets in 1981 were being utilized to only 80 percent of capacity. To use the existing fixed assets at full capacity, 1981 sales could have been as high as $500,000:

$$\frac{\text{Current sales}}{\text{Percent of capacity}} = \frac{\$400,000}{0.8} = \$500,000.$$

This suggests that Arinson's target fixed assets/sales ratio should be

$$\frac{\text{Fixed assets}}{\text{Sales}} = \frac{\$300,000}{\$500,000} = 0.6,$$

not the 0.75 that actually existed. Therefore, at the projected sales level of $600,000, Arinson will require fixed assets of only 0.6($600,000) = $360,000, up only $60,000 from the $300,000 currently on hand.[5]

We estimated earlier that Arinson would need an additional $231,000 of capital, and that at least $76,000 of this amount would have to be raised by selling common stock. However, that capital requirements estimate was based on the assumption that $450,000 of fixed assets would be required. If Arinson can attain a sales level of $600,000 with only $360,000 of fixed assets, then the external funds needed will decline by $90,000, to $141,000, and no new common equity will be required.

Computerized Financial Planning Models

Although the type of financial forecasting described in this chapter can be done by hand, most well-managed firms with sales greater than a few million dollars employ some type of computerized financial planning model. Such models can be programmed to show the effects of different sales levels, different ratios of sales to operating assets, and even different assumptions about sales prices and input costs (labor, materials, and so forth). Plans are then made regarding how financial requirements are to be met—through bank loans, thus increasing short-term notes payable; by selling long-term bonds; or by selling new common stock. Pro forma balance sheets and income statements are generated under the different financing plans, and earnings per share are projected, along with such risk measures as the current ratio, the debt/assets ratio, and the times interest earned ratio.

Depending on how these projections look, management may modify its initial plans. For example, the firm may conclude that its sales forecast must be cut because the requirements for external capital exceed the

---

[5] This $60,000 required new fixed assets could also be determined by noting (1) that sales could grow from $400,000 to $500,000 without any increase in fixed assets, but (2) that the sales increase from $500,000 to $600,000 would require new fixed assets of (FA/S)(ΔS) = 0.6($100,000) = $60,000.

firm's ability to raise money. Or, management may decide to reduce dividends and thus generate more funds internally. Alternatively, the company may decide to investigate production processes that require fewer fixed assets, or to consider the possibility of buying rather than manufacturing certain components, thus eliminating raw materials and work-in-process inventories, as well as certain manufacturing facilities.

In subsequent chapters we will look in detail at ways of analyzing policy changes such as those mentioned above. In all such considerations, the basic issue is the effect that a specific action will have on future earnings, on the riskiness of these earnings, and, hence, on the price of the firm's stock. Since computerized models help management assess these effects, such planning models are playing an ever increasing role in corporate management.[6]

Summary

This chapter described in broad outline how firms go about projecting their financial statements and determining their overall financial requirements. In brief, management establishes a target balance sheet based on the type of ratio analysis discussed in Chapter 6. Assuming that each balance sheet ratio is at the desired level and that the optimal levels for these ratios are stable, the *percentage of sales method* can be used to forecast the external financial requirements associated with any given increase in sales. If the balance sheet ratios are subject to change, as they will be if excess capacity exists, then each item in the projected balance sheet must be forecast separately.

The type of forecasting described here is important for several reasons. First, if the projected operating results look poor, management can "go back to the drawing board" and reformulate its plans for the coming year. Second, it is possible that the funds required to meet the sales forecast simply cannot be obtained. If so, it is obviously better to know this in advance and to scale back the projected level of operations. And third, even if the required funds can be raised, it is desirable to plan for the acquisition of these funds well in advance. As we shall see in later chapters, raising capital takes time and is expensive, and both time and money can be saved by careful forward planning.

---

[6] Corporations can develop their own computerized models, but excellent and easy-to-use planning models are also available from a number of specialized computer software companies. One such model—Interactive Financial Planning System (IFPS)—is installed on the computer system at the University of Florida. IFPS is also used by several hundred companies, including 3M Corporation, Shell Oil, and Florida Power & Light. Further discussion of computer models is deferred to Chapter 12, where their use in capital budgeting is considered.

7-1 Certain liability and net worth items generally increase spontaneously with increases in sales. Put a check ($\checkmark$) by those items that typically increase spontaneously:

Accounts payable   ____
Notes payable to banks   ____
Accrued wages   ____
Accrued taxes   ____
Mortgage bonds   ____
Common stock   ____
Retained earnings   ____
Marketable securities   ____

7-2 The following equation can, under certain assumptions, be used to forecast financial requirements:

$$\text{Additional funds needed} = \frac{A}{S}(\Delta S) - \frac{L}{S}(\Delta S) - MS_1(1 - d).$$

Under what conditions does the equation give satisfactory predictions, and when should it not be used?

7-3 Assume that an average firm in the office supply business has a 6 percent after-tax profit margin, a 40 percent debt/assets ratio, a turnover of 2 times, and a dividend payout ratio of 40 percent. Is it true that if such a firm is to have *any* sales growth ($g > 0$), it will be forced to sell either bonds or common stock; that is, it will need some nonspontaneous external capital, and this will be true even if g is very small?

7-4 Is it true that computerized corporate planning models were a fad during the 1970s, but, because of a need for flexibility in corporate planning, they have been dropped by most firms?

7-5 Suppose a firm makes the following policy changes. If the change means that external, nonspontaneous financial requirements for any rate of growth will increase, indicate this by a ($+$); indicate decreases by a ($-$); and indicate indeterminant and/or no effect by a (0). Think in terms of the immediate, short-run effect on funds requirements.

a. The dividend payout ratio is increased.   ____
b. The firm contracts to buy rather than make certain components used in its products.   ____
c. The firm decides to pay all suppliers on delivery, rather than after a thirty day delay, in order to take advantage of discounts for rapid payment.   ____
d. The firm begins to sell on credit; previously, all sales had been on a cash basis.   ____
e. The firm's profit margin is eroded by increased competition.   ____
f. Advertising expenditures are stepped up.   ____

g. A decision is made to substitute long-term mortgage bonds for short-term bank loans. _____

h. The firm begins to pay employees on a weekly basis; previously, it paid at the end of each month. _____

Self-Test Problems

ST7-1 J. Bildersee, Inc., has these ratios: A/S = 1.6; L/S = 0.4; profit margin = 0.10; and dividend payout ratio = 0.45 or 45%. Sales last year were $100 million. Assuming that these ratios will remain constant and that all liabilities increase spontaneously with increases in sales, what is the maximum growth rate Bildersee can achieve without having to employ nonspontaneous external funds?

ST7-2 Suppose Bildersee's financial consultants report (1) that the inventory turnover ratio is sales/inventory = 3 times versus an industry average of 4 times, and (2) that Bildersee could raise its turnover to 4 without affecting sales, the profit margin, or the other asset turnover ratios. Under these conditions, what amount of external funds would Bildersee expect to require during each of the next two years if sales grow at a rate of 20 percent per year?

Problems

7-1 A group of investors is planning to set up a new company to manufacture and distribute a novel type of running shoe. To help plan the new operation's financial requirements, you have been asked to construct a pro forma balance sheet for 12/31/82, the end of the first year of operations. Sales for 1982 are projected at $20 million, and the following are industry average ratios for athletic shoe companies.

Sales to common equity	5×
Current debt to equity	50%
Total debt to equity	80%
Current ratio	2.2×
Net sales to inventory	9×
Accounts receivable to sales	10%
Fixed assets to equity	70%
Profit margin	3%
Dividend payout ratio	30%

Pro Forma Balance Sheet, December 31, 1982 ($ in Millions)

Cash	$_____	Current debt	$_____
Accounts receivable	_____	Long-term debt	_____
Inventories	_____	Total debt	_____
Total current assets	_____	Equity	_____
Fixed assets	_____		
Total assets	$_____	Total claims	$_____

a. Complete the pro forma balance sheet on p. 258, assuming that 1982 sales are $20 million.

b. If our group supplies all the new firm's equity, how much capital will we be required to put up by 12/31/82?

7-2 Dandy Computers makes bulk purchases of small computers, stocks them in conveniently located warehouses, and then ships them to its chain of retail stores. Dandy's balance sheet as of 12/31/1981 is shown below (in millions of dollars):

Cash	$ 2.0	Accounts payable	$ 5.0
Receivables	15.0	Notes payable	10.0
Inventories	33.0	Accruals	5.0
Total current assets	$50.0	Total current liabilities	$20.0
Net fixed assets	20.2	Mortgage loan	3.4
		Common stock	8.4
		Retained earnings	38.4
Total assets	$70.2	Total liabilities and net worth	$70.2

Sales for 1981 were $200 million, while net income after taxes for the year was $5,670,000. Dandy paid dividends of $2,268,000 to common stockholders. The firm is operating at full capacity.

a. If sales are projected to increase by $50 million, or by 25 percent, during 1982, what are Dandy's projected external capital requirements?

b. Construct Dandy's pro forma balance sheet for 12/31/1982. Assume that all external capital requirements are met by bank loans and are reflected in notes payable.

c. Now calculate the following ratios, based on your projected 12/31/1982 balance sheet. Dandy's 1981 ratios and industry average ratios are shown below for comparison.

	Dandy Computers 12/31/82	Dandy Computers 12/31/81	Industry Average 12/31/81
Current ratio	_____	2.5×	3×
Debt/total assets	_____	33.3%	30%
Rate of return on net worth	_____	12.1%	12%

d. Now assume that Dandy grows by the same $50 million, but that the growth is spread over five years; that is, sales grow by $10 million each year.

1. Calculate total external financial requirements over the five year period.

2. Construct a pro forma balance sheet as of 12/31/1986, using notes payable as the balancing item.

3. Calculate the current ratio, debt/assets ratio, and rate of return on net worth as of 12/31/86.

   Hint: Be sure to use *total sales*, which amount to $1,150 million, to calculate retained earnings, but 1986 profits to calculate the rate of return on net worth; that is, (1986 profits)/(12/31/86 net worth).

e. Do the plans outlined in Parts c and d seem feasible to you? That is, do you think Dandy could borrow the required capital, and would the company be raising the odds on its bankruptcy to an excessive level in the event of some temporary misfortune?

7-3 The McCollough-Crum Company's 1981 sales were $24 million. The percentage of sales of each balance sheet item that varies directly with sales is given below:

Cash	3%
Receivables	20
Inventories	25
Net fixed assets	40
Accounts payable	15
Accruals	10
Profit rate (after taxes) on sales	5

The dividend payout ratio is 40 percent; the 12/31/1980 balance sheet account for retained earnings was $8.2 million; and both common stock and mortgage bonds are constant and equal to the amounts shown on the balance sheet below.

a. Complete the following balance sheet:

McCollough-Crum Company: Balance Sheet,
December 31, 1981 ($ in Thousands)

Cash	$	Accounts payable	$	
Receivables		Notes payable	2,200	
Inventories	_____	Accruals		
Total current assets		Total current liabilities		
Net fixed assets	_____	Mortgage bonds	2,000	
		Common stock	2,000	
		Retained earnings	_____	
		Total liabilities and		
Total assets	$_____	net worth	$_____	

b. Now suppose that 1982 sales increase by 10 percent over 1981 sales. How much additional external capital will be required? The company was operating at full capacity in 1981. Use Equation 7-1 to answer this question.

c. Develop a pro forma balance sheet for 12/31/1982. Assume that any required financing is borrowed as notes payable.

d. What would happen to external funds requirements under each of the following conditions? Answer in words, without calculations.

1. The profit margin went (i) from 5 percent to 6 percent, (ii) from 5 percent to 3 percent.

2. The dividend payout rate (i) was raised from 40 to 90 percent, (ii) was lowered from 40 to 20 percent.

3. Credit terms on sales were relaxed substantially, giving customers longer to pay.

4. The company had excess manufacturing capacity at 12/31/81.

7-4 Alabama Textile's 1981 sales were $72 million. The percentage of sales of each balance sheet item except notes payable, mortgage bonds, and common stock is given below:

Cash	4%
Receivables	25
Inventories	30
Net fixed assets	50
Accounts payable	15
Accruals	5
Profit margin (after taxes) on sales	5

The dividend payout ratio is 60 percent; the 12/31/1980 balance sheet account for retained earnings was $41.8 million; and both common stock and mortgage bonds are constant and equal to the amounts shown on the following balance sheet.

a. Complete the balance sheet on the next page.

b. Assume that the company was operating at full capacity in 1981 with regard to all items *except* fixed assets; had the fixed assets been used to full capacity, the fixed assets/sales ratio would have been 40 percent in 1981. By what percentage could 1982 sales increase over 1981 sales without the need for an increase in fixed assets?

c. Now suppose that 1982 sales increase by 20 percent over 1981 sales. How much additional external capital will be required? Assume that Alabama Textile cannot sell any fixed assets. (Hint: Equation 7-1 can no longer be used. You must develop a pro forma balance sheet as in

Alabama Textile: Balance Sheet, December 31, 1981 ($ in Thousands)

Cash	$		Accounts payable	$
Receivables			Notes payable	6,840
Inventories	————		Accruals	————
Total current assets			Total current liabilities	
Net fixed assets	————		Mortgage bonds	10,000
			Common stock	4,000
			Retained earnings	————
			Total liabilities and	
Total assets	$————		net worth	$————

Table 7-2.) Assume that any required financing is borrowed as notes payable.

d. Suppose the industry averages for receivables and inventories are 20 percent and 25 percent, respectively, and that Alabama Textile matches these figures in 1982 and then uses the funds released to reduce equity. (It could pay a special dividend out of retained earnings.) What would this do to the rate of return on year-end 1982 equity?

Solutions to Self-Test Problems

ST7-1 To solve this problem, we will use the following three equations:

$$\Delta S = S_0(g).$$
$$S_1 = S_0(1 + g).$$
$$AFN = (A/S)\Delta S - (L/S)\Delta S - M(1 - d)S_1.$$

Set AFN = 0, substitute in known values for A/S, L/S, M, d, and S_0, and then solve for g:

$$0 = 1.6(\$100g) - 0.4(\$100g) - 0.1(0.55)[\$100(1 + g)]$$
$$= \$160g - \$40g - 0.055(\$100 + \$100g)$$
$$= \$160g - \$40g - \$5.5 - \$5.5g$$
$$\$114.5g = \$5.5$$
$$g = \$5.5/\$114.5 = 0.048 = 4.8\% = \begin{matrix}\text{Maximum growth rate} \\ \text{without external financing.}\end{matrix}$$

ST7-2 Note that assets consist of cash, marketable securities, receivables, inventories, and fixed assets. Therefore, we can break the A/S ratio into its components, cash/sales, inventories/sales, and so forth. Then,

$$\frac{A}{S} = \frac{A - \text{Inventories}}{S} + \frac{\text{Inventories}}{S} = 1.6.$$

We know that the inventory turnover ratio is sales/inventories = 3 times, so inventories/sales = $^1/_3$ = 0.3333. Further, if the inventory turnover ratio could be increased to 4 times, then the inventory/sales ratio would fall to $^1/_4$ = 0.25, a difference of 0.3333 − 0.2500 = 0.0833. This, in turn, would cause the A/S ratio to fall from A/S = 1.6 to A/S = 1.6 − 0.0833 = 1.5167.

This change would have two effects: (1) it would change the AFN equation, and (2) it would mean that Bildersee currently has excessive inventories, so there could be some sales growth without any additional inventories. Therefore, we could set up the revised AFN equation, estimate the funds needed next year, and then subtract out the excess inventories currently on hand:

Present Conditions:

$$\frac{\text{Sales}}{\text{Inventories}} = \frac{\$100}{\text{Inventories}} = 3,$$

so

Current level of inventories = $100/3 = $33.3 million.

New Conditions:

$$\frac{\text{Sales}}{\text{Inventories}} = \frac{\$100}{\text{Inventories}} = 4,$$

so

New level of inventories = $100/4 = $25 million.

Therefore,

Excess inventories = $33.3 − $25 = $8.3 million.

Forecast of Funds Needed, 1st Year:

ΔS in first year = 0.2($100 million) = $20 million.

$$
\begin{aligned}
\text{AFN} &= 1.5167(\$20) - 0.4(\$20) - 0.1(0.55)(\$120) - \$8.3 \\
&= \$30.3 - \$8 - \$6.6 - \$8.3 \\
&= \$7.4 \text{ million.}
\end{aligned}
$$

Forecast of Funds Needed, 2nd Year:

ΔS in second year = 0.2($120 million) = $24 million.

$$
\begin{aligned}
\text{AFN} &= 1.5167(\$24) - 0.4(\$24) - 0.1(0.55)(\$144) \\
&= \$36.4 - \$9.6 - \$7.9 \\
&= \$18.9 \text{ million.}
\end{aligned}
$$

Selected References   The heart of successful financial planning is the sales forecast. On this key subject, see

Pan, Judy, Donald R. Nichols, and O. Maurice Joy, "Sales Forecasting Practices of Large U.S. Industrial Firms," *Financial Management,* Fall 1977, 72-77.

Pappas, James L., and Eugene F. Brigham, *Managerial Economics* (Hinsdale, Ill.: The Dryden Press, 1978).

Computer modeling is becoming increasingly important. For general references see

Carleton, W. T., C. L. Dick, Jr., and D. H. Downes, "Financial Policy Models: Theory and Practice," *Journal of Finance,* vol. 20 (December 1973), 691-709.

Francis, Jack Clark, and Dexter R. Rowell, "A Simultaneous Equation Model of the Firm for Financial Analysis and Planning," *Financial Management,* Spring 1978, 29-44.

Grinyer, P. H., and J. Wooller, *Corporate Models Today—A New Tool for Financial Management* (London: Institute of Chartered Accountants, 1978).

Pappas, James L., and George P. Huber, "Probabilistic Short-Term Financial Planning," *Financial Management,* vol. 2 (Autumn 1973), 36-44.

Traenkle, J. W., E. B. Cox, and J. A. Bullard, *The Use of Financial Models in Business* (New York: Financial Executives' Research Foundation, 1975).

For a detailed description of how one commercially available and widely used planning system operates, see

Interactive Financial Planning System: Users' Manual, Execucom Systems Corporation, 3409 Executive Center Drive, Austin, Texas 78731.

Working Capital Management

IV

Up to now we have discussed financial management in a generalized sense. In the remainder of the book we look at specific financial decisions, beginning in Part IV with decisions related to working capital management. Chapter 8 considers accounts receivable and inventories; Chapter 9 analyzes the management of cash and marketable securities; and Chapter 10 discusses the various types of short-term credit that can be used to finance current assets.

Accounts Receivable and Inventories

In Part III we saw (1) that a firm's assets are closely related to actual and projected sales, (2) that the various liability and equity accounts must be analyzed in terms of their relationships to assets, and (3) that risk, profitability, and consequently stock prices are all dependent upon decisions relating to acquiring and financing assets. However, this discussion was very general, and we looked more at industry averages than at specific economic determinants of the different types of assets. Now, in Part IV, we examine the optimal levels of current assets and current liabilities.

Working Capital Policy and Management

Before taking up the topics of primary interest in this chapter, accounts receivable and inventories, it is useful to examine in a general way the concepts of working capital and working capital management. We begin by defining the following key terms:

1. *Working capital,* sometimes called gross working capital, simply refers to current assets.[1]
2. *Net working capital* is defined as current assets minus current liabilities.
3. *Working capital policy* refers to basic policy decisions regarding target levels for each category of current assets, and to the financing of these assets.
4. *Working capital management* involves the administration, within policy guidelines, of current assets and current liabilities.

Whereas working capital *policy* relates to setting long-run targets, working capital *management* deals with the implementation of policy. Both are critically important. Working capital is used to make adjustments in operations as economic conditions change. If demand begins to rise or fall, the immediate response is in the working capital accounts, and the appropriateness of the response can spell success or failure for the firm. For example, when its sales began to decline in the late 1970s, Chrysler decided that the decline was only a temporary dip, so production levels were maintained. By the time it became clear that the "dip" was really a

---

[1] The term *working capital* originated with the old Yankee peddler, who would load up his wagon with goods, then go off on his route to peddle his wares. The merchandise was defined as his "working capital" because it was what he actually sold or "turned over" to produce his profits.

major recession, Chrysler had built up huge inventories of new cars. The company had borrowed heavily to finance this inventory buildup, and these loans had to be repaid. The only choice was to slash prices below costs in order to move the cars. This poor management of working capital resulted in hundreds of millions of dollars of losses, and to this time it is still unclear whether or not Chrysler will ever recover.

The types of credit available to finance current assets will be discussed in detail in Chapter 10. At this point, it is necessary only to know (1) that a major element of working capital policy and management relates to the financing of current assets and (2) that lining up sources of short-term credit, minimizing the cost of this credit, and making sure that it can be repaid on schedule is an important part of working capital operations.

With this background, we are now in a position to consider policy and management decisions relating to specific types of current assets and to the types of credit available to finance these assets. We begin with accounts receivable and inventories. In 1981, the typical manufacturing firm had approximately 21 percent of its total assets invested in receivables, and another 21 percent in inventories. With such a large percentage of its funds tied up in these two accounts, the effectiveness with which they are managed is obviously important to a firm's profitability and risk, and thus to its stock price.

Accounts Receivable

Most firms sell on credit. When goods are shipped, inventories are reduced, and an *account receivable* is created.[2] Eventually, the customer will pay the account, at which time receivables will decline and cash will increase.

The total amount of accounts receivable outstanding at any given time is determined by two factors: (1) the volume of credit sales and (2) the average length of time between sales and collections. For example, suppose someone opens a store on January 1 and, starting the first day, makes sales of $100 each day. Customers are given ten days in which to pay. At the end of the first day, accounts receivable will be $100; they will rise to $200 by the end of the second day; and by January 10, they will have risen to $10 \times $100 = $1,000$. On January 11, another $100 will be added to receivables, but payments for sales made on January 1 will

---

[2] Whenever goods are sold on credit, two accounts actually are created—an asset item entitled *accounts receivable* appears on the books of the selling firm, and a liability item called *accounts payable* appears on the books of the purchaser. At this point we are analyzing the transaction from the viewpoint of the seller, so we are concentrating on the variables under its control. We will examine the transaction from the viewpoint of the purchaser in Chapter 10, where we discuss accounts payable as a source of funds and consider the cost of these funds relative to the cost of funds obtained from other sources.

reduce receivables by $100, so total accounts receivable will remain constant at $1,000. In general, once the firm's operations are stable,

$$\text{Accounts receivable} = \text{Sales per day} \times \text{Length of collection period}$$
$$= \$100 \times 10 \text{ days} = \$1,000.$$

If either sales or the collection period changes, this change will be reflected in accounts receivable.

Notice that the $1,000 investment in receivables must be financed. To illustrate, suppose that when our firm started on January 1, the owner had put up $100 as common stock and used this money to buy the goods sold the first day. Thus, the initial balance sheet would be as follows:

Inventories	$100	Common equity	$100
Total assets	$100	Total claims	$100

At the end of the day, the balance sheet would look like this:[3]

Accounts receivable	$100		
Inventories	0	Common equity	$100
Total assets	$100	Total claims	$100

In order to remain in business, the owner must replenish inventories. To do so requires that $100 of goods be purchased, and this requires $100. Assuming the owner borrows the $100 from the bank, the balance sheet at the start of the second day will be as follows:

Accounts receivable	$100	Notes payable to bank	$100
Inventories	100	Common equity	100
Total assets	$200	Total claims	$200

---

[3] Of course, a profit might have been earned on the sales, but it would, for a retail business, amount to only about 2 percent, or $2. Also, the firm would need other assets such as cash, fixed assets, and a permanent stock of inventory. We abstract from these details so that we may focus on receivables.

At the end of the day, the inventories will have been converted to receivables, and the firm will have to borrow another $100 to restock for the third day.

This process will continue, provided the bank is willing to lend the necessary funds, until on the eleventh day the balance sheet reads as follows:

Accounts receivable	$1,000	Notes payable to bank	$1,000
Inventories	100	Common equity	100
Total assets	$1,100	Total claims	$1,100

This balance sheet is in a "steady state" condition—every day, $100 of receivables will be collected and the money will be used to finance the sales made that day. Thus, the balance sheet will remain stable until the situation changes.

Now suppose sales doubled, to $200 per day. After a brief transition period (ten days), the balance sheet would be as follows:

Accounts receivable	$2,000	Notes payable to bank	$2,100
Inventories	200	Common equity	100
Total assets	$2,200	Total claims	$2,200

Or, if sales had remained constant at $100 per day but the collection period had doubled from ten to twenty days, the balance sheet would have changed as follows:

Accounts receivable	$2,000	Notes payable to bank	$2,000
Inventories	100	Common equity	100
Total assets	$2,100	Total claims	$2,100

These examples should make it clear (1) that accounts receivable depend jointly on the level of sales and the collection period, and (2) that any increase in receivables must be financed in some manner. We assumed bank financing, but other possibilities include the firm's buying on credit itself (in which case the claim would be represented by accounts payable rather than notes payable), selling bonds, or selling more common stock.[4] The question of the best method of financing accounts receivable (and other current assets) is considered in Chapter 10. In the remainder of this chapter, we examine how the firm determines and attains the optimal level of receivables.

Credit Policy

As noted above, accounts receivable are equal to (Sales per day) × (Collection period). Both of these factors are influenced by a set of controllable factors called the firm's *credit policy*. The four credit policy variables are

1. the *credit period*, which is the length of time for which credit is granted;
2. the *credit standards*, which refers to the minimum financial strength of acceptable credit customers;
3. the firm's *collection policy*, which is measured by its toughness or laxity in following up on slow-paying accounts; and
4. any *discounts* given for early payment.

The credit manager has the responsibility for administering the credit policy. However, because of the pervasive importance of credit, the credit policy itself is established by the executive committee, which usually consists of the president and the vice-presidents in charge of finance, marketing, and production. If the credit policy is *eased* by lengthening the credit period, by relaxing credit standards, by following a less tough collection policy, or by offering cash discounts, then sales should increase: *Easing the credit policy stimulates sales.* However, if the credit policy is eased and sales do rise, then costs will also rise because more labor, more materials, and so on, will be required to produce more goods. Thus, the basic question that credit policy makers must answer is this: Will sales revenues rise more than costs, causing net income to increase, or will the increase in sales revenues be more than offset by higher costs?

The basic point of credit policy analysis is to provide an answer to this question, and the basic approach employed is called *incremental analysis*. In incremental analysis, we attempt to determine the increase or decrease in both sales and costs associated with a given easing or tightening of the credit policy. The difference between incremental sales and incremental costs is defined as *incremental profit*. If the expected incremental profit is positive, then the proposed credit policy change is a good one.

Incremental analysis is not a difficult concept, but care must be taken to insure that all the relevant costs and benefits of a proposed change are

---

[4] In time, profits will presumably be earned and reinvested in the business, but, with normal profit margins, external funds will be needed to support rapid growth. This point was discussed in Chapter 7 in connection with the Arinson Supply Company. Also, as is shown later in this chapter, only the *incremental costs* tied up in receivables (and inventories) must be financed.

considered. Generally, a credit policy change will affect these variables: (1) sales, (2) production costs associated with a higher or lower sales volume, (3) bad debt losses, (4) discount expenses, (5) the level of accounts receivable, hence the cost of the capital tied up in receivables, (6) the costs of administering the credit department, and (7) collection expenses. It is far from easy to estimate these factors. For example, to estimate the effect on sales of a given credit policy change requires a knowledge not only of how customers will respond but also of how the firm's competitors will react. Similarly, to estimate the effects on production costs involves a consideration of both variable costs per unit of output and the firm's capacity situation—incremental production costs will be far different if the firm is currently operating at full capacity than if excess capacity exists.

In this section, we examine the effects of changes in the credit period, while in the following three sections we consider credit standards, collection policy, and cash discounts. Throughout, we illustrate the situation with data on Judy-Rose Fashions, Inc.

Credit Period

Lengthening the Credit Period. Judy-Rose currently sells on a cash only basis. Since it extends no credit, the company has no funds tied up in receivables, no bad debt losses, and no credit expenses of any kind. On the other hand, its sales volume is lower than it would be if credit terms were offered. Judy-Rose is now considering extending credit on thirty day terms. Current sales are $100,000 per year, variable costs are 60 percent of sales, excessive productive capacity exists (so no new fixed costs will be incurred as a result of expanded sales), and the cost of new capital is 10 percent. Judy-Rose estimates that sales will increase to $150,000 per year if credit is extended.

We will need to set up some simple equations to analyze this credit policy change, so we begin by defining these terms and symbols:

S_0 = Judy-Rose's current sales = $100,000 per year.

ΔS = incremental sales = $50,000. Note that ΔS would be negative had Judy-Rose been selling on credit and then reduced the credit period.

V = variable costs as a percentage of sales = 60%. V includes the cost of administering the credit department and all other costs except bad debt losses and financing costs (interest charges) associated with carrying the investment in receivables. Costs of carrying inventories are included in V.

$1 - V = 1 - 0.6 = 0.4 = 40\%$ = contribution margin, or the percentage of each sales dollar that goes toward covering overhead and increasing profits. The contribution margin is somtimes referred to as the gross profit margin.

k = the cost of financing the investment in receivables = 10%. k is the firm's cost of new capital when the capital is used to finance receivables.

ACP_0 = average collection period prior to a change in credit policy. Since Judy-Rose sold for cash only, $ACP_0 = 0$.

ACP_N = new average collection period after the credit policy change = 30 days. Here we assume that all customers pay on time, so ACP = specified credit period. Generally, some customers pay late, so as a general rule ACP > specified credit period.

Given this information, we can now calculate values for the following:

ΔI = incremental change in the level of the firm's investment in accounts receivable.

ΔP = incremental change in profits.

To begin, recognize that although easing credit by lengthening the credit period stimulates sales, there is a cost to tying up funds in receivables. The investment in receivables will increase for two reasons: (1) old customers will now take longer to pay, and (2) new sales will result in new receivables. The incremental investment in receivables (ΔI) is calculated as follows:

$$\Delta I = \begin{bmatrix} \text{Increased investment} \\ \text{in receivables associated} \\ \text{with original sales} \end{bmatrix} + \begin{bmatrix} \text{Investment in} \\ \text{receivables associated} \\ \text{with new sales} \end{bmatrix}$$

$$= \begin{bmatrix} \text{Change in} \\ \text{collection period} \end{bmatrix}\begin{bmatrix} \text{Old sales} \\ \text{per day} \end{bmatrix} + \begin{bmatrix} V(ACP_N) \left(\dfrac{\text{Incremental sales}}{\text{per day}} \right) \end{bmatrix}$$

$$= (ACP_N - ACP_0)(S_0/360) + [V(ACP_N)(\Delta S/360)] \qquad (8\text{-}1)$$

$$= (30 - 0)(\$100{,}000/360) + 0.6[30(\$50{,}000/360)]$$

$$= \$8{,}333 + \$2{,}500$$

$$= \$10{,}833.$$

Note that the increased investment in accounts receivable (A/R) associated with old sales is based on the full amount of the receivables; that is, we do not multiply by V as we do for new sales. This difference reflects the facts (1) that the firm only invests its variable cost in *new* receivables, but (2) that it would have collected the *full sales price* on the old receivables earlier had it not made the credit policy change. There is an *opportunity cost* associated with the $8,333 additional investment in A/R from old sales and a *direct financing cost* associated with the $2,500 investment in A/R from new sales.

Given this information, we may now determine the incremental profit, ΔP, associated with the proposed credit period change:

$$\Delta P = \begin{bmatrix} \left(\begin{matrix} \text{New} \\ \text{sales} \end{matrix} \right)\left(\begin{matrix} \text{Contribution} \\ \text{margin} \end{matrix} \right) \end{bmatrix} - \begin{bmatrix} \text{Cost of carrying} \\ \text{new receivables} \end{bmatrix}$$

$$\begin{aligned} &= \Delta S(1 - V) - k(\Delta I) &&(8\text{-}2)\\ &= \$50,000(0.4) - 0.10(\$10,833)\\ &= \$20,000 - \$1,083\\ &= \$18,917. \end{aligned}$$

Since pretax profits are expected to increase by \$18,917, the credit policy change should be made.

Two simplifying assumptions which were made in our analysis should be noted: (1) we assumed that all customers paid on time (ACP = credit period), and (2) we assumed that no bad debt losses were incurred. The assumption of prompt payment can be relaxed quite easily. We simply use the actual average collection period (say forty days) rather than the credit period in Equation 8-1 to calculate the investment in receivables, and then use this new (and higher) value of ΔI in Equation 8-2 to calculate ΔP. Thus, if $ACP_N = 40$ days, then

$$\Delta I = [(40 - 0)(\$100,000/360)] + 0.6[40(\$50,000/360)]$$

$$= \$11,111 + \$3,333 = \$14,444,$$

and

$$\Delta P = [\$50,000(0.4)] - [0.10(\$14,444)]$$

$$= \$20,000 - \$1,444 = \$18,556.$$

Incremental profits are reduced slightly, but they are still positive, so the credit policy should still be relaxed.

Bad debts can be handled equally easily. First, recognize that bad debts do not affect our calculation of the firm's incremental investment in receivables (Equation 8-1). However, notice that bad debts do reduce profits, so Equation 8-2 must be modified. Assuming that 5 percent of all sales after the change (S_N) end up as bad debt losses ($B_N = 5\% = 0.05$), then we have

$$\Delta P = \binom{\text{New}}{\text{sales}}\binom{\text{Contribution}}{\text{margin}} - \binom{\text{Cost of carrying}}{\text{receivables}} - \binom{\text{Bad debt}}{\text{losses}}$$

$$\begin{aligned} &= \Delta S(1 - V) - k(\Delta I) - B_N(S_N)\\ &= \$50,000(0.4) - 0.10(\$14,444) - 0.05(\$150,000)\\ &= \$20,000 - \$1,444 - \$7,500\\ &= \$11,056. \end{aligned}$$

Bad debts reduce the expected incremental profits, but ΔP is still positive, so extending credit still appears to be a good idea.[5]

---

[5] If the company had been selling on credit initially and incurring bad debt losses, then we would have had to modify Equation 8-2 even further:

(continued)

Shortening the Credit Period. Now suppose that, a year after Judy-Rose began offering thirty day credit terms, management decides to consider the effects of shortening the credit period from thirty to twenty days. We assume that expected sales would decline by $20,000 per year from the current level of $150,000, so $\Delta S = -\$20,000$. We assume further that the bad debt percentage on these lost sales is 5 percent, the same as on the original sales, and that other values are as given in the preceding example.

We first calculate the incremental investment in receivables:

$$\Delta I = [ACP_N - ACP_0] [(S_0 + \Delta S)/360] + V[ACP_0 (\Delta S/360)] \qquad (8\text{-}3)$$
$$= [20 - 30][(\$150,000 - \$20,000)/360] + 0.6[30 (-\$20,000/360)]$$
$$= -\$3,611 - \$1,000$$
$$= -\$4,611.$$

Thus, reducing the credit period would result in a $4,611 reduction in the investment in receivables, consisting of a $3,611 decline in receivables of continuing customers and a $1,000 decline resulting from a reduced sales volume.

This information may now be used to analyze the profitability of the proposed change:

$$\Delta P = \Delta S(1 - V) - B_N(\Delta S) - k(\Delta I) \qquad (8\text{-}4)$$
$$= -\$20,000(0.4) - (0.05)(-\$20,000) - (0.10)(-\$4,611)$$
$$= -\$8,000 + \$1,000 + \$461$$
$$= -\$6,539.$$

Since the expected incremental profits are negative, the firm should not reduce its credit period from thirty to twenty days.

Other factors could be introduced into the analysis. For example, the company could consider a further easing of credit by extending the credit period to sixty days, or it could weigh the effects of a sales expansion so great that fixed assets, hence higher fixed costs, had to be added. Such additional factors complicate the analysis, but the basic principles are the same—just keep in mind that we are seeking to determine the *incremental*

$$\Delta P = \Delta S(1 - V) - k(\Delta I) - \Delta(\text{Bad debt losses})$$
$$= \Delta S(1 - V) - k(\Delta I) - [\text{New bad debt losses} - \text{Old bad debt losses}]$$
$$= \Delta S(1 - V) - k(\Delta I) - [B_N S_N - B_0 S_0].$$

In our example, $B_0 S_0 = 0$ because $B_0 = 0$. Notice that B_N is the *average* credit loss percentage on total new sales. Bad debts may be higher for new customers attracted by the credit terms than for old customers who take advantage of them, but B_N is an average of these two groups. Note, though, that at times it is convenient to keep the two groups separate and to define B_N as the bad debt percentage of the new sales only. We will see examples of this type later in the chapter.

sales revenues, the *incremental costs,* and consequently the *incremental net income* associated with a given change in credit policy.

The second element of the firm's credit policy relates to decisions about who will be granted credit. If the firm extended credit sales to only the strongest of customers, it would never have bad debt losses, nor would it incur much in the way of expenses for a credit department. On the other hand, it would probably be losing sales, and the profits that were foregone on these lost sales could be far larger than the costs that were avoided. Determining the optimal credit standards involves equating the incremental costs of credit to the incremental profits on the increased sales.

Credit Standards

Incremental costs include production and selling costs plus those costs associated with the "quality" of the marginal accounts, or *credit quality costs.* These costs include (1) default, or bad debt losses, (2) higher investigation and collection costs, and (3) higher costs of capital tied up in the additional receivables that result when customers are less creditworthy, pay their accounts more slowly, and so cause the average collection period to lengthen.

We have seen that a firm may change its credit standards either by *relaxing* them to increase sales or by *tightening* them to reduce both bad debt losses and slow-paying accounts. To illustrate the process, assume now that Judy-Rose Fashions currently sells on terms granting thirty days' credit, written as "net 30," and that the following conditions hold:

$S_0 = \$150,000 =$ original sales per year.
$V = 60\% =$ variable cost percentage.
$1 - V = 40\% =$ contribution margin.
$k = 10\% =$ cost of capital.
$ACP_0 = 40$ days $=$ original average collection period (10 days late).
$B_0 = 5\% =$ original bad debt loss percentage.

Assume that excess capacity still exists and that management is considering relaxing its credit standards to permit sales to some new customers who did not qualify for credit under the old standards. However, bad debt losses will also rise, as will the average collection period, because weaker customers generally pay more slowly than strong ones. Should the change be made?

We begin the analysis by estimating incremental sales, the average collection period for the new customers (ACP_N), and the new bad debt loss percentage (B_N). Assume these values have been estimated as follows:

$$\Delta S = \$50,000.$$
$$ACP_N = 60 \text{ days}.$$
$$B_N = 15\%.$$

Note that we are assuming no changes for the old customers—they continue with sales at the rate of $150,000 per year, $ACP_0 = 40$ days, and $B_0 = 5\%$.

With this information, we calculate the incremental investment in receivables as follows:

$$\Delta I = V(ACP_N)(\Delta S/360)$$
$$= 0.6(60)(\$50,000/360)$$
$$= \$5,000.$$

With ΔI calculated, we now find incremental profits:

$$\Delta P = \begin{pmatrix} \text{Increase in} \\ \text{gross profits} \end{pmatrix} - \begin{pmatrix} \text{Cost of carrying} \\ \text{new receivables} \end{pmatrix} - \begin{pmatrix} \text{Increased bad} \\ \text{debt losses} \end{pmatrix}$$

$$= (1 - V)(\Delta S) - k(\Delta I) - B_N(\Delta S)$$
$$= 0.4(\$50,000) - 0.10(\$5,000) - 0.15(\$50,000)$$
$$= \$20,000 - \$500 - \$7,500$$
$$= \$12,000.$$

Since profits are expected to increase, the analysis suggests that Judy-Rose should relax credit standards.

**Measuring
Credit Quality**

A key element in setting credit standards relates to the factors that determine the likelihood that a given customer will pay slowly or even end up as a bad debt loss. This is called *measuring credit quality*. To begin the analysis, we need to define *credit quality*. Perhaps the best way is in terms of the probability of default. These probability estimates are, for the most part, subjective estimates, but credit evaluation is a well-established practice, and a good credit manager can make reasonably accurate judgments of the probability of default by different classes of customers.

To evaluate credit risk, credit managers consider the five C's of credit: character, capacity, capital, collateral, and conditions:

1. *Character* refers to the probability that customers will *try* to honor their obligations. This factor is of considerable importance, because every credit transaction implies a *promise* to pay. Will debtors make an honest effort to pay their debts, or are they likely to try to get away with something? Experienced credit managers frequently insist that the moral factor is the most important issue in a credit evaluation.
2. *Capacity* is a subjective judgment of customers' ability to pay. It is gauged by their past records, supplemented by physical observation of customers' plants or stores, and their business methods.
3. *Capital* is measured by the general financial position of firms as indicated by a financial ratio analysis, with special emphasis on the risk

ratios—the debt/assets ratio, the current ratio, and the times interest earned ratio.

4. *Collateral* is represented by assets that customers may offer as security to obtain credit.

5. *Conditions* refers to the impact of general economic trends or to special developments in certain geographic regions or sectors of the economy that may affect customers' ability to meet their obligations.

Information on these five factors is obtained from the firm's previous experience with customers, supplemented by a well-developed system of external information-gathering groups.

Two major sources of external information are available. The first is the work of the *credit associations*, local groups which meet frequently and correspond with one another to exchange information on credit customers. These local groups have also banded together to create Credit Interchange, a system developed by the National Association of Credit Management for assembling and distributing information about debtors' past performances. The interchange reports show the paying records of different debtors, the industries from which they are buying, and the trading areas in which purchases are being made. The second source of external information is the work of the *credit-reporting agencies*, which collect credit information and sell it for a fee; the best known of these agencies are Dun & Bradstreet (D&B) and TRW, Incorporated. D&B, TRW, and other agencies provide factual data that can be used in credit analysis; they also provide ratings similar to those available on corporate bonds.[6]

Modern credit managers practice "management by exception." Under such a system, customers are first classified into five or six categories according to degree of risk, and then the credit manager concentrates time and attention on the weakest customers. For example, the following classes might be established:

Risk Class	Percentage of Uncollectible Credit Sales	Percentage of Customers in This Class
1	0-$\frac{1}{2}$%	60%
2	$\frac{1}{2}$-2	20
3	2-5	10
4	5-10	5
5	Over 10	5

[6] For additional information, see *Credit Management Handbook*, 2d ed., a publication of the National Association of Credit Management (Homewood, Ill.: Richard D. Irwin, 1965). Also, see Peter Nulty, "An Upstart Takes on Dun & Bradstreet," *Fortune*, April 9, 1979.

Firms in Class 1 might be extended credit automatically, and their credit status only reviewed once a year. Those in Class 2 might also receive credit (up to specified limits) automatically, but a ratio analysis of these firms' financial condition would be conducted more frequently (perhaps quarterly), and they would be moved down to Class 3 if their position deteriorated. Specific approvals might be required for credit sales to Classes 3 and 4, while sales to Class 5 might be on a COD (cash on delivery) basis only.

Managing a credit department requires fast, accurate, up-to-date information, and to help get such information, the National Association of Credit Management (a group with 43,000 member firms) persuaded TRW, Inc., to develop a computer-based, fully automated data retrieval system. Such a system is now in existence, and teletype credit reports are available within minutes. While Dun & Bradstreet's reports are more complete, they come in more slowly, through the U.S. mail. A typical credit report would include the following pieces of information:

1. A summary balance sheet and income statement.
2. A number of key ratios, with trend information.
3. Information obtained from the firm's suppliers telling whether it has been paying promptly or slowly or has failed to make payments.
4. A verbal description of the physical condition of the firm's operations.
5. A verbal description of the backgrounds of the firm's owners, including any previous bankruptcies, lawsuits, and the like.
6. A summary rating, going from A+ for the best credits down to F for those who are most likely to default.

Although a great deal of credit information is available, it must still be processed in a judgmental manner. The data and information systems can assist in making better credit decisions, but, in the final analysis, credit decisions are really exercises in informed judgment.

Collection Policy

Collection policy refers to the procedures the firm follows to collect past-due accounts. For example, a letter may be sent to such accounts when the bill is ten days past due; a more severe letter, followed by a telephone call, may be used if payment is not received within thirty days; and the account may be turned over to a collection agency after ninety days.

The collection process can be expensive in terms of both out-of-pocket expenditures and lost goodwill, but at least some firmness is needed to prevent an undue lengthening of the collection period and to minimize outright losses. Again, a balance must be struck between the costs and benefits of different collection policies.

Changes in collection policy influence sales, the collection period, the bad debt loss percentage, and the percentage of customers who take discounts. Accordingly, the effects of a change in collection policy should be analyzed within the framework of the equations developed above.

To illustrate how a proposed change in the collection policy should be analyzed, suppose that, after Judy-Rose begins to offer credit, its average collection period is sixty days, well above the thirty day terms offered, and bad debt losses amount to 5 percent of sales. What would be the effect on profits if Judy-Rose institutes a vigorous collection policy designed to reduce the ACP to thirty days and the bad debt loss percentage to 2 percent? The old and expected new conditions are shown below:

$$S_0 = \$150,000.$$
$$\Delta S = -\$10,000.$$
$$ACP_0 = \text{old collection period} = 60 \text{ days}.$$
$$ACP_N = \text{new collection period} = 30 \text{ days}.$$
$$B_0 = \text{bad debt loss percentage prior to change} = 5\%.$$
$$B_N = \text{bad debt loss percentage following change} = 2\%.$$
$$V = 60\% \text{ (unchanged)}.$$
$$k = 10\%.$$

We first determine the change in the investment in receivables:

$$\Delta I = (ACP_N - ACP_0) [(S_0 + \Delta S)/360] + V[ACP_0(\Delta S/360)]$$
$$= (30 - 60)(\$150,000 - \$10,000)/360 + 0.6[60(-\$10,000/360)]$$
$$= -\$11,667 - \$1,000$$
$$= -\$12,667.$$

Next, we determine the change in profits:

$$\Delta P = \begin{bmatrix} \text{Change in} \\ \text{gross profits} \end{bmatrix} + \begin{bmatrix} \text{Change in bad} \\ \text{debt losses} \end{bmatrix} - \begin{bmatrix} \text{Change in cost of} \\ \text{carrying receivables} \end{bmatrix}$$

$$= \Delta S(1 - V) + [B_0 S_0 - B_N(S_0 + \Delta S)] - k(\Delta I) \qquad (8\text{-}5)$$
$$= -\$10,000 (0.4) + [(0.05)(\$150,000) - (0.02)(\$140,000)]$$
$$\quad - (0.10)(-\$12,667)$$
$$= -\$4,000 + \$4,700 + \$1,267$$
$$= \$1,967.$$

Since the expected change in pre-tax profits is positive, Judy-Rose should institute the tougher collection policy.

Cash Discounts

The last element in the credit policy decision, cash discounts for early payment, can also be analyzed through the use of our equation set. For example, Judy-Rose Fashions might decide to change its credit terms from thirty days (net 30) to allow a 2 percent discount if payment is received within ten days (stated "2/10, net 30"). This change should produce two benefits: (1) it would attract new customers who consider discounts a type of price reduction, and (2) the discounts would cause a reduction in the average collection period, since some old customers would pay more promptly in order to take advantage of the discount. Offsetting these benefits is the dollar cost of the discounts taken. The optimal discount is established at the point where the costs and benefits are exactly offsetting.

To illustrate, suppose Judy-Rose is considering offering a 2 percent discount for payments made within ten days, which represents a change in credit terms from net 30 to 2/10, net 30. The following conditions currently exist or are expected to occur if the change is made:

S_0 = current gross sales = $150,000.
ΔS = increase in gross sales if discount is offered = $10,000.
D_0 = original discount = 0%.
D_N = new discount percentage = 2%.
ACP_0 = old average collection period = 30 days.
ACP_N = new average collection period = 20 days. The new ACP is based on the assumption that 50 percent of the customers will take discounts and pay on the tenth day and the remaining 50 percent will pay on the thirtieth day.
p_0 = percentage of customers who took discounts previously = 0%.
p_1 = percentage of customers who will take discounts under new policy = 50%.

The incremental investment in receivables is found as follows:

$$\Delta I = (ACP_N - ACP_0)\,(S_0/360) + V[ACP_N\,(\Delta S/360)]$$
$$= (20 - 30)(\$150,000/360) + 0.6[20(\$10,000/360)]$$
$$= -\$4,167 + \$333$$
$$= -\$3,834.$$

Thus, offering discounts will speed up collections and reduce the investment in receivables by $3,834.

The expected change in profits may now be analyzed as follows:[7]

$$\Delta P = \Delta S(1 - V) + [D_0 S_0 p_0 - D_N(S_0 + \Delta S)\,(p_1)] - k(\Delta I) \quad (8\text{-}6)$$
$$= \$10,000(0.4) - [(0.02)(\$160,000)(0.5)] - (0.1)(-\$3,834)$$
$$= \$4,000 - \$1,600 + \$383$$
$$= \$2,783.$$

Since the expected incremental pre-tax profits are positive, Judy-Rose should begin to offer discounts.

If sales are seasonal, a firm may use *seasonal dating* on discounts. For example, Jenson, Inc., is a swimsuit manufacturer which sells on terms

---

[7] We have simplified the analysis somewhat by assuming away bad debt losses, but this could be easily included in the analysis.

of 2/10, net 30, May 1 dating. This means that the effective invoice date is May 1, even if the sale was made back in January. If the discount is not taken by May 10, the full amount must be paid on May 30. Jenson produces throughout the year, but retail sales of bathing suits are concentrated in the spring and early summer, and offering seasonal datings induces some customers to stock up early, saving Jenson storage costs and also "nailing down sales."

Simultaneous Changes in Policy Variables

The preceding discussion has considered the effects of changes in credit policy one at a time. The firm could, of course, change several or all policy variables simultaneously. An almost endless variety of equations could be developed, depending on which policy variables are manipulated and on the assumed effects on sales, discounts taken, the collection period, bad debt costs, the existence of excess capacity, changes in credit department costs, changes in the variable cost percentage, and so on. The analysis would get "messy," and the incremental profit equation would be complex, but the principles we have developed could be used to handle any type of policy change.

Profit Potential in Carrying Accounts Receivable

Thus far we have emphasized the costs of carrying receivables. *However, if it is possible to sell on credit and also to assess a carrying charge on the receivables that are outstanding, then credit sales can actually be more profitable than cash sales.*[8] This is especially true for consumer durables (autos, appliances, clothing, and so on), but it is also true for certain types of industrial equipment. Thus, the General Motors Acceptance Corporation (GMAC) unit, which finances automobiles, is highly profitable, as is Sears Roebuck's credit subsidiary. Some encyclopedia companies are even reported to lose money on cash sales but to more than make up these losses from the carrying charges on their credit sales; obviously, such companies would rather sell on credit than for cash!

The carrying charges on outstanding credit are generally about 18 percent on an annual interest rate basis ($1\frac{1}{2}\%$ per month, so $1.5\% \times 12 = 18\%$). Until the 1980s, when short-term interest rates rose to unprecedented levels, having receivables outstanding that earned 18 percent was highly profitable.

Legal Considerations in Granting Credit

It is illegal, under the Robinson-Patman Act, for a firm to charge prices that discriminate among customers unless these differential prices are

---

[8] Where companies do a large volume of sales financing, they typically set up subsidiary companies called *captive finance companies* to do the actual financing. Thus, General Motors, Chrysler, and Ford all have captive finance companies, as do Sears Roebuck and Montgomery Ward. The reason for this is that consumer finance companies, because their assets are highly liquid, tend to use far more debt, and especially short-term debt, than manufacturers or retailers. Thus, if GM did not use a captive finance company, its balance sheet would show an exceptionally high debt ratio and a low current ratio. By setting up GMAC as a separate but wholly owned corporation, GM avoids distorting its own balance sheet, and this presumably helps it raise capital on more favorable terms.

cost-justified. The same holds true with regard to credit—it is illegal to offer more favorable credit terms to one customer or class of customers than to another, unless the differences are cost-justified.

Credit Instruments

Most credit is offered on *open account,* which means that the only formal evidence of credit is an invoice which the buyer signs to indicate that goods have been received. Then, the buyer and the seller each record the purchase in their books of account. Under certain circumstances, the selling firm may require the buyer to sign a *promissory note* evidencing the credit obligation. Promissory notes are useful (1) if the order is very large; (2) if the seller anticipates the possibility of trouble collecting, because a note is a stronger legal claim than a simple signed invoice; and (3) if the buyer wants a longer-than-usual time in which to pay for the order, because interest charges can be built into a promissory note.

Another instrument used in trade credit, especially in international trade, is the commercial draft. Here the seller draws up a draft—which is a cross between a check and a promissory note—calling for the buyer to pay a specific amount to the seller by a specified date. This draft is then sent to the buyer's bank, along with the shipping invoices necessary to take possession of the goods. The bank forwards the draft to the buyer, who signs it and returns it to the bank. The bank then delivers the shipping documents to its customer, who at this point can claim the goods. If the draft is a *sight draft,* then upon delivery of the shipping documents and acceptance of the draft by the buyer, the bank actually withdraws money from the buyer's account and forwards it to the selling firm. If the draft is a *time draft,* payable on a specific future date, then the bank returns it to the selling firm; in this case the draft is called a trade acceptance, and it amounts to a promissory note that the seller can hold for future payment or use as collateral for a loan. The bank, in such a situation, has served as an intermediary, making sure that the buyer does not receive title to the goods until the note (or draft) has been executed for the benefit of the seller.

A seller who lacks confidence in the ability or willingness of the buyer to pay off a time draft may refuse to ship without a guarantee of payment by the buyer's bank. Presumably, the bank knows its customer and for a fee will guarantee payment of the draft. In this instance, the draft is called a *banker's acceptance.* Such instruments are widely used, especially in foreign trade. They have a low degree of risk if guaranteed by a strong bank, and there is a ready market for acceptances, making it easy for the seller of the goods to sell the instrument to raise immediate cash. (Banker's acceptances are sold at a discount below face value, then paid off at face value when they mature, so the discount amounts to interest on the acceptance. The effective interest rate on a strong banker's acceptance is a little above the Treasury bill rate of interest.)

A final type of credit instrument that should be mentioned is the *con-*

ditional sales contract. With a sales contract, the seller retains legal ownership of the goods until the buyer has completed payment. This instrument is used primarily for sales of such items as machinery, dental equipment, and the like, which are often paid for on an installment basis. The significant advantage of a conditional sales contract is that the seller finds it easier to repossess the equipment in the event of default than it would be if title had passed, and this feature makes possible some credit sales that otherwise would not be feasible.

How Effective Is the Firm's Credit Policy?

It is apparent from the preceding sections that the optimal credit policy, hence the optimal level of accounts receivable, depends on the firm's own unique operating conditions. Thus, a firm with excess capacity and low variable production costs should extend credit more liberally and carry a higher level of accounts receivable than a firm operating at full capacity. However, even though optimal credit policies vary among firms or even for a single firm over time, it is still useful to analyze the effectiveness of the firm's credit policy in an overall, aggregate sense.

As we saw in connection with the du Pont analysis, an excessive investment in any asset account will lead to a low rate of return on net worth. For comparative purposes, we can focus on the average collection period as discussed in Chapter 6. There we saw that Carter Chemical Company's average collection period was forty-two days, compared to an industry average of thirty-six days. If Carter lowered its average collection period by six days to thirty-six days, this would mean a reduction of (6)($8,333,333) = $50 million in the amount of capital tied up in receivables. If the cost of funds tied up in receivables is 10 percent, this would mean a savings of $5 million per year, other things held constant.

The average collection period can also be compared to Carter's credit terms. Carter typically sells on terms of 1/10, net 30, so its customers, on average, are not paying their bills on time: the forty-two day average collection period is greater than the thirty day credit period. Note, however, that some of the customers could be paying within ten days to take advantage of the discount, while others could be taking much longer than forty-two days to pay. To check against this possibility, we use the *aging schedule,* which breaks down accounts receivable according to how long they have been outstanding. Carter Chemical's aging schedule is shown on the following page. Most of the accounts pay on schedule or after only a slight delay, but a significant number are over one month past due. This indicates that even though the average collection period is close to the thirty day credit period, Carter has quite a bit of capital tied up in slow-paying accounts, some of which may eventually result in losses.

Management should constantly monitor the firm's average collection period and its aging schedule in comparison with industry averages, recent trends, and the firm's credit terms to see how effectively the credit

Age of Account (Days)	Percent of Total Value of Accounts Receivable
0-10	52%
11-30	20
31-45	13
46-60	4
Over 60	11
Total	100%

department is operating. If the average collection period starts to lengthen, or if the aging schedule begins to show an increasing percentage of past due accounts, then the credit manager may not be enforcing the standards closely enough or the collection policy may be too lax. In any event, the ACP and the aging schedule are useful tools for reviewing the credit manager's performance.

Investors—both stockholders and bank loan officers—should pay close attention to accounts receivable management; otherwise, they could be misled by the current financial statements and later suffer serious losses on their investments. When a sale is made, the following events occur: (1) inventories are reduced by the cost of goods sold, (2) accounts receivable are increased by the sales price, and (3) the difference is recorded as a profit. If the sale is for cash, the profit is definitely earned, but if the sale is on credit, the profit is not actually earned unless and until the account is collected. Firms have been known to encourage "sales" to very weak customers in order to inflate reported profits. This could boost the stock price, at least until credit losses begin to lower earnings, at which time the stock price falls. An analysis along the lines suggested above would detect any such questionable practice, as well as any unconscious deterioration in the quality of accounts receivable. Such early detection could help both investors and bankers avoid losses.[9]

Inventory Management

Inventories, which may be classified as (1) *raw materials,* (2) *work-in-process,* and (3) *finished goods,* are an essential part of most business operations. Like accounts receivable, inventory levels depend heavily upon sales. However, whereas receivables build up *after* sales have been made, inventories must be acquired *ahead* of sales. This is a critical difference, and the necessity of forecasting sales before establishing target inventory levels makes inventory management a difficult task.

---

[9] Accountants are increasingly interested in these matters. Investors have sued several of the Big Eight accounting firms for substantial damages where (1) profits were overstated and (2) it could be shown that the auditors should have conducted an analysis along the lines described here and then should have reported the results to stockholders on the audited financial statements.

Some examples of typical inventory decisions will make clear the types of issues involved.

1. Retail clothing store. Glamour Galore Boutique must order bathing suits for summer sales in January, and it must take delivery by April to be sure of having enough suits to meet the heavy May-June demand. Bathing suits come in many styles, colors, and sizes. If the buyer stocks incorrectly, either in total or in terms of the style-color-size distribution, then the store will have trouble. It will lose potential sales if it stocks too few suits, and it will be forced to mark them down and take losses if it stocks too many or the wrong types.

The effects of inventory changes on the balance sheet are important. For simplicity, assume that Glamour Galore has a $100 base stock of inventories, financed by common stock. Its initial balance sheet is as follows:

Inventories (base stock)	$100	Common stock	$100
Total assets	$100	Total claims	$100

Now it anticipates a seasonal increase in sales of $300 and takes on additional inventories in that amount, financing them with a bank loan:

Inventories	$400	Notes payable to bank	$300
		Common stock	100
Total assets	$400	Total claims	$400

If everything works out as planned, sales will occur, inventories will be converted to cash, the bank loan can be retired, and the company will have earned a profit. The balance sheet, after a successful season, might look like this:

Cash and marketable securities	$ 50	Notes payable to bank	$ 0
Inventories (base stock)	100	Common stock	100
		Retained earnings	50
Total assets	$150	Total claims	$150

The company is now in a highly liquid position and is ready to begin a new season.

Now suppose the season had not gone well. Sales were slow, and as fall approached the balance sheet looked like this:

Inventories	$300	Notes payable to bank	$200
		Common stock	100
Total assets	$300	Total claims	$300

Suppose the bank insists on repayment of its loan, and it wants cash, not bathing suits. But if the bathing suits did not sell well in the summer, how will out-of-style suits sell in the fall? Assume that Glamour Galore is forced to mark the suits down to half price in order to sell them to raise cash to repay the bank loan. The result will be:

Cash	$150	Notes payable to bank	$200
		Common equity	(50)
Total assets	$150	Total claims	$150

At this point, Glamour Galore goes bankrupt. The bank gets the $150 of cash and takes a $50 loss on its loan. The stockholders are wiped out, and the company goes out of business.

2. Manufacturer. Now consider a different type of situation, that of Whirlwind Corporation, a well-established appliance manufacturer whose inventory position is shown below:

Raw materials	$200
Work-in-process	200
Finished goods	600
	$1,000

Suppose Whirlwind anticipates that the economy is about to get much stronger and that the demand for appliances is likely to rise sharply. If it is to share in the expected boom, Whirlwind will have to increase production. This means it will have to increase inventories, and, since the inventory increase will precede sales, additional financing will be required. The details are not shown here, but some liability account, perhaps notes payable, would have to be increased in order to support the inventory buildup.

Proper inventory management requires close coordination among the sales, purchasing, production, and finance departments. The sales/marketing department is generally the first to spot changes in demand. These changes must be worked into the company's purchasing and manufacturing schedules, and the financial manager must arrange any financing that will be needed to support the inventory buildup.

Improper coordination among departments, poor sales forecasts, or both can lead to disaster. For example, Varner Corporation, a manufacturer of electronic components, was recently forced into bankruptcy because of a poor system of internal controls. The company set its production schedules for 1981 on the basis of 1980 sales. However, sales for several key items dropped sharply during the first half of 1981. Production schedules were not adjusted downward, so both inventories and bank debt built up. By the time the situation was properly assessed, inventories of now obsolete components had risen to over $10 million. The situation was like this:

Cash	$ 1	Accounts payable	$ 3
Receivables	8	Notes payable to bank	15
Inventories: good	6	Total current liabilities	$18
bad	10	Long-term debt	10
Total current assets	$25	Common equity	7
Fixed assets	10		
Total assets	$35	Total claims	$35

The bank insisted upon payment of the note. Varner simply could not generate the necessary cash, so it was forced into bankruptcy.[10]

Inventory Models

Inventories are obviously necessary, but it is equally obvious that a firm will suffer if it has too much or too little inventory. How can we determine the *optimal* inventory level? One commonly used approach to determining optimal levels is the *Economic Ordering Quantity (EOQ) Model*, which is described in this section.

---

[10] As we shall see in Chapter 10, bank loans are generally written as ninety day notes. Thus, the loan must be repaid or renewed every ninety days. If the bank thinks the firm's situation has deteriorated, as Varner's had, it will refuse to renew. Then, if the firm cannot raise cash to repay the loan, it is bankrupt.

We begin the EOQ analysis by noting that the inventory of any item consists of a *working stock* and a *safety stock*. The working stock depends on the pattern of inflows and outflows, while the safety stock is designed to guard against unexpectedly high demand, delays in receiving shipments, or both. In this section we first analyze optimal working stocks, then go on to look at safety stocks.

Figure 8-1 illustrates the basic premise on which inventory theory is built. First, you should recognize that the average investment in inventories depends on how frequently orders are placed and the size of each order—if we order every day, average inventories will be much smaller than if we order once a year. Further, as Figure 8-1 shows, some of the firm's costs rise with larger orders: included here are warehousing costs, interest on funds tied up in inventory, insurance, and obsolescence. Other costs decline with larger orders and inventories: for example, lost profits on sales lost because of shortages, or the costs of production interruptions caused by inadequate inventories. If these two curves are added, the sum represents the total cost of ordering and holding inventories. The point where the total cost curve is minimized represents the Economic Order Quantity, or the EOQ, and this, in turn, determines the optimal average inventory level.

It can be shown that, under certain reasonable assumptions, the order quantity that minimizes the total cost curve in Figure 8-1, or the EOQ, can be found by use of the following formula:[11]

$$EOQ = \sqrt{\frac{2FS}{CP}}.\qquad(8\text{-}7)$$

Here,

EOQ = the economic ordering quantity, or the optimum quantity to be ordered each time an order is placed.
F = fixed costs of placing and receiving an order.
S = annual sales in units.
C = carrying cost expressed as a percentage of inventory value.
P = purchase price per unit of inventory.

The assumptions of the model, which will be relaxed shortly, include the following: (1) sales can be forecasted perfectly, (2) sales are evenly distributed throughout the year, and (3) orders are received with no delays whatever.

---

[11] The EOQ model is derived in Appendix 8A. In essence, the fixed costs of ordering inventory (including production set-up costs for a manufacturing operation) and of carrying it are expressed as a percentage of the dollar volume of inventory holdings. Next, these costs are added to form the total cost of ordering and carrying inventories. This total cost function is then differentiated, and the first derivative is set equal to zero to locate the minimum point on the total cost curve in Figure 8-1. Equation 8-7 results from this operation.

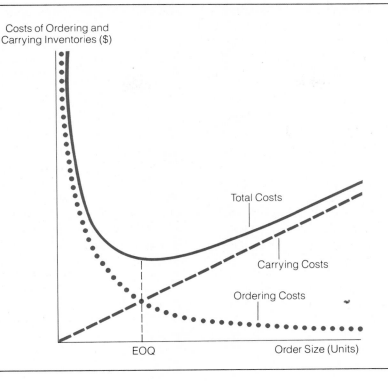

**Figure 8-1
Determination of the
Optimal Order Quantity**

To illustrate the EOQ model, consider the following data, supplied by Romantic Books, Inc., publisher of the classic novel, *Madame Boudoir:*

S = sales = 26,000 copies per year.

C = carrying cost = 20 percent of inventory value.[12]

P = purchase price per book to Romantic Books from a printing company = $6.1538 per copy. (The sales price is $9, but this is irrelevant for our purposes.)

F = fixed cost per order = $1,000. The bulk of this cost is the labor cost for setting the plates on the presses, as well as for setting up the binding equipment for the production run. The printer bills this cost separately from the $6.1538 cost per copy.

---

[12] In an unpublished study, the U.S. Department of Commerce estimated that, on the average, manufacturing firms have an annual cost of carrying inventories that equals 25 percent of original inventory cost. This percentage is broken down as follows: obsolescence, 8 percent; physical depreciation, 4 percent; interest, 9 percent; handling, 2.50 percent; property taxes, 0.50 percent; insurance, 0.25 percent; storage, 0.75 percent.

Substituting these data into Equation 8-7, we obtain

$$EOQ = \sqrt{\frac{2FS}{CP}}$$

$$= \sqrt{\frac{(2)(1,000)(26,000)}{(0.2)(6.1538)}}$$

$$= \sqrt{42,250,317}$$

$$= 6,500 \text{ copies.}$$

Average inventory holdings depend directly on the EOQ; this relationship is illustrated graphically in Figure 8-2. Immediately after an order is received, 6,500 copies are in stock. The usage rate, or sales rate, is 500

Figure 8-2
Inventory Position without Safety Stock

copies per week (26,000/52 weeks), so inventories are drawn down by this amount each week. Thus, the actual number of units held in inventory will vary from 6,500 books just after an order is received to zero just before an order arrives. On average, the number of units held will be 6,500/2 = 3,250 books. At a cost of $6.1538 per book, the average investment in inventories will be 3,250 × $6.1538 = $19,999.85 ≈ $20,000. If inventories are financed by bank loans, the loan will vary from a high of $40,000 to a low of $0.0, but the average amount outstanding over the course of a year will be $20,000.

Because a two week lead time is required for production and shipping, orders are placed when the stock falls to 1,000 copies, which is defined as the *order point*. Some procedure, perhaps computerized, should trigger an order when the stock hits this level. With a 6,500 beginning balance, a zero ending balance, and a uniform sales rate, inventories will average one-half the EOQ, or 3,250 copies, during the year.

Notice that the EOQ, hence average inventory holdings, rises with the square root of sales. Therefore, a given increase in sales will result in a less-than-proportionate increase in inventories, so the inventory/sales ratio will tend to decline as a firm grows. For example, Romantic Books' EOQ is 6,500 copies at an annual sales level of 26,000, and the average inventory is 3,250 copies, or $20,000. However, if sales increase by 100 percent, to 52,000 copies per year, the EOQ will rise only to 9,192, or by 41 percent, and the average inventory will rise by this same percentage. This suggests that there are economies of scale in the holding of inventories.[13]

Safety Stocks

If Romantic Books knew for certain that both the sales rate and the order lead time would never vary, it could operate exactly as shown in Figure 8-2. However, sales rates do change, and production and/or shipping delays are frequently encountered; to guard against these events, the company will carry additional inventories, or *safety stocks*.

The concept of a safety stock is illustrated in Figure 8-3. First, note that the slope of the sales line measures the expected rate of sales. The company *expects* sales of 500 copies per week, but let us assume a maximum likely sales rate of twice this amount, or 1,000 copies each week. It initially orders 7,500, the EOQ plus a safety stock of 1,000 copies. Subsequently, it reorders the EOQ, 6,500 copies, whenever the inventory level falls to 2,000 copies, the safety stock of 1,000 copies plus the 1,000 copies expected to be used while awaiting delivery of the order. Notice that the company could, over the two week delivery period, sell 1,000 copies a

---

[13] Note, however, that these scale economies relate to the particular item, not to the entire firm. Thus, a large publishing company with $500 million of sales might have a higher inventory/sales ratio than a much smaller publisher if the small house has only a few high-sales-volume books while the large house publishes a great many low-volume books.

Figure 8-3
Inventory Position with Safety Stock Included

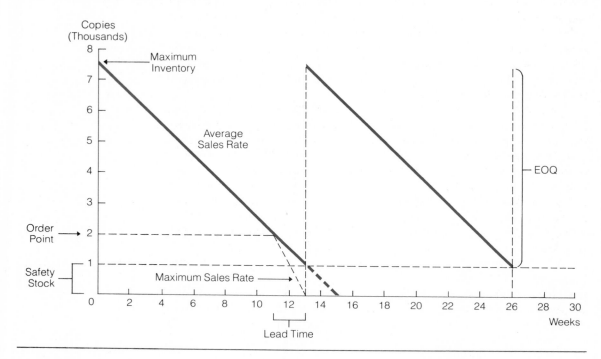

week, or double its normal expected sales. This maximum rate of sales is shown by the steeper dashed line in Figure 8-3. The condition that makes possible this higher maximum sales rate is the introduction of a safety stock of 1,000 copies.

The safety stock is also useful to guard against delays in receiving orders. The expected delivery time is two weeks; however, with a 1,000 copy safety stock, the company could maintain sales at the expected rate of 500 copies per week for an additional two weeks if production or shipping delays held up an order.

The optimum safety stock varies from situation to situation, but, in general, it *increases* with (1) the uncertainty of demand forecasts, (2) the costs (in terms of lost sales and lost goodwill) that result from inventory shortages, and (3) the probability of delays in receiving shipments. The optimum safety stock *decreases* with the cost of carrying the extra inventory.[14]

[14] For a more detailed discussion of safety stocks, see Arthur Snyder, "Principles of Inventory Management," *Financial Executive*, April 1964, 13-21. If we knew (1) the probability distribution of usage rates
(continued)

Moderate inflation—say, 3 percent per year—can largely be ignored for purposes of inventory management, but the higher the rate of inflation, the more important it is to consider this factor. If the rate of inflation in the types of goods the firm stocks tends to be relatively constant, it can be dealt with quite easily—simply deduct the expected annual rate of inflation from the carrying cost percentage, C, in Equation 8-7, and use this modified version of the EOQ model to establish the working stock.

The reason for making this deduction is that inflation causes the value of the inventory to rise, thus offsetting somewhat the effects of depreciation and other carrying cost factors. Since C will now be smaller, the calculated EOQ, hence the average inventory, will increase. However, the higher the rate of inflation, the higher are interest rates, and this factor will cause C to increase, thus lowering the EOQ and average inventories. On balance, there is no evidence that inflation either raises or lowers the optimal inventories of firms in the aggregate. Inflation should still be explicitly considered, however, for it will raise the individual firm's optimal holdings if the rate of inflation for its own inventories is above average (and is greater than the effects of inflation on interest rates), and vice versa.

Effects of Inflation on Inventory Management

Summary

The typical manufacturing firm has about 42 percent of its assets invested in inventories and receivables, so the management of these assets is obviously important. The investment in receivables is dependent on the firm's *credit policy*, and the four credit policy variables are these: (1) the *credit standards*, or the financial strength customers must exhibit in order to be granted credit, (2) the *credit period*, or length of time for which credit is extended, (3) *cash discounts* designed to encourage rapid payment, and (4) *collection policy*, which helps determine how long accounts remain outstanding. Credit policy has an important impact on the volume of sales, and the optimal credit policy involves a tradeoff between the costs inherent in various credit policies and the profits generated by higher sales. From a practical standpoint, it is impossible to determine the optimal credit policy in a mathematical sense—good credit management involves a blending of quantitative analysis and business judgment.

and (2) the probability distribution of order lead times, we could determine joint probabilities of stock-outs with various safety stock levels. With a safety stock of 1,000 copies, for example, the probability of a stock-out for *Madame Boudoir* might be 5 percent. If the safety stock is reduced to 500 copies, the stock-out probability might rise to 15 percent, while this probability might be reduced to 1 percent with a safety stock of 2,000 copies. If we had additional information on the precise cost of a stock-out, we could compare this with the cost of carrying larger safety stocks. The optimum safety stock is determined at the point where the marginal stock-out cost is equal to the marginal inventory carrying cost.

Inventory management centers around the balancing of a set of costs that increase with larger inventory holdings (storage costs, cost of capital, physical deterioration) and a set of costs that decline with larger holdings (ordering costs, lost sales, disruptions of production schedules). Inventory management has been quantified to a greater extent than most aspects of business. The EOQ model is one important part of most inventory systems. This model can be used to determine optimal order quantity, which, when combined with a specified safety stock, determines the average inventory level.

Questions

8-1 Is it true that when one firm sells to another on credit, the seller records the transaction as an account receivable while the buyer records it as an account payable, and that, disregarding discounts, the receivable typically exceeds the payable by the amount of profit on the sale?

8-2 What are the four elements in a firm's credit policy? To what extent can firms set their own credit policies as opposed to having to accept credit policies as dictated by "the competition"?

8-3 Suppose a firm makes a purchase and receives the shipment on February 1. The terms of trade as stated on the invoice read, "2/10, net 40, May 1 dating." What is the latest date on which payment can be made and the discount still be taken? What is the date on which payment must be made if the discount is not taken?

8-4 a. What is the "average collection period" for a firm whose sales are $2,880,000 per year and whose accounts receivable are $312,000? (Use 360 days per year.)

b. Is it true that if this firm sells on terms of 3/10, net 40, its customers probably all pay on time?

8-5 Is it true that if a firm calculates its average collection period, it has no need for an aging schedule?

8-6 Firm A had no credit losses last year, but 1 percent of Firm B's accounts receivable proved to be uncollectible and resulted in losses. Should Firm B fire its credit manager and hire A's?

8-7 Indicate by a (+), (−), or (0) whether each of the following events would probably cause accounts receivable (A/R), sales, and profits to increase, decrease, or to be affected in an indeterminant manner:

	A/R	Sales	Profits
a. The firm tightens its credit standards.	___	___	___
b. The terms of trade are changed from 2/10, net 30, to 3/10, net 30.	___	___	___
c. The terms are changed from 2/10, net 30, to 3/10, net 40.	___	___	___
d. The credit manager gets tough with past due accounts.	___	___	___

8-8 If a firm calculates its optimal inventory of widgets to be 1,000 units when the general rate of inflation is 2 percent, is it true that the optimal inventory (in units) will almost certainly rise if the general rate of inflation climbs to 10 percent?

8-9 Indicate by a ($+$), ($-$), or (0) whether each of the following events would probably cause average annual inventories (the sum of the inventories held at the end of each month of the year divided by 12) to rise, fall, or change in an indeterminant manner:

a. Our suppliers switch from delivering by train to air freight. _____

b. We change from producing to meet seasonal sales to steady year-round production. Sales peak at Christmas. _____

c. Competition in the markets in which we sell increases. _____

d. The rate of general inflation increases. _____

e. Interest rates rise; other things are constant. _____

ST8-1 The Celec Company expects to have sales of $20 million this year under current operating policies. Its variable costs as a percentage of sales is 0.8, and its cost of capital is 16 percent. Currently, Celec's credit policy is net 25 (no discount for early payment). However, its ACP is thirty days, and its bad debt loss percentage is 3 percent.

Self-Test Problem

The credit manager is considering five alternative proposals for changing Celec's credit policy. For each proposal find: (1) the expected change in investment in accounts receivable, ΔI; and (2) the incremental change in profits, ΔP, taking into consideration the anticipated changes in carrying costs for accounts receivable, the probable bad debt losses, and the discounts likely to be taken.

Proposal 1: *Lengthen the credit period* by going from net 25 to net 40. Anticipated effects:

$$\Delta S = \$2,000,000.$$
$$B_N = 6\% \text{ on } \Delta S.$$
$$B_0 = 3\% \text{ on } S_0 \text{ (no change for old sales)}.$$
$$ACP_N = 45 \text{ days (on all sales)}.$$

Proposal 2: *Shorten the credit period* by going from net 25 to net 20. Anticipated effects:

$$\Delta S = -\$2,000,000.$$
$$B_N = 1.5\% \text{ (on all sales)}.$$
$$ACP_N = 22 \text{ days}.$$

Note: Celec's other three proposed changes are given in Problem 8-3. Solutions for Proposals 1 and 2 are given at the end of the problems for this chapter.

Problems

8-1 Kim-Atkins, Inc., sells on terms of 2/10, net 30. Total sales for the year are $600,000. Forty percent of the customers pay on the tenth day and take discounts; the other 60 percent pay, on average, forty days after their purchases.

a. What is the average collection period?

b. What is the average investment in receivables?

c. What would happen to the average investment in receivables if Kim-Atkins toughened up on its collection policy, with the result that all nondiscount customers paid on the thirtieth day?

8-2 The Oh Drilling Company is considering changing its credit terms from 2/15, net 30, to 3/10, net 45. All of its sales are "credit sales," but 70 percent of the customers presently take the 2 percent cash discount; under the new terms this percentage is expected to decline to 65 percent. The average collection period is also expected to change under the new policy, from seventeen days at present to twenty days under the new plan. (Note: These averages are heavily weighted with customers who pay on the tenth day.)

Expected sales, before discounts are deducted, are $1,200,000 with the present terms, but they will rise to $1,350,000 if the new terms are used. Assume that Oh Drilling presently earns a 12 percent gross profit margin on sales, and that this margin will also apply after the change in credit policy. However, profits will be reduced somewhat if the new credit policy is put into effect because of additional credit-associated costs. Oh Drilling has a 12 percent opportunity cost, or cost of capital, for any additional funds tied up in receivables. Calculate the following items:

a. The increase in gross profits before credit costs.

b. The cost of increasing the cash discount.

c. The increased cost of carrying receivables.

d. The net change in pre-tax profits.

8-3 This problem extends the self-test problem. Read the basic problem and Proposals 1 and 2, and then analyze Proposals 3, 4, and 5.

Proposal 3: *Relax credit standards* and sell to less creditworthy customers. Anticipated effects:

$$\Delta S = \$2,000,000.$$
$$B_N = 6\% \text{ (on new sales only).}$$
$$ACP_N = 40 \text{ days (on new sales only).}$$

Proposal 4: *Tighten credit collection policy.* Anticipated effects:

$$\Delta S = -\$1,500,000.$$
$$B_N = 1.5\% \text{ (on all sales).}$$
$$ACP_N = 25 \text{ days (on all sales).}$$

Proposal 5: *Offer a discount for early payment.* Here we would allow a 2 percent discount for payment within ten days (i.e., 2/10, net 25). It is estimated that 50 percent of the customers would take discounts. Anticipated effects:

$$\Delta S = \$2,000,000.$$
$$B_N = 2\% \text{ (on all sales)}.$$
$$D_N = 2\%.$$
$$ACP_N = 0.5(10) + 0.5(30) = 20 \text{ days}.$$

8-4 The following relations for inventory costs have been established for the Mehta Service Corporation:

---

1. Orders must be placed in multiples of 200 units.
2. Annual sales are 600,000 units.
3. The purchase price per unit is $6.
4. Carrying cost is 25 percent of the purchase price of goods.
5. Cost per order placed is $40.
6. Desired safety stock is 20,000 units; this amount is on hand initially.
7. Three days are required for delivery.

---

a. What is the EOQ?
b. How many orders should Mehta place each year?
c. At what inventory level should a reorder be made?
d. Calculate the total cost of ordering and carrying inventories if the order quantity is (1) 4,000 units, (2) 5,600 units, or (3) 7,000 units. Keep separate the cost of carrying the "working inventory" versus the safety stock.
e. Construct a graph similar to Figure 8-1 based on your answer to Part d above.

8-5 King Keg, Inc., distributes keg beer to bars and restaurants in the Springfield, Missouri, area. Rob Moore, the owner-manager, is thinking of changing his credit terms from 2/15, net 30, to 3/15, net 45, in an effort to boost sales. Moore's main concern is the effect the change will have on his profits and financing needs. He asks you to help him analyze the effects of the change.

Moore's records are in terrible shape; he does not know exactly how many of his customers take the discount or when the others pay. He tells you, however, to assume that 60 percent of his accounts pay in fifteen days and take the discount, while the other 40 percent pay in thirty days.

a. Do Moore's assumptions about his collections seem realistic to you?
b. Assuming Moore's collection assumptions are correct, what is his average collection period? (Hint: Calculate a weighted average.)
c. Sales last year were 10,000 kegs at a price of $50 per keg. How much does Moore have in outstanding receivables, assuming his collections

data are correct? Use 360 days per year and disregard discounts in answering this question.

d. Moore buys kegs of beer for $35. He estimates that the change in credit policy will increase annual sales by 4,000 kegs, that 60 percent of his customers will continue to take discounts, and that the other customers will pay on time. Under these assumptions, what will happen to his average collection period and what will be the changes in accounts receivable?

e. Moore estimates that his inventory carrying costs are 20 percent and that his ordering costs are $200 per order. *Before* he changes his credit policy, what are (1) Moore's EOQ, (2) the number of orders he should place each year, and (3) his average inventory balance assuming a zero safety stock?

f. Assume Moore changes his credit policy, and sales increase according to his forecast. Calculate his new EOQ, his new number of orders, his new average inventory balance (in dollars), and the change in average inventory balance.

g. Assume Moore's general, administrative, and sales expenses (GA&S) amount to 20 percent of sales; that his income tax rate is 20 percent; and that he must borrow at a 10 percent interest rate the funds needed to carry his *added* receivables and inventory. (He currently has no debt outstanding.) Calculate his net income under the two credit policies. Use the income statement format shown below:

	Old	New
Gross sales		
Less discounts	_____	_____
Net sales		
Cost of goods sold	_____	_____
Gross profit		
GA&S		
Interest	_____	_____
Net profit before taxes		
Taxes at 20%	_____	_____
Net income after taxes	==============	==============

h. Should Moore change his credit policy? In answering this question, consider the reliability of the numerical answers you have developed and ways of improving the reliability factor.

Solution to Self-Test Problem

ST8-1 Proposal 1: *Lengthen credit period* such that

$$ACP_N = 45 \text{ days (on all sales).}$$
$$\Delta S = \$2,000,000.$$
$$B_N = 6\% \text{ on } \Delta S.$$
$$B_0 = 3\% \text{ on } S_0.$$

$$\Delta I = (ACP_N - ACP_0)(S_0/360) + V(ACP_N)(\Delta S/360)$$
$$= (45 - 30)(\$20,000,000/360) + 0.8(45)(\$2,000,000/360)$$
$$= \$833,333 + \$200,000$$
$$= \$1,033,333.$$

$$\Delta P = (1 - V)(\Delta S) - (B_N)(\Delta S) - k(\Delta I)$$
$$= (0.2)(\$2,000,000) - (0.06)(\$2,000,000) - (0.16)(\$1,033,333)$$
$$= \$400,000 - \$120,000 - \$165,333$$
$$= \$114,667.$$

Therefore, the change appears to be a good one if the assumptions are correct. Note: In the incremental profit equation we do not bring in bad debts on old sales because they are assumed to be unchanged. Had the lengthened credit period been assumed to lead to greater losses on old sales, the ΔP equation would have had to show Δ bad debts $= B_0 S_0 - B_N(S_0 + \Delta S)$.

Proposal 2: *Shorten the credit period* to net 20.

$$\Delta S = -\$2,000,000.$$
$$B_N = 1.5\% \text{ (on all sales)}.$$
$$ACP_N = 22 \text{ days}.$$

$$\Delta I = (ACP_N - ACP_0)[(S_0 + \Delta S)/360] + V(ACP_0)(\Delta S/360)$$
$$= (22 - 30)[\$18,000,000/360] + 0.8(30)(-\$2,000,000/360)$$
$$= -\$400,000 - \$133,333$$
$$= -\$533,333.$$

$$\Delta P = (1 - V)(\Delta S) + [B_0 S_0 - B_N(S_0 + \Delta S)] - k(\Delta I)$$
$$= (0.2)(-\$2,000,000) + [(0.03)(\$20,000,000) - (0.015)(\$18,000,000)]$$
$$- (0.16)(-\$533,333)$$
$$= -\$400,000 + (\$600,000 - \$270,000) + \$85,333$$
$$= \$15,333.$$

This change also looks profitable, but it conflicts with Proposal 1, which appears to be far more profitable, so Proposal 2 should be rejected in favor of Proposal 1.

Selected References

Three general references on credit policy at the applied level are

Beckman, T. N., and R. S. Foster, *Credits and Collections: Management and Theory* (New York: McGraw-Hill, 1969).

Christie, George N., and Albert E. Bracuti, *Credit Management* (Lake Success, N.Y.: Credit Research Foundation, 1981).

Cole, R. H., *Consumer and Commercial Credit Management,* (Homewood, Ill.: Irwin, 1972).

More analytical books which deal with both credit policy and inventory management include the following:

Mehta, Dileep R., *Working Capital Management* (Englewood Cliffs, N.J.: Prentice-Hall, 1974).

Smith, Keith V., *Management of Working Capital* (New York: West, 1974).

Some recent articles which address credit policy and receivables management include the following:

Atkins, Joseph C., and Yong H. Kim, "Comment and Correction: Opportunity Cost in the Evaluation of Investment in Accounts Receivable," *Financial Management*, Winter 1977, 71-74.

Dyl, Edward A., "Another Look at the Evaluation of Investment in Accounts Receivable," *Financial Management*, Winter 1977, 67-70.

Kim, Yong H., and Joseph C. Atkins, "Evaluating Investments in Accounts Receivable: A Wealth Maximizing Framework," *Journal of Finance*, vol. 33 (May 1978), 403-412.

Lewellen, Wilbur G., and Robert W. Johnson, "A Better Way to Monitor Accounts Receivable," *Harvard Business Review*, May-June 1972, 101-109.

Oh, John S., "Opportunity Cost in the Evaluation of Investment in Accounts Receivable," *Financial Management*, vol. 5 (Summer 1976), 32-36.

Roberts, Gordon S., and Jerry A. Viscione, "Captive Finance Subsidiaries: The Manager's View," *Financial Management*, vol. 10 (Spring 1981), 36-42.

Stone, Bernell K., "The Payments-Pattern Approach to the Forecasting and Control of Accounts Receivable," *Financial Management*, Autumn 1976, 65-82.

Walia, Tirlochan S., "Explicit and Implicit Cost of Changes in the Level of Accounts Receivable and the Credit Policy Decision of the Firm," *Financial Management*, Winter 1977, 75-78.

Weston, J. Fred, and Pham D. Tuan, "Comment on Analysis of Credit Policy Changes," *Financial Management*, vol. 9 (Winter 1980), 59-63.

Appendix 8A

The Basic Inventory Model

As we noted in Chapter 8, mathematical models have been applied to inventory management with perhaps better results than in any other area of business management. In this appendix we will see how the basic inventory model—the EOQ model—is developed.

Nature of the Problem

Recalling Figure 8-1, we note (1) that some costs associated with inventories decline as inventory holdings increase, (2) that other costs rise, and (3) that the total inventory-associated cost curve has a minimum point. The purpose of the basic inventory model is to locate this minimum and the economic order quantity (EOQ) which will lead to minimum costs. We will assume that the Norgaard Company expects to achieve a sales volume, S, of 1,000 widgets during the coming year, and that Norgaard is quite confident of hitting this target. Further, these sales are expected to be evenly distributed over the year, so inventories will decline smoothly and gradually. Widgets are purchased for $10 each. No inventory is on hand at the beginning of the year, and none will be held at year's end.

Under these circumstances, the Norgaard Company could place one order for Q = 1,000 units at the start of the year. If it did, the average inventory for the year, A, would be equal to

$$A = \frac{Q}{2} = \frac{S}{2} = \frac{1,000}{2} = 500 \text{ units.} \tag{8A-1}$$

Since widgets cost $10 each, the average investment in inventories would be $5,000.

Alternatively, Norgaard could place two orders for 500 each, in which case average inventories would be

$$A = \frac{500}{2} = 250,$$

or four orders of 250 each for an average inventory of 125, and so on. Inventory investment would decline correspondingly.

We can see that average inventories are a function of the number of orders placed per year, N. Specifically, when the number of orders placed is incorporated into the calculation, Equation 8A-1 becomes

$$A = \frac{S/2}{N}. \qquad (8A\text{-}1a)$$

By ordering more frequently (increasing N), Norgaard can reduce its average inventory further and further.

How far should inventory reductions be carried? Smaller inventories involve lower *carrying costs*—cost of capital tied up in inventories, storage costs, insurance, and so on—but since smaller average inventories imply more frequent orders, they involve higher *ordering costs*.

Classification of Costs

The first step in the process of building an inventory model is to specify those costs that rise and those that decline with higher levels of inventory. Table 8A-1 gives a listing of some typical costs that are associated with carrying inventories. In the table we have broken costs down into

**Table 8A-1
Costs Associated with Inventories**

Carrying costs

1. Cost of capital tied up
2. Storage costs
3. Insurance
4. Property taxes
5. Depreciation and obsolescence

Costs of running short

1. Loss of sales
2. Loss of customer goodwill
3. Disruption of production schedules

Shipping, receiving, and ordering costs

1. Cost of placing orders, including production set-up costs
2. Shipping and handling costs
3. Quantity discounts lost

three categories: those associated with carrying inventories, those associated with running short of inventory, and those associated with ordering and receiving inventories.

Although they may well be the most important element, we shall disregard the second category of costs—the costs of running short—at this point. These costs are taken account of by adding "safety stocks," as noted in Chapter 8. Further, we shall disregard quantity discounts, although it is easy enough to adjust the basic model to include discounts.[1] The costs that remain for consideration at this stage, then, are carrying costs and ordering costs.

Carrying Costs

Carrying costs generally rise in direct proportion to the average amount of inventory carried, and this is the case with the Norgaard Company. For example, Norgaard's cost of capital is 10 percent, and depreciation is estimated to amount to 5 percent per year. Lumping together these and Norgaard's other costs of carrying inventory produces a total cost of 25 percent of the investment in inventory. Defining the percentage cost as C, we can, in general, find the total carrying costs as the percentage carrying cost (C) times the price per unit (P) times the average number of units (A):

$$K = \text{Total carrying costs}$$
$$= (C)(P)(A). \tag{8A-2}$$

If Norgaard elects to order only once a year, average inventories will be $1,000/2 = 500$ units; the cost of carrying the inventory will be $0.25 \times \$10 \times 500 = \$1,250$. If the company orders twice a year, and, hence, has average inventories that are half as large, total carrying costs will decline to $625, and so on.

Shipping, Receiving, and Ordering Costs

Although carrying costs are entirely variable and rise in direct proportion to the average size of inventories, ordering costs consist of both a fixed and a variable component. For example, the costs of *placing* an order—interoffice memos, long-distance telephone calls, setting up a production run, and so on—are fixed costs, so the total cost of placing orders may simply be the cost of placing an order times the number of orders placed. Shipping and receiving costs, on the other hand, generally involve a fixed charge plus a variable charge per unit.[2]

---

[1] See A. Snyder, "Principles of Inventory Management," *Financial Executive*, April 1964.

[2] The fixed-versus-variable components in ordering costs can be confusing, so some elaboration on this point might be useful. First, *in toto*, ordering costs are considered to be a variable cost—if the firm does not place any orders, it does not incur any ordering costs. However, some of the costs of each order are fixed and some are variable. It is this fact—that a component of a *variable* cost is *fixed*—that occasionally causes confusion.

We can lump together all fixed costs of placing and receiving an order and define them as F. Norgaard's total fixed cost *per order*, for example, is \$100. The company's total variable cost of ordering, shipping, and receiving, which we define as V, depends on the number of units ordered, and it amounts to \$1.00 *per unit ordered*.

Combining the fixed and variable components of ordering costs, we obtain the following equation for R, the total cost of placing and receiving orders:

$$R = (F)(N) + (V)(S), \qquad\qquad (8A\text{-}3)$$

where F = fixed costs per order; N = number of orders placed; V = variable cost per unit ordered; and S = total number of units ordered during the year, which in this case equals the total sales in units.

Equation 8A-1a may be rewritten as N = S/2A, then substituted into Equation 8A-3 as follows:

$$R = F\left(\frac{S}{2A}\right) + (V)(S). \qquad\qquad (8A\text{-}4)$$

To illustrate, if F = \$100, S = 1,000, A = 250, and V = \$1.00, then R, the total ordering cost, is

$$R = \$100(2) + \$1(1,000) = \$1,200.$$

Total Inventory Costs

Total carrying costs (K) as defined in Equation 8A-2 and ordering costs (R) as defined in Equation 8A-4 may be combined to find total inventory costs (T) as follows:

$$\begin{aligned} T &= K + R \\ &= (C)(P)(A) + F\left(\frac{S}{2A}\right) + (V)(S). \qquad\qquad (8A\text{-}5) \end{aligned}$$

Recognizing that A = Q/2, or one half the size of each order quantity, Q, Equation 8A-5 may be rewritten as

$$\begin{aligned} T &= CP\left(\frac{Q}{2}\right) + F\left(\frac{S}{Q}\right) + (V)(S) \\ &= CP\left(\frac{Q}{2}\right) + \frac{F(S)}{Q} + (V)(S). \qquad\qquad (8A\text{-}6) \end{aligned}$$

The next step is to locate an optimal order quantity, or the value of Q that minimizes T. We find this optimal quantity, or the EOQ, by differentiating Equation 8A-6 with respect to Q, setting the derivative equal to zero, and obtaining[3]

$$EOQ = \sqrt{\frac{2FS}{CP}}. \tag{8A-7}$$

In the Norgaard case, we find the EOQ to be

$$EOQ = \sqrt{\frac{2(\$100)\,(1,000)}{(0.25)\,(\$10)}}$$

$$= \sqrt{\frac{200,000}{2.5}}$$

$$= \sqrt{80,000}$$

$$\approx 280 \text{ units.}$$

If this quantity is ordered four times a year ($1,000/280 \approx 4$), or every three months, total costs of ordering and carrying inventories, calculated from Equation 8A-6, will be

$$T = CP\left(\frac{Q}{2}\right) + \frac{FS}{Q} + VS$$

$$= \$2.50\,(140) + \frac{(\$100)(1,000)}{280} + \$1(1,000)$$

$$= \$350 + \$357 + \$1,000$$

$$= \$1,707.$$

This is the lowest possible cost of ordering and carrying the required amount of inventories.

Equation 8A-7 gives us the optimum, or cost minimizing, order quantity for given levels of sales (S), inventory carrying costs (C), and fixed

---

[3] Proof: Differentiate Equation 8A-6 with respect to Q and set equal to zero; then solve for Q:

$$\frac{\partial T}{\partial Q} = \frac{CP}{2} - \frac{FS}{Q^2} = 0$$

$$\frac{CP}{2} = \frac{FS}{Q^2}$$

$$Q^2 = \frac{2FS}{CP}$$

$$Q = \sqrt{\frac{2FS}{CP}}$$

order costs (F). Knowing the EOQ and continuing our assumption of zero beginning and ending inventory balances, we find the optimal average inventory as[4]

$$A = \frac{EOQ}{2} = \frac{280}{2} = 140.$$

Norgaard will, thus, have an average inventory investment of 140 units at $10 each, or $1,400.

---

[4] As noted in Chapter 8, there will also be a safety stock added to the average inventory as determined by the EOQ formula.

Cash and Marketable Securities

In the last chapter we examined the firm's investment in accounts receivable and inventories. To complete our analysis of current assets, we now turn to cash and marketable securities.

Cash Management

Approximately 1.5 percent of the average industrial firm's assets are held in the form of cash, which is defined as the total of bank demand deposits plus currency. However, cash balances vary widely not only among industries but also among the firms within a given industry, depending on the individual firms' specific conditions and on their owners' and managers' aversion to risk. In this section, we analyze the factors that determine firms' cash balances. These same factors, incidentally, apply to the cash holdings of individuals and nonprofit organizations, including government agencies.

Reasons for Holding Cash

Firms hold cash for four primary reasons:

1. *Transactions.* Cash balances are necessary to conduct business. Payments must be made in cash, and receipts are deposited in the cash account. Cash balances associated with routine payments and collections are known as *transactions balances*.
2. *Precaution.* Cash inflows and outflows are somewhat unpredictable, with the degree of predictability varying among firms and industries. Therefore, just as firms hold safety stocks of inventories, they also need to hold some cash in reserve for random, unforeseen fluctuations in inflows and outflows; these amounts are defined as *precautionary balances*. The less predictable the firm's cash flows, the larger the precautionary balances. However, if the firm has easy access to borrowed funds—that is, if it can borrow on short notice—then this reduces its need to hold cash for precautionary purposes. Also, as shall be noted later in this chapter, firms that would otherwise need large precautionary balances tend to hold highly liquid marketable securities; such holdings accomplish the same purposes as cash balances while providing income in the form of interest.
3. *Speculation.* Some cash balances may be held to enable the firm to take advantage of any bargain purchases that might arise; these are

defined as *speculative balances*. However, as with precautionary balances, firms today are more likely to rely on reserve borrowing power and on marketable securities portfolios than on actual cash holdings for speculative purposes.

4. *Compensation to banks for providing loans and services.* This type of balance, defined as a *compensating balance*, is discussed in detail later in this chapter.

Although the actual cash account can be thought of as consisting of transactions balances, speculative balances, precautionary balances, and compensating balances, we cannot calculate the amount needed for each type, add them together, and produce a total desired cash balance, because the same money serves all four purposes. Firms do, however, consider these four factors when establishing their target cash positions.

While there are good reasons for holding *adequate* cash balances, there is a strong reason for not holding *excessive* balances—cash is a nonearning asset, so excessive cash balances simply lower the total asset turnover, thereby reducing both the rate of return on net worth and the value of the stock. Thus, firms are very much interested in establishing procedures for increasing the efficiency of their cash management. If they can make their cash work harder, they can reduce cash balances.

The Cash Budget

The most important tool in cash management is the *cash budget*, a statement showing the firm's projected cash inflows and outflows over some specified period of time. Cash budgets can be constructed on a monthly, a weekly, or even a daily basis. Table 9-1 shows a monthly cash budget covering the last six months of 1981 for the Dayton Printing Company, a leading producer of greeting cards.

Dayton's birthday and get-well cards are sold year-round, but the bulk of the company's sales occurs during September, when retailers are stocking up for Christmas. All sales are made on terms that allow a cash discount for payments made within twenty days; if the discount is not taken, the full amount must be paid in forty days. However, like most other companies, Dayton finds that some of its customers delay payment up to ninety days. Experience shows that on 20 percent of the sales, payment is made during the month in which the sale is made; on 70 percent of the sales, payment is made during the second month after the sale; and on 10 percent of the sales, payment is made during the third month.

Rather than produce at a uniform rate throughout the year, Dayton prints cards immediately before they are required for delivery. Paper, ink, and other materials amount to 70 percent of sales and are bought the month before the company expects to sell the finished product. Its own purchase terms permit Dayton to delay payment on its purchases for one month. Accordingly, if July sales are forecast at $10 million, then pur-

Table 9-1
Dayton Printing Company: Worksheet and Cash Budget ($ in Thousands)

	May	June	July	Aug.	Sept.	Oct.	Nov.	Dec.	Jan.
Worksheet									
Sales (net of cash discounts)	$5,000	$5,000	$10,000	$15,000	$20,000	$10,000	$10,000	$5,000	$5,000
Collections									
During month of sale (20%)	1,000	1,000	2,000	3,000	4,000	2,000	2,000	1,000	
During first month after sale (70%)		3,500	3,500	7,000	10,500	14,000	7,000	7,000	
During second month after sale (10%)			500	500	1,000	1,500	2,000	1,000	
Total collections	$1,000	$4,500	$6,000	$10,500	$15,500	$17,500	$11,000	$9,000	
Purchases (70% of next month's sales)	$3,500	$7,000	$10,500	$14,000	$7,000	$7,000	$3,500		
Payments (one month lag)		$3,500	$7,000	$10,500	$14,000	$7,000	$7,000	$3,500	
Cash Budget									
(1) Collections			$6,000	$10,500	$15,500	$17,500	$11,000	$9,000	
(2) Payments									
(3) Purchases			$7,000	$10,500	$14,000	$7,000	$7,000	$3,500	
(4) Wages and salaries			750	1,000	1,250	750	750	500	
(5) Rent			250	250	250	250	250	250	
(6) Other expenses			100	150	200	100	100	50	
(7) Taxes					2,000			2,000	
(8) Payment for plant construction						5,000			
(9) Total payments			$ 8,100	$11,900	$17,700	$13,100	$ 8,100	$6,300	
(10) Net cash gain (loss) during month (Line 1 – Line 9)			($ 2,100)	($ 1,400)	($ 2,200)	$ 4,400	$ 2,900	$2,700	
(11) Cash at start of month if no borrowing is done			3,000	900	500	(2,700)	1,700	4,600	
(12) Cumulative cash (= cash at start plus gains or minus losses = Line 10 + Line 11)			$ 900	($ 500)	($ 2,700)	$ 1,700	$ 4,600	$7,300	
(13) Deduct target level of cash			2,500	2,500	2,500	2,500	2,500	2,500	
(14) Total loans outstanding to maintain $2,500 target cash balance			$ 1,600	$ 3,000	$ 5,200	$ 800	—	—	
(15) Surplus cash			—	—	—	—	$ 2,100	$4,800	

Note: 1. The amount shown on Line 11 for the first month, the $3,000 balance on July 1, is given. The values shown for each of the following months on Line 11 represent the "cumulative cash" as shown on Line 12 for the preceding month.

2. When the target cash balance of $2,500 (Line 13) is deducted from the cumulative cash balance (Line 12), if a negative figure results, it is shown on Line 14 as a required loan, while if a positive figure results, it is shown on Line 15 as surplus cash.

chases during June will amount to $7 million, and this amount will actually be paid in July.

Such other cash expenditures as wages and rent are given in the lower part of Table 9-1. The company must also make tax payments of $2 million on September 15 and on December 15, while payment for a new plant must be made in October. Assuming the company needs to keep a minimum cash balance of $2.5 million at all times, and that it has $3 million on July 1, what are Dayton's financial requirements for the period July through December?

The monthly cash requirements are worked out in Table 9-1. The top half of the table provides a worksheet for calculating collections on sales and payments on purchases. The first line in the worksheet gives the sales forecast for the period May through January; May and June sales are necessary to determine collections for July and August. Next, cash collections are given. The first line of this section shows that 20 percent of the sales during any given month are collected that month. The second line shows the collections on the prior month's sales: 70 percent of sales in the preceding month. The third line gives collections from sales two months earlier: 10 percent of sales in that month. The collections are summed to find the total cash receipts from sales during each month under consideration.

With the worksheet completed, the cash budget itself can be constructed. Receipts from collections are given on the top line. Next, payments during each month are summarized. The difference between cash receipts and cash payments is the net cash gain or loss during the month; for July there is a net cash loss of $2.1 million. The initial cash on hand at the beginning of the month is added to the net cash gain or loss during the month to obtain the cumulative cash that would be on hand if no financing were done; at the end of July, Dayton would have cumulative cash totaling $900,000.

The cumulative cash is next subtracted from the target cash balance, $2.5 million, to determine the firm's borrowing requirements or surplus cash, whichever the case may be. In July, Dayton expects to have cumulative cash as shown on Line 12 of $900,000. It has a target cash balance of $2.5 million. Thus, to maintain the target cash balance it must borrow $1.6 million by the end of July. Assuming that this amount is indeed borrowed, loans outstanding will total $1.6 million at the end of July.

This same procedure is used in the following months. Sales will expand seasonally in August. With the increased sales will come increased payments for purchases, wages, and other items. Receipts from sales will go up too, but the firm will still be left with a $1.4 million cash outflow during the month. The total financial requirements at the end of August will be $3 million, the cumulative cash plus the target cash balance. The $3 million is also equal to the $1.6 million needed at the end of July plus the $1.4 million cash deficit for August. Thus, loans outstanding will total $3 million at the end of August.

Sales peak in September, and the cash deficit during this month will amount to another $2.2 million. The total borrowing requirements through September will increase to $5.2 million. Sales, purchases, and payments for past purchases will fall markedly in October; collections will be the highest of any month because they reflect the high September sales. As a result, Dayton will enjoy a healthy $4.4 million cash surplus during October. This surplus can be used to pay off borrowings, so loans outstanding will decline by $4.4 million, to $800,000.

Dayton will have another cash surplus in November, which will permit it to eliminate completely the need for borrowing. In fact, the company is expected to have $2.1 million in surplus cash by the month's end, while another cash surplus in December will swell the extra cash to $4.8 million. With such a large amount of unneeded funds, Dayton's treasurer will doubtless want to invest in interest-bearing securities or put the funds to use in some other way.

Before concluding our discussion of the cash budget, we should make five additional points: (1) Our cash budget does not reflect interest on loans or income from the investment of surplus cash. This refinement could be added quite easily. (2) More important, if cash inflows and outflows are not uniform during the month, we could be seriously understating or overstating our financing requirements. For example, if all payments must be made on the fifth of each month, but collections come in uniformly throughout the month, then we would need to borrow much larger amounts than those shown in Table 9-1. In such a case, we would need to prepare cash budgets on a daily basis. (3) Since depreciation is a noncash charge, depreciation does not appear on the cash budget. (4) The cash budget represents a forecast, so all the values in the table are *expected* values. If actual sales, purchases, and so on are different from the forecasted levels, then our forecasted cash deficits and surpluses will also be incorrect. (5) Finally, we should note that the target cash balance would probably be adjusted over time, rising and falling with seasonal patterns and with longer-term changes in the scale of the firm's operations. Factors that influence the target cash balance are discussed in the following sections.

Other Procedures for Increasing the Efficiency of Cash Management

While a carefully prepared cash budget is a necessary starting point, there are other elements in a good cash management program. For example, the $2.5 million minimum cash balance in the preceding example—which represents a safety stock—could be reduced if Dayton could predict its inflows and outflows more precisely. Most firms do not know exactly when bills will come in or when payments will be received, and transactions balances must include a safety stock element to allow for a random increase in bills requiring payment at a time when receipts lag below expectations. Although we do not consider them in this book, statistical procedures are available to help improve cash flow forecasts, and the better the cash flow forecast, the lower the minimum cash balance.

Synchronizing Cash Inflows and Outflows. If you, as an individual, were to receive income on a daily basis instead of once a month, you could operate with a lower average checking account balance. If you could arrange to pay rent, tuition, and other charges on a daily basis, this would further reduce your required average cash balances. Exactly the same situation holds for business firms—by arranging things so that their cash receipts coincide with the timing of their cash outflows, firms can hold their transactions balances to a minimum. Recognizing this point, utility companies, oil companies, and others arrange to bill customers and to pay their own bills on a regular schedule throughout the month. In our cash budgeting example, if Dayton Printing could arrange a better synchronization of its cash inflows and outflows, it might be able to reduce somewhat its minimum cash balance, and therefore its required bank loans.

Speeding Collections of Checks Received and Slowing Collections of Checks Written. Another important aspect of cash management deals with processing the checks a company writes and receives. It is obviously inefficient to put checks received in a drawer and deposit them every week or so; no well-run business would follow such a practice. Similarly, cash balances are drawn down unnecessarily if bills are paid earlier than required. In fact, efficient firms go to great lengths to speed up the processing of incoming checks, thus putting the funds to work faster, and they try to stretch their own payments out as long as possible.

When a customer writes and mails a check, this *does not* mean that the funds are immediately available to the receiving firm. Most of us have deposited a check in our account and then been told that we cannot write our own checks against this deposit until the check clears. Our bank must (1) make sure that the check we deposited is good and (2) receive funds itself before releasing funds for us to spend.

As shown on the left side of Figure 9-1, quite a bit of time may be required for a firm to process incoming checks and obtain the use of the money. A check must first be delivered through the mails, then cleared through the banking system, before the money can be put to use. Checks received from customers in distant cities are especially subject to delays. First, possible mail delays can obviously cause problems. Second, clearing checks can also delay the effective use of funds received. Assume, for example, that we receive a check and deposit it in our bank. Our bank must present the check to the bank on which it was drawn. Only when this latter bank transfers funds to our bank are they available for us to use. Checks are generally cleared through the Federal Reserve System or through a clearinghouse set up by the banks in a particular city. Of

Figure 9-1
Diagram of the Check Clearing Process

Regular Process

Action	Time Required to Complete Action
Customer writes a check and mails it.	
	1–3 days
Firm A receives the check.	
	1 day
Firm A deposits the check in its own bank. It cannot use the money yet.	
	1 day
Firm A's bank sends the check to the Federal Reserve system for clearing.	
	1 day
The Federal Reserve processes the check. The bank on which it was drawn notifies the Fed that the check is "good," in which case the Fed transfers funds from the customer's bank to Firm A's bank. This process is faster if the two banks are located in the same city.	
	2 days
Firm A's bank notifies it that the check has cleared and the funds are now available for use.	

6–8 working days

Accelerated Process

Action	Time Required to Complete Action
Customer writes a check and mails it.	
	1 day
Check arrives at a lockbox in customer's city and is picked up by the bank, which starts the clearing process immediately.	
	1 day
Check is cleared through the local clearinghouse, or perhaps within the bank itself if the check was drawn on Firm A's own bank.	
	1 day
The bank notifies Firm A (by wire if the two are in different cities) that the check has cleared and the funds are available for use.	

3 working days

course, if the check is drawn on the bank of deposit, that bank merely transfers funds by bookkeeping entries from one of its depositors to another. The length of time required for other checks to clear is a function of the distance between the payer's and the payee's banks; in the case of private clearinghouses, it can range from one to three days. The maximum time required for checks to clear through the Federal Reserve System is two days.

The right side of Figure 9-1 shows how the process can be speeded up. First, to reduce mail and clearing delays, a *lockbox plan* can be used. Suppose a New York firm makes sales to customers all across the country. It can arrange to have its customers send payments to post office boxes (lockboxes) in their own local areas. A local bank will pick up the checks, have them cleared in the local area, and then transfer the funds by wire to the company's New York bank. In this way, collection time can be reduced by one to five days. Examples of freeing funds in the amount of $5 million or more by this method are not uncommon.

Just as expediting the collection process conserves cash, slowing down disbursements accomplishes the same thing by keeping cash on hand for longer periods. One obviously could simply delay payments, but this involves equally obvious difficulties. Firms have, in the past, devised rather ingenious methods for "legitimately" lengthening the collection period on their own checks, ranging from maintaining deposits in distant banks to using slow, awkward payment procedures. Since such practices are usually recognized for what they are, there are severe limits to their use.

The most widely publicized of these procedures in recent years is the use of drafts. While a check is payable on demand, a draft must be transmitted to the issuer, who approves it and deposits funds to cover it, after which it can be collected. Insurance companies often use drafts. In handling claims, for instance, Aetna can pay a claim by draft on Friday. The recipient cashes the draft at a local bank, which sends it on to Aetna's Hartford bank. It may be Wednesday or Thursday before the draft arrives. The bank then sends it to the company's accounting department, which has until 3 P.M. that day to inspect and approve it. Not until then does Aetna deposit funds in its bank to pay the draft.

Using Float. Float is defined as the difference between the balance shown in a firm's (or an individual's) checkbook and the balance on the bank's books. Suppose a firm writes, on the average, checks in the amount of $5,000 each day. It takes about six days for these checks to clear and to be deducted from the firm's bank account. Thus, the firm's own checking records show a balance $30,000 smaller than the bank's records. If the firm receives checks in the amount of $5,000 daily but loses only four days while these checks are being deposited and cleared, its own books have a balance that is, because of this factor, $20,000 larger than the bank's balance. Thus, the firm's net float—the difference between the $30,000 positive float and the $20,000 negative float—is $10,000.

If a firm's own collection and clearing process is more efficient than that of the recipients of its checks—and this is generally true of larger, more efficient firms—then the firm could show a *negative* balance on its own records and a *positive* balance on the books of its bank. Some firms indicate that they *never* have true positive cash balances. One large manufacturer of construction equipment stated that, while its account according to its bank's records shows an average cash balance of about $20 million, its *actual* cash balance is *minus* $20 million; it has $40 million of net float. Obviously, the firm must be able to forecast its positive and negative clearings accurately in order to make such heavy use of float.

Matching the Costs and Benefits Associated with Cash Management

Although a number of procedures may be used to hold down cash balance requirements, implementing these procedures is not a costless operation. How far should a firm go in making its cash operations more efficient? As a general rule, the firm should incur these expenses so long as marginal returns exceed marginal expenses.

For example, suppose that by establishing a lockbox system and increasing the accuracy of cash inflow and outflow forecasts, a firm can reduce its investment in cash by $1 million without increasing the risk of running short of cash. Further, suppose the firm borrows at a cost of 12 percent. The steps taken have released $1 million, which can be used to reduce bank loans and thus save $120,000 per year. If the costs of the procedures necessary to release the $1 million are less than $120,000, the move is a good one; if the costs exceed $120,000, the greater efficiency is not worth the cost. It is clear that larger firms, with larger cash balances, can better afford to hire the personnel necessary to maintain tight control over their cash positions. Cash management is one element of business operations in which economies of scale are present.

Very clearly, the value of careful cash management depends upon the costs of funds invested in cash, which in turn depend upon the current rate of interest. In the early 1980s, with interest rates at historic highs, firms have been devoting more care than ever to cash management.

Compensating Balances

Earlier in the chapter we listed compensating balance requirements as one of the major determinants of cash balances. Banks provide services to firms—they clear checks, operate lockbox plans, supply credit information, and the like. These services cost the bank money, so the bank must be compensated for rendering them.

Banks earn most of their income by lending money at interest, and most of the funds they lend are obtained in the form of deposits. If a firm maintains a deposit account with an average balance of $100,000, and if the bank can lend these funds at a net return of $8,000, then the account is, in a sense, worth $8,000 to the bank. Thus, it is to the bank's advantage to provide services worth up to $8,000 to attract and hold the account.

Banks determine first the costs of the services rendered to their larger customers and then the average account balances necessary to provide enough income to compensate for these costs. Firms often maintain these compensating balances in order to avoid paying cash service charges to the bank.[1]

---

[1] Compensating balance arrangements apply to individuals as well as to business firms. Thus, you

(continued)

Compensating balances are also required by some bank loan agreements. During periods when the supply of credit is restricted and interest rates are high, banks frequently insist that borrowers maintain accounts that average some percentage of the loan amount as a condition for granting the loan; 15 percent is a typical figure. If the balance is larger than the firm would otherwise maintain, then the effective cost of the loan is increased; the excess balance presumably "compensates" the bank for making a loan at a rate below what it could earn on the funds if they were invested elsewhere.[2]

Compensating balances can be established (1) as an *absolute minimum*, say $100,000, below which the actual balance must never fall, or (2) as a *minimum* average balance, perhaps $100,000, over some period, generally a month. The absolute minimum is a much more restrictive requirement, because the total amount of cash held during the month must be above $100,000 by the amount of the transactions balances. The $100,000 in this case is "dead money" from the firm's standpoint. The minimum average balance, however, could fall to zero one day provided it was $200,000 some other day, with the average working out to $100,000. Thus, the $100,000 in this case is available for transactions.

Statistics on compensating balance requirements are not available, but average balances are typical and absolute minimums rare for business accounts. Discussions with bankers, however, indicate that absolute balance requirements are less rare during times of extremely tight money such as prevailed during 1981.

Overdraft Systems

Most countries outside the United States use *overdraft systems*. In such systems depositors write checks in excess of their actual balances, and the bank automatically extends loans to cover the shortages. The maximum amount of such loans must, of course, be established beforehand. Although statistics are not available on the usage of overdrafts in the United States, a number of firms have worked out informal, and in some cases formal, overdraft arrangements. (Also, both banks and credit card companies regularly establish "cash reserve" systems for individuals.) Thus, the use of overdrafts has been increasing in recent years. If this trend continues, we can anticipate a further reduction of cash balances.

Establishing the Target Cash Balance

The firm's target cash balance is set as the larger of (1) its transactions balances plus precautionary (safety stock) balances or (2) its required compensating balances. Both the transactions balances and the precautionary balances depend upon the volume of business the firm does, the degree of uncertainty inherent in its forecasts of cash inflows and outflows, and

---

might get "free" checking services if you maintain a minimum balance of $200, but be charged 10 cents per check if your balance falls below $200 during the month.

[2] The interest rate effect of compensating balances is discussed further in Chapter 10.

its ability to borrow on short notice to meet cash shortfalls. Consider again the cash budget shown for Dayton Printing in Table 9-1. The target cash balance (or desired cash balance) is shown on Line 13 of the table. Other things held constant, the target cash balance would increase if Dayton expanded or decrease if Dayton contracted. Similarly, Dayton could afford to operate with a smaller target balance if it were more certain that inflows would come in as scheduled and that no unanticipated outflows such as might result from uninsured fire losses, lawsuits, and the like would occur. The higher the cash balance, the smaller the probability that reduced inflows or unexpected outflows will cause the firm to actually run out of cash.

Statistics are not available on whether transactions plus precautionary balances or compensating balances actually control most firms' target cash balances, but compensating balance requirements do often dominate, especially during periods of high interest rates and tight money.[3] Also, while our discussion of the target cash balance in this section has been more intuitive than rigorous, formal models designed to optimize cash holdings have been developed. Some of these models are discussed later in the chapter, after we consider the types of marketable securities that are available to the firm for holding "near-cash" assets which earn a return but which can be converted to cash very rapidly.

Cash Management in the Multidivisional Firm

The concepts, techniques, and procedures described thus far in the chapter must be extended when applied to large, national firms. Such corporations have plants and sales offices all across the nation (or the world), and they deal with banks in all of their operating territories. These companies must maintain the required compensating balance in each of their banks, and they must be sure that no bank account becomes overdrawn. Cash inflows and outflows are subject to random fluctuations, so, in the absence of close control and coordination, there would be a tendency for some accounts to have shortages while excess balances existed in others. Thus, a sound cash management program for such a multibank corporation necessarily includes provisions for keeping strict account of the level

---

[3] This point is underscored by an incident that occurred at a professional finance meeting. A professor presented a scholarly paper that used operations research techniques to determine "optimal cash balances" for a sample of firms. He then reported that actual cash balances of the firms greatly exceed "optimal" balances, suggesting inefficiency and the need for more refined techniques. The discussant of the paper made her comments short and sweet. She reported that she had written and asked the sample firms why they had so much cash; they uniformly replied that their cash holdings were set by compensating balance requirements. The model was useful to determine the optimal cash balance in the absence of compensating balance requirements, but it was precisely those requirements that determined actual balances. Since the model did not include compensating balances as a determinant of cash balances, its usefulness is questionable.

of funds in each account and for shifting funds between accounts so as to minimize the total corporate cash balance. Mathematical models and electronic connections between a central computer and each branch location have been developed to help with such situations, but a discussion of these topics would go beyond the scope of this book.

Marketable Securities

Sizable holdings of such short-term marketable securities as U.S. Treasury bills (T-bills) or bank certificates of deposit (CDs) are often reported on corporations' financial statements. The reasons for such holdings, as well as the factors that influence the choice of securities held, are discussed in this section.

Reasons for Holding Marketable Securities

Marketable securities typically provide much lower yields than firms' operating assets; for example, International Business Machines (IBM) recently held a multibillion dollar portfolio of marketable securities that yielded about 8 percent, while its operating assets provided a return of about 18 percent. Why would a company such as IBM have such large holdings of low-yielding assets? There are two basic reasons for these holdings: first, they serve as a substitute for cash balances, and, second, they are used as a temporary investment. These points are considered below.

Marketable Securities as a Substitute for Cash. Some firms hold portfolios of marketable securities in lieu of larger cash balances, liquidating part of the portfolio to increase the cash account when cash outflows exceed inflows. In such situations, the marketable securities could be a substitute for transactions balances, precautionary balances, speculative balances, or all three. In most cases, the securities are held primarily for precautionary purposes—most firms prefer to rely on bank credit to make temporary transactions or meet speculative needs, but they still hold some liquid assets to guard against a possible shortage of bank credit.

At the end of 1976, IBM had approximately $6 billion in marketable securities. This large liquid balance had been built up as a reserve for possible damage payments resulting from pending antitrust suits. When it became clear that IBM would win most of the suits, the liquidity need declined, and the company spent some of the funds on other assets, including repurchases of its own stock. This is a prime example of a firm's building up its precautionary balances to handle possible emergencies.

Marketable Securities Held as a Temporary Investment. Whenever a firm has over 1 or 2 percent of its total assets invested in marketable securities, chances are good that these funds represent a strictly temporary investment. Such temporary investments generally occur in one of the three situations described below:

1. *When the firm must finance seasonal or cyclical operations.* Firms engaged in seasonal operations frequently have surplus cash flows during part of the year and deficit cash flows during the other part. Such firms may purchase marketable securities during their surplus periods, then liquidate them when cash deficits occur. Other firms, particularly in capital goods industries, where fluctuations are violent, attempt to accumulate cash or near-cash securities during downturns in order to be ready to finance increases in assets when business returns to normal.

2. *When the firm must meet some known financial requirements.* If a major plant construction program is planned for the near future, or if a bond issue is about to mature, a firm may build up its marketable securities portfolio to provide the required funds. Furthermore, marketable securities holdings are frequently large immediately preceding quarterly corporate tax payment dates.

3. *When the firm has just sold long-term securities.* An expanding firm has to sell long-term securities (stocks or bonds) periodically. The funds from such sales can be invested in marketable securities, which can, in turn, be sold off to provide cash as it is needed to pay for operating assets.

Strategies Regarding Marketable Securities Holdings

Actually, each of the needs listed above can be met either by taking short-term loans or by holding marketable securities. Consider a firm such as Dayton Printing Company, which we discussed earlier, whose sales are growing over time but are fluctuating on a seasonal basis. As we saw from Dayton's cash budget (Table 9-1), the firm plans to borrow to meet seasonal needs. As an alternative financial strategy, Dayton could hold a portfolio of marketable securities, then liquidate these securities to meet its peak cash needs.

Figure 9-2 illustrates three alternative strategies for a firm such as Dayton. Under Plan A, Dayton would hold no marketable securities, relying completely on bank loans to meet seasonal peaks. Under Plan B, Dayton would stockpile marketable securities during slack periods, then sell these securities to raise funds for peak needs. Plan C is a compromise; under this alternative, the company would hold some securities, but not enough to meet all of its peak needs. Dayton actually follows Plan C.

There are advantages and disadvantages to each of these strategies. Plan A is clearly the most risky—the firm's current ratio is always lower than under the other plans, indicating that it might encounter difficulties either in borrowing the funds needed or in repaying the loan. On the other hand, Plan A requires no holdings of low-yielding marketable securities, and this will probably lead to a relatively high expected rate of return on both total assets and net worth.

Figure 9-2
Alternative Strategies for Meeting Seasonal Cash
Needs

Exactly the same types of choices are involved with regard to meeting such other known financial needs as plant construction, as well as in deciding to issue long-term securities before or after the actual need for the funds. Consolidated Edison, the electric utility serving New York City, can be used to illustrate the issues involved in timing the sale of long-term securities. Con Ed has a permanent, ongoing construction program, generating a continuous need for new outside capital. As we shall see in Chapters 13 and 14, there are substantial fixed costs involved in stock or bond flotations, so these securities are issued infrequently and in large amounts.

During the 1960s, Con Ed followed the practice of selling bonds and stock *before* the capital was needed, investing the proceeds in marketable securities, and then liquidating the securities to finance plant construction. Plan A in Figure 9-3 illustrates this procedure.

During the 1970s Con Ed encountered severe financial problems. It was forced to use up its liquid assets and to switch to its present policy of financing plant construction with short-term bank loans, then selling long-term securities to retire these loans when they have built up to some target level. This policy is illustrated by Plan B of Figure 9-3.

Plan A is the more conservative, less risky one. First, the company is minimizing its liquidity problems because it has no short-term debt hanging over its head. Second, it is sure of having the funds available to meet construction payments as they come due. On the other hand, firms generally have to pay higher interest rates when they borrow than the return

Figure 9-3
Alternative Methods of Financing a Continuous
Construction Program

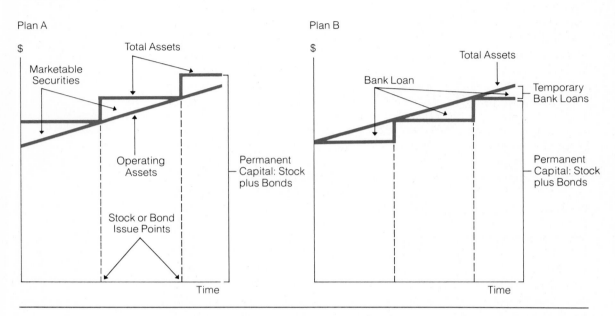

they receive on marketable securities, so following the less risky strategy does have a cost. Again, we are faced with a risk-return tradeoff.

It is difficult to "prove" that one strategy is better than another. In principle, the practice of holding marketable securities reduces the expected rate of return, but it also reduces k_s, the required rate of return on the firm's stock. Although we can quantify the costs of following more conservative policies—this cost is the average percentage differential between the return received on marketable securities and the interest rate paid on the long-term debt issued to purchase them—it is almost impossible to quantify the benefits of such a policy in terms of how much it reduces risk and how this risk reduction affects k_s. Accordingly, the basic policies with regard to securities holdings are generally set either on the basis of judgment or, as in the case of Con Ed, by circumstances beyond the company's control.

Factors Influencing the Choice of Securities

A wide variety of securities, differing in terms of default risk, interest rate risk, liquidity risk, and expected rate of return, are available to firms that do choose to hold marketable securities. In this section, we first consider the characteristics of different securities, then show how the financial manager selects the specific instruments held in the marketable securities portfolio. These same characteristics are, incidentally, as important for individuals' investment decisions as for businesses' decisions.

Default Risk. The risk that an issuer will be unable to make interest payments, or to repay the principal amount on schedule, is known as *default risk*. If the issuer is the U.S. Treasury, the default risk is negligible; thus, Treasury securities are regarded as being default-free. (Treasury securities are not completely free of risk; as we saw in Chapter 4, U.S. government bonds are subject to risk due to interest rate fluctuations, and they are also subject to loss of purchasing power due to inflation.) Corporate securities and bonds issued by state and local governments are subject to some degree of default risk. Several organizations (for example, Moody's Investment Services and Standard & Poor Corporation) "rate" bonds. They classify them on a scale from very high quality to highly speculative with a definite chance of going into default.[4] Ratings change from time to time. Thus, Chrysler's securities were given high ratings at one time, but the ratings were lowered as the company's financial position deteriorated.

Interest Rate Risk. We saw in Chapter 4 that bond prices vary with changes in interest rates. Further, the prices of long-term bonds are much more sensitive to shifts in interest rates than are prices of short-term securities—they have a much greater *interest rate risk*. Thus, if Dayton's treasurer purchased at par $1 million of twenty-five year U.S. Government bonds paying 9 percent interest, and if interest rates rose to 13.5 percent, the market value of the bonds would fall from $1 million to approximately $680,000—a loss of over 30 percent. (This actually happened from 1980 to 1981.) Had ninety day Treasury bills been held, the capital loss resulting from the change in interest rates would have been negligible.

Purchasing Power Risk. Another type of risk is *purchasing power risk,* or the risk that inflation will reduce the purchasing power of a given sum of money. Purchasing power risk, which is important both to firms and to individual investors during times of inflation, is generally regarded to be lower on assets whose returns can be expected to rise during inflation than on assets whose returns are fixed. Thus, real estate and common stocks are often thought of as being better "hedges against inflation" than are bonds and other fixed income securities.

Liquidity (or Marketability) Risk. An asset that can be sold on short notice for close to its quoted market price is defined as being highly liquid. If Dayton purchases $1 million of infrequently traded bonds of a relatively obscure company such as Bigham Pork Products, it will probably have to

---

[4]Bond ratings are discussed in detail in Chapter 13.

accept a price reduction to sell the bonds on short notice. On the other hand, if Dayton buys $1 million worth of U.S. Treasury bonds, or bonds issued by AT&T, General Motors, or Exxon, it will be able to dispose of them almost instantaneously at close to the quoted market price. These latter bonds are said to have very little *liquidity risk.*

Returns on Securities. As we know from our earlier study of the security market line, the higher a security's risk, the higher the required return on the security. Thus corporate treasurers, like other investors, must make a tradeoff between risk and return when choosing investments for their marketable securities portfolios. Since the liquidity portfolio is generally held for a specific known need, or else for use in emergencies, the firm might be financially embarrassed should the portfolio decline in value. Further, most nonfinancial corporations do not have investment departments specializing in appraising securities and determining the probability of their going into default. Accordingly, the marketable securities portfolio is generally confined to safe, highly liquid, short-term securities issued by either the U.S. government or the very strongest corporations. Given the purpose of the securities portfolio, treasurers are unwilling to sacrifice safety for higher rates of return.

The Term Structure of Interest Rates[5]

To manage the marketable securities portfolio properly, and also to make proper decisions regarding how to finance asset acquisitions, it is important to have a good understanding of the relationship between the interest rates on long-term and short-term securities. In Chapter 4 we saw that long-term bonds are exposed to greater risks from changing interest rates than are short-term securities. Further, it seems natural to expect the risk of default to be higher on long-term than on short-term debt. For both these reasons we would expect to find higher risks, hence higher returns, on long-term than on short-term bonds. In fact, this condition does generally hold, but at times short-term securities provide higher yields than long-term bonds. In February 1981, for example, ninety day U.S. Treasury bills yielded 15.5 percent versus a yield of only 12.9 percent on long-term Treasury bonds.

The relationship between yields and maturities is called the *term structure of interest rates,* and graphs of this relationship are defined as *yield curves.* Different yield curves exist at different points in time. The curves

---

[5] The term structure was discussed in some detail in Appendix 2A. The term structure discussion here in Chapter 9 is meant to be complete, but if you are not absolutely clear on the relationships, go back and read Appendix 2A.

for Treasury securities in June 1977 and in February 1981 are shown in Figure 9-4.[6]

Whether long-term yields are above or below short-term yields (that is, whether the yield curve slopes up or down) depends on three factors: (1) risk preferences, (2) supply and demand conditions in long-term versus short-term markets, and (3) expectations about future interest rates. The effects of these three factors are explained in the following section.

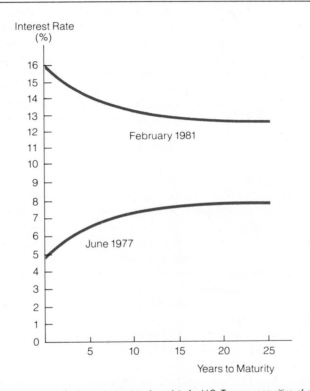

Figure 9-4
Yield Curves for U.S. Treasury Securities in 1977 and 1981

Note: These yield curves show the interest rate at a given date for U.S. Treasury securities of different maturities. Thus, on June 10, 1977, thirty day U.S. Treasury bills yielded 4.81 percent, one year certificates yielded 5.7 percent, five year notes yielded 6.8 percent, and so on. When the yield curve is upward sloping, investors obtain higher yields on bonds with long maturities, and conversely if the yield curve is sloping downward.

[6] A yield curve is applicable only to securities of a given risk class. Figure 9-4 relates to default-free U.S. Treasury securities. If yield curves for the debt of A-rated corporations in June 1977 and February 1981 were also plotted on Figure 9-4, they would have shapes similar to the curves shown in the graph, but they would be higher, denoting a higher interest rate for every maturity.

Risk Preferences. It was noted above that long-term bond prices are especially sensitive to changes in interest rates, and that chances of default are higher on long-term than on short-term securities. Therefore, if long-term and short-term securities had identical yields (and the yield curve were flat, or horizontal), lenders would prefer to hold short-term issues. People holding long-term bonds would sell them to buy short-term bonds, and this would drive short-term prices up and yields down, and conversely for long-term bonds. Accordingly, lender pressure would cause short-term rates to be relatively low, long-term rates to be relatively high, and the yield curve to slope upward, other things held constant.

At the same time, borrowers generally prefer to issue long-term bonds, because then they will not have to worry about interest rates rising or about having to renew their loans frequently. Accordingly, borrowers are willing to pay more for long-term than for short-term credit, and this too causes the yield curve to slope upward. *Thus, both lenders' and borrowers' preferences tend to produce relatively low rates on short-term securities, high rates on long-term bonds, and an upward sloping yield curve.* The higher yield on long-term as opposed to short-term debt arising from these preferences is known as a *maturity premium.*

Supply-Demand Conditions. Short-term debt capital is supplied largely by banks, while long-term debt is supplied mostly by pension funds and life insurance companies. At the same time, certain types of borrowers (home purchasers, as well as utilities, hospitals, and other organizations that have heavy fixed asset investments) are primarily interested in borrowing on a long-term basis, while other borrowers (individuals seeking consumer credit and business firms borrowing to finance inventories) are mainly interested in short-term credit. This suggests that the capital markets are *segmented.* Accordingly, if at a particular point in time demand is heavier in the short-term market, while capital is in more ample supply in the long-term market, this will tend to produce high short-term and low long-term rates, and a downward sloping yield curve. At other times the situation could be reversed, with market supply-demand conditions leading to an upward sloping curve. Thus, supply-demand conditions, coupled with market segmentation, can produce either upward or downward sloping yield curves.

Expectations about Future Interest Rates. The third factor affecting the yield curve is expectations about future interest rates. Suppose the yield curve is horizontal, with long- and short-term bonds providing identical yields—say, 8 percent. Now new statistics are reported, indicating an increase in the rate of inflation. You and everyone else think that the Federal Reserve will take action to combat inflation, and that this will result in higher future interest rates. If you had $1 million to invest, would you rather buy 8 percent, twenty year bonds or 8 percent bonds maturing in one month? Suppose you bought the twenty year bonds and interest rates rose to 10 percent. The value of the bonds would fall to $829,690.[7] Thus, you would incur a capital loss of $170,310 if you sold the bonds. If you did not sell, you would incur an opportunity loss of 2 percent, or $20,000, per year (with a present value of $170,310) by buying 8 percent bonds now rather than waiting until next month and buying 10 percent bonds.

On the other hand, if you invested the $1 million in the short-term bonds, you would earn 8 percent for one month, then still have the full $1 million to invest in bonds that would then yield 10 percent. Therefore, if interest rates were expected to rise, you and all other lenders would rather invest in short-term than in long-term bonds, as long as rates were the same on both types of bonds. Borrowers, meantime, would react in the opposite direction—they would want to borrow at 8 percent on a long-term basis to avoid paying the higher rates when they "rolled over," or renewed, their short-term loans. Thus, both lender and borrower pressures would rapidly produce a rising yield curve. *In general, other things held constant, the yield curve will be upward sloping if future rates are expected to rise, downward sloping if future rates are expected to fall, and flat if investors have no strong feelings about future changes in interest rates.*

You may also think of long-term rates as being an average (strictly speaking, a geometric average) of expected future short-term rates. For example, if the one year bill rate is 5 percent today, is expected to rise to 6 percent next year, and then is expected to go to 7 percent the following year, then the rate on three year bonds should be 6 percent—an investor could expect a 6 percent return by buying either a three year bond or a series of one year bills.

Empirical studies suggest that all three explanations of the slope of the yield curve—liquidity preference, market segmentation, and interest rate expectations—are valid, but at any given time one or the other factor dominates to actually determine the shape of the curve. Financial managers, and investors in general, must consider all three factors whenever they attempt to forecast future interest rates.

Table 9-2 provides a listing of the major types of investment securities available for investments, with yields as of June 10, 1977, and February 11, 1981. Depending on how long they will be held, the financial manager decides upon a suitable maturity pattern for the firm's holdings.

Securities Available for Investment of Surplus Cash

---

[7] Each bond originally sold at its $1,000 par value. The bond would fall in price to $80 (PVIFA$_{10\%,\ 20\ yrs.}$) + $1,000 (PVIF$_{10\%,\ 20\ yrs.}$) = $80(8.5136) + $1,000 (0.1486) = $829.69. This assumes annual compounding.

Table 9-2
Securities Available for Investment of Surplus Cash

Type of Security	Typical Maturity at Time of Issue	Approximate Yields		Appropriate to Hold as a Near-Cash Reserve
		June 10, 1977	Feb. 11, 1981	
U.S. Treasury bills	91 days to 1 year	4.8%	15.5%	Yes
U.S. Treasury notes[a]	3 to 5 years	6.8	13.6	Questionable
U.S. Treasury bonds	Up to 30 years	7.6	12.9	No
Commercial paper[b]	Varies; up to 270 days	5.5	16.5	Yes
Negotiable certificates of deposit with U.S. banks (CDs)	90 days	6.0	16.3	Yes
Money market mutual funds[c]	Instant liquidity	5.1	15.5	Yes
Eurodollar bank time deposits	Varies; up to 6 months	6.1	17.1	Questionable
Bonds of other corporations[d]	Varies; up to 40 years	8.2	14.3	No
State and local government bonds[e]	Varies; up to 30 years	5.7	10.4	No
Stocks of other corporations	Unlimited	Variable	Variable	No
Stock of the firm in question (treasury stock)	Unlimited	Variable	Variable	No

[a] U.S. agency notes and bonds are also available. These securities yield slightly more than U.S. Treasury securities. For example, in February 1981, long-term agency bonds yielded about 13.4 percent versus 12.9 percent for Treasury bonds.

[b] Commercial paper is short-term notes issued by the strongest corporations. These securities are discussed further in Chapter 10.

[c] Money market mutual funds are mutual funds that hold only short-term securities such as Treasury bills, CDs, and commercial paper. These funds provide instant liquidity, are safe, and are free from risk due to fluctuations in interest rates. They became popular in 1973, especially for individuals and smaller firms.

[d] The rate shown here is for AAA bonds. Yields are higher on more risky corporate bonds.

[e] The yield shown here is for AAA long-term municipal bonds. Interest on these bonds is exempt from federal income taxes; thus, the 1981 before-tax equivalent yield on a taxable bond for a taxpayer in the 50 percent bracket was 20.8 percent. (Before-tax equivalent yield = tax-free rate ÷ (1 − tax rate) = 10.4% ÷ 0.5 = 20.8%.)

Because their characteristics change with shifts in financial market conditions, it would be misleading to attempt to give detailed descriptions here.

The Baumol Model for Balancing Cash and Marketable Security Holdings

Earlier in the chapter, when we discussed Dayton Printing Company's cash budget, we took as a given the $2.5 million target cash balance. Subsequently, we discussed how the use of lockboxes, the synchronization of cash inflows and outflows, and so on can be used to reduce the size of the required cash balance. Now we shall consider a formal model for establishing a target cash balance.

William Baumol first noted that cash balances are in many respects similar to inventories, and that the EOQ inventory model developed in

Chapter 8 can be used to establish a target cash balance.[8] Baumol's model assumes (1) that the firm uses cash at a steady, predictable rate, say $1 million per week, and (2) that the firm's cash inflows from operations also occur at a steady, predictable rate, say $900,000 per week, so (3) that the firm's net cash outflows, or net need for cash, also occur at a steady rate, in this case, $100,000 per week.[9] Under these steady-state assumptions, the firm's cash position will resemble the situation shown in Figure 9-5, which is conceptually identical to the inventory position shown in Figure 8-2 in Chapter 8.

Figure 9-5
Cash Balances under the Baumol Model's Assumptions

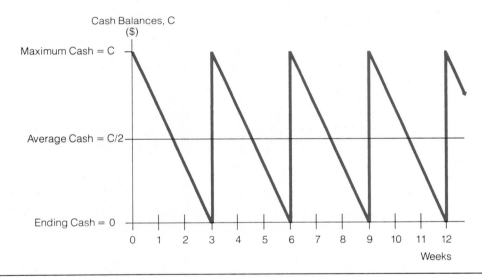

If our illustrative firm started at time 0 with a cash balance of C = $300,000, and its outflows exceeded its inflows by $100,000 per week, then (1) its cash balance would drop to zero at the end of Week 3, and

[8] William J. Baumol, "The Transactions Demand for Cash: An Inventory Theoretic Approach," *Quarterly Journal of Economics*, November 1952, 545-556.

[9] Our hypothetical firm is experiencing a $100,000 weekly cash shortfall, but this does not necessarily imply that it is headed for bankruptcy. The firm could, for example, be highly profitable and be enjoying high earnings, but be expanding so rapidly that it is experiencing chronic cash shortages that must be made up by borrowing or by selling common stock. See Chapter 7 for examples. Or, the firm could be in the construction business and therefore receive major cash inflows at wide intervals, but have net cash outflows of $100,000 per week between major inflows.

(2) its average cash balance would be C/2 = $300,000/2 = $150,000. Therefore, at the end of Week 3, the firm would have to replenish its cash balance, either by selling marketable securities if it has any or by borrowing.

If C were set at a higher level, say $600,000, then the cash supply would last longer (six weeks), and the firm would have to sell securities (or borrow) less frequently. Since a "transactions cost" must be incurred to sell securities (or borrow), establishing larger cash balances will lower the "ordering costs" associated with cash management. On the other hand, cash provides no income, so holding it causes the firm to incur an opportunity cost equal to the return that could have been earned on securities or other assets held in lieu of cash. Thus, we have the situation that is graphed in Figure 9-6, which is analogous to the one for inventories presented in Figure 8-1.

The optimal cash balance, C*, is found by use of the EOQ concepts described in Chapter 8:

$$EOQ = C^* = \sqrt{\frac{2FT}{k}}. \qquad (9-1)$$

Here

C^* = optimal cash holdings to be transferred from marketable securities or borrowed. $\frac{C^*}{2}$ = optimal average cash balance.

F = fixed costs of making a securities trade or of borrowing.

T = total amount of net new cash needed for transactions over the entire period (usually a year).

k = the opportunity cost of holding cash (equals rate of return foregone on marketable securities or the cost of borrowing to hold cash).

Suppose F = $150; T = 52 weeks × $100,000/week = $5,200,000; and k = 15% = 0.15. Then

$$C^* = \sqrt{\frac{2(\$150)\ (\$5,200,000)}{0.15}} = \$101,980.$$

Thus, the firm should sell securities in the amount of $101,980 when its cash balance approaches zero, thus building its cash balance back up to $101,980, and then repeat this process $5,200,000/$101,980 = 50.99 ≅ 51 times during the year, or about once a week. The firm's average cash balance would be about $101,980/2 = $50,990 ≅ $51,000.

Notice that the optimal cash balance increases less-than-proportionately with increases in transactions. For example, if transactions doubled, from $5,200,000 to $10,400,000 per year, average cash balances would in-

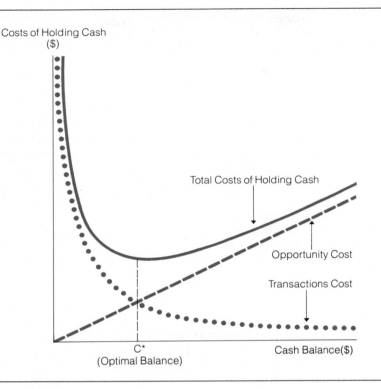

Figure 9-6
Determination of the
Optimal Cash Balance

Costs of Holding Cash
($)

Total Costs of Holding Cash

Opportunity Cost

Transactions Cost

C*
(Optimal Balance)

Cash Balance($)

crease by only 41 percent, from $51,000 to $72,000. This suggests that there are economies of scale in the holding of cash balances, and this, in turn, gives larger firms an edge over smaller ones.[10]

Of course, just as in the case of inventory holdings, the firm would probably want to hold a "safety stock" of cash designed to hold the probability of a cash shortage to some specified level. But, if the firm is able to sell securities or to borrow on short notice—and most larger firms can do so in a matter of just a couple of hours simply by making a telephone call—then the safety stock of cash can be quite low.

The Baumol model is obviously simplistic in many respects. Most important, it assumes relatively stable, predictable cash inflows and outflows, and it does not take account of any seasonal or cyclical trends. Other models have been developed to deal with uncertainty in the cash

---

[10] This edge may, of course, be more than offset by other factors—after all, cash management is only one aspect of running a business.

flows, and with trends.[11] Any of these models—including the Baumol model—can provide a useful starting point for establishing a target cash balance, but all of them have limitations and must be applied with a great deal of judgment.

Summary

The first topic covered in this chapter was *cash management*. We saw that the key element in any cash management system is the *cash budget*, which is a forecast of cash inflows and outflows during a given planning period. The cash budget shows whether the firm can expect a cash deficit, in which case plans must be made to obtain external capital; or a cash surplus, in which case plans should be made to invest the available funds. We also discussed ways of speeding up cash flows by the use of *lockboxes*, what *float* is and how it can be used to hold down bank loans, and *compensating balances*.

Our study of marketable securities began with a discussion of why securities are held—primarily, they are held (1) as a reserve for future contingencies, (2) to meet seasonal needs, with holdings being built up during the slack season and then liquidated when cash requirements are high, (3) to meet known future cash requirements such as construction progress payments or taxes, and (4) immediately after the sale of long-term securities. Given the motives for holding them, treasurers generally do not want to gamble by holding risky securities—safety is the watchword, and rarely will a treasurer sacrifice safety for the higher yields offered on risky securities.

The chapter also covered the *term structure of interest rates*, or the relationship between securities' yields and maturities. Generally, short-term securities offer lower yields than long-term securities, but this is not always the case. If the current level of rates is high by historic standards and is expected to fall, then short rates may be higher than long rates.

The final section of the chapter dealt with the Baumol model, one of several models designed to determine the optimal cash balance. These models are, generally, based on the standard EOQ inventory model, and they balance the opportunity cost of holding cash against the transactions costs associated with replenishing the cash account either by selling off marketable securities or by raising cash through the issuance of debt or equity securities.

[11] See M. H. Miller and D. Orr, "A Model of the Demand for Money by Firms," *Quarterly Journal of Economics,* August 1966, 413-435; P. A. Frost, "Banking Services, Minimum Cash Balances, and the Firm's Demand for Money," *Journal of Finance,* December 1970, 1029-1039; and H. G. Daellenbach, "Are Cash Management Optimization Models Worthwhile?" *Journal of Financial and Quantitative Analysis,* September 1974, 607-626.

9-1 What are the four principal reasons for holding cash? Can a firm estimate its target cash balance by summing the cash held to satisfy each of the four?

9-2 Explain how each of the following factors would probably affect a firm's target cash balance if all other factors are held constant.

a. The firm institutes a new billing procedure which better synchronizes its cash inflows and outflows.

b. The firm develops a new sales forecasting technique which improves its forecasts.

c. The firm reduces its portfolio of U.S. Treasury bills.

d. The firm arranges to use an overdraft system for its checking account.

e. The firm borrows a large amount of money from its bank, and it also begins to write far more checks than it did in the past.

f. Interest rates on Treasury bills rise from 5 percent to 10 percent.

9-3 In the cash budget shown in Table 9-1, is the projected maximum funds requirement of $5.2 million in September known with certainty, or should it be regarded as the expected value of a probability distribution? Consider how this peak would probably be affected by each of the following:

a. A lengthening of the average collection period.

b. An unanticipated decline in sales that occurred when sales were supposed to peak.

c. A sharp drop in sales prices required to meet competition.

d. A sharp increase in interest rates for a firm with a large amount of short-term debt outstanding.

9-4 Would a lockbox plan make more sense for a firm that makes sales all over the United States or for a firm with the same volume of business but concentrated in one city?

9-5 The yield curves shown in Figure 9-4 were constructed with data on the three U.S. Treasury securities shown in Table 9-2. In a recent *Wall Street Journal*, find yields on these same three types of securities today, and draw a third yield curve on Figure 9-4. Has the slope of the curve changed? Does its position indicate that most rates have risen or fallen?

9-6 What does the term *liquidity* mean? Which would be more important to a firm that held a portfolio of marketable securities as precautionary balances against the possibility of losing a major lawsuit—liquidity or rate of return? Explain.

9-7 Firm A's management is very conservative, while Firm B's managers are more aggressive. Is it true that, other things the same, Firm B would probably have larger holdings of marketable securities? Explain.

9-8 Is it true that *interest rate risk* refers to the risk that a firm will be unable to pay the interest on its bonds? Explain.

9-9 The curve describing the relationship between interest rates and term to maturity is known as the _____curve. Other things held constant, how would each of the following factors affect the slope and the general position of this curve? Indicate by a (+) if it would lead to an upward shift in the curve, a (−) if it would cause the curve to shift downward, or a (0) if it would have no effect or an indeterminant effect on the slope or position of the curve.

	Effect on the Yield Curve	
	Slope	Position
a. Investors perceive the risk of default to increase on securities with longer maturities; that is, they become increasingly uncertain about the more distant future.	_____	_____
b. Future interest rates are expected to fall.	_____	_____
c. The Federal Reserve pumps a large amount of money into the banking system.	_____	_____
d. Business firms begin a massive inventory buildup.	_____	_____
e. An inexpensive method of harnessing solar power is developed; this development leads to a decline in the expected rate of inflation.	_____	_____

9-10 Corporate treasurers, when selecting securities for portfolio investments, must make a tradeoff between higher risk and higher returns. Is it true that most treasurers are willing to assume a fairly high exposure to risk to gain higher expected returns?

9-11 Assume that the yield curve is horizontal. Now you and other investors receive information that suggests the economy is headed into a recession. You and most other investors think that the Fed will soon relax credit and that this will lead to a decline in short-term interest rates. Over the long run (the next five, ten, or fifteen years) people expect a fairly high rate of inflation, and they expect that this will keep long-term rates fairly high. Explain what all of this will probably do to the yield curve. Use a graph to illustrate your answer.

Problems

9-1 The McShane-Blarney Company is setting up a new bank account with the First National Bank. McShane-Blarney plans to issue checks in the amount of $2 million each day and to deduct them from its own records at the close of business on the day they are written. On average, the bank will receive and clear (that is, deduct from the firm's bank balance) the checks at 5 P.M. the fourth day after they are written. For example, a check written on Monday will be cleared on Friday afternoon. The firm's agreement with the bank requires it to maintain a $1.5 million average compensating balance; this is $500,000 greater than the cash balance the firm would otherwise have on deposit; that is, without the compensating balance, it would carry an average of $1 million.

a. Assuming that the firm makes deposits at 4 P.M. each day (and the bank includes the deposit in that day's transactions), how much must the firm deposit each day to maintain a sufficient balance on the day it opens the account, during the first four days after it opens the account, and once it reaches a "steady state"?

b. What ending daily balance should the firm try to maintain (1) on the bank's records and (2) on its own records?

c. Explain how net float can help increase the value of the firm's common stock.

9-2 Rick and Marlo Petteway recently leased space in the Southside Mall and opened a new business, Petteway's Coin Shop. Business has been good, but the Petteways have frequently run out of cash. This has necessitated late payment on certain orders, and this, in turn, is beginning to cause a problem with suppliers. The Petteways plan to borrow from the bank to have cash ready as needed, but first they need a forecast of just how much they must borrow. Accordingly, they have asked you to prepare a cash budget for the critical period around Christmas, when needs will be especially high.

Sales are made on a *cash basis only*. Petteway's purchases must be paid for the following month. The Petteways pay themselves a salary of $4,800 per month, and the rent is $2,000 per month. In addition, the Petteways must make a tax payment of $12,000 in December. The current cash on hand (on December 1) is $400, but the Petteways have agreed to maintain an average bank balance of $6,000—this is their target cash balance. (Disregard till cash, which is insignificant because the Petteways keep only a small amount on hand in order to lessen the chances of robbery.)

The estimated sales and purchases for December, January, and February are shown below. Purchases during November amounted to $140,000.

	Sales	Purchases
December	$160,000	$40,000
January	40,000	40,000
February	60,000	40,000

a. Prepare a cash budget for December, January, and February.

b. Now suppose the Petteways were to start selling on a credit basis on December 1, giving customers thirty days to pay. All customers accept these terms, and all other facts in the problem are unchanged. What would the company's loan requirements be at the end of December in this case? (Hint: The calculations required to answer this question are minimal.)

9-3 The Taussig Company is planning to request a line of credit from its bank.[12] The following sales forecasts have been made for 1982 and 1983:

May 1982	$ 750,000
June	750,000
July	1,500,000
August	2,250,000
September	3,000,000
October	1,500,000
November	1,500,000
December	375,000
January 1983	750,000

Collection estimates were obtained from the credit and collection department as follows: collected within the month of sale, 5 percent; collected the month following the sale, 80 percent; collected the second month following the sale, 15 percent. Payments for labor and raw materials are typically made during the month following the month in which these costs are incurred. Total labor and raw materials costs are estimated for each month as follows (payments are made the following month):

May 1982	$ 375,000
June	375,000
July	525,000
August	3,675,000
September	1,275,000
October	975,000
November	675,000
December	375,000

General and administrative salaries will amount to approximately $112,-500 a month; lease payments under long-term lease contracts will be $37,500 a month; depreciation charges are $150,000 a month; miscellaneous expenses will be $11,500 a month; income tax payments of $262,-

---

[12] A line of credit is an agreement that the bank will lend a specified sum of money to the company during a stated time period. Lines of credit are discussed extensively in Chapter 10. Also, note that this problem is adapted from *Cases in Managerial Finance*, 4th ed., Case 5.

500 will be due in both September and December; and a progress payment of $750,000 on a new research laboratory must be paid in October. Cash on hand on July 1 will amount to $550,000, and a minimum cash balance of $375,000 should be maintained throughout the cash budget period.

a. Prepare a monthly cash budget for the last six months of 1982.

b. Prepare an estimate of required financing (or excess funds) for each month during the same period, that is, the amount of money that the Taussig Company will need to borrow (or will have available to invest) each month.

c. Suppose receipts from sales come in uniformly during the month; that is, cash payments come in 1/30th each day, but all outflows are paid on the fifth of the month. Would this have an effect on the cash budget; that is, would the cash budget you have prepared be valid under these assumptions? If not, what could be done to make a valid estimation of financing requirements?

d. Taussig produces on a seasonal basis, just ahead of sales. Without making any calculations, discuss how the company's current ratio and debt ratio would vary during the year, assuming all financial requirements are met by short-term bank loans. Could changes in these ratios affect the firm's ability to obtain bank credit?

e. Now suppose a recession occurs, and sales fall below the forecasted, or budgeted, levels. However, the firm continues production according to the indicated plans. Also, because of the recession, customers delay payments, so the lag between sales and collections lengthens. What would all this do to the realized cash surpluses and deficits, and to the external funds requirements?

f. If you prepared the cash budget in Part a correctly, you show a surplus of $426,000 at the end of July. Suggest some alternative investments for this money. Be sure to consider long-term bonds versus short-term debt instruments, and the appropriateness of investing in common stock.

g. Would your choice of securities in Part f be affected if the cash budget showed continuous cash surpluses versus alternating surpluses and deficits?

9-4 Suppose the interest rate on one year Treasury bills purchased today (1/1/81) is 12 percent. You and other investors anticipate that a recession is on the horizon and that the T-bill rate will fall to 10 percent next year (1/1/82) and to 8 percent the following year (1/1/83). Your best guess as to T-bill rates from 1/1/84 on is 9 percent, which is based on an expected long-term inflation rate of 7 percent and a 2 percent real risk-free interest rate. Assuming that the expectations theory holds exactly, what is the approximate equilibrium interest rate for (1) five year Treasury bonds and (2) ten year Treasury bonds?

Selected References   Some key references on cash management include the following:

Baumol, William J., "The Transactions Demand for Cash: An Inventory Theoretic Approach," *Quarterly Journal of Economics,* vol. 65 (November 1952), 545-556.

Daellenbach, Hans G., "Are Cash Management Optimization Models Worthwhile?" *Journal of Financial and Quantitative Analysis,* vol. 9 (September 1974), 607-626.

Emery, Gary W., "Some Empirical Evidence on the Properties of Daily Cash Flow," *Financial Management,* vol. 10 (Spring 1981), 21-28.

Gitman, Lawrence J., D. Keith Forrester, and John R. Forrester, Jr., "Maximizing Cash Disbursement Float," *Financial Management,* Summer 1976, 15-24.

Gitman, Lawrence J., E. A. Moses, and I. T. White, "An Assessment of Corporate Cash Management Practices," *Financial Management,* vol. 8 (Spring 1979), 32-41.

Hill, Ned C., and K. D. Riener, "Determining the Cash Discount in the Firm's Credit Policy," *Financial Management,* Spring 1979, 68-73.

Maier, Steven F., David W. Robinson, and James H. Vander Weide, "A Short-Term Disbursement Forecasting Model," *Financial Management,* vol. 10 (Spring 1981), 9-20.

Maier, Steven F., and James H. Vander Weide, "A Practical Approach to Short-Run Financial Planning," *Financial Management,* vol. 7 (Winter 1978), 10-16.

Miller, Merton H., and Daniel Orr, "A Model of the Demand for Money by Firms," *Quarterly Journal of Economics,* vol. 80 (August 1966), 413-435.

Mullins, David Wiley, Jr., and Richard B. Homonoff, "Applications of Inventory Cash Management Models," *Modern Developments in Financial Management,* ed. Stewart C. Myers (New York: Praeger, 1976).

Stone, Bernell K., and Robert A. Wood, "Daily Cash Forecasting: A Simple Method for Implementing the Distribution Approach," *Financial Management,* Fall 1977, 40-50.

For more on the term structure of interest rates, see Appendix 2A and

Van Horne, James C., *Financial Markets and Flows* (Englewood Cliffs, N.J.: Prentice-Hall, 1978).

Financing Current Assets: Short-Term Credit

As we noted in Chapter 8, working capital management involves decisions relating to current assets, including decisions about how these assets are to be financed. The primary purposes of this chapter are (1) to discuss alternative strategies for financing working capital and (2) to examine the types of short-term credit that are available. Decisions in these two areas will affect both the firm's riskiness and its expected rate of return, hence its market value.

As defined in Chapter 8, the term *gross working capital* means total current assets, while *net working capital* means current assets minus current liabilities. The concept of working capital originated at a time when most industries were closely related to agriculture. Processors would buy crops in the fall, process them, sell the finished product, and end up just before the next harvest with relatively low inventories. Bank loans with maximum maturities of one year were used to finance both the purchase and the processing costs, and these loans were retired with the proceeds from the sale of the finished products.

Alternative Strategies for Financing Working Capital

This situation is depicted in Figure 10-1, where fixed assets are shown to be growing steadily over time, while current assets jump at harvest season, decline during the year, and end at zero just before the next crop is harvested. Short-term credit is used to finance current assets, and fixed assets are financed with long-term funds. Thus, the top segment of the graph deals with working capital.

The figure represents an idealized situation—actually, current assets build up gradually as crops are purchased and processed; inventories are drawn down less regularly; and ending inventory balances do not decline to zero. Nevertheless, the example does illustrate the general nature of the production and financing process, and working capital management consists of decisions relating to the top section of the graph—managing current assets and arranging the short-term credit used to finance them.

As the economy became less oriented toward agriculture, the production and financing cycles of "typical" businesses changed. Although seasonal patterns still existed, and business cycles also caused asset requirements to fluctuate, it became apparent that current assets rarely drop to zero. This realization led to the development of the idea of "permanent

**Figure 10-1
Fixed and Current
Assets and Their
Financing**

current assets," diagramed in Figure 10-2. As the figure is drawn, it maintains the traditional notion that permanent assets should be financed with long-term capital, while temporary assets should be financed with short-term credit.

The matching of asset and liability maturities as shown in Figures 10-1 and 10-2 was considered to be desirable because it minimizes the risk that the firm may be unable to pay off its maturing obligations. To illustrate, suppose a firm borrows on a one year basis and uses the funds obtained to build and equip a plant. Cash flows from the plant (profits plus depreciation) would almost never be sufficient to pay off the loan at the end of only one year, so the loan must be renewed. If for some reason the lender refuses to renew the loan, then the firm has problems.

**Figure 10-2
Fluctuating versus
Permanent Assets:
Exactly Matching
Maturities**

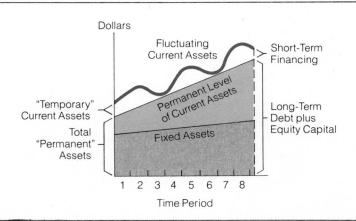

Had the plant been financed with long-term debt, however, cash flows over a longer time frame would have been sufficient to retire the loan, and the problem of renewal would not have arisen.

At the limit, a firm could attempt to match the maturity structure of its assets and liabilities exactly. Inventory expected to be sold in a few weeks could be financed with a short-term bank loan; a machine expected to last for five years could be financed by a five year loan; a twenty year building could be financed by a twenty year mortgage bond; receivables expected to be collected in twenty days could be financed by a twenty day bank loan; and so forth. Actually, of course, uncertainty about the lives of assets prevents this exact maturity matching. For example, a firm may finance inventories with a thirty day loan, expecting to sell the inventories and use the cash generated to retire the loan. But if sales are slow, the cash will not be forthcoming, and the use of short-term credit may cause a problem.

Figure 10-2 showed the situation for a firm that attempts to match asset and liability maturities. Such a policy could be followed, but firms may also follow other maturity-matching policies. Figure 10-3, for example, illustrates the situation for a firm that finances all of its fixed assets with long-term capital but part of its permanent current assets with short-term credit.[1]

The dashed line could even have been drawn *below* the line designating fixed assets, indicating that all the current assets and part of the fixed assets are financed with short-term credit; this would be a highly aggres-

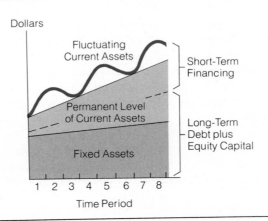

Figure 10-3
Fluctuating versus
Permanent Assets

---

[1] Firms generally have some short-term credit in the form of "spontaneous" funds—accounts payable and accruals (see Chapter 7). Used within limits, these constitute "free" capital, so virtually all firms employ at least some short-term credit at all times.

sive, nonconservative position, and the firm would be very much subject to potential loan renewal problems. However, as we shall see in the next section and later in the. chapter, short-term debt is often cheaper than long-term debt, so some firms may be willing to sacrifice safety for possibly higher profits.

As in Figure 10-4, the dashed line could also be drawn *above* the line designating permanent current assets, indicating that permanent capital

Figure 10-4
Fluctuating versus
Permanent Assets and
Liabilities

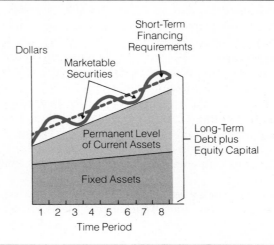

is being used to meet seasonal demands. In this case, the firm uses a small amount of short-term credit to meet its peak requirements, but it also meets a part of its seasonal needs by "storing liquidity" in the form of marketable securities during the off-season. The humps above the dashed line represent short-term financing; the troughs below the dashed line represent short-term security holdings. This would represent a very safe, conservative position.

Advantages and
Disadvantages of
Short-Term Credit

Although using short-term debt is generally riskier than using long-term debt, short-term credit does have some offsetting advantages. The pros and cons of financing with short-term debt are considered in this section.

Flexibility. If its needs for funds are seasonal or cyclical, a firm may not want to commit itself to long-term debt. Such debt can be repaid early, provided the loan agreement includes a prepayment provision, but, even so, prepayment penalties can be expensive. Accordingly, if a firm thinks its need for funds will diminish in the near future, it should choose short-term debt for the flexibility it provides.

Cost of Long-Term versus Short-Term Debt. In Chapter 9 we saw that the yield curve is often upward sloping, indicating that interest rates are lower on short-term than on long-term debt. When this situation exists, interest expense will be lower if the firm borrows on a short-term rather than a long-term basis.

Risk of Long-Term versus Short-Term Debt. Even though short-term debt is often less expensive than long-term debt, financing with short-term debt subjects the firm to more risk than does financing with long-term debt. This risk effect occurs for two reasons: (1) If a firm borrows on a long-term basis, its interest costs will be relatively stable over time, but if it borrows short-term, its interest expense will fluctuate widely, at times going quite high. For example, from 1977 to 1980, the short-term rate for large corporations went up more than three times, going from 6.25 percent to 21 percent. (2) If a firm borrows heavily on a short-term basis, it may find itself unable to repay this debt, and it may be in such a weak financial position that the lender will not extend the loan; thus, the firm could be forced into bankruptcy.

A good example of the riskiness of short-term debt is provided by Transamerica Corporation, a major financial services company. Transamerica's chairman noted in a recent interview that the company was moving aggressively to reduce its dependency on short-term loans whose costs vary with short-term interest rates:

Mr. Beckett said Transamerica has reduced its variable-rate loans by about $450 million over the past two years. "We aren't going to go through the enormous increase in debt expense again that had such a serious impact [on earnings]," he said. The company's earnings fell sharply because money rates rose to records. "We were almost entirely in variable-rate debt," he said, but currently out of total debt of slightly more than $1 billion, "about 65% is fixed rate and 35% variable. We've come a long way and we'll keep plugging away at it," he added.

Transamerica's earnings were badly depressed by the increase in short-term rates, but other companies were even less fortunate—they simply could not pay the interest charges, and this forced them into bankruptcy.[2]

Statements about the flexibility, cost, and riskiness of short-term versus long-term credit depend, to a large extent, on the nature of the short-

---

[2] Some academicians argue that while financial policy related to working capital affects a firm's *total risk*, it has a much smaller effect on *market or beta risk*. Hence, from its stockholders' point of view, the riskiness of a firm's working capital policy is not too important. Several comments are appropriate. First, it is difficult to prove this point one way or the other, but most authorities would probably argue that working capital policy *does* have a significant effect on beta risk. Second, by following a risky working capital policy, a firm can increase greatly the odds of bankruptcy or other types of financial distress, and this can lower its expected future profit stream at the same time that it raises the riskiness of the stream. This would have a double-barreled effect on the value of the firm.

term credit that is actually used. To make these distinctions clear, the major types of short-term credit are discussed in the following sections.

Accrued Wages and Taxes

Firms generally pay employees on a weekly, biweekly, or monthly basis, so the balance sheet will typically show some accrued wages. Similarly, the firm's own estimated income taxes, social security and income taxes withheld from employee payrolls, and sales taxes collected by the firm are generally paid on a weekly, monthly, or quarterly basis, so the balance sheet will typically show some accrued taxes.

As we saw in Chapter 7, accruals increase spontaneously as a firm's operations expand. Further, this type of debt is "free" in the sense that no interest must be paid on funds raised through accruals. However, a firm cannot ordinarily control its accruals: payrolls and the timing of wage payments are set by economic forces and by industry custom, while tax payment dates are established by law. Thus, firms use all the accruals they can, but they have little control over the level of these accounts.

Accounts Payable, or "Trade Credit"

Firms generally make purchases from other firms on credit, recording the debt as an *account payable*. Accounts payable, or *trade credit*, as it is commonly called, is the largest single category of short-term debt, representing about 40 percent of the current liabilities of nonfinancial corporations. This percentage is somewhat larger for smaller firms: because small companies often do not qualify for financing from other sources, they rely rather heavily on trade credit.[3]

Trade credit is a "spontaneous" source of financing in that it arises from ordinary business transactions. For example, suppose a firm makes average purchases of $2,000 a day on terms of net 30. On the average it will owe thirty times $2,000, or $60,000, to its suppliers. If its sales, and consequently its purchases, were to double, then its accounts payable would also double to $120,000. The firm would have spontaneously generated an additional $60,000 of financing. Similarly, if the terms of credit were extended from thirty to forty days, accounts payable would expand from $60,000 to $80,000. Thus, lengthening the credit period, as well as expanding sales and purchases, generates additional financing.

The Cost of Trade Credit

As we saw in Chapter 8 in connection with accounts receivable management, firms that sell on credit have a *credit policy* that includes setting the

---

[3] In a credit sale, the seller records the transaction as an *account receivable*, the buyer as an *account payable*. We examined accounts receivable as an asset investment in Chapter 8. Our focus in this chapter is on accounts payable, a liability item. We might also note that if a firm's accounts payable exceed its receivables, it is said to be *receiving net trade credit*, while if its receivables exceed its payables, it is *extending net trade credit*. Smaller firms frequently receive net credit; larger firms extend it.

terms of credit. For example, Carter Chemical Company's Textile Products division sells on terms of 2/10, net 30, meaning that a 2 percent discount is given if payment is made within ten days of the invoice date and that the full invoice amount is due and payable within thirty days if the discount is not taken.

Suppose Fall Mills, Inc., buys an average of $12 million of materials from Carter each year, less a 2 percent discount, or net purchases of $11,760,000/360 = $32,666.67 per day. For simplicity, suppose Carter Chemical is Fall Mills' only supplier. If Fall Mills takes the discount, paying at the end of the tenth day, its payables will average (10)($32,666.67) = $326,667; Fall Mills will, on average, be receiving $326,667 of credit from its only supplier, Carter Chemical Company.

Now suppose Fall Mills decides *not* to take the discount; what will happen? First, Fall Mills will begin paying invoices after thirty days, so its accounts payable will increase to (30)($32,666.67) = $980,000.[4] Carter Chemical will now be supplying Fall Mills with an *additional* $653,333 of credit. Fall Mills could use this additional credit to pay off bank loans, to expand inventories, to add fixed assets, to build up its cash account, or even to increase its own accounts receivable.

Fall Mills' new credit from Carter Chemical has a cost—Fall Mills is foregoing a 2 percent discount on its $12 million of purchases, so its costs will rise by $240,000 per year. Dividing this $240,000 by the additional credit, we find the implicit percentage cost of the added trade credit as follows:

$$\text{Percentage cost} = \frac{\$240,000}{\$653,333} = 36.7\%.$$

Assuming that Fall Mills can borrow from its bank (or from other sources) at an interest rate of less than 36.7 percent, it should not expand its payables by foregoing discounts.

The following equation may be used to calculate the approximate percentage cost, on an annual basis, of not taking discounts:

$$\text{Percentage cost} = \frac{\text{Discount percent}}{100 - \left(\begin{array}{c}\text{Discount}\\\text{percent}\end{array}\right)} \times \frac{360}{\left(\begin{array}{c}\text{Days credit}\\\text{is}\\\text{outstanding}\end{array}\right) - \left(\begin{array}{c}\text{Discount}\\\text{period}\end{array}\right)}. \quad (10\text{-}1)$$

---

[4] A question arises: Will accounts payable reflect gross purchases or purchases net of discounts? Although generally accepted accounting practices permit either treatment on the grounds that the difference is not material, most accountants prefer recording both inventories and payables net of discounts, then reporting the higher payments that result from not taking discounts as an additional expense. *Thus, we show accounts payable net of discounts even when the company does not expect to take the discount.*

The numerator of the first term, discount percent, is the cost per dollar of credit, while the denominator in this term (100 − discount percent) represents the funds made available by not taking the discount. The second term shows how many times each year this cost is incurred. To illustrate the equation, the cost of not taking a discount when the terms are 2/10, net 30, is computed as follows:[5]

$$\text{Cost} = \frac{2}{98} \times \frac{360}{20} = 0.0204 \times 18 = 0.367 = 36.7\%.$$

Notice also that the calculated cost can be reduced by paying late. Thus, if Fall Mills can get away with paying in sixty days rather than in the specified thirty, then the effective credit period becomes 60 − 10 = 50, and the calculated cost becomes

$$\text{Cost} = \frac{2}{98} \times \frac{360}{50} = 0.0204 \times 7.2 = 0.147 = 14.7\%.$$

In periods of excess capacity, firms may be able to get away with late payments, but they may also suffer a variety of problems associated with being a "slow payer" account. These problems are discussed later in the chapter.

The cost of additional trade credit resulting from not taking discounts can be worked out for other purchase terms. Some illustrative costs are shown below:

Credit Terms	Cost of Additional Credit If Cash Discount Not Taken
1/10, net 20	36%
1/10, net 30	18
2/10, net 20	73
3/15, net 45	37

---

[5] In compound interest terms, the rate is even higher. As discussed in Chapter 3, if interest is earned and paid during the year, and if interest is earned on interest, then the effective annual rate is increased over the rate with annual compounding. In the case of trade discounts, the discount amounts to interest, and with terms of 2/10, net 30, we have eighteen "interest periods" per year. The first term in our equation is (Discount percent)/(100 − Discount percent) = 0.02/(0.98) = 0.0204. This "interest rate" is "earned" eighteen times each year, so the effective annual rate cost of trade credit is

$$\text{Percentage cost} = (1.0204)^{18} - 1.0 = 1.438 - 1.0 = 43.8\%.$$

Thus, the 36.7% cost calculated above understates the cost of trade credit in a compound interest sense.

As these figures show, the cost of not taking discounts can be substantial. Incidentally, throughout the chapter we assume that payments are made either on the *last day* for taking discounts or on the last day of the credit period unless otherwise noted. It would be foolish to pay, say, on the fifth or twentieth day if the credit terms were 2/10, net 30.

A firm's policy with regard to taking or not taking discounts can have a significant effect on its financial statements. To illustrate, let us assume that Fall Mills is just beginning its operations. On the first day, it makes net purchases of $32,666.67. This amount is recorded on the balance sheet under accounts payable.[6] The second day it buys another $32,666.67. The first day's purchases are not yet paid for, so at the end of the second day accounts payable total $65,333.34. Accounts payable increase by another $32,666.67 the third day, to a total of $98,000, and after ten days accounts payable are up to $326,667.

Effects of Trade Credit on the Financial Statements

If Fall Mills takes discounts, then on the eleventh day it will have to pay for the $32,666.67 of purchases made on the first day, which will reduce accounts payable. However, it will buy another $32,666.67, which will increase payables. Thus, after the tenth day of operations, Fall Mills' balance sheet will level off, showing a balance of $326,667 in accounts payable, assuming the company pays on the tenth day in order to take discounts.

Now suppose Fall Mills decides not to take discounts. In this case, on the eleventh day it will add another $32,666.67 to payables, but it will not pay for the purchases made on the first day. Thus, the balance sheet figure for accounts payable will rise to $11 \times \$32,666.67 = \$359,333.37$. This buildup will continue through the thirtieth day, at which point payables will total $30 \times \$32,666.67 = \$980,000$. On the thirty-first day, it will buy another $32,667 of goods, which will increase accounts payable; but it will pay for the purchases made the first day, which will reduce payables. Thus, the balance sheet item "accounts payable" will stabilize at $980,000 after thirty days, assuming Fall Mills does not take discounts.

Table 10-1 shows Fall Mills' balance sheet, after it reaches a steady state, under the two trade credit policies. The assets are unchanged by this policy decision, and we also assume that accruals and common equity are unchanged. The differences show up in accounts payable and notes payable; when Fall Mills elects to take discounts and thus gives up some of the trade credit it otherwise could have obtained, it will have to raise $653,333 from some other source. It could have sold more common stock, or it could have used long-term bonds, but it chose to use bank credit, which has a 10 percent cost and is reflected in notes payable.

---

[6] Inventories also increase by $32,666.67, but we are not concerned with this account at this time.

Table 10-1
Fall Mills' Balance Sheet
with Different Trade
Credit Policies

A. Do Not Take Discounts; Use Maximum Trade Credit

Cash	$ 500,000	Accounts payable	$ 980,000
Receivables	1,000,000	Notes payable	0
Inventories	2,000,000	Accruals	500,000
Fixed assets	2,980,000	Common equity	5,000,000
	$6,480,000		$6,480,000

B. Take Discounts; Borrow from Bank

Cash	$ 500,000	Accounts payable	$ 326,667
Receivables	1,000,000	Notes payable (10%)	653,333
Inventories	2,000,000	Accruals	500,000
Fixed assets	2,980,000	Common equity	5,000,000
	$6,480,000		$6,480,000

Table 10-2 shows Fall Mills' income statement under the two policies. If the company does not take discounts, then its interest expense is zero, but it will have a $240,000 expense for "discounts lost." On the other hand, if it does take discounts, it incurs an interest expense of $65,333, but it also avoids the cost of discounts lost. Since discounts lost exceed the interest expense, the take-discounts policy results in the higher net income and, thus, in a higher value of the stock.

Table 10-2
Fall Mills' Income
Statement with Different
Trade Credit Policies

	Do Not Take Discounts	Take Discounts
Sales	$15,000,000	$15,000,000
Purchases	11,760,000	11,760,000
Labor and other costs	2,000,000	2,000,000
Interest	0	65,333
Discounts lost	240,000	0
Total costs	$14,000,000	$13,825,333
Net income before tax	1,000,000	1,174,667
Tax (40%)	400,000	469,867
Net income after tax	$ 600,000	$ 704,800

Components of Trade
Credit: Free versus
Costly

Based on the preceding discussion, trade credit can be divided into two components:

1. *Free trade credit,* which involves credit received during the discount period. For Fall Mills, this amounts to ten days of net purchases, or $326,667.[7]

---

[7] There is some question as to whether any credit is really "free," because the supplier will have a cost

(continued)

2. *"Costly" trade credit*, which involves credit in excess of the free credit. This credit has an implicit cost equal to the foregone discounts. Fall Mills could obtain $653,333, or twenty days' net purchases, of such credit at a cost of approximately 37 percent.

Financial managers should always use the free component, but they should use the costly component only after analyzing the cost of this capital and determining that it is less than the cost of funds obtained from other sources. Under the terms of trade found in most industries, the costly component will involve a relatively high percentage cost, so stronger firms will avoid using it.

Another point which may be made about trade credit is that firms sometimes can and do deviate from the stated credit terms, thus altering the percentage cost figures cited above. To illustrate, a California manufacturing firm that buys on terms of 2/10, net 30, makes a practice of paying in fifteen days (rather than ten) and still taking discounts. Its treasurer simply waits until fifteen days after receipt of the goods to pay, then writes a check for the invoiced amount less the 2 percent discount. The company's suppliers want its business, so they tolerate this practice. Similarly, a Wisconsin firm that also buys on terms of 2/10, net 30, does not take discounts, but it pays in sixty rather than in thirty days. As shown above, both practices reduce the cost of trade credit. Neither of these firms is "loved" by its suppliers, and neither could continue these practices in times when suppliers were operating at full capacity and had order backlogs, but these practices can and do reduce the costs of trade credit during times when suppliers have excess capacity.

Short-Term Bank Loans

Commercial banks, whose loans appear on firms' balance sheets as notes payable, are second in importance to trade credit as a source of short-term financing.[8] The banks' influence is actually greater than appears from the dollar amounts they lend, because banks provide *nonspontaneous* funds. As a firm's financing needs increase, it requests its bank to pro-

---

of carrying receivables which must be passed on to the customer in the form of higher prices. Still, where suppliers sell on standard terms such as 2/10, net 30, and where the base price cannot be negotiated downward for early payment, then for all intents and purposes the ten days of trade credit are indeed "free."

[8] There are two types of banks: (1) *Savings banks do not* make short-term loans to businesses. These banks accept mainly time deposits, and they invest heavily in residential mortgage loans. Savings banks are located principally in the Northeast and are very similar to savings and loan associations. (2) *Commercial banks do* accept demand deposits and *do* make short-term loans to both individuals and businesses. When the word "bank" is used in this book, it means a commercial bank unless otherwise specified. (There are also "investment banking houses," which are firms such as Merrill Lynch engaged in various aspects of the securities business. Investment bankers traditionally accept *no* regular deposits and make *no* regular loans. Investment bankers simply buy stocks and bonds issued by business firms for resale to investors. Investment banking is described in detail in Chapters 13 and 14.)

vide the additional funds. If the request is denied, often the firm is forced to slow down its rate of growth. Some features of bank loans are discussed below.

Maturity. Although banks do make longer-term loans, *the bulk of their lending is on a short-term basis*—about two-thirds of all bank loans mature in a year or less. Bank loans to businesses are frequently written as ninety day notes, so the loan must be repaid or renewed at the end of ninety days. Of course, if a borrower's financial position has deteriorated, the bank may well refuse to renew the loan. This can mean serious trouble for the borrower.

Promissory Note. When a bank loan is taken out, the agreement is executed by the signing of a promissory note. The note specifies (1) the amount borrowed; (2) the percentage interest rate; (3) the repayment schedule, which can involve either a lump sum or a series of installments; (4) any collateral that might be put up as security for the loan; and (5) any other terms and conditions to which the bank and the borrower may have agreed. When the note is signed, the bank credits the borrower's demand deposit with the amount of the loan. On the borrower's balance sheet, both cash and notes payable increase.

Compensating Balances. In Chapter 9, compensating balances were discussed in connection with the firm's cash account. As noted there, banks typically require that a regular borrower maintain an average checking account balance of 10 to 20 percent of the face amount of the loan. These compensating balances raise the effective interest rate. For example, if a firm needs $80,000 to pay off outstanding obligations, but it must maintain a 20 percent compensating balance, then it must borrow $100,000 to obtain a usable $80,000. If the stated interest rate is 8 percent, the effective cost is actually 10 percent: $8,000 divided by $80,000 equals 10 percent.[9]

Line of Credit. A line of credit is a formal or an informal understanding between the bank and the borrower indicating the maximum size loan the bank will allow the borrower. For example, on December 31 a bank loan officer may indicate to a financial manager that the bank regards the firm as being "good" for up to $80,000 for the forthcoming year. On January 10 the manager signs a promissory note for $15,000 for ninety days—this is called "taking down" $15,000 of the total line of credit. This

---

[9] Note, however, that the compensating balance may be set as a minimum monthly *average*; if the firm maintains this average anyway, the compensating balance requirement does not entail higher effective rates. Also, note that these *loan* compensating balances are added to any *service* compensating balances (discussed in Chapter 9) that the firm's bank may require.

amount is credited to the firm's checking account at the bank. Before repayment of the $15,000, the firm may borrow additional amounts up to a total outstanding at any one time of $80,000.

Revolving Credit Agreement. A *revolving credit agreement* is a formal line of credit often used by large firms. To illustrate, in 1981 Carter Chemical negotiated a revolving credit agreement for $100 million with a group of banks. The banks were formally committed for four years to lend Carter up to $100 million if the funds were needed. Carter, in turn, paid a commitment fee of one-quarter of one percent on the unused balance of the commitment to compensate the banks for making the funds available. Thus, if Carter did not take down any of the $100 million commitment during a year, it would still be required to pay a $250,000 fee. If it borrowed $50 million, the unused portion of the line of credit would fall to $50 million, and the fee would fall to $125,000. Of course, interest also had to be paid on the amount of money Carter actually borrowed. As a general rule, the rate of interest on "revolvers" is pegged to the prime rate (see next section), so the cost of the loan varies over time as interest rates vary. Carter's rate was set at prime plus 0.5 percent.

The cost of bank loans varies for different types of borrowers at a given point in time, and for all borrowers over time. Interest rates are higher for riskier borrowers. Rates are also higher on smaller loans because of the fixed costs of making and servicing loans. If a firm can qualify as a "prime risk" because of its size and financial strength, it can borrow at the *prime rate*, which is normally the lowest rate banks charge. Rates on other loans are scaled up from the prime rate.[10]

The Cost of Bank Loans

Bank rates vary widely over time depending on economic conditions and Federal Reserve policy. When the economy is weak, then (1) loan demand is usually slack and (2) the Fed also makes plenty of money available to the system. As a result, rates on all types of loans are relatively low. Conversely, when the economy is booming, loan demand is typically strong, and the Fed generally restricts the money supply—the result is high interest rates. As an indication of the kinds of fluctuations that can occur, the prime rate in 1974 varied from a low of 8.5 percent to a high of 12 percent, and it rose to 21 percent in 1980. Interest rates on other bank loans vary more or less with the prime rate.

---

[10] Each bank sets its own prime rate, but, because of competitive forces, most banks' prime rates are identical. Further, most banks follow the rate set by the large New York City banks, and they, in turn, generally follow the rate set by Citibank, New York City's largest. Citibank normally sets the prime rate each week at $1\frac{1}{4}$ to $1\frac{1}{2}$ percentage points above the average rate on large certificates of deposit (CDs) during the three weeks immediately preceding. CD rates represent the "price" of money in the open market, and they rise and fall with the supply and demand of money, so CD rates are "market-clearing" rates. By tying the prime rate to CD rates, the banking system insures that the prime rate will also be a market-clearing rate.

Interest rates on bank loans are calculated in three ways: as "simple" interest, as "discount" interest, and as "add-on" interest. These three methods are explained below.

Regular, or Simple, Interest. Exactly the type of interest rate we discussed in Chapters 3 and 4 is involved in simple interest. On the typical loan for $10,000 for one year at 9 percent, the borrower receives $10,000 now and repays $10,900 at the end of the year:

$$\text{Effective rate of interest on simple interest loan} = \frac{\text{Interest}}{\text{Amount borrowed}} = \frac{\$900}{\$10,000} = 9\%. \quad (10\text{-}2)$$

If the loan had been written for less than a year, say for ninety days, then the interest charge would have been calculated as follows, using 365 days per year:

Interest charge = (Interest rate per day)(Number of days)(Amount borrowed)
= (Annual rate/365)(90)($10,000)
= $221.92.

Thus, at the end of ninety days the borrower would have to repay the bank $10,221.92.[11]

Discount Interest. If the bank deducts the interest in advance (*discounts* the loan), the effective rate of interest is increased. On the $10,000 loan for 9 percent, the discount is $900, and the borrower obtains the use of only $9,100. The effective rate of interest is 9.9 percent versus 9 percent on a simple interest loan:

$$\text{Effective rate of interest on discounted loan} = \frac{\text{Interest}}{\text{Amount borrowed} - \text{Interest}}$$

$$= \frac{\$900}{\$9,100} = 9.9\%.$$

---

[11] People sometimes suggest this alternative way of calculating the amount to be repaid, and by implication the interest charge:

$$\text{Amount to be repaid} = \text{Principal } (1 + k_d)^{m/365}$$
$$= \$10,000(1.09)^{90/365}$$
$$= \$10,214.77.$$

Here, k_d is the simple interest rate and m is the number of days. This alternative method is *not* generally used, because it implicitly assumes that interest is earned on interest, an assumption that is inconsistent with annual compounding.

Alternatively,

$$\begin{array}{c}\text{Effective rate of interest} \\ \text{on discounted loan}\end{array} = \frac{\text{Interest rate (\%)}}{1.0 - \text{Stated interest rate (fraction)}} \qquad (10\text{-}3)$$

$$= \frac{9\%}{0.91} = 9.9\%.$$

Installment Loans: Add-On Interest. Banks (and other lenders) typically charge add-on interest on automobile and other types of installment loans for under about $10,000. The term *add-on* means that interest is calculated and added on to the funds received to determine the face amount of the note. To illustrate, suppose our $10,000 loan is to be repaid in twelve monthly installments. At a 9 percent add-on rate, the borrower pays a total interest charge of $900. Thus, the note signed is for $10,900. However, since the loan is paid off in installments, the borrower has the full $10,000 only during the first month, and by the last month eleven-twelfths of the loan will have been repaid. The borrower must pay $900 for the use of only about half the amount received, as the *average* amount of the original loan outstanding during the year is only about $5,000. Therefore, the effective rate on the loan is approximately 18 percent, calculated as follows:

$$\begin{array}{c}\text{Approximate interest rate} \\ \text{on installment loan}\end{array} = \frac{\text{Average annual interest}}{\text{Loan amount} \div 2} \qquad (10\text{-}4)$$

$$= \frac{\$900}{\$5,000} = 18\%.$$

The main point to note here is that interest is paid on the *original* amount of the loan, not on the amount actually outstanding (the declining balance), which causes the effective interest rate to be almost double the stated rate.[12]

[12] This is only an approximation of the true rate of interest. To determine the precisely correct effective annual percentage rate (APR) on the loan, we proceed as follows:

1. The total loan to be repaid is $10,000 plus $900 interest, which is added on to the amount borrowed, for a total of $10,900.
2. The monthly payment is $10,900 ÷ 12 = .$908.33.
3. The bank is, in effect, buying a twelve period annuity of $908.33 for $10,000, so $10,000 is the PV of the annuity. Expressed in equation form,

$$PV = \$10,000 = \sum_{t=1}^{12} \$908.33 \left[\frac{1}{1 + k_d} \right]^{t} \qquad (10\text{-}5)$$

4. This equation can be solved for k_d, which is the rate per month. Here k_d = 1.3513%.
5. The "true" APR is calculated as follows:

    True APR = $(1 + k_d)^{12} - 1.0 = (1.013513)^{12} - 1.0 = 1.175 - 1.0 = 17.5$ percent.

6. Under the truth-in-lending laws, banks, department stores, and other installment lenders are re-

(continued)

Suppose you had borrowed the $10,000 for three years at a 9 percent discount rate: what would the approximate interest rate have been? The total interest in dollars would have been (0.09)($10,000)(3) = $2,700, or $900 per year on average, and the average loan amount outstanding would have remained at $5,000, so the approximate interest rate would also remain the same, 18 percent.

Consumer Revolving Credit. Credit card companies, department stores, and banks grant consumers lines of credit up to specified limits. Interest is calculated each month on the outstanding balance, and this interest is added to the previous balance. Frequently, the rate is set at $1\frac{1}{2}$ percent per month, and the annual percentage rate (APR) is stated to be $12 \times 1\frac{1}{2} = 18\%$.[13]

Effective Interest Rates When Compensating Balances Apply. Compensating balances tend to raise the effective interest rate on bank loans. To illustrate this, suppose a firm needs $10,000 to pay for some equipment that it recently purchased. A bank offers to lend the company money at a 9 percent simple interest rate, but the company must maintain a compensating balance equal to 20 percent of the amount of the loan. If it did not take the loan, the firm would keep no deposits with the bank. What is the effective interest rate on the loan?

First, note that although the firm needs only $10,000, it must borrow $12,500, calculated as follows:[14]

$$\text{Amount of loan} = \frac{\text{Funds needed}}{1.0 - \text{Compensating balance percentage}} \tag{10-6}$$

$$= \frac{\$10,000}{0.8} = \$12,500.$$

quired to report the APR in boldface type on the face of all installment loan contracts. This is to prevent lenders from calling a loan with an effective rate of 17.5 percent a 9 percent loan. Note, however, that existing laws permit lenders to report as the APR either the 18% calculated by Equation 10-4 or the 17.5% calculated by Equation 10-5.

7. If an installment loan is paid off ahead of schedule, other complications arise. For a discussion of this point, see Dick Bonker, "The Rule of 78," *Journal of Finance*, June 1976, 877-888.

8. If the loan were for a period other than twelve months, Equation 10-5 would be modified to determine the true APR.

[13] Although the APR is said (legally, under the truth-in-lending laws) to be 18 percent, the "really true" rate in a compound interest sense is

$$(1.015)^{12} - 1.0 = 1.196 - 1.0 = 0.196 = 19.6\%.$$

[14] The logic behind Equation 10-6 is explained below:

Amount of loan = Amount needed + Compensating balance
= $10,000 + (0.2)(Amount of loan)
Amount of loan − 0.2(Amount of loan) = $10,000
Amount of loan (1 − 0.2) = $10,000
Amount of loan = $10,000/0.8 = $12,500
= (Funds needed)/(1 − Compensating balance).

The interest paid will be (0.09)($12,500) = $1,125, but the firm will only get the use of $10,000. Therefore, the effective interest rate is

$$\frac{\text{Effective}}{\text{interest rate}} = \frac{\text{Interest paid}}{\text{Funds actually used}} = \frac{\$1,125}{\$10,000} = 0.1125 = 11.25\%.$$

In general, we can use this formula to find the effective interest rate when compensating balances apply:

$$\frac{\text{Effective}}{\text{interest rate}} = \frac{\text{Stated interest rate}}{1.0 - \text{Compensating balance fraction}}. \qquad (10\text{-}7)$$

In our example,

$$\frac{\text{Effective}}{\text{interest rate}} = \frac{9\%}{1.0 - 0.2} = \frac{9\%}{0.8} = 11.25\%.$$

The analysis can be extended to the case where compensating balances are required and the loan is based on discount interest:

$$\frac{\text{Effective}}{\text{interest rate}} = \frac{\text{Stated interest rate}}{(1.0) - \left(\dfrac{\text{Compensating balance}}{\text{fraction}}\right) - \left(\dfrac{\text{Stated interest}}{\text{rate}}\right)}.$$

For example, if we needed $10,000 and were offered a loan with a stated interest rate of 9 percent, discount interest, with a 20 percent compensating balance, the effective interest rate would be

$$\text{Effective interest rate} = \frac{9\%}{1.0 - 0.2 - 0.09} = \frac{9\%}{0.71} = 12.68\%.$$

The amount that we would need to borrow would be

$$\text{Amount borrowed} = \frac{\$10,000}{1.0 - 0.2 - 0.09} = \$14,084.51.$$

We would use this $14,084.51 as follows:

To make the required payment	$10,000.00
Compensating balance (20% of $14,084.51)	2,816.90
Prepaid interest (9% of $14,084.51)	1,267.61
	$14,084.51

In our example, compensating balances and discount interest combined to push the effective rate of interest up from 9 percent to 12.68 percent. Note, however, that our analysis assumed that the compensating balance requirements forced the firm to increase its bank deposits.

Had the company had transactions balances which could be used to supply all or part of the compensating balances, the effective interest rate would have been less than 12.68 percent.

Choosing a Bank

Individuals whose only contact with their bank is through the use of its checking services generally choose a bank for the convenience of its location and the competitive cost of its checking service. However, a business that borrows from banks must look at other criteria, and a potential borrower seeking banking relations should recognize that important differences exist among banks. Some of these differences are considered below.

1. Banks have different basic policies toward risk. Some banks are inclined to follow relatively conservative lending practices; others engage in what are properly termed "creative banking practices." These policies reflect partly the personalities of officers of the bank and partly the characteristics of the bank's deposit liabilities. Thus, a bank with fluctuating deposit liabilities in a static community will tend to be a conservative lender, while a bank whose deposits are growing with little interruption may follow "liberal" credit policies. A large bank with broad diversification over geographic regions or among industries served can obtain the benefit of combining and averaging risks. Thus, marginal credit risks that might be unacceptable to a small bank or to a specialized unit bank can be pooled by a branch banking system to reduce the overall risks of a group of marginal accounts.

2. Some bank loan officers are active in providing counsel and in stimulating development loans to firms in their early and formative years. Certain banks have specialized departments to make loans to firms expected to grow and thus become more important customers. The personnel of these departments can provide much counseling to customers.

3. Banks differ in the extent to which they will support the activities of the borrower in bad times. This characteristic is referred to as the degree of *loyalty* of the banks. Some banks may put great pressure on a business to liquidate its loans when the firm's outlook becomes clouded, whereas others will stand by the firm and work diligently to help it get back on its feet. An especially dramatic illustration of this point was Bank of America's recent bail-out of Memorex Corporation. The bank could have forced Memorex into bankruptcy, but instead it loaned the company additional capital and helped it survive a bad period. Memorex's stock price subsequently rose on the New York Stock Exchange from $1.50 to $68, so Bank of America's help was indeed substantial.

4. Banks differ greatly in their degrees of loan specialization. Larger banks have separate departments specializing in different kinds of

loans—for example, real estate loans, installment loans, and commercial loans. Within these broad categories there may be a specialization by line of business, such as steel, machinery, or textiles. The strengths of banks are also likely to reflect the nature of the business and the economic environment in which they operate. For example, Texas banks have become specialists in lending to oil companies, while many midwestern banks are agricultural specialists. A firm can obtain more creative cooperation and more active support by going to the bank that has the greatest experience and familiarity with its particular type of business. The financial manager should therefore choose a bank with care. A bank that is excellent for one firm may be unsatisfactory for another.

5. The size of a bank can be an important factor. Since the maximum loan a bank can make to any one customer is generally limited to 10 percent of the bank's capital accounts (capital stock plus retained earnings), it will generally not be appropriate for large firms to develop borrowing relationships with small banks.

Commercial Paper

Commercial paper consists of unsecured promissory notes of large, strong firms and is sold primarily to other business firms, to insurance companies, to pension funds, and to banks. Although the amounts of commercial paper outstanding are much smaller than bank loans outstanding, this form of financing has grown rapidly in recent years.

Maturity and Cost

Maturities of commercial paper generally vary from two to six months, with an average of about five months.[15] The rates on commercial paper fluctuate with supply and demand conditions—they are determined in the marketplace and vary daily as conditions change. Typically, commercial paper rates range from $1\frac{1}{4}$ to $1\frac{1}{2}$ percentage points below rates on prime business loans. Also, since compensating balances are not required for commercial paper, the *effective* cost differential is still wider.[16]

Use

The use of commercial paper is restricted to a comparatively small number of concerns that are exceptionally good credit risks. Dealers prefer to handle the paper of concerns whose net worth is $10 million or more and whose annual borrowing exceeds $1 million.

---

[15] The maximum maturity without SEC registration is 270 days. Also, commercial paper can only be sold to "sophisticated" investors; otherwise, SEC registration would be required for shorter maturities as well.

[16] However, this factor is offset to some extent by the fact that firms issuing commercial paper are generally required by commercial paper dealers to have unused bank lines of credit to back up their outstanding commercial paper, and fees must be paid on these lines. In other words, to sell $1 million of commercial paper, a firm must have a line of credit available to pay off the paper when it matures, and commitment fees on this unused credit line (about $\frac{1}{2}$ percent) increase the effective cost of the paper.

Other Factors

One potential problem with commercial paper is that a debtor who is in temporary financial difficulty may receive little help, because commercial paper dealings are generally less personal than are bank relationships. Thus, banks are generally more able and willing to help a good customer weather a temporary storm than is a commercial paper dealer. On the other hand, using commercial paper permits a corporation to tap a wide range of credit sources, including banks outside its own area and industrial corporations across the country.

Use of Security in Short-Term Financing

Given a choice, it is ordinarily better to borrow on an unsecured basis, as the bookkeeping costs of secured loans are often high. However, weak firms may find (1) that they can borrow only if they put up some type of security to protect the lender, or (2) that by using some security they can borrow at a much lower rate.

Several different kinds of collateral can be employed—marketable stocks or bonds, land or buildings, equipment, inventory, and accounts receivable. Marketable securities make excellent collateral, but few firms hold portfolios of stocks and bonds. Similarly, real property (land and buildings) and equipment are good forms of collateral, but they are generally used as security for long-term loans. However, a great deal of secured short-term business borrowing involves the use of accounts receivable and inventories.

To understand the use of security, consider the case of a Gainesville hardware dealer who wanted to modernize and expand his store. He requested a $200,000 bank loan. After examining his business's financial statements, the bank indicated (1) that it would lend him a maximum of $100,000, and (2) that the interest rate would be 20 percent, discount interest, or an effective rate of 25 percent. The owner had a substantial personal portfolio of stocks, so he offered to put up $300,000 of high-quality stocks to support the $200,000 loan. The bank then granted the full $200,000 loan, and at a rate of only 18 percent, simple interest. The store owner might also have used his inventories or receivables as security for the loan, but processing costs would have been high.

In the past, state laws varied greatly with regard to the use of security in financing. Today, however, all states except Louisiana operate under a *Uniform Commercial Code*, which standardizes and simplifies the procedure for establishing loan security. The heart of the Uniform Commercial Code is the *Security Agreement*, a standardized document, or form, on which the specific assets that are pledged are stated. The assets can be items of equipment, accounts receivable, or inventories. Procedures for financing under the Uniform Commercial Code are described in Appendix 10A.

Summary

This chapter began with a discussion of the use of short-term or long-term debt to finance current assets. We saw that because short-term credit offers advantages of lower cost and greater flexibility, most firms use at least some current debt, in spite of the fact that short-term debt increases the firm's risk.

The chapter also examined the four major types of short-term credit available to a firm: (1) *accruals*, (2) *accounts payable, or "trade credit,"* (3) *bank loans*, and (4) *commercial paper*. Companies use accruals on a regular basis, but this usage is not subject to discretionary actions. The other types of credit are controllable, at least within limits.

Accounts payable may be divided into two components, *free trade credit* and *costly trade credit*. The cost of the latter is based on discounts lost, and it can be quite high. The financial manager should use all the free trade credit that is available, but costly trade credit should be used only if other credit is not available on better terms.

The third major source of short-term credit is the *commercial banking system*. Bank loans may be obtained as the need arises, or they may be obtained on a regular basis under a *line of credit*. There are three different kinds of interest charges on bank loans: (1) *simple interest*, (2) *discount interest*, and (3) *add-on interest* for installment loans. Banks often require borrowers to maintain *compensating balances*. If the required balance exceeds the balance the firm would otherwise maintain, a compensating balance raises the effective cost of a bank loan.

Commercial paper constitutes another important source of short-term credit, but it is available only to large, financially strong firms. Interest rates on commercial paper are generally below the prime bank rate, and the relative cost of paper is even lower when compensating balances on bank loans are considered. However, commercial paper does have disadvantages—if a firm that depends heavily on commercial paper experiences problems, its source of funds will immediately dry up. Commercial bankers are much more likely to help their customers ride out bad times.

Although we mentioned it only briefly in the chapter, short-term credit is often secured by inventories and accounts receivable. Techniques for using security to obtain short-term credit are discussed in the appendix to this chapter.

Questions

10-1 "Firms can control their accruals within fairly wide limits; depending on the cost of accruals, financing from this source will be increased or decreased." Discuss.

10-2 Is it true that both trade credit and accruals represent a spontaneous source of capital to finance growth? Explain.

10-3 Is it true that most firms are able to obtain some "free" trade credit, and that additional trade credit is often available, but at a cost? Explain.

10-4 Define each of the following terms:
   a. Promissory note.
   b. Compensating balance.
   c. Line of credit.
   d. Prime rate.
   e. Revolving credit agreement.
   f. Simple interest, discount interest, add-on interest, and APR.

10-5 What is commercial paper? Could Mamma and Pappa Gus's Corner Grocery borrow on commercial paper?

10-6 From the standpoint of the borrower, is long-term or short-term credit riskier? Explain.

10-7 If long-term credit exposes a borrower to less risk, why would people or firms borrow on a short-term basis?

10-8 Suppose that a firm can borrow at the prime rate and it can also sell commercial paper. (a) If the prime rate is 12 percent, what is a reasonable estimate for the cost of commercial paper? (b) If a substantial cost differential exists, why might a firm such as this one actually borrow from both markets?

Problems

10-1 Calculate the implicit cost of nonfree trade credit under the following terms, using Equation 10-1.
   a. 2/15, net 40.
   b. 3/10, net 20.
   c. 1/10, net 60.

10-2 a. If a firm buys under terms of 2/10, net 40, but actually pays after twenty days and *still takes the discount,* what is the cost of its nonfree trade credit?
   b. Does it receive more or less trade credit than it would if it paid within ten days?

10-3 Suppose a firm makes purchases of $2,400,000 per year under terms of 2/10, net 30. It takes discounts.
   a. What is the average amount of its accounts payable, net of discounts? (Assume the $2.4 million purchases are net of discounts; that is, gross purchases are $2,448,980, discounts are $48,980, and net purchases are $2.4 million. Also, use 360 days in a year.)
   b. Is there a cost of the trade credit it uses?
   c. If it did not take discounts, what would its average payables be, and what would be the cost of this nonfree trade credit?

10-4 You plan to borrow $10,000 from the bank. The bank offers to lend you the money at a 15 percent interest rate on a one year loan. What is the true, or effective, rate of interest for (a) simple interest, (b) discount interest, and (c) add-on interest, if the loan is a twelve month installment loan?

10-5 Deitz Corporation projects an increase in sales from $2 million to $3 million, but the company needs an additional $600,000 of assets to support this expansion. The money can be obtained from the bank at an interest rate of 14 percent discount interest. Alternatively, Deitz can finance the expansion by no longer taking discounts, thus increasing accounts payable. Deitz purchases under terms of 2/10, net 30, but it can delay payment for an additional thirty days, paying in sixty days and thus becoming thirty days past due, without a penalty at this time.

    a. Based strictly on an interest rate comparison, how should Deitz finance its expansion? Show your work.

    b. What additional qualitative factors should be considered in reaching a decision?

10-6 The Beedles Corporation had sales of $1.95 million last year and earned a 4 percent return, after taxes, on sales. Although its terms of purchase are twenty days, its accounts payable represent sixty days' purchases. The president of the company is seeking to increase the company's bank borrowings in order to become current (that is, have twenty days' payables outstanding) in meeting its trade obligations. The company's balance sheet is shown below:

    a. How much bank financing is needed to eliminate past-due accounts payable?

    b. Would you as a bank loan officer make the loan? Why?

Beedles Corporation
Balance Sheet

Cash	$ 25,000	Accounts payable	$ 300,000	
Accounts receivable	125,000	Bank loans	250,000	
Inventory	650,000	Accruals	125,000	
Current assets	$ 800,000	Current liabilities	$ 675,000	
Land and buildings	250,000	Mortgage on real estate	250,000	
Equipment	250,000	Common stock,		
		par 10 cents	125,000	
		Retained earnings	250,000	
		Total liabilities		
Total assets	$1,300,000	and net worth	$1,300,000	

10-7 K. J. Johnson & Sons sells on terms of 2/10, net 40. Sales last year were $6 million. Half of Johnson's customers pay on the tenth day and take discounts.

    a. If accounts receivable last year averaged $583,343, what is Johnson's average collection period *on nondiscount sales?*

    b. What rate of return is Johnson earning on its nondiscount receivables, where this rate of return is defined to be equal to the cost of this trade credit to the nondiscount customers?

10-8 Eiteman & Daughters, Inc., buys on terms of 1/10, net 30, but it has not been taking discounts and has actually been paying in sixty days rather than thirty days. Eiteman's balance sheet follows.

Cash	$ 50,000	Accounts payable[a]	$ 500,000
Accounts receivable	450,000	Notes payable	50,000
Inventories	750,000	Accruals	50,000
Total current assets	$1,250,000	Total current liabilities	$ 600,000
		Long-term debt	150,000
Fixed assets	750,000	Common equity	1,250,000
		Total liabilities	
Total assets	$2,000,000	and equity	$2,000,000

[a]Stated net of discounts, even though discounts may not be taken.

Now Eiteman's suppliers are threatening to stop shipments unless the company begins making prompt payments (that is, pays in thirty days or less). Eiteman can borrow on a one year note (call this a current liability) from its bank at a rate of 15 percent, discount interest, with a 20 percent compensating balance required. (All of the cash now on hand is needed for transactions; it cannot be used as part of the compensating balance.)

a. Determine what action Eiteman should take by (1) calculating the cost of nonfree trade credit, and (2) calculating the cost of the bank loan.
b. Based on your decision in Part a, construct a pro forma balance sheet. (Hint: You will need to include an account entitled "prepaid interest" under current assets.)

Selected References

For a further discussion of trade credit, see the credit policy texts referenced in Chapter 8. In addition, see

Moskowitz, L. A., *Modern Factoring and Commercial Finance* (New York: Thomas Y. Crowell, 1977).

For more on bank lending and commercial credit in general, see

Hayes, Douglas A., *Bank Lending Policies, Domestic and International* (Ann Arbor: Bureau of Business Research, University of Michigan, 1971).
Jessup, Paul F., *Modern Bank Management* (New York: West, 1980).
Reed, Edward W., Richard V. Cotter, Edward K. Gill, and Richard K. Smith, *Commercial Banking* (Englewood Cliffs, N.J.: Prentice-Hall, 1976).
Rose, Peter, and Donald R. Fraser, *Financial Institutions* (Dallas: Business Publications, 1980).
Stigum, M., *The Money Market: Myth, Reality, and Practice* (Homewood, Ill.: Irwin, 1978).

For a good discussion of the effective interest rate on installment loans, especially when they are paid off ahead of schedule, see

Bonker, Dick, "The Rule of 78," *Journal of Finance*, June 1976, 877-888.

Appendix 10A

Procedures for Securing Short-Term Loans

Procedures under the Uniform Commercial Code for using accounts receivable and inventories as security for short-term credit are described in this appendix. As noted in Chapter 10, secured short-term loans involve quite a bit of paperwork and other administrative costs; hence, they are relatively expensive. However, this is often the only type of financing available to weaker firms.

Accounts receivable financing involves either the pledging of receivables or the selling of receivables (factoring). The *pledging of accounts receivable* is characterized by the fact that the lender not only has a claim against the receivables but also has recourse to the borrower (seller); if the person or the firm that bought the goods does not pay, the selling firm must take the loss. In other words, the risk of default on the accounts receivable pledged remains with the borrower. Also, the buyer of the goods is not ordinarily notified about the pledging of the receivables. The financial institution that lends on the security of accounts receivable is generally either a commercial bank or one of the large industrial finance companies.

Factoring, or *selling accounts receivable*, involves the purchase of accounts receivable by the lender without recourse to the borrower (seller). With factoring, the buyer of the goods is typically notified of the transfer and makes payment directly to the lender. Since the factoring firm assumes the risk of default on bad accounts, it must do the credit checking. Accordingly, factors provide not only money but also a credit department for the borrower. Incidentally, the same financial institutions that make loans against pledged receivables also serve as factors. Thus, depending on the circumstances and the wishes of the borrower, a financial institution will provide either form of receivables financing.

Financing Accounts Receivable

The financing of accounts receivable is initiated by a legally binding agreement between the seller of the goods and the financing institution. The agreement sets forth in detail the procedures to be followed and the legal obligations of both parties. Once the working relationship has been established, the seller periodically takes a batch of invoices to the financing institution. The lender reviews the invoices and makes credit appraisals of the buyers. Invoices of companies that do not meet the lender's credit standards are not accepted for pledging.

The financial institution seeks to protect itself at every phase of the operation. Selection of sound invoices is the essential first step in safeguarding the financial institution. If the buyer of the goods does not pay the invoice, the lender still has recourse against the seller of the goods. However, if many buyers default, the seller firm may be unable to meet its obligation to the financial institution. Additional protection is afforded the lender in that the loan will generally be for less than 100 percent of the pledged receivables; for example, the lender may advance the selling firm only 75 percent of the amount of the pledged receivables.

Procedure for Pledging Accounts Receivable

The procedure for factoring is somewhat different from that for pledging. Again, an agreement between the seller and the factor is made to specify legal obligations and procedural arrangements. When the seller receives an order from a buyer, a credit approval slip is written and immediately sent to the factoring company for a credit check. If the factor does not approve the sale, the seller generally refuses to fill the order. This procedure informs the seller, prior to the sale, about the buyer's creditworthi-

Procedure for Factoring Accounts Receivable

ness and acceptability to the factor. If the sale is approved, shipment is made and the invoice is stamped to notify the buyer to make payment directly to the factoring company.

The factor performs three functions in carrying out the normal procedure as outlined above: (1) credit checking, (2) lending, and (3) risk bearing. The seller can select various combinations of these functions by changing provisions in the factoring agreement. For example, a small or a medium-sized firm can avoid establishing a credit department. The factor's service might well be less costly than a department that may have excess capacity for the firm's credit volume. At the same time, if the firm uses part of the time of a noncredit specialist to perform credit checking, then lack of education, training, and experience may result in excessive losses.

The seller may utilize the factor to perform the credit-checking and risk-taking functions but not the lending function. The following procedure is carried out on receipt of a $10,000 order. The factor checks and approves the invoices. The goods are shipped on terms of net 30. Payment is made to the factor, who remits to the seller. But assume that the factor has received only $5,000 by the end of the credit period. The $10,000 must still be remitted to the seller (less a fee, of course). If the remaining $5,000 is never paid, the factor sustains a $5,000 loss.

Now consider the more typical situation in which the factor performs a lending function by making payment in advance of collection. The goods are shipped and, even though payment is not due for thirty days, the factor immediately makes funds available to the seller. Suppose $10,000 worth of goods is shipped. The factoring commission for credit checking is $2\frac{1}{2}$ percent of the invoice price, or $250, and the interest expense is computed at a 9 percent annual rate on the invoice balance, or $75.[1] The seller's accounting entry is as follows:

Cash	$9,175	
Interest expense	75	
Factoring commission	250	
Reserve due from factor on collection of account	500	
Accounts receivable		$10,000

---

[1] Since the interest is only for one month, we take one-twelfth of the stated rate, 9 percent, and multiply this by the $10,000 invoice price:

$$\frac{1}{12} \times 0.09 \times \$10,000 = \$75.$$

Note that the effective rate of interest is really above 9 percent, because a discounting procedure is used and the borrower does not get the full $10,000. In many instances, however, the factoring contract calls for interest to be computed on the invoice price *less* the factoring commission and the reserve account.

The $500 due from factor on collection of account is a reserve established by the factor to cover disputes between sellers and buyers on damaged goods, goods returned by the buyers to the seller, and failure to make outright sale of goods. The reserve is paid to the selling firm when the factor collects on the account.

Factoring is normally a continuous process instead of the single cycle described above. The firm selling the goods receives orders; it transmits the purchase orders to the factor for approval; on approval, the goods are shipped; the factor advances the money to the seller; the buyers pay the factor when payment is due; and the factor periodically remits any excess reserve to the seller of the goods. Once a routine is established, a continuous circular flow of goods and funds takes place between the seller, the buyers of the goods, and the factor. Thus, once the factoring agreement is in force, funds from this source are *spontaneous*.

Accounts receivable pledging and factoring services are convenient and advantageous, but they can be costly. The credit-checking commission is 1 to 3 percent of the amount of invoices accepted by the factor. The cost of money is reflected in the interest rate (usually two to three percentage points over the prime rate) charged on the unpaid balance of the funds advanced by the factor. When risk to the factoring firm is excessive, it purchases the invoices (with or without recourse) at discounts from face value.

Cost of Receivables Financing

It cannot be said categorically that accounts receivable financing is always either a good or a poor method of raising funds for an individual business. Among the advantages is, first, the flexibility of this source of financing. As the firm's sales expand and more financing is needed, a larger volume of invoices is generated automatically. Because the dollar amounts of invoices vary directly with sales, the amount of readily available financing increases. Second, receivables or invoices provide security for a loan that a firm might otherwise be unable to obtain. Third, factoring provides the services of a credit department that might otherwise be available to the firm only under much more expensive conditions.

Evaluation of Receivables Financing

Accounts receivable financing also has disadvantages. First, when invoices are numerous and relatively small in dollar amount, the administrative costs involved may render this method of financing inconvenient and expensive. Second, the firm is using a highly liquid asset as security. For a long time, accounts receivable financing was frowned upon by most trade creditors. In fact, such financing was regarded as a confession of a firm's unsound financial position. It is no longer regarded in this light, and many sound firms engage in receivables pledging or factoring. However, the traditional attitude causes some trade creditors to refuse to sell on credit to a firm that is factoring or pledging its receivables, on the grounds that this practice removes one of the most liquid of the firm's assets and, accordingly, weakens the position of other creditors.

**Future Use of
Receivables
Financing**

We might make a prediction at this point: In the future, accounts receivable financing will increase in relative importance. Computer technology is rapidly advancing toward the point where credit records of individuals and firms can be kept in computer memory units. Systems have been devised so that a retailer can have a unit on hand that, when an individual's magnetic credit card is inserted into a box, gives a signal that the credit is "good" and that a bank is willing to "buy" the receivable created when the store completes the sale. The cost of handling invoices will be greatly reduced over present-day costs because the new systems will be so highly automated. This will make it possible to use accounts receivable financing for very small sales, and it will reduce the cost of all receivables financing. The net result will be a marked expansion of accounts receivable financing.

**Inventory
Financing**

A rather large volume of credit is secured by business inventories. If a firm is a relatively good credit risk, the mere existence of the inventory may be a sufficient basis for receiving an unsecured loan. If the firm is a relatively poor risk, the lending institution may insist upon security, which often takes the form of a *blanket lien* against the inventory. Alternatively, *trust receipts* or *field warehouse receipts* can be used to secure the loan. These methods of using inventories as security are discussed below.

**Blanket Inventory
Lien**

The blanket inventory lien gives the lending institution a lien against all inventories of the borrower. However, the borrower is free to sell inventories; thus the value of the collateral can be reduced.

Trust Receipts

Because of the weakness of the blanket lien for inventory financing, another kind of security is used—the trust receipt. A trust receipt is an instrument acknowledging that the borrower holds the goods in trust for the lender. When trust receipts are used, the borrowing firm, on receiving funds from the lender, conveys a trust receipt for the goods. The goods can be stored in a public warehouse or held on the premises of the borrower. The trust receipt states that the goods are held in trust for the lender or are segregated in the borrower's premises on behalf of the lender, and proceeds from the sale of goods held under trust receipts are transmitted to the lender at the end of each day. Automobile dealer financing is the best example of trust receipt financing.

One defect of trust receipt financing is the requirement that a trust receipt must be issued for specific goods. For example, if the security is bags of coffee beans, the trust receipts must indicate the bags by number. In order to validate its trust receipts, the lending institution would have to send someone to the premises of the borrower to see that the bag numbers are correctly listed. Furthermore, complex legal requirements of trust receipts require the attention of a bank officer. Problems are compounded if borrowers are widely separated geographically from the lender. To offset these inconveniences, *warehousing* has come into wide use as a method of securing loans with inventory.

Warehouse Financing

Like trust receipts, warehouse financing uses inventory as security. A *public warehouse* represents an independent third party engaged in the business of storing goods. Items which must age, such as tobacco and liquor, are often financed and stored in public warehouses. Sometimes a public warehouse is not practical because of the bulkiness of goods and the expense of transporting them to and from the borrower's premises. *Field warehouse* financing represents an economical method of inventory financing in which the warehouse is established at the place of the borrower. To provide inventory supervision, the lending institution employs a third party in the arrangement, the field warehousing company. This company acts as the control (or supervisory) agent for the lending institution.

Field warehousing is illustrated by a simple example. Suppose a potential borrower firm has stacked iron in an open yard on its premises. A field warehouse can be established if a field warehousing concern places a temporary fence around the iron and erects a sign stating: "This is a field warehouse supervised and conducted by the Smith Field Warehousing Corporation." These are minimal conditions, of course.

The example illustrates the two elements in the establishment of a warehouse: (1) public notification of the field warehouse arrangement and (2) supervision of the field warehouse by a custodian of the field warehouse concern. When the field warehousing operation is relatively small, the second condition is sometimes violated by hiring an employee of the borrower to supervise the inventory. This practice is viewed as undesirable by the lending institution, because there is no control over the collateral by a person independent of the borrowing concern.[2]

The field warehouse financing operation is described best by a specific illustration. Assume that a tomato cannery is interested in financing its operations by bank borrowing. The cannery has sufficient funds to finance 15 to 20 percent of its operations during the canning season. These funds are adequate to purchase and process an initial batch of tomatoes. As the cans are put into boxes and rolled into the storerooms, the cannery needs additional funds for both raw materials and labor. Because of

---

[2] This absence of independent control was the main cause of the breakdown that resulted in the huge losses connected with the loans to the Allied Crude Vegetable Oil Company. American Express Field Warehousing Company hired men from Allied's staff as custodians. Their dishonesty was not discovered because of another breakdown—the fact that the American Express touring inspector did not actually take a physical inventory of the warehouses. As a consequence, the swindle was not discovered until losses running into the hundreds of millions of dollars had been suffered. See N. C. Miller, *The Great Salad Oil Swindle* (Baltimore, Md.: Penguin Books, 1965), 72-77.

the cannery's poor credit rating, the bank decides that a field warehousing operation is necessary to secure its loans.

The field warehouse is established, and the custodian notifies the lending institution of the description, by number, of the boxes of canned tomatoes in storage and under warehouse control. Thereupon, the lending institution establishes for the cannery a deposit on which it can draw. From this point on, the bank finances the operations. The cannery needs only enough cash to initiate the cycle. The farmers bring more tomatoes; the cannery processes them; the cans are boxed, and the boxes are put into the field warehouse; field warehouse receipts are drawn up and sent to the bank; the bank establishes further deposits for the cannery on the basis of the receipts; the cannery can draw on the deposits to continue the cycle.

Of course, the cannery's ultimate objective is to sell the canned tomatoes. As the cannery receives purchase orders, it transmits them to the bank, and the bank directs the custodian to release the inventories. It is agreed that, as remittances are received by the cannery, they will be turned over to the bank. These remittances by the cannery pay off the loans made by the bank.

Typically, a seasonal pattern exists. At the beginning of the tomato harvesting and canning season, the cannery's cash needs and loan requirements begin to rise and reach a maximum at the end of the canning season. It is hoped that, well before the new canning season begins, the cannery has sold a sufficient volume to have paid off the loan completely. If for some reason the cannery has had a bad year, the bank may carry it over another year to enable it to work off its inventory.

Acceptable Products. In addition to canned foods, which account for about 17 percent of all field warehouse loans, many other product inventories provide a basis for field warehouse financing. Some of these are miscellaneous groceries, which represent about 13 percent; lumber products, about 10 percent; and coal and coke, about 6 percent. These products are relatively nonperishable and are sold in well-developed, organized markets. Nonperishability protects the lender if it should have to take over the security. For this reason, a bank would not make a field warehousing loan on perishables such as fresh fish. However, frozen fish, which can be stored for a long time, can be field warehoused. An organized market aids the lender in disposing of an inventory that it takes over. Banks are not interested in going into the canning or the fish business. They want to be able to dispose of an inventory with the expenditure of a minimum of time.

Cost of Financing. The fixed costs of a field warehousing arrangement are relatively high; such financing is therefore not suitable for a very small firm. If a field warehouse company sets up the field warehouse itself, it will typically set a minimum charge of about $350 to $600 a year, plus about 1 to 2 percent of the amount of credit extended to the borrower. Furthermore, the financing institution will charge an interest rate of two to three percentage points over the prime rate. An efficient field warehousing operation requires a minimum inventory of about $500,000.

Appraisal. The use of field warehouse financing as a source of funds for business firms has many advantages. First, the amount of funds available is flexible because the financing is tied to the growth of inventories, which in turn is related directly to financing needs. Second, the field warehousing arrangement increases the acceptability of inventories as loan collateral. Some inventories would not be accepted by a bank as security without a field warehousing arrangement. Third, the necessity for inventory control, safekeeping, and the use of specialists in warehousing has resulted in improved warehouse practices. The services of the field warehouse companies have often saved money for the firm in spite of the costs of financing mentioned above. The field warehouse company may suggest inventory practices which reduce the labor that the firm has to employ, and reduce inventory damage and loss as well. The major disadvantage of a field warehousing operation is the fixed cost element, which reduces the feasibility of this form of financing for small firms.

10A-1 The Fagan Company manufactures plastic toys. It buys raw materials, manufactures the toys in the spring and summer, and ships them to department stores and toy stores by late summer or early fall. Fagan factors its receivables. If it did not, Fagan's October 1981 balance sheet might appear as shown below:

Problem

				Fagan Company: Pro Forma Balance Sheet, October 31, 1981
Cash	$ 40,000	Accounts payable	$1,200,000	
Receivables	1,200,000	Notes payable	800,000	
Inventory	800,000	Accruals	80,000	
Total current assets	$2,040,000	Total current liabilities	$2,080,000	
		Mortgages	200,000	
		Common stock	400,000	
Fixed assets	800,000	Retained earnings	160,000	
Total assets	$2,840,000	Total claims	$2,840,000	

Fagan provides advanced dating on its sales; thus, its receivables are not due for payment until January 31, 1982. Also, Fagan would have been overdue on some $800,000 of its accounts payable if the above situation had actually existed.

Fagan has an agreement with a finance company to factor the receivables for the period October 31 through January 31 of each selling season. The factoring company charges a flat commission of 2 percent, plus 6 percent a year interest on the outstanding balance; it deducts a reserve of 8 percent for returned and damaged materials. Interest and commission are paid in advance. No interest is charged on the reserved funds or on the commission.

a. Show the balance sheet of Fagan on October 31, 1981, giving effect to the purchase of all the receivables by the factoring company and the use of the funds to pay accounts payable.

b. If the $1.2 million is the average level of outstanding receivables, and if they turn over four times a year (hence the commission is paid four times a year), what are the total dollar costs of financing and the effective annual interest rate?

Capital Budgeting: Investing in Fixed Assets

V

Capital budgeting is an exceptionally important subject. By definition, "fixed assets" are those which last for a number of years, so investment decisions of this type affect the course of a business for years into the future. Chapter 11 describes the basics of capital budgeting, while Chapter 12 explores the subject in more depth and considers in detail how the riskiness of different projects is evaluated.

11   The Basics of Capital Budgeting

In Part IV we analyzed decisions relating to current assets and current liabilities, or working capital management. Now we turn to investment decisions involving fixed assets, or the process called *capital budgeting*. The term *capital* refers to fixed assets used in production, while a *budget* is a plan detailing projected inflows and outflows during some future period. Thus, the *capital budget* outlines the planned expenditures on fixed assets, and *capital budgeting* is the whole process of analyzing projects and deciding whether they should be included in the capital budget.

Our treatment of capital budgeting is divided into two parts. First, Chapter 11 gives an overview of the process and explains the basic analysis necessary in capital budgeting. Then, in Chapter 12, we go on to consider other topics in capital budgeting, especially risk analysis.

Similarities between Capital Budgeting and Security Valuation

Fixed assets are, by definition, expected to provide cash flows for some years into the future. Thus, the discounting process, which is largely ignored in current asset analysis, is of critical importance in capital budgeting. In fact, the capital budgeting process involves exactly the same six conceptual steps that are used in security analysis as described in Chapters 4 and 5:

1. First, management estimates the expected cash flows from a given project, including the value of the asset at a specified terminal date. This is similar to estimating the future dividend or interest payment stream in security analysis.
2. Next, the riskiness of the projected cash flows must be estimated.
3. Then, given (a) the riskiness of a project's cash flows and (b) the general level of money costs in the economy as reflected in the riskless rate (R_F), the firm determines the appropriate discount rate, called the *cost of capital*, at which the project's cash flows are to be discounted. This is equivalent to finding the required rate of return on a stock or a bond as we did in Chapter 5.
4. Next, the expected cash flows are put on a present value basis to obtain an estimate of the asset's value to the firm. This is equivalent to finding the PV of expected future dividends.
5. The PV of the expected cash inflows is then compared to the cost of

the project; if the asset's present value exceeds its cost, the project should be accepted.

6. Finally, and very important, the effect of the capital budgeting process on the value of the firm is considered. If an individual investor identifies and invests in a stock or bond whose market price is less than its true value, then the value of the investor's portfolio will be increased. Similarly, if the firm identifies (or creates) investment opportunities with present values greater than their costs, the value of the firm will be increased. This increase in firm value from capital budgeting will be reflected in the growth factor, g, that we discussed in Chapters 4 and 5. Thus, there is a very direct link between capital budgeting and stock values: The more effective the firm's capital budgeting procedures, the higher its growth rate, hence the higher the price of its stock.

Ideas for Capital Projects

Even though the same concepts are involved in both capital budgeting and security analysis, there are major differences in the collection and analysis of data for the two types of investments. Most important, a set of stocks and bonds exists in the securities market, and investors select a portfolio from this set. *However, capital projects are created by the firm.* For example, a sales representative may report that customers are asking for a particular product that the company does not now produce. The sales manager then discusses the idea with people in the marketing research group to determine whether a sizable market exists for the proposed product. If it appears likely that a market does exist, cost accountants and engineers will be brought in to estimate production costs. If this type of investigation suggests that the product can be produced and sold to yield a sufficient profit, then the project will be undertaken.

A firm's growth and development, even its ability to remain competitive and to survive, depend upon a constant flow of new investment ideas. Accordingly, a well-managed firm will go to great lengths to develop good capital budgeting proposals. For example, the executive vice-president of a major corporation indicated that his company takes the following steps to generate projects:

Our R & D department is constantly searching for new products, or for ways to improve existing products. In addition, our Executive Committee, which consists of senior executives in marketing, production, and finance, identifies the products and markets in which our company will compete, and the Committee sets long-run targets for each division. These targets, which are formalized in the Corporation's strategic business plan, provide a general guide to the operating executives who must meet them. These executives then seek new products, set expansion plans for existing products, and look for ways to reduce production and distribution costs. Since bonuses and promotions are based in large part on each unit's ability to meet or exceed its targets, these economic incentives encourage our operating executives to seek out profitable investment opportunities.

While our senior executives are judged and rewarded on the basis of how well their units perform, people further down the line are given bonuses for specific suggestions, including ideas that lead to profitable investments. Additionally, a percentage of our corporate profit is set aside for distribution to nonexecutive employees. Our objective is to encourage lower level workers to keep on the lookout for good ideas, including those that lead to capital investments.

If a firm has capable and imaginative executives and employees, and if its incentive system is working properly, many ideas for capital investment will be advanced. Since some ideas will be good ones while others will not, procedures must be established for screening projects. Steps in the screening process are discussed in the following sections.

Project Classification

Analyzing capital expenditure proposals is not a costless operation—benefits can be gained from a careful analysis, but such an investigation does have a cost. For certain types of projects, a relatively refined analysis may be warranted; for others, cost/benefit studies may suggest that a simpler procedure should be used. Accordingly, firms frequently classify projects into the following categories:

1. *Replacement: Maintenance of Business.* Expenditures necessary to replace worn-out or damaged equipment are in this group.
2. *Replacement: Cost Reduction.* Expenditures to replace serviceable but obsolete equipment fall into this category. The purpose of these expenditures is to lower the cost of labor, materials, or other items such as electricity.
3. *Expansion of Existing Products or Markets.* Expenditures to increase output of existing products, or to expand outlets or distribution facilities in markets now being served, are included here.
4. *Expansion into New Products or Markets.* These are expenditures necessary to produce a new product, or to expand into a geographic area not currently being served.
5. *Safety and/or Environmental Projects.* Expenditures necessary to comply with government orders, labor agreements, or insurance policy terms are listed here. These expenditures are often called *mandatory investments,* or *non-revenue-producing projects.*
6. *Other.* This catch-all includes office buildings, parking lots, and so on.

In general, relatively simple calculations and only a few supporting documents are required for replacement decisions, especially maintenance-type investments in profitable plants. More detailed analysis is required for cost reduction replacements, for expansion of existing product lines, and for investments into new products or areas. Also, within each category, projects are broken down by their dollar costs: the larger the required investment, the more detailed the analysis and the higher the level of the officer who must authorize the expenditure. Thus, while a plant manager may be authorized to approve maintenance expenditures up to $10,000 on the basis of a relatively unsophisticated analysis, the full board of directors may have to approve decisions which involve either amounts over $1 million or expansions into new products or markets, and a very detailed, refined analysis will be required to support these decisions.

The most important, but also the most difficult, step in the analysis of a capital expenditure proposal is the estimation of the cash flows associated with the project—the outflows associated with building and equipping

Estimating the Cash Flows

Table 11-1
Carter Chemical Company: Estimated Investment Requirements for Compound X, 1982-1985

	1982	1983	1984	1985	Total
Required Investment (Supported by Engineering Estimate)					
Capital					
1. Land	$ 0	$ 0	$	$	$ 0
2. Land improvements	0	0			0
3. Buildings	475,000	511,000			986,000
4. Process equipment	1,000,000	1,702,000			2,702,000
5. Mobile equipment		75,000			75,000
Less: Investment tax credit	(102,570)	(160,430)			(263,000)
6. Subtotal	$1,372,430	$2,127,570			$3,500,000
Expenses					
7. Relocations	0	0			0
8. ———					
9. ———					
10. Subtotal	$	$	$	$	$
11. Total authorized	$1,372,430	$2,127,570			$3,500,000
Working Capital					
12. Accounts receivable	$	$ 742,500	$148,500	$ 99,000	$ 990,000
13. Raw materials inventory		157,500	31,500	21,000	210,000
14. Parts inventory		0	0	0	0
15. Goods in process		180,000	36,000	24,000	240,000
16. Finished materials inventory		202,500	40,500	27,000	270,000
17. Operating materials and supplies		112,500	22,500	15,000	150,000
18. Payables/accruals	( )	(270,000)	(54,000)	(36,000)	(360,000)
19. Net working capital	$	$1,125,000	$225,000	$150,000	$1,500,000
Total investment (Lines 11 + 19)					$5,000,000

the new facility and the annual cash inflows the project will produce after it goes into operation. A great many variables are involved in the cash flow forecast, and many individuals and departments participate in developing them. We cannot in this book fully develop the techniques and methodologies used in cash flow analysis, but an examination of Tables 11-1 through 11-4 will give an idea of what is entailed. The example used is taken from the files of a major industrial firm, which we shall call Carter Chemical Company. Carter's cash flow analysis for the Compound X project is typical of that used in all types of businesses with sales in excess of about $10 million.[1]

Table 11-1 summarizes the investment outlay required for the project. A total of $5 million is necessary: $3.5 million for land, buildings, and equipment, and $1.5 million for the net investment in working capital. These expenditures will be incurred over a four year period, from 1982 through 1985. The plant will be constructed and equipped in 1982 and 1983, while working capital will be built up during 1983, 1984, and 1985.

Table 11-2 shows a series of income statements detailing the expected cash flows during certain years of the project's projected fifteen year service life. Sales in both units and dollars are shown, after which the various types of expenses and taxes are deducted to produce the net income expected from the project as shown on the third line from the bottom. These incremental profits are *before* financing charges; the cost of the capital used to finance the project is accounted for when the cash flows are discounted to find their present value.[2] Depreciation, which is not a cash outlay, is added to profits to produce the bottom-line figures, the net cash flows from the project.[3]

The new plant will go into service in 1983, and it is expected to generate a net cash flow of $601,155 in that year. Cash flows are expected to climb during the next two years, as the plant is broken in and the market

---

[1] The company has eighteen printed forms upon which different types of information related to capital expenditures are submitted. Not all the forms are used for every investment decision, but most are used for larger projects. For the illustrative case, fifteen forms were completed, in addition to a great many worksheets, letters, memos, and so on that were developed in the course of analyzing the project. Firms do not make $5 million expenditures on the basis of a casual analysis, at least not if they wish to survive.

[2] The process of discounting a future cash flow has the effect of reducing it by an amount sufficient to cover the cost of the capital investment needed to produce the cash flow. Thus, if financing charges were included in the income statements given in Table 11-2, and if the net cash flows were later discounted, then we would be counting the financing costs twice.

[3] If the treatment of depreciation is not clear, recognize that net sales represent cash received, and that all items *except depreciation* represent cash outlays during the year. Thus, Carter expects to have net sales for cash of $4.5 million in 1983 and to incur *cash* costs for taxes and all costs shown *except* depreciation, so that $4.5 million cash from net sales, minus cash costs totaling $3,051,000 + $696,825 = $3,747,825, minus $151,020 income taxes, equals $601,155. The $601,155 cash flow is, of course, also equal to net income after tax plus depreciation.

Table 11-2
Carter Chemical Company: Cash Flow Analysis for Compound X

Profit Center: Textile Products
Location: Raleigh, N.C.
Title: Plant to Manufacture Compound X

			Estimated Profits and Cash Flows				
	1983	1984	1985	1986	Years 1987 through 1995 are not shown here.	1996	1997
Quantity shipped, tons	75,000	90,000	100,000	100,000		100,000	100,000
Gross sales, dollars	$4,564,000	$5,477,000	$6,085,000	$6,085,000		$6,085,000	$6,085,000
Less: Freight	46,000	55,000	61,000	61,000		61,000	61,000
Cash discounts	18,000	22,000	24,000	24,000		24,000	24,000
Total deductions	64,000	77,000	85,000	85,000		85,000	85,000
Net sales	$4,500,000	$5,400,000	$6,000,000	$6,000,000		$6,000,000	$6,000,000
Cost of sales							
Variable	$2,340,000	$2,880,000	$3,240,000	$3,240,000		$3,240,000	$3,240,000
Fixed, excluding depreciation and depletion	360,000	360,000	360,000	360,000		360,000	360,000
Break-in costs	351,000	144,000	—	—		—*	—
Total	3,051,000	3,384,000	3,600,000	3,600,000		3,600,000	3,600,000
Depreciation	437,550	408,380	379,210	350,040		58,290	29,120
Total cost of sales	$3,488,550	$3,792,380	$3,979,210	$3,950,040		$3,658,290	$3,629,120
Gross profit	$1,011,450	$1,607,620	$2,020,790	$2,049,960		$2,341,710	$2,370,880
Selling expenses	240,000	240,000	240,000	240,000		240,000	240,000
Advertising	130,000	105,000	90,000	90,000		90,000	90,000
Administrative	300,000	300,000	300,000	300,000		300,000	300,000
Provision for bad debts	26,825	31,325	34,325	34,325		34,325	34,325
Total: Selling, etc., costs	696,825	676,325	664,325	664,325		664,325	664,325
Net income before tax	314,625	931,295	1,356,465	1,385,635		1,677,385	1,706,555
State and federal income tax @ 48%	151,020	447,022	651,103	665,105		805,145	819,146
Net income	163,605	484,273	705,362	720,530		872,240	887,409
Add back depreciation	437,550	408,380	379,210	350,040		58,290	29,120
Net cash flow	$ 601,155	$ 892,653	$1,084,572	$1,070,570		$ 930,530	$ 916,529

Salvage value: buildings and machines = 0
Recovery of working capital = $1,500,000
Net cash flow, year 1997 = $2,416,529

is developed, but to decline thereafter because of rising taxes caused by declining deductions for depreciation.[4]

Table 11-3 lists the critical assumptions that were made in developing the cash flow estimates shown in Table 11-2. They are of key importance, for the most serious errors in capital budgeting are caused by incorrect assumptions about basic operating conditions. Mistakes in these basic assumptions will lead to incorrect cash flow forecasts and, consequently, to bad accept-reject decisions. For this reason, executives pay a great deal of attention to the basic assumptions used to generate expected cash flows.

**Table 11-3
Carter Chemical
Company: Key
Assumptions in the
Cash Flow Analysis
for Compound X**

1. It is assumed that the annual sales volume will be 100,000 tons by the third year. This is 10 percent of projected industry sales. These estimates are based on (a) the results of a test marketing program for our newly patented Compound X and (b) the market potential as projected for the next fifteen years by the Market Research Department.
2. The net sales price will be $60.00 per ton. This estimate is based on present competitive price levels as determined by the Marketing Department.
3. The assumed production rates, lost time, and labor crew requirements were estimated by the Production Department and are consistent with design speeds approved by the Engineering Department.
4. The assumed labor rates, fringe benefits, training, and availability are based on studies in the plant site area made by the Industrial Relations Department.
5. It is assumed that pollution control standards will not be increased.
6. Selling and advertising expenses, which were estimated by the Marketing Department, are based on other products sold to the textile industry.
7. The assumed percentages of general and administrative expenses are based on past experience.
8. Fuel costs are based on oil at $32 per barrel.
9. An inflation rate of 8 percent in labor and materials cost is expected. Sales prices will increase at this same rate.[a]
10. The $5 million of capital needed to undertake the project can be raised at an average cost (average of debt and equity) of 10 percent.

[a]Table 11-2 is, in effect, stated in 1982 dollars. In current dollars, sales and costs are both expected to rise by 8 percent per year. See Chapter 12 for more on inflation.

---

[4] Carter Chemical, like most firms, uses accelerated depreciation for tax calculations. This causes depreciation (a noncash charge) to be high early in the project's life, lower later on. The high initial depreciation results in lower taxes, hence in higher cash flows during the early years.

Two other points are worth mentioning here. First, people sometimes ask, "What happens to the cash flows shown at the bottom of Table 11-2?" The answer is that they go into Carter Chemical's coffers for payment of interest and dividends, as well as for reinvestment in other projects. The second point has to do with the recovery of working capital. As we saw in Chapter 7, some amount of working capital (inventories and receivables, less payables and accruals) must be held to support sales. In this case, the investment in net working capital is $1.5 million, and this investment must be maintained intact as long as operations continue. Thus, the $1.5 million net working capital will be needed until the plant closes in 1997. During that year, as operations are closed down, inventories will be sold off and not replaced, and receivables will be collected with no new ones created because sales will cease. Thus, during 1997 the $1.5 million of working capital will be converted to cash and, presumably, reinvested elsewhere in the company.

Profit Center: Textile Products
Location: Raleigh, North Carolina
Title: Construct Plant to Manufacture Compound X
Authorization Number: 550-0080-0001
Date: September 1981
Amount Requested: $5,000,000

**Table 11-4
Carter Chemical
Company: Authorization
for Expenditure**

Description of Request—Summary:

Construction of a plant in Raleigh for the manufacture of 100,000 tons of Compound X annually. This new product, used in the dyeing process for textile fibers, will be shipped from Raleigh primarily to the Southeastern United States.

After Approval—Estimated Start: January 1982, Completion: March 1983.

Benefits of Request—Summary:

The addition of Compound X to the existing products we sell to the textile industry will complete our product line and substantially improve our competitive position. The net present value ($2.3 million) is favorable, and the projected future product growth is large, so these returns could be bettered.

Classification of Project	**Return on Investment**	**Predicted Performance— First 10 Years**		
		Year	**Net Sales**	**Net Cash Flow**
☒ New Business	Net present value: $2,303,581			
☐ Expansion—Existing Business		1983	$4,500,000	$ 601,155
☐ Cost Reduction	Internal Rate of Return: 17%	1984	5,400,000	892,653
☐ Replacement		1985	6,000,000	1,084,572
☐ Quality		1986	6,000,000	1,070,570
☐ Safety/Environmental	Payback: (useful life, 15 yrs.) 5.25 Yrs.	1987	6,000,000	1,056,569
☐ _____		1988	6,000,000	1,042,567
		1989	6,000,000	1,028,565
		1990	6,000,000	1,014,564
	Breakeven percent of capacity: 46.2%	1991	6,000,000	1,000,543
		1992	6,000,000	986,551

Summary of Expenditures Proposed Expenditures:

	1982	1983	1984-85	Total
Capital	$1,372,430	$2,127,570	$ —	$3,500,000
Working Funds	—	1,125,000	375,000	1,500,000
Total Investment	$1,372,430	$3,252,570	$375,000	$5,000,000

Profit Center—Reviews and Approvals

Marketing _M.R._ Date _10/15/81_   Industrial Relations _W.T._ Date _9-12-81_

Production _C.M._ Date _10/8/81_   Cost Accounting _J.W._ Date _10/18/81_

Engineering _B.P._ Date _9/12/81_   Chief Operations Officer _____ Date _10/20/81_

(continued)

Corporate—Reviews and Approvals

Tax _____F.M._____ Date _11/2/81_   Chief Financial Officer _F.M._ Date _11/20/81_

Legal _____Q.C._____ Date _11/10/81_   President _____P.V.F._____ Date _11/25/81_

Director of
Capital
Budgeting _____D.O._____ Date _11-15-81_   Board of Directors _____C.L._____ Date _12-1-81_

Table 11-4 summarizes the analysis of the Compound X expenditure proposal; it provides information on the investment outlays, the projected cash flows from the project, and the expected profitability of the project (the "net present value" and "internal rate of return," which will be explained later in the chapter). Note also that the summary sheet has been reviewed by marketing, production, engineering, accounting, and industrial relations people at the profit center.[5] They must verify that they consider the cash flows, investment requirements, and so on to be reasonable estimates. If the project is undertaken and turns out to be unprofitable, these are the people who will be required to explain what went wrong, so they are careful in making their estimates. Note also that the project is reviewed at the corporate level. Since this is a major project, its approval must go all the way up to the board of directors. Had this project involved only $5,000, it could have been approved at the profit center level, and no initials would appear in the section headed "Corporate—Reviews and Approvals."

Methods Used to Evaluate Proposed Projects

A number of different methods are used to rank projects and to decide whether or not they should be accepted for inclusion in the capital budget. Three of the most commonly used are these:[6]

1. *Payback (or Payback Period).* This is the number of years required to return the original investment.
2. *Net Present Value (NPV).* This is the present value of future cash flows, discounted at the appropriate cost of capital, minus the cost of the investment. The NPV (and also the IRR) method is called a *discounted cash flow (DCF)* method.

---

[5] A *profit center* is an operating unit with responsibility for a given product line or geographic area. Carter Chemical has twelve profit centers, one of which is Textile Products.

[6] A number of "average rate of return" methods have been discussed in the literature and are used in practice. These methods are generally unsound and are rapidly being replaced by the methods considered here. Also, a "benefit/cost," or "profitability index," method is sometimes used. This method is described in Appendix 11C.

3. *Internal Rate of Return (IRR).* This is the discount rate that equates the present value of the expected future cash flows to the initial cost of the project. The IRR corresponds to the yield-to-maturity on a bond.

Future cash flows are, in all cases, defined as the expected annual net cash inflows from the investments. The nature and characteristics of the three methods are illustrated and explained below, where we use the cash flow data shown in Table 11-5 for Projects S and L to illustrate each method. For now, we assume that the projects are equally risky. Note that cash flows consist of both after-tax profits and depreciation, not profits alone. Also, most projects require both fixed assets and an addition to net working capital as in the Compound X case; the investment outlays in Table 11-5 include any necessary working capital, and the cash flow in the last year includes the return of these funds.

	Net Cash Flow (= Profit after Taxes plus Depreciation)		
Year		Project S	Project L
1		$ 500	$ 100
2		400	300
3		300	400
4		100	600
Total inflows		$1,300	$1,400
Investment outlay, or initial cost at Time 0		$1,000	$1,000

**Table 11-5
Cash Flows for
Projects S and L**

Payback Method

The payback period is defined as the number of years it takes a firm to recover its original investment from net cash flows. Since both projects cost $1,000, the payback period is $2^1/_3$ years for Project S and $3^1/_3$ years for Project L. If the firm were to require a payback of three years or less, Project S would be accepted, but Project L would be rejected. If the projects were *mutually exclusive*, S would be accepted over L because S has the shorter payback.[7] Thus, the payback method ranks S over L. Incidentally, the S stands for *short* and the L for *long*: Project S is a short-term project and L a long-term one in the sense that S's cash inflows tend to come sooner than L's.

[7] *Mutually exclusive* projects are alternative investments; if one project is taken on, the other must be rejected. For example, the installation of a conveyor belt system in a warehouse and the purchase of a fleet of fork trucks for the same warehouse would be mutually exclusive projects—accepting one implies rejection of the other. *Independent* projects are projects whose costs and revenues are independent of one another. For example, the Compound X project and the purchase of a corporate jet by Carter Chemical would represent independent projects.

Prior to the 1960s the payback was the most commonly used method for screening capital expenditure proposals. It is still widely used, but generally only for smaller replacement projects or as a risk indicator for larger projects. Some features of the payback, which indicate both its strengths and its weaknesses, are listed below:

1. *Ease of Calculation.* The payback is easy to calculate and apply. This was an important consideration in the precomputer, precalculator days.
2. *Ignores Returns beyond Payback Period.* One glaring weakness of the payback method is that it ignores cash flows beyond the payback period. Thus, Project L might have had a cash flow of $1,000 in Year 5, but this fact would not influence either the payback or a payback ranking of Projects S and L. Ignoring returns in the distant future means that the payback method is biased against long-term projects.
3. *Ignores Time Value of Money.* The timing of cash flows is obviously important, yet the payback method ignores the time value of money. A dollar in Year 3 is given the same weight as a dollar in Year 1.

Net Present Value (NPV) Method

As the flaws in the payback method were recognized, people began to search for methods of evaluating projects that would recognize that a dollar received immediately is preferable to a dollar received at some future date. This led to the development of *discounted cash flow (DCF)* techniques to take account of the time value of money. One such DCF technique is called the *net present value method. To implement this approach, find the present value of the expected net cash flows of an investment, discounted at an appropriate percentage rate, and subtract from it the initial cost outlay of the project.* If its net present value is positive, the project should be accepted; if negative, it should be rejected. If two projects are mutually exclusive, the one with the higher net present value should be chosen.

The equation for the net present value (NPV) is

$$
\begin{aligned}
NPV &= \left[\frac{CF_1}{(1 + k)^1} + \frac{CF_2}{(1 + k)^2} + \cdots + \frac{CF_n}{(1 + k)^n} \right] - C \\
&= \sum_{t=1}^{n} \frac{CF_t}{(1 + k)^t} - C \\
&= CF_1(PVIF_{k,1}) + CF_2(PVIF_{k,2}) + \cdots + CF_n(PVIF_{k,n}) - C.
\end{aligned}
\tag{11-1}
$$

Here, CF_1, CF_2, and so forth represent the annual receipts, or net cash flows; k is the appropriate discount rate, or the project's cost of capital; C is the initial cost of the project; and n is the project's expected life. The cost of capital, k, depends on the riskiness of the project, the level of interest rates in the economy, and several other factors. In this chapter we take k as a given, but it is discussed in detail in Chapter 15.

The net present values of Projects S and L are calculated in Table 11-6, using the procedures developed in Chapter 3. Assuming that they each have a 10 percent cost of capital, Project S has an NPV of $78.80, while L's NPV is $49.15. On this basis, both should be accepted if they are independent, but S should be the one chosen if they are mutually exclusive.

If costs are spread over several years, this must be taken into account. Suppose, for example, that a firm bought land in 1981, erected a building in 1982, installed equipment in 1983, and started production in 1984. One could treat 1981 as the base year, comparing the present value of the costs as of 1981 to the present value of the benefit stream as of that same date. Also, note that Equation 11-1 can be written with the summation beginning with $t = 0$ rather than $t = 1$:

$$NPV = \sum_{t=0}^{n} \frac{CF_t}{(1 + k)^t}. \qquad (11\text{-}1a)$$

In this alternative format, CF_0 is the initial investment, or cost, made at Time $t = 0$, and it is *negative*. The alternative format is especially useful for considering projects for which the investment costs are incurred over several years, as was true of Carter Chemical's Compound X project. Equation 11-1a is actually used later on in the chapter when we calculate the NPV for Compound X.

	Project S			Project L		
Year	Net Cash Flow	PVIF (10%)	PV of Cash Flow	Net Cash Flow	PVIF (10%)	PV of Cash Flow
1	$500	0.9091	$ 454.55	$100	0.9091	$ 90.91
2	400	0.8264	330.56	300	0.8264	247.92
3	300	0.7513	225.39	400	0.7513	300.52
4	100	0.6830	68.30	600	0.6830	409.80
	PV of inflows		$1,078.80	PV of inflows		$1,049.15
	Less cost		−1,000.00	Less cost		−1,000.00
	NPV_S =		$ 78.80	NPV_L =		$ 49.15

Table 11-6
Calculating the Net Present Values (NPVs) of Projects S and L

The value of a firm is a composite of the values of its parts. Thus, when a firm takes on a project with a positive NPV, the value of the firm should increase by the amount of the NPV. In our example, the value of the firm increases by $78.80 if it takes on Project S, but by only $49.15 if it takes on Project L. *The increase in the value of the firm from its capital budget for the year is the sum of the NPVs of all accepted projects.* Viewed in this manner, it is easy to see why S, which adds $78.80 to the value of the firm, is preferred to L, which adds only $49.15, and it is also easy to see the logic of the NPV approach.[8]

The Internal Rate of Return (IRR)

In Chapter 4 we examined procedures for finding the rate of return on a bond purchased and held as an investment. This rate of return is called the *yield-to-maturity* (YTM), and if a bond's YTM exceeds its required rate of return, then it represents a good investment. Exactly the same concepts are employed in capital budgeting when the internal rate of return method is used.

The internal rate of return (IRR) is the discount rate that equates the present value of the expected future cash flows, or receipts, to the initial cost of the project. The equation for calculating this rate is

$$\frac{CF_1}{(1 + r)^1} + \frac{CF_2}{(1 + r)^2} + \cdots + \frac{CF_n}{(1 + r)^n} - C = 0$$

$$\sum_{t=1}^{n} \frac{CF_t}{(1 + r)^t} - C = 0 \qquad (11\text{-}2)$$

$$CF_1(PVIF_{r,1}) + CF_2(PVIF_{r,2}) + \cdots + CF_n(PVIF_{r,n}) - C = 0.$$

Here we know the value of C and also the values of CF_1, CF_2, . . ., CF_n, but we do not know the value of r. Thus, we have an equation with one unknown, and we can solve for the value of r. *Some value of r will cause the sum of the discounted receipts to equal the initial cost of the project, making the equation equal to zero: This value of r is defined as the internal rate of return.* In other words, the solution value of r is the IRR.

Notice that the internal rate of return formula, Equation 11-2, is simply the NPV formula, Equation 11-1, solved for the particular discount rate that causes the NPV to equal zero. Thus, the same basic equation is used for both methods, but in the NPV method the discount rate, k, is specified and the NPV is found, while in the IRR method the NPV is specified to equal zero and the value of r that forces the NPV to equal zero is found.[9]

The internal rate of return may be found in a number of ways. Several methods are discussed in the following section.

---

[8] One important point should be noted here: If a new product competes with one of the firm's existing products, then this fact must be considered when analyzing the new project. In essence, we must reduce the net cash flows of the new project by the amount that the cash flows from the old project will be reduced. Thus, we end up with net *incremental* cash flows from the new project—the amount by which the *firm's* cash flows will be increased if the project is accepted.

[9] If costs are incurred over several years, Equation 11-2 must be modified in the same manner as the modified version of Equation 11-1, which is used to find the NPV (see Equation 11-1a). In fact, we can modify Equation 11-1a as follows: (1) set NPV = 0, and (2) replace k with r. Now solve for r; the solution value is the IRR. This equation, with the graphic method explained below, was used to determine the IRR for the Carter Chemical Compound X project, which was determined to be 17 percent.

Procedure 1: IRR with Constant Cash Inflows. If the cash flows from a project are constant, or equal in each year, then the project's internal rate of return can be found by a relatively simple process. In essence, such a project is an annuity: the firm makes an outlay, C, and receives a stream of cash flow benefits, CF_t, for a given number of years. The IRR for the project is found by applying Equation 3-5, discussed in Chapter 3.

To illustrate, suppose a project has a cost of $10,000 and is expected to produce cash flows of $1,627.45 a year for ten years. The cost of the project, $10,000, is the present value of an annuity of $1,627.45 a year for ten years, so applying Equation 3-5, we obtain

$$\frac{\text{Cost}}{\text{CF}} = \frac{\$10,000}{\$1,627.45} = 6.1446 = \text{PVIFA}_{k,n}.$$

Looking up PVIFA in Table A-2 in Appendix A (at the end of the book) across the row for Year 10, we find it located under the 10 percent column. Accordingly, 10 percent is the project's IRR. In other words, 10 percent is the value of r that would force Equation 11-2 to zero when CF is constant at $1,627.45 per year for ten years and C is $10,000. This procedure works only if the project has constant annual cash flows; if it does not, the IRR must be found by one of the methods discussed below.

Procedure 2: Trial and Error. In the trial and error method, we first compute the present value of cash flows from an investment, using a somewhat arbitrarily selected discount rate. Since the cost of capital for most firms is in the range of 10 to 20 percent, it is to be hoped that projects will promise a return of at least 10 percent. Therefore, 10 percent is a good starting point for most problems. Then we compare the present value so obtained with the investment's cost. Suppose the present value of the inflows is *larger* than the project's cost. What do we do now? We must *lower* the present value, and to do this we must *raise* the discount rate and go through the process again. Conversely, if the present value is lower than the cost, we lower the discount rate and repeat the process. We continue until the present value of the flows from the investment is approximately equal to the project's cost. *The discount rate that brings about this equality is defined as the internal rate of return.*

This calculation process is illustrated in Table 11-7 for the same Projects S and L that we analyzed earlier. First, the 10 percent interest factors are obtained from Table A-1 in Appendix A, at the end of the text. These factors are then multiplied by the cash flows for the corresponding years, and the present values of the annual cash flows are placed in the appropriate columns. Next, the present values of the yearly cash flows are summed to obtain the investment's total present value. Subtracting the cost of the project from this figure gives the net present value. Because the net present value of both investments is positive at the 10 percent rate, we increase the rate to 15 percent and try again. At this point the net present value of S is just below zero, which indicates that its internal rate of return is slightly less than 15 percent. L's net present value at 15 percent is well below zero, so its IRR is quite a bit less than 15 percent.

Table 11-7
Finding the Internal Rate of Return for Projects S and L

					Cash Flows (CF$_t$ Values)	
				Year	S	L
C = investment = $1,000.				1	$ 500	$ 100
				2	400	300
				3	300	400
				4	100	600
	Total cash flows				$1,300	$1,400

| | | 10% | | | 15% | |
| | | Present Value | | | Present Value | |
Year	PVIF	PV$_S$	PV$_L$	PVIF	PV$_S$	PV$_L$
1	0.9091	$ 454.55	$ 90.91	0.8696	$ 434.80	$ 86.96
2	0.8264	330.56	247.92	0.7561	302.44	226.83
3	0.7513	225.39	300.52	0.6575	197.25	263.00
4	0.6830	68.30	409.80	0.5718	57.18	343.08
Present value		$1,078.80	$1,049.15		$ 991.67	$ 919.87
Less cost		1,000.00	1,000.00		1,000.00	1,000.00
Net present value		$ 78.80	$ 49.15		$ (8.33)	$ (80.13)

These trials could be continued to obtain closer and closer approximations to the exact IRR, but, as noted below, procedures are available to speed up the process.

Procedure 3: Graphic Solution. The third method for finding IRRs involves plotting curves that show the relationship between a project's NPV and the discount rate used to calculate the NPV. Such a curve is defined as the project's *net present value profile;* profiles for Projects L and S are shown in Figure 11-1. To construct the graph, we first note that at a zero discount rate, the NPV is simply the total undiscounted cash flows less the cost of the project; thus, at a zero discount rate NPV$_S$ = $1,300 − $1,000 = $300, while NPV$_L$ = $400. These values are plotted as the vertical axis intercepts in Figure 11-1. Next, we calculate the projects' NPVs at three discount rates, say 5, 10, and 15 percent, and plot these values. (Since we have already calculated NPVs at 10 percent and 15 percent, we may take these values from Table 11-7.) The four points plotted on our graph are these:

Discount Rate	NPV$_S$	NPV$_L$
0%	$300.00	$400.00
5	180.42	206.50
10	78.80	49.15
15	(8.33)	(80.13)

When we connect these points, we have the net present value profiles.[10]

Since the IRR is defined as the discount rate at which a project's NPV equals zero, *the point where its net present value profile crosses the horizontal axis indicates the project's internal rate of return.* Figure 11-1 shows that IRR$_S$ is 14.5 percent, while IRR$_L$ is 11.8 percent. With graph paper and a sharp pencil, the graphic method yields reasonably accurate results.[11]

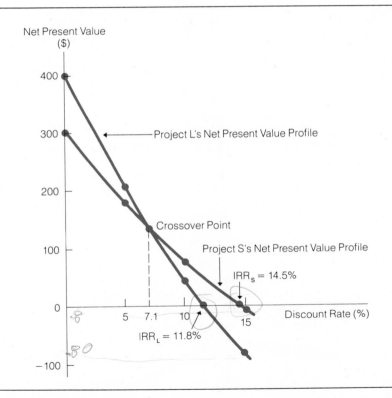

Figure 11-1
Net Present Value Profiles: NPVs of Projects S and L at Different Discount Rates

[10] Notice that the present value profiles are curved—they are *not* straight lines. Also, the NPVs approach the negative of the cost of the project as the discount rate increases without limit. The reason is that, at an infinitely high discount rate, the PV of the inflows would be zero, and NPV = 0 − Cost = −Cost. We should also note that under certain conditions the NPV profiles can cross the horizontal axis several times, or never cross it. This point is discussed in Appendix 11B.

[11] For all practical purposes, an IRR that is accurate to within about one-half percent is sufficient, given

(continued)

Procedure 4: Computer and Financial Calculator Solutions. Since internal rates of return can be calculated very easily by computers, many firms have computerized their capital budgeting processes and automatically generate IRRs, NPVs, and paybacks for all projects. Even some hand-held calculators are programmed to compute IRRs. Thus, business firms have no difficulty whatever with the mechanical side of capital budgeting.

Rationale and Use of the IRR Method

What is so special about the particular discount rate that equates a project's cost with the present value of its receipts? To answer this question, let us first assume that our firm obtains the $1,000 needed to take on Project S by borrowing from a bank at an interest rate of 14.5 percent. Since the internal rate of return on this particular project was calculated to be 14.5 percent, the same as the cost of the bank loan, the firm can invest in the project, use the cash flows generated by the investment to pay off the principal and interest on the loan, and come out exactly even on the transaction. This point is demonstrated in the following tabulation, which shows that Project S provides cash flows that are just sufficient to pay 14.5 percent interest on the unpaid balance of a bank loan, retire the loan over the life of the project, and end up with a balance that differs from zero only by a rounding error of thirty-two cents:

Beginning Investment (1)	Cash Flow (2)	Interest on the Loan at 14.5% (3) = 0.145 × (1)	Return of Capital (4) = (2) − (3)	Ending Balance (5) = (1) − (4)
$1,000.00	$500	$145.00	$355.00	$645.00
645.00	400	93.53	306.47	338.53
338.53	300	49.09	250.91	87.62
87.62	100	12.70	87.30	0.32

If the internal rate of return exceeds the cost of the funds used to finance the project, a surplus is left over after paying for the capital. This surplus accrues to the firm's stockholders, so taking on the project increases the value of the firm. If the internal rate of return is less than the cost of capital, taking on the project imposes a cost on existing stockholders, so in this case accepting the project would result in a reduction of value. It is this "breakeven" characteristic that makes us interested in the internal rate of return.[12]

the inaccuracy of the cash flow estimates. The calculations may be carried out to several decimal places, but for most projects this is spurious accuracy.

[12] This example illustrates the logic of the IRR method, but for technical correctness, the capital used to finance the project should be assumed to come from both debt and equity, not from debt alone. This point is discussed further in Chapter 15.

Continuing with our example of Projects L and S, if the firm has a cost of capital of 10 percent, the internal rate of return criterion indicates that if the projects are independent, both should be accepted—they both do better than "break even." If they are mutually exclusive, S ranks higher and should be accepted, while L should be rejected. If the cost of capital is 15 percent, both projects should be rejected.

NPV Rankings Depend on the Discount Rate

We saw in Figure 11-1 that each project's NPV declines as the discount rate increases. Notice in the figure that Project L has the higher NPV at low discount rates, while NPV_S is greater than NPV_L if the discount rate exceeds 7.1 percent. Notice also that Project L's NPV is "more sensitive" to changes in the discount rate than is NPV_S; that is, Project L's net present value profile has the steeper slope, indicating that a small change in k has a larger effect on NPV_L than on NPV_S.

To see why L has the greater sensitivity, recall first that the cash flows from S are received faster than those from L; in a payback sense, S is a short-term project, while L is a long-term project. This point is emphasized in Figure 11-2, which graphs the projects' cash flows over time.

Next, recall the equation for the NPV:

$$NPV = \frac{CF_1}{(1 + k)^1} + \frac{CF_2}{(1 + k)^2} + \frac{CF_3}{(1 + k)^3} + \frac{CF_4}{(1 + k)^4} - C.$$

Now notice that the denominators of the terms in this equation increase as k and t increase, and that the increase is exponential; that is, the effect

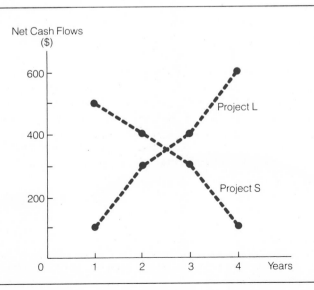

**Figure 11-2
Timing of Cash Flows: Cash Flow Patterns for Projects S and L**

of a higher k is more pronounced if t is larger. To understand this point more clearly, consider the following data:

PV of $100 due in 1 year, discounted at 5%	$95.24
PV of $100 due in 1 year, discounted at 10%	$90.91
Percentage decline in PV resulting from increased k	−4.5%
PV of $100 due in 10 years, discounted at 5%	$61.39
PV of $100 due in 10 years, discounted at 10%	$38.55
Percentage decline in PV resulting from increased k	−37.2%

Thus, if a project has most of its cash flows coming in early years, its NPV will not be lowered very much if the discount rate increases, but a project whose cash flows come later will be severely penalized by high discount rates. Accordingly, Project L, which has its largest cash flows in the later years, looks relatively good when the discount rate is low but bad when the rate is high, while Project S, which has relatively rapid cash flows, receives a less adverse impact from high discount rates.[13]

Application of the NPV and IRR Methods to Carter Chemical

Table 11-8 gives a time line that shows the timing of cash flows for Project X. The cash flows in this table were taken from Tables 11-1, 11-2, and 11-4. The project's NPV is calculated to be $2,303,581.

To see this, refer back to Carter Chemical's Project X, Tables 11-1 and 11-2. Carter used January 1, 1982, as $t = 0$. Further, Carter assumed that all the investment outlays reported in Table 11-1 would be incurred at the *beginning* of each year but that the cash inflows reported in Table 11-2 would be received at the *end* of the year in question. Thus, CF_0 = 1982 total expenditures = −$1,372,430; CF_1 = 1983 expenditures = −$2,127,570 − $1,125,000 = −$3,252,570; CF_2 = 1984 expenditures (incurred at the *beginning* of 1984) + 1983 inflows (assumed received at the *end* of 1983) = *minus* $225,000 *plus* $601,155 = +$376,155; CF_3 = 1984 inflows − $150,000 = $742,653, etc.; down to CF_{16} = 1997 inflows + return of working capital = $916,529 + $1,500,000 = $2,416,529. Inserting these values and k = 10% into Equation 11-1a resulted in the equation

$$NPV = -\frac{\$1,372,430}{(1.10)^0} - \frac{\$3,252,570}{(1.10)^1} + \frac{\$376,155}{(1.10)^2} + \cdots + \frac{\$2,416,529}{(1.10)^{16}}.$$

[13] The situation here is exactly like the one described for long- and short-term bonds in Figure 4-3, where we saw that the prices of long-term bonds are much more sensitive to interest rate changes than are short-term bond prices.

Table 11-8
Calculating the NPV for Project X

Year	1/1/82 t = 0	1/1/83 1	12/31/83 or 1/1/84 2	12/31/84 or 1/1/85 3	12/31/85 4	12/31/86 5	12/31/87 6	12/31/88 7	12/31/89 8	12/31/90 9
		(2,127,570) (1,125,000)	601,155 (225,000)	892,653 (150,000)						
Net Cash Flow	(1,372,430)	(3,252,570)	376,155	742,653	1,084,572	1,070,570	1,056,569	1,042,567	1,028,565	1,014,564

(Continuation of Time Line)

	12/31/91 10	12/31/92 11	12/31/93 12	12/31/94 13	12/31/95 14	12/31/96 15	12/31/97 16
							916,529 1,500,000 (Working Capital)
	1,000,543	986,551	972,535	958,519	944,503	930,530	2,416,529

$$
\begin{aligned}
NPV &= \sum_{t=0}^{16} \frac{\text{Net cash flow}_t}{(1+k)^t} = \frac{-\$1,372,430}{(1.10)^0} + \frac{-\$3,252,570}{(1.10)^1} + \cdots + \frac{\$2,416,529}{(1.10)^{16}} \\
&= -\$1,372,430 + (-\$3,252,570)(PVIF_{10\%, 1yr.}) + \cdots + (\$2,416,529)(PVIF_{10\%, 16yrs.}) \\
&= (1,372,430) + (2,956,586) + 310,704 + 557,732 + 740,763 + 664,824 + 595,905 + 534,837 + \\
&\quad 480,340 + 430,175 + 386,210 + 345,293 + 310,239 + 277,971 + 248,404 + 222,397 + 526,803 \\
&= \$2,303,581.
\end{aligned}
$$

When the inflows for all the years were plugged in, the NPV was found to be $2,303,581. This may look like a formidable arithmetic problem, but with Carter's computerized capital budgeting system, it can be solved almost instantaneously. It is not even much work with a hand calculator.

Carter Chemical's capital budgeting process is computerized, so the company actually found IRR_X on the computer. However, one could check the computer solution by use of the graphic method described above. Simply find the NPV at discount rates of 0 percent, 10 percent (which is $2,303,581), 15 percent, and 20 percent; plot the NPVs against their respective discount rates; connect the points to obtain an NPV profile; and recognize that the discount rate shown as the horizontal axis intercept is the IRR. In this case, $IRR_X = 17$ percent.

The Post-Audit

The final aspect of the capital budgeting process is the *post-completion audit*, or *post-audit*, which involves (1) a comparison of actual results to those predicted in the request for funds, and (2) an explanation of observed differences. Carter Chemical, for example, requires that the operating divisions send a monthly report for the first six months after a project such as that for Compound X goes into operation, and a quarterly report thereafter until the project's results are up to expectations. From then on, reports on it are handled like those of other operations.

The post-audit has several purposes, including the following:

1. *Improve Forecasts.* When decision makers systematically compare their projections to actual outcomes, there is a tendency for estimates to improve. Conscious or unconscious biases are observed and eliminated; new forecasting methods are sought as the need for them becomes apparent; and people simply tend to do everything better, including forecasting, if they know that their actions are being monitored.

2. *Improve Operations.* Businesses are run by people, and people can perform at higher or lower levels of efficiency. When a divisional team has made a forecast about a new installation, its members are, in a sense, putting their reputations on the line. If Carter Chemical's executives forecast annual sales of 100,000 tons of Compound X and a production cost of $45 per ton, then *because of the post-audit* these executives have every incentive to "make it happen." If costs are above predicted levels, sales below expectations, and so on, then executives in production, sales, and other areas will strive to improve operations and to bring results into line with forecasts.

The post-audit is not a simple process. There are a number of factors that can cause complications. First, we must recognize that each element of the cash flow forecast is subject to uncertainty, so a percentage of all projects undertaken by any reasonably venturesome firm will necessarily go awry. This fact must be considered when appraising the performances of the operating executives who submit capital expenditure requests. Second, projects sometimes fail to meet expectations for reasons beyond the control of the operating executives and for reasons that no one could realistically be expected to anticipate.[14] For example, the imposition of price controls in the 1970s adversely affected many projects for which price increases had been projected, and the quadrupling of oil prices in the mid 1970s hurt others. Third, it is often difficult to separate the operating results of one investment from those of a larger system. While the Compound X project stands alone and permits ready identification of costs and revenues, the actual cost savings that result from a replacement project may be very hard to measure. Fourth, if the post-audit process is not used with care, executives may be reluctant to suggest potentially profitable but risky projects. And fifth, the executives who were actually responsible for a given decision may have moved on by the time the results of the decision are known.

Because of these difficulties, some firms tend to play down the importance of the post-audit. However, observations of both businesses and governmental units suggest that the best-run and most successful organizations are the ones that put the greatest stress on post-audits. Accordingly, the post-audit is one of the most important elements in a good capital budgeting system.

Other Issues in Capital Budgeting

Thus far, the chapter has outlined the basic procedures used by most firms when making decisions about investments in fixed assets. However, capital budgeting is a very complex subject, and we have by no means dealt with all the important issues. Some of the significant ones that have not been covered are listed here and discussed very briefly to provide an indication of the types of questions that can arise when one actually becomes involved in the capital budgeting process.

1. *Growth is preferable to "expansion."* A firm's earnings per share, hence its dividends and stock price, can grow over time even if it invests in projects with zero (or even negative) NPVs. Recognize that a project's NPV will be negative if its IRR is less than the cost of capital. However, if the IRR is positive, and if the project is financed with retained earnings, then taking on the project will make some contribution to earnings, hence to earnings growth, even if the IRR is less than the cost of capital. This being the case, why not take on projects with

---

[14] Because of such uncertainties, many firms include in the "request for expenditure" package a list of key assumptions such as the one shown in Table 11-3. Top managers often have more information on national political and economic trends than do division managers, engineers, and lower-level people, and highlighting the key assumptions in a separate exhibit helps to better utilize top management's unique expertise.

zero or even negative NPVs, so long as the IRRs are positive? The reason has to do with stockholders' *opportunity costs,* or what stockholders could do with earnings if they were distributed rather than invested in projects which earn less than their cost of capital. This point is discussed further in Chapter 15. The conclusion reached there is that stockholders are served best by having the firm accept only projects with NPV > 0.

2. *Conflicts in project rankings occur under NPV and IRR.* Look again at Figure 11-1. Notice that if the cost of capital is lower than the crossover rate, 7.1 percent, the NPV method ranks Project L higher but the IRR method indicates that Project S is better. Thus, if L and S are mutually exclusive, then L will be chosen if the NPV method is used and the cost of capital is below the crossover rate, but S will be selected if the firm uses IRR. There will be no conflict if the cost of capital is above the crossover rate. The reasons for this potential conflict are discussed in Appendix 11A. The appendix also suggests that NPV is usually the better method and that conflicts should be resolved in favor of the project with the higher NPV.

3. *Multiple IRRs may be found.* Under certain conditions, more than one value of r solves Equation 11-2. Thus, a project can have more than one IRR. The reason for this situation is explained in Appendix 11B.

4. *The size of the capital budget can have an effect on the cost of capital.* Throughout this chapter, we have assumed that the firm's cost of capital is a given constant. However, as is shown in Chapter 15, the size of the capital budget can influence the cost of capital, hence the acceptability of specific projects.

5. *Capital may be rationed.* Firms occasionally set limits on the amount of money they will spend on fixed assets; this is called *capital rationing.* Thus, it is conceivable that a firm may end up with more projects having acceptable NPVs or IRRs than it is willing to finance. This situation is discussed in Chapter 12.

6. *Project risk must be taken into account.* Thus far, we have abstracted from the riskiness of different projects. This subject is taken up in Chapter 12.

7. *The cost of capital is critical.* The cost of capital, which is the discount rate used in the NPV method and the cutoff rate in the IRR method, is difficult to estimate, yet vital to the capital budgeting process. Methods for estimating the cost of capital are discussed in Chapter 15.

8. *Inflation must be dealt with.* The best procedure is to estimate inflation rates for the product's sales price and also for each cost item, and then to let these rates be reflected in the cash flows as shown in Table 11-2 for Compound X. Inflation is discussed in Chapter 12.

Capital budgeting is similar in principle to security valuation—future cash flows are estimated, risks are appraised and reflected in a cost of capital discount rate, all cash flows are put on a present value basis, and if a project's *net present value* (NPV) is positive, it is accepted. In outline form, the capital budgeting process centers around the following steps:

Summary

1. Ideas for projects are developed.
2. Projects are classified by type of investment: replacement, expansion of existing product lines, expansion into new markets, and "other."
3. The expected future cash flows from a project are estimated. This involves (a) estimating the investment outlay required for the project and (b) estimating the cash inflows over the project's projected life.
4. The riskiness inherent in the project is appraised. This important subject is taken up in Chapter 12.
5. The next step is to rank projects by their NPVs or IRRs, accepting those with NPV > 0 or IRR > the cost of capital.
6. The final step in a good capital budgeting system is the *post-audit*, which involves comparing actual to predicted results. Post-audits help get the best results from every accepted project; they also lead to improvements in the forecasting process and, hence, to better future capital budgeting decisions.

While this chapter has presented the basic elements of the capital budgeting process, there are many other aspects of this crucial topic. Some of the more important ones are discussed in the appendices to this chapter and in Chapters 12 and 15.

Questions

11-1 How is a project classification scheme (for example, replacement, expansion into new markets, and so forth) used in the capital budgeting process?

11-2 a. Why is the investment tax credit subtracted from expenditures on fixed assets in the top section of Table 11-1?

b. Why is working capital included in a capital budgeting analysis? Why are "payables/accruals" deducted from working capital? Would the working capital section of Table 11-1 need to be filled out if the project were for replacement rather than for expansion?

11-3 If Carter Chemical used straight line rather than sum-of-years'-digits depreciation, how would this affect (a) the total amount of depreciation, net income, and net cash flows over the project's expected life, (b) the timing of depreciation, net income, and net cash flows, and (c) the project's payback and NPV? (Depreciation is reviewed in Appendix 11D.)

11-4 Net cash flows rather than profits are listed in Table 11-4. What is the basis for this emphasis on cash flows as opposed to profits?

11-5 Explain why the NPV of a relatively long-term project, defined as one with a high percentage of its cash flows expected in distant future years, is more sensitive to changes in the cost of capital than is the NPV of a short-term project.

11-6 Explain why, if two mutually exclusive projects are being compared, the short-term project might have the higher ranking under the NPV criterion if the cost of capital is high, but the long-term project might be deemed better if the cost of capital is low. Would changes in the cost of capital ever cause a change in the IRR ranking of two such projects?

Self-Test Problem

ST11-1 Mountain States Chemical Company (MSC) is considering two mutually exclusive investments. Project A involves acquiring land, developing a new plant, operating the plant during the development of a major shale oil project, and then cleaning up residue at the site when the operation is completed. Here is a summary of the project's characteristics (dollars in millions):

1. A total of $50 has been spent thus far to investigate the feasibility of the process used in Project A.
2. Purchase land immediately at a cost of $300.
3. Put up a shale storage building at a cost of $400. This outlay is considered to occur at $t = 1$, that is, at the end of Year 1.
4. Install equipment at a cost of $200. This outlay is considered to occur at $t = 2$.
5. Bring in net working capital with a cost of $100. This outlay will occur at $t = 3$, that is, at the end of Year 3, and working capital will be recovered at the end of Year 6.
6. The plant will commence operations at the beginning of Year 4. Sales will be $1,500 per year, costs other than depreciation will be $600 per year. Assume cash flows from operations occur at the end of each year.
7. The operation will continue for three years. Depreciation will be by the straight line method and will be based on a three year useful life for depreciable assets. The building will have a salvage value of $100, the equipment of $50. The land will be donated to the state, and an additional $500 will have to be spent on the land to clean it up prior to the turnover; this expenditure and donation will occur at $t = 7$, that is, at the end of Year 7.
8. MSC's effective tax rate is 40 percent.
9. An investment tax credit of $3^1/_3$ percent applies to the buildings and equipment.

Project B has a net cost at $t = 0$ of $405.50 million and net cash flows after taxes of $134.25 million per year for six years.

a. Determine the annual net cash flows for Project A. Display these cash flows in the form of a time line.
b. Construct NPV profiles, on the same graph, for Projects A and B.
c. Determine each project's IRR.

d. Determine each project's payback.

e. You have not been given information on MSC's cost of capital. If you were told that the cost of capital is 10 percent, or 17 percent, how would this affect the choice between these two mutually exclusive projects? Had they been independent projects, how high could the cost of capital have risen before the projects were rejected?

11-1 Project M has a cost of $2,000, and its expected net cash inflows are $527.60 per year for five years.

Problems

a. What is the project's payback, to the closest year?

b. The cost of capital is 12 percent. What is the project's NPV?

c. What is the project's IRR? (Hint: Recognize that the project is an annuity.)

11-2 Project Z costs $20,000 and is expected to produce cash flows of $6,687.62 per year for five years.

a. What is the project's payback?

b. The cost of capital is 12 percent. What is its NPV?

c. What is the project's IRR? (Hint: Recognize that the project is an annuity.)

11-3 Two projects each involve an investment of $4,500. Cash flows (after-tax profits plus depreciation) are $3,000 a year for two years for Project S and $1,200 a year for six years for Project L.

a. Compute the net present value of each project if the firm's cost of capital is 0 percent and if it is 6 percent. NPVs for S at 10 percent and 20 percent, respectively, are $706.50 and $83.40, while NPVs for L at 10 percent and 20 percent are $726.36 and ($509.40).

b. Graph the present value profiles of the two projects, putting NPV on the Y axis and the cost of capital on the X axis, and use the graph to estimate each project's IRR.

c. Use a formula to calculate the internal rate of return for each project.

d. If these projects were mutually exclusive, which one would you select, assuming a cost of capital of (1) 8 percent, (2) 10.3 percent, or (3) 12 percent? Explain. (Note: In Chapter 12 we shall discuss "replacement chains," where projects such as these are extended out to a common life. For this problem, assume that the operation will terminate at the end of the project's life, making replacement chain analysis unnecessary.)

11-4 The net cash flows fc   rojects X and Y are shown on following page. Each project has a cost of $10,000, and the company uses a 12 percent cost of capital.

a. Calculate each project's payback.

b. Calculate each project's NPV at the 12 percent cost of capital.

c. Calculate each project's IRR. (Hint: Use the graphic method for Project X, and notice that Y is an annuity.)

d. Should X and/or Y be accepted if they are independent projects?

Year	Project X	Project Y
1	$6,500	$3,500
2	3,000	3,500
3	3,000	3,500
4	1,000	3,500

    e. Which project should be accepted if they are mutually exclusive?

    f. How might a change in the cost of capital produce a conflict between NPV and IRR? At what values of k would this conflict exist?

11-5 The Bey Burger Company is considering two mutually exclusive investments. Project A has a cost of $20,000 and will produce after-tax net cash flows of $3,752.21 per year for ten years. Project B also has a cost of $20,000, and it is expected to produce cash flows of $5,880.72 per year for five years.

    a. Assuming that Bey's average cost of capital is 12 percent, and that these two projects are both of average risk, which, if either, should Bey accept? (See note to Problem 11-3.)

    b. Now assume that Bey's cost of capital rises to 14 percent. What is your decision now? (Note: $NPV_B = \$189.10$.)

    c. Suppose Bey's cost of capital falls to 10 percent. How does this affect your decision? (Note: $NPV_B = \$2,292.63$.)

    d. Graph the two projects' NPV profiles. (Hint: At a zero cost of capital, $NPV_A = \$17,522.10$ and $NPV_B = \$9,403.60$.)

    e. Explain why Project A's NPV profile declines more rapidly than that of Project B. Also, explain the economic logic of why A is better at a low cost of capital, while B is better at a high capital cost.

11-6 F. Morrissey & Co. is considering the installation of a new production line for its rapidly expanding skate division. The line will have a cost of $100,000 and will be depreciated toward a zero salvage value over a five year period. The following income statements are expected to apply to the machine for each of its five operating years:

	Year 1	Year 2	Year 3	Year 4	Year 5
Sales	$100,000	$100,000	$100,000	$100,000	$100,000
Costs other than depreciation	71,667	71,667	71,667	71,667	71,667
Depreciation	33,333		20,000		6,667
Total costs	105,000		91,667		78,334
Income before taxes	(5,000)		8,333		21,666
Taxes (credit)	(2,000)		3,333		8,666
Net income after taxes	(3,000)		5,000		13,000
Add back depreciation	33,333		20,000		6,667
Net cash flow	$ 30,333		$ 25,000		$ 19,667

The company's cost of capital is 16 percent, and its tax rate is 40 percent.

a. Complete the table, assuming the company uses sum-of-years'-digits depreciation, and then calculate the project's net present value. (See Appendix 11D for depreciation calculation.)

b. What would the NPV have been if the company had used straight line depreciation?

c. Suppose a 10 percent investment tax credit had been applicable. How would this have affected your NPV calculations?

11-7 The Roenfeldt-Cooley Paper Company's director of capital budgeting is analyzing a proposal to build a pulp mill in eastern South Carolina. The following data have been developed thus far:

Land acquisition, cost incurred at start of Year 1 (t = 0)	$300,000
Plant construction, cost incurred at start of Year 2 (t = 1)	$700,000
Equipment purchase, cost incurred at start of Year 3 (t = 2)	$1,000,000
Net working capital, investment made at start of Year 4 (t = 3)	$400,000

A 10 percent investment tax credit is available on plant and equipment expenditures, but not on land costs. The credit is received at the beginning of the year in which the expenditure is made.

Operations will begin in Year 4 and will continue for ten years, through Year 13. Sales revenues and operating costs are assumed to come at the end of each year. Since the plant will be in operation for ten years, operating costs and revenues occur at the ends of Years 4 through 13 (t = 4 to 13). The following additional assumptions are made:

1. The plant and equipment will be depreciated over a ten year life, starting in Year 4. The buildings and equipment will be worthless after ten years' use, but Roenfeldt-Cooley expects to sell the land for $300,000 when the plant is closed down. Roenfeldt-Cooley uses straight line depreciation.
2. Roenfeldt-Cooley uses a cost of capital of 15 percent to evaluate projects such as this one.
3. Annual sales = 10,000 tons at $113.50 per ton. Annual sales revenues = $1,135,000.
4. Annual fixed operating costs *excluding* depreciation are $130,000.
5. Annual variable operating costs are $200,385, assuming the plant operates at full capacity.
6. Roenfeldt-Cooley's marginal income tax rate is 46 percent.

a. Calculate the project's NPV. Should Roenfeldt-Cooley accept this project?

b. Assuming constant sales prices and constant variable costs per unit, what will happen to the NPV if unit sales fall 10 percent below the forecast level?

Solution to Self-Test Problem

ST11-1 a. Develop Project A's cash flows:

$t = 0$ $-\$300$
$t = 1$ $-\$400 + 0.03333(\$400) = -\$400 + \$13.33 = -\$386.67$
$t = 2$ $-\$200 + 0.03333(\$200) = -\$200 + \$6.67 = -\$193.33$
$t = 3$ $-\$100$
$t = 4$ through 6:

Sales	$1,500	Building depreciation:
Costs without		
depreciation	−600	($400 − $100)/3 = $100/year
Depreciation	−150	
Gross profit	$ 750	Equipment depreciation:
Taxes (40%)	300	
Net income	$ 450	($200 − $50)/3 = $50/year
Plus depreciation	150	
Net cash flow	$ 600	

$t = 6$ Recovery of salvage:

	Buildings	$100
	Equipment	50
		$150

Recovery of net working capital: $100

$t = 7$ Donation of land to state: This donation is a tax deduction, so it reduces taxable income by $300 and saves taxes in the amount of (Tax rate) ($300) = (0.4) ($300) = $120. This $120 tax savings in Year 7 is considered to be an inflow attributable to this project.

Expenditure to clean up and restore land: The clean-up will cost $500, but it is a deductible expense. Therefore, it will have a net cash cost of $500 − [(Tax rate) ($500)] = $500 (1 − t) = $500 (0.6) = $300.

The net cash outflow at t = 7 is + $120 − $300 = −$180.
Note: The $50 that has already been spent is a sunk cost, hence does not enter this analysis. We are concerned only with *future* expenditures and the returns attributable to these expenditures.

Project A's cash flows can be displayed in the form of a time line:

0	1	2	3	4	5	6	7
−$300	−$386.67	−$193.33	−$100	+$600	+$600	+$600	+$120
						+$150	−$300
						+$100	−$180
						+$850	

b. Construct NPV profiles:

1. Always start by adding up the annual cash flows. This sum is the project's NPV at k = 0%.

$$\text{Project A: } \sum_{t=0}^{7} CF = -300 - 386.67 - 193.33 - 100$$
$$+ 600 + 600 + 850 - 180$$
$$= +\$890.$$

$$\text{Project B: } \sum_{t=0}^{6} CF = -405.5 + 6(134.25)$$
$$= \$400.$$

2. Next, calculate NPV at several discount rates—10 percent and 20 percent are two good ones to use. Notice that since Project A has several years of negative cash flows, we use the form of the NPV equation which starts with $t = 0$:

$$NPV_A = \sum_{t=0}^{7} CF_t(PVIF_{k,t}).$$

At 10%,

$$NPV_A = -300 - 386.67(0.9091) - 193.33(0.8264)$$
$$- 100(0.7513) + 600(0.6830) + 600(0.6209)$$
$$+ 850(0.5645) - 180(0.5132)$$
$$= \$283.37.$$

For Project B, which has a single cash outlay at $t = 0$ followed by a six year annuity, we would use this equation:

$$NPV_B = CF (PVIFA_{k,6}) - Cost.$$

At 10%,

$$NPV_B = 134.25(4.3553) - 405.50$$
$$= \$179.20.$$

Going through the same process, we find NPVs at other discount rates as listed below. Usually, 0 percent, 10 percent, and 20 percent are sufficient, but the more points plotted, the more accurate the NPV profile plot.

Discount rate	NPV_A	NPV_B
0%	$890.00	$400.00
10	283.37	179.20
20	−49.45	40.95
25	−156.83	−9.27

These data are plotted to form the NPV profile on the next page.

NPV Profiles for Projects A and B

c. Since Project B is an annuity, its IRR can be found as follows:

$$\text{Cost} = \text{Cash inflows (PVIFA}_{k,6}).$$
$$\text{PVIFA}_{k,6} = \$405.5/\$134.25$$
$$= 3.0205.$$

Look this factor up in Table A-2, going across the row for six payments. The factor 3.0205 is found in the column for 24 percent, so
$\text{IRR}_B = 24\%$. Note, though, that if the cost and/or cash flows had
been slightly different, the IRR would not have turned out to be a
whole number, so interpolation would have been necessary.

Note also that since the definition of the IRR is the discount rate
which causes NPV to equal zero, we can observe on the graph the
horizontal axis intercept. This intercept is the rate which causes NPV
= 0, so it is the IRR. By inspection, we see that $\text{IRR}_A \approx 18.1\%$ and
$\text{IRR}_B \approx 24\%$. Some financial calculators can be used to calculate IRRs
directly.

d. The payback is defined as the length of time it takes to recover the investment in a project. For Project B, payback is determined in the table below:

Year	Cash Flow	Cumulative CF
1	$134.25	$134.25
2	134.25	268.50
3	134.25	402.75
4	134.25	

$405.50 − 402.75 = $2.75 unrecovered after three years
$134.25/365 = 0.3678 = recovery per day
$2.75/0.3678 = 7.5 days to recover remainder.

Therefore, the payback period for Project B is three years and one week, which would be rounded to three years.

For Project A, the total "front-end" investment is $980 during t = 0 to t = 3. Net cash flows would be $600 in Years 4 and 5. After Year 4, the unrecovered investment would be $980 − $600 = $380. During Year 5, we can assume that cash flows are coming in at the rate of $600/365 = $1.6438 per day. Thus, it would take $380/$1.6438 = 231.2 days to recover the remaining balance, or 231.2/365 = 0.63 of a year. Therefore, full recovery of all front-end investment would be projected to occur 4.63 years after the first investment was made, so A's payback is 4.63 years.

e. The preferred ranking criterion is the NPV method. From the NPV profile graph, we see that the crossover rate is about 14.5 percent—at a cost of capital below 14.5 percent, $NPV_A > NPV_B$, so Project A would be selected, while if k > 14.5%, $NPV_B > NPV_A$, so B would be selected. At k = 10%, pick A, but at k = 17%, choose B.

Had A and B been independent projects, both A and B would be included in the capital budget if k were less than 18.1 percent, while B would be acceptable at any cost of capital below 24 percent.

Note: Additional aspects of this problem are brought out in appendix Problems 11A-2 and 11B-2, which get into (1) the fundamental difference between NPV and IRR, namely the assumptions implicit in each method about the firm's opportunity to invest cash flows from projects, and (2) multiple internal rates of return.

Selected References

For a deeper treatment of capital budgeting techniques, see

Bierman, Harold, Jr., and Seymour Smidt, *The Capital Budgeting Decision*, 4th ed. (New York: Macmillan, 1975).

Grant, E. L., W. G. Ireson, and R. S. Leavenworth, *Principles of Engineering Economy*, 6th ed. (New York: Ronald, 1976).

Levy, Haim, and Marshall Sarnat, *Capital Investment and Financial Decisions* (Englewood Cliffs, N.J.: Prentice-Hall, 1978).

Osteryoung, Jerome, *Capital Budgeting: Long-Term Asset Selection* (Columbus, Ohio: Grid, 1974).

For a discussion of strategic considerations in capital budgeting, see

Crum, R., and F. D. J. Derkinderen, eds., *Readings in Strategies for Corporate Investments* (New York: Pitman, 1980).

Three articles related directly to the materials in Chapter 11 and its appendices are

Bacon, Peter W., "The Evaluation of Mutually Exclusive Investments," *Financial Management,* Summer 1977, 55-58.

Kim, Suk H., and Edward J. Farragher, "Current Capital Budgeting Practices," *Management Accounting,* June 1981, 26-30.

Lewellen, Wilbur G., Howard P. Lanser, and John J. McConnell, "Payback Substitutes for Discounted Cash Flow," *Financial Management,* vol. 2 (Summer 1973), 17-23.

Other capital budgeting references are provided in Chapter 12.

Appendix 11A

Comparison of NPV and IRR Methods

In Chapter 11 we described the NPV and IRR methods, as well as the rationale behind their use in the capital budgeting process. In this appendix, we compare the two methods, showing (1) when they give similar accept/reject decisions, (2) when they produce conflicting decisions, and (3) why these conflicts arise. In the process, we shall see that NPV is conceptually superior to IRR and, hence, that when conflicts arise the NPV method is the one upon which to rely.[1]

Independent Projects

If two projects are independent, then the NPV and IRR criteria always lead to the same accept/reject decision—if NPV says accept, IRR also says accept. To see why this is so, look back at Figure 11-1 and notice (1) that the IRR criterion for acceptance is that the cost of capital (which is derived elsewhere and then used in capital budgeting) is less than (or to the left of) the IRR, and (2) that whenever the cost of capital is less than the IRR, the NPV is positive. Thus, for any cost of capital less than 11.8 percent, Project L is acceptable by both the NPV and the IRR criteria, while both methods reject the project if the cost of capital is greater than 11.8 percent. Project S—and all other independent projects under consideration—could be analyzed similarly.

---

[1] Because the NPV method is better than IRR, it is tempting to just explain NPV, state that it should be used as the general acceptance criterion, and go on to the next topic. However, since the IRR method was developed first, it is familiar to many top managers, and it is widely entrenched in industry. Therefore, it is important that students of business administration, and especially finance majors, thoroughly understand IRR and be prepared to explain why, at times, a project with a lower IRR may be preferable to one with a higher IRR.

Now assume that Projects L and S are *mutually exclusive,* not indepen-dent. Notice in Figure 11-1 that, so long as the cost of capital is *greater than* the crossover rate of 7.1 percent, NPV$_S$ is greater than NPV$_L$, and also that IRR$_S$ is greater than IRR$_L$. Therefore, for k greater than the cross-over rate of 7.1 percent, the two methods lead to the selection of the same project. However, if the cost of capital is *less than* the crossover rate, the NPV method ranks Project L higher, but the IRR method indicates that Project S is better. Thus, a conflict exists. NPV says choose L, while IRR says take S. Which answer is correct? The NPV method, since it selects the project which adds the most to the value of the firm, is the correct one. The reasons for these conflicts are set forth in the next sec-tion, where we discuss the underlying conditions that lead to conflicting rankings of mutually exclusive projects.

Mutually Exclusive Projects

NPV versus IRR conflicts cannot exist for independent projects, but for mutually exclusive projects there are two basic conditions under which the NPV and IRR may make conflicting choices. The first condition is that *project size* (or scale) differences exist, meaning that the cost of one project is larger than that of the other. The second condition is that *timing differ-ences* exist, meaning that the timing of cash flows from the two projects differs, with most of the cash flows from one project coming in the early years and most of the cash flows from the other project coming in the later years.

Reasons for Conflicts between NPV and IRR

With either size or timing differences, the firm will have different amounts of funds to invest in various years, depending on which of the two mutually exclusive projects it chooses. For example, if one project costs more than the other, then the firm will have more money at Time 0 to invest elsewhere if it selects the smaller project, while for projects of equal size, the one with the large early cash flows provides more funds for reinvestment. As we shall see, the NPV and IRR methods are based on different assumptions about how these differential cash flows are to be invested—this is called the reinvestment rate assumption—and it is a basic difference in their assumptions about the applicable reinvestment rate which gives rise to NPV/IRR conflicts.

Mutually exclusive projects often differ in size. For example, suppose a firm has the opportunity to buy a copper mine for $500,000. If it buys the mine, the company can get the ore to its smelter in two different ways. Plan S (the smaller project) calls for buying a fleet of trucks for $500,000, resulting in a total cost of the project of $500,000 + $500,000 = $1,000,000. Plan L (the larger project) calls for spending $4.5 million to install a conveyor-belt system for moving the ore, making the total cost $500,000 + $4,500,000 = $5,000,000. If trucks are used, then fuel, labor, and other operating costs will be much higher than with the conveyor

Project Size, or Scale

system. For simplicity, assume that the project will operate for only one year, after which the ore body will be exhausted. Assume also that after-tax net cash inflows, which occur at the end of the year, will be $1.28 million under Plan S but $6 million under Plan L. These cash inflows include salvage values.

Assuming that the company's cost of capital is 10 percent, we can find each project's NPV as follows:

$$NPV_S = \$1,280,000 \, (PVIF_{10\%,1 \text{ yr.}}) - \$1,000,000$$
$$= \$1,280,000 \, (0.9091) - \$1,000,000 = \$163,648.$$
$$NPV_L = \$6,000,000 \, (0.9091) - \$5,000,000 = \$454,600.$$

We can also find each project's IRR:

$$IRR_S: \$1,280,000 \, (PVIF_{k,1}) - \$1,000,000 = 0$$
$$PVIF_{k,1} = \$1,000,000/\$1,280,000 = 0.7813,$$
$$\text{which is the PVIF for 28\%, so } IRR_S = 28\%.$$
$$IRR_L: \$6,000,000 \, (PVIF_{k,1}) - \$5,000,000 = 0$$
$$PVIF_{k,1} = \$5,000,000/\$6,000,000 = 0.8333,$$
$$\text{which is the PVIF for 20\%, so } IRR_L = 20\%.$$

Thus, there is a conflict, with $NPV_L > NPV_S$, but $IRR_S > IRR_L$.

Given this conflict, which project should be accepted? If we assume that the cost of capital is constant, meaning that the firm can raise all the capital it wants at a cost of 10 percent, then the answer is L, the project with the higher NPV. The differential between the initial outlays on the two projects ($4 million) can be looked upon as an investment itself, Project Δ. That is, Project L can be broken down into two components, one equal to Project S, the other a residual project equal to a hypothetical Project Δ. The hypothetical investment has a "cost" of $4 million and a net present value equal to the differential between the NPVs of the first two projects, or $290,952. This is shown here:

Project	Cost	NPV
L	$5,000,000	$454,600
S	−1,000,000	−163,648
Δ	$4,000,000	$290,952

Since the hypothetical Project Δ has a positive net present value, it should be accepted. This amounts to accepting Project L.

To put it another way, Project L can be split into two components, one costing $1 million and having a net present value of $163,648, the other costing $4 million and having a net present value of $290,952. As each of the two components has a positive net present value, both should be accepted. But if Project S is accepted, the effect is to reject the second component of Project L, the hypothetical Project Δ. Since the IRR method selects Project S while the NPV method selects Project L, we conclude that the NPV method is preferable.[2]

NPV profiles for these two projects are shown in the left panel of Figure 11A-1. The crossover point for the two profiles is 18 percent, indicating that no NPV/IRR conflict occurs unless the cost of capital is less than 18 percent. In our example, k = 10%, so a conflict does occur.

Figure 11A-1
NPV Profiles of Mutually Exclusive Projects That Differ in Size and Timing

a. Large versus Small Projects

b. Long-Term versus Short-Term Projects

Timing of Cash Flows

Conflicts between NPV and IRR can also arise due to differences in the timing of projects' cash flows, even when the two projects cost exactly the same amount. To illustrate, suppose we are considering the purchase

[2] The matter of project size can be considered in more dramatic terms: Would a business that is able to raise all the capital it wants at a cost of 10 percent rather have a 100 percent rate of return on a $1 investment or a 95 percent return on a $1 million investment? The answer is obvious here, and the same principle applies in more realistic situations. Notice also that, under the assumption of unlimited capital at a constant cost, the existence of other projects is irrelevant to the choice between L and S. Any other projects that are "good" can be accepted and financed regardless of whether or not L or S is selected.

of timber rights in a forest for $1 million. If we were to log the property immediately according to Plan S (which is thus a short-term project), our expected cash flow would be $1.28 million at the end of Year 1. Alternatively, if we were to delay logging the property for ten years according to Plan L (which is a long-term project), the larger trees would produce a net cash inflow of $4,046,000 at the end of Year 10.

Assuming the cost of capital is 10 percent, we can find each project's NPV as follows:

$$NPV_S = \$1,280,000 \ (PVIF_{10\%,1}) - \$1,000,000$$
$$= \$1,280,000 \ (0.9091) - \$1,000,000 = \$163,648.$$
$$NPV_L = \$4,046,000 \ (0.3855) - \$1,000,000 = \$559,733.$$

We can also find each project's IRR:

$$IRR_S: \$1,280,000 \ (PVIF_{k,1}) - \$1,000,000 = 0$$
$$PVIF_{k,1} = \$1,000,000/\$1,280,000 = 0.7813,$$
which is the PVIF for 28%, so $IRR_S = 28\%$.
$$IRR_L: \$4,046,000 \ (PVIF_{k,10}) - \$1,000,000 = 0$$
$$PVIF_{k,10} = \$1,000,000/\$4,046,000 = 0.2472,$$
which is the PVIF for 15%, so $IRR_L = 15\%$.

Again, we find a conflict: Because of timing differences, $NPV_L > NPV_S$, but $IRR_S > IRR_L$.

In Chapter 11, we saw that high discount rates impose a greater penalty on distant cash flows than on near term cash flows. Therefore, long-term projects like Project L have NPV profiles which decline quite steeply relative to the NPV profiles of projects like S. The right panel of Figure 11A-1 illustrates this point for the two projects under consideration here. If the cost of capital is to the left of the crossover point, 13.7 percent, which it is since k = 10% in this case, then a conflict occurs between NPV and IRR.

Earlier, where our two projects differed in scale but the timing of their cash flows was the same, we set up a hypothetical Project Δ, which had a positive NPV, to show why the project with the larger basic NPV should be accepted. We can illustrate timing differences similarly. Project S provides a cash flow of $1,280,000 at the end of Year 1, while Project L has a cash flow of $4,046,000 at the end of Year 10. If we accept Project S, we get a cash flow of $1,280,000 at t = 1. If we accept Project L, we give up this Year 1 cash flow, which amounts to investing it, in order to get $4,046,000 at t = 10. Thus, our "timing difference" Project Δ has a cost of $1,280,000 at the end of Year 1 and a cash flow of $4,046,000 at the end of Year 10:

$$NPV_\Delta = \$4,046,000(PVIF_{10\%,10}) - \$1,280,000 \ (PVIF_{10\%,1})$$
$$= \$4,046,000 \ (0.3855) - \$1,280,000 \ (0.9091)$$
$$= \$1,559,733 - \$1,163,648 = \$396,085.$$

If we accept Project S, we are rejecting Project Δ, with its positive NPV of $396,085. Thus, we are foregoing a $396,085 increase in the value of the firm. Therefore, we should accept Project L.

In both our project size and our timing of cash flow examples, there are *cash flow differentials*. In the size example, we would have had an extra $4 million at t = 0 if we had taken the smaller project. In the timing example, we would have had an extra $1.28 million in Year 1 if we had taken the shorter-term project. The critical issue in resolving conflicts between mutually exclusive projects is this: At what rate can these differential cash flows be invested? *The use of the NPV method to compare projects implicitly assumes that the opportunity exists to reinvest the cash flows generated by a project at the cost of capital, while use of the IRR method implies the opportunity to reinvest at the IRR.* The cash flows may actually be withdrawn as dividends by the stockholders and spent on beer and pizza, but the assumption of a reinvestment opportunity is still implicit in the calculations. To demonstrate this, consider the following steps.

The Reinvestment Rate Assumption

Step 1. Notice that both the NPV and IRR methods involve the use of present value interest factors (PVIFs) in the solution process; for example, to determine the NPV, we multiply a series of cash flows by appropriate PVIFs, sum these products, subtract the initial cost, and the result is the NPV. Thus, the NPV method involves using present value tables, and the same thing holds for finding the IRR.

Step 2. Refer back to Chapter 3, Table 3-1 and Equation 3-2, and notice how present value tables are constructed. *The present value of any future sum is defined as the beginning amount which, when compounded at a specified and constant interest rate, will grow to equal the future amount over the stated time period.* From Table 3-1 we can see that the present value of $127.63 due in five years, when discounted at 5 percent, is $100 because $100, when interest earned is reinvested and compounded at 5 percent for five years, will grow to $127.63. Thus, compounding and discounting are reciprocal relationships, and the *very construction of PV tables implies a reinvestment process.*

Step 3. Since both the NPV and IRR methods involve the use of compound interest tables, and since the very construction of these tables involves an assumed reinvestment process, the concept of reinvestment opportunities underlies the two methods.

Step 4. The implicitly assumed reinvestment rate used in the NPV method is the cost of capital, k; that used in the IRR method is r, which is the IRR in the solution process. These are the rates built into the PVIFs.

Suppose the cash flows from a project are not reinvested but are used to pay dividends. No reinvestment is involved, yet an IRR for the project could still be calculated—does this show that the reinvestment assumption is not *always* implied in the IRR calculation? The answer is *no*; reinvestment itself is not necessarily assumed, but the *opportunity* for reinvestment *is* assumed. Because that assumption is made in the very construction of the PV tables, we simply could not define or interpret the concepts of NPV or IRR without it.

Which Reinvestment Rate Assumption Is Better?

We have seen that use of the NPV method implicitly assumes reinvestment, or at least the opportunity to reinvest, at the cost of capital, while the use of the IRR method assumes that the firm has the opportunity to reinvest a project's cash flows at the project's IRR. Which is the better assumption? We can arrive at the answer as follows:

1. Assume that the firm's cost of capital is 10 percent. Management can obtain all the funds it wants at this rate. This condition is expected to hold in the future.
2. Projects are evaluated at $k = 10\%$. All the projects with NPV > 0 are accepted. Plenty of capital is available to finance these projects, both now and in the future.
3. As cash flows come in from past investments, what will be done with them? If the good projects have already been accepted, the only projects left will have NPV < 0, so the cash flows can only be paid out to investors or, more likely, be used as a substitute for outside capital that costs 10 percent. *Thus, since the cash flows are expected to save the firm 10 percent, this is their opportunity cost reinvestment rate.*
4. The IRR method implicitly assumes reinvestment at the internal rate of return itself. Given a constant expected future cost of capital and ready access to capital markets, this assumption is incorrect.

Logically, we must come to the conclusion that the assumption of reinvestment at *the cost of capital implicit in the NPV method is the better assumption*. This, in turn, leads to a preference for the NPV method, at least for firms willing and able to obtain capital at a cost reasonably close to their current cost of capital.

Questions

11A-1 In what sense is a reinvestment rate assumption embodied in NPV and IRR calculations? What is the implicitly assumed reinvestment rate of each method?

11A-2 "Assume that a firm has no mutually exclusive projects, only independent ones; that its cost of capital is constant; and that all of its projects are normal in the sense of having an outflow followed by a stream of inflows. Under these conditions, the NPV and IRR methods will always result in identical capital budgets." Discuss the statement.

11A-3 "If a project's IRR is greater than the cost of capital, its NPV will always be greater than zero, and accepting the project will *always* increase the firm's value, assuming all projects are 'normal' in the sense that they have one or more negative cash flows followed by a series of positive cash flows." Discuss the statement.

Problems

11A-1 P. Hunt & Company is considering two mutually exclusive plans for extracting oil on property for which it has mineral rights. Both plans call for the expenditure of $10,000,000 to drill development wells, but under Plan A all the oil will be extracted in one year, producing a cash flow at t = 1 of $12,000,000, while under Plan B cash flows will be $1,750,000 per year for twenty years.

a. What are the annual cash flows that will be available to P. Hunt if it undertakes Plan B rather than Plan A?

b. If P. Hunt accepts Plan A, then invests the extra cash generated at the end of Year 1, what rate of return (reinvestment rate) would cause the cash flows from reinvestment to equal the cash flows from Plan B?

c. Suppose a company has a cost of capital of 10 percent. Is it logical to assume that it would take on all available independent projects (of average risk) with returns greater than 10 percent? Further, if all available projects with returns greater than 10 percent have already been taken, would this mean that cash flows from past investments would have an opportunity cost of only 10 percent, because all the firm could do with these cash flows would be to replace money that has a cost of 10 percent? Finally, does this imply that the cost of capital is the correct rate to assume for the reinvestment of a project's cash flows?

d. Construct NPV profiles for Plans A and B, identify each project's IRR, and indicate the crossover rate of return.

11A-2 The J. Pettijohn Brewing Company is considering two mutually exclusive expansion plans. Plan A calls for the expenditure of $50 million on a large-scale, integrated brewery which will provide an expected cash flow stream of $8 million per year for twenty years. Plan B calls for the expenditure of $15 million to build a somewhat less efficient, more labor intensive plant which has an expected cash flow stream of $3.4 million per year for twenty years. Pettijohn's cost of capital is 10 percent.

a. Calculate each project's NPV and IRR.

b. Set up a Project Δ by showing the cash flows (plus or minus) that will exist if Pettijohn goes with the large plant rather than the smaller plant. What are the NPV and the IRR for this Project Δ?

c. Graph the NPV profiles for Project A, Project B, and Project Δ.

d. Give a logical explanation, based on reinvestment rates and opportunity costs, as to why the NPV method is better than the IRR method when the firm's cost of capital is constant at some value such as 10 percent.

Appendix 11B

**Multiple Rates
of Return**

A problem that arises with the IRR method is that in solving the IRR Equation, 11B-1, it is possible to obtain more than one positive value of r:

$$0 = \frac{CF_1}{(1 + r)^1} + \frac{CF_2}{(1 + r)^2} + \cdots + \frac{CF_n}{(1 + r)^n} - C. \qquad (11B\text{-}1)$$

Notice that this equation is a polynomial of degree n. Therefore there are n different roots, or solutions, to the equation. All except one of the roots either are imaginary numbers or are negative when investments are "normal" (a normal investment is one that has one or more outflows (costs) followed by a series of inflows), so in the normal case only one positive value of r appears. If, however, a project calls for a large outflow either sometime during or at the end of its life, then it is a "nonnormal" project, and the possibility of multiple real roots arises.

To illustrate this problem, suppose the project calls for the expenditure of $1.6 million to develop a strip mine. The mine will produce a cash flow of $10 million at the end of Year 1. Then, at the end of Year 2, $10 million must be expended to restore the land to its original condition. Therefore, the project's cash flows are as follows:

Year end:	0	1	2
Cash flow:	− $1.6 million	+ $10 million	− $10 million.

These values can be substituted into Equation 11B-1 to derive the IRR for the investment:

$$0 = -\$1.6 \text{ million} + \frac{\$10 \text{ million}}{(1 + r)^1} - \frac{\$10 \text{ million}}{(1 + r)^2}.$$

NPV = 0 when r = 25% and also when r = 400%, so the IRR of the investment is both 25 and 400 percent. This relationship is graphically depicted in Figure 11B-1. Note that no dilemma would arise if the NPV method were used; we would simply use Equation 11-1, find the NPV, and use this for ranking.[1]

Another example of multiple internal rates of return occurred when a major California bank *borrowed* funds from an insurance company, then used these funds (plus an initial investment of its own) to buy a number of jet engines, which it then leased to a major airline. The bank expected to receive positive net cash flows (lease payments minus interest on the insurance company loan) for a number of years, then several large nega-

---

[1] Does this analysis suggest that the firm should try to *raise* its cost of capital to about 100 percent in order to maximize the NPV of the project? Certainly not. As we shall see later in the book, the firm should seek to *minimize* its cost of capital—this will maximize the price of its stock. Taking actions to raise the cost of capital might make this particular project look good, but these actions would be terribly harmful to the firm's more numerous "normal" projects. Only if the firm's cost of capital is high, in spite of efforts to keep it down, will the illustrative project have a high NPV.

Net Present Value
($ in Millions)

$$NPV = -\$1.6 + \frac{\$10}{(1 + k)} - \frac{\$10}{(1 + k)^2}$$

Discount Rate (%)

Figure 11B-1
Net Present Value as a
Function of Cost of
Capital

tive cash flows as it repaid the insurance company loan, and, finally, a large inflow from the sale of the engines when the lease expired.[2]

The bank discovered two IRRs and wondered which was correct. It could not ignore the IRR and use the NPV method, as the lease was already on the books; meanwhile, the bank's senior loan committee as well as the Federal Reserve Bank examiners wanted to know the return on the lease. The bank's solution called for compounding the cash flows—both positive and negative—at an assumed reinvestment rate of 9 percent, its average return on loans, to arrive at a compounded terminal value for the operation. Then the interest rate that equated this terminal sum to the bank's initial cost was called the IRR, or the rate of return on the lease. This procedure satisfied both the loan committee and the bank examiners.[3]

Problems

11B-1 A coal mining firm is considering opening a strip mine, the cost of which is $4.4 million. Cash flows will be $27.7 million, all coming at the end of

[2] The situation described here is a *leveraged lease*. See Chapter 22 for more on leveraged leases, and the Quantum Airlines Case in *Cases in Managerial Finance,* 4th edition, for a detailed discussion.

[3] For additional insights into the multiple root problem, see James C. T. Mao, *Quantitative Analysis of Financial Decisions* (New York: Macmillan, 1969), chapter 6, and William H. Jean, "On Multiple Rates of Return," *Journal of Finance,* March 1968, 187-192.

Year 1. The land must be returned to its natural state at a cost of $25 million, payable at the end of Year 2.

    a. Find the IRR(s). (Hint: Graph the project's *approximate* present value profile by finding NPV at 0, 9.2, 80.5, and 420 percent.)

    b. Should the project be accepted (1) if k = 8%, or (2) if k = 14%? Explain your reasoning.

    c. Can you think of some other capital budgeting situations where negative cash flows during or at the end of the project's life might lead to multiple IRRs?

11B-2 The Elton-Gruber Development Company has many excellent investment opportunities, but it has insufficient cash to undertake them all. Now Elton-Gruber is offered the chance to borrow $2 million from the Pacific City Retirement Fund at 10 percent, the loan to be repaid at the end of one year. Also, a "consulting fee" of $700,000 will be paid to Pacific City's mayor at the end of one year for helping to arrange the credit. Of the $2 million received, $1 million will be used immediately to buy an old city-owned hotel and convert it to a gambling casino. The other $1 million will be invested in other lucrative Elton-Gruber projects that otherwise would have to be foregone because of a lack of capital. For two years, all cash generated by the casino will be plowed back into the casino project. At the end of the two years the casino will be sold for $2 million.

    Assuming (1) the facts as given, (2) that the deal has been worked out in the sunshine and is completely legal, and (3) that cash from other Elton-Gruber Company operations will be available to make the required payments at the end of Year 1, under what rate of return conditions should Elton-Gruber accept the offer? Disregard taxes. (Hint: This problem involves multiple rates of return. First determine the cash flows associated with the casino project, then graph the project's NPV profile, and, finally, discuss the likelihood that the relevant discount rate is in the range where NPV > 0.)

Appendix 11C

The Profitability Index

Another method that is used fairly often to evaluate projects is the Profitability Index (PI), or the benefit/cost ratio, as it is sometimes called:

$$\text{PI} = \frac{\text{PV benefits}}{\text{Cost}} = \frac{\sum_{t=1}^{n} \dfrac{CF_t}{(1 + k)^t}}{\text{Cost}}. \qquad \text{(11C-1)}$$

The PI shows the *relative* profitability of any project, or the present value of benefits per dollar of cost.[1]

    As was true in the NPV versus IRR comparison, the NPV and PI

---

[1] If investment expenditures are incurred over several years, as they were in the Compound X example discussed in Chapter 11, then the denominator must be the present value of these outlays.

always make the same accept-reject decisions for independent projects. However, NPV and PI can give different project rankings, which presents problems when mutually exclusive projects are being compared. In Appendix 11A we compared Project L, which called for investing $5 million in a mine plus a conveyor-belt system for handling ore, with Project S, which called for an expenditure of only $1 million to do the same thing by employing a fleet of trucks. However, the conveyor-belt system had lower operating costs, so its cash flows were larger, and the net present values were found to be $454,600 for L and $163,648 for S. Using the NPV criterion, on the one hand, we would select Project L. On the other hand, if we compute the ratio of the present value of the returns (or benefits) of each project to its cost, we find S's ratio to be $1,280,000/$1,000,000 = 1.28 and L's ratio to be $5,454,600/$5,000,000 = 1.09. Thus, using the PI for our ranking, we would select Project S because it produces higher net returns per dollar invested.

Given this conflict, which project should be accepted? Alternatively stated: Is it better to use the net present value approach on an absolute basis (NPV) or on a relative basis (PI)? For a firm that seeks to maximize stockholders' wealth, the NPV method is better. Recall that the differential between the initial outlays of the two projects ($4,000,000) can be looked upon as an investment itself with an NPV equal to the differential in the NPVs of the two projects ($290,952). Thus, Project L can be broken down into two projects, one equal to Project S and one a residual project equal to the hypothetical Project Δ. Since both Projects S and Δ contribute positively to the value of the firm, they should both be accepted. This amounts to accepting Project L, the one chosen by the NPV method. Thus, we conclude that the NPV method leads to better decisions than the PI method.

11C-1   Project S has a cost of $10,000 and is expected to produce benefits (cash flows) of $3,000 per year for five years. Project L costs $25,000 and is expected to produce cash flows of $7,400 per year for five years. Calculate the two projects' NPVs, IRRs, and PIs, assuming a cost of capital of 12 percent. Which project would be selected, assuming they are mutually exclusive, using each ranking method? Which should actually be selected?

Problem

Depreciation is a deductible expense. Several different depreciation methods are permitted for tax purposes, and the choice of the tax depreciation method used can have a profound effect on a firm's tax liabilities and cash flows. The four principal methods of depreciation—straight line, sum-of-years'-digits, double declining balance, and units of production—and their effects on a firm's taxes are illustrated in this appendix. We will begin by assuming that a machine is purchased for $2,500 and has an estimated useful life of six years or 6,000 hours. It will have a scrap value

Appendix 11D

Depreciation

**Figure 11D-1
Double Declining
Balance versus Straight
Line Depreciation**

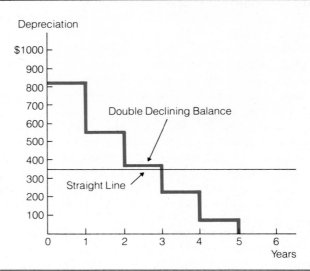

of $400 after six years of use or after 6,000 hours, whichever comes first. Table 11D-1 illustrates each of the four depreciation methods and compares the depreciation charges under each method over the six year period. Figure 11D-1 graphs the depreciation charges under straight line and double declining balance.

Straight Line

With the straight line method, a uniform annual depreciation charge of $350 a year is allowed. This figure is arrived at by simply dividing the economic life into the total cost of the machine minus the estimated salvage value:

**Table 11D-1
Comparison of
Depreciation Methods
for a Six Year, $2,500
Asset with a $400
Salvage Value**

Year	Straight Line	Double Declining Balance (DDB)	Sum-of-Years'-Digits (SYD)	Units of Production[a]
1	$ 350	$ 833	$ 600	$ 700
2	350	556	500	630
3	350	370	400	350
4	350	247	300	210
5	350	94[b]	200	140
6	350	—	100	70
Total	$2,100	$2,100	$2,100	$2,100

[a]The assumption is made that the machine is used the following number of hours: first year, 2,000; second year, 1,800; third year, 1,000; fourth year, 600; fifth year, 400; sixth year, 200.

[b]The maximum depreciation that can be taken is the value of cost minus salvage, or $2,100 in this example. Thus, $94 of depreciation in Year 5 exhausts the depreciation allowed under DDB.

$$\frac{\$2,500 \text{ cost} - \$400 \text{ salvage value}}{6 \text{ years}} = \$350 \text{ a year depreciation charge.}$$

If the estimated salvage value had been less than 10 percent of the original cost, it could have been ignored.

Double Declining Balance

The double declining balance (DDB) method of depreciation requires the application of a constant rate of depreciation each year to the undepreciated value of the asset at the close of the previous year. To calculate DDB depreciation, we first find the fraction $1/N$, where N is the life of the asset. In our example, $1/N = 1/6 = 0.1667$. This fraction is then doubled, to become 0.3333 in this case, and it is called the "depreciation rate." This rate is applied to the full purchase price of the machine, not to the cost less salvage value. Therefore, depreciation under the DDB method during the first year is calculated as follows:

$$0.3333 (\$2,500) = \$833.$$

Depreciation during the second year is calculated by applying the 33.33 percent rate (or 0.3333) to the undepreciated balance as follows:

$$0.3333(\$2,500 - \$833) = 0.3333(\$1,667) = \$556.$$

The process is continued for other years, until the total depreciation taken equals the cost of the asset less the estimated salvage value. Thus, in the illustrative case, the asset is fully depreciated during the fifth year.

The total amount of depreciation taken under the DDB method is equal to that under straight line, but under DDB the depreciation is taken faster, as it is under sum-of-years'-digits. Thus, DDB and sum-of-years'-digits are called *accelerated depreciation methods.*[1]

Sum-of-Years'-Digits

Under the sum-of-years'-digits (SYD) method, the yearly depreciation allowance is determined as follows:

1. Calculate the SYDs. In our example there is a total of 21 digits: $1 + 2 + 3 + 4 + 5 + 6 = 21$. This figure can also be arrived at by means of the sum of an algebraic progression equation, where N is the life of the asset:

$$\text{Sum} = N\left(\frac{N + 1}{2}\right)$$
$$= 6\left(\frac{6 + 1}{2}\right) = 21.$$

---

[1] It should also be noted that a firm may switch from DDB (or SYD) to straight line whenever it becomes advantageous to do so. The undepreciated balance, less the estimated salvage value, is divided by the remaining life to get the annual depreciation. If this value is larger than the DDB depreciation, then the switch should be made. In our example, it is not advantageous to switch. Had the salvage value been lower, then a switch would have been advantageous.

2. Divide the number of remaining years by the SYDs and multiply this fraction by the depreciable cost (total cost minus salvage value) of the asset:

$$\text{Year 1: } \left(\frac{6}{21}\right)(\$2,100) = \$600 \text{ depreciation}$$

$$\text{Year 2: } \left(\frac{5}{21}\right)(\$2,100) = \$500 \text{ depreciation}$$

$$\cdot$$
$$\cdot$$
$$\cdot$$

$$\text{Year 6: } \left(\frac{1}{21}\right)(\$2,100) = \$100 \text{ depreciation.}$$

Units of Production

Under the units of production method, the expected useful life of 6,000 hours is divided into the depreciable cost (purchase price minus salvage value) to arrive at an hourly depreciation rate of 35 cents. Since, in our example, the machine is run for 2,000 hours in the first year, the depreciation in that year is $700; in the second year it is $630, and so on. With this method, depreciation charges cannot be estimated precisely ahead of time; the firm must wait until the end of the year to determine what usage has been made of the machine and, hence, its depreciation.

Effect of Depreciation on Taxes Paid

The effect of the accelerated methods on a firm's income tax payment is easily demonstrated. In the first year, if the firm chooses to use the straight line method, only $350 may be deducted from its earnings to arrive at earnings before taxes (the amount of earnings to which the tax rate applies). However, using any one of the other three methods, the firm would have a much greater deduction and, therefore, a lower tax liability.

This point is illustrated in Table 11D-2, which shows the cash flows a hypothetical firm will generate if it uses straight line versus double declining balance depreciation. In Year 1, taxes are lower under DDB depreciation, hence cash flows are higher. However, the situation changes over time—in later years, the depreciation tax shelter declines in the DDB case, causing taxes to rise and cash flows to decline.

Over the entire six year period, total cash flows are the same for the two cases. However, since cash received sooner is more valuable than cash received later, a firm that uses accelerated depreciation and thus speeds up the cash flows from operations will have a higher value than a similar firm that uses straight line depreciation. Similarly, an asset that

	Straight Line	DDB
Year 1		
Sales (all cash)	$2,000	$2,000
Costs other than depreciation (all cash)	1,000	1,000
Depreciation (not a cash charge)	350	833
Total deductible costs	$1,350	$1,833
Taxable income	650	167
Taxes (assume a 40% rate)	$ 260	$ 67
Cash flow = Sales − Other costs − Taxes	$ 740	$ 933
Year 6		
Sales (all cash)	$2,000	$2,000
Costs other than depreciation (all cash)	1,000	1,000
Depreciation (not a cash charge)	350	—
Total deductible costs	$1,350	$1,000
Taxable income	650	1,000
Taxes (assume a 40% rate)	$ 260	$ 400
Cash flow = Sales − Other costs − Taxes	$ 740	$ 600

**Table 11D-2
Cash Flow Effects:
Straight Line versus
DDB Depreciation**

can be depreciated by an accelerated method will have a higher value than one that must be depreciated by straight line.[2]

Depreciable Lives

Different assets have different economic lives, or different periods over which it will be economically feasible to use the assets rather than to replace them with newer and more efficient ones. Replacements are discussed in Chapter 12. In the past, depreciation charges for tax purposes had to be based on asset lives which more or less approximated expected economic lives. However, the 1981 tax law permits assets to be written off for tax purposes over periods which are much shorter than their operating lives. In general, these are tax lives for various classes of assets:

3 years: Autos, light trucks, certain types of short-lived machinery and equipment

[2] Firms may report profit to stockholders using straight line depreciation even though they use an accelerated depreciation method for tax purposes. The difference between taxes actually paid during the year (the actual tax bill) and the taxes that would have been paid had the firm used straight line for tax purposes is reported on the income statement as "deferred taxes," and the accumulated deferred taxes over the years is reported on the balance sheet as a liability item. This treatment, which is called "normalization" for timing differences in the reporting of depreciation for tax and book purposes, would keep our illustrative firm from having to report lower income just because it elected to use accelerated depreciation for tax purposes.

5 years: Heavy trucks, aircraft, most types of production machinery and equipment, office furniture

10 years: Certain types of real estate with relatively short economic lives

15 years: Buildings, most public utility assets

The tax code spells out in detail what types of assets qualify for the different lives.

Note also that companies can, if they choose, elect to use *longer* lives than those specified in the Tax Code. A company which is currently unprofitable, but which expects to move into a profitable position in a few years, might elect to use longer depreciable lives.

Problem   11D-1

a. The Ajax Company acquires a machine tool that costs $50,000, has a five year life, and will have a zero salvage value. Calculate the depreciation schedule on the asset under the straight line, double declining balance, and sum-of-years'-digits methods.

b. Assume that Ajax earns $20,000 per year before depreciation and income taxes on the machine tool (sales − operating expenses = $20,000). What are Ajax's tax bill, profit after tax, and cash flow in Year 1 and Year 5 under (1) straight line and (2) sum-of-years'-digits depreciation? For convenience, assume the company pays a 20 percent tax rate on *all* taxable income.

c. Suppose the investment tax credit is currently 9 percent on assets with lives of eight years or longer, 6 percent on assets with lives of six or seven years, and 3 percent on assets with lives of four or five years. How would the ITC affect Ajax's tax situation? (Assume that Ajax will be able to use the calculated credit in full.)

d. Consider the question of Ajax's changing depreciation, for example, from DDB to SYD after two years, or from either DDB or SYD to straight line. (The IRS permits such switches under certain conditions.) Would a switch be appropriate for Ajax?

Risk and Other Topics in Capital Budgeting

Our discussion of capital budgeting in the last chapter was incomplete in that we did not consider four important topics: (1) asset replacement decisions, (2) the effects of inflation on capital budgeting analysis, (3) capital rationing, and (4), most important, the effects of risk on capital budgeting. These topics are covered in this chapter.

Carter Chemical Company's Compound X project was used in the last chapter to show how expansion projects are analyzed. As we mentioned there, Carter and other companies also make *replacement decisions*, and the analysis relating to replacement is somewhat different from that for expansion projects. These differences are illustrated with another Carter Chemical example, this time from the company's Plastics Division.

Replacement Decisions

A lathe for trimming molded plastics was purchased five years ago at a cost of $7,500. The machine had an expected life of fifteen years at the time it was purchased, and it was estimated then that its salvage value would be zero at the end of the fifteen years. The machine is being depreciated on a straight line basis, so its annual depreciation charge is $500, and its present book value is $5,000.

The division manager reports that a new machine can be purchased for $12,000 (including installation) which, over its ten year life, will reduce labor and raw materials usage sufficiently to cut operating costs from $7,000 to $4,000. This reduction in costs will cause before-tax profits to rise by $7,000 − $4,000 = $3,000 per year.

It is estimated that the new machine can be sold for $2,000 at the end of ten years; this is its estimated salvage value. The old machine's actual current market value is $1,000, which is well below its book value. Taxes are at a 46 percent rate and are paid quarterly, and the appropriate discount rate is 10 percent. An investment tax credit (ITC) of 10 percent of the purchase price can be used if the new machine is acquired. Net working capital requirements will also increase by $1,000. Should Carter buy the new machine?

Provided the annual cash flows are constant, as they are in this example, the worksheet presented in Table 12-1 can be used to analyze the project.[1] A line-by-line description of the table follows.

---

[1] If the cash flows are not level over the project's life, then it will be necessary to calculate after-tax

(continued)

**Table 12-1
Worksheet for
Replacement Analysis**

	Amount before Tax (1)	Amount after Tax (2)	Year Event Occurs (3)	PV Factor at 10% (4)	PV (5)
Net outflows at the time the investment is made: t = 0					
1. Cost of new equipment	$12,000	$12,000	0	1.0	$12,000
2. Salvage value of old equipment	(1,000)	(1,000)	0	1.0	(1,000)
3. Tax effect of sale of old equipment	(4,000)	(1,840)	0	1.0	(1,840)
4. Increase in net working capital	1,000	1,000	0	1.0	1,000
5. Investment tax credit	(1,200)	(1,200)	0	1.0	(1,200)
6. Total initial outflows (PV of costs)					$ 8,960
Net inflows over the project's life: t = 1 to 10					
7. Decrease in costs	$ 3,000	$ 1,620	1-10	6.1446	$ 9,954
8. Depreciation on new machine	1,000	—	—	—	—
9. Depreciation on old machine	(500)	—	—	—	—
10. Net change in tax savings from depreciation	500	230	1-10	6.1446	1,413
11. Estimated salvage value of new machine	2,000	2,000	10	0.3855	771
12. Return of working capital (if applicable)	1,000	1,000	10	0.3855	386
13. Total PV of cash inflows					$12,524
14. NPV = PV of inflows − PV of costs = $12,524 − $8,960 = $3,564.					

Line 1. The top section of the table, Lines 1 through 6, relates to cash flows which occur at (approximately) t = 0, the time the investment is made. Line 1 shows the purchase price of the machine, including any installation charges. No discounting is required, so the present value interest factor is 1.0.

Line 2. Here we show the price received from sale of old equipment. The parentheses denote that this amount is deducted when finding the net cash outflow at t = 0.

Line 3. Since the old equipment was sold at a loss, this reduces Carter's taxable income, hence its next quarterly income tax payment. The tax

savings for each year. This requires that income statements such as the one for Compound X in Chapter 11, Table 11-2, be set up.

savings is equal to (loss)(t) = ($4,000)(0.46) = $1,840, where t is the tax rate. The Tax Code defines this loss as an operating loss, not a capital loss, because it reflects the fact that inadequate depreciation was taken on the old asset. If there had been a profit on the sale (that is, if the sales price had exceeded book value), Line 3 would have shown taxes *paid*, a positive cash outflow. In the actual case, the equipment was sold at a loss, so no taxes were paid. In effect, Carter receives a tax credit of $1,840.

Line 4. The investment in additional net working capital (current assets required less spontaneous accounts payable and accruals) is shown here. This investment will be recovered at the end of the project's life. No taxes are involved. Also, as discussed in Chapter 8, the investment in receivables should reflect costs only, not profits.

Line 5. The ITC is equal to 10 percent of the purchase price.[2]

Line 6. Here we show the net cash outflow at the time the replacement is made. Carter writes a check for $12,000 to pay for the machine, and another $1,000 is invested in working capital, but these outlays are partially offset by the items on Lines 2, 3, and 5.

Line 7. The lower section of the table shows the *incremental future* cash flows, or benefits, that will result if the replacement is made. The first of these benefits is the reduction in operating costs shown in Column 1. This cost reduction increases cash flows because operating costs are reduced, but it also raises taxable income, hence income taxes payable. Therefore, the after-tax benefit is $3,000 − $3,000(t) = $3,000(1 − t) = $3,000(1 − 0.46) = $3,000(0.54) = $1,620. These benefits occur in Years 1-10, so the PV of this annuity is equal to $1,620(6.1446) = $9,954, the amount shown in the last column. Also, note that had the replacement resulted in an increase in sales in addition to the reduction in costs (if the new machine had been both larger and more efficient), then this amount would also be reported on Line 7. Alternatively, a separate line could be added.

Lines 8, 9, and 10. Lines 8 and 9 show the depreciation on the new and old machines, while Line 10 shows both the net addition to depreciation and the tax savings from this additional depreciation. Depreciation is not in itself a cash inflow—no one writes Carter a check for depreciation.

---

[2] If a company takes an ITC based on an expected life of seven or more years but then actually sells or retires the asset which gave rise to the ITC in, say, five years, then $1/3$ of the ITC must be repaid, or is "recaptured" by the government. If an ITC had been taken on the old machine when it was acquired five years ago, then part of this ITC would have to be repaid, and we would need to include another outflow element in the top section of Table 12-1. Congress can change these provisions.

However, the increase in depreciation does reduce Carter's taxes. The amount of the taxes saved by the increased depreciation is $500(t) = $500(0.46) = $230; this figure is shown in Column 2. The savings occur in Years 1-10, and the present value of this ten year annuity is $230(6.1446) = $1,413, the amount shown in Line 10, Column 5.

Note that the relevant cash flow is the tax savings on the *net increase* in depreciation, not the depreciation on the new equipment. Replacement decisions are based on *incremental* cash flows. Since we lose $500 of depreciation if we replace the old machine, the incremental or additional depreciation is only $1,000 − $500 = $500, so the incremental cash flow from taxes saved is $230.

Line 11. The estimated salvage value on the new machine at the end of its ten year life is $2,000. This is a return of capital, so no taxes are involved. The PV of the salvage value is $2,000(0.3855) = $771.

Line 12. An investment of $1,000 was made in net working capital at t = 0. This investment, like the salvage value, will be recovered when the project is terminated at the end of Year 10. Accounts receivable will be collected, inventories will be drawn down and not replaced, and the cash required to operate the facility will no longer be needed. The present value of the recovered working capital is $386.

Line 13. This line sums the PVs of the benefits.

Line 14. Here we calculate the net present value of the replacement project. The PV of the benefits exceeds the investment outlay, so the project has a positive NPV of $3,564. Therefore, the old machine should be replaced.

Comparing Projects with Unequal Lives

To simplify matters, our example of replacement decisions assumed that the new machine had a life equal to the remaining life of the existing one. Suppose, however, that we must choose between two mutually exclusive replacement alternatives that have *different* lives. For example, Machine S has an expected life of ten years, while L has a fifteen year life. The most typical procedure for solving problems of this type is to set up a series of *replacement chains* extending out to the "common denominator" year, that is, the year in which both alternatives would require replacement. For Machines S and L this would be Year 30, so it would be necessary to compare a three chain cycle for S, the ten year machine, with a two chain cycle for L, the fifteen year project.

To illustrate both the replacement chain problem and its solution, suppose we are considering the replacement of a fully depreciated printing press with a new one. The plant in which the press is used is profitable and is expected to continue in operation for many years. The old press could continue to be used indefinitely, but it is not as efficient as the new ones. Two replacement machines are available. Press A has a cost of $36,100, will last for five years, and will produce after-tax incremental cash flows of $9,700 per year for five years. Press B has a cost of $57,500, will last for ten years, and will produce net cash flows of $9,500 per year. Both the costs and performances of Presses A and B have been constant in recent years and are expected to remain constant in the future. The company's cost of capital is 10 percent.

Should the old press be replaced, and if so, with A or with B? To answer these questions, we first calculate A's NPV as follows:

$$NPV_A = \$9,700(3.7908) - \$36,100 = \$36,771 - \$36,100 = \$671.$$

B's NPV is:

$$NPV_B = \$9,500(6.1446) - \$57,500 = \$58,374 - \$57,500 = \$874.$$

These calculations suggest that the old press should indeed be replaced, and that Press B should be selected. However, the analysis is incomplete, and the decision to choose Press B is incorrect. If we choose Press A, we will have an opportunity to make a similar investment after five years, and this second investment will also be profitable. However, if we choose Press B, we will not have this second investment opportunity. Therefore, to make a proper comparison of Presses A and B, we must find the present value of Press A over a ten year period and compare it with Press B over the same ten years.

The NPV for Press B as calculated above is correct as it stands. For Press A, however, we must take three additional steps: (1) determine the NPV of the second Press A five years hence, (2) bring this NPV back to the present, and (3) sum these two component NPVs:

1. NPV_{A2} five years in future $= \$9,700(3.7908) - \$36,100 = \$671.$
2. PV of $NPV_{A2} = \$671(PVIF_{10\%,5 \text{ yrs.}}) = \$671(0.6209) = \$417.$
3. "True" $NPV_A = \$671 + \$417 = \$1,088.$

The "true" NPV of Press A, $1,088, can be compared with NPV_B. Since the value of the firm will increase by $1,088 if the old press is replaced by Press A versus only $874 for Press B, Press A should be selected.

Although our simple example illustrates why a chain analysis is necessary if mutually exclusive projects have different lives, in practice the arithmetic is generally more complex. For example, Press A might have had a life of eight years versus an eleven year life for B. This would require an analysis over eighty-eight years, the lowest common denominator of the two presses' lives. In such a situation, it is often simpler to use another

Equivalent Annual Annuity Method

procedure, the *equivalent annual annuity* method. Here we find the present value of each project assuming continuous replacement chains on out to infinity. Three steps are involved:

1. Find each project's NPV over its original life. For the printing press example, we found $NPV_A = \$671$ and $NPV_B = \$874$.
2. Divide the original NPV of each project by the annuity factor for the project's original life to obtain the equivalent annual annuity:

$$\text{Equivalent annual annuity, Press A} = NPV_A/PVIFA_{10\%,5 \text{ yrs.}}$$
$$= \$671/3.7908$$
$$= \$177.01.$$

$$\text{Equivalent annual annuity, Press B} = \$874/6.1446$$
$$= \$142.24.$$

Press A, in effect, provides an annuity of $177.01 per year for five years—such an annuity would be worth exactly 3.7908($177.01) = $671—while Press B provides an equivalent annuity of $142.24.

3. Assuming infinite replacement, these equivalent annual annuities will continue on out to infinity; that is, they will constitute perpetuities. Recognizing (from Chapter 3) that the value of a perpetuity is V = Annual receipt ÷ k, we can find the net present values of the infinite annuities provided by Presses A and B:

$$NPV_A = \$177.01/0.10 = \$1{,}770.10.$$
$$NPV_B = \$142.24/0.10 = \$1{,}422.40.$$

Since the infinite horizon NPV of A exceeds that of B, Press A should be accepted. Therefore, the equivalent annual annuity method leads to the same decision rule as the simple chain method—accept Press A.

Computationally, the equivalent annual annuity method is often easier to apply than the chain method. However, the chain method is often easier to explain to decision makers, and it does not require the assumption of an infinite time horizon. Also, note that Step 3 above is not really necessary for making the decision—we could have just chosen the project with the larger annual annuity. However, going on to Step 3 does point out by how much each project will increase the value of the firm.

Implications for Nonreplacement Decisions

Once students become aware of the replacement chain problem, they often ask this question: "Shouldn't replacement chains, or common life analysis, be used for *all* capital budgeting analysis, not just for replacement decisions? For example, if we were analyzing one project with a five year life and another with a ten year life, shouldn't we put them on a common time basis?" Not necessarily. For example, we could compare the NPV on Carter Chemical's fifteen year Compound X project with the

NPV on a ten year project in the company's building supply division. There would be no need whatever to put the projects on a common life basis—each project should be accepted if its NPV is positive or rejected if its NPV is negative, and these decisions are independent of one another. On the other hand, suppose Carter has two alternative ways to produce Compound X. Method 1 involves a plant that could be operated for fifteen years, while Method 2 involves a plant with a five year life. Assuming the market demand for the product is expected to last for fifteen years, then Method 2 must be evaluated over three five-year cycles when it is compared to Method 1. Otherwise, the analysis would be seriously biased against the plant with the shorter life.

As a general rule, (1) the replacement chain issue does not arise for independent projects, but (2) it can arise if mutually exclusive projects with different lives are being evaluated. However, it is not always appropriate to run the analysis out to a common denominator year—this depends on whether the operation will actually be continued. If the operation is likely to be continued, then the extension must be considered to avoid biasing the analysis against the project with the shorter life.

Inflation and Changing Equipment Performance in Replacement Analysis

One serious weakness of our replacement analysis is the fact that we have ignored possible inflation in the purchase price of future equipment—if inflation is expected to continue, then replacement equipment will have a higher price, and this should be incorporated into the analysis. However, there may be an offset to inflation—future generations of equipment like printing presses may have better performance characteristics and therefore may provide additional cost reductions. Also, some types of equipment—computers, for example—have had declining costs. The best way of handling these complications is to build expected inflation and/or possible efficiency gains directly into the cash flow estimates, and then use the replacement chain approach (but not the equivalent annual annuity method). The arithmetic is more complicated, but the concepts are exactly the same as in our examples.

Effects of Inflation on Capital Budgeting Analysis[3]

Inflation is a fact of life in the United States and most other nations, so it must be considered in any sound capital budgeting analysis. Several procedures are available for dealing with inflation. The two most frequently used methods are discussed in this section.

[3] For a formal discussion of this subject, see J. C. Van Horne, "A Note on Biases in Capital Budgeting Introduced by Inflation," *Journal of Financial and Quantitative Analysis*, January 1971; P. L. Cooley, R. L. Roenfeldt, and I. K. Chew, "Capital Budgeting Procedures under Inflation," *Financial Management*, Winter 1975; and "Cooley, Roenfeldt, and Chew vs. M. C. Findlay and A. W. Frankle," *Financial Management*, Autumn 1976. Also, note that Appendix 2A discusses in more depth the effect of inflation on interest rates.

To see how inflation enters the picture, suppose an investor lends $100 for one year at a rate of 5 percent. At the end of the year the investor will have $100(1.05) = $105.

Now suppose prices rise by 6 percent during the year. This means that the ending $105 will have a purchasing power, in terms of beginning-of-year values, of only $105/1.06 = $99. Thus, the investor will have lost $1, or 1 percent of the original purchasing power, in spite of having earned 5 percent interest: $105 at the end of the year will buy only as much in goods as $99 would have bought at the beginning of the year.

Investors recognize this problem, and, as we saw in Chapters 2 and 5, they incorporate expectations about inflation into the required rate of return. For example, suppose investors seek a *real rate of return* (k_r) of 8 percent on an investment with a given degree of risk. Suppose further that they anticipate an *annual rate of inflation* (i) of 6 percent. Then, in order to end up with the 8 percent real rate of return, the nominal rate of return, k_n, must be a value such that

$$1 + k_n = (1 + k_r)(1 + i), \tag{12-1}$$

or

$$
\begin{aligned}
k_n &= (1 + k_r)(1 + i) - 1 \\
&= 1 + k_r + i + k_r i - 1 \\
&= k_r + i + k_r i. \tag{12-1a}
\end{aligned}
$$

In words, the nominal rate (k_n) must be set equal to the real rate (k_r) plus the expected inflation (i) plus a cross-product term ($k_r i$). In our example,

$$
\begin{aligned}
k_n &= 0.08 + 0.06 + (0.08)(0.06) \\
&= 0.08 + 0.06 + 0.0048 \\
&= 0.1448 = 14.48\%.
\end{aligned}
$$

If the investor earns a nominal return of 14.48 percent on a $100 investment, the ending value, in real terms, will be

$$\$100(1.1448)/(1.06) = \$114.48/1.06 = \$108,$$

producing the required 8 percent real rate of return.

We can use these concepts to analyze capital budgeting under inflation. First, note that a project's NPV in the absence of inflation, where $k_r = k_n$ and CF_t = the net cash flow in Year t, is calculated as follows:

$$NPV = \sum_{t=1}^{N} \frac{CF_t}{(1 + k_n)^t} - Cost.$$

Now suppose we expect both sales prices and input costs to rise at the rate i, the same inflation rate that is built into the estimated cost of capital that we find in the capital markets. In this event, CF_t will increase annually at the rate i percent, producing this situation:

$$CF_t = \text{Actual cash flow}_t = \text{Inflation-free cash flow}_t(1 + i)^t.$$

For example, if we expected a net cash flow of $100 in Year 5 in the absence of inflation, then with a 5 percent rate of inflation, $CF_t = \$100(1.05)^5 = \$127.63$.

Now if net cash flows increase at the rate i per year, and if this same inflation factor is built into the cost of capital, then

$$NPV = \sum_{t=1}^{N} \frac{CF_t(1 + i)^t}{(1 + k_r)^t(1 + i)^t} - \text{Cost}.$$

Since the $(1 + i)^t$ terms in the numerator and denominator cancel, we are left with

$$NPV = \sum_{t=1}^{N} \frac{CF_t}{(1 + k_r)^t} - \text{Cost}.$$

Thus, whenever costs and sales prices are both expected to rise at the same inflation rate that investors have built into the cost of capital, then the inflation-adjusted NPV is identical to the inflation-free NPV.

If the cost of capital includes an inflation premium, as it typically does, but the cash flows are stated in current dollars, as they sometimes are, then the calculated NPV will be downward biased. The denominator will reflect inflation, but the numerator will not, and this produces the bias. If sales prices and all costs are expected to rise at exactly the same rate, then the bias can be corrected by having current cash flows increase at the inflation rate.

While it is often appropriate to assume that *variable costs* will rise at the same rate as sales prices, fixed costs, especially the depreciation associated with a project, generally increase at a lower rate. In this case, or in any situation where both revenues and all costs are not expected to rise at exactly the same rate of inflation as is built into the cost of capital, the best procedure is to build inflation into the basic cash flow component projections for each year. For example, in the Compound X example discussed in Chapter 11, the cash flows in Table 11-2 could have incorporated individual inflation rates for sales prices, wage rates, materials cost, overhead, and so on. If significant rates of inflation are projected, and if expected inflation rates for sales prices and input costs differ materially, such an adjustment must be made. This point is discussed later in the chapter, in connection with computerized capital budgeting analysis.

Capital budgeting under ordinary circumstances is, in essence, an application of a classic economic principle: A firm should expand to the point

Capital Rationing

where its marginal revenue is just equal to its marginal cost. When this rule is applied to the capital budgeting decision, marginal revenue is taken to be the percentage return on projects, while marginal cost is the firm's marginal cost of capital.

A simplified view of the concept is shown in Figure 12-1. Here we assume that the firm has five equally risky, independent investment op-

Figure 12-1
The Typical Capital Budgeting Situation

Note: If IRR > 10%, NPV is positive. Therefore, Projects A, B, and C have NPV > 0, while D and E have NPV < 0.

portunities which would cost in total $23 million. Its cost of capital is assumed to be constant at 10 percent, implying that the firm can raise all the money it wants at a cost of 10 percent. Under these conditions, the firm would accept projects A, B, and C, as they all have IRRs greater than the cost of capital, hence NPVs greater than zero. It would reject D and E because they have IRRs less than k, indicating negative NPVs. This decision would maximize the value of the firm and the wealth of its stock-holders.

Firms ordinarily operate in the manner depicted in the graph—they accept all independent projects having positive NPVs, reject those with negative NPVs, and choose between mutually exclusive investments on the basis of the higher NPV. However, a firm will occasionally set an absolute limit on the size of its capital budget that is less than the level of investment called for by the NPV (or IRR) criteria. This is called *capital rationing*.

The principal reason for such action is that some firms are reluctant to engage in external financing (borrowing, or selling stock). One management, recalling the plight of firms with substantial amounts of debt during the credit crunches of the early 1980s, may simply refuse to use debt. Another management, which has no objection to selling debt, may not want to sell equity capital for fear of losing some measure of voting control. Still others may refuse to use any form of outside financing, considering safety and control to be more important than additional profits. These are all cases of capital rationing, and they result in limiting the rate of expansion to a slower pace than would be dictated by "purely rational wealth-maximizing behavior."[4]

How should projects be selected under conditions of capital rationing? First, note that under conditions of true capital rationing, the firm's value is not being maximized: If management were maximizing, then it would move to the point where the marginal project's NPV was zero and capital rationing as defined would not exist. So, if a firm uses capital rationing, it has ruled out value maximization. The firm may, however, want to maximize value *subject to the constraint that the capital ceiling not be exceeded.* Following constrained maximization behavior will, in general, result in a

Project Selection under Capital Rationing

---

[4] We should make three points here. First, we do *not* necessarily consider a decision to hold back on expansion irrational. If the owners of a firm have what they consider to be plenty of income and wealth, then it might be quite rational for them to "trim their sails," relax, and concentrate on enjoying what they have already earned rather than on earning still more. Such behavior would not, however, be appropriate for a publicly owned firm.

The second point is that it is not correct to interpret as capital rationing a situation where the firm is willing to sell additional securities at the going market price but finds that it cannot because the market simply will not absorb more of its issues. Rather, such a situation indicates that the cost-of-capital curve is rising. If more acceptable investments are indicated than can be financed, then the cost of capital being used is too low and should be raised. This is discussed in chapter 15.

Third, firms sometimes set a limit on capital expenditures, not because of a shortage of funds, but because of limitations on other resources, especially managerial talent. A firm might, for example, feel that its personnel development program is sufficient to handle an expansion of no more than 10 percent a year, then set a limit on the capital budget to insure that expansion is held to that rate. This is not capital rationing—rather, it involves a downward reevaluation of project returns if growth exceeds some limit; that is, expected rates of return are, after some point, a decreasing function of the level of expenditures.

lower value than following unconstrained maximization, but some type of constrained maximization may produce reasonably satisfactory results. Linear programming is one method of constrained maximization that has been applied to capital rationing. Much work is going on in the area, and linear programming may, in the future, be widely applied in capital budgeting.

If a financial manager does face capital rationing, and if the constraint cannot be lifted, what can be done? The objective should be to select projects, subject to the capital rationing constraint, such that the sum of the projects' NPVs is maximized. Linear programming can be used, or, if there are not too many projects involved, one can simply enumerate all the sets of projects that meet the budget constraint and then select the set with the largest total NPV.[5]

The complexities involved in a capital rationing situation are indicated in Table 12-2. Here we assume that the firm is considering a total of eight potential projects. They are all independent, and they are equally risky. The firm has a 10 percent cost of capital, but management has decided to limit capital expenditures during the year to the amount of money that can be generated internally, $500,000. In the table, the projects are listed in the order of their NPVs, but their IRRs and profitability indices (PIs) are also shown.[6]

Table 12-2
Illustration of Capital Rationing

Project Number	Project Cost, or Outlay at t = 0	Project Life (Years)	Cash Flow per Year	NPV at 10% Cost of Capital	IRR	Profit-ability Index (PI)
1	$400,000	20	$58,600	$98,894	13.5%	1.25
2	250,000	10	55,000	87,951	17.7	1.35
3	100,000	8	24,000	28,038	17.3	1.28
4	75,000	15	12,000	16,273	13.7	1.22
5	75,000	6	18,000	3,395	11.5	1.05
6	50,000	5	14,000	3,071	12.4	1.06
7	250,000	10	41,000	1,927	10.2	1.01
8	250,000	3	99,000	−3,802	9.1	0.98

If it is to maximize the value of the firm, management must choose that set of projects with the greatest total NPV, but subject to the constraint that total expenditures must not exceed $500,000. With only eight

---

[5] For one interested in programming solutions to capital budgeting problems, a good starting point for further study is James C. T. Mao, *Quantitative Analysis of Financial Decisions* (New York: Macmillan, 1969).

[6] PI is simply the PV of the inflows divided by the cost. See Appendix 11C.

projects in total, we can try all different combinations and, by "brute force," determine the set which maximizes NPV. This set is optimal:

Project	Cost	NPV
2	$250,000	$ 87,951
3	100,000	28,038
4	75,000	16,273
5	75,000	3,395
	$500,000	$135,657

This analysis seems simple enough, but there are three factors which complicate it greatly in realistic situations:

1. Number of Projects. In the example we have only eight projects, so it is easy enough to simply list the various combinations whose costs do not exceed $500,000 and then see which combination provides the greatest total NPV. For a large firm with thousands of projects, this would be a tedious process, although computer programs are available to solve such problems. However, the other problems listed below are more serious.

2. Project Risk. In our example, we assume that the eight projects are equally risky, hence have the same cost of capital. If this were not the case, and if the number of projects were so large as to preclude hand analysis, then it would be difficult if not impossible to reach an optimal solution because the computer programs currently available cannot deal efficiently with projects having differential risk.

3. Multiple Time Constraints. Our example also assumed a single time period capital constraint. Yet, realistically, when capital rationing is practiced, the constraints usually extend out for several years. However, the funds available in future years depend on cash throw-offs from investments made in earlier years. Thus, the constraint in Year 2 depends on the investments made in Year 1, and so on. For example, we might have investment funds of $500,000 per year available from external sources for 1981 through 1985 plus, in 1982, the cash flows from investments made in 1981, and so on. To solve this type of multiperiod problem, we need information on investment opportunities in future years, not just on the opportunities in the current year, and the NPV we seek to maximize is the sum of the NPVs in each year over the time horizon being analyzed, say 1981 to 1985. In such a situation, we might even choose Project 8 in Table 12-2, in spite of its negative NPV, because it has rapid cash throw-offs. In fact, if excellent investment opportunities are expected to be available in 1982, 1983, and 1984, taking Project 8 might be part of the best long-run strategy.

A Better Approach to Capital Rationing

Our main conclusion thus far about capital rationing—which means deliberately foregoing projects with positive NPVs—is that practicing it is irrational for any firm which seeks to maximize the value of its stockholders' wealth. Also, while mathematical programming methods are available to help solve the simpler cases of capital rationing and thus to help management make the best of a bad situation, programming methods are really not capable of dealing with all the complexities encountered in the real world.

Fortunately, a better method exists for handling the types of situations that give rise to capital rationing. Usually, capital rationing occurs when the firm believes that it will encounter severe problems if it attempts to raise capital beyond some specified amount—for example, the interest rate it would have to pay would rise sharply if it attempted to increase its existing lines of credit. Such situations can be rationally handled by increasing the assigned cost of capital as the amount of capital raised increases. In effect, in terms of Figure 12-1 above, the marginal cost of capital (MCC) would begin to rise beyond some amount of capital, and this higher MCC should be used as the discount rate when determining a project's NPV. This discussion will be continued in Chapter 15, where we consider the MCC and its use in capital budgeting in some detail.

Risk Analysis in Capital Budgeting

Risk analysis is important in all financial decisions, including those relating to capital budgeting. As we saw in Chapter 5, the higher the risk associated with an investment, the higher the rate of return needed to compensate investors for assuming the risk. Procedures for both measuring project risk and incorporating it into the accept-reject decision are covered in this section.

Actually, two separate and distinct types of risk have been identified in capital budgeting: (1) *beta risk*, which measures risk only from the standpoint of an investor who holds a highly diversified portfolio, and (2) *total*, or *corporate*, *risk*, which looks at a firm's risk without considering the effects of its stockholders' own personal diversification.

Beta Risk

In Chapter 5 we examined the Capital Asset Pricing Model (CAPM) and developed the concept of the *beta coefficient* as an index of the riskiness of a particular stock relative to that of an average stock. As we saw, betas generally range from about 0.5 to about 1.5. Further, the beta of a portfolio of stocks is equal to the weighted average of the betas of the individual stocks in the portfolio, with the weights based on the number of dollars invested in each stock.

We also saw in Chapter 5 that the required rate of return on a company's stock (k) is equal to the riskless rate (R_F) plus a risk premium which is equal to the stock's beta coefficient (b) times the market risk premium ($k_M - R_F$):

$$k = R_F + b(k_M - R_F).$$

For example, consider the case of Erie Steel Company, an integrated steel producer operating in the Great Lakes region. Erie Steel's beta is 1.1, so if $R_F = 8\%$ and $k_M = 12\%$, then

$$k = 8\% + 1.1(4\%) = 12.4\%.$$

This suggests that stockholders are willing to give Erie money to invest if the company can earn 12.4 percent or more on this money. *Therefore, as a first approximation, Erie should invest in capital projects if and only if these projects have an expected return of 12.4 percent or more.*[7] In other words, Erie should use 12.4 percent as its discount rate to determine projects' NPVs, or as the "hurdle rate" if the IRR method is used.

Suppose, however, that taking on a particular project will change Erie's beta coefficient. For example, the company might be considering the construction of a fleet of barges to haul iron ore, and barge operations might have betas of 1.5 rather than 1.1. Since the corporation itself may be regarded as a "portfolio of assets," and since the beta of any portfolio is a weighted average of the betas of the individual assets, taking on the barge investment will cause the overall corporate beta to rise and to end up somewhere between the original beta of 1.1 and the barge division's beta of 1.5. The exact position will depend on the relative size of the investment in basic steel versus that in barges. If 80 percent of the total corporate funds were in basic steel and 20 percent were in barges, then the new beta would be $0.8(1.1) + 0.2(1.5) = 1.18$.

An increase in the beta coefficient will cause the stock price to decline *unless the increased beta is offset by a higher expected rate of return.* Specifically, the overall corporate cost of capital will rise to 12.72 percent:

$$k_{(new)} = 8\% + 1.18(4\%) = 12.72\%.$$

Therefore, to keep the barge investment from lowering the value of the firm, Erie's expected overall rate of return must rise from 12.4 percent to 12.72 percent.

If investments in basic steel earn 12.4 percent, how much must the barge investment earn in order for the new overall rate of return to equal

---

[7] To simplify things somewhat, we assume at this point that the firm uses only equity capital. If debt is used, then the cost of capital used must be a weighted average of the costs of debt and equity. This point is discussed at length in Chapters 15, 16, and 17.

12.72 percent? Let X be the required return on the barge investment, and then calculate the value of X as follows:

$$0.8(12.4\%) + 0.2(X) = 12.72\%$$
$$X = 14.0\%.$$

In summary, if Erie makes the barge investment, its beta will rise from 1.1 to 1.18; its overall required rate of return will rise from 12.4 percent to 12.72 percent; and it will achieve this new required rate if the barge investment earns 14 percent. If the barge investment has an expected return of more than 14 percent, taking it on will increase the value of Erie's stock. If the expected return is less than 14 percent, taking it on will decrease the stock's value. At an expected return of 14 percent, the barge project is a "breakeven" proposition in terms of its effect on the value of the stock.

This line of reasoning leads to the conclusion that, if the beta coefficient for each project could be determined, individual projects' costs of capital could be found as follows:

$$k_{(project)} = R_F + b_{(project)}(k_M - R_F).$$

Thus, for basic steel projects with b = 1.1, Erie should use 12.4 percent as the discount rate. The barge project should be evaluated at a 14 percent discount rate:

$$k_{(barge)} = 8\% + 1.5(4\%) = 8\% + 6\% = 14\%.$$

Figure 12-2
Using the Security Market Line Concept in Capital Budgeting

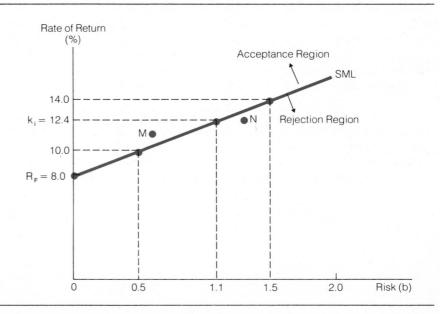

A low-risk project such as a new steel distribution center with a beta of only 0.5 would have a cost of capital of 10 percent:

$$k_{(center)} = 8\% + 0.5(4\%) = 10\%.$$

Figure 12-2 gives a graphic summary of these concepts as applied to Erie Steel. Note the following points:

1. The SML is the same as the Security Market Line developed in Chapter 5. It shows how investors are willing to make tradeoffs between risk as measured by beta and expected returns. The higher the risk, the higher the rate of return needed to compensate investors for bearing this risk, and the SML specifies the nature of this relationship.
2. Erie Steel initially had a beta of 1.1, so its required rate of return on average-risk investments was 12.4 percent.
3. High-risk investments like the barge line require higher rates of return, while low-risk investments like the distribution center have lower required rates of return. Note also that if Erie makes relatively large investments in either high- or low-risk projects, as opposed to those with average risks, both the corporate beta and the required rate of return on the common stock (k_s) will change.
4. If the expected rate of return on a given capital project lies *above* the SML, the expected rate of return on the project is more than enough to compensate for its risk, so it should be accepted. Conversely, if the project's rate of return lies *below* the SML, it should be rejected. Thus, Project M in Figure 12-2 is acceptable, while Project N should be rejected. N has a higher expected return than M, but the differential is not enough to offset N's much higher risk.

Corporate Risk versus Beta Risk

A particular project might have highly uncertain returns, yet taking it on might not affect the firm's beta coefficient at all. Recall that the beta coefficient reflects only that part of an investor's risk which cannot be eliminated by holding a large portfolio of stocks. Now suppose that 100 firms in the oil business each drill one wildcat well. Each company has $1 million of capital which it will invest in one well. If a firm strikes oil, then it will earn a profit of $1.4 million, while if it hits a dry hole, it will suffer a $1 million loss and go bankrupt. The probability of striking oil is 50 percent.

From the standpoint of the individual firms, this is a very risky business. Their expected rate of return is 20 percent, calculated as follows:

$$\begin{aligned}
\frac{\text{Expected rate}}{\text{of return}} &= \frac{\text{Expected profit}}{\text{Investment}} \\
&= \frac{0.5(-\$1 \text{ million}) + 0.5(+\$1.4 \text{ million})}{\$1 \text{ million}} \\
&= \frac{-\$500,000 + \$700,000}{\$1,000,000} = 20\%.
\end{aligned}$$

Note, however, that even though the expected return is 20 percent, there is a 50 percent probability of each firm's being wiped out.

Although the riskiness of each individual firm is high, if a stockholder constructs a portfolio consisting of one share of each of the 100 companies, the riskiness of this portfolio is not high at all. Some of the stocks will hit and do well, others will miss and go out of business, but the portfolio's return will be very close to the expected 20 percent. Therefore, since investors can diversify away the risks inherent in each of the individual companies, these risks are *not market-related* and so do not affect the companies' beta coefficients.[8]

With this background, *we may define the corporate risk of a capital budgeting project as the probability that the project will incur losses which will, at a minimum, destabilize the corporation's earnings and, at the extreme, cause it to go bankrupt.* A project with a high degree of corporate risk will not necessarily affect the firm's beta to any great extent; our oil drilling example demonstrates this point. On the other hand, if the riskiness of a project is not diversifiable, then the project may have a high degree of both corporate and beta risk. For example, suppose a firm decides to undertake a major expansion to build solar-powered autos. The firm is not sure if its technology will work on a mass production basis, so there are great risks in the venture. Management also estimates that the project will have a higher probability of success if the economy is strong, for then people will have the money to spend on buying the new autos. This means that the plant will tend to do well if other companies are also doing well, and to do badly if they do badly; hence the plant's beta coefficient will be high. A project like this will have a high degree of both corporate risk and beta risk.

Beta risk is obviously important because of beta's effect on the value of a firm's stock. At the same time, corporate risk is also important for two primary reasons:

1. Undiversified stockholders, including the owners of small businesses, are more concerned about corporate risk than about beta risk.
2. The firm's stability is important to its managers, workers, customers, suppliers, and creditors, and also to the community in which it operates. Firms that are in serious danger of bankruptcy, or even of suffering low profits and reduced output, have difficulty attracting and retaining good managers and workers. Also, both suppliers and

---

[8] Note also that if the 100 separate companies were merged, the combined company would not be very risky—it would drill lots of wells, losing on some and hitting on others, but it would earn a relatively steady profit. This helps explain why large oil (and other) companies are less risky than smaller companies, but it also explains why an investor who holds the stocks of many small companies may not have a riskier portfolio than someone who holds the stocks of large companies.

customers will be reluctant to depend on the weak firm, and it will have difficulty borrowing money except at high interest rates. These factors will tend to reduce the firm's profitability, hence the price of its stock.

We see, then, that corporate risk is also important even to well-diversified stockholders.

Measuring the risk inherent in capital projects is a difficult task. Studies suggest that most corporations give less weight to beta than to corporate risk, and that they consider beta risk only in terms of subjective evaluations, not by statistical and mathematical processes. Corporate risk, on the other hand, is given great weight in the capital budgeting process, and it is analyzed by both quantitative and qualitative methods. Some of these methods are discussed in this section.

Techniques for Measuring Corporate Risk

The starting point for analyzing corporate risk involves determining the uncertainty inherent in a project's cash flows. This analysis can be handled in a number of ways, ranging from informal judgments to complex economic and statistical analyses involving large-scale computer models. To illustrate what is involved here, refer back to Carter Chemical's Compound X project as described in Chapter 11. Most of the elements in Table 11-2, which gave the income statement projections for Compound X, are subject to uncertainty. For example, sales for 1983 are projected at 75,000 tons to be sold at a net price of $60 per ton, or $4.5 million in total. However, unit sales will probably be somewhat higher or lower than 75,000 tons, and the sales price might be different from $60 per ton. *In effect, these estimates are expected values taken from probability distributions, as are all the other figures shown in Table 11-2.* The distributions could be relatively "tight," with small standard deviations, or they could be "flat," denoting a great deal of uncertainty about the variable in question. For example, the 75,000 ton sales estimate for 1983 could have come from a distribution like A, B, or C in Figure 12-3. The more peaked the distribution, the higher the probability that actual sales will be close to the predicted level, hence the smaller the risk of the project.[9]

Intuitively, we know that every element in Table 11-2 represents an expected value taken from a distribution like one of those shown in Figure 12-3. We also know that if a key input variable such as tons sold changes, so will the project's NPV. *Sensitivity analysis indicates exactly how much NPV will change in response to a given change in an input variable, other things held constant.* Sensitivity analysis is sometimes called "what if" analysis be-

Sensitivity Analysis

---

[9] For convenience, we frequently use distributions that are approximately normal. While the assumption of normality is often appropriate, at times a skewed distribution is more realistic.

Figure 12-3
Probability Distributions for Tons of Compound X
Sold in 1983

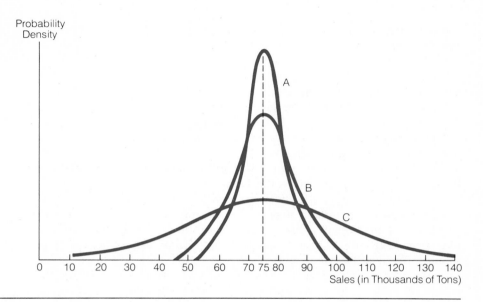

cause it answers questions such as this: "What if sales are only 75,000 units rather than 100,000? What will then happen to NPV?"

Sensitivity analysis begins with a *base case* situation. To illustrate the procedure, we shall consider the data given in Table 12-3, where projected income statements for Project Y, a $100,000 plant with a five year expected life, are shown. The values for unit sales, sales price, fixed and variable costs, and construction costs are the *most likely*, or *base case*, values, and the resulting $13,970 NPV is called the *base case NPV*. Now we begin asking a series of "what if" questions: "What if output is 20 percent below the forecasted level?" "What if sales prices fall?" "What if the construction cost is $120,000 rather than the expected $100,000?" *Sensitivity analysis is designed to answer questions such as these.*

In a sensitivity analysis, we change each variable by specific percentages above and below the base case value, calculate new NPVs (holding other things constant), and then plot the NPVs against the variable in question. Figure 12-4 shows Project Y's sensitivity graphs for a number of the key input variables. The slopes of the lines show how sensitive NPV is to changes in each of the inputs: the steeper the slope, the more sensitive the NPV is to changes in the variable.

Table 12-3
Project Y: Data on Project and Base Case
Analysis

Project cost: $100,000 expenditure at t = 0.
Salvage value: $15,000.
Expected life: 5 years.
Depreciation method: Straight line. Annual depreciation = ($100,000 − $15,000)/5
= $17,000.
Cost of capital: 10%.

Projected income statement, base case:

	Year 1	Year 2	Year 3	Year 4	Year 5
Sales (units)	3,000	3,000	3,000	3,000	3,000
Sales price	$75	$75	$75	$75	$75
Net sales	$225,000	$225,000	$225,000	$225,000	$225,000
Variable costs ($45.87/unit)	137,600	137,600	137,600	137,600	137,600
Fixed costs (except depreciation)	50,000	50,000	50,000	50,000	50,000
Depreciation	17,000	17,000	17,000	17,000	17,000
Total costs	$204,600	$204,600	$204,600	$204,600	$204,600
EBIT	$ 20,400	$ 20,400	$ 20,400	$ 20,400	$ 20,400
Federal and state taxes (48%)	9,792	9,792	9,792	9,792	9,792
Net income	$ 10,608	$ 10,608	$ 10,608	$ 10,608	$ 10,608
Add back: depreciation	17,000	17,000	17,000	17,000	17,000
salvage					15,000
Net cash flow	$ 27,608	$ 27,608	$ 27,608	$ 27,608	$ 42,608

NPV = $27,608 (PVIFA$_{10\%,5}$) + $15,000(PVIF$_{10\%,5}$) − $100,000
= $27,608(3.7908) + $15,000(0.6209) − $100,000
= $13,970.

If we were comparing two projects, other things held constant, the one with the steeper sensitivity lines would be regarded as riskier—a relatively small error in estimating variables such as demand for the product would produce a large error in the project's projected NPV. Thus, sensitivity analysis provides useful insights into the relative riskiness of different projects. It is interesting—and it should be frightening to management—to note that even a small decline in tons sold or the sales price, or a small rise in the variable cost per unit, would cause Project Y's NPV to change from positive to negative. Project Y has quite a bit of corporate risk.

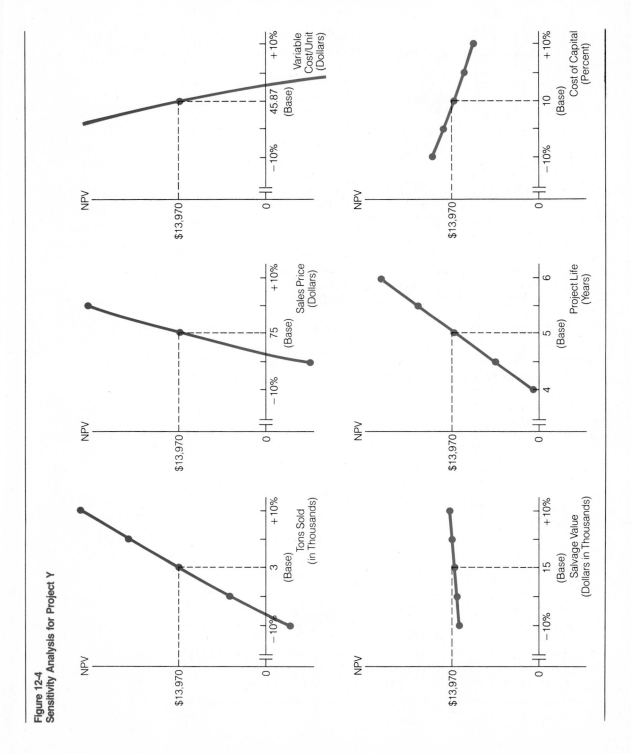

Figure 12-4
Sensitivity Analysis for Project Y

Although sensitivity analysis is widely used in industry, it does have some severe limitations. Consider, for example, a proposed coal mine whose NPV is highly sensitive to changes in both output and sales prices. Still, if a utility company has contracted to buy most of the mine's output at a fixed price per ton, plus inflation adjustments, then the mine venture may not be very risky in spite of the steep sensitivity lines. *In general, a project's risk depends on both (1) its sensitivity to changes in key variables and (2) the range of likely values of these variables—the variables' probability distributions.*

Computer simulation provides a means of tying together sensitivities and probability distributions to quantify a project's risk. The first step in a computer simulation is to specify a probability distribution for each of the key variables in the analysis. To illustrate, suppose we have determined that the probability distribution of the future unit sales of Compound Y is represented by Columns 1 and 2 of Table 12-4.[11] The expected value of units sold is 3,000, but sales can range from 2,000 to 4,000 units. The third column of Table 12-4 gives a range of random numbers associated with each sales estimate. Computers have stored in them (or they can generate) random numbers such as those given in Table 12-5. Notice that in Column 2 of Table 12-4 there is a 5 percent probability that sales will be as low as 2,000 units; therefore, 5 digits (0, 1, 2, 3, and 4) are assigned to this output (see Column 3 of Table 12-4). Twenty digits are assigned to an output of 2,500, and so on for the other possible outputs. If the distributions and associated random numbers have been specified for all the other key variables—sales price, unit variable costs, and construction costs, to name some—the computer simulation can begin. These are the steps involved:

Computer Simulation[10]

Table 12-4
Probability Distribution for Units Sold of Compound Y

Units Sold (1)	Probability (2)	Associated Random Numbers (3)
2,000	0.05	00-04
2,500	0.20	05-24
3,000	0.50	25-74
3,500	0.20	75-94
4,000	0.05	95-99
Expected value = 3,000		

[10] The concept of simulation analysis in capital budgeting was first reported by D. B. Hertz, "Risk Analysis in Capital Investments," *Harvard Business Review* (January-February 1964).

[11] Here we assume that sales are always in multiples of 500 and that there is no probability of sales below 2,000 or above 4,000 units. These simplifications are purely for illustrative purposes; actual simulation models need have no such restrictions. In fact, standard computer simulation software pack-

(continued)

1. The computer selects a random number for each uncertain variable (a different number for each variable). For example, it might select 44 for units sold; 17 for the sales price; and 16 for labor costs—these are the first three random numbers listed in Table 12-5.
2. Depending on the random number selected, a value is determined for each variable. The 44 associated with the units sold indicates in Table 12-4 that the appropriate number of units for use in the first run is 3,000. Had a 3 come up, then tons sold would have been 2,000, while if 99 had come up, then the designated tons sold would have been 4,000. Values for all the other variables are set in like manner.[12]
3. Once values have been established for all the variables, the computer generates a set of income statements and cash flows similar to the ones shown earlier in Table 12-3. (Table 12-3 is based on the expected values of the designated variables.) These cash flows are then discounted at the cost of capital (which may also be treated as a random variable), the value of the construction cost is subtracted, and the result is the net present value of the project on the computer's first run.

Table 12-5					44	17	16	58	01	79	83	86	19	62	06 76 50 03 10
Illustrative Table of Two					84	16	07	44	99	83	11	46	32	24	20 14 85 88 45
Digit Random Numbers					82	97	77	77	81	07	45	32	14	08	32 98 94 07 72

<table>
<tr><td>Table 12-5
Illustrative Table of Two
Digit Random Numbers</td><td>
44 17 16 58 01   79 83 86 19 62   06 76 50 03 10
84 16 07 44 99   83 11 46 32 24   20 14 85 88 45
82 97 77 77 81   07 45 32 14 08   32 98 94 07 72
50 92 26 11 97   00 56 76 31 38   80 22 02 53 53
83 39 50 08 30   42 34 07 96 88   54 42 06 87 98

40 33 20 38 26   13 89 51 03 74   17 76 37 13 04
96 83 50 87 75   97 12 25 93 47   70 33 24 03 54
88 42 95 45 72   16 64 36 16 00   04 43 18 66 79
33 27 14 34 09   45 59 34 68 49   12 72 07 34 45
50 27 89 87 19   20 15 37 00 49   52 85 66 60 44
</td></tr>
</table>

ages can very easily handle continuous normal distributions or distributions skewed in any manner. At the University of Florida we use a program called Interactive Financial Planning System (IFPS), which is available from Execucom Systems Corporation, Austin, Texas. IFPS is also used by several hundred large corporations and is on Control Data Corporation's time sharing system. One can learn to use this system (or others that are available) in a few days and then do the type of analysis described here very easily.

[12] Simulation models can be programmed to assume either independence or dependence among variables. In this simple example, we assume independence; however, in many real simulations it is more realistic to assume dependence. Thus, it might be assumed that if demand is weak and the figure for tons sold is relatively low, then prices will also be weak. Similarly, the sales price in one year can be completely independent of or dependent on the price in the preceding year, or it can be somewhat correlated with the previous year's price. Simulation programs such as the one used at the University of Florida (IFPS) can handle these issues with ease, although decision makers often have trouble specifying exactly how the different variables are related to one another.

4. The NPV generated on Run 1 is stored, and the computer then goes on to Run 2. Here a different set of random numbers, hence cash flows, is used. The NPV generated in Run 2 is then stored, and the model proceeds on out to perhaps 500 runs. Modern computers can complete this operation almost instantaneously for a cost of less than two dollars.
5. The stored NPVs (all 500 of them) are then printed out in the form of a frequency distribution, together with the expected NPV and the standard deviation of this NPV.[13]

The simulation process is summarized in Figure 12-5. Here we see (in graph form) the probability distributions of the key variables, a listing of the steps in the simulation process, and the NPV distribution that results when Compound Y is subjected to simulation analysis.

The significant advantage of simulation is that it shows us the range of possible outcomes if the project is accepted, not just a point estimate of the NPV. The expected NPV can be used as a measure of the project's profitability, while the variability of this NPV can be used to measure risk. To illustrate, assume that Project Y's expected NPV is \$13,970, and the standard deviation of this NPV, as calculated by the computer in the simulation, is $\sigma_{NPV} = \$8,250$. Some other Project Z has expected NPV = \$25,000 and $\sigma_{NPV} = \$30,000$. We can calculate the *coefficient of variation* of each of the projects' NPVs as follows:

$$\text{Coefficient of variation} = v = \frac{\text{Standard deviation}}{\text{Expected value}} = \frac{\sigma_{NPV}}{\text{Expected NPV}}.$$

$$v_Y = \frac{\$8,250}{\$13,970} = 0.59 \text{ for Project Y.}$$

$$v_Z = \frac{\$30,000}{\$25,000} = 1.20 \text{ for Project Z.}$$

The coefficient of variation is a standardized risk measure, and it can be used to compare the relative riskiness of projects which differ in size, such as Y and Z. (If standard deviations were compared, then a large project, which would have a large σ_{NPV} just because it had a large NPV, would generally appear riskier than a smaller project with a smaller NPV. Use of the coefficient of variation avoids this problem.) If Carter Chemical's average project had v = 1.0, then Project Y, with v = only 0.59, would appear to be less risky than most, while Project Z would be riskier than average. Thus, Y would appear to be eligible for evaluation with a relatively low cost of capital, while a higher than average cost should be used for Z.[14]

---

[13] The better computer programs give other information, such as IRR, σ_{IRR}, and payback. They also generate the data points required for a sensitivity analysis.

[14] Use of the coefficient of variation in risk analysis is discussed further in Appendices 12A and 12B.

Figure 12-5
Illustration of Simulation Analysis

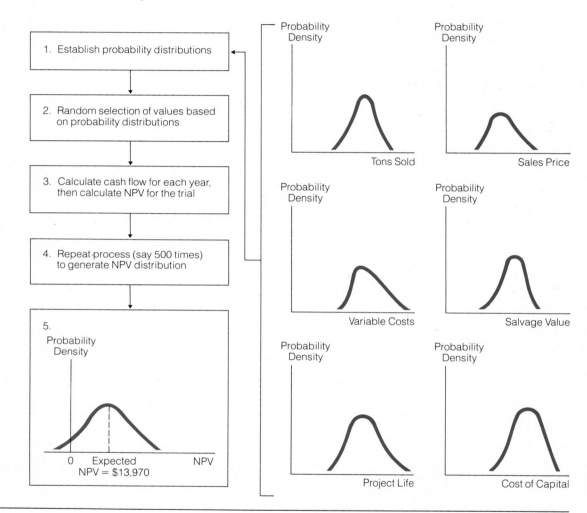

Limitations of Simulation Analysis

In spite of its obvious appeal, simulation analysis has not been as widely used in industry as one might think. Five major reasons for this lack of general acceptance are discussed here.

Cost versus Benefits. One reason that simulation is not more widely used has to do with its cost in relation to the benefits of its use. Until quite recently, developing a simulation model was a major undertaking that required a good deal of high-powered programming talent and a lot of expensive computer time. This is no longer true. Simulation software, and computer hardware, have been developed to the point where cost is not a major consideration, at least for the larger firms.

Time Lag. It generally takes a while for any new managerial technology to become widely accepted, and simulation analysis may be in this position. This point was made by several executives who reviewed this book.

Interdependencies among the Variables. The simulation process described above assumes that the variables are independent of one another. However, it may very well be that such variables as unit sales and sales prices are correlated. For example, if demand is weak, sales prices may also be depressed. This suggests that if a low value of tons sold is selected, a low value for the sales price should also be used.[15] Similarly, the simulation process described above assumes that the values of each variable, hence the bottom line cash flows, are independent over time. Yet in many situations it seems more reasonable to assume that high sales in the early years imply market acceptance, hence high sales in future years, rather than to assume that sales in one year are not correlated with sales levels in other years.

It is easy enough to incorporate any type of correlation among variables that one desires into a simulation analysis. However, it is *not* easy to specify what the correlations should be. Indeed, people who have tried to obtain such relationships from the operating executives who must estimate them have eloquently emphasized the difficulties involved.[16] Clearly, the problem is not insurmountable, as the use of simulation is growing rapidly. Still, it is important not to underestimate the difficulty of obtaining valid estimates of probability distributions and correlations among the variables.[17]

No Specific Decision Rule. A fourth problem with simulation analysis is that, even when a simulation analysis has been completed, no clear-cut

[15] This statement implies a *downward shift* in the demand curve for the product. However, one can also visualize *movement along a demand curve*, which would imply that low sales prices would be associated with high demand. The economics of the situation would determine the specific nature of the relationship, and making such determinations is the critical substantive ingredient of good capital budgeting simulation analysis.

[16] For an excellent discussion of this problem, see K. Larry Hastie, "One Businessman's View of Capital Budgeting," *Financial Management*, Winter 1974.

[17] Some critics use the terms GIGO and SWAG to describe simulation analysis. These terms are defined in the glossary.

decision rule emerges. We end up with an expected NPV and a distribution about this expected value, which we can use to judge the project's risk, but the analysis has no mechanism to indicate whether the profitability as measured by the expected NPV is sufficient to compensate for the risk as indicated by σ_{NPV} or v_{NPV}. This is in sharp contrast to the beta approach, where a project is specifically acceptable if its expected rate of return exceeds its beta-determined required rate of return.

Ignores Diversification. The fifth problem with simulation is that it ignores the effects of diversification, both within the firm and by investors in their personal portfolios. Thus, an individual project may have highly uncertain returns, but if those returns are not correlated with the returns on the firm's other assets, then the project may not be risky in the sense of destabilizing the firm as a whole. Similarly, if a project's returns are not correlated with the stock market, even a project with highly variable returns might not be regarded as risky by well-diversified stockholders, who are concerned with *market risk*, not with *total risk*.

Scenario Analysis: Optimistic, Pessimistic, and Most Likely Outcomes

Because of the problems associated with simulation analysis, especially the problem of dealing with correlations among the variables, firms often use a shorter version of simulation called *scenario analysis*. Here the operating executives pick a "bad" set of circumstances (low unit sales, low sales price, high variable cost/unit, high construction cost, etc.) and a "good" set. Perhaps each set might be selected on the basis that the probability of each variable being as high or as low as the indicated value is no more than 25 percent. The NPV under the "bad" and "good" conditions would be calculated and compared to the most likely, or base case, NPV.

Portfolio Effects within the Firm

As we noted in Chapter 5, a security might be quite risky if held in isolation, but not very risky if held as a part of a well-diversified portfolio. The same thing is true of capital budgeting—the returns on an individual project might be highly uncertain, but if the project is small relative to the total firm, and if its returns are not highly correlated with the firm's other assets, then the project may not be very risky in either the corporate or the beta sense.

Many firms do make serious efforts to diversify; often, this is a specific objective of the long-run strategic plan. For example, the oil companies have diversified into both nuclear energy and coal to broaden their operating bases, while real estate developers have diversified geographically to lessen the impact of a slowdown in one region. The major objective of many such moves is to stabilize earnings, reduce corporate risk, and thereby raise the value of the firm's stock.

Thus far we have seen that capital budgeting can affect a firm's beta risk, its corporate risk, or both. We have also seen that it is exceedingly difficult to quantify either effect. In other words, it is possible to reach the general conclusion that one project is riskier than another (in either the beta or the corporate sense), but it is difficult to develop a really good *measure* of project risk.

This lack of precision in measuring project risk makes it difficult to specify risk-adjusted rates of return, or costs of capital, with which to evaluate individual projects. As we shall see in Chapter 15, it is possible to estimate a firm's overall cost of capital reasonably accurately. Moreover, it is generally agreed that riskier projects should be evaluated with a higher cost of capital than the overall corporate cost, while a lower discount rate should be used for lower-risk projects. Unfortunately, there is no good way of specifying exactly *how much* higher or lower these discount rates should be; given the present state of the art, risk adjustments are necessarily judgmental and somewhat arbitrary.

Although the process is not exact, Carter Chemical (and many other companies) sets risk-adjusted discount rates for use in capital budgeting in a two step process: (1) divisional costs of capital are established for each of the major operating divisions, and (2) within divisions, all projects are classified into three categories—high-risk, average-risk, and low-risk. The cost of capital estimate obtained for each division depends on (1) the beta coefficient the division would have if it operated as an independent unit and (2) the amount of debt financing the division does. (Discussion of the calculations involved in estimating the cost of capital is deferred to Chapter 15.) Each of Carter's divisions then uses its basic cost of capital as the discount rate for average projects, reduces it by one percentage point when evaluating low-risk projects, and raises it by two percentage points for high-risk projects. For example, if a division's basic cost of capital is estimated to be 10 percent, then a 12 percent discount rate will be used for high-risk projects and a 9 percent rate for low-risk projects. Average-risk projects, which constitute about 80 percent of most divisions' capital budgets, are evaluated at the 10 percent corporate cost of capital. This procedure is not very elegant, but it does at least recognize that different divisions have different characteristics, hence different costs of capital, and it also recognizes differential project riskiness within divisions. Carter Chemical's financial staff feels that these adjustments are in the right direction and that they result in better decisions than would be obtained if no adjustments at all were made.

Risk-Adjusted Discount Rates and Divisional Cost of Capital

Summary

This chapter has dealt with four key issues in capital budgeting: equipment replacement decisions, inflation adjustments, capital rationing, and risk. The key to making good replacement decisions is to develop accurate estimates of *incremental* cash flows—how large an investment will the replacement entail, and what *net* savings will it produce? If the present value of the net savings exceeds the cost of the equipment, then the replacement should be undertaken. However, as noted in the chapter, if the various replacement alternatives have different lives, it is necessary to adjust to a common life. This adjustment can be made either by *replacement chains* or by using *equivalent annual annuities*.

Inflation exists in the U.S. and most other economies, and it must be dealt with in capital budgeting analysis. If inflation is ignored, this generally has the effect of not increasing the cash flows in the numerator of the NPV equation, but of unconsciously adjusting the denominator because market forces build inflation into the cost of capital. Thus, the net result of ignoring inflation is to create a downward bias in evaluating projects (that is, reject projects that should be accepted). The best way of correcting for the bias is to build price increases based on expected inflation rates directly into the cash flows. Computer programs for capital budgeting analysis make this adjustment relatively easy.

Capital rationing exists whenever the firm sets a specific limit on the size of its capital budget rather than expand the capital budget to the point where all projects with NPV > 0 are included. If capital rationing exists, then management should attempt to maximize the total NPV added subject to the constraint of not exceeding the available capital. Methods have been devised for dealing with capital rationing, but the best solution to this problem is simply to avoid it by (1) adjusting upward the cost of capital if capital costs indeed rise whenever the amount of capital increases beyond some point, and (2) then using this higher marginal cost of capital as the discount rate in an NPV project evaluation. This process is discussed in some depth in Chapter 15.

Our analysis of risk has focused on two issues: (1) the effect of a given project on the firm's beta coefficient *(beta risk)* and (2) the project's effect on the probability of bankruptcy *(corporate risk)*. Both types of risk are important. Beta risk directly affects the value of the firm's stock. Corporate risk affects the financial strength of the firm, and this, in turn, influences its ability to use debt, to maintain smooth operations over time, and to avoid crises that might consume the energy of the firm's managers and disrupt its employees, customers, suppliers, and community.

Both measuring risk and incorporating it into capital budgeting decisions involve judgment. It is possible to use techniques such as simulation and sensitivity analysis, but the assessment of risk in capital budgeting nonetheless remains a judgmental process.

Questions   **12-1** Look at Table 12-1, and answer these questions:

a. Why are the salvage values shown on Lines 2 and 11 not reduced for taxes?

b. Why is depreciation on the old machine deducted on Line 9?

c. What would happen if the new machine permitted a *reduction* in working capital?

d. Why are the cost savings on Line 7 reduced by multiplying the before-tax figure by $(1 - t)$, whereas the net depreciation figure on Line 10 is multiplied by t?

12-2 In what sense do the key assumptions listed in Table 11-3 in Chapter 11 represent points on probability distributions? Would it be more important to conduct a sensitivity analysis on input variables with peaked or with flat distributions?

12-3 Differentiate among (a) simulation analysis, (b) optimistic-pessimistic-most likely analysis, and (c) sensitivity analysis. If AT&T were considering two investments, one calling for the expenditure of $100 million to develop a satellite communications system, and the other involving the expenditure of $5,000 for a new truck, on which one would the company be more likely to use simulation?

12-4 Distinguish between the beta risk and the corporate risk of a project being considered for inclusion in the capital budget. Which type do you feel should be given the greater weight in capital budgeting decisions?

12-5 Why is it true, in general, that a failure to adjust expected cash flows for expected inflation biases the calculated NPV downward?

12-6 Suppose a firm is considering two mutually exclusive projects. One has a life of six years and the other a life of ten years. Would the failure to employ some type of replacement chain analysis bias an NPV analysis against one of the projects? Explain.

12-7 What is the best way to deal with capital rationing? Justify your answer.

12-8 If two projects had the same costs (both at t = 0), the same levels of expected cash flows in each year, the same expected lives, and the same standard deviations of expected cash flows in each year, under what conditions should they be evaluated with the same or with different costs of capital?

ST12-1 The Bower-Logue Corporation (BLC) currently uses an injection molding machine that was purchased two years ago. This old machine is being depreciated on a straight line basis toward a $500 salvage value, and it has six years of remaining life. Its current book value is $2,600, and it can be sold for $3,000 at this time.

Self-Test Problem

    BLC is offered a replacement machine which has a cost of $8,000, an estimated useful life of six years, and an estimated salvage value of $800. This machine would also be depreciated on a straight line basis, and a 6 2/3 percent tax credit would be applicable. The replacement machine would permit an output expansion, so sales would rise by $1,000 per year, yet the new machine's much greater efficiency would still cause operating expenses to decline by $1,500 per year. The new machine would require that inventories be increased by $2,000, but accounts payable would also increase by $500.

BLC's effective tax rate is 46 percent, and its cost of capital is 15 percent. Should it replace the old machine?

Problems

12-1 (Risk-adjusted discount rates) The Bey Burger Company's average cost of capital is 10 percent. The company is choosing between two mutually exclusive projects. Project B is of average risk, it has a cost of $20,000, and it has expected cash flows of $5,880.72 per year for five years. Project A is of above average risk, and management estimates that its cost of capital is 12 percent. A also costs $20,000, and it is expected to provide cash flows of $3,752.21 per year for ten years. Each project will terminate at the end of its designated life.

a. Calculate risk-adjusted NPVs for the two projects, and use these NPVs to choose between them. (Note: No new calculations are needed if you worked Problem 11-5 in Chapter 11.)

b. Explain how you could find a risk-adjusted discount rate for Project A that would make its risk-adjusted NPV_A equal to NPV_B when B is evaluated at a 10 percent cost of capital.

12-2 (Replacement) The Bankston Company is considering the purchase of a new machine tool to replace an obsolete one. The machine being used for the operation has both a tax book value and a market value of zero; it is in good working order and will last, physically, for at least an additional fifteen years. The proposed machine will perform the operation so much more efficiently that Bankston's engineers estimate that labor, material, and other direct costs of the operation will be reduced by $4,500 a year if it is installed. The proposed machine costs $24,000 delivered and installed, and its economic life is estimated to be fifteen years with a zero salvage value. The company expects to earn 14 percent on its investment after taxes (14 percent is the firm's cost of capital). The tax rate is 55 percent, and the firm uses straight line depreciation. Should Bankston buy the new machine? The investment tax credit does not apply.

12-3 (Replacement) Rentz Brewing Company is contemplating replacing one of its bottling machines with a newer and more efficient machine. The old machine has a book value of $100,000 and a remaining useful life of five years. The firm does not expect to realize any return from scrapping the old machine in five years, but if it were sold now to another firm in the industry, Rentz would receive $60,000 for it.

The new machine has a purchase price of $220,000, an estimated useful life of five years, and an estimated salvage value of $30,000. A 10 percent investment tax credit is in effect. The new machine is expected to economize on electric power usage, labor, and repair costs, and also to reduce defective bottles; in total, an annual saving of $50,000 will be realized if the new machine is installed. (Note: To calculate depreciation, assume that the salvage value *is* deducted from cost to get the depreciable cost.) The company is in the 40 percent tax bracket, has a 14 percent cost of capital, and uses straight line depreciation.

a. Should Rentz purchase the new machine? Support your answer.

b. In general, how would each of the following factors affect the investment decision, and how would each be treated? (Give verbal answers.)

   1. The expected life of the existing machine decreases.

   2. Improvements in the equipment to be purchased are expected to occur each year, and the result will be to increase the returns or expected savings from new machines over the savings expected with this year's model for every year in the foreseeable future.

12-4 (Replacement) Nantell Printing Company has an opportunity to purchase a new, more efficient printing press, Model 1982, to replace two presses now in use, Models 1964 and 1979. Nantell's vice-president in charge of purchasing has reported that the new press, Model 1982, will cost $62,500. It has an expected eight year useful life and a salvage value of $6,500 based on figures approved by the IRS. However, since Model 1982 represents a new generation of presses, it is predicted that the press will actually be sold for $7,500 at the end of its useful life. Use straight line depreciation.

From an examination of the company's books, you have determined that Model 1964 has been fully depreciated, while Model 1979, which was purchased three years ago for $62,000, is being depreciated over an original eleven year period toward an estimated salvage value of $7,000. The demand in the market for these older presses is such that Model 1964 could be sold today for $3,000 and Model 1979 for $20,000.

If the Model 1982 printing press is purchased, Nantell will be able to *decrease* inventories by $7,000, and accounts payable will decline by $4,000 for the duration of Model 1982's useful life. Model 1982 will generate annual inflows of $10,833 before tax. You have been asked to calculate the NPV for this project. Nantell's income tax rate is 40 percent, the capital gains tax rate is 30 percent, and Model 1982 is eligible for a 10 percent investment tax credit. The company's cost of capital is 14 percent. (Hint: Remember to treat capital gains and capital losses separately—they should not be netted out. Also, remember that recaptured depreciation is taxed at regular income tax rates: only sums received from the sale of equipment in excess of the original depreciable cost are taxed as capital gains.)

12-5 (Unequal lives) Station WJXT is considering the replacement of its old, fully depreciated sound mixer. Two new models are available. Mixer X has a cost of $216,600, a five year expected life, and after-tax cash flows (labor savings) of $58,200 per year. Mixer Y has a cost of $345,000, a ten year life, and after-tax cash flows of $63,400 per year. No new technological developments are expected, but mixer prices are falling because of competition from Japanese imports. In five years, mixer prices are expected to be only 75 percent of current prices. The cost of capital is 12 percent. If the replacement is to be made, it must be done now. Should WJXT replace the old mixer and, if so, with X or Y?

12-6 (Inflation adjustment) Nuclear Data, Inc. (NDI), a firm which manufactures monitoring equipment used in nuclear power plants, is considering a major expansion into equipment to measure sulphur dioxide emissions in coal-burning power plants. The cost of the expansion would be $10 million. The project would have a life of ten years, and its expected after-tax cash flows over this time are $1.5 million per year, in current dollars. NDI's after-tax cost of long-term capital is 15 percent for projects with this degree of risk. The average rate of inflation forecasted for the general economy over the next ten years is 9 percent, and NDI estimates that both its input costs and sales prices will rise at about this same rate. Should NDI undertake the project?

12-7 (Inflation adjustment) The Kose Corporation is considering an average-risk project that has a cost of $100,000. The project will produce 1,000 tons of output per year indefinitely. The current sales price is $127 per ton, and the current cost per ton (all variable) is $100. Kose is taxed at a rate of 50 percent. Both prices and costs are expected to rise at a rate of 5 percent per year. Kose uses only equity, and it has a cost of capital of 15 percent per year ($k = D_1/P_0 + g = 15\%$). Assume cash flows consist only of after-tax profits.

a. Should Kose accept the project? (Hint: The project is a perpetuity, so you must use the formula for a perpetuity to find the NPV.)

b. If total costs consist of a fixed cost of $10,000 per year and variable costs of $90 per unit, and if only the variable costs increase with inflation, would this make the project better or worse?

12-8 (CAPM approach to risk adjustments) Goodtread Rubber Company has two divisions: (1) the Tire Division, which manufactures tires for new autos; and (2) the Recap Division, which manufactures recapping materials that are sold to independent tire recapping shops throughout the U.S. Since auto manufacturing moves up and down with the general economy, the Tire Division's earnings contribution to Goodtread's stock price is highly correlated with returns on most other stocks. If the Tire Division were operated as a separate company, its beta coefficient would be about 1.60. The sales and profits of the Recap Division, on the other hand, tend to be counter-cyclical, as recap sales boom when people cannot afford to buy new tires. Recap's beta is estimated to be 0.40. Approximately 75 percent of Goodtread's corporate assets are invested in the Tire Division and 25 percent are in the Recap Division.

Currently, the rate of interest on Treasury securities is 10 percent, and the expected rate of return on an average share of stock is 15 percent. Goodtread uses only common equity capital, and it has no debt outstanding.

a. What is the required rate of return on Goodtread's stock?

b. What discount rate should be used to evaluate capital budgeting projects? Explain your answer fully, and, in the process, illustrate your answer with a project which costs $100,000, has a ten year life, and provides after-tax cash flows of $20,000 per year.

12-9 (Simulation for risk analysis) Hospital Supplies Corporation (HSC) manufactures medical products for hospitals, clinics, and nursing homes. HSC is considering introducing a new type of X-ray scanner designed to identify certain types of cancers in their early stages. There are a number of uncertainties about the proposed project, but the following data are felt to be reasonably accurate:

	Probability	Value	Random Numbers
Developmental costs	0.3	$2,000,000	00-29
	0.4	4,000,000	30-69
	0.3	6,000,000	70-99
Project life	0.2	3 years	00-19
	0.6	8 years	20-79
	0.2	13 years	80-99
Sales in units	0.2	100	00-19
	0.6	200	20-79
	0.2	300	80-99
Sales price	0.1	$13,000	00-09
	0.8	13,500	10-89
	0.1	14,000	90-99
Cost per unit (excluding developmental costs)	0.3	$ 5,000	00-29
	0.4	6,000	30-69
	0.3	7,000	70-99

HSC uses a cost of capital of 15 percent to analyze average-risk projects, 12 percent for low-risk projects, and 18 percent for high-risk projects. These risk adjustments reflect primarily the uncertainty about each project's NPV and IRR as measured by the coefficients of variation of NPV and IRR. HSC is in the 40 percent income tax bracket.

a. What is the expected IRR for the X-ray scanner project? Base your answer on the expected values of the variables. Also, assume the after-tax "profits" figure you develop is equal to annual cash flows. All facilities are leased, so depreciation may be disregarded. Can you determine the value of the σ_{IRR} short of actual simulation or a fairly complex statistical analysis?

b. Assume that HSC uses a 15 percent cost of capital for this project. What is the project's NPV? Could you estimate σ_{NPV} without either simulation or a complex statistical analysis?

c. Show the process by which a computer would perform a simulation analysis for this project. Use the random numbers in Table 12-5, start-ing with the 44 in the upper left corner for developmental costs, the 17 for project life, and so on, to illustrate the process with the first computer run. Actually calculate the first-run NPV and IRR. Assume that the cash flows for each year are *independent* of cash flows in other years. Also, assume that the computer operates as follows: (1) A de-velopmental cost and a project life are estimated for the first run. (2) Next, sales volume, sales price, and cost per unit are estimated and used to derive a first year cash flow. (3) Then the next three random numbers are used to estimate sales volume, sales price, and cost per unit for the second year, hence the second year's cash flow. (4) Cash flows for other years are developed similarly, on out to the first run's estimated life. (5) With the developmental cost and the cash flow stream established, NPV and IRR for the first run are derived and stored in the computer's memory. (6) The process is repeated to gen-erate perhaps 500 other NPVs and IRRs. (7) Frequency distributions for NPV and IRR are plotted by the computer, and the distributions' means and standard deviations are calculated to obtain the expected IRR and NPV, and σ_{IRR} and σ_{NPV}.

d. Does it seem a little strange to conduct a risk analysis such as the one done here *after* having already established a cost of capital for use in the analysis? What might be done to improve this situation?

e. In this problem we assumed that the probability distributions were all independent of one another. It would have been possible to use con-ditional probabilities where, for example, the probability distribution for cost per unit would vary from trial to trial, depending on the unit sales for the trial. Also, it would be possible to construct the simula-tion model such that the sales distribution in Year t would depend on the sales level attained in Year t $-$ 1. Had these modifications been made in this problem, do you think the standard deviation of the NPV distribution would have been larger (riskier) or smaller (less risky) than where complete independence is assumed?

f. Name two *major* difficulties not mentioned above that occur with the kind of analysis discussed in this problem.

Solution to Self-Test Problem

ST12-1 To solve this problem, set up a worksheet similar to Table 12-1, as illus-trated below. You will find that the old machine should be replaced.

Net outflows at t = 0:

	Amount before Tax	Amount after Tax	Year	PV Factor (15%)	PV
Purchase price	$8,000	$8,000	0	1.0	$8,000
ITC (6⅔%)	(533)	(533)	0	1.0	(533)

Net outflows at t = 0:

	Amount before Tax	Amount after Tax	Year	PV Factor (15%)	PV
Sale of old machine:					
Return of capital	(2,600)				
Profit (recapture of depreciation)	(400)[a]				
Tax on profit (46%)	184		0	1.0	(2,816)
Working capital					
Δ Inventory	2,000				
Δ A/P	(500)		0	1.0	1,500
Net investment outlay at t = 0					$6,151
Net inflows over project's life (t = 1 to 6):					
Increase in Sales	$1,000	$ 540	1-6	3.7845	$2,043
Reduction in Expenses	1,500	810	1-6	3.7845	3,065
Depreciation: new	1,200[b]				
old	350				
Δ Depreciation	850	391	1-6	3.7845	1,480
Salvage: new	800				
old	500				
Δ Salvage[c]	300	300	6	0.4323	130
Return of Working Capital	1,500	1,500	6	0.4323	648
					$7,366
Less investment outlay					6,151
Net present value					$1,215

[a] We can determine the depreciation on the old machine as follows:

$$\text{Depreciation} = \frac{\text{Book value} - \text{Salvage}}{\text{Life}} = \frac{\$2,600 - \$500}{6} = \$350 \text{ per year.}$$

Thus far, then, BLC has taken $2 \times \$350 = \$700$ of depreciation. If it sells the old machine for $3,000, the $400 gain over the current book value, $2,600, will be a recovery of depreciation and thus taxed at the 46 percent rate.

[b] Depreciation on the new machine:

$$\text{Depreciation} = \frac{\$8,000 - \$800}{6} = \$1,200 \text{ per year.}$$

[c] Recall that this worksheet is designed to cover *incremental* cash flows that will result from the replacement. If the replacement were not made, then BLC would have had $500 from the sale of the old machine in Year 6. This amount must be deducted to obtain the incremental cash flow from salvage in Year 6.

For further depth on replacement analysis, as well as other aspects of capital budgeting, see the Bierman and Smidt, the Grant, Ireson, and Leavengood, and the Levy and Sarnat texts referenced in Chapter 11.

Some important papers on the proper treatment of inflation in capital budgeting include the following:

Bailey, A. D., and D. L. Jensen, "General Price Level Adjustments in the Capital Budgeting Decision," *Financial Management,* vol. 6 (Spring 1977), 26-32.

Cooley, Philip L., Rodney L. Roenfeldt, and It-Keong Chew, "Capital Budgeting Procedures under Inflation," *Financial Management,* Winter 1975, 18-27.

Selected References

Findlay, M. Chapman, III, Alan W. Frankle, Philip L. Cooley, Rodney L. Roenfeldt, and It-Keong Chew, "Capital Budgeting Procedures under Inflation: Cooley, Roenfeldt, and Chew vs. Findlay and Frankle," *Financial Management,* Autumn 1976, 83-90.

Van Horne, James C., "A Note on Biases in Capital Budgeting Introduced by Inflation," *Journal of Financial and Quantitative Analysis,* vol. 6 (March 1971), 653-658.

The literature on risk analysis in capital budgeting is vast; here is a small but useful selection of papers that bear directly on the topics covered in this chapter:

Bower, Richard S., and J. M. Jenks, "Divisional Screening Rates," *Financial Management,* vol. 4 (Autumn 1975), 42-49.

Fama, E. F., "Risk-Adjusted Discount Rates and Capital Budgeting under Uncertainty," *Journal of Financial Economics,* vol. 5 (August 1977), 3-24.

Fuller, Russell J., and Halbert S. Kerr, "Estimating the Divisional Cost of Capital: An Analysis of Pure-Play Technique," *Journal of Finance,* forthcoming.

Hertz, David B., "Risk Analysis in Capital Investment," *Harvard Business Review,* January-February 1964, 95-106.

Lessard, Donald R., and Richard S. Bower, "An Operational Approach to Risk Screening," *Journal of Finance,* vol. 28 (May 1973), 321-338.

Myers, Stewart C., and Stuart M. Turnbull, "Capital Budgeting and the Capital Asset Pricing Model: Good News and Bad News," *Journal of Finance,* vol. 32 (May 1977), 321-333.

Robichek, Alexander A., "Interpreting the Results of Risk Analysis," *Journal of Finance,* vol. 30 (December 1975), 1384-1386.

Robichek, Alexander A., and James C. Van Horne, "Abandonment Value and Capital Budgeting," *Journal of Finance,* vol. 22 (December 1967), 577-590.

Weingartner, H. Martin, "Capital Rationing: *n* Authors in Search of a Plot," *Journal of Finance,* vol. 32 (December 1977), 1403-1431.

Additional references are contained in footnotes in the appendices to this chapter.

Appendix 12A

Probability Distributions

The concept of probability theory underlies many aspects of financial management, but its most frequent use is in the area of capital budgeting, especially in the rapidly growing simulation approach to capital budgeting. Therefore, it is important for people who are interested in understanding and using this important tool to understand the basics of probability analysis. This appendix is provided as an introduction and/or refresher on the subject.

In Chapter 5 we saw that probability distributions can be viewed in either of two ways: (1) as a series of *discrete values* represented by a bar chart, such as Figure 5-1, or (2) as a *continuous function* represented by a smooth curve, such as that in Figure 5-2. Actually, there is an important difference in the way these two graphs are interpreted. The probabilities associated with the outcomes in Figure 5-1 are given by the *height* of each bar, while in Figure 5-2 the probabilities must be found by calculating the *area* under the curve between points of interest. Suppose, for example, that we have the continuous probability distribution shown in Figure 12A-1. This can be treated as a normal curve, as introduced in Chapter 5, with a mean of 20 and a standard deviation of 5; x can be dollars, percentage rates of return, or any other unit. If we want to know the prob-

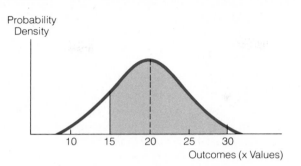

ability that an outcome will fall between 15 and 30, we must calculate the area beneath the curve between these points, or the shaded area in the diagram.

The area under the curve between 15 and 30 can be determined by integrating the curve over this interval or, since the distribution is normal, by reference to statistical tables of the area under the normal curve, which were used in constructing Table 12A-1.[1] To use this table, it is necessary only to know the mean and standard deviation of the distribution.[2]

z	Area from the Mean to the Point of Interest	Ordinate
0.0	0.0000	0.3989
0.5	0.1915	0.3521
1.0	0.3413	0.2420
1.5	0.4332	0.1295
2.0	0.4773	0.0540
2.5	0.4938	0.0175
3.0	0.4987	0.0044

Table 12A-1
Area under the Normal Curve

z is the number of standard deviations from the mean. Some area tables are set up to indicate the area to the left or right of the point of interest; in this book we indicate the area between the mean and the point of interest. A more complete set of values is given in Table A-5 at the end of the book.

[1] The equation for the normal curve is tedious to integrate, thus making the use of tables much more convenient. The equation for the normal curve is

$$f(x) = \frac{1}{\sqrt{2\pi\sigma^2}}\, e^{-(x-\mu)^2/2\sigma^2}$$

where π and e are mathematical constants; μ and σ denote the mean and standard deviation of the probability distribution, and x is any possible outcome.

[2] The procedure for calculating means and standard deviations was illustrated in Chapter 5.

The distribution to be investigated must first be standardized by using the following formula:

$$z = \frac{x - \mu}{\sigma}, \qquad (12A\text{-}1)$$

where z is the standardized variable, or the number of standard deviations from the mean,[3] x is the outcome of interest, and μ (pronounced "mu") and σ are the mean and standard deviation of the distribution, respectively. For our example, where we are interested in the probability that an outcome will fall between 15 and 30, we first normalize these points of interest using Equation 12A-1:

$$z_1 = \frac{15 - 20}{5} = -1.0; \; z_2 = \frac{30 - 20}{5} = 2.0.$$

The areas associated with these z values are found in Table 12A-1 to be 0.3413 and 0.4773.[4] This means that the probability is 0.3413 that the actual outcome will fall between 15 and 20, and 0.4773 that it will fall between 20 and 30. Summing these probabilities shows that the probability of an outcome falling between 15 and 30 is 0.8186, or 81.86 percent.

Suppose we were interested in determining the probability that the actual outcome will be greater than 15. We would first note that the probability is 0.3413 that the outcome will be between 15 and 20 and then observe that the probability is 0.5000 of an outcome greater than the mean, 20. Thus, the probability is $0.3413 + 0.5000 = 0.8413$, or 84.13 percent, that the outcome will exceed 15.

Illustrating the Use of Probability Concepts

Consider a situation with Project A and Project B, assuming three states of the economy: boom, normal, and recession.[5] We can attach a probability of occurrence to each state of the economy and estimate the returns that would occur under each state. This information is summarized in Table 12A-2.

The expected values of returns for A and B are calculated by Equation 12A-2,

$$\hat{k} = \sum_{i=1}^{n} k_i P_i, \qquad (12A\text{-}2)$$

[3] Note that if the point of interest is 1σ away from the mean, then $x - \mu = \sigma$, so $z = \sigma/\sigma = 1.0$. Thus, when $z = 1.0$, the point of interest is 1σ away from the mean; when $z = 2$, the value is 2σ, and so forth.

[4] Note that the negative sign on z_1 is ignored. Since the normal curve is symmetrical around the mean, the minus sign merely indicates that the point lies to the left of the mean.

[5] Throughout this appendix, we illustrate the concepts with discrete points that are assumed to represent points on continuous distribution functions. It would, of course, be possible to include more points, and thus more closely approximate the true continuous distribution, but we use only three points to simplify the arithmetic.

State of the Economy	Probability of This State, P_i	Return k_i		$k_i P_i$
Boom	0.3	25%		7.5%
Normal	0.4	15		6.0
Recession	0.3	5		1.5
	1.0		Expected value = $\hat{k}_A$ =	15.0%

Standard deviation = σ_A = 7.75%

State of the Economy	Probability of This State, P_i	Return k_i		$k_i P_i$
Boom	0.3	40%		12.0%
Normal	0.4	15		6.0
Recession	0.3	−10		−3.0
	1.0		Expected value = $\hat{k}_B$ =	15.0%

Standard deviation = σ_B = 19.36%

Table 12A-2
Means and Standard Deviations of Returns for Projects A and B

and the standard deviations of their respective returns are found by Equation 12A-3,

$$\sigma_i = \sqrt{\sum_{i=1}^{n}(k_i - \hat{k})^2 P_i}. \qquad (12A\text{-}3)$$

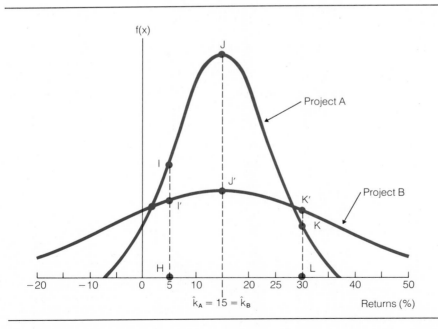

Figure 12A-2
Probability Distributions for Projects A and B

On the assumption that the returns from both projects are normally distributed, knowing the mean and the standard deviation as shown in Table 12A-2 permits us to graph probability distributions for these two projects as shown in Figure 12A-2.[6] The expected values of returns for both projects are 15 percent; however, the flatter graph of B indicates that it is the riskier project.

Suppose we want to determine the probabilities that the actual returns of Projects A and B will be in the interval of 5 to 30 percent. Using Equation 12A-1, we can calculate the respective probability distributions. The first step is to calculate the z values of the interval limits for the two.

Project A:

$$\text{Lower } z_1 = \frac{5 - 15}{7.75} = -1.29.$$

$$\text{Upper } z_2 = \frac{30 - 15}{7.75} = 1.94.$$

[6] Normal probability distributions can be constructed once the mean and standard deviation are known, using a table of *ordinates* of the normal curve. (See Column 3 of Table 12A-1.) The ordinate table gives relative *heights* of the probability curve f(x) at various z values rather than areas beneath the curve. Figure 12A-2 was constructed by plotting points at various z values according to the following formula:

$$f(x) = \frac{1}{\sigma} \times (\text{ordinate for z value}),$$

where the ordinate value is read from a table of ordinates.

For example, the points corresponding to the mean, +1 standard deviation, and +2 standard deviations for both projects are calculated as follows:

(1)	z (2)	Ordinate at z (3)	1/σ (4)	f(x) (5) = (3) × (4)	Height of Graph in Inches (6) = (5) × 100
Project A:					
mean = 15%	0	0.3989	1/7.75	0.0515	5.15
+1σ = 22.75	1	0.2420	1/7.75	0.0312	3.12
+2σ = 30.50	2	0.0540	1/7.75	0.0070	0.70
Project B:					
mean = 15%	0	0.3989	1/19.36	0.0206	2.06
+1σ = 34.36	1	0.2420	1/19.36	0.0125	1.25
+2σ = 53.72	2	0.0540	1/19.36	0.0028	0.28

Column 5 gives the relative heights of the two distributions, and Column 6 gives the height of the points, assuming that we have decided (for pictorial convenience) to let the curve for Project A be about five inches high at the mean. We would multiply all the values in Column 5 by 100 to get heights at different points in inches. Project B's graph would, of course, be only 2.06 inches at its mean versus

(continued)

Project B:

$$\text{Lower } z_1 = \frac{5 - 15}{19.36} = -0.52.$$

$$\text{Upper } z_2 = \frac{30 - 15}{19.36} = 0.77.$$

In Table A-5 at the end of the book, which gives a more complete table of z values, we find the areas under a normal curve for each of these four z values:

	z Value	Area
Project A:		
Lower z:	−1.29	0.4015
Upper z:	1.94	0.4738
	Total area =	0.8753 or 87.53%
Project B:		
Lower z:	−0.52	0.1985
Upper z:	0.77	0.2794
	Total area =	0.4779 or 47.79%

Thus, there is about an 88 percent chance that the actual return from Project A will lie in the interval of 5 to 30 percent and about a 48 percent probability that B's return will fall in this interval.

Now look back at Figure 12A-2 and observe the two areas that were just calculated. For Project A, the area bounded by HIJKL represents about 88 percent of the area under A's curve. For Project B, that area bounded by HI'J'K'L includes about 48 percent of the total area.

Suppose we ask these questions: What is the probability that the returns from Project A will be at least 10 percent? 20 percent? 30 percent? and so on. Obviously, there is a higher probability of their being at least 10 percent rather than 20 percent, 20 percent rather than 30 percent, and so on. In general, the most convenient way of expressing the answer to such "at least" questions is through the use of *cumulative probability distributions*. These distributions for Projects A and B are calculated in Table 12A-3 and plotted in Figure 12A-3.

Cumulative Probability

5.15 inches for Project A. Had we decided we wanted A's graph to be about 2½ inches high, we would have multiplied by 50 rather than 100, or by 200 if we wanted the height to be about ten inches.

**Table 12A-3
Cumulative Probability
Distributions for Returns
of Projects A and B**

Project Return	z Value	Cumulative Probability of Actual Return Being at Least Equal to the Indicated Return
Project A:		
−10%	−3.23	0.9990
0	−1.94	0.9738
10	−0.65	0.7422
15	0.00	0.5000
20	0.65	0.2578
30	1.94	0.0262
40	3.23	0.0010
Project B:		
−30%	−2.32	0.9898
−20	−1.81	0.9649
−10	−1.29	0.9015
0	−0.77	0.7794
10	−0.26	0.6026
15	0.00	0.5000
20	0.26	0.3974
30	0.77	0.2206
40	1.29	0.0985
50	1.81	0.0351

Notes:

1. $z = \dfrac{x - \mu}{\sigma} = \dfrac{-10 - 15}{7.75} = \dfrac{-25}{7.75} = -3.23$ for a return of −10%. See Table 12A-2 for data. Other z values are calculated similarly. Use Table A-5 at the end of the book to obtain areas associated with these z values.
2. The cumulative probability of obtaining a return at least as large as any specific return *less than* the mean (μ) is the area under the normal curve to the right of the point in question, and it is equal to 0.5000 plus the area between the point of interest and the mean. For example, for Project A, the cumulative probability of a return of at least −10 percent is 0.5000 + 0.4990 = 0.9990. The 0.4990 is taken as the largest value in Table A-5 at the end of the book.
3. The mean has a cumulative probability of 0.5000. Thus, the probability of a return of at least 15 percent is 0.5000, or 50 percent, for both Project A and Project B.
4. For returns *greater* than the mean, the cumulative probability is the area to the right of the return in question. This area is 0.5000 *less* the area between the mean and the point in question. Thus, for Project A, the probability of a return of at least 20 percent is 0.5000 − 0.2422 = 0.2578 = 25.78%.

Other Distributions

Thus far we have assumed that returns fit a probability distribution that is approximately normal. Many distributions do fit this pattern, and normal distributions are relatively easy to work with. Therefore, much of the work done on risk measurement assumes a normal distribution. However, other distributions are certainly possible; Figure 12A-4 shows distributions that are skewed to the right and left. For two possible investments with equal expected returns, $\hat{k}$, would an investor prefer a normal, left-skewed, or right-skewed distribution? A distribution skewed to the right, such as the one in Figure 12A-4a, would probably be chosen because the odds on a large loss are small, while there is some chance of

**Figure 12A-3
Cumulative Probability
Distributions for Returns
of Projects A and B**

Cumulative Probability of Returns
Being Equal to or Greater than
the Value on the X-Axis
(%)

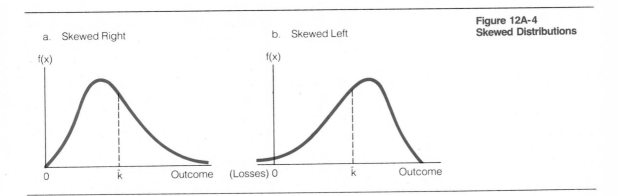

**Figure 12A-4
Skewed Distributions**

very high returns. For the left-skewed distribution there is little likelihood
of large gains but some possibility of large losses.

12A-1 The sales of the Systems Company for next year have the probability   **Problems**
distribution shown on the next page.
a. On graph paper, plot sales on the horizontal axis and probability of
sales on the vertical axis, using points from the distributions. Draw a

Probability	Sales (Millions)
0.1	$10
0.2	12
0.4	15
0.2	18
0.1	20

smooth curve connecting your plotted points. What can you say about this curve?

b. Compute the mean of the probability distribution.

c. Compute the standard deviation of the probability distribution.

d. Compute the coefficient of variation of the probability distribution ($v = \sigma/\mu$).

e. What is the probability that sales will exceed $16 million?

f. What is the probability that sales will fall below $13 million?

g. What is the probability that sales will be between $13 and $16 million?

h. What is the probability that sales will exceed $17 million?

12A-2 An insurance company offers to sell your firm a $1 million, one year term insurance policy on your corporate jet for a premium of $7,500. The probability that the plane will be lost in any twelve month period is 0.001.

a. What is the insurance company's expected gross profit from sale of the policy?

b. What is the insurance company's expected gain or loss if the probability of a $1 million loss is 0.01? Would the insurance company still offer your firm the same policy for the same premium? Explain.

12A-3 Suppose Project X has an expected cost (outlay at t = 1) of $1,000,000, but the standard deviation of this expected cost is $200,000.

a. What is the probability that the cost will exceed $1.2 million? $1.5 million? $2 million?

b. What is the probability that the cost will be in the range of $950,000 to $1,100,000?

c. Draw an accurate graph of this probability distribution.

d. Draw an accurate graph of the cumulative probability distribution, using on the vertical axis the probability that the cost is equal to or greater than the indicated amounts shown on the horizontal axis.

Appendix 12B

The Hillier Model

In Chapter 12 we considered risk analysis in capital budgeting in two basically different ways: (1) a CAPM-oriented approach which focuses on projects' betas and which is especially relevant for highly diversified stockholders, and (2) an approach called "corporate risk analysis," which considers each project's risk as it might be viewed by an undiversified stockholder, by the firm's management, and by others with a strong interest in the firm's survival.

In this appendix, we examine an analytical approach to corporate risk that was first presented by Frederick Hillier.[1] Hillier's approach is designed to produce the same type of probabilistic information as computer simulation, but analytically rather than by having the computer grind out a multitude of numbers. The strengths of the Hillier method are (1) that it provides us with insights into some of the fundamental determinants of project risk and (2) that under certain conditions, it is far easier to use than computer simulation.

The Setting for Risk Analysis

Most medium to large corporations must evaluate hundreds or even thousands of potential capital projects each year. Some of the projects are mutually exclusive while others are independent, and they differ in terms of size, timing of cash flows, and uncertainty of the cash flows (or riskiness). The NPV method as discussed in Chapter 11 can deal with the size and timing differences among projects, but it must be modified to deal with risk differences.

Suppose Carter Chemical Company has identified 5,000 potential investments for the coming year. Suppose, further, that Carter's treasurer has determined that the corporate cost of capital (a weighted average of the cost of debt and equity) is 10 percent. If a project is deemed to be of average risk, then its NPV should be found using the 10 percent corporate cost of capital as the discount rate. However, if the project is more or less risky than average, then a higher or lower discount rate should be used to calculate its NPV. Then, if "reasonable" risk-adjusted discount rates have been used, proper choices will be made among mutually exclusive projects, and correct accept/reject decisions will be made for independent projects.

If we have a fairly good idea about the potential variability of the cash flows in each year for each project, we can use either the Hillier method as it will be developed in this appendix or computer simulation to develop a "risk index" for each project. Then, projects whose riskiness is about average can be evaluated at the corporate cost of capital, and higher or lower rates can be used for higher or lower risk projects.

Hillier's Model with Independent Returns over Time

Suppose we are considering a project that involves an expansion of a particular product line. If we expand, the project is expected to produce cash flows of CF_0, CF_1, CF_2, . . . , CF_n at the end of Years 0, 1, 2, . . . , n. These cash flows are not known with certainty; they are random variables which we assume are normally distributed. Also, we assume that the yearly cash flows vary with the state of the economy,

[1] Frederick S. Hillier, "The Derivation of Probabilistic Information for the Evaluation of Risky Investments," *Management Science*, vol. 9 (April 1963), 443-457.

and that they are independent of one another. If we have an estimate of the probability distributions of the cash flows in each year, we can use two equations which were originally developed in Chapter 5 to calculate the expected value for each year and the standard deviation of each annual cash flow. Then we can use two new equations to calculate the project's NPV and the riskiness inherent in this NPV estimate. First, the terms used in the equations are summarized, and then the equations themselves are presented and discussed.

CF_{jt} = net cash flow (either a cost or a return) associated with the jth probability in Year t.

P_{jt} = probability of the jth cash flow in Year t.

$\widehat{CF}_t$ = expected net cash flow from the investment in the tth year, a weighted average weighted by probabilities.

σ_t = standard deviation of the expected cash flows in the tth year.

NPV = net present value of all expected cash flows over the n-year life of the investment.

k = appropriate rate of discount for the future cash flows; in this analysis, the proper value for k is the *riskless rate of return.*[2]

σ_{NPV} = standard deviation of the net present value of expected cash flows.

Here are the two Chapter 5 equations.

Expected net cash flow for Year t:

$$\widehat{CF}_t = \sum_{j=1}^{m} (CF_{jt}P_{jt}).$$
(12B-1)

Variation of expected cash flows for Year t:

$$\sigma_t = \left[\sum_{j=1}^{m} (CF_{jt} - \widehat{CF}_t)^2 P_{jt} \right]^{1/2}.$$
(12B-2)

Also, based on the expected values of the cash flows, we can calculate the expected NPV for the project as shown here.

Expected net present value of investment:

$$\widehat{NPV} = \sum_{t=0}^{n} \left[\frac{\widehat{CF}_t}{(1 + k)^t} \right].$$
(12B-3)

Further, if (1) the probability distribution (P_{jt}) is normally distributed and (2) the expected net cash flow in each Year t, $\widehat{CF}_t$, is independent of the

---

[2] Here we use the riskless rate of return to find a "first approximation" NPV. The σ of a project's first approximation NPV is used to determine its relative riskiness. Then, a subsequent adjustment is made for different degrees of risk. *But at this stage we are determining relative risk, not deciding how to choose among projects that differ in riskiness.*

cash flow in Year $(t - 1)$, then we can use a new equation to find the riskiness of the expected NPV, measuring riskiness by σ_{NPV} as calculated in Equation 12B-4, which we shall call "the Hillier equation for *independent* cash flows."

Variation of expected net present value of investment:[3]

$$\sigma_{NPV} = \left[\sum_{t=0}^{n} \frac{\sigma_t^{2}}{(1 + k)^{2t}} \right]^{1/2}. \qquad \text{(12B-4)}$$

Equation 12B-1 calculates the expected cash flows of an investment for a given Year t as a weighted average, the items to be averaged being the possible outcomes and the weights being the probabilities associated with each possible outcome for the year. Equation 12B-2 calculates the standard deviation of the expected cash flows in Year t. Equation 12B-3 discounts the expected cash flows over each year of the project's life to find its net present value, and Equation 12B-4 calculates the standard deviation of the expected net present value. The first two equations deal with the cash flows and risk for individual years, while the last two deal with cash flows and risk of the project as a whole. Note, however, that Equation 12B-4 holds only if cash flows are independent over time, that is, if the distribution of returns in Year t is unaffected by the actual cash flow outcome in Year $(t - 1)$. The situation where returns in Year t are correlated with returns in Year $(t - 1)$ is covered later in the appendix.

The use of the model can be explained by use of an example. Section I of Table 12B-1 shows that Project E requires a cash outlay, or a cost, at $t = 0$, and that it has inflows at the end of Years 1 and 2. Neither the cost nor the inflows are known with certainty—both depend on economic conditions. There are three possible states of the economy, each with a specific probability, and a cash flow is associated with each economic state. The expected cost of Project E is $400, and the expected inflows at the end of Years 1 and 2 are $250 and $240, respectively.

Application of the Model.

In Section II of the table we calculate the standard deviations of the cost and the cash inflows, and in Section III we find the NPV of the project, using the riskless rate $k = R_F = 8\%$ as the discount rate. Finally, in Section IV, we use the Hillier formula to calculate $\sigma_{NPV} = \$202.01$.

Based upon the computations made in Table 12B-1, we can make the following points:

1. If the cash flows were known with certainty and were equal to the expected values of $400 for the outflow and $250 and $240 for inflows in Years 1 and 2, then the NPV as calculated at the riskless discount rate would have an expected value of $37.24 and a standard deviation

[3] For a proof of Equation 12B-4, see Hillier, "The Derivation of Probabilistic Information."

Table 12B-1
Analysis of Project E

I. Calculation of Project E's Expected Cash Flows in Each Year:

State j	Probability (P_{jt}) of State j	Period 0 $(CF_0 = Cost)$	Period 1 $(CF_1 = Return)$	Period 2 $(CF_2 = Return)$
1 (Recession)	0.2	−$350	$ 0	−$ 10
2 (Normal)	0.6	−400	250	240
3 (Boom)	0.2	−450	500	490
$\sum_{j=1}^{3}(\widehat{CF}_{j0}P_{jt}) = \widehat{CF}_0 =$		−$400	$\widehat{CF}_1 = 250	$\widehat{CF}_2 = 240

II. Calculation of Standard Deviation of Each Year's Cash Flow:

$$\sigma_t = \left[\sum_{j=1}^{3}(CF_{jt} - \widehat{CF}_t)^2 P_{jt}\right]^{1/2}$$

$$\sigma_0 = [(-\$350 + \$400)^2(0.2) + (-\$400 + \$400)^2(0.6) + (-\$450 + \$400)^2(0.2)]^{1/2}$$
$$= \$31.62.$$

$$\sigma_1 = [(0 - \$250)^2(0.2) + (\$250 - \$250)^2(0.6) + (\$500 - \$250)^2(0.2)]^{1/2}$$
$$= \$158.11.$$

$$\sigma_2 = [(-\$10 - \$240)^2(0.2) + (\$240 - \$240)^2(0.6) + (\$490 - \$240)^2(0.2)]^{1/2}$$
$$= \$158.11.$$

III. Calculation of Project E's Expected NPV:

$$\widehat{NPV} = -\$400 + \frac{\$250}{(1.08)^1} + \frac{\$240}{(1.08)^2} = -\$400 + \$231.48 + \$205.76$$
$$= \$37.24.$$

IV. Calculation of Project E's Riskiness as Measured by σ_{NPV}:

$$\sigma_{NPV} = \left[\frac{\$1,000}{(1.08)^0} + \frac{\$25,000}{(1.08)^2} + \frac{\$25,000}{(1.08)^4}\right]^{1/2} = [\$1,000 + \$21,433 + \$18,376]^{1/2}$$
$$= \$202.01.$$

---

of zero. The project would have no risk, and it would clearly be acceptable because of its positive NPV.

2. However, because of the uncertainty about the cash flows, the firm cannot be sure of the expected NPV of $37.24. There is some probability that the realized NPV will be higher than the expected value, but there is also a probability that it will be lower. Because of this variability about the expected NPV, the project is considered risky; a measure of this risk is the standard deviation of the NPV, calculated to be $\sigma_{NPV} = \$202.01$.

3. This measure of risk can be used to develop a risk-adjusted discount rate, which would obviously be greater than the riskless rate, 8.0 percent. With the risk-adjusted discount rate, we could recalculate the

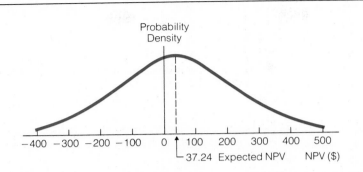

Figure 12B-1
Probability Distribution
of NPV for Project E

NPV of the project at the higher discount rate. If the NPV were still positive, the project would be accepted.

4. We could also calculate the cumulative distribution of NPV to help answer this question: What is the probability that the NPV will actually turn out to be negative? If this probability is high, then the firm would certainly want to use a high cost of capital to evaluate the project.

Figure 12B-2
Cumulative Probability
Distribution for Project E

Probability distribution graphs and cumulative distributions for Project E are shown in Figures 12B-1 and 12B-2. Figure 12B-1 shows that even though the expected NPV is positive, the probability distribution is relatively flat, so there is a high probability of a negative NPV. Figure 12B-2 gives the same information, but in a different format, and it indicates that there is a 58 percent probability that the NPV of Project E will be zero or greater, so there is a $100\% - 58\% = 42\%$ probability that the NPV will be negative.

Based on this information, one would probably conclude that Project E is unacceptable. The variability ($\sigma_{NPV} = \$202.01$) about the expected value ($\$37.24$) is very large, resulting in a high probability (42 percent) that the project would be a losing proposition. Also, if the risk-adjusted discount rate were set at 14.5 percent, the 8 percent risk-free rate plus a 6.5 percent risk premium based on the assessment of Project E's riskiness, then its expected NPV would fall below zero. The final decision must involve judgment, but at least an analysis such as this can contribute to the decision-making process.

Interdependent Returns over Time

The preceding section presented a general method for dealing with risk assuming that the cash flows of one period are independent of outcomes in other years and that the cash flows for a given year are normally distributed. These may not be bad assumptions for expansion projects whose returns vary with the business cycle, but they might not reflect the true situation in some other cases. Therefore, Hillier also developed a model for use where the expected net cash flows for different periods are correlated (for example, if cash flows in Year 1 are high, then cash flows in successive years are also likely to be high). This assumption is likely to be true for new ventures, where product acceptance or lack of acceptance will be signaled in Year 1. Hence, if sales in Year 1 are high, sales in subsequent years will be, too.[4]

In this section, we consider the case where all data are the same as in the Table 12B-1 example, except here the cash flows are assumed to be normally distributed and *perfectly positively* correlated (versus completely uncorrelated as in the last section). Under these assumptions, the ex-

[4] Models have also been developed where the cash flow stream is split into two parts, with one part of the cash flow being correlated over time and the other independent. Mathematical techniques are even available for dealing with nonnormal probability distributions, but these are generally too complex for practical applications. However, computer simulation as described in Chapter 12, as opposed to mathematical statistics as described in this appendix, can deal with nonnormal distributions at a practical level.

pected value of Project New Product's NPV is exactly the same as for independent cash flows, \$37.24. However, the standard deviation, σ_{NPV}, is now given by Equation 12B-5:[5]

$$\sigma_{NPV} = \sum_{t=0}^{n} \frac{\sigma_t}{(1 + k)^t}. \qquad (12B\text{-}5)$$

Referring back to Table 12B-1, Section II, for data on σ_t, we can use Equation 12B-5 to calculate the project's riskiness under the assumption of complete intertemporal dependence (or perfect positive correlation):

$$
\begin{aligned}
\sigma_{NPV} &= \frac{\sigma_0}{(1 + k)^0} + \frac{\sigma_1}{(1 + k)^1} + \frac{\sigma_2}{(1 + k)^2} \\
&= \frac{\$31.62}{(1.08)^0} + \frac{\$158.11}{(1.08)^1} + \frac{\$158.11}{(1.08)^2} \\
&= \$313.57.
\end{aligned}
$$

Note that the variability in Project New Product's NPV increases from $\sigma_{NPV} = \$202.01$ when cash flows were independent over time to \$313.57 when they are assumed to be perfectly correlated. This is logical because if a low cash flow occurs in Year 1, this same low result will also hold in all other years, so a very low NPV will result. The reverse would hold true if a good first year result occurred. Thus, the extreme values are far wider under the dependence assumption, and σ_{NPV} is, therefore, much larger.

Hillier has also worked out an equation for the case where a portion of the cash flow in each year is independent and the remainder is perfectly correlated. Again, the expected value of NPV would not change, but the standard deviation, σ_{NPV}, lies between the two extremes of independent and perfectly correlated cash flows. Although it is possible to deal mathematically with these more complicated cases, the more practical approach to capital budgeting under uncertainty is simulation analysis as described in Chapter 12. Standard software packages make it relatively easy to account for intertemporal dependence, as well as for correlations among sales prices, volume, and unit costs. From a pragmatic standpoint, simulation and/or sensitivity analysis seem to offer the best possibilities for dealing with risk analysis in capital budgeting. Still, models such as the ones developed here do provide useful insights into the problem of capital budgeting under uncertainty, and, as will be noted, they may be put to practical use.

---

[5] See Hillier, "The Derivation of Probabilistic Information," for the derivation of Equation 12B-5.

Using the Hillier Method to Develop Risk-Adjusted Discount Rates

Toward the end of Chapter 12, we discussed the use of simulation to develop risk-adjusted discount rates. The Hillier models could be used similarly. One would first use Equation 12A-4 or 12A-5, along with the risk-free rate, to obtain σ_{NPV}. The next step is to divide each project's σ_{NPV} by its expected NPV to obtain its coefficient of variation, v_{NPV}. The coefficient of variation can then be used as an index of relative risk and as a basis for setting risk-adjusted discount rates. These risk-adjusted discount rates can, in turn, be used to establish the final NPVs used to make accept/reject decisions.[6]

Problems

12B-1 Contra Corporation, a NYSE company, manufactures and distributes low-cost paints and other items for home repairs. Sales are more volatile than those of most corporations, and there is a tendency for business to expand cyclically in times like 1981, when unemployment was high and laid-off workers had time to "fix up" their homes. Contra's assets currently are $1 billion, and it is considering a project with this expected after-tax cash flow pattern (dollars in millions):

| | | Cash Flows | |
Probability	(Cost) Time 0	End of Year 1	End of Year 2
0.1	−$150	−$250	−$250
0.2	−175	0	0
0.4	−200	125	125
0.2	−225	250	250
0.1	−250	500	500
$\hat{X}$	?	$125	$125
σ	?	$185.40	$185.40

Assume that the risk-free rate is 8 percent, the average NYSE company has a cost of equity of 12 percent, Contra uses only equity financing, and the expected cash flows in Year t are not influenced by actual cash flows in Year (t − 1).

a. On a pure time value of money basis—before any adjustment is made

[6] In a recent article, Roger Bey pointed out another problem with the Hillier approach ("Calculating Means and Variances of NPVs When the Life of the Project is Uncertain," *Journal of Financial Research,* Fall 1980, 139-152). Hillier's method assumes that the projects' lives are known with certainty, and σ_{NPV} is based on this assumption. Bey showed that NPV is generally very sensitive to project life, and that if life is made a random variable, σ_{NPV} increases sharply. This phenomenon could lead to problems if Hillier's method were being used to compare the relative riskiness of projects whose lives have different degrees of uncertainty.

for risk—what is the project's NPV, its standard deviation (σ_{NPV}), and its coefficient of variation (v)?

b. Assume (1) that you are the portfolio manager for a pension fund which holds some Contra stock; (2) that the coefficient of variation for Contra's average capital project is v = 8, the same as that of an average NYSE firm; and (3) that the data contained in the problem are accurate. Would you want management to accept this project? Assume that it has approximately a +1.0 correlation with the firm's other assets. Why might management not want to accept the project? Explain your answer *carefully*. (Hint: Think what the name Contra, and the nature of the company's business, implies about its beta coefficient.)

c. How would your answer to the question in Part a have changed if the problem had stated that the actual cash flow in Year 2 was perfectly positively correlated with the cash flow in Year 1—that is, cash flows were *intertemporally dependent* rather than *intertemporally independent?*

12B-2 The financial vice-president for the Ace Manufacturing Company is analyzing the potential of a $1,500 investment in a new machine. His estimate of the cash flow distribution for the three year life of the machine is shown here. The cost is known with certainty, and the cash flows from year to year are independent of one another.

Period 1		Period 2		Period 3	
Probability	Cash Flow	Probability	Cash Flow	Probability	Cash Flow
0.10	$800	0.10	$800	0.20	$1,200
0.20	600	0.30	700	0.50	900
0.40	400	0.40	600	0.20	600
0.30	200	0.20	500	0.10	300

Probability distributions are assumed to be independent. Treasury bills are yielding 5 percent. To evaluate the investment, the vice-president has asked you to make the following calculations:

a. The expected net present value of the project.

b. The standard deviation of the expected NPV.

c. The probability that the net present value will be zero or less (assume that the distribution is normal and continuous).

d. The probability that the net present value will be greater than zero.

e. The probability that the net present value will be at least equal to the mean.

f. The profitability index of the expected value.

g. The probability that the profitability index will be (1) less than 1 or (2) greater than 2.

h. Would σ_{NPV} increase, decrease, or remain constant if the cash flows were (1) perfectly or (2) partially correlated with one another?

12B-3 The Golden Machine Tool Company is considering an investment in a project that requires an initial outlay of $3,000 with an expected cash flow generated over three periods as follows:

Period 1		Period 2		Period 3	
Probability	Cash Flow	Probability	Cash Flow	Probability	Cash Flow
0.10	$ 800	0.10	$ 800	0.20	$ 800
0.20	1,000	0.30	1,000	0.50	1,000
0.40	1,500	0.40	1,500	0.20	1,500
0.30	2,000	0.20	2,000	0.10	2,000

a. What is the expected net present value of this project? (Assume that the probability distributions are perfectly positively correlated and that Treasury bills are yielding 5 percent.)

b. Calculate the standard deviation of the expected value.

c. Find the probability that the net present value will be zero or less. (Assume that the distribution is normal and continuous.) What is the probability that the net present value will be greater than zero?

d. Calculate the profitability index of the expected value. What is the probability that the index will be (1) less than 1 and (2) greater than 2?

12B-4 The Acme Company has the following probability distributions for net cash flows during the first year for a potential project.

Probability	Cash Flow
0.50	$100
0.30	200
0.20	300

Performance of similar projects in the past has indicated that the net cash flow distributions are not independent. The level of demand and the related net cash flows experienced in Period 1 influence the achievements in Period 2 as shown on the next page.

a. If $200 is earned in Year 1, what is the probability that the second year's earnings will be $200 or less?

b. What is the probability that earnings for Year 1 will be $100 and for Year 2, $200?

If Year 1 = $100, the distribution for Year 2 is:

0.70	$100
0.20	200
0.10	300

If Year 1 = $200, the distribution for Year 2 is:

0.10	$100
0.60	200
0.30	300

If Year 1 = $300, the distribution for Year 2 is:

0.10	$100
0.20	200
0.50	300
0.20	400

c. What is the probability that the Acme Company will earn more than $300 on this project in the second year?
d. If earnings for the first year are $300, what is the probability that $200 or more will be earned the second year?
e. What is the probability that Acme will earn at least $600 over the life of the project?

Thus far in the book, whenever the expected future returns of two securities have had different degrees of risk, we have adjusted for this risk in the *denominator* of the present value equation by applying a higher discount rate to the more risky investment. However, we could also adjust for risk by altering the *numerator* of the present value equation. In this appendix we examine this second approach, then use it to reconsider the implications of adjusting for risk by altering discount rates.

Appendix 12C

Certainty Equivalents

The *certainty equivalent* method of security valuation follows directly from the concept of utility theory. Under the certainty equivalent (CE) approach, the investor must specify how much money is required with certainty to make this certain sum and the expected value (EV) of a risky sum equally attractive. To illustrate, suppose a rich eccentric offered you the following two choices:

Certainty Equivalent Adjustments

1. Flip a fair coin. If a head comes up, you receive $1 million, but if a tail comes up, you get nothing. The expected value of the gamble is $500,000 (= 0.5 × $1,000,000 + 0.5 × 0).
2. You do not flip the coin; you simply pocket $300,000 cash.

If you find yourself indifferent in regard to the two alternatives, then $300,000 is your certainty equivalent for the risky $500,000 expected return. In other words, the certain or riskless amount provides exactly the same utility as the risky alternative. Any certainty equivalent less than $500,000 indicates risk aversion. In general, if the certainty equivalent is less than the expected value of an investment, risk aversion is present, and the lower the certainty equivalent, the greater the risk aversion.

The certainty equivalent concept is illustrated in Figure 12C-1. The

**Figure 12C-1
Certainty Equivalent
Returns**

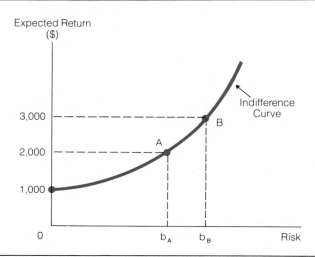

curve shows a series of risk-return combinations to which the decision maker is indifferent. For example, Point A represents an investment with a perceived degree of risk as measured by the risk coefficient, b_A, and with an expected dollar return of $2,000. The individual whose risk-return tradeoff function, or indifference curve, is shown here is indifferent with regard to a sure $1,000, an expected $2,000 with risk b_A, and an expected $3,000 with risk b_B.

Given the risk-return indifference curve of investors in general, we could determine security values as follows:

1. Substitute R_F for k in the denominator of the equation

$$\text{Value} = \sum_{t=1}^{n} \frac{R_t}{(1 + R_F)^{t'}} \qquad (12C\text{-}1)$$

where R_F is the discount rate applicable for riskless investments such as United States government bonds and R_t is the cash flow from the investment in each Year t.

2. Divide the certainty equivalent of a risky return by the risky return itself to obtain a *certainty equivalent adjustment factor*, α (pronounced "alpha"):

$$\alpha_A = \frac{\text{Certain return}}{\text{Risky return}} = \frac{\$1,000}{\$2,000} = 0.50 \text{ for } b_A, \text{ and} \qquad (12C\text{-}2)$$

$$\alpha_B = \frac{\$1,000}{\$3,000} = 0.33 \text{ for } b_B.$$

3. Conceptually, α values could be developed for all possible values of b. The range of α would be from 1.0 for $b = 0$ to a value close to zero for large values of b, assuming risk aversion.[1]

4. The risk-aversion functions of all individuals could, conceptually, be averaged to form a "market risk-aversion function." An example of such a function is shown in Figure 12C-2.

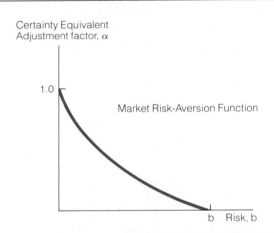

Certainty Equivalent
Adjustment factor, α

1.0

Market Risk-Aversion Function

b   Risk, b

**Figure 12C-2
Hypothetical Market
Risk-Aversion Function**

5. Given the market risk-aversion function and the degree of risk inherent in any risky return, the risky return could be replaced by its certainty equivalent:

$$\text{Certainty equivalent of } R_t = \alpha R_t. \qquad (12C\text{-}3)$$

[1] Of course, different individuals may have different α functions, depending on their degrees of risk aversion. Further, individuals' α functions shift over time as their personal situations—including age, wealth, and family status—change.

6. The valuation Equation 12C-1 could then be converted to Equation 12C-4, a model that explicitly accounts for risk:

$$\text{Value} = \sum_{t=1}^{n} \frac{R_t}{(1 + k)^t} = \sum_{t=1}^{n} \frac{\alpha_t R_t}{(1 + R_F)^t}. \qquad (12C\text{-}4)$$

In this form, the effects of different investments with different risks, b, and expected returns, R_t, can be appraised.

Certainty Equivalents versus Risk-Adjusted Discount Rates

Investment risk can be handled by making adjustments to the numerator of the present value equation (the certainty equivalent method) or to the denominator of the equation (the risk-adjusted discount rate method). The risk-adjusted rate method is the one most frequently used, probably because it is easier to estimate suitable discount rates than it is to derive certainty equivalent factors. However, Robichek and Myers have advocated the certainty equivalent approach as being theoretically superior to the risk-adjusted discount rate method.[2] Still, they, as well as H. Y. Chen, have shown that if risk is perceived to be an increasing function of time, then using a risk-adjusted discount rate is a theoretically valid procedure.[3]

[2] A. A. Robichek and S. C. Myers, "Conceptual Problems in the Use of Risk-Adjusted Discount Rates," *Journal of Finance*, vol. 21 (December 1966), 727-730.

[3] H. Y. Chen, "Valuation under Uncertainty," *Journal of Financial and Quantitative Analysis*, vol. 2 (September 1967), 313-326.

Long-Term Financing Decisions   VI

A decision to increase assets means that the firm must also raise new capital. In Part VI we examine (1) the types of long-term capital available to the firm and (2) the analysis employed when choosing among these types. We begin in Chapters 13 and 14 by examining the characteristics of bonds, preferred stock, and common stock. Chapter 15 shows how the costs of different types of capital are combined to form the weighted average cost of capital used in capital budgeting. Then, in Chapter 16, we consider the optimal mix of these securities, or the capital structure decision. The discussion of the optimal capital structure is extended in Chapter 17, where we review and evaluate the theories of capital structure that have appeared in the literature. Finally, Chapter 18 shows how the firm's investment opportunities and supply of capital schedule interact to determine dividend policy.

13

Long-Term Debt and Preferred Stock

Most firms find it both necessary and desirable to use long-term debt financing, and some also use preferred stock. There are many types of fixed-income securities: secured and unsecured, marketable and nonmarketable, convertible and nonconvertible, and so on. Different groups of investors favor different types of securities, and their tastes change over time. An astute financial manager knows how to "package" securities at a given point in time to attract the greatest possible number of potential investors, thereby keeping the firm's cost of capital to a minimum. This chapter first discusses long-term securities in general, then analyzes the three most important types of *fixed-income securities*—term loans, bonds, and preferred stocks. Later chapters deal with other types of long-term capital, while the proper mix of securities is discussed in Chapters 16 and 17.

Funded Debt

Funded debt is simply long-term debt. When a firm is said to be planning to "fund" its floating debt, it is planning to replace short-term debt with securities of longer maturity. Funding does not imply placing money with a trustee or other repository; it is simply part of the jargon of finance and means making debt long-term. Tampa Electric Company provides a good example of funding. This company has a continuous construction program. Typically, it uses short-term debt to finance construction expenditures. However, once short-term debt has built up to about $75 million, the company sells a stock or bond issue, uses the proceeds to pay off its bank loans, and starts the cycle again. The high flotation cost on a small security issue, discussed later in this chapter, makes this process desirable. (See Figure 9-3, Plan B, in Chapter 9 for a graphic view of the process of funding short-term debt.)

Term Loans

A *term loan* is a contract under which a borrower agrees to make payments of interest and principal, on specific dates, to a lender.[1] Term loans are usually negotiated directly between the borrowing firm and a financial

---

[1] If the interest and maturity payments are not met on schedule, the issuing firm is said to have *defaulted* and can then be forced into *bankruptcy*. See Chapter 21 for a discussion of bankruptcy.

institution—generally a bank, an insurance company, or a pension fund. Although the maturities of term loans vary from two to thirty years, most are for periods in the three to fifteen year range.

Term loans have three major advantages over publicly issued securities— *speed, flexibility,* and *low issuance costs.* Because they are negotiated directly between the lender and the borrower, formal procedures are minimized. The key provisions of the loan can be worked out much more quickly, and with more flexibility, than can those for a public issue, and it is not necessary for a term loan to go through the Securities and Exchange Commission (SEC) registration process (see Appendix 13A). A further advantage of term loans over publicly held debt securities has to do with future flexibility: If a bond issue is held by many different bondholders, it is difficult to obtain permission to alter the terms of the agreement, even though new economic conditions may make such changes desirable. With a term loan, the borrower generally can sit down with the lender and work out modifications in the contract.

Advantages of Term Loans

Most term loans are *amortized,* or paid off, in equal installments over the life of the loan. (At this point, you should review the discussion of amortization in Chapter 3.) The purpose of amortization is to have the loan repaid gradually over its life rather than fall due all at once. Amortization forces the borrower to retire the loan slowly; this protects both the lender and the borrower against the possibility that the borrower will not make adequate provisions for the loan's retirement during the life of the loan. Amortization is especially important whenever the loan is used to purchase a specific item of equipment; here the repayment schedule should be matched to the productive life of the equipment, with the payments being made from cash flows resulting from its use.

Amortization

The interest rate on a term loan can be either fixed for the life of the loan or variable. If it is fixed, the rate used will be close to the rate on bonds of equivalent maturity for companies of equivalent risk. If the rate is variable, it is usually set at a certain number of percentage points over the prime rate. Thus, when the prime rate goes up or down, so does the rate on the outstanding balance of the term loan. In 1981, over 70 percent of the dollar amount of term loans made by banks had floating rates, up from virtually zero in 1970. With the increased volatility of interest rates, arising from high and variable inflation rates, lenders are becoming increasingly reluctant to make long-term, fixed-rate loans.

Interest Rate

A bond is a long-term contract under which a borrower agrees to make payments of interest and principal, on specific dates, to the holder of the bond. While bonds have traditionally been issued with maturities of be-

Bonds

tween twenty and thirty years, in the 1980s shorter maturities, such as seven to ten years, have been used to an increasing extent. Although bonds are similar to term loans, a bond issue is generally advertised, offered to all investors (the "public"), and actually sold to many different investors. Indeed, thousands of individual and institutional investors may purchase bonds when a firm sells a bond issue, while there is generally only one lender in the case of a term loan.[2] With bonds, the interest rate is generally fixed, although in recent years there has been a sharp increase in the use of various types of floating rate bonds. There are a number of different types of bonds, the more important of which are discussed in this chapter.

Indenture and Trustee

An *indenture* is a legal document that spells out the rights of both the bondholders and the issuing corporation, and a *trustee* is an official (usually of a bank) who represents the bondholders and makes sure the terms of the indenture are carried out. The indenture may be several hundred pages in length, and it will cover such points as the conditions under which the issuer can pay off the bonds prior to maturity, the times-interest-earned ratio the issuer must maintain if it is to sell additional bonds, restrictions against the payment of dividends unless earnings meet certain specifications, and the like. The trustee monitors the situation and takes action on behalf of the bondholders in the event that the issuer violates any provision in the indenture.

The Securities and Exchange Commission (1) approves indentures and (2) makes sure that all indenture provisions are met before allowing a company to sell new securities to the public. Also, it should be noted that the indentures of most larger corporations were actually written back in the 1930s or 1940s, and that many issues of new bonds, all covered by this same indenture, have been sold down through the years. The interest rates on the bonds and perhaps their maturities will change from issue to issue, but bondholders' protections as spelled out in the indenture will be the same for all bonds in the class.[3] Some of the more important provisions in most indentures are discussed in the following sections.

Mortgage Bonds

Under a mortgage bond, the corporation pledges certain real assets as security for the bond. To illustrate, suppose $10 million is required to purchase land and to build a plant. Bonds in the amount of $4 million, secured by a mortgage on the property, are issued. If the company defaults on the bonds (that is, if it does not pay interest or required pay-

---

[2] However, for very large term loans, twenty or more financial institutions may form a syndicate to grant the credit. Also, it should be noted that a bond issue can be sold to one lender or to just a few; in this case, the bond is said to be "privately placed." Companies that place bonds privately do so for the same reasons that they use term loans—speed, flexibility, and low issuance costs.

[3] A firm will have different indentures for each of the major classes of bonds described in this chapter.

ments on the principal on time), the bondholders can foreclose on the plant and sell it to satisfy their claims. (Procedures for foreclosure are discussed later in this chapter and also in Chapter 21.)

If our illustrative company chose to, it could issue *second mortgage bonds* secured by the same $10 million plant. In the event of liquidation, the holders of these second mortgage bonds would have a claim against the property only after the first mortgage bondholders had been paid off in full. Thus, second mortgages are sometimes called *junior mortgages* because they are junior in priority to the claims of senior mortgages, or *first mortgage bonds*.

The first mortgage indentures of most major corporations were written twenty, thirty, forty, or more years ago. These indentures are generally "open-ended," meaning that new bonds may be issued from time to time under the existing indenture. However, the amount of new bonds that can be issued is virtually always limited to a specified percentage of the firm's total "bondable property," which generally includes all plant and equipment. For example, Savannah Electric can issue first mortgage bonds in total up to 60 percent of its fixed assets. If fixed assets totaled $200 million, and if the company had $100 million of first mortgage bonds outstanding, then it could, by the property test, issue another $20 million of bonds (60% of $200 million = $120 million).

In 1979, Savannah Electric could not issue any new first mortgage bonds at all because of another indenture provision: its times-interest-earned ratio was below 2.5 times, the minimum coverage that must be attained prior to the sale of new bonds. Thus, Savannah Electric passed the property test but failed the coverage test; hence, it could not issue first mortgage bonds. Since first mortgage bonds carry lower rates of interest, this restriction is a costly one.

Savannah Electric's neighbor, Georgia Power Company, has more flexibility under its indenture; its interest coverage requirement is only 2.0 times. In hearings before the Georgia Public Service Commission, it was suggested that Savannah Electric change its indenture coverage to 2.0 times so that it could issue more first mortgage bonds. This is simply not possible—the holders of the outstanding bonds would have to approve the change, and it is inconceivable that they would vote for a change that would seriously weaken their position!

Debentures

A debenture is an *unsecured* bond and, as such, provides no lien on specific property as security for the obligation. Debenture holders are, therefore, general creditors whose claims are protected by property not otherwise pledged. In practice, the use of debentures depends on the nature of the firm's assets and its general credit strength. If its credit position is exceptionally strong, the firm can issue debentures—it simply does not need specific security. American Telephone & Telegraph finances mainly through debentures; AT&T is such a strong corporation that it does not have to put up property as security for its debt issues. Debentures are also issued by companies in industries where it would not be practical to provide security through a mortgage on fixed assets. Examples of such industries are the large mail-order houses and the finance companies, which characteristically hold most of their assets in the form of inventory or receivables, neither of which is satisfactory security for a mortgage bond.

Subordinated Debentures

The term *subordinate* means "below," or "inferior." Thus, subordinated debt has claims on assets in the event of bankruptcy only after senior debt (usually mortgage bonds) has been paid off. Debentures may be subordinated to designated notes payable—usually bank loans—or to all other debt. In the event of liquidation or reorganization, holders of subordinated debentures cannot be paid until senior debt as named in the debentures' indenture has been paid. Precisely how subordination works, and how it strengthens the position of senior debt holders, is shown later in the chapter.

Zero (or Very Low) Coupon Bonds

Zero (or very low) coupon bonds are bonds offered at a substantial discount below their par values. In the spring of 1981, as this book was going to press, IBM, Alcoa, J. C. Penney, ITT, Cities Services, GMAC, Martin-Marietta, and a number of other companies sold over $2 billion of these bonds, and corporate treasurers all over the country were considering using them. To understand what they are, consider Penney's $200 million par value issue of bonds which (1) have no coupons and (2) pay no annual interest. These zero coupon bonds mature in eight years, in 1989, at which time holders will be paid $1,000. The bonds were sold at a discount of 66.753 percent below par, or for $332.47 per $1,000 bond, so someone who bought a bond for $332.47 in 1981 and held it until it matured in 1989 would receive a return of 14.25 percent (on a semiannual basis). Penney received $66,494,000, less underwriting expenses, for the issue, but it will have to pay back $200,000,000 in 1989.

The advantages to Penney include the following: (1) no cash outlays are required for either interest or principal until the bond matures; (2) these bonds have a relatively low yield-to-maturity (Penney would have had to pay approximately 15 percent versus the actual 14.25 percent had it issued regular coupon bonds at par); and (3) Penney receives an annual tax deduction equal to the yearly amortization of the discount ($667.53/8 = $83.44), which means that the bonds provide a positive cash flow over their life. There are also two disadvantages to Penney: (1) the bond is, in effect, simply not callable, so Penney cannot refund it if interest rates should fall, and (2) Penney will have a very large nondeductible cash outlay coming up in 1989.

There are two principal advantages to the purchasers—(1) they have no danger whatever of a call, and (2) they are guaranteed a "true" yield of 14.25 percent irrespective of what happens to interest rates—the holders of these bonds do not have to worry about having to reinvest coupons received at low rates if interest rates should fall, which would result in a "true" yield-to-maturity of less than 14.25 percent. This second feature is extremely important to pension funds, life insurance companies, and other institutions which make actuarial contracts based on assumed reinvestment rates; for such investors, the risk of declining interest rates, hence an inability to reinvest cash inflows at the assumed rates, is greater than the risk of an increase in rates and the accompanying fall in bond values.

To illustrate, suppose an insurance company or pension plan signed a contract to pay $100,000 in eight years in exchange for a lump sum premium of $35,056 today. The premium was based on the assumption that the company could invest the $35,056 at a return of 14 percent. If the $35,056 were invested in regular coupon bonds paying a 14 percent coupon rate, then the accumulated value eight years hence would be equal to the required $100,000 only if coupon payments could be invested at 14 percent over the next eight years. If interest rates were to fall, then the accumulated amount would fall short of the required $100,000. Note, however, that if the $35,056 were invested in a zero coupon bond, the company would end up with the required $100,000 irrespective of what happened to interest rates in the future. Thus, the insurance company or pension fund would have been "immunized" against a decline in interest rates.

One might think that there would be a tax advantage to the purchaser of a zero coupon bond in that income would come in the form of capital gains rather than interest income, but this is not true. The Internal Revenue Service has ruled that the amortization of original-issue discounts must be treated as ordinary income. Further, all zero coupon bonds must be registered, and the issuing corporation must send both the registered owner and the IRS a Form 1099 each year indicating the amount of the amortized discount. However, according to the investment bankers who have handled the underwritings, this is not a material issue, because these bonds have been sold exclusively to tax-exempt organizations, principally pension funds.[4] Yet, since pension funds are by far the largest purchasers of corporate bonds, the potential market for zero coupon bonds is by no means small.

To analyze a zero coupon bond and to compare it with a coupon bond, a corporate treasurer (or pension fund administrator) must employ the valuation models developed in Chapter 4. Consider again Penney's bonds. Penney will receive $332.47 per bond at $t = 0$. Also, Penney will

---

[4]This statement refers to sales within the U.S. According to reports, there is a strong market for zero coupon bonds of U.S. companies issued in Europe and the Far East.

have a tax deduction each year equal to the $83.44 amortization of the discount. This deduction will save taxes each year in the amount t(Deduction) = 0.46($83.44) = $38.38. Penney will have to make a payment of $1,000 at t = 8. Thus, the after-tax cash flow time line is as follows:

0	1	2	. . .	7	8
+$332.47	+$38.38	+$38.38		+$38.38	+$38.38
					−$1,000.00
					−$961.62

The discount rate which solves this equation is Penney's after-tax cost of debt capital from the zero coupon bond:

$$\frac{\$332.47}{(1 + k_d)^0} + \frac{\$38.38}{(1 + k_d)^1} + \cdots + \frac{\$38.38}{(1 + k_d)^7} - \frac{\$961.62}{(1 + k_d)^8} = 0.$$

The solution value for k_d is 7.6 percent (7.34 percent semiannually).

If Penney had sold a regular coupon bond, it would have had to pay about 15 percent, on a semiannual basis. Its after-tax semiannual interest payments would have been (Coupon/2)(1 − t) = $75(0.54) = $40.50, and its after-tax cost of debt would have been k_d = 8.1 percent:

$$\frac{\$1,000}{(1 + k_d/2)^0} - \frac{\$40.50}{(1 + k_d/2)^1} - \cdots - \frac{\$40.50}{(1 + k_d/2)^{15}} - \frac{\$1,040.50}{(1 + k_d/2)^{16}} = 0.$$

Thus, on an after-tax basis, it is clear that the zero coupon bond has a lower cost to Penney than would a regular coupon bond.[5]

For a purchaser, of course, the reverse is true. A tax-exempt bond buyer would receive the YTM, which is 14.25 percent for the zero coupon bond and 15.0 percent for the coupon bond. The purchasers apparently believe that total call protection and interest rate immunization are worth the 0.75 percentage point cost.

Other Types of Bonds

Several other types of bonds are used sufficiently often to warrant mention. First, *convertible bonds* are securities that are convertible into shares of common stock, at a fixed price, at the option of the bondholder. Con-

---

[5] Even if Penney could have sold a regular coupon bond at the same YTM as the zero coupon bond, 14.25 percent, there still would have been an after-tax cost advantage to the zero coupon bond. The after-tax cost of a regular coupon bond would have been 7.7 percent (versus 7.34 percent for the zero coupon bond):

$$\frac{\$1,000}{(1 + k_d/2)^0} - \frac{\$38.475}{(1 + k_d/2)^1} - \cdots - \frac{\$1,038.475}{(1 + k_d/2)^{16}} = 0.$$

This difference arises due to the fact that the zero coupon bond gets its interest tax shelter in advance of the cash outlay for interest, while for a regular bond the tax deduction and cash payment occur simultaneously.

vertibles are discussed in detail in Chapter 23. *Income bonds* are bonds that pay interest only when the interest is earned. Thus, these securities cannot bankrupt a company, but from an investor's standpoint they are riskier than "regular" bonds. Another type of bond that has been discussed in the United States, but not yet used here, is the *indexed or purchasing power bond*, which is popular in Brazil, Israel, and a few other countries long plagued by inflation. The interest rate paid on these bonds is based on an inflation index such as the consumer price index; interest paid rises when the inflation rate rises, thus protecting the bondholders against inflation. Mexico is using bonds whose interest rate is pegged to the price of oil to finance the development of its huge petroleum reserves; these bonds will probably be even better than regular indexed bonds, as oil prices are rising faster than other prices.

Two similar types of bonds that have been used in recent years are *floating rate bonds* and *bonds that are redeemable at par at the option of the holder*. Ordinarily, a bond's coupon interest payment is fixed when it is issued and remains fixed for the life of the bond. Floating rate bonds, which have been used by many companies, including Chase Manhattan, Citibank, and Gulf Oil, have interest payments that move up or down (generally within limits) as interest rates in general shift. Thus, the investor's interest income will vary (as will the borrower's interest expense), but the market value of the bond will not fluctuate as much as it would if the interest rate were fixed.

Bonds that are redeemable at the holder's option also protect the holder against a rise in interest rates. If rates rise, fixed rate bonds' prices decline. Should these redeemable bonds' prices go down due to rising rates, the holders would simply turn them in, receive the par value, and invest in new, high-rate bonds. Examples of such bonds include Transamerica's $50 million issue of twenty-five year, $8\frac{1}{2}$ percent bonds. The bonds are not callable by the company, and holders can turn them in for redemption at par on or after July 1984. If interest rates have risen, holders will turn in the bonds and reinvest the proceeds at a higher rate. This feature enabled Transamerica to sell the bonds with an $8\frac{1}{2}$ percent coupon at a time when other similarly rated bonds had yields of $8\frac{3}{4}$ percent.

Two more types of bonds that are being used increasingly are *development bonds* and *pollution control bonds*. State and local governments may set up *industrial development agencies* and *pollution control agencies*. These agencies are allowed, under certain circumstances, to sell *tax-exempt bonds*, making the proceeds available to corporations for specific uses deemed (by Congress) to be in the public interest. Thus, a Florida industrial development agency might sell bonds to provide funds for a paper company to build a plant in the West Florida area, where unemployment is high. Similarly, a Tampa pollution control agency might sell bonds to provide Tampa Electric Company or Tampa Steel with funds to be used to purchase pollution control equipment. In both cases, the income from the bonds would be tax exempt to the holders; hence, the bonds would sell at relatively low interest rates. Note, however, that these bonds are guaranteed by the corporation that will use the funds, not by a unit of government.

Bond Maturities

Bond maturities generally vary from five to forty years, although most have historically been in the twenty to thirty year range. However, during the 1980s there has been a pronounced trend toward shorter maturities as a result of volatile interest rates. As Figure 4-3 in Chapter 4 showed, long-term bond prices fall much more sharply than short-term bond prices if interest rates rise. Thus, during 1980, for example, when interest rates rose from 10 percent to over 14 percent, "safe" Bell System bonds declined in price by over 28 percent. Since investors who buy bonds are generally very much concerned with the safety of their investments, the 1980s experience has caused investors to be reluctant to buy long-term bonds. This, in turn, has led corporations to issue more bonds of shorter maturities. Therefore, during 1981, about half the fixed rate bonds that were issued had intermediate maturities—maturities in the seven to ten year range.[6]

Coverage Ratios

One of the key elements in the analysis of corporate bonds is *coverage*, which measures a firm's ability to meet interest and principal payments and thus avoid default. The most commonly used coverage ratio is the *times interest earned* (TIE). This ratio is defined below and illustrated with data for Carter Chemical Company (see Chapter 6 for the basic data):

$$\text{Times interest earned} = \frac{\text{Earnings before interest and taxes (EBIT)}}{\text{Interest}} = \frac{\$266}{\$66}$$

$$= 4.03 \text{ for Carter Chemical.}$$

$$\text{Industry average} = 6 \text{ times.}$$

The times-interest-earned ratio (TIE) depends on the level of interest payments, which in turn depends on the percentage of total capital represented by debt. For example, if Carter had used twice as much debt (with a corresponding reduction in equity), and if the interest rate had remained constant, then its interest charges would have been $66 \times 2 = $132. EBIT is not affected by changes in capital structure, so the increased use of debt would have lowered Carter's TIE to 2.02:

$$\text{TIE} = \frac{\$266}{\$132} = 2.02 \text{ times.}$$

---

[6] Floating rate bonds issued in 1981 tended to have maturities of twenty years or longer, but it was the floating rate feature which permitted companies to use these long maturities without paying very high interest rates.

As we shall see in Chapter 16, the times-interest-earned ratio is given careful consideration when a firm establishes its target capital structure. The pro forma, or projected, TIE that would result under different financing plans is calculated, and care is taken to insure that the use of debt does not lower the TIE to an unacceptable level.

Another ratio that is often used to measure a company's ability to service its debt is the *fixed charge coverage ratio*, defined and illustrated with data for Carter Chemical as follows:

$$\text{Fixed charge coverage ratio} = \frac{\text{EBIT} + \text{Lease payments}}{\text{Interest} + \left(\begin{array}{c}\text{Lease} \\ \text{payments}\end{array}\right) + \left(\dfrac{\text{Sinking fund payment}}{1 - \text{Tax rate}}\right)}$$

$$= \frac{\$266 + \$28}{\$66 + \$28 + [\$20/(1 - 0.4)]}$$

$$= 2.3 \text{ times for Carter Chemical.}$$

$$\frac{\text{Industry}}{\text{average}} = 2.5 \text{ times.}$$

Sinking funds are discussed later in this chapter, but, in essence, a sinking fund payment goes toward the retirement of the bond. Whereas interest and lease payments are tax deductible, sinking fund payments are not. Thus, the sinking fund payment in this equation is divided by (1 − tax rate) to find the before-tax income required to pay taxes and have enough left to make the sinking fund payment.

Although bankruptcy is discussed in detail in Chapter 21, it is nevertheless useful at this point to trace through the handling of bondholders' claims in the event a firm goes into bankruptcy and must be liquidated. The three cases described in Table 13-1 illustrate how different classes of debt are treated in a bankruptcy liquidation.[7]

Treatment of Bonds in the Event of Bankruptcy

Sinking Fund. A sinking fund is a provision that facilitates the orderly retirement of a bond issue (or, in some cases, an issue of preferred stock). Typically, the sinking fund provision requires the firm to retire a portion of the bond issue each year. On rare occasions, the firm is required to deposit money with a trustee, who invests the money and then uses the

Bond Repayment Provisions

---

[7] This company had no preferred stock outstanding, but suppose it had had $500 million of preferred and $500 million of common. In the first situation, the preferred would have been paid off in full, while the common would have been wiped out. Also, in this case, as in most where subordinated debentures are used, the debentures were issued as part of a "package deal." The banks agreed to supply credit in the form of notes payable *if and only if* the company would simultaneously issue debentures subordinated to the bank loans. The debentures' indenture stated that they were subordinated to the notes payable. The rate of interest on the debentures is, of course, higher than that on the bank debt because the debentures are riskier.

Table 13-1
Illustration of Bankruptcy: Payments to Senior
Debt, Other Debt, and Subordinated Debt ($ in Millions)

I. A total of $1,500 is available to meet claims.

	Book Value of Claims (1)	Percent of Total Debt (2)	Initial Allocations (3)	Actual Payments after Subordination Adjustment (4)	Percent of Original Claims Satisfied (5)
Accounts payable	$ 60	6%	$ 60	$ 60	100%
Notes payable to bank	100	10	100	100	100
Taxes and accrued wages	140	14	140	140	100
Mortgage bonds	500	50	500	500	100
Subordinated debentures (subordinated to notes payable)	200	20	200	200	100
Total debt	$1,000	100%	$1,000	$1,000	100%
Common equity	1,000		500	500	50%
Total	$2,000		$1,500	$1,500	75%

All debts are satisfied, and $500 is left for common equity.

II. A total of $750, including $600 realized from sale of plant and equipment, is available to meet claims.

	Book Value of Claims (1)	Percent of Total Debt (2)	Initial Allocations (3)	Actual Payments after Subordination Adjustment (4)	Percent of Original Claims Satisfied (5)
Accounts payable	$ 60	6%	$ 18.33	$ 18.33	30.55%
Notes payable to bank	100	10	30.56	91.67	91.67
Taxes and accrued wages	140	14	140.00	140.00	100.00
Mortgage bonds	500	50	500.00	500.00	100.00
Subordinated debentures	200	20	61.11	0.00	0.00
Total debt	$1,000	100%	$750.00	$750.00	75.00%
Common equity	1,000				0.00
Total	$2,000				37.50%

Basis of allocation in Case II:

1. The mortgage bonds receive $500 of the $600 obtained from sale of property. This satisfies their claim in full, and $500 is recorded in Column 3. This leaves $750 − $500 = $250 available for other claims.
2. By law, wages have first claim on the remaining available funds, and taxes have second priority. Thus, taxes and accrued wages receive $140. This amount is also shown in Column 3. At this point $250 − $140 = $110 is still available for other creditors, called "general creditors."
3. The claims of general creditors total $360, consisting of the following: accounts payable, $60; notes payable, $100; subordinated debentures, $200. Since there is only

$110 available to creditors with claims for $360, the general creditors receive $110/ $360 = 0.3056 per dollar of debt, so the figures shown for these creditors in Column 3 are 0.3056 times the amounts shown in Column 1.

4. The debentures are subordinated to the notes payable. This means that the debenture holders must turn over monies initially allocated to them until either the notes payable have been satisfied or the funds allocated to the debentures have been exhausted. Thus, the entire $61.11 allocated to the debentures is reallocated to the notes payable. In Column 4, Actual Payments, the notes payable are shown to receive $30.56 + $61.11 = $91.67, while the debenture holders receive nothing.

III. A total of $750, including $400 realized from sale of plant and equipment, is available to meet claims.

	Book Value of Claims (1)	Percent of Total Debt (2)	Initial Allocations (3)	Actual Payments after Subordination Adjustment (4)	Percent of Original Claims Satisfied (5)
Accounts payable	$ 60	6%	$ 27.40	$ 27.40	45.67%
Notes payable to bank	100	10	45.65	100.00	100.00
Taxes and accrued wages	140	14	140.00	140.00	100.00
Mortgage bonds	500	50	400 + 45.65	445.65	89.13
Subordinated debentures	200	20	91.30	36.95	18.48
Total debt	$1,000	100%	$750.00	$750.00	75.00%
Common equity	1,000				0.00
Total	$2,000				37.50%

Basis of allocation in Case III:

1. Mortgage bonds receive $400. Since the mortgage claim was $500, there is a deficiency of $100. The mortgage bondholders are classified as general creditors in the amount of $100, and $350 is available for other claims.
2. Taxes and wages receive $140 of the remaining $350.
3. After payment of taxes and wages, and $400 to the mortgage bonds, there remains $750 − $140 − $400 = $210. There are claims of $460 (accounts payable, notes payable, $100 deficiency of mortgage bonds, and debentures) against this amount, so the general creditors will receive $210/$460 = 0.4565 per dollar of claims. Multiplying 0.4565 by the amounts shown in Column 1 for accounts payable, notes payable, and debentures produces the amounts for the initial allocation in Column 3. Taxes and wages receive their full $140, while the mortgage bonds are allocated $400 + 0.4565 ($100).
4. The subordinated debentures must remit sufficient funds to the notes payable to satisfy the notes. Thus, $100 − $45.65 = $54.35 is transferred to notes payable. This completes the actual payments shown in Column 4.

---

accumulated sum to retire the bonds when they mature. Sometimes the stipulated sinking fund payment is tied to sales or earnings of the current year, but usually it is a mandatory fixed amount. If it is mandatory, a failure to meet the sinking fund requirement causes the bond issue to be thrown into default, which may force the company into bankruptcy. Obviously, then, a sinking fund can constitute a dangerous cash drain on the firm.

In most cases the firm is given the right to handle the sinking fund in either of two ways:

1. It may call in for redemption a certain percentage of the bonds at a stipulated price each year—for example, 2 percent of the total original amount of the issue at a price of $1,000. The bonds are numbered serially, and the ones called for redemption are determined by a lottery.
2. It may buy the required amount of bonds on the open market.

The firm will take whichever action results in the greatest reduction of outstanding bonds for a given expenditure. Therefore, if interest rates have risen and bond prices have fallen, the company will elect to use the option of buying bonds at a discount in the open market.

It must be recognized that the sinking fund may at times work to the detriment of bondholders. If, for example, the bond carries a 15 percent interest rate, and if yields on similar securities are 10 percent, then the bond will sell above par. A sinking fund call at par would thus greatly disadvantage some bondholders.

On balance, securities that provide for a sinking fund and continuing redemption are likely to be offered initially on a lower yield basis than are securities without such a fund. Since sinking funds provide additional protection to investors, bond issues which have them are likely to sell initially at higher prices; hence, they have a lower cost of capital to the issuer.

Call Provision. A call provision gives the issuing corporation the right to call the bond for redemption. If it is used, the call provision generally states that the company must pay an amount greater than the par value for the bond. The additional sum required is defined as the *call premium*. The call premium is typically set equal to one year's interest if the bond is called during the first year, with the premium declining at a constant rate each year thereafter. For example, the call premium on a $1,000 par value, twenty year, 8 percent bond would generally be $80 if it were called during the first year, $76 during the second year (calculated by reducing the $80, or 8 percent, premium by one-twentieth), and so on.

The call privilege is valuable to the firm but potentially detrimental to the investor, especially if the bond is issued in a period when interest rates are cyclically high. Accordingly, the interest rate on a new issue of callable bonds will exceed that on a new issue of noncallable bonds. For example, on March 1, 1981, Great Falls Power Company sold an issue of A-rated bonds to yield 14.375 percent. These bonds were callable immediately. On the same day, Midwest Electric sold an issue of A-rated bonds to yield 14.20 percent. Midwest's bonds were noncallable for ten years. (This is known as a *deferred call*.) Investors were apparently willing to accept a 0.175 percent lower interest rate on Midwest's bonds for the assurance that the relatively high (by historic standards) rate of interest would be earned for at least ten years. Great Falls, on the other hand, had to incur a 0.175 percent higher annual interest rate to obtain the option of calling the bonds in the event of a subsequent decline in interest rates. We discuss the analysis for determining when to call an issue in Appendix 13B.

Note that the call for refunding purposes is quite different from the call for sinking fund purposes. The call for sinking fund purposes generally has no call premium, but only a small percentage of the issue is callable each year.

Restrictive Covenants

A *restrictive covenant* is a provision in a bond indenture or term loan agreement that requires the issuer of the bond to meet certain stated conditions. Typical provisions include requirements that debt not exceed a specific percentage of total capital, that the current ratio be maintained above a specific level, that dividends not be paid on common stock unless earnings are maintained at a given level, and so on. Overall, these covenants are designed to insure, insofar as possible, that the firm does nothing to cause the quality of its bonds to deteriorate after they are issued.

The trustee is responsible for making sure the covenants are not violated, or for taking appropriate action if a violation occurs. What constitutes "appropriate action" varies with the circumstances. It might be that to insist on immediate compliance would result in bankruptcy and possibly large losses on the bonds. In such a case the trustee may decide that the bondholders would be better served by giving the company a chance to work out its problems and thus avoid bankruptcy.

Bond Ratings

Since the early 1900s, bonds have been assigned quality ratings that reflect their probability of going into default. The two major rating agencies are Moody's Investors Service and Standard & Poor's Corporation (S&P). These agencies' rating designations are shown in Table 13-2.

The triple A bonds are extremely safe, while the double A and single A bonds are also strong enough to be held in conservative portfolios.[8] The triple Bs are strong enough to be called "investment grade," and banks and other institutional investors are permitted by law to hold these bonds. Double B and lower bonds are speculations, with a significant probability of default; many financial institutions are prohibited from buying them.

---

[8] In the discussion to follow, reference to the S&P code is intended to imply the Moody code as well. Thus, for example, *triple B bonds* means both BBB and Baa bonds; *double B bonds*, both BB and Ba bonds. Chairman Bobby Pafford of the Georgia Public Service Commission came up with a new rating just after Savannah Electric's bonds were downgraded from Baa to Ba: the rating BAD.

**Table 13-2
Comparison of Bond
Ratings**

		High Quality		Investment Grade		Substandard		Speculative
Moody's		Aaa	Aa	A	Baa	Ba	B	Caa to D
S&P		AAA	AA	A	BBB	BB	B	CCC to D

Although the rating assignments are judgmental, they are based on both qualitative and quantitative factors, some of which are listed below:

1. Debt/assets ratio.
2. Times-interest-earned ratio.
3. Times fixed charges covered ratio.
4. Current ratio.
5. Mortgage provisions: Is the bond secured by a mortgage? If it is, and if the property has a high value in relation to the amount of bonded debt, the bond's rating is enhanced.
6. Subordination provisions: Is the bond subordinated to other debt? If so, it will be rated at least one notch below the rating it would have if it were not subordinated. Conversely, a bond with other debt subordinated to it will have a somewhat higher rating.
7. Guarantee provisions: Some bonds are guaranteed by other firms. If a weak company's debt is guaranteed by a strong company (usually the weak company's parent), then the bond will be given the strong company's rating.
8. Sinking fund: Does the bond have a sinking fund to insure systematic repayment? This feature is a plus factor to the rating agencies.
9. Maturity: Other things the same, a bond with a shorter maturity will be judged less risky than a longer-term bond, and this will be reflected in the rating.
10. Stability of sales and earnings.
11. Regulation: Is the company regulated, and could an adverse regulatory climate cause the company's economic position to decline? Regulation is especially important for utilities, airlines, railroads, and telephone companies.
12. Antitrust: Are any antitrust actions pending against the firm that could erode its position?
13. Overseas operations: What percentage of the firm's sales, assets, and profits are from overseas operations, and what is the political climate in the host countries?
14. Environmental factors: Is the firm likely to face heavy expenditures for pollution control equipment?
15. Pension liabilities: Does the firm have unfunded pension liabilities that could pose a future problem?
16. Labor unrest: Are there potential labor problems on the horizon that could weaken the firm's position?

17. Resource availability: Is the firm likely to face supply shortages that could force it to curtail operations?
18. Accounting policies: If a firm uses relatively conservative accounting policies, then its reported earnings will be of "higher quality" than if it used less conservative accounting procedures. Thus, conservative accounting policies are a plus factor in bond ratings.

Analysts at the rating agencies have consistently stated that no precise formula is used when setting a firm's rating—all the factors listed, plus others, are taken into account, but not in a mathematically precise manner. Statistical studies have borne out this contention. Researchers who have tried to predict bond ratings on the basis of quantitative data have had only limited success, indicating that the agencies do indeed use a good deal of subjective judgment when establishing a firm's rating.[9]

Bond ratings are very important both to firms and to investors for several reasons. First, a bond's rating is an indicator of its risk; hence, the rating has a direct, measurable influence on the bond's interest rate and the firm's cost of debt capital. Second, most bonds are purchased by institutional investors, not by individuals, and these institutions are generally restricted to investment-grade securities. Thus, if a firm's bonds fall below BBB, it will have a difficult time selling new bonds, as most of the potential purchasers will not be allowed to buy them.

Ratings also have an effect on the availability of debt capital. If an institutional investor buys BBB bonds and these bonds are subsequently downgraded to BB or lower, then (1) the institution's regulators will reprimand or perhaps impose restrictions on the institution if it continues to hold the bonds, but (2) since many other institutional investors cannot purchase the bonds, the institution that owns them will probably not be able to sell them except at a sizable loss. Because of this fear of downgrading, many institutions restrict their bond portfolios to at least A, or even AA, bonds. Some even confine purchases to AAA bonds. Thus, the lower a firm's bond rating, the smaller the group of available purchasers for its new issues.

As a result of their higher risk and more restricted market, lower-grade bonds have much higher required rates of return, k_d, than do high-grade bonds. Figure 13-1 illustrates this point. Throughout the twenty-nine years shown on the graph, U.S. Government bonds always have had the lowest yields, AAA have been next, and the BBB bonds have had the highest yields of the three types.

Figure 13-1 also shows that the gaps between yields on the three types of bonds vary over time; in other words, the cost differentials, or risk

[9] See G. E. Pinches and K. A. Mingo, "A Multivariate Analysis of Industrial Bond Ratings," *Journal of Finance*, March 1973.

Figure 13-1
Yields on U.S. Government Bonds, AAA
Corporates, and BBB Corporates, 1953-1981

Source: Federal Reserve Board, *Historical Chart Book*, 1979; and *Federal Reserve Bulletin*, January 1981.

premiums, fluctuate from year to year.[10] This point is highlighted in Table 13-3, which gives the yields on the three types of bonds, and the risk premiums for AAA and BBB bonds, in June 1963, in June 1975, and again in January 1981. All the yields were higher in the more recent years, but risk premiums also rose dramatically, causing an especially sharp increase in the rates on BBB bonds.

| | Long-Term Government Bonds (Default-free) (1) | AAA Corporate Bonds (2) | BBB Corporate Bonds (3) | Risk Premiums | | **Table 13-3** **Risk Premiums in 1963, 1975, and 1981** |
				AAA (4) = (2) − (1)	BBB (5) = (3) − (1)	
June 1963	4.00%	4.23%	4.84%	0.23%	0.84%	
June 1975	6.86	8.77	10.40	1.91	3.54	
January 1981	11.49	12.83	15.09	1.34	3.60	

Source: Federal Reserve Bulletins, December 1963, December 1975, and January 1981.

The Table 13-3 data are plotted in Figure 13-2 to show approximately what happened to risk premiums between 1963 and 1981.[11] First, the risk-less rate, or vertical axis intercept, rose almost $7\frac{1}{2}$ percentage points—this reflected the increase in realized and anticipated inflation. Second, the slope of the line also rose, indicating increased investor risk aversion, although the slope was less steep in 1981 than in 1975.

[10] The term *risk premium* ought to reflect only the difference in expected (and required) returns between two securities that results from differences in their risk. However, the difference between *yields-to-maturity* on different types of bonds consists of (1) a risk premium; (2) a liquidity, or marketability, premium, which reflects the fact that U.S. Treasury bonds are more readily marketable than corporates; (3) a call premium, because most treasury bonds are not callable, while corporate bonds are; and (4) a default premium which reflects the probability of loss on the corporate bonds. As an example of the latter point, suppose the yield-to-maturity on a BBB bond is 10 percent versus 7 percent on government bonds, but there is a 0.5 percent probability of default loss on the corporate bond. In this case, the expected return on the BBB bond is 9.5 percent, and the risk premium is 2.5 percent, not the full 3 percentage point difference in yields-to-maturity. Therefore, the risk premiums given in Table 13-3 overstate somewhat the true (but unobservable) risk premiums.

[11] The relationship graphed here is akin to the Security Market Line (SML) developed in Chapter 5, although bond ratings rather than beta coefficients are used to measure risk. A word about the scaling of the horizontal axis and about the placement of the points is in order. (1) We have shown a linear fit, although there is no theoretical reason to think that yields plotted against bond ratings are necessarily linear. (2) We have shown the interval on the horizontal axis between AAA and BBB to be equal to that between U.S. Government bonds and AAA, but this is an arbitrary scaling. (3) Finally, on a very accurate, large-scale graph it would be clear that the plotted points for the AAA and BBB bonds are not precisely on the straight lines shown in the graph; however, they are sufficiently close to warrant our analysis.

Attempts have been made to calculate beta coefficients for bonds and to plot bonds on the same Security Market Line that is used for common stocks. However, these results have not been successful—bonds do not plot on the same linear SML. See W. F. Sharpe, *Investments* (Englewood Cliffs, N.J.: Prentice-Hall, 1978), 246-252.

Figure 13-2
Relationship between
Bond Ratings and Bond
Yields, 1963, 1975, and
1981

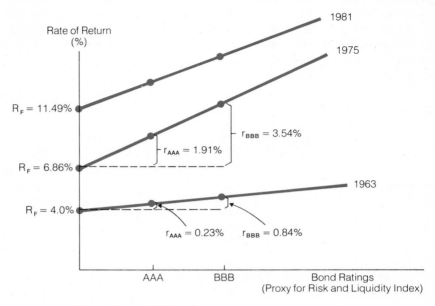

r_{AAA} = risk premium on AAA bonds.
r_{BBB} = risk premium on BBB bonds.

Source: Table 13-3.

Changes in Ratings

A change in a firm's bond rating will have a significant effect on its ability to borrow long-term capital, and on the cost of that capital. Rating agencies review outstanding bonds on a periodic basis, occasionally upgrading or downgrading a bond as a result of its issuer's changed circumstances. Also, an announcement of a new issue of bonds will trigger agency reviews and possibly lead to rating changes.[12]

If a firm's situation has deteriorated somewhat, but its bonds have not been reviewed and downgraded, then it may choose to use a term loan or short-term debt rather than finance through a public bond issue. This will perhaps postpone an agency review until the situation has improved. For example, a number of public utilities delayed bond issues in 1980 and 1981, financing with short-term debt until rate increases could be obtained to raise interest coverage ratios to acceptable levels. After rate increases were put into effect, the companies sold bonds and used the proceeds to retire the excess short-term debt.

---

[12] Rating agencies do review ratings without being prompted by the company, but most reviews associated with new issues are actually requested by the company. The investment bankers will make this a condition of the offering. A company must pay the agency to have its bonds rated.

Preferred Stock

Preferred stock is similar to bonds in some respects and similar to common stock in other ways. Preferred has a par value, usually either $25 or $100. The dividend is indicated either as a percentage of par, in dollars, or sometimes both ways. For example, Mississippi Power Company recently sold 150,000 shares of $100 par value preferred stock for a total of $15 million. This preferred had a stated dividend of $12 per share, so the preferred dividend yield was $12/$100 = 0.12, or 12 percent, at the time of issue. The dividend was set when the stock was issued; it will not be changed in the future. Therefore, if the market price of the stock changes from $100 after the issue date—as it certainly will—then the yield will go up or down. For example, if the market price rises to $120, the yield will fall to $12/$120 = 10 percent.

If the preferred dividend is not earned, the company does not have to pay it. However, most preferred issues are *cumulative*, meaning that the cumulative total of all unpaid preferred dividends must be paid before dividends can be paid on common stock. Unpaid preferred dividends are called *arrearages*.[13]

Even though nonpayment of preferred dividends will not bankrupt a company, corporations issue preferred with every intention of paying the dividends. Failure to pay the preferred dividend precludes payment of common dividends and, in addition, makes it virtually impossible for a firm to raise capital by selling bonds, more preferred, or common stock. However, having preferred stock outstanding does give a firm that experiences temporary problems a chance to overcome its difficulties; had bonds been used instead of preferred stock, the company might have been forced into bankruptcy. Thus, preferred stock is less risky than bonds from the viewpoint of the issuing corporation.

Investors, on the other hand, regard preferred stock as being riskier than bonds for two reasons: (1) preferred stockholders' claims are subordinated to bondholders' in the event of liquidation, and (2) bondholders are more likely to continue receiving income during hard times than are preferred stockholders. Accordingly, investors historically have required a higher rate of return on a given firm's preferred stock than on its bonds. However, the fact that preferred dividends are largely exempt from the corporate tax has made preferred stock attractive to corporate investors.[14] In recent years, high-grade preferred stock, on average, has sold on a lower yield basis than high-grade bonds. As an example, in February 1981, AT&T's preferred stock yielded about $11\frac{1}{2}$ percent, while its bonds provided a yield of 14 percent, or $2\frac{1}{2}$ percentage points *more* than its preferred. The tax treatment accounted for this differential; the after-tax

---

[13] Dividends in arrears do not earn interest; thus, arrearages do not increase in a compound interest sense. They only grow from continued nonpayment of the preferred dividend.

[14] Recall from Chapter 2 that 85 percent of dividends received by one corporation from another corporation is exempt from corporate income taxes.

yield to corporate investors was greater on the preferred stock than on the bonds.[15]

About half of all preferred stock issued in recent years is convertible into common stock. For example, a firm might issue preferred stock which stipulated that one share of preferred could be converted into three shares of common, at the option of the preferred stockholder. Convertibles are discussed at length in Chapter 23.

Preferred stock is generally similar to perpetual bonds in that it has no maturity date. However, many preferred shares do have a sinking fund provision; if the sinking fund called for the retirement of 1 percent of the issue each year, the issue would "mature" in a maximum of 100 years. Also, many preferred issues are callable by the issuing corporation. This feature, if exercised, will limit the life of the preferred.

Cost of Issuing Securities

Table 13-4 gives an indication of the flotation costs associated with public issues of bonds, preferred stocks, and common stocks. As the table shows, costs as a percentage of the proceeds are higher for stocks than

Table 13-4
Costs of Flotation, 1971-1972 (Costs Expressed as Percentage of Gross Proceeds)

Size of Issue ($ in Millions)	Bonds			Preferred Stock			Common Stock		
	Underwriting Commission	Other Expenses	Total Costs	Underwriting Commission	Other Expenses	Total Costs	Underwriting Commission	Other Expenses	Total Costs
Under 0.5	—	—	—	—	—	—	13.3	10.4	23.7
0.5-0.9	9.9	3.4	13.3	—	—	—	12.6	8.3	20.9
1.0-1.9	—	—	—	8.3	3.5	11.8	11.0	5.9	16.9
2.0-4.9	4.0	2.2	6.2	—	—	—	8.6	3.8	12.4
5.0-9.9	2.4	0.8	3.2	1.9	0.7	2.6	6.3	1.9	8.1
10.0-19.9	1.2	0.7	1.9	1.4	0.4	1.8	5.1	0.9	5.9
20.0-49.9	1.0	0.4	1.4	1.4	0.3	1.7	4.1	0.5	4.6
50.0 and over	0.9	0.2	1.1	1.4	0.2	1.6	3.3	0.2	3.5

Source: Securities and Exchange Commission, *Cost of Flotation of Registered Equity Issues, 1971-1972* (Washington, D.C.: U.S. Government Printing Office, December 1974). Because of rounding errors, totals may not equal the sum of the parts. Preferred stocks were used infrequently, as were bond issues of under $2 million. Therefore (1) all bond issues of under $2 million were lumped together, and (2) blanks are shown for several preferred stock categories because no issues in those size ranges were reported. These data are quite old, but periodic surveys by the author, plus discussions with both SEC officials and investment bankers, suggest that they still indicate the approximate cost of issuing securities. However, the percentage costs tend to rise somewhat when interest rates are cyclically high, indicating that money is in relatively tight supply, hence that investment bankers will have a relatively hard time placing issues with permanent investors.

[15] The after-tax yield on a 14 percent bond to a corporate investor paying a 46 percent marginal tax rate is $14(1 - t) = 14(0.54) = 7.56\%$. The after-tax yield on an 11.5 percent preferred stock is

(continued)

for bonds, and costs are higher for small than for large issues. The relationship between size of issue and flotation cost is due primarily to the existence of fixed costs—certain costs must be incurred regardless of the size of the issue, so the percentage flotation cost is quite high for small issues.

Data are not available on the costs involved in borrowing through term loans, but these costs are certainly lower than the costs of issuing bonds to the public.[16]

At this point, two questions are likely to come to mind: (1) Why are there so many different types of long-term securities? (2) Why would anybody ever be willing to purchase subordinated bonds or income bonds? The answers to both questions may be made clear by reference to Figure 13-3, which depicts the now familiar risk-return tradeoff function drawn to show the risk and the expected returns for the various securities of the

**Rationale
for the Use
of Different Types
of Securities**

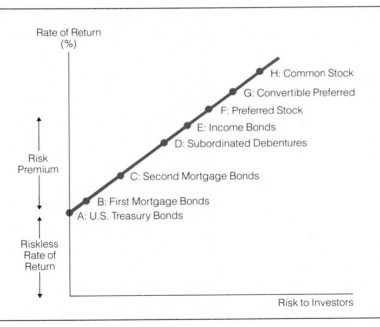

**Figure 13-3
Longstreet Company,
Risk and Expected
Returns on Different
Classes of Securities**

11.5(0.85) + 11.5(0.15)(0.54) = 10.71%. The situation for AT&T was unusual; typically a company's preferreds have yielded about 0.50 percentage points less than its bonds. Also, as a general rule, the stronger the company, the lower will be its preferred yield relative to its bond yield, and low-rated companies' preferreds will yield more than their bonds. See Appendix 4B for more on this.

[16] Additional material on the process of issuing securities to the public is contained in Appendix 13A and also in Chapter 14.

Longstreet Company. Longstreet's first mortgage bonds are somewhat riskier than U.S. Treasury bonds and sell at a somewhat higher expected return. The second mortgage bonds are even riskier and have a still higher expected return. Subordinated debentures, income bonds, and preferred stocks are all increasingly risky and have increasingly higher expected returns. Longstreet's common stock, the riskiest security the firm issues, has the highest expected return of any of its offerings.

Why does Longstreet issue so many different classes of securities? Why not just offer one type of bond plus common stock? The answer lies in the fact that different investors have different risk-return tradeoff preferences; to appeal to the broadest possible market, Longstreet must offer securities that interest as many different investors as possible. Also, different types of securities are most appropriate at different points in time. Used wisely, a policy of selling differentiated securities to take advantage of market conditions can lower a firm's overall cost of capital below what it would be if it issued only one class of debt and common stock.

Advantages and Disadvantages of Bonds and Preferred Stock

There are pros and cons to holding bonds and preferred stocks as investments, and also to their use as a means of financing by corporations. Some of these factors are considered below:

Income and Cost Are Limited. Regardless of how profitable the company is or may become, bondholders and preferred stockholders receive only a fixed, limited income. This is an advantage from the firm's standpoint, as more of the operating income is available for the common stockholders, but it is a distinct disadvantage to the bondholders or preferred stockholders.

Control. Typically, bondholders and preferred stockholders are not entitled to vote for directors—voting control lies in the hands of the common stockholders. Thus, when a firm is considering alternative means of financing, if the existing management group is concerned about losing voting control of the business, then selling bonds or preferred stock will have an advantage over financing with common stock. This point is covered in more detail in Chapter 14.

Taxes. Bond interest is a deductible expense to the issuing firm, so for a firm in the 46 percent tax bracket, the federal government in effect pays 46 percent of the interest charges on debt. Thus, bonds have an advantage over common and preferred stock to a corporation planning to raise new capital. (This point was covered in Chapter 2 and will be examined again in Chapters 15, 16, and 17.).

Risk. To the corporation, bonds or term loans, especially those with sinking funds or amortization payments, entail significantly more risk than do preferred or common stocks. Further, the shorter the maturity, the greater the risk. From the investor's viewpoint, however, bonds (or term loans) are safer.

Flexibility. The indenture provisions (restrictive convenants) on a long-term bond are generally much more stringent than they are either in a short-term credit agreement or for common or preferred stock. Hence, the firm may be subject to much more disturbing and crippling restrictions under a long-term debt arrangement than would be the case if it had borrowed on a short-term basis or had issued common or preferred stock.

Similarly, there is a limit on the extent to which funds can be raised through long-term debt. Generally accepted standards of financial policy dictate that the debt ratio must not exceed certain limits. When debt grows beyond these limits, its cost rises rapidly, or it may simply cease to be available.

Another significant point connected with flexibility relates to the ability to finance in times of economic stress. As a firm's fortunes deteriorate, it experiences great difficulties in raising capital. Further, in such times investors are increasingly concerned with the security of their investments, and they may refuse to advance funds to the firm except on the basis of well-secured loans. A firm that finances with debt during good times to the point where its debt/assets ratio is at the upper limits for its industry simply may not be able to finance at all during times of stress. Thus, corporate treasurers like to maintain some "reserve borrowing capacity"; this restrains their use of debt financing during "normal" times.

These points are always considered by firms planning new security issues. However, we will defer further consideration of the pros and cons of alternative securities until we have analyzed in the next chapter the other principal type of long-term capital—common stock.

Summary

This chapter described the characteristics, advantages, and disadvantages of the major types of long-term, fixed-income securities: *term loans, bonds,* and *preferred stocks.* The key difference between bonds and term loans is the fact that term loans are sold directly by a corporate borrower to between one and twenty lenders, while bonds are generally sold to many public investors through investment bankers. Preferred stocks are similar to bonds in that they offer a fixed return. However, preferred stock is less risky than bonds from the corporation's viewpoint because (1) the dividend does not have to be paid if it is not earned, and (2) nonpayment of preferred dividends will not bankrupt the firm. From the investors' standpoint, however, preferred stocks are riskier than bonds because

(1) firms are more likely to omit preferred dividends than to fail to pay interest, and (2) bonds have priority over preferred stock in the event of bankruptcy.

Appendix A to this chapter presents the procedures involved in issuing bonds and preferred stocks, while Appendix B examines the analysis that a firm should undertake when deciding whether to call a bond for refunding prior to its maturity date. Other types of long-term securities, including common stock, leases, and convertible bonds, are described in later chapters, and in Chapters 16 and 17 we discuss the *optimal mix of securities*, or the *capital structure decision*.

Questions

13-1 This chapter is *descriptive;* it is designed to describe the key features and terms of the markets for long-term debt and preferred stock. Any investor, or anyone concerned with the financial operations of a business, should understand and be able to define the following terms. If you do not understand them, look them up in the chapter or the glossary.

a. Bond
b. Term loan
c. Mortgage
d. Debenture
e. Convertible
f. Subordinated debenture
g. Income bond
h. Development bond
i. Pollution control bond
j. Indenture
k. Restrictive covenant
l. Call provision
m. Sinking fund
n. Amortization schedule
o. Funded debt
p. Preferred stock arrearage
q. Flotation costs
r. Floating rate bond

13-2 What effect would each of the following items have on the interest rate a firm must pay on a new issue of long-term debt? Indicate by a plus (+), minus (−), or zero (0) whether the factor will tend to raise, lower, or have an indeterminate effect.

	Effect on Interest Rate
a. The firm uses bonds rather than a term loan.	_____
b. The firm uses nonsubordinated debentures rather than first mortgage bonds.	_____
c. The firm makes its bonds convertible into common stock.	_____

d. The firm makes its debentures subordinated to its bank debt. What will the effect be

    (1) on the debentures?   _____

    (2) on the bank debt?   _____

    (3) on the average total debt?   _____

e. The firm sells income bonds rather than debentures.   _____

f. The firm must raise $100 million, all of which will be used to construct a new plant, and is debating the sale of mortgage bonds or debentures. If it decides to issue $50 million of each type, as opposed to $75 million of mortgage bonds and $25 million of debentures, how will this affect

    (1) the debentures?   _____

    (2) the mortgage bonds?   _____

    (3) the average cost of the $100 million?   _____

g. The firm is planning to raise $25 million of long-term capital. Its outstanding bonds yield 9 percent. If it sells preferred stock, how will this affect the yield on the outstanding debt?   _____

h. The firm puts a call provision on its new issue of bonds.   _____

i. The firm includes a sinking fund on its new issue of bonds.   _____

j. The firm's bonds are downgraded from A to BBB.   _____

13-3 Rank the following securities from lowest (1) to highest (10) in terms of their riskiness for an investor. All securities (except the government bond) are for a given firm. If you think two or more securities are equally risky, so indicate.

Rank
(10 = Highest Risk)

a. Income bond   _____

b. Subordinated debentures—noncallable   _____

c. First mortgage bond—no sinking fund   _____

d. Preferred stock   _____

e. Common stock   _____

f. U.S. Treasury bond   _____

g. First mortgage bond—with sinking fund   _____

h. Subordinated debentures—callable   _____

i. Amortized term loan   _____

j. Nonamortized term loan   _____

13-4 A sinking fund can be set up in one of two ways:

1. The corporation makes annual payments to the trustee, who invests the proceeds in securities (frequently government bonds) and uses the accumulated total to retire the bond issue at maturity.

2. The trustee uses the annual payments to retire a portion of the issue

each year, either calling a given percentage of the issue by a lottery and paying a specified price per bond or buying bonds on the open market, whichever is cheaper.

Discuss the advantages and disadvantages of each procedure from the viewpoint of both the firm and the bondholders.

Problems

13-1 Suppose a firm is setting up an amortized term loan. What are the annual payments for a $2 million loan under the following terms:
a. 8 percent, five years?
b. 8 percent, ten years?
c. 10 percent, five years?
d. 10 percent, ten years?

13-2 Set up an amortization schedule for a $1 million, three year, 9 percent term loan.

13-3 A company borrows $1 million on a three year, 9 percent, partially amortized term loan. The annual payments are to be set so as to amortize $700,000 over the loan's three year life, plus pay interest on the $300,000 nonamortized portion of the loan.
a. How large must each annual payment be? (Hint: Think of the loan as consisting of two loans, one fully amortized for $700,000 and one on which interest only is paid each year until the end of the third year.)
b. Suppose the firm requested a $1 million, 9 percent, three year loan with payments of $250,000 per year (interest plus some principal repayment) for the first two years, with the remainder to be paid off at the end of the third year. How large must the final payment be?

13-4 The Florida Tile Company has the following balance sheet:

Current assets	$2,800	A/P	$ 600
Fixed assets	1,500	N/P (to bank)	300
		Accrued taxes	100
		Accrued wages	100
		Total current liabilities	$1,100
		First mortgage bonds	$ 500
		Second mortgage bonds	500
		Total mortgage bonds	$1,000
		Subordinated debentures	600
		Total debt	$2,700
		Preferred stock	200
		Common equity	1,400
Total assets	$4,300	Total claims	$4,300

The debentures are subordinated (only) to the notes payable. If Florida Tile goes bankrupt and is liquidated, how much will each class of investors receive if a total of $2,000 results from sale of assets? Of this amount, $700 is derived from the sale of the fixed assets, which were pledged as security for the first and second mortgage bonds, and $1,300 is from the sale of current assets. (Note: Under the federal bankruptcy laws, $700 will be immediately allocated to the mortgage bonds, and $200 of the $1,300 from sale of current assets will be immediately allocated to accrued wages and taxes.)

13-5 A firm has the following balance sheet:

Current assets	$1,500,000	Bank debt	$ 300,000
Fixed assets	1,500,000	Trade credit	600,000
		Subordinated debentures	600,000
		Total debt	$1,500,000
		Common equity	1,500,000
Total assets	$3,000,000	Total claims	$3,000,000

If the debentures are subordinated only to the bank debt, and the firm goes bankrupt, how much will each class of investors receive under each of the following conditions?
a. A total of $2 million is received from sale of assets.
b. A total of $1.5 million is received from sale of assets.
c. A total of $1 million is received from sale of assets.
d. A total of $500,000 is received from sale of assets.
e. What is the significance of these findings for the banks, the trade creditors, the debenture holders, and the common stockholders?

13-6 Suppose U.S. Steel (USS) needed to raise $500 million, and its investment bankers indicated that ten year, zero coupon bonds could be sold at a YTM of 14 percent, while a 15 percent yield would be required on *annual* payment coupon bonds.
a. How many $1,000 par value bonds would USS have to sell under each plan?
b. What would be the YTM on each type of bond (1) to a holder who was tax exempt and (2) to a taxpayer in the 50 percent bracket?
c. What would be the after-tax cost of each type of bond to USS?
d. Why would investors be willing to buy the zero coupon bonds?
e. Why might USS turn down the zero coupon bonds?

13-7 The Montreal Development Company has just issued a $100 million, ten year, 8 percent bond. A sinking fund will retire the issue over its life. Sinking fund payments are of equal amounts and will be made semiannually, and the proceeds will be used to retire bonds immediately. Bonds can be called at par for sinking fund purposes, or the funds paid into the sinking fund can be used to buy bonds in the open market.

a. How large must each semiannual sinking fund payment be? (Note: You do *not* need to calculate a loan amortization payment; try $5 million, but explain *why* $5 million is the correct answer.)

b. What will happen, under the conditions of the problem thus far, to the company's debt service requirements per year for this issue over time?

c. Now suppose that Montreal Development had set its sinking fund so that equal *annual* amounts, payable at the end of each year, were paid into a sinking fund trust held by a bank, with the proceeds being used to buy government bonds that pay 6 percent interest. The payments, plus accumulated interest, must total $100 million at the end of ten years, and the proceeds will be used to retire the bonds at that time. How large must the annual sinking fund payment now be?

d. What are the annual cash requirements to cover bond service costs under this procedure? (Note: Under either procedure, interest must be paid on Montreal's outstanding bonds, but not on bonds that have been retired.)

e. What would have to happen to interest rates to cause the company to buy bonds on the open market rather than call them under the original sinking fund plan?

13-8 In 1936 the Canadian government raised $55 million by issuing perpetual bonds at a 3 percent annual rate of interest. Unlike most bonds issued today, which have a specific maturity date, these perpetual bonds can remain outstanding forever; they are, in fact, perpetuities.

At the time of issue, the Canadian government stated in the bond indenture that cash redemption was *possible* at face value ($100) on or after September 1966; in other words, the bonds were callable at par after September 1966. Believing that the bonds would in fact be called, many investors in the early 1960s purchased these bonds with expectations of receiving $100 in 1966 for each perpetual they held. In 1963 the bonds sold for $55, but a rush of buyers drove the price to just below the $100 par value by 1966. Prices fell dramatically, however, when the Canadian government announced that these perpetual bonds were indeed perpetual and would not be paid off. A new thirty year supply of coupons was sent to each bondholder, and the bonds' market price declined to $42 in December 1972.

Because of their severe losses, hundreds of Canadian bondholders formed the Perpetual Bond Association to lobby for face value redemption of the bonds. Government officials in Ottawa insisted that claims for face value payment were nonsense, that the bonds were clearly identified as perpetuals, and that they did not mature in 1966 or at any other time. One Ottawa official stated, "Our job is to protect the taxpayer. Why should we pay $55 million for less than $25 million worth of bonds?"

a. Would it make sense for a business firm to issue bonds such as the Canadian bonds described above? Would it matter if the firm was a proprietorship or a corporation?

b. If the United States government today offered a five year bond, a fifty year bond, a "regular perpetuity," and a Canadian-type perpetuity, what do you think the relative order of interest rates would be; that is, rank the bonds from the one with the lowest to the one with the highest rate of interest. Explain your answer.

c. 1. Suppose that because of pressure by the Perpetual Bond Association, you believed that the Canadian government would redeem this particular perpetual bond issue in five years. Which course of action would be more advantageous to you if you owned the bonds: (a) to sell your bonds today at $42 or (b) to wait five years and have them redeemed? Assume that similar risk bonds earn 8 percent today, and interest rates are expected to remain at this level for the next five years.

   2. If you had the opportunity to invest your money in bonds of similar risk, at what rate of return would you be indifferent between selling your perpetuals today or having them redeemed in five years; that is, what is the expected yield-to-maturity on the Canadian bonds? (Hint: You might want to consider the yield-to-maturity as being the IRR on the bonds and obtain a graphic solution to the IRR.)

d. Show, mathematically, the perpetuities' value if they yield 7.15 percent, pay $3 interest annually, and are considered as regular perpetuities. Show what would happen to the price of the bonds if the interest rate fell to 2 percent.

e. Are the Canadian bonds more likely to be valued as "regular perpetuities" if the going rate of interest is above or below 3 percent? Why?

f. Do you think the Canadian government would have taken the same action with regard to retiring the bonds if the interest rate had fallen rather than risen between 1936 and 1966?

g. Do you think the Canadian government was "fair" or "unfair" in its actions? Give pros and cons, and justify your reason for thinking that one outweighs the other.

Selected References

The chapters on fixed income securities in the investments textbooks listed in the Chapter 4 references provide more information on bonds and preferred stocks, as well as the markets in which they are traded. In addition, the following articles offer useful insights:

Backer, Morton, and Martin L. Gosman, "The Use of Financial Ratios in Credit Downgrade Decisions," *Financial Management,* vol. 9 (Spring 1980), 53-56.

Clark, John J., with Brenton W. Harries, "Some Recent Trends in Municipal and Corporate Securities Markets: An Interview with Brenton W. Harries, President of Standard & Poor's Corporation," *Financial Management,* vol. 5 (Spring 1976), 9-17.

Ferri, Michael G., "An Empirical Examination of the Determinants of Bond Yield Spreads," *Financial Management,* vol. 7 (Autumn 1978), 40-46.

Neuberger, Brian, and C. T. Hammond, "A Study of Underwriters' Experience with Unseasoned New Issues," *Journal of Financial and Quantitative Analysis*, March 1974, 165-177.

Pinches, George E., J. Clay Singleton, and Ali Jahankhani, "Fixed Coverage as a Determinant of Electric Utility Bond Ratings," *Financial Management*, vol. 7 (Summer 1978), 45-55.

Silvers, J. B., "Liquidity, Risk, and Duration Patterns in Corporate Financing," *Financial Management*, vol. 5 (Autumn 1976), 54-64.

Smith, Clifford W., and J. B. Warner, "On Financial Contracting: An Analysis of Bond Covenants," *Journal of Financial Economics*, June 1979, 117-161.

Weinsten, Mark I., "The Seasoning Process of New Corporate Bond Issues," *Journal of Finance*, vol. 33 (December 1978), 1343-1354.

Zwick, Burton, "Yields on Privately Placed Corporate Bonds," *Journal of Finance*, vol. 35 (March 1980), 23-29.

Appendix 13A

Procedures for Issuing Long-Term Debt and Preferred Stock

Long-term investment capital is supplied primarily by individuals who spend less than they earn. Most of these savings reach business borrowers through a *financial intermediary*, often called an *institutional investor*, such as a life insurance company, mutual fund, pension fund, savings and loan association, or bank. In the institutional market, savers transmit funds to the institutional investors, who in turn buy business securities or make loans to business firms. As we shall see in Chapter 14, individual investors are very important in the stock market, but institutional investors dominate the market for long-term debt. In this appendix, we examine the process by which firms issue long-term debt and preferred stock.

Direct (or Private) Placements

One obvious method of selling long-term debt is for the issuing firm and a potential lender (or perhaps a syndicate of two to twenty lenders) to simply sit down and hammer out an agreement under which the lender (virtually always a bank, insurance company, or pension fund) will lend money to the company. Such loans are called *term loans,* or *direct placements*. In recent years about one-third of all long-term debt raised by corporations has been directly placed, although the percentage varies from year to year.

Public Offerings by Investment Bankers

Most smaller ($10 million and less) long-term debt issues are privately placed, but if larger sums are involved, the amount of money may become too great for an individual institution or a small group of institutions to handle. Institutions seek wide diversification in their investment portfolios, so they are unwilling to purchase in its entirety a large issue such as the $1 billion debt issue IBM sold in October 1979. Thus, these larger issues are sold to "the public" by *investment bankers*, whose functions are described next.

Investment banking houses play two main roles in the security markets. First, they serve as intermediaries in the process of selling new securities—the investment bankers buy securities from the issuing firm and then sell them to ultimate purchasers. Second, investment banking houses help maintain a secondary market for securities after they have been issued—this is the *brokerage* side of investment banking. Thus, Merrill Lynch, Pierce, Fenner & Smith is an investment banking house which not only helps firms raise capital by issuing stocks and bonds, but also, through its brokerage operations, facilitates trading in these securities after their original issue. Since brokerage activities are concentrated primarily on common stocks rather than bonds, we shall defer analysis of that aspect of investment banking to Chapter 14.

Steps in Issuing a Bond

The following steps are involved in long-term debt financing. Although the steps do indicate the *approximate* sequence of events, this sequencing is not exact. In certain circumstances several of the steps may be reversed, or they may occur simultaneously.[1]

Step 1. The *approximate* amount of funds to be raised must be determined. The final decision on the amount of money to be raised is often reached after consultation with investment bankers and lenders.

Step 2. Whether the funds are to be raised as a private placement or in a public offering must be decided. Often this decision will be reached after discussions with insurance companies and other institutional investors who make term loans, and also with the investment bankers who would handle a public offering. Direct placements can be obtained faster and with lower issuing costs, so if the interest rates and other terms are comparable, firms generally opt for direct placements. However, lower rates can sometimes be obtained on public offerings, especially if the issue is a large one, so treasurers must investigate carefully the pros and cons of private placements versus public offerings.

Step 3. If the issue is to be a public offering, the firm must choose an investment banker. If the firm is well known and has issued securities in the past, it probably already has established relations with an investment banking firm. If the firm is going public for the first time, it will "shop" for a banker; low cost as well as a reputation for good service are key characteristics the firm will seek.

---

[1] The procedure described here relates to a *negotiated sale*. Alternatively, the firm could use a *competitive sale*, whereby it would simply inform all investment bankers that it wished to raise $X of money by selling twenty year bonds and then let the bankers bid competitively for the issue. The firm would award the issue to the banker who offered the best terms, that is, the lowest interest rate to the firm.

Step 4. Once the investment banker has been selected, the issuing firm and the banker meet and settle the key features of the issue—the exact size, maturity, type of security to be offered, call feature, sinking fund, and, of course, the interest rate and the fees the investment banker will charge.

Step 5. The interest rate depends primarily on (1) the firm's financial strength and (2) the rate of interest on outstanding bonds comparable to this issue. The investment banker can judge the firm's strength, and if it has bonds outstanding already, the rating agencies will have assigned them a rating. The interest rate also depends on the detailed terms of a bond issue—the rate will be lower if the bond is not callable, if it has a sinking fund, if it includes a mortgage, and if it has strong covenants designed to protect the bondholders' interests.

Step 6. The issue can be sold either on an *underwritten* basis or on a *best efforts* basis. In an underwriting, the banker actually purchases the issue from the firm, then sells the bonds to permanent investors. There may be an interval of time between the purchase and the resale, during which interest rates may rise, causing bond values to drop. For example, in October 1979, IBM sold $1 billion of debt securities. Interest rates rose dramatically during the underwriting period, causing the bonds' prices to fall. The investment bankers handling the issue lost about $10 million, but IBM did not have to worry about the risk of market price fluctuations while the investment bankers were selling the bonds. IBM had received its money. Since the investment banking firms often underwrite, or guarantee, the sale of the issue, investment bankers are sometimes called *underwriters*.

On a *best efforts* sale, the investment banking house does not guarantee the sale of the issue—it merely agrees to use its best efforts to help the corporation sell the bonds. Best efforts arrangements are employed primarily in two situations: (1) where the firm is so strong and prices the issue so attractively that it does not feel the need for the banker's guarantee, and (2) where the issue is so "shaky" that the bankers refuse to guarantee its sale. Actually, best efforts arrangements are more common in stock than in bond flotations—most bonds are sold on an underwritten basis.

Step 7. The selling procedures must be worked out. On large public offerings ($20 million or more), the investment banker will generally work with other bankers in a *syndicate*. The banking house that does the direct negotiations with the issuing firm is called the *lead* or *managing underwriter*. It manages the issue and coordinates the activities of the other investment bankers involved in the issue. On very large issues ($100 million or more), as many as 100 investment banking firms may be involved.

Step 8. The investment banker's compensation and other costs associated with the issue must be settled. Table 13-4 in the text gives an indication of the flotation costs associated with different types of securities.

Step 9. The investment bankers and the firm must clear the issue with the Securities and Exchange Commission (SEC), the government agency charged with making sure that investors are given valid information that is not misleading. A detailed report (the *registration statement*) must be filed with the SEC twenty days prior to the actual sale, and another report (the *prospectus*) must be made available to potential investors. These reports contain detailed financial information on the firm, indicate the key features of the issue, describe the firm's history and management, and indicate what the firm plans to do with the proceeds of the sale.

Step 10. The final phase of the operation is the actual sale of securities to the public. The investment bankers will have reached tentative agreements with at least some potential investors before the formal sale begins. The formal public offering is called "opening the books," an archaic term reflecting ancient customs of the investment banking trade. When the books are opened, the manager accepts subscriptions to the issue. If the demand is great, the books may be closed immediately and an announcement made that the issue is oversubscribed; the issue is said to "fly out the window." If the reception is weak, the books may remain open for an extended period. If the bankers completely misjudged the market, or if interest rates rose after the rate to the issuer had been settled, the bankers may have to cut the price of the bonds and take losses to move the issue. This happened with the IBM issue.

Suppose a company sold bonds or preferred stock at a time when interest rates were relatively high. Provided the issue was callable, as many are, the company could sell a new issue of low-yielding securities if and when interest rates dropped. It could then use the proceeds to retire the high-rate issue and thus reduce interest expenses. This is called a *refunding operation*. Refunding decisions actually involve two separate questions: (1) Is it profitable to recall an outstanding bond in the current period and to replace it with a new issue, and (2) even if refunding is currently profitable, would the expected value of the firm be increased even more if the refunding were postponed to a later date? We consider both questions in this appendix.[1]

Appendix 13B

Refunding Operations

---

[1] There has recently been a flurry of work on the pros and cons of refunding bond issues that have fallen to deep discounts as a result of a post-issue rise in interest rates. Although the issue has not been finally resolved, the tentative results suggest that bonds should not, in general, be refunded after a rise in rates; hence this topic is not discussed here. For a summary, see J. F. Weston and E. F. Brigham, *Managerial Finance*, 7th ed. (Hinsdale, Ill.: The Dryden Press, 1981), 839-843.

The decision to refund a security issue is analyzed in much the same manner as a capital budgeting expenditure. The costs of refunding—the investment outlays—are (1) the call premium paid for the privilege of calling the old issue and (2) the flotation costs incurred in selling the new issue. The annual benefits, in the capital budgeting sense, are the interest payments that are saved each year. For example, if interest expense on the old issue is $1 million while that on the new issue is $700,000, the $300,000 saving constitutes the annual benefits.

The net present value method is used to analyze the advantages of refunding—discount the future interest savings back to the present and compare this discounted value with the cash outlays associated with the refunding. *In the discounting process, the after-tax cost of the new debt, k_d, should be used as the discount factor.* The reason for this is that there is relatively little risk to the savings—their value is known with relative certainty, which is quite unlike the situation with cash flows in most capital budgeting decisions. The following example illustrates the calculations needed in a refunding decision.

The Carter Chemical Company has outstanding a $60 million, twenty-five year bond issue, carrying an 8 percent interest rate. This issue, which was sold five years ago, had flotation costs of $3 million, which the firm is currently amortizing on a straight line basis over the life of the issue. The bond indenture carries a call provision making it possible for the company to retire the bonds by calling them in at a 6 percent call premium. Investment bankers have assured the company that it could sell an additional $60 or $70 million worth of twenty year bonds at an interest rate of 6 percent. To ensure that the funds required to pay off the old debt will be available, the new bonds will be sold one month before the old issue is called, so for one month, interest must be paid on two issues. Predictions are that interest rates are unlikely to fall below 6 percent.[2] Flotation costs on the new issue will amount to $2.65 million. Carter's effective tax rate is 40 percent. Should the company refund the $60 million of bonds? The following steps outline the decision process, while Table 13B-1 summarizes it in worksheet form.

Step 1. Determine the investment outlay required to refund the issue.
a. Call premium:

$$\text{Before tax: } 0.06 \times \$60,000,000 = \$3,600,000.$$

$$\text{After tax: } \$3,600,000(1 - t) = \$3,600,000(0.6)$$

$$= \$2,160,000.$$

---

[2] The firm's management has estimated that interest rates will probably rise to center on 7 percent in the near future, with a standard deviation of $3/4$ percent. This implies that there is only a 9 percent chance (1.33 standard deviations from the mean) of future rates falling below 6 percent.

Although Carter must expend $3.6 million on the call premium, this is a deductible expense in the year the call is made. Since the company is in a 40 percent tax bracket, it saves $1.44 million in taxes. Therefore, the after-tax cost of the call is only $2,160,000.

b. Flotation costs on new issue:

Total flotation costs are $2.65 million. For tax purposes, flotation costs are amortized over the life of the new bond, or twenty years. Therefore, the annual tax deduction is

$$\frac{\$2,650,000}{20} = \$132,500.$$

Since Carter is in the 40 percent tax bracket, it has a tax saving of $132,500 times 0.4 = $53,000 a year for twenty years. This is an annuity of $53,000 for twenty years. The present value of this annuity, discounted at 3.6 percent, the after-tax cost of debt, is calculated as follows:[3]

$$
\begin{aligned}
\text{PV of tax saving} &= \text{PVIFA} \times \$53,000 \\
&= 14.085 \times \$53,000 \\
&= \$746,505.
\end{aligned}
$$

The net after-tax cost of new flotation costs is

New flotation costs	$2,650,000
PV of tax saving	−746,505
Net cost	$1,903,495

c. Flotation costs on old issue:

The old issue has an unamortized flotation cost of $2.4 million (20/25 × $3,000,000). This may be recognized immediately as an expense, thus creating an after-tax savings of $2,400,000(t) = $960,000. The firm will, however, lose a tax deduction of $120,000 a year for

---

[3] The cost of capital is developed in detail in Chapter 15. There we will see (1) that the cost of capital increases as the riskiness of the firm increases and (2) that there is a cost of debt, a cost of equity, and an "average cost of capital," which is a weighted average of the cost of debt and equity. Also, we will see that the relevant cost of debt is an *after-tax cost*, calculated as follows:

$$\text{After-tax cost of debt} = (\text{Interest rate})(1 - \text{Tax rate}) = (6\%)(0.6) = 3.6\%.$$

This calculation recognizes that interest is tax deductible, so the federal government, in effect, bears a portion of the cost of debt.

Since a 3.6 percent interest rate is not in the tables, how do we obtain PVIFA for 3.6 percent for twenty years? One way would be to interpolate. Alternatively, we could use the equation

$$\text{PVIFA} = \sum_{t=1}^{n} \frac{1}{(1+k)^t} = \frac{1 - \dfrac{1}{(1+k)^n}}{k} = 14.085.$$

twenty years, or an after-tax benefit of $48,000 a year. The present value of this lost benefit, discounted at 3.6 percent, is

$$
\begin{aligned}
\text{PV of } \textit{lost} \text{ benefit} &= \text{PVIFA} \times \$48,000 \\
&= 14.085 \times \$48,000 \\
&= \$676,080.
\end{aligned}
$$

The net after-tax effect of old flotation costs is thus

Tax savings on old flotation costs	($960,000)
PV of lost benefits of old flotation costs	676,080
Net after-tax effect of old flotation costs	($283,920)

d. Additional interest:[4]

One month "extra" interest on old issue, after taxes, is

$$
\text{Dollar amount} \times \tfrac{1}{12} \text{ of } 8\% \times (1 - \text{Tax rate}) = \text{Interest cost}
$$
$$
\$60,000,000 \times 0.0067 \times 0.6 = \$240,000.
$$

e. Total after-tax investment:

The total investment outlay required to refund the bond issue, which will be financed by debt, is thus

Call premium	$2,160,000
Flotation cost, new	1,903,495
Flotation cost, old	(283,920)
Additional interest	240,000
Total investment	$4,019,575

Step 2. Calculate the annual savings.

a. Old bond interest, after tax:

$$
\$60,000,000 \times 0.08 \times 0.6 = \$2,880,000
$$

b. New bond interest, after tax:[5]

$$
\$60,000,000 \times 0.06 \times 0.6 = \$2,160,000
$$

c. Annual savings: $ 720,000

---

[4] If the proceeds from the new issue are invested in short-term securities for one month, as they typically would be, this reduces the effect of the "extra" interest. For example, if the $60 million were invested to yield 4 percent, then the after-tax interest of $60,000,000 × $\tfrac{1}{12}$ of 4% × (1 − Tax rate) = $120,000 would be deducted from the $240,000 to obtain "net additional interest."

[5] The investment outlay (in this case, the $4,019,575) is usually raised by increasing the amount of the new bond issue. In the example given, the new issue would be $64,019,575, rounded to $64,020,000. However, the interest on the additional debt *should not* be deducted at Step 2 because the $4,019,575 is deducted at Step 4. If additional interest were deducted at Step 2, then interest would, in effect, be deducted twice.

Step 3. Find the present value of the annual savings:

a. Twenty year PVIFA at 3.6 percent = 14.085.

b. PV of $720,000 a year for twenty years:

$$14.085 \times \$720,000 = \$10,141,200.$$

Step 4. Conclusion: Since the present value of the receipts is $10,141,200, which exceeds the required investment of $4,019,575, the issue should be refunded.

Several other points are significant. First, since the $720,000 annual savings is an essentially riskless investment, its present value is found by discounting at the firm's least risky rate—its after-tax cost of debt. Second, since the refunding operation is advantageous to the firm, it must be disadvantageous to bondholders; they must give up their 8 percent bonds and reinvest in new ones yielding 6 percent. This points out the danger of the call provision to bondholders and explains why bonds without a call provision command higher prices than callable bonds.

Table 13B-1
Worksheet for the Bond Refunding Decision

	Amount before Tax	Amount after Tax	Year(s) Event Occurs	PV Factor at 3.6%	PV
Costs of Refunding at t = 0					
1. Call premium outflow	$3,600,000	$2,160,000	0	1.0	$2,160,000
2. Flotation cost on new issue	2,650,000	2,650,000	0	1.0	2,650,000
3. Tax savings on flotation cost amortization, new	(132,500)	(53,000)	1-20	14.085	(746,505)
4. Tax savings on old flotation cost expense	(2,400,000)	(960,000)	0	1.0	(960,000)
5. Tax benefits lost on old flotation cost	120,000	48,000	1-20	14.085	676,080
6. Extra interest on old issue	400,000	240,000	0	1.0	240,000
			Total after-tax investment =		$4,019,575
			(PV of investment)		
Savings over the Life of the New Issue: t = 1 to 20					
7. Interest on old bond	$4,800,000	$2,880,000			
8. Interest on new bond	3,600,000	2,160,000			
Net savings on interest, after tax	$1,200,000	$720,000	1-20	14.085	$10,141,200

$$\begin{aligned} \text{NPV} &= \text{PV of interest savings} - \text{PV of investment.} \\ &= \$10,141,200 - \$4,019,575 \\ &= \$6,121,625. \end{aligned}$$

Third, although it is not emphasized in the example, we assume that the firm raises the investment required to undertake the refunding operation (the $4,019,575) as debt. This should be feasible, as the refunding operation will improve the interest coverage ratio even though a larger amount of debt is outstanding.[6] Fourth, we set up our example in such a way that the new issue had the same maturity as the remaining life of the old issue. If the old bond has only a relatively short time to maturity (say, five to ten years), while the new bond will realistically have a much longer maturity (say, twenty-five to thirty years), then a "replacement chain" analysis like the one described in Chapter 12 should be used.

Problem   13B-1   The Wonder Corporation is considering whether to refund a $50 million, 11 percent coupon, twenty year bond issue which was sold five years ago. It is amortizing $2 million of flotation costs on the 11 percent bonds over the twenty year life of that issue. Wonder's investment bankers have indicated that the company could sell a new $50 million, fifteen year issue at an interest rate of $9^3/_4$ percent in today's market. Neither they nor Wonder's management sees much chance that interest rates will fall below $9^3/_4$ percent any time soon, but there is a chance that rates will increase.

A call premium of 5 percent would be required to retire the old bonds, and flotation costs on the new issue would amount to $3 million. Wonder's marginal tax rate is 40 percent. The new bonds would be issued one month before the old bonds were called, with the proceeds of the new issue being invested in short-term government securities with a 5 percent coupon during the interim period.

a. Calculate the NPV of the bond refunding. Should Wonder refund the old issue at this time? (Hint: The PVIFA of 5.85 percent for fifteen years is 9.8082.)

b. If the yield curve at this time were sharply downward sloping, how might this fact alter management's expectations about future interest rates and affect the decision to refund at this time?

Selected References
Ang, James S., "The Two Faces of Bond Refunding: Reply," *Journal of Finance*, vol. 33 (March 1978), 354-356.

————, "The Two Faces of Bond Refunding," *Journal of Finance*, vol. 30 (June 1975), 869-874.

Bowlin, Oswald D., "The Refunding Decision: Another Special Case in Capital Budgeting," *Journal of Finance*, vol. 21 (March 1966), 55-68.

---

[6] See A. R. Ofer and R. A. Taggart, "Bond Refunding: A Clarifying Analysis," *Journal of Finance*, March 1977, 21-30, for a discussion of how the method of financing the refunding affects the analysis. Ofer and Taggart prove that (1) if the refunding investment outlay is to be raised as debt, then the after-tax cost of debt is the proper discount rate, while (2) if these funds are to be raised as common equity, then the before-tax cost of debt is the proper rate. Since a profitable refunding will virtually always raise the firm's debt-carrying capacity (because total interest charges after the refunding will be lower than before the refunding), it is more logical to use debt than either equity or a combination of debt and equity to finance the operation.

Dyl, Edward A., and Michael D. Joehnk, "Refunding Tax Exempt Bonds," *Financial Management,* vol. 5 (Summer 1976), 59-66.

Emery, Douglas R., "Overlapping Interest in Bond Refunding: A Reconsideration," *Financial Management,* vol. 7 (Summer 1978), 19-20.

Harris, Robert S., "The Refunding of Discounted Debt: An Adjusted Present Value Analysis," *Financial Management,* vol. 9 (Winter 1980), 7-12.

Kalotay, A. J., "On the Advanced Refunding of Discounted Debt," *Financial Management,* vol. 7 (Summer 1978), 14-18.

Laber, Gene, "The Effect of Bond Refunding on Shareholder Wealth: Comment," *Journal of Finance,* vol. 34 (June 1979), 795-799.

———, "Implications of Discount Rates and Financing Assumptions for Bond Refunding Decisions," *Financial Management,* vol. 8 (Spring 1979), 7-12.

———, "Repurchases of Bonds through Tender Offers: Implications for Shareholder Wealth," *Financial Management,* vol. 7 (Summer 1978), 7-13.

Livingston, Miles, "Bond Refunding Reconsidered: Comment," *Journal of Finance,* vol. 35 (March 1980), 191-196.

———, "The Effect of Bond Refunding on Shareholder Wealth: Comment," *Journal of Finance,* vol. 34 (June 1979), 801-804.

Mayor, Thomas H., and Kenneth G. McCoin, "Bond Refunding: One or Two Faces?" *Journal of Finance,* vol. 33 (March 1978), 349-353.

Ofer, Ahron R., and Robert A. Taggart, Jr., " 'Bond Refunding Reconsidered': Reply," *Journal of Finance,* vol. 35 (March 1980), 197-200.

Riener, Kenneth D., "Financial Structure Effects of Bond Refunding," *Financial Management,* vol. 9 (Summer 1980), 18-23.

Yawitz, Jess B., and James A. Anderson, "The Effect of Bond Refunding on Shareholder Wealth: Reply," *Journal of Finance,* vol. 34 (June 1979), 805-809.

———, "The Effect of Bond Refunding on Shareholder Wealth," *Journal of Finance,* vol. 32 (December 1977), 1738-1746.

Zeise, Charles H., and Roger K. Taylor, "Advance Refunding: A Practitioner's Perspective," *Financial Management,* vol. 6 (Summer 1977), 73-76.

14   Common Stock

Common stock—or, for unincorporated businesses, the proprietors' or partners' capital—represents the ownership of the firm. In earlier chapters, we discussed the process by which stock prices are determined in the marketplace. Now we consider legal and accounting aspects of common stocks, the markets in which stock is traded, and the procedures involved when firms raise new capital by issuing additional shares of stock.

Balance Sheet Accounts and Definitions

Legal and accounting terminology is vital to both investors and financial managers if they are to avoid misinterpretations and possibly costly mistakes, so we begin our analysis of common stocks with a discussion of accounting and legal issues. Consider first Table 14-1, which shows the "common stockholders' equity" section of Carter Chemical Company's balance sheet; these data are reproduced from Table 6-2 in Chapter 6. Carter's owners, its stockholders, have authorized management to issue a total of 60 million shares, and management has, thus far, actually issued (or sold) 50 million shares. Each share has a *par value* of $1; this is the minimum amount for which new shares can be issued.[1]

Carter Chemical is an old company, established in 1873. Its initial equity capital consisted of 5,000 shares sold at the $1 par value, so on its first balance sheet the total stockholders' equity was $5,000. The additional paid-in capital and retained earnings accounts showed zero balances. Over the years, Carter retained earnings, and the firm issued new stock to raise capital from time to time. As we saw in Chapter 6, during

---

[1] A stock's par value is an arbitrary value that indicates the minimum amount of money stockholders have put up, or that they must put up in the event of bankruptcy. Actually, the firm could legally sell new shares at below par, but any purchaser would be liable for the difference between the issue price and the par value in the event the company went bankrupt. Thus, if Carter sold an investor 10,000 shares at 40 cents per share, for $4,000, the investor would have to put up an additional $6,000 if the company should later go bankrupt. This contingent liability effectively precludes the sale of new common stock at prices below par.

    Also, we should point out that firms are not required to establish a par value for their stocks. Thus, Carter could have elected to use "no par" stock, in which case the "common stock" and "additional paid-in capital" accounts could have been consolidated under one account called "common stock," which would show a balance of $150 million.

Common stock (60 million shares authorized, 50 million shares outstanding, $1 par)	$ 50,000,000
Additional paid-in capital	100,000,000
Retained earnings	750,000,000
Total common stockholders' equity (or common net worth)	$900,000,000

$$\text{Book value per share} = \frac{\text{Total common stockholders' equity}}{\text{Shares outstanding}}$$

$$= \frac{\$900,000,000}{50,000,000}$$

$$= \$18.$$

1981 Carter earned $120 million, paid $100 million in dividends, and retained $20 million. The $20 million was added to the $730 million accumulated retained earnings shown on the year-end 1980 balance sheet to produce the $750 million retained earnings at year-end 1981. Thus, since its inception in 1873, Carter has retained, or plowed back, a total of $750 million. This is money that belongs to the stockholders and that they could have received in the form of dividends. Instead, the stockholders chose to let management reinvest the $750 million in the business.

Now consider the $100 million additional paid-in capital. This account shows the difference between the stock's par value and what new stockholders paid when they bought newly issued shares. As noted above, Carter was formed in 1873 with 5,000 shares issued at the $1 par value; thus, the first balance sheet showed a zero balance for additional paid-in capital. By 1888, the company had demonstrated its profitability and was earning $0.50 per share. Further, it had built up the retained earnings account to a total of $10,000, so the total stockholders' equity was $5,000 of par value plus $10,000 of retained earnings = $15,000, and the book value per share was $15,000/5,000 shares = $3. Carter had also borrowed heavily, and, in spite of its retained earnings, the company's debt ratio had built up to an unacceptable level, precluding further use of debt without an infusion of equity.

The company had profitable investment opportunities, so, to take advantage of them, it decided to issue another 2,000 shares of stock. The market price at the time was $4 per share, which was eight times the 50 cent earnings per share (the price/earnings ratio was $8\times$). This $4 market value was also well in excess of the $1 par value, and also higher than the $3 book value per share, demonstrating that par value, book value, and market value are not directly related. Had the company lost money since its inception, it would have had *negative* retained earnings, the book value would have been below par, and the market price might well have been below book. After the 2,000 new shares had been sold to investors back in 1888, at a price of $4 per share, which was the market price then, Carter Chemical's partial balance sheet changed as shown below:

	Before Sale of Stock
Common stock (5,000 shares outstanding, $1 par)	$ 5,000
Additional paid-in capital	0
Retained earnings	10,000
Total stockholders' equity	$15,000
Book value per share = $15,000/5,000 =	$3.00

	After Sale of Stock
Common stock (7,000 shares outstanding, $1 par)	$ 7,000
Additional paid-in capital ($4 − $1) × 2,000 shares	6,000
Retained earnings	10,000
Total stockholders' equity	$23,000
Book value per share = $23,000/7,000 =	$3.29

Each share brought in $4, of which $1 represented the par value and $3 represented the excess of the sale price above par. Since 2,000 shares were involved, a total of $2,000 was added to common stock, while $6,000 was entered in additional paid-in capital. Notice also that book value per share rose from $3 to $3.29; whenever stock is sold at prices above book, the book value increases, and conversely if stock is sold below book.[2]

Similar transactions have taken place down through the years to produce the current situation, as shown on Carter's latest balance sheet in Table 6-2.[3]

---

[2] The effects on book value are not important for industrial firms, but they are *very* important for utility companies, whose allowable earnings per share are, in effect, determined by regulators as a percentage of book value. Thus, if a utility's stock is selling below book, and the company sells stock to raise new equity, this dilutes its book value and drives down its allowable earnings per share, which in turn drives down the market price. Most U.S. electric utilities' stocks sold below book during the late 1970s and early 1980s. They needed to raise large amounts of capital. Although this capital could not all be raised as debt, selling stock at below book tended to depress the market value of the stock still further. At this writing, the situation is posing a real problem for utility managers, who see a need to raise more capital to build the plants necessary to provide electricity in the future, but who cannot raise capital without depressing the prices of their companies' stocks, to the detriment of their stockholders.

[3] Stock dividends, stock splits, and stock repurchases (the reverse of stock issues) also affect the capital accounts. However, we shall defer a discussion of these topics until Chapter 18.

The common stockholders are the owners of the corporation, and as such they have certain rights and privileges. The most important of these are discussed in this section.

Control of the Firm

The stockholders have the right to elect the firm's directors, who in turn select the officers who manage the business. In a small firm, the major stockholder typically assumes the positions of president and chairman of the board of directors. In a large, publicly owned firm, the managers typically have some stock, but their personal holdings are insufficient to exercise voting control. Thus, the management of a publicly owned firm can be removed by the stockholders if the stockholder group decides the management is not effective.

Various state and federal laws stipulate how stockholder control is to be exercised. First, corporations must hold an election of directors periodically, usually once a year, with the vote taken at the annual meeting. Frequently, one-third of the directors are elected each year for a three year term. Each share of stock has one vote; thus, the owner of 1,000 shares has 1,000 votes. Stockholders can appear at the annual meeting and vote in person, or they can transfer their right to vote to a second party by means of an instrument known as a *proxy*. Management always solicits stockholders' proxies and usually gets them. However, if earnings are poor and stockholders are dissatisfied, an outside group may solicit the proxies in an effort to overthrow management and take over control of the business. This is known as a *proxy fight*.

The question of control has become a central issue in finance in recent years. The frequency of proxy fights has increased, as have attempts by one corporation to take over another by purchasing a majority of the outstanding stock. This latter action, which is called a *takeover*, is discussed in detail in Chapter 20. Managers who do not have majority control (over 50 percent) of their firms' stocks are very much concerned about takeovers, and many of them are attempting to get stockholder approval for changes in their corporate charters that would make takeovers more difficult. For example, a number of companies tried in 1981 to get their stockholders to agree (1) to elect only one-third of the directors each year (rather than to elect all directors each year) and (2) to require 75 percent of the stockholders (rather than 50 percent) to approve a merger. Managements seeking such changes generally indicate a fear of the firm's being picked up at a bargain price, but some stockholders wonder whether concern about their jobs might not be an even more important consideration.[4]

---

[4] One frequently used voting procedure, *cumulative voting*, is discussed in Appendix 14A.

The Right to Purchase New Stock: The Preemptive Right

Common stockholders often have the right, called the *preemptive right*, to purchase any additional shares sold by the firm. In some states, the preemptive right is made a part of every corporate charter; in others, it is necessary to insert the preemptive right specifically into the charter.

The purpose of the preemptive right is twofold. First, it protects the power of control of present stockholders. If it were not for this safeguard, the management of a corporation under criticism from stockholders could prevent stockholders from removing it from office by issuing a large number of additional shares and purchasing these shares itself. Management would thereby secure control of the corporation to frustrate the will of the current stockholders.

The second, and by far the more important, protection that the preemptive right affords stockholders regards dilution of value. For example, assume that 1,000 shares of common stock, each with a price of $100, are outstanding, making the total market value of the firm $100,000. An additional 1,000 shares are sold at $50 a share, or for $50,000, thus raising the total market value of the firm to $150,000. When the total market value is divided by the new total shares outstanding, a value of $75 a share is obtained. Thus, selling common stock at below market value would dilute the price of the stock and would be detrimental to present stockholders and beneficial to those who purchase the new shares. The preemptive right prevents such occurrences.[5]

Types of Common Stock

Although most firms have only one type of common stock, in some instances special classifications of stock are created to meet the special needs of the company. Generally, when different types of stock are used, one type is designated *Class A*, the second *Class B*, and so on. Small, new companies seeking to acquire funds from outside sources sometimes use different types of common stock. For example, stock designated Class A may be sold to the public, pay a dividend, and have full voting rights. The stock designated Class B, however, may be retained by the organizers of the company, and the legal terms may state that dividends will not be paid on it until the company has established its earning power by building up retained earnings to a designated level. By the use of classified stock, the public can take a position in a conservatively financed growth company without sacrificing income. In situations such as this, the Class B stock is often called *founders' shares* and given *sole* voting rights for a number of years. This permits the organizers of the firm to maintain complete control of the operations in the crucial early stages of the firm's development. At the same time, other investors are protected against excessive withdrawals of funds by the original owners.

---

[5] Procedures for issuing stock to existing stockholders, called a *rights offering*, are discussed in Appendix 14B.

Savannah Electric provides an example of yet another type of classification. This company has Class A common that pays a $1.34 annual dividend versus $1.20 for the Class B common. If earnings increase and the dividend on the Class B stock is raised to a level above $1.34, the Class A stockholders can convert to Class B. Conversion from A to B will occur automatically in 1984 if voluntary conversion has not occurred earlier. The reason for selling the Class A was quite simple—while Savannah needed money badly in the 1970s, it could not sell debt because of indenture restrictions, it could not sell preferred stock because of other restrictions, and it could not sell "regular" common because the market would not absorb it without depressing the price very badly. The Class A common was the only feasible alternative.

Note that "Class A," "Class B," and so on have no standard meanings. Most firms have no classified shares. Of the firms that do use classified shares, one may designate its Class B shares as founders' shares and its Class A shares as those sold to the public. Another firm can reverse these designations. Other firms, like Savannah Electric, can use the A and B designations for entirely different purposes.

The Market for Common Stock

Common stocks are bought by individual investors, by institutional investors (mutual funds, pension funds, insurance companies, university endowment funds, etc.), by foreign investors, and by corporate investors, including corporations formed specifically to invest in new, developing businesses.

Prior to the 1950s, the vast majority of the stock of U.S. corporations was owned by individual investors. More recently, a tremendous change in the way people save has greatly increased the proportion of stocks held by institutional investors, especially bank trust departments and insurance companies—both of which administer government and corporate pension funds—and mutual funds. Prior to 1950, relatively few corporations had pension plans, so people had to save for retirement on an individual basis. Now almost everyone is covered by a pension plan, and both employees and employers pay billions into these funds each year. Because much of this money has been invested in common stocks, today institutional investors own about 35 percent of the stock of major U.S. corporations. However, since the institutional investors are more active in the market than are individual investors, they account for about 77 percent of the trading activity in the stock market.

The stocks of smaller companies are generally owned by their management groups—such companies are called *closely held corporations*, or *closed corporations*. Most of the stock of larger firms is owned by a large number of investors not actively involved with management—these companies are known as *publicly held corporations*. The managers of most publicly held firms own some shares but not the 50 percent plus necessary for absolute voting control, although in some instances the managements of public companies do have voting control.

Types of Stock Market Transactions

We can classify stock market transactions into three distinct categories:

1. *Trading in the outstanding shares of established, publicly owned companies: the secondary market.* Carter Chemical Company has 50 million shares of stock outstanding. If the owner of 100 shares sells his or her stock, the trade is said to have occurred in the *secondary market*. Thus, the market for outstanding shares, or *used shares,* is defined as the secondary market. The company receives no new money when sales occur in the secondary market.

2. *Additional shares sold by established, publicly owned companies: the primary market.* If Carter Chemical decides to sell an additional one million shares to raise new equity capital, this transaction is said to occur in the primary market.[6]

3. *New public offerings by privately held firms: the primary market.* In 1975 the Coors Brewing Company, which was owned by the Coors family at the time, decided to sell some stock to raise capital needed for a major expansion program.[7] This type of transaction is defined as *going public*—whenever stock in a closely held corporation is offered to the public for the first time, the company is said to be going public. The market for stock that has recently gone public is often called the *new issue market.*

Firms can go public without raising any additional capital. For example, in its early days the Ford Motor Company was owned exclusively by the Ford family. When Henry Ford died, he left a substantial part of his stock to the Ford Foundation. When the Foundation later sold some of this stock to the general public, the Ford Motor Company went public, even though the company raised no capital in the transaction.

Markets for Outstanding Shares: The Stock Exchanges

There are two basic types of security markets—the *organized exchanges,* typified by the New York Stock Exchange, and the less formal *over-the-counter markets*. Since the organized exchanges have actual physical market locations and are easier to describe and understand, we shall consider them first.

The organized security exchanges are tangible, physical entities. Each of the larger ones occupies its own building, has specifically designated

---

[6] Recall that Carter has 60 million shares authorized but only 50 million shares are outstanding. Thus, the company has 10 million authorized but unissued shares. If it had no authorized but unissued shares, management could increase the authorized shares by obtaining stockholders' approval, which would generally be granted without any arguments.

[7] The stock Coors offered to the public was designated Class B, and it was nonvoting. The Coors family retained the founders' shares, called Class A stock, which carried full voting privileges.

members, and has an elected governing body—its board of governors. Members are said to have "seats" on the exchange, although everybody stands up. These seats, which are bought and sold, represent the right to trade on the exchange. In 1968, seats on the New York Stock Exchange (NYSE) sold at a record high of $515,000, but in 1979 they sold for as little as $40,000. They were back up to $220,000 in 1981.

Most of the larger stock brokerage firms own seats on the exchanges and designate one or more of their officers as members. The exchanges are open daily, with the members meeting in a large room equipped with telephones and other electronic equipment that enable each brokerage house member to communicate with the firm's offices throughout the country.

Like other markets, security exchanges facilitate communication between buyers and sellers. For example, Merrill Lynch, Pierce, Fenner & Smith, Inc. (the largest brokerage firm), might receive an order in its Atlanta office from a customer who wants to buy 100 shares of General Motors stock. Simultaneously, E. F. Hutton's Denver office might receive an order from a customer wishing to sell 100 shares of GM. Each broker communicates by wire with the firm's representative on the NYSE. Other brokers throughout the country are also communicating with their own exchange members. The exchange members with *sell orders* offer the shares for sale, and they are bid for by the members with *buy orders*. Thus, the exchanges operate as *auction markets*.[8]

Special procedures are available for handling large blocks of securities. For example, if General Motors, whose stock is already listed on the NYSE, plans to sell a new issue of stock, the exchange has facilities that make it easier for the market to absorb the new issue. Similarly, if a large mutual fund or pension fund wants to sell a large block of a listed stock, procedures are available that facilitate the sale without putting undue pressure on the stock price.

Stock Market Reporting. Securities traded on the organized security exchanges are called *listed securities*. (Other securities are known as *unlisted*, or *over-the-counter*, securities, and they are discussed later in this chapter.) Quite a lot of information is available dealing with transactions of both listed and unlisted securities, and the very existence of this information

---

[8] This discussion is highly simplified. The exchanges have members known as *specialists*, who facilitate the trading process by keeping an inventory of shares of the stocks in which they specialize. If a buy order comes in at a time when no sell order arrives, the specialist may sell off some inventory. Similarly, if a sell order comes in, the specialist will buy and add to inventory. The specialist sets a *bid price* (the price the specialist will pay for the stock) and an *asked price* (the price at which shares will be sold out of inventory). The bid and asked prices are set at levels designed to keep the inventory in balance. If many buy orders start coming in because of favorable developments, or sell orders because of unfavorable events, the specialist will raise or lower prices to keep supply and demand in balance.

reduces the uncertainty inherent in security investments. We cannot delve deeply into the matter of financial reporting—this is more properly the field of investment analysis—but it is useful to explain the basics of the stock market reporting system.

Table 14-2 is a section of the stock market page for stocks listed on the NYSE taken from the *Wall Street Journal*. For each stock listed, it provides

Table 14-2 Stock Market Transactions, February 18, 1981	52 Weeks		Stock	Div.	Yld %	P-E Ratio	Sales 100s	High	Low	Close	Net Chg.
	High	Low									
	15	$9^1/8$	AAR	.40	3.4	7	29	$11^3/4$	$11^1/2$	$11^5/8$	$+ \ ^3/8$
	$52^1/4$	$27^1/2$	ACF	2.50	4.8	10	223	$51^7/8$	$51^1/2$	$51^3/4$	$+ \ ^1/4$
	$24^1/2$	$11^1/2$	AMF	1.24	5.9	8	x777	$21^5/8$	21	$21^1/8$	. . . .
	$24^3/4$	$11^7/8$	AM Intl		. .	46	318	$12^1/8$	$d11^3/8$	$11^7/8$	$- \ ^1/8$
	$11^3/8$	$6^7/8$	APL		. .	. .	13	$7^3/8$	$7^1/4$	$7^3/8$	$+ \ ^1/8$
	$37^5/8$	$24^3/4$	ARA	1.94	5.9	6	42	$32^7/8$	$32^1/2$	$32^7/8$	$+ \ ^3/8$
	$91^1/2$	$35^5/8$	ASA	5a	10.	. .	588	$51^7/8$	$50^1/8$	$50^1/8$	$- 1^3/8$
	23	$8^1/2$	ATO	.60	3.4	6	135	18	$17^3/4$	$17^7/8$	$+ \ ^1/8$
	45	$18^1/4$	AVX	.32	1.1	17	67	$29^1/2$	29	$29^1/8$	$+ \ ^1/8$
	61	$34^1/8$	AbbtLb	1.20	2.0	17	642	59	$57^5/8$	59	$+ 1^3/8$

specific data on the trading that took place on February 18, 1981, as well as other, more general information. Similar information is available on stocks listed on the other exchanges, and also on stocks traded over the counter. Stocks are listed alphabetically, from AAR Industries to Zurn Industries; the data in Table 14-2 were taken from the top of the page. The two columns on the left show the highest and lowest prices at which the stocks have sold during the year; AAR, the first company shown, has traded in the range from $15 to $9^1/8$ (or from $15 to $9.125) during the past fifty-two weeks. The figure just to the right of the company's abbreviated name is the dividend expected for the year; AAR had a current indicated dividend rate of $0.40 per share and a dividend yield of 3.4 percent in 1981. Next comes the P/E ratio, followed by the volume of trading for the day; 2,900 shares of AAR stock were traded on February 18, 1981. Following the volume come the high and the low prices for the day, and then the closing price. On February 18, AAR traded as high as $11^3/4$ and as low as $11^1/2$, while the last trade was at $11^5/8$. The last column gives the change from the closing price on the previous day. AAR was up $^3/8$, or $0.375, so the previous close must have been $11^1/4$ (since $11^1/4 + \ ^3/8 = \$11^5/8$, the indicated closing price on February 18).

A set of footnotes always accompanies the stock market quotes, giving additional information about specific issues. Most of these notes refer to dividends, and they can best be understood after our discussion of this topic in Chapter 18, so we defer further comment on Table 14-2 until that chapter.[9]

In contrast to the organized security exchanges, the over-the-counter market is a nebulous, intangible organization. Perhaps an explanation of the term *over-the-counter* will help clarify exactly what this market is. The exchanges operate as auction markets—buy and sell orders come in more or less simultaneously, and the exchanges are used to match these orders. But if a stock is traded less frequently, perhaps because it is the stock of a new or a small firm, few buy and sell orders come in, and matching them within a reasonable length of time would be difficult. To avoid this problem, brokerage firms maintain an inventory of the stocks. They buy when individual investors wish to sell, and sell when investors want to buy. At one time the inventory of securities was kept in a safe, and when bought and sold, the stocks were literally passed over the counter.

Today, over-the-counter markets are defined as all facilities that provide for security transactions not conducted on the organized exchanges. These facilities consist primarily (1) of the relatively few dealers who hold inventories of over-the-counter securities and who are said to "make a market" in these securities and (2) of the thousands of brokers who act as agents in bringing these dealers together with investors. The dealers who make a market in a particular stock will, upon request, quote a price at which they are willing to buy the stock (the *bid* price) and a price at which they will sell shares (the *asked* price). The spread between bid and asked prices represents the dealer's markup, or profit.

In terms of numbers of issues, the majority of stocks are traded over the counter. However, because the stocks of larger companies are listed on the exchanges, it is estimated that two-thirds of the dollar volume of stock trading takes place on the exchanges. The situation is reversed in the bond market. Although the bonds of a number of the larger companies are listed on the NYSE bond list, over 95 percent of bond transactions take place in the over-the-counter market. The reason for this is that bonds typically are traded among the large financial institutions, for example, life insurance companies and pension funds, which deal in very large blocks of securities. It is relatively easy for the over-the-counter bond dealers to arrange the transfer of large blocks of bonds among the

Over-the-Counter Security Markets

---

[9] We should note that some shares listed on the NYSE are also traded on one or more regional exchanges. The *Wall Street Journal* reports trades of NYSE stocks made not only on the NYSE itself but also on the regional exchanges. Thus, if AAR were listed on both the NYSE and the Midwest Exchange, the 2,900 shares traded could have represented 2,000 shares traded on the NYSE and 900 shares traded on the Midwest Exchange. Similarly, the high, low, and closing prices could represent trades on either the NYSE or the Midwest Exchange.

relatively few holders of the bonds. It would be impossible to conduct similar operations in the stock market among the literally millions of large and small stockholders.

Some Trends in Security Trading Procedures

From the NYSE's inception in the 1800s until the 1970s, the vast majority of all stock trading occurred on the Exchange and was conducted by member firms. The Exchange established a set of minimum brokerage commission rates, and no NYSE member firm could charge a commission lower than the set rate. This was a monopoly, pure and simple. Finally, in the 1970s, the SEC, with strong prodding from the Antitrust Division of the Justice Department, forced the NYSE to abandon its fixed commissions. Commissions declined dramatically, falling in some cases as much as 80 percent from former levels. These changes were a boon for the investing public, but not for the brokerage industry. A number of brokerage houses went bankrupt, and others were forced to merge with stronger firms. Many Wall Street experts predict that, once the dust settles, the number of brokerage houses will have declined from literally thousands in the 1960s to perhaps twenty large, strong, nationwide companies.

Decision to List Stock

The exchanges have certain requirements that firms must meet before their stocks can be listed. These requirements relate to size of company, number of years in business, earnings record, number of shares outstanding, total market value, and the like. In general, requirements become more stringent as we move from the regional exchanges toward the NYSE.

The firm itself makes the decision to seek to list or not to list its securities on an exchange. Typically, the stocks of new and small companies are traded over the counter—there is simply not enough activity to justify the use of an auction market for such stocks. As the company grows, establishes an earnings record, expands the number of shares outstanding, and increases its list of stockholders, it may decide to apply for listing on one of the regional exchanges. For example, a Chicago company might list on the Midwest Stock Exchange, or a West Coast company might list its stock on the Pacific Coast Exchange. As the company grows still more, and as its stock becomes distributed throughout the country, it may seek a listing on the American Stock Exchange, the smaller of the two national exchanges. Finally, if it becomes one of the nation's leading firms, it could switch to the Big Board, the New York Stock Exchange.

Assuming a company qualifies, many people believe that listing is beneficial both to it and to its stockholders. Listed companies receive a certain amount of free advertising and publicity, and their status as a listed company enhances their prestige and reputation. This may have a beneficial effect on the sales of the products of the firm, and it probably is advantageous in terms of lowering the required rate of return on the common stock. Investors respond favorably to increased information, increased liquidity, and increased prestige. By providing investors with these services in the form of listing their companies' stocks, financial managers may lower their firms' costs of capital.

Issuing Common Stock

Suppose a firm has analyzed its investment opportunities, concluded that its profitable investments exceed its internally generated funds, and decided to float a stock issue to raise the needed capital. In this section we trace through the procedures for marketing the issue.

Choosing an Investment Banker. Most established firms will already have a working relationship with an investment banking firm. If not, or if the firm is not satisfied with the service it has been receiving, an underwriter must be selected.

Deciding Whether the Issue Should Be a Rights Offering. If the firm's stockholders have the preemptive right, then the stock must be offered to the existing stockholders. Otherwise, the firm, in consultation with its bankers, must decide whether to offer the stock to existing stockholders or to the general public. The complex technical issues which are involved in this decision are discussed in Appendix 14B.

Registration with the SEC. A registration statement must be filed with the SEC. This statement will be completed by the firm and its investment banker, with the aid of lawyers and accountants who specialize in security offerings. The statutes set a twenty day waiting period (which in practice may be shortened or lengthened by the SEC) during which time the SEC staff analyzes the registration statement to determine whether there are any omissions or misrepresentations of fact. The SEC may file exceptions to the registration statement or may ask for additional information from the issuing company or the underwriters during the examination period. During this period the investment bankers are not permitted to offer the securities for sale, although they may print preliminary prospectuses with all the customary information except the offering price.

Determining Flotation Costs. The firm and its investment bankers must agree on the banker's compensation, or the flotation cost involved in issuing the stock. As shown in Table 13-4 in Chapter 13, the costs of issuing common stock generally range from 23.7 percent of the issue price on small issues to 3.5 percent on issues involving stock with a value of over $50 million. Since the figures in the table are *averages*, the extremes are even wider—cases of flotation costs of 25 percent have been observed on very small offerings.

Flotation costs to the firm consist of two elements—compensation to the investment banker plus legal, accounting, printing, and other out-of-pocket costs borne by the issuer. In addition, if a firm is small and is going public for the first time, the underwriters may accept warrants as part of their compensation. (Warrants are options to buy stock; they are discussed in Chapter 23.) Assuming warrants are not involved, the investment banker's compensation consists of the *spread* between the price the company is paid for the stock and the price at which the stock is sold to the public, called the *offering price*. Naturally, the company wants to receive the highest possible price for the stock, so it bargains with the banker over both the offering price and the spread. The higher the offering price and the lower the spread, the more the company receives per share of stock sold; and the more it receives per share, the fewer the number of shares required to raise a given amount of money.

Setting the Offering Price. The offering price is not generally determined until the close of the registration period. There is no universally followed practice, but one common arrangement for a new issue of stock calls for the investment banker to buy the securities at a prescribed number of points below the closing price on the last day of registration. Suppose that in October 1981 the stock of Carter Chemical Company had a current price of $28.50 and that it had traded between $25 and $30 a share during the previous three months. Suppose further that Carter and its underwriter agreed that the investment banker would buy 10 million new shares at $1 below the closing price on the last day of registration. If the stock closed at $26 on the day the SEC released the issue, Carter would receive $25 a share. Typically, such agreements have an escape clause that provides for the contract to be voided if the price of the securities ends below some predetermined figure. In the illustrative case, this "upset" price might be set at $25 a share. Thus, if the closing price of the shares on the last day of registration had been $24.50, Carter would have had the option of withdrawing from the agreement.[10]

The investment banker will have an easier job if the issue is priced relatively low. The issuer of the securities naturally wants as high a price as possible. Some conflict of interest on price therefore arises between the investment banker and the issuer. If the issuer is financially sophisticated and makes comparisons with similar security issues, the investment banker will be forced to price close to the market.

The offering price may have to be set at a price substantially below the preoffering market price. Consider Figure 14-1, in which d_0 is the

---

[10] The type of arrangement described above holds, of course, only for additional offerings of stock of firms whose old stock was previously traded. When a company goes public for the first time, the investment banker and the firm must negotiate a price. Problem 14-1 illustrates this process.

**Figure 14-1
Estimated Demand
Curve for Carter
Chemical Company's
Common Stock**

estimated market demand curve for Carter Chemical stock and S_0 is the number of shares outstanding. Initially, there are 50 million shares outstanding, and the equilibrium price of the stock is $28.50. As we saw in Chapter 5, this price is found in accordance with the following equation:

$$P_0 = \frac{D_1}{k_s - g} = \frac{\$2}{0.12 - 0.05} = \$28.57 \approx \$28.50.$$

The values shown for D_1, k_s, and g are the *estimates of an average stockholder*. Some stockholders doubtlessly regard Carter as being less risky than others, hence assign it a lower value for k_s. Similarly, some stockholders will estimate the company's growth rate higher than others, so use g > 5 percent when calculating the stock's intrinsic value. Thus, there are some investors who think Carter's stock is worth more than $28.50 and others who think it is worth less, but the marginal investor thinks the stock is worth $28.50. Accordingly, this is its current price.

If Carter is to sell another 10 million shares of stock, it will have to either attract some investors who are apparently not willing to own the stock at the $28.50 price or else induce present stockholders to buy additional shares. There are two ways this can be accomplished: (1) by reducing the price of the stock or (2) by "promoting" or "advertising" the company and thus shifting the demand curve to the right.[11] If the demand curve does not shift at all, we see from Figure 14-1 that the only way the 10 million additional shares could be sold would be by setting the offering price at $26 per share. However, if the investment bankers can promote the stock sufficiently to shift the demand curve out to d_1, then the offering price can be set equal to the current market price, $28.50.[12]

The extent to which the demand curve can be shifted depends primarily on two factors: (1) what investors think the company can do with the money brought in by the stock sale, and (2) how effectively the brokers promote the issue. If investors can be convinced that the new money will be invested in highly profitable projects that will substantially raise earnings and the earnings growth rate, then the shift will occur, and the stock price may even go above $28.50. Even if investors do not radically change their expectations about the company's fundamental factors, the fact that thousands of stockbrokers telephone their clients with suggestions that they consider purchasing Carter's stock may shift the demand curve. The extent to which this promotion campaign is successful in shifting the demand curve depends, of course, upon the effectiveness of the investment banking firm. Therefore, Carter's financial manager's perceptions about the effectiveness of different investment bankers will be an important factor in the choice of an underwriter.

One final point is that *if pressure from the new shares drives down the price of the stock, all shares outstanding—not just the new shares—are affected.* Thus, if Carter's stock should fall from $28.50 to $26 as a result of the financing, and if the price should remain at this new level, then the company would incur a loss of $2.50 on each of the 50 million shares previously outstanding, or a total market value loss of $125 million. In a sense, this loss could be called a *flotation cost*, as it is a cost associated with the new issue. However, most observers feel that even though pressure may drive stock prices down immediately after a new issue is announced, demand curves do shift over time, so Carter Chemical would not be likely to suffer a permanent loss anywhere close to $125 million on an issue such as this one.

---

[11] It should be noted that investors can buy newly issued stock without paying normal brokerage commissions, and brokers are careful to point this out to potential purchasers. Thus, if an investor were to buy Carter stock at $28.50 in the regular market, the commission would be about 1 percent, or 28 cents per share. If the stock were purchased in an underwriting, this commission would be avoided.

It should also be noted that many academicians argue that the demand curve for a firm's stock is either horizontal or has only a slight downward slope. Most corporate treasurers, on the other hand, feel that there is a decided downward slope to the curve, especially if the sale occurs at a time when the stock is "out of favor" with the investing public. Recent empirical studies suggest that the demand curve, at least for utility stocks, does have a slight downward slope. See the Bowyer and Yawitz article listed in the references at the end of this chapter.

[12] The supply curve is a vertical line, first at 50 million and then, after the new issue, at 60 million.

The matter of flotation costs, including price pressure effects, is considered again in Chapter 15, where we calculate the marginal cost of capital and show how this cost is used in capital budgeting decisions.

Formation of an Investment Banking Group. Stocks are generally offered to the public the day after the issue is cleared by the SEC. Investors are required to pay for the stock within ten days, and the investment bankers must pay the issuing firm within four days of the time the offering officially begins. Typically, the bankers sell the stock within a day or two after the offering begins, but on occasion the bankers miscalculate, set the offering price too high, and are unable to move the issue. At still other times, the stock market declines during the offering period, forcing the bankers to reduce the price of the stock. In either instance, the firm receives the price that was agreed upon, and the bankers must absorb any losses that may be incurred.

Because they are exposed to large potential losses, investment bankers typically do not handle the purchase and distribution of issues single-handedly unless the issue is a very small one. If the sum of money involved is large and the risk of price fluctuation is substantial, investment bankers form *underwriting syndicates* in an effort to minimize the amount of risk each one carries.

In addition to the underwriting syndicate, on larger offerings still more investment bankers are included in the *selling group*, which handles the distribution of securities to individual investors. The selling group includes dealers who take relatively small participations, or shares of the total issue, from the members of the underwriting syndicate. Thus, the underwriters act as wholesalers, while members of the selling group act as retailers. The number of houses in a selling group depends partly upon the size of the issue; for example, the one for Communications Satellite Corporation consisted of 385 members.

Maintenance of the Secondary Market. In the case of a large, established firm such as Carter Chemical, the investment banking firm's job is finished once it has disposed of the stock and turned the net proceeds over to the issuing firm. However, in the case of a company going public for the first time, the investment banker is under some obligation to maintain a market in the shares after the issue has been completed. Such stocks are typically traded in the over-the-counter market, and the principal underwriter generally agrees to "make a market" in the stock so as to keep it reasonably liquid. The company wants a good market to exist for its stock, as do the stockholders. Therefore, if the banking house wants to do business with the company in the future, keep its own brokerage customers happy, and have future referral business, it will hold an inventory and help to maintain an active secondary market in the stock.

Regulation of Security Markets

The operations of investment bankers, exchanges, and over-the-counter markets are regulated by the Securities and Exchange Commission (SEC) and, to a lesser extent, by each of the fifty states. Certain rules apply to new securities, while others apply to securities traded in the secondary markets:

1. *Elements in the regulation of new issues by the SEC:*
    a. The SEC has jurisdiction over all interstate offerings to the public in amounts of $1,500,000 or more.
    b. Securities must be registered at least twenty days before they are publicly offered. The registration statement provides financial, legal, and technical information about the company. A prospectus summarizes this information for use in selling the securities. SEC lawyers and accountants analyze both the registration statement and the prospectus, and if the information is inadequate or misleading, the SEC will delay or stop the public offering.
    c. After the registration has become effective, the securities may be offered if accompanied by the prospectus. Preliminary or "red herring" prospectuses may be distributed to potential buyers during the waiting period.
    d. If the registration statement or prospectus contains misrepresentations or omissions of material facts, any purchaser who suffers a loss may sue for damages. Severe penalties may be imposed on the issuer, its officers, directors, accountants, engineers, appraisers, underwriters, and all others who participated in the preparation of the registration statement.
2. *Elements in the regulation of outstanding securities:*
    a. The SEC regulates all national securities exchanges. Companies whose securities are listed on an exchange must file reports similar to registration statements with both the SEC and the stock exchange and must provide periodic reports as well.
    b. The SEC has control over corporate *insiders*. Officers, directors, and major stockholders of a corporation must file monthly reports of changes in their holdings of the stock of the corporation. Any short-term profits from such transactions are payable to the corporation.
    c. The SEC has the power to prohibit manipulation by such devices as pools (aggregations of funds used to affect prices artificially) or wash sales (sales between members of the same group to record artificial transaction prices).
    d. The SEC has control over the proxy machinery and practices.
    e. Control over the flow of credit into security transactions is exercised by the Board of Governors of the Federal Reserve System. The Fed exercises this control through *margin requirements,* which stipulate the maximum percentage of the purchase price of a se-

curity that can be borrowed. If a great deal of margin borrowing has been going on, then a decline in stock prices can result in inadequate coverages, which forces the stockbrokers to issue *margin calls*, requiring investors either to put up more money or to have their margined stock sold to pay off their loans. Such forced sales further depress the stock market and can set off a downward spiral. To prevent this, the Fed controls the volume of margin borrowing.

3. *State regulations:*
   a. States have some control over the issuance of new securities within their boundaries. This control is usually exercised by a "Corporation Commissioner" or similar official.
   b. State laws relating to security sales are called "Blue Sky Laws" because they were put into effect to keep unscrupulous promoters from selling securities that offered the blue sky but actually had little or no asset backing.

In general, government regulation of securities trading is designed to insure that investors receive information that is as accurate as possible, that no one artificially manipulates (that is, drives up or down) the market price of a given stock, and that corporate insiders do not take advantage of their position to profit in their companies' stocks at the expense of other stockholders. Neither the SEC nor the state regulators can prevent investors from making foolish decisions or from having "bad luck," but they can and do help investors obtain the best data possible for making sound investment decisions.

Summary

Our discussions of common stock focused on these items: (1) the balance sheet treatment of common stock; (2) the legal rights of individual stockholders, especially their control of the firm; (3) the types of common stock that are in use (for example, founders' shares); (4) the market for common stocks; (5) the steps that a firm must go through when issuing new shares; and (6) the government's regulation of security markets. Cumulative voting and the use of rights when selling new issues of common stock are discussed in the appendices. The chapter is more descriptive than analytical, but a knowledge of the issues discussed here is essential to an understanding of finance.

Questions

14-1 This chapter is descriptive; it is designed to describe the key features and terms of the markets for common stock. Any investor, or anyone concerned with the financial operations of a business, should understand and be able to define the following terms. If you do not know what each term means, look it up in the chapter or in the glossary.

    a. Net worth

    b. Common equity

    c. Paid-in capital

    d. Book value per share

    e. Proxy; proxy fight

    f. Preemptive right

    g. Class A and Class B stock; founders' shares

    h. Closely held corporations versus publicly held corporations

    i. Secondary market; primary market

    j. Going public

    k. New issue market

    l. Organized exchanges

   m. Over-the-counter market

    n. Listed stock

    o. Flotation costs

    p. Offering price; spread

    q. Market pressure

    r. Shift in the stock demand curve

    s. SEC

14-2 Examine Table 14-1. Suppose Carter sold 2 million new shares, with the company netting $25 per share. Construct a pro forma statement of the equity accounts to reflect this sale.

14-3 Is it true that the "flatter," or more nearly horizontal, the demand curve for a particular firm's stock, the more important the role of investment bankers when the company sells a new issue of stock?

14-4 Company A has assets of $20 million, net income after taxes of $1 million, manufactures widgets, and is publicly owned. Company B is identical to A in every respect except that B's stock is all owned by its founder. If each firm sells stock to the public to raise $5 million of new money for corporate purposes, which will probably have the higher flotation cost? Why?

14-5 Draw an SML graph. Put dots on the graph to show (approximately) where you think a particular company's (a) common stock and (b) bonds would lie. Now put on a dot to represent a riskier company's stock.

Problem

14-1 The Callaway Company is a small jewelry manufacturer. The company has been successful and has grown. Now Callaway is planning to sell an issue of common stock to the public for the first time, and it faces the problem of setting an appropriate price on its common stock. The company and its investment bankers feel that the proper procedure is to select firms similar to it with publicly traded common stock and to make relevant comparisons.

    Several jewelry manufacturers are reasonably similar to Callaway with respect to product mix, size, asset composition, and debt/equity proportions. Of these, Sonnet and Mailers are most similar. Data are given below. When analyzing these data, assume that 1976 and 1981 were reasonably "normal" years for all three companies; that is, these years were neither especially good nor bad in terms of sales, earnings, and dividends. At the time of the analysis, R_F was 10 percent and k_M was 15 percent. Sonnet is listed on the American Exchange, and Mailers on the NYSE, while Callaway will be traded in the OTC market.

	Sonnet	Mailers	Callaway (Totals)
Earnings per share			
1981	$ 4.50	$ 7.50	$1,200,000
1976	3.00	5.50	816,000
Price per share			
1981	$36.00	$65.00	—
Dividends per share			
1981	$ 2.25	$ 3.75	$ 600,000
1976	1.50	2.75	420,000
Book value per share			
1981	$30.00	$55.00	$9,000,000
Market/book ratio			
1981	120%	118%	—
Total assets, 1981	$28 million	$ 82 million	$20 million
Total debt, 1981	$12 million	$ 30 million	$11 million
Sales, 1981	$41 million	$140 million	$37 million

a. Assume that Callaway has 100 shares of stock outstanding. Use this information to calculate earnings per share (EPS), dividends per share (DPS), and book value per share for Callaway.

b. Based on your answer to Part a, do you think Callaway's stock would sell at a price in the same "ballpark" as Sonnet's and Mailers's, that is, sell in the range of $25 to $100 per share?

c. Assuming that Callaway's management can split the stock so that the 100 shares could be changed to 1,000 shares, 100,000 shares, or any other number, would such an action make sense in this case? Why?

d. Now assume that Callaway did split its stock and has 400,000 shares. Calculate new values for EPS, DPS, and book value per share.

e. What can you say about the relative growth rates of the three companies?

f. What can you say about their dividend payout policies?

g. Return on equity (ROE) can be measured as EPS/book value per share, or as total earnings/total equity. Calculate ROEs for the three companies.

h. Calculate debt/total assets ratios for the three companies.

i. Calculate P/E ratios for Sonnet and Mailers. Are these P/Es consistent with the growth and ROE data? If not, what other factors could explain the relative P/E ratios?

j. Now determine a range of values for Callaway's stock, with 400,000 shares outstanding, by applying Sonnet's and Mailers's P/E ratios, price/dividends ratios, and price/book value ratios to your data for Callaway. For example, one possible price for Callaway's stock is (P/E Sonnet)(EPS Callaway) = (8) ($3) = $24 per share. Similar calculations would produce a range of prices based on both Sonnet and Mailers data.

k. Using the equation $k = D_1/P_0 + g$, find approximate k values for Sonnet and Mailers. Then use these values in the constant growth stock price model to find a price for Callaway's stock.

l. At what price do you think Callaway's shares should be offered to the public? You will want to find the *equilibrium price,* i.e., a price that will be low enough to induce investors to buy the stock, but not so low that it will rise sharply immediately after it is issued. Think about relative growth rates, ROEs, dividend yields, and total returns ($k = D/P + g$). Also, as you think about the appropriate price, recognize that when Howard Hughes let the Hughes Tool Company go public, different investment bankers proposed prices that ranged from $20 to $30 dollars per share. Hughes naturally accepted the $30 price, and the stock jumped to $40 almost immediately. Nobody's perfect!

m. Would your recommended price be different if the offering were by the Callaway family, selling some of their 400,000 shares, or if it were new stock authorized by the company? For example, another 100,000 shares could be authorized, which when issued would bring the outstanding shares up to 500,000, with 400,000 shares owned by the Callaways and 100,000 shares held by the public. If the Callaways sell their own shares, they receive the proceeds as their own personal funds. If the company sells newly issued shares, the company receives the funds and presumably uses the money to expand the business.

n. If the price you selected in Part l above were actually established as the price at which the stock would be offered to the public, approximately how much money, in total, would Callaway actually receive?

Selected References

For a wealth of facts and figures on a major segment of the stock market, see:

New York Stock Exchange, *Fact Book* (New York, published annually).

For both a description of the stock markets and some further facts and figures, see:

Francis, Jack C., *Investments: Analysis and Management* (New York: McGraw-Hill, 1980).
Reilly, Frank K., *Investment Analysis: Portfolio Management* (Hinsdale, Ill.: The Dryden Press, 1979).
Sharpe, William F., *Investments* (Englewood Cliffs, N.J.: Prentice-Hall, 1981).

For a discussion of the current state of investment banking and trends in the industry, see:

Hayes, S. L., "The Transformation of Investment Banking," *Harvard Business Review* (January-February 1979), 153-170.

Other good references on specific aspects of equity financing include the following:

Block, Stanley, and Marjorie Stanley, "The Financial Characteristics and Price Movement Patterns of Companies Approaching the Unseasoned Securities Market in the Late 1970s," *Financial Management*, vol. 9 (Winter 1980), 30-36.

Bowyer, J. W., and J. B. Yawitz, "The Effect of New Equity Issues on Utility Stock Prices," *Public Utilities Fortnightly*, May 22, 1980, 25-28.

Fabozzi, Frank J., "Does Listing on the Amex Increase the Value of Equity?" *Financial Management*, vol. 10 (Spring 1981), 43-50.

Logue, D. E., and R. A. Jarrow, "Negotiation versus Competitive Bidding in the Sale of Securities by Public Utilities," *Financial Management*, vol. 7 (Autumn 1978), 31-39.

Smith, C. W., "Alternative Methods for Raising Capital: Rights versus Underwritten Offerings," *Journal of Financial Economics*, December 1977, 273-307.

Appendix 14A

Cumulative Voting

Two methods of voting are employed to elect directors. Under one method, which is called *noncumulative voting*, each stockholder can vote for each directorship up for election. Thus, if you own 100 shares of stock and six directors are to be elected, you can cast 100 votes each for six different candidates. *Cumulative voting*, on the other hand, permits multiple votes for a single director. Thus, under a cumulative voting system, using our illustrative case, you could cast all of your 600 votes for *one* director. In other words, you can accumulate your votes and cast 600 votes for *one* director, instead of giving 100 votes to each of *six* directors. Cumulative voting is designed to enable a minority group of stockholders to obtain some voice in the control of the company by electing at least one director to the board.

The nature of cumulative voting is illustrated by use of the following formula:

$$n = \frac{d \times S}{D + 1}. \tag{14A-1}$$

n = number of shares required to elect a desired number of directors. If n solves to be a fraction, then round up, while if n is an integer, add 1.0.

d = number of directors the stockholder seeks to elect.

S = total number of shares of common stock outstanding and entitled to vote.[1]

D = total number of directors to be elected.

---

[1] An alternative that may be agreed to by the contesting parties is to define S as the number of shares *voted*, not *authorized to vote*. This procedure, which in effect gives each group seeking to elect directors the same percentage of directors as their percentage of the voted stock, is frequently followed. When it is used, a group that seeks to gain control with a minimum investment must estimate the percentage of shares that will be voted and then obtain control of more than 50 percent of that number.

The formula may be made more meaningful by an example. The ABC company will elect six directors. There are fifteen candidates and 100,000 shares entitled to vote. If a group desires to elect two directors, how many shares must it have?

$$n = \frac{2 \times 100,000}{6 + 1} = 28,572.$$

Observe the significance of the formula. Here, a minority group wishes to elect one-third of the board of directors. It can achieve its goal by owning less than one-third of the number of shares of stock.[2]

Alternatively, assuming that a group holds 40,000 shares of stock in this company (here n = 40,000), how many directors would it be possible for the group to elect, following the rigid assumptions of the formula? The formula can be used in its present form or can be solved for d and expressed as

$$d = \frac{n(D + 1)}{S}. \tag{14A-2}$$

Inserting the figures, the calculation would be

$$d = \frac{40,000 \times 7}{100,000} = 2.8.$$

The 40,000 shares could elect two and eight-tenths directors. Since directors cannot exist as fractions, the group can elect only two directors.

As a practical matter, suppose that in the above situation the total number of shares is 100,000. Hence 60,000 shares remain in other hands. The voting of all the 60,000 shares may not be concentrated. Suppose the 60,000 shares (cumulatively, 360,000 votes) not held by our group are distributed equally among ten candidates, 36,000 votes in total for each candidate. If our group's 240,000 votes are distributed equally for each of six candidates, we could elect all six directors even though we do not have a majority of the stock.

Actually, it is difficult to make assumptions about how the opposition votes will be distributed. What is shown here is a good example of game theory. One rule in the theory of games is to assume that your opponents will do the worst they can do to you and to counter with actions to minimize the maximum loss. This is the kind of assumption followed in the formula: If your opposition concentrates its votes in the optimum manner, what is the best you can do to work in the direction of your goal? Other plausible assumptions can be substituted if there are sufficient facts to support alternative hypotheses about the behavior of the opponents.

---

[2] Note also that at least 14,286 shares must be controlled to elect one director. As far as electing a director goes, any number less than 14,286 constitutes a useless minority.

If the preemptive right is contained in a particular firm's charter, then it must offer any new common stock to existing stockholders. If the charter does not prescribe a preemptive right, the firm has a choice of making the sale to its existing stockholders or to the public at large. If the sale is to the existing stockholders, the stock flotation is called a *rights offering*. Each stockholder is issued an option to buy a certain number of new shares, and the terms of the option are contained on a piece of paper called a *right*. Each stockholder receives one right for each share of stock held. The advantages and disadvantages of rights offerings are described in this appendix.

Several issues confront the financial manager who is deciding on the details of a rights offering. The various considerations can be made clear by the use of illustrative data on the Southeast Company, whose balance sheet and income statement are given in Table 14B-1.

Appendix 14B

The Use of Rights in Financing

Partial balance sheet (before sale of new stock)

	Total debt	$ 40,000,000
	Common stock	10,000,000
	Retained earnings	50,000,000
Total assets $100,000,000	Total liabilities and capital	$100,000,000

Partial income statement (before sale of new stock)

Earnings before interest and taxes	$20,000,000
Interest on debt	4,000,000
Income before taxes	16,000,000
Taxes (50% assumed)	8,000,000
Earnings after taxes	$ 8,000,000
Earnings per share (1,000,000 shares)	$8
Market price of stock (price/earnings ratio of 12.5)	$100

Table 14B-1
Southeast Company: Financial Statements before Rights Offering

Southeast earns $8 million after taxes and has 1 million shares outstanding, so earnings per share are $8. The stock sells at 12.5 times earnings, or for $100 a share. The company plans to raise $10 million of new equity funds through a rights offering and decides to sell the new stock to shareholders for $80 a share. The questions facing the financial manager are these:

1. How many rights will be required to purchase a share of the newly issued stock?
2. What is the value of each right?
3. What effect will the rights offering have on the price of the existing stock?

We will now analyze each of these questions.

Number of Rights Needed to Purchase a New Share

Southeast plans to raise $10 million in new equity funds and to sell the new stock at a price of $80 a share. Dividing the subscription price into the total funds to be raised gives the number of shares to be issued:

$$\text{Number of new shares} = \frac{\text{Funds to be raised}}{\text{Subscription price}} = \frac{\$10,000,000}{\$80}$$
$$= 125,000 \text{ shares.}$$

The next step is to divide the number of new shares into the number of previously outstanding shares to get the number of rights required to subscribe to one share of the new stock. Note that stockholders always get one right for each share of stock they own, so

$$\frac{\text{Number of rights needed to}}{\text{buy a share of the stock}} = \frac{\text{Old shares}}{\text{New shares}} = \frac{1,000,000}{125,000}$$
$$= 8 \text{ rights.}$$

Therefore, a stockholder will have to surrender eight rights plus $80 to receive one of the newly issued shares. Had the subscription price been set at $95 a share, 9.5 rights would have been required to subscribe to each new share; if the price had been set at $10 a share, only one right would have been needed.

Value of a Right

It is clearly worth something to be able to buy for less than $100 a share of stock selling for $100. The right provides this privilege, so the right must have a value. To see how the theoretical value of a right is established, we continue with the example of the Southeast Company, assuming that it will raise $10 million by selling 125,000 new shares at $80 a share.

First, notice that the *market value* of the old stock was $100 million: $100 a share times 1 million shares. (The book value is irrelevant.) When the firm sells the new stock, it brings in an additional $10 million. As a first approximation, we assume that the total market value of the common stock increases by exactly this $10 million. Actually, the market value of all the common stock will go up by more than $10 million if investors think the company will be able to invest these funds at a return substantially in excess of the cost of equity capital, but it will go up by less than $10 million if investors are doubtful of the company's ability to put the new funds to work profitably in the near future.

Under the assumption that market value exactly reflects the new funds brought in, the total market value of the common stock after the new issue will be $110 million. Dividing this new value by the new total number of shares outstanding, 1.125 million, we obtain a new market value of $97.78 a share. We see, then, that after the financing has been completed, the price of the common stock will have fallen from $100 to $97.78.

Since the rights give the stockholders the privilege of buying for only $80 a share of stock that will end up being worth $97.78, thus saving $17.78, is $17.78 the value of each right? The answer is *no*, because eight rights are required to buy one new share; we must divide $17.78 by 8 to get the value of each right. In the example, each right is worth $2.22.

Ex Rights

The Southeast Company's rights have a very definite value, and this value accrues to the holders of the common stock. What will be the price of the stock if it is traded during the offering period? This depends on who will receive the rights, the old owners or the new. The standard procedure calls for the company to set a "holder-of-record date," then for the stock to go *ex rights* four trading days prior to the holder-of-record date. If the stock is sold prior to the ex-rights date, it is sold *rights on;* that is, the new owner will receive the rights. If the stock is sold on or after the ex-rights date, the old owner will receive them. The exact time at which the stock goes ex rights is at the close of business (say 5 P.M.) on the fifth trading day before the holder-of-record date. The following tabulation indicates what is involved:

		Stock Price
Rights on	Nov. 9	$100.00
	Nov. 10	100.00
Ex-rights date:	Nov. 11	97.78
	Nov. 12	97.78
	Nov. 13	97.78
	Nov. 14	97.78
Holder-of-record date:	Nov. 15	97.78

On October 15, Southeast Company announced the terms of the new financing, stating that rights would be mailed out on December 1 to stockholders of record as of the close of business on November 15. Anyone buying the old stock on or before November 10 will receive the rights; anyone buying the stock on or after November 11 will *not* receive the rights. Thus, November 11 is the *ex-rights date;* before November 11 the stock sells *rights on.* In the case of Southeast Company, the *rights-on price* is $100, while the *ex-rights price* is $97.78.

Formula Value of a Right

Rights On

Equations have been developed for determining the value of rights without going through all the procedures described above. While the stock is still selling rights on, the value at which the rights will sell when they are issued can be found by use of the following formula:

$$\frac{\text{Value of}}{\text{one right}} = \frac{\text{Market value of stock, rights on } - \text{ Subscription price}}{\text{Number of rights required to purchase one share } + 1}.$$

$$R = \frac{M_0 - S}{N + 1}. \tag{14B-1}$$

Here

M_0 = rights-on price of the stock.
  S = subscription price.
  N = number of rights required to purchase a new share of stock.
  R = value of one right.

Substituting the appropriate values for the Southeast Company, we obtain

$$R = \frac{\$100 - \$80}{8 + 1} = \frac{\$20}{9} = \$2.22.$$

This agrees with the value of the rights we found by the long procedure.

Ex Rights

Suppose you are a stockholder in the Southeast Company. When you return to the United States from a trip to Europe, you read about the rights offering in the newspaper. The stock is now selling ex rights for $97.78 a share. How can you calculate the theoretical value of a right? Simply by using the following formula, which follows the logic described in preceding sections:

$$\frac{\text{Value of}}{\text{one right}} = \frac{\text{Market value of stock, ex rights } - \text{ Subscription price}}{\text{Number of rights required to purchase one share}}.$$

$$R = \frac{M_e - S}{N}. \tag{14B-2}$$

$$R = \frac{\$97.78 - \$80}{8} = \frac{\$17.78}{8} = \$2.22.$$

Here, M_e is the ex-rights price of the stock.[1]

---

[1] We developed Equation 14B-2 directly from the verbal explanation given in the section, "Value of a Right." Equation 14B-1 can then be derived from Equation 14B-2 as follows:

  1. Note that

$$M_e = M_0 - R. \tag{14B-3}$$

  2. Substitute Equation 14B-3 into Equation 14B-2, obtaining

$$R = \frac{M_0 - R - S}{N}. \tag{14B-4}$$

(continued)

Stockholders have the choice of exercising their rights or selling them. Those who have sufficient funds and want to buy more shares of the company's stock will exercise their rights. Others can sell theirs. In either case, provided the formula value of the right holds true, the stockholder will neither benefit nor lose by the rights offering. This statement can be illustrated by the position of an individual stockholder in the Southeast Company.

Effects on Position of Stockholders

Assume the stockholder had eight shares of stock before the rights offering. The eight shares each had a market value of $100 a share, so the stockholder had a total market value of $800 in the company's stock. If the rights are exercised, one additional share can be purchased at $80 a share, a new investment of $80. The total investment is now $880, and the investor owns nine shares of the company's stock, which, after the rights offering, has a value of $97.78 a share. The value of the stock is $880, exactly what is invested in it.

Alternatively, if the eight rights are sold at their value of $2.22 a right, the investor will receive $17.78, ending up with the original eight shares of stock plus $17.78 in cash. The original eight shares of stock now have a market price of $97.78 a share. This new $782.24 market value of the stock, plus the $17.78 in cash, is the same as the original $800 market value of the stock. From a purely mechanical or arithmetical standpoint, the stockholders neither benefit nor lose from the sale of additional shares of stock through rights. Of course, if they forget either to exercise or to sell the rights, or if brokerage costs of selling their rights are excessive, then stockholders can suffer losses. However, in general, the issuing firm makes special efforts to minimize brokerage costs, and adequate time is given to enable the stockholders to take some action, so their losses are minimal.

Notice that after a rights offering, the price of the company's stock will be lower than it was prior to the offering. Stockholders have not

---

3. Simplify Equation 14B-4 as follows, ending with Equation 14B-1.

$$R = \frac{M_0 - S}{N} - \frac{R}{N}$$

$$R + \frac{R}{N} = \frac{M_0 - S}{N}$$

$$R\left(\frac{N + 1}{N}\right) = \frac{M_0 - S}{N}$$

$$R = \frac{M_0 - S}{N} \cdot \frac{N}{N + 1}$$

$$R = \frac{M_0 - S}{N + 1}. \tag{14B-1}$$

This completes the derivation.

suffered a loss, however, because they receive the value of the rights. Thus, the stock price decline is similar in nature to a *stock split*, a process described in some detail in Chapter 18. The larger the underpricing in the rights offering, the greater the stock split effect—that is, the lower the final stock price. Thus, if a company wants to lower its price by a substantial amount, it will set the subscription price well below the current market price. If it does not want to lower the price very much, it will set the subscription price just enough below the current price to ensure that the market price will remain above the subscription price during the offering period and thus cause the new shares to be purchased and the new funds to come into the corporation.

Problems

14B-1 The common stock of Irving Development Company is selling for $55 in the market. The stockholders are offered one new share at a subscription price of $25 for every five shares held. What is the value of each right?

14B-2 American Appliance Company's common stock is priced at $72 a share in the market. Notice is given that stockholders may purchase one new share at a price of $40 for every seven shares held. You hold 120 shares at the time of notice.
a. At approximately what price will each right sell in the market?
b. Why will this be the approximate price?
c. What effect will the issuance of rights have on the original market price? Why?

14B-3 Jane Thompson has 300 shares of Piper Industries. The market price per share is $75. The company now offers stockholders one new share to be purchased at $60 for every four shares held.
a. Determine the value of each right.
b. Assume that Jane (1) uses 80 rights and sells the other 220, or (2) sells 300 rights at the market price you have calculated. Prepare a statement showing the changes in her position in each case.

The Cost of Capital 15

The cost of capital is critically important in finance for three main reasons. First, proper capital budgeting decisions require an estimate of the cost of capital. Second, many other types of decisions, including those related to leasing, to bond refunding, and to working capital policy, require estimates of the cost of capital. Finally, maximizing the value of a firm requires that the costs of all inputs, including capital, be minimized, and to minimize the cost of capital we must be able to calculate it.[1]

Our first topic in this chapter is the logic of the weighted average cost of capital. Next, we consider the costs of the major components of the capital structure. Then, we will see how the individual component costs are brought together to form a weighted average cost of capital. Finally, we will examine the relationship between capital budgeting and the cost of capital.

The Logic of the Weighted Average Cost of Capital

Suppose a particular firm's cost of debt is estimated to be 8 percent, its cost of equity is estimated to be 12 percent, and the decision has been made to finance next year's projects by selling debt. The argument is sometimes made that the cost of capital for these projects is 8 percent, because debt will be used to finance them. However, this position is incorrect. To finance a particular set of projects with debt implies that the firm is also using up some of its potential for obtaining new low-cost debt in the future. As expansion occurs in subsequent years, at some point the firm will find it necessary to use additional equity financing to prevent the debt ratio from becoming too large.

To illustrate, suppose the firm borrows heavily at 8 percent during 1981, using up its debt capacity in the process, to finance projects yielding 9 percent. In 1982 it has projects available that yield 11 percent, well above the return on 1981 projects, but it cannot accept these new projects because they would have to be financed with 12 percent equity money.

---

[1] The cost of capital is also vitally important in regulated industries, including electric, gas, telephone, railroad, and airline companies. In essence, regulatory commissions first measure a utility's cost of capital, then set prices so that the company will just earn this rate of return. If the estimate is too low, then the company will not be able to attract sufficient capital to meet long-run demands for service, and the public will suffer. If the estimate of capital costs is too high, customers will pay too much for service.

To avoid this problem, the firm should be viewed as an ongoing concern, and the cost of capital used in capital budgeting should be calculated as a weighted average, or composite, of the various types of funds it uses.

Basic Definitions

Capital components are the items on the right-hand side of the balance sheet: various types of debt, preferred stock, and common equity. Any net increase in assets must be financed by an increase in one or more capital components.

Capital is a necessary factor of production, and like any other factor, it has a cost. The cost of each component is defined as the *component cost* of that particular type of capital. For example, if the firm can borrow money at 8 percent, the component cost of debt is defined as 8 percent. Throughout most of this chapter, we concentrate on debt, preferred stock, retained earnings, and new issues of common stock. These are the major capital structure components, and their component costs are identified by the following symbols:

k_d = interest rate on the firm's new debt = component cost of debt, before tax.

$k_d(1 - t)$ = component cost of debt, after tax, where t is the marginal tax rate. $k_d(1 - t)$ is the debt cost used to calculate the weighted average cost of capital.

k_p = component cost of preferred stock.

k_s = component cost of retained earnings (or internal equity). This k_s is identical to the k_s developed in Chapter 5 and defined there as the required rate of return on common stock.

k_e = component cost of external capital obtained by issuing new common stock. As we shall see, it is necessary to distinguish between equity raised by retaining earnings versus that raised by selling new stock. This is why we distinguish between k_s and k_e.

k_a = an average, or composite, cost of capital. If a firm raises $1 of new capital to finance asset expansion, and if it is to keep its capital structure in balance (that is, if it is to keep the same percentage of debt, preferred stock, and common equity), then it will raise part of the dollar as debt, part as preferred stock, and part as common equity (with equity coming either as retained earnings or from the sale of new common stock).[2]

---

[2] Firms try to keep their debt, preferred, and common equity in balance, but they do not try to maintain any proportional relationship between the common stock and retained earnings accounts as shown on the balance sheet. Common equity is common equity, whether it is represented by common stock or by retained earnings.

k_a also reflects the riskiness of the firm's various assets as discussed in Chapter 12. If a firm uses risk-adjusted discount rates for different capital projects, the average of these rates, weighted by the sizes of the various investments, should equal k_a.

These definitions and concepts are explained in detail in the remainder of this chapter.

Cost of Debt

The component cost of debt used to calculate the weighted average cost of capital is the interest rate on debt, k_d, multiplied by $(1 - t)$, where t is the firm's tax rate:[3]

$$\text{Component cost of debt} = k_d(1 - t). \qquad (15\text{-}1)$$

For example, if a firm can borrow at an interest rate of 10 percent, and if it has a tax rate of 40 percent, then its after-tax cost of debt is 6 percent:

$$k_d(1 - t) = 10\%(0.6) = 6.0\%.$$

The reason for making the tax adjustment is as follows. The value of the firm's stock, which we want to maximize, depends on *after-tax* income. Interest is a deductible expense. The effect of this is that the federal government pays part of the interest charges. Therefore, to put the costs of debt and equity on a comparable basis, we adjust the interest rate downward to take account of the preferential tax treatment of debt.

Note that the cost of debt is the interest rate on *new* debt, not the interest rate on any old, previously outstanding debt. In other words, we are interested in the cost of new debt, or the *marginal* cost of debt. Our primary concern with the cost of capital is to use it in a decision-making process—the decision whether to obtain capital to make new investments. Whether the firm borrowed at high or low rates in the past is irrelevant for this purpose.[4]

Cost of Preferred Stock

The component cost of preferred stock used to calculate the weighted cost of capital (k_p) is the preferred dividend (D_p) divided by the net issuing price (P_n), or the price the firm receives after deducting flotation costs:

$$\begin{array}{c}\text{Component cost of} \\ \text{preferred stock}\end{array} = k_p = \frac{D_p}{P_n}. \qquad (15\text{-}2)$$

For example, suppose a firm has preferred stock that pays a $12 dividend per share and sells for $100 per share in the market. If it issues new shares of preferred, it will incur an underwriting (or flotation) cost of 2.5

---

[3] Note that the cost of debt is considered in isolation. The impact of debt on the cost of equity, as well as on future increments of debt, is treated when the weighted cost of a combination of debt and equity is derived. Also, flotation costs, or the costs of selling the debt, are ignored. Flotation costs for debt issues are generally quite low; in fact, most debt is placed directly with banks, insurance companies, pension funds, and the like, and involves no flotation costs.

[4] It should also be noted that the tax rate is zero for a firm with losses. Therefore, for a company that does not pay taxes, the cost of debt is not reduced; that is, in Equation 15-1 the tax rate equals zero, so the after-tax cost of debt is equal to the interest rate.

percent, or $2.50 per share, so it will net $97.50 per share. Therefore, the cost of preferred stock would be 12.31 percent:

$$k_p = \$12.00/\$97.50 = 12.31\%.$$

Note that no tax adjustments are made when calculating k_p because, unlike interest expense on debt, dividend payments on preferred stock are *not* tax deductible.

Cost of Retained Earnings, k_s

The costs of debt and preferred stock are based on the return investors require on these securities. *The cost of equity obtained by retaining earnings can be defined similarly; it is k_s, the rate of return stockholders require on the firm's common stock.*[5]

The required rate of return is equal to the riskless rate plus a risk premium: $k_s = R_F + \rho$. For stocks in equilibrium (which is the typical situation), the required rate of return is also equal to the expected rate of return, $\hat{k}_s$. In Chapters 4 and 5 we saw that the expected rate of return on a share of common stock depends, ultimately, on the dividends paid on the stock:

$$P_0 = \frac{D_1}{(1 + \hat{k}_s)} + \frac{D_2}{(1 + \hat{k}_s)^2} + \cdots. \tag{15-3}$$

Here P_0 is the current price of the stock; D_t is the dividend expected to be paid at the end of Year t; and $\hat{k}_s$ is the expected rate of return. If dividends are expected to grow at a constant rate, then, as we saw in Chapter 4, Equation 15-3 reduces to the following expression:

$$P_0 = \frac{D_1}{\hat{k}_s - g}. \tag{15-4}$$

We can solve for $\hat{k}_s$ to obtain the expected rate of return on common equity, which in equilibrium is also equal to the required rate of return:[6]

$$\hat{k}_s = \frac{D_1}{P_0} + \text{Expected g}. \tag{15-5}$$

---

[5] The term *retained earnings* can be interpreted to mean the balance sheet item "retained earnings," consisting of all the earnings retained in the business throughout its history, or it can mean the income statement item "additions to retained earnings." The income statement definition is used in the present chapter: *"Retained earnings" for our purpose here refers to that part of current earnings which is not paid out in dividends but, rather, is retained and reinvested in the business.*

[6] Note, however, that if a firm's growth rate is *not* expected to remain constant, then Equations 15-4 and 15-5 will not hold. In this case, it will be necessary to solve for k_s in the nonconstant growth formula developed in Chapter 4. Note also that dividends are actually paid quarterly, and D_1 is generally taken to be the dividends expected to be paid during the next four quarters. The model could be worked out on a quarterly basis, but in view of our uncertainty about the inputs, especially the growth rate, this refinement is not worth the effort.

Thus, investors expect to receive a dividend yield, D_1/P_0, plus a capital gain, g, for a total expected return of $\hat{k}_s$.

To illustrate, suppose a firm's stock sells for $21.73; its next expected dividend is $1.43; and its expected growth rate is 6.6 percent. The firm's expected and required rate of return, hence its cost of retained earnings, is 13.2 percent:

$$k_s = \hat{k}_s = \frac{\$1.43}{\$21.73} + 6.6\% = 6.6\% + 6.6\% = 13.2\%.$$

This 13.2 percent is the minimum rate of return that management must expect to earn to justify retaining earnings and plowing them back into the business rather than paying them out to stockholders as dividends. Henceforth in this chapter we assume that equilibrium exists and use the terms k_s and $\hat{k}_s$ interchangeably.

The logic behind assigning a cost of capital to retained earnings involves the *opportunity cost principle*. The firm's after-tax earnings literally belong to the stockholders. Bondholders are compensated by interest payments, while earnings belong to the common stockholders and serve to "pay the rent" on stockholders' capital. Management may either pay out earnings in the form of dividends or retain earnings and reinvest them in the business. *If management decides to retain earnings, there is an opportunity cost involved—stockholders could have received the earnings as dividends and invested these funds in other stocks, in bonds, in real estate, or in anything else. Thus, the firm must earn on the retained earnings at least as much as stockholders themselves could earn in alternative investments of comparable risk.*

What rate of return could stockholders expect to earn on equivalent risk investments? The answer is k_s. *Therefore, if the firm cannot invest retained earnings and earn at least k_s, then it should pay these funds to its stockholders and let them invest directly in other assets that do provide this return.*[7]

Cost of Newly Issued Common Stock, or External Equity, k_e

The cost of new common stock, or external equity capital, k_e, is higher than the cost of retained earnings, k_s, because of flotation costs involved in selling new common stock. What rate of return must be earned on funds raised by selling stock in order to make issuing new stock worthwhile? To put it another way, what is the cost of new common stock?

---

[7] One complexity in estimating the cost of retained earnings deals with the fact that dividends and capital gains are taxed differently. Retaining earnings rather than paying them out as dividends can convert ordinary income to capital gains. This point is discussed in Appendix 15A and also in chapters 16, 17, and 18.

For a firm with a constant growth rate, the answer is found by applying the following formula:

$$k_e = \frac{D_1}{P_0(1 - F)} + g. \qquad (15\text{-}6)$$

Here F is the percentage flotation cost incurred in selling the issue, so $P_0(1 - F)$ is the net price per share received by the company when it sells a new stock issue.[8]

Assuming that our illustrative firm's flotation cost is 10 percent, its cost of new outside equity is computed as follows:

$$k_e = \frac{\$1.43}{\$21.73 \, (1 - 0.10)} + 6.6\% = \frac{\$1.43}{\$19.56} + 6.6\%$$
$$= 7.3\% + 6.6\% = 13.9\%.$$

Investors require a return of $k_s = 13.2\%$ on the stock. However, because of flotation costs, the company must earn *more* than 13.2 percent on funds obtained by selling stock in order to provide this 13.2 percent. Specifically, if the firm earns 13.9 percent on funds obtained from new common stock issues, then earnings per share will not fall below previously expected earnings; its expected dividend can be maintained; and as a result of all this, the price per share will not decline. If the firm earns less than 13.9 percent, then earnings, dividends, and growth will fall below expectations, causing the price of the stock to decline. If it earns more, the price of the stock will rise.[9]

---

[8] Equation 15-6 is derived as follows:

Step 1. The old stockholders expect the firm to pay a stream of dividends, D_t. This dividend stream will be derived from existing assets. New investors will likewise expect to receive the same stream of dividends, D_t. For new investors to obtain this stream *without impairing the D_t stream of the old investors*, the new funds obtained from the sale of stock must be invested at a return high enough to provide a dividend stream whose present value is equal to the price the firm receives:

$$P_n = \sum_{t=1}^{\infty} \frac{D_t}{(1 + k_e)^t}. \qquad (15\text{-}7)$$

Here P_n is the net price to the firm, and $P_n = P_0(1 - F)$; D_t is the dividend stream to new stockholders; and k_e is the cost of new outside equity.

Step 2. When growth is a constant, Equation 15-7 reduces to

$$P_n = P_0(1 - F) = \frac{D_1}{k_e - g}. \qquad (15\text{-}7a)$$

Step 3. Equation 15-7a may be solved for k_e:

$$k_e = \frac{D_1}{P_0(1 - F)} + g. \qquad (15\text{-}6)$$

[9] On occasion, it may be useful to use another equation to calculate the cost of external equity:

$$k_e = \frac{\text{Dividend yield}}{(1 - F)} + g = \frac{D_1/P_0}{(1 - F)} + g. \qquad (15\text{-}6a)$$

Equation 15-6a is derived algebraically from 15-6, and it is useful when information on dividend yields, but not on dollar dividends and stock prices, is available.

It is obvious by now that the basic rate of return investors require on a firm's common equity, k_s, is a most important quantity. This required rate of return is the cost of retained earnings, and it forms the basis for the cost of capital obtained from new stock issues. How is this all-important quantity estimated? There are several methods, including (1) the *CAPM* approach, (2) the *bond yield plus risk premium* approach, and (3) the *dividend yield plus growth rate*, or *DCF*, approach.

Finding the Basic Required Rate of Return on Common Equity

The Capital Asset Pricing Model (CAPM) as developed in Chapter 5 can be used to help estimate k_s. To use the CAPM, we proceed as follows:

The CAPM Approach

Step 1. Estimate the riskless rate, R_F, generally taken to be either the U.S. Treasury bond rate or the thirty day Treasury bill rate.

Step 2. Estimate the stock's beta coefficient, b, and use this as an index of the stock's risk.

Step 3. Estimate the rate of return on "the market," or on an "average" stock. Designate this return k_M.

Step 4. Estimate the required rate of return on the firm's stock as follows:

$$k_s = R_F + b(k_M - R_F). \qquad (15\text{-}8)$$

The value $(k_M - R_F)$ is the risk premium on the average stock, while b is an index of the particular stock's own risk.

To illustrate the CAPM approach, assume that $R_F = 6\%$, $k_M = 10\%$, and $b = 0.7$ for a given stock. The stock's k_s is calculated as follows:

$$k_s = 6 + 0.7(10 - 6) = 6 + 2.8 = 8.8\%.$$

Had b been 1.8, indicating that the stock was riskier than average, k_s would have been

$$k_s = 6 + 1.8(4) = 6 + 7.2 = 13.2\%.$$

It should be noted that while the CAPM approach appears to yield accurate, precise estimates of k_s, we saw in Chapter 5 that there are several problems with it. There is uncertainty over whether to use long-term or short-term Treasury bonds for R_F; it is hard to estimate the beta that investors expect the company to have in the future; and it is hard to estimate the market risk premium. This latter problem is especially vexing in the 1980s, because the riskiness of stocks versus bonds has been changing, making the market risk premium unstable. This point was discussed in Appendix 5B.

Although it is essentially an *ad hoc*, subjective procedure, analysts often estimate a firm's cost of common equity by adding a risk premium of about 4 percentage points to the interest rate on the firm's long-term

Bond Yield plus Risk Premium Approach

debt. It is logical to think that firms with risky, low-rated, and consequently high-interest rate debt will also have risky, higher-cost equity, and the procedure of basing the cost of equity on readily observable debt cost utilizes this precept. For example, if an Aaa-rated firm's bonds yield 9 percent, then its cost of equity might be estimated as follows:

$$k_s = \text{Bond rate} + \text{Risk premium} = 9\% + 4\% = 13\%.$$

A Baa firm's debt might carry a yield of 11 percent, making its estimated cost of equity 15 percent:

$$k_s = 11\% + 4\% = 15\%.$$

This risk premium is a judgmental estimate, so the estimated value of k_s is also judgmental. Moreover, while a number of studies conducted in the past have indicated that the 4 percentage point premium is reasonably accurate for most companies, the increasingly volatile interest rates and bond prices experienced in the late 1970s and early 1980s seem to have increased the risk of bonds in relation to that of stock, thus compressing, or reducing, the risk premium. In 1980 and 1981, the premium of a company's stock over its own bonds fluctuated in the range of 2 to 4 percentage points.

Dividend Yield plus Growth Rate (or DCF) Approach

We know that stocks are typically in equilibrium, with the expected rate of return equal to the required rate. If the firm is expected to grow at a constant rate, then we can estimate k_s by the discounted cash flow (DCF) formula as follows:

$$k_s = \frac{D_1}{P_0} + \text{Expected dividend growth rate.}$$

If past growth rates in earnings and dividends have been relatively stable, and if investors appear to be projecting a continuation of past trends, then g may be based on the firm's historic growth rate. *However, if the company's growth has been abnormally high or low, either because of its own unique situation or because of general economic conditions, then investors will not project the past growth rate into the future.* In this case, g must be estimated in some other manner. Security analysts regularly make earnings and dividends growth forecasts, looking at such factors as projected sales, profit margins, and competitive factors. Someone making a cost of capital estimate can obtain such analysts' forecasts and use them as a proxy for the growth expectations of investors in general, then combine g with the current dividend yield, and estimate k_s as follows:

$$k_s = \frac{D_1}{P_0} + \text{Growth rate as projected by security analysts.}$$

Again, note that this estimate of k_s is based upon the assumption that g is expected to remain constant in the future. If this assumption is not correct, then it will be necessary to solve for k_s in the nonconstant growth model developed in Chapter 4.[10]

In practical work, it is best to use all three methods—CAPM, bond rate plus risk premium, and DCF—and then apply judgment when the methods produce different results. People experienced in estimating equity capital costs recognize that both careful analysis and some very fine judgments are required. *It would be nice to pretend that these judgments are unnecessary and to specify an easy, precise way of determining the exact cost of equity capital. Unfortunately, this is not possible. Finance is in large part a matter of judgment, and we simply must face this fact.*

As we shall see in Chapter 16, each firm has an optimum capital structure, which is that mix of debt, preferred, and common equity which causes its stock price to be maximized. Therefore, rational, value-maximizing firms establish *target capital structures* and raise new capital in a manner that will keep the actual capital structure on target over time. In the remainder of this chapter we will assume that the firm has identified its optimal capital structure, uses this optimum as the target, and finances so as to remain constantly on target. How the target is established will be examined in Chapters 16 and 17.

Combining Debt, Preferred, and Common Equity: Weighted Average, or Composite, Cost of Capital, k_a

The target proportions of debt, preferred, and common equity, along with the component costs of capital, are used to calculate the firm's overall or weighted average cost of capital, k_a. To illustrate, suppose Firm M has a target capital structure calling for 30 percent debt, 10 percent preferred stock, and 60 percent common equity. Its cost of debt, k_d, is 10.0 percent; its cost of preferred stock, k_p, is 12.0 percent; its cost of common equity from retained earnings, k_s, is 15.0 percent; and its marginal tax rate is 40 percent.

Now suppose the firm needs to raise $100. In order to keep its capital

---

[10] When the DCF method is used, we are implicitly assuming that the stock's price is in equilibrium, with $\hat{k}_s = D_1/P_0 + g = R_F + \text{Risk premium} = k_s$. Thus, the DCF and risk premium methods will, if all inputs are estimated correctly, produce identical cost of capital estimates. Also, as indicated above, growth rates may be estimated (1) by projecting past trends if there is reason to think these trends will continue or (2) by asking security analysts what growth rates they are projecting (or, alternatively, by looking up projected growth rates in such publications as *Value Line*, a financial service subscribed to by many investors). A third method involves projecting the firm's dividend payout ratio and the complement of this ratio, the *retention rate*, and then multiplying the retention rate by the company's projected rate of return on equity (ROE):

$$\text{Growth rate} = (\text{Retention rate})(\text{ROE}) = (1.0 - \text{Payout rate})(\text{ROE}).$$

If the retention rate is zero, meaning that all earnings are paid out as dividends, the growth rate will also be zero, while if the retention rate is 1.0, meaning the payout ratio is zero, the growth rate will be equal to the return on equity. Using this procedure assumes (1) that the future retention rate and ROE are expected to be stable, and (2) that competition is driving the NPV of new capital budgeting projects to zero. (If NPV > 0, a firm could pay out all earnings as dividends, finance new projects by selling common stock plus debt, and cause earnings and dividends to grow.) If these are not valid assumptions, then the procedure will not produce a correct estimate of the true growth rate.

structure on target, it must obtain $30 as debt, $10 as preferred, and $60 as common equity. (Common equity can come either from retained earnings or from the sale of new stock.) The weighted average cost of the $100, assuming the equity portion is from retained earnings, is calculated as follows:

Component	Weight	Component Cost	Product
Debt	0.30	6.0%[a]	1.8%
Preferred	0.10	12.0	1.2
Common equity	0.60	15.0	9.0
		Weighted average cost = k_a =	12.0%

[a]$k_d (1 - t) = 10\% (0.6) = 6.0\%$.

In equation format, we would have

$$k_a = W_d k_d (1 - t) + W_p k_p + W_s k_s \qquad (15\text{-}9)$$
$$= 0.3 (10\%)(0.6) + 0.1(12\%) + 0.6(15\%) = 12\%.$$

Here W_d, W_p, and W_s are the weights used for debt, preferred, and common equity.

Every dollar of new capital that Firm M obtains consists of 30 cents of debt with an after-tax cost of 6 percent, 10 cents of preferred with a cost of 12 percent, and 60 cents of common equity with a cost of 15 percent. The average cost of each whole dollar is 12.0 percent.

The weights could be based either on the accounting values shown on the firm's balance sheet or on the market values of the different securities. Inflation has caused true values to depart radically from stated accounting values in many instances, and when this is the case, firms should target on true values, which are closer to market values than to balance sheet figures. This point is discussed further in Chapter 16, but in the remainder of Chapter 15 we shall assume that the target capital structure is based on market values of debt, preferred, and common.

The Marginal Cost of Capital

The *marginal cost* of any item is the cost of another unit of that item; for example, the marginal cost of labor is defined as the cost of adding one additional worker. The marginal cost of labor might be $25 per person if ten workers are added, but $35 per person if the firm tries to hire 100 new workers, because it would be harder to find that many people willing and able to do the work. The same concept applies to capital. As the firm tries to attract more new dollars, the cost of each dollar will, at some point, rise. *Thus, the marginal cost of capital is defined as the cost of obtaining another dollar of new capital, and the marginal cost rises as more and more capital is raised.*

We can use Firm M to illustrate the marginal cost of capital concept. The company's market value capital structure and other data are given below:[11]

Debt	$ 3,000,000	30%
Preferred	1,000,000	10
Common equity (300,000 shares × $20 per share)	6,000,000	60
Total value	$10,000,000	100%

$P_0 = \$20$.

$D_0 = \$1.495 =$ dividends per share in the *last* period. D_0 has already been paid, so someone purchasing this stock today would *not* receive D_0. Rather, he or she would receive D_1, the *next* dividend.

---

[11] Firm M has only a negligible amount of payables and accruals, so these items were ignored. However, suppose the company had had $2,000,000 of payables/accruals in addition to $3,000,000 of interest-bearing debt. Payables/accruals could be handled in one of two ways:

1. Simply ignore these items on the grounds that, in the capital budgeting process, these spontaneously generated funds are netted out against the required investment outlay, then ignored in the cost of capital calculation. To illustrate, consider a retail firm thinking of opening a new store. According to customary practices, the firm should (a) estimate the required outlay, (b) estimate the net receipts (additions to profits) from the new store, (c) discount the estimated receipts at the cost of capital, and (d) accept the decision to open the new store only if the net present value of the expected revenue stream exceeds the investment outlay. The estimated accruals, trade payables, and other forms of credit that do not bear interest are deducted from the investment to determine the required outlay before making the calculation. This is exactly the procedure used by Carter Chemical and illustrated in Table 11-1, and it is what most companies actually do.

   For Firm M, we would have the following situation:

	Complete Capital Structure (1)	Relevant Capital Structure (2)	Percentage of Relevant Capital Structure (3)
Payables/accruals	$ 2,000,000	—	—
Debt (interest-bearing)	3,000,000	$ 3,000,000	30%
Preferred	1,000,000	1,000,000	10
Equity	6,000,000	6,000,000	60
Total market value	$12,000,000	$10,000,000	100%

The values in the third column would be used as the weights to determine the weighted average cost of capital. Payables/accruals are simply ignored.

2. Alternatively, we could bring payables/accruals into the calculation directly. Accruals virtually always have a zero cost, as do payables for firms that take all discounts offered. If a firm has discounts available but does not take them, then it would be necessary to divide payables into "free" and "costly" components, and to determine an interest cost on the costly trade credit.

g = 7 percent, and it is expected to remain constant.

$$k_s = \frac{D_1}{P_0} + g = \frac{D_0(1 + g)}{P_0} + g = \frac{\$1.495(1.07)}{\$20.00} + 0.07$$

$$= \frac{\$1.60}{\$20.00} + 0.07 = 0.08 + 0.07 = 0.15 = 15\%.$$

$k_d = 10$ percent.
$k_p = 12$ percent.
t = 40 percent.

Based on these data, the weighted average cost of capital, k_a, is 12 percent:

$$k_a = \left(\begin{array}{c}\text{Fraction}\\\text{of debt in}\\\text{capital}\\\text{structure}\end{array}\right) \left(\begin{array}{c}\text{Interest}\\\text{rate}\end{array}\right) (1 - \text{Tax rate})$$

$$+ \left(\begin{array}{c}\text{Fraction}\\\text{of preferred}\\\text{in capital}\\\text{structure}\end{array}\right) \left(\begin{array}{c}\text{Cost of}\\\text{preferred}\end{array}\right) + \left(\begin{array}{c}\text{Fraction of}\\\text{common equity}\\\text{in capital}\\\text{structure}\end{array}\right) \left(\begin{array}{c}\text{Cost of}\\\text{equity}\end{array}\right)$$

$$= 0.3(10\%)(0.6) + 0.1(12\%) + 0.6(15\%)$$
$$= 1.8\% + 1.2\% + 9.0\% = 12.0\%.$$

Since the firm's optimal capital structure calls for 30 percent debt, 10 percent preferred, and 60 percent equity, each new (or marginal) dollar will be raised as 30 cents of debt, 10 cents of preferred, and 60 cents of common equity. Otherwise, the capital structure would not stay on target. As long as Firm M's debt has an after-tax cost of 6 percent, its preferred has a cost of 12 percent, and its common equity has a cost of 15 percent, then its weighted average cost of capital will be 12 percent. Thus, each new dollar will be raised as 30 cents of debt, 10 cents of preferred, and 60 cents of equity, and each new (or marginal) dollar will have a weighted average cost of 12 percent.

The graph shown in Figure 15-1 is defined as Firm M's *marginal cost of capital schedule*. Here the dots represent dollars raised. Since each dollar of new capital has a cost of 12 percent, the marginal cost of capital (MCC) for Firm M is constant at 12 percent under the assumptions we have used thus far.[12]

Breaks, or Jumps, in the MCC Schedule

Could Firm M raise an unlimited amount of new capital at the 12 percent cost? The answer is no. As companies raise larger and larger sums during

[12] Firm M's MCC schedule in Figure 15-1 would be different (higher) if the company used any capital structure other than 30 percent debt, 10 percent preferred, and 60 percent equity. This point will be developed in chapter 16, but as a general rule, a different MCC schedule would exist for every possible capital structure, and the optimal structure is the one that produces the lowest MCC schedule.

Figure 15-1
Marginal Cost of Capital
Schedule (MCC) for
Firm M

Weighted Average Cost
of Capital: k_a = MCC(%)

MCC = k_a

a given time period, the costs of both the debt and the equity components begin to rise, and as this occurs, the weighted average cost of new dollars also rises. Thus, just as corporations cannot hire unlimited numbers of workers at a constant wage, neither can they raise unlimited amounts of capital at a constant cost. At some point, the cost of each new dollar will increase above 12 percent.

Where will this point occur for Firm M? As a first step to determining this point, recognize that, although the company has total capital (at market value) of $10 million, all of this capital was raised in the past, and all of it is invested in assets which are used in operations. Now suppose Firm M's capital budget calls for net expenditures of $1 million during 1982. This new (or marginal) capital will presumably be raised so as to maintain the 30/10/60 debt/preferred/common relationship. Therefore, the company will obtain $300,000 of debt, $100,000 of preferred, and $600,000 of common equity. The new equity could come from two sources: *(1) that part of this year's profits which management decides to retain in the business rather than use for dividends (but not from earnings retained in the past) or (2) the sale of new common stock.*

The debt will have an interest rate of 10 percent, or an after-tax cost of 6 percent. The preferred stock will have a cost of 12 percent. The cost of common equity will be k_s if the equity is obtained by retained earnings, but it will be k_e if the company must sell new common stock. Consider first the case where the new equity comes from retained earnings. Firm M's stock now sells for $20 per share; its last dividend (D_0) was $1.495; its expected growth rate is 7 percent; and its next expected dividend is $1.60. Thus, the expected and required rate of return on common equity, k_s, is estimated to be 15 percent:

$$k_s = \frac{D_1}{P_0} + g = \frac{\$1.60}{\$20} + 7\% = 8\% + 7\% = 15\%.$$

If the company expands so rapidly that its retained earnings for the year are not sufficient to meet its needs for new equity, forcing it to sell new common stock, and if the flotation cost of new stock is 10 percent, then its cost of equity will rise to 15.9 percent:

$$k_e = \frac{D_1}{P_0(1 - F)} + g = \frac{\$1.60}{\$20(0.9)} + 7\% = 15.9\%.$$

Firm M's weighted average cost of capital, using first new retained earnings (earnings retained this year, not in the past) and then new common stock, is shown in Table 15-1. We see that the weighted average cost of each dollar, or the marginal cost of capital, is 12 percent so long as retained earnings are used, but the average cost jumps to 12.5 percent as soon as the firm exhausts its retained earnings and is forced to sell new common stock.[13]

How much new capital can Firm M raise before it exhausts its retained earnings and is forced to sell new common stock; that is, where will the breaking point occur? Assume that the company expects to have total earnings of $840,000 for the year, and that it has a policy of paying out half of its earnings as dividends. Thus, the addition to retained earnings will be $420,000 during the year. How much *total financing*, debt and preferred, plus this $420,000 of retained earnings, can be done before the retained earnings are exhausted and the firm is forced to sell new common stock? In effect, we are seeking some amount, X, which is defined as a *breaking point* and which represents the total financing that can be done before Firm M is forced to sell new common stock. We know that

---

[13] In Chapter 7 we examined the amount of external capital a firm would need to acquire the assets necessary to meet different growth rates in sales. At relatively low growth rates, expansion could be financed by spontaneously generated debt and retained earnings, but at higher growth rates, external capital was needed. A similar situation exists here—if an analysis like that in chapter 7 indicated that Firm M would need no external equity, then its marginal cost of capital would be 12 percent. However, if its growth rate were so rapid as to require it to sell new common stock, then its marginal cost of capital would rise to 12.5 percent.

a. MCC when equity is from new retained earnings

Component	Weight	Component Cost	Product
Debt	0.3	6.0%	1.8%
Preferred	0.1	12.0	1.2
Common equity	0.6	15.0	9.0
	1.0	MCC = k_a =	12.0%

b. MCC when equity is from sale of new common stock

Component	Weight	Component Cost	Product
Debt	0.3	6.0%	1.8%
Preferred	0.1	12.0	1.2
Common equity	0.6	15.9	9.5
	1.0	MCC = k_a = 12.5%	

Table 15-1
Firm M's Marginal Cost of Capital Using (a) New Retained Earnings and (b) New Common Stock

60 percent of X will be the new retained earnings, which will amount to $420,000. Therefore

$$0.6X = \text{Retained earnings} = \$420,000.$$

Solving for X, we obtain

$$\text{Breaking point} = X = \frac{\text{Retained earnings}}{0.6} = \frac{\$420,000}{0.6} = \$700,000.$$

Thus, Firm M can raise a total of $700,000, consisting of $420,000 of retained earnings and $700,000 − $420,000 = $280,000 of new debt and preferred stock supported by these new retained earnings, without altering its capital structure:

New debt supported by retained earnings	$210,000	30%
Preferred stock supported by retained earnings	70,000	10
Retained earnings	420,000	60
Total expansion supported by retained earnings (= breaking point for retained earnings)	$700,000	100%

Figure 15-2 graphs Firm M's marginal cost of capital schedule. Each dollar has a weighted average cost of 12 percent until the company has

Figure 15-2
Marginal Cost of Capital
Schedule for Firm M
Using Both Retained
Earnings and New
Common Equity

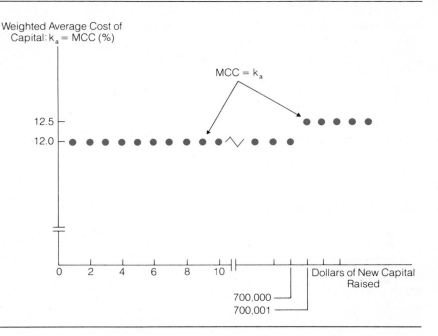

raised a total of $700,000. This $700,000 will consist of $210,000 of new debt with an after-tax cost of 6 percent, $70,000 of preferred stock with a cost of 12 percent, and $420,000 of retained earnings with a cost of 15 percent. However, if Firm M raises $700,001, the last dollar will contain 60 cents of equity *obtained by selling new common equity at a cost of 15.9 percent*, so k_a = MCC rises from 12 percent to 12.5 percent, as calculated in Table 15-1.

Other Breaks in the
MCC Schedule

There is a jump, or break, in Firm M's MCC schedule at $700,000 of new capital. Could there be other breaks in the schedule? Yes, there could be. For example, suppose Firm M can obtain only $300,000 of debt at a 10 percent interest rate, with additional debt costing 12 percent. This would result in a second breaking point in the MCC schedule at the point where the $300,000 of 10 percent debt is exhausted. At what amount of *total financing* would the 10 percent debt be used up? If we let Y represent the total financing at this second breaking point, then

$$0.3Y = \$300,000,$$

and solving for Y, we obtain

$$Y = \frac{10\% \text{ debt}}{0.3} = \frac{\$300,000}{0.3} = \$1,000,000 = \text{Breaking point for debt.}$$

Thus, there will be another break in the MCC schedule after Firm M has raised a total of $1 million. As we saw above, up to $700,000 the MCC is 12 percent, while just beyond $700,000 the MCC rises to 12.5 percent. Now we see that the MCC rises again, at $1,000,001, to 12.9 percent, as a result of the increase in k_d from 10 percent to 12 percent:

Component	Weight		Component Cost		Product
Debt	0.3	×	7.2[a]	=	2.2%
Preferred	0.1	×	12.0	=	1.2
Common	0.6	×	15.9	=	9.5
			k_a = MCC	=	12.9%

[a] 12%(1 − t) = 12%(0.6) = 7.2%, up from 6%.

In other words, the next dollar beyond $1 million will consist of 30 cents of 12 percent debt (7.2 percent after taxes), 10 cents of 12 percent preferred, and 60 cents of new common stock (retained earnings were used up much earlier), and this marginal dollar will have an average cost of 12.9 percent.

The effect of this new MCC increase is shown in Figure 15-3. We now have two breaks, one caused by using up all the retained earnings and the other caused by using up all the 10 percent debt. With the two breaks, we have three different MCCs: MCC_1 = 12% for the first $700,000 of new capital; MCC_2 = 12.5% in the interval between $700,000 and $1 million; and MCC_3 = 12.9% for all new capital beyond $1 million.[14]

There could, of course, be still more breaking points. For example, the interest rate on debt might rise again, from 12 to 14 percent, after the firm had used $400,000 of the 12 percent debt. In this case, the 14 percent debt would be used after $700,000 of lower-cost debt had been used: $300,000 of 10 percent debt plus $400,000 of 12 percent debt. Therefore, a new break would occur at $2,333,333:

$$\text{Break point for 14\% debt} = \frac{\$300,000 + \$400,000}{0.3} = \frac{\$700,000}{0.3} = \$2,333,333.$$

[14] When we use the term *weighted average cost of capital,* we are referring to k_a, which is the cost of one dollar raised partly as debt, partly as preferred, and partly as equity. One could also calculate the average cost of *all* capital the firm raises during a given year. For example, if Firm M raised $2 million, then the first $700,000 would have a cost of 12.0 percent, the next $300,000 would have a cost of 12.5 percent, and the last $1 million would have a cost of 12.9 percent. The entire $2 million would have an average cost of

$$(0.7/2)(12.0\%) + (0.3/2)(12.5\%) + (1/2)(12.9\%) = 12.53\%.$$

This particular cost of capital should not be used for any financial decisions; *it has no relevance in finance.*

Figure 15-3
Marginal Cost of Capital
Schedule for Firm M
Using Retained Earnings,
New Common Stock,
and Higher-Cost Debt

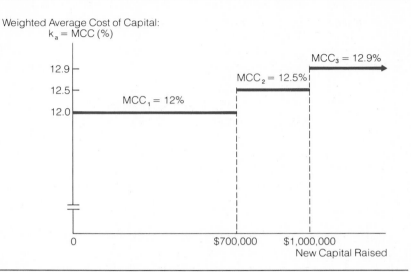

Other break points would occur if the interest rate continued to rise, if the cost of preferred stock rose, or if flotation costs increased above 10 percent as larger amounts of common stock were sold and thus pushed up the cost of common equity. In general, a break point will occur whenever the cost of one of the capital components rises, and the break point can be determined by this equation:

$$\text{Break point} = \frac{\begin{array}{c}\text{Total amount of lower cost}\\ \text{capital of a given type}\end{array}}{\begin{array}{c}\text{Fraction of this type of capital}\\ \text{in the capital structure}\end{array}}. \qquad (15\text{-}10)$$

The break point for the 14 percent debt above was found by an application of this formula.

We see, then, that numerous break points can occur. At the limit, we can even think of an MCC with so many breaking points that it rises almost continuously beyond some given level of new financing. Such an MCC schedule is shown in Figure 15-4.[15]

---

[15] The first breaking point is not necessarily the point where retained earnings are used up—it is possible that low-cost debt could be exhausted *before* retained earnings have been used up. For example, if Firm M had available only $150,000 of 10 percent debt, then Point Y would have occurred at

$$Y = \frac{\$150,000}{0.3} = \$500,000.$$

This is well before the break for retained earnings, which occurs at $700,000.

Weighted Average Cost of Capital:
k_a = MCC (%)

MCC

0   New Capital Raised

Figure 15-4
Smoothed, or
Continuous, Marginal
Cost of Capital Schedule

The easiest sequence for calculating MCC schedules is as follows:

1. Identify the points where breaks occur. A break will occur any time the cost of one of the capital components rises. (However, it is possible that two capital components could both increase at the same point.) Use Equation 15-10 to determine the exact break points.
2. Determine the cost of capital for each component in the intervals between breaks.
3. Calculate the weighted averages of these costs; the weighted averages are the MCCs in each interval. The MCC is constant within each interval, but it rises at each break point.

Notice that if there are n separate breaks, there will be n + 1 different MCCs. For example, in Figure 15-3 we see two breaks and three different MCCs. See the self-test problem for another illustration.

Before closing this section, we should note again that a different MCC schedule would result if a different capital structure were used. As we will establish in Chapter 16, the optimal capital structure produces the lowest MCC.

Now that we have calculated the MCC schedule, we can use it to determine the discount rate used in the capital budgeting process; *that is, we can use the MCC schedule to find the cost of capital for use in determining projects' net present values (NPVs) as discussed in Chapter 11.*

To understand how the MCC is used in capital budgeting, assume

Combining the MCC and the Investment Opportunity Schedules

that Firm M has three financial executives: a financial vice-president, a treasurer, and a director of capital budgeting. The financial VP asks the treasurer to develop the firm's MCC schedule, and the treasurer produces the schedule shown earlier in Figure 15-3.

Next, the financial VP asks the director of capital budgeting (DCB) to determine the dollar amounts of all projects that are potentially acceptable, using the IRR method (or using the NPV method at a number of different discount rates). The DCB has a listing of all the firm's potential projects, including the cost of each project and its projected annual net cash inflows. This listing is shown in Table 15-2. For example, Project A has a cost of $200,000 and is expected to produce inflows of $55,757 per year for five years, while Project B, which has a cost of $150,000, is expected to produce inflows of $33,917 per year for seven years. For simplicity, we assume now that all projects are independent, that they are equally risky, and that their risk is equal to that of the average existing asset in the firm.

Table 15-2
Potential Capital Budgeting Projects Available to Firm M

Project	Cost	Annual Inflows	Project Life (Years)	IRR, or Discount Rate at Which NPV = 0
A	$200,000	$ 55,757	5	12.2%
B	150,000	33,917	7	13.0
C	250,000	43,344	10	11.5
D	350,000	90,005	6	14.0
E	200,000	41,250	8	12.7
F	250,000	106,781	3	13.5

The DCB would first calculate each project's IRR as shown in the last column of Table 15-2, then plot the data given there as the Investment Opportunity Schedule (IOS) shown in Figure 15-5. The figure also reproduces Firm M's MCC schedule as developed by the treasurer and plotted in Figure 15-3. The IOS schedule shows how much money Firm M could profitably invest at different rates of return. If the cost of capital were *above* 14 percent, none of the available projects would have positive NPVs; hence none of them should be accepted. In this case, Firm M should simply not expand. If the cost of capital were 14 percent, Firm M should take on only Project D, and its capital budget would call for the company to raise and invest $350,000. If the cost of capital were 13.5 percent, the firm should take on Projects D and F, raising and investing a total of $600,000. Successively lower costs of capital call for larger and larger investment outlays.

Just how far down its IOS curve should Firm M go? That is, which of

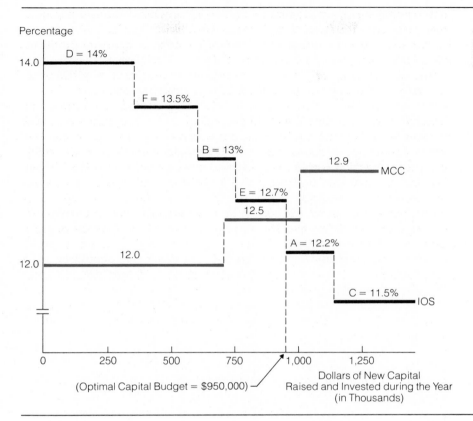

Figure 15-5
Combining Firm M's
MCC and IOS Curves to
Determine Its Optimal
Capital Budget

its available projects should it accept? *The answer is that Firm M should accept the four projects (D, F, B, and E) which have rates of return in excess of the cost of the capital that would be used to finance them.* Projects A and C should be rejected, because they would have to be financed with capital that has a cost of 12.9 percent, and at that cost of capital, A and C (1) have negative NPVs and (2) have IRRs that are below their costs of capital. Therefore, Firm M's capital budget should total $950,000.[16]

---

[16] People sometimes ask this question: "If we took Project A first, it would be acceptable, because its 12.2 percent return would exceed the 12 percent cost of money used to finance it. Why couldn't we do this?" The answer is that we are seeking, in effect, to maximize the *excess of returns over costs*, or the area that is above the MCC but below the IOS. We accomplish this by graphing (and accepting) the most profitable projects first.

Another question that sometimes arises is this: What would happen if the MCC cut through one of the projects? For example, suppose the second breaking point in the MCC schedule had occurred at $900,000 rather than at $1 million, so that the MCC cut through Project E. Should we then accept Project E? If Project E could be accepted in part, then we would take on only part of it. Otherwise, the answer would be determined by (1) finding the average cost of the funds needed to finance Project E

(continued)

The above analysis as summarized in Figure 15-5 reveals a very important point: *The cost of capital used in the capital budgeting process as discussed in Chapter 11 is actually determined at the intersection of the IOS and MCC schedules. If this intersection rate is used, then the firm will make correct accept/reject decisions, and its level of financing and investment will be optimal. If it uses any other rate, its capital budgeting will not be optimal.*

If Firm M had fewer good investment opportunities, then its IOS schedule would be shifted to the left, causing the intersection to occur at a lower level on the MCC curve. Conversely, if the firm had more and better investment opportunities, the IOS would be shifted to the right, and the intersection would have occurred at a higher MCC. Thus, we see that the discount rate used in capital budgeting is influenced by the set of projects that is available.

We have, of course, abstracted from differential project riskiness in this chapter: implicitly, we have assumed that all projects are equally risky. As noted in Chapter 12, the cost of capital used to evaluate riskier projects should be adjusted upward, while a lower rate should be used for projects with below average risk. The MCC as determined in Figure 15-5 should be used to find the NPVs of new projects that are about as risky as the firm's existing assets. This cost of capital should be adjusted up or down to find NPVs for projects with higher or lower risk than the average project.[17]

Some Problem Areas in Cost of Capital

A number of difficult issues relating to the cost of capital either have not been mentioned or else have been glossed over lightly thus far in the chapter. These topics are covered in advanced courses, but they deserve

(some of the money would cost 12.5 percent and some would cost 12.9 percent), and then (2) comparing the average cost of this money to the 12.7 percent return on the project. We should accept Project E if its return exceeds the average cost of the $200,000 needed to finance it. The self-test problem illustrates this point.

[17] One way of handling project risk in Figure 15-5 is as follows:

1. Determine the relative riskiness of each potential capital budgeting project. See Chapter 12.
2. If a project is of average risk, use k_a = MCC to calculate its NPV. If the project is riskier than average, calculate its NPV at a higher risk-adjusted rate, say MCC_R = 1.2(MCC). If the project is less risky than average, use, say, MCC_L = 0.8(MCC). Again, see Chapter 12.
3. Now have the DCB assume some high MCC, say 25 percent, and calculate each project's risk-adjusted NPV. In this case, no project's NPV is positive. The DCB next shifts the assumed MCC to some lower level, say 24 percent, and repeats the process. When the assumed MCC is 14 percent, then Project D has NPV = 0, so it is accepted and plotted on the graph. (This assumes that D is of average risk; had D's risk been less than average, then it would have been acceptable at a higher MCC of 14%/0.8 = 17.5 percent. Had it been of above average risk, D would have been acceptable at a corporate MCC of only 14%/1.2 = 11.7 percent. See the self-test problem.
4. As the assumed MCC is lowered, the different projects become acceptable and are plotted on the graph of Figure 15-5. Hence, we end up with a risk-adjusted IOS schedule. If this adjustment is not done, then it is possible that the IOS schedule will not show the various projects in proper perspective.

some mention now so that the reader may be alerted to potential dangers as well as provided with a preview of some of the matters dealt with in advanced finance courses.

1. The Effects of Personal Income Taxes. Our discussion of the cost of capital dealt with corporate income taxes, but we abstracted from personal income taxes. When we use the equation $k_s = D_1/P_0 + g$, we often assume that investors are indifferent between dividend yield and capital gains. However, dividends are taxed at ordinary tax rates, whereas capital gains are taxed at a lower rate. Hence, investors may favor capital gains (g) more than dividend yield (D_1/P_0). This, in turn, might cause the differential between the cost of retained earnings (k_s) and new common stock (k_e) to be greater than can be accounted for by flotation costs alone. (See Appendix 15A and Chapters 17 and 18.)

2. Depreciation-Generated Funds. The largest single source of capital for many firms is depreciation, yet we did not discuss the cost of funds from this source. In brief, depreciation cash flows can either be reinvested or returned to investors—stockholders *and* creditors. The cost of depreciation-generated funds is approximately equal to the weighted average cost of capital in the interval where capital comes from retained earnings and low-cost debt. (See Appendix 15A).

3. Deferred Taxes. Most companies show, as a liability, an item called "deferred taxes." Deferred taxes arise principally from accelerated tax depreciation and delays in payments of regular taxes. Deferrals can constitute an important source of funds for many companies. Since deferred taxes are, in effect, an interest-free loan from the federal government, they have a zero cost. Many companies include deferred taxes in the weighted average cost of capital calculation but give it a zero cost. If deferred taxes are material for a given company, some care should be exercised in how this issue is handled.

4. Privately Owned Firms. Our whole discussion of the cost of equity was related to publicly owned corporations, and we concentrated on the rate of return required by stockholders at large. There is a serious question as to how one should measure the cost of equity for a firm whose stock is not traded. Tax issues also become especially important in these cases. As a general rule, most authorities feel that the same principles of cost of capital estimation apply to both privately held and publicly owned firms, but the problems of obtaining input data are somewhat different.

5. Small Businesses. Small businesses are generally privately owned, making it difficult to estimate their cost of equity, and they also often obtain debt from government sources (the Small Business Administration). However, the same theoretical principles apply to large and small firms. See Chapter 24.

6. Measurement Problems. One cannot overemphasize the practical difficulties encountered in actually estimating the cost of equity. It is very difficult to obtain good input data for the CAPM, for g in the formula $k_s = D_1/P_0 + g$, and for the risk premium in the formula k_s = bond yield plus risk premium.

7. Costs of Capital for Projects of Different Riskiness. As noted in Chapter 12, a major difficulty arises when one attempts to assign different risk-adjusted discount rates to capital budgeting projects of differing degrees of riskiness.

8. Capital Structure Weights. In this chapter, we simply took as given the target capital structure, and we used this target to obtain the weights used to calculate k_a. As we shall see in Chapter 16, establishing the target capital structure is a major task in itself.

9. Dynamic Considerations. Capital budgeting and cost of capital estimates are a part of the *planning process*—they deal with ex ante, or estimated, data rather than ex post, or historical, data. Hence, we can be wrong about the location of the IOS and the MCC. For example, we can underestimate the MCC, hence accept projects that, with 20-20 foresight, we would have rejected. In a dynamic, changing world this is a real problem. Interest rates and money costs at the time plans are being laid and contracts to build plants are being let could be low, but six or eight months later money costs could have risen substantially. Thus, a project that formerly looked good could now look bad because we improperly estimated our MCC schedule. The example given in the next section illustrates the dynamic nature of the capital budgeting/cost of capital estimation process.

Although the listing of problem areas appears formidable, the state of the art in cost of capital estimation is really not in bad shape. The procedures outlined in this chapter can be used to obtain cost of capital estimates that are sufficiently accurate for practical purposes, and the problems listed here, in a sense, merely indicate the desirability of certain refinements. The refinements are not unimportant, but the problems identified certainly do not invalidate the usefulness of the procedures outlined in the chapter.

Amfac, Inc., is a large New York Stock Exchange company based in Honolulu. It operates six types of businesses (food processing, retailing, shipping, agriculture, hotels, and real estate development). Its sales are about $2 billion, and its net income is about $100 million. The central financial staff determines a corporate cost of capital, which the division managers must use to evaluate capital expenditure proposals.

On February 6, 1981, corporate headquarters notified all division managers that as a result of recent increases in money costs, all capital budgeting "hurdle rates"—the required rates of return on new projects—were being raised by two percentage points. The estimated average corporate cost of capital had risen from under 12 percent to just over 14 percent during the previous two years. Currently, Amfac's before-tax cost of debt is 14.15 percent; its cost of equity (estimated as the U.S. Treasury bond rate of 11.9 percent plus a 6.9 percent risk premium) is 18.8 percent; its tax rate is 46 percent; its capital structure consists of 42 percent debt and 58 percent equity; and, thus, its weighted average cost of capital is $0.42(14.15\%)(0.54) + 0.58(18.8\%) = 14.1\%$.

To account for differential project risk, Amfac adds risk premiums of up to six percentage points to riskier projects. The hurdle rate is set at 14 percent on cost reduction and maintenance projects (investments necessary to maintain its current sales levels), at 17 percent on projects to expand existing businesses, and at 20 percent on investments in new products or services. Amfac considers its six business groups to be equally risky and to have the same optimal capital structures. Therefore, each business group has the same basic cost of capital.

Both interest rates and the cost of equity, hence the average cost of capital, change daily, but Amfac and other firms adjust hurdle rates only periodically. For example, Amfac's February 1981 increase was the first change in two years, even though capital costs had been rising all during 1979 and 1980. It would not be administratively feasible to change hurdle rates on a daily, weekly, or even monthly basis, as this would unduly disrupt the planning process.

On the other hand, if capital costs change but hurdle rates are not adjusted, mistakes will be made. To illustrate, Amfac's controller acknowledges that the company's delay in raising hurdle rates in 1980 resulted in expenditures on several projects which should have been rejected. If capital costs continue to be as volatile in the future as they have been in the recent past, Amfac and other companies will have to make more frequent adjustments, in spite of the administrative problems such adjustments cause.

An Illustration: Amfac, Inc.[18]

[18] This section is based on an article that appeared in the February 23, 1981, issue of *Business Week*.

Summary

This chapter showed how the MCC schedule is developed and then used in the capital budgeting process. We began by discussing the process of estimating the cost of each capital structure component. The *cost of debt* is simply $k_d(1 - t)$. The first increment of *common equity* is raised by *retaining earnings*, whose cost, k_s, may be estimated in one of three ways: (1) by the CAPM equation, $k_s = R_F + b(k_M - R_F)$; (2) by the dividend growth model, $k_s = D_1/P_0 + g$; or (3) by adding a risk premium of about 4 percent to the firm's cost of long-term debt. Once retained earnings have been exhausted, the firm must sell new common stock, or *external equity*, whose cost is $k_e = D_1/[P_0(1 - F)] + g$ in the case of a constant growth stock.

The next task is to combine the component costs to form a *weighted average cost of capital*, k_a. The weights used to develop k_a should be based on the firm's target capital structure. If these weights are used, the stock price will be maximized and the cost of capital will simultaneously be minimized.

Capital typically has a higher cost if the firm expands beyond certain limits. This means that the MCC curve turns up beyond some point. We used the *breaking-point concept* to develop a step-function MCC schedule, which we then combined with the IOS schedule to determine both the optimal capital budget and the cost of capital that should be used in capital budgeting.

The concepts developed here are extended in Chapters 16 and 17, where we consider the effect of the capital structure on the cost of capital, and in Chapter 18, where we consider the optimal allocation of current earnings between dividends and retained earnings.

Questions

15-1 In what sense is the marginal cost of capital an average cost?

15-2 How would each of the following affect a firm's cost of debt, $k_d(1 - t)$; its cost of equity, k_s; and its average cost of capital, k_a? Indicate by a plus $(+)$, a minus $(-)$, or a zero (0) if the factor would raise, lower, or have an indeterminate effect on the items in question. Assume other things are held constant. Be prepared to justify your answer, but recognize that several of the parts probably have no single correct answer; these questions are to stimulate thought and discussion.

	Effect on		
	$k_d(1-t)$	k_s	k_a
a. The corporate tax rate is lowered.	_____	_____	_____
b. The Federal Reserve tightens credit.	_____	_____	_____
c. The firm uses more debt; that is, it increases the debt/assets ratio.	_____	_____	_____
d. The dividend payout ratio is increased.	_____	_____	_____

e. The firm doubles the amount of capital it raises during the year.   _____ _____ _____

f. The firm expands into a risky new area.   _____ _____ _____

g. The firm merges with another firm whose earnings are countercyclical to those of the first firm and to the stock market.   _____ _____ _____

h. The stock market falls drastically, and our firm's stock falls along with the rest.   _____ _____ _____

i. Investors become more risk averse.   _____ _____ _____

j. The firm is an electric utility with a large investment in nuclear plants. Several states propose a ban on nuclear power generation.   _____ _____ _____

15-3 Suppose a firm estimates its MCC and IOS schedules for the coming year and finds that they intersect at the point 10%, $10,000,000. What cost of capital should be used to evaluate average projects, high-risk projects, and low-risk projects?

15-4 The MCC and IOS schedules shown in Figure 15-5 could be thought of as "bands" rather than as lines to show that they are not known with certainty but, rather, are merely estimates of the true MCC and IOS schedules.

a. Do you think that the bands would be wider for the MCC or for the IOS schedule? In answering this question, visualize each point on the MCC and IOS schedules as being the expected value of a probability distribution.

b. For the IOS schedule, would the band, or confidence interval, associated with each project be identical? If not, what would this imply, and how might it affect the firm's capital budgeting analysis?

ST15-1 Laser Communications, Inc. (LCI), has the following capital structure, which it considers to be optimal:

**Self-Test
Problem**

Debt	25%
Preferred stock	15
Common equity	60
	100%

LCI's net income expected this year is $17,142.86; its established dividend payout ratio is 30 percent; its tax rate is 40 percent; and investors expect earnings and dividends to grow at a constant rate of 9 percent in the future. LCI paid a dividend of $3.60 per share last year, and its stock currently sells at a price of $60 per share. Treasury bonds yield 11 percent; an average stock has a 14 percent expected rate of return; and LCI's beta is 1.51.

LCI can obtain new capital as indicated below:

Common: New common stock would have a flotation cost of 10 percent for up to $6,000 of stock, and 20 percent for all common over $6,000.

Preferred: New preferred can be sold to the public at a price of $100 per share, with a dividend of $11. Flotation costs of $5 per share would be incurred for up to $3,750 of preferred, while these costs would rise to $10, or 10 percent, on all preferred over $3,750.

Debt: Up to $2,500 of debt can be sold at an interest rate of 12 percent; debt in the range of $2,501 to $5,000 must carry an interest rate of 14 percent; and all debt over $5,000 will have an interest rate of 16 percent.

LCI has the following investment opportunities:

Project	Cost at t = 0	Annual Net Cash Flow	Project Life	Raw IRR	Risk Adjustment Factor[a]	Risk-Adjusted IRR
A	$ 5,000	$1,095.60	7 years	12.0%	0.8	15.0%
B	5,000	1,577.21	5 years	17.4	1.2	14.5
C	5,000	1,085.09	8 years	14.2	1.0	14.2
D	10,000	1,894.74	10 years	13.7	1.0	13.7
E	10,000	2,713.92	6 years		1.2	

[a] LCI classifies each project as low-risk, average-risk, or high-risk and assigns a factor of 0.8, 1.0, and 1.2, respectively, to projects in the three risk classes. The raw IRR divided by the adjustment factor gives the risk-adjusted IRR for each project. The risk-adjusted IRRs make all projects comparable with respect to risk. Thus, Project A, which is a low-risk project, has a raw IRR of 12 percent and a risk-adjusted IRR of 12%/0.8 = 15%, and it ranks higher on a risk-adjusted basis than Project B, with a raw IRR of 17.4 percent and an adjusted IRR of 14.5 percent.

a. Find the breaking points in the MCC schedule.
b. Determine the component costs of capital for each capital structure component.
c. Calculate the weighted cost of capital (or the MCC) in the interval between each break in the MCC schedule.
d. Calculate the raw IRR and the risk-adjusted IRR for Project E.
e. Construct a graph showing the MCC and IOS schedules.
f. Which projects should LCI accept?

g. Suppose LCI estimated its corporate cost of capital to be 13.53 percent, which is an average of 13.16 percent and 13.9 percent, and then adjusted this rate by multiplying it by 1.2 for high-risk projects and by 0.8 for low-risk projects. Then, if it had potential Projects A, B, C, D, and E, and used the NPV method to evaluate them, which projects would it accept? Consider A to be low-risk, B and E to be high-risk, and C and D to be average-risk projects.

Problems

15-1 Calculate the after-tax cost of debt under each of the following conditions:
   a. Interest rate, 10%; tax rate, 0%.
   b. Interest rate, 10%; tax rate, 40%.
   c. Interest rate, 10%; tax rate, 60%.

15-2 XYZ Company's last dividend per share was $1; that is, $D_0 = \$1$. The stock sells for $20 per share. The expected growth rate is 5 percent. Calculate XYZ's cost of capital from retained earnings.

15-3 The Dorfman Company's EPS in 1981 was $2.00. EPS in 1976 was $1.3612. The company pays out 40 percent of its earnings as dividends, and the stock sells for $21.60.
   a. Calculate the growth rate in earnings. (Hint: This is a *five*-year growth period.)
   b. Calculate the *next* expected dividend per share, D_1. ($D_0 = 0.4(\$2) = \$0.80$.) Assume the past growth rate will continue.
   c. What is the cost of retained earnings, k_s, for the Dorfman Company?

15-4 Suppose the Celec Company has this *book value* balance sheet:

Current assets	$30,000,000	Current liabilities	$10,000,000
Fixed assets	50,000,000	Long-term debt	30,000,000
		Common equity:	
		Common stock	
		(1 million shares)	1,000,000
		Retained earnings	39,000,000
Total assets	$80,000,000	Total claims	$80,000,000

The current liabilities consist entirely of notes payable to banks, and the interest rate on this debt is 10 percent, the same as the rate on new bank loans. The long-term debt consists of 30,000 bonds, each of which has a par value of $1,000, carries a coupon interest rate of 6 percent, and matures in twenty years. The going rate of interest on new long-term debt, k_d, is 10 percent, and this is the present yield-to-maturity on the bonds. The common stock sells at a price of $60 per share. Calculate Celec's market value capital structure.

15-5 The Dorfman Company expects earnings of $10 million next year. Its dividend payout ratio is 40 percent, and its debt/value ratio is 60 percent. Dorfman uses no preferred stock.

a. What amount of retained earnings does Dorfman expect next year?

b. At what amount of financing will there be a breaking point in the MCC schedule?

c. If Dorfman can borrow $4 million at an interest rate of 8 percent, another $4 million at a rate of 9 percent, and additional debt at a rate of 10 percent, at what points will rising debt costs cause breaks in the MCC schedule?

15-6 The Dorfman Company's next expected dividend (D_1) is $0.864, its growth rate is 8 percent, and the stock now sells for $21.60. New stock can be sold at a price of $18.36.

a. What is Dorfman's percentage flotation cost, F?

b. What is Dorfman's cost of new common stock, k_e?

15-7 On January 1, the total market value of the Gould Company was $60 million. During the year, the company plans to raise and invest $30 million. The firm's present capital structure, shown below, is considered to be optimal. Assume that there is no short-term debt.

Debt	$30,000,000
Common equity	30,000,000
	$60,000,000

New bonds will have an 8 percent coupon rate and will be sold at par. Common stock, currently selling at $30 a share, can be sold to net the company $27 a share. Stockholders' required rate of return is estimated to be 12 percent, consisting of a dividend yield of 4 percent and an expected growth rate of 8 percent. (The next expected dividend is $1.20, so $1.20/$30 = 4%.) Retained earnings for the year are estimated to be $3 million (ignore depreciation). The marginal corporate tax rate is 40 percent.

a. Assuming all asset expansion (gross expenditures for fixed assets plus related working capital) is included in the capital budget, what is the dollar amount of the capital budget? (Ignore depreciation.)

b. To maintain the present capital structure, how much of the capital budget must be financed by common equity?

c. How much of the new common equity funds needed must be generated internally? Externally?

d. Calculate the cost of each of the common equity components.

e. At what level of capital expenditures will there be a break in the MCC schedule?

f. Calculate the MCC (1) below and (2) above the break in the schedule.

g. Plot the MCC schedule. Also, draw in an IOS schedule that is consistent with both the MCC schedule and the projected capital budget. Any IOS schedule that is consistent will do.

15-8 The following tabulation gives earnings per share figures for Template Manufacturing during the preceding ten years. The firm's common stock, 140,000 shares outstanding, is now selling for $50 a share, and the expected dividend for the current year (1982) is 50 percent of the 1981 EPS. Investors expect past trends to continue, so g may be based on the earnings growth rate.

Year	EPS
1972	$2.00
1973	2.16
1974	2.33
1975	2.52
1976	2.72
1977	2.94
1978	3.18
1979	3.43
1980	3.70
1981	4.00

The current interest rate on new debt is 8 percent. The firm's marginal tax rate is 40 percent. The firm's capital structure, considered to be optimal, is as follows:

Debt	$ 3,000,000
Common equity	7,000,000
	$10,000,000

a. Calculate the after-tax cost of new debt and of common equity, assuming new equity comes only from retained earnings. Calculate the cost of equity as $k_s = D_1/P_0 + g$.

b. Find the marginal cost of capital, again assuming no new common stock is sold.

c. How much can be spent for capital investments before external equity must be sold? (Assume that retained earnings available for 1982 investment are 50 percent of 1981 earnings. Obtain 1981 earnings by multiplying 1981 EPS by the shares outstanding.)

d. What is the marginal cost of capital (cost of funds raised in excess of the amount calculated in Part c) if new common stock can be sold to the public at $50 a share to net the firm $45 a share? The cost of debt is constant.

15-9 Haslem Enterprises has the following capital structure, which it considers to be optimal under the present and forecasted conditions:

Debt (long-term only)	30%
Common equity	70
Total capital	100%

For the coming year, management expects to realize net earnings of $105,000. The past dividend policy of paying out 50 percent of earnings will continue. Present commitments from its banker will allow Haslem to borrow according to the following schedule:

Loan Amount	Interest Rate
$0 to $42,000	8%
$42,001 and above	12%

The company's tax rate is 40 percent, the current market price of its stock is $50 per share, its *last* dividend was $1.85 per share, and the expected growth rate is 8 percent. External equity (new common) can be sold at a flotation cost of 15 percent.

The firm has the following investment opportunities for the next period:

Project	Cost	Annual Cash Flows	Project Life	IRR Schedule
A	$ 75,000	$15,629	8 years	13.0
B	100,000	15,582	10 years	9.0
C	50,000	15,775	4 years	
D	25,000	14,792	2 years	12.0
E	50,000	12,858	6 years	

Management asks you to help them determine what projects (if any) should be undertaken. You proceed with this analysis by answering the following questions as posed in a logical sequence:

a. How many breaks are there in the MCC schedule?

b. At what dollar amounts do the breaks occur, and what causes them?

c. What is the weighted average cost of capital, k_a, in each of the intervals between the breaks?

d. What are the IRR values for Projects C and E?

e. Graph the IOS and MCC schedules.

f. Which projects should Haslem's management accept?

g. What implicit assumptions about project risk are embodied in this problem? If you learned that Projects E, A, and D were of above-average risk, yet Haslem chose the projects which you indicated in Part f, how would this affect the situation?

h. The problem stated that Haslem pays out 50 percent of its earnings as dividends. In words, how would the analysis change if the payout ratio were changed to zero, 100 percent, or somewhere in between?

15-10 In October, 1981, Builtwell Construction Company executives were working on their budget for 1982. Builtwell expects to have the following *book value* capital structure on December 31, 1981:

Debt	$12,000,000
Preferred stock (25,000 shares)	2,500,000
Common stock (1,000,000 shares)	5,000,000
Retained earnings	10,000,000
	$29,500,000

Earnings per share have grown steadily over the past seven years, from $1.65 in 1974 to $3.00 projected for 1981. The investment community expects growth to continue, but at a slower rate; the average past growth rate of 9 percent has recently dropped to 5 percent, and it is expected to remain constant at this level. Based on a 5 percent growth rate, the stock now sells at a price/earnings ratio of 6×. The last dividend, D_0, was $1.88; it is expected to increase at the new 5 percent growth rate.

Builtwell's preferred stock, which was issued several years ago, has a book value of $100 per share, and it pays a dividend of $9. The yield currently on preferred stock of this degree of risk is 11.25 percent.

The debt consists of $12,000,000 of $1,000 par, twenty year bonds with a 7 percent coupon, payable semiannually. These bonds were issued seven years ago, hence have thirteen years remaining to maturity. The yield-to-maturity for these bonds is currently 9.227 percent.

The addition to retained earnings projected for 1981 is $1,026,000.[19] These funds will be available during the 1982 budget year. The corporate tax rate, including state income taxes, is 60 percent.

Assuming that the capital structure relations developed in Part a below are maintained, new securities can be sold at the following costs:

Bonds

1. Up to and including $3 million of new bonds, 10 percent cost to the company (after flotation adjustment) on these bonds.
2. From $3.01 to $5 million of new bonds, 10.5 percent cost to the company on this increment of bonds.
3. Over $5 million of new bonds, 14 percent cost to the company on this increment of bonds.

Preferred

1. Additional preferred stock can be sold to investors at a price of $100 per share (which is par value) with a coupon of 11.25 percent, but the company will incur a 5 percent flotation cost, hence will net only $95 per share.

Common

Additional common equity can be obtained as follows:

1. Up to $3 million of new common stock can be sold at the current market price, with a flotation cost of 5 percent.
2. Over $3 million of new common stock will be sold at the current market price, but it will have a flotation cost of 15 percent.

Based on this data, answer the following questions:
  a. Find Builtwell's market value capital structure, rounded to the nearest million dollars. (Hint: PVIF for 4.6135%, 26 periods = 0.3095, and PVIFA = 14.9660.)
  b. At what dollar amounts of new capital will breaks occur in the MCC schedule?
  c. Calculate the MCC in the interval between each of these breaks, and then plot the MCC schedule.
  d. Assume that the company has the following investment opportunities. They are all indivisible; that is, they must be accepted in total or else rejected. In addition, Projects A and A' are mutually exclusive; that is, only one, if either, may be accepted. All of the projects have a one year life. Dollars are in millions:

---

[19]
$$1981 \text{ DPS} = D_1 = (\$1.88)(1.05) = \$1.974.$$
$$\text{Retained earnings} = (\text{EPS} - \text{DPS}) \times 1,000,000 \text{ shares}$$
$$= (\$3.00 - \$1.974)(1,000,000) = \$1,026,000.$$

Project	t = 0 Investment Cost	t = 1 Expected Year End After-Tax Cash Flow
A	$ 4	$ 4.600
A'	2	2.336
B	3	3.420
C	15	16.995
D	1	1.130
E	1	1.115

Develop the Investment Opportunity Schedule and determine which projects will be accepted. (Hints: (1) Draw an MCC schedule and *two* IOS schedules (one including A and the other A') on the same graph; (2) draw a graph with NPV profiles for A and A'; and (3) consider the choice between A and A' in the light of these two graphs, noting that the corporation's MCC (the cost of the *next* dollar raised, which is a *point* on the MCC *schedule*) is constant at 13.4 percent regardless of whether A or A' is chosen.

e. Builtwell receives some new information which leads management to revise downward the expected cash inflow on Project C from $16,995,000 to $16,800,000. How will this affect the ranking of the projects and the accept/reject decision? (Hint: You need to construct a new IOS schedule on a graph which also shows the MCC schedule.)

f. (Note: This question deals with differential project risk. The specific solution requires a familiarity with material developed in Appendix 12B, so the question should be omitted unless Appendix 12B has been covered.) To this point, our evaluation has ignored the relative riskiness of the potential projects. There will, however, be uncertainty surrounding the cash flows of the projects. Below are the subjective probability distributions for Projects A and A'. The cash flows are assumed to be intertemporally independent, and to be random variables which are normally distributed.

State	Probability of State j	Project A Period 0 (cost)	Project A Period 1 (return)	Project A' Period 0 (cost)	Project A' Period 1 (return)
Recession	0.2	− $2	$2.6	− $1.8	$2.166
Normal	0.6	− 4	4.6	− 2.0	2.366
Boom	0.2	− 6	6.6	− 2.2	2.566

1. Using the Hillier model coefficient of variation as the measure of risk, which project is riskier? (The risk-free rate is 7 percent.)
2. Suppose Builtwell uses risk-adjusted discount rates to evaluate projects according to the following schedule:

Coefficient of Variation (Range at Risk-Free Rate)	Discount Rate
$v \leq 3.0$ (low-risk projects)	11% (average cost less 2%)
$3.0 < v \leq 6.0$ (average-risk projects)	13% (assumed average cost of capital)[a]
$v > 6.0$ (high-risk projects)	15% (average cost plus 2%)

[a]The average cost of capital would normally be based upon your analysis in Parts a through e, but for purposes of this question *assume* that the average cost of capital for the corporation has been determined to be 13 percent.

If the coefficients of variation for Projects B, C, D, and E are 7.1, 4.6, 2.1, and 3.5, respectively, what projects will be in Builtwell's optimal capital budget, and what will be the total amount of capital expenditures? (The cash flows for Project C are assumed to be those originally determined; that is, disregard Part e above.)

Solution to Self-Test Problem

ST 15-1   a. A breaking point will occur each time a low-cost type of capital is used up. We establish the breaking points as follows, after first noting that LCI has $12,000 of retained earnings.

$$
\begin{aligned}
\text{Retained earnings} &= (\text{Total earnings})(1.0 - \text{Payout}) \\
&= (\$17,142.86)(0.7) \\
&= \$12,000.
\end{aligned}
$$

Capital Used Up	Breaking Point Calculation	Break Number
Retained earnings	$BP_{RE} = \dfrac{RE}{\text{Equity fraction}} = \dfrac{\$12,000}{0.60} = \$20,000.$	②
10% flotation common	$BP_{10\%E} = \dfrac{RE + \text{Equity at 10\% flotation}}{\text{Equity fraction}}$ $= \dfrac{\$12,000 + \$6,000}{0.60} = \$30,000.$	④
5% flotation preferred	$BP_{5\%P} = \dfrac{\text{Preferred at 5\% flotation}}{\text{Preferred fraction}}$ $= \dfrac{\$3,750}{0.15} = \$25,000.$	③

Capital Used Up	Breaking Point Calculation	Break Number
12% debt	$BP_{12\%D} = \dfrac{12\% \text{ debt}}{\text{Debt fraction}} = \dfrac{\$2,500}{0.25} = \$10,000.$	①
14% debt	$BP_{14\%D} = \dfrac{12\% \text{ debt} + 13\% \text{ debt}}{\text{Debt fraction}}$ $= \dfrac{\$2,500 + \$2,500}{0.25} = \$20,000.$	②

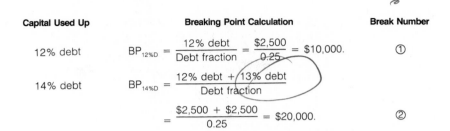

Summary of Breaking Points

1. There are three common equity costs, hence two changes, hence two equity-induced breaks in the MCC. There are two preferred costs, hence one preferred break. There are three debt costs, hence two debt breaks.

2. The numbers in the right column of the above table designate the sequential order of the breaks. Note that the second debt break and the break for retained earnings both occur at $20,000.

3. The breaks themselves are summarized below:

Break Number	Total Dollars of Capital Raised	Cause of Break
1	$10,000	Used up 12% debt and went to 14% debt.
2	$20,000	This break is caused by two factors: (1) used up retained earnings and (2) used up 14% debt.
3	$25,000	Used up preferred with F = 5%.
4	$30,000	Used up common with F = 10%.

b. Component costs within indicated total capital intervals:

Retained Earnings ($0 to $20,000)[a]

$$\text{Dividend growth model: } k_s = \frac{D_1}{P_0} + g = \frac{D_0(1 + g)}{P_0} + g$$

$$= \frac{\$3.60(1.09)}{\$60} + 0.09$$

$$= 0.0654 + 0.09 = \quad 15.54\%.$$

(continued)

Common with F = 10% ($20,000 to $30,000)

$$k_e = \frac{D_1}{P_0(1.0 - F)} + g = \frac{\$3.924}{\$60(0.9)} + 9\% = \qquad 16.27\%.$$

Common with F = 20% (Over $30,000)

$$k_e = \frac{\$3.924}{\$60(0.8)} + 9\% = \qquad 17.18\%.$$

Preferred with F = 5% ($0 to $25,000)

$$k_p = \frac{\text{Preferred dividend}}{P_n} = \frac{\$11}{\$100(0.95)} = \qquad 11.58\%.$$

Preferred with F = 10% (Over $25,000)

$$k_p = \frac{\$11}{\$100(0.9)} = \qquad 12.22\%.$$

Debt at k_d = 12% ($0 to $10,000)

$$k_d(1 - t) = 12\%(0.6) = \qquad 7.20\%.$$

Debt at k_d = 14% ($10,000 to $20,000)

$$k_d(1 - t) = 14\%(0.6) = \qquad 8.40\%.$$

Debt at k_d = 16% (Over $20,000)

$$k_d(1 - t) = 16\%(0.6) = \qquad 9.60\%.$$

[a] We could also calculate k_s by the CAPM method:

$$k_s = R_F + b(k_M - R_F) = 11\% + 1.51(14\% - 11\%) = 15.53\%.$$

If the dividend growth model and the CAPM had not given consistent results, further analysis would have been necessary to determine which k_s estimate was better. Here we will use 15.54 percent.

c. MCC calculations within indicated total capital intervals:

(1) $0 to $10,000 (Debt = 7.2%, Preferred = 11.58%, and RE = 15.54%):

$$MCC = k_a = w_d(k_d)(1 - t) + w_p(k_p) + w_e(k_s)$$
$$= 0.25(7.2\%) + 0.15(11.58\%) + 0.60(15.54\%) = 12.86\%.$$

(2) $10,001 to $20,000 (Debt = 8.4%, Preferred = 11.58%, and RE = 15.54%):

$$MCC = k_a = 0.25(8.4\%) + 0.15(11.58\%) + 0.60(15.54\%) = 13.16\%.$$

(3) $20,001 to $25,000 (Debt = 9.6%, Preferred = 11.58%, and Equity = 16.27%):

$$MCC = k_a = 0.25(9.6\%) + 0.15(11.58\%) + 0.60(16.27\%) = 13.90\%.$$

(4) $25,001 to $30,000 (Debt = 9.6%, Preferred = 12.22%, and Equity = 16.27%):

$$MCC = k_a = 0.25(9.6\%) + 0.15(12.22\%) + 0.60(16.27\%) = 14.00\%.$$

(5) Over $30,000 (Debt = 9.6%, Preferred = 12.22%, and Equity = 17.18%):

$$MCC = k_a = 0.25(9.6\%) + 0.15(12.22\%) + 0.60(17.18\%) = 14.54\%.$$

d. IRR calculation for Project E:

$$\text{PVIFA}_{k,6} = \frac{\$10,000}{\$2,713.92} = 3.6847.$$

This is the factor for 16 percent, so raw $\text{IRR}_E = 16\%$.
Adjusted $\text{IRR}_E = 16\%/1.2 = 13.3\%$.

e. See the graph of the MCC and IOS schedules for LCI.

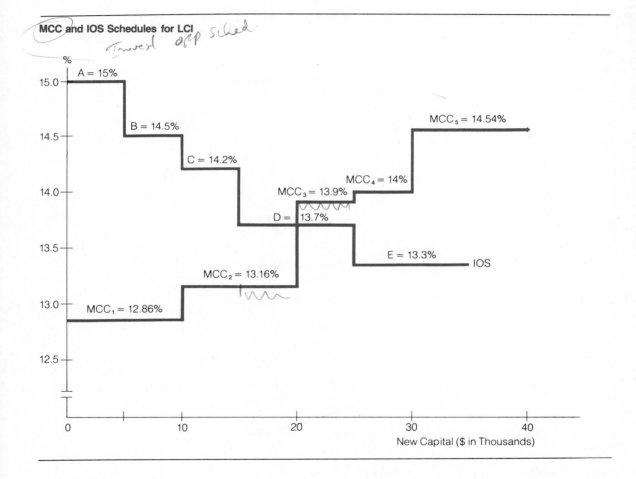

f. LCI clearly should accept Projects A, B, and C. It should also accept Project D, because the average cost of the $10,000 needed to finance D is

$$\left(\frac{\$5,000}{\$10,000}\right)(13.16\%) + \left(\frac{\$5,000}{\$10,000}\right)(13.90\%) = 13.53\%,$$

$13.53 < 13.70$

while $IRR_D = 13.70\%$. Therefore, $NPV_D > 0$, so accepting D would increase the value of the firm.

The firm's capital budget would total $25,000.

g. We first calculate the risk-adjusted discount rates:

Low risk (A only):	$k = 0.8(13.53\%)$	$= 10.824\%.$
Average risk (C and D):	$k = 13.53\%.$	
High risk (B and E):	$k = 1.2(13.53\%)$	$= 16.236\%.$

If you have a financial calculator, you can estimate NPVs directly. Otherwise, use the formula at the top of Table A-2 to develop PVIFAs, and proceed as follows:

$$
\begin{aligned}
NPV_A &= PVIFA_{10.824\%,7 \text{ yrs.}}(\$1{,}095.60) - \$5{,}000 \\
&= 4.7391(\$1{,}095.60) - \$5{,}000 \\
&= \$192.16. \\
NPV_B &= \$135.95. \\
NPV_C &= \$113.97. \\
NPV_D &= \$67.17. \\
NPV_E &= (\$62.12).
\end{aligned}
$$

Thus, the NPV method, using a corporate cost of capital and risk-adjusted costs of capital for the individual projects, leads to the same decision as the IRR method, because our projects were assumed to be independent.

As an operating procedure, a firm can estimate its MCC schedule, make an informed estimate of its IOS schedule *without actually analyzing individual projects*, observe the intersection of the MCC and IOS schedules, use the intersection MCC as the corporate cost of capital, and proceed to analyze individual projects using the risk-adjusted NPV method. The graph above would be smoothed out, rather than showing the breaks, for both the MCC and the IOS. In our example, this smoothing would result in an MCC of about 13.50 percent, which is very close to the 13.53 percent we used.

Selected References

The weighted average cost of capital as described in this chapter is widely used in both industry and academic circles. It has been criticized on several counts, but to date it has withstood the challenges. See the following articles:

Arditti, Fred D., and Haim Levy, "The Weighted Average Cost of Capital as a Cutoff Rate: A Critical Examination of the Classical Textbook Weighted Average," *Financial Management*, Fall 1977, 24-34.

Beranek, William, "The Weighted Average Cost of Capital and Shareholder Wealth Maximization," *Journal of Financial and Quantitative Analysis*, March 1977, 17-32.

Boudreaux, Kenneth J., and Hugh W. Long; John R. Ezzell and R. Burr Porter; Moshe Ben-Horim; and Alan C. Shapiro, "The Weighted Average Cost of Capital: A Discussion," *Financial Management,* vol. 8 (Summer 1979), 7-23.

Reilly, Raymond R., and William E. Wacker, "On the Weighted Average Cost of Capital," *Journal of Financial and Quantitative Analysis,* January 1973, 123-126.

Appendix 11C of the second edition of this book also analyzed the use of a weighted average cost of capital versus a project-specific cost.

Some other works that are relevant include these:

Alberts, W. W., and S. H. Archer, "Some Evidence on the Effect of Company Size on the Cost of Equity Capital," *Journal of Financial and Quantitative Analysis,* vol. 8 (March 1973), 229-242.

Chen, Andrew, "Recent Developments in the Cost of Debt Capital," *Journal of Finance,* June 1978, 863-883.

Gordon, Myron J., and L. I. Gould, "The Cost of Equity Capital with Personal Income Taxes and Flotation Costs," *Journal of Finance,* vol. 33 (September 1978), 1201-1212.

Gordon, Myron J., and P. J. Halpern, "Cost of Capital for a Division of a Firm," *Journal of Finance,* vol. 29 (September 1974), 1153-1163.

Myers, S. C., "Interactions of Corporate Financing and Investments Decisions—Implications for Capital Budgeting," *Journal of Finance,* vol. 29 (March 1974), 1-25.

Nantell, Timothy J., and C. Robert Carson, "The Cost of Capital as a Weighted Average," *Journal of Finance,* December 1975, 1343-1355.

Additional references on the cost of capital are cited in Chapters 16, 17, and 18, which deal with the effects of financial leverage and dividend policy on the cost of capital.

Appendix 15A

Some Unresolved Issues on the Cost of Capital

In this appendix we will show how some of the issues glossed over earlier can affect the cost of capital calculation. The purpose here is as much to raise questions as to answer them, yet the material has important practical implications. Moreover, anyone engaged in financial management must understand all the implications underlying the practical, rule-of-thumb procedures that the financial manager will necessarily be forced to follow.

Cost of Retained Earnings

Whenever a firm retains a portion of its net income rather than pay it out in dividends, there is an "opportunity cost" to the stockholders. If the firm in question has a required rate of return of 12 percent on its stock (that is, $k_s = 12\%$), then presumably its shareholders could have invested the retained earnings, had they been paid out in dividends, in other firms of similar risk and received a 12 percent return. This 12 percent is, under certain assumptions, the opportunity cost of retained earnings. The two assumptions are (1) that the stockholders pay no income tax on dividends and (2) that they incur no brokerage costs when reinvesting dividend receipts.[1] *To the extent that these assumptions are not met, the opportunity cost*

---

[1] There is also a question of whether investors prefer to receive their rewards from stock investments in the form of dividends or as capital gains. The question is considered in some detail in Chapter 18, but here it is assumed that investors are indifferent between dividends and capital gains.

of retained earnings, hence the cost of capital from retained earnings, is lower than the cost of new common stock. The following example is an illustration.

The ABC Company has net earnings of $1 million, and all of its stockholders are in the 30 percent marginal tax bracket. Management estimates that under present conditions the stockholders' required rate of return is 12 percent. If the earnings are paid out as dividends, the recipients will pay income taxes, then reinvest the proceeds in the stock of similar firms and obtain a 12 percent return. The brokerage costs to the stockholders will average 3 percent of the new investments. What rate of return must be earned internally to provide the stockholders with incremental earnings equal to what they would receive externally?

1. After-tax proceeds of dividend payment

$$= \$1,000,000 - \text{Personal taxes}$$
$$= \$1,000,000 - \$300,000$$
$$= \$700,000.$$

2. Net investment after brokerage costs

$$= \$700,000 - \text{Brokerage}$$
$$= \$700,000 - \$21,000$$
$$= \$679,000.$$

3. Earnings on new investment $= (679,000)(0.12) = \$81,480$.
4. Internal rate of return, k_r, necessary to provide stockholders with incremental income of $81,480:

$$\$81,480 = (\$1,000,000)(k_r)$$
$$k_r = 8.148\%.$$

5. If the firm is able to earn 8.148 percent on retained earnings, the stockholders will be as well off as they would be if all earnings were paid out and then reinvested to yield 12 percent.
6. Therefore, the internal opportunity cost, or the required rate of return on retention-financed investments, is less than the stockholders' required rate of return and may be calculated as follows:

$$k_r = k_s(1 - T)(1 - B),$$

where k_r is the required return on retention-financed investments, k_s is the stockholders' required rate of return, T is the stockholders' marginal tax rate, and B is the percentage brokerage cost. In the example being considered,

$$k_r = 0.12(0.7)(0.97) = 0.08148, \text{ or } 8.148\%.$$

This procedure actually involves an overstatement. The retained earnings will give rise to an increase in the price of the stock; if the investors sell it, their profits will be subject to a capital gains tax. The capital gains tax rate is lower than the rate applicable to dividends (generally); also, as this tax is deferred, it has a lower present value.

Two limiting cases can be applied. First, it can be assumed that the stockholders never sell the stock, passing it on to their heirs, who do the same, *ad infinitum*. In this case the procedures in the example are correct. At the other limit, it can be assumed that the investors hold the stock for the minimum holding period (one year) to receive long-term capital gains tax treatment, then sell the stock and pay a tax at 40 percent of their normal tax rate. In this case, the value of T for the example should be 12 percent, and the resultant cost of retained earnings is computed to be

$$k_r = 0.12(0.88)(0.97) = 0.102, \text{ or } 10.2\%$$

The correct figure probably lies somewhere between these two extremes, but there is no way of knowing exactly where.

The example shows that, in general, the required rate of return on retention-financed investment, k_r, is less than the investors' required rate of return, k_s, by the amount of brokerage costs on reinvested dividend receipts and by stockholders' marginal tax rates. But suppose there are many stockholders, and their marginal tax rates range from zero to 70 percent. Now what should be done? There simply is no one correct answer. One could use one-half the average marginal tax rate of individual stockholders in general—it has averaged about 40 percent in recent years[2]—the maximum capital gains tax, or the tax rate of the controlling stockholder, or one could try to estimate the average tax rate of all the firm's stockholders and use 40 percent of that number.[3]

The decision rules in this section apply, to the extent that they are valid at all, only to a firm that is not selling new stock. If investors require $k_s = 12\%$, then they would not buy new stock of a firm that was reinvesting earnings at $k_r < k_s$. Reinvestment at the rate k_r might be the best we can do, but we would certainly not put any new external equity into the firm.

---

[2] Vincent Jolivet, "The Weighted Average Marginal Tax Rate on Dividends Received by Individuals in the U.S.," *American Economic Review*, June 1966.

[3] Another equation for determining a tax-and-brokerage adjusted cost of retained earnings is the following:

$$k_r = k_s \left[\frac{(1 - B)(1 - T_p)}{(1 - T_g)} \right].$$

Here T_p is the personal tax on dividend income and T_g is the tax on capital gains. Using our illustrative values, we find k_r as follows:

$$k_r = 12 \left[\frac{(0.97)(0.7)}{0.88} \right] = 12(0.7716) = 9.3\%. \tag{15A-1}$$

Thus, this estimate of k_r lies between our extreme cases, 8.1 percent and 10.2 percent. See W. G. Lewellen, *The Cost of Capital* (Belmont, Calif.: Wadsworth, 1969), chapter 5, for a discussion of the logic behind this formula.

Stock Purchases

Under certain circumstances, the procedure discussed in the preceding section is invalid or, at least, unnecessary. If k_s, the market-determined rate of return on the stock of the firm in question or of firms in the same risk class, is 12 percent, and if the firm can buy its own or similar stocks to yield 12 percent, then this sets a lower limit on project returns. The firm would never invest in assets yielding less than 12 percent, the value of k_s, because it can obtain this yield on market securities.

Several points make this line of reasoning questionable. First, a company whose stock is not publicly traded cannot buy its own stock on the open market. Second, privately held firms could not buy large amounts of the stock of publicly owned firms without the Internal Revenue Service stepping in and imposing penalties under the improper accumulation of retained earnings tax (see Chapter 2). Third, publicly owned companies that can legally buy their own stock on the open market under certain conditions are frequently averse to doing so, because such purchases amount to admitting that they are unable to generate acceptable projects. Also, if a firm engages in large-scale purchases of its own stock, it will probably run the price up and the yield down during the period in which it is making the acquisition.[4]

The question of open-market purchases has never been investigated in a satisfactory manner.[5] We are convinced that many firms, especially privately owned companies, cannot use open-market purchases (or mergers either) to avoid the effects of personal taxes on dividends; at least for these companies, the cost of retained earnings is somewhat lower than the basic required rate of return. In our own experience, we have seen situations in which the stockholders of closely held firms were in high tax brackets and, therefore, directed the firms to make internal investments at rates of return less than the expected market returns on common stock for precisely the reasons outlined here. Further, we find it difficult to question their logic and their judgment that their cost of retained earnings is less than their external required rate of return. Certainly, the cost of external equity is higher than the cost of retained earnings because of flotation and other transactions costs.

Cost of Depreciation-Generated Funds

The very first increment of internal funds used to finance any year's capital budget is depreciation-generated funds. In their statements of sources and uses of funds, corporations generally show depreciation charges to be one of the most important sources of funds, if not the most important. For capital budgeting purposes, should depreciation be considered "free"

---

[4] See Chapter 18 for an extended discussion of stock repurchases.

[5] H. Bierman and R. West discuss some of the theoretical issues in "The Acquisition of Stock by the Corporate Issuer," *Journal of Finance*, vol. 21 (December 1966), 687-696, as do the prior papers cited in their article. The important empirical questions are unresolved at this time.

capital; should it be ignored completely; or should a charge be assessed against it? The answer is that a charge should indeed be assessed against these funds, and that this cost is approximately equal to the average cost of capital before outside equity is used.

The reasoning here is that the firm could, if it so desired, distribute the depreciation-generated funds to its stockholders and creditors, the parties who financed the assets in the first place. For example, if $10 million of depreciation-generated funds were available, the firm could either reinvest them or distribute them. If they are to be distributed, the distribution must be to both bondholders and stockholders in proportion to their shares of the capital structure; otherwise the capital structure will change. Obviously, this distribution should take place if the funds cannot be invested to yield the cost of capital, but retention should occur if the internal rate of return exceeds the cost of capital. Since the cost of depreciation-generated funds is equal to the average cost of capital, depreciation does not enter the calculation of the average cost of capital.

Depreciation does, however, affect the cost of capital *schedule* in a very significant way. Consider Figure 15-3 in Chapter 15. The cost of capital schedule begins to rise once the total amount of funds raised goes beyond $700,000. However, if depreciation is considered to be a source of funds available for capital budgeting purposes, then the flat part of the curve would be extended out by the amount of the depreciation. In the example, if depreciation amounted to $1 million, then the cost of capital schedule would begin to rise at $1.7 million rather than at $700,000.

What difference does all this make, and should we be concerned with a cost of capital schedule that includes or excludes depreciation? If we are concerned with the effects of *net increases* in assets, then the schedule without depreciation is appropriate. However, if we are concerned with gross capital expenditures—including replacement as well as expansion investments—then the schedule that includes depreciation is the relevant one.[6]

Problems

15A-1 Ed Smidt, treasurer of Collins Mills, Inc., is reviewing his firm's cost of capital calculations. He has been using a weighted average cost, with k_s = 15%. Collins can generate all the equity that it requires through retained earnings, so Smidt has not needed to estimate a value for k_e. However, he is concerned over the matter of personal taxes and their effects on the cost of retained earnings.

Walker Collins, the firm's principal stockholder, who is in the 70 percent tax bracket, owns 42 percent of the outstanding stock. The remaining 58 percent is owned by other members of the Collins family, by the man-

[6] For a further discussion of the role of depreciation in the MCC schedule, see the Union Telecommunications Case in E. F. Brigham et al., *Cases in Managerial Finance*, 4th ed. (Hinsdale, Ill.: Dryden Press, 1980).

agement team, by institutional investors (including some pension funds which pay no taxes), and by the general public.

Smidt recently conducted a survey of Collins' stockholders and learned, among other things, that the average tax rate—averaging in the 70 percent bracket owners with the 0 percent institutions—is 45 percent. Further, he estimates that, if Walker Collins or other stockholders receive dividends and then reinvest them in other stocks, they will pay brokerage charges and other transactions costs of about 3 percent.

a. What cost of retained earnings should Smidt use in developing Collins Mills' weighted average cost of capital for capital budgeting purposes?

b. Assume that Collins Mills is financed with only equity capital. If the company has the opportunity to invest in a project with an expected return of 10 percent, should it do so? Assume that the project has a beta risk of 1.2, which is exactly the same as that of Collins' stock.

15A-2 Paula Solinger, financial vice-president of the Dayton Publishing Company, is in the process of estimating a projected MCC schedule for 1982. The following data have been developed for use in this projection:

k_d = 9% for all new debt,
k_s = 12%,
k_e = 13%,
Estimated retained earnings for 1982 = $10 million,
Estimated depreciation for 1982 = $5 million,
Effective corporate tax rate = t = 40%, and
Target debt/value ratio = 30%.

Also, Solinger notes that Dayton's existing debt consists of 7 percent bonds, which may be called without penalty at any time.

a. Develop Dayton's MCC schedule. (Hint: Look for breaks to occur at $5 million and at $19.29 million, but show *why* these breaks occur.) Include depreciation in your MCC schedule.

b. What should Dayton's total capital budget be under each of the following investment opportunity schedules?

1. $2 million at an 11 percent IRR, $6 million at a 9 percent IRR.

2. $6 million at an 11.5 percent IRR, $2 million at a 9.5 percent IRR.

3. $10 million at a 12 percent IRR, $8 million at an 11 percent IRR, and $5 million at a 10 percent IRR.

c. What dividend policy should Dayton follow under Part b(1)?

Capital Structure Decisions 16

In Chapter 15, when we calculated the weighted average cost of capital for use in capital budgeting, we took the capital structure weights as given. However, if the weights were changed, this could have an effect on the calculated cost of capital and consequently could change the set of acceptable projects. Also, if the capital structure were changed, this would affect the riskiness inherent in the firm's common stock and thus affect k_s and consequently P_0. Therefore, the choice of a capital structure, or the mix of securities used to finance the firm, is a potentially important decision.

As we shall see, the firm analyzes a number of factors, then establishes a *target capital structure*. This target may change over time as conditions vary, but at any given moment the firm's management does have a specific capital structure in mind, and individual financing decisions should be consistent with this target. If the actual debt ratio is below the prescribed ratio, expansion capital will probably be raised by issuing debt, while stock will probably be sold if the debt ratio is above the target level.

Capital structure policy involves a choice between risk and expected returns. Using more debt raises the riskiness of the firm's earnings stream, but more debt generally means a higher expected rate of return. Higher risk tends to lower the stock's price, but a higher expected rate of return raises it. *The optimal capital structure strikes a balance between these risks and returns and thus maximizes the price of the stock.*

Types of Risk

In Chapter 5, when we examined risk from the viewpoint of the individual investor, we distinguished between market risk, which is measured by the firm's beta coefficient, and total risk, which includes both the beta risk and an element of risk which can be eliminated by diversification. Then, in Chapter 12, we examined risk from the viewpoint of the corporation, and we considered how capital budgeting decisions affect the riskiness of the firm. There we again distinguished between beta risk (the effect of a project on the firm's beta) and corporate risk (the effect of the project on the firm's total risk).

Now we introduce two new dimensions of risk: (1) *business risk*, or the riskiness of the firm's operations if it used no debt, and (2) *financial risk*, the additional risk placed on the common stockholders as a result of the firm's decision to use debt.[1] Conceptually, the firm has a certain amount of risk inherent in its operations—this is its business risk. When it uses debt, it partitions this risk and concentrates most of it on one class of investors—the common stockholders. However, the common stockholders are compensated by a higher expected return.

Business Risk

Business risk, which is defined as the uncertainty inherent in projections of future *operating income,* or *earnings before interest and taxes (EBIT),* is the single most important determinant of a firm's capital structure. Figure 16-1 gives some clues about Carter Chemical's business risk. The top graph shows the trend in EBIT over the past eleven years; this gives both security analysts and Carter's management an idea of the degree to which EBIT has varied in the past and might vary in the future. The bottom graph shows a subjectively estimated probability distribution of Carter's EBIT for 1981. The estimate was made at the beginning of 1981, and the expected value of $275 million was read from the trend line in Figure 16-1a. As the graphs indicate, actual EBIT in 1981 fell below the expected value.

Carter's past fluctuations in EBIT were caused by many factors— booms and recessions in the national economy, successful new products introduced both by Carter and by its competitors, labor strikes, price controls, fires in Carter's major plants, and so on. Similar events will doubtless occur in the future, and when they do, EBIT will rise or fall. Further, there is always the possibility that a long-term disaster might strike, permanently depressing the company's earning power; for example, a competitor could introduce a new product that might permanently lower Carter's earnings.[2]

This element of uncertainty regarding Carter's future operating income is defined as the company's *basic business risk.* Business risk varies not only from industry to industry but also among firms in a given industry. Further, business risk can change over time. For example, the electric utilities were regarded for years as having little business risk, but a combination of events in the 1970s altered the utilities' situation, produced sharp declines in their operating income, and greatly increased the industry's business risk. Now, food processors and grocery retailers are frequently given as examples of industries with low business risks, while cyclical manufacturing industries such as steel are regarded as having es-

---

[1] Using preferred stock also adds to financial risk. To simplify matters somewhat, in this chapter we shall consider only debt and common equity.

[2] Two examples of "safe" industries that turned out to be risky are the railroads just before automobiles, airplanes, and trucks took away most of their business, and Western Union just before telephones came on the scene. Numerous individual companies have been hurt, if not destroyed, by antitrust actions, fraud, or plain old bad management.

a. Trend in Earnings before Interest and Taxes (EBIT)

Figure 16-1
Carter Chemical
Company: Trend in
EBIT, 1971-1981, and
Subjective Probability
Distribution of EBIT,
1981

b. Subjective Probability Distribution of EBIT

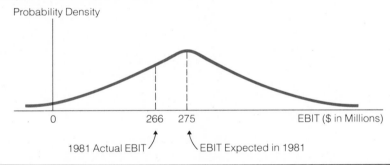

pecially high business risks. Also, smaller companies, and those that are dependent on a single product, are often regarded as having a high degree of business risk.[3]

Business risk depends on a number of factors, the more important of which include the following:

1. *Demand variability*. The more stable the demand for a firm's products, other things held constant, the lower its business risk.

---

[3] We have avoided any discussion of market versus company-specific risk in this section. We note now (1) that any action which increases business risk will generally increase a firm's beta coefficient but (2) that a part of business risk as we define it will generally be company-specific, hence subject to elimination by diversification by the firm's stockholders. This point is discussed at some length later in the chapter.

2. *Sales price variability.* Firms whose products are sold in highly volatile markets are exposed to more business risk than similar firms whose output prices are more stable.

3. *Input price variability.* Firms whose input prices are highly uncertain are exposed to a high degree of business risk.

4. *Ability to adjust output prices for changes in input prices.* Some firms are better able to raise their own output prices when input costs rise than are others. The greater the ability to adjust output prices, the lower the degree of business risk, other things held constant. This factor has become increasingly important during the past few years because of inflation.

5. *The extent to which costs are fixed: operating leverage.* If a high percentage of a firm's costs are fixed, hence do not decline when demand falls off, then it is exposed to a relatively high degree of business risk. This point is discussed at length in the next section.

Each of these factors is determined partly by the firm's industry characteristics, but each of them is also controllable to some extent. For example, most firms can, through their marketing policies, take actions to stabilize both unit sales and sales prices. However, this stabilization may require firms to spend a great deal on advertising and/or price concessions in order to get their customers to commit to purchase fixed quantities at fixed prices in the future. Similarly, firms such as Carter Chemical may reduce the volatility of future input costs by negotiating long-term labor and materials supply contracts, but they may have to agree to pay prices above the current spot price level to obtain these contracts.[4]

Operating Leverage

As was noted above, business risk depends in part on the extent to which a firm builds fixed costs into its operations—if fixed costs are high, even a small decline in sales can lead to a large decline in EBIT, so, other things held constant, the higher a firm's fixed costs, the greater its business risk. Higher fixed costs are generally associated with more highly automated, capital intensive firms and industries. Also, businesses that employ highly skilled workers who must be retained and paid even during recessions have relatively high fixed costs.

If a high percentage of a firm's total costs are fixed costs, then the firm is said to have a high degree of operating leverage. In physics, leverage implies the use of a lever to raise a heavy object with a small force. In politics, if people have leverage, their smallest word or action can accomplish a lot. *In business terminology, a high degree of operating leverage, other things held*

---

[4] For example, in 1981 utilities could buy coal in the spot market for about $40 per ton. Under a five year contract, coal cost about $60 per ton. Clearly, the price for reducing uncertainty was high!

constant, implies that a relatively small change in sales results in a large change in operating income.

Figure 16-2 illustrates the concept of operating leverage by comparing the results that a new firm can expect if it uses different degrees of operating leverage. Plan A calls for a relatively small amount of fixed charges—here the firm would not have much automated equipment, so its depreciation, maintenance, property taxes, and so on would be low. Note, however, that under Plan A the total cost line has a relatively steep

**Figure 16-2
Illustration of Operating
Leverage**

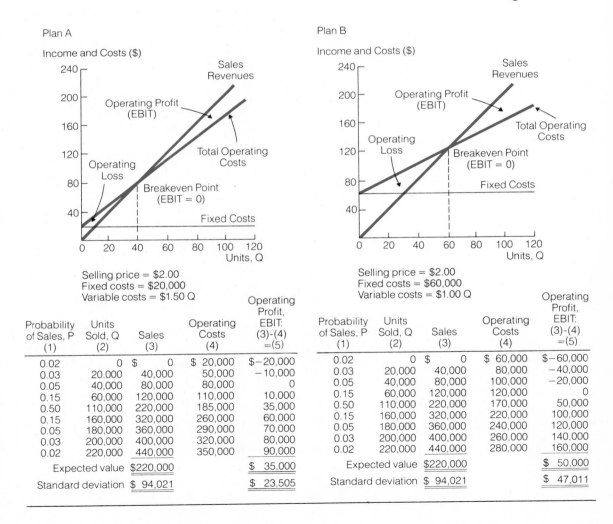

Probability of Sales, P (1)	Units Sold, Q (2)	Sales (3)	Operating Costs (4)	Operating Profit, EBIT: (3)-(4) =(5)
0.02	0	$ 0	$ 20,000	$−20,000
0.03	20,000	40,000	50,000	−10,000
0.05	40,000	80,000	80,000	0
0.15	60,000	120,000	110,000	10,000
0.50	110,000	220,000	185,000	35,000
0.15	160,000	320,000	260,000	60,000
0.05	180,000	360,000	290,000	70,000
0.03	200,000	400,000	320,000	80,000
0.02	220,000	440,000	350,000	90,000
Expected value	$220,000			$ 35,000
Standard deviation	$ 94,021			$ 23,505

Probability of Sales, P (1)	Units Sold, Q (2)	Sales (3)	Operating Costs (4)	Operating Profit, EBIT: (3)-(4) =(5)
0.02	0	$ 0	$ 60,000	$−60,000
0.03	20,000	40,000	80,000	−40,000
0.05	40,000	80,000	100,000	−20,000
0.15	60,000	120,000	120,000	0
0.50	110,000	220,000	170,000	50,000
0.15	160,000	320,000	220,000	100,000
0.05	180,000	360,000	240,000	120,000
0.03	200,000	400,000	260,000	140,000
0.02	220,000	440,000	280,000	160,000
Expected value	$220,000			$ 50,000
Standard deviation	$ 94,021			$ 47,011

slope, indicating that variable costs per unit are higher than they would be if the firm used more leverage. Plan B calls for a higher level of fixed costs. Here the firm uses automated equipment (with which one operator can turn out a few or many units at the same labor cost) to a much larger extent. The breakeven point is higher under Plan B: Breakeven occurs at 40,000 units under Plan A versus 60,000 units under Plan B.[5]

How does operating leverage affect business risk? *Other things held constant, the higher a firm's operating leverage, the higher its business risk.* This point is demonstrated in Figure 16-3, where we show how probability distributions for EBIT under Plans A and B are developed.

The top section of Figure 16-3 gives the probability distribution of sales. This distribution, which is taken from the tabular information contained in Figure 16-2, depends on how demand for the product varies, not on whether the product is manufactured by Plan A or by Plan B. Therefore, the same sales probability distribution applies to both production plans, and expected sales are $220,000, but with a range from zero to about $500,000, under either plan.

We can use the information on the sales probability distribution, together with the operating profit (EBIT) at each sales level as shown in Column 5 of the tables in the lower part of Figure 16-2, to develop probability distributions for EBIT under Plans A and B. The calculations are shown in the tabular section of Figure 16-2, and the resulting distributions for both sales and EBIT are shown in Figure 16-3. Plan B has a higher expected level of EBIT, but it also entails a much higher probability of large losses. Clearly, Plan B, the one with more fixed costs and a higher degree of operating leverage, is riskier. *In general, holding other things constant, the higher the degree of operating leverage, the greater the degree of business risk as measured by variability of EBIT.*

To what extent can firms control their operating leverage? For the most part, operating leverage is determined by technology. Electric utilities, telephone companies, airlines, steel mills, and chemical companies simply *must* have heavy investments in fixed assets; this results in high fixed costs and operating leverage. Grocery stores, on the other hand, generally have significantly lower fixed costs, hence lower operating leverage. Still, all firms have some control over their operating leverage. For example, an electric utility can expand its generating capacity by building either a nuclear reactor or a coal-fired plant. The nuclear generator would

---

[5] Algebraic procedures for determining breakeven points and for analyzing operating leverage are discussed in Appendix 16A. The formula is

$$\text{Breakeven quantity} = \text{Fixed cost}/(\text{Price} - \text{Variable cost}),$$

or

$$Q = F/(P - V).$$

For Plan A, $Q = 40,000$ units, while for Plan B, $Q = 60,000$ units.

Figure 16-3
Analysis of Business
Risk

a. Sales Probability Distribution

b. EBIT Probability Distribution

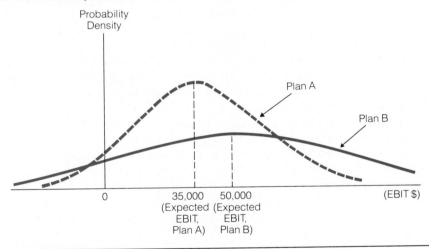

require a larger investment, hence higher fixed costs, but its variable operating costs would be relatively low. The coal plant, on the other hand, would require a smaller investment and would have lower fixed costs, but the variable costs (for coal) would be high. Thus, by its capital budgeting decisions a utility (or any other company) can influence its operating leverage, hence it basic business risk.

The concept of operating leverage was, in fact, originally developed for use in making capital budgeting decisions. Alternative methods for

producing a given product often have different degrees of operating leverage, hence different breakeven points and different degrees of risk.
Carter Chemical and other companies regularly undertake a type of
breakeven analysis (the sensitivity analysis discussed in Chapter 12) as a
part of their capital budgeting processes. Still, once a corporation's operating leverage has been established, the degree of this leverage influences
its capital structure decisions. This point is covered next.

Financial Leverage

Whereas operating leverage refers to the use of fixed operating costs,
*financial leverage refers to the use of fixed charge securities—debt and preferred
stock.* In this section, we show how financial leverage affects a firm's return on equity and the riskiness of this return. Subsequently, we examine
the effects of financial leverage on earnings per share and the price of the
firm's stock.

Conceptually, the firm has a certain amount of risk inherent in its
operations—this is its business risk, which is defined as the uncertainty
inherent in projections of future EBIT. If a firm uses debt, or financial
leverage, this concentrates its business risk on the stockholders. For example, suppose ten people decide to form a corporation to manufacture
solar fuel cells. There is a certain amount of business risk in the operation. If the firm is capitalized only with common equity, and if each person buys 10 percent of the stock, then the investors all share the business
risk equally. However, suppose the firm is capitalized with 50 percent
debt and 50 percent equity, with five of the investors putting up their
capital as debt and the other five putting up their money as equity. In
this case, the investors who put up the equity will have to bear all of the
business risk, so the common stock will be twice as risky as it would
have been had the firm been financed only with equity. Thus, the use of
debt concentrates the firm's business risk on its stockholders.[6]

---

[6] Two additional points should be made about business risk. First, in Chapter 5 we learned that *beta*
(or *market*) risk is the risk that is relevant to most stockholders. Therefore, a firm can be risky in a
business risk sense (that is, there can be great uncertainty about its future EBIT), but if its returns are
not perfectly correlated with those of other firms, then the stock may still be regarded as being not very
risky by diversified investors. In other words, a part of any firm's business risk is company-specific, or
unsystematic, risk. Since company-specific risk can be eliminated by diversification, an investor who
holds a stock in isolation must bear his or her share of the entire business risk of the firm. By definition,
however, well-diversified stockholders render "irrelevant" the company-specific portion of the firm's
business risk. Still, the high correlation among the returns on different firms permits us to state as a
generality that most increases in business risk result in higher systematic, or beta, risk, and so have an
adverse effect even on well-diversified investors. See B. Lev, "On the Association between Operating
Leverage and Risk," *Journal of Financial and Quantitative Analysis,* September 1974, 627-642, and
W. H. Beaver and J. Manegold, "The Association between Market-Determined and Accounting-Deter-
mined Measures of Systematic Risk: Some Further Evidence," *Journal of Financial and Quantitative
Analysis,* June 1975, 231-284.

Second, even though debt has a prior claim on the firm's assets and income, under extremely bad
business conditions, debtholders can still suffer losses. Therefore, debtholders cannot be totally protected against business risk.

To illustrate this concentration, consider a firm with an expected EBIT of $4 million and assets of $20 million. We first divide EBIT by the dollar amount of assets required to produce the EBIT, obtaining *the rate of return on assets* (ROA), which in this case is ROA = $4/$20 = 0.20 = 20%. If the company had no debt, then (1) its assets would be equal to its equity, (2) its return on equity (ROE) would be equal to its return on assets (ROA), and (3) its equity would be exactly as risky as the assets.

Now suppose that the firm decides to change its capital structure by issuing $10 million of debt which carries a 15 percent interest rate and then using these funds to retire equity. Its expected return on equity (which would now be only $10 million) would rise from 20 percent to 25 percent:

Expected EBIT (unchanged)	$4,000,000
Interest (15% on $10 million of debt)	1,500,000
Income available to common (zero taxes)	$2,500,000

Expected ROE = $2,500,000/$10,000,000 = 25%.

Thus, the use of debt would "leverage" expected ROE up from 20 percent to 25 percent.

However, financial leverage also increases risk to the equity investors. For example, suppose EBIT actually turned out to be $2 million rather than the expected $4 million. If the firm had not used debt, then ROE would have declined from 20 percent to 10 percent, but if the firm had used debt, then ROE would have fallen from 25 percent to only 5 percent:

	Zero Debt	$10 Million of Debt
Actual EBIT	$2,000,000	$2,000,000
Interest (15%)	0	1,500,000
Income available to common (zero taxes)	$2,000,000	$ 500,000
Actual ROE:		
$2,000,000/$20,000,000 =	10%	
$500,000/$10,000,000 =		5%

The effect of leverage on the firm's ROE is illustrated in Figure 16-4. The two lines in the top graph show the level of ROE that would exist at different levels of ROA with two different capital structures. For example, if the firm used zero debt, then if ROA were 20 percent, ROE would also be 20 percent, while if ROA fell to 10 percent, ROE would likewise fall to 10 percent. However, as we saw in the preceding illustration, if the firm used $10 million (or 50 percent of its $20 million total capital) as debt, then a 20 percent ROA would produce a 25 percent ROE, but if ROA declined from 20 percent to 10 percent, then ROE would plummet to 5 percent. Thus, when financial leverage is used, ROE is more sensitive to changes in ROA.[7]

The lower panel of Figure 16-4 shows the effects of leverage on the firm's probability distribution of ROE. With zero debt, the company would have an expected ROE of 20 percent, the same as its expected ROA, and a relatively tight distribution. With $10 million of debt, the expected ROE would be 25 percent, but the ROE distribution would be much flatter, indicating a larger standard deviation of returns (σ_{ROE}) and a more risky situation for the equity investors.

Our conclusions from this analysis may be stated as follows:

1. The use of debt generally increases the expected ROE.
2. σ_{ROA} is a measure of business risk, while σ_{ROE} is a measure of the risk borne by stockholders. $\sigma_{ROE} = \sigma_{ROA}$ if the firm does not use any financial leverage, but if the firm does use debt, then $\sigma_{ROE} > \sigma_{ROA}$, indicating that business risk is being concentrated on the stockholders.
3. The difference between σ_{ROA}, which is the risk that stockholders would bear if no financial leverage were used, and σ_{ROE}, the risk stockholders actually face, is a measure of the risk-increasing effects of financial leverage:

$$\text{Risk from financial leverage} = \sigma_{ROE} - \sigma_{ROA}.$$

Of course, σ_{ROE} is the total risk which stockholders must bear, and a portion of this risk can be eliminated through diversification. However,

---

[7] If more debt—say $15 million—were used, the ROE line would be even steeper, while if $5 million of debt were used, the line would be between the two shown in Figure 16-4. The lines would all intersect at the point where ROE = ROA = 15%, showing that if ROA = k_d, then leverage has no effect on ROE. Note also that the vertical axis intercept shows the fixed interest cost that must be borne by the stockholders; that is, at the intercept, the ROA is zero, but interest must be paid, and this interest must come out of the stockholders' share of the business, hence it produces an accounting loss and a 15 percent negative return to stockholders. The stockholders' loss would be greater or smaller if the firm used a greater or lesser amount of debt. For example, if the firm used only $5 million of debt, then the stockholders would have a 7.5 percent negative return if ROA were zero.

Note also that we have assumed away taxes. If taxes were introduced, the effect would be to lower the ROE. For example, if the tax rate were 50 percent, then the ROE lines in the top panel of Figure 16-4 would shift downward so that the lines would intersect at ROA = 15%, ROE = 7.5%.

Figure 16-4
Effects of Financial
Leverage on ROE

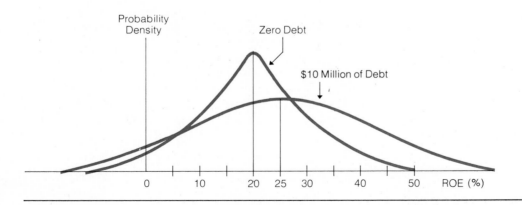

as was noted earlier, the firm's beta coefficient is highly correlated with its σ_{ROE}, so any action such as increasing financial leverage which raises σ_{ROE} will also raise beta.[8]

Forsyth Products Company

We saw in the preceding section that financial leverage raises both risk and expected returns. Increased risk tends to lower the price of a firm's stock, but a higher expected rate of return raises it. When management chooses a capital structure, it seeks to strike that balance between risk and return which will maximize the price of the firm's stock. In this section, we illustrate how capital structure decisions are made in practice.

Forsyth Products Corporation (FPC) was founded in 1975 to produce a new type of roofing stapler used in the construction industry. The stapler was invented and patented by Charles Forsyth, FPC's founder. Forsyth also owns most of the stock, and the company has no debt. Its assets are carried at a book value of $1 million; hence, its common equity also has a balance sheet value of $1 million. See Table 16-1. However, these balance sheet figures are not very meaningful because (1) the asset figures do not include any value for patents and (2) the fixed assets were purchased several years ago at preinflationary prices.

Charles Forsyth will retire shortly, and he is planning to sell his interest in the company to the public. As a part of the planning process, the question of capital structure has arisen: Should the firm continue the policy of using no debt, or should it start using financial leverage? And if it does decide to substitute debt for equity, how far should it go?[9] As in all such decisions, the correct answer is that *it should choose that capital structure which maximizes the value of the company.* If the company's total market value is maximized, so will be the price of its stock, and its cost of capital will simultaneously be minimized.

To simplify the analysis, we assume that the long-run demand for FPC's products is not expected to grow; hence, its EBIT is expected to continue at $4 million. (However, future sales may turn out to be different from the expected level, so EBIT may actually differ from $4 million.) Also, since the company has no need for new capital, all of its income

---

[8] Robert S. Hamada has developed an equation which directly relates a firm's beta to its financial leverage:

$$b_L = b_U[1 + (1 - t)(D/S)].$$

Here, b_L is the beta of a leveraged firm; b_U is the beta of an otherwise identical unleveraged firm; t is the firms' tax rate; and D and S represent the market values of the firms' debt and equity securities. Hamada's equation is based on the assumption that the Modigliani-Miller model described in Chapter 17 holds exactly. Since the pure MM model does not hold exactly, the Hamada equation is only an approximation. See R. S. Hamada, "The Effect of the Firm's Capital Structure on the Systematic Risk of Common Stocks," *Journal of Finance*, vol. 27 (May 1972), 435-452.

[9] Such a change is called a *recapitalization*.

Table 16-1
Data on Forsyth Products Corporation

I. Balance Sheet on 12/31/81

Current assets	$ 500,000	Debt	$	0
Net fixed assets	500,000	Common equity		
		(1.0 million shares outstanding)		1,000,000
Total assets	$1,000,000	Total claims		$ 1,000,000

II. Income Statement for 1981

Sales		$20,000,000
Fixed operating costs	$ 4,000,000	
Variable operating costs	12,000,000	16,000,000
Earnings before interest and taxes (EBIT)		$ 4,000,000
Interest		0
Taxable income		$ 4,000,000
Taxes (40%)		1,600,000
Net income after taxes		$ 2,400,000

III. Other Data

1. Earnings per share = EPS = $2,400,000/1,000,000 shares = $2.40.
2. Dividends per share = DPS = $2,400,000/1,000,000 shares = $2.40.
3. Book value per share = $1,000,000/1,000,000 shares = $1.
4. Market price per share = P_0 = $20. Thus, the stock sells at 20 times its book value.
5. Price/earnings ratio = P/E = $20/2.40 = 8.33 times.
6. Dividend yield = DPS/P_0 = $2.40/$20 = 12%.

will be paid out as dividends, and its earnings and dividends are not expected to grow.

Now assume that FPC's financial manager consults with investment bankers and learns that debt can be sold, but the more debt used, the riskier the debt, hence the higher the interest rate (k_d) will be. Also, the company learns that the more debt it uses, the greater the riskiness of its stock, hence the higher will be its required rate of return on equity (k_s). Estimates of k_d, beta, and k_s at different debt levels are given in Table 16-2, and Figure 16-5 presents these data in graph form.

Given the data in Tables 16-1 and 16-2, we can determine FPC's total market value at different capital structures and then use this information to establish its stock price. These equations are used in the analysis:

$$V = D + S. \tag{16-1}$$

$$S = \frac{\text{Net income after taxes}}{k_s} = \frac{(\text{EBIT} - k_dD)(1 - t)}{k_s}. \tag{16-2}$$

$$P_0 = \frac{DPS}{k_s} = \frac{EPS}{k_s} \text{ when DPS = EPS and } g = 0. \qquad (16\text{-}3)$$

$$k_a = (D/V)(k_d)(1 - t) + (S/V)(k_s). \qquad (16\text{-}4)$$

Here, V is the total market value of the firm, D is the market value of the debt, S is the market value of the stock, DPS is the dividends per share, and all other terms are as defined in Chapter 15.

Table 16-2
FPC's Cost of Debt and Equity at Different Levels of Debt

Amount Borrowed[a] (1)	Interest Rate on All Debt, k_d (2)	Estimated Beta Coefficient of Stock, b (3)	Required Rate of Return on Stock, k_s[b] (4)
$ 0	—	1.50	12.0%
2,000,000	8.0%	1.55	12.2
4,000,000	8.3	1.65	12.6
6,000,000	9.0	1.80	13.2
8,000,000	10.0	2.00	14.0
10,000,000	12.0	2.30	15.2
12,000,000	15.0	2.70	16.8
14,000,000	18.0	3.25	19.0

[a] The firm is unable to borrow more than $14 million because of limitations on interest coverage in its corporate charter.

[b] We assume that R_F = 6% and k_M = 10%. Therefore, at zero debt, k_s = 6% + 1.5(10% − 6%) = 6% + 6% = 12%. Other values of k_s are calculated similarly.

Equation 16-1 is simply a definition which recognizes that the total value of the firm is equal to the value of the debt plus the value of the equity. Equation 16-2 has what amounts to an income statement laid out horizontally in the numerator, and, since the firm is not growing, its net income is a constant. Hence, the net income represents a perpetuity, so the present value of the net income, which is the value of the stock, may be found by dividing by k_s.[10] Equation 16-3 is derived from 16-2 by dividing both sides by n, the number of shares outstanding, to put things on

[10] To derive Equation 16-2, first note that the numerator is, in essence, an income statement written out horizontally as an equation rather than vertically as in accounting statements:

$$\underbrace{\text{Sales} - \frac{\text{Operating}}{\text{expenses}}}_{\text{EBIT}} - \underbrace{\text{Interest}}_{k_d D} - \underbrace{\text{Taxes}}_{T} = \text{Net income available to common}$$

Taxes are equal to $(EBIT - k_d)t$, so

$$(EBIT - k_d D) - (EBIT - k_d D)t = \text{Net income to common}$$
$$(EBIT - k_d D)(1 - t) = \text{Net income to common.}$$

Since all income is paid out as dividends, and since no growth is expected, the stock is a perpetuity

(continued)

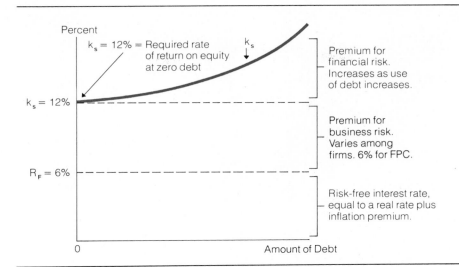

**Figure 16-5
Required Rate of Return
on FPC's Equity**

a per share basis. Finally, Equation 16-4 is simply the formula for the weighted average cost of capital as developed in Chapter 15.

We first substitute values for k_d, D, and k_s into Equation 16-2 to obtain values for S, the common equity, at each level of D, then sum S and D to find the total value of the firm. Table 16-3 was developed by this process. The values shown in Columns 1, 2, and 3 were taken from Table 16-2, while those in Column 4 were obtained by solving Equation 16-2 at different debt levels. The values for the firm given in Column 5 were obtained by summing Columns 1 and 4: D + S = V.

To see how the stock prices shown in Column 6 were developed, visualize this series of events:

1. Initially, FPC has no debt. Its value is $20 million, or $20 for each of its 1 million shares. (See the top line of Table 16-3.)
2. Management decides to change the capital structure. This decision is announced—legally, the firm *must* make an explicit announcement or run the risk of having stockholders sue the directors. (See Appendix 18A for a discussion of recapitalization through stock repurchases.)
3. The values shown in Columns 1 through 5 of Table 16-3 are estimated as described above. The major institutional investors, and the large brokerage companies which advise individual investors, have analysts just as capable of making these estimates as the firm's manage-

whose value can be found as follows:

$$S = \frac{Dividends}{k_s} = \frac{(EBIT - k_d D)(1 - t)}{k_s}. \qquad (16\text{-}2)$$

Table 16-3
Value of FPC and Its
Cost of Capital at
Different Levels of Debt

Value of Debt (D) (Millions) (1)	k_d (2)	k_s (3)	Value of Stock (S) (Millions) (4)	Value of Firm (V) (Millions) (5)	Stock Price (P) (6)	D/V (7)	k_a (8)
$ 0	8.0%	12.0%	$20.000	$20.000	$20.00	0.0%	12.0%
2.0	8.0	12.2	18.885	20.885	20.89	9.6	11.5
4.0	8.3	12.6	17.467	21.467	21.47	18.6	11.2
6.0	9.0	13.2	15.727	21.727	21.73 (Max.)	27.6	11.0 (Min.)
8.0	10.0	14.0	13.714	21.714	21.71	36.8	11.1
10.0	12.0	15.2	11.053	21.053	21.05	47.5	11.4
12.0	15.0	16.8	7.857	19.857	19.86	60.4	12.1
14.0	18.0	19.0	3.160	17.160	17.16	81.6	12.3

Notes:

1. Values shown in Columns 1 through 3 were taken from Table 16-2.
2. Values for S in Column 4 were found by use of Equation 16-2:

$$S = \frac{\text{Net income after taxes}}{k_s} = \frac{(EBIT - k_dD)(1 - t)}{k_a}. \qquad (16\text{-}2)$$

For example, at D = $0,

$$S = \frac{(\$4.0 - 0)(0.6)}{0.12} = \frac{\$2.4}{0.12} = \$20.0 \text{ million},$$

while at D = $6.0,

$$S = \frac{[\$4.0 - 0.09(6.0)](0.6)}{0.132} = \frac{\$2.076}{0.132} = \$15.727 \text{ million}.$$

3. Values for V in Column 5 were obtained as the sum of D + S. For example, at D = $6.0, V = $6.0 + $15.727 = $21.727 million.
4. The stock prices shown in Column 6 are equal to the value of the firm as shown in Column 5 divided by the original number of shares outstanding, which in this case is 1 million. The logic behind this statement is explained in the text.
5. Column 7 is found by dividing Column 1 by Column 5. For example, at D = $6, D/V = $6/$21.727 = 27.6%.
6. Column 8 is found by use of Equation 16-4. For example, $k_a = (D/V)(k_d)(1 - t) + (S/V)k_s = (0.276)(9\%)(0.6) + (0.724)(13.2\%) = 11.0\%$.

ment. They would start making their own estimates as soon as FPC announced the planned change in leverage, and they would presumably reach the same conclusions as the FPC analysts.

4. FPC's stockholders initially own the entire company. (There are not yet any bondholders.) They see, through their advisor-analysts, that very shortly the value of the enterprise will rise from $20 million to some higher amount, presumably the maximum attainable, or $21,727,000. Thus, they anticipate that the value of the firm will increase by $1,727,000.

5. This additional $1,727,000 will accrue to the firm's stockholders. Since there are 1 million shares of stock, each share will rise in value by $1.73, or from $20 to $21.73.

6. This price increase will occur *before* the transaction is completed. Sup-

pose, for example, that the stock price remained at $20 after the announcement of the recapitalization plan. Shrewd investors would recognize that the stock's price will soon go up to $21.73, and they would place orders to buy at any price below $21.73. This buying pressure would quickly run the price up to $21.73, at which point it would remain constant. Thus, $21.73 is defined as the *equilibrium stock price* for FPC once the decision has been made to recapitalize.

7. The firm sells $6 million of bonds at a cost of 9 percent. This money is used to buy stock at the market price, which is now $21.73, so 276,116 shares are repurchased:

$$\text{Shares repurchased} = \frac{\$6,000,000}{\$21.73} = 276,116.$$

8. The value of the stock after the 276,116 shares have been repurchased and retired is $15,727,000, as shown in Column 4 of Table 16-3. There are 1,000,000 − 276,116 = 723,884 shares still outstanding, so the value per share of the remaining stock is

$$\text{Value per share} = \frac{\$15,727,000}{723,884} = \$21.73.$$

This confirms our earlier calculation of the equilibrium stock price.

9. The same process was used to find stock prices at other capital structures; these prices are given in Column 6 of Table 16-3. *Since the maximum price occurs when FPC uses $6 million of debt, its optimal capital structure calls for $6 million of debt.*

10. In this example, it was assumed that EBIT would decline from $4 million to $3.52 million if the firm's debt rose to $14 million. The reason for the decline is that, at this level of debt, managers and employees would be worried about the firm's failing and about losing their jobs; suppliers would not sell to the firm on favorable credit terms; orders would be lost because of customers' fears that the company might go bankrupt and thus be unable to deliver; and so on. EBIT is generally independent of financial leverage, but at an extreme degree of leverage, EBIT is adversely affected.

11. Quite obviously, the situation in the real world is much more complex, and less exact, than this example suggests. Most important, different investors will have different estimates for EBIT and k_s, and hence will form different expectations about the equilibrium stock price. This means that the firm may have to pay more than $21.73 to repurchase the 276,116 shares, or perhaps that the shares can be bought at a lower price. These changes would cause the optimal amount of debt to be somewhat higher or lower than $6 million. Still, $6 million represents our best guess as to the optimal level, hence it is the level we should use as our target capital structure.

12. The average cost of capital for the various levels of debt is shown in

**Figure 16-6
Relationship between
FPC's Capital Structure,
Cost of Capital, and
Stock Price**

Column 8 of Table 16-3. It can be seen that the minimum cost of capital (11.0%) corresponds to the level of debt at which the value of the firm and its stock price are maximized, $6.0 million.

The stock price and cost of capital relationships developed in Table 16-3 are graphed in Figure 16-6. Here we see that FPC's stock price is maximized and its weighted average cost of capital is minimized at a D/V ratio of 27.6 percent.[11]

Further Analysis of Leverage and Stock Prices

We can use the concepts developed above to examine the effects of debt on stock prices under two somewhat different conditions: (1) where the firm goes from zero debt to some positive level of debt, and (2) where the firm changes its debt from one non-zero level to some other level. Such effects are analyzed with this new equation:

$$P = \frac{\text{Ending value of firm} - \text{Beginning amount of debt}}{\text{Beginning number of shares}}. \quad (16\text{-}5)$$

Here the beginning amount of debt would be zero for a debt-free company but some positive number for firms with debt. In Equation 16-5, there is a different ending value and a different P at each level of debt.

Example 1. Suppose we wish to determine what would happen to FPC's stock price if it went from zero debt to $4 million of debt. This requires us to find V and P with $4 million of debt:

$$V = D + S$$
$$= D + \frac{(\text{EBIT} - k_d D)(1 - t)}{k_s}$$
$$= \$4,000,000 + \frac{(\$4,000,000 - \$332,000)(0.6)}{0.126}$$
$$= \$4,000,000 + \$17,466,667 = \$21,466,667.$$

$$P = \frac{\text{Ending value} - \text{Beginning debt}}{\text{Beginning shares}}$$
$$= \frac{\$21,466,667 - \$0}{1,000,000}$$
$$= \$21.47, \text{ versus } \$20 \text{ with zero debt.}$$

[11] Notice that the leverage ratio, D/V, is expressed in *market value*, not book value (D/A), terms. FPC does, of course, have some given amount of assets, so we could calculate the D/A ratio with the optimal amount of debt. However, all of the analysis used to establish the optimal amount of debt must be based on market values.

As explained above, this stock price would exist *as soon as investors learned of the recapitalization plans, before the plans were actually carried out.* Stockholders would recognize that the company will have a value of $21,466,667 very shortly, and this value will belong entirely to them because presently there is no debt outstanding. Note also that management must inform all stockholders of the planned recapitalization. If you were a stockholder, you would certainly not be willing to sell your stock back to the company at $20 per share, only to see the stock price then rise to $21.47. You and the other stockholders would insist on receiving as much if you sold your stock as you would end up with if you chose not to sell it.[12]

Once the plan has been carried out, the shares outstanding will decline from 1,000,000 to 813,694.

$$n_1 = n_0 - \text{Shares repurchased}$$

$$= n_0 - \frac{\text{Incremental debt}}{\text{Price per share}}$$

$$= 1,000,000 - \frac{\$4,000,000}{\$21.47}$$

$$= 1,000,000 - 186,306 = 813,694 \text{ shares after repurchase.}$$

Check on stock price:

$$P = \frac{\text{New value of equity}}{\text{New shares outstanding}} = \frac{S_1}{n_1} = \frac{\$17,466,667}{813,694} = \$21.47.$$

Had we made similar calculations, but used $6 million of debt, the resulting stock price would have been $21.73 as shown in Table 16-3.

Example 2. Now assume that we are analyzing another company, called Firm D, which has exactly the same characteristics as FPC with $4 million of debt. What would happen to Firm D's stock price if it increased its leverage from $4 million to $6 million of debt? Assume that its old debt must be retired if new debt is issued, so the entire $6 million of debt will have a cost of 9 percent (from Table 16-2). Firm D has these initial values:

$$\text{Original debt} = \$4 \text{ million.}$$
$$\text{Original shares} = 813,694.$$
$$\text{Original value} = \$21,466,667.$$
$$\text{Original price} = \$21.47.$$

---

[12] Indeed, if you and other stockholders were silly enough to sell at $20 per share, then the $4 million of debt could be used to buy and retire even more shares, so the remaining shares would be worth even more than $21.47. In fact, the stock would, under these conditions, be worth $21.83:

(continued)

The new equilibrium value will be

$$V = \$6,000,000 + \frac{(\$4,000,000 - \$540,000)(0.6)}{0.132}$$
$$= \$6,000,000 + \$15,727,272 = \$21,727,272,$$

and the new equilibrium price will be

$$P = \frac{\text{New value} - \text{Beginning debt}}{\text{Beginning shares}} = \frac{\$21,727,272 - \$4,000,000}{813,694}$$
$$= \frac{\$17,727,272}{813,694} = \$21.79.$$

Thus, Firm D can increase the value of its stock from \$21.47 to \$21.79 by increasing its leverage from \$4 million to \$6 million.[13]

Although management's primary focus is on stock prices, the effect of capital structure changes on earnings per share is also of interest. Table 16-4 shows how expected EPS varies with changes in financial leverage. The top third of the table begins with a probability distribution of sales, then shows EBIT at sales of \$10 million, \$20 million, and \$30 million. Notice that here *EBIT is assumed not to depend on financial leverage.*[14]

The Effect of Financial Leverage on EPS

$$P = \frac{\$17,466,667}{1,000,000 - (\$4,000,000/\$20)} = \$21.83.$$

Of course, you might be afraid that the recapitalization plan would fall through, so you might be willing to sell out for slightly less than \$21.47, figuring that, say, \$21 in the hand is better than \$21.47 in the bush.

[13] Notice the slight difference in equilibrium stock prices at \$6 million of debt for FPC and Firm D: \$21.73 versus \$21.79. This difference demonstrates two important facts: (1) if FPC could move to its optimal capital structure in stages, it would repurchase shares at a lower average price than the equilibrium price of \$21.73, and (2) if it could buy back shares at a lower price, its final price would be higher because more shares could be repurchased for a given expenditure (debt raised), hence fewer shares would be outstanding in the end.

[14] As we discuss in detail in Chapter 17, capital structure does at times affect EBIT. First, if debt levels are excessive, the firm will probably not be able to finance at all if its earnings are low at a time when interest rates are high. This could lead to stop-start operations and/or to the necessity of passing up good investment opportunities. Second, a weak financial situation brought on by too much debt could cause a firm to lose contracts. For example, companies such as General Motors examine closely the financial strength of potential suppliers, and if they are so weak that they might not be able to deliver materials as called for in the contract, they simply will not get the business. Third, financially strong companies are able to bargain hard with unions as well as other suppliers; weaker companies may have to give in simply because they do not have the financial resources to carry on the fight. And fourth, a company with so much debt that bankruptcy is a serious threat will have difficulty attracting and retaining managers and employees, or will have to pay them premium salaries. People value job security, and financially weak companies simply cannot provide such protection. For all these reasons, it is not totally correct to state that a firm's financing policy does not affect its operating income, and on this basis we estimate that FPC's EBIT would fall from \$4 million to \$3.52 million if the level of debt rose to \$14 million.

Table 16-4
FPC's EPS at Different
Amounts of Debt ($ in
Millions except per
Share Figures)

Probability of Indicated Sales	0.2	0.6	0.2
Sales	$10.00	$20.00	$30.00
Fixed costs	4.00	4.00	4.00
Variable costs (60% of sales)	6.00	12.00	18.00
Total costs (except interest)	$10.00	$16.00	$22.00
Earnings before interest and taxes (EBIT)	$ 0.00	$ 4.00	$ 8.00
Zero Debt			
Less interest	$ 0.00	$ 0.00	$ 0.00
Earnings before taxes	0.00	4.00	8.00
Less taxes (40%)	0.00	1.60	3.20
Net income after taxes	$ 0.00	$ 2.40	$ 4.80
Earnings per share on 1 million shares (EPS)	$ 0.00	$ 2.40	$ 4.80
Expected EPS		$ 2.40	
Standard deviation of EPS[a]		$ 1.52	
$10 Million of Debt			
Less interest (0.12 × $10,000,000)	$ 1.20	$ 1.20	$ 1.20
Earnings before taxes	(1.20)	2.80	6.80
Less taxes (40%)[b]	(0.48)	1.12	2.72
Net income after taxes	($ 0.72)	$ 1.68	$ 4.08
Earnings per share on 524,940 shares (EPS)[c]	($ 1.37)	$ 3.20	$ 7.77
Expected EPS		$ 3.20	
Standard deviation of EPS[a]		$ 2.90	

[a]Procedures for calculating the standard deviation are discussed in Chapter 5.

[b]Assume tax credit on losses.

[c]Shares outstanding is determined as follows:

$$\text{Shares} = \text{Original shares} - \frac{\text{Debt}}{\text{Stock price}} = 1,000,000 - \frac{\text{Debt}}{\text{Stock price}},$$

where the stock price is taken from Table 16-3, Column 6. With $10 million of debt, P = $21.05. After the recapitalization, 524,940 shares will remain outstanding:

$$\text{Shares} = 1,000,000 - \frac{\$10,000,000}{\$21.05} = 524,940.$$

EPS figures can also be calculated using this formula:

$$\text{EPS} = \frac{(\text{EBIT} - k_d D)(1 - t)}{\text{Original shares} - \text{Debt/Price}}.$$

For example, at D = $10 million,

$$\text{EPS} = \frac{(4,000,000 - 0.12 \times 10,000,000)(0.6)}{1,000,000 - \$10,000,000/\$21.05} = \frac{\$1,680,000}{524,940} = \$3.20.$$

The middle third of Table 16-4 shows the situation if FPC continues to use no debt. Net income after taxes is divided by the 1 million shares outstanding to calculate EPS. If sales are as low as $10 million, EPS will be zero, but EPS will rise to $4.80 at sales of $30 million.

The EPS at each sales level is next multiplied by the probability of that sales level to calculate the expected EPS, which is $2.40 if FPC uses no debt.[15] We also calculate the standard deviation of EPS to get an idea of the firm's risk at a zero debt ratio: $\sigma_{EPS} = \$1.52$.[16]

The lower third of the table shows the financial results that would occur if the company decided to use $10 million of debt. The interest rate on the debt, 12 percent, is taken from Table 16-2. With $10 million of 12 percent debt outstanding, the company's interest expense in Table 16-4 is $1.2 million per year. This is a fixed cost, and it is deducted from EBIT as calculated in the top section. Next, taxes are taken out, and we work on down to the EPS figures that will result at each sales level. With $10 million of debt, EPS will be −$1.37 if sales are as low as $10 million; it will rise to $3.20 if sales are $20 million; and it will soar to $7.77 if sales are as high as $30 million.

The EPS distributions under the two financial structures are graphed in Figure 16-7. Although expected EPS is much higher if the firm uses financial leverage, the graph makes it clear that the risk of low or even negative EPS is also higher if debt is used.

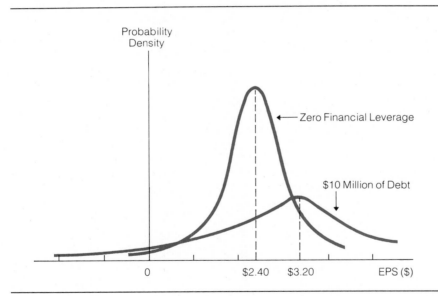

**Figure 16-7
Probability Distribution
of EPS for FPC with
Different Amounts of
Financial Leverage**

[15] Expected EPS = 0.2(0.0) + 0.6($2.40) + 0.2($4.80) = $2.40.

[16] See Chapter 5 for a review of procedures for calculating standard deviations. Also, it should be noted that it is sometimes useful to go one step further in this analysis and to calculate the *coefficient of variation*, which is the standard deviation of EPS divided by expected EPS:

Coefficient of variation = (σ_{EPS})/(Expected EPS) = $1.52/$2.40 = 0.63.

The advantage of the coefficient of variation is that it permits better comparisons when the mean values of EPS vary, as they do here. Still, for illustrative purposes we shall use standard deviations rather than coefficients of variation.

Table 16-5
FPC's Expected EPS and Standard Deviation with Different Degrees of Financial Leverage[a]

Debt	Expected EPS	Standard Deviation of EPS
$ 0	$2.40	$1.52
2,000,000	2.55	1.68
4,000,000	2.70	1.87
6,000,000	2.87	2.09
8,000,000	3.04	2.40
10,000,000	3.20	2.90
12,000,000	3.30	3.83
14,000,000	3.26	5.20

[a]Values for zero and $10 million of debt are taken from Table 16-4. Values at other debt levels were calculated similarly.

These relationships between expected EPS, risk, and financial leverage are extended in Table 16-5 and Figure 16-8. Here we see that expected EPS rises for a while as the use of debt increases; interest charges rise, but a smaller number of shares outstanding as debt is substituted for equity still causes EPS to increase. However, EPS peaks when $12 million of debt is used. Beyond this amount, interest rates rise rapidly and EBIT

Figure 16-8
Relationship between FPC's Expected EPS, Risk, and Financial Leverage

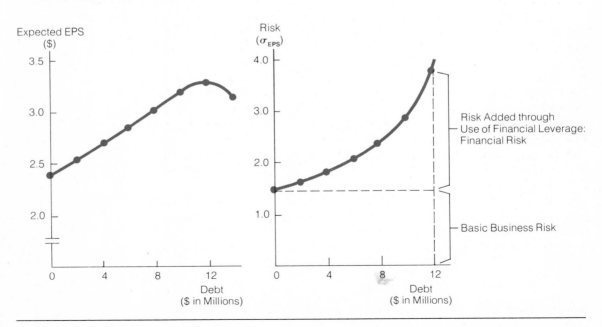

begins to fall, so that EPS is depressed in spite of the falling number of shares outstanding. Risk, as measured by the standard deviation of EPS, rises continuously and at an increasing rate as debt is substituted for equity.

We see, then, that using leverage involves a risk-return tradeoff—higher leverage increases expected earnings per share (at least for a while), but using more leverage also increases the firm's risk. It was this increasing risk that caused k_s to increase in Table 16-2 at higher amounts of financial leverage.

EPS versus Stock Prices

Using the example of FPC, we have seen how financial leverage affects both stock prices and EPS. In each case, we saw that the variable we are interested in (stock price or EPS) first rises with leverage, then hits a peak, and finally declines. Does the same amount of debt maximize both price and EPS? The answer is *no*. As we can see in Figure 16-9, FPC's stock price is maximized with $6 million of debt, while expected EPS is maximized by using $12 million of debt. *Since management is primarily interested in maximizing the value of the stock, the optimal capital structure calls for the use of $6 million of debt.*

Taxes, Bankruptcy Costs, and the Value of the Firm

Why does the expected stock price first rise as the firm begins to use financial leverage, then hit a peak, and finally decline when leverage becomes excessive? This pattern occurs primarily because of *corporate income taxes* and *bankruptcy-related costs*. Since interest on debt is tax deductible, the more debt a firm has, the greater the proportion of its operating income that flows through to investors, hence the higher the value of the firm. On the other hand, the larger the debt, the greater the risk of bankruptcy. At very high levels of debt, the odds are very great that bankruptcy will occur, and if this happens, lawyers may end up with almost as much of the firm's assets as do the investors.[17]

Figure 16-10, which is taken from Chapter 17, illustrates this concept. With zero debt, the firm's value is V_0. As it begins to use debt, the total market value (and consequently the stock price) begins to rise because of the tax shelter benefits of debt. Prior to D_1, potential bankruptcy costs are insignificant. However, at D_1 investors begin to worry about the effects of debt, so potential bankruptcy costs begin to offset the debt tax shelter benefits. At D_2, the marginal tax shelter benefits are equal to marginal potential bankruptcy costs, and the value of the firm is maximized. Beyond D_2, potential bankruptcy costs more than offset the benefits of ad-

---

[17] See Chapter 21 for a discussion of bankruptcy costs. Also, as noted earlier, the threat of potential bankruptcy can have a severe adverse effect on a firm's operations and income, hence on its value.

**Figure 16-9
Relationship between
FPC's Expected EPS
and Stock Price**

ditional debt, so further increases in leverage reduce the firm's value. Thus, D_2 represents the optimal capital structure.

This entire concept—including (1) why the tax shelter benefits cause a linear increase in value, (2) the specific elements that make up "bankruptcy-related costs," and (3) the effects of personal income taxes on capital structure decisions—is discussed in Chapter 17, "Theory of Capital Structure."

Figure 16-10
Effect of Leverage on the
Value of the Firm

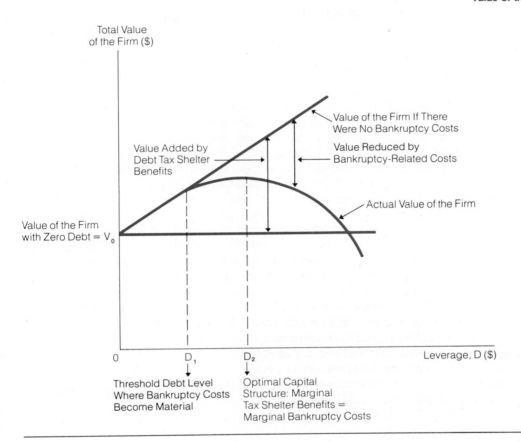

There are some difficult problems with the type of analysis described in the preceding sections, including the following:

1. Because of the difficulties in determining exactly how equity capital-ization rates (k_s values) are affected by different degrees of financial leverage, management rarely, if ever, has sufficient confidence in this type of analysis to use it as the sole determinant of the target capital structure.[18]

Other Factors Influencing the Capital Structure Decision

[18] The statistical relationship between k_s and financial leverage has been studied extensively by use of both cross-sectional and time series data. In the cross-sectional studies, a sample of firms is analyzed, with multiple regression techniques used in an attempt to "hold constant" all factors other than financial leverage that might influence k_s. The general conclusion of the cross-sectional studies is that k_s rises as leverage increases, but statistical problems preclude us from specifying the functional relationship with much confidence.

(continued)

2. Many firms are not publicly owned. If the owners plan never to have the firm go public, then potential market value data are irrelevant. However, an analysis based on market values for a privately owned firm is useful if the owner is interested in knowing how the market value of the firm would be affected by leverage should the decision be made to go public.

3. Even for publicly owned firms, the managers may be more or less "conservative" than the average stockholder, hence may set a somewhat different target capital structure than the one that would maximize the stock price. The managers of a publicly owned firm would never admit this, for unless they owned voting control, they would quickly be removed from office. However, in view of the uncertainties about what constitutes the value-maximizing structure, management could always say that the target capital structure employed is, in its judgment, the value-maximizing structure, and it would be difficult to prove otherwise.

4. Managers of large firms, especially those providing vital services such as electricity or telephones, have a responsibility to provide *continuous* service, so they must refrain from using leverage to the point where the firm's long-run viability is endangered. Long-run viability may conflict with short-run stock price maximization.[19]

5. Our formal analysis was restricted to the case of a no-growth firm. Models have been developed for the growth case, but they are quite complex. In view of the input requirements for even the simple no-growth model, and the still greater ones for the growth model, it is unrealistic to think that a precisely accurate optimal capital structure can really be identified.[20]

For all of these reasons, managers are very much concerned with the effects of financial leverage on the risk of bankruptcy, so an analysis of this factor is an important input in the capital structure decision. Accordingly, managements give considerable weight to such ratios as the *times-interest-earned ratio* (TIE). The lower this ratio, the higher the probability that a firm will default on its debt and be forced into bankruptcy.

In the time series studies, a single firm's k_s is analyzed over time in an attempt to see how it changes in response to changes in its debt ratio, or, perhaps, how it changes in relation to changes in the economy. Here again, "other things" do not remain constant, so it is impossible to specify exactly how k_s is affected by financial leverage.

[19] Recognizing this fact, most public service commissions require utilities to obtain their approval before issuing long-term securities, and Congress has empowered the SEC to supervise the capital structures of public utility holding companies. However, in addition to concern over the firms' safety, which suggests low debt ratios, both managers and regulators recognize a need to keep all costs as low as possible, including the cost of capital. Since a firm's capital structure affects its cost of capital, regulatory commissions and utility managers try to select capital structures that minimize the cost of capital, subject to the constraint that the firm's solvency is not endangered.

[20] Ezra Solomon, *The Theory of Financial Management* (New York: Columbia University Press, 1963).

Amounts of Debt ($ in Millions)	Expected TIE[a]	
$ 0	Undefined	
2	25.0	
4	12.1	
6	7.4	
8	5.0	
10	3.3	
12	2.2	

**Table 16-6
Expected Times-Interest-Earned Ratio at Different Amounts of Debt**

[a]$TIE = \dfrac{EBIT}{Interest}$

Example: $TIE = \dfrac{\$4,000,000}{\$1,200,000} = 3.3$ at $10 million of debt.

Data are from Tables 16-1 and 16-2.

Table 16-6 shows how FPC's expected TIE ratio declines as the use of debt increases. When only $2 million of debt is used, the expected TIE is a high 25 times, but the interest coverage ratio declines rapidly as debt rises. Note, however, that these coverages are the expected values—the actual TIE will be higher if sales exceed the expected $20 million level, but lower if sales fall below $20 million.

The variability of the TIE ratios is highlighted in Figure 16-11, which shows the probability distributions of the ratios at $8 million and $12 million of debt. The expected TIE is much higher if only $8 million of debt is used. Even more important, with more debt there is a much higher prob-

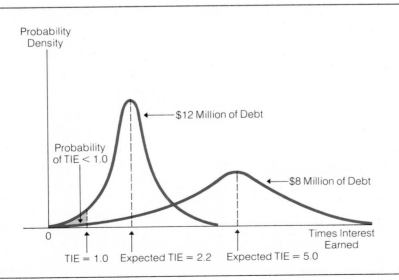

**Figure 16-11
Probability Distributions of Times-Interest-Earned Ratios for FPC with Different Capital Structures**

ability of a TIE of less than 1.0, the level at which the firm is not earning enough to meet its required interest payment and is thus seriously exposed to the threat of bankruptcy.

Checklist for Capital Structure Decisions

In addition to the problems discussed above, the firm must also consider the following factors, which have an important, though hard to measure, bearing on the choice of a target capital structure:

1. Sales Stability. If its sales are relatively stable, a firm can safely take on more debt and incur higher fixed charges than can a company with unstable sales. Utility companies, because of their stable demand, have thus been able to undertake more debt financing than have industrial firms.

2. Asset Structure. Firms whose assets are suitable as security for loans tend to use debt rather heavily. Thus, real estate companies tend to be highly leveraged, while companies involved in technological research employ less debt.

3. Operating Leverage. Other things the same, a firm with less operating leverage is better able to employ financial leverage. Appendix 16A shows how operating and financial leverage interact to determine the overall impact of a decline in sales on operating income and net cash flows.

4. Growth Rate. Other things the same, faster growing firms must rely more heavily on external capital (see Chapter 7). Further, the flotation costs involved in selling common stock exceed those incurred when selling debt. Thus, rapidly growing firms tend to use somewhat more debt than do slower-growth companies.

5. Profitability. One often observes that firms with very high rates of return on investment use relatively little debt. Although there is no theoretical justification for this fact, the practical reason seems to be that very profitable firms such as IBM, 3M, and Xerox simply do not need to do much debt financing—their high rates of return enable them to do most of their financing with retained earnings.

6. Taxes. Interest is a deductible expense, while dividends are not deductible. Hence, the higher a firm's corporate tax rate, the greater the advantage of using debt. This point is developed in more detail in Chapter 17.

7. Control. The effect that debt or stock financing might have on a management's control position may influence its capital structure decision. If management has voting control (over 50 percent of the stock) but is not in a position to buy any more stock, debt may be the choice for new financings. On the other hand, a management group that is not concerned about voting control may decide to use equity rather than debt if the firm's financial situation is so weak that the use of debt might subject the firm to serious risk of default; if the firm goes into default, the managers will almost surely lose their jobs. However, if too little debt is used, management runs the risk of a takeover attempt; here some other company or management group tries to persuade stockholders to turn over control to the new group, which may plan to boost earnings and stock prices by using financial leverage. In general, control considerations do not necessarily suggest the use of debt or equity, but if management is at all insecure, the effects of capital structure on control will certainly be taken into account.

8. Management Attitudes. In the absence of proof that one capital structure will lead to higher stock prices than another, management can exercise its own judgment about a proper capital structure. Some managements tend to be more conservative than others and thus use less debt than the average firm in their industry, while for other managements the reverse is true.

9. Lender and Rating Agency Attitudes. Regardless of managers' own analyses of the proper leverage factors for their firms, there is no question but that lenders' and rating agencies' attitudes are frequently important determinants of financial structures. In the majority of cases, the corporation discusses its financial structure with lenders and rating agencies, and gives much weight to their advice. But when management is so confident of the future that it seeks to use leverage beyond the norms for its industry, lenders may be unwilling to accept such debt increases, or may do so only at a high price.

10. Market Conditions. Conditions in the stock and bond markets undergo both long- and short-run changes which can have an important bearing on a firm's optimal capital structure. For example, during the credit crunch in the winter of 1981, there was simply no market at any "reasonable" interest rate for new long-term bonds rated below A. Low-rated companies that needed capital were forced to go to the stock market or to the short-term debt market. Actions such as this could represent either permanent changes in target capital structures or temporary departures from stable targets, but the important point is that stock and bond market conditions do influence the type of securities used for a given financing.

11. The Firm's Internal Condition. A firm's own internal conditions also have a bearing on its target capital structure. For example, suppose a firm has just successfully completed an R&D program and projects higher earnings in the immediate future. However, the new earnings are not yet anticipated by investors, hence are not reflected in the price of the stock. This company would not want to issue stock—it would prefer to finance with debt until the higher earnings materialize and are reflected in the stock price, at which time it might want to sell an issue of common stock, retire the debt, and return to its target capital structure.

Variations in Capital Structures among Firms

As might be expected, wide variations in the use of financial leverage occur both among industries and among the individual firms in each industry. Table 16-7 illustrates this point. Retailers make heavy use of debt, especially short-term debt used to carry inventories. Manufacturing companies as a group use less debt, especially short-term debt. Within manufacturing, small firms with limited access to the stock market employ the most debt, and again the bulk of their liabilities are short-term. The majority of the debt shown for small manufacturers represents trade credit, although the data in the table are not broken down enough to indicate this.

Table 16-7
Capital Components as a Percentage of Total Capital, 1981

	Current Liabilities	Long-Term Debt	Total Liabilities	Equity
Retail trade	37%	23%	60%	40%
Manufacturing (all sizes)	33	17	50	50
Assets under $5 million	35	19	54	46
Assets over $5 million	32	17	49	51
Selected manufacturing industries				
Aircraft	56	12	68	32
Electrical machinery	35	19	55	45
Steel	24	31	55	45
Drugs	21	19	40	60

Source: Federal Trade Commission, *Quarterly Financial Reports.*

Financing mixes also vary widely among manufacturing sectors. Aircraft companies are highly leveraged, borrowing heavily on a short-term basis to finance the construction of airplanes. Because of their long production cycle, aircraft manufacturers have large work-in-process inventories that must be financed. Aircraft manufacturers receive advances from their customers, and these advances are shown as current liabilities. Like the aircraft companies, manufacturers of electrical equipment also have long construction periods—for example, nuclear reactors take years to build—and short-term credit is often used to finance this construction. The drug companies, on the other hand, do not use much debt. Their production period is short, and the uncertainties inherent in an industry that is both oriented toward research and development and exposed to lawsuits arising from adverse reactions to its products render the heavy use of leverage unwise.[21]

Summary

In this chapter, we examined the effects of financial leverage on stock prices, earnings per share, and the cost of capital. Our conclusions here are consistent with generally accepted capital structure theory as it is developed in the following chapter.

The analysis suggests that some *optimal capital structure* exists which simultaneously maximizes the firm's total market value and its stock price while minimizing its average cost of capital. However, although it is theoretically possible to determine the optimal capital structure, as a practical matter we cannot estimate this structure with precision. Accordingly, financial executives generally treat the optimal capital structure as a range—for example, 40 to 50 percent debt—rather than as a precise point such as 45 percent. Also, financial executives analyze the effects of different capital structures on expected earnings per share and interest coverage ratios, rather than concentrate exclusively on imprecisely estimated market values. Firms also tend to analyze such factors as sales stability, asset structure, effects on control, and so on, and the final target capital structure is more judgmentally than rigorously determined.

This discussion is extended in the next chapter, where we review the major developments in the theory of finance. A study of the theory will provide a deeper understanding of the factors that determine the optimal capital structure. As we shall see, the primary advantage of debt is the tax shelter it provides—corporate income transmitted to investors as interest payments on debt is not subject to corporate income taxes. The primary disadvantages of debt are associated with costs that arise as a result of actual or potential bankruptcy. The optimal capital structure involves a trade-off between these tax advantages and potential bankruptcy costs.

Questions

16-1 What is the uncertainty inherent in projections of future operating income called?

16-2 Firms with relatively high nonfinancial fixed costs are said to have a high degree of what?

---

[21] It should be noted that Table 16-7 is based on accounting (or book) values. Stated on a market value basis, the results would be somewhat different. Most important, the equity percentage would rise because most stocks sell at prices higher than their book values. If inflation continues in the 1980s at the same rate as in the 1970s, one could expect to find (1) book value of equity ratios as in Table 16-7 declining but (2) market value ratios remaining about constant.

16-3 "One type of leverage affects both EBIT and EPS. The other type affects only EPS." Explain what the statement means.

16-4 What is the relationship between *market* (or beta) risk and leverage?

16-5 Why is the following statement true? "Other things being the same, firms with relatively stable sales are able to carry relatively high debt ratios."

16-6 Why do public utility companies usually pursue a different financial policy from that of retail firms?

16-7 Some economists believe that swings in business cycles will not be as wide in the future as they have been in the past. Assuming that they are correct in their analysis, what effect might this added stability have on the types of financing used by firms in the United States? Would your answer be true for all firms?

16-8 Why is EBIT generally considered to be independent of financial leverage? Why might EBIT actually be influenced by financial leverage at high debt levels?

16-9 If a firm with no debt could buy back and retire its stock at the initial price, would this result in a higher final stock price than the procedure outlined in the chapter? Would it be fair for a firm to buy back its stock without telling stockholders that stock was being repurchased?

16-10 How might increasingly volatile inflation rates, interest rates, and bond prices affect the optimal capital structure for corporations?

16-11 If a firm went from zero debt to successively higher levels of debt, why would you expect its stock price to first rise, then hit a peak, and then begin to decline?

16-12 Why is the debt level that maximizes a firm's expected EPS generally higher than the debt level that maximizes its stock price?

Self-Test Problems

ST16-1 Gentry Motors, Inc., produces turbine generators which sell for $P = \$100,000$. Gentry's fixed costs are $2,000,000; 50 generators are produced and sold each year; profits total $500,000; and Gentry's assets (all equity financed) are $5,000,000. Gentry estimates that it can change its production process, adding $4,000,000 to investment and $500,000 to fixed operating costs. This change will (1) reduce variable costs (VC) per unit by $10,000 and (2) increase output by 20 units, but (3) the sales price on all units will have to be lowered to $95,000 to permit sales of the additional output. Gentry has tax loss carry-forwards that cause its tax rate to be zero, and its cost of capital is 15 percent. Gentry uses no debt.
   a. Should Gentry make the change?
   b. Would Gentry's operating leverage increase or decrease if it made the change? What about its breakeven point?
   c. Would the new situation have more or less business risk than the old one?

ST16-2 Suppose, some years later, Gentry Motors is in this situation: (1) EBIT = $4,000,000; (2) tax rate = $t = 35\%$; (3) value of debt = $D = \$2,000,000$; (4) $k_d = 10\%$; (5) $k_s = 15\%$; (6) shares of stock outstanding = $N =$

600,000. Gentry's market is stable, and it expects no growth, so all earn-ings are paid out as dividends. The debt consists of perpetual bonds.

a. What is the total market value of Gentry's stock (S), its price per share (P_0), and the firm's total market value (V)?

b. What is Gentry's weighted average cost of capital, k_a?

c. Gentry can increase its debt by $8 million, to a total of $10 million, using the new debt to buy back and retire some of its shares. Its interest rate on all debt will be 12 percent (it will have to call and refund the old debt), and its cost of equity will rise from 15 percent to 17 percent. EBIT will remain constant. Should Gentry change its capital structure?

d. If Gentry did not have to refund the $2 million of old debt, how would this have affected things? Assume the new and the old debt are equally risky, with $k_d = 12\%$, but the coupon rate on the old debt is 10 percent.

e. What is Gentry's TIE coverage ratio under the original condition and under the conditions in Part c?

16-1 a. Given the following information, calculate the expected value and standard deviation for Firm C's EPS. $EPS_A = \$3.40$, $\sigma_A = \$2.41$, $EPS_B = \$2.80$, $\sigma_B = \$1.97$.

	Probability				
	0.1	0.2	0.4	0.2	0.1
Firm A: EPS_A	($1.00)	$1.20	$3.40	$5.60	$7.80
Firm B: EPS_B	($0.80)	$1.00	$2.80	$4.60	$6.40
Firm C: EPS_C	($1.60)	$0.90	$3.40	$5.90	$8.40

b. Discuss the relative riskiness of the three firms' earnings.

16-2 ABC, Inc., has no debt outstanding, and its financial position is given by the following data:

Assets (book = market)	$3,000,000
EBIT	$500,000
Cost of equity (k_s)	10%
Stock price (P_0)	$15
Shares outstanding (N)	200,000
Tax rate (t)	40%

The firm is considering selling bonds and simultaneously repurchasing some of its stock. If it uses $900,000 of debt, its cost of equity (k_s) will increase to 11 percent to reflect the increased risk. Bonds can be sold at a cost (k_d) of 7 percent.

a. What effect would this use of leverage have on the value of the firm?

b. What would be the price of ABC's stock?

c. What happens to the firm's earnings per share after the recapitalization? (Assume all earnings are paid out as dividends.)

16-3 The following data reflect the current financial condition of Crowell Corporation:

Value of debt (book value = market value)	$ 1,000,000
Market value of equity (P_0 × shares)	5,257,143
Total value of firm	$ 6,257,143
Sales, last 12 months	$12,000,000
Variable operating costs (50% of sales)	6,000,000
Fixed operating costs	5,000,000
Tax rate (t)	40%

At the current level of debt, the cost of debt (k_d) is 8 percent and the cost of equity (k_s) is 10.5 percent. Management questions whether or not the capital structure is optimal, so the financial vice-president has been asked to consider the possibility of issuing $1 million of additional debt and using the proceeds to repurchase stock. It is estimated that if the leverage were increased by raising the level of debt to $2 million, the interest rate on new debt would rise to 9 percent and k_s would rise to 11.5 percent. (The old 8 percent debt would remain outstanding.)

a. Should Crowell increase its debt to $2 million? (Hint: Compare the current value of the firm [V] to its value at the higher level of debt. Use the following formula, and assume [1] that the old bonds are senior to the new bonds and [2] that the value of the old debt remains at $1 million.)

$$V = D + \frac{(EBIT - I)(1 - t)}{k_s}$$

$$= D + \frac{[EBIT - 8\%(\text{Old debt}) - 9\%(\text{New debt})](1 - t)}{k_s}.$$

b. If the firm decided to increase its level of debt to $3 million, its cost of the additional $2 million of debt would be 12 percent, and k_s would rise to 15 percent. The original 8 percent debt would again remain outstanding. What level of debt should the firm choose: $1 million, $2 million, or $3 million?

c. The market price of Crowell Corporation's stock was originally $20 per share. Calculate the new equilibrium stock prices at debt levels of $2 million and $3 million.

d. Calculate the firm's earnings per share if it uses debt of $1 million, $2 million, and $3 million. Assume that the firm pays out all of its earnings as dividends. If you find that EPS increases with more debt, does this mean that the firm should choose to increase its debt to $3 million, or possibly higher?

e. What would happen to the value of the old bonds if Crowell used more leverage and the old bonds were not senior to the new bonds?

16-4 Penn Paints, Inc., has a total market value of $100 million, consisting of 1 million shares selling for $50 per share and $50 million of 10% perpetual bonds now selling at par. The company's EBIT is $15 million, and its tax rate is 30 percent. Penn Paints can change its capital structure by either increasing its debt to $70 million or decreasing it to $30 million. If it decides to *increase* its use of leverage, it must call its old bonds and issue new ones with a 12 percent coupon. If it decides to *decrease* its leverage, it will call in its old bonds and replace them with new 8 percent coupon bonds. The company will sell or repurchase stock at the new equilibrium price to complete the capital structure change.

Penn Paints pays out all earnings as dividends; hence, its stock is a zero growth stock. If it increases leverage, k_s will be 16 percent. If it decreases leverage, k_s will be 13 percent.

a. What is the cost of equity to Penn Paints at present? (Hint: $k_s = D/P + g$, with $g = 0$, where D = dividends per share.)

b. Should Penn Paints change its capital structure? Explain, and show your work.

c. Suppose the tax rate is changed to 60 percent. This would lower after-tax income and also cause a decline in the price of the stock and the value of the equity, other things held constant. Calculate the new stock price (at $50 million of debt).

d. Continue the scenario of Part c, but now re-examine the question of the optimal amount of debt. Does the tax rate change affect your decision about the optimal use of financial leverage?

e. How would your analysis of the capital structure change be modified if Penn Paints' presently outstanding debt could not be called, and did not have to be replaced, that is, if the $50 million of 10 percent debt continued even if the company issued new 12 percent bonds?

ST16-1 a. 1. Determine the variable cost per unit at present, VC:

Solutions to Self-Test Problems

$$Profit = P(Q) - FC - VC(Q)$$
$$\$500,000 = (\$100,000)(50) - \$2,000,000 - VC(50)$$
$$50VC = \$2,500,000$$
$$VC = \$50,000.$$

2. Determine the new profit level if the change is made:

$$\text{New profit} = P_2(Q_2) - FC_2 - VC_2(Q_2)$$
$$= \$95,000(70) - \$2,500,000 - (\$50,000 - \$10,000)(70)$$
$$= \$1,350,000.$$

3. Determine the incremental profit:

$$\Delta\text{Profit} = \$1,350,000 - \$500,000 = \$850,000.$$

4. Estimate the approximate rate of return on the new investment:

$$\text{ROI} = \frac{\Delta\text{Profit}}{\Delta\text{Investment}} = \frac{\$850,000}{\$4,000,000} = 21.25\%.$$

Since the ROI exceeds the 15 percent cost of capital, this analysis suggests that Gentry should go ahead with the change.

b. If we measure operating leverage by the ratio of fixed costs to total costs at the expected output, then the change would increase operating leverage:[22]

$$\text{Old: } \frac{FC}{FC + VC(Q)} = \frac{\$2,000,000}{\$2,000,000 + \$2,500,000} = 44.44\%.$$

$$\text{New: } \frac{\$2,500,000}{\$2,500,000 + \$2,800,000} = 47.17\%.$$

The change would also increase the breakeven point:

$$\text{Breakeven, old: } P(Q) = FC + VC(Q)$$

$$Q_{BE} = \frac{FC}{P - VC} = \frac{\$2,000,000}{\$100,000 - \$50,000} = 40 \text{ units.}$$

$$\text{Breakeven, new: } Q_{BE} = \frac{\$2,500,000}{\$95,000 - \$40,000} = 45.45 \text{ units.}$$

c. It is impossible to state unequivocally whether the new situation would have more or less business risk than the old one. We would need information on both the sales probability distribution and the uncertainty about variable input costs in order to make this determi-

---

[22] However, one could measure operating leverage in other ways (see Appendix 16A). The old "degree of operating leverage" is

$$\text{DOL} = \frac{Q(P - VC)}{Q(P - VC) - F} = \frac{50(\$50,000)}{50(\$50,000) - \$2,000,000} = 5.0.$$

The new DOL, at the expected sales level of 70, is

$$\text{DOL} = \frac{70(\$95,000 - \$40,000)}{70(\$55,000) - \$2,500,000} = 2.85.$$

The problem here is that we have changed both output and the sales price, so the DOLs are not really comparable.

nation. However, since a higher breakeven point, other things held constant, is more risky, the change in breakeven points—and also the higher percentage of fixed costs—suggests that the new situation is more risky.

ST16-2   a.

$$S = \frac{[EBIT - k_d(D)](1 - t)}{k_s}$$

$$= \frac{[\$4,000,000 - 0.10(\$2,000,000)](0.65)}{0.15} = \$16,466,667.$$

$$P_0 = S/N = \$16,466,667/600,000 = \$27.44.$$

$$V = D + S = \$2,000,000 + \$16,466,667 = \$18,466,667.$$

b.

$$k_a = (D/V)(k_d)(1 - t) + (S/V)(k_s)$$

$$= \left(\frac{\$2,000,000}{\$18,466,667}\right)(10\%)(0.65) + \left(\frac{\$16,466,667}{\$18,466,667}\right)(15\%)$$

$$= 14.08\%.$$

c. Under the new capital structure,

$$S = \frac{[\$4,000,000 - 0.12(\$10,000,000)](0.65)}{0.17} = \$10,705,882.$$

$$V = \$10,000,000 + \$10,705,882 = \$20,705,882.$$

The new value of the firm will thus be \$20,705,882. This value belongs to the *present* stockholders and bondholders, so we may calculate the new equilibrium price of the stock, P_{new}:

$$P_{new} = \frac{V_{new} - D_{old}}{N_{old}} = \frac{\$20,705,882 - \$2,000,000}{600,000} = \$31.1765.$$

Check: Shares repurchased $= \dfrac{\Delta Debt}{P_{new}} = \dfrac{\$8,000,000}{\$31.1765} = 256,604.$

$$P_{new} = \frac{S_{new}}{N_{new}} = \frac{\$10,705,882}{600,000 - 256,604} = \$31.1765.$$

$$k_a = \left(\frac{\$10,000,000}{\$20,705,882}\right)(12\%)(0.65) + \left(\frac{\$10,705,882}{\$20,705,882}\right)(17\%) = 12.56\%.$$

Thus, the proposed capital structure change would increase the value of the firm and the price of the stock, and lower the cost of capital. Therefore, Gentry should increase its use of financial leverage. Of course, it is possible that some amount of debt other than \$10,000,000 would result in an even higher value, but we do not have enough information to make this determination.

d. Offhand, we would expect the value of the equity and the price of the stock to rise. We would also expect the value of the old debt to decline. Further, the following will be the case:

$$S = \frac{[EBIT - I_{old} - I_{new}](1 - t)}{k_s}$$

$$= \frac{[\$4,000,000 - 0.10(\$2,000,000) - 0.12(\$8,000,000)](0.65)}{0.17}$$

$$= \$10,858,824.$$

Value of debt = Old debt + New debt
= $200,000/0.12 + $8,000,000 = $9,666,667.

Value of the firm = V = D + S
= $9,666,667 + $10,858,824
= $20,525,491.

$$P_{new} = \frac{\text{New total value} - \text{New value of old debt}}{\text{Old shares outstanding}}$$

$$= \frac{\$20,525,491 - (\$200,000/0.12)}{600,000} = \$31.43.$$

In this case, the old stockholders gain from the use of increased leverage, and they also extract a further benefit from the old bondholders. This illustrates why bond indentures place restrictions on the sale of future debt issues.

e.
$$TIE = \frac{EBIT}{I}.$$

$$\text{Original TIE} = \frac{\$4,000,000}{\$200,000} = 20 \text{ times.}$$

$$\text{New TIE} = \frac{\$4,000,000}{\$1,200,000} = 3.33 \text{ times.}$$

Selected References

Chapter 16 dealt with the actual determination of capital structure policy, so the references given here are oriented more toward applications than theory. Chapter 17 contains references on the theory of capital structure.

Donaldson's work on the setting of debt targets is old but still relevant:

Donaldson, Gordon, *Corporate Debt Capacity* (Boston: Division of Research, Harvard Business School, 1961).

———, "New Framework for Corporate Debt Capacity," *Harvard Business Review*, vol. 40 (March-April 1962), 117-131.

———, "Strategy for Financial Emergencies," *Harvard Business Review*, vol. 47 (November-December 1969), 67-79.

Definitive references on the empirical relationship among capital structure and (1) the cost of debt, (2) the cost of equity, (3) earnings, and (4) the price of a firm's stock are virtually nonexistent. Statistical problems make the precise estimation of these relationships extraordinarily difficult, if not impossible. Probably the best way to get a feel for the issues involved is to obtain a set of the cost of capital testimonies filed in a major utility rate case—such testimony is available from state public utility commissions, the Federal Communications Commission, the Federal Energy Regulatory Commission, and utility companies themselves. For an academic discussion of the issues, see

Caks, John, "Corporate Debt Decisions: A New Analytical Framework," *Journal of Finance,* vol. 33 (December 1978), 1297-1315.

Gordon, Myron J., *The Cost of Capital to a Public Utility* (East Lansing, Michigan: Division of Research, Graduate School of Business Administration, Michigan State University, 1974).

Hamada, Robert S., "The Effect of the Firm's Capital Structure on the Systematic Risk of Common Stocks," *Journal of Finance,* vol. 27 (May 1972), 435-452.

Masulis, R. W., "The Effects of Capital Structure Change on Security Prices: A Study of Exchange Offers," Study Center in Managerial Economics and Finance, UCLA, December 1978.

Shalit, Sol S., "On the Mathematics of Financial Leverage," *Financial Management,* vol. 4 (Spring 1975), 57-66.

Shiller, Robert J., and Franco Modigliani, "Coupon and Tax Effects on New and Seasoned Bond Yields and the Measurement of the Cost of Debt Capital," *Journal of Financial Economics,* September 1979, 297-318.

Appendix 16A

Interrelationship between Financial and Operating Leverage

In our discussion of operating leverage in Chapter 16 we made no mention of financial leverage, and when we discussed financial leverage, the degree of operating leverage was assumed to be given. Actually, the two types of leverage are interrelated. For example, if FPC could *reduce* its degree of operating leverage, then it could probably *increase* its use of financial leverage. On the other hand, if it decided to use more operating leverage, then its optimal capital structure would probably call for a lower debt ratio. Thus, there is a tradeoff between operating risk and financial risk.

The theory of finance has not been developed to the point where one can simultaneously determine the optimal levels of operating and financial leverage. However, we can get a better understanding of how operating and financial leverage interact through an analysis of the *degree of leverage.* The degree of operating leverage (DOL) is defined as the percentage change in operating profits associated with a given percentage change in sales volume. Equation 16A-1 can be used to calculate the degree of operating leverage:[1]

---

[1] Equation 16A-1 is developed as follows. The change in output is defined as ΔQ. Fixed costs are constant, so the change in profits is $\Delta Q(P - V)$, where P is the price per unit and V the variable cost

(continued)

$$\text{Degree of operating} \atop \text{leverage at Point Q} = \frac{Q(P - V)}{Q(P - V) - F}. \qquad (16A\text{-}1)$$

$$\text{DOL} = \frac{S - VC}{S - VC - F}. \qquad (16A\text{-}1a)$$

Here Q is units of output, P is the average sales price per unit of output, V is the variable cost per unit, F is fixed operating costs, S is sales in dollars, and VC is total variable costs. Equation 16A-1a may also be thought of as the *contribution margin* divided by EBIT.

Applying Equation 16A-1a to data from FPC at a sales level of $20 million as shown in Table 16-4, we find its degree of operating leverage to be 2.0, so an X percent increase in sales will produce a 2X percent increase in EBIT.

$$\text{DOL} = \frac{\$20,000,000 - \$12,000,000}{\$20,000,000 - \$12,000,000 - \$4,000,000}$$
$$= \frac{\$8,000,000}{\$4,000,000} = 2.0.$$

Operating leverage affects earnings before interest and taxes (EBIT), while financial leverage affects earnings after interest and taxes, or the earnings available to common stockholders. In terms of Table 16-4, operating leverage affects the top section of the table, financial leverage the lower sections. Thus, if FPC had more operating leverage, its fixed costs would be higher than $4 million, its variable cost ratio would be lower than 60 percent of sales, and earnings before interest and taxes would vary with sales to a greater extent. Financial leverage takes over where operating leverage leaves off, further magnifying the effect on earnings per share of a change in the level of sales. For this reason, operating leverage is sometimes referred to as *first-stage leverage* and financial leverage as *second-stage leverage*.

---

per unit. The initial profit is Q(P − V) − F, so the percentage change in profit is

$$\frac{\Delta Q(P - V)}{Q(P - V) - F}.$$

The percentage change in output is ΔQ/Q, so the ratio of the change in profits to the change in output is

$$\text{DOL} = \frac{\dfrac{\Delta Q(P - V)}{Q(P - V) - F}}{\dfrac{\Delta Q}{Q}} = \left(\frac{\Delta Q(P - V)}{Q(P - V) - F}\right)\left(\frac{Q}{\Delta Q}\right) = \frac{Q(P - V)}{Q(P - V) - F}. \qquad (16A\text{-}1)$$

In economic terms, the DOL is an *arc elasticity*. Note also that the derivation of the DOL formula assumes that P and V are constant; they do not change with changes in output.

The *degree of financial leverage* (DFL) is defined as the percentage change in earnings available to common stockholders that is associated with a given percentage change in earnings before interest and taxes (EBIT). An equation has been developed as an aid in calculating the degree of financial leverage for any given level of EBIT and interest charges, I:[2]

Degree of Financial Leverage

$$\text{Degree of financial leverage} = \frac{\text{EBIT}}{\text{EBIT} - \text{I}}. \qquad (16\text{A-2})$$

For FPC at sales of $20 million and an EBIT of $4 million, the degree of financial leverage with $10 million of debt is

$$\text{DFL at \$10 million of debt} = \frac{\$4,000,000}{\$4,000,000 - \$1,200,000}$$

$$= 1.43.$$

Therefore, a 100 percent increase in EBIT would result in a 100(1.43) = 143% increase in earnings per share. If no debt were used, the degree of financial leverage would be 1.0, so a 100 percent increase in EBIT would produce a 100 percent increase in EPS. Table 16-4 confirms these statements; a 100 percent increase in EBIT, from $4 million to $8 million, produces a 100 percent increase in EPS if zero debt is used, but a 143 percent increase if $10 million of debt is used.

[2] The equation is developed as follows:

1. Notice that EBIT = Q(P − V) − F.

2. Earnings per share (EPS) $= \dfrac{(\text{EBIT} - \text{I})(1 - t)}{n}$, where EBIT is earnings before interest and taxes, I is interest paid, t is the corporate tax rate, and n is the number of shares outstanding.

3. I is a constant, so ΔEPS, the change in EPS, is

$$\Delta\text{EPS} = \frac{\Delta\text{EBIT}(1 - t)}{n}.$$

4. The percentage change in EPS is the change in EPS over the original EPS, or

$$\frac{\dfrac{\Delta\text{EBIT}(1 - t)}{n}}{\dfrac{(\text{EBIT} - \text{I})(1 - t)}{n}} = \frac{\Delta\text{EBIT}}{\text{EBIT} - \text{I}}.$$

5. The degree of financial leverage is the percentage change in EPS over the percentage change in EBIT, so

$$\text{Degree of financial leverage} = \text{DFL} = \frac{\dfrac{\Delta\text{EBIT}}{\text{EBIT} - \text{I}}}{\dfrac{\Delta\text{EBIT}}{\text{EBIT}}} = \frac{\text{EBIT}}{\text{EBIT} - \text{I}}.$$

6. This equation must be modified if the firm has preferred stock outstanding.

Combining Operating and Financial Leverage

We have seen that operating leverage causes a change in sales volume to have a magnified effect on EBIT, and if financial leverage is superimposed on operating leverage, changes in EBIT will have a magnified effect on earnings per share. Therefore, if a firm uses a considerable amount of both operating leverage and financial leverage, even small changes in the level of sales will produce wide fluctuations in EPS.

Equation 16A-1 for the degree of operating leverage can be combined with Equation 16A-2 for financial leverage to show the total leveraging effect of a given change in sales on earnings per share:[3]

$$\text{Degree of total leverage (DTL)} = \frac{Q(P - V)}{Q(P - V) - F - I}.$$

$$\text{DTL} = \frac{S - VC}{S - VC - F - I}. \qquad (16A\text{-}3)$$

For FPC at sales of $20 million, the degree of total leverage, using $10 million of debt, is 2.86:

$$
\begin{aligned}
\text{Degree of total leverage (DTL)} &= \frac{\$20,000,000 - \$12,000,000}{\$20,000,000 - \$12,000,000 - \$4,000,000 - \$1,200,000} \\[2mm]
&= \frac{\$8,000,000}{\$2,800,000} = 2.86.
\end{aligned}
$$

We can use the degree of total leverage (DTL) to find the new earnings per share (EPS_1) for a given percentage increase in sales (% Δ sales) as follows:

$$
\begin{aligned}
EPS_1 &= EPS_0 + EPS_0[(DTL)(\% \Delta \text{ sales})] \\
&= EPS_0[1.0 + (DTL)(\% \Delta \text{ sales})].
\end{aligned}
$$

---

[3] Equation 16A-3 is developed as follows:

1. Recognize that EBIT = $Q(P - V) - F$, then rewrite Equation 16A-2 as follows:

$$\frac{EBIT}{EBIT - I} = \frac{Q(P - V) - F}{Q(P - V) - F - I} = \frac{S - VC - F}{S - VC - F - I}. \qquad (16A\text{-}2a)$$

2. The degree of total leverage is equal to the degree of operating leverage times the degree of financial leverage, or Equation 16A-1 times Equation 16A-2a:

$$\text{Degree of total leverage} = (\text{Equation 16A-1})(\text{Equation 16A-2a})$$

$$
\begin{aligned}
DTL &= \left(\frac{Q(P - V)}{Q(P - V) - F}\right)\left(\frac{Q(P - V) - F}{Q(P - V) - F - I}\right) \\[2mm]
&= \frac{Q(P - V)}{Q(P - V) - F - I} = \frac{S - VC}{S - VC - F - I} \\[2mm]
&= DOL \times DFL. \qquad (16A\text{-}3a)
\end{aligned}
$$

For example, a 50 percent increase in sales, from \$20 million to \$30 million, would cause EPS_0 (\$3.20 as shown in Table 16-4) to increase to \$7.78:

$$EPS_1 = \$3.20\ [1.0 + (2.86)(0.50)]$$
$$= \$3.20\ [2.43]$$
$$= \$7.78.$$

This figure agrees with the one for EPS_1 worked out in Table 16-4 except for a one cent rounding error.

The usefulness of the degree of leverage concept lies in the facts that it (1) enables us to specify the precise effect of a change in sales volume on earnings available to common stock and (2) permits us to show the interrelationship between operating and financial leverage. The concept can be used to show the owner or manager of a business, for example, that a decision to automate and to finance new equipment with bonds will result in a situation wherein a 10 percent decline in sales will produce a 50 percent decline in earnings, whereas a different operating and financial leverage package will be such that a 10 percent sales decline will cause earnings to decline by only 20 percent. Having the alternatives stated in this manner gives the decision maker a better idea of the ramifications of the possible actions.[4]

16A-1 In public utility rate cases, a utility's riskiness is a key issue, as utilities are supposed to be allowed to earn the same rate of return on common equity as "unregulated firms of comparable risk." The difficulty is specifying in quantitative terms the riskiness of utilities and nonutilities. Do you see how the degree of leverage concepts (DOL, DFL, and DTL) might be used as indicators of risk in a rate case? **Question**

16A-1 a. Refer back to Figure 16-2. Calculate the degree of operating leverage for Plans A and B at sales of \$120,000 and \$160,000. At sales of \$80,000, DOL_A = undefined (or ∞) and DOL_B = -2.0, while at sales of \$240,000, DOL_A = 1.50 and DOL_B = 2.0. **Problems**

    b. Is it true that the DOL is approximately equal to infinity just above the breakeven point, implying that a very small increase in sales will produce a huge percentage increase in EBIT, but that DOL declines when calculated at higher levels of sales?

    c. Is it true for all sales levels where DOL > 0 for both plans that DOL_B < DOL_A? Explain.

    d. Assume that Plans A and B can be financed in either of the two fol-

---

[4] The concept is also useful for investors. If firms in an industry are classified as to their degrees of total leverage, an investor who is optimistic about prospects for the industry might favor those firms with high leverage, and vice versa if industry sales are expected to decline.

lowing ways: (1) No debt; (2) $90,000 of debt at 10 percent. Calculate the DFL for Plan A at sales of $120,000 and $160,000. The DFLs for Plan B at these sales levels with debt are 0 and 1.82, respectively.

e. Calculate the degree of total leverage (DTL) under Plan A with debt at sales of $120,000 and $160,000. The DTLs under Plan B at these sales levels are -6.67 and 7.27, respectively.

f. Several of the degree of leverage figures were negative; for example, DTL_B at $S = \$120,000$ in Part e was -6.67. Does a negative degree of leverage imply that an increase in sales will *lower* profits?

16A-2 Varifixed Corporation will begin operations next year producing a single product to be priced at $8 per unit. Varifixed has a choice of two methods of production: Method A, with variable costs of $3 per unit and $400,000 of fixed costs, and Method B, with variable costs of $5 per unit and fixed costs of $200,000. In anticipation of beginning operations, the firm has acquired $1,000,000 in assets of which $300,000 is financed by debt. The current cost of debt (k_d) to Varifixed is 10 percent. Analysis of the two methods requires the following calculations: (1) unit contribution margins under each method, (2) breakeven points for each method, and (3) level of sales in units at which the firm should be indifferent between the two methods with respect to expected earnings.

The sales forecast for the coming year is 150,000 units. Under which method would profits be most adversely affected if sales did not reach expected levels? Given the present debt of the firm, which method would produce the greatest percentage increase in earnings per share for a given increase in EBIT? What is the maximum debt ratio under Method A which would produce the same degree of total leverage as for Method B? If the management of the firm is risk averse, which method of production will most likely be selected? (Hint: Let $DTL_A = DTL_B$ and then solve for I.)

Theory of Capital Structure*

In Chapter 16 we discussed the types of factors and analyses firms consider when they make capital structure decisions. In our discussion, we noted that the optimal capital structure is determined as a tradeoff between the tax shelter benefits of debt versus the costs associated with potential bankruptcy. Now we delve more deeply into these interactions as they have been developed in theoretical works on capital structure. As we shall see, the theory cannot enable us to locate an exact optimal capital structure, so capital structure decisions remain judgmental rather than precise mathematical calculations. However, because the theory can help us to identify more clearly the key factors which determine the optimal structure, an understanding of the theory is important to financial decision makers.

Theories of Capital Structure

A number of theories have been set forth regarding how leverage affects the value of a firm and its cost of capital. These theories address two basic questions: (1) Can a firm increase the wealth of its stockholders by replacing some of its equity with debt? (2) If so, exactly how much debt should it use?

In order to answer these questions, we need to consider several valuation equations; the key terms used in these equations are as follows:

- S = market value of the common stock (price per share times number of shares outstanding).
- D = market value of the debt. (For simplicity, we shall ignore preferred stock and assume that the firm uses only one class of debt, which is a perpetuity.)
- V = total market value of the firm = $D + S$.
- EBIT = earnings before interest and taxes, also called net operating income (NOI).
- k_d = interest rate on debt.
- k_s = cost of equity, or required rate of return on common equity.
- k_a = weighted average cost of capital.
- t = corporate tax rate.

* This chapter was coauthored with Dilip K. Shome.

Assume that our illustrative company, Firm B, is paying out all of its earnings as dividends, hence is in a no-growth situation.[1] In this case Firm B's dividends represent a perpetuity, and the total market value of its common stock (S) may be found by this equation:[2]

$$S = \frac{\text{Dividends}}{k_s} = \frac{\text{Net income}}{k_s}$$

$$= \frac{(\text{EBIT} - k_d D)(1 - t)}{k_s}. \qquad (17\text{-}1)$$

The numerator gives the net income after taxes available to common stockholders, which we assume is all paid out as dividends, while the denominator is the cost of common equity. We shall use this equation shortly to show how changes in the amount of debt financing affect the value of the firm's stock.

Next, recall that the weighted average cost of capital was developed in Chapter 15 as follows:

$$k_a = w_d k_d (1 - t) + w_s k_s$$

$$= \left(\frac{D}{V}\right)\left(k_d(1 - t)\right) + \left(\frac{S}{V}\right)k_s. \qquad (17\text{-}2)$$

We will use Equation 17-2 shortly to show how changes in the debt level affect the firm's average cost of capital.

Note that we could find the value of the firm as a whole, V, by first using Equation 17-1 to find the value of the equity, then adding the value of the debt: V = S + D. Alternatively, we could solve Equation 17-2 for V to develop Equation 17-3 for obtaining the firm's value:[3]

$$V = \frac{\text{EBIT}(1 - t)}{k_a}. \qquad (17\text{-}3)$$

---

[1] We assume a no-growth situation in order to simplify the analysis. If we assumed growth, we would reach exactly the same conclusions, but the algebra would be much more complicated. See Ezra Solomon, *The Theory of Financial Management* (New York: Columbia University Press, 1963).

[2] Equation 17-1 was derived in Chapter 16, where it was designated Equation 16-2.

[3] Equation 17-3 is obtained from Equation 17-1 as follows. First, we solve Equation 17-2 for V:

$$V = \frac{Dk_d(1 - t) + Sk_s}{k_a}.$$

The first term in the numerator is the after-tax dollars paid to the bondholders, which may be expressed as I(1 − t) = I − It, where I is dollars of interest paid, while the second term is the income remaining for stockholders, (EBIT − I)(1 − t) = EBIT − I − t(EBIT) + It. Combining these terms and canceling, we produce Equation 17-3:

$$V = \frac{I - It + \text{EBIT} - I - t(\text{EBIT}) + It}{k_a}$$

$$= \frac{\text{EBIT} - t(\text{EBIT})}{k_a}$$

$$= \frac{\text{EBIT}(1 - t)}{k_a}. \qquad (17\text{-}3)$$

Equation 17-3 finds the value of the firm by capitalizing the after-tax operating income at the firm's weighted average cost of capital, k_a.[4]

We will use Equations 17-1, 17-2, and 17-3 to examine the way changes in capital structure affect the firm's value and cost of capital. This is our task in the remainder of the chapter.

NI versus NOI

The earliest formal work on the theory of capital structure was that of David Durand, who identified two extreme positions that had been taken by writers up to that time:[5] (1) the *Net Income (NI) Approach*, and (2) the *Net Operating Income (NOI) Approach*. For convenience, we first examine the NI and NOI theories under the assumption of a zero tax rate. Later on, we introduce taxes. Note that Equations 17-1, 17-2, and 17-3 apply to both theories—the differences lie in the values for k_s and k_a that are assumed to exist and are therefore inserted into the equations. The following conditions hold for our illustrative company, Firm B:

1. Firm B currently has no debt; it is an all equity company.
2. Expected EBIT = $4,000,000. This amount is not expected to increase over time, so Firm B is in a no-growth situation.
3. Firm B pays out all of its after-tax income as dividends.
4. Firm B has a zero tax rate, so t = 0. This assumption is later dropped.
5. If Firm B begins to use debt, it can borrow at a rate k_d = 8%. This borrowing rate is constant and is independent of the amount of debt used. Any money raised by selling debt will be used to retire common stock, so the assets of Firm B will remain constant.
6. Firm B's beta coefficient is b = 1.5; the riskless rate is R_F = 6%; and the return on an average stock is k_M = 10%. Therefore, for Firm B,

$$\begin{aligned} k_s &= R_F + b\,(k_M - R_F) \\ &= 6\% + 1.5\,(10\% - 6\%) \\ &= 6\% + 1.5\,(4\%) \\ &= 12\%, \end{aligned}$$

which is a constant under NI assumptions. However, k_s increases with leverage under the NOI theory.[6]

The Net Income Theory (NI)

Under the NI approach, both the interest on debt (k_d) and the cost of equity capital (k_s) are assumed to be independent of leverage; that is,

---

[4] The term *capitalizing* means "finding the present value of," and *capitalization rate* means "discount rate." These terms are used frequently in finance, especially in the valuation of corporations.

[5] See D. Durand, "Costs of Debt and Equity Funds for Business: Trends and Problems of Measurement," *Conference on Research in Business Finance*, National Bureau of Economic Research, New York, 1952.

[6] Under the NI theory, k_s is a constant and does not increase with leverage. This implies, in a CAPM framework, that beta is also independent of leverage. NOI assumes that k_s, hence beta, increases with leverage.

they are constant regardless of how much debt the firm uses. If debt is cheaper than equity, and if k_d and k_s are both constant, then the average cost of capital (k_a) must decline as the firm uses more and more of the cheaper debt. Further, this cost of capital decline must cause an increase in the value of the firm. Thus, the NI theory implies that k_a declines and V rises as the firm increases its use of debt. (Figure 17-1 graphs the NI situation.)

To illustrate, the value of Firm B's stock with zero debt may be found by applying Equation 17-1:

$$S = \frac{(EBIT - k_d D)(1 - t)}{k_s}$$
$$= \frac{(\$4 \text{ million} - 0)(1 - 0)}{0.12}$$
$$= \$4 \text{ million}/0.12 = \$33.33 \text{ million.}$$

The total market value, V, may then be found as $V = D + S = 0 + \$33.33$ million $= \$33.33$ million. The company's weighted average cost of capital, using Equation 17-3, is 12 percent:

$$k_a = \left(\frac{D}{V}\right)\left(k_d(1 - t)\right) + \left(\frac{S}{V}\right)k_s$$
$$= 0 + \left(\frac{\$33.33 \text{ million}}{\$33.33 \text{ million}}\right)\left(12\%\right) = 12\%.$$

Now suppose Firm B sells $10 million of 8 percent debt and uses the proceeds to reduce equity. The value of its stock would, under the NI assumptions, change as follows:

$$S = \frac{[\$4 \text{ million} - 0.08(\$10 \text{ million})](1 - 0)}{0.12}$$
$$= \frac{\$3.2 \text{ million}}{0.12}$$
$$= \$26.67 \text{ million.}$$

Its total market value would rise from $33.33 million to $36.67 million:

$$V = D + S = \$10 \text{ million} + \$26.67 \text{ million} = \$36.67 \text{ million.}$$

Finally, B's weighted average cost of capital would decline from 12 percent to 10.91 percent:

$$k_a = \left(\frac{\$10 \text{ million}}{\$36.67 \text{ million}}\right)\left(8\%\right) + \left(\frac{\$26.67 \text{ million}}{\$36.67 \text{ million}}\right)\left(12\%\right)$$
$$= 2.18\% + 8.73\%$$
$$= 10.91\%.$$

Thus, under the NI assumptions, the use of $10 million of debt would (1) cause Firm B's value to increase from $33.33 million to $36.67 million, and

(2) cause its average cost of capital to decline from 12 percent to 10.91 percent.

To determine the general effects of leverage under the NI assumptions, we can work through the equations with other amounts of debt; the results are shown in Table 17-1 and plotted in Figure 17-1. As the figure shows, under the NI theory, the firm's value continuously increases and its cost of capital continuously decreases until it has 100 percent debt. Thus, if the NI assumptions were valid, the logical conclusion would be that Firm B should be financed with virtually 100 percent debt.[7]

In the preceding section we saw that the NI approach is based on the assumption that net income to common is capitalized at a constant rate (k_s = constant), while k_a declines with leverage. These assumptions are reversed under the NOI theory: NOI assumes that k_a = constant while k_s increases with leverage:

The Net Operating Income Theory (NOI)

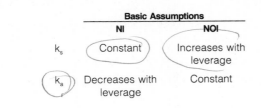

	Basic Assumptions	
	NI	NOI
k_s	Constant	Increases with leverage
k_a	Decreases with leverage	Constant

Under both theories, it is assumed that the cost of debt (k_d) is a constant.

We can now apply the NOI method to Firm B to obtain its value and cost of capital at various debt levels. First, recall that Firm B currently has $k_s = R_F + b (k_M - R_F) = 12\%$. Second, note that with debt equal to zero, the weighted average cost of capital must also be $k_a = k_s = 12\%$. Third, since k_a is assumed to be a constant, $k_a = 12\%$ regardless of how much debt Firm B uses. Fourth, EBIT is also a constant and is equal to $4 million. Therefore, assuming at this point that the tax rate is zero, we can find Firm B's value at any debt level by use of Equation 17-3:

$$V = \frac{\text{EBIT } (1 - t)}{k_a} = \frac{\$4 \text{ million } (1.0)}{0.12} = \$33.333 \text{ million.}$$

[7] Someone might notice that the value of the stock declines from $33.33 million to $26.67 million as Firm B substitutes $10 million of debt for equity, and ask if this is really better for the stockholders. The answer is yes. To see why, suppose you were the sole owner of Firm B in its unlevered position. Now you have the firm sell $10 million of debt and simultaneously use the new cash to pay yourself a $10 million tax-free return-of-capital dividend. You now have a net worth of $10 million cash + $26.67 million stock = $36.67 million total, so you've gained $3.34 million from the firm's use of debt. The relative effects would be the same if you owned 1 percent or any other fraction of the company. This point was discussed at length in Chapter 16.

Table 17-1
Effects of Leverage:
NI, Zero Taxes
($ in Millions)

D (1)	k_d (2)	k_s (3)	S (4)	V (D + S) (5)	k_a (6)	D/V (7)
$ 0	8.0%	12.0%	$33.333	$33.333	12.00%	0.00%
5	8.0	12.0	30.000	35.000	11.43	14.29
10	8.0	12.0	26.667	36.667	10.91	27.27
15	8.0	12.0	23.333	38.333	10.43	39.13
20	8.0	12.0	20.000	40.000	10.00	50.00
30	8.0	12.0	13.333	43.333	9.23	69.23
40	8.0	12.0	6.667	46.667	8.57	85.71
50	8.0	12.0	0.000	50.000	8.00	100.00

Now suppose that Firm B decides to use $10 million of debt. By definition, V = D + S, so S = V − D. Therefore, with V constant at $33.333 million, the value of the equity when the firm has $10 million of debt must be $23.333 million:

$$S = V - D = \$33.333 - \$10 = \$23.333 \text{ million.}$$

The value of the stock at other debt levels could be calculated similarly.

Now consider what must be happening to the cost of equity, k_s, as the level of debt rises. If we solve Equation 17-1 for k_s, we obtain this expression:

$$k_s = \frac{(EBIT - k_d D)(1 - t)}{S}. \qquad (17\text{-}1a)$$

At D = 0, we obtain

$$k_s = \frac{[\$4 \text{ million} - 0.08 (0)] (1.0)}{\$33.333 \text{ million}}$$

$$= \frac{\$4 \text{ million}}{\$33.333 \text{ million}}$$

$$= 0.12 = 12\%,$$

while at D = $10 million, we obtain

$$k_s = \frac{[\$4 \text{ million} - 0.08 (\$10 \text{ million})] (1.0)}{\$23.333 \text{ million}}$$

$$= \frac{\$3.20 \text{ million}}{\$23.33 \text{ million}}$$

$$= 13.71\%.$$

For consistency, we would expect the average cost of capital to be constant at k_a = 12% for D = $0 and D = $10 million. This is indeed the case:

At D = $0,

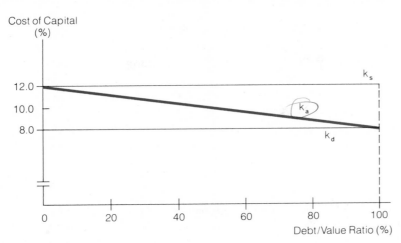

Figure 17-1
Effects of Leverage: NI,
Zero Taxes

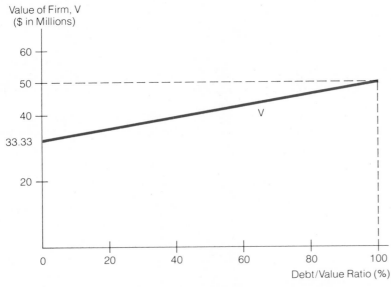

$$k_a = D/V \ (k_d) + S/V \ (k_s)$$

$$= \left(\frac{0}{\$33.333 \ \text{million}} \right) \left(8\% \right) + \left(\frac{\$33.333 \ \text{million}}{\$33.333 \ \text{million}} \right) \left(12\% \right) = 12\%,$$

and at D = \$10 million,

$$k_a = \left(\frac{\$10 \ \text{million}}{\$33.333 \ \text{million}} \right) \left(8\% \right) + \left(\frac{\$23.333 \ \text{million}}{\$33.333 \ \text{million}} \right) \left(13.71\% \right)$$

$$= 2.40\% + 9.60\% = 12.00\%.$$

Other values of S, V, k_s, and k_a are shown in Table 17-2 and are plotted in Figure 17-2. Here we see, in contrast with the NI values in Figure 17-1, that under the NOI theory leverage has no effect on either the firm's average cost of capital or its total market value. Thus, under the NOI conditions in a world with no corporate taxes, capital structure decisions are unimportant.[8]

Table 17-2
Effects of Leverage: NOI, Zero Taxes ($ in Millions)

D (1)	k_d (2)	k_s (3)	S (4)	V (D + S) (5)	k_a (6)	D/V (7)
$ 0	—	12.00%	$33.33	$33.33	12.00%	0.00%
5	8.0%	12.71	28.33	33.33	12.00	15.00
10	8.0	13.71	23.33	33.33	12.00	30.00
15	8.0	15.27	18.33	33.33	12.00	45.00
20	8.0	18.00	13.33	33.33	12.00	60.00
25	8.0	24.00	8.33	33.33	12.00	75.00
30	8.0	48.00	3.33	33.33	12.00	90.00

The Modigliani-Miller Model

As we saw in the preceding section, the NI theory suggests that firms interested in maximizing their value should move toward 100 percent debt, while the NOI theory suggests that capital structure simply does not matter, as a firm's value is independent of capital structure. Both theories are obviously artificial and incomplete because they assume a zero corporate tax rate, among other things. We will relax the tax assumption shortly, but first, in a zero tax world, which theory is more logical, NI or NOI?

In what has been called the single most important financial research paper ever published, Franco Modigliani and Merton Miller (MM) addressed this issue.[9] To begin, MM made these assumptions:

[8] It is also worth noting at this point that the NI approach assumes implicitly that beta is independent of leverage, while the NOI approach assumes that beta increases with leverage. Knowing the values of k_s from Table 17-2, and using the CAPM equation solved for beta, we could find the implied beta at D = 0, D = $10 million, and other values:

$$k_s = R_F + b (k_M - R_F).$$
$$b = \frac{k_s - R_F}{k_M - R_F}.$$

At D = $0, b = (12% − 6%)/(10% − 6%) = 6%/4% = 1.5.
At D = $10 million, b = (13.71% − 6%)/(10% − 6%) = 1.93.

Thus, acceptance of the NOI method implies acceptance of the proposition that beta increases with leverage, while acceptance of the NI theory implies that beta is independent of leverage.

[9] See F. Modigliani and M. H. Miller, "The Cost of Capital, Corporation Finance and the Theory of Investment," *American Economic Review,* vol. 48 (June 1958), 261-297; and "The Cost of Capital, Corporation Finance and the Theory of Investment: Reply," *American Economic Review,* vol. 49 (Sep-

(continued)

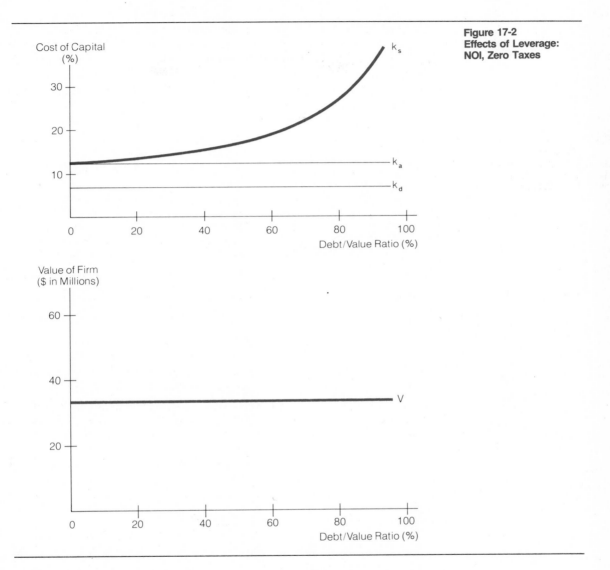

**Figure 17-2
Effects of Leverage:
NOI, Zero Taxes**

1. Firms' business risk can be measured (by σ_{EBIT}), and firms with the same degree of business risk are said to be in a *homogeneous business risk class*.

tember 1958), 655-669; "Taxes and the Cost of Capital: A Correction," *American Economic Review*, vol. 53 (June 1963), 433-443; and "Reply," *American Economic Review*, vol. 55 (June 1965), 524–527. In a 1979 survey of Financial Management Association members, the original MM article was judged to have had the greatest impact on the field of finance of any work ever published. See Philip L. Cooley and J. Louis Heck, "Significant Contributions to Finance Literature," *Financial Management*, vol. 10 (Summer 1981), 23-33.

2. All present and prospective investors have identical estimates of each firm's average future EBIT; that is, investors have *homogeneous expectations* about expected future corporate earnings and the riskiness of these earnings.

3. Stocks and bonds are traded in *perfect capital markets*. This assumption implies, among other things, (a) that there are no brokerage costs and (b) that investors (individuals and institutions) can borrow at the same rate as corporations.

4. The debt of firms and individuals is riskless, so the interest rate on debt is the risk-free rate. Further, this situation holds regardless of how much debt a firm (or an individual) issues.

5. There are *no corporate taxes*. This assumption is later dropped, but the others are not.

Based on these assumptions, MM advanced and then proved two propositions. The propositions are stated below, then proved in the next section.

Proposition I. The value of the firm is established by capitalizing net operating income (NOI = EBIT) at a rate appropriate for the firm's risk class:

$$V = \frac{\text{EBIT}}{k_a}.$$

Proposition I is identical to the NOI hypothesis.

Proposition II. The cost of equity is equal to a constant average cost of capital plus a risk premium which depends on the degree of financial leverage:

$$k_s = k_a + \text{Risk premium}$$
$$= k_a + (k_a - k_d)\,(D/S).$$

Proposition II states that as the firm's use of debt increases, its cost of equity also rises, and in an exactly specified manner.

The two MM propositions imply that the inclusion of more debt in the capital structure will not increase the value of the firm because the benefits of cheaper debt will be exactly offset by an increase in the cost of equity. *Thus, the basic MM hypothesis is that, in a world without taxes, the value of a firm and its cost of capital are completely unaffected by its capital structure.*

Proof of the MM Hypothesis

MM use an *arbitrage proof* to support their propositions. They show that, under their assumptions, if two companies differ only (1) in the way they are financed and (2) in their total market values, then investors will sell shares of the overvalued firm, buy those of the undervalued firm, and continue this process until the companies have exactly the same market value. To illustrate, assume that two firms, Firm L (for levered) and Firm

U (for unlevered), are identical in all important respects except financial structure: Firm L has $4 million of 7.5 percent debt, while Firm U is all equity financed. Both firms have EBIT = $900,000, and σ_{EBIT} is the same for both firms, so they are in the same risk class. In the initial situation, before any arbitrage occurs, assume that both firms have an equity capitalization rate of $k_s = 10\%$.

Under these conditions, and assuming that the NI approach is correct, the following situation would exist:

Firm U:

$$\text{Value of Firm U's stock} = S_U = \frac{EBIT - k_dD}{k_s} = \frac{\$900,000 - 0}{0.10} = \$9,000,000.$$

$$\text{Total market value of Firm U} = V_U = D_U + S_U = \$0 + \$9,000,000 = \$9,000,000.$$

Firm L:

$$\text{Value of Firm L's stock} = S_L = \frac{\$900,000 - 0.075\,(\$4,000,000)}{0.10} = \$6,000,000.$$

$$\text{Total market value of Firm L} = V_L = D_L + S_L = \$4,000,000 + \$6,000,000 = \$10,000,000.$$

Thus, before arbitrage the value of the levered company, Firm L, exceeds that of unlevered Firm U.

MM argue that this is a disequilibrium situation which cannot persist. To see why, suppose that you owned 10 percent of L's stock, with an investment of $600,000. According to MM, you could increase your total investment income, without increasing your financial risk, by (1) selling your stock in L for $600,000, (2) borrowing an amount equal to 10 percent of L's debt ($400,000), and then (3) buying 10 percent of U's stock for $900,000. Notice that you would receive $1 million from sale of your 10 percent of L's stock plus your borrowing, and you would be spending only $900,000 on U's stock, so you would have $100,000 in uncommitted funds.

Now consider your income position:

Old income:	10% of L's $600,000 equity income		$60,000
New income:	10% of U's $900,000 equity income	$90,000	
	Less 7.5% interest on $400,000 loan	−30,000	$60,000

Thus, your net investment income from common stock would be exactly the same as before, but you would have $100,000 left over for investment elsewhere, say in riskless treasury bonds. Therefore, the total return on your $600,000 net worth would rise. Further, your risk, according to MM, would be the same as before—you would have simply substituted $400,000 of "homemade" leverage for your share of Firm L's corporate leverage.

MM argue that this arbitrage process would actually occur, with sales of L's stock driving its price down and purchases of U's stock driving its price up, until the market values of the two firms were equal. Until this equality was established, there would be gains to be had from switching from one stock to the other, so the profit motive would force the equality to be reached. When equilibrium was established, the NOI conditions would be fulfilled, and the values of Firms L and U, and their average costs of capital, would be equal. Thus, according to Modigliani and Miller, V and k_a must be independent of capital structure under equilibrium conditions.

The Modigliani-Miller View with Taxes

When taxes are introduced, MM derive a new set of conditions. With corporate taxes, they conclude that the levered firm will have a higher value because interest on debt is a deductible expense, hence more of the operating income flows through to investors. Specifically, MM demonstrate that the value of the levered firm (V_L) exceeds that of the unlevered firm (V_U) by an amount equal to the present value of the tax savings (tD) that arises from the use of debt. Their proof follows.

First, consider two firms that are identical in all respects except capital structure. Firm U has no debt in its capital structure, while L uses debt. Expected EBIT is identical for each firm. Under these assumptions, the operating cash flows available to Firm U's investors, CF_U, are calculated as

$$CF_U = EBIT\,(1 - t),\qquad(17\text{-}4)$$

while the cash flows to Firm L's investors are

$$CF_L = (EBIT - k_dD)\,(1 - t) + k_dD,\qquad(17\text{-}5)$$

which can be rewritten as follows:[10]

$$CF_L = EBIT\,(1 - t) + tk_dD.\qquad(17\text{-}5a)$$

[10] The first term to the right of the equal sign in Equation 17-5 is the income available to stockholders, while the second term is income available to bondholders. CF_L is the total income available to all investors. Equation 17-5 can be restated as follows:

$$
\begin{aligned}
CF_L &= EBIT - k_dD - EBIT(t) + tk_dD + k_dD \\
&= EBIT - EBIT(t) + tk_dD \\
&= EBIT(1 - t) + tk_dD.
\end{aligned}\qquad(17\text{-}5a)
$$

The first term in Equation 17-5a, or EBIT $(1 - t)$, is identical to U's income, while the second term, tk_dD, represents the tax savings that occur because interest is deductible.

The value of the unlevered firm, V_U, may be determined by capitalizing its annual net income after corporate taxes, $CF_U = EBIT(1 - t)$, at its cost of equity:

$$V_U = \frac{EBIT\ (1 - t)}{k_s}. \tag{17-6}$$

The value of the levered firm, on the other hand, is found by capitalizing both parts of its after-tax earnings. MM argue that because L's "regular" earnings stream is precisely as risky as the income of Firm U, it should be capitalized at the same rate, k_s. However, the tax savings will occur so long as interest on the debt is paid, so the tax savings are exactly as risky as the firm's debt, hence should be discounted at the rate k_d. Thus, we obtain Equation 17-7 for Firm L's value:

$$\begin{aligned} V_L &= \frac{EBIT\ (1 - t)}{k_s} + \frac{tk_dD}{k_d} \\ &= \frac{EBIT\ (1 - t)}{k_s} + tD. \end{aligned} \tag{17-7}$$

Since the first term in Equation 17-7, $EBIT(1 - t)/k_s$, is identical to V_U in Equation 17-6, we may also express V_L as follows:

$$V_L = V_U + tD. \tag{17-8}$$

Thus, the value of the levered firm is above that of the unlevered company, and the differential increases as the use of debt goes up.[11]

We can illustrate the MM model with the data given earlier for Firm B. When Firm B has zero debt, its value is $20 million as found by applying Equation 17-6:

$$\begin{aligned} V_U &= \frac{EBIT(1 - t)}{k_s} \\ &= \frac{\$4\ \text{million}\ (0.6)}{0.12} \\ &= \$20.0\ \text{million}. \end{aligned}$$

With $10 million of debt, by Equation 17-8 we see that total market value rises to $24 million:

$$\begin{aligned} V_L &= V_U + tD \\ &= \$20\ \text{million} + 0.4\ (\$10\ \text{million}) \\ &= \$24\ \text{million}, \end{aligned}$$

[11] MM presented an arbitrage proof of the valuation equation with taxes. This proof is similar to the without-tax arbitrage proof, so it is not included here.

and the value of Firm B's stock must be $14 million:

$$S = V - D$$
$$= \$24 \text{ million} - \$10 \text{ million}$$
$$= \$14 \text{ million.}$$

We can also find Firm B's cost of equity (k_s) and its weighted average cost of capital (k_a) at debt of $10 million:

$$k_s = \frac{(EBIT - k_dD)\,(1 - t)}{S}$$
$$= \frac{[\$4 \text{ million} - (\$10 \text{ million})\,(0.08)]\,(1 - 0.4)}{\$14 \text{ million}}$$
$$= 0.1371 = 13.71\%,$$

and

$$k_a = (D/V)\,k_d\,(1 - t) + (S/V)\,k_s$$
$$= (\$10 \text{ million}/\$24 \text{ million})\,(8\%)\,(0.6)$$
$$\quad + (\$14 \text{ million}/\$24 \text{ million})\,(13.71\%)$$
$$= 10\%.$$

Alternatively, we could have found k_a as

$$k_a = \frac{EBIT\,(1 - t)}{V} = \frac{\$4 \text{ million}\,(0.6)}{\$24 \text{ million}}$$
$$= 0.10 = 10\%.$$

Firm B's value and cost of capital at other debt levels are shown in Table 17-3 and plotted in Figure 17-3. Here we see that in an MM world with taxes, financial leverage does matter—the value of the firm is maximized, and its cost of capital is minimized, if it uses virtually 100 percent debt financing.[12]

---

[12] In the limiting case, where the firm used 100 percent debt financing, the bondholders would own the entire company, hence they would have all of the business risk. (Up until this point, MM assume that the stockholders have all of the risk.) If the bondholders have all of the risk, then the capitalization rate on the debt should be equal to the equity capitalization rate at zero debt, $k_d = k_s = 12\%$.

The income stream to the stockholders in the all-equity case was $CF_U = \$4{,}000{,}000\,(1 - t) = \$2{,}400{,}000$, and the value of the firm was

$$V_U = \frac{\$2{,}400{,}000}{0.12} = \$20{,}000{,}000.$$

With all debt, the entire $4,000,000 of EBIT would be used to pay interest charges: k_d would be 12%, so $I = 0.12\,(\$33{,}333{,}333) = \$4{,}000{,}000$. Therefore, taxes would be zero, and investors (bondholders) would get the entire $4,000,000 of operating income; they would not have to share it with the government. Thus, at 100 percent debt, the value of the firm would be

$$V_L = \frac{\$4{,}000{,}000}{0.12} = \$33{,}333{,}333.$$

There is, of course, a transition problem in all this—MM assume that $k_d = 8\%$ regardless of how much debt the firm has until debt reaches 100 percent, at which point k_d jumps to 12 percent, the cost of equity. As we shall see later in the chapter, k_d realistically rises more or less continuously as the use of financial leverage increases.

Table 17-3
Effect of Leverage on Value and Cost of Capital: MM with Taxes

D (Million $) (1)	V (Million $) (2)	S (Million $) (3)	$\frac{D}{V}$ (4)	k_d (5)	k_s (6)	k_a (7)
$ 0	$20.00	$20.00	0.00%	8.0%	12.00%	12.00%
5	22.00	17.00	22.73	8.0	12.71	10.91
10	24.00	14.00	41.67	8.0	13.71	10.00
15	26.00	11.00	57.69	8.0	15.27	9.23
20	28.00	8.00	71.43	8.0	18.00	8.57
25	30.00	5.00	83.33	8.0	24.00	8.00
30	32.00	2.00	93.75	8.0	48.00	7.50
33.33[a]	33.33	0.00	100.00	12.0	—	12.00

[a]The case of 100 percent debt is the theoretically limiting case. See Footnote 12 for a discussion.

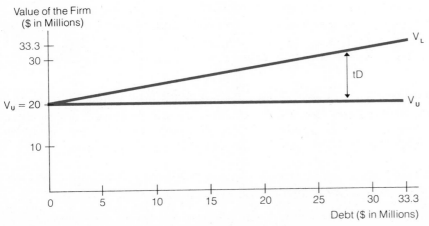

Figure 17-3
Effect of Leverage on Value and Cost of Capital: MM with Taxes

Criticisms of the MM Hypothesis

MM's conclusions follow logically from their initial assumptions—if their assumptions are correct, then their conclusions must be reached. Therefore, people who disagree with the MM theory generally attack them on the grounds that their assumptions are unrealistic. Some of the main objections are listed below:

1. The MM analysis implies that personal and corporate leverage are perfect substitutes. However, an individual investing in a levered firm has less loss exposure, or a more *limited liability*. In our illustration of the MM arbitrage argument, only the $600,000 invested in Firm L could be lost if the firm were to go bankrupt. However, someone who engaged in arbitrage transactions and switched to a "homemade" leveraged position in Firm U could lose $900,000. This would tend to restrain investors from engaging in arbitrage.

2. In the MM analysis, brokerage costs are assumed away, making the switch from L to U costless. However, brokerage and other transactions costs do exist, and they too impede the arbitrage process.

3. Restrictions on institutional investors may also retard the arbitrage process. Institutional investors dominate the stock markets today, but most institutional investors are prohibited from engaging in "homemade" leverage.

4. MM assume that corporations and investors can borrow at the same rate. Although major institutional investors could probably borrow at the corporate rate, institutions are generally not allowed to borrow to buy securities. Most individual investors probably must borrow at higher rates than those paid by corporations. Therefore, lower interest rates on corporate borrowings could prevent the arbitrage solution from working out to the exact MM solution.

5. MM do not take account of personal income taxes, thereby implicitly assuming a zero personal tax rate. However, as noted later in the chapter, Miller has addressed this issue.

6. MM assume that the cost of debt does not increase as the use of debt increases. This is, obviously, a worrisome assumption, and relaxing it leads to some alterations in the "pure MM conclusions."

Relaxing the MM Assumptions

The MM conclusion that firms can maximize their values by using virtually 100 percent debt financing follows logically from their assumptions. However, their assumptions are not completely correct, so we must relax them to see how debt affects value under real world conditions.

Bankruptcy Costs

As we shall see in Chapter 21, quite a few firms go bankrupt each year. When bankruptcy occurs, several things happen:

1. Bankrupt firms are generally forced to sell assets at abnormally low

prices. For example, we often hear of someone buying assets in a bankruptcy sale for say $1 million and then, a few months later, selling them for $2 or $3 million.

2. Arguments between claimants may delay the liquidation of assets, thus leading to physical deterioration and/or obsolescence of inventories and fixed assets. Bankruptcy cases can take many years to settle, and during this time machinery rusts, buildings are vandalized, inventories become obsolete, and the like.

3. Lawyer's fees, court costs, and administrative expenses absorb part of the firm's value. These costs are significant, but they are not as large as the first two cost elements.

All things considered, the costs associated with bankruptcy are high. Further, bankruptcy can only occur if a firm has debts—no debt-free firm has ever gone bankrupt. *Therefore, the greater the use of debt financing, and the larger the fixed interest charges, the greater the probability that a decline in earnings will lead to bankruptcy, and, hence, the higher the probability of a bankruptcy-related loss of value.*

An increase in the probability of bankruptcy lowers the current value of a firm and raises its cost of capital. To see why, suppose Firm B would incur bankruptcy costs of $7 million if it failed at some future date, and the *present value* of this possible future cost is $5 million. Suppose, further, the probability of bankruptcy increases with leverage, causing the expected costs of bankruptcy to rise from zero at zero debt to $4.75 million at $30 million of debt as shown:

Amount of debt	$0	$5 Million	$10 Million	$20 Million	$30 Million
Probability of bankruptcy	0.0	0.05	0.15	0.50	0.95
PV of expected costs of bankruptcy ($5 million times the indicated probability)	$0	$250,000	$750,000	$2,500,000	$4,750,000

These expected bankruptcy costs must be subtracted from the values calculated in Table 17-3 to find the firm's value at various degrees of leverage—they would reduce the values of V and S in Columns 2 and 3, and, as a result, would raise k_s and k_a in Columns 6 and 7. For example, at $20 million of debt we would obtain the values in Table 17-4. These changes would, of course, then have carry-through effects on Figure 17-3—most important, they would reduce the decline of the k_a line and also reduce the slope of the V_L line. We shall modify Figure 17-3 for bankruptcy costs shortly, but it is useful to first look at other factors which also affect the graph.

**Table 17-4
Effects of
Bankruptcy**

	Table 17-3 Values at D = \$20 Million with Bankruptcy Effects Ignored: Pure MM	Table 17-3 Values at D = \$20 Million with Bankruptcy Effects Considered: Modified MM[13]
V	\$28.00	\$28.00 − \$2.5 = \$25.5
S	\$ 8.00	\$ 8.00 − \$2.5 = \$ 5.5
k_s	18.00%	26.18%
k_a	8.57%	9.41%

**Effects of
Leverage on the
Cost of Debt**

MM assume that k_d is a constant irrespective of how much debt a firm uses. This is not realistic—as the debt ratio rises, so will the interest rate on that debt. This will not affect EBIT, but it will cause a reduction in S and consequently in V, and this in turn will cause k_s and k_a to rise. Thus, recognizing that k_d increases with leverage causes several elements in Figure 17-3 to change.

**Effects of
Financial Leverage
on Operating Income
(EBIT)**

Modigliani and Miller assumed that EBIT is a constant and is independent of the degree of financial leverage. This assumption is correct if the firm uses only a moderate amount of debt, but if debt becomes excessive, expected EBIT will fall for a number of reasons. First, firms with high debt ratios find it difficult to obtain operating capital when money gets tight or when the economy is weak. Such firms may have to pass up favorable investment opportunities or even curtail normal operations because of financial problems.

Another problem faced by firms with excessive leverage is that, when times are bad, management may have to devote most of its time and energies to raising the capital needed for survival rather than to running the company. Chrysler Corporation in recent years is an example. Whereas General Motors' management was supervising the design and production of automobiles, Chrysler's top managers were literally running around the world trying to obtain the capital the firm needed to survive.

Firms whose excessive debt places them in danger of bankruptcy also

---

[13] Apply Equations 17-1a and 17-2, respectively, to find k_s and k_a:

$$k_s = \frac{(EBIT - k_dD)\,(1 - t)}{S} = \frac{[\$4 - 0.08\,(\$20)]\,(1 - 0.4)}{\$5.5} = 26.18\%.$$

$$\begin{aligned} k_a &= (D/V)\,(k_d)\,(1 - t) + (S/V)\,(k_s) \\ &= (10/25.5)\,(8\%)\,(0.6) + (5.5/25.5)\,(26.18\%) \\ &= 3.76\% + 5.65\% = 9.41\%. \end{aligned}$$

have a problem retaining good managers, employees, and customers. For example, Chrysler is reported to have lost some of its best (and consequently most mobile) managers and other employees to sounder firms where future employment is more assured. At the same time, many potential Chrysler customers have bought other makes of cars because they were afraid of what might happen if Chrysler went bankrupt.

Another factor which has an effect on the firm's income stream at high debt levels is *agency costs*, the costs associated with dealings between a firm's stockholders and its bondholders. In the absence of restrictions, a firm's management might take actions that would benefit stockholders at the expense of bondholders. For example, if Firm B were to sell only a small amount of debt, then this debt would have relatively little risk, hence a high bond rating and a low interest rate. Yet, having sold the low-risk debt, Firm B could then issue more debt. This would raise the risks faced by *all bondholders*, causing k_d to rise and the original bondholders to suffer capital losses. Well-designed bond indenture covenants could help curb this potential abuse, but suppose Firm B decided to restructure its assets, selling off assets with low business risk and acquiring assets that were more risky but that had higher expected rates of return. If things worked out well, the stockholders would benefit. If things went sour, most of the loss in a highly leveraged firm would fall on the bondholders. In other words, "Heads, the stockholders win; tails, the bondholders lose."

Agency Costs

Because of the possibility that stockholders would try to take advantage of bondholders in these and other ways, bonds are protected by restrictive covenants as discussed in Chapter 13. These covenants hamper the corporation's legitimate operations to some extent, and, further, the company must be monitored to insure that the covenants are being obeyed. The costs of lost efficiency plus monitoring are what we mean by the term "agency costs," and the existence of these costs reduces the advantage of debt.[14]

In a pure MM world with corporate taxes, the value of a firm would rise continuously as the firm moved from zero debt toward 100 percent debt: $V_L = V_U + tD$, with the rising component of value (tD) resulting directly from the shelter provided by the debt interest. However, (1) the present value of potential future bankruptcy, (2) the effects of high leverage and

Value and the Cost of Capital with Bankruptcy and Related Costs

---

[14] See Michael C. Jensen and William H. Meckling, "Theory of the Firm: Managerial Behavior, Agency Costs, and Ownership Structure," *Journal of Financial Economics*, vol. 3 (October 1976), 305-360.

a weak balance sheet on expected future EBIT, and (3) agency costs all combine to reduce the value of the firm if it uses too much debt:

$$V_L = V_U + tD - \begin{pmatrix} \text{PV of} \\ \text{expected} \\ \text{bankruptcy} \\ \text{costs} \end{pmatrix} - \begin{pmatrix} \text{Reduction in} \\ \text{value from} \\ \text{lower EBIT} \end{pmatrix} - \begin{pmatrix} \text{Reduction in} \\ \text{value from} \\ \text{agency costs} \end{pmatrix}. \quad (17\text{-}9)$$

In graph form, the relationship expressed in this equation is shown in Figure 17-4. The tax shelter effect totally dominates until the debt ratio reaches Point A. After Point A, bankruptcy and related costs become increasingly important, offsetting some of the tax advantages. At Point B, the marginal tax shelter benefits of additional debt are exactly offset by the disadvantages of debt, and beyond Point B the disadvantages outweigh the tax benefits.

The tax benefits (tD) can be estimated relatively precisely, but the value reduction resulting from potential bankruptcy, lower expected EBIT, and agency costs cannot be measured with much precision at all.[15]

Figure 17-4
Net Effect of Leverage
on the Value of the Firm

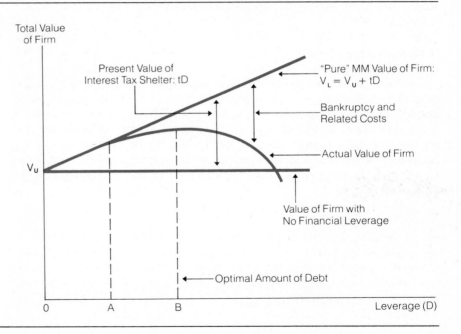

---

[15] Even the tax benefits may be different from tD. If brokerage and other transactions costs, a higher interest rate on personal versus corporate debt, concerns about limited liability, and so on, impede arbitrage, then (1) corporate leverage would be better than "homemade" leverage, (2) the slope of the

We know these costs must increase as leverage rises, but we do not know the exact functional relationship. Further, the functional relationship almost certainly varies among firms and industries. For example, if Firm A had less business risk than Firm B, then Firm A could carry more debt before the threat of bankruptcy and/or reduced expected EBIT became serious problems. Thus, Firm A could afford to use more debt and to take advantage of more interest tax shelter than Firm B. Similarly, if one firm uses assets which make good collateral for mortgage bonds, it can have a higher debt ratio without having to worry too much about "agency" costs, while another firm which uses most of its capital for research and development, hence has fewer mortgageable assets, would have a lower optimal debt ratio.

It should also be apparent that for a given firm, more debt can be used to finance some types of assets than others. Thus, if a drug firm were raising $10 million to support genetic engineering research and another $10 million to build a general purpose office complex, it would be easier to obtain debt financing for the office complex than for the research program. The office project is said to have a greater "debt-carrying capacity." Some consideration should be given to this fact, in the capital budgeting process, if it is thought to be important in individual cases.[16]

Thus far we have considered only the effects of corporate income taxes—we have not considered personal taxes at all. Can personal income taxes affect the optimal capital structure enough to merit consideration? The answer is yes. To illustrate, suppose you (or you and a group of investors) decide to establish a company, and $100,000 of capital is required. A 20 percent before-tax return on assets is expected; that is, ROA = 20%. Disregarding bankruptcy considerations for the moment, you should put up your $100,000 in the manner that would result in your receiving the largest cash flows after both corporate and personal taxes. If you supply capital as debt, you will receive payments in the form of interest. If you

Personal Income Taxes

---

line labeled "Pure MM Value" in Figure 17-4 would be increased, and (3) this would increase the optimal debt ratio for the firm. However, as we shall see in the next section, personal income taxes offset these factors to some extent, and thus decrease the optimal capital structure somewhat.

[16] This idea has led some researchers to suggest that each capital budgeting project should be analyzed separately, with the project's NPV being split into an operating PV, found by discounting after-tax operating income at the equity capitalization rate for an all equity firm, k_s, plus the PV of a tax shelter equal to tD, where D is the amount of debt used to finance the project:

$$NPV_{project} = \frac{EBIT_{project}\ (1\ -\ t)}{k_s} + tD_{project} - Cost_{project}.$$

This approach is conceptually appealing but of limited practical value, primarily because firms are generally viewed as entities, and they raise capital in lumps to support a wide variety of projects. Further, the nebulous nature of bankruptcy and related costs makes it difficult enough to specify an optimal debt level for a firm, let alone for a single project.

put up equity, your receipts will come as dividends, as capital gains, or as some of each.

If we define t_c as the corporate tax rate and t_p as the personal tax rate, then cash flows after all taxes can be found as follows:

$$\begin{aligned}
\text{Expected after-tax} \atop \text{cash flow} &= (\text{ROA}) \left(\begin{matrix} \text{Amount of} \\ \text{investment} \end{matrix}\right) (1 - t_c)(1 - t_p) \qquad (17\text{-}10) \\
&= 0.2\,(\$100,000)\,(1 - t_c)(1 - t_p) \\
&= \$20,000\,(1 - t_c)(1 - t_p).
\end{aligned}$$

Now assume that the corporate tax rate is 46 percent, your personal tax rate on interest and dividends is 70 percent, your tax rate on capital gains is 28 percent, and you will take long-term capital gains as they occur by selling part of your stock. (You will, however, keep your $100,000 investment intact.) Your expected after-tax cash flows under several different scenarios are as follows:

Capital Structure and Payout	Expected After-Tax Cash Flow
100% debt: (Here, $t_c = 0$ because all income is paid out as interest.)	CF = $20,000 (1.0) (0.3) = $6,000.
100% equity, 0% dividend payout:	CF = $20,000 (0.54) (0.72) = $7,776.
100% equity, 100% dividend payout:	CF = $20,000 (0.54) (0.30) = $3,240.

100% equity,
39.15% dividend payout:
	CF = $20,000 (0.54) (0.6085) (0.72)
	     + $20,000 (0.54) (0.3915) (0.3)
	     = $4,732 + $1,268 = $6,000.

The effective total tax rate, which combines the corporate and personal tax rates, is 70 percent in the 100 percent debt case, 61.1 percent in the case of 100 percent equity with only capital gains, 83.8 percent in the case of 100 percent equity with only dividend income, and 70 percent in the case of 100 percent equity with a mix of dividend and capital gains income.[17]

Had we assumed that you were in the zero rather than the 70 percent personal tax bracket, that either the corporate or the personal tax rates

---

[17] Effective total tax rate = Taxes/EBIT
                             = (EBIT − CF)/EBIT.

Example: 100 percent equity, 100 percent payout: ($20,000 − $3,240)/$20,000 = 83.8%.

were changed, or that a different dividend payout policy was followed, the net effects of corporate leverage would have changed. In general, the following points apply:

1. If all investors were in the zero personal tax bracket, then the original MM analysis with taxes still would be appropriate.
2. If the personal tax rates on both debt and equity income were identical, then again the original MM tax position would apply.
3. However, if capital gains are taxed at a lower rate than interest and dividends, and if a part of the equity return is received as capital gains, then the personal tax advantage of equity financing will offset some of the advantages of corporate debt financing. In terms of Figure 17-4, the effect would be to reduce somewhat the slope of the line labeled "'Pure' MM Value," and thereby lower the optimal debt ratio.

The third situation is undoubtedly the one that applies in reality—personal tax advantages of equity offset some of the advantages of corporate debt financing.

Miller's Model

In his 1976 Presidential Address to the American Finance Association, Merton Miller introduced the ideas discussed above and developed Equation 17-11 to show how leverage affects value when both personal and corporate taxes are taken into account:[18]

$$V_L = V_U + \left[1 - \frac{(1 - t_c)(1 - t_{ps})}{(1 - t_{pD})} \right] D. \qquad (17\text{-}11)$$

The second term on the right replaces the term tD in the original MM work; and t_c is the corporate tax rate, t_{ps} is the personal tax rate on income from stocks, and t_{pD} is the personal tax rate on interest income from debt. The tax rate on stock, t_{ps}, is a weighted average of the tax on dividends and the tax on capital gains.

If the personal tax rates on debt and equity returns are equal (that is, if $t_{ps} = t_{pD}$), then Equation 17-11 reduces to $V_L = V_U + t_c D$, the original MM position. Miller himself concluded, for reasons set forth in his article, that tax rates are probably such that $(1 - t_c)(1 - t_{ps}) = (1 - t_{pD})$, which causes the second term on the right in Equation 17-11 to go to zero, V_L to equal V_U, and leverage to have no effect on the value of the firm or its cost of capital. In other words, he concluded that the personal tax advantages of equity probably just about offset the corporate tax advantages of debt. His analysis suggested that there is an optimal capital structure for all firms in the aggregate, but that one capital structure is as good as any other for an individual firm.

[18] M. H. Miller, "Debt and Taxes," *Journal of Finance*, May 1977, 261-275.

Others have extended and tested Miller's analysis. Generally, these extensions suggest that Miller's conclusion that there is no advantage whatever from the use of corporate debt is unwarranted. In all probability, based on the most recently available empirical evidence, the product $(1 - t_c)(1 - t_{ps})$ is less than $(1 - t_{pD})$, a condition which gives rise to some tax advantage to the use of corporate debt.[19] However, the tax advantages of debt are clearly less than were implied in the original MM tax article.

The Current View of Financial Leverage

The great contribution of MM and their followers is that they clarified the sources of the benefits and costs of using debt—taxes, bankruptcy costs, EBIT effects, and agency costs. Prior to MM, we simply had no capital structure theory, and no way of rationally considering just how much debt a firm should use. The current (1981) view of most authorities is captured in Figure 17-5.[20] The top graph shows the relationship between the debt ratio and the cost of debt, the cost of equity, and the average cost of capital. Both k_s and $k_d(1 - t)$ rise steadily with increases in leverage, but the rate of increase accelerates at higher debt levels, reflecting the increased likelihood of bankruptcy and its related costs. The weighted average cost first declines, then hits a minimum at D/V*, and then begins to rise. Note, however, that the k_a curve is shaped more like a shallow bowl than like a sharp V, indicating that over a fairly wide range the debt ratio does not have a pronounced effect on the average cost of capital.

The bottom graph in Figure 17-5 shows the general relationship between the value of the firm and its debt ratio. This graph is based on Figure 17-4. Notice that the same debt ratio which minimizes the weighted average cost of capital also maximizes the firm's value. Thus, the optimal capital structure can be defined in terms of cost minimization or value maximization, for the same capital structure does both.

Empirical Relationships

There is very little disagreement in either business or academic circles that the general situation as described in Figure 17-5 is correct. However, there is a great deal of disagreement over (1) whether arbitrage can work exactly as MM suggest to produce the tax shelter benefit tD; (2) the sig-

---

[19] See R. H. Litzenberger, "Debt, Taxes, and Incompleteness: A Survey," (Paper presented at the Thirty-ninth Annual Meeting of the American Finance Association, Denver, September 1980), for an excellent analysis of the theoretical and empirical work that has followed Miller's "Debt and Taxes."

[20] In the literature there is set forth a position called "the traditional view," which means the view of people prior to MM. Unfortunately, before MM, writers simply were not very specific, so it is hard to tell what they thought. It is interesting to note, though, that when MM and their followers drew graphs of "the traditional view," they looked very much like what we now call "the current view."

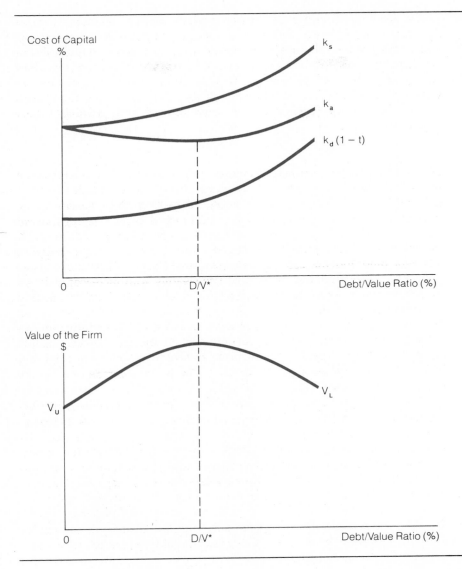

Figure 17-5
Effect of Leverage on
Value and Cost of
Capital: The Current
View

nificance of bankruptcy costs; (3) the extent to which agency costs and other factors lower EBIT as leverage increases; and (4) the precise effects of personal taxes.

The problem is not a theoretical one; it is an empirical (or statistical) one. We are simply not able to measure the relevant variables accurately enough to ascertain the true relationships. We can, of course, determine the values of V, D, and S, and we can get a reasonably good "fix" on k_d

and k_s for a given firm with a given capital structure. However, we cannot determine with much precision what would happen to these values if the firm changed its capital structure, at least not for firms whose capital structures are "reasonable." The studies cited at the end of this chapter describe some of the research that has attempted to resolve the empirical problems, but a careful review of this work leads one to conclude that determining the optimal capital structure necessarily involves a great deal of judgment.

Summary

In this chapter we examined the major elements of the theory of capital structure. We saw that two early theories—Net Income (NI) and Net Operating Income (NOI)—were advanced to explain the relationship between leverage and the firm's value and cost of capital. Using NI and NOI as a starting point, Franco Modigliani and Merton Miller (MM) added a tax effect and then developed a formal model which supported the NOI theory and led to the conclusion that the use of leverage lowers a firm's cost of capital and raises its value, with both results flowing directly (and only) from the tax savings attributable to the fact that interest is a deductible expense.

The basic MM theory (with corporate taxes) led to the conclusion that firms should use virtually 100 percent debt financing. However, MM's analysis was based on some unrealistic assumptions, and it also ignored (1) bankruptcy costs, (2) agency costs, (3) the harmful effects of excessive leverage on expected EBIT, and (4) personal taxes. When these factors are taken into account, we conclude that each firm does have an optimal capital structure which simultaneously maximizes its value and minimizes its cost of capital.

Although a great deal of empirical work has been done on the exact relationship between leverage, value, and cost of capital, it has not produced definitive results. While the research has established that there are benefits to be had from going from zero to some positive level of debt, or from an extremely high debt ratio to a somewhat more moderate amount of debt, the research has not been able to pinpoint the optimal amount of debt. Therefore, establishing the target capital structure remains a matter of informed judgment.

Questions

17-1 Explain why "agency costs" would probably be more of a problem for a small firm that is heavily engaged in R&D than for a large public utility.

17-2 Draw graphs which illustrate (1) NOI, (2) NI, and (3) "the current view" of the relationship between leverage, value, and the cost of capital.

17-3 Use Equation 17-3 to explain why the capital structure which maximizes a firm's value must also minimize its weighted average cost of capital.

17-4 The stock of XYZ Company is currently selling at its low for the year, but management feels that the stock price is only temporarily depressed because of investor pessimism. The firm's capital budget this year is so large that the use of new outside equity is contemplated. However, management does not want to sell new stock at the current low price and is therefore considering a departure from its "optimal" capital structure by borrowing the funds it would otherwise have raised in the equity markets. Does this seem to be a wise move?

17-5 Explain, in words, how MM use the arbitrage process to prove the validity of the NOI approach. Also, list the major MM assumptions and explain why each of these assumptions is necessary in the arbitrage proof.

17-6 A utility company is supposed to be allowed to charge prices high enough to cover all costs, including its cost of capital. Public service commissions are supposed to take actions to stimulate companies to operate as efficiently as possible in order to keep costs, hence prices, as low as possible. In the mid-1960s, AT&T's debt ratio was about 33 percent. Some people (M. J. Gordon in particular) argued that a higher debt ratio would lower AT&T's cost of capital and permit it to charge lower rates for telephone service. Gordon thought an optimal debt ratio for AT&T was about 50 percent. How would people who believe in the NI, NOI, MM, and MM with bankruptcy cost theories react to this controversy?

Problems

17-1 Companies U and L are identical in every respect except that U is unlevered while L has $10 million of 5 percent bonds outstanding. Assume (1) that all of the MM assumptions are met, (2) that the tax rate is 40 percent, (3) that EBIT is $2 million, and (4) that the equity capitalization rate for Company U is 10 percent.
   a. What value would MM estimate for each firm?
   b. Suppose V_U = $8 million and V_L = $18 million. According to MM, do these represent equilibrium? If not, explain the process by which equilibrium will be restored. No calculations are necessary.

17-2 Company L and Company U are in the same risk class and are identical in every respect except that Company L is levered, while Company U is not. Company L has $3 million in 5 percent bonds outstanding. Both firms earn 10 percent *before interest and taxes* on their $5 million of total assets. Assume perfect capital markets, rational investors, and so on; a tax rate of 60 percent; and a capitalization rate of 10 percent for an all equity company.
   a. Compute the values of Firms L and U using the net income (NI) approach.
   b. Compute the value of each firm using the net operating income (NOI) approach.
   c. Using the NOI approach, calculate the after-tax weighted average cost of capital, k_a, for Firms L and U. Which of those two firms has an optimal capital structure according to the NOI approach? Why?
   d. According to the NOI approach, the values for Firms L and U computed in Part a above are not in equilibrium. If a situation like this

exists, an investor in the overvalued firm can, through the arbitrage process, secure the same income at lower cost. Assuming that you own 1 percent of L's stock, show the process which will give you the same amount of income but at less cost. At what point would this process stop? (Hint: Sell your holdings in L and use personal leverage equal to 0.01(1 − t)(L's debt). Buy 1 percent of U's stock. Now compare your income and risk versus that in your original position.)

e. Company U wants to change its capital structure by introducing debt. Management believes that the cost of equity to the firm will take the form

$$k_s = R_F + r_1 + r_2,$$

where

k_s = the cost of equity.

R_F = the after-tax riskless interest rate, currently at about 6 percent.

r_1 = a premium demanded from the firm as a result of its particular business activity, currently estimated to be 4 percent.

r_2 = a premium demanded as a result of the firm's financial leverage.

Management believes that the premium, r_2, can be approximated by taking the firm's *debt/value* ratio, squaring it, and multiplying by 0.10 to give the additional percentage points of premium required by the market. Management also feels that the firm's cost of debt is a function of the debt ratio, and estimates that this function is approximately equal to the following schedule:

Debt/Value Ratio	After-Tax Cost of Debt
0%	0.05
20	0.05
30	0.06
40	0.07
60	0.12

Is there an optimal capital structure for Firm U? If so, what is the approximate value of the optimal debt/equity ratio? Could you state that the value of the firm is strictly in accordance with the following equation?

$$V_L = V_U + Dt.$$

17-3 Overseas Enterprises, Incorporated, is just about to commence operations as an international trading company. The firm will have book assets of $10 million, and it expects to earn a 20 percent return on these assets before taxes. However, because of certain tax arrangements with foreign governments, OEI will actually pay no taxes; that is, its tax rate will be zero. Management is trying to decide how to raise the required $10 million. It is known that the capitalization rate for an all equity firm in this business is 10 percent; that is, $k_s = 10\%$ for an all equity operation. Further, OEI can borrow at a rate $k_d = 6\%$. Part of the management team believes the NI theory of valuation is the correct one, while others are convinced that the NOI theory is valid.

a. What will be the value of the firm if it uses no debt and also if it uses $6 million of 6 percent debt, according to both the NI and the NOI advocates?

b. For capital budgeting purposes, what would OEI's cost of capital be under each of the two theories?

c. What would happen to the value of the firm, to k_a, and to k_s according to each theory if the amount of debt were increased from $6 million to $9 million? to $19 million?

d. Graph the relationship between the debt ratio and V, D, and S, and also k_d, k_s, and k_a, for both NI and NOI. What do these graphs suggest about the importance of capital structure decisions?

e. Which theory do MM support? What are their two propositions?

f. What are MM's major assumptions? How do MM use these assumptions to prove their two propositions, and thus to "prove" that NOI is correct? Illustrate with the data given in the basic problem, assuming that OEI uses $6 million of debt and gets an initial value of $V_L = \$22.4$, but also assuming that some other firm in the same risk class is identical in every respect except that it uses only equity and has a value of $V_U = \$20$ million. Assume that you own 10 percent of the leveraged firm, OEI, and show how you could raise your income without raising your risk if this situation existed.

g. What are the major criticisms of the MM theory as we have expressed it thus far?

h. Assume the initial facts of the problem ($k_d = 6\%$, EBIT = $2 million, $k_{sU} = 10\%$), but now assume that a 40 percent corporate tax rate exists. Find the new values for OEI with zero debt and with $6 million of debt, using the MM formulas.

i. What are the values of k_a and k_s at debt levels of D = 0, D = $6 million, D = $10 million, and D = $20 million? Plot the relationships between the value of the firm and the debt ratio, and between the cost of capital and the debt ratio.

j. How would each of these factors tend to change the values you plotted in your graph?

1. The interest rate on debt increases as the debt ratio rises.
2. At higher levels of debt, the probability of bankruptcy rises. This causes a reduction in expected EBIT.

17-4 Until recently, Zenith Company carried a triple A bond rating and was strong in every respect. However, a series of problems has afflicted the firm. It is currently in severe financial distress, and its ability to make future payments on outstanding debt is questionable. If the firm were forced into bankruptcy at this time, the common stockholders would almost certainly be wiped out. Although Zenith has limited financial resources, its cash flows (primarily from depreciation) are sufficient to support one of two mutually exclusive investments, each costing $150 million. These projects have the same market (or systematic) risk, but different total risk as measured by the variance of returns. Each project has the following after-tax cash flows:

	Annual Cash Inflows	
Probability	Project A	Project B
0.5	$30,000,000	$10,000,000
0.5	$35,000,000	$50,000,000

Zenith's weighted average cost of capital is 15 percent regardless of which project it chooses. Each project has an expected life of ten years.

a. What is the expected cash inflow from each project?
b. Which project has the greater total risk?
c. Which project would you choose if you were a Zenith stockholder? Why?
d. Which project would the bondholders prefer to see management select? Why?
e. If the choices conflict, what "protection" do the bondholders have against the firm's making a decision that is contrary to their interests?
f. Who bears the cost of this "protection"? How is this cost related to leverage and the optimal capital structure?

17-5 Nadir Incorporated is an unlevered firm, and it has constant expected operating earnings (EBIT) of $2 million per year. Nadir's tax rate is 40 percent, and its market value is $V = S = 12 million. Management is considering the use of debt. (Debt would be issued and used to buy back stock, so the size of the firm would remain constant.) Since interest expense is tax deductible, the value of the firm would tend to increase as debt is added to the capital structure, but there would be an offset in the form of a rising risk of bankruptcy. The firm's analysts have estimated, as an approximation, that the present value of any future bankruptcy cost is $8 million, and that the probability of bankruptcy would increase with leverage according to the following schedule:

Value of debt (millions):	$2.5	$5.0	$7.5	$10.0	$15.0	$20.0
Probability of failure:	0%	1.25%	2.5%	6.25%	31.25%	75.0%

a. What is Nadir's cost of equity and average cost of capital at this time?
b. According to the "pure" MM after-tax valuation model, what is the optimum level of debt?
c. What is the optimal capital structure when bankruptcy costs are included?
d. Plot the value of the firm, with and without bankruptcy costs, as a function of the level of debt.

17-6 Baxter, Incorporated, currently has no debt. An in-house research group has just been assigned the job of determining whether the firm should change its capital structure. Because of the importance of the decision, management has also hired the investment banking firm of Stanley Morgan to conduct a parallel analysis of the situation. Mr. Smith, the in-house analyst, who is well-versed in modern finance theory, has decided to carry out the analysis using the MM framework. Mr. Jones, the Stanley Morgan consultant, who has a good knowledge of capital market conditions and is confident of his ability to predict the firm's debt and equity costs at various levels of debt, has decided to estimate the optimal capital structure as that structure which minimizes the firm's weighted average cost of capital. The following data are relevant to both analyses:

> EBIT = $4 million per year, in perpetuity.
> Tax rate = 40%.
> Dividend payout ratio = 100%.
> Current required rate of return on equity = 12%.

The cost of capital schedule predicted by Mr. Jones follows:

	At a Debt Level of ($ in Millions)							
	$0	$2	$4	$6	$8	$10	$12	$14
Cost of Debt (%)	8.0	8.0	8.3	9.0	10.0	11.0	13.0	16.0
Cost of Equity (%)	12.0	12.25	12.75	13.0	13.15	13.40	14.65	17.0

The following are additional data acquired by Mr. Smith:

> Present value of bankruptcy costs = $8 million.

	At a Debt Level of ($ in Millions)							
	$0	$2	$4	$6	$8	$10	$12	$14
Probability of bankruptcy	0	0	0.05	0.07	0.10	0.17	0.47	0.90

a. What level of debt would Mr. Jones and Mr. Smith recommend as optimal?

b. Comment on the similarities and differences in their recommendations.

Selected References

The body of literature on capital structure—and the number of potential references—is huge. Therefore, only a sampling can be given here. For an extensive review of the recent literature, as well as a detailed bibliography, see:

Beranek, William, "Research Directions in Finance," *Quarterly Review of Business and Economics,* Spring 1981, 6-24.

The major theoretical works on capital structure theory, in the order of their appearance, include the following:

Durand, David, "Costs of Debt and Equity Funds for Business: Trends and Problems of Measurement," *Conference on Research in Business Finance* (New York: National Bureau of Economic Research, 1952).

Modigliani, Franco, and Merton H. Miller, "The Cost of Capital, Corporation Finance and the Theory of Investment," *American Economic Review,* vol. 48 (June 1958), 261-297.

———, "The Cost of Capital, Corporation Finance and the Theory of Investment: Reply," *American Economic Review,* vol. 49 (September 1958), 655-669. "Taxes and the Cost of Capital: A Correction," *American Economic Review,* vol. 53 (June 1963), 433-443. "Reply," *American Economic Review,* vol. 55 (June 1965), 524-527.

Hamada, R. S., "Portfolio Analysis, Market Equilibrium, and Corporation Finance," *Journal of Finance,* vol. 24 (March 1969), 13-32.

These works and others are discussed in an integrated framework in:

Fama, Eugene F., and Merton H. Miller, *The Theory of Finance* (New York: Holt, Rinehart and Winston, 1972).

The addition of personal taxes into capital structure analysis has been dealt with in these articles:

Gordon, Myron J., and L. I. Gould, "The Cost of Equity Capital with Personal Income Taxes and Flotation Costs," *Journal of Finance,* vol. 33 (September 1978), 1201-1212.

Miller, Merton H., "Debt and Taxes," *Journal of Finance,* May 1977, 261-276.

Some other references of note include the following:

Conine, Thomas E., Jr., "Debt Capacity and the Capital Budgeting Decision: Comment," *Financial Management,* vol. 9 (Spring 1980), 20-22.

Ferri, Michael G., and Wesley H. Jones, "Determinants of Financial Structure: A New Methodological Approach," *Journal of Finance,* vol. 34 (June 1979), 631-644.

Flath, D., and C. R. Knoeber, "Taxes, Failure Costs and Optimal Industry Capital Structure," *Journal of Finance,* vol. 35 (March 1980), 89-117.

Jensen, Michael C., and William H. Meckling, "Theory of the Firm: Managerial Behavior, Agency Costs and Ownership Structure," *Journal of Financial Economics,* vol. 3 (October 1976), 305-360.

Lee, Wayne Y., and Henry H. Barker, "Bankruptcy Costs and the Firm's Optimal Debt Capacity: A Positive Theory of Capital Structure," *Southern Economic Journal,* vol. 43 (April 1977), 1453-1465.

Martin, John D., and David F. Scott, "Debt Capacity and the Capital Budgeting Decision: A Revisitation," *Financial Management,* vol. 9 (Spring 1980), 23-26.

Schneller, Meir I., "Taxes and the Optimal Capital Structure of the Firm," *Journal of Finance,* vol. 35 (March 1980), 119-127.

Taggart, Robert A., Jr., "Taxes and Corporate Capital Structure in an Incomplete Market," *Journal of Finance,* vol. 35 (June 1980), 645-659.

Warner, J. B., "Bankruptcy Costs: Some Evidence," *Journal of Finance,* vol. 32 (May 1977), 337-348.

18　Dividend Policy

Dividend policy involves the decision to pay out earnings or to retain them for reinvestment in the firm. Our basic stock price model, $P_0 = D_1/(k_s - g)$, shows that a policy of paying out more cash dividends will raise D_1, which will tend to increase the price of the stock. However, raising cash dividends means that less money is available for reinvestment, and plowing back less earnings into the business will lower the expected growth rate and depress the price of the stock. Thus, dividend policy has two opposing effects, and *the optimal policy is the one that strikes a balance between current dividends and future growth and thereby maximizes the price of the firm's stock.*

A number of factors influence dividend policy. Included are the differential tax rates on dividends and capital gains, the investment opportunities available to the firm, alternative sources of capital, and stockholders' preferences for current versus future income. The major goal of this chapter is to show how these and other factors interact to determine the optimal dividend policy.

The Residual Theory of Dividends

In the preceding chapters on capital budgeting and the cost of capital, we indicated that, generally, the cost of capital and investment opportunity schedules must be combined before the cost of capital can be established. In other words, the optimum capital budget, the marginal cost of capital, and the marginal rate of return on investment are determined *simultaneously.* In this section we use this framework to develop what is called *the residual theory of dividends,* which states that a firm should follow these four steps: (1) determine the optimal capital budget; (2) determine the amount of equity needed to finance that budget; (3) use retained earnings to supply this equity to the extent possible; and (4) pay dividends only if more earnings are available than are needed to support the capital budget. The word *residual* implies "left over," and the residual theory states that dividends should be paid only out of leftover earnings.

The basis of the theory is that *investors prefer to have the firm retain and reinvest earnings rather than pay them out in dividends if the return on reinvested earnings exceeds the rate of return the investors could obtain on other investments of comparable risk.* If the corporation can reinvest retained earnings at a 20 percent rate of return, while the best rate stockholders can obtain if the earnings are passed on in the form of dividends is 12 percent, then stockholders would prefer to have the firm retain the profits.

We saw in Chapter 15 that the cost of retained earnings is an *opportunity cost* that reflects rates of return available to equity investors. If a firm's stockholders could buy other stocks of equal risk and obtain a 12 percent dividend-plus-capital-gain yield, then 12 percent is the firm's cost of retained earnings. The cost of new outside equity raised by selling common stock is higher because of the costs of floating the issue.

Most firms have a target capital structure that calls for at least some debt, so new financing is done partly with debt and partly with equity. As long as the firm finances at the optimum point, using the proper amounts of debt and equity, and provided it uses only internally generated equity (retained earnings), its marginal cost of each new dollar of capital will be minimized. Internally generated equity is available for financing a certain amount of new investment; beyond this amount, the firm must turn to more expensive new common stock. At the point where new stock must be sold, the cost of equity and, consequently, the marginal cost of capital, rises.

These concepts, which were developed in Chapter 15, are illustrated in Figure 18-1 with data from the Erie Steel Company. Erie has a marginal cost of capital of 10 percent as long as retained earnings are available, but MCC begins to rise at the point where new stock must be sold. Erie has $60 million of earnings and a 40 percent optimum debt ratio. Provided it does not pay cash dividends, Erie can make net investments (investments in addition to asset replacements financed from deprecia-

Figure 18-1
Marginal Cost of Capital

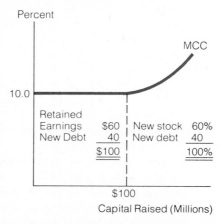

tion) of $100 million, consisting of $60 million from retained earnings plus $40 million of new debt supported by the retained earnings, at a 10 percent marginal cost of capital. Therefore, its marginal cost of capital is constant at 10 percent up to $100 million of capital. Beyond $100 million, the marginal cost of capital rises as the firm begins to use more expensive new common stock. Of course, if Erie does not retain all of its earnings, the MCC will begin to rise before $100 million. For example, if Erie retained only $30 million, then the MCC would begin to rise at $30 million retained earnings + $20 million debt = $50 million.

Now suppose Erie's director of capital budgeting constructs an Investment Opportunity Schedule and plots it on a graph. The investment opportunity schedules for three different years—one for a good year (IOS_G), one for a normal year (IOS_N), and one for a bad year (IOS_B)—are shown in Figure 18-2. IOS_G shows that Erie can invest more money, and at

Figure 18-2
Investment Opportunity
(or IRR) Schedules

higher rates of return, than it can when the investment opportunities are as given by IOS_N and IOS_B.

In Figure 18-3 we combine the investment opportunity schedules with the cost of capital schedule. The point where the IOS curve cuts the MCC curve defines the proper level of new investment. When investment opportunities are relatively bad (IOS_B), the optimum level of investment is $40 million; when opportunities are normal (IOS_N), $70 million should be

Figure 18-3
Interrelation among Cost of Capital, Investment Opportunities, and New Investment

invested; and when opportunities are relatively good (IOS_G), Erie should make new investments in the amount of $150 million.

Consider the situation where IOS_G is the appropriate schedule. Erie has $60 million in earnings and a 40 percent target debt ratio. Thus, it can finance $100 million, consisting of $60 million of retained earnings plus $40 million of new debt, at a cost of 10 percent if it retains all of its earnings. If it pays out part of the earnings in dividends, then it will have to begin using expensive new common stock earlier than need be, so the MCC curve will rise before it otherwise would. *This suggests that under the conditions of IOS_G, Erie should retain all of its earnings. According to the residual theory, its payout ratio should be zero.*

Under the conditions of IOS_N, however, Erie should invest only $70 million. How should this investment be financed? First, notice that if it retains the full amount of its earnings, $60 million, it will need to sell only $10 million of new debt. However, if Erie retains $60 million and sells only $10 million of new debt, it will move away from its target capital structure. To stay on target, Erie must finance 60 percent of the required $70 million by equity—retained earnings—and 40 percent by debt; this means retaining $42 million and selling $28 million of new debt. Since Erie retains only $42 million of its $60 million total earnings, it must distribute the residual, $18 million, to its stockholders. Thus, its optimal payout ratio is $18 million/$60 million = 30 percent.

Under the conditions of IOS_B, Erie should invest only $40 million. Because it has $60 million in earnings, it could finance the entire $40 million out of retained earnings and still have $20 million available for dividends. Should this be done? Under our assumptions, this would not be a good decision, because Erie would move away from its optimal capital structure. To stay at the 40 percent target debt/assets ratio, Erie must retain $24 million of earnings and sell $16 million of debt. When the $24 million of retained earnings is subtracted from the $60 million total earnings, Erie is left with a residual of $36 million, the amount that should be paid out in dividends. Thus, the payout ratio as prescribed by the residual theory is 60 percent.

Is Dividend Policy Really Relevant?

It has been asserted that dividend policy has no effect either on the price of a firm's stock or on its cost of capital; that is, that dividend policy is irrelevant. The principal proponents of this view are Merton Miller and Franco Modigliani (MM).[1] MM prove their position in a theoretical sense, but only under the assumptions that (1) there are no personal or corporate income taxes, (2) there are no stock flotation costs, and (3) the "pure MM leverage theory" is correct. Since these assumptions are clearly not true, dividend policy may be and probably is relevant in the sense that it influences stock prices and the cost of capital.

However, MM's analysis does make it quite clear that the residual theory is only a starting point in establishing a dividend policy. Other factors must also be taken into account. Some of these factors are discussed in the next section.

Factors That Influence Dividend Policy

By definition, the optimal dividend policy is the one that maximizes the price of a firm's stock. Suppose Erie Steel has the cost of capital schedule shown in Figure 18-3, and IOS_N is the applicable set of investment opportunities. Under these conditions, the residual theory indicates that Erie should pay out 30 percent of its earnings. What would happen if Erie set a different dividend policy? How would this affect the price of the firm's stock?

Consider the options open to Erie. The firm could change its dividend policy by increasing or by decreasing the payout ratio, but either action would necessitate other changes in corporate policy. Thus, if Erie *raises* its dividends, it must do one of the following: (1) reduce its level of investment below $70 million, thereby foregoing profitable projects; (2) sell common stock to replace the retained earnings, thus incurring unnecessary flotation costs; or (3) replace the retained earnings with additional debt, thus moving away from the optimal capital structure. On the other hand, if Erie *reduces* its dividends, it must also (1) increase its capital bud-

---

[1] Merton H. Miller and Franco Modigliani, "Dividend Policy, Growth, and the Valuation of Shares," *Journal of Business*, vol. 34 (October 1961), 411-433.

get, which would involve accepting unprofitable projects, or (2) use the extra retained earnings as a substitute for new debt, which would cause a departure from the target capital structure.

It would therefore appear that the dividend policy as determined by the residual theory is the only dividend policy that will maximize the price of the firm's stock. However, a critical assumption is embodied in the residual theory—it assumes that k_s, the rate of return investors require on the stock, is not affected by the firm's dividend policy. In the case of Erie Steel, the residual theory implicitly assumes that so long as the company maintains its 40 percent debt ratio, k_s remains constant at 13.3 percent. This implies that investors are indifferent between dividends and capital gains, and that

$$k_s = D_1/P_0 + g = 13.3\%$$

for any combination of dividend yield and capital gains yield.

The question of whether or not dividend policy affects the cost of equity has been hotly debated in academic circles. Myron Gordon and John Lintner, on the one hand, have argued that k_s increases as the dividend payout ratio is reduced. They say, in effect, that investors value a dollar of expected dividends more highly than a dollar of expected capital gains.[2] Miller and Modigliani, on the other hand, have argued that k_s is independent of dividend policy, which implies that investors are indifferent between dividends and capital gains.[3]

Figure 18-4 presents two graphs which highlight the arguments. The left panel shows the Miller-Modigliani position. Here the company has $k_s = D_1/P_0 + g = 13.3\%$ for any dividend policy: The equilibrium return, k_s, is assumed to be a constant regardless of whether it comes entirely as dividend yield, entirely as expected capital gains, or as a combination of the two. Dividends may be less risky than expected capital gains, but capital gains are taxed at a lower rate, and MM assume that these two effects offset one another.

The right panel shows the Gordon-Lintner view. They argue that the greater risk of possible capital gains more than offsets the tax benefits of gains over dividends, so investors are willing to accept a lower total return (k_s) if it has a heavier dividend yield component. In other words, Gordon-Lintner assume that more than 1 percent of additional g is required to offset a 1 percent reduction of dividend yield.

---

[2] M. J. Gordon, "Optimal Investment and Financing Policy," *Journal of Finance*, May 1963, 264-272; and J. Lintner, "Dividends, Earnings, Leverage, Stock Prices, and the Supply of Capital to Corporations," *Review of Economics and Statistics*, August 1962, 243-269. In essence, Gordon and Lintner argue that dividends are regarded by investors as being less risky than the potential future capital gains produced by retained earnings, and this risk differential causes k_s to be a function of payout.

[3] M. H. Miller and F. Modigliani, "Dividend Policy, Growth, and the Valuation of Shares." MM argue that investors tend to reinvest dividends in stocks of the same or equally risky companies, hence dividends are really about as risky as retained earnings. They call the Gordon-Lintner argument "the bird in the hand fallacy."

Figure 18-4
The Modigliani-Miller and Gordon-Lintner Dividend
Hypotheses

a. Dividends Are Irrelevant (MM)

b. Dividends Are Relevant: Investors Like Dividends (Gordon-Lintner)

Attempts have been made to test the MM and Gordon-Lintner hypotheses.[4] In theory, one could take a sample of companies which have different dividend policies, hence different dividend yield and growth rate components, and plot them on graphs such as those shown in Figure 18-4. If the points all plotted on the line in the left graph so that the slope of the resulting regression line was -1.0, this would support the MM indifference hypothesis. If the points all plotted on the line in the right graph so that the slope was less negative than -1.0 (say -0.8), this would support the Gordon-Lintner hypothesis. In fact, when this is done with real companies, the slope of the regression line is found to be about -1.0. This seems to refute Gordon-Lintner, but statistical difficulties prevent us from saying that this really *proves* that MM are right, and that dividend policy does not affect k_s. There are two problems here. First, for a valid statistical test, things other than dividend policy must be held constant; that is, the sample companies must differ only with respect to

[4] See E. F. Brigham and M. J. Gordon, "Leverage, Dividend Policy, and the Cost of Capital," *Journal of Finance*, March 1968, 85-104.

their dividend policy. And second, we must be able to measure the expected growth rates for the sample firms with a high degree of accuracy. These conditions do not hold. We simply cannot find a set of publicly owned firms that differ only with respect to dividend policy, and we cannot get precise estimates of investors' expected growth rates. Therefore, we cannot determine empirically what effect, if any, dividend policy has on the cost of equity. However, the research that has been done does provide us with a good starting point for analyzing dividend policy decisions.

The factors which influence dividend policy may be grouped into four broad categories: (1) constraints on dividend payments, (2) investment opportunities, (3) availability and cost of alternative sources of capital, and (4) effects of dividend policy on the required rate of return, k_s. Each of these categories has several subparts. They are all discussed below.

1. Bond Indentures. Debt contracts generally restrict dividend payment to earnings generated after the loan was granted. Also, debt contracts often stipulate that no dividends can be paid unless the current ratio, the times-interest-earned ratio, and other safety ratios exceed stated minimums.

Constraints

2. Impairment of Capital Rule. Dividend payments cannot exceed the balance sheet item "retained earnings." This is a legal restriction known as the impairment of capital rule, and it is designed to protect creditors. ("Liquidating dividends" can be paid out of capital, but they must be indicated as such, and they must not reduce capital below limits stated in the debt contract.)

3. Availability of Cash. Cash dividends can only be paid with cash. Thus, a shortage of cash in the bank can restrict dividend payments. However, unused borrowing capacity can offset this factor.

4. Penalty Tax on Improperly Accumulated Earnings. To prevent wealthy individuals from using corporations to avoid personal taxes, the tax code provides for a special surtax on improperly accumulated income (see Chapter 2). Thus, if the IRS can demonstrate that the dividend payout ratio is being deliberately held down to help stockholders avoid personal taxes, the firm is subject to heavy penalties.

5. Location of the IOS Schedule. If the relevant IOS schedule in Figure 18-3 is far to the right, this will tend to produce a low payout, and conversely if the IOS is far to the left. Also, the steeper the slope of the IOS, the more important it is to use the payout prescribed by the residual theory.

Investment Opportunities

6. Possibility of Accelerating or Delaying Projects. If the firm can accelerate or postpone projects, this will permit more flexibility in its dividend policy.

Alternative Sources of Capital

7. Cost of Selling New Stock. If a firm wishes to finance a given level of investment, it can obtain equity by retaining earnings or by selling new common stock. If flotation costs are high, k_e will be well above k_s, making it much better to finance through retention versus sale of new common stock (see Chapter 15). If flotation costs are low, then dividend policy will be less important. Flotation costs must include underwriting costs and underpricing caused by a downward sloping demand curve for new stock (see Chapter 14). Flotation costs differ among firms (for example, they are higher for small firms). Hence, the importance of dividend policy and the optimal policy vary among firms.

8. Control. If management is concerned about maintaining control, it may be reluctant to sell new stock, hence may retain more earnings than it otherwise would. This factor is most important for small, closely held firms.

9. Capital Structure Flexibility. A firm can finance a given level of investment with debt or equity. As we saw above, if stock flotation costs are low, dividend policy is less important because equity can be raised by retaining earnings or by selling new stock. A similar situation holds for debt policy. If the firm is willing to adjust its debt ratio, it can maintain a constant dollar dividend by using a variable debt ratio. The shape of the average cost of capital curve (left panel in Figure 18-1) determines the practical extent to which the debt ratio can be varied. If the average cost of capital curve is relatively flat over a wide range, then dividend policy is less critical than it is if the curve has a distinct minimum.

Effects of Dividend Policy on k_s

10. Capital Gains Tax Rate. Dividends are taxed at federal rates up to 70 percent, plus additional state taxes. The tax on capital gains is generally limited to 28 percent. This makes wealthy investors tend to prefer capital gains to dividends. To the extent that this factor is important, k_s will be smaller the lower the payout, other things held constant. If k_s does vary with the dividend payout, then the MCC curves in Figures 18-1 and 18-3 are not constant as shown, but vary depending on the payout. This could invalidate the residual theory and require more complex decision rules. In general, tax effects should cause the optimal payout to be *lower* than that suggested by the simple residual theory.

Large, publicly owned firms have stockholders whose tax brackets range from zero (for some retirees and institutional investors such as pension funds) to about 80 percent (for wealthy individuals). This makes it difficult to accommodate all stockholders and thus creates a problem—for which group of stockholders should dividend policy be set? To the extent that stockholders can shift their investments among firms, a firm can set any specific policy, then have stockholders who do not like this policy sell to other investors who do. Thus, the firm will attract a certain clientele of stockholders. However, switching may be inefficient because of (1) brokerage costs, (2) the possibility that selling stockholders must pay capital gains taxes, and (3) a possible shortage of investors who like the firm's newly stated dividend policy.

11. Stockholders' Desire for Current versus Future Income. Some stockholders desire current income; retired individuals and university endowment funds are examples. Other stockholders have no need for current investment income and simply reinvest any dividends received, after first paying income taxes on the dividend income. If the firm retains and reinvests income, rather than paying dividends, those stockholders who need current income will be disadvantaged. They will presumably receive capital gains, but they will be forced to sell off some of their shares to obtain cash. This will involve brokerage costs, which are relatively high unless large sums are involved. Also, some institutional investors (or trustees for individuals) may be precluded from selling stock and then "spending capital." Stockholders who are saving rather than spending dividends will, of course, have to incur brokerage costs to reinvest their dividends. (However, as we note in a later section, many firms today have automatic dividend reinvestment plans which minimize the expense of reinvestment.)

Investors can, of course, switch companies if they own stock in a firm whose dividend policy differs from the policies they desire. This is another example of the "clientele effect," and the same three constraints on switching noted in Item 10 apply.

12. Risk of Dividends versus Risk of Capital Gains. It has been argued that investors regard returns coming in the form of dividends as being less risky than capital gains returns. Others disagree. If someone receives dividends, then turns around and reinvests them in the same firm or one of similar risk, there would appear to be little difference in risk between this operation and having the company retain and reinvest the earnings in the first place. This question has been subjected to statistical studies, but without conclusive results.

13. Information Content of Dividends. It has been observed that an increase in the dividend (for example, the annual dividend per share is raised from $2 to $2.50) is often accompanied by an increase in the price of the stock, while a dividend cut generally leads to a stock price decline. This suggests to some that investors like dividends more than capital gains. However, MM argue differently. They state that corporations are always reluctant to cut dividends, so firms do not raise dividends unless they anticipate higher, or at least stable, earnings in the future. Thus, a dividend increase is a signal to investors that the firm's management forecasts good future earnings. Conversely, a dividend reduction signals that management is forecasting poor earnings in the future. Thus, MM state that a change in dividend policy is not important in the sense of showing that investors prefer dividends to retained earnings; the fact that price changes follow dividend actions simply indicates to them that there is an important *information content* in dividend announcements. Like most other aspects of dividend policy, empirical studies on this topic have been inconclusive. There clearly is some information content in dividend announcements, but it may or may not be the complete explanation for the stock price changes that follow increases or decreases in dividends.

14. Legal Listing. New York and certain other important states have a list of stocks of good, solid companies which can be purchased by certain fiduciary institutions—this is called the "legal list." Institutional investors not subject to the legal list still consider it and often refuse to buy stocks that are not included. Being on the legal list increases the demand for a firm's stock, so companies like to be on it. Since one criterion for inclusion on the legal list is the absence of dividend reductions, companies try very hard to maintain stable dividend policies.

The fourteen points discussed above are considered by financial executives when they are establishing their firms' dividend policies, but the only real generalizations we can make are these:

1. The optimal dividend policy for a firm is influenced by many factors. Some suggest a higher payout than would be called for by the residual theory, while others suggest a lower optimal payout.
2. Much research has been done on dividend policy, but many points are still unresolved. Researchers are far from being able to specify a precise model for establishing corporate dividend policy.

Although no one has been able to construct a usable model for finding an optimal dividend policy, the residual theory does at least provide a good starting point, and we do have a checklist of factors to consider before finalizing the dividend policy. Later in the chapter we shall return to the process of establishing a dividend policy, but first we must take up three other components of dividend policy—actual payment procedures, stock splits, and stock dividends.

Dividend Payment Procedures

Corporations tend to use one of three major dividend payment procedures. These alternatives are discussed in this section.

Constant, or Steadily Increasing, Dividend per Share. Some firms set a specific annual dividend per share and then maintain it, increasing the annual dividend only if it seems clear that future earnings will be sufficient to allow the dividend to be maintained. A corollary of the policy is this rule: *Avoid ever reducing the annual dividend.* The fact that many corporations do in fact follow, or attempt to follow, such a policy lends support to the information content hypothesis of Modigliani and Miller (Item 13 in the preceding section).

A stable payment policy is illustrated in Figure 18-5 with data for the Walter Watch Company over a thirty year period. Initially, earnings were $2 and dividends were $1 a share, so the payout ratio was 50 percent. Earnings rose for four years, while dividends remained constant; thus, the payout ratio fell during this period. During 1955 and 1956, earnings fell substantially; however, the dividend was maintained and the payout rose above the 50 percent target. During the period between 1956 and 1960, earnings experienced a sustained rise. Dividends were held constant for a time, while management sought to determine whether the earnings increase would be permanent. By 1961, it was apparent that the earnings gain would be maintained, so dividends were raised in three steps to reestablish the 50 percent target payout. During 1965, a strike caused earnings to fall below the regular dividend. Expecting the earnings decline to be temporary, management maintained the dividend. Earnings fluctuated on a fairly high plateau from 1966 through 1972, during which time dividends remained constant. A new increase in earnings permitted management to raise the dividend in 1973 to reestablish the 50 percent payout ratio.

**Figure 18-5
Walter Watch Company:
Dividends and Earnings
over Time**

A variant of this policy is the "stable growth rate" policy. Here the firm sets a target growth rate for dividends, say 6 percent per year, and strives to increase dividends by this amount each year. Obviously, earnings must be growing at a reasonably steady rate for this to be feasible. This policy is especially practicable during an inflationary period; hence in the 1970s and 1980s it became very popular.

There are several rationales for these policies. First, given the existence of the information content idea, a fluctuating payment policy might lead to fluctuating stock prices, which in turn could lead to a high k_s. Second, stockholders who use dividends for current consumption want to be able to count on receiving dividends on a regular basis, so irregular dividends might lower demand for the stock. Third, a stable dividend policy is most consistent with the requirements for legal listing. Fourth, even though the optimal payout (in the residual theory sense) might vary somewhat from year to year, delaying some investment projects, departing from the target capital structure during a particular year, or even selling common stock might all be preferable to cutting the dividend or reducing its growth rate. Finally, setting a steady dividend growth rate will confirm investors' estimates of the g-factor and thus enhance the price of the stock; that is, investors will think of the stock as a "growth stock."

Constant Payout Ratio. A very few firms follow a policy of paying out a constant percentage of earnings. Earnings will surely fluctuate, so following this policy necessarily means that the dollar amount of dividends will fluctuate. For reasons discussed in the preceding section, this policy is not likely to maximize a firm's stock price. However, before its bankruptcy, Penn Central Railroad did follow the policy of paying out one-half its earnings: "A dollar for the stockholders and a dollar for the company," as one director put it. Logic like this could drive any company to bankruptcy!

Low Regular Dividend plus Extras. The low regular dividend plus a year-end extra is a compromise between the first two policies. It gives the firm flexibility, but it leaves investors somewhat uncertain about what their dividend will be. Still, if a firm's earnings and cash flows are quite volatile, using extra dividends may well be its best choice. The directors can set a relatively low regular dividend—low enough that it can be maintained even in low-profit years or in years when a considerable amount of reinvestment is needed—and then supplement it with an extra dividend in years when excess funds are available. General Motors, whose earnings fluctuate widely from year to year, has long followed the practice of supplementing its regular dividend with an extra dividend paid at the end of the year, when its profits and investment requirements are known.

The Actual Payment

Dividends are normally paid quarterly. For example, AT&T paid dividends of $5.40 during 1981, $1.35 each quarter. In common financial language, we say that AT&T's *regular quarterly dividend* is $1.35, or that its *regular annual dividend* is $5.40. The actual payment procedure is as follows:

1. *Declaration date*. The directors meet, say on November 15, and declare the regular dividend. On this date, the directors issue a statement similar to the following: "On November 15, 1981, the directors of the XYZ Company met and declared the regular quarterly dividend of 50 cents a share, plus an extra dividend of $1.00 a share, payable to holders of record on December 15, payment to be made on January 2, 1982."

2. *Holder-of-record date*. At the close of business on the *holder-of-record date*, December 15, the company closes its stock transfer books and makes up a list of the shareholders as of that date. If XYZ Company is notified of the sale and transfer of some stock before 5 P.M. on December 15, the new owner receives the dividend. However, if notification is received on or after December 16, the old stockholder gets the dividend check.

3. *Ex dividend date*. Suppose Jean B buys 100 shares of stock from John S on December 13. Will the company be notified of the transfer in time to list B as the new owner and, thus, pay the dividend to her? To avoid conflict, the stock brokerage business has set up a convention of declaring that the right to the dividend remains with the stock until four business days prior to the holder-of-record date; on the fourth day before the record date, the right to the dividend no longer goes with the shares. The date when the right to the dividend leaves the stock is called the *ex dividend date*. In this case, the ex dividend date is four days prior to December 15, or December 11:

	Dec. 10
Ex dividend date:	Dec. 11
	Dec. 12
	Dec. 13
	Dec. 14
Holder-of-record date:	Dec. 15

Therefore, if B is to receive the dividend, she must buy the stock by December 10. If she buys it on December 11 or later, S will receive the dividend.

The total dividend, regular plus extra, amounts to $1.50, so the ex dividend date is important. Barring fluctuations in the stock market, we would normally expect the price of a stock to drop by approximately the amount of the dividend on the ex dividend date. Thus, if XYZ closed at $51\frac{1}{2}$ on December 10, it would probably open at about $50 on December 11.

4. *Payment date*. The company actually mails the checks to the holders of record on January 2, the payment date.

Dividend Reinvestment Plans[5]

During the 1970s most of the larger companies instituted *Dividend Reinvestment Plans*, or DRPs, whereby stockholders can automatically reinvest dividends received in the stock of the paying corporation. *There are two types of DRPs: one involves only stock that is already outstanding, while the other involves newly issued stock.* In either case, the stockholder must pay income taxes on the amount of the dividends, even though stock rather than cash is received.

Under the first type of plan, the stockholder elects either to continue receiving dividend checks or to have the dividend used to buy more stock in the corporation. If the stockholder elects reinvestment, a bank (Citibank of New York is the leader), acting as trustee, takes the total funds available for reinvestment (less a fee), purchases the corporation's stock on the open market, and allocates the shares purchased to the participating stockholders' accounts on a *pro rata* basis. The transactions costs of buying shares (brokerage costs) are low because of volume purchases, so these plans benefit small stockholders who do not need cash dividends for current consumption.

The other type of DRP provides for dividends to be invested in *newly issued stock; hence, these plans raise new capital for the firm.* AT&T, Florida Power & Light, Union Carbide, and many other companies had such plans in effect in 1981, using them to raise substantial amounts of new equity capital. No fees are charged to stockholders, and many companies offer stock at a discount of 5 percent below the actual market price. The companies absorb these costs as a tradeoff against flotation costs that would be incurred on stock sold through investment bankers rather than through the dividend reinvestment plans. Discussions with corporate treasurers suggest that many other companies are seriously considering establishing or switching to new-stock DRPs.[6]

Stock Repurchases

As an alternative to cash dividends, a firm may distribute income to stockholders by *repurchasing its own stock.* For example, in July 1981, Gulf Oil announced plans to buy back 10 million shares of its common stock. Gulf's stock was selling for about $30 per share when the repurchase plans were formulated. Subsequently, it rose to $37.50. Gulf's chairman, Jerry McAfee, noted (1) that the stock's book value was $51 per share and

---

[5] See R. H. Pettway and R. P. Malone, "Automatic Dividend Reinvestment Plans," *Financial Management*, Winter 1973, 11-18, for an excellent discussion of the topic.

[6] One interesting aspect of DRPs is that they are forcing corporations to reexamine their basic dividend policies. A high participation rate in a DRP suggests that stockholders might be better off if the firm simply reduced cash dividends, as this would save stockholders some personal income taxes. Quite a few firms are surveying their stockholders to learn more about their preferences and to find out how they would react to a change in dividend policy. A more rational approach to basic dividend policy decisions may emerge from this research.

(2) that the replacement value of Gulf's assets was about $130 per share. Thus, in management's view, the stock was underpriced and represented an attractive investment.

Other reasons for distributing corporate income through repurchase rather than as cash dividends include these: (1) it avoids the high personal tax rate on cash dividends, and (2) it permits those stockholders who want cash to acquire it by selling some of their shares back to the firm, while stockholders who do not want cash may simply keep their shares. Since fewer shares will be outstanding after the repurchase, earnings per share and consequently the price of the remaining shares should increase.

The principal disadvantages of repurchases are (1) they are usually done on an irregular basis, so a stockholder cannot depend on income from this source; and (2) if regular repurchases were made, there is a good chance that the Internal Revenue Service (or Congress) would rule that the repurchases were simply a tax avoidance scheme and would assess penalty tax rates. Stock repurchase operations are discussed in more detail in Appendix 18A.

Stock Dividends and Stock Splits

Another aspect of dividend policy is the concept of stock dividends and stock splits. The rationale for stock dividends and splits can best be explained through an example; we use Carter Chemical Company to illustrate.

As Carter Chemical continues to grow and to retain earnings, its book value per share will also grow. More important, earnings per share and the market price per share will rise. Suppose only a few thousand shares were outstanding. After some years of growth, each share would have a very high EPS and DPS. If a "normal" P/E ratio were applied to the stock, the derived market price might be so high that few people could afford to buy even one share. This would limit demand for the stock, thus keeping the total market value of the firm below what it would be if more shares, at lower prices, were outstanding.

Although there is little empirical evidence to support the contention, there is nevertheless a widespread belief in financial circles that an *optimal price range* exists for stocks. *Optimal* means that, if the price is in this range, the price/earnings ratio will be maximized. Many observers, including Carter Chemical's management, feel that the best range for most stocks is from $20 to $80 per share. Accordingly, if at some future point the price of Carter's stock rose to $80, management would probably declare a *two-for-one stock split*, thus doubling the number of shares outstanding, halving the earnings and dividends per share, and thereby lowering the price of the stock. Each stockholder would have more shares, but each share would be worth less. If the post-split price were $40, Carter's stockholders would be exactly as well off as they were before the split. If the price of the stock were to stabilize above $40, stock-holders would be better off. Stock splits can be of any size. For example, the stock could be split two-for-one, three-for-one, 1.5-for-one, or in any other way.[7]

Stock dividends are similar to stock splits in that they divide the pie into smaller slices without affecting the fundamental position of the company. On a 5 percent stock dividend, the holder of 100 shares would receive an additional five shares (without cost); on a 20 percent stock dividend, the same holder would receive twenty new shares; and so on. Again, the total number of shares is increased, so earnings, dividends, and the price per share all decline.

If a firm wants to reduce the price of its stock, should a stock split or a stock dividend be used? Stock splits are generally used after a sharp price run-up, when a large price reduction is sought. Stock dividends are frequently used on a regular annual basis to keep the stock price more or less constrained. For example, if a firm's earnings and dividends are growing at about 10 percent per year, the price would tend to go up at about that same rate, and it would soon be outside the desired trading range. A 10 percent annual stock dividend would maintain the stock price within the optimal trading range.

Although the economic effects of stock splits and dividends are virtually identical, accountants treat them somewhat differently. On a two-for-one split, the shares outstanding are doubled, and the stock's par value is halved. This treatment is shown in Table 18-1, Section 2, for Carter Chemical, using a pro forma 1985 balance sheet. With a stock dividend, the par value is not reduced, but an accounting entry is made transferring capital from retained earnings to common stock and to paid-in capital. The transfer from retained earnings is calculated as follows:

$$\begin{pmatrix} \text{Dollars} \\ \text{transferred from} \\ \text{retained} \\ \text{earnings} \end{pmatrix} = \begin{pmatrix} \text{Number} \\ \text{of shares} \\ \text{outstanding} \end{pmatrix}\begin{pmatrix} \text{Percentage} \\ \text{of the} \\ \text{stock dividend} \end{pmatrix}\begin{pmatrix} \text{Market} \\ \text{price of} \\ \text{the stock} \end{pmatrix}.$$

For example, if Carter Chemical, selling at $80, declared a 20 percent stock dividend, the transfer would be

$$\text{Dollars transferred} = (50 \text{ million})(0.2)(\$80) = \$800,000,000.$$

As shown in Section 3 of Table 18-1, of this $800 million transfer, $10 million is recorded in common stock and $790 million in additional paid-in capital. Retained earnings are reduced to $1.05 billion.[8]

---

[7] *Reverse splits*, which reduce the shares outstanding, can even be used; for example, a company whose stock sells for $5 might employ a one-for-five reverse split, exchanging one new share for five old shares and raising the value of the shares to about $25, which is within the "acceptable" range.

[8] Note that Carter could not pay a stock dividend that exceeded 46.25 percent; a stock dividend of that percentage would exhaust the retained earnings. Thus, a firm's ability to declare stock dividends is constrained by the amount of its retained earnings.

| **Table 18-1** Carter Chemical Company: Stockholders' Equity Accounts, Pro Forma 12/31/1985 |

1. Before a stock split or a stock dividend:

Common stock (60 million shares authorized, 50 million outstanding, $1 par)	$ 50,000,000
Additional paid-in capital	100,000,000
Retained earnings	1,850,000,000
Total common stockholders' equity	$2,000,000,000

2. After a two-for-one stock split:

Common stock (120 million shares authorized, 100 million outstanding, $0.50 par)	$ 50,000,000
Additional paid-in capital	100,000,000
Retained earnings	1,850,000,000
Total common stockholders' equity	$2,000,000,000

3. After a 20 percent stock dividend:

Common stock (60 million shares authorized, 60 million outstanding, $1 par)[a]	$ 60,000,000
Additional paid-in capital[b]	890,000,000
Retained earnings[b]	1,050,000,000
Total common stockholders' equity	$2,000,000,000

[a]Shares outstanding are increased by 20 percent, from 50 million to 60 million.
[b]A transfer equal to the market value of the new shares is made from retained earnings to additional paid-in capital and common stock:

$$\text{Transfer} = (50 \text{ million shares})(0.2)(\$80) = \$800 \text{ million.}$$

Price Effects

Several empirical studies have examined the effects of stock splits and stock dividends on stock prices.[9] The findings of the Barker study are presented in Table 18-2. When stock dividends were associated with a cash dividend increase, the value of the company's stock six months after the ex dividend date had risen by 8 percent. On the other hand, where stock dividends were not accompanied by cash dividend increases, stock values fell by 12 percent, which approximated the percentage of the average stock dividend.

These data seem to suggest that stock dividends are seen for what they are—simply additional pieces of paper—and that they do not represent true income. When stock dividends are accompanied by higher earnings and cash dividends, investors bid up the value of the stock. However, when stock dividends are not accompanied by increases in earnings and cash dividends, the dilution of earnings and dividends per

[9] C. A. Barker, "Evaluation of Stock Dividends," *Harvard Business Review*, vol. 36 (July-August 1958), 99-114. Barker's study has been replicated several times in recent years, and his results are still valid—they have withstood the test of time. Another excellent study, using an entirely different methodology yet reaching similar conclusions, is that of E. Fama, L. Fisher, M. C. Jensen, and R. Roll, "The Adjustment of Stock Prices to New Information," *International Economic Review*, February 1969, 1-21.

Table 18-2
Price Effects of Stock
Dividends

	Price at Selected Dates (in Percentages)		
	Six Months prior to Ex Dividend Date	At Ex Dividend Date	Six Months after Ex Dividend Date
Cash dividend increase	100	109	108
No cash dividend increase	100	99	88

share causes the price of the stock to drop by about the same percentage as the stock dividend. The fundamental determinants of price are the underlying earnings and dividends per share.

Establishing a Dividend Policy: Some Illustrations

Many factors interact to determine a firm's optimal dividend policy. Moreover, since these interactions are too complex to permit the development of a rigorous model for use as a guide to dividend policy, firms are forced to consider their dividend policies in a relatively subjective manner. Some illustrations of how dividend policies are actually set are given below.

Erie Steel Company

Erie analyzed its situation in terms of the residual theory as shown in Figure 18-3. The residual theory suggested a dividend of $1.80 per share during 1982, or a 30 percent payout ratio. Erie's stock is widely held, and a number of tax-exempt institutions are important stockholders. A questionnaire to its stockholders revealed no strong preferences for dividends versus capital gains. Erie's long-range planning group projected a cost of capital and a set of investment opportunities during the next three to five years that are similar to those shown for this year.

Based on this information, Erie's treasurer recommended to the board of directors that it establish a dividend of $1.80 for 1982, payable 45 cents quarterly. The 1981 dividend was $1.70, so the $1.80 represents an increase of about 6 percent. The treasurer also reported to the board that, in the event of an unforeseen earnings downturn, the company could obtain additional debt to meet its capital expenditure requirements. The board accepted the treasurer's recommendation and in December of 1981 declared a dividend of 45 cents per share, payable January 15, 1982. The board also announced its intention of maintaining this dividend for the balance of 1982.

Watkins Electronics

Watkins Electronics has a residual theory position that resembles IOS_G in Figure 18-3. This suggests that no dividend be paid. Watkins has, in fact, paid no dividend since its inception in 1972, even though it has been continuously profitable and earnings have recently been growing at a 25 percent rate. Informal conversations with the firm's major stockholders, all of whom are in high tax brackets, suggest that they neither expect nor want dividends—they would prefer to have the firm retain earnings, have good earnings growth, and provide capital gains which are taxed at relatively low rates. The stock now sells for $106 per share. Watkins's treasurer recommended a three-for-one split, no cash dividend, and a future policy of declaring an annual stock dividend geared to earnings for the year. The board of directors concurred.

Midwest Electric has an acute need for new equity capital. The company has a major expansion program under way and absolutely must come up with the money to meet construction payments. The debt ratio is high, and if the times-interest-earned ratio falls any lower (1) the company's bonds will be downgraded, and (2) it will be barred by bond indenture provisions from further debt issues. These facts suggest a cut in dividends from the $2.50 per share paid last year. However, the treasurer knows that many of the stockholders rely on dividends for current living expenses, so if dividends are cut, these stockholders may be forced to sell, thus driving down the price of the stock. This would be especially bad in view of the treasurer's forecast that there will be a need to sell new common stock during the coming year. (New outside equity would be needed even if the company totally eliminated the dividend.) The treasurer is aware that many other utilities face a similar problem. Some have cut their dividends, and their stock prices invariably have fallen by amounts ranging from 30 to 70 percent.

Midwest Electric Company

Midwest's earnings were forecast to increase from $3.33 to $3.50. The treasurer recommended that the dividend be raised from $2.50 to $2.70, with the dividend increase being announced a few weeks before the company floated a new stock issue. The hope was that this action would cause the price of the stock to increase, after which the company could sell a new issue of common stock at a better price.

NAO's 1981 dividend was $2.45 per share, up from $2.30 in 1980. Both dividend figures represented about 50 percent of earnings, and this payout was consistent with a residual theory analysis. The company's growth rate in EPS and DPS had been in the 5 to 10 percent range during the past few years, and management had projected a continuation of this trend. The financial vice-president foresaw a cash flow problem in 1982—earnings were projected to increase in line with the historical average, but an especially large number of good investment opportunities (along with some unprofitable, but required, pollution control expenditures) were expected. A preliminary analysis using the residual theory suggested that the dividend in 1982 should be cut back sharply, if not eliminated.

North American Oil (NAO)

The financial vice-president quickly rejected this cutback, recommending instead a 6 percent *increase* in the dividend, to $2.60. He noted that the company could easily borrow funds during the coming year to meet its capital requirements. The debt ratio would rise somewhat above the target, but the firm's average cost of capital curve is relatively flat, and cash flows from the 1982 investments should permit a reduction in the debt ratio over the next few years. The vice-president felt that it was more important to maintain the steady growth in dividends than to adhere strictly to the target debt ratio.

Summary

Dividend policy involves the decision to pay out earnings or to retain them for reinvestment in the firm. Any change in dividend policy has both favorable and unfavorable effects on the price of the firm's stock. Higher dividends mean higher cash flows to investors, which is good, but lower future growth, which is bad. The optimal dividend policy balances these opposing forces and maximizes the price of the stock.

We identified a number of factors that bear on dividend policy, including these: legal constraints such as bond indenture provisions, the firm's investment opportunities, the availability and cost of funds from other sources (new stock and debt), tax rates, stockholders' desire for current income, and the "information effect" of dividend changes. Because of the large number of factors that bear on dividend policy, and also because the relative importance of these factors changes over time and across companies, it is impossible to develop a precise, generalized model for use in establishing dividend policy. Firms can, however, consider the *residual theory model,* along with other factors, in reaching a judgment as to the most appropriate dividend policy.

Firms tend to use one of three payment policies: (1) a stable or continuously increasing dollar dividend per share; (2) a low regular dividend plus extras that depend on annual earnings; and (3) a constant payout ratio, which will cause the dollar dividend to fluctuate. Most firms follow the first policy, a few use the second, and almost none use the third. Also, we noted that many firms today are using dividend reinvestment plans to help stockholders reinvest dividends at minimal brokerage costs, and some firms use stock repurchase plans in lieu of more cash dividends.

Stock splits and stock dividends were also discussed. Our conclusion was that these actions may be beneficial if the firm's stock price is quite high, but otherwise they have little effect on the value of the firm.

Questions

18-1 As an investor, would you rather invest in a firm that has a policy of maintaining (a) a constant payout ratio, (b) a constant dollar dividend per share, or (c) a constant regular quarterly dividend plus a year-end extra when earnings are sufficiently high or corporate investment needs are sufficiently low? Explain your answer.

18-2 How would each of the following changes probably affect aggregate (that is, the averages for all corporations) payout ratios? Explain your answers.

a. An increase in the personal income tax rate.

b. A liberalization in depreciation policies for federal income tax purposes.

c. A rise in interest rates.

d. An increase in corporate profits.

e. A decline in investment opportunities.

18-3 Discuss the pros and cons of having the directors formally announce what a firm's dividend policy will be in the future.

18-4 Most firms would like to have their stock selling at a high P/E ratio and also have an extensive public ownership (many different shareholders). Explain how stock dividends or stock splits may be compatible with these aims.

18-5 What is the difference between a stock dividend and a stock split? As a stockholder, would you prefer to see your company declare a 100 percent stock dividend or a two-for-one split? Assume that either action is feasible.

18-6 "The cost of retained earnings is less than the cost of new outside equity capital. Consequently, it is totally irrational for a firm to sell a new issue of stock and to pay dividends during the same year." Discuss this statement.

18-7 Would it ever be rational for a firm to borrow money in order to pay dividends? Explain.

18-8 Union representatives have presented arguments similar to the following: "Corporations such as General Foods retain about one-half their profits for financing needs. If they financed by selling stock instead of by retaining earnings, they could cut prices substantially and still earn enough to pay the same dividend to their shareholders. Therefore, their profits are too high." Evaluate this statement.

18-9 "Executive salaries have been shown to be more closely correlated to the size of the firm than to its profitability. If a firm's board of directors is controlled by management instead of by outside directors, this might result in the firm's retaining more earnings than can be justified from the stockholders' point of view." Discuss the statement, being sure (a) to use Figure 18-3 in your answer and (b) to explain the implied relationship between dividend policy and stock prices.

Problems

18-1 Barter Corporation declares a 4 percent stock dividend and a cash dividend of $0.40 per share. The cash dividend is paid on old shares *plus* shares received in the stock dividend. Construct a pro forma balance sheet giving effect to these actions; use one new balance sheet that incorporates both actions. The stock sells for $25 per share. A condensed version of the Barter Corporation's balance sheet as of December 31, 1981, before the dividends, follows:

Cash	$ 50,000,000	Debt	$1,000,000,000
Other assets	1,950,000,000	Common stock	
		(60 million shares authorized, 50	
		million shares outstanding, $1 par)	50,000,000
		Paid-in capital	200,000,000
		Retained earnings	750,000,000
	$2,000,000,000		$2,000,000,000

18-2   Wheezy Tobacco Company has for many years enjoyed a moderate but stable growth in sales and earnings. However, cigarette consumption and, consequently, Wheezy's sales have been falling off recently, partly because of a national awareness of the dangers of smoking to health. Anticipating further declines in tobacco sales for the future, Wheezy's management hopes eventually to move almost entirely out of the tobacco business and, instead, to develop a new, diversified product line in growth-oriented industries.

Wheezy has been especially interested in the prospects for pollution-control devices—its research department has already done much work on problems of filtering smoke. Right now, the company estimates that an investment of $24 million is necessary to purchase new facilities and begin operations on these products, but the investment could return about 18 percent within a short time. Other investment opportunities total $9.6 million and are expected to return about 12 percent.

The company has been paying a $2.40 dividend on its 6 million shares outstanding. The announced dividend policy has been to maintain a stable dollar dividend, raising it only when it appears that earnings have reached a new, permanently higher level. The directors might, however, change this policy if reasons for doing so are compelling. Total earnings for the year are $22.8 million, common stock is currently selling for $45, and the firm's current leverage ratio (debt/assets ratio) is 45 percent. Current costs of various forms of financing are listed below:

New bonds, 7%
New common stock sold at $45 to yield the firm $41
Investors' required rate of return on equity, 9%
Tax rate, 50%

a. Calculate the marginal cost of capital above and below the point of exhaustion of retained earnings for Wheezy, both with and without the dividend.
b. How large should Wheezy's capital budget be for the year?

c. What is an appropriate dividend policy for Wheezy? How should the capital budget be financed?

d. How might risk factors influence Wheezy's cost of capital, capital structure, and dividend policy?

e. What assumptions, if any, do your answers to the above make about investors' preference for dividends versus capital gains, that is, investors' preferences regarding the D_1/P_0 and g components of k?

Selected References

Dividend policy is another area that has been studied extensively by academicians. The first major academic work, and still a classic, is Lintner's analysis of how corporations actually set their dividend payment policies:

Lintner, John, "Distribution of Incomes of Corporations among Dividends, Retained Earnings, and Taxes," *American Economic Review*, vol. 46 (May 1956), 97-113.

The effects of dividend policy on stock prices and capital costs have been examined by many researchers. The classic theoretical argument that dividend policy is important, and that stockholders like dividends, was set forth by Gordon, while Miller and Modigliani (MM) developed the notion that dividend policy is not important:

Gordon, Myron J., "Dividends, Earnings and Stock Prices," *Review of Economics and Statistics*, vol. 41 (May 1959), 99-105.

Miller, Merton H., and Franco Modigliani, "Dividend Policy, Growth, and the Valuation of Shares," *Journal of Business*, vol. 34 (October 1961), 411-433.

Many researchers have both extended Gordon's and MM's theoretical arguments and attempted to test the effects of dividend policy in a variety of ways. Although statistical problems have precluded definitive conclusions, the following articles, among others, have helped to clarify the issues:

Brennan, Michael, "Taxes, Market Valuation, and Corporate Financial Policy," *National Tax Journal*, Spring 1975, 417-427.

Hayes, Linda S., "Fresh Evidence That Dividends Don't Matter," *Fortune*, May 4, 1981, 351-354.

Lewellen, Wilbur G., Kenneth L. Stanley, Ronald C. Lease, and Gary G. Schlarbaum, "Some Direct Evidence on the Dividend Clientele Phenomenon," *Journal of Finance*, vol. 33 (December 1978), 1385-1399.

Litzenberger, R. H., and K. Ramaswamy, "The Effect of Personal Taxes and Dividends on Capital Asset Prices: Theory and Empirical Evidence," *Journal of Financial Economics*, vol. 7 (June 1979), 163-195.

Mukherjee, Tarun K., and Larry M. Austin, "An Empirical Investigation of Small Bank Stock Valuation and Dividend Policy," *Financial Management*, vol. 9 (Spring 1980), 27-31.

Pettit, R. R., "Taxes, Transactions Costs and the Clientele Effect of Dividends," *Journal of Financial Economics*, vol. 5 (December 1977), 419-436.

For an excellent review of both the theoretical and the empirical literature (along with another test of the alternative theories), see

Vanderheiden, Paul A., *Dividend Level and Variability: Effects on Stock Returns*, Ph.D. dissertation, University of Florida, 1980.

On stock dividends and splits, see

Baker, W. Kent, and Patricia L. Gallagher, "Management's View of Stock Splits," *Financial Management*, vol. 9 (Summer 1980), 73-77.

Copeland, Thomas E., "Liquidity Changes Following Stock Splits," *Journal of Finance*, vol. 34 (March 1979), 115-141.

On repurchases, see

Finnerty, Joseph E., "Corporate Stock Issue and Repurchase," *Financial Management*, vol. 4 (Autumn 1975), 62-71.

Stewart, Samuel S., Jr., "Should a Corporation Repurchase Its Own Stock?" *Journal of Finance*, vol. 31 (June 1976), 911-921.

Appendix 18A

Stock Repurchases as an Alternative to Dividends

Treasury stock is the name given to common stock that has been repurchased by the issuing firm, and the acquisition of treasury stock represents an alternative to the payment of dividends. If some of the outstanding stock is repurchased, fewer shares will remain outstanding; and, assuming the repurchase does not adversely affect the firm's earnings, the earnings per share of the remaining shares will increase. This increase in earnings per share should result in a higher market price per share, so capital gains will have been substituted for dividends.

Many companies have been repurchasing their stock in recent years. Most repurchases amount to a few million dollars, but IBM, in the largest repurchase on record, bought 2,546,000 of its shares at a price of $280 per share, or $713 million in total. In another large repurchase, Gulf Oil bought back $338 million of its stock.

The effects of a repurchase are illustrated by American Development Corporation (ADC), which earned $4.4 million in 1981. Of this amount, 50 percent, or $2.2 million, had been allocated for distribution to common shareholders. There were 1,100,000 shares outstanding, and the market price was $20 a share. ADC could use the $2.2 million to repurchase 100,000 of its shares through a tender offer for $22 a share, or it could pay a cash dividend of $2 a share.[1]

The effect of the repurchase on the EPS and market price per share of the remaining stock can be determined in the following way:

1. Current EPS $= \dfrac{\text{Total earnings}}{\text{Number of shares}} = \dfrac{\$4.4 \text{ million}}{1.1 \text{ million}} = \$4$ per share.

2. Current P/E ratio $= \dfrac{\$20}{\$4} = 5 \times$.

3. EPS after repurchase of 100,000 shares $= \dfrac{\$4.4 \text{ million}}{1 \text{ million}} = \$4.40$ per share.

4. Expected market price after repurchase $= (P/E)(EPS) = (5)(\$4.40) = \$22$ per share.

[1] Stock repurchases are commonly made in three ways. First, a publicly owned firm can simply buy its own stock through a broker on the open market. Second, it can issue a *tender* under which it permits stockholders to send in (that is, "tender") their shares to the firm in exchange for a specified price per share. When tender offers are made, the firm generally indicates that it will buy up to a specified

(continued)

It should be noticed from this example that investors would receive benefits of $2 a share in any case, either in the form of a $2 cash dividend or a $2 increase in stock price. This result occurs because we assumed (1) that shares could be repurchased at exactly $22 a share and (2) that the P/E ratio would remain constant. If shares could be bought for less than $22, the operation would be even better for *remaining* stockholders, but the reverse would hold if ADC paid more than $22 a share. Furthermore, the P/E ratio might change as a result of the repurchase operation, rising if investors viewed it favorably, falling if they viewed it unfavorably. Some factors that might affect P/E ratios are considered next.

Advantages of Repurchases from the Stockholder's Viewpoint

1. Profits earned on repurchases are taxed at the capital gains rate, whereas a dividend distribution would be taxed at the stockholder's marginal tax rate. This is significant. For example, it has been estimated that, on the average, stockholders pay a tax of about 45 percent on marginal income. Since the capital gains tax rate is generally only 40 percent of the ordinary tax rate, the typical shareholder clearly benefits, other things the same, if the distribution is in the form of a stock repurchase rather than a dividend. Teledyne, a $3 billion conglomerate, earns about $400 million per year, and it has not paid a cash dividend in twenty years. Profits are, however, used to repurchase stock and thus stimulate growth. Teledyne's stock has risen from $4 in 1975 to $150 in 1981, so the company is doing something right!
2. The stockholder has a choice—to sell or not to sell. On the other hand, with a dividend, one must accept the payment and pay the tax.
3. A qualitative advantage advanced by market practitioners is that repurchase can often remove a large block of stock overhanging the market.

Advantages of Repurchases from Management's Viewpoint

1. Studies have shown that dividends are "sticky" in the short run because managements are reluctant to raise dividends if the new dividend cannot be maintained in the future—managements dislike cutting cash dividends. Hence, if the excess cash flow is thought to be only *temporary*, management may prefer to "conceal" the distribution in the form of share repurchases rather than to declare a cash dividend they believe cannot be maintained.

---

number of shares within a specified time period (usually about two weeks); if more shares are tendered than the company wishes to purchase, then purchases are made on a *pro rata* basis. Finally, the firm can purchase a block of shares from one large holder on a negotiated basis. If the latter procedure is employed, care must be taken to insure that this one stockholder does not receive preferential treatment not available to other stockholders.

2. Repurchased stock can be used for acquisitions or released when stock options are exercised. Discussions with financial managers indicate that it is frequently more convenient and less expensive to use repurchased stock than newly issued stock for these purposes, and also when convertibles are converted or warrants exercised.

3. If directors have large holdings themselves, they may have especially strong preferences for repurchases rather than dividend payments because of the tax factor.

4. Repurchases can be used to effect large-scale changes in capital structure. For example, at one time American Standard had virtually no long-term debt outstanding. The company decided that its optimal capital structure called for the use of considerably more debt, but even if it had financed *only* with debt it would have taken years to get the debt ratio up to the newly defined optimal level. What could the company do? It sold long-term debt and used the proceeds to repurchase its common stock, thus producing an instantaneous change in its capital structure.

5. Treasury stock can be resold in the open market if the firm needs additional funds.[2]

Disadvantages of Repurchases from the Stockholder's Viewpoint

1. Stockholders may not be indifferent between dividends and capital gains, and the price of the stock might benefit more from cash dividends than from repurchases. Cash dividends are generally thought of as being relatively dependable, but repurchases are not. Further, if a firm announced a regular, dependable repurchase program, the improper accumulation tax that will be discussed would probably become more of a threat. However, Teledyne has apparently had no problems in this regard, but Teledyne's repurchases are somewhat irregular, which may make a difference.

2. The *selling* stockholders may not be fully aware of all the implications of a repurchase or may not have all pertinent information about the corporation's present and future activities. For this reason, firms generally announce a repurchase program before embarking on it.

3. The corporation may pay too high a price for the repurchased stock, to the disadvantage of remaining stockholders. If the shares are inactive, and if the firm seeks to acquire a relatively large amount of its stock, the price may be bid above a maintainable price and then fall after the firm ceases its repurchase operations.

---

[2] Another interesting use of stock repurchases was St. Joe Minerals' strategy of repurchasing its own stock to thwart an attempted takeover. In 1981 Seagram Company was attempting to acquire a controlling interest in St. Joe through a tender offer of $45 a share. St. Joe's management countered with a tender offer of its own for 7 million shares at $60 per share, to be financed by the sale of several divisions plus borrowings. As this book goes to press, the ploy seems to be working—St. Joe's management has thus far retained control.

**Disadvantages
of Repurchases
from Management's
Viewpoint**

1. Some people have argued that firms which repurchase substantial amounts of stock often have poorer growth rates and fewer good investment opportunities than ones that do not. Thus, these people feel that announcing a repurchase program is like announcing that management cannot locate good investment projects. One could argue that instituting a repurchase program should be regarded in the same manner as announcing a higher dividend payout, but if repurchases are regarded as indicating especially unfavorable growth opportunities, then repurchases can have an adverse impact on the firm's image, and also on the price of its stock. There is, however, little empirical support for this position.

2. Repurchases might involve some risk from a legal standpoint. If the Internal Revenue Service can establish that the repurchases are primarily for the avoidance of taxes on dividends, then penalties may be imposed on the firm under the improper accumulation of earnings provision of the Tax Code. Actions have been brought against privately held companies under Section 531, but we know of no case where such an action has been brought against a publicly owned firm, even though some firms have retired over one-half of their outstanding stock. Also, the SEC may raise serious questions if it appears that the firm may be manipulating the price of its shares.

**Conclusion
on Stock
Repurchases**

When all the pros and cons on stock repurchases are totaled, where do we stand? The conclusions may be summarized as follows:

1. Repurchases on a regular, systematic, dependable basis, like quarterly dividends, may not be feasible because of uncertainties about the tax treatment of such a program and uncertainties about such things as the market price of the shares, how many shares would be tendered, and so forth.

2. However, repurchases do offer some significant tax advantages over dividends, so this procedure should be given careful consideration on the basis of the firm's own unique situation.

3. Repurchases can be especially valuable to make a significant shift in the capital structure within a short period.

Problem

18A-1 Gemstone, Inc., has earnings this year of $16.5 million, 50 percent of which is required to take advantage of the firm's excellent investment opportunities. The firm has 206,250 shares outstanding, selling currently at $320 a share. Greg Beaumont, a major stockholder (18,750 shares), has expressed displeasure with a great deal of managerial policy. Management has approached him about selling his holdings back to the firm, and he has expressed a willingness to do this at a price of $320 a share. Assuming that the market uses a constant P/E ratio of 4 in valuing the stock, should the firm buy Beaumont's shares? Assume that dividends will not be paid on Beaumont's shares if they are repurchased. (Hint: Calculate the ex dividend price of the stock with and without the repurchase, and add to these values the dividends received to determine the remaining stockholders' value per share.)

Special Topics in Financial Management

VII

Parts I through VI developed the basic framework of financial management. However, we have deferred several important topics that can best be analyzed on an integrated basis using the analytical tools developed in Chapters 1 through 18. Chapter 19 covers multinational finance; Chapter 20 deals with mergers; Chapter 21 takes up bankruptcy and reorganization; Chapter 22 examines leasing; Chapter 23 covers warrants, convertibles, and options; and Chapter 24 focuses on the financial problems of small businesses.

19 Multinational Finance*

Almost 25 percent of U.S. manufacturing firms' assets are located abroad, and a similar percentage of their income is derived from foreign sources. Further, international investment is growing more rapidly than domestic investment for American firms in the aggregate. This growth, which is highlighted in the left panel of Figure 19-1, has been caused primarily by the high rates of return available on foreign investments, especially in developing nations, as shown in the right panel.

A firm that operates in two or more nations is defined as a *multinational corporation*. Such a company has a base corporation in one country (the *parent company*) and operates branches and subsidiaries throughout the world. Its shares are normally owned mostly, if not entirely, by residents of the parent company's country. Although there has been much talk recently in the United States about foreigners, especially those from the OPEC countries, buying control of U.S. real estate and corporations, the fact of the matter is that multinational companies based in the U.S. invest far more money abroad than do those based in any other country in the world. In fact, the United States has more assets abroad than do Britain, Japan, West Germany, Canada, and Switzerland combined. General Electric has television assembly plants in Mexico, South Korea, and Singapore; IBM has computer hardware manufacturing and servicing subsidiaries in many parts of Europe and the Far East; Caterpillar produces tractors and farm equipment in the Middle East, Europe, the Far East, and Africa. American executives increasingly travel and live abroad, and American multinational corporations have come to exert significant economic and political influence in many parts of the world.[1]

Companies actually move into multinational operations for a number of specific reasons. First, a good many of our present multinational firms commenced their international operations because raw materials were located abroad; this is true of oil, mining, and some food processing companies. Other firms expanded overseas in order to obtain an outlet for

* This chapter was coauthored with Professor Hai Hong of the Graduate School of Management, Northwestern University.

[1] Some of the political influence of multinational corporations is of dubious desirability and has aroused Congressional disapproval. Examples include the ITT affair in Chile, as well as the Lockheed scandals in Japan and the Netherlands.

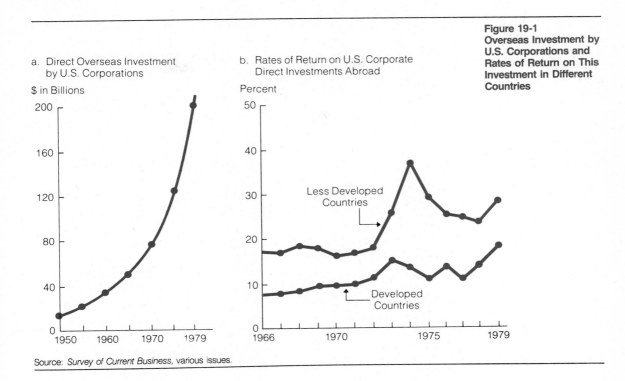

a. Direct Overseas Investment
   by U.S. Corporations

$ in Billions

b. Rates of Return on U.S. Corporate
   Direct Investments Abroad

Percent

Figure 19-1
Overseas Investment by
U.S. Corporations and
Rates of Return on This
Investment in Different
Countries

Source: *Survey of Current Business,* various issues.

their finished products. Frequently, the latter firms first set up sales offices, then developed manufacturing plants when it became clear that the market would support such plants. Still other firms have moved their manufacturing facilities overseas in order to take advantage of low production costs in cheap labor areas; the electronics and textile companies are good examples. Finally, banks, accounting firms, and other service corporations have expanded overseas both to better serve their primary customers and to take advantage of profitable new investment opportunities.

The study of multinational finance takes traditional managerial finance as its starting point, then builds on the models of capital budgeting, cost of capital, and working capital management discussed earlier in this book. However, multinational financial management must also take into account international differences in financial markets and institutions. Accordingly, this chapter is divided into four major sections: (1) foreign exchange rates and the international monetary system, (2) procedures for analyzing foreign investments, (3) the financial management of foreign assets, and (4) international capital markets.

Exchange Rates and the International Monetary System

An *exchange rate* designates the number of units of a given currency that can be purchased for one unit of another currency. Exchange rates for the leading trading partners of the United States appear in the *Wall Street Journal* each day. See, for example, the rates given on December 1, 1980, as shown in Table 19-1.

Table 19-1
Illustrative Exchange Rates, December 1, 1980

	U.S. Dollars Required to Buy One Unit of Foreign Currency (1)	Number of Units of Foreign Currency per U.S. Dollar (2)
British pound	$2.3530	0.4251
Canadian dollar	0.8385	1.1926
Dutch guilder	0.4753	2.1035
French franc	0.2222	4.5010
Greek drachma	0.0217	46.0405
Indian rupee	0.1282	7.8003
Italian lira	0.001086	920.8103
Japanese yen	0.004593	217.7226
Mexican peso	0.0432	23.1482
Norwegian krone	0.1968	5.0800
Saudi Arabian riyal	0.3012	3.3201
Singapore dollar	0.4767	2.0975
South African rand	1.3335	0.7499
Spanish peseta	0.0129	77.7605
Swedish krona	0.2292	4.3630
Swiss franc	0.5702	1.7535
Venezuelan bolivar	0.2330	4.2925
West German mark	0.5148	1.9423

Note: Column 2 equals 1.0 divided by Column 1.
Source: *Wall Street Journal*, December 2, 1980.

Recent History of the World Monetary System

From the end of World War II until August 1971, the world was on a *fixed exchange rate system* administered by the International Monetary Fund (IMF). Under this system, the U.S. dollar was linked to gold ($35 per ounce), and other currencies were then tied to the dollar. Exchange rates between other currencies and the dollar were controlled within narrow limits. For example, in 1964 the British pound was fixed at 2.80 dollars for one pound, with a 1 percent permissible fluctuation about this rate:

	Value of the Pound (Exchange Rate in Dollars per Pound)
Upper limit (+1%)	2.828
Official rate	2.800
Lower limit (−1%)	2.772

Fluctuations occurred because of changes in the supply of and demand for pounds. The demand for pounds tended to increase whenever Britain's exports exceeded its imports—people in other nations had to buy more pounds to pay for British goods than they received in payment for their shipments to Britain. This increased demand for pounds, in turn, tended to drive up their price relative to other currencies—for example, more dollars would have to be paid for each pound. Under the fixed exchange rate system, this increase in value was, of course, subject to the 1 percent upper limit.[2]

The demand for a currency, hence exchange rate fluctuations, also depended on capital movements. For example, suppose interest rates in Britain were higher than those in the United States. Americans would buy pounds with dollars, then use those pounds to purchase high-yielding British securities. This would tend to drive up the price of pounds.[3]

Finally, there are always international speculators (who include the Arab money managers and the Swiss, as well as the treasurers of major U.S. corporations) who buy pounds whenever they expect the value of the pound to rise relative to other currencies.

Prior to 1972, these fluctuations were kept within the narrow 1 percent limit by regular intervention of the British government in the market. When the value of the pound was falling, the Bank of England would step in and buy pounds, offering gold or foreign currencies in exchange. These government purchases would push up the pound rate. Conversely, when the pound rate was too high, the Bank of England would sell pounds. The central banks of other countries operated similarly.

With the approval of the IMF, a country could *devalue* its currency if it experienced persistent difficulty over a long period in preventing its exchange rate from falling below the lower limit, and if its central bank was running out of the gold and other currencies which could be used to

---

[2] For example, the dollar value of the pound might move up from $2.800 to $2.828. This increase in the value of the pound would mean that British goods would now be more expensive in export markets. For example, a box of candy costing one pound in England would rise in price in the U.S. from $2.80 to $2.828. Conversely, U.S. goods would be cheaper in England. For example, the British could now buy goods worth $2.828 for one pound, whereas before the exchange rate change, one pound would only buy merchandise worth $2.80. These price changes would, of course, tend to *reduce* British exports and *increase* imports, and this, in turn, would lower the exchange rate because people in other nations would be buying fewer pounds to pay for English goods. However, the 1 percent limit severely constrained the market's ability to reach an equilibrium between trade balances and exchange rates.

[3] Such capital inflows would also tend to drive down British interest rates. If rates were high in the first place because of efforts by the British monetary authorities to curb inflation, then the international currency flows would have helped thwart that effort. This is one of the reasons why domestic and international economics are so closely linked.

A good example of this occurred during the summer of 1981. In an effort to curb inflation, the Reagan administration pushed U.S. interest rates to record levels. This, in turn, caused an outflow of capital from European nations to the U.S. The Europeans were suffering from a severe recession and wanted to keep interest rates down in order to stimulate investment, but the U.S. policy made this difficult because of the ease of international capital flows.

buy its own currency and thus prop up its price. For just these reasons, the British pound was devalued from $2.80 per pound to $2.50 per pound in 1967. This lowered the price of British goods in the U.S. and elsewhere and raised the prices of foreign goods in Britain, thus stopping the British export deficit which was putting pressure on the pound in the first place. Conversely, a nation with an export surplus and a strong currency might *revalue* its currency upwards, as West Germany did twice in the 1960s.

Today's Floating Exchange Rate System

Devaluations and revaluations occurred only rarely before 1971. They were usually accompanied by severe international financial repercussions, partly because nations tended to postpone these needed measures until economic pressures had built up to explosive proportions. For this and other reasons, the old international monetary system came to a dramatic close in the early 1970s, when the U.S. dollar, the foundation upon which all other currencies were anchored, was cut loose from gold and, in effect, allowed to "float."

Under a system of *floating exchange rates,* currency prices are allowed to seek their own levels without much governmental intervention. The present world monetary system is known as a *managed floating system:* major world currency rates move (float) with market forces, unrestricted by any internationally agreed-upon limits. However, the central bank of each country does intervene in the foreign exchange market, buying and selling its currency to smooth out exchange rate fluctuations to some extent. Each central bank also tries to keep its average exchange rate at a level deemed desirable by its government's economic policy. This is important, because exchange rates have a profound effect on the levels of imports and exports, which in turn influence the level of domestic employment. For example, if a country were having a problem with excess unemployment, then its central bank might encourage a decline in the value of its currency. This would cause its goods to be cheaper in world markets and thus stimulate exports, production, and domestic employment. Conversely, the central bank of a country that was operating at full capacity and experiencing inflation might try to raise the value of its currency in order to reduce exports and increase imports. However, under the current floating rate system, such intervention can affect the situation only temporarily—market forces will prevail in the long run.

Figure 19-2 shows how German marks, Japanese yen, and British pounds moved in comparison to the dollar from 1960 through 1980. Until 1971, when the fixed rate system was terminated, rates were quite stable. The pound's fluctuations against the dollar were too small to even show up on the graph prior to 1967, when a devaluation occurred. The mark was revaluated upward in 1961 and again in 1969. The yen was stable until 1971, when the dollar was allowed to float. The pound has drifted down, while the yen and especially the mark have risen against the dollar since 1971. The root cause of these divergent trends has been the strength

**Figure 19-2
Changes in the Value of
Marks, Yen, and
Pounds Relative to the
Value of the Dollar,
1960-1980**

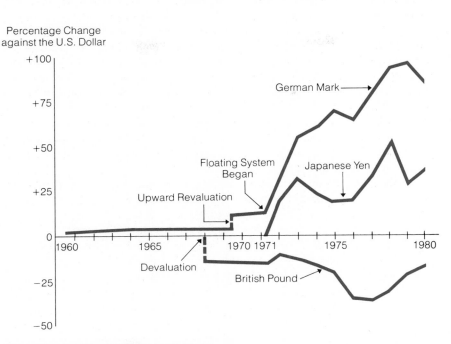

Percentage Change
against the U.S. Dollar

Source: *International Financial Statistics*, various issues.

of the British, German, and Japanese economies relative to that of the United States, and the relative inflation rates in the four countries. This point is discussed in detail in a later section.

Trading in Foreign Exchange

Importers, exporters, and tourists, as well as governments, buy and sell currencies in the foreign exchange market. For example, when a U.S. trader imports automobiles from West Germany, payment will probably be made in German marks. The importer buys marks (through its bank) in the foreign exchange market, much as one buys common stocks on the New York Stock Exchange or pork bellies on the Chicago Mercantile Exchange. However, while stock and commodity exchanges have organized trading floors, the foreign exchange market consists of a network of brokers and banks based in New York, London, Tokyo, and other financial centers. Most buy and sell orders are conducted by cablegram and telephone.[4]

---

[4] For a more detailed account of foreign exchange trading and money market instruments for financing foreign trade, see R. Rodriguez and E. Carter, *International Financial Management* (Englewood Cliffs, N.J.: Prentice-Hall, 1979), chapters 5 and 6.

Spot Rates and Forward Rates

The exchange rates shown earlier in Table 19-1 are known as *spot rates*, which means the rate paid for delivery of the currency "on the spot" or, really, two days after the day of the trade. For most of the world's major currencies, it is also possible to buy (or sell) currency for delivery at some agreed-upon future date, usually 30, 90, or 180 days from the day the transaction is negotiated. This rate is known as the *forward exchange rate*. For example, if a U.S. firm must make payment to a Swiss firm in ninety days, the U.S. firm's treasurer can buy Swiss francs today for delivery in ninety days, paying the ninety day forward rate. Forward rates are exactly analogous to futures prices on commodity exchanges, where contracts are drawn up for wheat or corn to be delivered at agreed-upon prices at some future date.

When the forward rate is above the current spot rate, the forward rate is said to be at a *premium*; conversely, when the forward rate is below the spot rate, it is said to be at a *discount*. Table 19-2 shows forward rates for British pounds and Swiss francs on December 1, 1980, along with spot rates from Table 19-1, which have been included for comparison. Note that forward rates on both pounds and francs sell at a premium. The reason for this premium will be explained shortly.

Table 19-2
Illustrative Spot and Forward Exchange Rates, December 1, 1980

	British Pounds	Swiss Francs
Spot rate	$2.3520	$0.5702
30 day forward	2.3629	0.5770
90 day forward	2.3757	0.5881
180 day forward	2.3855	0.6023

Source: *Wall Street Journal*, December 2, 1980.

Why do individuals and corporations buy or sell forward currencies? The main reason is that forward markets provide protection against future changes in exchange rates. For example, suppose that on December 1, 1980, a U.S. jeweler buys watches from a Swiss manufacturer for one million Swiss francs. Payment is to be made in Swiss francs ninety days after the goods are shipped, or on March 1, so the Swiss firm is extending trade credit for ninety days. The Swiss franc has been strong recently, and the U.S. firm is afraid that the trend will continue. If the franc appreciates rapidly, more dollars will be required to buy the million francs, and the profits on the watches will be lost. Still, the U.S. firm does not want to forego the trade credit, so it protects itself by buying one million ninety day forward francs for $0.5881 × 1,000,000, or $588,100. When payment comes due on March 1, regardless of the spot rate on this day, the U.S.

firm can obtain the needed Swiss francs at the agreed-upon price. The U.S. firm is said to have *covered its trade payments.*[5]

Relative inflation rates, or the rates of inflation in foreign countries compared to that at home, have many implications for multinational financial decisions. Obviously, relative inflation rates will greatly influence production costs at home and those abroad. Equally important, they have a dominant influence not only on relative interest rates but also on exchange rates. Both relative interest rates and exchange rates influence the methods chosen by multinational corporations for financing their foreign investments, and both of these factors have a major impact on the profitability of foreign investments.

The currencies of countries with higher inflation rates than that of the U.S. tend to depreciate against the dollar. Some countries where this is the case are Britain, Italy, Mexico, and all the South American nations. On the other hand, the currencies of countries such as West Germany, Switzerland, and Japan, which have had less inflation than the U.S., have appreciated relative to the dollar. *In fact, a foreign currency will, on average, depreciate at a percentage rate approximately equal to the amount by which its inflation rate exceeds our own.*[6]

Relative inflation rates are also reflected in interest rates. The interest rate in any country is largely determined by its inflation rate; this point was made in Chapters 2 and 5. Therefore, countries currently experiencing higher rates of inflation than the U.S. also tend to have higher interest rates, while the reverse is true for countries with lower inflation rates.

It is tempting for the treasurer of a multinational corporation to borrow in countries with the lowest interest rates. However, this is not always the best strategy. For example, suppose interest rates in West Germany are lower than those in the U.S. because of Germany's lower inflation rate. A U.S. multinational firm could save interest by borrowing in Germany, but the German exchange rate can be expected to appreciate in the future, causing annual interest and principal payments on this debt to cost an increasing number of dollars over time. Thus, the lower interest rate could be more than offset by losses from currency appreciation. Sim-

[5] This example was first worked out in the summer of 1977, then updated in December 1980. At the earlier exchange rate, the watches had a dollar cost of $402,000. Three and one-half years later, this cost rose to $588,100, or by 46 percent, strictly because of the declining value of the dollar. These increases were being matched in other European countries, making European goods and services, including vacations, increasingly expensive for Americans. Conversely, American goods and services were becoming cheaper for Europeans.

[6] This is known as the Purchasing Power Parity Theorem. Some recent studies have shown that this theorem holds quite well over the long run (five years or more), but over the short run the relationship is much less accurate. This is because factors other than inflation are also important in the short run, especially the activities of the national governments in trying to support their exchange rates at some desired levels. Some evidence on this is given in R. Aliber and C. Stickney, "Accounting Exposures of Foreign Exchange: The Long and the Short of It," *Accounting Review* (January 1975), 44-57.

ilarly, one should not expect multinational corporations to avoid borrowing in a country like Brazil where interest rates are very high, because future depreciation of the Brazilian cruzeiro might well make such borrowing relatively inexpensive.

Procedures for Analyzing Potential Foreign Investments

Although the same basic principles of investment analysis apply to both foreign and domestic operations, there are some key differences. First, *cash flow analysis is much more complex for overseas investments*. Most multinational firms set up a separate subsidiary in each foreign country in which they operate. *The relevant cash flows are the dividends and royalties repatriated by each subsidiary to the parent company. These cash flows must be converted to the currency of the parent company and thus are subject to future exchange rate changes.* In other words, General Motors' German subsidiary may make a profit of 100 million marks in 1980 and again in 1981, but the value of these profits to GM will depend on the dollar/mark exchange rate: How many *dollars* is 100 million marks worth?

Dividends and royalties are normally taxed by both foreign and domestic governments. Furthermore, a foreign government may restrict the amount and nature of the cash flows that may be *repatriated* to the parent company. For example, some governments place a ceiling, stated as a percentage of the company's net worth, on the amount of cash dividends that may be paid by a subsidiary to its parent company. Such restrictions are normally intended to force multinational firms to reinvest earnings in the foreign country, although they are sometimes imposed to prevent large currency outflows which might destabilize exchange rates. Finally, depreciation cash flows of the subsidiary are usually not directly available to the parent company, since they are not part of the earnings from which dividends are paid. This can be an important consideration, as we shall see later in the chapter.

In addition to the complexities of the cash flow analysis, *the cost of capital may be different for a foreign project than for an equivalent domestic project because foreign projects may be more or less risky*. A higher risk could arise from two primary sources: (1) exchange risk and (2) sovereign risk, while a lower risk might result from international diversification.

Exchange risk refers to the fact that exchange rates fluctuate. This increases the inherent uncertainty about cash flows to the parent. In other words, foreign projects have an added risk element relating to what the basic cash flows will be worth in the parent company's home currency. As we shall see later, it is generally possible to "hedge" against exchange rate fluctuations, but it may not be possible to hedge completely, and, in addition, the costs of hedging must be added to the basic cost of capital.

Sovereign risk refers both to the possibility of expropriation and to unanticipated restrictions of cash flows to the parent company, such as tighter controls on repatriation of dividends or higher taxes. The risk of expropriation of U.S. assets abroad is small in traditionally friendly and stable countries such as Britain or Switzerland. However, in the East European countries and in most parts of the developing world of Latin America, Africa, and the Far East, the risk may be substantial. Recent expropriations include those of ITT and Anaconda Copper in Chile, Gulf Oil in Bolivia, Occidental Petroleum in Libya, International Petroleum in Peru, and many companies in both Cuba and Iran.

The combined impact of exchange and sovereign risks, as well as such "regular" risk factors as the stability and predictability of product markets, labor supplies, and governmental regulations, can be summarized as the "investment climate" of a foreign country. A recent survey of the investment climates in countries all over the world, which appeared in a leading Japanese business journal, is shown in Table 19-3. The countries are

	Sociopolitical and Investment Climate	Risk Rating	Table 19-3 The Risks of Foreign Investments in Various Countries
West Germany	94	AAA	
United States	95	AAA	
Canada	91	AA	
France	90	AA	
Australia	83	AA	
Sweden	90	AA	
Netherlands	90	AA	
Saudi Arabia	83	AA	
Belgium	94	A	
Spain	83	A	
Britain	87	A	
New Zealand	83	A	
Italy	78	A	
Singapore	80	BBB	
Portugal	79	BBB	
Brazil	77	BBB	
Mexico	76	BBB	
Malaysia	64	BBB	
Indonesia	65	BBB	
Philippines	68	BBB	
Argentina	70	BB	
Chile	79	BB	
Kenya	72	BB	
Pakistan	63	BB	
South Korea	54	BB	
Peru	60	BB	
Thailand	54	BB	
Egypt	30	BB	
India	23	B	

Source: *Nikkei Business*, reprinted in the *Far Eastern Economic Review*, March 18, 1977, 88. Iran was listed as an A-rated country in 1977; its rating recently has been lowered greatly.

rated in descending order from AAA to B, in much the same way that Moody's rates corporate bonds for risk of default. These ratings, or other procedures as established by an individual multinational corporation, may be used as a basis for estimating the costs of capital for capital budgeting purposes in each country in which the firm operates.

Although exchange and sovereign risks would typically increase the cost of capital of foreign projects as compared with domestic ones, the benefits of international diversification may tend to lower the cost of capital for a foreign project. Operating conditions in the U.S. and foreign nations are not perfectly correlated—international economies are, to some extent, similar to the situation shown in Figure 5-6 in Chapter 5, so the returns on a corporation's "portfolio of assets" may be more stable if it is diversified internationally. More will be said about international diversification later in the chapter, but it can have the effect of holding down the cost of capital on foreign capital budgeting projects.

An Illustration of Multinational Capital Budgeting

The principles of capital budgeting in a multinational setting can be illustrated by International Electronics Corporation's analysis of a proposed plant in Bratina to assemble television sets for sale in Bratina and other South American countries. If the plant is built, a new IEC subsidiary will be incorporated in Bratina. It will be financed only with common stock, all of which will be owned by the parent company.

The cost of capital used to analyze the plant was established by the methods described in Chapter 15 and is assumed to be 15 percent. Bratina has a 20 percent corporate income tax, and there is no withholding tax on dividends paid.

While there are no restrictions on dividend repatriations, depreciation cash flows may not be repatriated except when the company is liquidated or sold. The investment, to be made in January 1982, consists almost entirely of plant and equipment, and the cost will be 50 million Bratinian cruzes. Because of the nature of the television industry and the Bratinian

---

Table 19-4 Projected Cash Flows, 1982-1986 (Millions of Bratinian Cruzes)

	1982	1983	1984	1985	1986
Revenues	50.0	55.0	60.0	65.0	70.0
Operating cost	30.0	30.0	35.0	35.0	40.0
Depreciation	5.0	5.0	5.0	5.0	5.0
Income before tax	15.0	20.0	20.0	25.0	25.0
Bratinian tax	3.0	4.0	4.0	5.0	5.0
Net income	12.0	16.0	16.0	20.0	20.0
Dividends repatriated	12.0	16.0	16.0	20.0	20.0
U.S. tax	4.5	6.0	6.0	7.5	7.5
After-tax dividend	7.5	10.0	10.0	12.5	12.5

market, IEC bases its analysis on a time horizon of only five years. At the end of the five years (in 1986), it is assumed that the operation will have a terminal value of 25 million cruzes. Table 19-4 summarizes the projected income statements.

The parent corporation receives a *tax credit* from the U.S. government for taxes paid by its subsidiary to the foreign government. The amount of the credit depends on the dividend payout ratio of the subsidiary. With a 100 percent payout, which the Bratinian subsidiary has used, the parent corporation pays the difference between the U.S. tax rate (assumed to be 50 percent) and the Bratinian tax rate of 20 percent. Thus, the U.S. tax each year amounts to an additional 30 percent of the net income for that year. For example, in the 1982 column of Table 19-4 we see that if the subsidiary earned 15 million cruzes before tax, it would pay a Bratinian tax of 20 percent, or 3 million cruzes, and a U.S. tax of 50 − 20 = 30%, or 4.5 million cruzes.[7]

Since the cash flows from depreciation cannot be repatriated until the company is liquidated at the end of 1986, they will be invested in Bratinian government bonds to earn tax-exempt interest at the rate of 8 percent. The accumulated and interest-compounded depreciation cash flow at the termination of the project is shown in Table 19-5 to be 29.333 million cruzes.

Year of Depreciation	Amount (Millions of Cruzes)	Future Value Interest Factor at 8 Percent	Terminal Value in 1986 (Millions of Cruzes)
1982	5.0	1.3605	6.802
1983	5.0	1.2597	6.299
1984	5.0	1.1664	5.832
1985	5.0	1.0800	5.400
1986	5.0	1.0000	5.000
		Total	29.333

Table 19-5
Depreciation Cash Flows

[7] Often a foreign subsidiary will not pay out all of its income, but will retain a portion of it for new investments. Also, the foreign government may levy a withholding tax on repatriated dividends. The U.S. tax computation is somewhat more complicated then. The following formula may be used in this more general case. Net U.S. tax = $pE[t_{US} - t_F - (1 - t_F)t_D]$. Here, p is the foreign subsidiary's dividend payout ratio; E is the gross foreign income before taxes; t_F and t_{US} are the foreign and U.S. income tax rates; and t_D is the foreign withholding tax rate on repatriated dividends (Bratina has no such withholding tax). Note that U.S. taxes are collected only on the portion of income that is repatriated. (If payout, p, = 0, no U.S. taxes are paid.) This works as an incentive for multinational corporations to reinvest earnings for the growth of the foreign subsidiary. It also explains why U.S. oil companies and other multinationals often have very low U.S. taxes in relation to reported income.

If the net tax computed from the above formula is negative, this deficit can be used to offset U.S. taxes on income from other foreign subsidiaries in any part of the world. For a more detailed explanation of multinational taxation, see the U.S. Tax Reform Act of 1976, or Price Waterhouse, *U.S. Corporations Doing Business Abroad* (New York: Price Waterhouse, 1976).

The next steps in the analysis are: (1) to convert the annual cash flows from cruzes to dollars and (2) to find the net present value of the project. These steps are shown in Table 19-6. Column 1 gives the annual cash flows in cruzes. In 1982 through 1985, dividends represent the only cash flow, but the 1986 cash flow of 66.833 million cruzes consists of dividends (12.5 million cruzes), the estimated sale price of the fixed assets (25 million cruzes), and the interest-accumulated depreciation cash flows (29.333 million cruzes).

Table 19-6
Cash Flows to Parent Company and the Parent's NPV

	Cash Flows (Millions of Cruzes) (1)	Exchange Rate (2)	Cash Flows (Millions of Dollars) (3)	PVIF at 15 Percent (4)	PV of Cash Flows (Millions of Dollars) (5)
1982	7.500	5.00	$ 1.500	0.8696	$ 1.304
1983	10.000	5.25	1.905	0.7561	1.440
1984	10.000	5.51	1.815	0.6575	1.193
1985	12.500	5.79	2.159	0.5718	1.235
1986	66.833	6.08	10.992	0.4972	5.465
				Total	$10.637
		Less initial investment of 50 million cruzes at 5 cruzes per dollar			(10.000)
				NPV of project =	$ 0.637

The estimated exchange rates are shown in Column 2. The current rate, five cruzes to the dollar, is expected to hold during 1982, but the cruze is expected to depreciate thereafter at a rate of 5 percent per year.

Dividing the cash flows in cruzes (Column 1) by the exchange rates (Column 2) gives the expected cash flows in dollars as shown in Column 3. The dollar cash flows are converted to a present value basis in Column 5, and the sum of the annual PV cash flows is $10.637 million. By subtracting the initial cost of the project, $10 million, from the PV of the inflows, we obtain the project's NPV, $637,000. Since its NPV is positive, the project should be accepted.[8]

Strategic Considerations in Analyzing Foreign Investments

Although we have emphasized the financial aspects of foreign investments, nonfinancial or *strategic* considerations often dominate the decision. For example, if Ford were to set up production in Peru, General Motors might feel compelled to do the same in order not to lose its position in the South American automobile market. Similarly, many U.S. companies are establishing operations in Hong Kong, not so much be-

---

[8] The project's IRR is 16.9 percent, which exceeds the 15 percent cost of capital, so the IRR criterion also indicates acceptance.

cause of the profit prospects of a Hong Kong branch but, rather, to be in a position to move rapidly if China is opened to U.S. firms on a wide scale. Because of many unknown economic factors in foreign investment, top management may not trust the "numbers" and may decide that it simply cannot sit idly by while a major competitor expands and preempts a potentially important market. Under these circumstances, financial analysis is used only as a rough screening device to eliminate ventures that are obviously unprofitable.[9]

The political ramifications of foreign investment are another strategic consideration. In recent years, labor unions have increasingly opposed U.S. multinational investments abroad. The unions and their supporters in Congress claim that such investments "export" U.S. jobs and capital—U.S. citizens lose jobs to foreigners who work for U.S. subsidiaries abroad, and the outflow of U.S. dollars to finance the investments tends to weaken the dollar in foreign exchange markets. Regardless of the merits of such criticisms, a multinational corporation's management must weigh carefully the investment benefits to the company versus possible reprisals against domestic operations by labor unions or unfriendly politicians.[10]

Sources of Funds for Foreign Investments

In the preceding example, we assumed that the foreign subsidiary would obtain all of its capital as common equity supplied by the parent. Several other sources of funds exist, including (1) sale of common stock to local residents, (2) borrowing from local residents, and (3) borrowing in world financial markets.

Selling common stock to residents of foreign countries has both advantages and disadvantages. For example, it can result in loss of control of the subsidiary if the parent company owns less than 50 percent of the shares. Some countries require majority ownership by local residents. This allows them to have some control over major decisions made by corporations operating within their boundaries, and it also enables them to retain part of the companies' profits. However, this is not necessarily bad from the point of view of the multinational corporation—local participation may be a desirable feature in countries with less stable governments, since it provides an incentive for the local residents to exert pressure against the threat of expropriation or other interference. Similar protection is obtained by borrowing funds in the subsidiary's country. If

---

[9] See A. Yair, "The Foreign Investment Decision Process" (Boston: Harvard Business School, Division of Research, 1966); and A. Stonehill and L. Nathanson, "Capital Budgeting and the Multinational Corporation." *California Management Review*, Summer 1968. An excellent survey of motives for foreign investments may be found in G. Ragazzi, "Theories of the Determinants of Foreign Investments," *IMF Staff Papers*, March 1966.

[10] The Burke-Hartke Bill (1972) threatened to remove tax credits for U.S. multinational corporations and to limit the flow of investment funds abroad. For an interesting debate on the economic issues, see "The Foreign Trade and Investment Act of 1972: Three Points of View," *Columbia Journal of World Business*, March-April 1972.

the subsidiary company is highly leveraged and obtains this debt from local sources, expropriation will result in only minimal losses to the parent.

Aside from protecting against expropriation, borrowing locally may be advantageous if local sources of funds in the foreign country offer attractive interest rates. In comparing foreign and domestic interest rates, however, one must be careful to take into account expected future changes in the exchange rate. As was pointed out earlier, a country with interest rates lower than those in the United States has a currency that is likely to appreciate, causing the number of dollars required to meet interest and principal payments to increase over time and to offset the lower foreign interest rate.

The decision to use local or parent country financing necessarily depends in part on projections of future trends in foreign exchange rates. Because such projections are not always accurate, using foreign debt may be riskier than using domestic debt. With the growth of multinational corporations and the uncertainties of world inflation and floating rates, corporate treasurers are making increasing use of expertise offered by commercial bankers, who make such projections and advise firms on the best way to meet their foreign currency requirements. It should come as no surprise to learn that the international divisions have been among the fastest-growing departments of the larger banks in recent years.[11]

Management of Foreign Assets

The *Wall Street Journal* recently reported that TRW, a major aerospace and electronics conglomerate, was losing $300,000 in earnings every time the German mark moved up 1 percent against the dollar. This happened because TRW's West German subsidiary had about $30 million worth of debt denominated in marks. Since the interest and principal on the debt had to be paid in marks, a 1 percent appreciation of the mark meant that, in terms of U.S. dollars, the company had to pay more dollars to buy the marks needed to service the debt. For example, the average exchange rate of marks for dollars was 0.516 dollars per mark in November, but it had appreciated by 1.36 percent to 0.523 dollars per mark by December. The mark debt account of TRW would therefore appear as shown on the next page.

The increase in the dollar equivalent of foreign debt is reported as an *income loss item* under accounting standards introduced in 1976 by the Financial Accounting Standards Board (FASB #8). Such a loss is known

---

[11] Local borrowing is also advantageous in the sense of hedging against the impacts of exchange rate fluctuations on the parent corporation's reported profits, because if the assets and liabilities of a foreign subsidiary are denominated in the same currency, exchange rate-induced profit fluctuations are minimized. This point is covered later in the section entitled "FASB #8."

Month	Mark Rate ($/Mark)	Debt in Marks	Debt in Dollars
November	0.516	72,115,384	$37,211,538
December	0.523	72,115,384	37,716,346
	Increase in dollar value of debt		$ 504,808

as a *translation loss*, since it arises from "translating" financial statements from a foreign currency to U.S. dollars.[12]

Had TRW held only *monetary assets* (defined as cash, marketable securities, and accounts receivable) denominated in marks, its position would have been reversed: an appreciation of the mark would have produced a translation gain, while a depreciation would have led to losses. Had TRW both held monetary assets and owed money denominated in marks, then the difference between these two items would be its *net monetary position*. The net position indicates whether or not the company will have a translation gain or loss as a result of exchange rate fluctuations, that is, whether the company has exchange rate loss *exposure*.

Companies such as TRW operate on a worldwide basis, and they have positive net monetary positions in some countries and negative positions in others. Thus, TRW might have translation losses in Germany but translation gains in other countries, and its consolidated, or corporate, position could show either a gain or a loss. *Under FASB #8, the net corporate translation gain or loss must be reported through the income statement each quarter.* For firms with large foreign operations, translation losses can significantly lower earnings per share and thus have an adverse effect on stock prices. Therefore, multinational corporations have devised a number of ways to minimize the likelihood of translation losses. These techniques are discussed in the following paragraphs.

As noted above, an exposure to losses due to changing exchange rates is called *foreign exchange exposure*. It exists whenever the amounts of monetary assets and liabilities denominated in each foreign currency are not in exact balance. Monetary instruments like TRW's debt are obviously exposed, as are monetary assets such as cash held as marks. *Nonmonetary assets* can also be exposed. For example, if the French subsidiary of Goodyear carries an inventory of tires in Paris, the dollar value of these tires could change if the French franc is depreciated. The actual change in the tires' value will depend on where they are sold and on the contracts governing these sales. If all the tires are to be shipped to the United

Foreign Exchange Exposure

---

[12] Note, however, that if the German mark had depreciated against the dollar, TRW would have made a *translation gain*.

States at a predetermined dollar price, then a French devaluation would cause no loss in real value. But if the tires are to be sold to French consumers at a fixed French franc price, the dollar value of the inventory would fall. If the sales price is not fixed, and if the weakening of the franc results in a rise in French consumer prices, then the tires may be sold at franc prices high enough to produce the same number of dollars as was anticipated before the devaluation. We see, then, that the effect of depreciation on the dollar value of nonmonetary assets is difficult to determine.

If a multinational firm's income is to be reported properly to investors, the effects of changes in the value of assets and liabilities must be analyzed properly. Yet, since it is extremely difficult to determine the effects of changes in currency values on assets such as tires, finding the proper reporting method is a complex, difficult task.

FASB #8

Before FASB #8 was introduced by the accounting profession in 1976, multinational corporations accounted for their translation gains and losses in a variety of ways, often in the manner that best helped them present a good profit picture. FASB #8 has—at the moment—standardized accounting practices as follows:

1. All *monetary assets and liabilities,* including accounts payable and accounts receivable, must be translated at the exchange rate that prevails at the end of the reporting period, which is called the *current rate.* Thus, even for a stable firm, the reported value of these items changes each quarter if exchange rates fluctuate, causing fluctuations in reported earnings unless the net monetary position is zero.
2. All *inventories* must be translated at the exchange rate that prevailed at the time the goods were placed in inventory, which is called the *historic rate.*
3. All *fixed assets* must be translated at *historic rates.*
4. *Sales revenues* are translated at *current rates.* Therefore, if the value of the foreign currency (say francs) appreciates, a given volume of franc sales will have a higher dollar translation value. However, the inventories sold to produce those sales are translated at the lower historic rate. Thus, the result in this instance would be high reported profits generated by the exchange rate change.

Many multinational corporations have complained that reporting translation gains and losses in this manner makes their earnings volatile and subject to the vagaries of exchange rate fluctuations. Exchange rates may rise one quarter, then fall the next, and the corporation's income will rise and fall in concert, even though sales and other fundamental aspects of the operation may have been stable. FASB #8 is especially troublesome for a company like W. R. Grace, whose foreign subsidiaries (1) finance their inventories with local short-term debt and (2) have very little long-term debt. The company has argued that its exposure in current assets (inventories) approximately cancels out its exposure in current liabilities (debt). Therefore, it has no net *economic exposure,* and its *real economic income* is insensitive to exchange rate changes. However, under FASB #8 a depreciation in a foreign currency requires Grace's subsidiary in the foreign country to report a translation gain on debt in the quarter in which currency depreciation occurs. Then, in subsequent quarters when goods produced during that quarter are sold, the recorded cost of goods sold is translated at the higher historic rate, and the subsidiary's profits shrink. Thus, because under FASB #8 sales are translated into dollars at the current rate while costs of goods sold are translated at the historic rate, large swings in reported income can occur, and this will make the company look less stable than it really is.

Proposed Change in FASB #8. Because of the problems noted above, in 1981 the Financial Accounting Standards Board considered making a major change in FASB #8. The proposed change, as set forth by the FASB in its "Exposure Draft" dated August 28, 1980, included these features:

1. The distinction between monetary assets and other assets would become rather unimportant.

2. All translations would occur at the *current exchange rate* as of the date a financial statement is prepared. Thus, the term *historic exchange rate* would no longer be meaningful.

3. In preparing the parent company's consolidated balance sheet, the foreign subsidiary's balance sheet (all assets and liabilities) would be translated into U.S. dollars at the current exchange rate.

4. Revenues and expenses (including the cost of goods sold) would be translated (approximately) at the average exchange rate that prevailed during the reporting period (for example, a quarter for a quarterly earnings report). This would avoid the major problem under the current FASB #8, since the change would tend to stabilize the profit contribution of a foreign subsidiary, hence the parent company's reported income.

5. The cumulative effects of exchange rate changes on the value of a parent company's investment in a foreign subsidiary would be reported by the parent, either as a separate statement or in the notes to its financial statements. For example, suppose the German subsidiary of a U.S. firm had, on 1/1/82, (1) assets valued at 100 million dollars and 200 million marks, (2) liabilities denominated in marks with a value of 50 million dollars and 100 million marks, and (3) a net worth of 50 million dollars and 100 million marks, all based on an exchange rate of $1 to 2 marks. Now suppose that during 1982 the value of the mark doubled, to $1 to 1 mark. The subsidiary's new net worth, under the proposed version of FASB #8, would be $200 million assets − $100

million debt = $100 million net worth. The $50 million increase in net worth would not be reported as income, but it would be reported as a note or in some other form in the 1982 annual report. Continuing, if the mark depreciated during 1983, a negative net worth effect would be shown as a note in the 1983 annual report, along with the cumulative effect of 1982 plus 1983. This cumulation would continue until the German subsidiary was liquidated or it was agreed (by the firm's management and auditors) that the valuation change was permanent.[13]

The proposed new method of accounting amounts to adopting a *net investment view* of the foreign subsidiary as opposed to an individual asset and liability view. The net investment concept recognizes that the parent company has a net investment in a foreign business whose foreign currency earnings benefit the parent company by the dollar value of those earnings. It is based on the assumption that the accounts of the foreign business, expressed in terms of its own currency, best represent the performance of the business, and that all of its assets and liabilities should therefore be translated using the current exchange rate.

If FASB #8 is actually revised—and in 1981 this appeared likely—then the TRW problem described earlier will disappear, and the hedging operations discussed below will become somewhat less important. Multinational companies will still have to worry about long-run trends in exchange rates, but they will not have to fear that short-run exchange rate fluctuations will make the parent company's earnings appear to be less stable than they really are.

Hedging Exposures

Suppose the financial manager of a multinational corporation has an estimate of the firm's exchange exposure in each country in which it operates. What actions can be taken to reduce the exposure? Consider our previous example of TRW's debt of 72 million German marks. If the financial manager fears an appreciation of the mark, all of TRW's German debt could be retired and replaced by borrowing in U.S. dollars. However, this would be desirable only if dollar funds are available at acceptable interest rates. Alternatively, the financial manager could use *forward contracts* in the foreign exchange market.

In November, the spot rate on marks was 0.5160 dollars per mark, and the thirty day forward rate was 0.5180 dollars per mark. To see how forward contracts can be used to protect against exchange rate risk, suppose that in late November TRW's financial manager is worried about the mark appreciating by December 31. TRW could enter into a contract to buy marks on December 31 at the forward price, 0.5180 dollars per mark.

---

[13] Note, however, that an exception to this procedure applies in the case of actual trading in foreign currencies; gains or losses here would be reported through the income statement.

Suppose that by December 31 the spot price had risen to 0.5230. TRW could buy marks at the contractual price of 0.5180, sell them at the higher spot price of 0.5230, and earn a profit of $360,577:

On December 31 the forward contract becomes due.
Buy 72,115,384 marks at the agreed-upon price of $0.5180/mark. $37,355,769

Sell 72,115,384 marks at the spot price of $0.5230/mark.   37,716,346

Profit in dollars $ 360,577

This profit would largely offset the $504,808 increase in TRW's German debt as previously computed. The difference of $144,231 is TRW's *hedging cost*.[14]

A number of other methods of hedging against exchange losses on different types of liabilities and assets are available, but to discuss them would go well beyond the scope of this book.[15] The important points, for our purpose, are: (1) fluctuating exchange rates can cause earnings fluctuations for multinational corporations, but (2) for a price, the financial manager can buy protection against this risk in the form of various types of hedges. In a world of floating exchange rates, managing assets and liabilities located all across the globe presents quite a challenge. The financial manager at corporate headquarters must not only anticipate currency realignments in each country, but also coordinate hedging strategies in all these countries.

International Capital Markets

Direct foreign investment by U.S. multinational corporations is one way for Americans to invest in world markets. Another way is to purchase stocks, bonds, or various money market instruments issued in foreign countries. U.S. citizens actually do invest substantial amounts in the stocks and bonds of large corporations in Europe, and to a lesser extent

---

[14] Note that this hedging cost is independent of the spot price on December 31. To illustrate this, suppose the spot rate had been much higher, say $0.600/mark. By going through the same calculations as before, we can readily show that the increase in TRW's German debt would have been $5,913,461 and its profit from the forward mark transaction $6,057,692. This again implies a hedging cost of $144,231. For this cost, the financial manager has protected the company completely against all possible appreciation of the mark between November 30 and December 31. The company is said to be in a *fully hedged position* in the German mark over this period. In general, the hedging cost is given by this formula: (Forward price − Spot price) × (Amount of debt). Check to see that this formula gives a cost of $144,231.

[15] For a professional account of various strategies, see A. R. Prindl, *Foreign Exchange Risk* (New York: Wiley, 1976); and D. Eiteman and A. Stonehill, *Multinational Business Finance* (Reading, Mass.: Addison-Wesley, 1979), chapter 11.

in the Far East and South America. They also buy securities issued by foreign governments. Such investments in foreign capital markets are known as *portfolio investments* (and distinguished from *direct investments* by U.S. corporations in physical assets).

Eurodollars

Whenever a U.S. dollar is placed in a time deposit in a European bank, including a European branch of a U.S. bank, a *Eurodollar* is created. For example, Eurodollars would be created if a French wine exporter received a $100,000 payment (in dollars) for a shipment to the United States and then deposited the check in a Paris bank's time deposit (rather than exchanging the dollars for francs). Eurodollars are also created when a U.S. resident places dollar time deposits in any commercial bank located in Europe.

Eurodollars can be used to conduct transactions throughout Europe—indeed, throughout the world. American firms, including banks, borrow in the Eurodollar market, as do the Japanese, South Americans, and Africans. It is estimated that the total quantity of Eurodollars in 1980 approximated $200 billion, but no one knows the exact figure.[16]

Eurodollar Interest Rates

Eurodollars are always held in interest-bearing accounts. Thus, the French wine exporting firm would receive interest on its deposit balances. The interest rate paid on these deposits depends (1) on the bank's lending rate, as the interest a bank earns on loans determines its willingness and ability to pay interest on deposits, and (2) on rates of return available on U.S. money market instruments, for if rates in the U.S. are above Eurodollar deposit rates, these funds will be sent back and invested in the U.S., while if Eurodollar deposit rates are significantly above U.S. rates, more dollars will be sent to Europe, and this inflow will drive rates there down.[17]

International Bond Markets

The Eurodollar market is essentially a short-term market—most loans and deposits are for less than one year. However, there are also two important types of international bond markets: foreign bonds and Eurobonds.

---

[16] It should be noted that today U.S. dollar deposits in any part of the world outside the U.S. are called Eurodollars. It is also interesting to note that Eurodollars were first created by the Russians in Paris in the 1940s. The Russians wanted to use dollars to conduct trade with parties who did not want to be paid in Russian currency. At the same time, the Russians did not want to leave dollar balances in U.S. banks for fear these balances would be taken over and used to pay off defaulted Czarist bonds. Thus, they decided to purchase dollars, leave them on deposit in a Paris bank, and use them to conduct trade.

The idea of Eurodollars expanded rapidly thereafter. The dollar was, at that time, a strong and stable currency, which made it ideal for international trade. Gold had been used earlier to settle international balances, but it is much simpler to make electronic transfers of bank accounts than to ship gold bullion.

[17] April 1981 Eurodollar deposit rates were approximately $1\frac{1}{4}$ percentage points above domestic rates on bank time deposits of the same maturity: 13 percent for one month CDs versus $14\frac{1}{4}$ percent on Eurodollar deposits.

Foreign bonds are bonds sold by a foreign borrower but denominated in the currency of the country in which the issue is sold. Examples would include a U.S. firm selling a bond denominated in Swiss francs in Switzerland, or a Canadian government bond denominated in dollars floated in the U.S. The term *Eurobonds* is used to designate any bond sold in some country *other than* the one in whose currency the bond is denominated. Examples would include a British firm's issue of pound bonds sold in France, a Ford Motor Company issue denominated in dollars and sold in West Germany, or a German firm's sale of mark bonds in Switzerland.

Over half of all Eurobonds are denominated in dollars; bonds in German marks and Dutch guilders account for most of the rest. Although centered in Europe, Eurobonds are truly international. Their underwriting syndicates include investment bankers from all parts of the world, and the bonds are sold to investors not only in Europe but also in such faraway places as Bahrain and Singapore. Thus, multinational corporations, together with international financial institutions and national governments, play an important role in mobilizing capital in all parts of the world to finance production and economic growth. For better or for worse, this has resulted in great interdependence among world economies.

One reason for investing in foreign securities is to obtain *global diversification*. To see what is involved, consider Figure 19-3, which develops a capital market line (CML) such as the one developed in Figure 5A-7. The shaded area represents the feasible set of portfolios of risky assets; R_F represents the rate of return on (domestic) riskless assets;[19] M_D is the domestic market portfolio; and M_G is the *global market portfolio*, which contains foreign as well as domestic securities. Since returns on foreign securities are not perfectly correlated with those on domestic securities, including foreign assets in the portfolio shifts the boundary or feasible set of portfolios upward and to the left. This has the effect of rotating the CML upward, from CML_D to CML_G. This, in turn, permits an investor to move from portfolio P_1, on indifference curve I_1, to portfolio P_2, on the higher indifference curve I_2. P_2 contains a combination of domestic and foreign stocks and riskless domestic government securities, and it is better than P_1 in that it provides a higher expected return for any given level of risk.[20]

International Portfolio Diversification[18]

[18] This section can be omitted without loss of continuity. Appendix 5A is essential to an understanding of this material.

[19] Note that even foreign treasury bills are risky because of exchange risk. Thus, there are no riskless foreign securities when their returns are translated into dollars.

[20] For more on international diversification, see B. Solnik, "Why Not Diversify Internationally Rather Than Domestically?" *Financial Analysts' Journal*, July-August 1974; and D. Lessard, "World, Country, and Industrial Relationships in Equity Returns," *Financial Analysts' Journal*, January-February 1976.

Figure 19-3
Portfolio Analysis with
Global Diversification

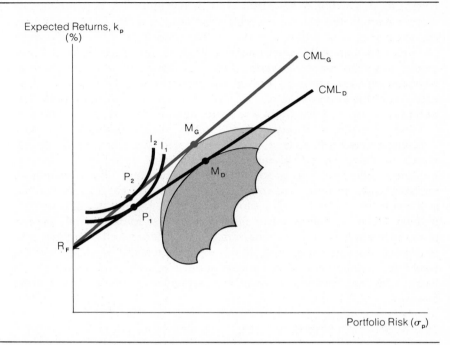

Summary

As the world economy becomes more integrated, the role of multinational firms is ever increasing, and new companies are joining the ranks of the multinationals every day. Although the same basic principles of financial management apply to multinational corporations as to domestic ones, the financial manager of a multinational firm faces a much more complex task. The primary problem, from a financial standpoint, is the fact that cash flows must cross national boundaries. These flows may be constrained in various ways, and, equally important, their value in dollars may rise or fall depending on exchange rate fluctuations. This means that the multinational manager must be constantly aware of the many complex interactions among national economies and the effects of these interactions on multinational operations.

World capital markets allow people from different countries to invest in the productive resources of other countries. Americans buy the stocks and bonds of foreign corporations, and foreigners in turn buy American securities. More efficient investments are possible for everyone due to the diversification opportunities offered through these markets.

Because of the central role of the U.S. dollar in international commerce, large markets have developed for U.S. dollar deposits (Eurodollars) and dollar-denominated bonds (Eurobonds) in Europe and Asia. These markets represent important sources of capital for multinational corporations.

Financial management in a multinational firm is both important and challenging. The risks of international operations are high, but so are the potential rewards. In a world economy that grows more interdependent each year, the multinational manager can look forward to an ever expanding role in corporate decision making.

19-1 Under the fixed exchange rate system, what was the currency against which all other currency values were defined? **Questions**

19-2 Exchange rates fluctuate under both the fixed exchange rate and floating exchange rate systems. What, then, is the difference between the two systems?

19-3 If the French franc depreciates against the U.S. dollar, can a dollar buy more or fewer French francs as a result?

19-4 If the United States imports more goods from abroad than it exports, foreigners will tend to have a surplus of U.S. dollars. What will this do to the value of the dollar with respect to foreign currencies? What is the corresponding effect on Arab investments in the U.S.?

19-5 Why do U.S. corporations build manufacturing plants abroad when they can build them at home?

19-6 Most firms require higher rates of return on foreign projects than on identical projects located at home. Why?

19-7 What is a Eurodollar? If a French citizen deposits $10,000 in Chase Manhattan Bank in New York, have Eurodollars been created? What if the deposit is made in Barclay's Bank in London? Chase Manhattan's Paris branch?

19-8 Explain how FASB #8 affects the reported profits of multinational corporations headquartered in the United States. What changes in FASB #8 have been proposed (by the FASB), and what would these proposed changes do to reported profits?

19-1 If British pounds sold for U.S. $1.70 per pound, what should dollars sell for in pounds per dollar? **Problems**

19-2 Suppose one French franc could be purchased in the foreign exchange market for twenty cents today. If the franc appreciated 10 percent tomorrow against the dollar, how many francs would a dollar buy tomorrow?

19-3 After all foreign and U.S. taxes, a United States corporation expects to receive two pounds of dividends per share from a British subsidiary this year. The exchange rate at the end of the year is expected to be $1.80 per pound, and the pound is expected to depreciate 5 percent against the dollar each year for an indefinite period. The dividend (in pounds) is expected to grow at 10 percent a year indefinitely. The parent U.S corporation owns 10 million shares of the subsidiary. What is the present value of its equity ownership of the subsidiary? Assume a cost of equity capital of 12 percent for the subsidiary.

19-4 You are the financial vice-president of International Widgets, Inc., head-quartered in Miami, Florida. All shareholders of International Widgets live in the United States. Earlier this month you obtained a loan of 10 million Canadian dollars from a bank in Toronto to finance the construction of a new plant in Montreal. At the time the loan was received, the exchange rate was 98 U.S. cents to the Canadian dollar. By the end of the month, it has unexpectedly dropped to 94 cents. Has your company made a gain or loss as a result, and by how much?

19-5 The Smith-Capone Corporation of Chicago manufactures typewriters for the world market. In early 1982, the company's board of directors requests the international planning department of the company to evaluate a proposal for setting up a wholly owned subsidiary in Paralivia, a country of 50 million people in South America. The subsidiary will make typewriters for the Paralivian market. Paralivia is a rapidly developing country which has effectively invested its rich oil revenues to support a growing industrial economy. Currently, it imports all of its typewriters from abroad, and Smith-Capone is expected to capture a large portion of this market.

Political sentiment in Paralivia regarding foreign investments has been somewhat lukewarm because such investments have overtones of foreign economic control. Not long ago the government passed a law requiring all foreign investments to pass to local ownership after six years or less. Paralivia recently adopted a parliamentary system of government after twenty years of military dictatorship under General Francisco, but the transition of power was peaceful. Mr. Gordon Lidder, chairman of the board of Smith-Capone, has expressed concern about the stability of the new government, but "usually reliable" CIA sources indicate that the government has popular support and is unlikely to be toppled for at least five to ten years.

The following financial information on the proposed project is available:

Paralivian Currency: Because the inflation rate in Paralivia is about 5 percent higher than that in the United States, the Paralivian *ringo* is expected to depreciate relative to the dollar by about 5 percent a year. In 1983, when the investment will be made, the exchange rate is expected to be 2 ringos per dollar.

Investment: The estimated investment to be made in 1983 is 60 million ringos in inventory, plant, and equipment. The parent corporation, Smith-Capone, will provide all the capital in the form of equity in the subsidiary. The project will begin to generate earnings in 1984. At the

end of six years (1989) all plant and equipment will be sold to the Paralivian government for 20 million ringos. This amount of money, plus all
accumulated cash, will be repatriated as a liquidating dividend.

Repatriation: Only dividends may be repatriated by the subsidiary to the
parent company. Cash flows from depreciation may not be repatriated
except as part of the liquidating dividend in 1989. However, these cash
flows can, in the meantime, be invested in local money market instruments to yield a 15 percent tax-free return.

Taxes: The Paralivian corporate income tax rate is 25 percent. There is also
a 10 percent withholding tax on dividends. The United States tax rate is
50 percent on the gross earnings of the foreign subsidiary. However, the
parent company gets a tax credit for taxes already paid to foreign governments. In the case of the liquidating dividend, the tax treatment is quite
different. The Paralivian government will not tax this dividend. Smith-
Capone has obtained a ruling from the Internal Revenue Service of the
United States that the liquidating dividend will not be taxed by the U.S.
government either.

Cost of Capital: Based on the sovereign and exchange risk characteristics of
Paralivia, Smith-Capone gives Paralivia a BB rating and requires a rate of
return of 20 percent on equity.

Projected Demand, Costs, and Exchange Rates:

Year	Demand for Typewriters (Thousands)	Price (Ringos)	Unit Variable Operating Cost (Ringos)	Exchange Rate (Ringos per Dollar)
1984	50	1,000	400	2.1
1985	55	1,000	420	2.2
1986	60	1,100	440	2.3
1987	70	1,100	460	2.4
1988	80	1,200	490	2.5
1989	90	1,200	540	2.6

Fixed Cost: Depreciation expense is 10 million ringos per year. Consider
this to be the only fixed cost of the project.

Use the information given above to answer the following questions:
a. Excluding the liquidating dividend, estimate the after-tax dividend received by the parent company each year.
b. Estimate the liquidating dividend, remembering that blocked depreciation flows are reinvested at 15 percent.
c. What is your recommendation for the project? (Consider its NPV and
   specify any other relevant considerations.)

Selected References   Useful texts and other books that describe international financial management in some detail include, among others, the following:

Aggarwal, Raj Kumar, *The Management of Foreign Exchange: Optimal Policies of a Multinational Company* (New York: Arno Press, 1980).

Aliber, Robert Z., *Exchange Risk and Corporate International Finance* (New York: Wiley, 1978).

Eiteman, David K., and Arthur I. Stonehill, *Multinational Business Finance* (Reading, Mass.: Addison-Wesley, 1979).

Lessard, Donald R., ed., *International Financial Management, Theory and Application* (New York: Warren, Gorham & Lamont, 1979).

Rodriguez, Rita M., and E. Eugene Carter, *International Financial Management* (Englewood Cliffs, N.J.: Prentice-Hall, 1979).

For more on capital budgeting by multinational firms, see

Oblak, David J., and Roy J. Helm, Jr., "Survey and Analysis of Capital Budgeting Methods Used by Multinationals," *Financial Management,* vol. 9 (Winter 1980), 37-41.

Shapiro, Alan C., "Capital Budgeting for the Multinational Corporation," *Financial Management,* vol. 7 (Spring 1978), 7-16.

Papers dealing with exchange rate risk include the following:

Calderon-Rossell, Jorge R., "Covering Foreign Exchange Risks of Single Transactions," *Financial Management,* vol. 8 (Autumn 1979), 78-85.

Eaker, Mark R., "Covering Foreign Exchange Risks: Comment," *Financial Management,* vol. 9 (Winter 1980), 64-65.

Feiger, George, and Bertrand Jacquillat, "Currency Option Bonds, Puts and Calls on Spot Exchange and the Hedging of Contingent Foreign Earnings," *Journal of Finance,* vol. 34 (December 1979), 1129-1139.

Goodman, Stephen H., "Foreign Exchange-Rate Forecasting Techniques: Implications for Business and Policy," *Journal of Finance,* vol. 34 (May 1979), 415-427.

Regarding decisions as to the use of financing outside the parent company's home country, see

Eaker, Mark R., "Denomination Decision for Multinational Transactions," *Financial Management,* vol. 9 (Autumn 1980), 23-29.

Folks, William R., Jr., and Ramesh Advani, "Raising Funds with Foreign Currency," *Financial Executive,* vol. 48 (February 1980), 44-49.

Severn, Alan K., and David R. Meinster, "The Use of Multicurrency Financing by the Financial Manager," *Financial Management,* vol. 7 (Winter 1978), 45-53.

Other recent works of interest include these:

Elliott, J. W., "The Expected Return to Equity and International Asset Prices," *Journal of Financial and Quantitative Analysis,* vol. 13 (December 1978), 987-1002.

Meadows, Edward, "How the Euromarket Fends Off Global Disaster," *Fortune,* September 24, 1979, 122-135.

Shapiro, Alan C., "Financial Structure and Cost of Capital in the Multinational Corporation," *Journal of Financial and Quantitative Analysis,* vol. 13 (June 1978), 211-226.

Mergers and Divestitures 20

Most corporate growth occurs through *internal expansion*, which takes place when the firm's existing divisions grow through normal capital budgeting activities. However, the most dramatic growth and, often, the largest increases in firms' stock prices are the result of *mergers*, one subject of this chapter.[1] Also, the conditions of corporate life often change over time, and as a result firms occasionally find it desirable to sell off major divisions to other firms which can better utilize the divested assets. This topic is also discussed in the chapter.

The primary motivation for mergers is to increase the value of the combined enterprise. If Companies A and B merge to form Company C, and if C's value exceeds that of A and B taken separately, then *synergy* is said to exist.[2] Such a merger is beneficial to both A's and B's stockholders. Synergistic effects can arise from three sources: (1) *operating economies* resulting from economies of scale in production or distribution; (2) *financial economies*, including either a higher P/E ratio, a lower cost of debt, or a greater debt capacity; and (3) *increased market power* due to reduced competition. Operating and financial economies are socially desirable, but mergers that reduce competition are both undesirable and illegal.[3]

When two firms begin merger negotiations, or when one firm begins thinking about acquiring another, one of the first considerations is antitrust: Is the Justice Department likely to try to block the merger, and

Economic Implications of Mergers

---

[1] As we use the term, *merger* means any combination that forms one economic unit from two or more previous ones. For legal purposes there are distinctions between the various ways these combinations can occur, but our emphasis is on fundamental business and financial aspects of mergers or acquisitions.

[2] If synergy exists, then the whole is greater than the sum of the parts. Synergy is also called the "2 plus 2 equals 5 effect." The distribution of the synergistic gain between A's and B's stockholders is determined by negotiation. This point is discussed later in the chapter.

[3] In the 1880s and 1890s, many mergers occurred in the United States, and some of them were rather obviously directed toward gaining market power rather than increasing operating efficiency. As a result, Congress passed a series of acts designed to insure that mergers are not used as a method of reducing competition. The principal acts include the Sherman Act (1890), the Clayton Act (1914), and the Celler Act (1950). These acts make it illegal for firms to combine in any manner if the combination tends to lessen competition. The acts are administered by the Antitrust Division of the Justice Department and by the Federal Trade Commission.

would it be able to do so? If the answer to either part of this question is yes, then chances are high that the merger will be aborted because of the legal expenses involved in fighting the Justice Department.

Types of Mergers

Economists classify mergers into four groups: (1) horizontal, (2) vertical, (3) congeneric, and (4) conglomerate. A *horizontal merger* occurs when, for example, one widget manufacturer acquires another, or one retail food chain merges with a second—that is, when one firm combines with another in its same line of business. An example of a *vertical merger* is a steel producer's acquisition of an iron or coal mining firm or an oil producer's acquisition of a petrochemical company. Congeneric means "allied in nature or action"; hence, a *congeneric merger* involves related enterprises, but not producers of the same product (horizontal) or firms in a producer-supplier relationship (vertical). Examples of congeneric mergers include banks' acquisitions of leasing companies, as well as insurance companies' takeovers of mutual fund management companies. *Conglomerate mergers* occur when unrelated enterprises combine; Mobil Oil's acquisition of Montgomery Ward illustrates a conglomerate merger.

Operating economies (and also anticompetitive effects) are at least partially dependent on the type of merger involved. Vertical and horizontal mergers generally provide the greatest operating benefits, but they are also the ones most likely to be attacked by the Justice Department. In any event, it is useful to think of these economic classifications when analyzing the feasibility of a prospective merger.

Level of Merger Activity

There have been four major periods of merger activity in the United States. The first was in the late 1800s, when consolidations occurred in oil, steel, tobacco, and other basic industries. The second was in the 1920s, when the stock market boom helped financial promoters consolidate firms in a number of industries, including utilities and communication companies. The third was in the 1960s, when conglomerate mergers were the rage. And the fourth is with us right now (1981).

The 1980s' "merger mania" has been sparked by three factors: (1) the relatively depressed condition of the stock market (for example, the Dow Jones index in 1981 was below its 1968 level), (2) the unprecedented level of inflation that existed during the 1970s and early 1980s, and (3) the Reagan administration's stated view that "bigness is not necessarily bad" and its more tolerant attitude toward mergers. The depressed stock market, combined with inflation—which has caused the true value of assets (mineral resources, land, buildings, and machinery) to be far greater than book values—has enabled companies to acquire assets more cheaply by purchasing the stocks of other companies than by obtaining assets directly.

Financial historians have not yet compiled the statistics and done the analysis necessary to compare the 1980s' merger wave with the earlier ones, but it is virtually certain to surpass in importance the ones of the 1920s and 1960s, and to approach if not surpass that of the 1890s. As an example, as this book was going into final production (Summer 1981), these mergers were in process or had just been completed:

1. *Conoco,* which has book value assets of $11 billion and is the fourteenth largest company in the world, is the target of Mobil (second largest in the United States, third in the world), du Pont (fifteenth in the United States, thirty-eighth in the world), and Seagram (a large Canadian company). This merger alone will almost surpass in dollar amount the previous record annual total ($12 billion in 1968). Conoco's stock sold for about $50 just before the bidding for it started; the bid price is now up to over $100 per share. Conoco's oil and coal reserves and its plant and equipment are worth far more than their book values. If Mobil wins, this will be a horizontal merger. If du Pont wins, it will be a vertical merger (du Pont uses petroleum in its production processes). And if Seagram wins, it will be a conglomerate merger. The Justice Department will not fight a merger with Seagram or du Pont, but it might well fight a merger with Mobil. Thus, although Mobil has made the highest bid ($115 per share), du Pont is the current favorite with a bid of $98; stockholders are choosing the du Pont bid over that of Mobil because they are afraid the Mobil merger would be blocked and Conoco's stock would then fall below the level of the du Pont bid price.

   Regardless of who wins, this is a *hostile merger*—Conoco's management would rather have had the company remain an independent entity. Obviously, though, this is not to be, and Conoco's top managers will soon be working for someone else (or out of a job). This is a good illustration of a point made in Chapter 1, namely that managers have a very strong motivation to operate in a manner that will maximize the value of their firms' stock. Otherwise, they could find themselves in the same boat as Conoco's managers.

2. *Teleprompter,* which is the largest cable TV company, is likely to be acquired by Westinghouse for $646 million. Since Westinghouse owns TV stations and a cable business, this would be partly a horizontal merger and partly a vertical one. Westinghouse may have to divest itself of the Teleprompter cable systems that are within the same geographic area as Westinghouse's TV stations in order to gain federal approval of the merger.

3. *Iowa Beef,* the largest meat processing company, is likely to be acquired by Occidental Petroleum for $800 million. This is a conglomerate merger; Occidental is seeking greater diversification.

4. *Colt Industries* (which makes guns, among other things) is being sought

for acquisition by Penn Central for $1.4 billion, or $100 per share versus a price of $45 shortly before the merger announcement. Penn Central has close to $2 billion of tax loss carry-forwards, so if it acquires Colt, Colt's earnings will be, in effect, tax-free for years. This tax situation makes Colt more valuable as a subsidiary of Penn Central than it would be if operated as a separate company or as a part of a company without tax loss carry-forwards.

5. *Schlitz*, once the largest U.S. brewer, has been losing both money and market share. By 1980 it had become only the fourth largest brewer, with a market share of 8.5 percent, and in 1981 it seemed to be on a collision course with bankruptcy. Schlitz's troubles arose from its poor marketing strategy, a problem which it seems unable to conquer. G. Heileman, the sixth largest brewer, with a 1980 market share of 7.5 percent, has been better managed, and its sales have been growing rapidly. (Heileman's ROE in 1980 was 27.3 percent; Schlitz has been losing money lately.) Because of its successful marketing programs, Heileman needs more brewing capacity, while because of its poor sales performance, Schlitz has 50 percent excess capacity. In July 1981, Heileman offered to buy Schlitz's common stock for $494 million. If the takeover attempt is successful, Heileman will be acquiring capacity at an effective cost of $19 per barrel versus a construction cost of about $50 per barrel. The merger would also make Heileman the third largest brewer in the nation. Although the Reagan Justice Department has taken the position that "bigness is not necessarily badness," it may oppose the merger if in its judgment such a merger would substantially reduce competition in the industry. Rumors on Wall Street suggest that other brewers may enter the bidding for Schlitz; in view of the wide disparity between Schlitz's reproduction cost and the price Heileman is offering, this would not be surprising.

These are just a few examples of the mergers that have been occurring recently. At this time, there is no way of knowing just how far the current merger wave will carry us or what its ultimate effects will be. In the remainder of the chapter, we shall explore the mechanics of mergers and procedures for evaluating the merits of a given merger.

Procedures for Combining Firms

In the vast majority of merger situations, one firm (generally the smaller of the two) is acquired by another company. Occasionally the acquired firm will initiate the action, but it is much more common for a firm to seek acquisitions than to seek to be acquired.[4] Following convention, we

---

[4] However, if a firm is in financial difficulty, if the managers are old and do not feel that suitable replacements are on hand, or if the firm needs the support (often the capital) of a larger company, then it may seek to be acquired.

shall call a company that seeks to acquire another the *acquiring company* and the one which it seeks to acquire the *target company*.

Once an acquiring company has identified a possible acquisition, it must establish a suitable price, or range of prices, that it is willing to pay. With this in mind, the acquiring firm's managers must decide how to approach the target company's managers. If the acquiring firm has reason to believe the target company's management will approve the merger, then it will simply propose a merger and, it is to be hoped, work out some suitable terms. Then the two management groups will issue statements to their stockholders recommending that they approve the merger. Assuming that the stockholders do approve, the acquiring firm will simply buy the target company's shares from its stockholders, paying for them either with its own shares (in which case the target company's stockholders become stockholders of the acquiring company) or with cash. Situations in which the terms of the merger are approved by both management groups are called *friendly mergers*.

Under other circumstances, the target company's management may resist the merger. Perhaps it feels that the price offered for the stock is too low, or perhaps the target firm's management simply wants to maintain its independence. In either case, the target firm's management is said to be *hostile*, and the acquiring firm must make a direct appeal to the target firm's stockholders. In hostile mergers, the acquiring company generally makes a *tender offer*, in which it asks the stockholders of the firm it is seeking to control to submit, or "tender," their shares in exchange for a specified price. The price is generally stated as so many dollars per share of the stock to be acquired, although it can be stated in terms of shares of stock in the acquiring firm. The tender offer is a direct appeal to stockholders, so it need not be approved by the management of the target firm. Tender offers are not new, but the frequency of their use has increased greatly in recent years.[5]

Tenneco's acquisition of Kern County Land Company can be used to illustrate how a tender offer works. Kern was a relatively old, conservatively managed company whose assets consisted largely of oil properties and agricultural land, together with some manufacturing subsidiaries. Many informed investors believed that Kern's assets had a potential long-run value in excess of its current market price. Occidental Petroleum, a relatively aggressive company, made an investigation of Kern's assets and decided to make a cash tender offer for the stock. At that time, Kern's market price on the New York Stock Exchange was about $60 a share, while the price Occidental decided to offer Kern's stockholders was $83.50 a share. According to Kern's management, Occidental's executives got in touch with them over the weekend and stated that a tender offer would be made the following Monday.

[5] Tender offers can be friendly, with the target firm's management recommending that stockholders go ahead and tender their stock.

Because Occidental's published statements indicated that it felt Kern's low market value was partly the result of an unimaginative management, Kern's executives could anticipate being fired if Occidental's takeover bid was successful. Naturally, they resisted it. Kern's president wrote a letter to the stockholders condemning the merger; the letter was also published as an advertisement in the *Wall Street Journal*. His position was that Kern's stock was worth more than Occidental Petroleum had offered, and that stockholders should not sell out for $83.50.

How would Kern's stockholders react to these statements? In the first place, the stock had been selling at about $60 a share, and they were now offered $83.50 cash per share. With this differential, stockholders would certainly accept the offer unless Kern's management could do something to keep the price above $83.50. What Kern did was to obtain "marriage proposals" from a number of other companies called "white knights." Kern's management reported to the newspapers—while Occidental's tender offer was still outstanding—that it had received a substantial number of proposals calling for the purchase of Kern's stock at prices substantially in excess of $83.50. This kept stockholders from tendering to Occidental.

The offer Kern's management finally recommended—and presumably the one giving Kern's stockholders the highest price—was from Tenneco Corporation. Tenneco, the winning white knight, offered one share of convertible preferred stock worth about $105 for each share of Kern's stock. Further, since the merger involved an exchange of stock rather than cash, Kern's stockholders would not have to pay capital gains tax on this stock at the time of the exchange. (Had they accepted Occidental's offer, the difference between $83.50 and the cost of their stock when they purchased it would have been taxable income.) Also, according to newspaper reports, Tenneco planned to keep Kern's existing management after the merger was completed.

Financial Analysis of a Proposed Merger

In theory, merger analysis is quite simple. The acquiring firm simply performs a capital budgeting analysis to determine whether the present value of the expected future income from the merger exceeds the price paid for the target company. The target company's stockholders, on the other hand, should accept the proposal if the price offered exceeds the present value of the firm's expected future cash flows, assuming that it operates independently. However, some difficult issues are involved: (1) it is necessary for the acquiring company to estimate the cash flow benefits that will be obtained from the acquisition; (2) it is necessary to determine what effect, if any, the merger will have on the required rate of return on equity; and (3) having estimated the benefits of the merger, it is necessary for the acquiring and target firms' managers and stockholders to bargain over how to share these benefits.

From the standpoint of financial analysis, there are two basic types of mergers:

1. *Operating mergers,* in which the operations of two companies are integrated with the expectation of obtaining synergistic effects. The Schlitz-Heileman case is a good example of an operating merger.
2. *Pure financial mergers,* in which the merged companies will not be operated as a single unit and from which no operating economies are expected. Colt–Penn Central illustrates a pure financial merger.

Of course, mergers may actually combine these two features. Thus, if Mobil acquired Conoco, this would be primarily an operating merger; it would be a financial merger if Seagram won the prize; and if du Pont should emerge the victor, the merger would be partly operating and partly financial.

In a pure financial merger, the postmerger cash flows are simply the sum of the expected cash flows of the two companies if they are to continue to operate independently. However, if the two firms' operations are to be integrated, then accurate projected cash flow statements, which are absolutely essential to sound merger decisions, will be difficult to construct.

The basic rationale for any operating merger is synergy. Del Monte Corporation provides a good example of a series of well thought out, successful operating mergers. Del Monte successfully merged and integrated numerous small canning companies into a very efficient, highly profitable organization. It used standardized production techniques to increase the efficiency of all its plants, a national brand name and national advertising to develop customer loyalty, a consolidated distribution system, and a centralized purchasing office that obtained substantial discounts from volume purchases. Because of these economies, Del Monte became perhaps the most efficient and profitable canning company, and its merger activities helped make possible the size that produced these economies. Consumers also benefited, because Del Monte's efficiency enabled the company to sell high quality products at relatively low prices.

An example of poor pro forma analysis that resulted in a disastrous merger is the consolidation of the Pennsylvania and New York Central Railroads. The premerger analysis was highly misleading. It failed to reveal the fact that certain key elements in the two rail systems were incompatible and hence could not be meshed together. Rather than gaining synergistic benefits, the combined system actually incurred additional overhead costs that helped lead to its bankruptcy.

It is impossible to generalize further about the construction of pro forma statements except to say that, in planning operating mergers, *the development of pro forma statements is the single most important aspect* of the merger analysis.[6]

Postmerger Market Values

Once the postmerger income statement has been estimated, the next step is to project the postmerger market price of the acquiring firm's stock. This, in turn, involves two steps: (1) estimating postmerger earnings per share and (2) estimating the postmerger price/earnings ratio. Since earnings per share depend on the terms of the merger (how much the acquiring firm pays for the acquired company), this topic is examined next.

Terms of the Merger

The terms of a merger include two important elements. (1) Who will control the combined enterprise? (2) How much will the acquiring firm pay for the acquired company?

Postmerger Control. The employment/control situation is of vital interest when a small, owner-managed firm sells out to a larger concern. The owner-manager may be anxious to retain a high position and also be concerned about keeping operating control of the organization after the merger. Thus, these points are likely to be stressed during the merger negotiations.[7] When a publicly owned firm not controlled by its managers is merged into another company, the acquired firm's management also is worried about its postmerger position. If the acquiring firm agrees to keep the old management, then management may be willing to support the merger and recommend its acceptance to the stockholders. If the old management is to be removed, then it will probably resist the merger, as Kern's management did in the example described earlier in the chapter.

The Price Paid. The second key element in a merger is the price to be paid for the acquired company—the cash or shares of stock to be given in exchange for the firm. If the merger is to be for cash, the analysis is similar to a regular capital budgeting analysis: The incremental earnings are estimated; a discount rate is applied to find the present value of these

---

[6] It should be noted that firms heavily engaged in mergers have "acquisition departments" whose functions include (1) seeking suitable merger candidates and (2) taking over and integrating acquired firms into the parent corporation. The first step involves developing both pro forma statements and a plan for making the projections materialize. The second step involves (1) streamlining operations of the acquired firm, if necessary, and (2) instituting a system of controls that will permit the parent to effectively manage the new division and to coordinate its operation with those of other units.

[7] The acquiring firm may also be concerned about this point, especially if the acquired firm's management is quite good. A condition of the merger may be that the management team agree to stay on for a period such as five years after the merger, and, further, that they agree not to start a new, competing business. Also, the price paid may be contingent on the acquired firm's performance subsequent to the merger. For example, when International Holdings acquired Walker Products, the price set was 100,000 shares of International Holdings stock at the time the deal was closed plus an additional 10,000 shares each year for the next three years *provided Walker Products earned at least $500,000 during each of these years*. Since Walker's managers owned the stock and would receive the bonus, they had incentive to stay on and to help the firm meet its targets.

earnings; and, if the present value of the future incremental earnings exceeds the price to be paid for the acquired firm, then the merger is approved. Thus, only if the acquired firm is worth more to the acquiring firm than its market value as a separate entity will the merger be feasible. Obviously, the acquiring firm tries to buy at as low a price as possible, while the acquired firm tries to sell out at the highest possible price. The final price is determined by negotiations, with the side that negotiates better capturing most of the incremental value. *The larger the synergistic benefits, the more room there is for bargaining and the higher the probability that the merger will actually be consummated.*[8]

If the merger calls for an exchange of stock, then the key issue is the *exchange ratio (ER), which is the number of shares the acquiring firm gives for each of the acquired firm's shares.* For example, when Emhart Industries acquired USM, 1.125 shares of Emhart were exchanged for each USM share; thus, the exchange ratio was 1.125. The three factors that have the greatest influence on the exchange ratio—current earnings, projected future earnings, and market prices—are discussed next.

Earnings per Share. Suppose the acquiring company (Firm A) earns $4.53 per share, while the target company (Firm T) has EPS = $3.49, and the companies are equally risky. On the basis of relative earnings, the exchange ratio would be set at $3.49/$4.53 = 0.77. This means that 77 shares of Firm A's stock would be exchanged for every 100 shares of Firm T's stock. An exchange on this basis would leave each stockholder's postmerger earnings unchanged. For example, the holder of 100 shares of T would receive 77 shares of A. The premerger earnings would have been 100 × $3.49 = $349, while the postmerger earnings would be 77 × $4.53 = $349.

Projected Future Earnings. The above arrangement would be appropriate if (1) there were no synergistic effects, and (2) the firms had identical growth rates. However, when the merger is expected to produce higher earnings, or when the firms' EPS growth rates differ, it is more appropriate to set the exchange ratio on the basis of *expected future EPS rather than historic EPS.*

First, consider the same case with no synergy but with the additional information that Firm A has been growing and is expected to continue to grow at a 6 percent rate, while T's growth rate is 4 percent. On the basis of the latest reported earnings, the exchange ratio would be

---

[8] It has been estimated that, of all merger negotiations seriously begun, only about one-third actually result in merger. Also, note that in a contested merger situation as exists with Conoco, the company that offers the most will make the acquisition. Presumably, du Pont, Mobil, and Seagram have all analyzed Conoco's value to them, and they will bid up close to that value. The company that will gain the greatest synergistic benefits should bid the most.

$3.49/\$4.53 = 0.77$. However, on the basis of next year's projected earnings, the ratio would be $\$3.49(1.04)/\$4.53(1.06) = \$3.63/\$4.80 = 0.756$. Further, on the basis of earnings five years hence, the exchange ratio would be $\$4.25/\$6.06 = 0.701$. Thus, a problem exists—on the basis of future earnings, the exchange ratio varies depending on how far into the future earnings are projected.

When possible synergistic effects are considered, it becomes even more difficult to use current earnings as a basis for the exchange ratio. Suppose, for example, that Firm A's EPS = $\$4.53$, Firm T's EPS = $\$3.49$, and no growth is expected. If the merger terms are based on relative EPS, then, as we have seen, the ratio will be set at 0.77, and both firms' stockholders will have the same postmerger earnings. Thus, EPS for Firm A, the surviving company, will remain at $\$4.53$. However, let us assume that synergistic effects are present, and on the basis of a 0.77 exchange ratio, A's postmerger EPS will rise to $6. This will benefit both T's and A's stockholders—the holder of 100 shares of T will now have earnings of $77 \times \$6 = \$462$ versus $\$349$ before the merger, while a 100 share owner of A will have $100 \times \$6 = \$600$ versus $\$453$ without the merger.

Accordingly, if synergy is anticipated, then A can realistically pay more for T than 0.77 shares, while T's stockholders can accept less than 0.77 shares and still come out ahead. To calculate this "breakeven exchange ratio" from Firm A's standpoint, we apply the following formula:

$$ER_A = \frac{TE - EPS_A(N_A)}{EPS_A(N_T)}. \tag{20-1}$$

Here ER_A is the maximum exchange ratio which will prevent dilution of Firm A's EPS; TE equals the consolidated total earnings (A's old earnings + T's old earnings + synergistic earnings); EPS_A is A's old EPS; N_A is the number of shares of A's stock outstanding before the merger; and N_T is the number of shares of T's stock outstanding before the merger.[9]

Suppose the following conditions exist:

$$N_T = 300 \text{ shares,}$$
$$N_A = 1,000 \text{ shares (before the merger),}$$
$$EPS_A = \$4.53, \text{ and}$$
$$TE = \$4,530 + \$1,047 + \$2,000 = \$7,577.$$

---

[9] Equation 20-1 is developed by finding the ER that keeps A's new EPS equal to its old EPS:

$$\text{New EPS} = \text{Old EPS} = \frac{TE}{N_A + N_T(ER)}.$$

Solving for ER produces Equation 20-1, with EPS_A being equal to A's old EPS.

The $2,000 included in TE represents synergistic earnings. Substituting into Equation 20-1, we obtain

$$\text{ER}_A = \frac{\$7,577 - \$4.53(1,000)}{\$4.53(300)} = \frac{\$3,047}{\$1,359} = 2.24 \text{ shares.}$$

Thus, A can give as many as 2.24 of its shares for each share of T without causing a dilution in its EPS:

$$\text{Old EPS} = \$4.53.$$

$$\text{New EPS} = \frac{\$7,577}{1,000 + 300(2.24)} = \frac{\$7,577}{1,672} = \$4.53.$$

Any lower exchange ratio will increase A's EPS.

A similar analysis can be conducted from the standpoint of T's stockholders to determine just how low the exchange ratio can be set without diluting T's stockholders' earnings. This minimum ratio is equal to the following:[10]

$$\text{ER}_T = \frac{\text{EPS}_T N_A}{\text{TE} - N_T \text{EPS}_T}. \tag{20-2}$$

Substituting into Equation 20-2, we find the minimum ratio acceptable to T's stockholders to be 0.534:

$$\text{ER}_T = \frac{\$3.49(1,000)}{\$7,577 - 300(\$3.49)} = \frac{\$3,490}{\$6,530} = 0.534.$$

If this ratio is used, A's postmerger EPS will be

$$\text{EPS}_A = \frac{\text{TE}}{N_A + \text{ER}(N_T)} = \frac{\$7,577}{1,000 + 160} = \$6.53.$$

The holder of 100 old shares of T would have had total earnings of 100 × $3.49 = $349. After the merger, if the exchange ratio is set at 0.534, the total earnings still will be $349: 53.4 shares × $6.53 = $349.

We see, then, that if no basic growth is expected, but synergy is present, our hypothetical merger should have an exchange ratio in the range of 0.53 to 2.24. The greater the synergistic effects, the wider the range of

---

[10] Equation 20-2 is developed as follows: We are seeking to set Old EPS_T = New EPS_T. New EPS_T = new EPS_A (ER), so $\text{EPS}_A = \text{EPS}_T/\text{ER}$, where EPS_A is the new, *postmerger* EPS. Footnote 9 also gave an equation for EPS_A, and we can set these two equations equal to one another:

$$\text{EPS}_A = \frac{\text{EPS}_T}{\text{ER}} = \frac{\text{TE}}{N_A + N_T \text{ER}}.$$

We can now solve for ER:

$$\text{ER}_T = \frac{\text{EPS}_T N_A}{\text{TE} - N_T \text{EPS}_T}. \tag{20-2}$$

the exchange ratio. Obviously, the acquiring firm will want to set the exchange ratio as low as possible, while the target firm will want to use the upper end of the range. The actual exchange ratio will be determined by the bargaining process, but with such a wide range as this one, the merger would almost certainly take place.

Either the acquiring or the target company could be in the stronger bargaining position, hence capture most of the synergistic benefits. For example, if the acquiring company were the only company whose operations blended with those of the target in a manner that would produce synergy, then it would probably set an exchange ratio close to the lower end of the range. On the other hand, if the target were a mining or oil producing company that would fit in well with many of the larger oil companies, then it could probably hold out for an exchange ratio close to the upper limit.

Market Values. Current and future earnings, risk, growth rates, potential synergistic effects, and a host of other factors are embodied in a firm's market price, so in many respects relative market prices represent the best basis for setting exchange ratios. Suppose, for example, that Firm A sells for $40 per share, while T's current price is $30. On the basis of market values, the exchange ratio would be set at $30/$40 = 0.75.

If no synergistic effects are likely, or if T's synergistic value to potential acquiring firms is already reflected in its price, then the actual exchange ratio will probably be based on relative market values. However, if T's price reflects only its "stand alone" value, but it could enjoy substantially higher profits if combined with another company, then the actual exchange ratio could be set well above the market value ratio. Most of the larger mergers in 1981 involved premiums of 50 percent or more over the pre-announcement price of the target firm's shares. Thus, du Pont and Conoco stock sold at about the same price before Conoco became a target, yet du Pont has bid 1.7 of its shares for each Conoco share (an ER of 1.7, and a 90 percent premium over Conoco's pre-merger price).

Illustration of a Merger Analysis

To illustrate how a merger might be analyzed, consider the proposed merger between Consolidated Enterprises and Target Technology, Inc. Consolidated Enterprises has been growing at a rate of about 5 percent per year, while Target Technology's past and projected future growth rate is 20 percent. Consolidated's total after-tax earnings are $50 million, or $4 for each of its 12.5 million shares; Target's latest earnings were $3 million, or $2 for each of its 1.5 million shares. Consolidated pays a $2 dividend, while Target pays $1 per share. Consolidated's current market price is $30 per share, and Target's is $20 per share.

When they began considering a possible merger, Consolidated's analysts first assumed that no synergistic effects would occur but that the combined companies would grow at a 5.85 percent rate, calculated as follows:[11]

	Total Earnings	Percentage Weights	Growth Rate	Product
Consolidated Enterprises	$50,000,000	0.9434	5%	4.717%
Target Technology	3,000,000	0.0566	20	1.132
	$53,000,000	1.0000		
Weighted average growth rate				5.849%

Next, the Consolidated analysts considered possible exchange ratios (ER). On the basis of *current* earnings, ER = $2/$4 = 0.5 shares of Consolidated given up for each share of Target Technology. On the basis of *future* earnings, the ratio would increase; for example, if earnings projected out five years were used, then the exchange ratio would be about 1.0:

$$ER = (1.20)^5(\$2)/(1.05)^5(\$4)$$
$$= 2.4883(\$2)/1.2763(\$4)$$
$$= \$4.98/\$5.11 = 0.975 \cong 1.0.$$

On the basis of relative market prices, the exchange ratio would be set at $20/$30 = 0.667, and EPS would be $53/(12.5 + 0.667 × 1.5) = $3.93.

The Consolidated analysts then projected earnings per share for each of the next five years under the alternative exchange ratios. This projection was made by first estimating total corporate earnings of the combined firm for each year, then dividing by the number of shares outstanding, which differs depending on the exchange ratio used. Figure 20-1 gives a plot of Consolidated's EPS assuming no merger and also assuming a merger based on current market prices. As the graph shows, Consolidated's EPS would decline immediately after the merger, assuming no synergy and a 0.667 exchange ratio, but in the future EPS would grow more rapidly than it would have without the merger.

Using other exchange ratios, other earnings growth rates, and synergistic effects, we could derive many other EPS patterns. Because so many factors are involved, it is difficult to generalize about postmerger earnings per share. However, one important generalization should be made: *If a*

[11] Notice that, if the merger were analyzed next year, Target Technology's weight would be larger, hence the weighted average rate would be increased. In fact, if the growth rates of the two components were maintained after the merger, the growth rate of the combined enterprise would change each year, rising from 5.85 percent the first year and approaching 20 percent as the number of years since the merger increased. Target Technology could not, however, maintain a 20 percent growth rate indefinitely; if it did, it would eventually surpass the Gross National Product!

**Figure 20-1
EPS Projections
for Consolidated
Enterprises**

firm with a high P/E ratio buys a firm with a lower P/E ratio, and the exchange ratio is based on current market prices, then the acquiring firm will obtain an immediate increase in EPS. Conversely, if a low P/E ratio company buys a high P/E firm, there will be an immediate dilution in EPS. This point is borne out by the Consolidated-Target merger analysis. Consolidated had a lower P/E ratio ($30/$4 = 7.5×) than Target Technology ($20/$2 = 10×), and this relationship led to the initial dilution in Consolidated's EPS as shown in Figure 20-1.[12] *In effect, Consolidated would be diluting its current EPS in order to obtain a higher future EPS growth rate.*

Target Technology's stockholders will have a higher level of current earnings at the market value exchange ratio:

Old earnings per 100 shares owned:	100 × $2 = $200.
New earnings per 100 shares formerly owned:	100(0.667)($3.93) = $262.

They will, of course, be giving up some of their future growth opportunities.

Operating Synergy. The analysis thus far is all based on the assumption of no operating synergies. However, Consolidated and Target Technology

---

[12] The extent of this earnings dilution or increase depends on the size of the target company relative to that of the acquiring firm—the larger the target, the greater the earnings increase or decrease.

may complement one another. For example, Target's metallurgical scientists may be able to improve Consolidated's product line, or Consolidated's unused plant may be utilized by Target Technology. If synergy does occur, it could partially or completely offset the initial dilution and also result in an increase in the postmerger growth rate.

The Postmerger Market Price: Estimating a P/E Ratio. After developing estimates of the postmerger EPS, the next task is to estimate a P/E ratio and then to apply this P/E ratio to the earnings estimate to obtain a *predicted postmerger market price.* The postmerger P/E ratio will reflect investors' estimates of the merged company's risk and growth prospects. If investors feel that Consolidated and Target Technology, as a combined enterprise, will be less risky because of diversification effects, then the P/E ratio may rise. Similarly, if investors think that the postmerger growth rate will be more reflective of Target Technology's situation, this too will enhance the P/E ratio.

The resulting P/E ratio might be the same as Consolidated's old ratio, 7.5 times. If this ratio is applied to an EPS of $3.93, the resulting price is $29.48. In this case, Consolidated's postmerger price would have declined from the old $30 level. On the other hand, if investors applied Target Technology's P/E of 10 to the combined company, then the postmerger stock price would be $39.30.

Several points should be clear from this brief discussion. First, Consolidated should acquire Target Technology if and only if the acquisition will raise Consolidated's stock price. Second, the postmerger price will reflect both the final EPS, which will depend on the exchange ratio and on possible synergistic effects, and the final P/E ratio, which will depend on investors' appraisal of the combined firm's risk and growth prospects. If a firm's analysts are good at estimating these factors, they will have a record of good acquisitions; otherwise, their merger program will not be successful.

Investment Bankers' Role in Mergers

The investment banking community is involved with mergers in a number of ways: (1) helping to arrange mergers, (2) helping target companies resist mergers, and (3) helping to establish the cash prices or exchange ratios for mergers. In each of these cases, the investment bankers are not motivated just by a desire to help others—activities associated with mergers pay very well. For example, the investment bankers who arranged RCA's acquisition of C.I.T. Financial earned fees of $5.8 million, and if du Pont wins the contest for Conoco, its investment banker, First Boston, will earn fees of over $15 million. Morgan Stanley, Conoco's investment banker, will earn fees of about $15 million regardless of who wins. No wonder investment banking houses are making top offers to finance graduates!

Arranging Mergers. The major investment banking firms have merger and acquisition groups that are generally set up within their corporate finance departments. (Corporate finance departments offer advice, as opposed to underwriting services, to business firms.) Members of these groups strive to keep aware of firms with excess cash that might want to buy other firms, and of firms that might be willing to be bought. Also, if a firm—say an oil company—decided to expand into coal mining, then it might enlist the aid of an investment banker in locating and then negotiating with a target coal company.

Fighting Off Mergers. Target firms that do not want to be acquired may enlist the help of an investment banking firm, along with a law firm that specializes in helping to block mergers. Defenses include such tactics as trying to convince the target firm's stockholders that the price being offered is too low, raising antitrust issues in hopes that the Justice Department will intervene, repurchasing stock in the open market in an effort to push the price above that being offered by the potential acquirer, and seeking a "white knight" that is more acceptable to the target firm's management to compete with the potential acquirer.

Establishing a Price. If a friendly merger is being worked out between two firms' managements, it is important to be able to prove that the agreed-upon price is a fair one. Otherwise, the stockholders of one company or the other may sue to block the merger. Therefore, in many large mergers each side will engage an investment banking firm to evaluate the target company and to help establish the fair price. For example, General Electric employed Morgan Stanley to determine a fair price for Utah International in their $2 billion merger.

Even if the merger is not friendly, investment bankers may still be asked to help establish a price. If a surprise tender offer is to be made, the acquiring firm will want to know the lowest price at which it might be able to acquire the stock, while the target firm may seek help in "proving" that the price being offered is too low.[13]

Effects of Accounting Practices on Reported Profits

Although a detailed discussion of accounting is best left to accounting courses, at least some mention should be made of alternative accounting treatments of merged firms and their effects on reported profits. Mergers are handled in either of two basic ways: (1) as a *pooling of interests* or (2)

---

[13] Such investigations must obviously be done in secret, for if someone knew that Company A was thinking of offering say $50 per share for Company T, which was currently selling at $35 per share, then huge profits could be made. The biggest scandal to hit Wall Street in 1981 was the disclosure that a member of Morgan Stanley's merger group was himself buying the stock of target companies which he was analyzing for others. His purchases, of course, raised the prices of the stocks and thus caused his clients to pay more than they would otherwise have had to pay.

as a *purchase*. The method used can have a significant effect on the post-merger reported profits, and this, in turn, can influence the desirability of the merger.

In a pooling of interests, the consolidated balance sheet is constructed by simply adding together the balance sheets of the merged companies. Table 20-1 shows the essential elements of the consolidated balance sheet after Firms A and B have merged under a pooling of interests. This final balance sheet holds, regardless of how many shares Firm A gave up to acquire Firm B. (In a pooling, shares, not cash, must be exchanged.)

Pooling of Interests

**Table 20-1
Pooling of Interests
Accounting**

	Firm A	Firm B	Merged Firm: A
Current assets	$ 50	$25	$ 75
Fixed assets	50	25	75
Total assets	$100	$50	$150
Debt	$ 40	$20	$ 60
Common equity	60	30	90
Total liabilities and net worth	$100	$50	$150

Purchase Accounting

Under purchase accounting, the acquiring firm is assumed to have "bought" the acquired company much as it would buy any capital asset, paying for it with cash, debt, or stock of the acquiring company. If the price paid is exactly equal to the net asset value (total assets minus liabilities), then the consolidated balance sheet is similar to that under pooling. Otherwise, there is an important difference. If the price paid exceeds the net asset value, then assets are increased to reflect the price actually paid, while if the price paid is less than the net asset value, then assets are written down when preparing the consolidated balance sheet.

Table 20-2 illustrates purchase accounting, using the same data as for the pooled companies. Note that Firm B's net asset value is $30, which is also its reported common equity value. This $30 could reflect the correct market value (which is determined by the firm's earning power), but net asset, or book value, could also be more or less than the market value. Three situations are considered. First, in Column 3 we assume that Firm A gives cash or stock worth $20 for Firm B. Thus, B was apparently overvalued, and A pays less than B's net asset value. The overvaluation could be in either fixed or current assets; we assume that fixed assets are overvalued. Accordingly, we reduce both B's fixed assets and its common equity by $10 before constructing the consolidated balance sheet shown

Table 20-2
Purchase Accounting

	Firm A (1)	Firm B (2)	Firm A after the Merger[a]		
			$20 Paid (3)	$30 Paid (4)	$50 Paid (5)
Current assets	$ 50	$25	$ 75	$ 75	$ 80
Fixed assets	50	25	65[b]	75	80
Goodwill[c]	0	0	0	0	10
	$100	$50	$140	$150	$170
Debt	$ 40	$20	$ 60	$ 60	$ 60
Equity	60	30	80[d]	90	110[e]
	$100	$50	$140	$150	$170

[a] The price paid is the *net* asset value, that is, total assets minus debt.

[b] Assume Firm B's fixed assets are written down to $15 before constructing the consolidated balance sheet.

[c] "Goodwill" refers to the excess paid for a firm over and above the appraised value of the physical assets purchased. Goodwill represents payment both for intangibles such as patents and also for "organization value" that might arise from having an effective sales force.

[d] Firm B's common equity is reduced by $10 prior to consolidation to reflect the fixed asset write-off.

[e] Firm B's equity is increased prior to consolidation to reflect the above-book purchase price.

in Column 3. Next, in Column 4 we assume that A pays exactly the net asset value for B. In this case, pooling and purchase accounting would produce identical balance sheets. Finally, in Column 5 we assume that A pays more than net asset value for B: $50 is paid for $30 of net assets. This excess is assumed to be partly attributed to undervalued assets (land, buildings, and machinery, and also inventories worth more because of inflation); to reflect this fact, current and fixed assets are each increased by $5. In addition, we assume that $10 of the $20 excess is due to a superior sales organization, or some other intangible factor, and post this excess as "goodwill." B's common equity is correspondingly increased by $20, and this is reflected in the consolidated common equity account.

Income Statement Effects

There can be a significant difference in reported profits under the two accounting methods. If asset values are increased, this must be reflected in higher depreciation charges (and also in a higher cost of goods sold if inventories are written up). This reduces reported profits. Also, goodwill represents the excess paid for a firm over its adjusted net asset value. This excess, in turn, is paid because of the acquired firm's superior earning power, which will, presumably, be eroded over time as patents expire, as new firms enter the industry, and so on. Thus, the accountants (in Accounting Principles Board Opinion #17) require that goodwill be written off, or "amortized," with the write-off period corresponding to the expected life of the superior earning power but in no case more than forty years.

Goodwill is certainly not a trivial issue. For example, Philip Morris, Inc., recently acquired Seven-Up for a price of $520 million; approximately $390 million of this represented goodwill. Table 20-3 illustrates the effects of goodwill write-off by showing the income statements for Firms A and B before the merger and for Firm A after the merger. For the purchase, we assume that A purchased B for $50, creating $10 of goodwill and $10 of higher physical asset value. Further, we assume that this $20 will be written off over ten years.[14] As Column 4 indicates, writing off goodwill and higher asset values under purchase accounting causes reported profits to be lower than under pooling.

	Premerger		Postmerger: Firm A		Table 20-3 Income Effects of Pooling versus Purchase Accounting
	Firm A (1)	Firm B (2)	Pooling (3)	Purchase (4)	
Sales	$100	$50	$150	$150	
Operating costs	72	36	108	109[a]	
Operating income	$ 28	$14	$ 42	$ 41	
Interest (10%)	4	2	6	6	
Taxable income	$ 24	$12	$ 36	$ 35	
Taxes (50%)	12	6	18	17.5	
Earnings after tax	$ 12	$ 6	$ 18	$ 17.5	
Goodwill write-off	0	0	0	1[b]	
Net income	$ 12	$ 6	$ 18	$ 16.5	
EPS[c]	$ 2	$ 2	$ 2	$ 1.83	

[a] Operating costs are $1 higher than they otherwise would be to reflect the higher reported costs caused by the physical asset markup at the time of purchase.

[b] $10 of increased goodwill ÷ 10 years = $1 write-off per year.

[c] Firm A had six shares and Firm B three shares before the merger. A gives one of its shares for each of B's, so A has nine shares outstanding after the merger.

The write-off of goodwill is also reflected in earnings per share. In our hypothetical merger, we assume that nine shares exist in the consolidated firm. (Six of these shares went to A's stockholders, three to B's.) Under pooling, EPS = $2, while under purchase, EPS = $1.83. Further, the greater the amount of goodwill, the larger the write-off and the more significant the dilution in reported earnings per share. This fact causes managers to prefer pooling to purchase accounting.

---

[14] The write-off of goodwill is not a deduction for income tax purposes, but the other excess write-offs are deductible. Also, "negative goodwill" is eliminated at the time of the merger, so negative goodwill cannot be used to increase reported profits in later years.

**Requirements
for Pooling**

Six conditions must be met before the pooling method may be used:

1. The acquired firm's stockholders must maintain an ownership position in the surviving firm.
2. The basis of accounting for the assets of the acquired entity must remain unchanged.
3. Only independent interests may be combined; each entity must have had autonomy for two years prior to the initiation of the plan to combine, and no more than 10 percent ownership of voting common stock may be held as intercorporate investments.
4. The combination must be effected in a single transaction; contingent payouts are not permitted in poolings, but they may be used in purchases.
5. The acquiring corporation may issue only common stock identical to its outstanding voting common stock in exchange for substantially all the voting common stock of the other company; "substantially" is defined as 90 percent.
6. The combined entity cannot dispose of a significant portion of the assets of the combined companies for two years after the merger.

If all of these conditions are met, then the combination is, in a sense, a "merger among equals," and a pooling of interests has occurred. In contrast, a purchase involves (1) new owners, (2) an appraisal of the acquired firm's physical assets with a restatement of the balance sheet to reflect these values, and (3) the possible creation of goodwill.[15]

Holding Companies

Holding companies date from 1889, when New Jersey became the first state to pass a law permitting corporations to be formed for the sole purpose of owning the stocks of other companies. Many of the advantages and disadvantages of holding companies are identical to the advantages and disadvantages of large-scale operations already discussed in connection with mergers and consolidations. Whether a company is organized on a divisional basis or with the divisions kept as separate companies does not affect the basic reasons for conducting a large-scale, multiproduct, multiplant operation. However, the holding company form of large-scale operations has some distinct advantages and disadvantages over those of completely integrated divisionalized operations.

**Advantages of
Holding Companies**

Control with Fractional Ownership. Through a holding company operation, a firm may buy 5, 10, or 50 percent of the stock of another corporation.

---

[15]See APB Opinions 16 and 17.

Such fractional ownership may be sufficient to give the acquiring company effective working control or substantial influence over the operations of the company in which it has acquired stock ownership. Working control is often considered to entail more than 25 percent of the common stock, but it can be as low as 10 percent if the stock is widely distributed. One financier says that the attitude of management is more important than the number of shares owned, adding that "if they think you can control the company, then you do." In addition, control on a very slim margin can be held through friendship with large stockholders outside the holding company group.

Isolation of Risks. Because the various operating companies in a holding company system are separate legal entities, the obligations of any one unit are separate from those of the other units. Catastrophic losses incurred by one unit of the holding company system are therefore not transmitted as claims on the assets of the other units.

Although this is a customary generalization, it is not completely valid. First, the parent company may feel obligated to make good on the subsidiary's debts, even though it is not legally bound to do so, in order to keep its good name and thus retain customers. Examples of this would include American Express's payment of over $100 million in connection with a swindle that was the responsibility of one of its subsidiaries, and United California Bank's coverage of its Swiss affiliate's multimillion dollar fraud in the 1970s. Second, a parent company may feel obligated to supply capital to an affiliate in order to protect its initial investment; General Public Utilities' continued support of its affiliate's Three Mile Island nuclear plant is an example. And, third, when lending to one of the units of a holding company system, an astute loan officer may require a guarantee or a claim on the assets of the parent or of other elements in the holding company system. To some degree, therefore, the assets in the various elements of a holding company are joined.

Partial Multiple Taxation. Provided the holding company owns at least 80 percent of a subsidiary's voting stock, the Internal Revenue Service permits the filing of consolidated returns, in which case dividends received by the parent are not taxed. However, if less than 80 percent of the stock is owned, returns may not be consolidated, but 85 percent of the dividends received by the holding company may be deducted. With a tax rate of 46 percent, this means that the effective tax rate on intercorporate dividends is 6.9 percent. This partial double taxation somewhat offsets the benefits of holding company control with limited ownership, but whether the penalty of 6.9 percent of dividends received is sufficient to offset other possible advantages is a matter that must be decided in individual situations.

Disadvantages of Holding Companies

Ease of Enforced Dissolution. It is relatively easy for the U.S. Department of Justice to require dissolution by disposal of stock ownership of a holding company operation it finds unacceptable. For instance, du Pont was required to dispose of its 23 percent stock interest in General Motors Corporation, acquired in the early 1920s. Because there was no fusion between the corporations, there were no difficulties, from an operating standpoint, in requiring the separation of the two companies. However, if complete amalgamation had taken place, it would have been much more difficult to break up the company after so many years, and the likelihood of forced divestiture would have been reduced.

Leverage in Holding Companies

The holding company vehicle has been used to obtain huge degrees of financial leverage. In the 1920s, several tiers of holding companies were established in the electric utility and other industries. In those days, an operating company might have $100 million of assets, financed by $50 million of debt and $50 million of equity. A first-tier holding company might own the stock (its only asset) and be financed with $25 million of debt and $25 million of equity. A second-tier holding company, which owned the stock of the first-tier company, might be financed with $12.5 million of debt and $12.5 million of equity. The system could be extended, but with only two holding companies, we see that $100 million of operating assets are controlled at the top by $12.5 million of equity, and that these assets must provide enough cash income to support $87.5 million of debt. *This holding company system is highly leveraged, even though the individual components only have 50 percent debt/asset ratios.* Because of this *consolidated leverage,* even a small decline in profits at the operating company level could bring the whole system down like a house of cards.[16]

Divestitures

Although corporations do more buying than selling of productive facilities, a good bit of selling does occur. Some recent examples include the following:

1. Esmark, a holding company which owns Swift, Playtex, and a number of other major divisions, recently sold its Vickers Energy Company subsidiary for approximately $1 billion. People thought of Esmark as a meat packing, consumer products company, and its stock price reflected this image, not that of a company with huge holdings of valuable oil reserves. Thus, Esmark's stock was undervalued, and it was

---

[16] Excessive leverage through holding companies caused problems for the electric utilities during the 1930s. Accordingly, Congress passed a law regulating utility holding companies and specifically forbidding them from issuing debt for the purpose of buying the stock of operating electric utilities. The same situation does not exist in the telephone industry. Therefore, telephone holding companies (such as AT&T) can and do sell bonds and use the proceeds to buy stock in operating companies. The purpose is to obtain capital at the lowest overall cost.

in danger of a Conoco-type takeover bid. Selling Vickers helped Esmark raise its market value from $19 in 1980 to $55 in 1981.

2. Outlet is a NYSE company which owns a number of TV and radio stations, plus 236 department stores and women's specialty stores. Radio and TV are growth industries and command high P/E ratios, but because of its involvement in retail operations, Outlet was regarded by investors as being a retailer. That adversely affected its price. It is now selling off its retail stores, and its stock rose from 12\frac{1}{2}$ in 1980 to $40 in 1981.

3. ITT, in a move to streamline and rationalize its holdings, divested itself of twenty-seven separate companies, with a value of $1.2 billion, during 1979 and 1980. Some of these divisions were suffering losses and holding down the parent company's earnings, while others simply no longer fitted into ITT's corporate strategy. Also, ITT has a debt ratio that many would regard as excessive, and it used the proceeds from these sales to reduce debt.

4. International Paper (IP) recently sold its Canadian subsidiary to Canadian Pacific for $1.1 billion. IP plans to spend $4 billion during the next five years on its capital budgeting program, and the sale of the Canadian unit will help finance these expenditures.

5. IU International, a multimillion dollar conglomerate listed on the NYSE, recently spun off two major subsidiaries—Gotaas-Larson, an $800 million ocean shipping company involved in petroleum products transportation, and Canadian Utilities, an electric utility. IU also owned (and retained) some major trucking companies (Ryder and PIE), manufacturing facilities, and agribusiness operations. The original idea was to combine highly cyclical businesses such as ocean shipping with stable ones such as utilities, and thereby gain overall corporate stability through diversification. However, the strategy did not work. According to management, IU's very diversity kept it from being assigned to any particular industrial classification, so security analysts tended not to follow the company and therefore did not recommend it to investors. (Analysts tend to concentrate on an industry, and they do not like to recommend, or investors do not like to invest in, a company they do not understand.) As a result, IU had a low P/E ratio and a low market price. After the spin-off, IU's stock price rose from $10 to $25.

6. Borg-Warner sold its auto after-market parts division to Echlin Manufacturing for Echlin stock worth $65 million. Echlin's primary business is auto parts (NAPA), and the presumption is that Echlin can operate these assets more effectively than can Borg-Warner.

These examples illustrate the varied reasons for divestitures. Sometimes an operation simply fits better into one company than another—the Borg-Warner/Echlin transaction is an example. Sometimes the market does not properly recognize the value of a firm's assets when they are held as part of a conglomerate—the Esmark and Outlet cases are examples. Sometimes a company needs the capital that can be obtained from an asset sale to support other operations—International Paper is an example. If IU International's management is correct, there are also cases where a corporation becomes so complex and so diverse that analysts and investors just do not understand it and consequently ignore it. Finally, the ITT example illustrates the fact that business is dynamic—conditions change, corporate strategies change in response, and, as a result, firms alter their "asset portfolios" by both acquisitions and divestitures.

Summary

A merger involves the consolidation of two or more firms. Mergers can provide economic benefits through economies of scale, but they also have the potential for reducing competition, and for this reason they are carefully regulated by governmental agencies.

In most mergers, one company (the *acquiring firm*) initiates action to take over another (the *target firm*). The acquiring company must analyze the situation and determine the value of the target company. Often there will be *operating economies,* or *synergistic benefits,* which will raise the earnings of the combined enterprise over the sum of the earnings of the two separate companies. In this circumstance, the merger is potentially beneficial to both sets of stockholders, but the two firms' managers and stockholders must agree as to how the net benefits will be shared. This all boils down to how much the acquiring company is willing to pay, either in cash or in shares of its own stock, for the target company. There are various methods for determining an appropriate price.

In a merger, one firm disappears. However, an alternative is for one firm to buy all or a majority of the common stock of another and to run the acquired firm as an operating subsidiary. When this occurs, the acquiring firm is said to be a *holding company.* Holding company operations have both advantages and disadvantages. The major advantage is the fact that control can often be obtained for a smaller cash outlay. The disadvantages include tax penalties and the fact of incomplete ownership.

Questions

20-1 Define the following terms:
   a. Synergy
   b. Tender offer
   c. Exchange ratio
   d. Holding company
   e. Operating company
   f. Purchase versus pooling

20-2 Four economic classifications of mergers are (a) horizontal, (b) vertical, (c) conglomerate, and (d) congeneric. Explain what each of these terms means, and explain its importance in merger analysis with regard to (1) the likelihood of Justice Department intervention and (2) possibilities for operating synergy.

20-3 Firm A wants to acquire Firm B. Firm B's management thinks the merger is a good idea. Might a tender offer be used?

20-4 Distinguish between operating mergers and pure financial mergers.

20-5 Several years ago the SEC and the New York Stock Exchange each issued sets of rulings on disclosure of information which, in effect, required that firms disclose that they have entered into merger discussions as soon as they start such discussions. Since the previous procedure had been to delay disclosure until it was evident that there was a reasonably good expectation the merger under discussion would actually go through (and not to bring the matter up at all if the merger died in the early stages), it can safely be predicted that, in a statistical sense, a larger percentage of prospective mergers will be "abandoned" in the future than in the past.

  a. Why do you think the new rulings were put into effect?

  b. Will the new rulings have any adverse effects? Why?

20-6 Suppose that AT&T's twenty-one operating subsidiaries such as Pacific Telephone and Southern Bell all had preferred stock, bonds, and publicly owned common stock outstanding. (Actually, some have preferred outstanding; all issue bonds; and AT&T owns 100 percent of the common stock of most of the operating telephone subsidiaries and a large fraction of that of the others.) AT&T's major asset is its stock in the operating telephone companies, but the parent company does own in its own right certain long distance telephone equipment, a manufacturing subsidiary (Western Electric), and Bell Labs.

  Given this information, describe the relative riskiness of investments in the common, preferred, and bonds both of AT&T itself (the parent) and of the operating subsidiaries. Assume that all the operating assets are equally risky.

20-7 Philip Morris, Inc., recently acquired Seven-Up Corporation for $520 million. Seven-Up had a book value of equity of $130 million. Do you think Philip Morris's management would prefer to treat the merger as a pooling or as a purchase? Would your reaction be the same if the book value had been $520 million and the price paid $130 million?

20-8 Two large, publicly owned firms are contemplating a merger. No operating synergy is expected, but returns on the two firms are not perfectly positively correlated, so σ_{EBIT} would be reduced for the combined corporation. One group of consultants argues that this risk reduction is sufficient grounds for the merger. Another group thinks that this type of risk reduction is irrelevant because stockholders could already hold the stock of both companies and thus gain the risk reduction benefits of merger. Whose position is correct?

20-1 The Hilltop Hotels are negotiating a merger with the Doze Inn Motel chain. Consider the following table:

Problems

	EPS	D_0	g	P_0	Number of Common Shares
Hilltop	$3.00	$1.50	8%	$53.55	5 million
Doze Inn	1.00	0.90	3	11.61	1 million

Establish the appropriate exchange ratio
a. based on current EPS.
b. based on EPS in five years.
c. based on current market values.
d. to maintain Hilltop's current EPS.
e. to maintain Doze Inn's current EPS.
Note: For Parts d and e, assume that incremental earnings attributable to synergy equal $2 million.

20-2 Morris Sisters' Cafeterias hopes to acquire Davidson's Cafeterias through a merger. Davidson's management will consider the offer only if the price is high and management can stay on in its present capacity.

Morris Sisters' expects to gain operating efficiency from the merger through purchasing, advertising, and distribution economies. It estimates that if the two chains had been operating jointly during the year that just ended, earnings would have totaled $21 million.

a. Using the table that follows, calculate exchange ratios based on: (1) market values, (2) most recent earnings per share, (3) a comparison of Morris Sisters' most recent EPS and the expected postmerger EPS, and (4) a comparison of Davidson's most recent earnings with its expected postmerger earnings.

	EPS	DPS	g	P_0	Number of Shares
Morris Sisters'	$2.50	$2.00	6%	$40	6 million
Davidson's	1.80	0.90	2	18	2 million

b. Irrespective of your answers to Part a, assume that Morris Sisters' agrees to a one-for-one exchange of shares. Calculate the expected postmerger EPS.
c. Assume a postmerger P/E of 15. Now calculate the expected postmerger market price and compare it to next year's expected price without a merger. Should Morris Sisters' acquire Davidson's?

20-3 Beti's Boutique wishes to acquire Jan's Jeans for $250,000. Beti expects the incremental earnings to be $45,000 for ten years. She has also calculated her marginal cost of capital for this investment to be 12 percent. Conduct a capital budgeting analysis for Beti to determine whether or not she should purchase Jan's shop.

20-4 Southern Bakery is being acquired by the Royal Crumb Cookie Company. Their premerger balance sheets are as follows:

Southern Bakery

Current assets	$ 750	Debt	$ 875
Fixed assets	1,125	Common equity	1,000
Total assets	$1,875	Total liabilities and net worth	$1,875

Royal Crumb Cookie Company

Current assets	$1,500	Debt	$2,000
Fixed assets	1,625	Common equity	1,125
Total assets	$3,125	Total liabilities and net worth	$3,125

a. Construct the postmerger balance sheet for Royal Crumb Cookie Company assuming the acquisition is a pooling of interests.

b. Assume the merger in Part a was a purchase rather than a pooling of interests. Royal Crumb bought Southern for $2,000. Now construct the postmerger balance sheet.

c. The following are Southern Bakery's and Royal Crumb's premerger income statements. Calculate postmerger net income and EPS for both purchase and pooling. Assume a one-for-one stock exchange was made and that goodwill will be written off over a twenty-five year expected life.

	Southern	Royal Crumb
Sales	$ 750	$1,300
Operating costs	488	830
Operating income	$ 262	$ 470
Interest	100	200
Taxable income	$ 162	$ 270
Taxes	81	135
Earnings after taxes	$ 81	$ 135
Goodwill write-off	0	0
Net income	$ 81	$ 135
Common shares	60	100
EPS	$1.35	$ 1.35

Appendix 20A

**Using Mergers
to Create an
Illusion of Growth**

As noted in Chapter 20, if a company with a high P/E ratio buys a firm with a lower P/E, then an increase in the acquiring firm's EPS results from the merger. If a firm carries out a series of such mergers, this activity will produce a pattern of rising earnings per share, even though no real growth in operating income exists. This illusion of growth, in turn, can lead to an overvaluation of the firm's stock, and this overvaluation may continue so long as the firm continues to buy low P/E companies.

This point is illustrated by the data in Table 20A-1. In Section 1, we see that Firm A experienced a 20 percent growth rate in after-tax earnings from 1977 to 1979. However, its growth period is over, and, without mergers, total income would level out at $10 million and EPS at $1. Investors, however, do not know that Firm A's growth is over, so the stock has a P/E of 16 and is priced at $16 per share.

In 1980, A merges with B, a no-growth company that earns $1 per

**Table 20A-1
Merger Analysis:
Growth Illusion**

1. Net Income after Taxes of Firms A, B, C, and D:

	A	B	C	D	Consolidated
1977	$ 6,944,444	$5,000,000	$7,500,000	$11,250,000	$30,694,444
1978	8,333,333	5,000,000	7,500,000	11,250,000	32,083,333
1979	10,000,000	5,000,000	7,500,000	11,250,000	33,750,000
1980	10,000,000	5,000,000	7,500,000	11,250,000	33,750,000
1981	10,000,000	5,000,000	7,500,000	11,250,000	33,750,000
1982	10,000,000	5,000,000	7,500,000	11,250,000	33,750,000

2. Assumptions and Basic Premerger Data
   a. P/E ratios: A's P/E = 16.
      Other firms' P/Es = 8.
   b. Exchange ratio (ER): Based on market values.
   c. Shares of acquired companies: Equal to earnings.
   d. Other companies' EPS = $1.
   e. Other companies' prices = $8.

3. Earnings per Share and Price Calculations
   a. 1980: Merge with B.
      $P_A = \$16 = 16 \times \$1.$
      $P_B = \$8 = 8 \times \$1.$
      ER = $8/$16 = 0.5.
      Δ shares = 0.5(5 million) = 2.5 million.
      New EPS = ($10 + $5)/(10 + 2.5) = $1.20.
      New price = $1.20 × 16 = $19.20.
   b. 1981: Merge with C.
      $P_A = \$19.20.$
      $P_C = \$8.$
      ER = 0.4167.
      Δ shares = 0.4167(7.5 million) = 3.125 million.
      New EPS = ($10 + $5 + $7.5)/(12.5 + 3.125) = $22.5/15.625 = $1.44.
      New price = $23.04.

c. 1982: Merge with D.

P_A = $23.04.

P_D = $8.

ER = 0.3472.

Δ shares = 0.3472(11.25 million) = 3.906 million.

New EPS = ($10 + $5 + $7.5 + $11.25)/(15.625 + 3.906) =
$33.75/19.531 = $1.73.

New price = $27.68.

4. Calculated Earnings per Share for Firm A:

	A	**B**	**C**	**D**	**Consolidated**
1977	$0.69	$1.00	$1.00	$1.00	$1.57
1978	0.83	1.00	1.00	1.00	1.64
1979	1.00	1.00	1.00	1.00	1.73
1980	$EPS_A = \$1.20$		1.00	1.00	1.73
1981		$EPS_A = \$1.44$		1.00	1.73
1982			$EPS_A = \$1.73$		

5. Growth rate in EPS for A only: $1.73/$0.69 = 2.5072 = FVIF for 20%.

Growth rate in consolidated EPS: $1.73/$1.57 = 1.1019 = FVIF for 2%.

---

share and sells for $8, or 8 times earnings. The exchange ratio is based on relative market price, so ER = $8/$16 = 0.5. Therefore, A gives up 0.5 shares for each of B's 5 million shares, or 2.5 million shares in total. This produces the following 1980 EPS for the now enlarged Firm A:

$$EPS = \frac{A's\ earnings + B's\ earnings}{A's\ shares + Shares\ given\ for\ B}$$
$$= \frac{\$10,000,000 + \$5,000,000}{10,000,000 + 2,500,000}$$
$$= \$1.20.$$

Thus, as shown in Section 3a, A's earnings per share for 1980 increase by 20 percent over 1979 EPS. Without the merger, EPS would have been $1, with zero growth.

Because A's 20 percent historic EPS growth rate was maintained, the P/E remains at 16 times. Now, in 1981, A buys C, another no-growth company similar to B except that C is 50 percent larger than B. Working through the arithmetic, we see in Section 3b that, because of the merger, A's 1981 EPS rises to $1.44, so the 20 percent growth rate is again maintained. Although there is no real growth in any of the companies—operating earnings are flat—the fact that A started off with a high P/E ratio and then bought a series of low P/E ratio companies has produced growth in its EPS. Note, however, that A must buy increasingly larger firms to maintain this growth.

Now suppose the merger string is broken at some point—for example, the Justice Department blocks a particular merger. (As the mergers get larger, there is increasing danger of Justice Department intervention.) A's EPS growth rate would fall to zero, and analysts would examine the company closely. This would probably cause the P/E ratio to decline, and if the P/E ratio dropped back to $8\times$, the norm for a no-growth company, then A could no longer play the merger game to obtain growth in EPS, and A's 1982 stock price would fall from the $27.68 shown in Section 3c to $1.73 \times 8 = $13.84.

Exactly this kind of thing happened during the conglomerate boom of the 1960s, and it has also occurred, though on a smaller scale, in the 1980s. In a very real sense, the growth obtained is illusory—it is not the kind of real growth that can be sustained. Buying stock in a firm that is using mergers to report growing EPS is very much like buying a chain letter; it can work out okay, but you had better know what you are doing, and you had better get in and out before the bubble bursts!

Selected References

Brenner, Menachem, and David H. Downes, "A Critical Evaluation of the Measurement of Conglomerate Performance Using the Capital Asset Pricing Model," *Review of Economics and Statistics,* vol. 61 (May 1979), 292-296.

Elgers, Pieter T., and John J. Clark, "Merger Types and Shareholder Returns: Additional Evidence," *Financial Management,* vol. 9 (Summer 1980), 66-72.

Firth, Michael, "The Profitability of Takeovers and Mergers," *Economic Journal,* vol. 89 (June 1979), 316-328.

Gahlon, James M., and Roger D. Stover, "Diversification, Financial Leverage, and Conglomerate Systematic Risk," *Journal of Financial and Quantitative Analysis,* vol. 14 (December 1979), 999-1013.

Hong, Hai, G. Mandelker, and R. S. Kaplan, "Pooling versus Purchase: The Effects of Accounting for Mergers on Stock Prices," *Accounting Review,* January 1978, 31-47.

Kummer, Donald R., and J. Ronald Hoffmeister, "Valuation Consequences of Cash Tender Offers," *Journal of Finance,* vol. 33 (May 1978), 505-516.

Mueller, Dennis C., "The Effects of Conglomerate Mergers: A Survey of the Empirical Evidence," *Journal of Banking and Finance,* vol. 1 (December 1977), 315-347.

Myers, Stewart C., "Introduction: A Framework for Evaluating Mergers," in Stewart C. Myers, ed., *Modern Developments in Financial Management* (New York: Praeger, 1976).

Salter, Malcolm S., and Wolf A. Weinhold, "Diversification via Acquisition: Creating Value," *Harvard Business Review,* vol. 56 (July-August 1978), 166-176.

Shrieves, Ronald E., and Donald L. Stevens, "Bankruptcy Avoidance as a Motive for Merger," *Journal of Financial and Quantitative Analysis,* vol. 14 (September 1979), 501-515.

Steiner, Peter O., *Mergers: Motives, Effects, Policies* (Ann Arbor, Mich.: University of Michigan Press, 1975).

Bankruptcy and Reorganization*   21

Thus far, the text has dealt with issues faced by growing, successful enterprises. However, many firms encounter financial difficulties, and some actually fail. An understanding of business failures, their causes, and their possible remedies is important to financial managers of successful as well as potentially unsuccessful firms, for the managers of the successful firms must know their rights and how to enforce them. There are several instances in which the failure of another firm may affect a successful one: (1) sales and profits, as well as accounts receivable owed to a firm, may be lost when a major customer fails; (2) the flow of incoming materials may be interrupted when a supplier fails; and (3) an increased share of the market may become available when a competitor fails. At the same time, the financial manager of a failing firm must know how to ward off the firm's total collapse and thereby reduce losses. The ability to do this often means the difference between the firm's forced liquidation and its rehabilitation and eventual success.

Failure

Failure can be interpreted in several ways, depending on the problems involved or the situation facing the firm. For the sake of clarity, it is necessary to define the following terms:

Economic Failure. Failure in an economic sense signifies that a firm's revenues do not cover its total costs, including its cost of capital.

Business Failure. This term is used by Dun & Bradstreet, which is the major compiler of failure statistics, to include any business that has terminated with a resultant loss to creditors.[1]

Technical Insolvency. A firm can be considered technically insolvent if it cannot meet its current obligations as they fall due. Technical insolvency denotes a lack of liquidity and may be only temporary.

---

*This chapter was coauthored by Arthur L. Herrmann of the University of Hartford.

[1] Dun & Bradstreet, Inc., *The Failure Record*. This publication is updated annually.

Insolvency in Bankruptcy. A firm is insolvent in bankruptcy when its total liabilities exceed the true valuation of its assets. This is usually a more serious condition than technical insolvency, and it often leads to liquidation of the firm.

Legal Bankruptcy. Although many people use the term *bankrupt* to refer to any firm that has "failed," a firm is not *legally bankrupt* unless (1) it has failed according to criteria established by the Federal Bankruptcy Act and (2) it has been adjudged bankrupt by a federal court. Bankruptcy is a legal procedure for liquidating or reorganizing a business, with the liquidation or reorganization being carried out under special courts of law. Bankruptcy can be either *voluntary*, with the debtor petitioning the court, or *involuntary*, with the creditors petitioning the court and proving that the debtor is not paying debts as they mature.

Causes of Failure

The causes of financial failure are numerous, and they vary from situation to situation. However, it is useful to isolate the major underlying causes in order to avoid them if possible, or to correct them in the event a reorganization is necessary. A recent Dun & Bradstreet compilation assigned percentage values to these causes as follows:

Cause of Failure	Percentage of Total
Neglect	2.0
Fraud	1.5
Disaster	0.9
Management incompetence	93.1
Unknown	2.5
	100.0

Management incompetence includes the failure to anticipate and then to adjust to recessions and unfavorable industry trends. This is logical, since managements should plan ahead and be prepared for both booms and recessions. Further, case studies show that financial difficulties are usually the result of a series of errors, misjudgments, and interrelated weaknesses that can be attributed directly or indirectly to management, and signs of potential financial distress are generally evident before the firm actually fails. Research to isolate and identify the causes of business failure, and thus to predict or prevent it, is extremely important.[2] A number

---

[2] Much of the current academic work in this area is based on writings by Edward I. Altman: *Corporate Bankruptcy in America* (Lexington, Mass.: Heath Lexington Books, 1972) and "Financial Ratios, Discriminant Analysis, and the Prediction of Corporate Bankruptcy," *Journal of Finance*, vol. 23 (September 1968), 589-609. See Appendix A to Chapter 6 for further discussion of Altman's work.

of financial remedies are available to management when it becomes aware of the imminence or occurrence of insolvency. These remedies are described later in this chapter.

The Failure Record

How widespread is business failure in the United States? In Table 21-1 we see that a fairly large number of businesses fail each year, although the failures in any one year are not a large percentage of the total business population. In 1980, for example, there were 11,742 business failures (as defined by Dun & Bradstreet), but this was only 0.47 percent of all business firms. It is interesting to note that while the failure rate per 10,-000 businesses fluctuates with the economy, the average liability per failure has tended to increase over time. This is due both to inflation and to an increase in the number of multimillion dollar bankruptcies in recent years (see Table 21-2).

Table 21-1
Historical Failure Rate: Experience of United States Businesses

Years	Number of Failures	Average Failure Rate (per 10,000 concerns)	Average Liability per Failure
1857-1968 (average per year)	11,233	87	$ 28,292
1900-1968 (average per year)	13,659	70	32,889
1946-1968 (average per year)	11,089	42	61,101
1959-1969 (average per year)	13,881	54	84,724
1970	10,748	44	175,638
1971	10,326	42	185,641
1972	9,566	38	209,099
1973	9,345	36	245,912
1974	9,915	38	307,937
1975	11,432	42	383,152
1976	9,628	35	312,762
1977	7,919	28	390,872
1978	6,619	24	355,946
1979	7,564	28	352,637
1980	11,742	47	394,744

Sources: Edward I. Altman, *Corporate Bankruptcy in America* (Lexington, Mass.: Heath Lexington Books, 1972); Dun & Bradstreet, *The Failure Record* (1973), and *The Monthly Failure Report* (May 1976); U.S. Department of Commerce, *Survey of Current Business* (February 1981).

While bankruptcy is more frequent among smaller firms, it is clear from Table 21-2 that large firms are not immune to bankruptcy. These data actually understate the financial problems among larger firms because, as Altman notes, mergers or governmental intervention are generally used as an alternative to outright bankruptcy except in cases of fraud or where the failing company is too large to be absorbed by another firm. The decision to give federal aid to Chrysler is one excellent illustra-

Table 21-2
The Ten Biggest
Bankruptcies

	Liabilities	Date
Penn Central	$3.3 billion	June 1970
W. T. Grant	$1 billion	Oct. 1975
W. Judd Kassuba and related and controlled businesses	$420 million	Dec. 1973
Investors Funding	$379 million	Oct. 1974
U.S. Financial Services	$300 million	July 1973
Equity Funding	$200 million	April 1973
Interstate Dept. Stores	$195.6 million	May 1974
Fidelity Mortgage Investors	$182.4 million	Jan. 1975
Daylins Dept. Stores	$155.2 million	Feb. 1975
Chicago, Rock Island & Pacific	$97.8 million	March 1975

Source: *New York Times*, October 12, 1975, section 3, p. 16.

tion. Also, in recent years the Federal Home Loan Bank System has arranged the absorption of several very large "problem" savings and loan associations by sound institutions, and the Federal Reserve System has done the same thing for banks. Several United States government agencies, principally the Defense Department, were able to "bail out" Lockheed when it otherwise would have failed, and the "shotgun marriage" of Douglas Aircraft and McDonnell was designed to prevent Douglas's failure. Merrill Lynch took over Goodbody & Company, which would otherwise have gone bankrupt and would have frozen the accounts of its 225,000 customers while the bankruptcy settlement was worked out. This would have panicked investors across the country, so the New York Stock Exchange member firms put up $30 million as an inducement to get Merrill Lynch to keep Goodbody from folding. Similar instances could be cited in other industries.

Why do government and industry seek to avoid bankruptcy among larger firms? There are many reasons. In the case of the financial institutions, the main one is to prevent an erosion of confidence. With Lockheed and Douglas, the Defense Department wanted not only to maintain viable suppliers but also to avoid disrupting local communities. Even when "the public interest" is not at stake, the fact that bankruptcy is a very expensive process gives private industry strong incentives to avoid out-and-out bankruptcy. The costs and complexities of bankruptcy are discussed in subsequent sections of this chapter, but first some less formal and less expensive remedies and legal actions are examined.

Extension and Composition

In the case of a fundamentally sound company whose financial difficulties appear to be temporary, the creditors generally prefer to work directly with the company and help it recover and reestablish itself on a sound financial basis. Such voluntary plans usually involve *extension,* which postpones the date of required payment of past-due obligations, and *composition,* by which the creditors voluntarily *reduce* their claims on the debtor. Both procedures are designed to keep the debtor in business and to avoid court costs. Although creditors do not obtain immediate payment and may still suffer losses, they often recover more money, and sooner, than if one of the formal procedures had been followed. Also, chances are good that a customer will be preserved.

The start of an extension or a composition is a meeting between the failing firm and its creditors. The creditors appoint a committee consisting of four or five of the largest creditors, plus one or two of the smaller ones. This meeting is typically arranged and conducted by an adjustment bureau associated with the local credit managers' association.[3] Once the decision has been reached that the case can be worked out, the bureau assigns investigators to make an exhaustive report. Then the bureau and the creditors' committee use the facts of the report to formulate a plan for adjustment of claims. Another meeting between the debtor and the creditors is then held in an attempt to work out an extension or a composition, or a combination of the two. Several meetings may be required to reach final agreements.

At least three conditions are usually necessary to make an extension or a composition feasible: (1) the debtor must be a good moral risk, (2) the debtor must show an ability to make a recovery, and (3) general business conditions must be favorable to recovery.

Creditors prefer *extension* because it provides for payment in full. The debtor buys current purchases on a cash basis and pays off the past balance over an extended time. In some cases, creditors may agree not only to extend the time of payment but also to subordinate existing claims to vendors extending new credit during the period of the extension. The creditors must have faith that the debtor will solve its problems.

In a *composition,* a reduced cash settlement is made. Creditors receive in cash from the debtor a uniform percentage of the amounts owed them. The cash received, which may be as low as 10 cents on the dollar, is taken as full settlement of the debt. Bargaining will take place between the debtor and the creditors over the savings that result from avoiding costs associated with the bankruptcy: costs of administration, legal fees, investigators, and so on. In addition to escaping such costs, the debtor gains in that the stigma of bankruptcy may be avoided; as a result, the debtor may be induced to part with most of the savings that result from avoiding a formal bankruptcy.

---

[3] There is a nationwide group called the National Association of Credit Management, which consists of bankers and industrial companies' credit managers. This group sponsors research on credit policy and problems, conducts seminars on credit management, and operates local chapters in cities throughout the nation. These local chapters frequently operate adjustment bureaus.

Often the bargaining process will result in a compromise involving both an extension and a composition. For example, the settlement may provide for a cash payment of 25 percent of the debt immediately, plus six future installments of 10 percent each, for a total payment of 85 percent. Installment payments are usually evidenced by notes, and creditors will also seek protective controls.

These voluntary settlements are informal and simple. They are also relatively inexpensive because investigating, legal, and administrative expenses are held to a minimum. Thus, voluntary procedures result in the largest return to creditors. In addition, the almost-bankrupt business may be saved to continue as a future customer. One possible disadvantage is that the debtor is left to manage the business. This situation may result in an erosion of assets, but there are numerous controls available to protect the creditors. It should also be noted that small creditors may play a nuisance role by insisting on payment in full. As a consequence, settlements typically provide for payment in full for claims under $500 or $1,000. If a composition is involved and all claims under $500 are paid, all creditors will receive a base of $500 plus the agreed-upon percentage for the balance of their claims.

Reorganization

If the situation is such that informal procedures are not feasible, then it may become necessary to use more formal procedures. The first of these is a *reorganization*, which is a court-approved attempt to keep a company alive by changing its capital structure and thereby reducing its interest expenses and its debt repayment schedules. It is like composition or extension, but the legal formalities are much more involved. Regardless of the legal procedure followed, reorganization processes have certain features in common.

1. The firm is insolvent either because it is unable to meet cash obligations as they come due (technical insolvency) or because claims on the firm exceed the value of its assets (insolvency in bankruptcy). Hence, some modifications in the nature or the amount of the firm's obligations must be made—fixed charges must be reduced or at least stretched out. The procedure may include scaling down interest charges, converting short-term debt into long-term debt, converting debt into common stock, or simply writing off some claims against the company.

2. Firms in financial trouble almost always let their properties run down, and they generally deplete their liquid assets. Therefore, in most reorganizations new funds must be raised to increase working capital and to rehabilitate property.

3. The operating and managerial causes of the difficulty must be discovered and eliminated.

The procedures involved in a reorganization are highly legalistic and are, in fact, best understood by attorneys who specialize in bankruptcy and reorganization. However, there are some general principles with which all financial managers should be familiar. As noted above, a reorganization requires a scaling down of claims, and in any reorganization two conditions must be met: (1) the scaling down must be fair to all parties, and (2) there must be a reasonably high probability of successful rehabilitation and profitable future operations. These are the standards of *fairness* and *feasibility*, which are analyzed further later in the chapter.

Bankruptcy proceedings begin when a debtor is unable to meet scheduled payments to creditors. At that time these central issues arise:

Federal Bankruptcy Laws

1. Is the inability to meet scheduled debt payments a temporary problem of technical insolvency, or is it a permanent problem caused by asset values and earning power's having fallen below debt obligations (insolvency in bankruptcy)?

2. If the problem is a temporary one, then a simple extension which enables the firm to recover and to satisfy everyone will be worked out. However, if basic long-run asset values have truly declined, then economic losses have occurred. In this event, who shall bear the losses? Two theories exist: (1) the *absolute priority doctrine*, which states that claims must be paid in strict accordance with the priority of each claim, regardless of the consequence to other claimants, and (2) the *relative priority doctrine*, which is more flexible and which gives a more balanced consideration to all claimants.

3. Is the company "worth more dead than alive," i.e., would the business be more valuable if it were maintained and continued in operation or if it were liquidated and sold off in pieces? Under the absolute priority doctrine, liquidations are more likely because this generally permits senior creditors to be paid off sooner, but often at the expense of junior creditors and stockholders. Under the relative priority doctrine, senior creditors are more likely to be required to wait for payment in order to increase the chances of providing some returns to junior creditors and stockholders.

4. Who should control the firm while it is being liquidated or rehabilitated? Should the existing management be left in control, or should a *trustee* be placed in charge of operations?

These are the issues that are addressed in the federal bankruptcy statutes.

Our bankruptcy laws were first enacted in 1898, were modified substantially in 1938, and then were changed radically in the Bankruptcy Reform Act of 1978. The 1978 act was designed primarily to streamline and speed up proceedings. During the 1970s, as bankruptcies became larger and more complex, it was simply taking too long to conclude bankruptcy proceedings, so Congress changed the law to speed things up. Also, the new bankruptcy act represented a shift from the absolute priority doctrine toward the relative priority doctrine. (These doctrines should be thought of as a continuum, not as absolute points. The new law represents a movement along the continuum, not a jump from one polar position to the other.)

The new bankruptcy law consists of eight odd-numbered chapters. (The even-numbered ones were eliminated by Congress in the rewrite, and the numerals were changed from Roman to Arabic.) Chapters 1, 3, and 5 contain general provisions applicable to the other chapters. Chapter 7 governs liquidations; Chapter 9 provides for financially distressed municipalities; Chapter 11 is the business reorganization chapter; Chapter 13 covers the adjustment of debts for "individuals with regular income"; and Chapter 15 sets up a system of trustees who help administer the new act. All bankruptcy cases filed after October 1, 1979, are governed by this new code.

Prior to passage of the new bankruptcy act, reorganizations in bankruptcy were of two types: either Chapter XI proceedings, which were voluntary reorganizations originated by the existing management, or Chapter X proceedings, which were involuntary, were originated by creditors, and called for a court-appointed trustee to restructure completely the finances of the firm or else to liquidate it. Long, drawn-out court fights occurred over whether the proceedings should be conducted under Chapter X or Chapter XI.

The new bankruptcy code combines the old Chapters X and XI into a single procedure (the new Chapter 11) which is more flexible and which provides more scope for informal negotiations between a company and its creditors and stockholders. Under the new act, a case is started by the filing of a petition with the bankruptcy court. The petition may be either voluntary or involuntary; that is, it may be filed either by the firm's management or by its creditors. A committee of unsecured creditors is then appointed by the court to negotiate with management for a reorganization, which may include the restructuring of debt and other claims against the firm. A trustee may be appointed by the court if it is in the best interests of the creditors and stockholders; otherwise, the existing management may stay in office. Under the new Chapter 11, if no fair and feasible reorganization can be worked out, the firm will be liquidated under the procedures spelled out in Chapter 7 of the act.

Financial Decisions in Reorganization

When a business becomes insolvent, a decision must be made whether to dissolve the firm through *liquidation* or to keep it alive through *reorganization*. Fundamentally, this decision depends on a determination of the value of the firm if it is rehabilitated versus the value of the assets if they are sold off individually. The procedure that promises higher returns to the creditors and owners will be adopted. Often the greater indicated value of the firm in reorganization, compared with its value in liquidation, is used to force a compromise agreement among the claimants in a reorganization, even when each group feels that its relative position has not been treated fairly in the reorganization plan. Both the SEC and the courts are called upon to determine the *fairness* and the *feasibility* of proposed plans of reorganization.

The basic doctrine of fairness states that claims must be recognized in the order of their legal and contractual priority. Carrying out this concept of fairness in a reorganization involves the following steps:

Standards of Fairness

1. Future sales must be estimated.
2. Operating conditions must be analyzed so that the future earnings on sales can be predicted.
3. The capitalization rate to be applied to these future earnings must be determined.
4. This capitalization rate must be applied to the estimated future earnings to obtain an indicated value for the company.
5. Provision for distribution to the claimants must then be made.

The meaning and content of these procedures may best be set out by the use of an example of reorganization involving the Edison Paper Corporation.[4] Table 21-3 gives Edison's balance sheet as of March 31, 1981.

**Table 21-3
Edison Paper Corporation: Balance Sheet, March 31, 1981
($ in Millions)**

Assets	
Current assets	$ 3.50
Net property	12.50
Miscellaneous	0.70
Total assets	$16.70

Liabilities and capital	
Accounts payable	$ 1.00
Taxes	0.25
Notes payable	0.25
Other current liabilities	1.75
7½% first-mortgage bonds, due 1995	6.00
9% subordinated debentures, due 1990	7.00
Common stock ($1 par)	1.00
Paid-in capital	3.45
Retained earnings	(4.00)
Total liabilities and capital	$16.70

[4] This example is based on an actual reorganization, although the company name has been changed and the numbers have been changed slightly to simplify the analysis.

The company had been suffering losses running to $2.5 million a year, and, as will be made clear in the following discussion, the asset values in the March 31, 1981, balance sheet are overstated. Since the firm was insolvent, it filed a petition with a federal court for reorganization under Chapter 11 of the Bankruptcy Act. The court, in accordance with the law, appointed a disinterested trustee. On June 13, 1981, the trustee filed with the court a plan of reorganization, which was subsequently analyzed by the SEC.

The trustee found that the company could not be internally reorganized and concluded that the only feasible program would be to combine Edison with an established producer of paper containers and wrappers. Accordingly, the trustee solicited the interest of a number of paper companies. Late in July 1981, National Paper Company showed an interest in Edison. On August 3, 1981, National made a formal proposal to take over Edison's $6 million of $7\frac{1}{2}$ percent first-mortgage bonds, to pay the $250,000 taxes owed by Edison, and to pay 40,000 shares of National Paper common stock to the company. Since the stock had a market price of $75 a share, the value of the stock was equivalent to $3 million. Thus, National Paper was offering $3 million, plus the $6 million loan takeover and the $250,000 taxes—a total of $9.25 million on assets that had a net book value of $16.7 million.

Trustee's Plan. The trustee's plan, based on 40,000 shares at $75 equaling $3 million, is shown in Table 21-4. As in all Chapter 11 plans, the secured creditors' claims are paid in full (in this case the mortgage bonds are taken over by National Paper). However, the total claims of the unsecured creditors equal $10 million, with only $3 million available. Thus,

---

**Table 21-4
Edison Paper
Corporation:
Trustee's Plan**

Prior Claims	Amount	Receives
Taxes	$ 250,000	Cash paid by National Paper
Mortgage bonds, 7½%, 1995	6,000,000	Bonds assumed by National Paper

Trustee's plans for remainder of claims:
Valuation based on 40,000 shares at $75 equals $3 million, or 30 percent of $10 million liabilities.

Other Claims	Original Amount	30% × Amount of Claim	Claim after Subordination	Number of Shares of Common Stock
Notes payable	$ 250,000	$ 75,000	$ 250,000	3,333
General unsecured creditors	2,750,000	825,000	825,000	11,000
Subordinated debentures	7,000,000	2,100,000	1,925,000	25,667
	$10,000,000	$3,000,000	$3,000,000	40,000

each claimant would be entitled to receive 30 percent before the adjustment for subordination. Before this adjustment, holders of notes payable would receive 30 percent of their $250,000 claim, or $75,000. However, the debentures are subordinated to the notes payable, so an additional $175,000 must be transferred to notes payable from the subordinated debentures. In the last column of Table 21-4 the dollar claims of each class of debt are restated in terms of the number of shares of National Paper common stock received by each class of unsecured creditors.

The Securities and Exchange Commission evaluated the proposal from the standpoint of fairness. The SEC began by estimating the value of Edison Paper (Table 21-5). After a survey and discussion with various experts, it arrived at estimated sales of $25 million a year. It further estimated that the profit margin on sales would equal 6 percent, thus giving indicated future earnings of $1.5 million a year.

Table 21-5
Edison Paper Corporation: SEC Evaluation

Estimated sales of Edison Paper Corporation	$25,000,000	per year
Earnings at 6 percent of sales	1,500,000	
Value with P/E ratio of 8 times earnings	12,000,000	
Mortgage bonds assumed	6,000,000	
Net value	$ 6,000,000	

Claims	Amount	Claim	Claim after Subordination
Taxes	$ 250,000	$ 250,000	$ 250,000
Notes payable	250,000	143,750	250,000[a]
General unsecured creditors	2,750,000	1,581,250	1,581,250
Subordinated debentures (subordinate to notes payable)	7,000,000	4,025,000	3,918,750[a]
Totals	$10,250,000	$6,000,000	$6,000,000
Total available	$ 6,000,000		
Percentage of claims[b]	57.5%		

[a] Notes payable must be satisfied before subordinated debentures receive anything.
[b] ($6,000,000 − $250,000)/($10,250,000 − $250,000).

The SEC analyzed price/earnings ratios for comparable paper companies and arrived at 8 times future earnings for a capitalization factor. Multiplying 8 by $1.5 million gave an indicated total value of the company of $12 million. Since the mortgage bonds assumed by National Paper totaled $6 million, a net value of $6 million was left for the other claims. This value is double that of the 40,000 shares of National Paper stock offered for the remainder of the company. Because the SEC felt that the value of these claims was $6 million rather than $3 million, it concluded that the trustee's plan for reorganization did not meet the test of fairness. Note that under both the trustee's plan and the SEC plan, the holders of common stock were to receive nothing, which is one of the risks of ownership, while the holders of the first-mortgage bonds were to be paid in full.

National Paper was told of the SEC's conclusions and asked to increase the number of shares it offered. National refused, and no other paper company offered to acquire Edison. Because no better alternative offer could be obtained, and the only alternative to the trustee's plan was liquidation (with a lower realized value), National Paper's proposal was accepted despite the SEC's disagreement with the valuation.

Standard of Feasibility

The primary test of feasibility in a reorganization is whether the fixed charges after reorganization will be adequately covered by earnings. Adequate coverage generally requires an improvement in earnings or a reduction of fixed charges, or both. Among the actions that must generally be taken are the following:

1. Debt maturities are usually lengthened, and some debt is usually converted into equity.
2. When the quality of management has been substandard, a new team must be given control of the company.
3. If inventories have become obsolete or depleted, they must be replaced.
4. Sometimes the plant and the equipment must be modernized before the firm can operate and compete successfully on a cost basis.
5. Reorganization may also require an improvement in production, marketing, advertising, and other functions.
6. It is sometimes necessary to develop new products or markets to enable the firm to move from areas where economic trends are poor into areas with more potential for growth or at least stability.

To illustrate how the feasibility tests are applied, let us refer again to the Edison Paper Corporation example. The SEC observed that in the reorganization National Paper Company would take over the properties of the Edison Paper Corporation. It judged that the direction and aid of National Paper would remedy the production deficiencies that had troubled Edison Paper. Whereas the debt/assets ratio of Edison Paper had become unbalanced, National Paper went into the purchase with only a moderate amount of debt. After consolidation, National Paper's total debt would be approximately $17.5 million versus total assets of more than $63 million, or a very reasonable debt ratio of about 27 percent.

National Paper's net income before interest and taxes had been running at a level of approximately $15 million. The interest on its long-term debt would be $1.5 million and, taking short-term borrowings into account, would total a maximum of $2 million a year. The $15 million profit before interest and taxes would therefore provide a 7.5 times coverage of fixed charges; this exceeds the norm of 5 times for the industry.

Notice that the question of feasibility would have been irrelevant (from the standpoint of the SEC) had National Paper offered $3 million in cash rather than in stock, and had it offered to pay off the bonds rather than take them over. It is the SEC's function to protect the interests of Edison Paper's creditors. Since they are being forced to take common stock or bonds guaranteed by another firm, the SEC must look into the feasibility of the transaction. If National Paper had made a cash offer, however, the feasibility of its own operation after the transaction was completed would have been none of the SEC's concern.

Liquidation can occur in two ways: (1) through an *assignment*, which is a liquidation procedure that does not go through the courts, or (2) through a formal *bankruptcy* carried out under the jurisdiction of a special court. Liquidation should occur when the business is worth more dead than alive, or when the possibilities of restoring profitability are so remote that the creditors run a high risk of loss if operations are continued.

Liquidation Procedures

Assignment is an informal procedure for liquidating debts, and it usually yields creditors a larger amount than they would receive in a formal bankruptcy. An assignment calls for title to the debtor's assets to be transferred to a third person, known as an *assignee* or *trustee*. The assignee is instructed to liquidate the assets through a private sale or a public auction, and then to distribute the proceeds among the creditors on a pro rata basis. The assignment does not automatically discharge the debtor's obligations. However, the debtor may write on the check to each creditor the requisite legal language to make endorsement of the check acknowledgment of full settlement of the claim.

Assignment

Assignment has some advantages over bankruptcy through the courts, which involves more time, legal formality, and expense. The assignee has more flexibility in disposing of property than does a bankruptcy trustee. Action can be taken sooner, before the inventory becomes obsolete or the machinery rusts, and, since the assignee is often familiar with the channels of trade in the debtor's business, better results may be achieved. However, an assignment does not automatically result in a full and legal discharge of all the debtor's liabilities, nor does it protect the creditors against fraud. Both of these problems can be overcome by formal bankruptcy proceedings, which are discussed in the following section.

The Federal Bankruptcy Act serves three important functions during a liquidation: (1) It provides safeguards against fraud by the debtor. (2) It

Liquidation in Bankruptcy

provides for an equitable distribution of the debtor's assets among the creditors. (3) It allows insolvent debtors to discharge all their obligations and to start new businesses unhampered by a burden of prior debt. However, liquidation is time-consuming, it can be costly, and it results in the extinction of the business.

The distribution of assets in a liquidation under Chapter 7 of the 1978 act is governed by the following priority of claims:

1. *Secured creditors, from the proceeds of the sale of specific property pledged for a lien or a mortgage.* If the proceeds from the sale of property do not fully satisfy the secured creditors' claims, the remaining balance is treated as a general creditor claim. See Item 8 that follows.[5]
2. *Trustee's costs to administer and operate the bankrupt estate.*
3. *Expenses incurred after an involuntary case has begun but before a trustee is appointed.*
4. *Wages due workers if earned within three months prior to the filing of the petition in bankruptcy.* The amount of wages is not to exceed $2,000 per person.
5. *Claims for unpaid contributions to employee benefit plans.* These claims, plus wages in Item 4, are not to exceed the $2,000 per wage-earner limit.
6. *Unsecured claims for customer deposits, not to exceed a maximum of $900 per individual.*
7. *Taxes due the United States, state, county, and any other government agency.*
8. *General or unsecured creditors.* Trade credit, unsecured loans, the unsatisfied portion of secured loans, and debenture bonds are classed as general creditors. Holders of subordinated debt also fall into this category, but they must turn over required amounts to the holders of senior debt.
9. *Preferred stock.*
10. *Common stock.*

To illustrate how this priority of claims works, consider the balance sheet of Wallace, Inc., shown in Table 21-6. Assets total $90 million. The claims are indicated on the right-hand side of the balance sheet. Note that the debentures are subordinated to the notes payable to banks.

---

[5] When a firm or individual who goes bankrupt has a bank loan, the bank will attach any deposit balances and use them to offset the loan balances. This is called, in legal terms, "the right of offset." The loan agreement may stipulate that the bank has a first-priority claim against any deposits. If so, the deposits are used to offset all or part of the bank loan. In this case, the banks will not have to share the deposits with other creditors. Compensating balances are often designated as being security against a loan. If the bank has no explicit claim against deposits, the bank will attach the deposits and hold them for the general body of creditors, including the bank itself. Without an explicit statement in the loan agreement, the bank does not receive preferential treatment with regard to attached deposits.

Now assume that the assets are sold. The assets as reported in the balance sheet in Table 21-6 are greatly overstated—they are, in fact, worth less than half of the $90 million at which they are carried. The following amounts are realized on liquidation:

Current assets	$28,000,000
Net property	5,000,000
Total receipts	$33,000,000

The order of priority for payment of claims is shown in Table 21-7. The first mortgage is paid from the net proceeds of $5 million from the sale of fixed property, leaving $28 million available to other creditors. Next come the fees and expenses of administration, which are typically about 20 percent of gross proceeds; in this example they are assumed to be $6 million. Next in priority are wages due workers, which total $700,000. The total amount of taxes to be paid is $1.3 million. Thus far, the total of claims paid from the $33 million is $13 million, leaving $20 million for the general creditors.

The claims of the general creditors total $40 million. Since $20 million is available, claimants would each receive 50 percent of their claims before the subordination adjustment. This adjustment requires that the subordinated debentures turn over to the notes payable all amounts received

				Table 21-6
Current assets	$80,000,000	Accounts payable	$20,000,000	**Wallace, Inc.:**
Net property	10,000,000	Notes payable		**Balance Sheet**
		(due bank)	10,000,000	
		Accrued wages, 1,400 at $500	700,000	
		U.S. taxes	1,000,000	
		State and local taxes	300,000	
		Current debt	$32,000,000	
		First mortgage	$ 6,000,000	
		Second mortgage	1,000,000	
		Subordinated debentures[a]	8,000,000	
		Long-term debt	$15,000,000	
		Preferred stock	2,000,000	
		Common stock	26,000,000	
		Paid-in capital	4,000,000	
		Retained earnings	11,000,000	
		Total equity	$43,000,000	
Total assets	$90,000,000	Total claims	$90,000,000	

[a] Subordinated to $10 million notes payable to the First National Bank.

until the notes are satisfied. In this situation, the claim of the notes payable is $10 million, but only $5 million is available; the deficiency is therefore $5 million. After transfer by the subordinated debentures of $4 million, there remains a deficiency of $1 million, which will be unsatisfied.

Table 21-7
Wallace, Inc.: Order of Priority of Claims

Distribution of Proceeds on Liquidation:

1. Proceeds of sale of assets	$33,000,000
2. First mortgage, paid from sale of net property	5,000,000
3. Fees and expenses of administration of bankruptcy	6,000,000
4. Wages due workers earned three months prior to filing of bankruptcy petition	700,000
5. Taxes	1,300,000
6. Available to general creditors	$20,000,000

Claims of General Creditors	Claim (1)	Application of 50 Percent (2)	After Subordination Adjustment (3)	Percentage of Original Claims Received (4)
Unsatisfied portion of first mortgage	$ 1,000,000	$ 500,000	$ 500,000	92
Unsatisfied portion of second mortgage	1,000,000	500,000	500,000	50
Notes payable	10,000,000	5,000,000	9,000,000	90
Accounts payable	20,000,000	10,000,000	10,000,000	50
Subordinated debentures	8,000,000	4,000,000	0	0
	$40,000,000	$20,000,000	$20,000,000	56

Notes:
1. Column 1 is the claim of each class of creditor. Total claims equal $40 million.
2. From Line 6 in the upper section of the table we see that $20 million is available. This sum, divided by the $40 million of claims, indicates that general creditors will receive 50 percent of their claims. This is shown in Column 2.
3. The debentures are subordinated to the notes payable. Four million dollars is transferred from debentures to notes payable in Column 3.
4. Column 4 shows the results of dividing the Column 3 figure by the original amount given in Table 21-6, except for the first mortgage, where $5 million paid on sale of property is included. The 56 percent total figure includes the first mortgage transactions; that is, ($20,000,000 + $5,000,000) ÷ ($40,000,000 + $5,000,000) = 56%.

Note that 90 percent of the bank claim is satisfied, whereas only 50 percent of other unsecured claims will be satisfied. These figures illustrate the usefulness of the subordination provision to the security to which the subordination is made. Since no other funds remain, the claims of the holders of preferred and common stocks are completely wiped out.

Studies of the proceeds in bankruptcy liquidations reveal that unsecured creditors receive, on the average, about 15 cents on the dollar, while common stockholders generally receive nothing.[6]

Summary

The major cause of business failure is incompetent management. Bad managers should, of course, be removed as promptly as possible, but if failure has occurred, a number of remedies are open to the interested parties.

The first question to be answered is whether the firm is better off "dead or alive"—whether it should be liquidated and sold off piecemeal or be rehabilitated. If the company is basically sound, the debtor and the creditors may work out a voluntary plan for its recovery. Legal procedures are always costly, especially in the case of a business failure. Therefore, if it is at all possible, both the debtor and the creditors are better off if matters can be handled on an informal basis rather than through the courts. The informal procedures used in rehabilitation are (1) *extension,* which postpones the date of settlement, and (2) *composition,* which reduces the amount owed.

If voluntary settlement through extension or composition is not possible, the matter is thrown into the courts. If the court decides on *reorganization* rather than *liquidation,* it will appoint a trustee (1) to control the firm going through reorganization and (2) to prepare a formal plan for reorganization. The plan, which for large firms must be reviewed by the SEC, must meet the standards of *fairness* to all parties and be *feasible* in the sense that the reorganized enterprise will stand a good chance of surviving instead of being thrown back into the bankruptcy courts.

The application of standards of fairness and feasibility developed in this chapter can help determine the probable success of a particular plan for reorganization. The concept of fairness involves the estimation of sales and earnings and the application of a capitalization rate to earnings to determine the appropriate distribution to each claimant.

---

[6] Pension plan liabilities may also have a bearing on bankruptcy settlements. Pension plans are of two types, *funded* and *unfunded.* Under a funded plan, the firm makes cash payments to an insurance company or to a trustee (generally a bank), who then uses these funds (and interest earned on them) to pay retirees' pensions. Under an unfunded plan, the firm is obligated to make payments to retirees, but it does not provide cash in advance. Most plans are actually partially funded—some money has been paid in advance, but not enough to provide full pension benefits to all employees.

If a firm goes bankrupt, the funded part of the pension plan remains intact and is available for retirees, but what about the unfunded amount? Do employees have a claim against the firm's assets for unfunded pension liabilities? Prior to 1974, employees had no explicit claim, but under the Employees' Retirement Income Security Act of 1974, up to 30 percent of the equity (common and preferred) is earmarked for employees' pension plans. This means, in effect, that the funded portion of a bankrupt firm's pension plan is secured but that the unfunded portion ranks with the stockholders and behind the creditors. Thus, if the proceeds from a liquidation were just sufficient to cover debts, neither stockholders nor unfunded pensioners would receive anything. If funds remained after payment of debts, 30 percent would be allocated to the pension plan.

The feasibility test examines the ability of the new enterprise to carry the fixed charges resulting from the reorganization plan. The quality of management and the company's assets must be assured. Production and marketing may also require improvement.

Finally, where liquidation is regarded as the only solution to the debtor's insolvency, the creditors should adopt procedures that will net them the largest recovery. *Assignment* of the debtor's property is the cheaper and the faster procedure. Furthermore, there is more flexibility in disposing of the debtor's property and thus providing larger returns. *Bankruptcy* provides formal procedures for liquidation to safeguard the debtor's property from fraud. It also provides equitable distribution to the creditors. Nonetheless, it is a long and cumbersome process, and unless the trustee is closely supervised by the creditors, the debtor's property may be poorly managed during bankruptcy proceedings. The debtor does, however, obtain a full legal release from liability.

Questions

21-1 "A certain number of business failures is a healthy sign. If there are no failures, this is an indication (a) that entrepreneurs are overly cautious, hence not as inventive and as willing to take risks as a healthy, growing economy requires, (b) that competition is not functioning to weed out inefficient producers, or (c) that both situations exist." Discuss this statement.

21-2 How could financial analysis be used to forecast the probability of a given firm's failure? Assuming that such analysis is properly applied, could it always predict failure?

21-3 Why do creditors usually accept a plan for financial rehabilitation rather than demand liquidation of the business?

21-4 Would it be possible to form a profitable company by merging two companies, both of which are business failures? Explain.

21-5 Distinguish between a reorganization and a bankruptcy.

21-6 Would it be a sound rule to liquidate whenever the liquidation value is above the value of the corporation as a going concern? Discuss.

21-7 Why do liquidations usually result in losses for the creditors or the owners, or both? Would partial liquidation or liquidation over a period limit their losses? Explain.

21-8 Are liquidations likely to be more common for public utility, railroad, or industrial corporations? Why?

Problems

21-1 The financial statements of the Carleton Publishing Company for 1981 follow. A recapitalization plan is proposed in which each share of the $6 preferred will be exchanged for one share of $2.40 preferred (stated value, $37.50) plus one 8 percent subordinated income debenture (stated principal, $75). The $10.50 preferred would be retired from cash.

a. Show the pro forma balance sheet (in millions of dollars) giving effect to the recapitalization and showing the new preferred at its stated value and the common stock at its par value.

b. Present the pro forma income statement (in millions of dollars carried to two decimal places).

c. How much does the firm increase income available to common stock by the recapitalization?

d. How much larger are the required pre-tax earnings after the recapitalization compared to the situation before the change? Required earnings are the amount that is just enough to meet fixed charges (debenture interest and/or preferred dividends).

Carleton Publishing Company: Balance Sheet, December 31, 1981 ($ in Millions)

Current assets	$120	Current liabilities		$ 42
Investments	48	Advance payments for subscriptions		78
Net fixed assets	153	Reserves		6
Goodwill	15	$6 preferred stock, $112.50 par		
		(1,200,000 shares)		135
		$10.50 preferred stock, no par		
		(60,000 shares, callable at $150)		9
		Common stock, par value of $1.50		
		(6,000,000 shares outstanding)		9
		Retained earnings		57
Total assets	$336	Total claims		$336

Carleton Publishing Company: Consolidated Statement of Income and Expense, Year Ended December 31, 1981 ($ in Millions)

Operating income		$540.0
Operating expense		516.0
Net operating income		$ 24.0
Other income		3.0
Other expense		0.0
Earnings before income tax		$ 27.0
Income tax at 50 percent		13.5
Income after taxes		$ 13.5
Dividends on $6 prior preferred stock	$7.2	
Dividends on $10.50 preferred stock	0.6	7.8
Income available for common stock		$ 5.7

e. How is the debt/assets ratio affected by the recapitalization? (Debt includes advances for subscriptions.)

f. Would you vote for the recapitalization if you were a holder of the $6 prior preferred stock?

21-2 At the time it defaulted, Rexford Forge had net current assets valued on its books at $20 million and net fixed assets valued at $25 million. At the time of final settlement its debts were as follows:

Current liabilities	$12 million
First-mortgage bonds	10 million
Second-mortgage bonds	5 million
Debenture bonds	4 million

None of the current liabilities have preferences in liquidation as provided for in the bankruptcy laws, and none have been secured by pledge of assets.

Assume that the amount shown for each of the four classes of liabilities includes all unpaid interest to the date of settlement. The fixed assets were pledged as security for the first-mortgage bonds and repledged for the second-mortgage bonds. Determine the appropriate distribution of the proceeds of liquidation under the following conditions:

a. Liquidation of current assets realizes $18 million, and $7 million is obtained from fixed assets.

b. Liquidation of current assets realizes $9 million, and $4 million is obtained from fixed assets.

Case

Case Number 36, Putnam Hardware, in *Cases in Managerial Finance,* is an excellent supplement to this chapter.

Selected References

Altman, Edward I., "Financial Ratios, Discriminant Analysis and the Prediction of Corporate Bankruptcy," *Journal of Finance,* vol. 23 (September 1968), 589-609.

Altman, Edward I., R. G. Haldeman, and P. Narayanan, "Zeta Analysis: A New Model to Identify Bankruptcy Risk of Corporations," *Journal of Banking and Finance,* vol. 1 (June 1977), 29-54.

Altman, Edward I., and Arnold W. Sametz, *Financial Crises: Institutions and Markets in a Fragile Environment* (New York: Wiley, 1977).

Collins, Robert A., "An Empirical Comparison of Bankruptcy Prediction Models," *Financial Management,* vol. 9 (Summer 1980), 52-57.

Dun & Bradstreet, Inc., New York, *The Failure Record,* updated annually.

Harris, Richard, "The Consequences of Costly Default," *Economic Inquiry,* October 1978, 477-496.

Miller, Danny, "Common Syndromes of Business Failure," *Business Horizons,* December 1977, 43-53.

Warner, Jerold B., "Bankruptcy Costs: Some Evidence," *Journal of Finance,* May 1977, 337-347.

U.S. Department of Commerce, Washington, D.C., *Survey of Current Business,* updated monthly.

Leasing

Firms generally own fixed assets and report them on their balance sheets, but it is the *use* of buildings and equipment that is important, not their ownership *per se*. One way of obtaining the use of facilities and equipment is to buy them, but an alternative is to lease them. Prior to the 1950s, leasing was generally associated with real estate—land and buildings. Today, however, it is possible to lease virtually any kind of fixed asset, and in 1981 about 20 percent of all new capital equipment acquired by businesses was financed through a lease arrangement.

Conceptually, as we show in this chapter, leasing is quite similar to borrowing, so leasing provides financial leverage. In effect, a lease is a type of debt.[1] Leasing takes several different forms, the three most important of which are (1) *sale and leaseback* arrangements, (2) *operating leases*, and (3) straight *financial or capital leases*.

Sale and Leaseback

Under a sale and leaseback arrangement, a firm owning land, buildings, or equipment sells the property to a financial institution and simultaneously executes an agreement to lease the property back for a specified period under specific terms. The financial institution could be an insurance company, a commercial bank, a specialized leasing company, or an individual investor. The lease is an alternative to a mortgage.

Note that the seller, or *lessee*, immediately receives the purchase price put up by the buyer, or *lessor*.[2] At the same time, the seller-lessee retains the use of the property. This parallel to borrowing is carried over to the lease payment schedule. Under a mortgage loan arrangement, the financial institution would receive a series of equal payments just sufficient to amortize the loan and to provide the lender with a specified rate of return on investment. Under a sale and leaseback arrangement, the lease payments are set up in exactly the same manner—the payments are sufficient to return the full purchase price to the investor, plus a stated return on the investment.

---

[1] Some instructors will prefer to cover this chapter immediately after Chapter 13, which deals with long-term debt. If this is done, it will be necessary to discuss separately the after-tax cost of debt.

[2] The term *lessee* is pronounced "less-ee," not "lease-ee," and *lessor* is pronounced "less-or."

Operating Leases

Operating leases, sometimes called service leases, provide for both *financing* and *maintenance*. IBM is one of the pioneers of the operating lease contract. Computers and office copying machines, together with automobiles and trucks, are the primary types of equipment involved in operating leases. These leases ordinarily call for the lessor to maintain and service the leased equipment, and the cost of the maintenance is built into the lease payments.

Another important characteristic of operating leases is the fact that they are frequently *not fully amortized*. In other words, the payments required under the lease contract are not sufficient to recover the full cost of the equipment. However, the lease contract is written for a period considerably less than the expected life of the leased equipment, and the lessor expects to recover all costs either in subsequent renewal payments or through disposal of the leased equipment.

A final feature of operating leases is that they frequently contain a *cancellation clause* giving the lessee the right to cancel the lease and return the equipment before the expiration of the basic lease agreement. This is an important consideration to the lessee, for it means that the equipment can be returned if it is rendered obsolete by technological developments or is simply no longer needed.

Financial, or Capital, Leases

A financial lease, sometimes called a capital lease, is one that (1) does *not* provide for maintenance service, (2) is *not* cancellable, and (3) *is* fully amortized (that is, the lessor receives rental payments equal to the full price of the leased equipment). The typical arrangement involves the following steps:

Step 1. The firm that will use the equipment (the lessee) selects the specific items it requires and negotiates the price and delivery terms with the manufacturer.

Step 2. The user firm then arranges with a bank or a leasing company (the lessor) to buy the equipment from the manufacturer or the distributor. When the equipment is purchased, the user firm simultaneously executes an agreement to lease the equipment from the financial institution. The terms of the lease call for full amortization of the financial institution's investment, plus a rate of return on the unamortized balance close to the percentage rate the lessee would have to pay on a secured term loan. For example, if the lessee would have to pay 10 percent for a term loan, then a rate of about 10 percent would be built into the lease contract. The lessee is generally given an option to renew the lease at a reduced rental on expiration of the basic lease. However, the basic lease usually cannot be canceled unless the financial institution is completely paid off. Also, the lessee generally pays the property taxes and insurance on the leased property. Since the lessor receives a return *after*, or *net of*, these payments, this type of lease is often called a "net, net" lease.

Financial leases are almost the same as sale and leaseback arrangements, the major difference being that the leased equipment is new and the lessor buys it from a manufacturer or a distributor instead of from the user-lessee. A sale and leaseback may, then, be thought of as a special type of financial lease. Both sale and leaseback arrangements and financial leases are analyzed in the same manner.

The full amount of the annual lease payment is a deductible expense for income tax purposes *provided the Internal Revenue Service agrees that a particular contract is a genuine lease and not simply an installment loan called a lease*. This makes it important that a lease contract be written in a form acceptable to the Internal Revenue Service. The following are the major factors that are examined to determine whether a given contract is likely to be classified as a bona fide lease transaction from the standpoint of the IRS:

Internal Revenue Service Requirements for a Lease

1. The term, or years involved in the lease, must be less than 75 percent of the life of the asset; otherwise the lease is likely to be regarded as a sale for tax purposes.
2. The rent must provide a reasonable rate of return to the lessor in relation to rates of return on loans.
3. The renewal option must be bona fide, and this requirement can best be met by giving the lessee the first option to meet an equal bona fide outside offer.
4. There should be no repurchase option; if there is, the lessee should merely be given parity with an equal outside offer.

The reason for the IRS's concern about these factors is that without restrictions a company could set up a "lease" transaction calling for very rapid payments, *which would be tax deductions*. The effect would be to depreciate the equipment over a much shorter period than its useful life. For example, suppose a firm planned to acquire a $2 million printing press which had a twenty year depreciable life. If straight line depreciation were used, the annual depreciation charges would be $100,000, and if the firm were in the 46 percent tax bracket, the depreciation would provide a tax saving of $46,000 per year for twenty years, or $920,000 in total. At a 15 percent discount rate, the present value of the $46,000 annual tax savings would be $287,929.

Now suppose the firm could acquire the press through a three year lease arrangement with a leasing company for payments of $666,666.67 per year with a $1 purchase option. If the $666,666.67 payments were treated as lease payments, they would be fully deductible, hence would provide a tax saving of 0.46($666,666.67) = $306,666.67 per year for three years, with a present value of $PVIFA_{15\%,3\,yrs.}$ ($306,666.67) = $700,181 versus a PV of only $289,929 for the depreciation shelters. Thus, the lease payments and the depreciation both provide the same total amount of tax savings ($920,000), but the savings come in much faster, hence have the higher PV, with the three year lease. Therefore, if any contract could be called a lease and given tax treatment as a lease, then the timing of the tax shelters could be speeded up as compared to depreciation tax shelters. This would benefit the firm, but it would be costly to the government. For this reason, the IRS has established the rules described above for defining a lease for tax purposes.

Even though leasing can be used only within limits to speed up the effective depreciation schedule, there are times when very substantial tax benefits can be derived from a leasing arrangement. For example, if the firm which will use the equipment has been experiencing losses and therefore has no tax liabilities, then it cannot use the investment tax credit. In this case, a leasing company can buy the equipment, receive the tax credit, and then share the savings with the lessee by charging lower rental payments. This will be discussed in detail later in the chapter, but the point to be made now is that if firms are to obtain tax benefits from leasing, the lease contract must be written in a manner that will qualify it as a true lease under IRS guidelines. If there is any question about the legal status of the contract, the financial manager must be sure to have the firm's lawyers and accountants check the latest IRS regulations.[3]

Effects of Leasing on a Firm's Balance Sheet

Leasing is often called "off balance sheet" financing, because, under certain conditions, neither the leased assets nor the liabilities under the lease contract appear on a firm's balance sheet. This point is illustrated in Table 22-1 by the balance sheets of two hypothetical firms, A and B. Initially, the balance sheets of both firms are identical, and they both have debt ratios of 50 percent. Next, they each decide to acquire assets costing $100. Firm A borrows $100 to make the purchase, so both an asset and a liability go on its balance sheet, and its debt ratio is increased to 75 percent. Firm B leases the equipment. The lease may call for fixed charges as high as or even higher than the loan, and the obligations assumed under the lease can be equally or more dangerous from the standpoint of financial analysis, but the firm's debt ratio will remain at 50 percent.

To correct this problem, the Financial Accounting Standards Board issued FASB #13, which requires that, for an unqualified audit report, firms entering

---

[3] There is a possibility that these provisions will be revised as a result of the income tax changes likely to be passed in 1981. As this book goes to press, Congress appears likely to provide major tax reductions, including business tax reductions. There is concern that certain firms will, because of their circumstances, not have sufficient income to utilize all of their tax credits and other benefits. Congress may require the IRS to relax its rules concerning the definition of a lease for tax purposes to help these firms lease and thereby utilize their credits.

Table 22-1
Balance Sheet Effects of Leasing

Before Asset Increase				After Asset Increase							
Firms A and B				Firm A, Which Borrows and Buys				Firm B, Which Leases			
		Debt	$ 50			Debt	$150			Debt	$ 50
Total		Equity	50	Total		Equity	50	Total		Equity	50
assets	$100		$100	assets	$200		$200	assets	$100		$100

into financial (or capital) leases must restate their balance sheets to report the leased asset under fixed assets and the present value of the future lease payments as a debt.[4] This process is called *capitalizing the lease,* and its net effect is to cause Firms A and B to have similar balance sheets, both of which will, in essence, resemble the one shown for Firm A.

The logic behind FASB #13 is as follows. If a firm signs a lease contract, its obligation to make lease payments is just as binding as are payments under a loan agreement—the failure to make lease payments can bankrupt a firm just as fast as the failure to make principal and interest payments on a loan. Therefore, for all intents and purposes, a financial lease is identical to a loan.[5] This being the case, if a firm signs a lease agreement, this has the effect of raising its effective debt ratio and changing its true capital structure. Therefore, if the firm had previously established a target capital structure, and if there is no reason to think that the optimal capital structure has changed, then using lease financing requires additional equity support in exactly the same manner as does debt financing.

If disclosure of the lease in our Table 22-1 example were not made, then Firm B's investors could be deceived into thinking that its financial position is stronger than it really is. Thus, even before FASB #13 was issued in 1976, firms were required to disclose the existence of long-term leases in footnotes to their financial statements. At that time, it was debated as to whether or not investors recognized fully the impact of leases and, in effect, would see that Firms A and B were in essentially the same financial position. Some people argued that leases were not fully recognized, even by sophisticated investors. If this were the case, then leasing

---

[4] FASB #13, *Accounting for Leases* (November 1976). This document spells out in detail the conditions under which the lease must be capitalized and the procedures for capitalizing it.

[5] There are, however, certain legal differences between loans and leases. In the event of liquidation in bankruptcy, a lessor is entitled to recover the leased asset, and if the value of the asset is less than the required payments under the lease, the lessor can enter a claim (as a general creditor) for one year's rental payments. In a reorganization, the lessor receives the asset plus three years' rentals if needed to cover the value of the lease. The lender under a secured loan arrangement has rights as described in Chapter 21. It is not possible to state, as a general rule, whether a supplier of capital is in a stronger position as a secured creditor or as a lessor. Usually, one position would be regarded as being about as good as the other at the time the financial arrangements are being made.

could alter the capital structure decision in a really significant manner—a firm could increase its true leverage through a lease arrangement with a smaller effect on its cost of conventional debt (k_d) and on its cost of equity (k_s). These benefits would accrue to existing investors at the expense of new investors who were, in effect, deceived by the fact that the firm's balance sheet did not reflect its true liability situation.

The question of whether investors were truly deceived was debated but never resolved. Those who believe strongly in efficient markets thought that investors were not deceived and that footnotes were sufficient, while those who question market efficiency felt that leases should be capitalized. FASB #13 represents a compromise between these two positions, though one that is tilted heavily toward those who favor capitalization.

A lease is classified as a capital lease, hence capitalized and shown directly on the balance sheet, if one or more of the following conditions exist:

1. Under the terms of the lease, ownership of the property is effectively transferred from the lessor to the lessee.
2. The lessee can purchase the property at less than its true market value when the lease expires.
3. The lease runs for a period equal to or greater than 75 percent of the asset's life. Thus, if an asset has a ten year life and the lease is written for eight years, the lease must be capitalized.
4. The present value of the lease payments is equal to or greater than 90 percent of the initial value of the asset, less any tax credit taken by the lessor.[6]

These rules, together with strong footnote disclosure rules for operating leases, should certainly be sufficient to insure that no one will be fooled by lease financing, and thus that leases will be regarded as debt and will have the same effects as debt on k_d and k_s. Therefore, leasing is not likely to permit a firm to use more financial leverage than could be obtained with conventional debt.

Evaluating Lease Proposals

In the typical case, the events leading to a lease arrangement follow the sequence that will be described. There is a great deal of uncertainty regarding the theoretically correct way to evaluate lease versus purchase decisions, and some very complex decision models have been developed to aid in the analysis. However, the simple analysis given here is the best approach for most decisions.

1. The firm decides to acquire a particular building or piece of equip-

---

[6] The discount rate used to calculate the PV of the lease payments must be the lower of (1) the rate used by the lessor to establish the lease payments (this rate is discussed later in the chapter) or (2) the rate of interest the lessee would have to pay for new debt with a maturity equal to that of the lease.

ment; this decision is based on regular capital budgeting procedures. The decision to acquire the machine is not at issue in the typical lease analysis—this decision was made previously as part of the capital budgeting process. In a lease analysis, we are concerned simply with whether to obtain the use of the machine by lease or by purchase. However, if the effective cost of the lease is substantially lower than the cost of debt—and, as explained later in this chapter, this could occur for several reasons, including the situation where the lessor is able to utilize the investment tax credit but the lessee is not—then the cost of capital used in capital budgeting would have to be recalculated, and, perhaps, projects formerly deemed unacceptable might become acceptable.

2. Once the firm has decided to acquire the asset, the next question is how to finance its acquisition. Well-run businesses do not have excess cash lying around, so new assets must be financed in some manner.

3. Funds to purchase the asset could be obtained by borrowing, or the asset could be leased. Also, we assume that the lease will be capitalized and will have the same capital structure effect as the loan would have.

As indicated at the beginning of this chapter, a lease is comparable to a loan in the sense that the firm is required to make a specified series of payments and that failure to meet these payments can result in bankruptcy. Thus, the most appropriate comparison is between lease financing and debt financing. The lease versus borrow-and-purchase analysis is illustrated with data on the Carter Chemical Company. The following conditions are assumed:

1. Carter plans to acquire equipment with a cost of $10,715,000, delivered and installed.

2. An investment tax credit of $715,000, which is approximately $6^2/_3$ percent, applies. Thus, the net financing required if Carter borrows and buys is $10 million.

3. Carter can borrow the required $10 million on a 10 percent loan to be amortized over five years. Therefore, the loan will call for payments of $2,637,965.60 per year, calculated as follows:

$$\text{Payment} = \frac{\$10,000,000}{\text{PVIFA}_{(10\%,5\text{ yrs.})}} = \frac{\$10,000,000}{3.7908} = \$2,637,965.60.$$

4. The equipment will definitely be used for five years, at which time its estimated salvage value is $715,000. If the operation is profitable, Carter will continue to use the equipment. If not, the equipment will be sold, presumably at its estimated salvage value.

5. Carter can lease the equipment for five years at a rental charge of $2,791,670 per year, but the lessor will own it at the expiration of the lease. (The lease payment schedule is established by the potential lessor, and Carter can accept it, reject it, or negotiate.) Carter plans to

continue using the equipment after the lease has ended, so a purchase arrangement will have to be negotiated with the lessor. We assume that Carter will be able to buy the equipment at its estimated salvage value, $715,000.

6. The lease contract calls for the lessor to maintain the equipment. If Carter borrows and buys, it will have to bear the cost of maintenance, which will be performed by the equipment manufacturer at a fixed contract rate of $500,000 per year.

7. Carter uses the sum-of-years'-digits depreciation method, and for this analysis we assume that its effective tax rate is 40 percent.

Table 22-2 shows the steps involved in the analysis. Columns 2 through 10 are devoted to the costs of borrowing and buying. Within this set, Columns 2 through 5 give the loan amortization schedule; Column 6 shows the maintenance expense; and Column 7 gives depreciation charges. Tax-deductible expenses—interest, maintenance, and depreciation—are summed and shown in Column 8, while Column 9 gives the taxes saved because Carter has these deductions. Column 10 summarizes the preceding columns and gives the annual net cash outflows that Carter will incur if it borrows and buys the equipment.

The lease payments are $2,791,670 per year; this rate, which includes maintenance, was established by the prospective lessor and offered to Carter Chemical. If Carter accepts the lease, the full $2,791,670 will be a deductible expense, so the after-tax cost of the lease will be calculated as follows:

$$
\begin{aligned}
\text{After-tax cost} &= \text{Lease payment} - \text{Tax savings} \\
&= \text{Lease payment} - (\text{Tax rate})\,(\text{Lease payment}) \\
&= \text{Lease payment}\,(1 - \text{Tax rate}) \\
&= \$2{,}791{,}670(1 - 0.4) \\
&= \$1{,}675{,}000.
\end{aligned}
$$

This amount is shown in Column 11, Years 1 through 5.

Notice the last entry in Column 11, the $715 shown under Year 5. This represents the $715,000 expected Year 5 purchase price. We include this amount as a cost of leasing because Carter Chemical will almost certainly want to continue the operation and thus will be forced to purchase the equipment from the lessor. If we assume that the operation will not be continued, then we should put the $715 into Column 10 as an inflow; that is, it would have a minus sign because it would then be an inflow in an outflow column.

The next step is to compare the net cost of owning with the net cost of leasing. However, we must first put the annual cash flows of leasing and borrowing on a common basis. This requires converting them to present values, which brings up the question of the proper rate at which to discount the costs. In Chapter 5, we saw that the riskier the cash flow,

Table 22-2
Carter Chemical Company: Lease versus Purchase Analysis ($ in Thousands)

	Applicable to Net Cost of Owning									Applicable to Lease	Comparative Costs		
	Loan Amortization Schedule												
Year (1)	Total Payment (2)	Interest (3)	Amortization Payment (4)	Remaining Balance (5)	Maintenance Cost (6)	Depreciation (7)	Tax-Deductible Expense = 3 + 6 + 7 (8)	Tax Savings = (0.4)(8) (9)[a]	Cash Outflow If Owned = 2 + 6 − 9 (10)	Lease Cost after Tax = (1 − 0.4) (Lease Cost) (11)	PVIFs for 6% (12)	Present Value of the Cost of Owning = 10 × 12 (13)[a]	Present Value of the Cost of Leasing = 11 × 12 (14)[a]
1	$ 2,638	$1,000	$ 1,638	$8,362	$500	$ 3,333	$4,833	$1,933	$1,205	$1,675	0.9434	$1,137	$1,580
2	2,638	836	1,802	6,560	500	2,667	4,003	1,601	1,537	1,675	0.8900	1,368	1,491
3	2,638	656	1,982	4,578	500	2,000	3,156	1,262	1,876	1,675	0.8396	1,575	1,406
4	2,638	458	2,180	2,398	500	1,333	2,291	916	2,222	1,675	0.7921	1,760	1,327
5	2,638	240	2,398	0	500	667	1,407	563	2,575	1,675	0.7473	1,924	1,252
5[b]	—	—	—	—	—					715	0.7473	—	534
	$13,190	$3,190	$10,000			$10,000						$7,764	$7,590

Net advantage to leasing = $7,764 − $7,590 = $174

[a] Figures in Columns 9, 13, and 14 are rounded to the nearest thousand dollars.

[b] Two lines are shown for Year 5 in order to account for the salvage value, $715,000.

Notes:

1. The net advantage to leasing could be calculated by subtracting Column 11 from Column 10, then discounting these differences. This procedure is more efficient, hence preferable in actual practice, but the procedure used here is better for explanatory purposes.

2. Leases often involve payments at the *beginning* of the period rather than at the end. Also, a "down payment" may be required under either the lease or the loan. In either event, it would be necessary to set up a "0" year to show payments made at Time zero. Also, if payments were to be made monthly, quarterly, or semiannually, the table would have to show more rows.

3. For a sale-and-leaseback analysis of existing property, the situation often involves such items as capital gains taxes paid when the property is sold, use of some of the sales proceeds to pay off an existing mortgage, payment of a finder's fee, and the like. In such cases, a "t = 0" row must be added to the table, and the after-tax consequences of these t = 0 cash flows must be reported, as appropriate, in Column 10 or 11.

the higher the discount rate used to find present values. This same principle was observed in our discussion of capital budgeting, and it also applies in lease analysis. Just how risky are the cash flows under consideration here? Most of them are relatively certain, at least compared to the types of cash flow estimates that were developed in capital budgeting. For example, the loan payment schedule is set by contract, as is the lease payment schedule. The depreciation expenses are also established and not subject to change, and the $500,000 annual maintenance cost is fixed by contract as well. The tax savings are somewhat uncertain, but they will be as projected so long as Carter's effective tax rate remains at 40 percent. The residual value is the least certain of the cash flows, but even here Carter's management is fairly certain it will want to acquire the property, hence will incur the $715,000 outlay in Year 5.

Since the cash flows under the lease and under the borrow-and-purchase alternatives are both relatively certain, they should be discounted at a relatively low rate. Most analysts recommend that the company's cost of debt be used, and this rate seems reasonable in this instance. Further, since all the cash flows are on an after-tax basis, *the after-tax cost of debt, which is 6 percent, should be used.* Accordingly, we multiply the cash outflows in Columns 10 and 11 by the 6 percent PVIFs given in Column 12. The resulting present values are shown in Columns 13 and 14; when these columns are summed, we have the net present values of the costs of owning and leasing. The financing method that produces the smaller present value of costs is the one that should be selected. The example shown in Table 22-2 indicates that leasing has the advantage over buying: The present value of the costs of leasing is $174,000 less than that of buying. In this instance, it is to Carter Chemical's advantage to lease.[7]

---

[7] The more complicated methods for analyzing leasing generally address the issue of what discount rate should be used to discount the cash flows. Conceptually, we could assign a separate discount rate to each individual cash flow component (the columns in Table 22-2), then find the present values of each of the cash flow components, and finally sum these PVs to determine the net advantage or disadvantage of leasing. This approach has been taken by Myers, Dill, and Bautista (MDB) ("Valuation of Financial Lease Contracts," *Journal of Finance,* June 1976, 799-819), among others. MDB correctly note that procedures like the one presented in this chapter are valid only if (1) leases and loans are viewed by investors as being equivalent and (2) all cash flows are equally risky, hence should be discounted at the same rate. Regarding the first point, the assumption is valid today for virtually all financial leases, and even where it is not, no one knows how to properly adjust for any capital structure effects that leases might have. (MDB, and others, have presented an adjustment formula, but it is based on the assumption that the Modigliani-Miller leverage argument, with no bankruptcy costs, is correct. Since the pure MM model is *not* correct, the MDB formula is highly questionable.) Regarding the second point, it is generally believed that all of the cash flows in Table 22-2 except the salvage value are of about the same degree of risk, at least to the extent that we are able to evaluate risk.

Regarding the application of the discount rate to the salvage value, advocates of multiple discount rates often point out that the salvage value is more uncertain than are the other cash flows and thus recommend discounting it at a higher rate. This would have the effect, in Table 22-2, of lowering the PV of the cost of leasing and thereby making the lease appear even more favorable. However, corporate managers would argue that this conclusion is incorrect. The $715,000 salvage value is an esti-

(continued)

The basic method of analysis set forth in Table 22-2 is sufficient to handle most situations. However, certain factors warrant additional comment.

Factors That Affect Leasing Decisions

Estimated Residual Value

It is important to note that the lessor owns the property at the expiration of a lease. The value of the property at the end of the lease is called its *residual value*. Superficially, it would appear that where residual values are large, owning would have an advantage over leasing. However, this apparent advantage of owning is subject to substantial qualification. If residual values are large, as they will be for certain types of equipment and also if land is involved, competition between leasing companies and other financial sources, as well as competition among leasing companies themselves, will force leasing rates down to the point where potential residual values are fully recognized in the lease contract rates. Thus, the existence of residual values on equipment is not likely to result in materially lower costs of owning.

Increased Credit Availability

As noted earlier, leasing is sometimes said to have an advantage for firms seeking the maximum degree of financial leverage. First, it is sometimes argued that firms can obtain more money for longer terms under a lease arrangement than under a secured loan agreement for the purchase of a specific piece of equipment. Second, since some leases do not appear on the balance sheet, lease financing has been said to give the firm a stronger appearance in a *superficial* credit analysis and thus to permit the firm to use more leverage than it could use if it did not lease.

There is probably some truth to these claims for smaller firms. However, now that large firms are required to capitalize major leases and report them on their balance sheets, this point is of questionable validity for them.

Investment Tax Credit and Accelerated Depreciation

The investment tax credit, discussed in Chapter 2, can be taken only if the firm's profits and taxes exceed a certain level. If a firm is unprofitable, or if it is expanding so rapidly and generating such large tax credits that it cannot use them all, then it may be worthwhile for it to enter a lease arrangement. Here the lessor (a bank or leasing company, or a wealthy individual) will take the credit and give the lessee a corresponding reduction in lease charges. Railroads and airlines have been large users of leas-

mate—it could be higher or lower, and the greater the uncertainty about its actual level, the greater the risk to which Carter's future profits are subject. Therefore, if the analysis is to properly reflect the riskiness of the salvage value, one could argue that the greater the variability about the future salvage value, the *lower* the discount rate that should be used to evaluate it! This problem is confused still further because, in a CAPM sense, all cash flows could be equally risky even though individual items like the salvage value might have more or less total variability than others.

For all these reasons, most analysts use only one discount rate—the after-tax cost of debt—to evaluate the cash flows in a lease analysis.

ing for this reason in recent years, as have industrial companies faced with particular situations. Anaconda, for example, recently financed most of the cost of a $138 million aluminum plant through a lease arrangement. Anaconda had suffered a $356 million tax loss when Chile expropriated its copper mining properties, and the carry-forward of this loss would hold taxes down for years. Thus, Anaconda could not use the tax credit associated with the new plant. By entering a lease arrangement, Anaconda was able to pass the tax credit on to the lessors, who in turn agreed to accept lower lease payments than would have existed under a loan arrangement. Anaconda's financial staff estimated that financial charges over the life of the plant would be $74 million less under the lease arrangement than under a borrow-and-buy plan.

Accelerated depreciation has the same type of effect as the tax credit. A firm that is suffering losses and not paying taxes cannot benefit from accelerated depreciation on new equipment. However, if the equipment is sold to a lessor who is in a high tax bracket, then the tax advantage of accelerated depreciation can be captured, and part of it can be returned to the lessee in the form of lower rental payments.

Tax considerations—the investment tax credit and accelerated depreciation—are probably the dominant motives behind most financial leases that are written today.

Leveraged Leases

Historically, only two parties have been involved in lease transactions—the lessor, who puts up the money, and the lessee. In recent years, however, a new type of lease, the *leveraged lease*, has come into widespread use. Under a leveraged lease, the lessor arranges to borrow part of the required funds. The Anaconda lease described above was set up as a leveraged lease. A group of banks and an auto company provided about $38 million of equity and were the owner-lessors. These owner-lessors borrowed the balance of the required funds from Prudential, Metropolitan, and Aetna—large insurance companies—giving these lenders a first mortgage on the plant. The banks and the auto company received not only the investment tax credit but also the tax shelter associated with accelerated depreciation on the plant. However, they also had to bear most of the risk that Anaconda would default on the lease payments because their position was junior to that of the insurance companies, which had a first mortgage on the plant.

Such leveraged leases, often with wealthy individuals who seek tax shelters acting as owner-lessors, are an important part of the financial scene today. Incidentally, whether or not a lease is leveraged is not important to the lessee; from the lessee's standpoint, the method of analyzing a proposed lease is unaffected by whether or not the lessor borrows part of the required capital.

Thus far we have considered leasing from the lessee's viewpoint. It is also useful to analyze the transaction as the lessor sees it: Is the lease a good investment for the party who must put up the money? (The lessor will generally be a specialized leasing company, a bank or a bank affiliate, an individual or group of individuals, or a manufacturer such as IBM that uses leasing as a sales tool.) The potential lessor obviously needs this information, and it is also useful for the prospective lessee to know how profitable the lease is to the lessor: Lease terms can often be negotiated, so it helps to have an idea of the other party's position.

Analysis of a Lease from the Lessor's Viewpoint

The lessor's analysis involves (1) determining the net cash outlay, which is usually the invoice price of the leased equipment less any investment tax credit and/or lease payments made in advance; (2) determining the periodic cash inflows, which consist of the lease payments minus both income taxes and the lessor's maintenance expense; (3) estimating the *residual value* of the property when the lease expires; and (4) determining whether the present value of the inflows exceeds the lessor's net cost of buying the equipment.

To illustrate the lessor's analysis, we assume the same facts as for the Carter Chemical lease. Further, we assume this situation: (1) The potential lessor is a wealthy individual whose current income is in the form of interest, and whose marginal federal plus state income tax rate, t_i, is 70 percent. (2) The investor can buy bonds that have a 10 percent yield-to-maturity, providing an after-tax yield of $(10\%)(1 - t_i) = (10\%)(0.3) = 3\%$. This is the after-tax return the investor will obtain if the lease investment is not made. (3) The bonds the investor would buy are about as risky as the cash flows expected under the lease. (4) The investor will, under the lease, receive the same investment tax credit as Carter Chemical, and the same depreciation schedule will also be applicable.

The lease analysis from the investor's standpoint is developed in Table 22-3. Here we see that the lease as an investment has a net present value of $305,000; on a present value basis, the investor who invests in the lease rather than in the 10 percent bonds is better off by this amount. This indicates that the investor should be willing to write the lease. We also show in the table that the lease provides the investor with an after-tax rate of return of 4.19 percent versus an after-tax return of 3 percent on alternative investments; thus, the IRR method of analysis confirms that the investor should write the lease. Since we saw earlier that the lease is also advantageous to Carter Chemical, the transaction should be completed.[8]

---

[8] Another point that should be noted here relates to the investment tax credit. Under 1981 IRS regulations, an individual investor may not take the credit if the lease is written for more than one-half the economic life of the equipment. Also, the tax credit can either be taken by the lessor or be passed back to the lessee. These points are ignored in the example.

The example in Table 22-3 is not set up as a leveraged lease. However, it would be possible for the lessor to borrow all or part of the required $10 million, making the transaction a leveraged lease. In this event, it would be necessary to add a set of columns to Table 22-3 to show the loan amortization schedule. The interest component of this schedule would represent another tax deduction, while the loan repayments would constitute an additional cash outlay. The "initial cost" would also be reduced by the amount of the loan. With these changes made, a new NPV and IRR could be calculated and used to evaluate whether or not the lease represents a good investment.

Table 22-3
Lease Analysis from Lessor's Viewpoint
($ in Thousands)

Year (1)	Lease Payment (2)	Maintenance Expense (3)	Depreciation (4)	Taxes = $(2 - 3 - 4)t_i$ (5)	Net Cash Flow = $(2 - 3 - 5)$ (6)	PVIFs at 3 Percent (7)	PV of After-Tax Cash Flows (8)
1	$ 2,791.67	$ 500	$ 3,333	$ (729)	$ 3,021	0.9709	$ 2,933
2	2,791.67	500	2,667	(263)	2,555	0.9426	2,408
3	2,791.67	500	2,000	204	2,088	0.9151	1,911
4	2,791.67	500	1,333	671	1,621	0.8885	1,440
5	2,791.67	500	667	1,137	1,155	0.8626	996
5	—	—	—	—	715	0.8626	617
	$13,958.35	$2,500	$10,000	$1,020	$11,155		$10,305
						Less cost	10,000
					NPV of the lease investment =		$ 305

Notes:

1. The investment tax credit is deducted from the equipment purchase price to produce the "cost" of $10,000,000 shown in Column 8.
2. We could calculate the rate of return (IRR) on the lease; this simply involves solving for r in the following equation:

$$NPV = 0 = \sum_{t=1}^{5} \frac{\text{Net cash flows under lease plan}}{(1 + r)^t} - \$10,000,000.$$

The cash flows are taken from Column 6 in Table 22-3, and the solution value of r is 4.19 percent. Thus, the lease has an after-tax rate of return to this 70 percent tax rate investor of 4.19 percent, which exceeds the 3 percent after-tax return on 10 percent loans (or bonds). So, using either the IRR or the NPV method, the lease would appear to be a good investment.

Typically, leveraged leases provide the lessor with higher expected rates of return (IRRs) and higher NPVs per dollar of invested capital than unleveraged leases. However, the riskiness of such leases is also higher for the same reason that any leveraged investment is riskier. Since leveraged leases are a relatively new development, no standard methodology has been developed for analyzing them in a risk-return framework. However, sophisticated lessors are now developing simulations similar to those described in Chapter 12 for use in analyzing the riskiness inherent in a lease transaction. Then, given the apparent riskiness of the lease investment, the lessor can decide whether the returns built into the contract are sufficient to compensate for the risk involved.

Summary

This chapter analyzed the three major types of leases: (1) *operating leases*, (2) *sale and leaseback plans*, and (3) *financial leases for new assets*. Operating leases generally provide both for the financing of an asset and for its maintenance, while both sale and leaseback plans and regular financial leases usually provide only financing and are alternatives to debt financing.

Financial leases (and sale and leaseback plans) are evaluated by a cash flow analysis. We start with the assumption that an asset will be acquired, and that the acquisition will be financed either by debt or by a lease. Next, we develop the annual net cash outflows associated with each financing plan. Finally, we discount the two sets of outflows at the company's after-tax cost of debt and choose the alternative with the lower present value of costs.

Leasing sometimes represents "off balance sheet" financing, which permits firms to obtain more financial leverage if they employ leasing than if they use straight debt. This was formerly cited as a major reason for leasing. Today, however, taxes are the primary reason for the growth of financial leasing. Leasing permits the tax shelters (deductible expenses and the ITC) to be transferred from the user of an asset to the supplier of capital, and if these parties are in different tax brackets, both can benefit from the lease arrangement.

Questions

22-1 Distinguish between operating leases and financial leases. Would you be more likely to find an operating lease employed for a fleet of trucks or for a manufacturing plant?

22-2 Would you be more likely to find that lessees are in high or low income tax brackets as compared to lessors?

22-3 Commercial banks moved heavily into equipment leasing during the early 1970s, acting as lessors. One major reason for this invasion of the leasing industry was to gain the benefits of accelerated depreciation and the investment tax credit on lease equipment. During this same period, commercial banks were investing heavily in municipal securities, and they were also making loans to real estate investment trusts (REITs). In the mid 1970s, these REITs got into such serious difficulty that many banks suffered large losses on their REIT loans. Explain how its investments in municipal bonds and REITs could reduce a bank's willingness to act as a lessor.

22-4 One alleged advantage of leasing voiced in the past is that it kept liabilities off the balance sheet, thus making it possible for a firm to obtain more leverage than it otherwise could have. This raised the question of whether or not both the lease obligation and the asset involved should be capitalized and shown on the balance sheet. Discuss the pros and cons of capitalizing leases and the related assets.

22-5 Suppose there were no IRS restrictions on what constituted a valid lease. Explain, in a manner that a legislator might understand, why some restrictions should be imposed.

22-6 What is a leveraged lease? What are the advantages and disadvantages of such leases from the standpoint of (a) the lessee, (b) the equity investor in the lease, and (c) the supplier of the debt capital?

22-7 In the summer of 1981, as this book was going to press, the Congress was discussing major tax law changes that would (1) permit equipment to be depreciated over a shorter period, (2) lower corporate tax rates, and (3) increase the investment tax credit. Discuss how each of these potential changes would affect the volume of leasing (versus conventional debt) in the U.S. economy.

Problems

22-1 University Leasing, Inc., which specializes in business financing in the Minneapolis-St. Paul area, is setting up a financial lease with Memorial Stadium, Inc. The lease will cover ice machines, pizza ovens, popcorn poppers, and cola dispensers which have a total cost of $200,000. The lease runs for five years. What is the annual lease payment based on a 9 percent interest rate? (Nine percent is simply the rate used to establish the lease payments. It is not the rate of return to the lessor.)

22-2 Two furniture manufacturing companies, Henri-Don and Roy Hill, began operations with identical balance sheets. A year later, both required additional manufacturing capacity at a cost of $50,000. Henri-Don obtained a five year, $50,000 loan at an 8 percent interest rate from its bank. Roy Hill, on the other hand, decided to lease the required $50,000 capacity from Furniture Financers for five years at 8 percent. The balance sheet for each company, before the asset increases, is shown below:

		Debt	$ 50,000
		Equity	100,000
Total assets	$150,000	Total	$150,000

a. Show the balance sheets for both firms after the asset increase, and calculate each firm's debt ratio.

b. Show how Roy Hill's balance sheet would look immediately after the financing if it capitalized the lease.

c. Would the rate of return on (1) assets and (2) equity be affected by the choice of financing? How?

22-3 S&W Processing Company must install $1,000,000 of new machinery in its Iowa gasohol plant. It can obtain a bank loan for 70 percent of the required amount. Alternatively, a Chicago investment banking firm which represents a group of rock stars believes that it can arrange for a lease financing plan. Assume that these facts apply:

1. The equipment will be depreciated by the sum-of-years'-digits method over a three year period toward a $200,000 estimated salvage value.
2. An investment tax credit (ITC) of 10 percent is allowed to encourage investment in this type of equipment.
3. Estimated maintenance expenses are $50,000 per year.
4. S&W's tax rate is 20 percent. However, because it has so much ITC carry-forward, it will be unable to utilize the ITC.
5. If the money is borrowed, the bank loan will be for $700,000, at 14 percent, amortized in three equal installments at the end of each year.
6. The tentative lease terms call for payments of $320,000 per year for three years. However, one-half of the payment for the third year must be made in advance. The potential lessors are in the 70 percent tax bracket, and if they do not invest in this project, they will invest in taxable bonds that yield 15 percent. Under the proposed lease terms, the lessee must pay for insurance, property taxes, and maintenance (the lease is net, net, net).
7. S&W must use the equipment if it is to continue in business, so it will almost certainly want to acquire the property at the end of the lease. If it does, then under the lease terms it can purchase the machinery at its fair market value at that time. The best estimate of this market value is the $200,000 salvage value, but it could be much higher or lower under certain circumstances.

To assist management in making the proper lease-versus-buy decision, you are asked to answer the following questions:

a. Assuming that the lease can be arranged, should S&W lease or borrow and buy the equipment? Explain.
b. Does it appear likely that the investment banker will be able to get the rock stars to agree to accept the terms of the proposed lease? Explain.
c. Does it seem that either party would be getting a better deal than the other under the proposed lease terms? How might one side or the other attempt to increase its advantage? In the economy, would you expect there to be an "equilibrium" set of lease terms relative to interest rates?
d. Consider the $200,000 estimated salvage value. Is it appropriate to discount it at the same rate as the other cash flows? What about the other cash flows; are they all equally risky?

22-4 Green Gardens, a manufacturer of lawn care and gardening products, has decided to expand production of its gardening tools division. The equipment necessary for expanded production can be either purchased or leased. The purchase plan requires Green Gardens to obtain a loan of $100,000 at a 10 percent interest rate, the loan to be amortized in level payments over a five year period. The lease provides $100,000 worth of equipment for five years, with the payment ($25,046) based on an 8 percent interest rate. If the equipment is acquired through the borrow-and-purchase arrangement, maintenance costs of $4,000 per year must be borne by Green Gardens. However, the lessor will assume these costs if Green Gardens decides to lease. As a proprietorship, Green Gardens is taxed at Joe Green's personal income tax rate of 20 percent.

The equipment will be depreciated by the sum-of-years'-digits method, and it is expected to have a $25,000 salvage value after five years. It is assumed that Green Gardens will purchase the equipment at the expiration of the lease for $25,000. The lessor is Rachel Walsh, the famous actress, whose marginal income is taxed at a 70 percent rate. She could invest the $100,000 in taxable investments with risk similar to the lease yielding 10 percent before tax. The same depreciation schedule would apply for either Miss Walsh or Mr. Green.

a. Develop an exhibit analyzing Green Gardens' lease-versus-purchase alternatives following the format of Table 22-2. (Use PVIFA = 3.7908 to calculate the loan payment, and round to the nearest dollar.)

b. Suppose a 5 percent investment tax credit applies, that because of his low taxes and investment tax credits on other investments, Mr. Green cannot use it, and, further, that Miss Walsh can. How could this fact affect Mr. Green's cost analysis? No calculations are necessary.

22-5 Minute-Ma'am operates a chain of retail grocery stores in the Southeast. In a move to increase distribution efficiency, the company has decided to modernize its warehouse facilities and equipment. Additional warehouse space will be rented, but the equipment—delivery trucks, fork lifts, and the like—must be financed. The equipment will cost a total of $10,000,000 and will be depreciated on a straight line basis over a five year expected life. The salvage value of the equipment is estimated to be $500,000, and the marginal tax rate is 40 percent. The cost of maintaining the equipment will average $20,000 per year over the five year period.

One method of financing the equipment, Plan A, calls for a five year, 10 percent, amortized term loan, to be secured by the equipment itself. Plan B calls for Minute-Ma'am to purchase the equipment, then sell it and lease it back over a five year period to yield the lessor 9 percent before taxes on his investment. The lessor is a wealthy investor whose income is derived primarily from interest and dividends; his marginal tax rate is 60 percent, and his before-tax return on capital averages $7\frac{1}{2}$ percent on investments similar in risk and maturity to the lease. Thus, $7\frac{1}{2}$ percent is the before-tax rate the investor could expect to earn if he simply maintained his existing investment portfolio. The lease would be written on a "net, net, net" basis, which means that all operating expenses, including maintenance, property taxes, and insurance, would be paid by the lessee, Minute-Ma'am. The investor would use the same depreciation schedule as would Minute-Ma'am.

a. Calculate the net advantage to leasing for Minute-Ma'am. Remember to include the tax-adjusted maintenance cost as an outflow to the lessee.

b. Would this be a good investment from the lessor's standpoint? Would the internal rate of return on the lease investment exceed the expected return on the investor's existing portfolio?

c. Discuss the matter of discount rates used to evaluate the lease from the lessee's standpoint. Just how sensitive is the outcome of the analysis to the discount rate used; that is, in this instance, is the discount rate selected likely to have a material bearing on the lease-versus-purchase decision?

Selected References

Athanasopoulos, Peter J., and Peter W. Bacon, "The Evaluation of Leveraged Leases," *Financial Management*, vol. 9 (Spring 1980), 76-80.

Bower, Richard S., "Issues in Lease Financing," *Financial Management*, vol. 2 (Winter 1973), 25-34.

Dyl, Edward A., and Stanley A. Martin, Jr., "Setting Terms for Leveraged Leases," *Financial Management*, vol. 6 (Winter 1977), 20-27.

Gaumnitz, Jack E., and Allen Ford, "The Lease or Sell Decision," *Financial Management*, vol. 7 (Winter 1978), 69-74.

Gordon, Myron J., "A General Solution to the Buy or Lease Decision: A Pedagogical Note," *Journal of Finance*, vol. 29 (March 1974), 245-250.

Idol, Charles R., "A Note on Specifying Debt Displacement and Tax Shield Borrowing Opportunities in Financial Lease Valuation Models," *Financial Management*, vol. 9 (Summer 1980), 24-29.

Levy, Haim, and Marshall Sarnat, "Leasing, Borrowing, and Financial Risk," *Financial Management*, vol. 8 (Winter 1979), 47-54.

Lewellen, Wilbur G., Michael S. Long, and John J. McConnell, "Asset Leasing in Competitive Capital Markets," *Journal of Finance*, vol. 31 (June 1976), 787-798.

Miller, Merton H., and Charles W. Upton, "Leasing, Buying, and the Cost of Capital Services," *Journal of Finance*, vol. 31 (June 1976), 761-786.

Olsen, Robert A., "Lease versus Purchase or Lease versus Borrow: Comment," *Financial Management*, vol. 7 (Summer 1978), 82-83.

Perg, Wayne F., "Leveraged Leasing: The Problem of Changing Leverage," *Financial Management*, vol. 7 (Autumn 1978), 47-51.

Roberts, Gordon S., and Arthur C. Gudikunst, "Equipment Financial Leasing Practices and Costs: Comment," *Financial Management*, vol. 7 (Summer 1978), 79-81.

Warrants, Convertibles, and Options

23

When we discussed long-term financing in Part VI, we concentrated on common stock, preferred stock, and various types of debt.[1] In this chapter, we see how the use of warrants and convertibles can make a company's securities attractive to an even broader range of investors, thereby increasing the supply of capital and decreasing its cost. Reducing the cost of capital will, of course, help to maximize the value of the firm's stock. Warrants and convertibles are rapidly gaining popularity, so a knowledge of these instruments is especially important today. We also examine briefly the rapidly growing options market, which is attractive to many investors.

Warrants

A warrant is an option to buy a stated number of shares of stock at a specified price. Generally, warrants are distributed with debt, and they are used to induce investors to buy a firm's long-term debt at a lower interest rate than would otherwise be required. For example, when Trans Pacific Airlines (TPA) wanted to sell $50 million of twenty year bonds in 1974, the company's investment bankers informed the financial vice-president that the bonds would be difficult to sell and that an interest rate of 14 percent would be required. However, as an alternative, the bankers suggested that investors might be willing to buy the bonds at a rate as low as $10^{3}/_{8}$ percent if the company would offer thirty warrants with each $1,000 bond, each warrant entitling the holder to buy one share of common stock at a price of $22 per share. The stock was selling for $20 per share at the time. The warrants would expire in 1984 if not exercised previously.

Why would investors be willing to buy Trans Pacific's bonds at a yield of only $10^{3}/_{8}$ percent just because warrants were also offered as part of the package? To answer this question, we must first see how warrants are valued in the market.

---

[1] If the instructor desires, this chapter may be covered immediately after Chapter 14, "Common Stock."

Warrants have both an "exercise," or "formula," value, which is equal to the value of the warrant if it were exercised today, and an actual price that is determined in the marketplace. The formula value is found with the following equation:

Formula Value of a Warrant

$$\begin{pmatrix} \text{Formula,} \\ \text{or exercise,} \\ \text{value} \end{pmatrix} = \left(\begin{array}{c} \text{Market price} \\ \text{of common} \\ \text{stock} \end{array} - \begin{array}{c} \text{Option} \\ \text{price} \end{array} \right) \times \left(\begin{array}{c} \text{Number of shares} \\ \text{each warrant entitles} \\ \text{owner to purchase} \end{array} \right).$$

For instance, a TPA warrant entitles the holder to purchase one share of common stock at $22 a share. If the market price of the common stock rose to $64.50, the formula value of the warrant would be

$$(\$64.50 - \$22) \times 1.0 = \$42.50.$$

The formula gives a negative value when the stock is selling for less than the option price. For example, if TPA stock is selling for $20, the formula value of the warrants is minus $2.

Generally, warrants actually sell at prices above their formula values. When TPA stock sold for $20, the warrants had a formula value of minus $2 but were selling at a price of $8. This represented a premium of $10 above the formula value.

Actual Price of a Warrant

TPA stock rose substantially after the bonds with warrants were issued in 1974. A set of TPA stock prices, together with actual and formula warrant values, is given in Table 23-1 and plotted in Figure 23-1. At any stock price below $22, the formula value of the warrants is negative; beyond $22, each $1 increase in the price of the stock brings with it a $1 increase in the formula value of the warrants. The actual market price of the warrants lies above the formula value at each price of the common stock. Notice, however, that the premium of market price over formula value declines as the price of the common stock increases. For example, when the common stock sold for $22 and the warrants had a zero formula value, their actual price, and the premium, was $9. As the price of the stock rises, the *formula value* of the warrants matches the increase dollar for dollar, but the *market price* of the warrants generally climbs less rapidly, and the premium declines. The premium is $9 when the stock sells for $22 a share, but it declines to $1 by the time the stock price has risen to $75 a share. Beyond this point the premium seems virtually to disappear.

Why does this pattern exist? Why should the warrant ever sell for more than its formula value, and why does the premium decline as the price of the stock increases? The answer lies in the speculative appeal of warrants—they enable an individual to gain a high degree of personal leverage when buying securities. To illustrate, suppose TPA warrants sold for exactly their formula value. Now suppose you were thinking of

Table 23-1
Formula and Actual Values of TPA Warrants at Different Market Prices of Common Stock

Price of Stock	Formula Value	Actual Warrant Price	Premium
$ 20.00	$ -2.00	$ 8.00	$10.00
22.00	0.00	9.00	9.00
23.00	1.00	9.75	8.75
24.00	2.00	10.50	8.50
33.67	11.67	17.37	5.70
52.00	30.00	32.00	2.00
75.00	53.00	54.00	1.00
100.00	78.00	78.50	0.50
150.00	128.00	Not available	—

investing in the company's common stock at a time when it is selling for $22.01 a share. If you buy a share and the price rises to $44.02 in a year, you would have made a 100 percent capital gain. However, had you bought the warrants at their formula value (1 cent when the stock sells for $22.01), your capital gain would have been $22.01 on a 1 cent investment, or 220,000 percent! At the same time, your total loss potential with the warrant would be only 1 cent, while the potential loss from the purchase of the stock would be $22.01. The huge capital gains potential, combined with the loss limitation, is clearly worth something—the exact amount it is worth to investors is the amount of the premium.

But why does the premium decline as the price of the stock rises? The

Figure 23-1
Formula and Actual Values of TPA Warrants at Different Common Stock Prices

answer is that both the leverage effect and the loss protection feature decline at high stock prices. For example, if you were thinking of buying the stock when its price was $75 a share, the formula value of the warrants would be $53. If the stock price doubled to $150, the formula value of TPA warrants would go from $53 to $128. The percentage capital gain on the stock would still be 100 percent, but the percentage gain on the warrant would now be only 142 percent versus 220,000 percent in the earlier case. Moreover, notice that the potential loss on the warrant is much greater when the warrant is selling at high prices. These two factors, the declining leverage impact and the increasing danger of losses, explain why the premium diminishes as the price of the common stock rises.

Remember that the TPA bonds, if issued as straight debt, would have carried a 14 percent interest rate. However, with warrants attached, the bonds could be sold to yield $10^3/_8$ percent. Remember also that with the stock selling at $20 per share, each of the 30 warrants attached to each bond sold for $8, making the warrants that come with each bond worth $30(\$8) = \$240$.

Initial Price of Bond with Warrants

    Someone buying the bonds at their $1,000 initial offering price would thus be receiving a package consisting of a $10^3/_8$, twenty year bond and thirty warrants worth $240. Since the going interest rate on bonds as risky as those of TPA is 14 percent, we can find the straight-debt value of the bonds as follows:

$$\text{Value} = \sum_{t=1}^{20} \frac{\$103.75}{(1.14)^t} + \frac{\$1,000}{(1.14)^{20}}$$
$$= \$103.75(\text{PVIFA}_{14\%,20}) + \$1,000(\text{PVIF}_{14\%,20})$$
$$= \$103.75(6.6231) + \$1,000(0.0728)$$
$$= \$687.15 + \$72.80 = \$759.95.$$

Thus, a person buying the bonds in the initial underwriting would pay $1,000 and receive in exchange a straight bond worth about $760 plus warrants worth about $240:

$$\begin{matrix}\text{Price paid for bond} \\ \text{with warrants}\end{matrix} = \begin{matrix}\text{Straight-debt} \\ \text{value of bond}\end{matrix} + \begin{matrix}\text{Value of} \\ \text{warrants}\end{matrix}$$
$$= \$760 + \$240$$
$$= \$1,000.$$

In the past, warrants have generally been used by small, rapidly growing firms as "sweeteners" when selling either debt or preferred stocks. Such firms are frequently regarded by investors as being highly risky. Their bonds could be sold only if they were willing to pay extremely high rates of interest and to accept very restrictive indenture provisions. To avoid this, firms such as Trans Pacific often offered warrants along with the

Use of Warrants in Financing

bonds. In the 1970s, however, AT&T raised $1.57 billion by selling bonds with warrants. This was the largest financing of any type ever undertaken by a business firm, and it marked the first use ever of warrants by a large, strong corporation.[2]

Getting warrants along with bonds enables investors to share in the company's growth, if it does in fact grow and prosper; therefore, investors are willing to accept a lower bond interest rate and less restrictive indenture provisions. A bond with warrants has some characteristics of debt and some characteristics of equity. It is a hybrid security that provides the financial manager with an opportunity to expand the firm's mix of securities, appealing to a broader group of investors, and, thus, possibly lowering the firm's cost of capital.

Warrants can also bring in additional funds. The option price is generally set at from 10 to 30 percent above the market price of the stock at the time of the bond issue. If the firm does grow and prosper, and if its stock price rises above the option price at which shares may be purchased, warrant holders will surrender their warrants and buy stock at the stated price. There are several reasons for this. (1) Warrant holders will *surely* surrender warrants and buy stock if the warrants are about to expire with the market price of the stock above the option price. (2) Warrant holders will tend to surrender *voluntarily* and buy if the company raises the dividend on the common stock by a sufficient amount. No dividend is earned on the warrant, so it provides no current income. However, if the common stock pays a high dividend, it provides an attractive dividend yield. This induces warrant holders to exercise their option to buy the stock. (3) Warrants sometimes have *stepped-up option prices*, which prod owners into exercising them. For example, the Williamson Scientific Company has warrants outstanding with an option price of $25 until December 31, 1984, at which time the option price rises to $30. If the price of the common stock is over $25 just before December 31, 1984, many warrant holders will exercise their options before the stepped-up price takes effect.

Virtually all warrants today are *detachable*. Thus, after a bond with attached warrants is sold, the warrants can be detached and traded separately from the bond. Further, when these warrants are exercised, the bond issue remains outstanding, so the warrants bring in additional funds to the firm.

---

[2] It is also interesting to note that before the AT&T issue, the New York Stock Exchange had a policy against listing warrants. The NYSE's stated policy was that warrants could not be listed because they were "speculative" instruments rather than "investment" securities. When AT&T issued warrants, however, the Exchange changed its policy and agreed to list warrants that met certain specifications. Many other warrants have since been listed.

One desirable feature of warrants is that they generally bring in funds only when they are needed. If the company grows, it will probably need new equity capital. At the same time, growth will cause the price of the stock to rise, the warrants to be exercised, and the firm to obtain additional cash. If the company is not successful and cannot profitably employ additional money, the price of its stock will probably not rise sufficiently to induce exercise of the options.

Convertibles

Convertible securities are bonds or preferred stocks that can be exchanged for common stock at the option of the holder and under specified terms and conditions. Unlike the exercise of warrants, which brings in additional funds to the firm, converting a bond does not bring in additional capital: Debt on the balance sheet is simply replaced by common stock. Of course, this reduction of the debt ratio will make it easier to obtain additional debt capital, but this is a separate action.

One of the most important provisions of a convertible bond is the number of shares of stock a bondholder receives upon conversion, defined as the *conversion ratio, R*. Related to the conversion ratio is the *conversion price, P_c*, which is the effective price paid for the common stock when conversion occurs. The relationship between the conversion ratio and the conversion price is illustrated by the Adams Engine Company's convertible debentures, issued at their $1,000 par value in 1980. At any time prior to maturity on July 1, 2000, a debenture holder can turn in a bond and receive in its place twenty shares of common stock; therefore, $R = 20$. The bond has a par value of $1,000, so the holder is giving up this amount upon conversion. Dividing the $1,000 par value by the twenty shares received gives a conversion price of $50 a share:

$$\text{Conversion price} = P_c = \frac{\text{Par value of bond}}{\text{Shares received}},$$

or

$$P_c = \frac{\$1,000}{R} = \frac{\$1,000}{20} = \$50.$$

Therefore,

$$R = \frac{\$1,000}{P_c} = \frac{\$1,000}{\$50} = 20 \text{ shares.}$$

Once R is set, this establishes the value of P_c, and vice versa.

Like warrant option prices, the conversion price is characteristically set at from 10 to 30 percent above the prevailing market price of the common stock at the time the convertible issue is sold. Exactly how the conversion price is established can best be understood after examining some of the reasons firms use convertibles.[3]

Advantages of Convertibles

Convertibles offer advantages to corporations as well as to individual investors by functioning in the following two ways:

1. *As a "sweetener" when selling debt.* Convertibles, like bonds with warrants, offer a company the chance to sell investors debt with lower interest rates and less restrictive covenants in exchange for a chance to share in potential capital gains.

2. *To sell common stock at prices higher than those currently prevailing.* Many companies actually want to sell common stock, not debt, but feel that the price of their stock is temporarily depressed. Management may know, for example, that earnings are depressed because of a strike but think that they will snap back during the next year and pull the price of the stock up with them. To sell stock now would require giving up more shares to raise a given amount of money than management thinks is necessary. However, setting the conversion price 10 to 30 percent above the present market price of the stock will require giving up 10 to 30 percent fewer shares when the bonds are converted than would be required if stock were sold directly at this time.

Notice, however, that management is counting on the stock's price rising above the conversion price to make the bonds attractive in conversion. If the stock price does not rise and conversion does not occur, then the company is saddled with debt.

How can the company be sure that conversion will occur when the price of the stock rises above the conversion price? Typically, convertibles

---

[3] Generally, the conversion price and ratio are fixed for the life of the bond, although sometimes a stepped-up conversion price is used. Litton Industries' convertible debentures, for example, were convertible into 12.5 shares until 1972; they can be exchanged into 11.76 shares from 1972 until 1982, and 11.11 shares from 1982 until they mature in 1987. The conversion price thus started at $80, rose to $85, then will go to $90. Litton's convertibles, like most, are callable at the option of the company.

Another factor that may cause a change in the conversion price and ratio is a standard feature of almost all convertibles—the clause protecting the convertible against dilution from stock splits, stock dividends, and the sale of common stock at prices below the conversion price. The typical provision states that if common stock is sold at a price below the conversion price, then the conversion price must be lowered (and the conversion ratio raised) to the price at which the new stock was issued. Also, if the stock is split, or if a stock dividend is declared, the conversion price must be lowered by the percentage amount of the stock dividend or split. For example, if Adams Engine were to have a two-for-one stock split, the conversion ratio would automatically be adjusted to 40 and the conversion price lowered to $25. If this protection were not contained in the contract, a company could completely thwart conversion by the use of stock splits and dividends. Warrants are similarly protected against dilution.

The standard protection against dilution from selling new stock at prices below the conversion price can, however, get a company into trouble. For example, Litton Industries' stock fell to $2.75 in 1975. Thus, Litton would have had to give the bondholders a tremendous advantage by lowering the conversion price from $85 to $2.75 if it had wanted to sell new common stock. Problems such as this must be kept in mind by firms considering the use of convertibles or bonds with warrants. (Note: By April 1981, Litton's stock was back up to $75 per share.)

contain a call provision that enables the issuing firm to force bondholders to convert. Suppose the conversion price is $50, the conversion ratio is 20, the market price of the common stock has risen to $60, and the call price on the convertible bond is $1,050. If the company calls the bond, bondholders can either convert into common stock with a market value of $1,200 or allow the company to redeem the bond for $1,050. Naturally, bondholders prefer $1,200 to $1,050, so conversion occurs. The call provision therefore gives the company a means of forcing conversion, provided the market price of the stock is greater than the conversion price.

From the standpoint of the issuer, convertibles have two important disadvantages. (1) Although the convertible bond does give the issuer the opportunity to sell common stock at a price 10 to 30 percent higher than the price at which it could otherwise be sold, if the common stock greatly increases in price, the issuing firm may find that it would have been better off if it had waited and simply sold the common stock. (2) If the company truly wants to raise equity capital, and if the price of the stock does not rise sufficiently after the bond is issued, then the company is stuck with debt. This debt will, however, have a low interest rate.

Disadvantages of Convertibles

Suppose Adams Engine is thinking of issuing twenty year convertible bonds at a price of $1,000 per bond; this $1,000 would also be the maturity (and par) value. The bonds would pay a 10 percent annual coupon interest rate, or $100 per year. Each bond could be converted into twenty shares of stock, so the conversion price is $1,000/20 = $50. The stock now pays a dividend of $2.80 and sells at $35 per share; this price is expected to grow at a rate of 8 percent per year. Therefore, $k_s = D_1/P_0 + g = $ $2.80/$35 + 8\% = 8\% + 8\% = 16\%$. If the bonds had not been made convertible, they would have had a yield of 13 percent, given their riskiness and the yields on other bonds. The convertible bonds would not be callable for ten years. After ten years, they could be called at a price of $1,050, with this price declining by $5 per year. If after ten years the conversion value exceeds the call price by at least 20 percent, management will probably call the bonds.

Model of a Convertible Bond

Figure 23-2 shows what both investors and the company would expect to happen over time:

1. The horizontal line at M = $1,000 represents the par (and maturity) value. Also, $1,000 is the price at which the bond is initially offered to the public.

2. The bond is protected against call for ten years. It is initially callable at a price of $1,050, and the call price declines thereafter by $5 per year. Thus, the call price is represented by the solid section of the line V_0M''.

3. Since the convertible has a 10 percent coupon rate, and since the

**Figure 23-2
Model of a Convertible
Bond**

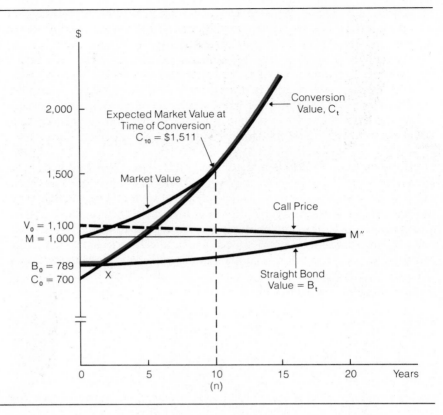

yield on a nonconvertible bond of similar risk was stated to be 13 percent, the "straight bond" value of the convertible, B, must be less than par. At the time of issue, it is actually $789:

$$B_0 = \sum_{t=1}^{20} \frac{\$100}{(1.13)^t} + \frac{\$1,000}{(1.13)^{20}} = \$789.$$

Note, however, that the bond's straight debt value must be $1,000 just prior to maturity, so the bond value rises over time. B_t follows the line B_0M'' in the graph.

4. The bond's initial *conversion value*, or the value of the stock the investor would receive if the bond were converted at $t = 0$, is $700: Conversion value = $P_0 \times R = \$35 \times 20$ shares = $700. Since the stock price is expected to grow at an 8 percent rate, the conversion value of the bond is also expected to rise over time. For example, in Year 5 it should be $P_5 \times R = \$35(1.08)^5(20) = \$1,029$. The expected conversion value, over time, is given by the line C_t in Figure 23-2.

5. The actual market price of the bond must always be equal to or greater than the higher of its straight debt value or its conversion value. If the market price were below the straight bond value, people who wanted bonds would recognize it as a bargain and buy it as a bond. If the market price were below the conversion value, people would buy the bond, convert it to stock, and sell the stock at a profit. Therefore, the higher of the bond value and conversion value curves in the graph represents a "floor price" for the bond. In Figure 23-2, the floor price is represented by the heavy line B_0XC_t.

6. In fact, the bond's market value will typically exceed its floor value. It will exceed the straight bond value because the conversion possibility is worth something—a 10 percent bond with conversion possibilities is worth more than a 10 percent bond without this option. The actual price will typically exceed the conversion value because holding the convertible is safer than holding the common stock—the stock can fall to zero, but the convertible bond will not fall below its straight bond value. We cannot say exactly where the market value line will lie, but it will be above the floor set by the straight bond and conversion value lines.

7. At some point, the market value line will hit the conversion value line. This convergence will occur for two reasons. First, the stock will pay higher and higher dividends as the years go by, but the interest payments on the convertible are fixed. For example, Adams Engine's convertibles would pay $100, while the dividends on the twenty shares received upon conversion would initially be 20($2.80) = $56. However, at an 8 percent growth rate, the dividends after ten years would be up to $120.90, while the interest would still be $100. Thus, at some point rising dividends will push against fixed interest payments and cause investors to convert voluntarily. Second, the market value of the bond cannot get very far above both the conversion value and the call price without exposing investors to the danger of a call. For example, suppose that ten years after issue (when the bonds were callable) the market value was $1,600, the conversion value was $1,500, the call price was $1,050, and you had just bought ten bonds for $16,000, when the company suddenly called the bonds. You would have lost $100 per bond, or $1,000! Recognizing this danger, investors simply will not pay much of a premium over the higher of the call or the conversion value. Therefore, in the example, we assume that the market value line hits the conversion value line in Year 10, when the bond becomes callable.

8. n represents the year when investors expect conversion to occur, either voluntarily because of rising dividends or because the company calls the convertibles to strengthen its balance sheet by substituting equity for debt. In this example, we assume that n = 10.

9. An investor can find the expected rate of return on the bond, k_c, which is an "internal rate of return," by solving for k_c in the following equation:

$$\text{Price paid for bond} = \$1,000 = \sum_{t=1}^{n} \frac{\$100}{(1 + k_c)^t} + \frac{\text{Expected market value at time of conversion}}{(1 + k_c)^n}.$$

Since $n = 10$ and the expected market value at Year 10 is $1,511, we can substitute into the equation and solve for k_c, which turns out to be 12.8 percent:[4]

$$\$1,000 = \sum_{t=1}^{10} \frac{\$100}{(1 + k_c)^t} + \frac{\$1,511}{(1 + k_c)^{10}}$$
$$= \$100(\text{PVIFA}_{12.8\%,10}) + \$1,511(\text{PVIF}_{12.8\%,10})$$
$$= \$100(5.4699) + \$1,511(0.2999)$$
$$= \$1,000.$$

10. The return on a convertible is expected to come partly from interest and partly from capital gains. The interest component is relatively assured, while the capital gains component is more risky. On a straight bond, all of the return is expected from interest. Therefore, a convertible's expected yield is more risky than that of a straight bond, so k_c should be larger than the cost of straight debt, k_d. Thus, the yield on Adams Engine's convertibles (k_c) should lie between its cost of straight debt ($k_d = 13\%$) and its cost of common stock ($k_s = 16\%$). Investment bankers use the type of model described here, plus a knowledge of the market, to set the terms (conversion ratio and coupon interest rate) so that the bond will just "clear the market" at its $1,000 offering price. In this example, these conditions do not hold— the expected rate of return on the convertible is only 12.8 percent, which is less than the cost of straight debt. Therefore, the terms on the bond must be made more attractive to investors. Adams Engine could either increase the coupon interest rate to something above 10 percent, raise the conversion ratio above 20 (and thereby lower the conversion price from $50 to something closer to the current $35 market price of the stock), or use a combination of these two such that the expected rate of return on the convertible ends up between 13 and 16 percent.[5]

---

[4] k_c is like an internal rate of return. It can be solved graphically, by trial and error, or with a financial calculator.

[5] For a more complete discussion of how this model can be used to structure the terms of a convertible offering, see E. F. Brigham, "An Analysis of Convertible Debentures," *Journal of Finance*, March 1966.

The Winchester Company, an electronic circuit and component manufacturer with assets of $60 million, illustrates a typical case in which convertibles proved useful. Winchester's profits had been depressed as a result of its heavy expenditures on research and development for a new product. This situation held down the growth rate of earnings and dividends; the price/earnings ratio was only 18 times, as compared with an industry average of 22. At the current $2 earnings per share and P/E of 18, the stock was selling for $36 a share. The Winchester family owned 70 percent of the 1.5 million shares outstanding, or 1.05 million shares. It wanted to retain majority control but could not buy more stock.

The heavy R&D expenditures had resulted in the development of a new type of printed circuit that management believed would be highly profitable. A total of $25 million was needed to build and equip new production facilities, but profits were not expected to flow into the company for some eighteen months after construction on the new plant was started. Winchester's debt amounted to $27 million, or 45 percent of assets, well above the 25 percent industry average. Its debt indenture provisions restricted the company from selling additional debt unless the new debt was subordinated to outstanding debt.

Investment bankers informed J. H. Winchester, Jr., the financial vice-president, that subordinated debentures could not be sold at any reasonable interest rate unless they were convertible or had warrants attached. Convertibles or bonds with warrants could be sold with a 5 percent coupon interest rate if the conversion price or warrant option price was set at 15 percent above the market price of $36, or at $41 a share. Alternatively, the investment bankers were willing to buy convertibles or bonds with warrants at a $5\frac{1}{2}$ percent interest rate and a 20 percent conversion premium, or a conversion (or exercise) price of $43.50. If the company wanted to sell common stock directly, it could net $33 a share.

Which of the alternatives should Winchester have chosen? First, note that if common stock were used, the company would have to sell 757,576 shares ($25 million divided by $33). Combined with the 450,000 shares already held outside the family, this amounts to approximately 1.2 million shares versus the Winchester holdings of 1.05 million. Thus, the family would lose majority control if common stock were sold.

If the 5 percent convertibles or bonds with warrants were used and the bonds were converted or the warrants exercised, 609,756 new shares would be added. Combined with the old 450,000, the outside interest would then be 1,059,756, so again the Winchester family would lose majority control. However, if the $5\frac{1}{2}$ percent convertibles or bonds with warrants were used, then after conversion or exercise only 574,713 new shares would be created. In this case, the family would have 1,050,000 shares versus 1,024,713 for outsiders; absolute control would be maintained.

Decisions on Use of Warrants and Convertibles

In addition to assuring control, using the convertibles or warrants would also benefit earnings per share in the long run—the total number of shares would be less because fewer new shares would be issued to get the $25 million, so earnings per share would be higher. Before conversion or exercise, however, the firm would have a considerable amount of debt outstanding. Adding $25 million would raise the total debt to $52 million against new total assets of $85 million, so the debt ratio would be over 61 percent versus the 25 percent industry average. This could be dangerous. If delays were encountered in bringing the new plant into production, if demand failed to meet expectations, if the company experienced a strike, if the economy went into a recession—if any of these things occurred— the company would be extremely vulnerable because of the high debt ratio.

In the actual case, the decision was made to sell the $5\frac{1}{2}$ percent convertible debentures. Two years later, earnings climbed to $3 a share, the P/E ratio to 20, and the price of the stock to $60. The bonds were called, but, of course, conversion occurred. After conversion, debt amounted to approximately $27.5 million against total assets of $87.5 million (some earnings had been retained), so the debt ratio was down to a more reasonable 31 percent.

Convertibles were chosen rather than bonds with warrants for the following reason. If a firm has a high debt ratio and its near-term prospects are favorable, it can anticipate a rise in the price of its stock and thus be able to call the bonds and force conversion. Warrants, on the other hand, have a stated life, and even though the price of the firm's stock rises, the warrants may not be exercised until near their expiration date. If, subsequent to the favorable period (during which convertibles could have been called), the firm encounters less favorable developments and the price of its stock falls, the warrants may lose their value and may never be exercised. The heavy debt burden will then become aggravated. Therefore, the use of convertibles gives the firm greater control over the timing of future capital structure changes. This factor is of particular importance to the firm if its debt ratio is already high in relation to the risks of its line of business.

Reporting Earnings If Warrants or Convertibles Are Outstanding

If warrants or convertibles are outstanding, a firm could theoretically report earnings per share in three ways:

1. *Simple EPS*, where earnings available to common stockholders are divided by the average number of shares actually outstanding during the period.
2. *Primary EPS*, where earnings available are divided by the average number of shares that would have been outstanding if warrants and convertibles "likely to be converted in the near future" had actually

been exercised or converted. Accountants have a formula which basically compares the conversion or option price with the actual market value of the stock to determine the likelihood of conversion, and they also add interest on the convertible bonds back into earnings.

3. *Fully diluted EPS,* which is similar to primary EPS except that *all* warrants and convertibles are assumed to be exercised or converted, regardless of the likelihood of exercise or conversion.

Simple EPS is virtually never reported by firms which have warrants or convertibles likely to be exercised or converted—the SEC requires that primary and fully diluted earnings be shown. For firms with large amounts of option securities outstanding, there can be a substantial difference between the two EPS figures. The purpose of the provision is, of course, to give investors a more accurate picture of the firm's true profit position.

Options

An option is a contract which gives its holder the right to buy (or sell) an asset at some predetermined price within a specified period of time. Thus, a warrant is an option, and so, too, are the stock options that corporations give their key executives as an incentive-based form of compensation. In the cases of both warrants and executive stock options, the options are created by the company and given up in exchange for something of value to the firm (low interest rate debt or better executive performance).

However, in recent years a new and rapidly growing market has developed for options created by individuals as opposed to issuing corporations. For example, if someone owned 100 shares of IBM stock, which in November 1980 sold for 66\frac{1}{2}$, that stockholder could give (or sell) to someone else the right to buy the 100 shares at any time during the next six months at a price of, say, $70 per share. (The $70 is called the "striking price.") Such options are actually offered, and they are traded on a number of stock exchanges, the Chicago Board Options Exchange (CBOE) being the oldest and largest. On November 6, 1980, IBM six month, $70 options sold on the CBOE for $4.75. Thus, for $4.75 × 100 = $475 you could buy an option giving you the right to purchase 100 shares of IBM at a price of $70 per share anytime during the next six months. If the stock price stayed below $70 during that period, you would lose your $475, but if it rose to $150, then your $475 investment would have grown to ($150 − $70)(100) = $8,000! That translates into a very healthy rate of return. Incidentally, if the stock did go up, you would probably not actually buy the stock—the writer of the option would just pay you your profit.

An option to *buy* stock such as we have just described is termed a *call option.* One can also buy an option to *sell* stock—these are called *put op-*

tions. For example, suppose you think that IBM's price is going to decline from its current level of $66½ sometime during the next six months. For $5.625 you could buy a six month put option giving you the right to sell one share (which you would not necessarily own) at a price of $70 ($70 is the striking price). If you bought a 100 share contract for $562.50 and IBM fell to $40, you would make ($70 − $40)(100) = $3,000, less the $562.50 you paid for the put option.

Options trading is one of the "hottest" financial activities in the U.S. today. The leverage involved makes it possible for speculators with just a few dollars to make a fortune almost overnight. Also, investors with sizable portfolios can sell options on their stocks and make the value of the option (less brokerage commissions) even if the stock's price remains constant.[6] Still, perhaps those who have profited most from the development of options trading are security brokers, who earn commission income on such trades.[7]

Corporations such as IBM on whose stock options are written have nothing to do with the options market. The corporations do not raise money in the options market or have any direct transactions in it. Option holders do not vote for corporate directors (unless they exercise their options to purchase the stock, which few actually do). There have been studies by the SEC and others as to whether options trading stabilizes or destabilizes the stock market, and whether it helps or hinders corporations seeking to raise new capital. The studies have not been conclusive one way or the other. In any event, options trading is here to stay, and many regard it as the most exciting game in town.[8]

Summary

Both warrants and convertibles are forms of options used to finance business firms. The use of such long-term options is encouraged by an economic environment in which either recessions or booms can occur. The senior position of the securities protects against recessions, while the option feature offers the opportunity for participation in rising stock markets.

Both convertibles and warrants are used as "sweeteners." The option privileges they grant may make it possible for small companies to sell

---

[6] An investor who sells options against stock held in a portfolio is said to be selling *covered options.* Options sold without the stock to back them up are called *naked options.*

[7] On a sparkling, sunny day sometime back, a famous stockbroker took a client to the New York Yacht Club for lunch. The broker pointed out one trim yacht and said it belonged to Broker A, nodded toward the one moored next to it, which was even longer, and said it belonged to Broker B, and so on. When he had finished, his guest turned to him and asked plaintively, "But where are the *clients'* yachts?"

[8] Formal, mathematical models have been developed to aid in the valuation of options. See F. Black and M. Scholes, "The Pricing of Options and Corporate Liabilities," *Journal of Political Economy* (May-June 1973), 637-654. Also, see any of the investments texts listed in the Chapter 4 references for a simplified explanation of the Black-Scholes model.

debt or preferred stock that otherwise could not be sold. For large companies, the "sweeteners" result in lower costs of the securities sold.

The conversion of bonds by their holders does not provide additional funds to the company. The exercise of warrants does provide such funds. The conversion of securities results in reduced debt ratios. The exercise of warrants also strengthens the equity position, but it still leaves the debt or preferred stock on the balance sheet. A firm with a high debt ratio should probably choose to use convertibles rather than senior securities carrying warrants. A firm with a moderate or low debt ratio may choose to employ warrants.

In the past, larger and stronger firms tended to favor convertibles over bonds with warrants, so most warrants were issued by smaller, weaker concerns. AT&T's use of warrants in its $1.57 billion financing has caused other large firms to reexamine their positions on warrants, and warrants have come into increasing use since that time.

Partly because of investors' interest in warrants and convertibles, a new market in pure options was developed during the 1970s. Option contracts are created by investors, not by the firms whose securities are involved in option contracts. The corporations themselves do not raise capital from the sale of these options and, in fact, have no direct involvement with this market.

Questions

23-1 Why do warrants typically sell at prices higher than their formula values?

23-2 What effect does the trend in stock prices (subsequent to issue) have on a firm's ability to raise funds (a) through convertibles and (b) through warrants?

23-3 If a firm expects to have additional financial requirements in the future, would you recommend that it use convertibles or bonds with warrants? What factors would influence your decision?

23-4 How does a firm's dividend policy affect each of the following?
   a. The value of long-term warrants.
   b. The likelihood that convertible bonds will be converted.
   c. The likelihood that warrants will be exercised.

23-5 Evaluate the following statement: "Issuing convertible securities represents a means by which a firm can sell common stock at a price above the existing market."

23-6 Why do corporations often sell convertibles on a rights basis?

23-7 Suppose a company simultaneously issues $50 million of convertible bonds with a coupon rate of 10 percent and $50 million of straight bonds with a coupon rate of 14 percent. Both bonds have the same maturity. Does the fact that the convertible issue has the lower coupon rate suggest that it is less risky than the straight bond? Explain.

Problems

23-1 a. Coit Industries, Inc., has warrants outstanding that permit the holders to purchase one share of stock per warrant at a price of $25. Calculate the formula value of Coit's warrants if the common sells at each of the following prices: (1) $20, (2) $25, (3) $30, (4) $100.

b. At what approximate price do you think the warrants would actually sell under each condition indicated above? What premium is implied in your price? Your answer is a guess, but your prices and premiums should bear reasonable relationships to one another.

c. How would each of the following affect your estimates of the warrants' prices and premiums in Part b?

1. The life of the warrant.
2. Expected variability (σ_p) in the stock's price.
3. The expected growth rate in the stock's EPS.
4. The company announces a change in dividend policy: Whereas it formerly paid no dividends, henceforth it will pay out *all* earnings as dividends.

d. Assume Coit's stock now sells for $20 per share. The company wants to sell some twenty year, annual interest, $1,000 par value bonds. Each bond will have attached fifty warrants, each exercisable into one share of stock at an exercise price of $25. Coit's straight bonds yield 12 percent. Regardless of your answer to Part b above, assume that the warrants will have a market value of $3 when the stock sells at $20. What coupon interest rate, and dollar coupon, must the company set on the bonds-with-warrants if they are to clear the market? Round to the nearest dollar or percentage point.

23-2 The Valley Forge Foundry was planning to finance an expansion in the summer of 1982. The principal executives of the company were agreed that an industrial company such as theirs should finance growth by means of common stock rather than by debt. However, they felt that the price of the company's common stock did not reflect its true worth, so they decided to sell a convertible security. They considered a convertible debenture but feared the burden of fixed interest charges if the common stock did not rise in price to make conversion attractive. They decided on an issue of convertible preferred stock, which would pay a dividend of $2.10 per share.

The common stock was selling at $42 a share at the time. Management projected earnings for 1982 at $3 a share and expected a future growth rate of 10 percent a year in 1982 and beyond. It was agreed by the investment bankers and the management that the common stock would sell at 14 times earnings, the current price/earnings ratio.

a. What conversion price should be set by the issuer? The conversion ratio will be 1.0; that is, each share of convertible preferred can be converted into one share of common. Therefore, the convertible's par value (and also the issue price) will equal the conversion price as a percentage over the current market price of the common. Your answer will be a guess, but make it a reasonable one.

b. Should the preferred stock include a call provision? Why?

23-3 In June 1976, U.S. Steel sold $400 million of convertible bonds, the largest issue on record. The bonds had a twenty-five year maturity, a $5^{3}/_{4}$ percent coupon rate, and were sold at their $1,000 par value. The conversion price was set at $62.75 against a current price of $55 per share of common. The bonds were subordinated debentures, and they were given an A rating; straight nonconvertible debentures of the same quality yielded about $8^{3}/_{4}$ percent at the time.

    a. Calculate the premium on the bonds, i.e., the percentage excess of the conversion price over the current stock price.

    b. What is U.S. Steel's annual interest savings on the convertible issue versus a straight debt issue?

    c. Look up U.S. Steel's current stock price in the paper. Based on this price, do you think it likely that the bonds would have been converted? (Calculate the value of the stock one would receive by converting a bond.)

    d. The bonds originally sold for $1,000. If interest rates on A-rated bonds had remained constant at $8^{3}/_{4}$ percent, what do you think would have happened to the price of the convertible bonds? (Note: Bond prices are quoted daily in the *Wall Street Journal* as well as in major newspapers, so you can look up the price of U.S. Steel's bonds to check your answer.)

    e. Now suppose the price of U.S. Steel's common stock had fallen from $55 on the day the bonds were issued to $20 at present. (At the time this problem was written, that is exactly what had happened.) Suppose also that the rate of interest had fallen from $8^{3}/_{4}$ to $5^{3}/_{4}$ percent. (This had not happened when the problem was being written—the interest rate on A-rated bonds was about 11 percent.) Under these conditions, what do you think would have happened to the price of the bonds?

    f. Set up a graphic model to illustrate how investors must have felt about the U.S. Steel convertibles in 1976. How well were these expectations realized?

23-4 The Dirk Manufacturing Company has grown rapidly during the past five years. Recently its commercial bank urged the company to consider increasing permanent financing. Its bank loan under a line of credit has risen to $250,000, carrying 8 percent interest. Dirk has been thirty to sixty days late in paying trade creditors.

Discussions with an investment banker have resulted in the decision to raise $500,000 at this time. Investment bankers have assured Dirk that the following alternatives are feasible (flotation costs will be ignored):

Alternative 1. Sell common stock at $8.

Alternative 2. Sell convertible bonds at an 8 percent coupon, convertible into 100 shares of common stock for each $1,000 bond (that is, the conversion price is $10 per share).

Alternative 3. Sell debentures at an 8 percent coupon, each $1,000 bond carrying 100 warrants to buy common stock at $10.

Tom O'Brien, the president, owns 80 percent of the common stock of Dirk Manufacturing Company and wishes to maintain control of the company. One hundred thousand shares are outstanding. The following additional information is given.

Dirk Manufacturing Company: Balance Sheet

		Current liabilities	$400,000
		Common stock, par $1.00	100,000
		Retained earnings	50,000
	Total assets $550,000	Total claims	$550,000

Dirk Manufacturing Company: Income Statement

Sales	$1,100,000
All costs except interest	990,000
Gross profit	$ 110,000
Interest	20,000
Profit before taxes	$ 90,000
Taxes at 50%	45,000
Profits after taxes	$ 45,000
Shares	100,000
Earnings per share	$0.45
Price/earnings ratio	19×
Market price of stock	$8.55

a. Show the new balance sheet under each alternative. For Alternatives 2 and 3, show the balance sheet after conversion of the debentures or exercise of the warrants. Assume that one-half of the funds raised will be used to pay off the bank loan and one-half to increase total assets.

b. Show O'Brien's control position under each alternative, assuming that he does not purchase additional shares.

c. What is the effect on earnings per share of each alternative, if it is assumed that profits before interest and taxes will be 20 percent of total assets?

d. What will be the debt ratio under each alternative?

e. Which of the three alternatives would you recommend to O'Brien, and why?

23-5 Magnetic Couplers, Inc. (MCI), needs to raise $25 million to put a new disk coupler into production. MCI's straight, nonconvertible debentures currently yield 14 percent. Its stock sells for $30 per share; the last dividend was $2; and the expected growth rate is 9 percent. Investment bankers have tentatively proposed that MCI raise the $25 million by issuing convertible debentures. These convertibles would have a $1,000 par value, carry a coupon rate of 10 percent, have a twenty year maturity, and be convertible into twenty shares of stock. The bonds would be noncallable for five years, after which they would be callable at a price of $1,075; this call price would decline by $5 per year in Year 6 and each year thereafter. Management has called convertibles in the past (and presumably it will call them again in the future), once they were eligible for call, when the bonds' conversion value was about 20 percent above the bonds' par value (not their call price).

a. Draw an accurate graph similar to Figure 23-2 representing the expectations set forth above.

b. What is the expected rate of return on the proposed convertible issue?

c. Do you think that these bonds could be successfully offered to the public at par? That is, does $1,000 seem to be an equilibrium price in view of the stated terms? If not, suggest the type of change that would have to be made to cause the bonds to trade at $1,000 in the secondary market, assuming no change in capital market conditions.

d. Suppose the projections outlined above work out on schedule for two years, but then MCI begins to experience extremely strong competition from Dutch firms. As a result, MCI's expected growth rate drops from 9 percent to zero. Assume that the dividend at the time of the drop is $2.38. The company's credit strength is not impaired, and its value of k_s is also unchanged. What would happen (1) to the stock price and (2) to the convertible bond's price? Be as precise as you can.

Selected References

Alexander, Gordon J., and Roger D. Stover, "Pricing in the New Issue Convertible Debt Market," *Financial Management,* vol. 6 (Fall 1977), 35-39.

———, "The Effect of Forced Conversions on Common Stock Prices," *Financial Management,* vol. 9 (Spring 1980), 39-45.

Alexander, Gordon J., Roger D. Stover, and David B. Kuhnau, "Market Timing Strategies in Convertible Debt Financing," *Journal of Finance,* vol. 34 (March 1979), 143-155.

Black, Fischer, "Fact and Fancy in the Use of Options," *Financial Analysts' Journal,* July-August 1975, 36-41.

Black, Fischer, and Myron Scholes, "The Valuation of Option Contracts and a Test of Market Efficiency," *Journal of Finance,* vol. 27 (May 1972), 399-417.

Brigham, Eugene F., "An Analysis of Convertible Debentures: Theory and Some Empirical Evidence," *Journal of Finance,* vol. 21 (March 1966), 35-54.

Galai, Dan, and Mier I. Schneller, "The Pricing of Warrants and the Value of the Firm," *Journal of Finance,* vol. 33 (December 1978), 1333-1342.

Ingersoll, J. E., "A Contingent Claims Valuation of Convertible Securities," *Journal of Financial Economics,* May 1977, 289-322.

———, "An Examination of Corporate Call Policies on Convertible Securities," *Journal of Finance,* vol. 32 (May 1977), 463-478.

Smith, C. W., Jr., "Option Pricing: A Review," *Journal of Financial Economics,* vol. 3 (January 1976), 3-51.

What is a "small" business? Definitions vary, but the U.S. Small Business Administration (SBA), the federal agency charged with encouraging the formation and growth of small businesses, uses the following classifications:

1. *Manufacturing.* Whether a manufacturer is defined as a small business depends on the number of employees it has, with the cutoff varying from industry to industry. An apparel company with fewer than 500 employees is classified as small, but so is an aircraft company with fewer than 1,500 employees.

2. *Retail trade.* Retail stores are classified on the basis of sales, with the limits depending on the type of store. A department store is defined as small if its sales are under $7.5 million, whereas the cutoff for an apparel store is $2.5 million.

3. *Service.* Service organizations are also classified on the basis of sales. For most categories, the cutoff point is $2 million.

Based on these definitions, about 93 percent of all U.S. businesses are small; however, these firms generate only about 11.5 percent of total sales in the economy. Even though small firms are overwhelmed by large ones in terms of their contribution to gross national product, small businesses do play a vital role in our economy—they represent a major spawning ground for the new ideas that lead to industrial progress. The very nature of large corporations makes it difficult for them to devote the resources— especially the managerial talent—necessary to develop and exploit truly revolutionary new ideas. The top managements of the A&Ps, IBMs, and du Ponts are typically so involved in their complex business plans, corporate strategies, and hierarchical structures that they have little time to expend on developing the potential in, say, convenience stores, fast food operations, personal computers, genetic engineering, and the like. Therefore, small business entrepreneurs on the lookout for more efficient ways of doing business have created such corporate giants as McDonald's, Apple Computer, Genentech, Seven-Eleven, and H&R Block.

The survival rate for new businesses is quite low. A Commerce Department study indicated that 37 percent of all new businesses fold within six months, 46 percent within $1\frac{1}{2}$ years, 74 percent within five years, and

81 percent within ten years. The losses incurred by these firms are unknown, but clearly the road to possible riches is strewn with corpses!

Some argue that there is no need to study small business as a separate topic because the same general principles of financial management apply to both large and small firms. However, small firms do face problems that are somewhat different from those confronting larger businesses, and the goals of a small firm are likely to be oriented more toward the aspirations of an individual entrepreneur rather than toward investors in general. Also, the characteristics of the money and capital markets create special problems for small firms, and, as noted above, a governmental agency, the U.S. Small Business Administration, exists to help small firms with their financing problems. This chapter presents some of the key factors in small business finance.

The life cycle of an industry or firm is often depicted as an S-shaped curve, as shown in Figure 24-1. The four stages in the life cycle are described as follows:

Life Cycle of the Firm

1. *Experimentation stage.* Sales and profits grow slowly following the introduction of a new product or firm.
2. *Exploitation stage.* The firm enjoys rapid growth of sales and high profitability, as market acceptance of its product accelerates, and as it expands to meet this vigorous demand.
3. *Maturity.* The rate of growth of sales begins to slow down; growth is dependent in large part on replacement demand.
4. *Decline.* The firm faces new competitive products, technological and managerial obsolescence, and saturation of demand for its goods.

Although it is an oversimplification, Figure 24-1 does provide a useful framework for analysis. The situation represented by the four stage life cycle concept is based on a number of assumptions. For example, it assumes competent management in the growth stages and a lack of management foresight prior to the decline phase. Obviously, one of manage-

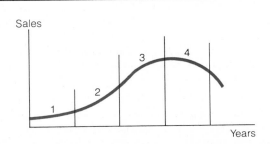

Figure 24-1
Hypothetical Life Cycle
of a Typical Firm

ment's primary goals is to prolong Stage 2 and to completely forestall Stage 4, and a great many firms are apparently successful in this endeavor. We shall discuss other aspects of the firm's life cycle later, giving special attention to the types of financing employed at each stage.

Traditional Small Business Industries

Some firms are small because the nature of the industry dictates that small enterprises are more efficient than large ones, while other firms are small primarily because they are new companies—either new entrants to established industries or new enterprises in developing industries. These two types of small firms face fundamentally different situations, and they have vastly different problems and opportunities. Traditional small businesses are discussed in the remainder of this section, while the special characteristics and problems of firms with growth potential are examined later in the chapter.

Characteristics of Traditional Small Firms

The industries or segments of industries in which small businesses predominate exhibit three common characteristics: (1) a localized market, (2) low capital requirements, and (3) relatively simple technology. Because these characteristics lead to heavy dependence on one person, problems often arise:

1. The key individual may not possess the full range of managerial skills required. For instance, the owner may be good in sales but unable to handle employees well, to keep adequate accounting records, to maintain financial control systems, or to deal adequately with other administrative tasks.
2. In a small business run by one key person, the control system tends to be informal, direct, and personal. If the business grows, the span of responsibilities may become excessive for the entrepreneur.
3. Because of the owner's preoccupation with the pressing problems of day-to-day operations, planning for the future is often inadequate. Firms where this is the case merely react to changes that have already occurred rather than anticipate or even bring about change. Such firms are, of course, more often hurt than helped by competitive shifts or fluctuations in the economic environment.
4. A relatively high degree of managerial training, experience, and breadth are necessary, yet often lacking; preoccupied with the present, the typical small-firm entrepreneur simply does not plan for management succession. As was noted in Chapter 21, Dun & Bradstreet data indicate that more failures are caused by the lack of competent management than by any other factor.

Profitability of Small Firms

Most studies show that running a small business is anything but a picnic. Owners often put in sixty or more hours per week, have all of their capital tied up in a risky undertaking, face nerve-racking problems, and earn less than the minimum wage for their efforts.

In the face of such discouraging statistics, why do people open their own businesses? The reasons vary. Some want to stake their career on an idea that they think may lead to extreme wealth—they do not want the measured advancement and security a position with a large corporation offers.[1] They hope to beat the odds; any community, large or small, has a group of very successful small business people who, while perhaps not millionaires, can afford $200,000 homes, country club memberships, and periodic trips abroad, not to mention sending their children to college in style. Others go into business for themselves not so much in hopes of getting rich as for the personal satisfaction and freedom of being their own boss. Most do not regard the time spent working in their own firms as drudgery; there are many tasks to be performed in running a small enterprise, and the work can be both interesting and challenging.

The typical small business, even the successful one, cannot look to the general capital markets for funds. If the firm owns any real estate, it may be able to obtain a mortgage from a bank or a savings and loan. Equipment may perhaps either be purchased under a term loan or be leased. After the business has survived for a few years, bank financing may be available on a seasonal basis, but not for permanent growth capital. Trade credit will typically represent the bulk of outside financing available to the firm.

Financial ratio analysis will be of major and overriding importance to the small firm. Such analysis, on a regular basis, is essential to ascertain whether the firm is operating efficiently. Whereas a larger, stronger firm may have the financial strength to fall below its industry standards and still recover, the small firm has less margin for error. Thus, anyone running a small firm is well advised to look at trends in its financial ratios and to compare them with industry standards. This point is discussed in more detail later in the chapter.

Working capital management is also of overwhelming importance for most small firms. Because the amount of funds available is limited, liquidity is crucial. Trade credit appears to be an easy way of obtaining funds, yet even trade credit is obtained on terms that generally call for payment within thirty days. Since inventories typically represent a large percentage of total assets, a small firm's inventory policy must also be stressed. Large firms usually offer credit, so to meet competition, small firms may also have to extend credit. The large firm is likely to have an established credit department, but how does the small firm evaluate credit risks? What vol-

Financing the Traditional Small Firm

[1] To illustrate, Apple Computer was started in 1976. Steve Jobs, one of its founders, was twenty-one at the time. Five years later, after the company went public, Jobs's stock was worth $200 million.

ume of accounts receivable can be built up without endangering both the solvency and the liquidity of the business? These are critical questions for the manager of a small business.

Current liability management is also important for the small firm. Although trade credit is relatively easy to obtain, it is often very costly. If discounts are available but not taken, the effective interest rate on such credit can be extremely high—as we know, not taking discounts on terms of 2/10, net 30 implies a 37 percent interest rate. Also, there is a temptation to be consistently slow in making payments, but this involves dangers: Suppliers may refuse to extend any credit whatever, or they may quote higher prices.

In summary, three areas of finance are of the utmost importance to firms in traditional small business industries. *First*, the proprietor must rely on internal financing (retained earnings) to a greater extent than would the management of a larger firm. *Second*, the proprietor must be a jack-of-all-trades and master of *all* if the business is to survive in the long run. *Third*, working capital management is critical to the small entrepreneur, for if a breakdown occurs here, the firm will not remain solvent, and it will go out of business.

Franchising

Many traditional small businesses are today moving toward franchise operations. Examples include McDonald's, Burger King, Midas Mufflers, Mr. Transmission, Hilton Hotels, Holiday Inn, and thousands more. Franchising represents a device whereby the training and experience required for a particular line of business is supplied to the proprietor on a rental contract basis. Sometimes the franchise also includes the use of a valuable name developed through national advertising and uniform standards (McDonald's), or of a special service (Holiday Inn's reservation service). Or, through bulk buying, the franchisor may be able to sell supplies to the franchisee at lower costs than would otherwise be available.

The typical arrangement calls for the franchisee (1) to construct a facility that meets the franchisor's specifications, (2) to pay the franchisor a one-time fee of, say, $10,000 for a license to operate in a given territory, (3) to send personnel to one of the franchisor's established locations for pre-opening training, and (4) to pay the franchisor a continuing fee of, say, 2 percent of sales revenues for continuing support. Each franchisee must also agree to operate in accordance with specified procedures and to permit regular inspections, for the maintenance of high, uniform standards is essential to the entire operation—one rotten franchise can spoil the whole barrel.

Most newly organized franchise operations require their franchisees to put up a substantial amount of "front money," mainly for buildings, inventory, and other start-up costs. Indeed, one reason for franchising rather than simply opening branch facilities is that there are much lower capital requirements for the parent organization, as capital is supplied by many individual entrepreneurs. However, once the franchisor becomes established and has developed lines of credit, the franchise-granting firm may reverse the process and supply capital to new operators (who are often promising but dollar-poor employees of existing franchisees).

Franchising can be very profitable to both the franchisor and the franchisees. It can project the franchisor from just another small business into a huge, national corporation, and it can give the franchisees a huge advantage over their competitors—how would you like to be the owner-operator of Ma & Pa's Motel and see the Holiday Inn construction crew pull up across the street? On the other hand, as many erstwhile franchise operators know, obtaining a franchise is not necessarily the road to riches—in many such arrangements, the owner of the franchised operation may be required to pay an excessive price for the trademark, specialty inputs, supplies, and managerial advice. As in most other aspects of business, franchising decisions should be based on a careful analysis of all the facts.

The Small Firm with Growth Potential

The second broad category of small business is the new firm with potential for substantial growth. Typically, such a firm has developed a new product or an innovative way of providing an old service: The personal computer industry is a good example of the former, while franchised hamburgers and other food operations illustrate the latter. In this section, we discuss the financial aspects of potential growth companies from inception until the business has matured enough to go public. The significant financial aspects of each stage of the life cycle will be set out as a guide to the establishment and development of the new small business enterprise.

Stage 1: Experimentation Period

As indicated above and shown in Figure 24-1, in the first stage of its life cycle, the firm is experimenting and working to establish itself. During this period, management must lay the foundation for future growth, realizing that growth occurs either because the firm can increase its share of the market or because of industry expansion. Market share expansion is difficult due to the reaction of existing firms, and even if the industry is growing, management must recognize that every product and industry has a life cycle. Hence, supernormal growth, whatever its cause, will continue for only a finite period.

Particularly in new industries, it is important that the firm identify the techniques needed to succeed in its line of business. When the auto industry was maturing, dealership organizations and the availability of repair parts and service were the critical factors to the success of individual firms. In the computer industry, a backup of software, marketing, and maintenance personnel is vital.

Like the owner of a firm in a traditional small business, a growth company entrepreneur must have a knowledge not only of products and markets, but also of the standard administrative tools essential for effective management in any line of business. Financial planning and control processes are especially important, and financial ratio analysis should be used to develop standards for determining the broad outlines of the balance sheet and the income statement, as well as for guidelines to help identify developing problem areas.

Planning for growth is an essential ingredient of success. Initially, such planning will emphasize the expansion of existing operations; later in the firm's life cycle, it must consider possible movement into new product lines. A basic decision that must be made, whatever type of expansion occurs, is to choose between using more or less highly automated productive processes. Standard breakeven analysis can be employed to measure how changing sales levels will affect the firm's risk and return characteristics.

Stage 2: Exploitation and Rapid Growth Period

After its inception, a successful firm with growth potential will enter Stage 2 of its financial cycle. Here, the firm has achieved initial success—it is growing rapidly and is reasonably profitable. Cash flows and working capital management have become increasingly important. Also, at this stage the firm will have an extraordinary need for additional outside financing; as we saw in Chapter 7, the need for external funds is a function of the firm's growth rate, so in Stage 2 large amounts of external funds are required. This necessitates good financial planning, for otherwise a shortage of capital may throttle the firm's growth opportunities.

Firms in Stage 2 have an especially difficult time obtaining equity capital because they are not large enough to go public, and relatively little is known about them. Typically, they are entering new areas about which little information is available. There may be great potential, but large risks are also involved, and for every glowing success story there are many instances of failure. In addition, even after an innovative growth firm has been established, there are continued pressures because of the financial problems noted above. Also, demonstrated success will stimulate imitators, so growth projections must take into account the influx of new firms and the likelihood of a declining market share and increased competitive pressures. Furthermore, high profits may lead to excessive industry expansion, which will be followed by excess capacity, which in turn will cause problems for every firm in the industry. For all these reasons, the small, rapidly growing firm's existence is precarious, even when the product market opportunities upon which it was conceived are sound.

The combination of high risks and profit potential inherent in Stage 2 firms has led to the development of *venture capital suppliers*—wealthy individuals, partnerships, or corporations whose business is supplying risk capital to small growth companies. When a new business makes an application for financial assistance from a venture capital firm, it receives a rigorous examination. Some development companies use their own staffs for this investigation, while others depend on a board of advisers acting in the capacity of consultants. A high percentage of applications is rejected, but if the application is approved, funds are provided. Venture capital companies generally take an equity position in the firms they finance, but they may also extend debt capital. However, when loans are made, they generally involve convertibles or warrants, or are tied in with the purchase of stock by the investment company.

Venture capital companies perform a continuing and active role in the enterprise. Typically, they do not insist on voting control, but they usually have at least one member on the board of directors of the new enterprise. The matter of control has *not* been one of the crucial considerations in investment companies' decisions to invest—indeed, if the management of a small business is not sufficiently strong to make sound policy decisions, the venture capital firm is not likely to be interested in the first place. The investment company does, however, want to maintain continuous contact, to provide management counsel, and to monitor the progress of its investment.

Another distinctive feature of the venture capital firm stems from its ownership by wealthy individuals. (Laurance Rockefeller, for example, is a leading venture capitalist.) For tax reasons, such people are interested in receiving their income in the form of capital gains rather than dividend income. They are, therefore, in a position to take larger risks. Further, special provisions of the tax laws make equity investments in small businesses (as defined by the tax code) especially interesting. First, as noted in Chapter 2, it is possible to set up a small business as a Subchapter S corporation, yet have it taxed as a partnership or a proprietorship, so that operating losses, tax credits, and so on can be passed through to the investor and used to offset ordinary income. Second, while it is generally possible to offset only $2,000 of ordinary income with capital losses, if the losses are on a small business as defined by the tax code, up to $50,000 per year of ordinary income may be offset. This provides a powerful inducement for wealthy investors to invest in small businesses.

To illustrate the tax loss advantage, suppose an investor who is in the 75 percent federal-plus-state income tax bracket on ordinary income and in the 28 percent bracket on long-term capital gains is considering a $50,000 investment in the stock of a small business. The company is judged to have a 50 percent probability of being worth $110,000 after a year and a 50 percent probability of being worth zero. On a before-tax basis, the expected rate of return on the investment is only 10 percent:

$$\begin{array}{c} \text{Expected} \\ \text{before-tax} \\ \text{rate of} \\ \text{return} \end{array} = \frac{0.5(\$110,000) + 0.5(\$0)}{\$50,000} - 1.0 = 0.10 = 10\%.$$

This is not a very good return on an investment that appears to be quite risky. However, consider the after-tax situation:

$$
\begin{aligned}
\begin{matrix} \text{Expected} \\ \text{after-tax} \\ \text{rate of} \\ \text{return} \end{matrix} &= \frac{0.5 \left[\begin{matrix} \text{Invested} \\ \text{capital} \end{matrix} + \begin{matrix} \text{After-tax} \\ \text{gains} \end{matrix} \right] + 0.5 \left[\begin{matrix} \text{Tax shelter} \\ \text{from loss} \end{matrix} \right]}{\text{Invested capital}} - 1.0 \\[2em]
&= \frac{0.5\,[\$50{,}000 + \$60{,}000(1.0 - 0.28)] + 0.5[\$50{,}000(0.75)]}{\$50{,}000} - 1.0 \\[1.5em]
&= \frac{\$46{,}600 + \$18{,}750}{\$50{,}000} - 1.0 = 30.7\%.
\end{aligned}
$$

A 30.7 percent after-tax return for a 75 percent bracket investor is not bad at all, especially if the investor takes a position in a number of different small businesses and thus diversifies away some of the risk that exists in each individual stock.

It is possible for corporations as well as individuals to benefit from small business investments. Therefore, in recent years many large, well-established corporations have invested both money and know-how in small businesses. Corporations with their own venture capital companies include General Electric, Texaco, Citicorp, and Xerox. Other established companies have invested heavily in new businesses in emerging technologies; for example, in recent years Dow, Monsanto, Shell Oil, and Standard of California have been among the many corporate investors in new genetic engineering firms such as Genentech, Cetus, and Genex Corporation. The founders of small, new firms are usually specialists, frequently technical people who need both money and help with administrative services such as accounting, finance, production, and marketing. The small firm's owners contribute entrepreneurship, special talents, a taste for risk taking, and "the willingness to work eighteen hours a day for peanuts—or maybe for millions." The major corporations have found that there is a mutual advantage in cooperative ventures with such individuals.

Another important source of venture capital financing for small business is the Small Business Investment Company (SBIC). To assist small companies in overcoming their very real disadvantages in the capital markets, in 1958 Congress passed the Small Business Investment Company Act, which empowered the Small Business Administration (SBA) to license and regulate SBICs and to provide them with financial assistance. A minimum of $150,000 in private capital is required for the licensing of an SBIC, and this amount can be doubled by selling subordinated debentures to the SBA (at interest rates generally below those prevailing in the market).

In their operations, SBICs have followed two policies similar to those of investment development or venture capital companies: (1) Their investments are generally made by the purchase of convertible securities or bonds with warrants, thus giving the SBICs a residual equity position in the companies to which funds are provided. (2) SBICs emphasize management counsel, for which a fee is charged.[2]

If Stage 2 growth continues long enough, the firm will experience increasing pressures to add large amounts of equity capital, and its owners may desire to establish a market for their own personal stock holdings. At this point, a full assessment of the critical step in a firm's life—that of "going public"—must be made.

Going Public

Going public leads to four fundamental changes: (1) The firm moves from informal, personal control to a system of formal controls, and the need for financial techniques such as ratio analysis and the du Pont system of financial control greatly increases. (2) Information must be reported on a timely basis to the outside investors, even though the founders may continue to have majority control. (3) The firm must have a breadth of management in all areas if it is to operate its expanded business effectively. (4) The publicly owned firm typically draws on a board of directors to help formulate sound plans and policies; the board should include representatives of the public owners and other external interest groups to aid the management group in carrying out its broader responsibilities.

The valuation process is particularly important at the time the firm goes public: At what price will stock be sold to new outside investors? In analyzing the investment value of the small and growing firm, some significant differences in capital costs between large and small firms should be noted:

1. It is especially difficult to obtain reliable estimates of the cost of equity capital for small, privately owned firms.
2. Because of the risks involved, the required rate of return tends to be high for small firms. However, portfolio effects from a pooling of risks can reduce this factor somewhat for publicly owned small firms.
3. Tax considerations are generally quite important for privately owned companies that are large enough to consider going public, as the owner-managers are probably in the top personal tax brackets. This factor can cause the effective after-tax cost of retained earnings to be considerably lower than the after-tax cost of new outside equity.[3]
4. Flotation costs for new security issues, especially new stock issues, are much higher for small than for large firms. This factor, as well as the relatively high after-tax cost of new outside equity noted above in Item

---

[2] The larger SBICs have staffs similar to those of holding companies or conglomerates; these staffs provide assistance, for a fee, to the firms in which the SBICs have invested.

[3] See Appendix 15A.

3, causes the marginal cost of capital curve for small firms to rise rapidly once retained earnings have been exhausted.

5. The timing of the decision to go public is very important because the demand for new public offerings tends to change markedly over time. As a result, a new company with a given set of financial statements and prospects might be worth two or even three times as much in a strong market as in a weak one. For example, Apple Computer went public in December 1980, at a price of $22 per share, which represented a P/E ratio of 92 times. In 1975, when the new issue market was weak, it probably would have commanded a P/E ratio in the 10 to 20 range. Thus, the founders had to give up a far smaller share of the stock to raise new equity capital than they would have if the company had gone public a few years earlier.

Of course, the small firm is not always free to choose when it will go public. Companies often have a slight head start over their larger competitors—as Apple and Wang Labs (a leading word processor manufacturer) had over IBM and Xerox—and they must forge ahead rapidly or else watch the market they have developed be picked off by another firm. Clearly, large amounts of capital are needed to keep pace, and the company may not have the luxury of waiting for a strong market before going public.

Note also that equity infusions also make it easier and less expensive to raise debt capital. During periods of tight money and high interest rates, financial institutions, especially commercial banks, find that the quantity of funds demanded exceeds the supply available at "reasonable" rates. One important method employed to ration credit is to raise credit standards. At such times, both a stronger balance sheet and a longer and more stable profitability record are required in order to qualify for bank credit. Since financial ratios for small and growing firms tend to be less strong, such firms bear the brunt of credit restraint. Obviously, the small firm that goes public and raises equity capital before a money squeeze occurs is in a better position to ride out a tight money period. This firm has already raised some of its needed capital, and its equity cushion enables it to present a stronger picture to the banks, thus helping it to obtain additional capital in the form of debt.

Small Business Administration

It is clear that small firms face difficulties in obtaining capital, and in recognition of this fact, the federal government set up the Small Business Administration (SBA).[4] The SBA operates a number of different programs. One was discussed above in connection with the formation and growth of SBICs. Another, the Business Loan Program, provides funds

---

[4] The SBA also helps small companies obtain a fair share of government contracts, and it administers training programs of various types designed to help small entrepreneurs.

for construction, machinery, equipment, and working capital.[5] Loans under this program, which are available only when small businesses are unable to obtain funds on reasonable terms from private sources, are of two types: (1) direct loans and (2) participation loans. In a *direct loan*, the SBA simply makes a loan to a small business borrower. In a *participation loan*, the SBA lends part of the funds, while a bank or other private lending institution advances the balance. Under a participation loan, a portion of the funds advanced by the private party may be guaranteed by the SBA. The maximum amount the SBA may lend to any borrower is $350,000; this maximum applies to either a direct loan or the SBA's portion of a participation loan. Since SBA loans or guarantees are advantageous to the business recipient, the definition of what constitutes a small business is important. As noted earlier, the definition varies depending on the industry.[6]

The key factors in small business financing are summarized briefly in Table 24-1, which sets forth the financing patterns at the firm's four stages of development. In its formative stage, the new small firm must rely most heavily on personal savings, trade credit, and government agencies. During its period of rapid growth, internal financing will become an important source for meeting its financing requirements, although continued reliance will be placed on trade credit. At this stage, its record of accomplishment makes it possible to obtain bank credit to finance seasonal needs, and if the loan can be paid off on an amortized basis over two or three years, the firm may qualify for a term loan as well. If it has the potential for really strong growth, the firm may also be able to attract equity from a venture capital company.

A particularly successful firm may reach Stage 3, where going public becomes feasible. This leads to access to the broader money and capital markets, and it represents a true coming-of-age for the small firm. Even at this point, however, the firm must look ahead, analyzing its products

Financing Patterns

---

[5] In addition to the Business Loan Program, the SBA administers a number of other programs, including the following: (1) Equal Opportunity Loan Program, designed specifically for disadvantaged persons who wish to start or expand an existing business; (2) Development Company Loan Program, which is used to help attract businesses to geographic areas in need of economic stimulation; (3) Displaced Business Loan Program, designed to help small businesses that are forced to relocate because of urban renewal or similar events; (4) Disaster Loan Program, designed to aid both businesses and homeowners who suffer losses as a consequence of some natural disaster; (5) Lease Guarantee Program, designed to help small businesses obtain rental space in the commercial real estate market; (6) Revolving Line-of-Credit Program, designed to aid small building contractors; (7) Surety Bonding Program, designed to aid small business people who must post performance bonds when seeking contracts; and (8) Minority Enterprise SBIC Program, designed to stimulate SBICs whose clients are minority-owned firms.

[6] A great deal of additional information on the SBA and its various programs may be obtained directly from the Small Business Administration, Washington, D.C., or from regional SBA offices.

Table 24-1
Financing Patterns at Four Stages of a Firm's
Development

Stage	Financing Pattern
1. Formation	Personal savings, trade credit, government agencies
2. Rapid growth	Internal financing, trade credit, bank credit, venture capital
3. Growth to maturity	Going public, money and capital markets
4. Maturity and industry decline	Internal financing, share repurchase, diversification, mergers

and their prospects. Because every product has a life cycle, the firm must be aware that without the continuous development of new products, growth will cease, and eventually the firm will decline. Accordingly, as Stage 4 approaches, the firm must plan for the possibility of share repurchases, mergers, or other long-term strategies. The best time to do this is while the firm still has energy, momentum, and a high price/earnings ratio—in Stage 3.

Survey and Analysis of Small Business Financial Practices

As noted earlier in this chapter and also in Chapter 21, small businesses have a very high mortality rate, and the cause of their demise is usually management incompetence. In order to gain insights into the financial expertise of small business managers, and also to obtain data on the potential gains from operating at industry averages with regard to key financial ratios, Bernie Grablowsky and Dexter R. Rowell (GR) conducted a survey and analysis of small business firms in the Norfolk, Virginia, area.[7] They focused on cash, receivables, and inventory management, on capital budgeting, and on financing sources. Among their findings are the following:

1. Only 30 percent of the firms surveyed prepared a cash budget, and only 34 percent made a conscious effort to speed up cash collections and/or to slow disbursements.

2. Approximately 95 percent of the firms that sold on credit had no credit-checking procedure and, consequently, offered credit to anyone who asked for it. Also, only 52 percent enforced a late payment charge, while 34 percent did not even have a formal process for aging accounts receivable. As a result of this poor credit and receivables management, bad debts averaged a high 1.75 percent of sales and ranged up to 10 percent of sales for some firms whose management was particularly poor.

---

[7] Bernie Grablowsky and Dexter R. Rowell, *Small Business Financial Management: Theory and Practice* (Norfolk, Va.: Old Dominion University, 1980).

3. Although most of the respondents had over 30 percent of their capital invested in inventory, only 6 percent of them used a quantitative method such as EOQ for optimizing inventory, and 54 percent did not even employ an inventory control system that permitted them to generate information on inventory turnover, reorder points, ordering costs, or carrying costs.

4. Most of the small businesses in the sample did generally take discounts (69 percent), and many even borrowed to do so (51 percent). However, 22 percent of the firms apparently never took discounts, and a high 40 percent of the respondents were unaware of the true cost of not taking discounts, as they indicated that the cost of discounts foregone on terms of 2/10, net 30, is only 2 percent.

5. Over 50 percent of the respondents used no formal criteria such as NPV, IRR, or even payback to evaluate capital budgeting projects.

6. Equity came primarily from the owner's own account, and the only other source of significant amounts of long-term capital was the banking system. No planning of capital sources or efforts to tap other sources of long-term capital were observed in most of the firms.

Based on these findings, GR concluded (1) that "most small business managers are primarily involved with day-to-day survival of the firm" and (2) that these managers do not personally have the expertise to design and operate satisfactory planning and control systems.

Grablowsky and Rowell then addressed the question of whether or not it would pay the owners of small businesses to hire regular employees or consultants to help with planning and control. For this phase of their study, they examined the modified du Pont system as set forth in Chapter 6, Figure 6-4. On the assumption that the owner-managers of small businesses are interested in maximizing their firms' ROAs and ROEs, they demonstrated the improvements in these two target variables that would occur if the principal control variables (cash/sales, average collection period, and inventory turnover) were shifted from the poorest quartile of firms in the industry as reported by Dun & Bradstreet to the highest quartile. Some dramatic potential improvements were evident, especially in the area of accounts receivable management but also with respect to inventory and cash management. The data were not designed to provide information on how improvements in either capital budgeting or capital structure would have affected ROA and ROE, but one could hypothesize that the benefits would have been substantial.

Of course, GR recognized that costs would be incurred to install and operate better planning and control systems, and that economies of scale would make such expenditures more effective for the larger of the small firms. However, their general conclusion was that except possibly for the very smallest firms, the probable gains from expenditures on better financial management far exceeded their costs.

Summary

Our coverage of small business finance has focused on the formation and growth of the small firm, and on some of the special problems it faces in raising capital. We have not considered in detail the areas of working capital management, capital budgeting, leverage, or many other important topics. This omission is deliberate—these topics were all covered earlier in the book, and the principles and methods already discussed are applicable to large and small firms alike. Of course, there are economies of scale in the use of some of the more sophisticated techniques; hence it may not pay to apply them in a small firm. Also, there is less need for certain types of financial controls in the small firm—the owner-manager simply does not need to worry about the formal ways to insure coordination between different parts of the firm that are essential in a large, multiproduct, multiplant corporation. On the other hand, the small firm has less room for error, and the manager must have a broader range of expertise than any single executive in a large corporation.

Questions

24-1 Identify the four stages in a typical firm's life cycle, and describe the major sources of capital for firms in each stage.

24-2 What is a venture capital firm?

24-3 What tax provisions make investing in small business especially desirable for investors in high tax brackets?

24-4 Assume that your family owns a successful campground located close to a major interstate highway. You are considering affiliating with one of the national campground franchise organizations such as KOA. Discuss the pros and cons of such an affiliation. Might it be feasible for you to franchise others?

24-5 Would you expect the dividend policy of a "typical" small firm to be the same or different from that of a "typical" large firm? Explain.

24-6 Would you expect to find greater use of operating leverage in large or small firms? Explain.

Problem

24-1 Contact a small firm in your city. Identify the firm's strengths and weaknesses through a ratio analysis. Then report how the various topics covered in the book might be used to help the firm operate with maximum efficiency.

Cases

The following cases from Brigham et al., *Cases in Managerial Finance*, 4th edition (Hinsdale, Ill.: The Dryden Press, 1980) are especially recommended for use with Chapter 24: Rio Wood Products, Component Controls Corporation, and Cromwell Courts.

Selected References

Archer, S. H., and L. G. Faerber, "Firm Size and the Cost of Externally Secured Equity Capital," *Journal of Finance*, vol. 21 (March 1966), 69-83.

Brigham, E. F., and K. V. Smith, "The Cost of Capital to the Small Firm," *Engineering Economist*, Fall 1967, 1-26.

Casey, William J., *Chairman's Report of the SBA Task Force on Venture and Equity Capital for Small Business* (Washington, D.C.: U.S. Small Business Administration, January 1977), 1-21.

Financial Research Associates, *Financial Studies of the Small Business* (Arlington, Va.: Financial Research Associates, 1976).

Huntsman, Blaine, and James P. Hoban, Jr., "Investment in New Enterprise: Some Empirical Observations on Risk, Return, and Market Structure," *Financial Management,* vol. 9 (Summer 1980), 44-51.

Kellogg, Douglas E., "How to Buy a Small Manufacturing Business," *Harvard Business Review,* September-October 1975, 92-102.

Mukherjee, Tarun K., and Larry M. Austin, "An Empirical Investigation of Small Bank Stock Valuation and Dividend Policy," *Financial Management,* vol. 9 (Spring 1980), 27-31.

Rossiter, Bruce G., and Gene I. Miller, "Financing the New Enterprise," in *The Treasurer's Handbook,* edited by J. Fred Weston and Maurice B. Goudzwaard (Homewood, Ill.: Dow Jones-Irwin, 1976), 861-900.

Walker, Ernest W., ed., *The Dynamic Small Firm: Selected Readings* (Austin, Tex.: Austin Press, 1975).

Walker, Ernest W., and J. William Petty, II, "Financial Differences between Large and Small Firms," *Financial Management,* vol. 7 (Winter 1978), 61-68.

Appendix A
Mathematical Tables

Table A-1
Present Value of $1: $PVIF_{k,n} = 1/(1 + k)^n$

Period	1%	2%	3%	4%	5%	6%	7%	8%	9%	10%
1	.9901	.9804	.9709	.9615	.9524	.9434	.9346	.9259	.9174	.9091
2	.9803	.9612	.9426	.9246	.9070	.8900	.8734	.8573	.8417	.8264
3	.9706	.9423	.9151	.8890	.8638	.8396	.8163	.7938	.7722	.7513
4	.9610	.9238	.8885	.8548	.8227	.7921	.7629	.7350	.7084	.6830
5	.9515	.9057	.8626	.8219	.7835	.7473	.7130	.6806	.6499	.6209
6	.9420	.8880	.8375	.7903	.7462	.7050	.6663	.6302	.5963	.5645
7	.9327	.8706	.8131	.7599	.7107	.6651	.6227	.5835	.5470	.5132
8	.9235	.8535	.7894	.7307	.6768	.6274	.5820	.5403	.5019	.4665
9	.9143	.8368	.7664	.7026	.6446	.5919	.5439	.5002	.4604	.4241
10	.9053	.8203	.7441	.6756	.6139	.5584	.5083	.4632	.4224	.3855
11	.8963	.8043	.7224	.6496	.5847	.5268	.4751	.4289	.3875	.3505
12	.8874	.7885	.7014	.6246	.5568	.4970	.4440	.3971	.3555	.3186
13	.8787	.7730	.6810	.6006	.5303	.4688	.4150	.3677	.3262	.2897
14	.8700	.7579	.6611	.5775	.5051	.4423	.3878	.3405	.2992	.2633
15	.8613	.7430	.6419	.5553	.4810	.4173	.3624	.3152	.2745	.2394
16	.8528	.7284	.6232	.5339	.4581	.3936	.3387	.2919	.2519	.2176
17	.8444	.7142	.6050	.5134	.4363	.3714	.3166	.2703	.2311	.1978
18	.8360	.7002	.5874	.4936	.4155	.3503	.2959	.2502	.2120	.1799
19	.8277	.6864	.5703	.4746	.3957	.3305	.2765	.2317	.1945	.1635
20	.8195	.6730	.5537	.4564	.3769	.3118	.2584	.2145	.1784	.1486
21	.8114	.6598	.5375	.4388	.3589	.2942	.2415	.1987	.1637	.1351
22	.8034	.6468	.5219	.4220	.3418	.2775	.2257	.1839	.1502	.1228
23	.7954	.6342	.5067	.4057	.3256	.2618	.2109	.1703	.1378	.1117
24	.7876	.6217	.4919	.3901	.3101	.2470	.1971	.1577	.1264	.1015
25	.7798	.6095	.4776	.3751	.2953	.2330	.1842	.1460	.1160	.0923
26	.7720	.5976	.4637	.3607	.2812	.2198	.1722	.1352	.1064	.0839
27	.7644	.5859	.4502	.3468	.2678	.2074	.1609	.1252	.0976	.0763
28	.7568	.5744	.4371	.3335	.2551	.1956	.1504	.1159	.0895	.0693
29	.7493	.5631	.4243	.3207	.2429	.1846	.1406	.1073	.0822	.0630
30	.7419	.5521	.4120	.3083	.2314	.1741	.1314	.0994	.0754	.0573
35	.7059	.5000	.3554	.2534	.1813	.1301	.0937	.0676	.0490	.0356
40	.6717	.4529	.3066	.2083	.1420	.0972	.0668	.0460	.0318	.0221
45	.6391	.4102	.2644	.1712	.1113	.0727	.0476	.0313	.0207	.0137
50	.6080	.3715	.2281	.1407	.0872	.0543	.0339	.0213	.0134	.0085
55	.5785	.3365	.1968	.1157	.0683	.0406	.0242	.0145	.0087	.0053

Table A-1
(continued)

Period	12%	14%	15%	16%	18%	20%	24%	28%	32%	36%
1	.8929	.8772	.8696	.8621	.8475	.8333	.8065	.7813	.7576	.7353
2	.7972	.7695	.7561	.7432	.7182	.6944	.6504	.6104	.5739	.5407
3	.7118	.6750	.6575	.6407	.6086	.5787	.5245	.4768	.4348	.3975
4	.6355	.5921	.5718	.5523	.5158	.4823	.4230	.3725	.3294	.2923
5	.5674	.5194	.4972	.4761	.4371	.4019	.3411	.2910	.2495	.2149
6	.5066	.4556	.4323	.4104	.3704	.3349	.2751	.2274	.1890	.1580
7	.4523	.3996	.3759	.3538	.3139	.2791	.2218	.1776	.1432	.1162
8	.4039	.3506	.3269	.3050	.2660	.2326	.1789	.1388	.1085	.0854
9	.3606	.3075	.2843	.2630	.2255	.1938	.1443	.1084	.0822	.0628
10	.3220	.2697	.2472	.2267	.1911	.1615	.1164	.0847	.0623	.0462
11	.2875	.2366	.2149	.1954	.1619	.1346	.0938	.0662	.0472	.0340
12	.2567	.2076	.1869	.1685	.1372	.1122	.0757	.0517	.0357	.0250
13	.2292	.1821	.1625	.1452	.1163	.0935	.0610	.0404	.0271	.0184
14	.2046	.1597	.1413	.1252	.0985	.0779	.0492	.0316	.0205	.0135
15	.1827	.1401	.1229	.1079	.0835	.0649	.0397	.0247	.0155	.0099
16	.1631	.1229	.1069	.0930	.0708	.0541	.0320	.0193	.0118	.0073
17	.1456	.1078	.0929	.0802	.0600	.0451	.0258	.0150	.0089	.0054
18	.1300	.0946	.0808	.0691	.0508	.0376	.0208	.0118	.0068	.0039
19	.1161	.0829	.0703	.0596	.0431	.0313	.0168	.0092	.0051	.0029
20	.1037	.0728	.0611	.0514	.0365	.0261	.0135	.0072	.0039	.0021
21	.0926	.0638	.0531	.0443	.0309	.0217	.0109	.0056	.0029	.0016
22	.0826	.0560	.0462	.0382	.0262	.0181	.0088	.0044	.0022	.0012
23	.0738	.0491	.0402	.0329	.0222	.0151	.0071	.0034	.0017	.0008
24	.0659	.0431	.0349	.0284	.0188	.0126	.0057	.0027	.0013	.0006
25	.0588	.0378	.0304	.0245	.0160	.0105	.0046	.0021	.0010	.0005
26	.0525	.0331	.0264	.0211	.0135	.0087	.0037	.0016	.0007	.0003
27	.0469	.0291	.0230	.0182	.0115	.0073	.0030	.0013	.0006	.0002
28	.0419	.0255	.0200	.0157	.0097	.0061	.0024	.0010	.0004	.0002
29	.0374	.0224	.0174	.0135	.0082	.0051	.0020	.0008	.0003	.0001
30	.0334	.0196	.0151	.0116	.0070	.0042	.0016	.0006	.0002	.0001
35	.0189	.0102	.0075	.0055	.0030	.0017	.0005	.0002	.0001	*
40	.0107	.0053	.0037	.0026	.0013	.0007	.0002	.0001	*	*
45	.0061	.0027	.0019	.0013	.0006	.0003	.0001	*	*	*
50	.0035	.0014	.0009	.0006	.0003	.0001	*	*	*	*
55	.0020	.0007	.0005	.0003	.0001	*	*	*	*	*

*The factor is zero to four decimal places.

Mathematical Tables

Table A-2
Present Value of an Annuity of $1 per Period for *n* Periods: $PVIFA_{k,n} = \sum_{t=1}^{n} \dfrac{1}{(1+k)^t}$

$$= \dfrac{1 - \dfrac{1}{(1+k)^n}}{k}$$

Number of Payments	1%	2%	3%	4%	5%	6%	7%	8%	9%
1	0.9901	0.9804	0.9709	0.9615	0.9524	0.9434	0.9346	0.9259	0.9174
2	1.9704	1.9416	1.9135	1.8861	1.8594	1.8334	1.8080	1.7833	1.7591
3	2.9410	2.8839	2.8286	2.7751	2.7232	2.6730	2.6243	2.5771	2.5313
4	3.9020	3.8077	3.7171	3.6299	3.5460	3.4651	3.3872	3.3121	3.2397
5	4.8534	4.7135	4.5797	4.4518	4.3295	4.2124	4.1002	3.9927	3.8897
6	5.7955	5.6014	5.4172	5.2421	5.0757	4.9173	4.7665	4.6229	4.4859
7	6.7282	6.4720	6.2303	6.0021	5.7864	5.5824	5.3893	5.2064	5.0330
8	7.6517	7.3255	7.0197	6.7327	6.4632	6.2098	5.9713	5.7466	5.5348
9	8.5660	8.1622	7.7861	7.4353	7.1078	6.8017	6.5152	6.2469	5.9952
10	9.4713	8.9826	8.5302	8.1109	7.7217	7.3601	7.0236	6.7101	6.4177
11	10.3676	9.7868	9.2526	8.7605	8.3064	7.8869	7.4987	7.1390	6.8052
12	11.2551	10.5753	9.9540	9.3851	8.8633	8.3838	7.9427	7.5361	7.1607
13	12.1337	11.3484	10.6350	9.9856	9.3936	8.8527	8.3577	7.9038	7.4869
14	13.0037	12.1062	11.2961	10.5631	9.8986	9.2950	8.7455	8.2442	7.7862
15	13.8651	12.8493	11.9379	11.1184	10.3797	9.7122	9.1079	8.5595	8.0607
16	14.7179	13.5777	12.5611	11.6523	10.8378	10.1059	9.4466	8.8514	8.3126
17	15.5623	14.2919	13.1661	12.1657	11.2741	10.4773	9.7632	9.1216	8.5436
18	16.3983	14.9920	13.7535	12.6593	11.6896	10.8276	10.0591	9.3719	8.7556
19	17.2260	15.6785	14.3238	13.1339	12.0853	11.1581	10.3356	9.6036	8.9501
20	18.0456	16.3514	14.8775	13.5903	12.4622	11.4699	10.5940	9.8181	9.1285
21	18.8570	17.0112	15.4150	14.0292	12.8212	11.7641	10.8355	10.0168	9.2922
22	19.6604	17.6580	15.9369	14.4511	13.1630	12.0416	11.0612	10.2007	9.4424
23	20.4558	18.2922	16.4436	14.8568	13.4886	12.3034	11.2722	10.3711	9.5802
24	21.2434	18.9139	16.9355	15.2470	13.7986	12.5504	11.4693	10.5288	9.7066
25	22.0232	19.5235	17.4131	15.6221	14.0939	12.7834	11.6536	10.6748	9.8226
26	22.7952	20.1210	17.8768	15.9828	14.3752	13.0032	11.8258	10.8100	9.9290
27	23.5596	20.7069	18.3270	16.3296	14.6430	13.2105	11.9867	10.9352	10.0266
28	24.3164	21.2813	18.7641	16.6631	14.8981	13.4062	12.1371	11.0511	10.1161
29	25.0658	21.8444	19.1885	16.9837	15.1411	13.5907	12.2777	11.1584	10.1983
30	25.8077	22.3965	19.6004	17.2920	15.3725	13.7648	12.4090	11.2578	10.2737
35	29.4086	24.9986	21.4872	18.6646	16.3742	14.4982	12.9477	11.6546	10.5668
40	32.8347	27.3555	23.1148	19.7928	17.1591	15.0463	13.3317	11.9246	10.7574
45	36.0945	29.4902	24.5187	20.7200	17.7741	15.4558	13.6055	12.1084	10.8812
50	39.1961	31.4236	25.7298	21.4822	18.2559	15.7619	13.8007	12.2335	10.9617
55	42.1472	33.1748	26.7744	22.1086	18.6335	15.9905	13.9399	12.3186	11.0140

Table A-2
(continued)

Number of Payments	10%	12%	14%	15%	16%	18%	20%	24%	28%	32%
1	0.9091	0.8929	0.8772	0.8696	0.8621	0.8475	0.8333	0.8065	0.7813	0.7576
2	1.7355	1.6901	1.6467	1.6257	1.6052	1.5656	1.5278	1.4568	1.3916	1.3315
3	2.4869	2.4018	2.3216	2.2832	2.2459	2.1743	2.1065	1.9813	1.8684	1.7663
4	3.1699	3.0373	2.9137	2.8550	2.7982	2.6901	2.5887	2.4043	2.2410	2.0957
5	3.7908	3.6048	3.4331	3.3522	3.2743	3.1272	2.9906	2.7454	2.5320	2.3452
6	4.3553	4.1114	3.8887	3.7845	3.6847	3.4976	3.3255	3.0205	2.7594	2.5342
7	4.8684	4.5638	4.2883	4.1604	4.0386	3.8115	3.6046	3.2423	2.9370	2.6775
8	5.3349	4.9676	4.6389	4.4873	4.3436	4.0776	3.8372	3.4212	3.0758	2.7860
9	5.7590	5.3282	4.9464	4.7716	4.6065	4.3030	4.0310	3.5655	3.1842	2.8681
10	6.1446	5.6502	5.2161	5.0188	4.8332	4.4941	4.1925	3.6819	3.2689	2.9304
11	6.4951	5.9377	5.4527	5.2337	5.0286	4.6560	4.3271	3.7757	3.3351	2.9776
12	6.8137	6.1944	5.6603	5.4206	5.1971	4.7932	4.4392	3.8514	3.3868	3.0133
13	7.1034	6.4235	5.8424	5.5831	5.3423	4.9095	4.5327	3.9124	3.4272	3.0404
14	7.3667	6.6282	6.0021	5.7245	5.4675	5.0081	4.6106	3.9616	3.4587	3.0609
15	7.6061	6.8109	6.1422	5.8474	5.5755	5.0916	4.6755	4.0013	3.4834	3.0764
16	7.8237	6.9740	6.2651	5.9542	5.6685	5.1624	4.7296	4.0333	3.5026	3.0882
17	8.0216	7.1196	6.3729	6.0472	5.7487	5.2223	4.7746	4.0591	3.5177	3.0971
18	8.2014	7.2497	6.4674	6.1280	5.8178	5.2732	4.8122	4.0799	3.5294	3.1039
19	8.3649	7.3658	6.5504	6.1982	5.8775	5.3162	4.8435	4.0967	3.5386	3.1090
20	8.5136	7.4694	6.6231	6.2593	5.9288	5.3527	4.8696	4.1103	3.5458	3.1129
21	8.6487	7.5620	6.6870	6.3125	5.9731	5.3837	4.8913	4.1212	3.5514	3.1158
22	8.7715	7.6446	6.7429	6.3587	6.0113	5.4099	4.9094	4.1300	3.5558	3.1180
23	8.8832	7.7184	6.7921	6.3988	6.0442	5.4321	4.9245	4.1371	3.5592	3.1197
24	8.9847	7.7843	6.8351	6.4338	6.0726	5.4510	4.9371	4.1428	3.5619	3.1210
25	9.0770	7.8431	6.8729	6.4642	6.0971	5.4669	4.9476	4.1474	3.5640	3.1220
26	9.1609	7.8957	6.9061	6.4906	6.1182	5.4804	4.9563	4.1511	3.5656	3.1227
27	9.2372	7.9426	6.9352	6.5135	6.1364	5.4919	4.9636	4.1542	3.5669	3.1233
28	9.3066	7.9844	6.9607	6.5335	6.1520	5.5016	4.9697	4.1566	3.5679	3.1237
29	9.3696	8.0218	6.9830	6.5509	6.1656	5.5098	4.9747	4.1585	3.5687	3.1240
30	9.4269	8.0552	7.0027	6.5660	6.1772	5.5168	4.9789	4.1601	3.5693	3.1242
35	9.6442	8.1755	7.0700	6.6166	6.2153	5.5386	4.9915	4.1644	3.5708	3.1248
40	9.7791	8.2438	7.1050	6.6418	6.2335	5.5482	4.9966	4.1659	3.5712	3.1250
45	9.8628	8.2825	7.1232	6.6543	6.2421	5.5523	4.9986	4.1664	3.5714	3.1250
50	9.9148	8.3045	7.1327	6.6605	6.2463	5.5541	4.9995	4.1666	3.5714	3.1250
55	9.9471	8.3170	7.1376	6.6636	6.2482	5.5549	4.9998	4.1666	3.5714	3.1250

Table A-3
Future Value of \$1 at the End of n Periods: $FVIF_{k,n} = (1 + k)^n$

Period	1%	2%	3%	4%	5%	6%	7%	8%	9%	10%
1	1.0100	1.0200	1.0300	1.0400	1.0500	1.0600	1.0700	1.0800	1.0900	1.1000
2	1.0201	1.0404	1.0609	1.0816	1.1025	1.1236	1.1449	1.1664	1.1881	1.2100
3	1.0303	1.0612	1.0927	1.1249	1.1576	1.1910	1.2250	1.2597	1.2950	1.3310
4	1.0406	1.0824	1.1255	1.1699	1.2155	1.2625	1.3108	1.3605	1.4116	1.4641
5	1.0510	1.1041	1.1593	1.2167	1.2763	1.3382	1.4026	1.4693	1.5386	1.6105
6	1.0615	1.1262	1.1941	1.2653	1.3401	1.4185	1.5007	1.5869	1.6771	1.7716
7	1.0721	1.1487	1.2299	1.3159	1.4071	1.5036	1.6058	1.7138	1.8280	1.9487
8	1.0829	1.1717	1.2668	1.3686	1.4775	1.5938	1.7182	1.8509	1.9926	2.1436
9	1.0937	1.1951	1.3048	1.4233	1.5513	1.6895	1.8385	1.9990	2.1719	2.3579
10	1.1046	1.2190	1.3439	1.4802	1.6289	1.7908	1.9672	2.1589	2.3674	2.5937
11	1.1157	1.2434	1.3842	1.5395	1.7103	1.8983	2.1049	2.3316	2.5804	2.8531
12	1.1268	1.2682	1.4258	1.6010	1.7959	2.0122	2.2522	2.5182	2.8127	3.1384
13	1.1381	1.2936	1.4685	1.6651	1.8856	2.1329	2.4098	2.7196	3.0658	3.4523
14	1.1495	1.3195	1.5126	1.7317	1.9799	2.2609	2.5785	2.9372	3.3417	3.7975
15	1.1610	1.3459	1.5580	1.8009	2.0789	2.3966	2.7590	3.1722	3.6425	4.1772
16	1.1726	1.3728	1.6047	1.8730	2.1829	2.5404	2.9522	3.4259	3.9703	4.5950
17	1.1843	1.4002	1.6528	1.9479	2.2920	2.6928	3.1588	3.7000	4.3276	5.0545
18	1.1961	1.4282	1.7024	2.0258	2.4066	2.8543	3.3799	3.9960	4.7171	5.5599
19	1.2081	1.4568	1.7535	2.1068	2.5270	3.0256	3.6165	4.3157	5.1417	6.1159
20	1.2202	1.4859	1.8061	2.1911	2.6533	3.2071	3.8697	4.6610	5.6044	6.7275
21	1.2324	1.5157	1.8603	2.2788	2.7860	3.3996	4.1406	5.0338	6.1088	7.4002
22	1.2447	1.5460	1.9161	2.3699	2.9253	3.6035	4.4304	5.4365	6.6586	8.1403
23	1.2572	1.5769	1.9736	2.4647	3.0715	3.8197	4.7405	5.8715	7.2579	8.9543
24	1.2697	1.6084	2.0328	2.5633	3.2251	4.0489	5.0724	6.3412	7.9111	9.8497
25	1.2824	1.6406	2.0938	2.6658	3.3864	4.2919	5.4274	6.8485	8.6231	10.834
26	1.2953	1.6734	2.1566	2.7725	3.5557	4.5494	5.8074	7.3964	9.3992	11.918
27	1.3082	1.7069	2.2213	2.8834	3.7335	4.8223	6.2139	7.9881	10.245	13.110
28	1.3213	1.7410	2.2879	2.9987	3.9201	5.1117	6.6488	8.6271	11.167	14.421
29	1.3345	1.7758	2.3566	3.1187	4.1161	5.4184	7.1143	9.3173	12.172	15.863
30	1.3478	1.8114	2.4273	3.2434	4.3219	5.7435	7.6123	10.062	13.267	17.449
40	1.4889	2.2080	3.2620	4.8010	7.0400	10.285	14.974	21.724	31.409	45.259
50	1.6446	2.6916	4.3839	7.1067	11.467	18.420	29.457	46.901	74.357	117.39
60	1.8167	3.2810	5.8916	10.519	18.679	32.987	57.946	101.25	176.03	304.48

Table A-3
(continued)

Period	12%	14%	15%	16%	18%	20%	24%	28%	32%	36%
1	1.1200	1.1400	1.1500	1.1600	1.1800	1.2000	1.2400	1.2800	1.3200	1.3600
2	1.2544	1.2996	1.3225	1.3456	1.3924	1.4400	1.5376	1.6384	1.7424	1.8496
3	1.4049	1.4815	1.5209	1.5609	1.6430	1.7280	1.9066	2.0972	2.3000	2.5155
4	1.5735	1.6890	1.7490	1.8106	1.9388	2.0736	2.3642	2.6844	3.0360	3.4210
5	1.7623	1.9254	2.0114	2.1003	2.2878	2.4883	2.9316	3.4360	4.0075	4.6526
6	1.9738	2.1950	2.3131	2.4364	2.6996	2.9860	3.6352	4.3980	5.2899	6.3275
7	2.2107	2.5023	2.6600	2.8262	3.1855	3.5832	4.5077	5.6295	6.9826	8.6054
8	2.4760	2.8526	3.0590	3.2784	3.7589	4.2998	5.5895	7.2058	9.2170	11.703
9	2.7731	3.2519	3.5179	3.8030	4.4355	5.1598	6.9310	9.2234	12.166	15.916
10	3.1058	3.7072	4.0456	4.4114	5.2338	6.1917	8.5944	11.805	16.059	21.646
11	3.4785	4.2262	4.6524	5.1173	6.1759	7.4301	10.657	15.111	21.198	29.439
12	3.8960	4.8179	5.3502	5.9360	7.2876	8.9161	13.214	19.342	27.982	40.037
13	4.3635	5.4924	6.1528	6.8858	8.5994	10.699	16.386	24.758	36.937	54.451
14	4.8871	6.2613	7.0757	7.9875	10.147	12.839	20.319	31.691	48.756	74.053
15	5.4736	7.1379	8.1371	9.2655	11.973	15.407	25.195	40.564	64.358	100.71
16	6.1304	8.1372	9.3576	10.748	14.129	18.488	31.242	51.923	84.953	136.96
17	6.8660	9.2765	10.761	12.467	16.672	22.186	38.740	66.461	112.13	186.27
18	7.6900	10.575	12.375	14.462	19.673	26.623	48.038	85.070	148.02	253.33
19	8.6128	12.055	14.231	16.776	23.214	31.948	59.567	108.89	195.39	344.53
20	9.6463	13.743	16.366	19.460	27.393	38.337	73.864	139.37	257.91	468.57
21	10.803	15.667	18.821	22.574	32.323	46.005	91.591	178.40	340.44	637.26
22	12.100	17.861	21.644	26.186	38.142	55.206	113.57	228.35	449.39	866.67
23	13.552	20.361	24.891	30.376	45.007	66.247	140.83	292.30	593.19	1178.6
24	15.178	23.212	28.625	35.236	53.108	79.496	174.63	374.14	783.02	1602.9
25	17.000	26.461	32.918	40.874	62.668	95.396	216.54	478.90	1033.5	2180.0
26	19.040	30.166	37.856	47.414	73.948	114.47	268.51	612.99	1364.3	2964.9
27	21.324	34.389	43.535	55.000	87.259	137.37	332.95	784.63	1800.9	4032.2
28	23.883	39.204	50.065	63.800	102.96	164.84	412.86	1004.3	2377.2	5483.8
29	26.749	44.693	57.575	74.008	121.50	197.81	511.95	1285.5	3137.9	7458.0
30	29.959	50.950	66.211	85.849	143.37	237.37	634.81	1645.5	4142.0	10143.
40	93.050	188.88	267.86	378.72	750.37	1469.7	5455.9	19426.	66520.	*
50	289.00	700.23	1083.6	1670.7	3927.3	9100.4	46890.	*	*	*
60	897.59	2595.9	4383.9	7370.1	20555.	56347.	*	*	*	*

*FVIF > 99,999.

Table A-4
Sum of an Annuity of $1 per Period for n Periods: $FVIFA_{k,n} = \sum_{t=1}^{n} (1 + k)^{n-t}$

$$= \frac{(1 + k)^n - 1}{k}$$

Number of Periods	1%	2%	3%	4%	5%	6%	7%	8%	9%	10%
1	1.0000	1.0000	1.0000	1.0000	1.0000	1.0000	1.0000	1.0000	1.0000	1.0000
2	2.0100	2.0200	2.0300	2.0400	2.0500	2.0600	2.0700	2.0800	2.0900	2.1000
3	3.0301	3.0604	3.0909	3.1216	3.1525	3.1836	3.2149	3.2464	3.2781	3.3100
4	4.0604	4.1216	4.1836	4.2465	4.3101	4.3746	4.4399	4.5061	4.5731	4.6410
5	5.1010	5.2040	5.3091	5.4163	5.5256	5.6371	5.7507	5.8666	5.9847	6.1051
6	6.1520	6.3081	6.4684	6.6330	6.8019	6.9753	7.1533	7.3359	7.5233	7.7156
7	7.2135	7.4343	7.6625	7.8983	8.1420	8.3938	8.6540	8.9228	9.2004	9.4872
8	8.2857	8.5830	8.8923	9.2142	9.5491	9.8975	10.259	10.636	11.028	11.435
9	9.3685	9.7546	10.159	10.582	11.026	11.491	11.978	12.487	13.021	13.579
10	10.462	10.949	11.463	12.006	12.577	13.180	13.816	14.486	15.192	15.937
11	11.566	12.168	12.807	13.486	14.206	14.971	15.783	16.645	17.560	18.531
12	12.682	13.412	14.192	15.025	15.917	16.869	17.888	18.977	20.140	21.384
13	13.809	14.680	15.617	16.626	17.713	18.882	20.140	21.495	22.953	24.522
14	14.947	15.973	17.086	18.291	19.598	21.015	22.550	24.214	26.019	27.975
15	16.096	17.293	18.598	20.023	21.578	23.276	25.129	27.152	29.360	31.772
16	17.257	18.639	20.156	21.824	23.657	25.672	27.888	30.324	33.003	35.949
17	18.430	20.012	21.761	23.697	25.840	28.212	30.840	33.750	36.973	40.544
18	19.614	21.412	23.414	25.645	28.132	30.905	33.999	37.450	41.301	45.599
19	20.810	22.840	25.116	27.671	30.539	33.760	37.379	41.446	46.018	51.159
20	22.019	24.297	26.870	29.778	33.066	36.785	40.995	45.762	51.160	57.275
21	23.239	25.783	28.676	31.969	35.719	39.992	44.865	50.422	56.764	64.002
22	24.471	27.299	30.536	34.248	38.505	43.392	49.005	55.456	62.873	71.402
23	25.716	28.845	32.452	36.617	41.430	46.995	53.436	60.893	69.531	79.543
24	26.973	30.421	34.426	39.082	44.502	50.815	58.176	66.764	76.789	88.497
25	28.243	32.030	36.459	41.645	47.727	54.864	63.249	73.105	84.700	98.347
26	29.525	33.670	38.553	44.311	51.113	59.156	68.676	79.954	93.323	109.18
27	30.820	35.344	40.709	47.084	54.669	63.705	74.483	87.350	102.72	121.09
28	32.129	37.051	42.930	49.967	58.402	68.528	80.697	95.338	112.96	134.20
29	33.450	38.792	45.218	52.966	62.322	73.639	87.346	103.96	124.13	148.63
30	34.784	40.568	47.575	56.084	66.438	79.058	94.460	113.28	136.30	164.49
40	48.886	60.402	75.401	95.025	120.79	154.76	199.63	259.05	337.88	442.59
50	64.463	84.579	112.79	152.66	209.34	290.33	406.52	573.76	815.08	1163.9
60	81.669	114.05	163.05	237.99	353.58	533.12	813.52	1253.2	1944.7	3034.8

Table A-4
(continued)

Number of Periods	12%	14%	15%	16%	18%	20%	24%	28%	32%	36%
1	1.0000	1.0000	1.0000	1.0000	1.0000	1.0000	1.0000	1.0000	1.0000	1.0000
2	2.1200	2.1400	2.1500	2.1600	2.1800	2.2000	2.2400	2.2800	2.3200	2.3600
3	3.3744	3.4396	3.4725	3.5056	3.5724	3.6400	3.7776	3.9184	4.0624	4.2096
4	4.7793	4.9211	4.9934	5.0665	5.2154	5.3680	5.6842	6.0156	6.3624	6.7251
5	6.3528	6.6101	6.7424	6.8771	7.1542	7.4416	8.0484	8.6999	9.3983	10.146
6	8.1152	8.5355	8.7537	8.9775	9.4420	9.9299	10.980	12.135	13.405	14.798
7	10.089	10.730	11.066	11.413	12.141	12.915	14.615	16.533	18.695	21.126
8	12.299	13.232	13.726	14.240	15.327	16.499	19.122	22.163	25.678	29.731
9	14.775	16.085	16.785	17.518	19.085	20.798	24.712	29.369	34.895	41.435
10	17.548	19.337	20.303	21.321	23.521	25.958	31.643	38.592	47.061	57.351
11	20.654	23.044	24.349	25.732	28.755	32.150	40.237	50.398	63.121	78.998
12	24.133	27.270	29.001	30.850	34.931	39.580	50.894	65.510	84.320	108.43
13	28.029	32.088	34.351	36.786	42.218	48.496	64.109	84.852	112.30	148.47
14	32.392	37.581	40.504	43.672	50.818	59.195	80.496	109.61	149.23	202.92
15	37.279	43.842	47.580	51.659	60.965	72.035	100.81	141.30	197.99	276.97
16	42.753	50.980	55.717	60.925	72.939	87.442	126.01	181.86	262.35	377.69
17	48.883	59.117	65.075	71.673	87.068	105.93	157.25	233.79	347.30	514.66
18	55.749	68.394	75.836	84.140	103.74	128.11	195.99	300.25	459.44	700.93
19	63.439	78.969	88.211	98.603	123.41	154.74	244.03	385.32	607.47	954.27
20	72.052	91.024	102.44	115.37	146.62	186.68	303.60	494.21	802.86	1298.8
21	81.698	104.76	118.81	134.84	174.02	225.02	377.46	633.59	1060.7	1767.3
22	92.502	120.43	137.63	157.41	206.34	271.03	469.05	811.99	1401.2	2404.6
23	104.60	138.29	159.27	183.60	244.48	326.23	582.62	1040.3	1850.6	3271.3
24	118.15	158.65	184.16	213.97	289.49	392.48	723.46	1332.6	2443.8	4449.9
25	133.33	181.87	212.79	249.21	342.60	471.98	898.09	1706.8	3226.8	6052.9
26	150.33	208.33	245.71	290.08	405.27	567.37	1114.6	2185.7	4260.4	8233.0
27	169.37	238.49	283.56	337.50	479.22	681.85	1383.1	2798.7	5624.7	11197.9
28	190.69	272.88	327.10	392.50	566.48	819.22	1716.0	3583.3	7425.6	15230.2
29	214.58	312.09	377.16	456.30	669.44	984.06	2128.9	4587.6	9802.9	20714.1
30	241.33	356.78	434.74	530.31	790.94	1181.8	2640.9	5873.2	12940.	28172.2
40	767.09	1342.0	1779.0	2360.7	4163.2	7343.8	22728.	69377.	*	*
50	2400.0	4994.5	7217.7	10435.	21813.	45497.	*	*	*	*
60	7471.6	18535.	29219.	46057.	*	*	*	*	*	*

*FVIFA > 99,999.

Table A-5
Values of the Standard Normal Distribution Function

z	0.00	0.01	0.02	0.03	0.04	0.05	0.06	0.07	0.08	0.09
0.0	.0000	.0040	.0080	.0120	.0160	.0199	.0239	.0279	.0319	.0359
0.1	.0398	.0438	.0478	.0517	.0557	.0596	.0636	.0675	.0714	.0753
0.2	.0793	.0832	.0871	.0910	.0948	.0987	.1026	.1064	.1103	.1141
0.3	.1179	.1217	.1255	.1293	.1331	.1368	.1406	.1443	.1480	.1517
0.4	.1554	.1591	.1628	.1664	.1700	.1736	.1772	.1808	.1844	.1879
0.5	.1915	.1950	.1985	.2019	.2054	.2088	.2123	.2157	.2190	.2224
0.6	.2257	.2291	.2324	.2357	.2389	.2422	.2454	.2486	.2517	.2549
0.7	.2580	.2611	.2642	.2673	.2704	.2734	.2764	.2794	.2823	.2852
0.8	.2881	.2910	.2939	.2967	.2995	.3023	.3051	.3078	.3106	.3133
0.9	.3159	.3186	.3212	.3238	.3264	.3289	.3315	.3340	.3365	.3389
1.0	.3413	.3438	.3461	.3485	.3508	.3531	.3554	.3577	.3599	.3621
1.1	.3643	.3665	.3686	.3708	.3729	.3749	.3770	.3790	.3810	.3830
1.2	.3849	.3869	.3888	.3907	.3925	.3944	.3962	.3980	.3997	.4015
1.3	.4032	.4049	.4066	.4082	.4099	.4115	.4131	.4147	.4162	.4177
1.4	.4192	.4207	.4222	.4236	.4251	.4265	.4279	.4292	.4306	.4319
1.5	.4332	.4345	.4357	.4370	.4382	.4394	.4406	.4418	.4429	.4441
1.6	.4452	.4463	.4474	.4484	.4495	.4505	.4515	.4525	.4535	.4545
1.7	.4554	.4564	.4573	.4582	.4591	.4599	.4608	.4616	.4625	.4633
1.8	.4641	.4649	.4656	.4664	.4671	.4678	.4686	.4693	.4699	.4706
1.9	.4713	.4719	.4726	.4732	.4738	.4744	.4750	.4756	.4761	.4767
2.0	.4773	.4778	.4783	.4788	.4793	.4798	.4803	.4808	.4812	.4817
2.1	.4821	.4826	.4830	.4834	.4838	.4842	.4846	.4850	.4854	.4857
2.2	.4861	.4864	.4868	.4871	.4875	.4878	.4881	.4884	.4887	.4890
2.3	.4893	.4896	.4898	.4901	.4904	.4906	.4909	.4911	.4913	.4916
2.4	.4918	.4920	.4922	.4925	.4927	.4929	.4931	.4932	.4934	.4936
2.5	.4938	.4940	.4941	.4943	.4945	.4946	.4948	.4949	.4951	.4952
2.6	.4953	.4955	.4956	.4957	.4959	.4960	.4961	.4962	.4963	.4964
2.7	.4965	.4966	.4967	.4968	.4969	.4970	.4971	.4972	.4973	.4974
2.8	.4974	.4975	.4976	.4977	.4977	.4978	.4979	.4979	.4980	.4981
2.9	.4981	.4982	.4982	.4982	.4984	.4984	.4985	.4985	.4986	.4986
3.0	.4987	.4987	.4987	.4988	.4988	.4989	.4989	.4989	.4990	.4990

z is the number of standard deviations from the mean. Some area tables are set up to indicate the area to the left or right of the point of interest; in this book we indicate the area between the mean and the point of interest.

Appendix B

We present here some of the intermediate steps and final answers to selected end-of-chapter problems. These are provided to aid the student in determining whether he or she is on the right track in the solution process. The primary limitation of this approach is that some of the problems may have *more than one* correct solution, depending upon which of several equally appropriate assumptions are made in the solution. Furthermore, there are often differences in answers due to rounding errors or other computational considerations. Many of the problems involve some verbal discussion as well as numerical calculations. This verbal material is *not* presented here.

2-1	$68,150.
2-2	a. $72,750; b. $9,200; c. $1,380.
2A-1	Expected rate on 1-year bills one year from now = 6.86%.
2A-2	a. 8.375%; c. 2-year bond rate = 12.995%, 10-year bond rate = 9.181%.
2A-3	Approximately 6%.
3-2	a. $325.78; c. $122.78.
3-3	a. 7 years; b. 5 years.
3-5	a. $1,228.92; c. $1,000.
3-8	Approximately 15%.
3-10	c. 5%; d. 9%.
3-14	9%.
3-15	a. $23,184.70.
3-16	b. $273.72; d. $225.36.
3-17	b. $145.68.
3-22	a. $54,732; b. $2,769.
3-23	$2,827.
3-24	a. $763,709; c. $59,427.
3A-1	a. $28,803; c-1. 10.25%; c-2. 10.52%.
4-1	a-2. $1,080.57; b-3. $982.19.
4-2	a-1. Approximately 8%.
4-3	a. $1,233.04; b. $905.50.
4-4	a. D_3 = $1.16; b. $2.74; d. $21.00.
4-5	b. 5%.
4-6	a-1. $4.52; a-3. $9.55.
4-7	c. $852.41; f-1. 5.23%.
4-8	$21.60.

4-10   a. $P_0 = \$36.46$; Dividend yield $= 6.86\%$; Capital gains yield $= 7.16\%$.

5-1   a. 17%; b. $\sigma_A = 12.85\%$.
5-2   a. 15.6%; c-1. $k_A = 17.0\%$; d-2. $k_A = 13.0\%$.
5-3   d-1. $\$150,000$; d-2. 15%.
5-5   a. Old $\underline{P_0 = \$45.53}$.
5-6   a. $k_C = 10.6\%$; b. New $P_C = \$22.73$.
5-7   a. $k_i = 7\% + b_i\,(5\%)$; c. $k_D = 19.5\%$.
5-9   b. $k_i = 10\% + b_i\,(5\%)$; c. $k_A = 15\%$; $k_B = 12.5\%$.
5A-2   a. $\hat{k}_A = 15\%$; $\sigma_A = 12.8\%$; b. Invest 71.53% in A; e. Invest 40% in A; h. $b_A = 0.74$.

6-1   a. ROE $= 4.8\%$; ROA $= 3\%$; ACP $= 36$ days.
6-2   a. ROE $= 7.1\%$; ROA $= 5\%$; ACP $= 30$ days.
6-3   a. Total sources $= \$117$ million; b. Net increase in working capital $= \$12$ million.
6-5   a. DPS growth rate $= 10\%$ to 12%, depending on procedure used.
6-6   ACP $= 30$ days.

7-1   a. Total assets $= \$7.2$ million; b. $\$3,580,000$.
7-2   a. $\$10,797,500$; c. Current ratio $= 1.88$ times;
d-1. $-\$4,511,500$; d-3. Return on net worth $= 10.7\%$.
7-3   a. Total assets $= \$21,120,000$; b. $\$720,000$.
7-4.   a. Total assets $= \$78,480,000$; b. 25%; c. Total assets $= \$86,976,000$.

8-1   a. 28 days; c. $\$36,666.74$.
8-2   a. $\$18,000$; d. $\$6,395$.
8-3   Proposal 3: $\Delta P = \$251,556$; Proposal 5: $\Delta P = \$414,667$.
8-4   a. $5,600$ units; c. $25,000$ units.
8-5   b. 21 days; d. ACP $= 27$ days; e-1. 756 units; e-3. Average inventory $= \$13,230$.

9-1   b-1. $\$1,500,000$; b-2. $-\$6,500,000$.
9-2   b. $\$164,400$.
9-3   a. Surplus in July $= \$426,000$; Loan in October $= \$133,500$.
9-4 9.6%; 9.3%.

10-1   b. 111%; c. 7.3%.
10-2   a. 36.73%.
10-3   a. $\$66,667$; c. $\$200,000$; 36.73%.
10-4   b. 17.6%; c. 24%, or 26.62%, or 30%, depending on procedure.
10-5   a. Loan interest rate $= 16.28\%$.
10-6   a. $\$200,000$.
10-7   a. 60 days; b. 14.69%.
10-8   a-1. 18.18%; a-2. 23.08%.

10A-1   a. Total assets = $1,752,200; b. Total costs = $160,800; 15.12%.

11-1   b. −$98.11; c. 10%.
11-2   b. $4,107.53; c. 20%.
11-3   c. IRR_S = 21.525%; IRR_L = 15.341%.
11-4   a. X = $2^1/_6$ years; c. IRR_Y = 15%.
11-5   a. NPV_A = $1,200.74; c. NPV_A = $3,055.83.
11-6   b. −$18,142; c. NPV = −$5,572.
11-7   a. PV of inflows = $1,691,812; NPV = $14,224; b. Annual net cash flow = $462,223; NPV = −$152,298.
11A-1   b. 16.07%; d. IRR_A = 20%; IRR_B = 16.7%.
11A-2   b. NPV of Project Δ = $4,162,560.
11B-2   Net cash flow at t=0: +$1,000,000; Net cash flow at t=1: −$2,900,000.
11D-1   b-2. Net cash flow in Year 1 = $19,333.

12-2   PV of inflows = $17,843.10.
12-3   a. PV of outflows = $122,000; NPV = $21,293.
12-4   PV of outflows = $20,650; NPV = $12,197.
12-5   Total NPV_X = $20,065.
12-6   NPV = $1,040,200.
12-8   a. 16.5%.
12-9   a. Annual cash flow = $900,000; b. NPV = $38,570.
12A-1   b. $15 million; e. 38.7%; g. 38.5%.
12A-2   a. $6,500.
12B-1   a. Expected NPV = $22.91 million.
12B-3   a. Expected NPV = $664; c. Probability that NPV will be greater than zero = 73.24%.

13-1   a. $500,914.17; d. $325,489.05.
13-2   R = $395,053.92; I_1 = $90,000; I_2 = $62,545.15.
13-4 $300 to notes payable; $250 to subordinated debentures.
13-5   d. 100%, 33%, 0%, 0%.
13-6   a. 1,853,637; b-2. YTM on a zero-coupon bond = 6.51%; YTM on an annual payment bond = 7.50%.
13-7   c. $7,586,793.
13-8   c-2. 24%; d. $41.96; $150.
13B-1   a. NPV = $20,403.

14-1   j. $24.00 to $27.00.
14B-1 $5.00.
14B-3   a. $3.00.

15-1   b. 6%.
15-3   c. 12%.
15-5   b. $15 million.
15-6   a. 15%; b. 12.71%.
15-7   b. $15,000,000; e. $6,000,000.

15-8 b. 9.84%; c. $400,000.

15-9 b. 1st breaking point = $75,000; c. MCC above 2nd break = 11.05%.

15-10 a. 33.3% debt, 6.7% preferred, 60% common; b. 1st breaking point = $1,710,000, 2nd breaking point = $6,710,000.

15A-2 a. MCC_1 = 9.66%, MCC_3 = 10.72%; b-2. $6 million.

16-2 a. V = $3,283,636; b. $16.42.

16-3 b. V = $5,720,000 at $3 million of debt; d. EPS = $2.33 at $2 million of debt.

16-4 a. 14%; c. $28.57.

16A-1 a. DOL_A = 3.0; 2.0; e. DTL_A = 30.0; 3.64.

16A-2 Breakeven volume = 80,000 for A, 66,667 for B.

17-1 a. V_U = $12 million; V_L = $16 million.

17-2 a. V_U = $2,000,000; V_L = $4,400,000; c. 5.26%; 10%.

17-4 b. σ_A = $2,500; σ_B = $20,000.

17-5 a. k_s = k_a = 10%; c. Optimal debt level = $12.5 million.

17-6 a. Mr. Smith: D = $10 million, V = $22.64 million, Mr. Jones: D = $10 million, V = $22.99 million.

18-1 Total assets = $1,979,200,000.

18-2 b. $33,600,000.

19-1 0.5882 pounds per dollar.

19-3 $514,290,000.

19-5 a. NPV of regular dollar dividend = $21,590,000; b. Total value = 107.54 million ringos.

20-1 c. ER ≈ 0.2168; e. ER ≈ 0.2941.

20-2 b. $2.625.

20-3 NPV = $4,259.

21-1 a. Total assets = $327 million; e. D/A(before) = 35.7%; D/A(after) = 64.2%.

21-2 a. Current liabilities = $9,000,000; First-mortgage bonds = $9,250,000.

22-1 $51,417.85.

22-3 a. PV cost of owning = $865,548; b. NPV of lease investment to lessor = $65,742.

22-4. a. Annual payment = $26,380 (borrow and buy); Annual payment = $25,046 (lease); Net advantage to leasing = $3,170.

23-1 a-3. $5; a-4. $75; b. P_S = $20; Warrant = $2; Premium = $7.

23-2 a. $46.20 to $50.40.

23-4 a. Alternative 1: Total assets = $800,000; b. Percent ownership, Alternative 2 = 53%; c. EPS, Alternative 3 = $0.73.

23-5 b. 11.65%; d-1. New stock price = $14.63.

Appendix C
Selected Equations

$k = RR + I.$ **Appendix 2A**

$\dfrac{\text{Average}}{\text{inflation rate}} = [(1 + I_1)(1 + I_2) \ldots (1 + I_n)]^{1/n} - 1.0.$

$FV_n = PV(1 + k)^n$ 　　　　$FVIFA_{k,n} = \dfrac{(1 + k)^n - 1}{k}.$ **Chapter 3**
$ = PV(FVIF_{k,n}).$

$PV = FV_n[1/(1 + k)]^n$
$ = FV_n(PVIF_{k,n}).$ 　　　$PVIFA_{k,n} = \dfrac{1 - \dfrac{1}{(1 + k)^n}}{k}.$

$APR = \left(1 + \dfrac{k_{nom}}{m}\right)^m - 1.0.$ 　　$PV = FV_n\left(\dfrac{1}{1 + \dfrac{k_{nom}}{m}}\right)^{mn}.$

$FV_n = PV\left(1 + \dfrac{k_{nom}}{m}\right)^{mn}.$ 　　$V = \dfrac{R}{k}.$

$S_n = R\displaystyle\sum_{t=1}^{n}(1 + k)^{n-t}$ 　　$A_n = R\displaystyle\sum_{t=1}^{n}\left(\dfrac{1}{1 + k}\right)^t$

$ = R(FVIFA_{k,n}).$ 　　　$ = R(PVIFA_{k,n}).$

$FV_n = (PV)e^{kn}.$ 　　　$PV = (FV_n)e^{-kn}.$

$V = \displaystyle\sum_{t=1}^{n}I\left(\dfrac{1}{1 + k_d}\right)^t + M\left(\dfrac{1}{1 + k_d}\right)^n$ 　　$D_t = D_0(1 + g)^t.$ **Chapter 4**

$ = I(PVIFA_{k_d,n}) + M(PVIF_{k_d,n}).$ 　　$P_0 = \dfrac{D_1}{k_s - g}.$

$\text{Approximate YTM} = \dfrac{I + (M - V)/n}{(M + V)/2}.$ 　　$\hat{k}_s = \dfrac{D_1}{P_0} + g.$

$k = R_F + b(k_M - R_F).$ 　　$\hat{k} = \displaystyle\sum_{i=1}^{n}P_ik_i.$ **Chapter 5**

$b_p = \displaystyle\sum_{j=1}^{n}x_jb_j.$ 　　　$\sigma = \sqrt{\displaystyle\sum_{i=1}^{n}(k_i - k)^2P_i}.$

$$\sigma_P = \sqrt{x^2\sigma_A^2 + (1 - x)^2\sigma_B^2 + 2x(1 - x)\, r_{AB}\sigma_A\sigma_B}.$$

Chapter 6

$$\frac{\text{Current}}{\text{ratio}} = \frac{\text{Current assets}}{\text{Current liabilities}}.$$

$$\frac{\text{Fixed asset}}{\text{turnover}} = \frac{\text{Sales}}{\text{Net fixed assets}}.$$

$$\text{ACP} = \frac{\text{Receivables}}{\text{Sales per day}} = \frac{\text{A/R}}{\text{Sales/360}}.$$

$$\frac{\text{Profit}}{\text{margin}} = \frac{\text{Net profit after taxes}}{\text{Sales}}.$$

$$\text{ROA} = \frac{\text{Net profit after taxes}}{\text{Total assets}}.$$

$$\text{ROE} = \frac{\text{Net profit after taxes}}{\text{Common equity}}.$$

$$\text{M/B ratio} = \frac{\text{Price per share}}{\text{Book value per share}}.$$

$$\text{ROA} = \frac{\text{Profit}}{\text{margin}} \times \frac{\text{Total asset}}{\text{turnover}}.$$

$$\frac{\text{Quick}}{\text{ratio}} = \frac{\text{Current assets} - \text{Inventory}}{\text{Current liabilities}}.$$

$$\frac{\text{Inventory}}{\text{turnover}} = \frac{\text{Sales}}{\text{Inventory}}.$$

$$\frac{\text{Total asset}}{\text{turnover}} = \frac{\text{Sales}}{\text{Total assets}}.$$

$$\frac{\text{Debt}}{\text{ratio}} = \frac{\text{Total debt}}{\text{Total assets}}.$$

$$\text{TIE} = \frac{\text{EBIT}}{\text{I}}.$$

$$\text{P/E ratio} = \frac{\text{Price per share}}{\text{Earnings per share}}.$$

$$\text{ROE} = \text{ROA} \times \frac{\text{Assets}}{\text{Common equity}}.$$

Chapter 7

$$\text{AFN} = \text{A/S}(\Delta S) - \text{L/S}(\Delta S) - \text{MS}_1(1 - d).$$

$$EOQ = \sqrt{\frac{2FS}{CP}}.$$

Changing credit standards:

$$\Delta I = V[ACP_N(\Delta S/360)].$$
$$\Delta P = \Delta S(1 - V) - B_N(\Delta S) - k(\Delta I).$$

Lengthening credit period:

$$\Delta I = (ACP_N - ACP_0)(S_0/360) + V[ACP_N(\Delta S/360)].$$

Shortening credit period:

$$\Delta I = (ACP_N - ACP_0)[(S_0 + \Delta S)/360] + V[ACP_0(\Delta S/360)].$$
$$\Delta P = \Delta S(1 - V) - B_N(\Delta S) - k(\Delta I).$$

Changing discounts:

$$\Delta I = (ACP_N - ACP_0)(S_0/360) + V[ACP_N(\Delta S/360)].$$
$$\Delta P = \Delta S(1 - V) + [B_0S_0 - B_N(S_0 + \Delta S)]$$
$$+ [D_0S_0p_0 - D_N(S_0 + \Delta S)(p_1)] - k(\Delta I).$$

Changing collection policy:

$$\Delta I = (ACP_N - ACP_0)[(S_0 + \Delta S)/360] + V[ACP_0(\Delta S/360)].$$
$$\Delta P = \Delta S(1 - V) + [B_0S_0 - B_N(S_0 + \Delta S)] - k(\Delta I).$$

$$C^* = \sqrt{\frac{2FT}{k}}.$$

$$\frac{\text{Percentage}}{\text{cost}} = \frac{\text{Discount}}{100 - \text{Discount percent}} \times \frac{360}{\text{Days credit is outstanding} - \text{Discount period}}.$$

Installment loan: $\dfrac{\text{Approximate}}{\text{rate}} = \dfrac{\text{Average annual interest}}{\text{Loan}/2}.$

Discount loan with compensating balance:

$$\frac{\text{Effective}}{\text{rate}} = \frac{\text{Interest}}{\text{Amount borrowed} - \text{Interest} - \text{Compensating balance}}.$$

$$APR = (1 + k_d)^{12} - 1.0.$$

Chapter 11

$$\text{NPV} = \sum_{t=1}^{n} \frac{CF_t}{(1 + k)^t} - C \qquad\qquad \text{IRR: } \sum_{t=1}^{n} \frac{CF_t}{(1 + r)^t} - C = 0.$$

$$= \sum_{t=1}^{n} CF_t(PVIF_{k,t}) - C. \qquad\qquad \sum_{t=1}^{n} CF_t(PVIF_{r,t}) - C = 0.$$

$$\text{PI} = \frac{\text{PV benefits}}{\text{Cost}} = \frac{\sum_{t=1}^{n} \dfrac{CF_t}{(1 + k)^t}}{\text{Cost}}.$$

Chapter 12

$$\text{NPV} = \sum_{t=0}^{n} \frac{CF_t(1 + i)^t}{(1 + k_r)^t (1 + i)^t}.$$

$$z = \frac{x - \mu}{\sigma}. \qquad\qquad \sigma_{\text{NPV}} = \left[\sum_{t=0}^{n} \frac{\sigma_t^2}{(1 + k)^{2t}} \right]^{1/2}.$$

Chapter 13

$$\text{FCC} = \frac{\text{EBIT} + \text{Lease payments}}{I + \text{Lease payments} + \dfrac{\text{Sinking fund payments}}{1 - t}}.$$

Appendix 14B

$$R = \frac{M_o - S}{N + 1}. \qquad\qquad R = \frac{M_e - S}{N}.$$

Chapter 15

$$k_d \text{ after-tax} = k_d (1 - t). \qquad\qquad k_e = \frac{D_1}{P_0(1 - F)} + g.$$

$$k_p = D_p/P_n. \qquad\qquad k_a = W_d(k_d)(1 - t) + W_s(k_s \text{ or } k_e) + W_p(k_p).$$

$$\text{Breaking point} = \frac{\$ \text{ of low cost capital}}{\begin{array}{c}\% \text{ of this type of capital}\\ \text{in capital structure}\end{array}}.$$

Chapter 16

$$Q = \frac{F}{P - V}. \qquad\qquad V = D + S.$$

$$S = \frac{(\text{EBIT} - k_dD)(1 - t)}{k_s} \qquad\qquad k_a = (D/V)(k_d)(1 - t) + (S/V)(k_s).$$

$$\text{DTL} = \frac{Q(P - V)}{Q(P - V) - F - I}. \qquad\qquad \text{DFL} = \frac{\text{EBIT}}{\text{EBIT} - I}.$$

$$\text{DOL} = \frac{Q(P - V)}{Q(P - V) - F}.$$

$$\text{DTL} = (\text{DOL})(\text{DFL}).$$
$$\text{EPS}_1 = \text{EPS}_0 [1 + (\text{DTL})(\%\Delta S)].$$

$$V_U = \frac{EBIT\ (1\ -\ t)}{k_s} \qquad V_L = \frac{EBIT\ (1\ -\ t)}{k_s} + tD.$$

$$\text{Expected after-tax cash flow} = (ROA) \begin{pmatrix} \text{Amount of} \\ \text{investment} \end{pmatrix} (1\ -\ t_c)\ (1\ -\ t_p).$$

$$V_L = V_U + tD.$$

$$V_L = V_U + \left[1 - \frac{(1\ -\ t_c)\ (1\ -\ t_{pS})}{(1\ -\ t_{pD})} \right] D.$$

$$ER_A = \frac{TE\ -\ EPS_A\ (N_A)}{EPS_A\ (N_t)}.$$

$$V_w = (P_0\ -\ P_s)\ (N).$$

$$P_c = M/R.$$

$$V_0 = \sum_{t\ =\ 1}^{n} \frac{I}{(1\ +\ k_c)^t} + \frac{P_0(1\ +\ g)^n R}{(1\ +\ k_c)^n}.$$

Glossary

Absolute Priority Doctrine In bankruptcy proceedings, the doctrine that states that claims must be paid in strict accordance with the priority of each claim, regardless of the consequence to other claimants.

Accelerated Depreciation Depreciation methods that write off the cost of an asset at a faster rate than the write-off under the straight line method. The three principal methods of accelerated depreciation are: (1) sum-of-years'-digits, (2) double declining balance, and (3) units of production.

Accruals Continually recurring short-term liabilities. Examples are accrued wages, accrued taxes, and accrued interest.

Add-on Interest Interest calculated and added to funds received to determine the face amount of the note.

Agency Costs The costs associated with monitoring management's actions to insure that these actions are consistent with contractual agreements among management, stockholders, and debtholders.

Aging Schedule A report showing how long accounts receivable have been outstanding. It gives the percent of receivables now past due and the percent past due by, for example, one month, two months, or other periods.

Amortization Schedule A schedule that shows precisely how a loan will be repaid. The schedule gives the required payment on each specific date and a breakdown of the payment showing how much of it constitutes interest and how much constitutes repayment of principal.

Amortize To liquidate on an installment basis; an amortized loan is one in which the principal amount of the loan is repaid in installments during the life of the loan.

Annual Percentage Rate (APR) The effective annual rate of interest being charged on a credit agreement. The APR may differ from the stated rate.

Annual Report A report, issued annually by corporations to their stockholders, which contains basic financial statements as well as management's opinion of the past year's operations and prospects for the future.

Annuity A series of payments of a fixed amount for a specified number of years.

Annuity, Deferred A series of payments of a fixed amount for a specified number of periods where the payments occur at the end of the period. Also called *ordinary annuity*.

Annuity Due A series of payments of a fixed amount for a specified number of periods where the payments occur at the beginning of the period.

Arbitrage The process of selling overvalued and buying undervalued assets so as to bring about an equilibrium where all assets are properly valued.

Arrearage Overdue payment; frequently, an omitted dividend on preferred stock.

Asked Price The price at which a dealer or specialist in securities will sell shares of stock out of inventory.

Assignment A relatively inexpensive way of liquidating a failing firm that does not involve going through the courts.

Automatic Dividend Reinvestment (ADR) An arrangement whereby stockholders automatically reinvest their dividends in the stock of the paying corporation.

Average Collection Period Accounts receivable divided by credit sales per day. It represents the average length of time a firm must wait after making a sale before receiving cash.

Balloon Payment When a debt is not fully amortized, the final payment that is larger than the preceding payments.

Banker's Acceptance A promissory note by a business debtor arising out of a business transaction; a bank, by endorsing, assumes the obligation of payment at the due date. The debtor has a deposit at the bank that will be charged for the amount plus interest.

Bankruptcy A legal procedure for formally liquidating a business, carried out under the jurisdiction of courts of law.

Bankruptcy Reform Act of 1978 Legislation enacted to speed up and streamline bankruptcy proceedings. This law represents a shift to a relative priority doctrine of creditors' claims.

Basis Points Percentage points times 100; for example, 2.5 percentage points equals 250 basis points.

Bearer Bond Possession of a bearer bond is primary evidence of its ownership. Opposite of "registered bond."

Benefit/Cost Ratio Profitability index.

Beta Coefficient A measurement of the extent to which the returns on a given stock move with the stock market.

Beta Risk Risk of a firm measured from the standpoint of an investor who holds a highly diversified portfolio.

Bid Price The price a dealer or specialist in securities will pay for a stock.

Blue Sky Laws State laws that prevent the sale of securities that have little or no asset backing.

Bond A long-term debt instrument.

Book Value The accounting value of an asset. The book value of a share of common stock is equal to the common equity (common stock plus paid-in capital plus retained earnings) of the corporation divided by the number of shares of stock outstanding.

Breakeven Analysis An analytical technique for studying the relationships among fixed cost, variable cost, and profits. A breakeven *chart* graphically depicts the nature of breakeven analysis. The breakeven *point* represents the volume of sales at which total costs equal total revenues (that is, profits equal zero).

Business Failure Condition when a business has terminated with a loss to creditors.

Business Risk The basic risk inherent in a firm's operations. Business risk plus financial risk resulting from the use of debt equals total corporate risk.

Call (1) An option to buy (or "call") a share of stock at a specified price within a specified period. (2) The process of redeeming a bond or preferred stock issue before its normal maturity.

Call Premium The amount in excess of par value that a company must pay when it calls a security.

Call Price The price that must be paid when a security is called. The call price is equal to the par value plus the call premium.

Call Privilege A provision incorporated into a bond or a share of preferred stock that gives the issuer the right to redeem (call) the security at a specified price.

Call Provision A provision in a bond contract that gives the issuer the right to redeem the bonds under specified terms prior to the normal maturity date.

Capital Asset An asset with a life of more than one year that is not bought and sold in the ordinary course of business.

Capital Asset Pricing Model (CAPM) A model based on the proposition that any stock's required rate of return is equal to the riskless rate of return plus its risk premium.

Capital Budgeting The process of planning expenditures on assets whose returns are expected to extend beyond one year.

Capital Gains Profits on capital assets.

Capital Gains Yield In any year, the capital gains yield is equal to the capital gain during the year divided by the beginning price.

Capital Intensity The amount of assets required to produce a dollar of sales.

Capital Losses Losses on the sale of capital assets.

Capital Market Line A graphical representation of the relationship between risk and the required rate of return.

Capital Rationing A situation where a constraint is placed on the total size of the capital investment during a particular period.

Capital Structure The percentage of each type of capital used by the firm—debt, preferred stock, and common equity. (Common equity consists of common stock, paid-in capital, and retained earnings.)

Capitalization Rate A discount rate used to find the present value of a series of future cash receipts. Sometimes called *discount rate.*

Capitalize In finance: to find the present value of a stream of cash flows. In accounting: to reflect costs on the balance sheet rather than charge them off through the income statement, as to capitalize major repairs to a fixed asset.

Carry-back; Carry-forward For income tax purposes, losses that can be carried backward or forward to reduce federal income taxes.

Cash Budget A schedule showing cash flows (receipts, disbursements, and net cash) for a firm over a specified period.

Certainty Equivalents The amount of cash (or rate of return) that someone would require *with certainty* in order to be indifferent between this certain sum (or rate of return) and a risky sum (or rate of return).

Characteristic Line A linear least squares regression line that shows the relationship between an individual security's return and returns on "the market." The slope of the characteristic line is the beta coefficient.

Charter A formal legal document which describes the scope and nature of a corporation and defines the rights and duties of its stockholders and managers.

Chattel Mortgage A mortgage on personal property (not real estate). A mortgage on equipment would be a chattel mortgage.

Closely Held Corporation A corporation that is not publicly owned; a corporation owned by a few individuals who are typically associated with the management of the firm. Also called a *closed corporation.*

Coefficient of Variation Standard deviation divided by the mean.

Collateral Assets that are used to secure a loan.

Commercial Paper Unsecured, short-term promissory notes of large firms, usually issued in denominations of $100,000 or more. The rate of interest on commercial paper is typically somewhat below the prime rate of interest.

Commitment Fee The fee paid to a lender for a formal line of credit.

Company-Specific Risk That part of a security's risk associated with random events; such risk can be eliminated by proper diversification.

Compensating Balance A required minimum checking account balance that a firm must maintain with a commercial bank. The balance is generally equal to 15 to 20 percent of the amount of loans outstanding. Compensating balances can raise the effective rate of interest on bank loans.

Composite Cost of Capital A weighted average of the component costs of debt, preferred stock, and common equity. Also called the *weighted average cost of capital,* it reflects the cost of each additional dollar raised, not the average cost of all capital the firm has raised throughout its history.

Composition An informal method of reorganization in which creditors voluntarily reduce their claims on the debtor firm.

Compound Interest An interest rate that is applicable when interest in succeeding periods is earned not only on the initial principal but also on the accumulated interest of prior periods.

Compounding The arithmetic process of determining the final value of a payment or series of payments when compound interest is applied.

Conditional Sales Contract A method of financing new equipment by paying it off in installments over a one to five year period. The seller retains title to the equipment until payment has been completed.

Congeneric Merger A merger between firms in the same general industry, where the merger partners are neither customers nor suppliers of one another. The term was first used in connection with mergers between financial institutions, as, for example, when a bank holding company acquired a mortgage service company or a leasing company.

Conglomerate Merger A merger between companies in different industries. If a grocery chain acquired a steel company, then a conglomerate corporation would result.

Consol Bond A perpetual bond issued by England in 1814 to consolidate past debts; in general, any perpetual bond.

Consolidated Tax Return An income tax return that combines the income statements of several affiliated firms.

Continuous Compounding (Discounting) As opposed to discrete compounding, a situation where interest is added continuously rather than at discrete points in time.

Conversion Price The effective price paid for common stock when the stock is obtained by converting either convertible preferred stocks or convertible bonds. For example, if a $1,000 bond is convertible into twenty shares of stock, the conversion price is $50 (= $1,000/20).

Conversion Ratio or Conversion Rate The number of shares of common stock that may be obtained by converting a convertible bond or share of convertible preferred stock.

Convertibles Securities (generally bonds or preferred stocks) that are exchangeable at the option of the holder for common stock of the issuing firm.

Correlation Coefficient A measurement of the degree of relationship between two variables.

Cost of Capital The discount rate that should be used in the capital budgeting process.

Coupon Rate The stated rate of interest on a bond.

Covenant Detailed clause in loan agreements, designed to protect lenders. It includes such items as limits on total indebtedness, restrictions on dividends, minimum current ratio, and similar provisions.

Covered Options Options sold by an investor against stock held in a portfolio.

Cumulative Dividends A protective feature on preferred stock that requires all past preferred dividends to be paid before any common dividends are paid.

Cumulative Voting A method of voting for corporate directors which permits multiple votes for a single director. This can enable a minority group of shareholders to obtain some voice in the control of the company.

Current Ratio Current assets divided by current liabilities. This ratio indicates the extent to which the claims of short-term creditors are covered by assets expected to be converted to cash in the near future.

Cut-off Point In the capital budgeting process, the minimum rate of return on acceptable investment opportunities.

Debenture A long-term debt instrument that is not secured by a mortgage on specific property.

Debt Ratio Total debt divided by total assets.

Default The failure to fulfill a contract; generally, the failure to pay interest or principal on debt obligations.

Default Risk Risk that an issuer of securities will not be able to make interest payments or repay the principal amount on schedule.

Degree of Leverage The percentage increase in profits resulting from a given percentage increase in sales. The degree of leverage may be calculated for financial leverage, operating leverage, or both combined.

Devaluation The process of reducing the value of a country's currency stated in terms of other currencies; for example, the British pound might be devalued from $2.30 for one pound to $2.00 for one pound.

Development Bond Bond sold by a government agency to raise funds to be used for economic development in a specific geographic region. Typically, a corporation agrees to build a plant in a local area, and the area's development agency sells tax-exempt bonds, uses the proceeds to build the plant to the company's specifications, leases the plant to the company, and uses the lease payments to service the bond.

Discount Rate The interest rate used in the discounting process; sometimes called *capitalization rate.*

Discounted Cash Flow (DCF) Techniques Methods of ranking investment proposals, including (1) internal rate of return method, (2) net present value method, and (3) profitability index or benefit/cost ratio.

Discounting The process of finding the present value of a series of future cash flows. Discounting is the reverse of compounding.

Discounting of Accounts Receivable Short-term financing where accounts receivable are used as collateral to secure a loan. The lender does not *buy* the accounts receivable but simply uses them as collateral for the loan. Also called *pledging of accounts receivable.*

Dividend Yield The ratio of the current dividend to the current price of a share of stock.

du Pont System A system of analysis designed to show the relationships among return on investment, asset turnover, and the profit margin.

EBIT Abbreviation for *earnings before interest and taxes.*

Economic Failure Condition that exists when a firm's revenues do not cover its total costs, including its cost of capital.

Economic Ordering Quantity (EOQ) The optimum (least cost) quantity of inventory which should be ordered.

Efficient Markets Hypothesis The hypothesis that securities are typically in equilibrium—that they are fairly priced in the sense that the price reflects all publicly available information on the security.

Efficient Portfolio The portfolio of securities that provides the highest possible expected return for any degree of risk or the lowest degree of risk for any expected return.

EPS Abbreviation for *earnings per share.*

Equilibrium A situation in which there is no systematic tendency for change. If a security is in equilibrium, then there is no pressure for its price to change.

Equity The net worth of a business, consisting of capital stock, capital (or paid-in) surplus, earned surplus (or retained earnings), and, occasionally, certain net worth reserves. *Common equity* is that part of the total net worth belonging to the common stockholders. *Total equity* includes preferred stockholders. The terms *common stock, net worth,* and *common equity* are frequently used interchangeably.

Equivalent Annual Annuity The NPV of a project over its original life divided by the annuity factor for the original life. The equivalent annual annuity provides a means of comparing mutually exclusive projects of unequal lives.

Eurobond A bond sold in a country other than the one in whose currency the bond is denominated.

Eurodollar A United States dollar on deposit in a foreign bank—generally, but not necessarily, a European bank.

Ex Ante Before the fact. Opposite of ex post.

Ex Dividend Date The date on which the right to the current dividend no longer accompanies a stock. (For listed stock, the ex dividend date is four working days prior to the date of record.)

Ex Post After the fact. Opposite of ex ante.

Ex Rights The date on which stock purchase rights are no longer transferred to the purchaser of the stock.

Exchange Rate The number of units of a given currency that can be purchased for one unit of another currency.

Exchange Ratio In mergers, the number of shares the acquiring firm must give for each of the acquired firm's shares.

Excise Tax A tax on the manufacture, sale, or consumption of specified commodities.

Exercise Price The price that must be paid for a share of common stock when it is bought by exercising a warrant.

Expectations Theory The theory that long-term interest rates are determined by investors' expectations about future short-term rates.

Expected Return The return someone expects to realize from an investment. The expected return is the mean value of the probability distribution of possible returns.

Expected Value The weighted average of all possible outcomes, where the weights are the probabilities of all expected outcomes.

Extension An informal method of reorganization in which the creditors voluntarily postpone the date of required payment on past-due obligations.

External Funds Funds acquired through borrowing or by selling new common or preferred stock.

Factoring A method of financing accounts receivable under which a firm sells its accounts receivable (generally without recourse) to a financial institution (the "factor").

Feasible Set Hypothetical set of all possible portfolios; also known as *the attainable set*.

Federal Reserve System The central banking system in the United States.

Field Warehousing A method of financing inventories in which a "warehouse" is established at the place of business of the borrowing firm.

Financial Accounting Standards Board (FASB) A private (nongovernment) agency which functions as an accounting standards–setting body.

Financial Institutions Establishments that handle monetary affairs, including insurance companies, commercial banks, savings and loans, leasing companies, and institutional investors.

Financial Intermediation Financial transactions conducted through a financial institution which brings together savers and those who need capital so that savings can be redistributed into their most productive uses.

Financial Lease A lease that does not provide for maintenance services, is not cancellable, and is fully amortized over its life. Also called a *capital lease*.

Financial Leverage The ratio of total debt to total assets. There are other measures of financial leverage, especially ones that relate cash inflows to required cash outflows. In this book, either the debt/total asset ratio or the debt/total market value ratio is generally used to measure leverage.

Financial Risk The portion of total corporate risk over and above basic business risk that results from using debt.

Financial Structure The entire right-hand side of the balance sheet—the way a firm is financed.

Fixed Charges Costs that do not vary with the level of output, especially fixed financial costs such as interest, lease payments, and sinking fund payments.

Fixed Exchange Rate System World monetary system in existence prior to 1971 under which the value of the U.S. dollar was tied to gold and the values of the other currencies were pegged to the U.S. dollar.

Float The amount of funds tied up in checks that have been written but are still in process and have not yet been collected.

Floating Exchange Rates Exchange rates not fixed by government policy ("pegged") but instead allowed to "float" up or down in accordance with supply and demand. When market forces are allowed to function, exchange rates are said to be floating.

Floating Rate Bond A bond whose interest rate fluctuates with shifts in interest rates.

Flotation Cost The cost of issuing new stocks or bonds.

Foreign Bond A bond sold by a foreign borrower but denominated in the currency of the country in which it is sold.

Foreign Exchange Exposure Exposure to losses due to fluctuating exchange rates.

Forward Exchange Rate An agreed-upon price at which two currencies are to be exchanged at some future date.

Founders' Shares Classified stock that has sole voting rights and restricted dividends. Owned by the firm's founders.

Franchise A device for small business whereby training, experience, and perhaps a valuable name or supplies are provided by a larger company for a fee.

Fully Diluted EPS Earnings available to common stockholders divided by the average number of shares which would have been outstanding if all warrants and convertibles had been exercised or converted, regardless of the likelihood of their exercise or conversion.

Funded Debt Long-term debt.

Funding The process of replacing short-term debt with long-term securities (stocks or bonds).

Future Value (FV) The amount to which a payment or series of payments will grow by a given future date when compounded by a given interest rate. FVIF = future value interest factor.

GIGO One of the fundamental laws of computer science, it stands for "Garbage In, Garbage Out." The term has now been broadened and applied to all aspects of financial analysis. *See* the SWAG method for obtaining inputs to a GIGO system.

Going Public The sale of stock by a closely held corporation (or its principal stockholders) to the public at large.

Goodwill Intangible assets of a firm established by the excess of the price paid for the going concern over the value of its assets.

Hedging Process of protecting oneself against loss due to future price changes.

Historic Rate of Return Dividend yield plus capital gain or minus capital loss that actually occurred for a given stock in a given year.

Holder-of-Record Date The date on which registered security owners are entitled to receive the forthcoming cash or stock dividend.

Holding Company A corporation which owns the common stocks of other corporations.

Horizontal Merger The combination of two firms which produce the same type of goods or service, for example, the merger between two shoe retailing chains or two shoe manufacturers.

Hurdle Rate In capital budgeting, the minimum acceptable rate of return on a project. If the expected rate of return is below the hurdle rate, the project is not accepted. The hurdle rate should be the marginal cost of capital, adjusted for the project's risk.

Impairment of Capital Legal restriction to protect creditors. It limits dividend payments to retained earnings.

Improper Accumulation Earnings retained by a business for the purpose of enabling stockholders to avoid personal income taxes.

Income Bond A bond that pays interest to bondholders only if the interest due is earned.

Incremental Cash Flow Net cash flow attributable to an investment project.

Incremental Cost of Capital The average cost of the increment of capital raised during a given year.

Indenture A formal agreement between the issuer of a bond and the bondholders.

Inflation Premium A premium for anticipated or expected inflation that investors add to the pure rate of return.

Insolvency The inability to meet maturing debt obligations.

Interest Factor (IF) Numbers found in compound interest and annuity tables. Usually called FVIF or PVIF.

Interest Rate Risk Risk to which investors are exposed due to changing interest rates.

Internal Financing Funds made available for capital budgeting and working capital expansion through the normal operations of the firm. Internal financing is approximately equal to retained earnings plus depreciation.

Internal Rate of Return (IRR) The rate of return on an asset investment, calculated by finding the discount rate that equates the present value of future cash flows to the cost of the investment.

Intrinsic Value The value of an asset which, in the mind of the analyst, is justified by the facts, often as distinguished from the asset's current market price and/or its book value.

Investment Banker One who underwrites and distributes new investment securities; more broadly, one who helps business firms obtain financing.

Investment Opportunity Schedule (IOS) A listing, or graph, of the firm's investment opportunities ranked in order of the projects' rates of return.

Investment Tax Credit A specified percentage of the dollar amount of new investments in each of certain categories of assets which business firms can deduct as a credit against their income taxes.

Legal List A list of securities in which mutual savings banks, pension funds, insurance companies, and other fiduciary institutions are permitted to invest.

Leverage Factor The ratio of debt to total assets.

Leveraged Lease Lease under which the lessor arranges to borrow a portion of the required funds.

Lien A lender's claim on assets that are pledged for a loan.

Line of Credit An arrangement whereby a financial institution (bank or insurance company) commits itself to lend up to a specified maximum amount of funds during a specified period. Sometimes the interest rate on the loan is specified; at other times, it is not. Sometimes a commitment fee is imposed for obtaining the line of credit.

Liquidation Dissolving a firm through the sale of its assets.

Liquidity A firm's position with respect to cash and marketable securities versus its short-term debt, reflecting its ability to meet maturing obligations. For an individual asset, it is the ability to sell the asset at a reasonable price on short notice.

Liquidity Preference Theory The theory which states that investors generally prefer short-term debt to long-term and, therefore, must be compensated by a premium (called a "liquidity" or "maturity" premium) to invest in long-term bonds.

Listed Securities Securities traded on an organized security exchange.

Lockbox Plan A procedure used to speed up collections and to reduce float.

Margin—Profit on Sales The *profit margin* is the percentage of profit after tax to sales.

Margin—Securities Business The buying of stocks or bonds on credit, known as *buying on margin*.

Marginal Cost The cost of an additional unit. The marginal cost of capital is the cost of an additional dollar of new funds.

Marginal Efficiency of Capital A schedule showing the internal rate of return on investment opportunities.

Marginal Revenue The additional gross revenue produced by selling one additional unit of output.

Marginal Tax Rate The tax rate applicable to the last unit of income.

Market Risk The part of a security's risk that cannot be eliminated by diversification. It is measured by the beta coefficient.

Market Segmentation Theory The theory that capital markets are segmented and that the yield curve is determined by the relative supply and demand for short- and long-term funds.

Merger Any combination that forms one company from two or more previously existing companies.

Money Market Financial market in which funds are borrowed or lent for short periods. (The money market is distinguished from the capital market, which is the market for long-term funds.)

Money Market Fund A mutual fund which invests in short-term, low-risk securities such as Treasury bills and bank certificates of deposit.

Mortgage A pledge of designated property as security for a loan.

Multiple Discriminant Analysis (MDA) A statistical technique similar to regression analysis that can be used to evaluate financial ratios.

Naked Options Options sold by an investor without any stock to back them up.

Net Present Value (NPV) Method A method of ranking investment proposals. The NPV is equal to the present value of future returns, discounted at the marginal cost of capital, minus the present value of the cost of the investment.

Net Worth The capital and surplus of a firm—capital stock, capital surplus (paid-in capital), earned surplus (retained earnings), and, occasionally, certain reserves. For some purposes, preferred stock is included; generally, *net worth* refers only to the common stockholders' position.

New Issue Market The market that consists of stocks of companies that have just gone public.

Nominal Interest Rate The contracted, or stated, interest rate, undeflated for price level changes.

Objective Probability Distribution Probability distribution determined by statistical procedures using actual data.

Offering Price Price at which common stock is sold to the public.

Operating Company A subsidiary of a holding company.

Operating Leverage The extent to which fixed costs are used in a firm's operation. Breakeven analysis is used to measure the extent to which operating leverage is employed.

Operating Merger A merger in which the operations of two companies are integrated with the expectation of achieving synergistic benefits.

Opportunity Cost The rate of return on the best *alternative* investment available—the highest return that will *not* be earned if the funds are invested in a particular project. For example, the opportunity cost of *not* investing in Bond A (which yields 8 percent) might be 7.99 percent, which could be earned on Bond B.

Option A contract giving the holder the right to buy or sell an asset at some predetermined price within a specified period of time.

Ordinary Income Income from normal operations but specifically excluding income from the sale of capital assets.

Organized Security Exchanges Formal organizations having tangible, physical locations and conducting auction markets in designated ("listed") investment securities. The New York Stock Exchange is an organized security exchange.

Overdraft System A system where a depositor may write checks in excess of the balance, with the bank automatically extending a loan to cover the shortage.

Over-the-Counter Market All facilities that provide for trading in unlisted securities—those not listed on organized exchanges. The over-the-counter market is typically viewed as a "telephone market," since most business is conducted by telephone.

Paid-in Capital The funds received in excess of par value when a firm sells stock. Paid-in capital can also be increased when a company declares a stock dividend. Often called *additional paid-in capital*.

Par Value The nominal or face value of a stock or bond.

Payback Period The length of time required for the net revenues of an investment to return the cost of the investment.

Payout Ratio The percentage of earnings paid out in the form of dividends.

Pegging A market stabilization action taken by the manager of an underwriting group during the offering of new securities. Pegging is done by continually placing orders to buy at a specified price in the market.

Percentage of Sales Method Method of forecasting financial requirements by expressing various balance sheet items as a percentage of sales, then multiplying these percentages by expected future sales to construct *pro forma* balance sheets.

Perpetuity A stream of equal future payments expected to continue forever.

Pledging of Accounts Receivable Short-term borrowing from financial institutions where the loan is secured by accounts receivable. Also called *discounting of accounts receivable*.

Pollution Control Bond Bonds similar to development bonds but whose proceeds are used by a company to purchase pollution abatement equipment. *See also* Development Bond.

Pooling of Interest An accounting method for combining the financial statements of two firms that merge. Under the pooling-of-interest procedure, the assets of the merged firms are simply added to form the balance sheet of the surviving corporation. This method is different from the "purchase" method, where goodwill is put on the balance sheet to reflect a premium (or discount) paid in excess of book value.

Portfolio Effect The extent to which the variation in returns on a combination of assets (a "portfolio") is less than the sum of the variations of the individual assets.

Portfolio Theory Theory that deals with the selection of optimal portfolios—portfolios that provide the highest possible return for any specified degree of risk.

Post-audit A comparison of the actual and expected results for a given capital project.

Precautionary Balance Cash balance held in reserve for random, unforeseen fluctuations in inflows and outflows.

Preemptive Right A provision contained in the corporate charter and bylaws that gives holders of common stock the right to purchase on a pro rata basis new issues of common stock (or securities convertible into common stock).

Preferred Stock Long-term equity security paying a fixed dividend.

Present Value (PV) The value today of a future payment, or stream of payments, discounted at the appropriate discount rate.

Pressure The effect on the price of a stock when a company sells a substantial block of new stock. The sale may tend to temporarily depress the price of outstanding shares.

Price/Earnings (P/E) Ratio The ratio of price to earnings, which shows the dollar amount investors will pay for $1 of current earnings. Faster-growing or less risky firms typically have higher P/E ratios than either slower-growing or more risky firms.

Price-Level Adjustment A restatement of a financial statement to adjust for the effects of general or specific price-level changes.

Primary EPS Earnings available to common stockholders divided by the average number of shares that would have been outstanding if warrants and convertibles likely to be converted in the near future had actually been exercised or converted.

Prime Rate A published rate of interest which commercial banks charge very large, strong corporations.

Pro Forma A financial statement that shows how an actual statement will look if certain specified assumptions are realized. *Pro forma* statements may be either future or past projections. A backward *pro forma* statement may be used when two firms are planning to merge and want to show what their consolidated financial statements would have looked like if they had been merged in preceding years.

Probability Distribution Listing of all possible outcomes or events, with a probability (the chance of the event's occurrence) assigned to each outcome.

Profit Center A unit of a large, decentralized firm that has its own investments and for which a rate of return on investment can be calculated.

Profit Margin The ratio of profits after taxes to sales.

Profitability Index (PI) The present value of future returns divided by the present value of the investment outlay.

Progressive Tax A tax that requires a higher percentage payment on higher incomes. The personal income tax in the United States, which has been at a rate of 14 percent on the lowest increments of income to 70 percent on the highest increments, is progressive.

Prospectus A document issued for the purpose of describing a new security issue. The Securities and Exchange Commission (SEC) examines prospectuses to insure that statements contained in them are not false or misleading.

Proxy A document giving one person the authority or power to act for another. Typically, the authority in question is the power to vote shares of common stock.

Purchase In mergers, the situation where a large firm acquires a smaller one.

Purchasing Power Risk Risk that inflation will reduce the purchasing power of a given sum of money.

Put An option to sell a specific security at a specified price within a designated period. Opposite of a call.

Quick Ratio Current assets minus inventory, divided by current liabilities. Sometimes called *acid test*.

Rate of Return The internal rate of return on an investment.

Recourse Arrangement A term used in connection with accounts receivable financing. A firm may sell its accounts receivable to a financial institution under a recourse agreement. If the accounts receivable cannot be collected, the selling firm must repurchase them from the financial institution.

Rediscount Rate The rate of interest at which a bank may borrow from a Federal Reserve Bank.

Refunding Sale of new debt securities to replace an old debt issue.

Registered Security A security whose ownership is recorded by its issuer.

Registration Statement Statement of facts filed with the SEC about a company planning to issue securities.

Regression Analysis A statistical procedure for predicting the value of one (dependent) variable on the basis of knowledge about one or more other (independent) variables.

Reinvestment Rate The rate of return at which cash flows from an investment are reinvested. The reinvestment rate may or may not be constant from year to year.

Relative Priority Doctrine In bankruptcy proceedings, a flexible approach to the priority of creditors' claims, giving balanced consideration to all claimants.

Reorganization The situation where the assets of a financially troubled firm are restated to reflect their current market value and the firm's financial structure is restated to reflect any changes on the asset side of the statement. Under a reorganization the firm continues in existence, whereas under bankruptcy the firm is liquidated and ceases to exist.

Replacement Chain Method of comparing the NPVs of mutually exclusive projects with unequal lives. The method is used by carrying the analysis out to a common denominator year.

Required Rate of Return The rate of return that stockholders expect to receive on common stock investments.

Residual Theory of Dividends The theory that dividends paid should equal the excess of earnings over retained earnings necessary to finance the optimal capital budget.

Residual Value The value of leased property at the end of the lease term.

Restrictive Covenant Provision in debt contracts, including bond indentures, that constrains the actions of a borrower.

Retained Earnings That portion of earnings not paid out in dividends. The figure that appears on the balance sheet is the sum of retained earnings for each year throughout the company's history.

Return on Common Equity Income available to common stockholders divided by common equity.

Revolving Credit Agreement Formal line of credit extended to a firm by a bank.

Right A short-term option to buy a specified number of shares of a new issue of securities at a designated "subscription" price.

Rights Offering A securities flotation offered to existing stockholders.

Risk The probability that actual future returns will be below expected returns. Risk is measured by standard deviation or coefficient of variation of expected returns or by the beta coefficient.

Risk-Adjusted Discount Rate The discount rate that applies to a particular risky (uncertain) stream of income; the riskless rate of interest plus a risk premium appropriate to the level of risk attached to the particular income stream.

Risk Aversion A dislike for risk. Investors who are averse to risk have higher required rates of return for securities with higher risk.

Risk Premium The difference between the required rate of return on a particular risky asset and the rate of return on a riskless asset with the same expected life.

Risk, Relevant Risk of a security that cannot be diversified away, or market risk. In theory, risk premiums should apply only to relevant risk.

Risk-Return Tradeoff Function *See* Capital Market Line.

Risk, Total The total of market and nonmarket risk of a security.

Safety Stock Additional inventories carried to guard against changes in sales rates or production/shipping delays.

Sale and Leaseback An operation whereby a firm sells land, buildings, or equipment to a financial institution and simultaneously leases the property back for a specified period under specific terms.

Salvage Value The value of a capital asset at the end of a specified period. It is the current market price of an asset being considered for replacement in a capital budgeting problem.

Scenario Analysis Short version of simulation, where bad and good sets of financial circumstances are compared to a most likely, or base, case NPV.

Seasoned Issue Outstanding bonds, or bonds which have been on the market for a while.

Secondary Market In investment terminology, the "market" in which stocks are traded after they have been issued by corporations. When a company sells a new issue of stock, the transaction is considered a "primary market transaction."

Securities and Exchange Commission (SEC) The U.S. government agency that regulates the issuance and trading of stocks and bonds.

Securities, Junior Securities that have lower priority in claims on assets and income than other securities (senior securities). For example, preferred stock is junior to debentures, but debentures are junior to mortgage bonds. Common stock is the most junior of all corporate securities.

Securities, Senior Securities having claims on income and assets that rank higher than certain other securities (junior securities). For example, mortgage bonds are senior to debentures, but debentures are senior to common stock.

Security Market Line The line that shows the relationship between risk and rates of return for individual securities.

Selling Group A group of stock brokerage firms formed for the purpose of distributing a new issue of securities; part of the investment banking process.

Sensitivity Analysis Simulation analysis in which key variables are changed one at a time and the resulting change in the rate of return is observed. Typically, the rate of return is more sensitive to changes in some variables than to changes in others.

Service Lease A lease under which the lessor maintains and services the asset. Also called an *operating lease*.

Short Selling Selling a security that is not owned by the seller at the time of the sale. The seller borrows the security from a brokerage firm and must at some point repay the brokerage firm by buying the security on the open market.

Simulation A technique whereby probable future events are simulated on a computer. Estimated rates of return and risk indexes can be generated.

Sinking Fund A required annual payment designed to amortize a bond or a preferred stock issue. The sinking fund may be held in the form of cash or marketable securities, but more generally the money put into the fund is used to retire some of the securities in question each year.

Small Business Administration (SBA) A government agency organized to aid small firms with their financing and other problems.

Social Responsibility The idea that businesses should be partly responsible for the welfare of society at large.

Sovereign Risk Risk of expropriation of a foreign subsidiary's assets by the host country and of unanticipated restrictions on cash flows to the parent.

Specialists Members of the stock exchange who facilitate the trading process by keeping an inventory of shares of the stocks in which they specialize.

Speculative Balance Cash balance that is held to enable the firm to take advantage of any bargain purchases that might arise.

Spot Rate The effective exchange rate for a foreign currency for delivery on (approximately) the current day. Distinguished from the forward rate.

Spread The difference between the price a security dealer offers to pay for securities (the "bid" price) and the price at which the dealer offers to sell them (the "asked" price).

Standard Deviation A statistical measurement of the variability of a set of observations.

Standard of Fairness In bankruptcy or reorganization, claims must be recognized in the order of their legal and contractual priority.

Standard of Feasibility Test made by the SEC during a reorganization to determine whether fixed charges would be covered by earnings, hence whether the reorganized company will be viable.

Stock Dividend A dividend paid in additional shares of stock rather than cash. It involves a transfer from retained earnings to the capital stock account; therefore, stock dividends are limited by the amount of retained earnings.

Stock Repurchase A means by which a firm distributes income to stockholders by buying back shares of its own stock, thereby decreasing shares outstanding, increasing EPS, and increasing the price of the stock.

Stock Split An accounting action to increase the number of shares outstanding; for example, in a 3-for-1 split, shares outstanding are tripled and each stockholder receives three new shares for each one formerly held. Stock splits involve no transfer from retained earnings to the capital stock account.

Subchapter S Section of the Internal Revenue Code that allows certain small business corporations to be taxed as either proprietorships or partnerships rather than as corporations.

Subjective Probability Distributions Probability distributions determined through subjective procedures without the use of statistics.

Subordinated Debenture A bond having a claim on assets only after the senior debt has been paid off in the event of liquidation.

Subscription Price The price at which a security may be purchased in a rights offering.

Supernormal Growth Part of the life cycle of a firm when its growth is much faster than that of the economy as a whole.

SWAG, or SWAG Method A method of obtaining data (generally quantitative) such as subjective probability distributions, when these data are not otherwise obtainable. SWAG stands for "Scientific Wild A—Guess." The SWAG method is often used to obtain inputs for GIGO analysis.

Synergy A situation where the whole is greater than the sum of its parts. In a synergistic merger, the postmerger earnings exceed the sum of the separate companies' premerger earnings.

Takeover The acquisition of one firm by another over the opposition of the acquired firm's management.

Tangible Assets Physical assets as opposed to intangible assets such as goodwill and the stated value of patents.

Target Company A company which another firm, generally a larger one, wants to acquire through merger.

Tender Offer A situation where one firm offers to buy the stock of another by going directly to the stockholders, frequently over the opposition of the management of the target company.

Term Loan A loan, generally obtained from a bank or insurance company, with a maturity greater than one year. Term loans are generally amortized.

Term Structure of Interest Rates Relationship between yields and maturities of securities.

Terminal Value The value of an asset at the end of its economic life; the terminal value includes all cash flows generated by the asset over its life, compounded at an assumed reinvestment rate. The value of an asset today is the present value of its terminal value discounted at its cost of capital.

Times Interest Earned Earnings before interest and taxes divided by interest charges. This ratio measures the ability of the firm to meet its annual interest charges.

Trade Credit Interfirm debt arising through credit sales and recorded as an account receivable by the seller and as an account payable by the buyer.

Transactions Balance Cash balance associated with payments and collections; the balance necessary to conduct day-to-day business.

Translation Loss Loss resulting from translating financial statements from a foreign subsidiary's currency to the parent's currency.

Treasury Stock Common stock that has been repurchased by the issuing firm.

Trend Analysis Analysis of a firm's financial ratios over time in order to determine the improvement or deterioration of the financial situation.

Trust Receipt An instrument acknowledging that the borrower holds certain goods in trust for the lender. Trust receipt financing is used in financing inventories for automobile dealers, construction equipment dealers, appliance dealers, and other dealers in expensive durable goods.

Trustee The representative of bondholders who acts in their interest and facilitates communication between them and the issuer. Typically these duties are handled by a department of a commercial bank.

Underwriting (1) The entire process of issuing new corporate securities. (2) The insurance function of bearing the risk of adverse price fluctuations during the period in which a new issue of stocks or bonds is being distributed.

Underwriting Syndicate A syndicate of investment firms formed to spread the risk associated with the purchase and distribution of a new issue of securities. The larger the issue, the greater the number of firms typically involved in the syndicate.

Unlisted Securities Securities that are traded in the over-the-counter market.

Utility Theory A body of theory dealing with the relationships among money income, utility (or happiness), and the willingness to accept risks.

Venture Capital Risk capital supplied to small companies by wealthy individuals, partnerships, or corporations, usually in return for an equity position in the firm.

Vertical Merger A company's acquisition of one of its suppliers or one of its customers.

Warrant A long-term option to buy a stated number of shares of common stock at a specified price. The specified price is generally called the *exercise price*.

Weighted Cost of Capital A weighted average of the component costs of debt, preferred stock, and common equity. Also called the *composite cost of capital*.

Working Capital A firm's investment in short-term assets—cash, short-term securities, accounts receivable, and inventories. *Gross working capital* is a firm's total current assets. *Net working capital* is current assets minus current liabilities. If the term *working capital* is used without further qualification, it generally refers to gross working capital.

Working Capital Policy Basic policy decisions regarding target levels for each category of current assets, and for the financing of these assets.

Yield The rate of return on an investment; the internal rate of return.

Yield Curve Graph of the relationship between the yields and maturities of a security.

Yield-to-Maturity Rate of interest earned on a bond if it is held to maturity.

Zero Coupon Bond A bond that pays no annual interest, but which sells at a discount below par and therefore provides compensation to investors in the form of capital appreciation.

Index